Field Guide to the Songbirds of South America

Mildred Wyatt-Wold Series in Ornithology

FIELD GUIDE TO
THE SONGBIRDS OF SOUTH AMERICA
THE PASSERINES

Robert S. Ridgely and Guy Tudor

In association with
The Academy of Natural Sciences of Philadelphia
and
World Land Trust–US

University of Texas Press   AUSTIN

The publication of this book was made possible by a generous contribution from the University of Texas Press Advisory Council.

Printed in China
First edition, 2009

Requests for permission to reproduce material from this work should be sent to:
Permissions
University of Texas Press
P.O. Box 7819
Austin, TX 78713-7819
www.utexas.edu/utpress/about/bpermission.html

♾ The paper used in this book meets the minimum requirements of ANSI/NISO Z39.48-1992 (R1997) (Permanence of Paper).

Library of Congress Cataloging-in-Publication Data

Ridgely, Robert S., 1946–
Field guide to the songbirds of South America : the passerines / Robert S. Ridgely and Guy Tudor. — 1st ed.
     p.   cm. — (Mildred Wyatt-Wold series in ornithology)
Includes bibliographical references and index.
ISBN 978-0-292-71748-0 (cloth : alk. paper) —
ISBN 978-0-292-71979-8 (pbk. : alk. paper)
1. Passeriformes—South America—Identification.
2. Songbirds—South America—Identification.
I. Tudor, Guy, 1934–   II. Title.
QL696.P2R53   2009
598.8098—dc22
                            2008052476

CONTENTS

PREFACE

With the publication of Volume II of *The Birds of South America* in 1994, we were faced with a choice of how best to proceed. The University of Texas Press proposed producing a more compact, single-volume work covering all of South America's passerine birds—a more portable book than the first two volumes, one designed more for use in the field. GT was enthused, but it must be admitted that RSR preferred to move ahead on our planned Volume III of the series, one that would cover families from the pigeons through the woodpeckers. With the appearance of this volume, it will be clear who was the more persuasive.

As seems so often to be the case, the effort took far longer than either of us envisioned. Truth be told, much of the fault for this lies with RSR, for whom the press of other activities has become truly overwhelming during the past decade. In particular, the drive to see *The Birds of Ecuador* through to completion and publication (achieved in 2001) consumed an inordinate amount of his time; in addition, and especially since the late 1990s, his bird conservation activities have become a major priority and responsibility. GT, having long since completed his artistic efforts for this work, had to be patient, while at the same time attempting to keep RSR's feet to the fire.

We hope, now that the book finally is in your hands, that the wait was worth it. We like the completed effort, and—despite the appearance of a number of single-country bird books in recent years—we remain convinced that there still is a role for publications that provide a broader perspective, dealing with the avifaunas of much larger areas. Producing this volume gave us the opportunity to update and revise our treatments where this was required, revisions that reflect the extraordinary amount of new information that has come to light during the last 15+ years. And yes, we do still intend to forge ahead with Volume III. That volume likely will be organized somewhat differently from Volumes I and II, and a new cast of characters may become involved, at least to some extent, but we do still want to do it. All we need is sufficient time and energy. Meanwhile, now it's back to a focus on bird conservation work, at least for RSR, and we hope that you, our readers, will recognize that conservation must come as the highest priority of all.

Acknowledgments

Many organizations and individuals have assisted us during this volume's long preparation. The majority did so as well during the preparation of Volumes I and II of *The Birds of South America*, and we remain grateful for their help. In particular let us single out the following:

Among the organizations, the following stand out as the most important:

The Academy of Natural Sciences of Philadelphia, RSR's institutional home for many years, though he departed it several years ago to pursue his growing interest in international conservation; in particular to Jim and Joli Stewart, and Jim and Jean Macaleer, for their steadfast support over the years.

The American Museum of Natural History in New York City, which GT has used as his source of specimen material for many decades, and which always permitted us unparalleled access to its renowned collection of study skins.

The National Audubon Society, which supported RSR during his initial move into the conservation world, and which, we hope, will continue to increase its presence in the international sphere.

The American Bird Conservancy, RSR's next institutional home; though young, it is now arguably the most effective bird-focused conservation organization in the United States, having made significant progress on numerous important issues, domestic and international, over the past few years.

BirdLife International, the premier international bird conservation organization (formerly the International Council for Bird Preservation), with which RSR has had both formal and informal ties over many years.

World Land Trust–U.S., a small but very successful organization that focuses on private land protection efforts in Middle and South America and with which RSR is now associated as Deputy Director.

The John D. and Catherine T. MacArthur Foundation, which funded RSR's crucial field investigations in Ecuador for over four years in the early 1990s.

World Wildlife Fund—U.S., which provided the initial support that got us started on *The Birds of South America*.

Among the individuals, our gratitude extends to virtually all of those men and women mentioned in the introductions of Volumes I and II of *The Birds of South America*. A few of them have been particularly helpful over the past decade or so, and we would like to single out David J. Agro, the late Paul Coopmans, Paul Greenfield, Steve Howell, Mark Robbins, Francisco Sornoza, Andrew Whittaker, and Kevin Zimmer. The following additional individuals have also been of assistance to us in one way or another during the past decade: Maria Allen, David Ascanio, Eustace Barnes, Juan Mazar Barnett, Louis Bevier, Braulio Carlos, Sally Conyne, Peter English, John Gwynne, A. Bennett Hennessey, Mitch Lysinger, John and the late Ruth Moore, Lelis Navarrete, Ricardo Parrini, Nate Rice, Nigel Simpson, and Barry Walker. A particular note of appreciation is due Terry Clarke for his untiring efforts in overseeing the design and production of this book's map and plate pages. We thank all of you, and RSR wishes to express his particular gratitude to his wonderful wife, Peg, for permitting him to devote so much time to this and other aspects of his work.

Robert S. Ridgely
Guy Tudor
February 2007

Field Guide to the Songbirds of South America

INTRODUCTION

Plan of the Book

It will be evident that this volume on the passerine birds of South America (or songbirds), designed to be a field guide, has been organized entirely differently from Volumes I and II of *The Birds of South America*. Its geographic scope remains the same, with all continental islands being included (e.g., Trinidad and Tobago, Juan Fernández, Fernando do Noronha), but not oceanic archipelagos (e.g., the Galápagos and South Georgia). All of GT's illustrations from the original two books are here, and figures of 406 new species have been inserted in their proper taxonomic sequence (or as close to it as could be managed, within cost restraints). Almost all these figures depict species that were not originally included. A very few show distinctly different plumages of a species already included (usually a different subspecies, sometimes the other sex). The presentation has been completely reorganized, with the original 83 plates expanded to 121. Even with the additional illustrations, a few species still are not pictured, but these gaps are now far fewer than in the original two volumes, mainly involving species closely similar to one that is depicted, species with very limited geographic ranges, and certain boreal migrants. There are full text accounts for a total of 1,981 species. As before, a few species that occur only as vagrants are given even less coverage, only being mentioned under the species they most resemble.

As an example, Plate 1 now incorporates coverage of two furnariid groups, the miners and the horneros. Ten miner species are depicted, two of them newly illustrated species (Grayish and Puna), with only one now left unillustrated (the scarce and range-restricted Creamy-rumped). For the horneros, five species are now depicted, one of them new (Lesser), leaving three of them unillustrated (the Bay and two species recently separated from the similar Pale-legged, Caribbean and Pacific).

Originally we intended to arrange the species accounts on the text pages surrounding the plate on which those species were illustrated, but ultimately this proved a bit too complicated. We thus opted instead to arrange the book in the more or less standard way for bird books of this genre, with all plates clustered together as a unit. Inspired by the arrangement in Rasmussen and Anderton's wonderful *Birds of South Asia: The Ripley Guide,* we opted to place the species distribution maps on the pages opposite the plates, an arrangement that we hope will prove to be convenient for users in the field. Unfortunately, space limitations prevented us from including any text material here.

The number of species in each family is given in parentheses following that family's heading. The species accounts have all information combined into one paragraph. Genera with more than one species are introduced by a brief paragraph that outlines generic characters; where practicable, information is presented here and then not repeated in the species accounts (such as the generalization that all hornero species build mud nests).

Following the bird's length (given in both inches and centimeters), each account begins with a summary of that species' *abundance, habitat, and range;* if the species migrates, this is also noted here. An indication of the species' *elevational preference* follows. Bearing this introductory information in mind is vital; yes, range extensions are still being made, but most are now minor. If your initial identification turns out not to be in the stated range, then odds are that your first determination was in error.

Next, where necessary, comes a summary of *taxonomic or nomenclatural changes* subsequent to that found in *The Birds of South America.* The scientific names of such species are followed by an asterisk (*), and supporting details have been presented in "Notes on Taxonomy and English Names," beginning on page 685. We have attempted to keep abreast of taxonomic changes as they develop and are (usually) published, and to be evenhanded in deciding which forms merit recognition as species and which do not. Debate is ongoing concerning many of these issues, and such debate will certainly continue; there often is no "correct" course. Even less is there agreement on the higher-order relationships of many bird groups, especially at the family level. Much information relating to this topic has appeared in the last few decades, yet many questions remain to be resolved. Much of this work appeared too late to be reflected in this book's organization, but where possible it is referred to. We should expressly note that we have opted to adhere to the decisions on English names and taxonomy that were put forward, after a number of years of deliberation, by the standing committee set up under the auspices of the International Ornithological Congress to make recommendations on a standardized list of names for the world's birds. This list was recently published (Gill and Wright 2006). Although we do not necessarily agree with every decision (e.g., "American Bare-eyed Thrush" and "American Cliff Swallow"), given our personal involvement with this effort (on the Neotropical Committee), it seems only appropriate that we accede to its decisions. In point of fact, apart from a shift in the way some group names are constructed (particularly the elimination of most hyphens, e.g., "Slaty Antshrike" as opposed to "Slaty-Antshrike" and "Seedfinch" as opposed to "Seed-Finch"), the number of changes to English names used in *The Birds of South America* is minimal. One significant difference, however, is the decision to continue to include diacritical marks (accents) in English bird names, where these names reflect a word in the Spanish or Portuguese languages (e.g., Marañón or Várzea).

Plumage descriptions have been reduced to the basics, omitting those points judged minor or less evident. The most important salient points are indicated in *italics*. Males are described first, with, as needed, females and any juvenale plumages described in relation to them. If there is significant geographic variation in plumage, the illustrated subspecies is the one described, with differences in other subspecies noted subsequently. Subspecific names have not been given; rather, the range of that subspecies (or group of subspecies) is indicated in **boldface**. Subspecific names can be found in the two *Birds of South America* volumes. For species in which more than one subspecies has been illustrated, these are denoted by an "A" or a "B" both in the text and on the plate. *Comparisons* with the species most likely to cause confusion follow.

A brief characterization of the species' *general behavior* comes next, together with a transcription of its *voice,* generally just its primary vocalization (or song). Commercially available cassette tapes, CDs, and even DVD-ROMs with recordings of the vocalizations of many species are now available for many areas. Learning to recognize bird voices is hard for most people. Although there is nothing like actually hearing (ideally in the field) a bird's vocalization in order to fix it in one's mind, we still find it worthwhile to transcribe bird voices phonetically, and we hope that our transcriptions will prove helpful.

Last in the species account, where applicable, we indicate *ranges beyond South America.*

As noted above, after much debate we opted not to position our *distribution maps* on the outside margin adjacent to each species account, but rather to place these maps on the pages facing the plates. RSR has spent an inordinate amount of time over the past two decades attempting to keep up with the flood of new information on bird distribution, in a multitude of publications; in addition, he has undertaken extensive travels and research of his own (with, at least some of the time, GT's company). As much of these data as feasible have been incorporated into these maps. We are confident that the maps represent as accurate a generalized interpretation of South American bird ranges as exists. This distribution information (including the specific locality points from which our generalized ranges have been drawn) is now being stored digitally, and we would be remiss not to mention here the invaluable assistance that RSR has received in this endeavor from his "map crew": Maria Allen, David Agro, Terry Clarke, Andrew Couturier (and Bird Studies Canada), Jamie Stewart, and Bruce Young (and NatureServe). Also, it should again be noted that the initial hard-copy paper maps that started this whole process, drawn up some 25 years ago, were assembled by our old friend and colleague, the late William Brown.

An astonishing amount of new information on all aspects of Neotropical ornithology has come to light over the past quarter-century, an explosion of knowledge that no one could have anticipated. If anything, it is now accelerating with the proliferation of Web sites, "gray literature" bird lists, etc. Though at times it has seemed almost overwhelming, we have included as much of this new information as was practicable within the confines of our rather rigid format and the limited amount of space available. Where the information here differs from that presented in *The Birds of South America,* it should be assumed that what is given here is more up-to-date and correct.

Over the course of the past nearly 40 years (!), RSR has had the good fortune to have encountered the vast majority of Neotropical birds. This experience, usually long-term and repeated, forms the backbone of this work (though some species remain elusive). GT's exposure to South America's birds has, unfortunately, been much less sustained, but his ability nonetheless to capture a bird's essence in his artwork remains a widely recognized marvel. Photographs and study skins are of course essential, but it is GT's genius that he has been able to portray our birds as accurately as he has. We both have benefited from information provided by numerous other individuals who share our passion for Neotropical birds, and we will always be grateful to them. We should expressly state that if a point of information presented here is not derived from our own experience, the individual responsible is credited at the appropriate point. We hope and presume that what we present is correct, but of course we take responsibility for any errors should it not be. Please let us know!

The cutoff date for new information to be incorporated into this volume was late 2006.

Conservation

In part because bird conservation efforts have become such a major part of RSR's life during the past decade, we would be remiss not to include at least a brief personal assessment of where bird conservation efforts in South America stand at present and what we hope to achieve in the next few decades.

First, the last few decades have seen a quantum leap in the quantity and the quality of information available on a multitude of bird conservation issues. Most notably these involve efforts to determine more accurately the status of species considered to be at risk, information that has been amassed by the ever-growing numbers of talented field observers and summarized by the staff of what is now called BirdLife International in a series of useful publications, in particular Collar et al. 1992 and BirdLife International 2000. These two publications present accurate and up-to-date summaries of the species at greatest risk of extinction: where their remnant populations persist, what factors have caused their decline, and what steps can be taken to ensure their survival and (one hopes) to increase their population size. Some of this information has been employed in what has turned out to be the very useful process of identifying, on a country-by-country basis, areas of maximum importance to birds, sites that are now universally called Important Bird Areas (usually simply IBAs). Such areas have been selected for a variety of reasons, employing standardized criteria including their importance for rare species, for long-distance migrants, and so on. Although the designation in and of itself confers no actual protection status, it can and should lead to increased awareness (individual, organizational, and governmental) of the importance of these sites to birds, thereby lessening the likelihood that they will be altered and their importance compromised. Focusing on the most critically endangered species of all (not only birds, but other taxa as well), in 2002 an international consortium of conservation groups began to coalesce, under the banner of the

Alliance for Zero Extinction, to focus attention on species found wholly or predominantly at single sites. This effort to halt extinction, although perhaps literally unachievable, has begun to acquire some momentum, and our hope is that it continue to do so.

Given the existence now of such detailed information on the status of birds, there is no longer any real excuse for not doing something about the dire straits so many species are in. Nothing is stopping us, except apathy and the discouraging sense, all too common in the developed world, that the situation is hopeless (especially in the tropics), that no effective actions can be taken to stem the extinction tide threatening to overwhelm our wonderful blue and green globe. Happily, developments demonstrating that this premise of hopelessness is false have begun to take form and gather in strength. It is especially encouraging that much of the impetus now is coming from Latin Americans themselves, a possibility that could not have been dreamed of a few decades ago. Also encouraging is that private organizations are playing an important role in this effort; organizations and individuals now seem less willing to sit back complacently and wait for some government or international entity to deal with the extinction crisis and other problems that are bearing down.

In South America, private groups such as ProAves Colombia in Colombia, Fundación Jocotoco in Ecuador, ECOAN in Peru, Armonia in Bolivia, Guyra Paraguay in Paraguay, AvesArgentinas in Argentina, SaveBrasil and Biodiversitas in Brazil, and numerous others have sprung up and are gradually strengthening. Though their institutional strategies may differ, all are beginning to achieve significant conservation success in their respective countries. BirdLife International is associated with many of these groups and is playing a key role in the coordination of their activities by hosting regional conferences and by supporting publications. In recent years the Neotropical Bird Club has come to play a role as well, not only by publishing the journal *Cotinga* but also increasingly by supporting direct conservation efforts.

We applaud and delight in these efforts. They give one hope, especially now that our own country, the United States, seems so totally to have abdicated its former leadership role in environmental matters both domestic and global. But we must emphasize that what all the private groups mentioned above (and many others besides) need most are the financial resources to do what they now know needs to be done. Such groups universally operate on a shoestring, typically in an environment in which charitable giving is not the social norm. We thus encourage all our readers, especially readers in the so-called First World, where such giving tends to be much more frequent, to support one or more of these organizations directly, through donations either financial or in-kind. These groups are accomplishing a lot already, and with additional resources, they could do so much more. In particular, if you care enough about South American birds to travel a long way to see them and to pay a considerable sum to do so, *it is also your responsibility to contribute toward the efforts being made to protect them.* Please do so.

HOW TO USE THE RANGE MAPS

Unlike some recent guides which utilize *map colors* to show *seasonal* status, our map colors here are simply a coding device for depicting more than one species per map. See the legends below.

In some cases, there were *too many* species for just one map page. These are "carried over" to a following full *map spread*, to face the *beginning* of the *next* plate. Note red arrows at (➤) bottom.

Maps of South America and all countries will be found on the *last three* pages of the color plates section.

Normally the range of only one bird species is shown per map. Its distribution is depicted in **green**.

Arrows are used to help indicate smaller isolated areas of distribution.

6 Plain Antvireo
Dysithamnus mentalis
p.338

If the species occurs as an austral migrant, that area is depicted in a **paler green**.

Vagrant localities are shown by **black dots**.

4 Southern Martin
Progne elegans
p.521

In some cases it became necessary to show the distribution of two species on one map. The distribution of the second species, usually smaller, is shown in **violet blue** – this unless the range of the second species is so small that we judged it necessary to be in **red**.

9 Musician Wren
Cyphorhinus arada
p.535
10 ● Song Wren
C. phaeocephalus
p.535

In a few cases it was necessary to show three species on one map. In these cases the third is shown in **red**, the second is shown in **violet blue** and the primary is shown in **green**.

15 Rufous-capped Spinetail
Synallaxis ruficapilla p.276
● Bahia Spinetail
S. whitneyi p.276
● Pinto's Spinetail
S. infuscata p.277

Very limited distributions are frequently shown in **red**, even when there is only one species per map.

8 ● Yellow-green Bush Tanager
Chlorospingus flavovirens
p.602

The ranges of boreal migrant species are always shown in **pale blue**.

Vagrant localities are again shown by **black dots**.

13 Blackpoll Warbler
Dendroica striata
p.565

PLATE 1   MINERS & HORNEROS

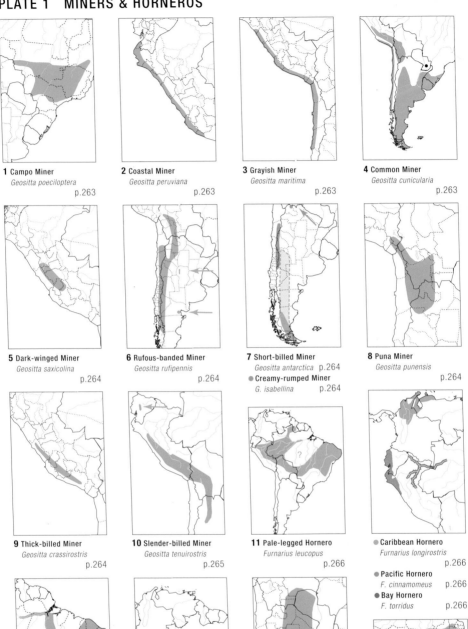

1 Campo Miner
Geosinta poeciloptera
p.263

2 Coastal Miner
Geositta peruviana
p.263

3 Grayish Miner
Geositta maritima
p.263

4 Common Miner
Geositta cunicularia
p.263

5 Dark-winged Miner
Geositta saxicolina
p.264

6 Rufous-banded Miner
Geositta rufipennis
p.264

7 Short-billed Miner
Geositta antarctica p.264
● Creamy-rumped Miner
G. isabellina   p.264

8 Puna Miner
Geositta punensis
p.264

9 Thick-billed Miner
Geositta crassirostris
p.264

10 Slender-billed Miner
Geositta tenuirostris
p.265

11 Pale-legged Hornero
Furnarius leucopus
p.266

● Caribbean Hornero
Furnarius longirostris
p.266

● Pacific Hornero
F. cinnamomeus   p.266
● Bay Hornero
F. torridus   p.266

12 Band-tailed Hornero
Furnarius figulus
p.267

13 Lesser Hornero
Furnarius minor
p.267

14 Crested Hornero
Furnarius cristatus
p.267

15 Rufous Hornero
Furnarius rufus
p.267

1

PLATE 2 EARTHCREEPERS, CACHOLOTES, etc.

1 Scale-throated Earthcreeper
Upucerthia dumetaria
p.267

2 Plain-breasted Earthcreeper
Upucerthia jelskii
p.268

White-throated Earthcreeper
Upucerthia albigula
p.268

3 Buff-breasted Earthcreeper
Upucerthia validirostris
p.268

4 Striated Earthcreeper
Upucerthia serrana
p.268

5 Rock Earthcreeper
Upucerthia andaecola
p.268

6 Straight-billed Earthcreeper
Upucerthia ruficaudus
p.268

7 Chaco Earthcreeper
Upucerthia certhioides
p.269

Bolivian Earthcreeper
Upucerthia harterti
p.269

8 Band-tailed Eremobius
Eremobius phoenicurus
p.269

9 Crag Chilia
Chilia melanura
p.269

10 Gray-crested Cacholote
Pseudoseisura unirufa
p.270

Caatinga Cacholote
Pseudoseisura cristata
p.270

11 Brown Cacholote
Pseudoseisura lophotes
p.270

12 White-throated Cacholote
Pseudoseisura gutturalis
p.270

PLATE 3   CINCLODES

1 Blackish Cinclodes
Cinclodes antarcticus
p.270

2 Dark-bellied Cinclodes
Cinclodes patagonicus
p.271

3 Chilean Seaside Cinclodes
Cinclodes nigrofumosus
p.271

4 Peruvian Seaside Cinclodes
Cinclodes taczanowskii
p.271

5 Gray-flanked Cinclodes
Cinclodes oustaleti
p.271

Olrog's Cinclodes
Cinclodes olrogi
p.271

6 Bar-winged Cinclodes
Cinclodes fuscus
p.271

7 Stout-billed Cinclodes
Cinclodes excelsior
p.272

● Royal Cinclodes
Cinclodes aricomae
p.272

8 Córdoba Cinclodes
Cinclodes comechingonus
p.272

9 Long-tailed Cinclodes
Cinclodes pabsti
p.272

10 White-winged Cinclodes
Cinclodes atacamensis
p.272

11 White-bellied Cinclodes
Cinclodes palliatus
p.273

3

PLATE 4 *Synallaxis* SPINETAILS, etc.

1 Great Spinetail
Siptornopsis hypochondriaca
p.273

2 White-browed Spinetail
Hellmayrea gularis
p.273

3 Necklaced Spinetail
Synallaxis stictothorax
p.274

● Chinchipe Spinetail
S. chinchipensis p.274

4 Rufous Spinetail
Synallaxis unirufa p.274
5 ● Black-throated Spinetail
S. castanea p.274
6 ● Rusty-headed Spinetail
S. fuscorufa p.274

7 Russet-bellied Spinetail
Synallaxis zimmeri p.274
8 ● Apurímac Spinetail
S. courseni p.275

Silvery-throated Spinetail
Synallaxis subpudica
p.275

9 Azara's Spinetail
Synallaxis azarae
p.275

10 Pale-breasted Spinetail
Synallaxis albescens
p.275

11 Spix's Spinetail
Synallaxis spixi
p.275

12 Sooty-fronted Spinetail
Synallaxis frontalis
p.275

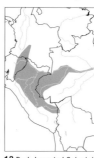

13 Dark-breasted Spinetail
Synallaxis albigularis
p.276

Slaty Spinetail
Synallaxis brachyura
p.276

14 Cinereous-breasted Spinetail
Synallaxis hypospodia
p.276

15 Rufous-capped Spinetail
Synallaxis ruficapilla p.276
● Bahia Spinetail
S. whitneyi p.276
● Pinto's Spinetail
S. infuscata p.277

16 Cabanis's Spinetail
Synallaxis cabanisi p.277
17 ● Dusky Spinetail
S. moesta p.277

McConnell's Spinetail
Synallaxis macconnelli
p.277

PLATE 5   SPINETAILS, RUSHBIRD, REEDHAUNTERS, etc.

1 Plain-crowned Spinetail
Synallaxis gujanensis
           p.277
● Marañón Spinetail
S. maranonica   p.277

2 White-lored Spinetail
Synallaxis albilora
           p.278
● Araguaia Spinetail
S. simoni   p.278

3 Gray-bellied Spinetail
Synallaxis cinerascens
           p.278

4 White-bellied Spinetail
Synallaxis propinqua
           p.278

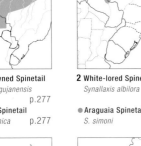

5 Stripe-breasted Spinetail
Synallaxis cinnamomea
           p.278

6 Blackish-headed Spinetail
Synallaxis tithys
           p.278

7 Ruddy Spinetail
Synallaxis rutilans
           p.279

8 Chestnut-throated Spinetail
Synallaxis cherriei
           p.279

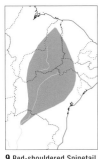

9 Red-shouldered Spinetail
Gyalophylax hellmayri
           p.279

10 Chotoy Spinetail
Schoeniophylax phryganophilus
           p.279

11 Wren-like Rushbird
Phleocryptes melanops
           p.280

12 Bay-capped Wren-Spinetail
Spartonoica maluroides
           p.280

13 Curve-billed Reedhaunter
Limnornis curvirostris
           p.280

14 Straight-billed Reedhaunter
Limnoctites rectirostris
           p.280

15 Ochre-cheeked Spinetail
Synallaxis scutata
           p.281

16 White-whiskered Spinetail
Synallaxis candei p.281
17 ● Hoary-throated Spinetail
S. kollari   p.281

PLATE 6 *Cranioleuca* SPINETAILS, etc.

1 Pink-legged Graveteiro
Acrobatornis fonsecai
p.281

2 Creamy-crested Spinetail
Cranioleuca albicapilla
p.281

3 Light-crowned Spinetail
Cranioleuca albiceps
p.282
4 ● Marcapata Spinetail
C. marcapatae p.282

5 Red-faced Spinetail
Cranioleuca erythrops
p.282
● Streak-capped Spinetail
C. hellmayri p.282

6 Crested Spinetail
Cranioleuca subcristata
p.282
7 ● Tepui Spinetail
C. demissa p.282

8 Ash-browed Spinetail
Cranioleuca curtata
p.283

9 Baron's Spinetail
Cranioleuca baroni
p.283
10 ● Line-cheeked Spinetail
C. antisiensis p.283

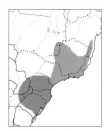

11 Pallid Spinetail
Cranioleuca pallida
p.283
12 ● Olive Spinetail
C. obsoleta p.283

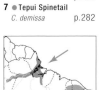

13 Gray-headed Spinetail
Cranioleuca semicinerea
p.283
14 ● Scaled Spinetail
C. muelleri p.284

15 Speckled Spinetail
Cranioleuca gutturata
p.284

16 Sulphur-bearded Spinetail
Cranioleuca sulphurifera
p.284

17 Stripe-crowned Spinetail
Cranioleuca pyrrhophia
p.284
● Inquisivi Spinetail
C. henricae p.284

18 Rusty-backed Spinetail
Cranioleuca vulpina
p.284

Parker's Spinetail
Cranioleuca vulpecula
p.285

19 Yellow-chinned Spinetail
Certhiaxis cinnamomeus
p.285

20 Red-and-white Spinetail
Certhiaxis mustelinus
p.285

PLATE 7   TIT-SPINETAILS, THISTLETAILS, etc.

1 Thorn-tailed Rayadito
Aphrastura spinicauda
p.285
● Masafuera Rayadito
A. masafuerae   p.286

2 Des Murs's Wiretail
Sylviorthorhynchus desmursii
p.286

3 Andean Tit-Spinetail
Leptasthenura andicola
p.286

4 Rusty-crowned Tit-Spinetail
Leptasthenura pileata
p.286
● White-browed Tit-Spinetail
L. xenothorax   p.287

5 Streak-backed Tit-Spinetail
Leptasthenura striata
p.287

6 Plain-mantled Tit-Spinetail
Leptasthenura aegithaloides
p.287

7 Tufted Tit-Spinetail
Leptasthenura platensis
p.287

8 Brown-capped Tit-Spinetail
Leptasthenura fuliginiceps
p.287

9 Tawny Tit-Spinetail
Leptasthenura yanacensis
p.287

10 Araucaria Tit-Spinetail
Leptasthenura setaria
p.288

11 Striolated Tit-Spinetail
Leptasthenura striolata
p.288

12 Ochre-browed Thistletail
Schizoeaca coryi
p.288
● Perijá Thistletail
S. perijana   p.288

13 White-chinned Thistletail
Schizoeaca fuliginosa
p.288

14 Mouse-colored Thistletail
Schizoeaca griseomurina
p.289
15 ● Eye-ringed Thistletail
S. palpebralis   p.289

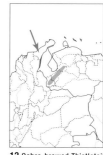

16 Vilcabamba Thistletail
Schizoeaca vilcabambae
p.289
● Puna Thistletail
S. helleri   p.289

17 Black-throated Thistletail
Schizoeaca harterti
p.289

7

PLATE 8 CANASTEROS, etc.

1 Itatiaia Spinetail
Oreophylax moreirae
p.289

● Cipó Canastero
Asthenes luizae   p.290

2 Rusty-vented Canastero
Asthenes dorbignyi
p.290

● Pale-tailed Canastero
A. huancavelicae   p.290

3 Dark-winged Canastero
Asthenes arequipae
p.290

● Berlepsch's Canastero
A. berlepschi   p.290

4 Steinbach's Canastero
* *Asthenes steinbachi*
p.291

5 Short-billed Canastero
Asthenes baeri
p.291

6 Sharp-billed Canastero
Asthenes pyrrholeuca
p.291

7 Patagonian Canastero
Asthenes patagonica
p.291

8 ● Dusky-tailed Canastero
A. humicola   p.291

9 Cordilleran Canastero
Asthenes modesta
p.292

10 Streak-throated Canastero
Asthenes humilis
p.292

11 ● Cactus Canastero
A. cactorum   p.292

12 Canyon Canastero
Asthenes pudibunda p.292

13 ● Rusty-fronted Canastero
A. ottonis   p.292

● Maquis Canastero
A. heterura   p.293

14 Streak-backed Canastero
Asthenes wyatti
p.293

Puna Canastero
Asthenes sclateri
p.293

15 Hudson's Canastero
Asthenes hudsoni
p.293

16 ● Austral Canastero
A. anthoides   p.293

17 Scribble-tailed Canastero
Asthenes maculicauda
p.294

18 Many-striped Canastero
Asthenes flammulata
p.294

19 Line-fronted Canastero
Asthenes urubambensis
p.294

● Junín Canastero
A. virgata   p.294

PLATE 9   SOFTTAILS, THORNBIRDS & ALLIES

1 ● Orinoco Softtail
Thripophaga cherriei
p.294

2 Striated Softtail
Thripophaga macroura
p.295

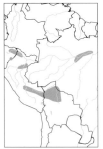

3 Plain Softtail
Thripophaga fusciceps
p.295

Russet-mantled Softtail
Thripophaga berlepschi
p.295

4 Streak-fronted Thornbird
Phacellodomus striaticeps
p.295

5 Rufous-fronted Thornbird
Phacellodomus rufifrons p.295
● Plain Thornbird
P. inornatus   p.296

6 Little Thornbird
Phacellodomus sibilatrix
p.296

7 Greater Thornbird
Phacellodomus ruber
p.296

8 Freckle-breasted Thornbird
Phacellodomus striaticollis
p.296

9 Spot-breasted Thornbird
Phacellodomus maculipectus
p.297

10 Chestnut-backed Thornbird
Phacellodomus dorsalis
p.297

11 Orange-eyed Thornbird
Phacellodomus erythrophthalmus
p.297

12 Red-eyed Thornbird
Phacellodomus ferrugineigula
p.297

13 Canebrake Groundcreeper
Clibanornis dendrocolaptoides
p.297

14 Lark-like Brushrunner
Coryphistera alaudina
p.297

15 Firewood-gatherer
Anumbius annumbi
p.298

PLATE 10   SMALL ARBOREAL FURNARIIDS

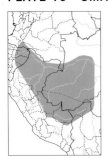

1 Orange-fronted Plushcrown
Metopothrix aurantiaca
p.298

2 Double-banded Graytail
Xenerpestes minlosi   p.298
3 ● Equatorial Graytail
X. singularis   p.298

4 Spectacled Prickletail
Siptornis striaticollis   p.299
5 ● Star-chested Treerunner
Margarornis stellatus   p.299

6 Pearled Treerunner
Margarornis squamiger
p.299

7 Rusty-winged Barbtail
Premnornis guttuligera
p.299

8 Spotted Barbtail
Premnoplex brunnescens p.299
● White-throated Barbtail
P. tatei   p.300

9 Roraiman Barbtail
Roraimia adusta   p.300
10 ● Great Xenops
Megaxenops parnaguae p.300

11 White-throated Treerunner
Pygarrhichas albogularis
p.300

12 Rufous-tailed Xenops
Xenops milleri
p.300

13 Streaked Xenops
Xenops rutilans
p.301

Slender-billed Xenops
Xenops tenuirostris
p.301

14 Plain Xenops
Xenops minutus
p.301

15 Sharp-billed Treehunter
Heliobletus contaminatus
p.301

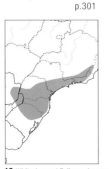

16 White-browed Foliage-gleaner
Anabacerthia amaurotis
p.302

17 Montane Foliage-gleaner
Anabacerthia striaticollis
p.302

Scaly-throated Foliage-gleaner
Anabacerthia variegaticeps
p.302

10

PLATE 11 TREEHUNTERS & *Syndactyla* FOLIAGE-GLEANERS

1 Streaked Tuftedcheek
Pseudocolaptes boissonneautii
p.302

2 Pacific Tuftedcheek
Pseudocolaptes johnsoni
p.303

3 Flammulated Treehunter
Thripadectes flammulatus
p.303

Peruvian Treehunter
Thripadectes scrutator
p.303

4 Striped Treehunter
Thripadectes holostictus
p.303

5 Black-billed Treehunter
Thripadectes melanorhynchus
p.303

6 Streak-capped Treehunter
Thripadectes virgaticeps
p.304

7 Uniform Treehunter
Thripadectes ignobilis
p.304

8 Lineated Foliage-gleaner
Syndactyla subalaris
p.304

9 Guttulated Foliage-gleaner
Syndactyla guttulata
p.304

10 Buff-browed Foliage-gleaner
Syndactyla rufosuperciliata
p.305

11 Rufous-necked Foliage-gleaner
Syndactyla ruficollis
p.305

12 Pale-browed Treehunter
Cichlocolaptes leucophrus
p.305

PLATE 12 *Philydor* FOLIAGE-GLEANERS & ALLIES

1 Peruvian Recurvebill
Simoxenops ucayalae
p.305

Bolivian Recurvebill
Simoxenops striatus
p.305

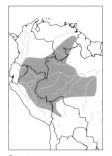

2 Eastern Woodhaunter
Hyloctistes subulatus
p.306

Western Woodhaunter
Hyloctistes virgatus
p.306

3 Chestnut-winged Hookbill
Ancistrops strigilatus
p.306

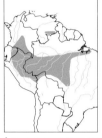

4 Chestnut-winged Foliage-gleaner
Philydor erythropterum
p.306

5 Buff-fronted Foliage-gleaner
Philydor rufum
p.307

6 Ochre-breasted Foliage-gleaner
Philydor lichtensteini
p.307

7 Rufous-rumped Foliage-gleaner
Philydor erythrocercum
p.307

8 Rufous-tailed Foliage-gleaner
Philydor ruficaudatum
p.307

9 Planalto Foliage-gleaner
Syndactyla dimidiata
p.308

10 Cinnamon-rumped Foliage-gleaner
Philydor pyrrhodes
p.308

Slaty-winged Foliage-gleaner
Philydor fuscipenne
p.308

11 Black-capped Foliage-gleaner
Philydor atricapillus
p.308

● Alagoas Foliage-gleaner
Philydor novaesi
p.308

PLATE 13 *Automolus* FOLIAGE-GLEANERS & ALLIES

1 Chestnut-crowned Foliage-
gleaner
Automolus rufipileatus
p.308

2 Olive-backed Foliage-
gleaner
Automolus infuscatus
p.309

Pará Foliage-gleaner
Automolus paraensis
p.309

3 White-eyed Foliage-gleaner
Automolus leucophthalmus
p.309

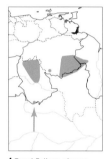

4 Tepui Foliage-gleaner
Automolus roraimae
p.309

5 Buff-throated Foliage-gleaner
Automolus ochrolaemus
p.309

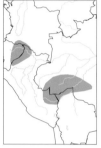

6 Brown-rumped Foliage-gleaner
Automolus melanopezus
p.310

7 Ruddy Foliage-gleaner
Automolus rubiginosus
p.310

8 Henna-hooded Foliage-gleaner
Hylocryptus erythrocephalus
p.310

9 Henna-capped Foliage-gleaner
Hylocryptus rectirostris
p.310

PLATE 14 *Anabazenops* FOLIAGE-GLEANERS, LEAFTOSSERS, etc.

1 White-collared Foliage-gleaner
Anabazenops fuscus
p.311

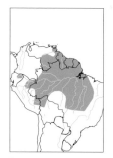

2 Bamboo Foliage-gleaner
Anabazenops dorsalis
p.311

3 Point-tailed Palmcreeper
Berlepschia rikeri
p.311

4 Rufous-breasted Leaftosser
Scelerurus scansor
p.312

5 Tawny-throated Leaftosser
Sclerurus mexicanus
p.312

6 Scaly-throated Leaftosser
Sclerurus guatemalensis
p.312

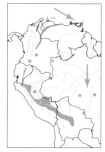

7 Gray-throated Leaftosser
Sclerurus albigularis
p.312

8 Short-billed Leaftosser
Sclerurus rufigularis
p.313

9 Black-tailed Leaftosser
Sclerurus caudacutus
p.313

10 Sharp-tailed Streamcreeper
Lochmias nematura
p.313

14

PLATE 15 *Dendrocincla* WOODCREEPERS, etc.

1 Tyrannine Woodcreeper
Dendrocincla tyrannina
p.314

2 Plain-brown Woodcreeper
Dendrocincla fuliginosa
p.314

3 Plain-winged Woodcreeper
Dendrocincla turdina
p.314

4 Ruddy Woodcreeper
Dendrocincla homochroa
p.315

3 White-chinned Woodcreeper
Dendrocincla merula
p.315

4 Long-tailed Woodcreeper
Deconychura longicauda
p.315

5 Spot-throated Woodcreeper
Deconychura stictolaema
p.315

6 Wedge-billed Woodcreeper
Glyphorynchus spirurus
p.316

7 Olivaceous Woodcreeper
Sittasomus griseicapillus
p.316

8 Long-billed Woodcreeper
Nasica longirostris
p.316

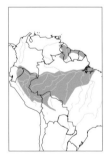

9 Cinnamon-throated Woodcreeper
Dendrexetastes rufigula
p.316

PLATE 16 *Xiphorhynchus* WOODCREEPERS, etc.

1 Straight-billed Woodcreeper
Xiphorhynchus picus
p.317

Zimmer's Woodcreeper
Xiphorhynchus kienerii
p.317

2 Striped Woodcreeper
Xiphorhynchus obsoletus
p.317

3 Ocellated Woodcreeper
Xiphorhynchus ocellatus
p.317

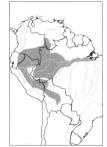

4 Elegant Woodcreeper
Xiphorhynchus elegans
p.318
● Spix's Woodcreeper
X. spixii p.318

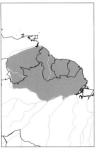

5 Chestnut-rumped Woodcreeper
Xiphorhynchus pardalotus
p.318

6 Buff-throated Woodcreeper
Xiphorhynchus guttatus
p.318
● Cocoa Woodcreeper
X. susurrans p.319

7 Olive-backed Woodcreeper
Xiphorhynchus triangularis
p.319

8 Spotted Woodcreeper
Xiphorhynchus erythropygius
p.319

9 Black-striped Woodcreeper
Xiphorhynchus lachrymosus
p.319

10 Lesser Woodcreeper
Xiphorhynchus fuscus
p.320

11 Lineated Woodcreeper
Lepidocolaptes albolineatus
p.320

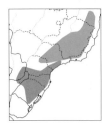

12 Scaled Woodcreeper
Lepidocolaptes squamatus
p.320
● Scalloped Woodcreeper
L. falcinellus
p.320

13 Montane Woodcreeper
Lepidocolaptes lacrymiger
p.321

14 Streak-headed Woodcreeper
Lepidocolaptes souleyetii
p.321

15 Narrow-billed Woodcreeper
Lepidocolaptes angustirostris
p.321

PLATE 17   LARGE WOODCREEPERS

1 Bar-bellied Woodcreeper
Hylexetastes stresemanni
p.321

2 Uniform Woodcreeper
Hylexetastes uniformis
p.322

3 Red-billed Woodcreeper
Hylexetastes perrotii
p.322

4 Hoffmann's Woodcreeper
Dendrocolaptes hoffmannsi
p.322

5 Amazonian Barred
Woodcreeper
Dendrocolaptes certhia
p.322

Northern Barred
Woodcreeper
Dendrocolaptes sanctithomae
p.322

6 Black-banded Woodcreeper
Dendrocolaptes picumnus
p.323

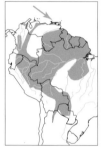

7 Planalto Woodcreeper
Dendrocolaptes platyrostris
p.323

8 White-throated
Woodcreeper
Xiphocolaptes albicollis
p.323

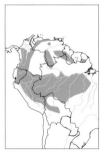

9 Strong-billed Woodcreeper
*Xiphocolaptes
promeropirhynchus*
p.323

10 Moustached Woodcreeper
Xiphocolaptes falcirostris
p.324

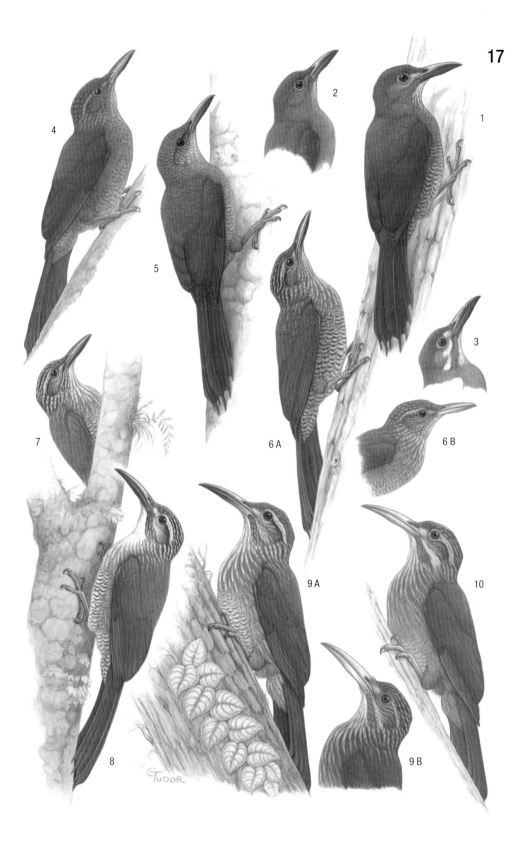

17

PLATE 18 LARGE WOODCREEPERS & SCYTHEBILLS

1 Great Rufous Woodcreeper
Xiphocolaptes major
                    p.324

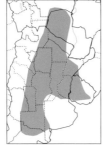

2 Scimitar-billed Woodcreeper
Drymornis bridgesii
                    p.324

3 Greater Scythebill
Campylorhamphus pucherani
                    p.325

4 Brown-billed Scythebill
Campylorhamphus pusillus
                    p.325

5 Curve-billed Scythebill
Campylorhamphus procurvoides
                    p.325

6 Red-billed Scythebill
Campylorhamphus trochilirostris
                    p.325

7 Black-billed Scythebill
Campylorhamphus falcularius
                    p.326

18

PLATE 19   "FASCIATED" & "GREAT" ANTSHRIKES

1 Fasciated Antshrike
Cymbilaimus lineatus
p.327

Bamboo Antshrike
Cymbilaimus sanctaemariae
p.327

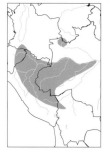

2 Undulated Antshrike
Frederickena unduligera
p.327

3 Black-throated Antshrike
Frederickena viridis
p.328

4 Tufted Antshrike
Mackenziaena severa
p.328

5 Large-tailed Antshrike
Mackenziaena leachii
p.328

6 Spot-backed Antshrike
Hypoedaleus guttatus
p.328

7 Great Antshrike
Taraba major
p.329

8 Giant Antshrike
Batara cinerea
p.329

1 ♀

♂

2 Imm. ♂

3 ♂

♂

4 ♀

6 ♂

5 ♂

7 ♂

8 A ♂

8 B ♀

GUDOR

PLATE 20   *Sakesphorus* & OTHER ANTSHRIKES

1 Black-throated Antshrike
Frederickena viridis
p.328

2 Great Antshrike
Taraba major
p.329

3 White-bearded Antshrike
Biatas nigropectus
p.329

4 Black-crested Antshrike
Sakesphorus canadensis
p.329

5 Collared Antshrike
Sakesphorus bernardi
p.330

6 Silvery-cheeked Antshrike
Sakesphorus cristatus
p.330

7 Black-backed Antshrike
Sakesphorus melanonotus
p.330

8 Band-tailed Antshrike
Sakesphorus melanothorax
p.330

9 Glossy Antshrike
Sakesphorus luctuosus
p.330

10 ● Speckled Antshrike
Xenornis setifrons
p.331

PLATE 21 *Thamnophilus* ANTSHRIKES

1 Blackish-gray Antshrike
Thamnophilus nigrocinereus
p.331

2 Castelnau's Antshrike
Thamnophilus cryptoleucus
p.331

3 Black Antshrike
Thamnophilus nigriceps
p.331

4 Cocha Antshrike
Thamnophilus praecox
p.332

5 White-shouldered Antshrike
Thamnophilus aethiops
p.332

6 Barred Antshrike
Thamnophilus doliatus
p.332

Chapman's Antshrike
Thamnophilus zarumae
p.332

7 Bar-crested Antshrike
Thamnophilus multistriatus
p.333

8 Rufous-winged Antshrike
Thamnophilus torquatus
p.333

9 Lined Antshrike
Thamnophilus tenuepunctatus
p.333

10 Chestnut-backed Antshrike
Thamnophilus palliatus
p.333

11 Rufous-capped Antshrike
Thamnophilus ruficapillus
p.333

1A ♀
1B ♀
1A ♂
2 ♂
3 ♀
4 ♀
4 ♂
5A ♀
5A ♂
5B ♂

8 ♂
6 ♀
7 ♂
9 ♂
9 ♀
10 ♂
11 C ♀
11 A ♂
11 B ♂

TUDOR

PLATE 22 *Thamnophilus* & OTHER ANTSHRIKES

1 Uniform Antshrike
Thamnophilus unicolor
p.334

2 Upland Antshrike
Thamnophilus aroyae
p.334

3 Plain-winged Antshrike
Thamnophilus schistaceus
p.334

4 Mouse-colored Antshrike
Thamnophilus murinus
p.334

5 Eastern Slaty Antshrike
Thamnophilus punctatus
p.334

Western Slaty Antshrike
Thamnophilus atrinucha
p.335

Natterer's Slaty Antshrike
Thamnophilus stictocephalus
p.335

Bolivian Slaty Antshrike
Thamnophilus sticturus
p.335

Planalto Slaty Antshrike
Thamnophilus pelzelni
p.335

Sooretama Slaty Antshrike
Thamnophilus ambiguus
p.335

6 Amazonian Antshrike
Thamnophilus amazonicus
p.335

● Acre Antshrike
Thamnophilus divisorius
p.336

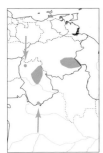

7 Streak-backed Antshrike
Thamnophilus insignis
p.336

8 Variable Antshrike
Thamnophilus caerulescens
p.336

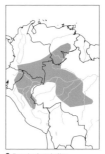

9 Pearly Antshrike
Megastictus margaritatus
p.336

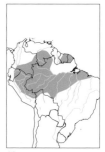

10 Spot-winged Antshrike
Pygiptila stellaris
p.336

22

PLATE 23 *Thamnomanes* ANTSHRIKES, ANTVIREOS, etc.

1 Dusky-throated Antshrike
Thamnomanes ardesiacus
p.337

2 Saturnine Antshrike
Thamnomanes saturninus
p.337

3 Bluish-slate Antshrike
Thamnomanes schistogynus
p.337

4 Cinereous Antshrike
Thamnomanes caesius
p.337

5 Russet Antshrike
Thamnistes anabatinus
p.338

6 Plain Antvireo
Dysithamnus mentalis
p.338

7 Spot-breasted Antvireo
Dysithamnus stictothorax
p.338

8 White-streaked Antvireo
Dysithamnus leucostictus
p.339

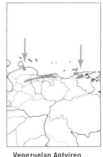

Venezuelan Antvireo
Dysithamnus tucuyensis
p.339

9 Plumbeous Antvireo
Dysithamnus plumbeus
p.339

10 Rufous-backed Antvireo
Dysithamnus xanthopterus
p.339

11 Spot-crowned Antvireo
Dysithamnus puncticeps
p.339

12 Bicolored Antvireo
Dysithamnus occidentalis
p.339

PLATE 24 *Myrmotherula* ANTWRENS I

1 Pygmy Antwren
Myrmotherula brachyura
p.340

2 Moustached Antwren
Myrmotherula ignota
p.340

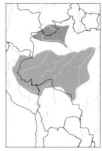

3 Sclater's Antwren
Myrmotherula sclateri
p.340
● Yellow-throated Antwren
M. ambigua
p.340

4 Amazonian Streaked Antwren
Myrmotherula multostriata
p.341

5 Guianan Streaked Antwren
Myrmotherula surinamensis
p.341
● Pacific Antwren
M. pacifica
p.341

6 Cherrie's Antwren
Myrmotherula cherriei
p.341

Klages's Antwren
Myrmotherula klagesi
p.341

7 Stripe-chested Antwren
Myrmotherula longicauda
p.342

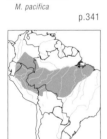

8 Plain-throated Antwren
Myrmotherula hauxwelli
p.342

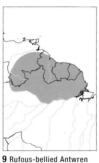

9 Rufous-bellied Antwren
Myrmotherula guttata
p.342

10 Star-throated Antwren
Myrmotherula gularis
p.342

11 Checker-throated Antwren
Myrmotherula fulviventris
p.342

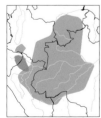

12 Stipple-throated Antwren
Myrmotherula haematonota
p.343
 Yasuní Antwren
M. fjeldsaai
p.343

13 Foothill Antwren
Myrmotherula spodionota
p.343

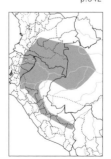

14 Rufous-tailed Antwren
Myrmotherula erythura
p.343

15 White-eyed Antwren
Myrmotherula leucophthalma
p.343
16 ● Brown-bellied Antwren
M. gutturalis
p.344

PLATE 25 *Myrmotherula* ANTWRENS II

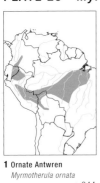

1 Ornate Antwren
Myrmotherula ornata
p.344

2 Slaty Antwren
Myrmotherula schisticolor
p.344

3 Río Suno Antwren
Myrmotherula sunensis
p.344

4 White-flanked Antwren
Myrmotherula axillaris
p.345

5 Silvery-flanked Antwren
Myrmotherula luctuosa
p.345

6 Salvadori's Antwren
Myrmotherula minor
p.345

7 Band-tailed Antwren
Myrmotherula urosticta
p.345

8 Long-winged Antwren
Myrmotherula longipennis
p.345

9 Ihering's Antwren
Myrmotherula iheringi
p.346

● Rio de Janeiro Antwren
Myrmotherula fluminensis
p.346

10 Gray Antwren
Myrmotherula menetriesii
p.346

11 Leaden Antwren
Myrmotherula assimilis
p.346

12 Unicolored Antwren
Myrmotherula unicolor
p.346

● Alagoas Antwren
Myrmotherula snowi
p.347

13 Yungas Antwren
Myrmotherula grisea
p.347

14 Plain-winged Antwren
Myrmotherula behni
p.347

25

1 A ♂

1 C ♀

♂ 2

♀

3 ♂

1 B ♂

5 ♂

6 ♂

4 ♂

1 A ♀

♀

♀ 7 ♂

♀ 8

♂ 9

♀ 10 B ♂

11 ♂

12 ♀

♂

10 A ♀

13

♂

10 A ♂

♀

14 ♂

PLATE 26 *Terenura* & *Herpsilochmus* ANTWRENS

1 Streak-capped Antwren
Terenura maculata p.347
2 ● Orange-bellied Antwren
T. sicki p.347

3 Ash-winged Antwren
Terenura spodioptila p.347
● Chestnut-shouldered Antwren
T. humeralis p.348

4 Rufous-rumped Antwren
Terenura callinota
p.348

5 Yellow-rumped Antwren
Terenura sharpei
p.348

6 Large-billed Antwren
Herpsilochmus longirostris
p.348
7 ● Pectoral Antwren
H. pectoralis
p.349

8 Ancient Antwren
Herpsilochmus gentryi
p.349

9 Caatinga Antwren
Herpsilochmus sellowi
p.349

10 Black-capped Antwren
Herpsilochmus atricapillus
p.349

Bahia Antwren
Herpsilochmus pileatus
p.349

● Creamy-bellied Antwren
Herpsilochmus motacilloides
p.349
● Ash-throated Antwren
H. parkeri p.350

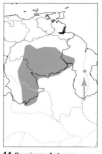

11 Roraiman Antwren
Herpsilochmus roraimae
p.350

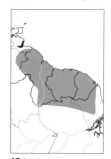

12 Todd's Antwren
Herpsilochmus stictocephalus
p.350

13 Spot-tailed Antwren
Herpsilochmus sticturus
p.350
● Dugand's Antwren
H. dugandi
p.350

14 Spot-backed Antwren
Herpsilochmus dorsimaculatus
p.350

15 Rufous-winged Antwren
Herpsilochmus rufimarginatus
p.351

16 Yellow-breasted Antwren
Herpsilochmus axillaris
p.351

26

PLATE 27 *Drymophila* ANTBIRDS & *Formicivora* ANTWRENS

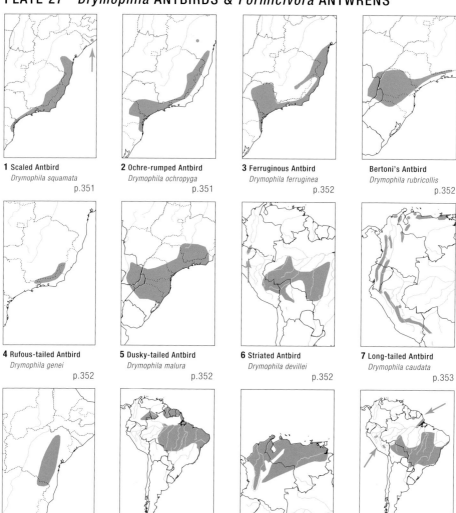

1 Scaled Antbird
Drymophila squamata
p.351

2 Ochre-rumped Antbird
Drymophila ochropyga
p.351

3 Ferruginous Antbird
Drymophila ferruginea
p.352

Bertoni's Antbird
Drymophila rubricollis
p.352

4 Rufous-tailed Antbird
Drymophila genei
p.352

5 Dusky-tailed Antbird
Drymophila malura
p.352

6 Striated Antbird
Drymophila devillei
p.352

7 Long-tailed Antbird
Drymophila caudata
p.353

8 Narrow-billed Antwren
Formicivora iheringi
p.353

9 Southern White-fringed Antwren
Formicivora grisea
p.353

Northern White-fringed Antwren
Formicivora intermedia
p.353

10 Rusty-backed Antwren
Formicivora rufa
p.354

11 Black-bellied Antwren
Formicivora melanogaster
p.354

12 Serra Antwren
Formicivora serrana p.354
● **Restinga Antwren**
F. littoralis p.354

13 ● Black-hooded Antwren
Formicivora erythronotos
p.354

● Marsh Antwren
Stymphalornis acutirostris
p.354

PLATE 28 *Cercomacra* ANTBIRDS, etc.

1 Gray Antbird
Cercomacra cinerascens
p.355

2 Dusky Antbird
Cercomacra tyrannina
p.355

Willis's Antbird
Cercomacra laeta
p.355

Parker's Antbird
Cercomacra parkeri
p.355

3 Rio de Janeiro Antbird
Cercomacra brasiliana
p.355

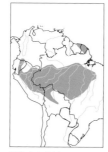

4 Black Antbird
Cercomacra serva
p.356

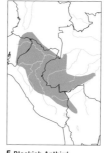

5 Blackish Antbird
Cercomacra nigrescens
p.356

6 Manu Antbird
Cercomacra manu
p.356

7 Jet Antbird
Cercomacra nigricans
p.356

8 Bananal Antbird
Cercomacra ferdinandi
p.356

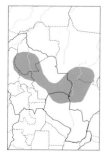

9 Mato Grosso Antbird
Cercomacra melanaria
p.357

Rio Branco Antbird
Cercomacra carbonaria
p.357

10 Dot-winged Antwren
Microrhopias quixensis
p.357

PLATE 29   FIRE-EYES, BUSHBIRDS, etc.

1 White-backed Fire-eye
Pyriglena leuconota
p.357

2 White-shouldered Fire-eye
Pyriglena leucoptera
p.358

● Fringe-backed Fire-eye
Pyriglena atra
p.358

3 Slender Antbird
Rhopornis ardesiacus
p.358

4 Stripe-backed Antbird
Myrmorchilus strigilatus
p.358

5 Black Bushbird
Neoctantes niger
p.358

6 Recurve-billed Bushbird
Clytoctantes alixii
p.359

7 ● Rondônia Bushbird
Clytoctantes atrogularis
p.359

PLATE 30 *Myrmoborus, Hylophylax* & ALLIED ANTBIRDS

1 White-browed Antbird
Myrmoborus leucophrys
p.359

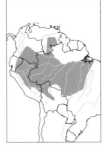

2 Black-faced Antbird
Myrmoborus myotherinus
p.359

3 Ash-breasted Antbird
Myrmoborus lugubris
p.360

4 Black-tailed Antbird
Myrmoborus melanurus
p.360

5 Banded Antbird
Dichrozona cincta
p.360

6 Spot-backed Antbird
Hylophylax naevius
p.360

Spotted Antbird
Hylophylax naevioides
p.361

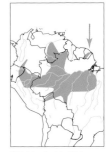

7 Dot-backed Antbird
Hylophylax punctulatus
p.361

8 Scale-backed Antbird
Hylophylax poecilinotus
p.361

9 Warbling Antbird
Hypocnemis cantator
p.361

10 Yellow-browed Antbird
Hypocnemis hypoxantha
p.362

11 Black-and-white Antbird
Myrmochanes hemileucus
p.362

12 Band-tailed Antbird
Hypocnemoides maculicauda
p.362

Black-chinned Antbird
Hypocnemoides melanopogon
p.362

13 Silvered Antbird
Sclateria naevia
p.362

PLATE 31 *Percnostola, Schistocichla,* & *Myrmeciza* ANTBIRDS

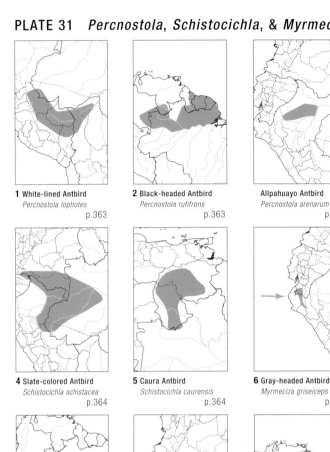

1 White-lined Antbird
Percnostola lophotes
p.363

2 Black-headed Antbird
Percnostola rufifrons
p.363

Allpahuayo Antbird
Percnostola arenarum
p.363

3 Spot-winged Antbird
Schistocichla leucostigma
p.363

4 Slate-colored Antbird
Schistocichla schistacea
p.364

5 Caura Antbird
Schistocichla caurensis
p.364

6 Gray-headed Antbird
Myrmeciza griseiceps
p.364

7 Yapacana Antbird
Myrmeciza disjuncta
p.364

8 Southern Chestnut-tailed Antbird
Myrmeciza hemimelaena
p.365

Northern Chestnut-tailed Antbird
Myrmeciza castanea
p.365

9 Black-throated Antbird
Myrmeciza atrothorax
p.365

Gray-bellied Antbird
Myrmeciza pelzelni
p.365

10 Ferruginous-backed Antbird
Myrmeciza ferruginea
p.365

11 Scalloped Antbird
Myrmeciza ruficauda
p.366

12 Squamate Antbird
Myrmeciza squamosa
p.366

13 White-bibbed Antbird
Myrmeciza loricata
p.366

PLATE 32 *Myrmeciza* ANTBIRDS & ALLIES

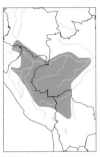

1 Plumbeous Antbird
Myrmeciza hyperythra
p.366

2 Immaculate Antbird
Myrmeciza immaculata
p.366

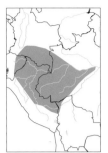

3 Sooty Antbird
Myrmeciza fortis
p.367

4 White-shouldered Antbird
Myrmeciza melanoceps
p.367

5 Goeldi's Antbird
Myrmeciza goeldii
p.367

6 White-bellied Antbird
Myrmeciza longipes
p.367

7 Chestnut-backed Antbird
Myrmeciza exsul
p.367

8 Esmeraldas Antbird
Myrmeciza nigricauda
p.368

Dull-mantled Antbird
Myrmeciza laemosticta
p.368

9 Stub-tailed Antbird
Myrmeciza berlepschi
p.368

10 Bare-crowned Antbird
Gymnocichla nudiceps
p.368

11 Wing-banded Antbird
Myrmornis torquata
p.369

PLATE 33 "PROFESSIONAL" ANT-FOLLOWING ANTBIRDS

1 White-plumed Antbird
Pithys albifrons
p.369

White-masked Antbird
Pithys castaneus
p.369

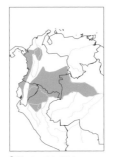

2 Bicolored Antbird
Gymnopithys leucaspis
p.369

3 Rufous-throated Antbird
Gymnopithys rufigula
p.370

4 White-throated Antbird
Gymnopithys salvini
p.370

Lunulated Antbird
Gymnopithys lunulatus
p.370

5 White-breasted Antbird
Rhegmatorhina hoffmannsi
p.370

6 Harlequin Antbird
Rhegmatorhina berlepschi
p.370

7 Bare-eyed Antbird
Rhegmatorhina gymnops
p.370

8 Chestnut-crested Antbird
Rhegmatorhina cristata
p.371

9 Hairy-crested Antbird
Rhegmatorhina melanosticta
p.371

10 Pale-faced Antbird
Skutchia borbae
p.371

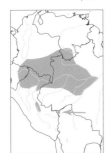

11 Reddish-winged Bare-eye
Phlegopsis erythroptera
p.371

12 Black-spotted Bare-eye
Phlegopsis nigromaculata
p.371

13 Ocellated Antbird
Phaenostictus mcleannani
p.372

PLATE 34   ANTTHRUSHES & *Pittasoma* ANTPITTAS

1 Black-faced Antthrush
Formicarius analis
p.373

Panama Antthrush
Formicarius hoffmanni
p.373

2 Rufous-breasted Antthrush
Formicarius rufipectus
p.373

3 Rufous-capped Antthrush
Formicarius colma
p.374

4 Black-headed Antthrush
Formicarius nigricapillus
p.374

5 Rufous-fronted Antthrush
Formicarius rufifrons
p.374

6 Short-tailed Antthrush
Chamaeza campanisona
p.374

7 Schwartz's Antthrush
Chamaeza turdina
p.374

8 Rufous-tailed Antthrush
Chamaeza ruficauda
p.375

Cryptic Antthrush
Chamaeza meruloides
p.375

9 Striated Antthrush
Chamaeza nobilis
p.375

10 Barred Antthrush
Chamaeza mollissima
p.375

11 Rufous-crowned Antpitta
Pittasoma rufopileatum
p.376

Black-crowned Antpitta
Pittasoma michleri
p.376

PLATE 35 *Grallaria* ANTPITTAS I

1 ● Santa Marta Antpitta
Grallaria bangsi
p.377

● Cundinamarca Antpitta
Grallaria kaestneri
p.377

2 Chestnut-crowned Antpitta
Grallaria ruficapilla
p.377

3 Watkins's Antpitta
Grallaria watkinsi
p.377

4 Stripe-headed Antpitta
Grallaria andicolus
p.377

5 Ochre-striped Antpitta
Grallaria dignissima
p.378

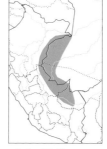

Elusive Antpitta
Grallaria eludens
p.378

6 Great Antpitta
Grallaria excelsa
p.378

7 Giant Antpitta
Grallaria gigantea
p.378

8 Undulated Antpitta
Grallaria squamigera
p.378

9 Plain-backed Antpitta
Grallaria haplonota
p.378

10 Variegated Antpitta
Grallaria varia
p.379

11 Scaled Antpitta
Grallaria guatimalensis
p.379

● Moustached Antpitta
Grallaria alleni
p.379

● Táchira Antpitta
Grallaria chthonia
p.379

PLATE 36 *Grallaria* ANTPITTAS II

1 Tawny Antpitta
Grallaria quitensis
p.379

2 Rufous-faced Antpitta
Grallaria erythrotis
p.380

3 Rufous Antpitta
Grallaria rufula
p.380

Chestnut Antpitta
Grallaria blakei
p.380

4 Gray-naped Antpitta
Grallaria griseonucha
p.380

5 Bicolored Antpitta
Grallaria rufocinerea
p.380

6 Chestnut-naped Antpitta
Grallaria nuchalis
p.380

Pale-billed Antpitta
Grallaria carrikeri
p.381

7 Yellow-breasted Antpitta
Grallaria flavotincta
p.381

8 White-bellied Antpitta
Grallaria hypoleuca
p.381

9 Rusty-tinged Antpitta
Grallaria przewalskii p.381
● Bay Antpitta
Grallaria capitalis p.381

10 Red-and-white Antpitta
Grallaria erythroleuca
p.382

11 White-throated Antpitta
Grallaria albigula
p.382

12 ● Jocotoco Antpitta
Grallaria ridgelyi
p.382

13 ● Brown-banded Antpitta
Grallaria milleri
p.382

PLATE 37 SMALLER ANTPITTAS

1 Thrush-like Antpitta
Myrmothera campanisona
p.382

2 Tepui Antpitta
Myrmothera simplex
p.383

3 Spotted Antpitta
Hylopezus macularius p.383
● **Masked Antpitta**
H. auricularis   p.383

4 Streak-chested Antpitta
Hylopezus perspicillatus
p.383

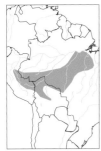

5 Amazonian Antpitta
Hylopezus berlepschi
p.383

6 White-lored Antpitta
Hylopezus fulviventris
p.384
● **Thicket Antpitta**
H. dives
p.384

7 White-browed Antpitta
Hylopezus ochroleucus
p.384

8 Speckle-breasted Antpitta
Hylopezus nattereri
p.384

9 Hooded Antpitta
Grallaricula cucullata
p.384

10 Slate-crowned Antpitta
Grallaricula nana
p.385

11 Crescent-faced Antpitta
Grallaricula lineifrons
p.385

12 Ochre-breasted Antpitta
Grallaricula flavirostris
p.385

13 Rusty-breasted Antpitta
Grallaricula ferrugineipectus
p.385

14 Leimebamba Antpitta
Grallaricula leymebambae
p.385

15 Peruvian Antpitta
Grallaricula peruviana
p.385
● **Ochre-fronted Antpitta**
G. ochraceifrons
p.386

16 Scallop-breasted Antpitta
Grallaricula loricata
p.386

PLATE 38   GNATEATERS, CRESCENTCHESTS, etc.

1 Chestnut-crowned Gnateater
Conopophaga castaneiceps
p.387

2 Slaty Gnateater
Conopophaga ardesiaca
p.387

3 Rufous Gnateater
Conopophaga lineata
p.387

4 Black-cheeked Gnateater
Conopophaga melanops
p.387

5 Ash-throated Gnateater
Conopophaga peruviana
p.388

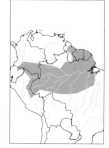

6 Chestnut-belted Gnateater
Conopophaga aurita
p.388

7 Hooded Gnateater
Conopophaga roberti
p.388

8 Black-bellied Gnateater
Conopophaga melanogaster
p.388

9 Spotted Bamboowren
Psilorhamphus guttatus
p.389

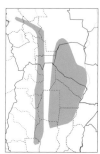

10 Olive-crowned Crescentchest
Melanopareia maximiliani
p.390

11 Collared Crescentchest
Melanopareia torquata
p.390

12 Elegant Crescentchest
Melanopareia elegans
p.390

● Marañón Crescentchest
Melanopareia maranonica
p.390

PLATE 39 LARGER TAPACULOS

1 Black-throated Huet-huet
Pteroptochos tarnii
p.392

Chestnut-throated Huet-huet
Pteroptochos castaneus
p.392

2 Moustached Turca
Pteroptochos megapodius
p.392

3 Chucao Tapaculo
Scelorchilus rubecula
p.393

4 White-throated Tapaculo
Scelorchilus albicollis
p.393

5 Crested Gallito
Rhinocrypta lanceolata
p.393

6 Sandy Gallito
Teledromas fuscus
p.393

7 Slaty Bristlefront
Merulaxis ater
p.394

● Stresemann's Bristlefront
Merulaxis stresemanni
p.394

8 Rusty-belted Tapaculo
Liosceles thoracicus
p.394

9 Ocellated Tapaculo
Acropternis orthonyx
p.394

PLATE 40 SMALLER TAPACULOS: *Scytalopus*, etc.

1 Ochre-flanked Tapaculo
Eugralla paradoxa
p.394

2 Ash-colored Tapaculo
Myornis senilis
p.395

3 Large-footed Tapaculo
Scytalopus macropus
p.395

4 Blackish Tapaculo
Scytalopus latrans
p.395

5 Unicolored Tapaculo
Scytalopus unicolor
p.395
● Tschudi's Tapaculo
S. acutirostris
p.395

Trilling Tapaculo
Scytalopus parvirostris
p.396

6 Bolivian White-crowned Tapaculo
Scytalopus bolivianus
p.396

Northern White-crowned Tapaculo
Scytalopus atratus
p.396

7 ● **Santa Marta Tapaculo**
Scytalopus sanctaemartae
p.396

8 Long-tailed Tapaculo
Scytalopus micropterus
p.396

Rufous-vented Tapaculo
Scytalopus femoralis
p.396

9 Mérida Tapaculo
Scytalopus meridanus p.396
● Caracas Tapaculo
S. caracae p.396
● Brown-rumped Tapaculo
S. latebricola p.397

Spillmann's Tapaculo
Scytalopus spillmanni
p.397

Chusquea Tapaculo
Scytalopus parkeri
p.397

Nariño Tapaculo
Scytalopus vicinior
p.397

● Stiles's Tapaculo
Scytalopus stilesi
p.397
● Upper Magdalena Tapaculo
S. rodriguezi p.397

continued on the next map page ⟶

PLATE 40 continued   SMALLER TAPACULOS: *Scytalopus*, etc.

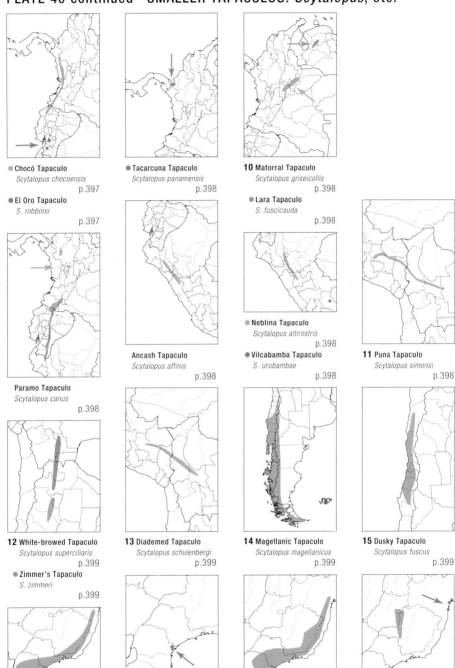

● Chocó Tapaculo
Scytalopus chocoensis
p.397

● El Oro Tapaculo
S. robbinsi
p.397

Paramo Tapaculo
Scytalopus canus
p.398

● Tacarcuna Tapaculo
Scytalopus panamensis
p.398

Ancash Tapaculo
Scytalopus affinis
p.398

10 Matorral Tapaculo
Scytalopus griseicollis
p.398

● Lara Tapaculo
S. fuscicauda
p.398

● Neblina Tapaculo
Scytalopus altirostris
p.398

● Vilcabamba Tapaculo
S. urubambae
p.398

11 Puna Tapaculo
Scytalopus simonsi
p.398

12 White-browed Tapaculo
Scytalopus superciliaris
p.399

● Zimmer's Tapaculo
S. zimmeri
p.399

13 Diademed Tapaculo
Scytalopus schulenbergi
p.399

14 Magellanic Tapaculo
Scytalopus magellanicus
p.399

15 Dusky Tapaculo
Scytalopus fuscus
p.399

16 Mouse-colored Tapaculo
Scytalopus speluncae
p.399

● Marsh Tapaculo
Scytalopus iraiensis
p.399

17 White-breasted Tapaculo
Scytalopus indigoticus
p.399

18 Brasília Tapaculo
Scytalopus novacapitalis
p.400

● Bahia Tapaculo
S. psychopompus
p.400

PLATE 41 *Zimmerius* & *Phyllomyias* TYRANNULETS, etc.

1 Mouse-colored Tyrannulet
Phaeomyias murina
p.401

Tumbesian Tyrannulet
Phaeomyias tumbezana
p.401

2 Southern Beardless Tyrannulet
Camptostoma obsoletum
p.401

3 Yellow-crowned Tyrannulet
Tyrannulus elatus
p.401

4 Brown-capped Tyrannulet
Ornithion brunneicapillus
p.401

5 White-lored Tyrannulet
Ornithion inerme
p.401

6 Golden-faced Tyrannulet
Zimmerius chrysops
p.403

● Loja Tyrannulet
Zimmerius flavidifrons p.403
● Peruvian Tyrannulet
Z. viridiflavus
p.403

7 Bolivian Tyrannulet
Zimmerius bolivianus
p.403
● Mishana Tyrannulet
Z. villarejoi
p.403

8 Slender-footed Tyrannulet
Zimmerius gracilipes
p.403

Red-billed Tyrannulet
Zimmerius cinereicapilla
p.404

9 Venezuelan Tyrannulet
Zimmerius improbus
p.404
● Paltry Tyrannulet
Z. vilissimus
p.404

10 Sooty-headed Tyrannulet
Phyllomyias griseiceps
p.404

11 Gray-capped Tyrannulet
Phyllomyias griseocapilla
p.405

12 Planalto Tyrannulet
Phyllomyias fasciatus
p.405

continued on the next map page ———➤

PLATE 41 continued   *Zimmerius* & *Phyllomyias* TYRANNULETS, etc.

13 Sclater's Tyrannulet
Phyllomyias sclateri
p.405

14 Plumbeous-crowned Tyrannulet
Phyllomyias plumbeiceps
p.405

15 Ashy-headed Tyrannulet
Phyllomyias cinereiceps
p.405

16 Rough-legged Tyrannulet
Phyllomyias burmeisteri
p.406

White-fronted Tyrannulet
Phyllomyias zeledoni
p.406

17 Greenish Tyrannulet
Phyllomyias virescens
p.406

Reiser's Tyrannulet
Phyllomyias reiseri
p.406

● Urich's Tyrannulet
Phyllomyias urichi
p.406

18 Tawny-rumped Tyrannulet
Phyllomyias uropygialis
p.406

19 Black-capped Tyrannulet
Phyllomyias nigrocapillus
p.407

20 Gray-and-white Tyrannulet
Pseudelaenia leucospodia
p.407

PLATE 42 *Serpophaga, Mecocerculus* TYRANNULETS, etc.

1 Greater Wagtail-Tyrant
Stigmatura budytoides
p.407
● Caatinga Wagtail-Tyrant
S. gracilis
p.407

2 Lesser Wagtail-Tyrant
Stigmatura napensis
p.408
● Bahia Wagtail-Tyrant
S. bahiae
p.408

3 White-crested Tyrannulet
Serpophaga subcristata
p.408

4 White-bellied Tyrannulet
Serpophaga munda
p.408

5 River Tyrannulet
Serpophaga hypoleuca
p.408

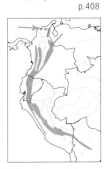

6 Sooty Tyrannulet
Serpophaga nigricans
p.409

7 Torrent Tyrannulet
Serpophaga cinerea
p.409

8 Pale-tipped Inezia
Inezia caudata
p.409
● Amazonian Inezia
I. subflava
p.409

9 Slender-billed Inezia
Inezia tenuirostris
p.409

10 Plain Inezia
Inezia inornata
p.409

11 White-tailed Tyrannulet
Mecocerculus poecilocercus
p.410

Buff-banded Tyrannulet
Mecocerculus hellmayri
p.410

12 Rufous-winged Tyrannulet
Mecocerculus calopterus
p.410

13 White-banded Tyrannulet
Mecocerculus stictopterus
p.410

14 Sulphur-bellied Tyrannulet
Mecocerculus minor
p.411

15 White-throated Tyrannulet
Mecocerculus leucophrys
p.411

PLATE 43 TACHURIS, DORADITOS, TIT-TYRANTS, etc.

1 Bearded Tachuri
Polystictus pectoralis
p.411

2 Gray-backed Tachuri
Polystictus superciliaris
p.411

3 Rufous-sided Pygmy-Tyrant
Euscarthmus rufomarginatus
p.412

4 Tawny-crowned Pygmy-Tyrant
Euscarthmus meloryphus
p.412

5 Subtropical Doradito
Pseudocolopteryx acutipennis
p.412

6 Dinelli's Doradito
Pseudocolopteryx dinelliana
p.412

7 Warbling Doradito
Pseudocolopteryx flaviventris
p.412

8 Crested Doradito
Pseudocolopteryx sclateri
p.413

9 Sharp-tailed Grass Tyrant
Culicivora caudacuta
p.413

10 Many-colored Rush Tyrant
Tachuris rubrigastra
p.413

11 Tufted Tit-Tyrant
Anairetes parulus
p.413
● Juan Fernández Tit-Tyrant
A. fernandezianus
p.414

12 Yellow-billed Tit-Tyrant
Anairetes flavirostris
p.414

13 Pied-crested Tit-Tyrant
Anairetes reguloides
p.414
● Black-crested Tit-Tyrant
A. nigrocristatus
p.414

14 ● Ash-breasted Tit-Tyrant
Anairetes alpinus
p.414

15 Agile Tit-Tyrant
Uromyias agilis
p.415

16 Unstreaked Tit-Tyrant
Uromyias agraphia
p.415

43

PLATE 44 *Suiriri* & *Elaenia* ELAENIAS

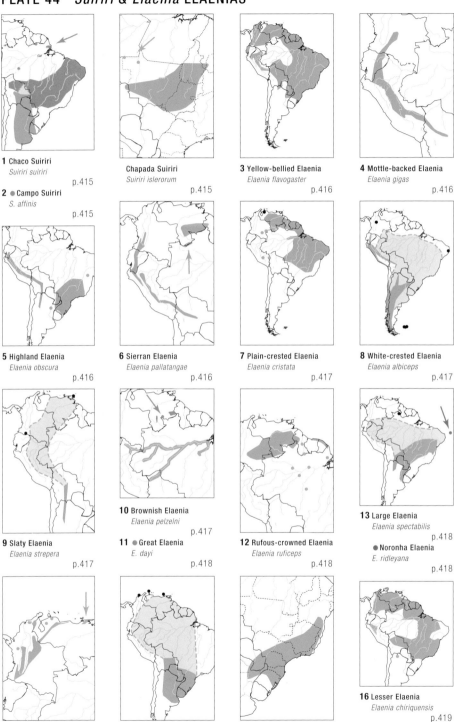

1 Chaco Suiriri
Suiriri suiriri
                                    p.415
2 ● Campo Suiriri
S. affinis
                                    p.415

Chapada Suiriri
Suiriri islerorum
                                    p.415

3 Yellow-bellied Elaenia
Elaenia flavogaster
                                    p.416

4 Mottle-backed Elaenia
Elaenia gigas
                                    p.416

5 Highland Elaenia
Elaenia obscura
                                    p.416

6 Sierran Elaenia
Elaenia pallatangae
                                    p.416

7 Plain-crested Elaenia
Elaenia cristata
                                    p.417

8 White-crested Elaenia
Elaenia albiceps
                                    p.417

9 Slaty Elaenia
Elaenia strepera
                                    p.417

10 Brownish Elaenia
Elaenia pelzelni
                                    p.417
11 ● Great Elaenia
E. dayi
                                    p.418

12 Rufous-crowned Elaenia
Elaenia ruficeps
                                    p.418

13 Large Elaenia
Elaenia spectabilis
                                    p.418
● Noronha Elaenia
E. ridleyana
                                    p.418

14 Mountain Elaenia
Elaenia frantzii
                                    p.418

15 Small-billed Elaenia
Elaenia parvirostris
                                    p.418

Olivaceous Elaenia
Elaenia mesoleuca
                                    p.419

16 Lesser Elaenia
Elaenia chiriquensis
                                    p.419
● Caribbean Elaenia
E. martinica
                                    p.419

44

PLATE 45 *Myiopagis* ELAENIAS, *Mionectes* FLYCATCHERS, etc.

1 Yellow-crowned Elaenia
Myiopagis flavivertex
p.419

2 Forest Elaenia
Myiopagis gaimardii
p.420

3 Gray Elaenia
Myiopagis caniceps
p.420

● **Foothill Elaenia**
Myiopagis olallai
p.420

4 Greenish Elaenia
Myiopagis viridicata
p.420

5 Pacific Elaenia
Myiopagis subplacens
p.421

6 Southern Scrub Flycatcher
Sublegatus modestus
p.421

7 ● **Northern Scrub Flycatcher**
S. arenarum
p.421

Amazonian Scrub Flycatcher
Sublegatus obscurior
p.421

8 Sepia-capped Flycatcher
Leptopogon amaurocephalus
p.422

9 Slaty-capped Flycatcher
Leptopogon superciliaris
p.422

10 Rufous-breasted Flycatcher
Leptopogon rufipectus
p.422

● **Inca Flycatcher**
L. taczanowskii
p.422

11 Olive-striped Flycatcher
Mionectes olivaceus
p.422

12 Streak-necked Flycatcher
Mionectes striaticollis
p.423

13 Ochre-bellied Flycatcher
Mionectes oleagineus
p.423

McConnell's Flycatcher
Mionectes macconnelli
p.423

14 Gray-hooded Flycatcher
Mionectes rufiventris
p.423

PLATE 46 *Phylloscartes* TYRANNULETS, BRISTLE TYRANTS, etc.

1 Yellow Tyrannulet
Capsiempis flaveola
p.423

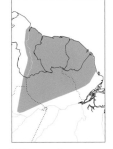

2 Olive-green Tyrannulet
Phylloscartes virescens
p.424

● Bahia Tyrannulet
Phylloscartes beckeri
p.424
● Alagoas Tyrannulet
P. ceciliae
p.424

3 Ecuadorian Tyrannulet
Phylloscartes gualaquizae
p.424

4 Mottle-cheeked Tyrannulet
Phylloscartes ventralis
p.425

● Restinga Tyrannulet
Phylloscartes kronei
p.425

5 ● Rufous-browed Tyrannulet
Phylloscartes superciliaris
p.425

6 Black-fronted Tyrannulet
Phylloscartes nigrifrons
p.425

7 Rufous-lored Tyrannulet
Phylloscartes flaviventris
p.425

Cinnamon-faced Tyrannulet
Phylloscartes parkeri
p.425

Minas Gerais Tyrannulet
Phylloscartes roquettei
p.426

8 Bay-ringed Tyrannulet
Phylloscartes sylviolus
p.426

9 Serra do Mar Tyrannulet
Phylloscartes difficilis
p.426

10 Oustalet's Tyrannulet
Phylloscartes oustaleti
p.426

11 São Paulo Tyrannulet
Phylloscartes paulista
p.426

continued on the next map page ⟶

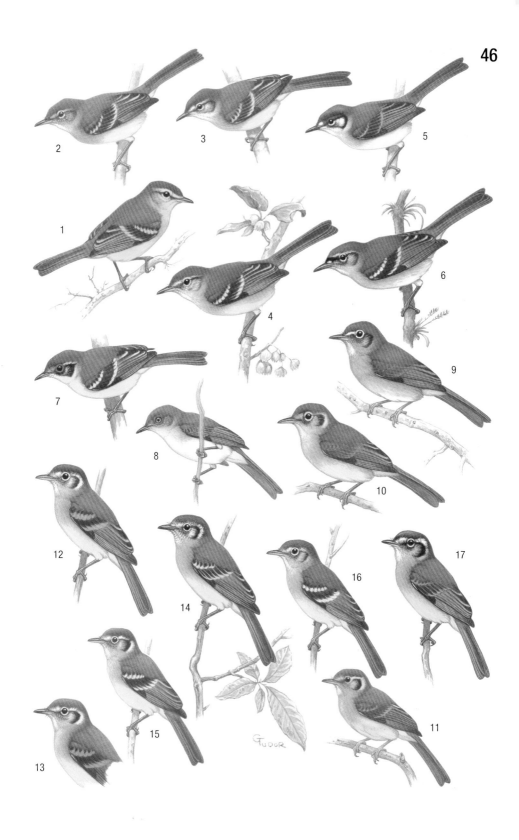

12 Variegated Bristle Tyrant
Pogonotriccus poecilotis
p.427

13 Chapman's Bristle Tyrant
Pogonotriccus chapmani
p.427

14 Marble-faced Bristle Tyrant
Pogonotriccus ophthalmicus
p.427

15 Venezuelan Bristle Tyrant
Pogonotriccus venezuelanus
p.427

16 Spectacled Bristle Tyrant
Pogonotriccus orbitalis
p.427

● Antioquia Bristle Tyrant
Pogonotriccus lanyoni
p.428

17 Southern Bristle Tyrant
Pogonotriccus eximius
p.428

PLATE 47 PYGMY-TYRANTS, TODY-TYRANTS, etc.

1 Short-tailed Pygmy-Tyrant
Myiornis ecaudatus
p.428

Black-capped Pygmy-Tyrant
Myiornis atricapillus
p.428

2 Eared Pygmy-Tyrant
Myiornis auricularis
p.428

3 White-bellied Pygmy-Tyrant
Myiornis albiventris
p.428

4 Southern Bentbill
Oncostoma olivaceum
p.429

5 Scale-crested Pygmy-Tyrant
Lophotriccus pileatus
p.429

6 Double-banded Pygmy-Tyrant
Lophotriccus vitiosus
p.429

7 Helmeted Pygmy-Tyrant
Lophotriccus galeatus
p.429
● Long-crested Pygmy-Tyrant
L. eulophotes   p.430

8 Pale-eyed Pygmy-Tyrant
Lophotriccus pilaris
p.430

9 Pearly-vented Tody-Tyrant
Hemitriccus margaritaceiventer
p.430

● Pelzeln's Tody-Tyrant
Hemitriccus inornatus p.430

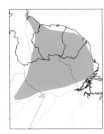

10 Boat-billed Tody-Tyrant
Hemitriccus josephinae
p.430

11 Stripe-necked Tody-Tyrant
Hemitriccus striaticollis
p.431

Johannes's Tody-Tyrant
Hemitriccus iohannis
p.431

12 Black-throated Tody-Tyrant
Hemitriccus granadensis
p.431

13 Buff-throated Tody-Tyrant
Hemitriccus rufigularis
p.431

continued on the next map page ⟶

PLATE 47 continued   PYGMY-TYRANTS, TODY-TYRANTS, etc.

14 White-eyed Tody-Tyrant
Hemitriccus zosterops
p.431

White-bellied Tody-Tyrant
Hemitriccus griseipectus
p.432

Snethlage's Tody-Tyrant
Hemitriccus minor
p.432

Zimmer's Tody-Tyrant
Hemitriccus minimus
p.432

Yungas Tody-Tyrant
Hemitriccus spodiops
p.432

15 Buff-breasted Tody-Tyrant
Hemitriccus mirandae
p.432
● Kaempfer's Tody-Tyrant
H. kaempferi
p.432

● Cinnamon-breasted Tody-Tyrant
Hemitriccus cinnamomeipectus
p.433

16 Fork-tailed Tody-Tyrant
Hemitriccus furcatus
p.433

17 Eye-ringed Tody-Tyrant
Hemitriccus orbitatus
p.433

18 Hangnest Tody-Tyrant
Hemitriccus nidipendulus
p.433

19 Drab-breasted Bamboo-Tyrant
Hemitriccus diops   p.433

20 Brown-breasted Bamboo-Tyrant
Hemitriccus obsoletus
p.433

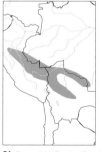

21 Flammulated Bamboo-Tyrant
Hemitriccus flammulatus
p.434

22 Bronze-olive Pygmy-Tyrant
Pseudotriccus pelzelni
p.434

Hazel-fronted Pygmy-Tyrant
Pseudotriccus simplex
p.434

23 Rufous-headed Pygmy-Tyrant
Pseudotriccus ruficeps
p.434

47

PLATE 48 TODY-FLYCATCHERS, ANTPIPITS, etc.

1 Ruddy Tody-Flycatcher
Poecilotriccus russatus
p.435

2 Ochre-faced Tody-Flycatcher
Poecilotriccus plumbeiceps
p.435

3 Rusty-fronted Tody-Flycatcher
Poecilotriccus latirostris
p.435

4 Smoky-fronted Tody-Flycatcher
Poecilotriccus fumifrons
p.435

● Buff-cheeked Tody-Flycatcher
Poecilotriccus senex
p.435

5 Slate-headed Tody-Flycatcher
Poecilotriccus sylvia
p.435

6 Spotted Tody-Flycatcher
Todirostrum maculatum
p.436

7 Yellow-lored Tody-Flycatcher
Todirostrum poliocephalum
p.436

8 Common Tody-Flycatcher
Todirostrum cinereum
p.436

Maracaibo Tody-Flycatcher
Todirostrum viridanum
p.436

9 Black-headed Tody-Flycatcher
Todirostrum nigriceps
p.436

10 Painted Tody-Flycatcher
Todirostrum pictum
p.437

11 Yellow-browed Tody-Flycatcher
Todirostrum chrysocrotaphum
p.437

continued on the next map page ⟶

PLATE 48 continued   TODY-FLYCATCHERS, ANTPIPITS, etc.

12 Golden-winged Tody-Flycatcher
Poecilotriccus calopterus
p.437

13 Black-backed Tody-Flycatcher
Poecilotriccus pulchellus
p.437

14 Black-and-white Tody-Flycatcher
Poecilotriccus capitalis
p.437

15 White-cheeked Tody-Flycatcher
Poecilotriccus albifacies
p.438

16 Rufous-crowned Tody-Flycatcher
Poecilotriccus ruficeps
p.438

● Lulu's Tody-Flycatcher
Poecilotriccus luluae
p.438

17 Black-chested Tyrant
Taeniotriccus andrei
p.438

18 Ringed Antpipit
Corythopis torquatus
p.439

Southern Antpipit
Corythopis delalandi
p.439

PLATE 49   SPADEBILLS

1 White-crested Spadebill
Platyrinchus platyrhynchos
p.439

2 Cinnamon-crested Spadebill
Platyrinchus saturatus
p.439

3 Yellow-throated Spadebill
Platyrinchus flavigularis
p.440

4 Golden-crowned Spadebill
Platyrinchus coronatus
p.440

5 White-throated Spadebill
Platyrinchus mystaceus
p.440

6 Russet-winged Spadebill
Platyrinchus leucoryphus
p.440

PLATE 50 FLATBILLS, ROYAL FLYCATCHERS, etc.

1 Yellow-olive Flatbill
Tolmomyias sulphurescens
p.441

Orange-eyed Flatbill
Tolmomyias traylori
p.441

2 Zimmer's Flatbill
Tolmomyias assimilis p.441
● Yellow-margined Flatbill
T. flavotectus p.441

3 Gray-crowned Flatbill
Tolmomyias poliocephalus
p.441

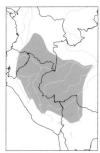

4 Olive-faced Flatbill
Tolmomyias viridiceps
p.442

5 Ochre-lored Flatbill
Tolmomyias flaviventris
p.442

6 Olivaceous Flatbill
Rhynchocyclus olivaceus
p.442

● Pacific Flatbill
Rhynchocyclus pacificus
p.442
● Eye-ringed Flatbill
R. brevirostris p.442

7 Fulvous-breasted Flatbill
Rhynchocyclus fulvipectus
p.442

8 Large-headed Flatbill
Ramphotrigon megacephalum
p.443

Dusky-tailed Flatbill
Ramphotrigon fuscicauda
p.443

9 Rufous-tailed Flatbill
Ramphotrigon ruficauda
p.443

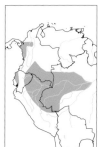

10 Brownish Twistwing
Cnipodectes subbrunneus
p.443

11 Amazonian Royal Flycatcher
Onychorhynchus coronatus
p.444

12 Pacific Royal Flycatcher
Onychorhynchus occidentalis
p.444
● Northern Royal Flycatcher
O. mexicanus p.444

13 Atlantic Royal Flycatcher
Onychorhynchus swainsoni
p.444

50

PLATE 51 *Myiophobus* & *Myiobius* FLYCATCHERS, etc.

1 Cinnamon Flycatcher
Pyrrhomyias cinnamomeus
p.444

2 Orange-crested Flycatcher
Myiophobus phoenicomitra
p.445

3 Flavescent Flycatcher
Myiophobus flavicans
p.445

● Unadorned Flycatcher
M. inornatus
p.445

4 Roraiman Flycatcher
Myiophobus roraimae
p.445

5 Orange-banded Flycatcher
Myiophobus lintoni
p.445

6 Handsome Flycatcher
Myiophobus pulcher
p.446

7 Ochraceous-breasted Flycatcher
Myiophobus ochraceiventris
p.446

8 Bran-colored Flycatcher
Myiophobus fasciatus
p.446

9 Olive-chested Flycatcher
Myiophobus cryptoxanthus
p.446

10 Ornate Flycatcher
Myiotriccus ornatus
p.447

11 Whiskered Myiobius
Myiobius barbatus
p.447

12 Yellow-rumped Myiobius
Myiobius mastacalis
p.447

Sulphur-rumped Myiobius
Myiobius sulphureipygius
p.447

13 Black-tailed Myiobius
Myiobius atricaudus
p.447

14 Tawny-breasted Myiobius
Myiobius villosus
p.448

15 Ruddy-tailed Flycatcher
Terenotriccus erythrurus
p.448

1 B

2 ♂

5 ♂

1 A

3 ♂

6 ♂

4 ♂

7 ♂

8

A ♂

B ♀

9 ♂

13 ♂

A

14 ♂

10

12 ♀

B

11 ♂

15

PLATE 52 TUFTED FLYCATCHERS, PEWEES & ALLIES

1 Northern Tufted Flycatcher
Mitrephanes phaeocercus
p.448

2 Olive Tufted Flycatcher
Mitrephanes olivaceus
p.448

3 Euler's Flycatcher
Lathrotriccus euleri
p.448

4 Gray-breasted Flycatcher
Lathrotriccus griseipectus
p.449

● Black-billed Flycatcher
Aphanotriccus audax
p.449

Acadian Flycatcher
Empidonax virescens
p.449

Willow Flycatcher
Empidonax traillii
p.449

Alder Flycatcher
Empidonax alnorum
p.449

5 Fuscous Flycatcher
Cnemotriccus fuscatus
p.450

6 Blackish Pewee
Contopus nigrescens
p.450

● White-throated Pewee
C. albogularis
p.450

7 Tropical Pewee
Contopus cinereus
p.450

● Tumbes Pewee
C. punensis
p.451

Eastern Wood Pewee
Contopus virens
p.451

Western Wood Pewee
Contopus sordidulus
p.451

8 Smoke-colored Pewee
Contopus fumigatus
p.451

9 Olive-sided Flycatcher
Contopus cooperi
p.451

10 Black Phoebe
Sayornis nigricans
p.452

11 Vermilion Flycatcher
Pyrocephalus rubinus
p.452

PLATE 53   CHAT-TYRANTS & ALLIES

1 Tumbes Tyrant
Tumbezia salvini
p.452

2 Patagonian Tyrant
Colorhamphus parvirostris
p.452

3 ● Blackish Chat-Tyrant
Ochthoeca nigrita
p.453

4 Slaty-backed Chat-Tyrant
Ochthoeca cinnamomeiventris
p.453

5 Maroon-belted Chat-Tyrant
Ochthoeca thoracica
p.453

6 Yellow-bellied Chat-Tyrant
Ochthoeca diadema
p.453

7 Golden-browed Chat-Tyrant
Ochthoeca pulchella
p.453

8 Jelski's Chat-Tyrant
Ochthoeca jelskii
p.453

9 Crowned Chat-Tyrant
Ochthoeca frontalis
p.454

Kalinowski's Chat-Tyrant
Ochthoeca spodionota
p.454

10 Rufous-breasted Chat-Tyrant
Ochthoeca rufipectoralis
p.454

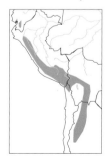

11 White-browed Chat-Tyrant
Ochthoeca leucophrys
p.454

Piura Chat-Tyrant
Ochthoeca piurae
p.454

12 D'Orbigny's Chat-Tyrant
Ochthoeca oenanthoides
p.455

13 Brown-backed Chat-Tyrant
Ochthoeca fumicolor
p.455

53

PLATE 54 SHRIKE-TYRANTS, BUSH TYRANTS, etc.

1 Lesser Shrike-Tyrant
Agriornis murinus
p.455

2 Black-billed Shrike-Tyrant
Agriornis montanus
p.455

3 White-tailed Shrike-Tyrant
Agriornis andicola
p.456

4 Great Shrike-Tyrant
Agriornis lividus
p.456

5 Gray-bellied Shrike-Tyrant
Agriornis micropterus
p.456

6 Rufous-bellied Bush Tyrant
Myiotheretes fuscorufus
p.456

7 Smoky Bush Tyrant
Myiotheretes fumigatus
p.456

8 Streak-throated Bush Tyrant
Myiotheretes striaticollis
p.457

● Santa Marta Bush Tyrant
Myiotheretes pernix
p.457

9 Rufous-webbed Bush Tyrant
Polioxolmis rufipennis
p.457

10 Red-rumped Bush Tyrant
Cnemarchus erythropygius
p.457

11 Cliff Flycatcher
Hirundinea ferruginea
p.457

PLATE 55 GROUND TYRANTS & ALLIES

1 Drab Water Tyrant
Ochthornis littoralis
p.458

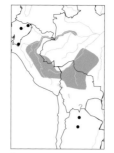

2 Little Ground Tyrant
Muscisaxicola fluviatilis
p.458

3 Spot-billed Ground Tyrant
Muscisaxicola maculirostris
p.458

4 White-fronted Ground Tyrant
Muscisaxicola albifrons
p.459

5 White-browed Ground Tyrant
Muscisaxicola albilora
p.459

6 Paramo Ground Tyrant
Muscisaxicola alpinus
p.459

7 Plain-capped Ground Tyrant
Muscisaxicola griseus
p.459

Cinereous Ground Tyrant
Muscisaxicola cinereus
p.459

8 Puna Ground Tyrant
Muscisaxicola juninensis
p.459

9 Rufous-naped Ground Tyrant
Muscisaxicola rufivertex
p.460

10 Ochre-naped Ground Tyrant
Muscisaxicola flavinucha
p.460

11 Black-fronted Ground Tyrant
Muscisaxicola frontalis
p.460

12 Cinnamon-bellied Ground Tyrant
Muscisaxicola capistratus
p.460

13 Dark-faced Ground Tyrant
Muscisaxicola maclovianus
p.460

14 Short-tailed Field Tyrant
Muscigralla brevicauda
p.461

15 Chocolate-vented Tyrant
Neoxolmis rufiventris
p.461

PLATE 56 MONJITAS & ALLIES

1 Rusty-backed Monjita
Xolmis rubetra
                              p.461

Salinas Monjita
Xolmis salinarum
                              p.461

2 Fire-eyed Diucon
Xolmis pyrope
                              p.461

3 Gray Monjita
Xolmis cinereus
                              p.462

4 White Monjita
Xolmis irupero
                              p.462

5 Black-crowned Monjita
Xolmis coronatus
                              p.462

6 White-rumped Monjita
Xolmis velatus
                              p.462

7 Black-and-white Monjita
Heteroxolmis dominicanus
                              p.462

8 Yellow-browed Tyrant
Satrapa icterophrys
                              p.463

9 Cattle Tyrant
Machetornis rixosa
                              p.463

10 Streamer-tailed Tyrant
Gubernetes yetapa
                              p.463

11 Shear-tailed Gray Tyrant
Muscipipra vetula
                              p.463

1 ♂
2
3
4 ♂
5
6
7 ♂
8 ♂
9
10
11
♀

GTUDOR

PLATE 57 *Knipolegus* TYRANTS & BLACK TYRANTS

1 Cinereous Tyrant
Knipolegus striaticeps
p.463

2 Rufous-tailed Tyrant
Knipolegus poecilurus
p.464

3 Andean Tyrant
Knipolegus signatus
p.464

4 Hudson's Black Tyrant
Knipolegus hudsoni
p.464

5 White-winged Black Tyrant
Knipolegus aterrimus
p.464

São Francisco Black Tyrant
Knipolegus franciscanus
p.465

6 Blue-billed Black Tyrant
Knipolegus cyanirostris
p.465

7 Amazonian Black Tyrant
Knipolegus poecilocercus
p.465

8 Riverside Tyrant
Knipolegus orenocensis
p.465

9 Crested Black Tyrant
Knipolegus lophotes
p.466

10 Velvety Black Tyrant
Knipolegus nigerrimus
p.466

PLATE 58 NEGRITOS, WATER TYRANTS & OTHER TYRANTS

1 Long-tailed Tyrant
Colonia colonus
p.466

2 Austral Negrito
Lessonia rufa
p.466

3 Andean Negrito
Lessonia oreas
p.466

4 Spectacled Tyrant
Hymenops perspicillatus
p.467

5 White-headed Marsh Tyrant
Arundinicola leucocephala
p.467

6 Pied Water Tyrant
Fluvicola pica
p.467

7 Black-backed Water Tyrant
Fluvicola albiventer
p.467

8 Masked Water Tyrant
Fluvicola nengeta
p.467

9 Strange-tailed Tyrant
Alectrurus risora
p.468

10 Cock-tailed Tyrant
Alectrurus tricolor
p.468

1 A ♂

1 B ♀

2 ♂

♂

♂

♀

3

♂

♀

4 ♂

♀

5 ♀

6

7

8

5 ♂

9 ♂

10 ♀

10 ♂

TUDOR

PLATE 59 ATTILAS, *Myiarchus* FLYCATCHERS, etc.

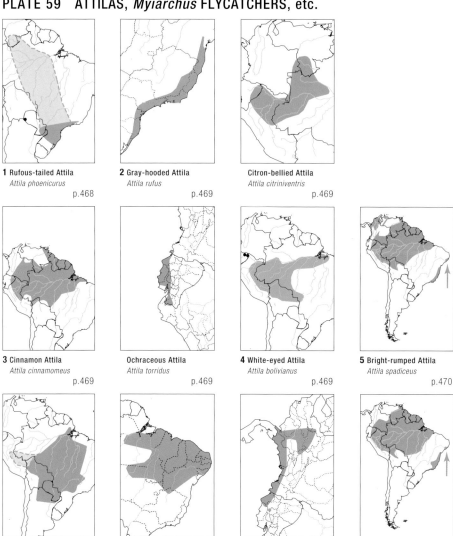

1 Rufous-tailed Attila
Attila phoenicurus
p.468

2 Gray-hooded Attila
Attila rufus
p.469

Citron-bellied Attila
Attila citriniventris
p.469

3 Cinnamon Attila
Attila cinnamomeus
p.469

Ochraceous Attila
Attila torridus
p.469

4 White-eyed Attila
Attila bolivianus
p.469

5 Bright-rumped Attila
Attila spadiceus
p.470

6 Rufous Casiornis
Casiornis rufus
p.470

7 Ash-throated Casiornis
Casiornis fuscus
p.470

8 Rufous Mourner
Rhytipterna holerythra
p.470

9 Grayish Mourner
Rhytipterna simplex
p.471

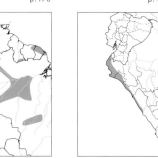

10 Pale-bellied Mourner
Rhytipterna immunda
p.471

11 Rufous Flycatcher
Myiarchus semirufus
p.471

12 Brown-crested Flycatcher
Myiarchus tyrannulus
p.471

Great Crested Flycatcher
Myiarchus crinitus
p.472

continued on the next map page ⟶

59

PLATE 59 continued ATTILAS, *Myiarchus* FLYCATCHERS, etc.

13 Swainson's Flycatcher
Myiarchus swainsoni
p.472

14 Short-crested Flycatcher
Myiarchus ferox
p.472

Panama Flycatcher
Myiarchus panamensis
p.472

Venezuelan Flycatcher
Myiarchus venezuelensis
p.472

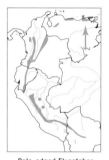

15 Sooty-crowned Flycatcher
Myiarchus phaeocephalus
p.472

Pale-edged Flycatcher
Myiarchus cephalotes
p.473

Apical Flycatcher
Myiarchus apicalis
p.473

16 Dusky-capped Flycatcher
Myiarchus tuberculifer
p.473

17 Eastern Sirystes
Sirystes sibilator
p.473

Western Sirystes
Sirystes albogriseus
p.473

PLATE 60 KISKADEES, *Myiozetes* FLYCATCHERS & ALLIES

1 Boat-billed Flycatcher
Megarynchus pitangua
p.474

2 Great Kiskadee
Pitangus sulphuratus
p.474

3 Lesser Kiskadee
Philohydor lictor
p.474

4 White-bearded Flycatcher
Phelpsia inornata
p.474

5 Dusky-chested Flycatcher
Myiozetetes luteiventris
p.475

6 Social Flycatcher
Myiozetetes similis
p.475

7 Rusty-margined Flycatcher
Myiozetetes cayanensis
p.475

8 Gray-capped Flycatcher
Myiozetetes granadensis
p.475

9 Three-striped Flycatcher
Conopias trivirgatus
p.476

10 Lemon-browed Flycatcher
Conopias cinchoneti
p.476

11 Yellow-throated Flycatcher
Conopias parvus
p.476

White-ringed Flycatcher
Conopias albovittatus
p.476

continued on the next map page —→

PLATE 60 continued   KISKADEES, *Myiozetes* FLYCATCHERS & ALLIES

12 Baird's Flycatcher
Myiodynastes bairdii
p.476

13 Golden-crowned Flycatcher
Myiodynastes chrysocephalus
p.477

14 Streaked Flycatcher
Myiodynastes maculatus
p.477

Sulphur-bellied Flycatcher
Myiodynastes luteiventris
p.477

15 Piratic Flycatcher
Legatus leucophaius
p.477

16 Variegated Flycatcher
Empidonomus varius
p.478

17 Crowned Slaty Flycatcher
Griseotyrannus
aurantioatrocristatus
p.478

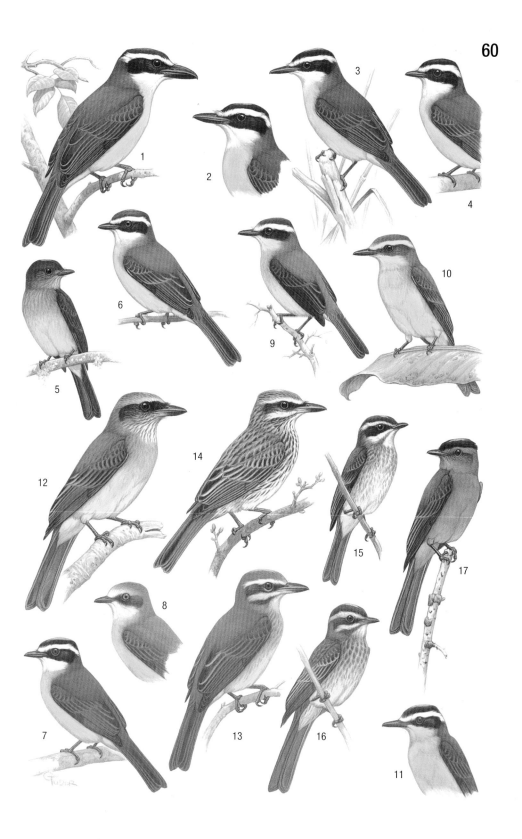

PLATE 61 KINGBIRDS & TITYRAS, etc.

  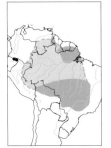

1 Sulphury Flycatcher
Tyrannopsis sulphurea
p.478

2 Tropical Kingbird
Tyrannus melancholicus
p.478

3 White-throated Kingbird
Tyrannus albogularis
p.479

 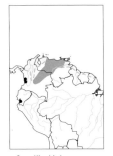  

4 Snowy-throated Kingbird
Tyrannus niveigularis
p.479

Gray Kingbird
Tyrannus dominicensis
p.479

5 Eastern Kingbird
Tyrannus tyrannus
p.479

6 Fork-tailed Flycatcher
Tyrannus savana
p.479

7 Black-crowned Tityra
Tityra inquisitor
p.481

8 Masked Tityra
Tityra semifasciata
p.481

9 Black-tailed Tityra
Tityra cayana
p.481

PLATE 62 XENOPSARIS & BECARDS

1 White-naped Xenopsaris
Xenopsaris albinucha
p.482

2 Green-backed Becard
Pachyramphus viridis
p.482

3 Yellow-cheeked Becard
Pachyramphus xanthogenys
p.482

4 Barred Becard
Pachyramphus versicolor
p.482

5 Glossy-backed Becard
Pachyramphus surinamus
p.483

6 White-winged Becard
Pachyramphus polychopterus
p.483

7 Black-capped Becard
Pachyramphus marginatus
p.483

8 Black-and-white Becard
Pachyramphus albogriseus
p.483

9 Chestnut-crowned Becard
Pachyramphus castaneus
p.484

10 Slaty Becard
Pachyramphus spodiurus
p.484

11 Cinereous Becard
Pachyramphus rufus
p.484

12 Cinnamon Becard
Pachyramphus cinnamomeus
p.484

13 One-colored Becard
Pachyramphus homochrous
p.484

14 Crested Becard
Pachyramphus validus
p.485

15 Pink-throated Becard
Pachyramphus minor
p.485

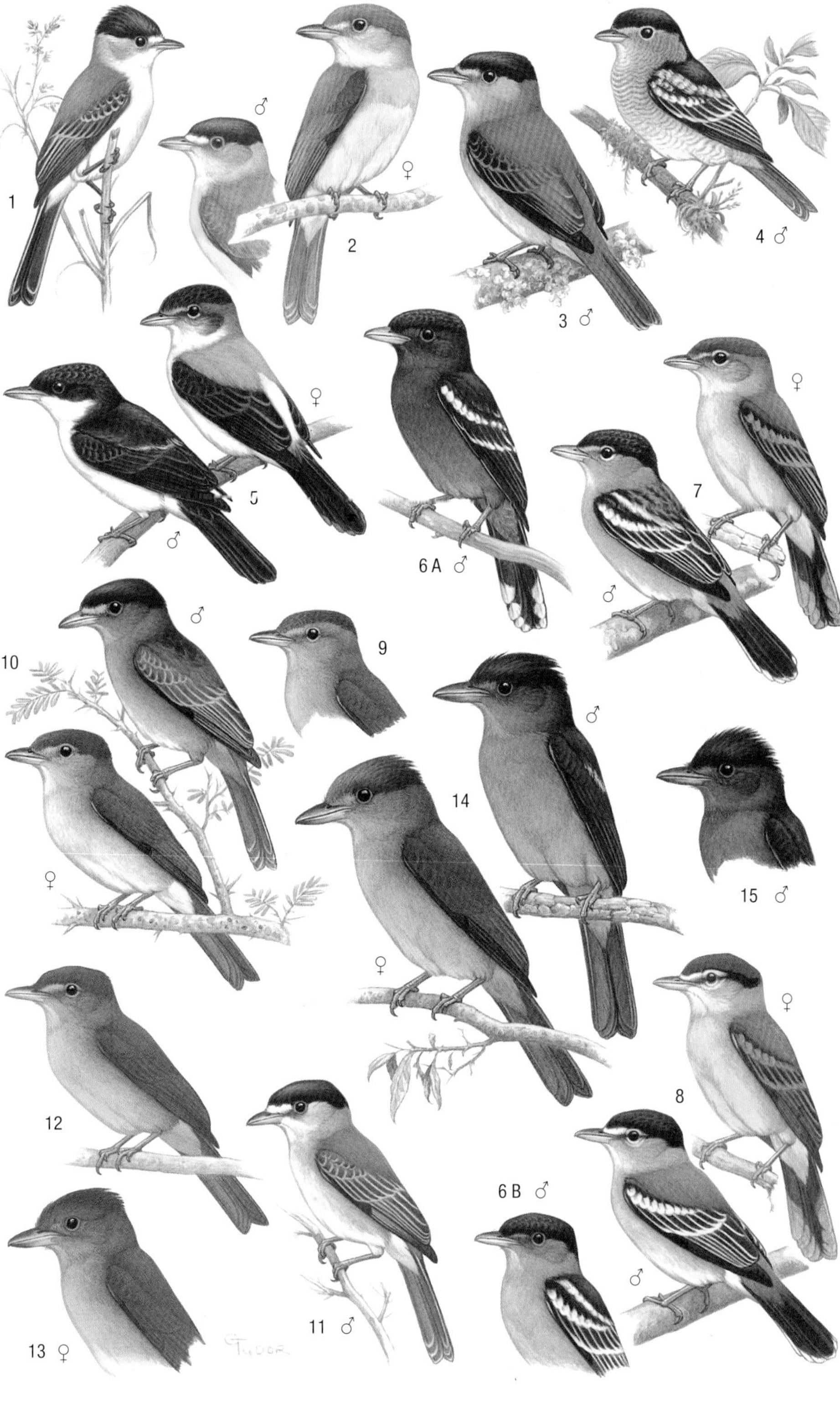
1
♂
♀
2
3 ♂
4 ♂
♀
5
♂
6 A ♂
♀
7
♂
♂
10
9
♀
14
♂
15 ♂
♀
♀
8
12
6 B ♂
♂
11 ♂
13 ♀

PLATE 63 *Schiffornis*; *Neopelma*, *Heterocercus* MANAKINS, etc.

1 Broad-billed Sapayoa
Sapayoa aenigma
　　　　　　　　　p.486

2 Greenish Schiffornis
Schiffornis virescens
　　　　　　　　　p.486

3 Thrush-like Schiffornis
Schiffornis turdina
　　　　　　　　　p.486

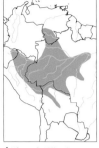

4 Várzea Schiffornis
Schiffornis major
　　　　　　　　　p.486

5 Dwarf Tyrant-Manakin
Tyranneutes stolzmanni
　　　　　　　　　p.488
6 ● Tiny Tyrant-Manakin
T. virescens
　　　　　　　　　p.488

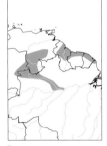

7 Saffron-crested Tyrant-
Manakin
Neopelma chrysocephalum
　　　　　　　　　p.488

8 Wied's Tyrant-Manakin
Neopelma aurifrons
　　　　　　　　　p.489

Serra do Mar Tyrant-Manakin
Neopelma chrysolophum
　　　　　　　　　p.489

9 Pale-bellied Tyrant-Manakin
Neopelma pallescens
　　　　　　　　　p.489

10 Sulphur-bellied Tyrant-
Manakin
Neopelma sulphureiventer
　　　　　　　　　p.489

11 Wing-barred Piprites
Piprites chloris
　　　　　　　　　p.489

12 Black-capped Piprites
Piprites pileata
　　　　　　　　　p.490

13 Cinnamon Neopipo
Neopipo cinnamomea
　　　　　　　　　p.490

14 Flame-crested Manakin
Heterocercus linteatus
　　　　　　　　　p.490

15 Yellow-crested Manakin
Heterocercus flavivertex
　　　　　　　　　p.490

16 Orange-crested Manakin
Heterocercus aurantiivertex
　　　　　　　　　p.490

2

5

7

8

1 ♂

3

6 ♂

9

4

10

11 A

12 ♂

13

14 ♀

14 ♂

11 B

12 ♀

15 ♂

16 ♂

TUDOR

PLATE 64 "TRUE" MANAKINS I

1 White-bearded Manakin
Manacus manacus
p.491

2 Golden-collared Manakin
Manacus vitellinus
p.491

3 White-throated Manakin
Corapipo gutturalis
p.491

4 White-ruffed Manakin
Corapipo leucorrhoa
p.491

5 Pin-tailed Manakin
Ilicura militaris
p.491

6 Golden-winged Manakin
Masius chrysopterus
p.492

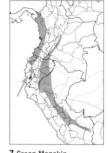

7 Green Manakin
Xenopipo holochlora
p.492

8 Yellow-headed Manakin
Xenopipo flavicapilla
p.492

9 Jet Manakin
Xenopipo unicolor
p.492

10 Olive Manakin
Xenopipo uniformis
p.492

11 Black Manakin
Xenopipo atronitens
p.493

12 Lance-tailed Manakin
Chiroxiphia lanceolata
p.493

13 Yungas Manakin
Chiroxiphia boliviana
p.493

14 Blue-backed Manakin
Chiroxiphia pareola
p.493

15 Blue Manakin
Chiroxiphia caudata
p.493

16 Helmeted Manakin
Antilophia galeata
p.494

17 ● Araripe Manakin
Antilophia bokermanni
p.494

PLATE 65 "TRUE" MANAKINS II

1 Western Striped Manakin
Machaeropterūs striolatus
p.494

● **Eastern Striped Manakin**
M. regulus
p.494

2 Fiery-capped Manakin
Machaeropterus pyrocephalus
p.494

3 Club-winged Manakin
Machaeropterus deliciosus
p.495

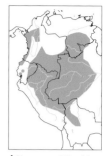

4 Blue-crowned Manakin
Lepidothrix coronata
p.495

5 Cerulean-capped Manakin
Lepidothrix coeruleocapilla
p.495

6 ● **Blue-rumped Manakin**
L. isidorei
p.495

7 White-fronted Manakin
Lepidothrix serena
p.496

Orange-bellied Manakin
Lepidothrix suavissima
p.496

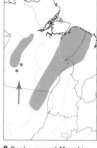

8 Opal-crowned Manakin
Lepidothrix iris
p.496

● **Golden-crowned Manakin**
L. vilasboasi
p.496

9 Snow-capped Manakin
Lepidothrix nattereri
p.496

10 White-crowned Manakin
Pipra pipra
p.496

11 Round-tailed Manakin
Pipra chloromeros
p.497

● **Red-capped Manakin**
P. mentalis
p.497

12 Scarlet-horned Manakin
Pipra cornuta
p.497

13 Golden-headed Manakin
Pipra erythrocephala
p.497

14 ● **Red-headed Manakin**
P. rubrocapilla
p.497

15 Wire-tailed Manakin
Pipra filicauda
p.498

16 Band-tailed Manakin
Pipra fasciicauda
p.498

17 Crimson-hooded Manakin
Pipra aureola
p.498

PLATE 66   SHARPBILL, PURPLETUFTS & MAINLY BRAZILIAN COTINGAS

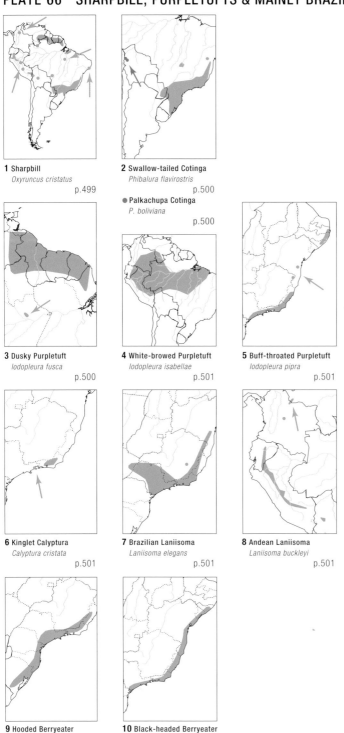

1 Sharpbill
Oxyruncus cristatus
p.499

2 Swallow-tailed Cotinga
Phibalura flavirostris
p.500
● Palkachupa Cotinga
P. boliviana
p.500

3 Dusky Purpletuft
Iodopleura fusca
p.500

4 White-browed Purpletuft
Iodopleura isabellae
p.501

5 Buff-throated Purpletuft
Iodopleura pipra
p.501

6 Kinglet Calyptura
Calyptura cristata
p.501

7 Brazilian Laniisoma
Laniisoma elegans
p.501

8 Andean Laniisoma
Laniisoma buckleyi
p.501

9 Hooded Berryeater
Carpornis cucullata
p.502

10 Black-headed Berryeater
Carpornis melanocephala
p.502

PLATE 67   ANDEAN COTINGAS & PLANTCUTTERS

1 Red-crested Cotinga
Ampelion rubrocristata
p.502

2 Chestnut-crested Cotinga
Ampelion rufaxilla
p.502

3 White-cheeked Cotinga
Zaratornis stresemanni
p.502

4 Bay-vented Cotinga
Doliornis sclateri
p.503

● Chestnut-bellied Cotinga
Doliornis remseni
p.503

5 Scaled Fruiteater
Ampelioides tschudii
p.503

6 White-tipped Plantcutter
Phytotoma rutila
p.503

7 Peruvian Plantcutter
Phytotoma raimondii
p.504

8 Rufous-tailed Plantcutter
Phytotoma rara
p.504

PLATE 68 FRUITEATERS

1 Barred Fruiteater
Pipreola arcuata
p.504

2 Green-and-black Fruiteater
Pipreola riefferii
p.504

3 Band-tailed Fruiteater
Pipreola intermedia
p.505

4 Black-chested Fruiteater
Pipreola lubomirskii
p.505

5 Masked Fruiteater
Pipreola pulchra
p.505

Orange-breasted Fruiteater
Pipreola jucunda
p.505

6 Golden-breasted Fruiteater
Pipreola aureopectus
p.505

7 Handsome Fruiteater
Pipreola formosa
p.505

8 Scarlet-breasted Fruiteater
Pipreola frontalis
p.506

9 Fiery-throated Fruiteater
Pipreola chlorolepidota
p.506

10 Red-banded Fruiteater
Pipreola whitelyi
p.506

PLATE 69 LOWLAND COTINGAS: *Cotinga*, *Xipholena*, etc.

1 Purple-throated Cotinga
Porphyrolaema porphyrolaema
p.506

2 Banded Cotinga
Cotinga maculata
p.507

Blue Cotinga
Cotinga nattererii
p.507

3 Purple-breasted Cotinga
Cotinga cotinga
p.507

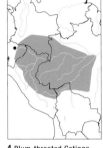

4 Plum-throated Cotinga
Cotinga maynana
p.507

5 Spangled Cotinga
Cotinga cayana
p.507

6 Pompadour Cotinga
Xipholena punicea
p.508

7 White-winged Cotinga
Xipholena atropurpurea
p.508

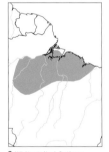

8 White-tailed Cotinga
Xipholena lamellipennis
p.508

9 Black-tipped Cotinga
Carpodectes hopkei
p.508

10 Black-faced Cotinga
Conioptilon mcilhennyi
p.508

PLATE 70   PIHAS & ALLIES

1 Cinereous Mourner
Laniocera hypopyrra
p.509

2 Speckled Mourner
Laniocera rufescens
p.509

3 Gray-tailed Piha
Snowornis subalaris
p.509

4 Olivaceous Piha
Snowornis cryptolophus
p.509

5 Rufous Piha
Lipaugus unirufus
p.510

6 Screaming Piha
Lipaugus vociferans
p.510

7 Rose-collared Piha
Lipaugus streptophorus
p.510

8 ● Chestnut-capped Piha
Lipaugus weberi
p.510

9 Scimitar-winged Piha
Lipaugus uropygialis
p.511

Dusky Piha
Lipaugus fuscocinereus
p.511

10 Cinnamon-vented Piha
Lipaugus lanioides
p.511

11 Black-and-gold Cotinga
Tijuca atra
p.511

● Gray-winged Cotinga
Tijuca condita
p.511

1 Imm.

6

5

3 ♂

7 ♂

8

11 ♀

9

11 ♂

4 ♂

10

2 ♂

GTUDOR

PLATE 71 FRUITCROWS, UMBRELLABIRDS & ALLIES

1 Bare-necked Fruitcrow
Gymnoderus foetidus
p.512

2 Purple-throated Fruitcrow
Querula purpurata
p.512

3 Red-ruffed Fruitcrow
Pyroderus scutatus
p.512

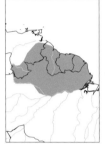

4 Crimson Fruitcrow
Haematoderus militaris
p.512

5 Capuchinbird
Perissocephalus tricolor
p.513

6 Amazonian Umbrellabird
Cephalopterus ornatus
p.513

7 Long-wattled Umbrellabird
Cephalopterus penduliger
p.513

1 ♂

2 ♂

3

4 ♂

6 ♂

5

1 ♀

4 ♀

7 ♂

GTUDOR

PLATE 72   BELLBIRDS, RED COTINGAS & COCKS-OF-THE-ROCK

1 White Bellbird
Procnias albus
                      p.513

2 Bare-throated Bellbird
Procnias nudicollis
                      p.514

3 Bearded Bellbird
Procnias averano
                      p.514

4 Black-necked Red Cotinga
Phoenicircus nigricollis
                      p.514

5 Guianan Red Cotinga
Phoenicircus carnifex
                      p.515

6 Guianan Cock-of-the-rock
Rupicola rupicola
                      p.515

7 Andean Cock-of-the-rock
Rupicola peruvianus
                      p.515

1 ♀

1 ♂

2 ♂

3 ♀

3 ♂

4 ♂

6 ♂

6 ♀

5 ♀

5 ♂

7 ♂

7 ♀

GTUDOR

PLATE 73 MAINLY "BLUE" JAYS

1 White-collared Jay
Cyanolyca viridicyanus
p.516

2 Black-collared Jay
Cyanolyca armillata
p.516

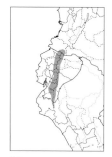

3 Turquoise Jay
Cyanolyca turcosa
p.516

4 Beautiful Jay
Cyanolyca pulchra
p.516

5 Purplish Jay
Cyanocorax cyanomelas
p.517

6 Azure Jay
Cyanocorax caeruleus
p.517

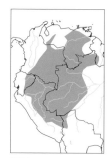

7 Violaceous Jay
Cyanocorax violaceus
p.517

PLATE 74 "WHITE-BELLIED" JAYS

1 Azure-naped Jay
Cyanocorax heilprini
p.517

2 Plush-crested Jay
Cyanocorax chrysops
p.517

Black-chested Jay
Cyanocorax affinis
p.518

3 Curl-crested Jay
Cyanocorax cristatellus
p.518

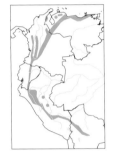

4 Inca Jay
Cyanocorax yncas
p.518

5 White-tailed Jay
Cyanocorax mystacalis
p.518

6 White-naped Jay
Cyanocorax cyanopogon
p.518

7 Cayenne Jay
Cyanocorax cayanus
p.519

PLATE 75 MARTINS & BOREAL MIGRANT SWALLOWS

1 Brown-chested Martin
Progne tapera
p.520

2 Gray-breasted Martin
Progne chalybea
p.520

3 Purple Martin
Progne subis
p.520

4 Southern Martin
Progne elegans
p.521

Peruvian Martin
Progne murphyi
p.521

Caribbean Martin
Progne dominicensis
p.521

5 Sand Martin
Riparia riparia
p.521

6 American Cliff Swallow
Petrochelidon pyrrhonota
p.521

7 Barn Swallow
Hirundo rustica
p.522

1 A

2 ♂

4 ♂

1 B

2

4 ♀

3 ♂

5

3 ♀

7 A

6

7 B

PLATE 76 SWALLOWS

1 White-winged Swallow
Tachycineta albiventer
p.522

2 Tumbes Swallow
Tachycineta stolzmanni
p.522

3 White-rumped Swallow
Tachycineta leucorrhoa
p.522

4 Chilean Swallow
Tachycineta meyeni
p.522

Tree Swallow
Tachycineta bicolor
p.523

5 Brown-bellied Swallow
Notiochelidon murina
p.523

6 Blue-and-white Swallow
Notiochelidon cyanoleuca
p.523

7 Pale-footed Swallow
Notiochelidon flavipes
p.523

8 White-thighed Swallow
Neochelidon tibialis
p.524

9 White-banded Swallow
Atticora fasciata
p.524

10 Black-collared Swallow
Atticora melanoleuca
p.524

11 Southern Rough-winged
Swallow
Stelgidopteryx ruficollis
p.524

12 Tawny-headed Swallow
Alopochelidon fucata
p.525

13 Andean Swallow
Haplochelidon andecola
p.525

14 Chestnut-collared Swallow
Petrochelidon rufocollaris
p.525

PLATE 77   DONACOBIUS; *Campylorhynchus & Cinnycerthia* WRENS

1 Black-capped Donacobius
Donacobius atricapilla
p.526

2 Bicolored Wren
Campylorhynchus griseus
p.527

3 Thrush-like Wren
Campylorhynchus turdinus
p.527

4 Fasciated Wren
Campylorhynchus fasciatus
p.527

Band-backed Wren
Campylorhynchus zonatus
p.528

5 White-headed Wren
Campylorhynchus albobrunneus
p.528

6 Stripe-backed Wren
Campylorhynchus nuchalis
p.528

7 Rufous Wren
Cinnycerthia unirufa
p.528

8 Peruvian Wren
Cinnycerthia peruana
p.528

Sepia-brown Wren
Cinnycerthia olivascens
p.529

9 Fulvous Wren
Cinnycerthia fulva
p.529

PLATE 78   *Thryothorus* WRENS

1 Whiskered Wren
Thryothorus mystacalis
p.529

2 Plain-tailed Wren
Thryothorus euophrys   p.529
● Inca Wren
T. eisenmanni
p.529

3 Sooty-headed Wren
Thryothorus spadix
p.530

4 Black-bellied Wren
Thryothorus fasciatoventris
p.530

5 Bay Wren
Thryothorus nigricapillus
p.530

6 Moustached Wren
Thryothorus genibarbis
p.530

7 Coraya Wren
Thryothorus coraya
p.530

8 Stripe-throated Wren
Thryothorus leucopogon
p.530

9 Speckle-breasted Wren
Thryothorus sclateri
p.531

10 Rufous-breasted Wren
Thryothorus rutilus
p.531

11 Buff-breasted Wren
Thryothorus leucotis
p.531

Fawn-breasted Wren
Thryothorus guarayanus
p.531

12 Long-billed Wren
Thryothorus longirostris
p.531

13 Superciliated Wren
Thryothorus superciliaris
p.531

14 Rufous-and-white Wren
Thryothorus rufalbus   p.532
● Niceforo's Wren
T. nicefori   p.532

15 Gray Wren
Thryothorus griseus
p.532

PLATE 79   SMALL WRENS

1 Gray-mantled Wren
Odontorchilus branickii
p.532

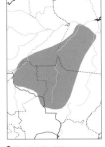

2 Tooth-billed Wren
Odontorchilus cinereus
p.532

3 Grass Wren
Cistothorus platensis
p.532

● Mérida Wren
Cistothorus meridae
p.533
● Apolinar's Wren
C. apolinari
p.533

4 Mountain Wren
Troglodytes solstitialis
p.533
● Santa Marta Wren
T. monticola
p.533

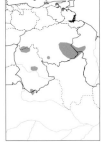

Tepui Wren
Troglodytes rufulus
p.533

5 Southern House Wren
Troglodytes musculus
p.534
● Cobb's Wren
T. cobbi
p.534

6 White-breasted Wood Wren
Henicorhina leucosticta
p.534

7 Gray-breasted Wood Wren
Henicorhina leucophrys
p.534
● Munchique Wood Wren
Henicorhina negreti
p.534

8 ● Bar-winged Wood Wren
Henicorhina leucoptera
p.534

9 Musician Wren
Cyphorhinus arada
p.535
10 ● Song Wren
C. phaeocephalus
p.535

11 Chestnut-breasted Wren
Cyphorhinus thoracicus
p.535

12 Southern Nightingale-Wren
Microcerculus marginatus
p.535

13 Wing-banded Wren
Microcerculus bambla
p.536

14 Flutist Wren
Microcerculus ustulatus
p.536

PLATE 80   SOLITAIRES, *Catharus* THRUSHES, etc.

1 Andean Solitaire
Myadestes ralloides
p.537

● Varied Solitaire
Myadestes coloratus
p.537

2 White-eared Solitaire
Entomodestes leucotis
p.537

3 Black Solitaire
Entomodestes coracinus
p.538

4 Rufous-brown Solitaire
Cichlopsis leucogenys
p.538

5 Swainson's Thrush
Catharus ustulatus
p.538

Gray-cheeked Thrush
Catharus minimus
p.538

Veery
Catharus fuscescens
p.538

6 Orange-billed Nightingale-Thrush
Catharus aurantiirostris
p.539

7 Spotted Nightingale-Thrush
Catharus dryas
p.539

8 Slaty-backed Nightingale-Thrush
Catharus fuscater
p.539

9 Plumbeous-backed Thrush
Turdus reevei
p.540

10 Marañón Thrush
Turdus maranonicus
p.540

PLATE 81 MAINLY MONTANE THRUSHES

1 Pale-eyed Thrush
Turdus leucops
p.540

2 Yellow-legged Thrush
Turdus flavipes
p.540

3 Glossy-black Thrush
Turdus serranus
p.540

4 Great Thrush
Turdus fuscater
p.541

5 Chiguanco Thrush
Turdus chiguanco
p.541

6 Austral Thrush
Turdus falcklandii
p.541

7 Black-hooded Thrush
Turdus olivater
p.541

8 Chestnut-bellied Thrush
Turdus fulviventris
p.542

PLATE 82 LOWLAND & FOOTHILL THRUSHES

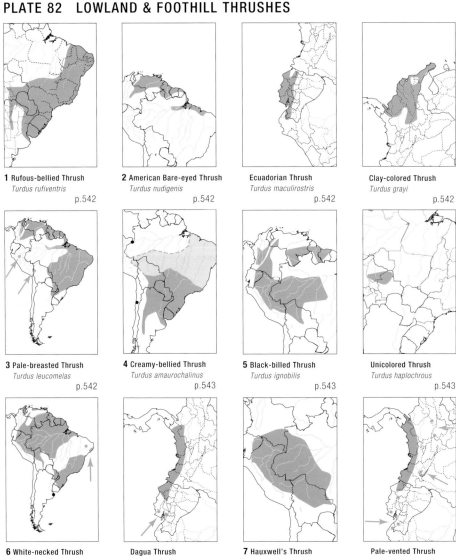

1 Rufous-bellied Thrush
Turdus rufiventris
p.542

2 American Bare-eyed Thrush
Turdus nudigenis
p.542

Ecuadorian Thrush
Turdus maculirostris
p.542

Clay-colored Thrush
Turdus grayi
p.542

3 Pale-breasted Thrush
Turdus leucomelas
p.542

4 Creamy-bellied Thrush
Turdus amaurochalinus
p.543

5 Black-billed Thrush
Turdus ignobilis
p.543

Unicolored Thrush
Turdus haplochrous
p.543

6 White-necked Thrush
Turdus albicollis
p.543

Dagua Thrush
Turdus daguae
p.543

7 Hauxwell's Thrush
Turdus hauxwelli
p.543

Pale-vented Thrush
Turdus obsoletus
p.544

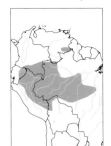

8 Lawrence's Thrush
Turdus lawrencii
p.544

9 Cocoa Thrush
Turdus fumigatus
p.544

10 Andean Slaty Thrush
Turdus nigriceps
p.544

11 Eastern Slaty Thrush
Turdus subalaris
p.544

PLATE 83   DIPPERS & MOCKINGBIRDS

1 White-capped Dipper
Cinclus leucocephalus
p.546

2 Rufous-throated Dipper
Cinclus schulzi
p.546

3 Tropical Mockingbird
Mimus gilvus
p.547

4 Chalk-browed Mockingbird
Mimus saturninus
p.547

5 Long-tailed Mockingbird
Mimus longicaudatus
p.547

6 White-banded Mockingbird
Mimus triurus
p.548

7 Brown-backed Mockingbird
Mimus dorsalis
p.548

8 Patagonian Mockingbird
Mimus patagonicus
p.548

9 Chilean Mockingbird
Mimus thenca
p.548

● Pearly-eyed Thrasher
Margarops fuscatus
p.548

PLATE 84   GNATWRENS, GNATCATCHERS & PIPITS, etc.

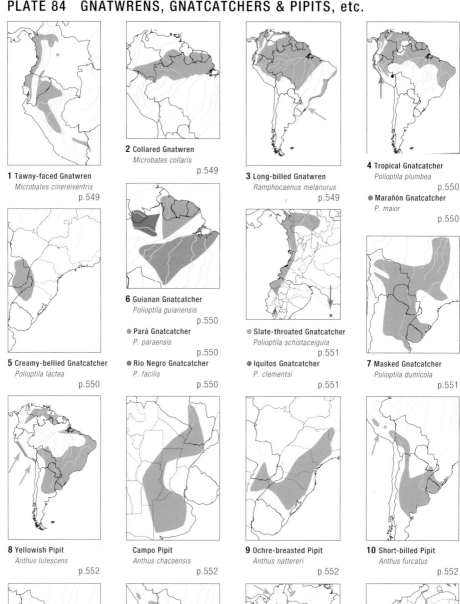

1 Tawny-faced Gnatwren
Microbates cinereiventris
p.549

2 Collared Gnatwren
Microbates collaris
p.549

3 Long-billed Gnatwren
Ramphocaenus melanurus
p.549

4 Tropical Gnatcatcher
Polioptila plumbea
p.550
● **Marañón Gnatcatcher**
P. maior
p.550

5 Creamy-bellied Gnatcatcher
Polioptila lactea
p.550

6 Guianan Gnatcatcher
Polioptila guianensis
p.550
● **Pará Gnatcatcher**
P. paraensis
p.550
● **Rio Negro Gnatcatcher**
P. facilis
p.550

● **Slate-throated Gnatcatcher**
Polioptila schistaceigula
p.551
● **Iquitos Gnatcatcher**
P. clementsi
p.551

7 Masked Gnatcatcher
Polioptila dumicola
p.551

8 Yellowish Pipit
Anthus lutescens
p.552

Campo Pipit
Anthus chacoensis
p.552

9 Ochre-breasted Pipit
Anthus nattereri
p.552

10 Short-billed Pipit
Anthus furcatus
p.552

11 Hellmayr's Pipit
Anthus hellmayri
p.553

12 Correndera Pipit
Anthus correndera
p.553

13 Paramo Pipit
Anthus bogotensis
p.553

14 Horned Lark
Eremophila alpestris
p.554

PLATE 85 VIREOS

1 Rufous-browed Peppershrike
Cyclarchis gujanensis
p.555

2 Black-billed Peppershrike
Cyclarchis nigrirostris
p.555

3 Slaty-capped Shrike-Vireo
Vireolanius leucotis
p.555

4 Yellow-browed Shrike-Vireo
Vireolanius eximius
p.556

Yellow-throated Vireo
Vireo flavifrons
p.556

5 Red-eyed Vireo
Vireo olivaceus
p.556

5 Red-eyed Vireo
Vireo olivaceus
p.556

Black-whiskered Vireo
Vireo altiloquus
p.556

● Noronha Vireo
Vireo gracilirostris
p.557

6 Yellow-green Vireo
Vireo flavoviridis
p.557

7 Brown-capped Vireo
Vireo leucophrys
p.557

● Chocó Vireo
Vireo masteri
p.557

8 Rufous-crowned Greenlet
Hylophilus poicilotis
p.557

Gray-eyed Greenlet
Hylophilus amaurocephalus
p.558

9 Scrub Greenlet
Hylophilus flavipes
p.558

Olivaceous Greenlet
Hylophilus olivaceus
p.558

continued on the next map page ⟶

PLATE 85 continued   VIREOS

10 Lemon-chested Greenlet
Hylophilus thoracicus
p.558

11 Tepui Greenlet
Hylophilus sclateri
p.558

12 Gray-chested Greenlet
Hylophilus semicinereus
p.558

13 Ashy-headed Greenlet
Hylophilus pectoralis
p.558

14 Dusky-capped Greenlet
Hylophilus hypoxanthus
p.559

Brown-headed Greenlet
Hylophilus brunneiceps
p.559

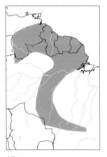

15 Buff-cheeked Greenlet
Hylophilus muscicapinus
p.559

16 Golden-fronted Greenlet
Hylophilus aurantiifrons
p.559

17 Rufous-naped Greenlet
Hylophilus semibrunneus
p.559

18 Lesser Greenlet
Hylophilus decurtatus
p.559

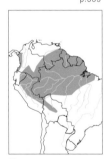

19 Tawny-crowned Greenlet
Hylophilus ochraceiceps
p.560

PLATE 86 WHITESTARTS, YELLOWTHROATS, MIGRANT WARBLERS, etc.

 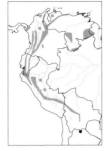  

1 Rose-breasted Chat
Granatellus pelzelni
p.561

2 Slate-throated Whitestart
Myioborus miniatus
p.561

3 Golden-fronted Whitestart
Myioborus ornatus
p.561

4 Spectacled Whitestart
Myioborus melanocephalus
p.562

5 White-fronted Whitestart
Myioborus albifrons
p.562
6 ● Yellow-crowned Whitestart
M. flavivertex
p.562

7 Tepui Whitestart
Myioborus castaneocapillus
p.562
● Paria Whitestart
M. pariae
p.562

● White-faced Whitestart
Myioborus albifacies
p.562
● Guaiquinima Whitestart
M. cardonai
p.562

8 Brown-capped Whitestart
Myioborus brunniceps
p.563

9 Southern Yellowthroat
Geothlypis velata
p.563
● Masked Yellowthroat
G. aequinoctialis
p.563

Black-lored Yellowthroat
Geothlypis auricularis
p.563

10 Olive-crowned Yellowthroat
Geothlypis semiflava
p.563

Common Yellowthroat
Geothlypis trichas
p.563

11 Tropical Parula
Parula pitiayumi
p.564

Golden-winged Warbler
Vermivora chrysoptera
p.564

Tennessee Warbler
Vermivora peregrina
p.564

12 ● Mangrove Warbler
Dendroica petechia
p.565
● Yellow Warbler
D. aestiva
p.565

continued on the next map page ⟶

PLATE 86 continued   MIGRANT WARBLERS

13 Blackpoll Warbler
Dendroica striata
p.565

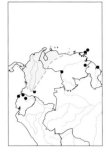

Bay-breasted Warbler
Dendroica castanea
p.565

Cerulean Warbler
Dendroica cerulea
p.565

Chestnut-sided Warbler
Dendroica pensylvanica
p.566

Black-throated Green Warbler
Dendroica virens
p.566

14 Blackburnian Warbler
Dendroica fusca
p.566

Cape May Warbler
Dendroica tigrina
p.566

Yellow-rumped Warbler
Dendroica coronata
p.566

Black-throated Blue Warbler
Dendroica caerulescens
p.567

Black-and-white Warbler
Mniotilta varia
p.567

15 Mourning Warbler
Oporornis philadelphia
p.567

Connecticut Warbler
Oporornis agilis
p.567

Kentucky Warbler
Oporornis formosus
p.567

16 American Redstart
Setophaga ruticilla
p.568

Prothonotary Warbler
Protonotaria citrea
p.568

Louisiana Waterthrush
Seiurus motacilla
p.569

17 Canada Warbler
Wilsonia canadensis
p.568

Hooded Warbler
Wilsonia citrina
p.568

18 Northern Waterthrush
Seiurus noveboracensis
p.568

Ovenbird
Seiurus aurocapilla
p.569

PLATE 87 *Basileuterus* WARBLERS

1 Gray-throated Warbler
Basileuterus cinereicollis
p.569
2 ● Gray-and-gold Warbler
B. fraseri
p.569

6 Citrine Warbler
Basileuterus luteoviridis
p.570

10 Two-banded Warbler
Basileuterus bivittatus
p.571
● Roraiman Warbler
B. roraimae
p.572

14 Flavescent Warbler
Basileuterus flaveolus
p.572

3 ● Gray-headed Warbler
Basileuterus griseiceps
p.569

7 Black-crested Warbler
Basileuterus nigrocristatus
p.571
● Pale-legged Warbler
B. signatus
p.570

11 Golden-crowned Warbler
Basileuterus culicivorus
p.572

15 White-striped Warbler
Basileuterus leucophrys
p.573

4 Three-banded Warbler
Basileuterus trifasciatus
p.570

8 Russet-crowned Warbler
Basileuterus coronatus
p.571
● White-lored Warbler
B. conspicillatus
p.571

12 White-bellied Warbler
Basileuterus hypoleucus
p.572

16 White-rimmed Warbler
Basileuterus leucoblepharus
p.573

5 Chocó Warbler
Basileuterus chlorophrys
p.570
● Cuzco Warbler
B. chrysogaster
p.570

9 Three-striped Warbler
Basileuterus tristriatus
p.571
● Santa Marta Warbler
B. basilicus
p.571

13 Chestnut-capped Warbler
Basileuterus delatrii
p.572
● Pirre Warbler
B. ignotus
p.572

17 Buff-rumped Warbler
Basileuterus fulvicauda
p.573
18 ● Riverbank Warbler
B. rivularis
p.573

PLATE 88 FLOWERPIERCERS

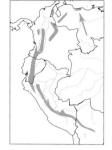

1 Bluish Flowerpiercer
Diglossa caerulescens
p.574

2 Masked Flowerpiercer
Diglossa cyanea
p.574

3 Indigo Flowerpiercer
Diglossa indigotica
p.575

4 Golden-eyed Flowerpiercer
Diglossa glauca
p.575

5 Greater Flowerpiercer
Diglossa major   p.575
● Scaled Flowerpiercer
D. duidae   p.575

6 Black Flowerpiercer
Diglossa humeralis
p.575

7 Glossy Flowerpiercer
Diglossa lafresnayii
p.575

8 Moustached Flowerpiercer
Diglossa mystacalis
p.575

9 Gray-bellied Flowerpiercer
Diglossa carbonaria
p.576

10 Black-throated Flowerpiercer
Diglossa brunneiventris
p.576

11 Mérida Flowerpiercer
Diglossa gloriosa
p.576

● Chestnut-bellied Flowerpiercer
Diglossa gloriosissima
p.576

12 White-sided Flowerpiercer
Diglossa albilatera
p.576

13 ● Venezuelan Flowerpiercer
Diglossa venezuelensis
p.576

14 Rusty Flowerpiercer
Diglossa sittoides
p.577

PLATE 89   PLUSHCAP, ANDEAN CONEBILLS, etc.

1 Plushcap
Catamblyrhynchus diadema
p.577

2 Pardusco
Nephelornis oneilli
p.577

3 Tit-like Dacnis
Xenodacnis parina
p.577

4 Giant Conebill
Oreomanes fraseri
p.577

5 Blue-backed Conebill
Conirostrum sitticolor
p.578

6 Cinereous Conebill
Conirostrum cinereum
p.578

7 Tamarugo Conebill
Conirostrum tamarugense
p.578

8 White-browed Conebill
Conirostrum ferrugineiventre
p.578

9 Rufous-browed Conebill
Conirostrum rufum
p.578

10 Capped Conebill
Conirostrum albifrons
p.579

PLATE 90 DACNISES & HONEYCREEPERS

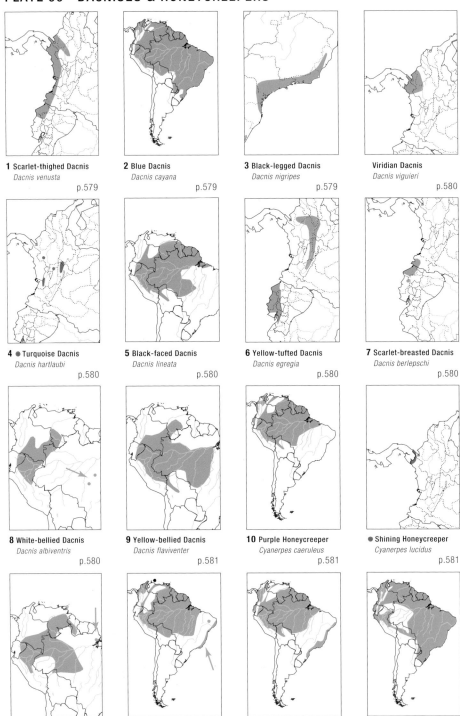

1 Scarlet-thighed Dacnis
Dacnis venusta
p.579

2 Blue Dacnis
Dacnis cayana
p.579

3 Black-legged Dacnis
Dacnis nigripes
p.579

Viridian Dacnis
Dacnis viguieri
p.580

4 ● Turquoise Dacnis
Dacnis hartlaubi
p.580

5 Black-faced Dacnis
Dacnis lineata
p.580

6 Yellow-tufted Dacnis
Dacnis egregia
p.580

7 Scarlet-breasted Dacnis
Dacnis berlepschi
p.580

8 White-bellied Dacnis
Dacnis albiventris
p.580

9 Yellow-bellied Dacnis
Dacnis flaviventer
p.581

10 Purple Honeycreeper
Cyanerpes caeruleus
p.581

● Shining Honeycreeper
Cyanerpes lucidus
p.581

11 Short-billed Honeycreeper
Cyanerpes nitidus
p.581

12 Red-legged Honeycreeper
Cyanerpes cyaneus
p.581

13 Green Honeycreeper
Chlorophanes spiza
p.582

14 Bananaquit
Coereba flaveola
p.583

90

PLATE 91 SMALLER TANAGERS & LOWLAND CONEBILLS

1 Orange-headed Tanager
Thlypopsis sordida
p.584

2 Buff-bellied Tanager
Thlypopsis inornata
p.584

3 Rufous-chested Tanager
Thlypopsis ornata
p.584

Brown-flanked Tanager
Thlypopsis pectoralis
p.584

4 Fulvous-headed Tanager
Thlypopsis fulviceps
p.584

5 Rust-and-yellow Tanager
Thlypopsis ruficeps
p.584

6 White-eared Conebill
Conirostrum leucogenys
p.585

7 Chestnut-vented Conebill
Conirostrum speciosum
p.585

8 Pearly-breasted Conebill
Conirostrum margaritae
p.585

9 ● Bicolored Conebill
Conirostrum bicolor
p.585

10 Scarlet-and-white Tanager
Erythrothlypis salmoni
p.585

11 Yellow-backed Tanager
Hemithraupis flavicollis
p.586

12 Guira Tanager
Hemithraupis guira
p.586

13 Rufous-headed Tanager
Hemithraupis ruficapilla
p.586

14 Hooded Tanager
Nemosia pileata
p.586

15 Cherry-throated Tanager
Nemosia rourei
p.586

PLATE 92 *Chlorochrysa* & ANDEAN *Tangara* TANAGERS

1 Multicolored Tanager
Chlorochrysa nitidissima
p.587

2 Glistening-green Tanager
Chlorochrysa phoenicotis
p.587

3 Orange-eared Tanager
Chlorochrysa calliparaea
p.587

4 Golden-hooded Tanager
Tangara larvata
p.587

5 Blue-necked Tanager
Tangara cyanicollis
p.588

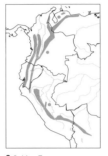

6 Golden Tanager
Tangara arthus
p.588

7 Saffron-crowned Tanager
Tangara xanthocephala
p.588

8 Beryl-spangled Tanager
Tangara nigroviridis
p.588
● Green-naped Tanager
T. fucosa
p.588

9 Golden-eared Tanager
Tangara chrysotis
p.588

10 Golden-naped Tanager
Tangara ruficervix
p.589

11 Blue-and-black Tanager
Tangara vassorii
p.589

12 Metallic-green Tanager
Tangara labradorides
p.589

13 Flame-faced Tanager
Tangara parzudakii
p.589

14 Blue-browed Tanager
Tangara cyanotis
p.589

92

PLATE 93 *Tangara* TANAGERS, etc.

1 Gray-and-gold Tanager
Tangara palmeri
p.590

2 Rufous-throated Tanager
Tangara rufigula
p.590

3 Plain-colored Tanager
Tangara inornata
p.590

4 Silver-throated Tanager
Tangara icterocephala
p.590

5 Rufous-cheeked Tanager
Tangara rufigenis
p.590

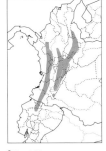

6 Scrub Tanager
Tangara vitriolina
p.590

● Green-capped Tanager
Tangara meyerdeschauenseei
p.590

7 Burnished-buff Tanager
Tangara cayana
p.591

8 Chestnut-backed Tanager
Tangara preciosa
p.591

9 Black-backed Tanager
Tangara peruviana
p.591

10 Black-capped Tanager
Tangara heinei
p.591

● Sira Tanager
Tangara phillipsi
p.591

11 Silver-backed Tanager
Tangara viridicollis
p.591

12 Straw-backed Tanager
Tangara argyrofenges
p.592

13 Black-headed Tanager
Tangara cyanoptera
p.592

14 Golden-collared Honeycreeper
Iridophanes pulcherrimus
p.592

PLATE 94 LOWLAND *Tangara* TANAGERS

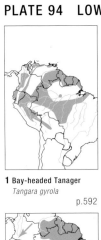

1 Bay-headed Tanager
Tangara gyrola
p.592

2 Rufous-winged Tanager
Tangara lavinia
p.592

3 Blue-whiskered Tanager
Tangara johannae
p.593

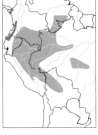

4 Green-and-gold Tanager
Tangara schrankii
p.593

● Emerald Tanager
T. florida
p.593

5 Spotted Tanager
Tangara punctata
p.593

Speckled Tanager
Tangara guttata
p.593

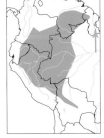

6 Yellow-bellied Tanager
Tangara xanthogastra
p.593

7 Dotted Tanager
Tangara varia
p.594

8 Masked Tanager
Tangara nigrocincta
p.594

9 Paradise Tanager
Tangara chilensis
p.594

10 Opal-crowned Tanager
Tangara callophrys
p.594

11 Opal-rumped Tanager
Tangara velia
p.594

12 Turquoise Tanager
Tangara mexicana
p.595

● White-bellied Tanager
T. brasiliensis
p.595

13 Green-headed Tanager
Tangara seledon
p.595

14 ● Seven-colored Tanager
T. fastuosa
p.595

15 Red-necked Tanager
Tangara cyanocephala
p.595

16 Gilt-edged Tanager
Tangara cyanoventris
p.595

17 Brassy-breasted Tanager
Tangara desmaresti
p.596

PLATE 95 EUPHONIAS

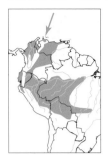

1 Thick-billed Euphonia
Euphonia laniirostris
p.596

2 Violaceous Euphonia
Euphonia violacea
p.596

3 Green-chinned Euphonia
Euphonia chalybea
p.596

4 Fulvous-vented Euphonia
Euphonia fulvicrissa
p.597

5 Finsch's Euphonia
Euphonia finschi
p.597

6 White-vented Euphonia
Euphonia minuta
p.597

7 Purple-throated Euphonia
Euphonia chlorotica
p.597

● Trinidad Euphonia
Euphonia trinitatis
p.597
● Velvet-fronted Euphonia
E. concinna
p.598

8 Orange-bellied Euphonia
Euphonia xanthogaster
p.598
● Tawny-capped Euphonia
E. anneae
p.598

9 Orange-crowned Euphonia
Euphonia saturata
p.598

10 Golden-rumped Euphonia
Euphonia cyanocephala
p.598

11 White-lored Euphonia
Euphonia chrysopasta
p.598

12 Rufous-bellied Euphonia
Euphonia rufiventris
p.599

13 Chestnut-bellied Euphonia
Euphonia pectoralis
p.599
14 ● Golden-sided Euphonia
E. cayennensis
p.599

15 Plumbeous Euphonia
Euphonia plumbea
p.599

16 Bronze-green Euphonia
Euphonia mesochrysa
p.599

PLATE 96 CHLOROPHONIAS, SWALLOW TANAGER & BUSH TANAGERS

1 Yellow-collared Chlorophonia
Chlorophonia flavirostris
p.600

2 Blue-naped Chlorophonia
Chlorophonia cyanea
p.600

3 Chestnut-breasted Chlorophonia
Chlorophonia pyrrhophrys
p.600

4 Swallow Tanager
Tersina viridis
p.600

5 Black-backed Bush Tanager
Urothraupis stolzmanni
p.601

6 Common Bush Tanager
Chlorospingus ophthalmicus
p.601

● Tacarcuna Bush Tanager
Chlorospingus tacarcunae
p.601

● Pirre Bush Tanager
Chlorospingus inornatus
p.601

7 Ashy-throated Bush Tanager
Chlorospingus canigularis
p.601

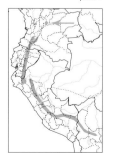

8 ● Yellow-green Bush Tanager
Chlorospingus flavovirens
p.602

9 Dusky Bush Tanager
Chlorospingus semifuscus
p.602

10 Yellow-whiskered Bush Tanager
Chlorospingus parvirostris
p.602

11 Yellow-throated Bush Tanager
Chlorospingus flavigularis
p.602

PLATE 97 *Hemispingus*, etc.

1 Gray-hooded Bush Tanager
Cnemoscopus rubrirostris
p.602

2 Black-capped Hemispingus
Hemispingus atropileus
p.603

3 White-browed Hemispingus
Hemispingus auricularis
p.603

4 Orange-browed Hemispingus
Hemispingus calophrys
p.603

5 ● Parodi's Hemispingus
Hemispingus parodii
p.603

6 Superciliaried Hemispingus
Hemispingus superciliaris
p.603

7 Oleaginous Hemispingus
Hemispingus frontalis
p.604

8 Black-headed Hemispingus
Hemispingus verticalis
p.604

9 Drab Hemispingus
Hemispingus xanthophthalmus
p.604

10 Three-striped Hemispingus
Hemispingus trifasciatus
p.604

11 Gray-capped Hemispingus
Hemispingus reyi
p.604

12 Black-eared Hemispingus
Hemispingus melanotis
p.604

13 Piura Hemispingus
Hemispingus piurae
p.605
● Western Hemispingus
H. ochraceus
p.605

14 Rufous-browed Hemispingus
Hemispingus rufosuperciliaris
p.605

15 ● Slaty-backed Hemispingus
Hemispingus goeringi
p.605

97

PLATE 98 MOUNTAIN TANAGERS & ALLIES I

1 Purplish-mantled Tanager
Iridosornis porphyrocephalus
p.605

2 Yellow-throated Tanager
Iridosornis analis
p.605

3 Golden-collared Tanager
Iridosornis jelskii
p.606

4 Yellow-scarfed Tanager
Iridosornis reinhardti
p.606

5 Golden-crowned Tanager
Iridosornis rufivertex
p.606

6 Blue-winged Mountain Tanager
Anisognathus somptuosus
p.606

7 Lacrimose Mountain Tanager
Anisognathus lacrymosus
p.606
8 ● Santa Marta Mountain Tanager
A. melanogenys
p.607

9 Scarlet-bellied Mountain Tanager
Anisognathus igniventris
p.607

10 Black-chinned Mountain Tanager
Anisognathus notabilis
p.607

11 ● Orange-throated Tanager
Wetmorethraupis sterrhopteron
p.607

12 Moss-backed Tanager
Bangsia edwardsi
p.607

13 Golden-chested Tanager
Bangsia rothschildi
p.607

● Black-and-gold Tanager
Bangsia melanochlamys
p.608

14 ● Gold-ringed Tanager
Bangsia aureocincta
p.608

98

PLATE 99   MOUNTAIN TANAGERS & ALLIES II

1 Buff-breasted Mountain Tanager
Dubusia taeniata
p.608

2 Chestnut-bellied Mountain Tanager
Delothraupis castaneoventris
p.608

3 Grass-green Tanager
Chlorornis riefferii
p.609

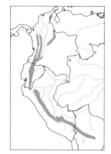

4 Hooded Mountain Tanager
Buthraupis montana
p.609

5 Black-chested Mountain Tanager
Buthraupis eximia
p.609

6 ● Golden-backed Mountain Tanager
Buthraupis aureodorsalis
p.609

7 Masked Mountain Tanager
Buthraupis wetmorei
p.609

8 White-capped Tanager
Sericossypha albocristata
p.610

PLATE 100 *Thraupis* TANAGERS, etc.

1 Fawn-breasted Tanager
Pipraeidea melanonota
p.610

2 Slaty Tanager
Creurgops dentatus
p.610

3 Rufous-crested Tanager
Creurgops verticalis
p.610

4 Blue-and-yellow Tanager
Thraupis bonariensis
p.610

5 Blue-capped Tanager
Thraupis cyanocephala
p.611

6 Palm Tanager
Thraupis palmarum
p.611

7 Golden-chevroned Tanager
Thraupis ornata
p.611

8 Blue-gray Tanager
Thraupis episcopus
p.611

9 Sayaca Tanager
Thraupis sayaca
p.612

Glaucous Tanager
Thraupis glaucocolpa
p.612

10 Azure-shouldered Tanager
Thraupis cyanoptera
p.612

PLATE 101 *Piranga* & *Ramphocelus* TANAGERS, etc.

1 Lowland Hepatic Tanager
Piranga flava
p.612

2 Highland Hepatic Tanager
Piranga lutea
p.612

3 Summer Tanager
Piranga rubra
p.613

Scarlet Tanager
Piranga olivacea
p.613

4 White-winged Tanager
Piranga leucoptera
p.613

5 Red-hooded Tanager
Piranga rubriceps
p.613

6 Masked Crimson Tanager
Ramphocelus nigrogularis
p.614

7 Silver-beaked Tanager
Ramphocelus carbo
p.614

8 Brazilian Tanager
Ramphocelus bresilius
p.614

9 Huallaga Tanager
Ramphocelus melanogaster
p.614

Crimson-backed Tanager
Ramphocelus dimidiatus
p.614

10 Flame-rumped Tanager
Ramphocelus flammigerus
p.614

11 Lemon-rumped Tanager
Ramphocelus icteronotus
p.615

12 Vermilion Tanager
Calochaetes coccineus
p.615

101

PLATE 102 LOWLAND & FOOTHILL TANAGERS: *Chlorothraupis*, *Habia*, etc.

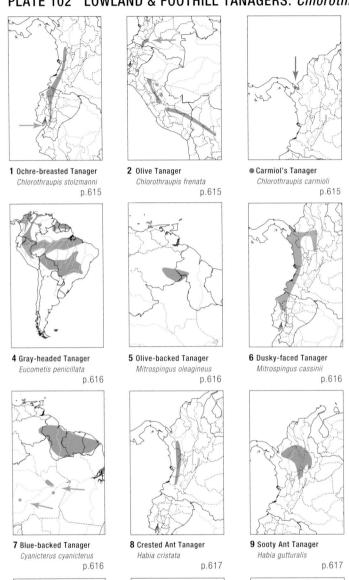

1 Ochre-breasted Tanager
Chlorothraupis stolzmanni
p.615

2 Olive Tanager
Chlorothraupis frenata
p.615

● Carmiol's Tanager
Chlorothraupis carmioli
p.615

3 Lemon-spectacled Tanager
Chlorothraupis olivacea
p.616

4 Gray-headed Tanager
Eucometis penicillata
p.616

5 Olive-backed Tanager
Mitrospingus oleagineus
p.616

6 Dusky-faced Tanager
Mitrospingus cassinii
p.616

7 Blue-backed Tanager
Cyanicterus cyanicterus
p.616

8 Crested Ant Tanager
Habia cristata
p.617

9 Sooty Ant Tanager
Habia gutturalis
p.617

10 Red-crowned Ant Tanager
Habia rubica
p.617

Red-throated Ant Tanager
Habia fuscicauda
p.617

11 Rosy Thrush-Tanager
Rhodinocichla rosea
p.618

PLATE 103 *Tachyphonus* TANAGERS & ALLIES

1 Scarlet-browed Tanager
Heterospingus xanthopygius
p.618

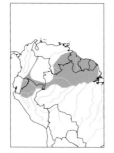

2 Fulvous Shrike-Tanager
Lanio fulvus
p.618

3 White-winged Shrike-Tanager
Lanio versicolor
p.618

4 White-shouldered Tanager
Tachyphonus luctuosus
p.619

5 Fulvous-crested Tanager
Tachyphonus surinamus
p.619

6 Flame-crested Tanager
Tachyphonus cristatus
p.619

7 Yellow-crested Tanager
Tachyphonus rufiventer
p.619

8 Tawny-crested Tanager
Tachyphonus delatrii
p.619

9 Red-shouldered Tanager
Tachyphonus phoenicius
p.619

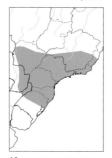

10 Ruby-crowned Tanager
Tachyphonus coronatus
p.620

11 White-lined Tanager
Tachyphonus rufus
p.620

2 ♂

5 ♀

5A ♂

1 ♂

♀

3

5 B ♂

4 ♂

6 ♀

7 ♂

4 ♀

6 ♂

9 ♀

♂

10

8 ♀

♀

11 ♀

9 ♂

TUDOR

PLATE 104   MAINLY "BRAZILIAN" TANAGERS

1 Brown Tanager
Orchesticus abeillei
p.620

2 Diademed Tanager
Stephanophorus diadematus
p.620

3 Olive-green Tanager
Orthogonys chloricterus
p.621

4 Black-goggled Tanager
Trichothraupis melanops
p.621

5 Chestnut-headed Tanager
Pyrrhocoma ruficeps
p.621

6 Cinnamon Tanager
Schistochlamys ruficapillus
p.621

7 Black-faced Tanager
Schistochlamys melanopis
p.621

8 Shrike-like Tanager
Neothraupis fasciata
p.622

9 White-rumped Tanager
Cypsnagra hirundinacea
p.622

10 Black-and-white Tanager
Conothraupis speculigera
p.622

● Cone-billed Tanager
Rhynchothraupis mesoleuca
p.623

11 Red-billed Pied Tanager
Lamprospiza melanoleuca
p.623

12 Magpie Tanager
Cissopis leverianus
p.623

13 Scarlet-throated Tanager
Compsothraupis loricata
p.623

104

PLATE 105   SALTATORS

1 Buff-throated Saltator
Saltator maximus
p.624

2 Green-winged Saltator
Saltator similis
p.624

3 Orinocan Saltator
Saltator orenocensis
p.624

4 Streaked Saltator
Saltator striatipectus
p.625

5 Grayish Saltator
Saltator coerulescens
p.625

6 Thick-billed Saltator
Saltator maxillosus
p.625

7 Black-winged Saltator
Saltator atripennis
p.625

8 Black-cowled Saltator
Saltator nigriceps
p.625

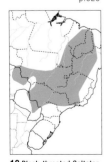

9 Golden-billed Saltator
Saltator aurantiirostris
p.626

10 Black-throated Saltator
Saltator atricollis
p.626

11 Rufous-bellied Saltator
Saltator rufiventris
p.626

12 Masked Saltator
Saltator cinctus
p.626

PLATE 106   CARDINALS & ARBOREAL GROSBEAKS

1 Red-capped Cardinal
Paroaria gularis
p.626

2 Crimson-fronted Cardinal
Paroaria baeri
p.627

3 Yellow-billed Cardinal
Paroaria capitata
p.627

4 Red-crested Cardinal
Paroaria coronata
p.627

5 Red-cowled Cardinal
Paroaria dominicana
p.627

6 Vermilion Cardinal
Cardinalis phoeniceus
p.627

7 Yellow Cardinal
Gubernatrix cristata
p.628

8 Black-backed Grosbeak
Pheucticus aureoventris
p.628

9 Southern Yellow Grosbeak
Pheucticus chrysogaster
p.628

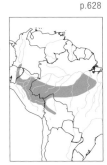

Rose-breasted Grosbeak
Pheucticus ludovicianus
p.628

10 Red-and-black Grosbeak
Periporphyrus erythromelas
p.629

11 Slate-colored Grosbeak
Saltator grossus
p.629

12 Black-throated Grosbeak
Saltator fuliginosus
p.629

13 Yellow-shouldered Grosbeak
Parkerthraustes humeralis
p.629

14 Yellow-green Grosbeak
Caryothraustes canadensis
p.629

106

PLATE 107 GRASSQUITS, "BLUE" GROSBEAKS, SEEDFINCHES, etc.

1 Blue-black Grassquit
Volatinia jacarina
p.630

2 Sooty Grassquit
Tiaris fuliginosus
p.630

Black-faced Grassquit
Tiaris bicolor
p.630

3 Dull-colored Grassquit
Tiaris obscurus
p.631

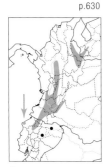

4 Yellow-faced Grassquit
Tiaris olivaceus
p.631

5 White-naped Seedeater
Dolospingus fringilloides
p.631

6 Crimson-breasted Finch
Rhodospingus cruentus
p.631

7 Blue-black Grosbeak
Cyanocompsa cyanoides
p.631

8 Ultramarine Grosbeak
Cyanocompsa brissonii
p.632

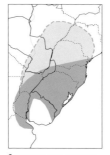

9 Glaucous-blue Grosbeak
Cyanoloxia glaucocaerulea
p.632

Indigo Bunting
Passerina cyanea
p.632

10 Blue Finch
Porphyrospiza caerulescens
p.632

11 Slaty Finch
Haplospiza rustica
p.633

12 Uniform Finch
Haplospiza unicolor
p.633

continued on the next map page ⟶

PLATE 107 continued   GRASSQUITS, SEEDFINCHES, etc.

13 Blackish-blue Seedeater
Amaurospiza moesta
p.633

Blue Seedeater
Amaurospiza concolor
p.633

● Carrizal Seedeater
Amaurospiza carrizalensis
p.634

14 Lesser Seedfinch
Oryzoborus angolensis
p.634

15 Great-billed Seedfinch
Oryzoborus maximiliani
p.634

Black-billed Seedfinch
Oryzoborus atrirostris
p.634

Large-billed Seedfinch
Oryzoborus crassirostris
p.634

PLATE 108 *Sporophila* SEEDEATERS

1 Black-and-white Seedeater
Sporophila luctuosa
p.635

2 Yellow-bellied Seedeater
Sporophila nigricollis
p.635

● Hooded Seedeater
Sporophila melanops
p.635

3 Drab Seedeater
Sporophila simplex
p.635

4 Rusty-collared Seedeater
Sporophila collaris
p.636

5 Caquetá Seedeater
Sporophila murallae
p.636

Wing-barred Seedeater
Sporophila americana
p.636

Variable Seedeater
Sporophila corvina
p.636

6 Lined Seedeater
Sporophila lineola
p.636

Lesson's Seedeater
Sporophila bouvronides
p.637

7 White-throated Seedeater
Sporophila albogularis
p.637

8 Double-collared Seedeater
Sporophila caerulescens
p.637

9 Parrot-billed Seedeater
Sporophila peruviana
p.637

10 Chestnut-throated Seedeater
Sporophila telasco
p.637

11 White-bellied Seedeater
Sporophila leucoptera
p.637

continued on the next map page ⟶

PLATE 108 continued   *Sporophila* SEEDEATERS

12 Buffy-fronted Seedeater
Sporophila frontalis
p.638

13 Slate-colored Seedeater
Sporophila schistacea
p.638

Temminck's Seedeater
Sporophila falcirostris
p.638

Gray Seedeater
Sporophila intermedia
p.638

14 Plumbeous Seedeater
Sporophila plumbea
p.638

15 Capped Seedeater
Sporophila bouvreuil
p.639

16 Tawny-bellied Seedeater
Sporophila hypoxantha
p.639

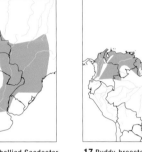

17 Ruddy-breasted Seedeater
Sporophila minuta
p.639

18 Rufous-rumped Seedeater
Sporophila hypochroma
p.639

Black-and-tawny Seedeater
Sporophila nigrorufa
p.640

19 Black-bellied Seedeater
Sporophila melanogaster
p.640

20 Chestnut-bellied Seedeater
Sporophila castaneiventris
p.640

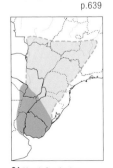

21 Marsh Seedeater
Sporophila palustris
p.640

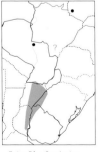

Entre Ríos Seedeater
Sporophila zelichi
p.640

22 Chestnut Seedeater
Sporophila cinnamomea
p.640

23 Dark-throated Seedeater
Sporophila ruficollis
p.641

108

PLATE 109 *Arremon* SPARROWS, BRUSHFINCHES, etc.

1 Pectoral Sparrow
Arremon taciturnus
p.641

2 ● Half-collared Sparrow
A. semitorquatus
p.641

● São Francisco Sparrow
A. franciscanus
p.641

3 Saffron-billed Sparrow
Arremon flavirostris
p.641

4 Golden-winged Sparrow
Arremon schlegeli
p.642

5 Orange-billed Sparrow
Arremon aurantiirostris
p.642

6 Black-capped Sparrow
Arremon abeillei
p.642

7 Bay-crowned Brushfinch
Atlapetes seebohmi
p.642

8 Slaty Brushfinch
Atlapetes schistaceus
p.642

● Cuzco Brushfinch
A. canigenis
p.643

9 White-winged Brushfinch
Atlapetes leucopterus
p.643

10 White-headed Brushfinch
Atlapetes albiceps
p.643

● Pale-headed Brushfinch
A. pallidiceps
p.643

11 Rusty-bellied Brushfinch
Atlapetes nationi
p.643

12 Rufous-eared Brushfinch
Atlapetes rufigenis
p.643

● Apurímac Brushfinch
A. forbesi
p.644

● Black-spectacled Brushfinch
Atlapetes melanopsis
p.644

13 Stripe-headed Brushfinch
Buarremon torquatus
p.644

Black-headed Brushfinch
Buarremon atricapillus
p.644

14 Chestnut-capped Brushfinch
Buarremon brunneinuchus
p.644

15 ● Tanager Finch
Oreothraupis arremonops
p.644

PLATE 110 *Lysurus* FINCHES, BRUSHFINCHES

1 Olive Finch
Lysurus castaneiceps
p.645

● **Sooty-faced Finch**
L. crassirostris
p.645

5 Rufous-naped Brushfinch
Atlapetes latinuchus
p.645

8 Chocó Brushfinch
Atlapetes crassus
p.646

● **Tricolored Brushfinch**
A. tricolor
p.646

12 Tepui Brushfinch
Atlapetes personatus
p.647

2 Yellow-throated Brushfinch
Atlapetes gutturalis
p.645

6 Gray-eared Brushfinch
Atlapetes melanolaemus
p.646

● **Vilcabamba Brushfinch**
A. terborghi
p.646

9 Pale-naped Brushfinch
Atlapetes pallidinucha
p.646

13 ● **Dusky-headed Brushfinch**
Atlapetes fuscoolivaceus
p.647

3 Moustached Brushfinch
Atlapetes albofrenatus
p.645

Bolivian Brushfinch
Atlapetes rufinucha
p.646

10 Ochre-breasted Brushfinch
Atlapetes semirufus
p.646

14 ● **Yellow-headed Brushfinch**
Atlapetes flaviceps
p.647

4 ● **Santa Marta Brushfinch**
Atlapetes melanocephalus
p.645

7 White-rimmed Brushfinch
Atlapetes leucopis
p.646

11 Fulvous-headed Brushfinch
Atlapetes fulviceps
p.647

15 Yellow-striped Brushfinch
Atlapetes citrinellus
p.647

PLATE 111   INCA FINCHES, *Catamenia* SEEDEATERS, SIERRA FINCHES, etc.

1 Slender-billed Finch
Xenospingus concolor
p.647

2 Cinereous Finch
Piezorhina cinerea
p.647

3 Great Inca Finch
Incaspiza pulchra
p.648

4 Rufous-backed Inca Finch
Incaspiza personata
p.648

Gray-winged Inca Finch
Incaspiza ortizi
p.648

5 Buff-bridled Inca Finch
Incaspiza laeta
p.648

6 ● Little Inca Finch
Incaspiza watkinsi
p.648

7 Plain-colored Seedeater
Catamenia inornata
p.649

8 Paramo Seedeater
Catamenia homochroa
p.649

9 Band-tailed Seedeater
Catamenia analis
p.649

10 Andean Boulder Finch
Idiopsar brachyurus
p.649

11 Plumbeous Sierra Finch
Phrygilus unicolor
p.650

12 Ash-breasted Sierra Finch
Phrygilus plebejus
p.650

13 Band-tailed Sierra Finch
Phrygilus alaudinus
p.650

111

PLATE 112   SIERRA FINCHES & ALLIES

1 Band-tailed Sierra Finch
Phrygilus alaudinus
p.650

2 Carbonated Sierra Finch
Phrygilus carbonarius
p.650

3 Mourning Sierra Finch
Phrygilus fruticeti
p.651

4 Patagonian Sierra Finch
Phrygilus patagonicus
p.651

5 Gray-hooded Sierra Finch
Phrygilus gayi
p.651

Peruvian Sierra Finch
Phrygilus punensis
p.651

6 Black-hooded Sierra Finch
Phrygilus atriceps
p.652

7 Red-backed Sierra Finch
Phrygilus dorsalis
p.651

White-throated Sierra Finch
Phrygilus erythronotus
p.652

8 White-winged Diuca Finch
Diuca speculifera
p.652

9 Common Diuca Finch
Diuca diuca
p.652

10 White-bridled Finch
Melanodera melanodera
p.653

11 Yellow-bridled Finch
Melanodera xanthogramma
p.653

PLATE 113   WARBLING FINCHES & ALLIES

1 Ringed Warbling Finch
Poospiza torquata
p.653

2 Collared Warbling Finch
Poospiza hispaniolensis
p.653

3 Cinereous Warbling Finch
Poospiza cinerea
p.654

4 Black-capped Warbling Finch
Poospiza melanoleuca
p.654

5 Black-and-rufous Warbling Finch
Poospiza nigrorufa
p.654

6 Red-rumped Warbling Finch
Poospiza lateralis
p.654

7 Cinnamon Warbling Finch
Poospiza ornata
p.654

8 Bay-chested Warbling Finch
Poospiza thoracica
p.654

9 Rusty-browed Warbling Finch
Poospiza erythrophrys
p.655

Rufous-breasted Warbling Finch
Poospiza rubecula
p.655

10 Black-and-chestnut Warbling
Finch
Poospiza whitii
p.655

11 Rufous-sided Warbling Finch
Poospiza hypochondria
p.655

12 Plain-tailed Warbling Finch
Poospiza alticola
p.655

13 Bolivian Warbling Finch
Poospiza boliviana
p.655

14 Tucumán Mountain Finch
Compsospiza baeri
p.656

15 ● Cochabamba Mountain Finch
C. garleppi
p.656

16 Chestnut-breasted Mountain Finch
Poospizopis caesar
p.656

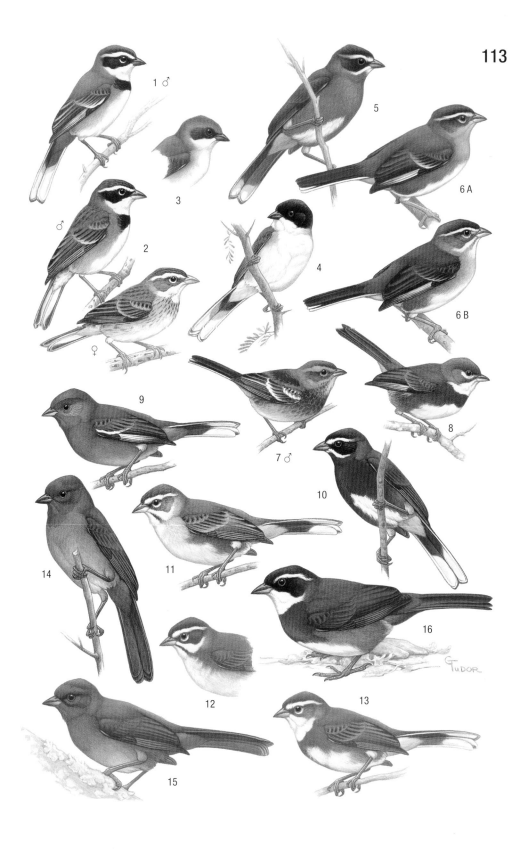

PLATE 114 YELLOWFINCHES, "GRASS" SPARROWS & DICKCISSEL

1 Sulphur-throated Finch
Sicalis taczanowskii
p.656

2 Saffron Finch
Sicalis flaveola
p.656

3 Orange-fronted Yellowfinch
Sicalis columbiana
p.657

4 Stripe-tailed Yellowfinch
Sicalis citrina
p.657

5 Grassland Yellowfinch
Sicalis luteola
p.657

Raimondi's Yellowfinch
Sicalis raimondii
p.657

6 Bright-rumped Yellowfinch
Sicalis uropygialis
p.657

7 Citron-headed Yellowfinch
Sicalis luteocephala
p.658

8 Puna Yellowfinch
Sicalis lutea
p.658

9 Greenish Yellowfinch
Sicalis olivascens
p.658

10 Greater Yellowfinch
Sicalis auriventris
p.658

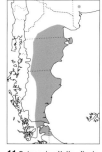

11 Patagonian Yellowfinch
Sicalis lebruni
p.658

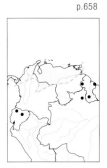

12 Dickcissel
Spiza americana
p.659

13 Yellow-browed Sparrow
Ammodramus aurifrons
p.659

14 Grassland Sparrow
Ammodramus humeralis
p.659

● Grasshopper Sparrow
Ammodramus savannarum
p.659

PLATE 115 "OPEN COUNTRY" SPARROWS & FINCHES

1 Stripe-capped Sparrow
Aimophila strigiceps
p.660

2 Tumbes Sparrow
Aimophila stolzmanni
p.660

3 Black-striped Sparrow
Arremonops conirostris
p.660

4 Rufous-collared Sparrow
Zonotrichia capensis
p.660

Tocuyo Sparrow
Arremonops tocuyensis
p.660

5 Coal-crested Finch
Charitospiza eucosma
p.661

6 Black-masked Finch
Coryphaspiza melanotis
p.661

7 Pale-throated Serra Finch
Embernagra longicauda
p.661

8 Great Pampa Finch
Embernagra platensis
p.661

9 Wedge-tailed Grassfinch
Emberizoides herbicola
p.662

● Duida Grassfinch
Emberizoides duidae
p.662

10 Lesser Grassfinch
Emberizoides ypiranganus
p.662

11 Long-tailed Reedfinch
Donacospiza albifrons
p.662

12 Many-colored Chaco Finch
Saltatricula multicolor
p.662

13 Black-crested Finch
Lophospingus pusillus
p.663

14 Gray-crested Finch
Lophospingus griseocristatus
p.663

15 Gray Pileated Finch
Coryphospingus pileatus
p.663

16 Red Pileated Finch
Coryphospingus cucullatus
p.663

PLATE 116 MEADOWLARKS, MARSHBIRDS, etc.

1 Eastern Meadowlark
Sturnella magna
p.664

2 Long-tailed Meadowlark
Sturnella loyca
p.664

3 Pampas Meadowlark
Sturnella defilippii
p.664

4 Peruvian Meadowlark
Sturnella bellicosa
p.665

4 White-browed Blackbird
Sturnella superciliaris
p.665

Red-breasted Blackbird
Sturnella militaris
p.665

5 Bobolink
Dolichonyx oryzivorus
p.665

6 Oriole Blackbird
Gymnomystax mexicanus
p.665

7 Scarlet-headed Blackbird
Amblyramphus holosericeus
p.666

8 Yellow-rumped Marshbird
Pseudoleistes guirahuro
p.666

9 Brown-and-yellow Marshbird
Pseudoleistes virescens
p.666

PLATE 117   BLACKBIRDS & COWBIRDS

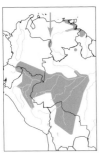

1 Velvet-fronted Grackle
Lampropsar tanagrinus
p.666

2 Chopi Blackbird
Gnorimopsar chopi
p.667

Forbes's Blackbird
Curaeus forbesi
p.667

3 Austral Blackbird
Curaeus curaeus
p.667

4 Screaming Cowbird
Molothrus rufoaxillaris
p.667

5 Shiny Cowbird
Molothrus bonariensis
p.667

● **Bronze-brown Cowbird**
M. armenti
p.668

6 Giant Cowbird
Molothrus oryzivorus
p.668

7 Baywing
Agelaioides badius
p.668

8 Bolivian Blackbird
Agelaioides oreopsar
p.668

9 Scrub Blackbird
Dives warszewiczi
p.668

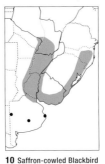

10 Saffron-cowled Blackbird
Xanthopsar flavus
p.669

11 Yellow-hooded Blackbird
Chrysomus icterocephalus
p.669

12 Chestnut-capped Blackbird
Chrysomus ruficapillus
p.669

13 Yellow-winged Blackbird
Agelasticus thilius
p.669

14 Unicolored Blackbird
Agelasticus cyanopus
p.670

15 ● **Pale-eyed Blackbird**
Agelasticus xanthophthalmus
p.670

PLATE 118 GRACKLES & ORIOLES

1 Carib Grackle
Quiscalus lugubris
p.670

2 Great-tailed Grackle
Quiscalus mexicanus
p.670

3 Golden-tufted Mountain Grackle
Macroagelaius imthurni
p.670

Colombian Mountain Grackle
Macroagelaius subalaris
p.671

4 Red-bellied Grackle
Hypopyrrhus pyrohypogaster
p.671

5 Moriche Oriole
Icterus chrysocephalus
p.671

6 Epaulet Oriole
Icterus cayanensis
p.671

7 Yellow-backed Oriole
Icterus chrysater
p.672

8 Venezuelan Troupial
Icterus icterus
p.672

9 Orange-backed Troupial
Icterus croconotus p.672
● Campo Troupial
I. jamacaii p.672

10 Baltimore Oriole
Icterus galbula
p.672

Orchard Oriole
Icterus spurius
p.672

11 White-edged Oriole
Icterus graceannae
p.673

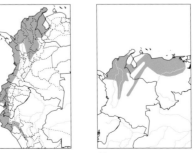

12 Yellow-tailed Oriole
Icterus mesomelas
p.673

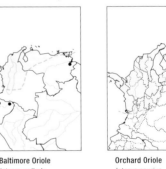

13 Orange-crowned Oriole
Icterus auricapillus
p.673

14 Yellow Oriole
Icterus nigrogularis
p.673

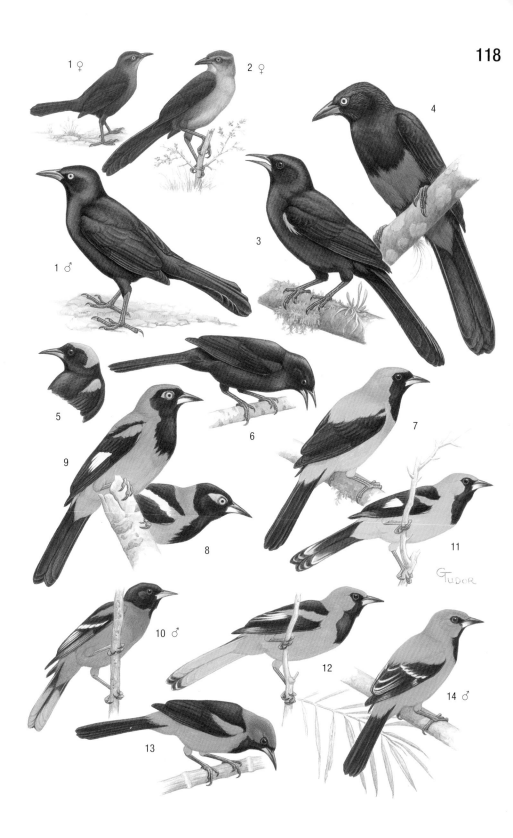

PLATE 119 CACIQUES, OROPENDOLAS etc.

1 Epaulet Oriole
Icterus cayanensis
p.671

2 Yellow-billed Cacique
Amblycercus holosericeus
p.673

3 Ecuadorian Cacique
Cacicus sclateri
p.674

Selva Cacique
Cacicus koepckeae
p.674

4 Solitary Cacique
Cacicus solitarius
p.674

5 Red-rumped Cacique
Cacicus haemorrhous
p.674

6 Subtropical Cacique
Cacicus uropygialis
p.674

Scarlet-rumped Cacique
Cacicus microrhynchus
p.675

7 Yellow-rumped Cacique
Cacicus cela
p.675

8 Golden-winged Cacique
Cacicus chrysopterus
p.675

9 Northern Mountain Cacique
Cacicus leucoramphus
p.675

10 Southern Mountain Cacique
Cacicus chrysonotus
p.675

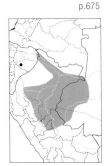

11 Band-tailed Oropendola
Ocyalus latirostris
p.676

12 Crested Oropendola
Psarocolius decumanus
p.677

PLATE 120 OROPENDOLAS

1 Chestnut-headed Oropendola
Zarhynchus wagleri
p.676

2 Casqued Oropendola
Clypicterus oseryi
p.676

3 Green Oropendola
Psarocolius viridis
p.676

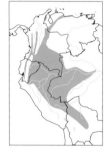

4 Crested Oropendola
Psarocolius decumanus
p.677

5 Russet-backed Oropendola
Psarocolius angustifrons
p.677

6 Dusky-green Oropendola
Psarocolius atrovirens
p.677

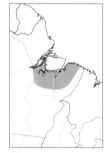

7 Olive Oropendola
Psarocolius yuracares
p.677

8 Pará Oropendola
Psarocolius bifasciatus
p.678

9 Black Oropendola
Psarocolius guatimozinus
p.678

● Baudó Oropendola
Psarocolius cassini
p.678

3 ♂

7 ♂

1 ♂

4

5 A ♂

♂

♀

4 ♂

8 ♂

2 ♂

9 ♂

5 B ♂

6 ♂

GTUDOR

PLATE 121 SISKINS & VARIOUS INTRODUCED SPECIES

1 Hooded Siskin
Carduelis magellanica
p.679

Olivaceous Siskin
Carduelis olivacea
p.679

Saffron Siskin
Carduelis siemeradzkii
p.679

2 Thick-billed Siskin
Carduelis crassirostris
p.679

3 Yellow-faced Siskin
Carduelis yarrellii
p.680

4 Black-chinned Siskin
Carduelis barbata
p.680

5 Andean Siskin
Carduelis spinescens
p.680

6 Red Siskin
Carduelis cucullata
p.680

7 Yellow-rumped Siskin
Carduelis uropygialis
p.680

8 Black Siskin
Carduelis atrata
p.680

9 Yellow-bellied Siskin
Carduelis xanthogastra
p.681

10 Lesser Goldfinch
Carduelis psaltria
p.681

European Goldfinch
Carduelis carduelis
p.681

European Greenfinch
Carduelis chloris
p.681

11 Common Waxbill
Estrilda astrild
p.682

● Black-headed Munia
Lonchura malacca
p.682

● **Java Sparrow**
Padda oryzivora
p.682

House Sparrow
Passer domesticus
p.683

● **Village Weaver**
Ploceus cucullatus
p.683

● **Common Starling**
Sturnus vulgaris
p.683

SOUTH AMERICA – ECUADOR, COLOMBIA, VENEZUELA, GUIANAS, PERU, BOLIVIA

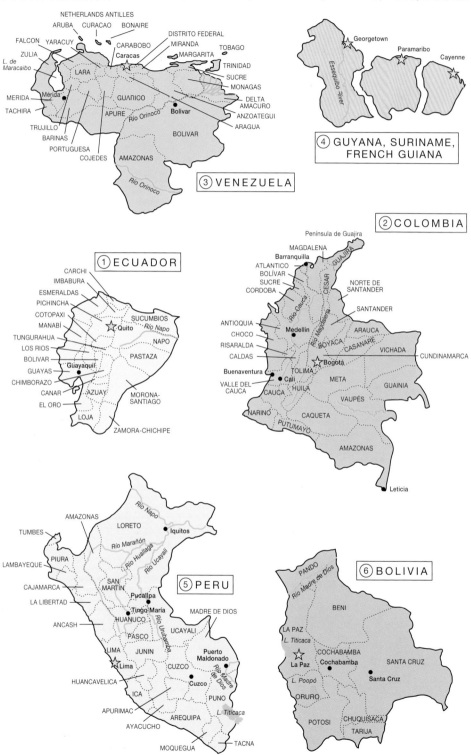

NETHERLANDS ANTILLES
ARUBA   CURACAO   BONAIRE
FALCON   YARACUY
ZULIA
L. de
Maracaibo
LARA
MERIDA
Mérida
TACHIRA
TRUJILLO
BARINAS
PORTUGUESA
COJEDES

DISTRITO FEDERAL
MIRANDA
CARABOBO
Caracas
MARGARITA
GUARICO
APURE   Río Orinoco   Bolivar
AMAZONAS
Río Orinoco

TOBAGO
TRINIDAD
SUCRE
MONAGAS
DELTA
AMACURO
ANZOATEGUI
ARAGUA
BOLIVAR

③ VENEZUELA

Georgetown
Essequibo River
Paramaribo
Cayenne

④ GUYANA, SURINAME,
FRENCH GUIANA

② COLOMBIA

Península de Guajira
MAGDALENA
Barranquilla
ATLANTICO
BOLÍVAR
SUCRE
CORDOBA
ANTIOQUIA
Medellín
CHOCO
RISARALDA
CALDAS
Buenaventura
VALLE DEL
CAUCA
GUAJIRA
CESAR
NORTE DE
SANTANDER
SANTANDER
ARAUCA
Río Cauca
Río Magdalena
BOYACA   CASANARE
CASANARE
VICHADA
CUNDINAMARCA
Bogotá
TOLIMA
Cali
HUILA
CAUCA
NARIÑO
CAQUETA
PUTUMAYO
META
VAUPÉS
GUAINIA
AMAZONAS
Leticia

① ECUADOR

CARCHI
IMBABURA
ESMERALDAS
PICHINCHA
COTOPAXI
MANABÍ
TUNGURAHUA
LOS RIOS
BOLIVAR
GUAYAS
CHIMBORAZO
CANAR
EL ORO
LOJA
SUCUMBIOS
Quito   Río Napo
NAPO
PASTAZA
Guayaquil
AZUAY
MORONA-
SANTIAGO
ZAMORA-CHICHIPE

⑤ PERU

AMAZONAS
TUMBES
PIURA
LAMBAYEQUE
CAJAMARCA
LA LIBERTAD
ANCASH
LIMA
Lima
HUANCAVELICA
ICA
APURIMAC
AYACUCHO
MOQUEGUA
Río Napo
LORETO   Iquitos
Río Marañón
Río Huallaga
Río Ucayali
SAN
MARTÍN
Pucallpa
Tingo María
HUANUCO
PASCO
JUNIN
CUZCO
Cuzco
Río Urubamba
UCAYALI
MADRE DE DIOS
Puerto
Maldonado
Río Madre de Dios
PUNO
L. Titicaca
AREQUIPA
TACNA

⑥ BOLIVIA

PANDO
Río Madre de Díos
BENI
LA PAZ
L. Titicaca
La Paz
COCHABAMBA
Cochabamba
SANTA CRUZ
Santa Cruz
L. Poopó
ORURO
POTOSI
CHUQUISACA
TARIJA

BRAZIL, PARAGUAY, CHILE, ARGENTINA, URUGUAY

RORAIMA

AMAPA

Marajó Island

Rio Negro

PARA

⑦ BRAZIL

Rio Amazonas

Manaus

Santarém

Belém

RIO GRANDE DO NORTE

AMAZONAS

Rio Juruá

Rio Purus

Rio Madeira

Rio Tapajós

Rio Xingu

PARA

Rio Araguaia

Rio Tocantins

MARANHAO

CEARA

PIAUI

PARAIBA

PERNAMBUCO

RONDONIA

Bananal Island

Rio Tocantins

ALAGOAS

MATO GROSSO

Rio Paraguay

Cuiabá

BAHIA

Rio São Francisco

SERGIPE

Salvador

GOIAS

⑨ CHILE

BRASILIA ☆

TARAPACA

JUJUY

MINAS GERAIS

MATO GROSSO DO SUL

ESPIRITO SANTO

ANTOFAGASTA

FORMOSA

Rio Paraná

SAO PAULO

RIO DE JANEIRO

SALTA

Salta

MISIONES

PARANA

São Paulo

Rio de Janeiro

TUCUMAN

Tucumán

CHACO

ATACAMA

CATAMARCA

SANTIAGO DEL ESTERO

SANTA FE

CORRIENTES

SANTA CATARINA

⑧ PARAGUAY

LA RIOJA

Córdoba

Rio Paraná

RIO GRANDE DO SUL

ALTO PARAGUAY

COQUIMBO

SAN JUAN

ENTRE RIOS

BOQUERON

CONCEPCION

ACONCAGUA

SAN LUIS

CORDOBA

Filadelfia

AMAMBAY

SANTIAGO

O'HIGGINS

Santiago

Buenos Aires ☆

Rio Paraguay

SAN PEDRO

COLCHAGUA

MENDOZA

PRESIDENTE HAYES

CANINDEYU

CURICO

LA PAMPA

BUENOS AIRES

ALTO PARANA

TALCA

MAULE

LINARES

NUBLE

NEUQUEN

Asunción ☆

CORDILLERA

CAAGUAZU

CONCEP-CION

BIO-BIO

RIO NEGRO

CENTRAL

PARAGUARI

GUAIRA

CAAZAPA

ARAUCO

MALLECO

Bariloche

NEEMBUCU

ITAPUA

CAUTIN

Valdez Peninsula

Montevideo ☆

MISIONES

OSORNO

VALDIVIA

CHILOE

LLANQUI-HUE

CHUBUT

⑪ URUGUAY

AYSEN

SANTA CRUZ

⑩ ARGENTINA

FALKLAND ISLANDS

TIERRA DEL FUEGO

MAGALLANES

Ushuaia

SOUTH AMERICA

SOUTH AMERICA

CARIBBEAN SEA

NETHERLANDS ANTILLES
ARUBA CURACAO BONAIRE   TRINIDAD   TOBAGO

Caracas

L. de Maracaibo

Río Cauca

Río Magdalena

Bogotá

VENEZUELA

Río Orinoco

Río Orinoco

GUYANA
SURINAME

Georgetown

Paramaribo
Cayenne

Essequibo River

**FRENCH
GUIANA**

PANAMA

COLOMBIA

Río Negro

BRAZIL

ATLANTIC OCEAN

ILHA FERNANDO
DE NORONHA

☆Quito

ECUADOR

Río Napo

Río Amazonas

Río Marañón

Río Huallaga

Río Ucayali

Río Urubamba

Río Juruá

Río Purús

Río Madeira

Río Tapajós

Río Xingú

Río Tocantins

Río Araguaia

Río Tocantins

Río São Francisco

Río Madre de Dios

PERU

☆Lima

L.Titicaca
☆La Paz

L. Poopó

BOLIVIA

BRAZIL

Brasília
☆

PACIFIC OCEAN

Río Paraguay

PARAGUAY

Río Paraná

BRAZIL

Río Paraguay

Asunción☆

CHILE

ISLAS
JUAN FERNANDEZ

Río Paraná

Santiago☆

ARGENTINA

URUGUAY☆
Buenos Aires Montevideo

FALKLAND ISLANDS

MINERS AND LEAFTOSSERS: SCLERURIDAE

These two genera have recently been recognized as forming a family separate from the Furnariidae, where they were traditionally placed. They are united in the placement of their nests at the end of long burrows dug into the ground. Note that the leaftossers are on pp. 312–313.

Geositta

Plain, *short-tailed,* terrestrial furnariids of open, arid terrain in *Andes and s. South America,* with one species in the cerrado. Most miners are similar, so focus on their *bill shape, breast streaking* (if present), and any *rump and tail pattern.* Many species have *rufous in wings, obvious in flight.* They run in bursts, pausing abruptly; their rearparts are often bobbed. Miners typically nest in burrows dug into the ground.

Campo Miner

Geositta poeciloptera*   PLATE 1(1)

12.5 cm (5″). Uncommon and somewhat erratic and local in *campos and cerrado of interior s. Brazil and adjacent ne. Bolivia and ne. Paraguay.* 500–1400 m. *Short-tailed.* Brown above with a narrow buff superciliary; wings dusky with *rufous in flight feathers* (obvious in flight), *tail rufous with broad black subterminal band.* Throat white; below dull buff, breast flammulated brown. No other miner occurs with the Campo. Could conceivably be confused with Rufous Hornero, though their habitats and habits differ markedly. Miner is terrestrial and usually inconspicuous, crouching when approached, then flushing abruptly and often flying off some distance. Normally found singly or in pairs, but given favorable conditions (it strongly favors recently burned areas) can be temporarily numerous. Song, usually given during a hovering display flight, a simple repeated "zhliip" or "zh-zh-zh-leép."

Coastal Miner

Geositta peruviana   PLATE 1(2)

14 cm (5½″). Locally common in barren, often desertlike areas in *w. Peru* (Tumbes to Ica), usually where sandy and *often along immediate coast.* To 700 m. *Pale sandy brownish above* with a narrow whitish superciliary; wings dusky *with*

pale edging and tawny-buff in flight feathers, tail pale grayish buff and dusky. *Uniform whitish below. Occurs at lower elevations than its congeners,* but overlaps with the similar Grayish Miner, which differs in being grayer above (including wings and tail) and having pinkish buff on flanks. Cf. also Short-tailed Field Tyrant. Mostly terrestrial, running rapidly in short bursts, then pausing; perches on walls, even low buildings. Song a musical twittering, usually given while hovering.

Grayish Miner

Geositta maritima   PLATE 1(3)

14 cm (5½″). Uncommon in open, barren (often rocky) areas from *w. Peru* (Ancash) *to n. Chile* (Atacama). To 2900 m in Chile. Resembles Coastal Miner, and where they overlap usually outnumbered by it. Grayish can occur in hilly desert terrain with little or no vegetation. Differs in being *grayer above* (including wings, which *show no pale buff in flight*) and having a darker tail (with narrow whitish margin but *no pale area toward base*); *flanks pinkish buff* (Coastal all white below). Behavior much as in Coastal Miner.

Common Miner

Geositta cunicularia   PLATE 1(4)

14–15 cm (5½–6″). *Widespread and locally common* on open plains, hillsides, and sandy areas (including coastal dunes) with sparse grassy vegetation from cen. Peru (north in Andes to Junín, along coast to Ica) and extreme s. Brazil (north to coastal Santa Catarina) to n. Tierra del Fuego. To 4800 m in Peru. *Bill slightly decurved.* In **Peru, Bolivia, and n. Chile altiplano** (illustrated) grayish brown above with buffyish superciliary; *flight feathers mainly pale rufous* and *tail dusky with creamy buff base* (both most prominent in flight). Below buffy whitish *with blurry brownish breast streaking.* **Austral birds** are duller with less rufous in wings and smaller pale tail base; breast streaking bolder. **Coastal birds of s. Peru and n. Chile** smaller, and sandier above and whiter below. In far south, cf. Short-billed Miner; in altiplano, cf. Puna Miner. Coastal and Grayish Miners lack pale tail base. Mainly terrestrial and usually inconspicuous, foraging quietly in pairs or alone; sometimes perch on fences and low shrubs. Nonbreeders can gather in small groups. Song, usually given in flight, a slow trilled series of quite musical notes (sharper in far southern birds).

Dark-winged Miner

Geositta saxicolina　　　　　PLATE 1(5)

16.5 cm (6½"). Fairly common on sparsely vegetated, rocky slopes in *high Andes of cen. Peru* (w. Pasco to e. Lima and Huancavelica). 4000–4900 m. Grayish brown above with *cinnamon-buff forehead, superciliary, and face; wings uniform dusky brown* (showing *no rufous* in flight), *basal half of tail creamy buff* (conspicuous in flight). *Uniform pale buff below.* Common Miner lacks buff on face and in flight shows obvious rufous in wings; it favors less precipitous terrain. Conspicuous, often resting on boulders and foraging on grassy or bare areas, wagging its rearparts; found singly or in pairs. Perched birds give a pretty, melodic "cheecheechee-chi-chi-chi-chi."

Rufous-banded Miner

Geositta rufipennis　　　　　PLATE 1(6)

17–18 cm (6¾–7"). Locally fairly common on rocky slopes with sparse vegetation in Andes from w. Bolivia (La Paz) to s. Chile (Aysén) and s. Argentina (nw. Santa Cruz). 2500–4500 m in Bolivia, but much lower southward. A fairly large miner but bill short. Brownish above with pale buffyish superciliary; *flight feathers rufous with a blackish border, prominent in flight; tail rufous with a broad black subterminal band.* Below dingy buffyish, *flanks often pinkish cinnamon.* Cf. range-restricted Creamy-rumped Miner. Behavior much as in other miners, though often seems more confiding; when not breeding can be more gregarious. Often wags rearparts. Song a long series of musical trills interspersed with sharper notes, e.g., "treetreetreetree-trrr-treetreetreetree," given at rest or in a display flight.

Creamy-rumped Miner

Geositta isabellina

18 cm (7"). Rare to uncommon and local on rocky slopes with scattered grassy areas in *high Andes of cen. Chile* (Atacama to Talca) *and adja-*

cent Argentina (San Juan and Mendoza), a few wintering northward. 3000–4500 m, lower in austral winter. Resembles Rufous-banded Miner but bill longer and more decurved, *more uniform flight feathers* (duller rufous with a less obvious dusky border), and *creamy whitish rump and uppertail-coverts* (contrasting with blackish terminal tail). Behavior much as in Rufous-banded Miner but much less numerous and seems never to be gregarious. Voice similar but without the trills (A. Jaramillo).

Short-billed Miner

Geositta antarctica　　　　　PLATE 1(7)

15.5 cm (6"). Locally fairly common on barren steppes with short grass and scattered low bushes, also sandier areas near coast, in *extreme s. Argentina* (north to Santa Cruz) *and extreme s. Chile* (Magallanes); during austral winter migrates north in Argentina. To 1000 m. Resembles Common Miner but differs in its *shorter and straighter bill,* uniform brownish wings (*no rufous showing, even in flight*), and more mottled breast (sympatric Commons are distinctly *streaked* there). Behavior much as in Common Miner. Rather different song, most often given while at rest, a simpler "weetuk-weetuk-weetuk-weetuk-weetuk."

Puna Miner

Geositta punensis　　　　　PLATE 1(8)

14.5 cm (5¾"). Fairly common on open, often quite barren, plains in *high Andes from extreme s. Peru* (Moquegua and Puno) *to n. Chile* (Atacama) *and nw. Argentina* (Catamarca). Mostly 3500–4900 m. Resembles Common Miner. Puna is slightly smaller with a marginally shorter bill; paler and sandier above with a more cinnamon tail base; and whiter below *without Common's breast streaking.* Behavior and voice much the same.

Thick-billed Miner

Geositta crassirostris　　　　　PLATE 1(9)

17–17.5 cm (6¾–7"). *Uncommon and local on rocky slopes with scattered bushes and cacti in Andes of w. Peru* (Lima to Arequipa). 500–800 m in coastal lomas, and 2000–3000 m (may not occur at intermediate elevations). *Bill heavy and rather decurved; legs whitish.* Above dark brown with narrow whitish superciliary, *mantle feathers edged paler with scaly effect;* flight feathers with rufous (visible mainly as a band in flight), tail mainly rufous basally with blackish subterminal band. Below grayish white, breast mottled dusky. Distinctive in its restricted range. Forages singly and in pairs, often on lichen-encrusted boulders. Song a series of 10 drawn-out wheezy notes, at first rising, then falling and slowing.

Slender-billed Miner

Geositta tenuirostris   PLATE 1(10)

18.5–19 cm (7¼–7½″). Uncommon on puna and drier paramo grasslands and adjacent fields, frequently near watercourses, in *Andes of n. Ecuador,* and from *n. Peru* (Cajamarca) *to nw. Argentina* (Catamarca). 2500–4600 m. *Long, thin, somewhat decurved bill* (recalling an earthcreeper). Above pale brown with buff superciliary; *pale wing-bars,* and *flight feathers and tail mainly rufous* (showing mainly in flight). Below pale buffyish with *blurry brownish breast streaking.* No other miner has such a long, slender bill; Common Miner has shorter bill, conspicuous pale basal tail. Earthcreepers (with similar sickle-shaped bills) are longer-tailed, lack breast streaking and wing-bars. Found singly or in pairs, walking on the ground with a waddling gait; meadows with short grass are favored. Sometimes forages with groups of other Andean birds (e.g., yellowfinches). During display, ♂ circles above its territory while pouring forth a simple, often long-continued "jee-jee-jee . . ."; also sings while on the ground.

OVENBIRDS: FURNARIIDAE

A large and diverse group of insectivorous birds that reaches its greatest diversity in s. South America and the Andes, ranging in both forested and open environments. None is especially colorful (shades of brown and rufous predominate), and many species are skulking birds, though vocalizations are often loud and distinctive. Identification can be difficult. Nest structure and placement vary greatly, the most notable nests being large and constructed of sticks; others are fabricated entirely from mud.

Furnarius

Chunky, short-tailed, vaguely thrushlike birds with *long legs* that range widely across *the more open parts of the S. Am. lowlands,* horneros are some shade of rufous or brown and most sport a bold eyebrow. Many (especially Argentina's national bird, the Rufous Hornero) are well known from their *distinctive oven-shaped mud nests with a side entrance,* placed on a horizontal branch or fence post; Rufous Hornero "ovens" are much more conspicuous than those of the other species.

Pale-legged Hornero
Furnarius leucopus   PLATE 1(11)
17 cm (6¾"). Fairly common in semiopen areas and woodland and forest borders from w. Amazonia to e. Brazil. To about 1100 m. *Legs pale, dull flesh;* bill also pale. *Mostly bright orange-rufous above* with contrasting dusky crown and bold white superciliary. Throat white; *rich cinnamon-buff below.* Less numerous Bay Hornero is darker both above and below, and its crown lacks contrast with upperparts. The similar Band-tailed Hornero (locally sympatric) is duller below, usually shows blackish on tail. Seen singly or in pairs, walking on the ground where it picks at or probes into soil, favoring areas near water; perches freely on low branches. Arresting song, a fast descending series of loud notes that slows toward end.

Caribbean Hornero
*Furnarius longirostris**
16.5–17 cm (6½–6¾"). Fairly common in open and semiopen areas and woodland borders in n. Colombia and nw. Venezuela (east to e. Falcón). To 600 m. Formerly treated as a race of Pale-legged Hornero (no overlap); differs in its *grayer crown. The only hornero in its small range.* Behavior much as in Pale-legged Hornero, though tends to range more often in the open, regularly walking on roads and around ranch buildings. Song a series of "jew" notes 4–5 seconds long, often run into a stutter; less explosive than in Pale-legged (or Pacific) Horneros.

Pacific Hornero
*Furnarius cinnamomeus**
19 cm (7½"). Common and widespread in a variety of open and semiopen habitats, even in built-up areas, from w. Ecuador (w. Esmeraldas) *to nw. Peru* (Ancash); spreading with deforestation. To 2300 m in Ecuadorian Andes. Formerly treated as a race of Pale-legged Hornero (no overlap), differing in its *considerably larger size,* longer and heavier bill, *yellow iris,* and *much whiter underparts. The only hornero in its range.* Much more numerous and conspicuous than either the Pale-legged or Caribbean Horneros, strutting boldly in the open, frequently on or along roads and around houses. Song a loud, almost raucous series of piercing notes that slows and drops in pitch, sometimes given more or less in unison by a pair.

Bay Hornero
Furnarius torridus
18–18.5 cm (7–7¼"). *Rare and local in riparian woodland and on river islands in upper Amazonia.* To 1100 m. Sometimes called Pale-billed Hornero. Resembles Pale-legged Hornero, but larger and markedly more saturated color in plumage; *above rufous-chestnut* with *crown virtually con-*

color and a less prominent, grayer superciliary; *below mainly rufous.* Behavior much as in Pale-legged Hornero, though seems to stay in cover more. Song like Pale-legged's but faster-paced.

Band-tailed Hornero
Furnarius figulus   PLATE 1(12)
16.5 cm (6½"). Fairly common in semiopen areas, gardens, and woodland borders, usually near water, in *ne. and lower Amaz. Brazil.* To 600 m. *Legs grayish.* In **lower Amazon drainage** (illustrated) cinnamon-rufous above with *contrasting dark brown crown and cheeks* and bold white superciliary; primaries blackish, and *tail feathers variably tipped black.* Throat whitish; *drab buffyish below.* In **ne. Brazil** has *crown nearly concolor rufous-brown.* Pale-legged Hornero (widely sympatric) is brighter generally, and it has a more contrasting white throat; its legs are paler, and it never shows black on tail (though it does show more black along wing's leading edge than is seen in Band-tailed). Seen singly or in pairs, walking on the ground with head nodding back and forth. Feeds by picking at or probing into the ground or grass, sometimes flicking aside leaves, but perches freely on fences and low tree limbs. Song an explosive series of notes that gradually slows and descends in pitch.

Lesser Hornero
Furnarius minor   PLATE 1(13)
15 cm (6"). Uncommon on or near ground in low woodland and early-succession scrub in *river islands along Amazon River and some of its major tributaries upriver to e. Ecuador and ne. Peru.* Below 300 m. *Small and dull. Legs gray.* Above dull rufous with brownish gray crown and whitish superciliary. Throat white; below buffyish. Other sympatric horneros (e.g., Pale-legged and Bay) are larger and brighter. Band-tailed's Amaz. race is similar but is more richly colored below with a more contrasting throat, usually black on tail-tip. Walks on the ground, generally within cover though at times emerging to edge. Song a fast and descending series of high-pitched (compared with other horneros), shrill "kee" notes.

Crested Hornero
Furnarius cristatus   PLATE 1(14)
15.5 cm (6"). Fairly common in chaco scrub and woodland, and in cleared areas around houses, in *se. Bolivia* (Chuquisaca and Tarija), *w. Paraguay, and n. Argentina* (south to San Luis and Entre Ríos). To 1000 m. Unmistakable, with *prominent*

crest. Above brown with whitish lores and rufescent forehead; tail rufous. Throat white; below pale buffyish, midbelly whiter. Rufous Hornero is markedly larger and lacks the crest. Behavior similar to that species, but Crested generally less numerous and confiding. Song and calls shriller and higher-pitched.

Rufous Hornero
Furnarius rufus   PLATE 1(15)
18–20 cm (7–8"). *Locally abundant and widespread* in open and semiopen areas, often around houses, from Bolivia and e. Brazil to cen. Argentina; less numerous in ne. Brazil. Mostly below 1000 m, but in Bolivia to over 3000 m. *Very plain.* In **most of range** (illustrated) above rufous brown with a slightly grayer crown and pale lores. Below paler buffy brown, throat and midbelly whiter. In **ne. Brazil** brighter and buffier below, crown more grayish. In chaco area, cf. Crested Hornero (obviously crested). *A numerous and familiar bird across much of its range,* with unique bold demeanor. Struts about mainly on the ground, though also perching freely on fences and in trees. Song a loud and abrupt series of harsh notes that rises, then subsides; it is often given by a pair more or less in unison.

Upucerthia

Fairly large, plain terrestrial furnariids found in *open and semiopen areas principally in the Andes* (though one species extends onto Patagonian plains). Most are characterized by a *long and decurved bill* (sickle-shaped in a few). Nests are typically placed in burrows dug into banks.

Scale-throated Earthcreeper
Upucerthia dumetaria   PLATE 2(1)
21.5 cm (8½"). Fairly common on shrubby Patagonian steppes in cen. and s. Argentina, and in cen. and s. Chile; less numerous in montane scrub in Andes north to w. Bolivia (La Paz) and extreme s. Peru (Puno); in winter a few migrate north to ne. Argentina and Uruguay. To 3900 m. *Long, slender, strikingly decurved bill.* Brown to grayish brown above with narrow whitish superciliary; a little rufous in flight feathers, and *outer tail feathers prominently tipped whitish* (most evident in flight). Buffy whitish below, throat whiter with *throat and chest variably scaled dusky. The only earthcreeper showing scaling on foreneck or pale tail-tips.* Found singly or in pairs, usually

skulking on or near the ground, in or near cover, though at times one will perch atop a shrub. Birds hopping on the ground frequently cock their tail. Song a spritely and rather musical "tr, tr, trreetree-treetrritrritrri."

Plain-breasted Earthcreeper
Upucerthia jelskii   PLATE 2(2)
19–19.5 cm (7½–7¾"). Fairly common on shrubby slopes with boulders and grassy or bare areas in *high Andes from cen. Peru* (Ancash) *to extreme n. Chile* (Arica) *and nw. Argentina* (Salta and Jujuy). Mostly 3500–4500 m. *Long, slender bill strikingly decurved.* In **most of range** (illustrated) light brown above with narrow buffyish superciliary; a little rufous in flight feathers, tail mostly rufous. *Below uniform dull buff* (more grayish in **cen. Peru**). Buff-breasted Earthcreeper is larger with a longer bill, slightly buffier below. Cf. also range-restricted White-throated Earthcreeper. Behavior much as in Scale-throated Earthcreeper: sneaky, often hiding among rocks or under bushes, but sometimes feeds more or less in the open, probing into loose soil. Favors ravines. Song a dry trill, recalling a canastero, often given while perched atop a rock or bush.

White-throated Earthcreeper
Upucerthia albigula
19.5 cm (7¾"). Uncommon and local on sparsely vegetated slopes and along arid quebradas in *Andes from sw. Peru* (Ayacucho) *to extreme n. Chile* (Arica). 2500–4000 m. Resembles more numerous Plain-breasted Earthcreeper (with which it is locally sympatric, though White-throated typically ranges at lower elevations). Differs in having more extensive rufous in flight feathers, more contrasting whiter throat, a more pronounced and whiter superciliary, and more contrasting rufous-chestnut tail. Behavior much as in Plain-breasted Earthcreeper; song also similar though tending to be more musical and slower, e.g., "cht, cht, ch-ch-chchchchi-chichi."

Buff-breasted Earthcreeper
Upucerthia validirostris   PLATE 2(3)
20–21 cm (8–8¼"). Fairly common on shrubby slopes with boulders and grassy or bare areas in *Andes of nw. Argentina* (Salta to n. Mendoza and w. Córdoba). Mostly 2500–4000 m. Resembles Plain-breasted Earthcreeper, replacing that species southward. Differs in its *larger size, even longer bill*, more rufous in wings, and slightly buffier underparts. Behavior and voice much as in Plain-breasted Earthcreeper.

Striated Earthcreeper
Upucerthia serrana   PLATE 2(4)
20.5 cm (8"). Uncommon on rocky shrubby slopes and in Polylepis woodland patches in *Andes of w. Peru* (Cajamarca to Huancavelica). Mostly 2800–4200 m. Bill fairly long and decurved (but less extreme than in previous four species). Above grayish brown with a narrow whitish superciliary and *pale shaft streaking on crown and upper back; wings and tail contrasting rufous.* Throat white, below grayish brown *with prominent whitish streaking.* Plain-breasted Earthcreeper has a longer, more decurved bill; *it lacks streaking.* Found singly or in pairs, hopping on the ground with tail usually held cocked; sometimes moves up into shrubs and low trees. Song a harsh trill with several introductory notes, "keep kip kip trrrrrrrr-r-r-r" (J. Fjeldså and N. K. Krabbe).

Rock Earthcreeper
Upucerthia andaecola   PLATE 2(5)
18.5 cm (7¼"). Uncommon on rocky hillsides with scattered bushes and in ravines in *Andes from w. Bolivia* (La Paz) *to nw. Argentina* (Catamarca) *and adjacent Chile.* 2600–4200 m. Bill only slightly decurved. Above brown with *narrow buff superciliary;* some rufous in primaries; *tail uniform rufous.* Below pale buffyish with *dusky streaking on sides and flanks* (sometimes extending across breast as well). Straight-billed Earthcreeper's bill is indeed straighter; *its streaking below is whitish* (not dark streaking on a paler ground color). Cf. also certain canasteros (all with shorter bills). Found singly or in pairs, hopping on the ground or among boulders; rarely away from rocky places. Tail usually cocked, though the angle is not as acute as is typical of Straight-billed. Song, often delivered from atop a rock or shrub, a series of piercing notes, e.g., "vee-vee-vee-vee-vee-vi-veet?," sometimes with a sputter at end; higher-pitched than Straight-billed.

Straight-billed Earthcreeper
Upucerthia ruficaudus   PLATE 2(6)
18.5 cm (7¼"). Locally fairly common on rocky slopes and in ravines in *Andes from s. Peru* (Arequipa) *to cen. Chile* (Santiago) *and w. Argentina* (Chubut); less numerous southward. Mostly 2300–4300 m, but locally to 1300 m in s. Argentina. *Bill nearly straight.* Above pale brown with narrow whitish superciliary; some rufous in flight feathers; *tail mostly rufous, but its inner webs are blackish.* Throat and chest white, breast and belly *pale brownish with blurry whitish streaking.* Rock Earthcreeper has a slightly more decurved bill,

buffier superciliary, more uniform underparts (lacking Straight-billed's white-bibbed effect) on which streaking is dark and is confined to sides; its tail is completely rufous. Cf. also certain canasteros (with shorter bills, etc.). Found singly or in pairs, and generally secretive, hopping or running among boulders and usually keeping out of sight; *tail almost always held cocked high, sometimes as much as 90° or even slightly forward.* Song, often delivered from the ground, a loud and fast series of ringing notes that rises at first, then fades toward end.

Chaco Earthcreeper
*Upucerthia certhioides**   PLATE 2(7)
17 cm (6¾"). *Uncommon in chaco woodland and scrub,* especially where undergrowth is dense, from extreme s. Bolivia (se. Santa Cruz) to w. Paraguay and n. and cen. Argentina (south locally to La Pampa and e. Río Negro). To 1700 m. This and the Bolivian Earthcreeper have been separated in the genus *Ochetorhynchus.* Bill slightly decurved. Above brown with *rufous forehead* and narrow buff to rufous superciliary; some rufous in flight feathers and tail. *Throat white; below pale grayish brown. No other earthcreeper occurs in the chaco lowlands.* Band-tailed Eremobius is streaked below, lacks rufous forehead, etc. Found singly or in pairs, foraging both on the ground and in dense low scrub; except when singing, often difficult to observe. Song a series of 6–10 loud penetrating notes, e.g., "cheeé-cheeé-cheeé-cheeé-cheéw," reminiscent of a thornbird and rather unlike other earthcreepers (except for Bolivian).

Bolivian Earthcreeper
*Upucerthia harterti**
17 cm (6¾"). Uncommon on or near ground in deciduous woodland and scrub in *Andes of w. Bolivia* (s. La Paz to Tarija). 1400–2950 m. Resembles Chaco Earthcreeper (no overlap), but *lacks* rufous forehead; paler below (hence its white throat contrasts *less*); superciliary always buff. Behavior as in Chaco, though Bolivian seems more terrestrial; it favors quebradas and areas with terrestrial bromeliads. Song similar to Chaco's, though often longer, then a seemingly endless series of "chyip" notes. Call a repeated sharp "cheeyp."

Band-tailed Eremobius
*Eremobius phoenicurus**   PLATE 2(8)
18 cm (7"). *Uncommon on arid shrubby Patagonian steppes in s. Argentina* (Neuquén and Río

Negro south) *and extreme s. Chile* (ne. Magallanes). To 1200 m. Often called Band-tailed Earthcreeper. Bill straight. Above grayish brown with *white superciliary* and rufescent cheeks; *tail black with basal half of all but central feathers rufous-chestnut.* Throat white; below dull grayish, *streaked white on breast and flanks.* Scale-throated Earthcreeper is larger and has much longer decurved bill as well as scaling on foreneck. Straight-billed Earthcreeper (an Andean bird) has mainly rufous tail, buffier underparts. Mainly terrestrial, running rapidly on the ground and keeping to cover; forages by probing into loose soil and rock crevices. The tail is usually held cocked at an acute angle. Singing birds may take a prominent perch; song a short and fast trill that sometimes ends with an emphasized "wheeék" note or a series of such notes. Nest a mass of twigs, very different from the typical earthcreepers.

Crag Chilia
Chilia melanura   PLATE 2(9)
18.5 cm (7¼"). Uncommon and local on *steep rocky slopes and around cliffs in Andes of cen. Chile* (Atacama to Colchagua). Mostly 1200–2500 m. *Bill straight,* lower mandible with pale base. Above dark brown with narrow white superciliary and *contrasting rufous rump, uppertail-coverts, and crissum; tail mainly blackish. Throat and breast sharply white,* belly brown. More strikingly patterned than most other similar-looking furnariids, and not likely confused in its limited range and habitat; cf. Straight-billed Earthcreeper. Favors areas with sparse or no vegetation. Found singly and in pairs, hopping and scampering on the ground and among rocks, flying but little; often cocks its tail at an acute angle. Foraging birds mainly pick and probe on rocks but also sometimes feed at cactus flowers. Usually sings from atop a boulder; song a short series of piercing "teet" notes, more jumbled at the start and finish.

Pseudoseisura

Large brown or rufous furnariids, most with *prominent bushy crests,* with primarily allopatric ranges in the semiopen or open terrain in e. and s. South America. Cacholotes are known for their *raucous, far-carrying calls* and *conspicuous huge stick nests.*

Gray-crested Cacholote

*Pseudoseisura unirufa**   PLATE 2(10)

23 cm (9″). Fairly common in borders of gallery woodland, islands of woodland in seasonally flooded savannas, and in trees around buildings in *n.* (mainly Beni) *and far e. Bolivia, sw. Brazil, and extreme n. Paraguay.* To 500 m. Now considered a separate species from the following one; formerly called Rufous Cacholote. Iris yellow. *Expressive bushy crest. Uniform cinnamon-rufous* with *gray usually showing in crest.* Gray-crested does not overlap with the Caatinga Cacholote; otherwise unmistakable. Mainly arboreal, though sometimes drops to the ground when feeding, often hopping or walking with an unsteady, almost lurching gait. Pairs are regularly seen around their very large conspicuous stick nests. Their loud and unmistakable vocalizations are given frequently, usually as a duet and often while a pair lingers near their nest. The presumed ♂ gives a descending series of "chup" notes that accelerates into a long-continued churring, while the presumed ♀ gives a fast series of "che" notes. It's a complex and jumbled effort, and gradually winds down to a stuttered stop.

Caatinga Cacholote

*Pseudoseisura cristata**

23 cm (9″). Locally fairly common in caatinga woodland and semiopen areas, sometimes even where overgrazed, in *ne. Brazil* (south to Minas Gerais). To 600 m. Now considered a separate species from the preceding, which it resembles; the Caatinga's bill is a bit longer, and the plumage slightly paler and brighter, *showing no gray in crest* (there may be a little in young birds). The two species do not overlap. Behavior much as in Gray-crested, but Caatinga is more often in small groups, and at least at times has helpers at the nest. Its loud vocalizations are basically similar, though the individual notes are delivered more slowly.

Brown Cacholote

Pseudoseisura lophotes   PLATE 2(11)

26 cm (10¼″). Fairly common in chaco woodland and scrub, and in monte and espinilho woodland, from *se. Bolivia* (s. Santa Cruz) *to Uruguay and cen. Argentina* (e. Río Negro). To 900 m. Iris yellow. *Expressive bushy crest. Above brown,* crest feathers grayer and darker; rump and tail dark rufous. Face and throat rufous; below brown, feathers scaled paler (most pronounced in Argentina; more obscure northward). Gray-crested Cacholote (no known over-

lap) is smaller and much brighter rufous overall. White-throated Cacholote is much more grayish overall. Behavior much as in Gray-crested, but somewhat more terrestrial. Its raucous vocalizations, usually given as a duet, differ in being even harsher and more grating; they typically do not accelerate into a stutter or chatter.

White-throated Cacholote

Pseudoseisura gutturalis   PLATE 2(12)

24 cm (9½″). Uncommon in arid shrubby Patagonian and Andean scrub in *w. and cen. Argentina* (Salta to n. Santa Cruz). To 2900 m. Crest shorter than in other cacholotes, often not evident at all. Above dull grayish to grayish brown. *Small throat patch white outlined below by black;* below grayish to sandy brown. Brown Cacholote is somewhat larger, with a longer crest, and browner overall with a rufescent tail; it lacks white and black on throat. Behavior much as in other cacholotes; White-throated is particularly terrestrial, capable of running rapidly on the ground (with less lurching than the others). Its loud raucous voice recalls Brown Cacholote.

Cinclodes

Sturdy furnariids found *primarily in the Andes* (several range along rocky coastlines), with one species (Long-tailed) isolated in se. Brazil. Cinclodes are *fond of the vicinity of water,* moving or still, fresh or salt. Most species show a *white to rufous wing-band,* obvious in flight and lacking in the somewhat similar (though even plainer) earthcreepers, whose bills tend to be more decurved. Their tails are often cocked. Nests are placed in a hole or burrow, most often dug into a bank but also in walls or old buildings.

Blackish Cinclodes

Cinclodes antarcticus   PLATE 3(1)

19–20 cm (7½–8″). Local along *rocky coasts* and on gravel beaches in *extreme s. Chile and Argentina; most numerous on small islands and Falklands,* avoiding areas where introduced predators are present. Yellowish base of lower mandible in **Chilean** birds (not Falklands). *Uniform dark sooty to sooty brown* (browner on **Falklands**), throat slightly paler. Hardly to be confused in its limited range and habitat. Can be astonishingly tame, sometimes even hopping about at your feet; forages mainly on insects and marine invertebrates found in kelp mats and on rocks. Song a loud, often long-continued series of sharp staccato notes interspersed with more musical trills, sometimes given in flight, but also when perched while flapping its wings.

Dark-bellied Cinclodes
Cinclodes patagonicus   PLATE 3(2)
20.5 cm (8″). Fairly common *near water* (fresh and salt) from *cen. and s. Chile* (Antofogasta) *and w. Argentina* (Mendoza) *to Tierra del Fuego.* To 2500 m in Chile. *Dusky gray above* with a *bold white superciliary;* buff wing-band shows mainly in flight, outer tail feathers tipped buff. Throat and sides of neck white flecked dusky; *below gray, breast distinctly streaked white.* The similar Gray-flanked Cinclodes is markedly smaller with a finer bill; its midbelly is whiter, contrasting with flanks. Chilean Seaside Cinclodes is darker and much browner, lacks such a bold white brow. An attractive cinclodes that often cocks its tail; it usually ranges in pairs that patrol streams and lakeshores, sometimes coasts. Song an arresting "pur-r-r-ree-pree-pree-pree-tr-r-r-r-r-r-r"; frequent call a sharp "tjit," often given in flight.

Chilean Seaside Cinclodes
Cinclodes nigrofumosus   PLATE 3(3)
21.5 cm (8½″). Locally fairly common on *rocky coastlines of n. and cen. Chile* (Arica to Osorno). Sometimes called simply the Seaside Cinclodes. *Dark sooty brown above* with *narrow pale superciliary;* a rufous-buff wing-band shows mainly in flight, outer tail feathers tipped buff. *Throat and sides of neck white;* below brown streaked with white, especially on breast. The similar Peruvian Seaside Cinclodes replaces this species northward, with no known overlap. Dark-bellied Cinclodes is somewhat smaller and grayer generally, with a more prominent white superciliary. True to its name, this species never occurs away from the immediate coast, foraging singly or in pairs on rocks, favoring surf-exposed areas. Sometimes partially cocks tail. Song an extended trill, often accompanied by flaring wings open and shut; it is usually given as the bird perches atop a boulder.

Peruvian Seaside Cinclodes
Cinclodes taczanowskii   PLATE 3(4)
21.5 cm (8½″). Locally fairly common on *rocky coastlines of cen. and s. Peru* (Ancash to Tacna). Sometimes called Surf Cinclodes. Resembles Chilean Seaside Cinclodes, replacing that species northward (no overlap). Not quite so dark; *white*

on throat less extensive and less contrasting, pale streaking below less extensive, superciliary narrower, and *wing-covert tips pale buff.* Behavior much as in the Chilean species, and equally tied to rocky coastlines. Often tame.

Gray-flanked Cinclodes
Cinclodes oustaleti   PLATE 3(5)
16.5–17 cm (6½–6¾″). Uncommon in open rocky or grassy areas, often near streams, in *Andes from n. Chile* (Antofogasta) *and w. Argentina* (Mendoza) *south to Tierra del Fuego;* breeds in mountains, retreating downslope, some to the coast, during winter; also resident on Juan Fernández Islands off Chile. To 3000 m. *Dusky gray above* with a narrow white superciliary; a *buff wing-band* shows mainly in flight, outer tail feathers tipped buff. Throat white flecked dusky; breast and flanks grayish, *breast irregularly spotted and streaked white, flanks more or less contrasting with whitish midbelly.* Dark-bellied Cinclodes is larger with a longer and heavier bill, more conspicuous brow, cleaner white breast streaks, and less contrasting flanks. Sympatric race of Bar-winged Cinclodes is browner above with a buffier superciliary, lacks breast streaking and contrasting flanks, and has whiter tail corners. Behavior similar to Dark-bellied Cinclodes, though Gray-flanked is less closely tied to the vicinity of water and never seems to be as numerous.

Olrog's Cinclodes
*Cinclodes olrogi**
17 cm (6¾″). Uncommon in open grassy and rocky areas, most often along streams, on *sierras of w. Argentina* (w. Córdoba and ne. San Luis). 1600–2800 m, descending in winter. Resembles Gray-flanked Cinclodes (no overlap) but has *striking white wing-band.* Córdoba Cinclodes (sympatric, and more numerous) has a rufous wing-band and less mottled or scaled breast. Differs from sympatric White-winged Cinclodes in its smaller size, rufous-buff (not white) tail corners, and breast markings (underparts more smoothly dark in White-winged). Behavior much as in Gray-flanked Cinclodes, but more tied to vicinity of water.

Bar-winged Cinclodes
Cinclodes fuscus   PLATE 3(6)
17–17.5 cm (6¾–7″). *Widespread and often common* in open, grassy or rocky areas in Andes from w. Venezuela (Lara) south to Tierra del Fuego, also in Patagonia; in winter southern breeders migrate north into Chile and Argentina, a few

as far as s. Paraguay and s. Brazil. To 5000 m. In **southern part of range** (A) grayish brown above with a buffy whitish superciliary; cinnamon-buff wing-band shows mainly in flight, outer tail feathers tipped buffy whitish. Throat whitish (sometimes scaled dusky); below grayish brown. **Andean races** are browner (less gray) generally; from **Peru to n. Chile and nw. Argentina** (B) has a *whitish wing-band,* from **Ecuador northward** (C) has a *rufous wing-band. Generally the most numerous cinclodes.* From Ecuador north, cf. Stout-billed Cinclodes. Southward in Andes, cf. White-winged Cinclodes (larger, with longer and blacker tail, more rufescent back, striking white wing-band and tail corners). Gray-flanked Cinclodes is darker generally, has a whiter superciliary and some streaking below (Bar-winged is plain below). Usually in pairs and often confiding, foraging on the ground and rocks, frequently near water but also in drier areas and along roads. Flight swift, usually low to the ground; often cocks tail jauntily upon alighting. Song a brief, high-pitched trill, often given with wings upraised and flapped exuberantly, sometimes in a display flight.

Stout-billed Cinclodes
Cinclodes excelsior　　　　PLATE 3(7)
20.5 cm (8"). Locally fairly common in paramo, open shrubby areas, and *Polylepis* woodland patches in *Andes of Colombia and Ecuador* (south to Azuay). 3300–5000 m. *Bill rather long, heavy, and markedly decurved.* Above dark brown with a whitish superciliary; rufous-buff wing-band shows mainly in flight, outer tail feathers tipped dull buff. Throat whitish scaled dusky; below buffy whitish, browner on sides, *breast with obvious brownish scaling.* Bar-winged Cinclodes is smaller with a finer, shorter, and straighter bill; it shows less scaling below. Behavior much as in the generally more numerous Bar-winged, though less tied to presence of water; more frequent in areas with shrubs and low trees, regularly perching in them. At higher elevations Stout-billed often outnumbers Bar-winged. Feeding birds probe into loose or moist soil. Song a rising trill, "tr-r-r-r-r-reeet," usually uttered during a wing-flapping display. Distinctive call a sharp "keeu."

Royal Cinclodes
Cinclodes aricomae
20.5 cm (8"). *Very rare and local in patches of Polylepis woodland in Andes of s. Peru* (Apurímac to Puno) *and w. Bolivia* (La Paz). 3600–

4700 m. Resembles Stout-billed Cinclodes (geographically distant), but with *considerably darker and browner belly,* buffier superciliary, and a *more conspicuous rufous wing-band.* Cf. smaller and slimmer Bar-winged Cinclodes, which in Royal's range has a whitish wing-band and is not so dark. Behavior (and apparently voice) much as in Stout-billed; Royal seems, however, to be much shyer and more confined to the interior of *Polylepis* woodland; threatened by continued cutting of that woodland.

Córdoba Cinclodes
Cinclodes comechingonus　　　PLATE 3(8)
17 cm (6¾"). Common in open grassy and rocky areas on *sierras of w. Argentina* (w. Córdoba and ne. San Luis); in winter some move north to Tucumán and Santiago del Estero. 1600–2400 m when breeding, lower in winter. Resembles southern race of Bar-winged Cinclodes, differing in its *deep rufous wing-band* (not cinnamon-buff) and *mostly yellowish lower mandible.* Sympatric Olrog's Cinclodes has an obvious white wing-band. Bar-winged does not breed sympatrically with Córdoba Cinclodes, but does occur with it during austral winter. Behavior of the two is similar, as is the voice, though song is rather more complex.

Long-tailed Cinclodes
Cinclodes pabsti　　　　PLATE 3(9)
21.5 cm (8½"). Uncommon in open grasslands, usually near water, in *extreme se. Brazil* (se. Santa Catarina and ne. Rio Grande do Sul). 750–1700 m. *Large.* Brown above with white superciliary; *wing-coverts and flight feathers tipped and edged cinnamon-buff;* outer tail feathers tipped cinnamon-buff. Throat white; below pale buffy brownish. *The only cinclodes in its restricted range.* Bar-winged Cinclodes could, however, occur here as a vagrant during winter; it is markedly smaller, with a shorter tail and a plainer closed wing (showing much less edging), and has a dusky-scaled throat. This cinclodes is so large that in a quick view it can even be taken for a Chalk-browed Mockingbird. Behavior much as in Bar-winged and other cinclodes.

White-winged Cinclodes
Cinclodes atacamensis　　　PLATE 3(10)
21 cm (8¼"). Uncommon to locally common *along streams* in grassy and shrubby terrain in Andes from cen. Peru (Ancash and Pasco) to w. Argentina (Mendoza; also on sierras of w. Córdoba and ne. San Luis). Mostly 2200–

4500 m, but lower in Argentina. Bill quite long. In **Andes** (A) *above rufous brown with white superciliary; broad pure white wing-band and patch on primary-coverts* especially conspicuous in flight; *tail blackish with white corners.* Throat white; below pale buffy grayish, flanks browner. On **Argentinian sierras** (B) darker brown above and grayer below (hence the white throat contrasts more). Sympatric Bar-winged Cinclodes is smaller with a shorter bill, less rufescent above with buffier superciliary, and much less white shows on closed wing; especially on flushing birds, note Bar-winged's shorter brown (not blackish, hence less contrasting) tail. Behavior much as in Bar-winged and other cinclodes, but more confined to vicinity of clear running water.

White-bellied Cinclodes
Cinclodes palliatus PLATE 3(11)
24 cm (9½"). *A large and rare cinclodes found very locally on and around cushion bogs in high Andes of cen. Peru* (Junín, Lima, and Huancavelica). 4400–5000 m. *Unmistakable.* Crown pale grayish, otherwise rich rufous brown above; *broad white wing-band conspicuous in flight* and visible even on closed wing; tail blackish with white tail corners. *Snowy white below.* Vaguely recalls a mockingbird, none of which occur anywhere near so high. Ranges in highly dispersed pairs that are conspicuous in the open terrain it favors, though it also can disappear for protracted periods (into holes?), then suddenly reappear in plain sight. Usually seen hopping on open bogs, but also forages on surrounding rocky slopes. The tail is almost always held cocked, often at an acute angle, and can even be angled sideways.

Great Spinetail
Siptornopsis hypochondriaca PLATE 4(1)
18.5 cm (7¼"). *Rare and local in arid montane scrub in upper Río Marañón valley of nw. Peru* (Cajamarca, La Libertad, and n. Ancash). 2150–2800 m. *Large* and *long-tailed.* Brown above with a *long white superciliary* and *blackish lores and auriculars;* lesser wing-coverts rufous. *White below* with *bold streaking on breast and down sides.* **Juvenile** less streaked below. Similarly patterned Necklaced and Chinchipe Spinetails are much smaller; they occur at lower elevations. Baron's Spinetail, almost as large, has rufous crown, wings, and tail; it occurs in more wooded habitats. Usually in pairs, foraging mainly as it hops along larger horizontal limbs, often cocking tail; overall comportment recalls a *Campylorhynchus*

wren (and occurs with Fasciated). Sometimes also drops to the ground. Apparent song a loud, explosive, reeling trill that slows into a variable number of sputtered notes. Call a distinctively doubled "jt-jeét," like a *Forpus* parrotlet.

White-browed Spinetail
Hellmayrea gularis PLATE 4(2)
13–13.5 cm (5–5¼"). A *small, short-tailed* spinetail found in *undergrowth of upper montane forest* in Andes from w. Venezuela (Trujillo) to cen. Peru (Junín). 2400–3700 m. In **Colombia and Ecuador** (illustrated) rufous brown above, tail mostly rufous, with *superciliary, lores, and throat white. Below buffy brown.* In **Venezuela** more grayish below; in **Peru** brighter and more cinnamon below. Can be confused with Mountain Wren (also rufescent and short-tailed), though the wren lacks white on face. Rufous Spinetail has a much longer tail, and also lacks white facial markings. Found singly or in pairs, generally apart from mixed flocks, and usually inconspicuous (though sometimes unwary of the observer). Feeds by probing into moss and dead leaves. Song a series of *Cranioleuca*-like, high-pitched notes ending in a trill, e.g., "chiyt-chit-chit-chit-chi-chi-chichichichichichi."

Synallaxis

A *difficult* genus of obscure slender furnariids with short wings and *often quite long, double-pointed tails, Synallaxis* spinetails occupy undergrowth in a variety of forested and semiopen habitats across all but southernmost South America. They can be hard to identify to species and are hard to see well; pay attention to *their often characteristic voices,* as many will be heard for every one seen. Many species show a *contrasting rufous crown* and rufous on wings, and most have a throat patch that often becomes more conspicuous (blacker) when they sing. *Tail color can be important,* rufous in some species but grayish or brown in others. Nests are globular structures of sticks with a tubular entrance on the side. There is some dispute as to generic limits; our first two species (Necklaced and Chinchipe) may deserve to be separated, and three depicted on Plate 5 (Ochre-cheeked, White-whiskered, and Hoary-throated) were formerly often separated in *Poecilurus* (and sometimes still are).

Necklaced Spinetail
Synallaxis stictothorax PLATE 4(3)
12.5 cm (5"). *Fairly common in arid scrub and deciduous woodland borders from sw. Ecuador* (Manabí) *to nw. Peru* (La Libertad). Below 300 m. In **most of Ecuador** (illustrated) is brownish above with forehead streaked black and white and a *narrow white superciliary,* rump more rufescent. Wings mostly rufous; tail rufous, inner web of central pair of feathers blackish, *with bicolored effect.* Below white, *purest on throat,* with *fine dusky streaking across breast.* In **Peru and extreme s. Ecuador** tail almost entirely rufous. Not likely confused in its restricted range and habitat, but cf. Chinchipe Spinetail in Río Marañón drainage (no overlap). Can look vaguely wrenlike (e.g., Superciliated). Usually in pairs, gleaning in foliage and more arboreal than other *Synallaxis,* thus easier to observe and often not at all shy. Most frequent song a series of sputtering notes, loud at first, then slowing and trailing off, e.g., "ch-ch-chéh-chéh-chéh-cheh-cheh-ch-ch-ch, ch, chch," sometimes given as a duet. Regularly vocalizes when perched near (or even in) its conspicuous ball-shaped nest.

Chinchipe Spinetail
Synallaxis chinchipensis
13.5 cm (5¼"). *Locally fairly common in deciduous woodland and borders in upper Río Marañón drainage of nw. Peru* (Cajamarca). To 700 m. Resembles Necklaced Spinetail of Pacific lowlands (no overlap) but slightly larger with a longer bill. Has a *much less prominent, buffier superciliary* and *breast spotted dusky* (not streaked); flanks grayish (not buff). Chinchipe's tail pattern is bicolored as in northern race of Necklaced. Great Spinetail has a similar pattern but is *much* larger, etc.; it occurs in the Peruvian Andes. Behavior recalls Necklaced Spinetail, but even more arboreal (thus *Cranioleuca*-like); voice also similar.

Rufous Spinetail
Synallaxis unirufa PLATE 4(4)
17–18 cm (6¾–7"). Uncommon in undergrowth of upper montane forest and borders in *Andes from w. Venezuela* (Trujillo) *to s. Peru* (Cuzco). 1700–3200 m. Rather long tail. In **most of range** (illustrated) *uniform bright rufous* with contrasting black lores. **Sierra de Perijá** birds are paler, more cinnamon. Resembles the more gregarious Rufous Wren, though the wren differs in showing faint barring on wings and its tail is shorter, more rounded. Also cf. Sepia-brown Wren. No overlap with similar Black-throated Spinetail. Favors

stands of *Chusquea* bamboo, where pairs and family groups hop and clamber about, tending to remain within dense cover where they are hard to see well or for long; most often independent of mixed flocks. Heard more often than seen. Song a simple, rather shrill "kweeík" or "kueék" or, less frequently, "kuh-kweeík" with a querulous upslurred effect, often steadily repeated.

Black-throated Spinetail
Synallaxis castanea PLATE 4(5)
18.5 cm (7¼"). Fairly common in undergrowth of montane forest and borders in *mountains of n. Venezuela* (Aragua to Miranda). 1300–2200 m. Resembles paler (Perijá) race of Rufous Spinetail (no overlap), but has a distinctive *contrasting black throat;* tail slightly longer and more rounded. In Venezuela the Rufous Spinetail ranges only in the Andes. Behavior much as in Rufous Spinetail, though seems less skulking. Voice very different; often given by both members of a pair, the call is a fast staccato "ke-che-che-che-che" followed by a louder "ker-cheé-cheé."

Rusty-headed Spinetail
Synallaxis fuscorufa PLATE 4(6)
17 cm (6¾"). Fairly common in undergrowth of montane forest and borders on *Santa Marta Mts. of n. Colombia.* Mostly 2000–3000 m. *Mostly bright rufous,* slightly paler below, with black lores; *back and rump contrasting grayish olive,* also flanks. Not likely confused, the only *Synallaxis* occurring at high elevations on the Santa Martas. Forages mainly in pairs, tending to hop higher above the ground than most other *Synallaxis;* sometimes accompanies small understory flocks. Frequent song a short nasal "di-dit-du" (S. Hilty).

Russet-bellied Spinetail
Synallaxis zimmeri PLATE 4(7)
16.5 cm (6½"). *Rare and local in montane scrub on west slope of Andes in nw. Peru* (La Libertad at Llaguén, and on slopes of Cordillera Negra in Ancash). 2100–2900 m. *Head gray* with narrow, broken whitish eye-ring, back olivaceous brown; rump and extensive area on wings rufous; outer tail feathers mostly rufous. Throat pale grayish; *below uniform pinkish rufous.* Not likely confused in its limited range. Forages in pairs or small family groups, usually not accompanying other birds. Song a fast, snarling "quik-quik" (J. Fjeldså and N. K. Krabbe).

Apurímac Spinetail
Synallaxis courseni   PLATE 4(8)

19 cm (7½"). Locally common in undergrowth and borders of montane forest, woodland, and borders in *Andes of s. Peru* (Apurímac). 2450–3500 m. Resembles much more widespread Azara's Spinetail but darker and *tail notably longer and brownish dusky* (not rufous). The two species apparently do not occur together, though range of Azara's is close. Behavior, including vocalizations, as in Azara's (J. Fjeldså and N. K. Krabbe).

Silvery-throated Spinetail
Synallaxis subpudica

19 cm (7½"). Fairly common in montane forest and woodland borders, overgrown clearings, and hedgerows in *Andes of ne. Colombia* (Boyacá and Cundinamarca). Mostly 2000–3200 m. Resembles geographically distant Apurímac Spinetail but more olivaceous brown generally (not so gray); Silvery-throated likewise has a *very long grayish brown tail*. The throat is really not very silvery. Recalls Azara's Spinetail, though Azara's has a *rufous tail*. Behavior much as in Azara's Spinetail, though Silvery-throated seems less furtive and is easier to see. Song a fast, coalescing series of chattered notes that drop in pitch, recalling a *Cranioleuca*, e.g., "chí-chi-chi-che-che-che-chu-chu-chu."

Azara's Spinetail
Synallaxis azarae   PLATE 4(9)

17–17.5 cm (6¾–7"). *Common and widespread* in montane forest borders, lighter woodland, clearings, and hedgerows in *Andes from w. Venezuela* (s. Lara) *to nw. Argentina* (Catamarca). Mostly 1500–3000 m northward; mainly 500–1500 m southward. Rather long tail. In **most of range** (A) olive brown above with *contrasting rufous crown* and brownish frontlet; *wings and tail also rufous.* Throat black scaled white; below whitish (northward) to grayish, darkest in s. Peru and nw. Bolivia. In **s. Bolivia and nw. Argentina** (B) has a *buff superciliary,* pale underparts. *Azara's is easily the most frequently recorded Andean Synallaxis.* In ne. Colombia, cf. Silvery-fronted Spinetail; in s. Peru, cf. Apurímac Spinetail; in s. Bolivia, cf. Sooty-fronted Spinetail. Though often heard, tends to be furtive and hard to see. Occurs singly or in pairs, creeping in dense vegetation such as bracken ferns, usually close to the ground; most often not with mixed flocks. Even singing birds are rarely in the open. Song, delivered at intervals through the day, an often endlessly repeated,

sharp "kuh-kweeé." Less often gives a *Scytalopus*-like series of notes, "kakakakakaka. . . ."

Pale-breasted Spinetail
Synallaxis albescens   PLATE 4(10)

16–16.5 cm (6¼–6½"). *Widespread and often common* in open grassy areas with scattered bushes, shrubby areas, and locally in arid scrub, marshes, and on river islands from n. and e. Colombia and Venezuela to n. and e. Bolivia, e. Brazil, and n. Argentina (La Pampa and Buenos Aires); absent from most of Amazonia. Mostly below 1500 m. Olive to grayish brown above with a dusky frontlet and rufous crown; *wing-coverts rufous, remainder of wing and tail brownish. Below whitish* with dusky throat flecking. Cinereous-breasted and Dark-breasted Spinetails are darker and grayer below; these and the Pale-breasted occur together only marginally, with voices of all three differing markedly. Furtive behavior much as in other *Synallaxis,* likewise heard far more often than seen. Characteristic, often incessantly repeated song a nasal, husky "weé-bzü," occasionally also some chatters. Also: Costa Rica and Panama.

Spix's Spinetail
Synallaxis spixi   PLATE 4(11)

16 cm (6¼"). Common in woodland borders and shrubby areas in *se. Brazil region* (north to e. Bahia). To 2000 m. Olive brown above with an *entirely rufous crown* (*no* dark frontlet) and mostly rufous wings; long tail grayish brown. *Mostly gray below,* throat flecked black and mid-belly paler. Cinereous-breasted Spinetail (minimal overlap) has a shorter, less pointed tail and a dusky frontlet; its voice differs markedly. Pale-breasted Spinetail favors more open habitats; it too has a frontlet and also is much paler below. Rufous-capped Spinetail has a yellow streak below its rufous crown and a shorter rufous tail. Behavior similar to numerous other *Synallaxis,* creeping about within dense cover (sometimes in extensive fern growth), emerging most often when singing. Song a constantly reiterated "whít, di-di-dit," recalling Dark-breasted Spinetail.

Sooty-fronted Spinetail
Synallaxis frontalis   PLATE 4(12)

16–16.5 cm (6¼–6½"). Fairly common and widespread in undergrowth and borders of woodland, chaco scrub, monte, and overgrown pastures from *w. Bolivia* (s. La Paz and Cochabamba) *and ne. Brazil to cen. Argentina* (La Pampa) *and Uruguay.* To 2500 m in Bolivia.

Olive brown above with sooty frontlet and a rufous crown; wings and tail also rufous. Throat whitish flecked black, breast pale grayish, mid-belly whitish. Pale-breasted Spinetail (often sympatric) has a brownish tail, as does the more local Cinereous-breasted; all three of these spinetails show a similar sooty front. Azara's Spinetail, which also is rufous-tailed, shows a buff brow in its area of overlap with Sooty-fronted (Bolivia). Sooty-fronted favors more wooded habitats than Pale-breasted Spinetail, though they can occur more or less together. Forages in pairs, with rather skulking behavior like most other *Synallaxis*. Song a sharp "ka-kweé," recalling Azara's Spinetail.

Dark-breasted Spinetail
Synallaxis albigularis   PLATE 4(13)
15.5 cm (6"). *Common in grassy pastures, shrubby clearings and borders, and younger woodland (including river islands) in w. Amazonia.* Mostly below 1500 m. Above olive brown with rufous crown and dark frontlet; wing-coverts also rufous; *rather short, spiky tail grayish brown.* Throat white scaled black; *below gray* (darker northward), midbelly whitish. Dusky and Cabanis's Spinetails are darker generally, more uniform below, and have rufous-chestnut tails; they are more forest-based. Slaty Spinetail occurs only *west* of Andes. Cinereous-breasted Spinetail (limited overlap at best) is similar, but its crown is slightly duller, gray on foreneck decidedly duller, and tail somewhat longer and more rounded. Habits similar to other *Synallaxis*. Frequent vocalizing attests to its high numbers, which continue to increase because of ongoing forest destruction. Though often hard to see, singing birds sometimes perch in the open. Song a fast "whít, di-di-di," regularly given during heat of day.

Slaty Spinetail
Synallaxis brachyura
15.5–16 cm (6–6¼"). Common in shrubby forest and woodland borders, clearings, and gardens from *w. Colombia to extreme nw. Peru* (Tumbes). To 2000 m in Colombia. Resembles Dark-breasted Spinetail (found only *east* of Andes), but somewhat longer-tailed, and darker and grayer generally. In most of range the *only Synallaxis* present, and thus easily recognized by its contrasting rufous crown and wing-coverts. Pale-breasted Spinetail is much whiter below; Azara's Spinetail mainly occurs at higher elevations and has a much longer rufous tail; both of these differ markedly in voice. Slaty is somewhat

less skulking than other *Synallaxis*, foraging higher above the ground and occasionally even emerging from dense cover. Song a low-pitched, throaty churring often introduced by a few notes, e.g., "ch-ch-chirrrr"; the "chirrrr" can be given alone. Also: Honduras to Panama.

Cinereous-breasted Spinetail
Synallaxis hypospodia   PLATE 4(14)
15.5 cm (6"). Fairly common but *local* in low shrubby areas and woodland borders, usually near water, from *e. Peru to ne. Brazil.* To 700 m. Resembles slightly larger Sooty-fronted Spinetail (sometimes seen with it), but its *shorter tail is dull dark brown* (not rufous). Pale-breasted Spinetail, also brownish-tailed, is whiter below. The voices of all three of these spinetails differ markedly. Spix's Spinetail has a completely rufous crown (*no* frontlet) and spikier tail; their ranges overlap barely if at all. Dark-breasted Spinetail is especially similar to Cinereous-breasted (even their voices are much alike), but its range barely overlaps; Dark-breasted's breast is indeed a darker gray, and its tail is shorter and spikier. Behavior as in Sooty-fronted and various other *Synallaxis*, like them heard more often than seen. Song a fast series of chippered notes that coalesce into a trill, e.g. "chew, chew-chee-chee-chee-ee-ee-ee-ee-ee-ee-ee-ee-ee-eu."

Rufous-capped Spinetail
Synallaxis ruficapilla   PLATE 4(15)
16 cm (6¼"). *Locally common in undergrowth and borders of humid forest and woodland in se. Brazil region* (north to Minas Gerais and Espírito Santo). To 1400 m. *Crown bright rufous, bordered below by a yellowish buff streak* and dusky cheeks; *above brown, most of wings and rather short tail rufous-chestnut.* Throat silvery grayish, breast pale grayish, belly pale ochraceous. A relatively colorful spinetail, not likely confused in range; no overlap with the similar Bahia Spinetail. Cf. Spix's Spinetail. Usually in pairs, hopping and creeping about close to the ground in dense undergrowth; *shows a strong predilection for bamboo.* Only infrequently with mixed flocks. Oft-heard song a somewhat nasal, fast "di-di-di-reét" phrase, sometimes repeated interminably.

Bahia Spinetail
*Synallaxis whitneyi**
16 cm (6¼"). *Very local (but can be common) in undergrowth and especially borders of montane forest and woodland in e. Brazil (s. Bahia and ne.*

Minas Gerais). 500–1000 m. Closely resembles Rufous-capped Spinetail (no overlap), but differs in its *dark gray underparts*. Behavior much as in that species, though Bahia Spinetail seems much less closely tied to bamboo. Song an often rapidly repeated pair of nasal notes, sometimes sounding jumbled (especially when both members of a pair are vocalizing); it is much less distinctly patterned than in Rufous-capped Spinetail.

Pinto's Spinetail
Synallaxis infuscata

16 cm (6¼"). *Rare and local in borders of humid forest and woodland in ne. Brazil* (Alagoas and Pernambuco). To 500 m. Resembles Rufous-capped Spinetail (no overlap), differing in essentially lacking the buff streak behind eye and *more uniform dark gray underparts*. Behavior much as in Rufous-capped, though Pinto's seems to be more of an edge species and is very much less numerous. It now seems to be declining even in the few areas that support remnant forest habitat. Song a sharp and nasal "enk-enk" or "enk-enk-enk."

Cabanis's Spinetail
Synallaxis cabanisi   PLATE 4(16)

15.5 cm (6"). Uncommon in thick undergrowth of borders of humid forest and woodland along *eastern base of Andes from cen. Peru* (Huánuco) *to w. Bolivia* (Cochabamba). 200–1350 m. *Dark and obscure.* In **Peru** (illustrated) brown above with *all-rufous crown*, dusky face; wings mainly rufous; *rather short, often frayed tail rufous-chestnut.* Throat mixed gray and black (whiter in malar area); below grayish olive brown. In **Bolivia** paler overall, and dingier buff below. Dusky Spinetail (no overlap) has a dusky frontlet. Dark-breasted Spinetail, more a bird of clearings and with very different voice, has a brown tail and dusky frontlet. Usually in pairs that creep and hop furtively in dense undergrowth near the ground, sometimes in *Gynerium* cane. Hard to see, but often reveals its presence by vocalizing. Song an abrupt and nasal "nyap" or "nyap-nyap."

Dusky Spinetail
Synallaxis moesta   PLATE 4(17)

15.5 cm (6"). Uncommon and local in dense undergrowth at edge of humid forest and woodland along *eastern base of Andes from e. Colombia to n. Peru* (n. San Martín), sparingly out into adjacent lowlands. 200–1350 m. Resembles Cabanis's Spinetail (replacing it northward; no

overlap), differing in having a *broad dusky frontlet*. Birds from **Ecuador and Peru** (illustrated) are also markedly darker and grayer, especially below. The more numerous Dark-breasted Spinetail's longer tail is brown (not rufous-chestnut); it favors grassy clearings and has very different voice. Cf. also Marañón Spinetail. Furtive behavior much as in Cabanis's Spinetail; in some areas Dusky favors patches of bamboo. Gives a low-pitched nasal chattering or churring, "rha-a-a-a-a-a-a."

McConnell's Spinetail
Synallaxis macconnelli

15.5 cm (6"). Uncommon and local in dense undergrowth at edge of humid forest and woodland in *ne. South America,* mainly on tepui slopes and in hilly terrain. Mostly 500–1900 m. Resembles geographically distant Cabanis's Spinetail, though like the Dusky Spinetail (no overlap), McConnell's has a *dusky frontlet;* moreover, it lacks whitish in malar area. Its sneaky behavior is much the same as theirs. Song a low-pitched, gravelly "kr-r-r-r-r krk," the last note soft.

Plain-crowned Spinetail
Synallaxis gujanensis   PLATE 5(1)

16–16.5 cm (6¼–6½"). Fairly common in dense undergrowth of várzea and riparian woodland and scrub, often on islands, *from Amazonia to the Guianas.* To 1200 m in Colombia. Probably more than one species. *Head grayish brown,* back olive brown; *wings and tail rufous. Below dingy buff,* whitest on throat. *Lacks* the rufous on crown and black on throat shown by many other *Synallaxis.* White-bellied Spinetail (often with it on Amazon islands) has a black throat patch and gray breast. Rusty-backed and Parker's Spinetails have upperparts *entirely* rufous. Skulking, foraging on or near the ground and favoring areas with *Gynerium* cane and *Cecropia*-dominated woodland. Usually in pairs that keep in contact through their frequent calling. Generally not with flocks. Distinctive call a leisurely "keé, kuh" repeated at intervals of several seconds; in se. Peru and Bolivia a rather different "cheeu, ka-kweek" resembling White-lored Spinetail. Often vocalizes through heat of day.

Marañón Spinetail
Synallaxis maranonica

15.5 cm (6"). Uncommon and local in undergrowth of deciduous and semihumid forest and woodland in *Río Marañón drainage of extreme s. Ecuador* (s. Loja) *and extreme nw. Peru*

(n. Cajamarca). 500–1500 m. Resembles Plain-crowned Spinetail (no overlap) but *markedly darker, grayer, and more uniform on head and below;* tail shorter with rounder rectrices. Easily recognized in its limited range from the *lack* of rufous on head and black on throat. Behavior as in Plain-crowned Spinetail; if not singing, equally hard to see. Call a very slow-paced, nasal "kieeuuw . . . keeeu," often with at least 5–10 seconds between phrases.

White-lored Spinetail
Synallaxis albilora   PLATE 5(2)
16 cm (6¼"). Locally common in undergrowth of deciduous and gallery woodland and riparian shrubbery in *sw. Brazil* (s. Mato Grosso and w. Mato Grosso do Sul) *and adjacent Bolivia and Paraguay.* Mostly below 500 m. Resembles Plain-crowned Spinetail (no overlap) but has a browner back (hence its grayish head contrasts more), *prominent white lores,* and *mostly bright ochraceous underparts.* Not likely confused in its limited range. Ochre-cheeked Spinetail has a more rufous back, black throat patch, and much more prominent superciliary. Behavior much as in Plain-crowned Spinetail, but because of its more open habitat, White-lored is easier to observe. Song a sharp and piercing "keeeu, kit-kweeit," given at a leisurely pace.

Araguaia Spinetail
*Synallaxis simoni**
16 cm (6¼"). *Locally fairly common in riparian thickets in cen. Amaz. Brazil* (along Rio Araguaia from Ilha do Bananal upstream). Below 200 m. Often considered conspecific with White-lored Spinetail. Its back is more uniform rufous and underparts whiter. Behavior similar, but song more nasal, usually a single note, "kweeu" (not sliding up).

Gray-bellied Spinetail
Synallaxis cinerascens   PLATE 5(3)
14 cm (5½"). *Uncommon and local in humid forest and woodland undergrowth in se. Brazil region* (north to Minas Gerais and Espírito Santo). To 1300 m. Above olive brown, grayer on face; wing-coverts and tail rufous. Chin white, patch on lower throat black; *below nearly uniform gray.* Spix's Spinetail (also mainly gray below) has rufous crown and a longer, grayish brown tail; Spix's inhabits more open, shrubbier terrain. This *small* spinetail is less often at edge than most of its congeners. Forages singly or in pairs, usually not with flocks; inconspicuous and not

apt to be found unless it is vocalizing. Distinctive song a thin, piercing "wheeeyt? beeeyt" or "wheeeyt bu-beeeyt."

White-bellied Spinetail
Synallaxis propinqua   PLATE 5(4)
16 cm (6¼"). *Locally fairly common in early-succession scrub on river islands in Amazonia upriver to e. Ecuador and ne. Peru.* To 300 m. Above grayish brown with *contrasting rufous wings and tail,* tail feathers frayed and pointed. *Large black patch on lower throat* (sometimes conspicuous); *breast gray,* midbelly white. Plain-crowned Spinetail *lacks* black on throat and is drab buff below (no gray); it favors undergrowth in woodland. White-bellied is especially numerous in dense growth of young *Gynerium* cane and scattered bushes. There single birds or pairs creep about on or near the ground, rarely leaving cover and hard to see. Oft-heard song a strange, low-pitched and nasal "ch-r-r-r-r-r-r-r." Also gives a slower, scratchy "krreenh-kreeenh-kre-kre-kre-kre-kre"; agitated birds can accelerate this into a *Laterallus*-like churr.

Stripe-breasted Spinetail
Synallaxis cinnamomea   PLATE 5(5)
14–15 cm (5½–6"). Fairly common in undergrowth of humid forest borders, secondary woodland, and deciduous woodland in *n. Venezuela* (east to Sucre) *and ne. Colombia.* Mostly below 1500 m. In **Venezuela** (illustrated) dull brown above with a buff superciliary; wings mostly rufous, tail dull chestnut. *Throat streaked black and white; below buff crisply streaked dusky.* In **ne. Colombia** more rufescent above (especially on face) with a rufous superciliary, and *below mostly rufous with blurry fulvous streaking.* On **Trinidad** dark brown above with *no* superciliary, blacker throat, and underparts dull olive brown with *little streaking;* on **Tobago** paler and more olivaceous brown, with some blurry buff streaking on breast. *A unique Synallaxis in being streaked below.* Skulking behavior much as in congeners, creeping about in pairs in dense undergrowth and thickets. Song a repeated "chík, kweeik?; chík, kweeik?; chík, kweeik? . . ." often protracted.

Blackish-headed Spinetail
Synallaxis tithys   PLATE 5(6)
14.5 cm (5¾"). *Now uncommon and local in undergrowth of deciduous forest and woodland from sw. Ecuador* (Manabí) *to extreme nw. Peru* (Tumbes). To 1100 m in Ecuador. *Head and neck*

dark gray, blacker on foreface; olivaceous gray above, *wing-coverts bright cinnamon-rufous; tail sooty.* Throat black, malar area grizzled white; below gray, paler on midbelly. An attractive *Synallaxis,* not likely confused in its small range, where the only other typical *Synallaxis* is the very different Slaty Spinetail (with rufous crown, etc.). Necklaced Spinetail displays entirely different behavior and appearance. Usually in pairs that hop on or near the ground, favoring dense tangles; inconspicuous unless vocalizing. Distinctive song a short, dry, ascending trill, "t-t-t-t-t-trit?," repeated every few seconds.

Ruddy Spinetail
Synallaxis rutilans   PLATE 5(7)
14.5–15 cm (5¾–6"). *Generally uncommon and local in dense undergrowth of terra firme forest from Amazonia to the Guianas.* To 1200 m in Venezuela. *Dark and richly colored.* In nw. Amazonia (A) *mostly rich rufous-chestnut* with *black lores* and a *black throat patch,* wings duskier; rather short and often frayed tail black; belly brownish gray. In ne. Amazonia similar but *more olivaceous above.* Most divergent in e. Amaz. Brazil (east of Rio Tocantins); here most birds (B) are *more or less uniform dark brownish gray* with black throat and tail and *contrasting rufous wing-coverts,* but a few look like northeastern birds and still others are intermediate. The rarer Chestnut-throated Spinetail is similar but browner above, and it never shows Ruddy's black throat patch (though this can be hard to see in the field). Chestnut-throated favors more secondary habitats and bamboo, and the two species differ vocally. Usually in pairs, foraging on or near the ground, often around treefalls where it inspects tangles and leaf litter; quite skulking. Sometimes follows understory flocks. Song a rapidly repeated and insistent "keé-kawów" or "keé-kow" phrase, at times continued interminably.

Chestnut-throated Spinetail
Synallaxis cherriei   PLATE 5(8)
14 cm (5½"). *Unaccountably local;* rare to fairly common in undergrowth of secondary woodland and humid forest borders, locally also in *Guadua* bamboo, from e. *Ecuador and adjacent Colombia to Amaz. Brazil.* 300–1100 m. In Peru (illustrated) has *face, throat, and breast orange-rufous* with dusky lores and grayish belly. Hindcrown and upperparts olivaceous brown; tail blackish. In Ecuador and adjacent Colombia darker and more rufescent brown above, the belly darker and

more contrasting. Birds from Brazil resemble those from Peru. Ruddy Spinetail always has a black throat patch (though this often is hard to see); its upperparts are more rufous, and it shows less contrast below. Behavior much as in Ruddy Spinetail, though Chestnut-throated is more a bird of secondary growth and edge; why it has not increased in response to all the forest clearing of recent decades remains a mystery. Rapidly repeated song a rather froglike "trrrr tuuít, trrrr tuuít, . . ." often long-continued.

Red-shouldered Spinetail
Gyalophylax hellmayri   PLATE 5(9)
18 cm (7"). *Locally not uncommon in arid scrub and undergrowth of low deciduous woodland in interior ne. Brazil* (Piauí to w. Pernambuco, Bahia, and nw. Minas Gerais). To 500 m. *Iris yellow-orange. Mostly uniform dingy brownish gray* with a large black throat patch; *wing-coverts contrasting bright rufous-chestnut; rather long tail blackish.* In general comportment recalls various *Synallaxis* spinetails, though Red-shouldered is *larger and darker;* Pale-breasted and Sooty-fronted Spinetails (both rather different) are sympatric. Forages mainly in pairs, skulking in dense growth and emerging from heavy cover mainly when vocalizing at and soon after dawn. Most frequent vocalization a "ka-chew, ka-chew, ka-chew, . . ." sometimes continuing for long periods. Apparent song a loud and abrupt chirring that becomes a stutter and gradually fades away.

Chotoy Spinetail
Schoeniophylax phryganophilus   PLATE 5(10)
19–22 cm (7½–8¾"). Fairly common in semiopen areas with scattered trees and bushes, gallery woodland, and gardens from *nw. Bolivia* (Beni) *and sw. and interior e. Brazil to ne. Argentina* (n. Buenos Aires). To 600 m. *Boldly patterned. Tail extremely long, spiky, and graduated.* Crown chestnut, superciliary white; *above sandy brown boldly streaked blackish.* Lesser wing-coverts rufous-chestnut; tail grayish brown. Chin yellow, patch on lower throat black, malar area white; *chest band cinnamon;* below mainly whitish. Ne. Brazil birds are smaller. The Chotoy has a much longer tail than any *Synallaxis,* none of which is streaked above; its overall shape brings to mind a tit-spinetail, though these are very different in color pattern and behavior. More arboreal than any *Synallaxis,* the attractive Chotoy is found in pairs and small groups; they clamber about inside leafy cover and usually remain out of sight.

They often range near water or around houses and construct conspicuous large stick nests. Chotoy is named for its most frequent call, a distinctive, low-pitched gurgling or chortling "cho-cho-cho-cho-chchchchchchchch."

Wren-like Rushbird
Phleocryptes melanops PLATE 5(11)

13.5–14.5 cm (5¼–5¾"). Often *common in reed-beds from nw. Peru* (Lambayeque) *to Chile, s. Argentina, and extreme se. Brazil* (north to coastal Santa Catarina); a few migrate to s. Paraguay in austral winter. Occurs in both brackish and freshwater and (like the Many-colored Rush Tyrant, often seen with it) from sea level to at least 4300 m. A small chunky furnariid. In **most of range** (illustrated) crown dark brown (forehead more rufous) with a *bold buffy whitish superciliary;* back streaked black, brownish, and white. Wings blackish *with conspicuous rufous markings; tail fairly short,* mostly brown and black and tipped whitish. Below buffy whitish. **Altiplano birds of Peru, Bolivia, and nw. Argentina** are larger and longer-billed. Few similar birds occur in the rushbird's restricted habitat. Bay-capped Wren-Spinetail has a much longer and more pointed tail, rufous crown, etc. Though usually inconspicuous, rushbirds can be locally abundant, and they are not particularly shy. Northern observers will be struck by its similarity to the Marsh Wren (*Cistothorus palustris*) of North America and to some Old World *Acrocephalus* warblers. Feeds singly and in pairs among reeds, often hopping onto mud or floating vegetation. Most frequent call a fast mechanical ticking that often continues for several minutes.

Bay-capped Wren-Spinetail
Spartonoica maluroides PLATE 5(12)

14–14.5 cm (5½–5¾"). *Uncommon and local in marshes* with extensive sedge and low reed growth (in both fresh and brackish water) *and adjacent wet grasslands in n. and cen. Argentina* (Chaco and Corrientes to Mendoza and La Pampa), *Uruguay, and extreme s. Brazil* (Rio Grande do Sul). To 900 m. Iris whitish. *Crown rufous, above sandy brown with bold black streaking;* wings with cinnamon area on flight feathers; mostly brown *tail long and strongly graduated with feathers pointed.* Below whitish, tinged buff on flanks. Hudson's Canastero (regularly sympatric) is similar but has a streaked crown (with *no* rufous) and buffier underparts with flank streaking. Sulphur-bearded Spinetail is *un-streaked above,* also lacks rufous crown, etc. Cf.

also much shorter-tailed Grass Wren. Typically a shy bird, hard to observe and rarely perching in the open for long. Flushed birds fly a short distance, then pitch back in, like as not disappearing. Somewhat easier to observe when singing, then sometimes lingering in the open. Distinctive song a very dry, mechanical reeling trill that lasts 2–3 seconds.

Limnornis and *Limnoctites*

Two marsh-loving furnariids found locally in *se. South America, both species with rather long bills* and dull plumage.

Curve-billed Reedhaunter
Limnornis curvirostris PLATE 5(13)

16–16.5 cm (6¼–6½"). *Locally fairly common in reedbeds,* especially where extensive and where they fringe large coastal lagoons, *from extreme se. Brazil* (Rio Grande do Sul) *to ne. Argentina* (Buenos Aires). Below 100 m. *Rather long, slightly decurved bill. Brown above* with *white superciliary;* wings and *fairly short tail* more rufescent. Essentially white below. Straight-billed Reedhaunter has a straighter bill, grayer upperparts, and a narrower and spikier tail. Found singly or in pairs, creeping about within the reeds (which it never seems to leave) and often hard to see. Distinctive loud song often delivered from a prominent vantage point during breeding season, a fast series of harsh, strident notes that rise at first and then slide down and weaken, e.g., "dr-rrrrrrri-di-di-di-dr-rrrrreuw."

Straight-billed Reedhaunter
Limnoctites rectirostris PLATE 5(14)

16 cm (6¼"). *Local and uncommon in marshes of extreme se. Brazil* (s. Santa Catarina and Rio Grande do Sul), *Uruguay, and ne. Argentina* (south to n. Buenos Aires). To 1100 m in Brazil. *Long, virtually straight bill.* Grayish brown above, *grayest on crown,* with narrow whitish superciliary; wings and tail rufous, *tail rather long, graduated, and pointed.* Essentially white below. Curve-billed Reedhaunter is heavier-bodied though shorter-tailed, has an obvious curve to its bill, and is browner (less grayish) above. Usually inconspicuous, occurring in pairs that creep about in dense marsh vegetation. As with so many furnariids, most easily seen when singing, then often mounting to a semi-exposed perch. Song a series of high-pitched notes on an even pitch, ending in a trill, e.g., "tsi-tsi-tsi-tsi-tsi-tititititititi."

Ochre-cheeked Spinetail
*Synallaxis scutata**   PLATE 5(15)
15.5 cm (6″). Uncommon and rather local in undergrowth of deciduous forest and woodland and borders of more humid forest from *e. Brazil to e. Bolivia* (mainly from Santa Cruz south; also an isolated population in La Paz foothills), *nw. Argentina, and extreme n. Paraguay.* To 1700 m in Bolivia. In **Brazil except for Mato Grosso** (illustrated) has crown and upper back grayish brown, *bold white superciliary; otherwise rufous above.* Chin white, *prominent patch on lower throat black;* mostly buff below. From **Mato Grosso south and west,** back and rump olive brown (only wings and tail rufous). White-lored Spinetail *lacks* an obvious superciliary and has more extensively ochraceous underparts (*no black on throat*). Forages in pairs, hopping about in thickets, usually on or near the ground. Does not associate with mixed flocks. Song (often given, and usually how the species is detected) a shrill "tweeeyt, yo-weét?" with a leisurely cadence; often repeated for protracted periods.

White-whiskered Spinetail
*Synallaxis candei**   PLATE 5(16)
16 cm (6¼″). *Fairly common in arid scrub and undergrowth in deciduous woodland in n. Colombia and nw. Venezuela* (east to Falcón and n. Lara). To 1100 m. In **most of range** (illustrated) *bright rufous above* with dark gray crown, *rufous postocular stripe,* and *black cheeks;* distal half of tail black. *Malar area and chin boldly white, lower throat black;* below mostly cinnamon. In **Colombia's Río Magdalena valley** lacks the postocular stripe, and white malar area less extensive (so entire head looks black), has browner back. Handsome and essentially unmistakable in range. Usually forages in pairs, often hopping on the ground with tail held partially cocked. Song a distinctly enunciated "kee, kee-kee" (sometimes a triplet at the end) that can be repeated quite rapidly.

Hoary-throated Spinetail
*Synallaxis kollari**   PLATE 5(17)
15.5 cm (6″). *Rare and local in undergrowth of gallery woodland in extreme n. Brazil* (Roraima) *and adjacent Guyana.* Below 200 m. Resembles White-whiskered Spinetail (no overlap), differing in its paler crown, *grayish* (not black) *cheeks and upper throat, entirely rufous tail* (no black tip), and *black and white flecking on throat and malar area.* Behavior similar to Ochre-cheeked and White-whiskered Spinetails, though seems decidedly less numerous even in seemingly ideal

habitat. Song a steadily repeated pair of sharp notes, "kee-ki?"

Pink-legged Graveteiro
*Acrobatornis fonsecai**   PLATE 6(1)
14 cm (5½″). A *very distinctive and only recently discovered arboreal furnariid,* locally not uncommon in cacao plantations and in the canopy and borders of humid forest and woodland in *e. Brazil* (s. Bahia and extreme ne. Minas Gerais). To 550 m. *Legs and lower mandible pink. Mostly dark gray, somewhat paler below,* with pale gray superciliary and mottled back streaking; wings and tail blackish edged paler, tail strongly graduated and spiky. **Juvenile** *mostly tawny,* with duskier crown, wings, and tail. Gray plumage of adult unique among furnariids found anywhere near this species' range (recalling only the *Xenerpestes* graytails). Cf. Olive Spinetail. Usually in pairs, often moving with loose, mixed flocks comprising a variety of other arboreal birds. Forages primarily by hitching, often acrobatically, along smaller limbs and on twigs. Song a long series of enunciated chippered notes that accelerates into an extended reeling trill, lasting up to 10 or so seconds.

Cranioleuca

A large, homogeneous group of small furnariids found widely in forested and wooded habitats across South America, with diversity highest in the Andes. *Cranioleuca* spinetails differ from *Synallaxis* in being *shorter-tailed* and *more arboreal,* looking like little foliage-gleaners. They tend to be more conspicuous than *Synallaxis,* not skulking in undergrowth, and they accompany mixed flocks much more often. They are, however, generally less vocal.

Creamy-crested Spinetail
Cranioleuca albicapilla   PLATE 6(2)
17 cm (6¾″). *Fairly common in semiarid montane scrub and woodland and patches of Polylepis-dominated woodland in Andes of s. Peru* (Junín to Cuzco). 2500–3600 m. *Bill pale.* **Northern birds** (illustrated) have *creamy white crown* (feathers often raised into a *bushy crest*) and postocular stripe; above brownish olive, wing-coverts and tail rufous. Throat white, below pale buffy grayish. **Further south** (Cuzco and Apurímac) crown and underparts buffier. Marcapata Spinetail is smaller with a black bill and black-margined rufous or white crown; it inhabits

montane forest (not semiarid woodland). Found singly or in pairs, hitching along branches and probing into moss, bark crevices, and epiphytes. Frequently given song a loud and descending series of semimusical notes, e.g., "tch, tch, chee-chee-cheechee-ee-ee-ee-ee-ew."

Light-crowned Spinetail
Cranioleuca albiceps   PLATE 6(3)
15.5 cm (6"). Fairly common in lower growth and borders of montane forest on *east slope of Andes from extreme s. Peru* (Puno) *to w. Bolivia* (w. Santa Cruz). 2400–3300 m. **Northern birds** (south to La Paz; illustrated) have *crown white or whitish bordered with black;* superciliary and sides of head dark olive grayish; above otherwise bright rufous. Below dark olive grayish. In **southern birds** crown *rich buff.* In an unusual parallel, Marcapata Spinetail also has two races with differing crown colors; it has a whiter superciliary and a whiter throat. The two species are not known to range together. Active behavior much as in Creamy-crested Spinetail, though Light-crowned more often accompanies mixed flocks. Favors areas with bamboo. Song a series of shrill notes that descend and fade away.

Marcapata Spinetail
Cranioleuca marcapatae   PLATE 6(4)
16 cm (6¼"). Uncommon in lower growth and borders of montane forest on *east slope of Andes in s. Peru* (Cuzco). 2400–3400 m. In **most of range** (illustrated) *crown rufous outlined with black, narrow superciliary whitish,* sides of head and neck grayish; otherwise rufous above. Throat white, below dull buffy grayish. On the remote **Cordillera Vilcabamba** crown *white.* Cf. the similar Light-crowned Spinetail (found farther south). Ash-browed Spinetail, also rufous-crowned, is smaller and lacks the rufous back and black crown outline; it ranges at lower elevations. Behavior and voice as in Light-crowned Spinetail.

Red-faced Spinetail
Cranioleuca erythrops   PLATE 6(5)
14 cm (5½"). Fairly common in canopy and borders of foothill and montane forest and woodland on *west slope of Andes in w. Colombia and w. Ecuador* (south to Guayas and Azuay). Mostly 700–1600 m. **Adult** has *rufous crown and face;* otherwise olive brown above, wings and tail rufous. Throat whitish; below dull brownish or grayish olive. **Juvenile** lacks rufous on face, but shows a narrow buff eyebrow and some

ochraceous below. **Immature** seems to acquire rufous first on crown, and may then retain the superciliary. Line-cheeked Spinetail replaces this species southward in w. Ecuador; it shows a clean-cut rufous crown and a bolder, whiter superciliary. Found singly or in pairs, foraging actively with mixed flocks, usually remaining well above the ground. Hitches along branches, probing into bark crevices and rummaging in epiphytes and tangles; rarely gleans from leaves. Song a fast, spritely series of shrill notes ending in a trill and fading. Also: Costa Rica and Panama.

Streak-capped Spinetail
Cranioleuca hellmayri
14 cm (5½"). Common in subcanopy and borders of montane forest and woodland in *Santa Marta Mts. of n. Colombia;* also recently recorded once on Sierra de Perijá of w. Venezuela. Mostly 1600–3000 m. *Iris pale. Crown rufous streaked black,* short superciliary white; above olive brown, wings and tail rufous. Throat whitish, below pale smoky grayish. No other *Cranioleuca* ranges on the Santa Martas; cf. Rusty-headed Spinetail (a *Synallaxis*). Arboreal behavior similar to many other *Cranioleuca,* including Crested; song also similar, though perhaps averages shorter.

Crested Spinetail
Cranioleuca subcristata   PLATE 6(6)
14 cm (5½"). Common in subcanopy and borders in a variety of forested and wooded habitats in *mountains of n. Venezuela,* less numerous in *Andes of w. Venezuela and ne. Colombia* (south to Boyacá). Mostly 400–1600 m. Despite name, *not "crested." Bill pinkish.* Olive brown above with *faint black crown streaks* and *indistinct pale superciliary;* wings and tail rufous. Below dingy pale olivaceous brown. Though dull, not likely confused in its range, as it is the only *Cranioleuca* present there. Arboreal behavior much as in many other *Cranioleuca;* hops and twists on branches, in viny growth, and in foliage. Frequently accompanies mixed flocks. Song a series of high-pitched shrill notes that accelerates into a trill, similar to that of many congeners.

Tepui Spinetail
Cranioleuca demissa   PLATE 6(7)
14.5 cm (5¾"). Fairly common in subcanopy and borders of montane forest and borders and gallery woodland on *tepuis of s. Venezuela area.* 1100–2450 m. Resembles Ash-browed Spinetail (no overlap) but *distinctly grayer below.* The

only *Cranioleuca* in range, and as such should be readily recognized. Cf. McConnell's Spinetail (a *Synallaxis*). Arboreal, flocking behavior, and high-pitched shrill song much as in its congeners.

Ash-browed Spinetail
Cranioleuca curtata   PLATE 6(8)

14.5 cm (5¾"). Fairly common in canopy and borders of foothill and lower montane forest and woodland on *east slope of Andes from n. Colombia* (Santander) *to w. Bolivia* (Cochabamba). Mostly 900–2000 m. *Crown rufous-chestnut with indistinct grayish superciliary; above olive brown, wings and tail rufous-chestnut. Throat whitish; below dull brownish olive. Striking immature has superciliary, sides of head and neck, and most of underparts orange-ochraceous.* Line-cheeked Spinetail's range comes close to this species', though it never reaches the actual *east* slope where Ash-browed takes over; Line-cheeked has a bolder, whiter superciliary and is paler below. Cf. also Montane Foliage-gleaner. Arboreal behavior and voice as in Red-faced Spinetail.

Baron's Spinetail
Cranioleuca baroni   PLATE 6(9)

16.5–17.5 cm (6½–7"). *Locally fairly common in montane forest and woodland, also in Polylepis-dominated woodland, in Andes of n. and cen. Peru* (Cajamarca and Amazonas to Lima and Pasco). Mostly 2300–4000 m. A *large Cranioleuca*. **Southern birds** (illustrated) have crown rufous with narrow white superciliary, streaked cheeks; above brownish gray, wings and tail rufous. *Throat and chest white,* pale grayish below, sides rather mottled. **Northward from Ancash** more olivaceous above and less mottled below. Line-cheeked Spinetail (no overlap) is similarly patterned but smaller and browner above, buffier below. Cf. also the rare Great Spinetail. Found singly or in pairs, sometimes with small mixed flocks, creeping on branches and searching epiphytes, moss clumps, and bark. Song similar to other *Cranioleuca*, but can have a more musical (less shrill) quality.

Line-cheeked Spinetail
Cranioleuca antisiensis   PLATE 6(10)

14.5 cm (5¾"). *Fairly common in montane forest, woodland, and scrub in Andes from sw. Ecuador* (Azuay) *to ne. Peru* (Lambayeque and Cajamarca). Mostly 900–2500 m. *Crown rufous bordered below by narrow white superciliary,* cheeks indistinctly streaked; above olivaceous brown,

wings and tail rufous. Throat whitish; below dull buffy brownish. Basically distinctive in its limited range. In w. Ecuador, cf. Red-faced Spinetail (juveniles of which show a buff superciliary). Ash-browed Spinetail occurs only on actual east slope of Andes. Behavior similar to Red-faced and Ash-browed Spinetails, though Line-cheeked is more tolerant of habitat disturbance and thus more often forages closer to the ground in shrubbier terrain. Has a variety of chippering and scolding calls, e.g., "tsi-chík," used as contact notes. Song a fast series of loud shrill notes typically ending in a trill and fading.

Pallid Spinetail
Cranioleuca pallida   PLATE 6(11)

14 cm (5½"). Fairly common in canopy and borders of montane and semihumid forest and woodland in *se. Brazil* (s. Goiás and Minas Gerais to e. São Paulo). 700–2150 m. *Crown rufous, bold whitish superciliary, otherwise olive brown above, wings and tail rufous. Throat whitish, below pale buffy brownish.* Olive Spinetail replaces this species southward, with no known overlap; *it lacks the rufous crown.* Behavior and high-pitched shrill song much as in other arboreal *Cranioleuca* spinetails.

Olive Spinetail
Cranioleuca obsoleta   PLATE 6(12)

14 cm (5½"). Fairly common in canopy and borders of humid forest and woodland, also in Araucaria-dominated woodland, in *se. Brazil area* (north to s. São Paulo). To 1400 m. *Drab and uniform. Brownish olive above with whitish superciliary; wing-coverts (only) and tail rufous. Pale drab buffy olivaceous below.* Pallid Spinetail *(which occurs north of Olive's range, with no known overlap)* differs in its rufous crown and entirely rufous wing. Cf. also Stripe-crowned Spinetail, which replaces Olive to south and west. Behavior and high-pitched shrill song much as in other arboreal *Cranioleuca* spinetails.

Gray-headed Spinetail
Cranioleuca semicinerea   PLATE 6(13)

14 cm (5½"). Uncommon and local in subcanopy and borders of forest and woodland (both humid and deciduous) in *ne. Brazil* (south to s. Goiás and n. Minas Gerais). To 800 m. *Bill pinkish.* In **most of range** (illustrated) *head and neck pale ashy gray,* forehead and superciliary whiter, becoming *dingy pale grayish below;* above otherwise entirely rufous. In **s. Goiás** darker on crown and ear-coverts and with a more promi-

nent superciliary. No other *Cranioleuca* spinetail occurs with this distinctive species. Behavior and voice similar to many other arboreal *Cranioleuca*, though Gray-headed seems more often to forage apart from mixed flocks.

Scaled Spinetail
Cranioleuca muelleri   PLATE 6(14)

16 cm (6¼"). *Local and apparently uncommon in várzea forest of Brazil along the lower Amazon River* (upriver to near Manaus). Below 150 m. Above like much better known Speckled Spinetail. Below dull buffy whitish, *feathers of throat and breast edged dark olive, giving a coarse, scaled appearance.* Speckled Spinetail (locally sympatric) is smaller and more black-speckled or streaked below. Behavior apparently similar to Speckled.

Speckled Spinetail
Cranioleuca gutturata   PLATE 6(15)

14.5 cm (5¾"). Uncommon in lower growth and mid-levels of humid forest and borders from *w. and cen. Amazonia to s. Venezuela and the Guianas.* Locally to 1100 m. Iris yellow. Dark olive brown above with rufous-chestnut crown and narrow buff superciliary; wings and tail rufous-chestnut. Chin yellowish; *below dull buff thickly speckled with blackish on breast,* speckles fading on belly. In most of range readily known by its unique speckled underparts; cf. Scaled Spinetail (restricted to lower Amazon) and Orinoco Softtail (only in s. Venezuela). Found singly or in pairs, often accompanying mixed understory flocks. Hops along larger branches and trunks and scuttles into vine tangles, probing into vegetation and dead leaf clusters. For a spinetail not very vocal. Song a short series of very high-pitched piercing notes, "tsee-tsee-tsee-tsee-tsee-tsee."

Sulphur-bearded Spinetail
Cranioleuca sulphurifera   PLATE 6(16)

15 cm (6"). *Locally fairly common in marshes in extreme se. Brazil* (s. Rio Grande do Sul), *Uruguay, and e. Argentina* (south to e. Río Negro). To 300 m. Iris orangy. Above olive brown with whitish superciliary; wing-coverts rufous and *patch in flight feathers buff* (showing as a stripe in flight); outer tail feathers rufescent. *Small patch of yellow on throat;* below whitish, *foreneck narrowly streaked gray. No other Cranioleuca inhabits marshes.* Stripe-crowned Spinetail ranges in nearby shrubbery; it has crown streaking, a bolder superciliary, pure white foreneck. Yellow-chinned Spinetail is much more rufous

above. Cf. also the streakier Bay-capped Wren-Spinetail and Hudson's Canastero, and the reedhaunters. Often hard to see, except in the early morning when birds may perch atop low bushes or grass clumps. Distinctive song an up-slurred trill followed by a fast series of harsher notes, e.g., "d-d-d-r-r-i-i, dirip, dirip, dirip, drip drip dreeuw drreuw."

Stripe-crowned Spinetail
Cranioleuca pyrrhophia   PLATE 6(17)

14.5 cm (5¾"). *Common and widespread* in canopy and borders of forest and woodland, and in a variety of scrubby situations (including chaco) from *w. Bolivia* (La Paz) *and extreme s. Brazil* (Rio Grande do Sul) *to cen. Argentina* (Neuquén and Río Negro). To 3100 m in Bolivia. In **most of range** (illustrated) *crown obviously streaked buff and blackish* with a *broad white superciliary,* whitish face, and blackish post-ocular line; above grayish brown with rufous wing-coverts and tail. *Mostly whitish below.* In **Bolivia** browner above with more extensive crown streaking. Olive Spinetail is smaller and much drabber below and on superciliary; it lacks crown streaking. Little Thornbird shows only inconspicuous streaking on forehead, has a fainter superciliary and browner wings and tail; cf. also Streak-fronted Thornbird. Behavior (including voice) similar to many other *Cranioleuca,* though this attractive species seems tamer and is often easier to observe.

Inquisivi Spinetail
*Cranioleuca henricae**

14.5 cm (5¾"). *Fairly common but very local in arid intermontane woodland in highlands of w. Bolivia* (known only from Inquisivi in La Paz). 2500–2900 m. A recently described species. Has been called Bolivian Spinetail. Resembles Ash-browed Spinetail (no overlap, occurs only on east slope of Andes), differing in bolder and whiter superciliary and grayer underparts. Stripe-crowned Spinetail has extensive crown streaking, is whiter below. Behavior and voice much as in other arboreal *Cranioleuca.*

Rusty-backed Spinetail
Cranioleuca vulpina   PLATE 6(18)

14–14.5 cm (5½–5¾"). *Fairly common to common and widespread* in shrubby thickets and undergrowth of gallery forest from Venezuela and ne. Colombia to s. Brazil (Mato Grosso do Sul and Santa Catarina). To at least 600 m. Parker's Spinetail of Amazonia is now regarded as a separate species. In **most of range** (illustrated) uniform *rufous above* with grayish cheeks and a narrow superciliary. *Below drab buffy grayish.* **Ne. Brazil** birds are brighter cinnamon-rufous above, paler and buffier below. Parker's Spinetail is whiter below, especially on its throat. Cf. also *Certhiaxis* spinetails. Usually in pairs, foraging in dense tangled growth and hard to observe well or for very long; sometimes moves with small loose flocks. Often occurs in seasonally flooded areas; in any case, almost invariably near water. Song a fairly long, fast series of descending nasal chortling notes, initially better enunciated, e.g., "kwee-kwee-kwee-kweh-kweh-kweh-kwakwakwakwakwakwa," often given by both members of a pair more or less simultaneously. The song is most often given at quite long intervals.

Parker's Spinetail
Cranioleuca vulpecula*
14 cm (5¼"). Fairly common in undergrowth of low woodland and early-succession scrub on *islands in Amazon River and its tributaries upriver to e. Ecuador and ne. Peru.* Below 400 m. Formerly considered conspecific with Rusty-backed Spinetail, which it resembles aside from its *whiter underparts, especially on throat.* In some areas the two species occur together, though Parker's favors younger, earlier-succession habitats. Yellow-chinned and Red-and-white Spinetails are longer-billed and even whiter below. Parker's forages in pairs in shrubbery and dense low undergrowth and generally does not move with mixed flocks. It is quite vocal, giving a variety of vocalizations including an accelerating, descending series of nasal notes that ends in a chortle, e.g., "tew-tew-tew-tew-trrrrrr."

Certhiaxis

Two sharply **bicolored** spinetails of open habitats in the lowlands, always near water. They are longer-billed than *Cranioleuca.*

Yellow-chinned Spinetail
Certhiaxis cinnamomeus   PLATE 6(19)
14–14.5 cm (5½–5¾"). *Common and widespread* in marshes and adjacent grassy and shrubby areas, around pond and lake margins, along ditches, and locally even in mangroves *from n. Colombia and Venezuela to n. Argentina.* To 500 m. In **most of range** (illustrated) *above bright reddish brown, rufous on wings and tail,* with an indistinct pale grayish superciliary and dusky lores and postocular line. *Below white,*

chin spot pale yellow (very inconspicuous). In **n. Colombia and nw. Venezuela** has a dusky frontlet. In most of range this clean-cut, attractive spinetail is easily known by its bicolored, rufous and white, appearance. Along the Amazon, cf. the similar Red-and-white Spinetail. Rusty-backed and Parker's Spinetails are dingier below. Conspicuous for a marsh bird, often feeding in the open on floating vegetation or in low bushes near water. Vocal, calling at intervals through day (even when hot and sunny); most frequent song a harsh and loud churring rattle reminiscent of certain *Laterallus* crakes.

Red-and-white Spinetail
Certhiaxis mustelinus   PLATE 6(20)
14 cm (5½"). *Uncommon and local in grassy areas and adjacent shrubbery on islands in Amazon River upriver to ne. Peru.* Below 150 m. *Bright rufous above* with *contrasting black lores. Immaculate white below* (no yellow chin spot). Cf. Yellow-chinned Spinetail (not as bright above, nor as pure white below, and bill slightly shorter). Behavior similar to Yellow-chinned, though Red-and-white is much more confined to seasonally flooded grassy areas. Most frequent song is quite different, a repeated and sharply emphasized "chu-chéh."

Aphrastura

Two small, easily recognized furnariids, one of them widespread in forest and woodland in *s. South America,* the other rare on the remote Juan Fernández Islands.

Thorn-tailed Rayadito
Aphrastura spinicauda   PLATE 7(1)
14–14.5 cm (5½–5¾"). *Common in a variety of forested and wooded habitats from cen. Chile* (Coquimbo) *and adjacent Argentina* (north to Neuquén) *to Tierra del Fuego.* Mostly below 1750 m. Unmistakable, and one of the more numerous birds of far southern forests. *Head black with long broad buff superciliary;* brown above becoming *rufous on rump and tail, tail with narrow protruding shafts;* wings blackish with *prominent buff markings.* Below whitish (bright pale ochraceous on **Chile's Chiloé Island**). The energetic rayadito is often found in groups (largest during winter) around which small mixed flocks coalesce. They forage actively at all levels, inspecting foliage, branches, and trunks, often cocking their tail; behavior recalls that of holarctic tits (*Parus* spp.), and rayaditos are often equally bold. Gives

a variety of calls, the most frequent a short dry "trrrrrreet," sometimes protracted and interspersed by "tic" notes; also a scolding "tsii-tsii-tsii-tsii. . . ."

Masafuera Rayadito
Aphrastura masafuerae

16.5 cm (6½"). *Now very rare on Isla Alejandro Selkirk in the Juan Fernández Islands off Chile.* 600–1300 m. Larger, with longer tail than the mainland species, and much duller plumage. Differs in having head dusky brown with *broad superciliary dull buffy grayish,* and drab buffy grayish underparts. Impossible to confuse; Juan Fernández Tit-Tyrant occurs only on Isla Robinson Crusoe. Not a well-known bird. Ranges in pairs in dense fern-dominated understory, with acrobatic behavior much as in Thorn-tailed Rayadito. Often gives a churring call.

Des Murs's Wiretail
Sylviorthorhynchus desmursii   PLATE 7(2)

19–23 cm (7½–9"). *Uncommon in bamboo-dominated undergrowth of humid forest and woodland in cen. and s. Chile* (Aconcagua to Magallanes) *and adjacent Argentina* (w. Neuquén to w. Santa Cruz). To 1200 m. Unmistakable, with *extraordinarily long, narrow, and filamentous central tail feathers. Rufous brown above,* crown and wings most rufescent, with narrow buffy whitish superciliary. *Below buff,* whiter on midbelly. The wiretail's tail feathers are so thin that they often can be hard to see in the field; however, no other similar bird occurs with it. Forages singly or in pairs, usually skulking and hard to see (in part because its favored habitat is so dense). Song, given fairly often during breeding season, a repeated rollicking phrase preceded by several husky notes, e.g., "zhree-zhree, ch-dreuw, ch-dreuw, ch-dreuw, ch-dreuw-ch-dreuw."

Leptasthenura

A distinctive group of *slender, very long-tailed furnariids,* some of them prominently crested, found *mainly in scrub and woodland patches at higher elevations in the Andes;* a few species occur in s. South America. Their tails are graduated, with *very pointed feathers.* Tit-spinetails forage actively in foliage, often hanging upside down; they are easy to observe.

Andean Tit-Spinetail
Leptasthenura andicola   PLATE 7(3)

16.5–17 cm (6½–6¾"). Fairly common in shrubby paramo, low treeline woodland, and patches of *Polylepis*-dominated woodland in *Andes from w. Venezuela* (s. Trujillo) *to w. Bolivia* (La Paz); less numerous south of Ecuador. Mostly 3000–4500 m. *Crown streaked black and rufous, bold superciliary white;* above dark brown, back streaked white, outer tail feathers white-edged. Below brown *extensively streaked white* (streaking especially bold in **Peru and Bolivia**). In **Colombia's E. Andes and Santa Marta Mts.** has rufous patch in primaries, less streaking on belly. *The only tit-spinetail found north of Peru; no other shows as much streaking.* Streak-backed, Rusty-crowned, and White-browed Tit-Spinetails all have streaking on back, but on underparts it is confined to foreneck. Many-striped Canastero also has streaky plumage, but has rufous in wings, a shorter tail. Found in pairs or small groups, at times accompanying loose mixed flocks, foraging restlessly and sometimes hanging upside down as they inspect foliage and bark for insects. Song a hesitating series of high-pitched short trills, e.g., "trrrr . . . trrr . . ."; also "tzik" or "tzi-dik" calls.

Rusty-crowned Tit-Spinetail
Leptasthenura pileata   PLATE 7(4)

17 cm (6¾"). Fairly common in montane scrub and woodland patches (including *Polylepis*-dominated woodland) in *Andes of Peru* (s. Cajamarca to Huancavelica and Ayacucho). Mostly 2500–4000 m. In **Lima** (A) has *crown uniform rufous* with narrow white superciliary; above brownish streaked whitish; wings brownish dusky with ashy patch, tail feathers edged paler. *Throat and upper chest white boldly checkered black,* below pale grayish buff. **Ayacucho and Huancavelica** birds are more streaked (above and below). **North of Lima** (B) shows black streaking in crown. Birds with solid rufous crowns are unique in this regard aside from the range-restricted White-browed Tit-Spinetail (no overlap). Northward in Peru, where Rusty-crowned's crown shows streaking, resembles Streak-backed Tit-Spinetail (usually at lower elevations), though that species has a rufous patch in primaries and is less boldly marked on foreneck. Behavior and voice much as in Andean Tit-Spinetail.

White-browed Tit-Spinetail
Leptasthenura xenothorax
17 cm (6¾"). Now rare and local in patches of Polylepis woodland in Andes of s. Peru (Apurímac and Cuzco). 3800–4500 m. Resembles Rusty-crowned Tit-Spinetails that have a solid rufous crown. Differs in being plain smoky grayish below (no mottling or streaking), with even sharper black checkering on foreneck. This most handsome of the tit-spinetails does not occur with Rusty-crowned; the only tit-spinetail found with it is the very different Tawny. Behavior and voice much as in Andean Tit-Spinetail; threatened by continued cutting of its always limited habitat.

Streak-backed Tit-Spinetail
Leptasthenura striata   PLATE 7(5)
16.5–17 cm (6½–6¾"). Locally fairly common in montane scrub and patches of *Polylepis*-dominated woodland in *Andes from w. Peru* (Ancash) *to n. Chile* (Tarapacá). Mostly 2000–4000 m. Sometimes called Streaked Tit-Spinetail. *Crown streaked black and rufous,* narrow superciliary white; above brown, back streaked whitish; *wings with large patch of rufous in primaries,* outer tail feathers white-edged. *Below mottled pale grayish,* throat usually with fine black streaking. Andean Tit-Spinetail overlaps with this species locally, though mainly occurring at higher elevations; it is darker overall and more boldly streaked (especially below). Rusty-crowned Tit-Spinetail *lacks* the rufous patch in wing and is more boldly black-speckled on foreneck. Plain-mantled Tit-Spinetail has a plain, *unstreaked* back. Behavior and voice much as in Andean Tit-Spinetail.

Plain-mantled Tit-Spinetail
Leptasthenura aegithaloides   PLATE 7(6)
16–16.5 cm (6¼–6½"). Fairly common and widespread in low scrub, rocky ravines with scattered shrubs, and (in Chile) matorral from *s. Peru* (Arequipa) *and w. Bolivia* (La Paz) *south through Chile and much of w. and s. Argentina* (to n. Isla Grande). To about 4000 m in Andes of Bolivia and n. Chile, but mostly below 2500 m. Probably more than one species. In **most of range** (illustrated) has crown streaked cinnamon and dusky, narrow white superciliary, and whitish streaking on nape; *otherwise plain brownish gray on mantle;* wings with cinnamon-rufous patch in flight feathers; outer tail feathers edged whitish. *Throat white,* its sides and upper chest faintly streaked dusky; below pale buffy grayish. In **altiplano of Bolivia and adjacent countries**

larger and buffier below. Tufted Tit-Spinetail always shows a conspicuous crest; other vaguely similar tit-spinetails (e.g., Streak-backed, Rusty-crowned) all have streaking on mantle. Ranges in pairs or small groups, clambering about in shrubs and low trees, sometimes dropping to grass or even to the ground. Song in Argentina an irregular (sometimes long-continued) series of sharp high-pitched, scratchy notes and trills, e.g., "skwee, tzee-tzee-tzi-ti-ti."

Tufted Tit-Spinetail
Leptasthenura platensis   PLATE 7(7)
16–16.5 cm (6¼–6½"). Fairly common in lighter woodland (including monte) and adjacent scrub in *w. and s. Paraguay, n. and cen. Argentina* (south to Chubut), *Uruguay, and adjacent Brazil* (sw. Rio Grande do Sul). To 1000 m. Resembles Plain-mantled Tit-Spinetail but has a *distinct bushy crest, completely speckled throat* (not pure white in the middle), and pale cinnamon (not whitish) in outer tail feathers. Behavior and voice similar to Plain-mantled; Tufted is more of a woodland bird (less often in semiopen, scrubby situations), and its vocalizations are weaker and higher-pitched than Plain-mantled's in Argentina.

Brown-capped Tit-Spinetail
Leptasthenura fuliginiceps   PLATE 7(8)
16.5 cm (6½"). Locally fairly common in patches of low woodland, arid montane scrub, and ravines in *Andes from w. Bolivia* (La Paz) *to w. Argentina* (Mendoza and w. Córdoba). Mostly 2000–3300 m. Above sandy brown with *contrasting rufous brown crown* (usually raised into a *short bushy crest*) and buffyish superciliary; *wings and tail rufous.* Below dingy buff. The longer-billed Tawny Tit-Spinetail lacks the crest and capped effect and is more richly colored below. Behavior much as in Andean Tit-Spinetail. Call a high-pitched series of sputtered notes.

Tawny Tit-Spinetail
Leptasthenura yanacensis   PLATE 7(9)
16.5 cm (6½"). Local and uncommon in patches of *Polylepis* woodland and scrub in *Andes from w. Peru* (Ancash in the Cordillera Blanca) *to extreme nw. Argentina* (n. Jujuy and n. Salta). 2900–4600 m, lowest in Argentina. Bill rather long. *Above tawny brown,* more rufous on forecrown and with buff superciliary; wings duskier, feathers broadly edged rufous; rather long tail rufous. *Below uniform bright ochraceous.* Brown-capped Tit-Spinetail (sometimes sympatric)

has a stubbier bill and looks crested and dark-capped; it is duller below. Cf. also certain of the plainer canasteros, e.g., Canyon and Maquis; these differ behaviorally. Behavior similar to other tit-spinetails. Song a simple trill, "tree-ee-ee-ee," lasting around 2 seconds; also various chattered calls.

Araucaria Tit-Spinetail
Leptasthenura setaria   PLATE 7(10)
17 cm (6¾"). *Fairly common in* Araucaria-*dominated forest and woodland in se. Brazil* (Rio de Janeiro to n. Rio Grande do Sul) *and ne. Argentina* (Misiones). To 2200 m. *Boldly patterned and prominently crested.* Crown black with fine white streaking and a narrow white superciliary; *upperparts contrasting rufous-chestnut,* more blackish on wings; tail very long and mostly rufous-chestnut. Throat and upper chest flecked dusky, below ochraceous. Striolated Tit-Spinetail lacks the crest, has streaked (not rufous) back. Forages at all heights, almost always in *Araucaria* trees (including plantations), usually well above the ground and therefore sometimes hard to see. High-pitched, descending trilled song typical of genus.

Striolated Tit-Spinetail
Leptasthenura striolata   PLATE 7(11)
16–16.5 cm (6¼–6½"). *Fairly common in a variety of wooded and shrubby habitats in se. Brazil* (e. Paraná to n. Rio Grande do Sul). 500–1500 m. Crown black streaked rufous with indistinct whitish superciliary; *above brown streaked buffy-ish;* rufous patch in flight feathers, tail mostly rufous. Dull buff below, foreneck speckled brown. Only other sympatric tit-spinetail is the very different Araucaria, which is black-crowned and crested, has an unstreaked rufous-chestnut mantle, and is largely confined to *Araucaria* trees themselves. Other tit-spinetails that show back streaking are found in Andes. Behavior and high-pitched voice (e.g., "tsi-tsi-tsi-tsitsitsi") comparable to other tit-spinetails.

Schizoeaca

Small furnariids with *long and strongly graduated tails,* the feathers (especially at tips) frayed, found in *woodland undergrowth near treeline in the Andes.* The various species have *entirely allopatric distributions* and are here presented proceeding from north to south. *Interspecific variation is subtle,* primarily involving dorsal color, the presence or absence of an eye-ring and superciliary, and chin patch color. Behavior of all thistletails is similar. They are found singly or in pairs, most often independent of flocks (sometimes loosely associated), hopping and fluttering through dense vegetation, often with tail partially cocked. Occasionally drop to the ground. Flight always brief and weak. Although not especially shy, thistletails are often hard to see well or for long because their favored habitat is so dense; only rarely does one linger in the open for long. They glean for insects from foliage and twigs.

Ochre-browed Thistletail
Schizoeaca coryi   PLATE 7(12)
18 cm (7"). Locally fairly common in dense undergrowth of low montane woodland and forest borders, most often near treeline, and shrubby paramo in *Andes of w. Venezuela* (Trujillo to n. Táchira). Mostly 3400–4100 m, a few lower. Olive brown above with *contrasting ochre superciliary, face, and chin patch.* Below drab grayish. White-chinned Thistletail, occurring to the south (no overlap), lacks ochre on face and is much more rufescent above. Song a high-pitched thin trill that accelerates and descends slightly.

Perijá Thistletail
Schizoeaca perijana
19 cm (7½"). *Sierra de Perijá on Colombia-Venezuela border;* habitat and status unknown, but likely similar to other thistletails. 3000–3400 m. Olive brown above, crown slightly grayer and with indistinct grayish superciliary and narrow whitish eye-ring. Chin patch ochre; below drab brownish gray. *The only thistletail on the Sierra de Perijá.* Behavior and voice unknown, but presumably as in its congeners.

White-chinned Thistletail
Schizoeaca fuliginosa   PLATE 7(13)
18.5–19 cm (7¼–7½"). Uncommon in undergrowth of shrubby woodland near and just below treeline and in patches of *Polylepis-*dominated woodland in *Andes from extreme sw. Venezuela* (sw. Táchira) *to cen. Ecuador* (n. Morona-Santiago), and in *n. Peru* (Amazonas south of Río Marañón to Huánuco). Mostly 2800–3500 m, down to 2400 m in Peru. In **most of range** (illustrated) *chestnut brown above* with *narrow white eye-ring* and *short pale grayish postocular. Gray below* with *white chin patch.* In **Huánuco, Peru,** has a whiter postocular and some whitish streaking on lower throat and breast.

Mouse-colored Thistletail (occurring between the disjunct parts of White-chinned range) is duller and more olivaceous above with virtually no postocular. Eye-ringed Thistletail (ranging south of White-chinned) has orange-rufous chin patch and no postocular. Voice somewhat higher-pitched than Ochre-browed Thistletail.

Mouse-colored Thistletail
Schizoeaca griseomurina   PLATE 7(14)
18.5–19 cm (7¼–7½"). Uncommon in undergrowth of shrubby woodland near and just below treeline and in patches of *Polylepis*-dominated woodland in *Andes from cen. Ecuador* (Azuay and s. Morona-Santiago) *to n. Peru* (Piura and n. Cajamarca). Mostly 2800–4000 m. *Olivaceous brown above* with *conspicuous white eye-ring* and vaguer grayish postocular stripe. Grayish below with whitish chin patch. White-chinned Thistletail is much more rufescent above and has a more obvious whitish postocular. Song starts more slowly than Ochre-browed, with several well-enunciated rising notes before ending in a high-pitched trill.

Eye-ringed Thistletail
Schizoeaca palpebralis   PLATE 7(15)
18.5–19 cm (7¼–7½"). Reportedly fairly commmon in undergrowth of shrubby woodland *near treeline* on *east slope of Andes in cen. Peru* (Junín). About 3000–3700 m. *Chestnut brown above* with *conspicuous white eye-ring.* Gray below with *orange-rufous chin patch.* White-chinned Thistletail (occurring just to north) has whitish chin patch and whitish postocular. Vilcabamba Thistletail (occurring to south) is more olivaceous above and has *no* eye-ring. Not well known, but habits and voice presumably as in its congeners.

Vilcabamba Thistletail
Schizoeaca vilcabambae   PLATE 7(16)
18.5–19 cm (7¼–7½"). Reportedly fairly common in undergrowth of shrubby woodland *near treeline on east slope of Andes in s. Peru* (n. Ayacucho and w. Cuzco). 2800–3500 m. In **Ayacucho** (illustrated) olive brown above with at most a vague grayish postocular (and *no* eye-ring). Grayish below with *rufous chin patch.* In **Cuzco,** chin patch smaller and paler and with *underparts scaled whitish.* Eye-ringed Thistletail (found just to north) is more rufescent above and has a prominent eye-ring. Puna Thistletail is also more rufescent above and has blackish on lower throat. Poorly known, but habits and voice presumably as in its congeners.

Puna Thistletail
Schizoeaca helleri
18 cm (7"). Uncommon in undergrowth of shrubby woodland and borders *near treeline on east slope of Andes from s. Peru* (Cuzco) *to extreme w. Bolivia* (w. La Paz). 2800–3600 m. Resembles Vilcabamba Thistletail (occurring to north), differing in its more rufescent upperparts, very small rufous chin patch, *blackish lower throat flecked with gray,* and *absence of* scaly effect on underparts. Black-throated Thistletail (found to the south) has more ochreous on face, a white chin patch, and lower throat more solid black. Song an accelerating chipper, lacking Black-throated Thistletail's rattled effect.

Black-throated Thistletail
Schizoeaca harterti   PLATE 7(17)
18 cm (7"). Fairly common in undergrowth of woodland and borders *near treeline on east slope of Andes in w. Bolivia* (La Paz to w. Santa Cruz). Mostly 2500–3400 m. In **La Paz** (illustrated) brown above, more rufescent on crown and tail, with narrow whitish eye-ring and narrow buffy whitish postocular; *face washed ochraceous.* Chin patch whitish, *lower throat blackish;* below dull grayish. In **Cochabamba and Santa Cruz** shows more ochraceous on face. Puna Thistletail (found to north) is duller overall with a less marked facial pattern. Song a rattled trill that accelerates and rises slightly, ending in a sputter.

Itatiaia Spinetail
Oreophylax moreirae   PLATE 8(1)
19 cm (7½"). *Fairly common but very local in areas with low shrubs and coarse grass in higher mountains of se. Brazil* (cen. Minas Gerais at Caraça to extreme ne. São Paulo at Itatiaia). 1900–2800 m. Above olivaceous brown with faint buffyish superciliary; *tail more rufescent, very long and strongly graduated, with feathers pointed and somewhat frayed.* Chin patch orange-rufous; below pale buffyish. Confusion in its limited range unlikely; Spix's Spinetail can occur with it but is quite different (rufous on crown, etc.). Cf. also Cipó Canastero (no known overlap). Usually in pairs, hopping on or near the ground in dense vegetation; inconspicuous except when singing, then often mounting to the top of a bush or rock. Song a jumbled series of fast notes that ends in a chippered trill, e.g., "whyee-whee-whee-dwee-dwee-dwee-didididididididiu."

Asthenes

Small, usually long-tailed furnariids found in open and semiopen grassy or shrubby terrain, principally in the Andes (some species occur in Patagonia or the chaco). Primarily terrestrial, canasteros are often shy and hard to see well, which makes it even more difficult to distinguish the many species that closely resemble each other. Watch for the following key points: the presence or absence of streaking, above and/or below; the presence of a chin patch, usually orange-rufous (absent in a few species, and in a few individuals of others); and the extent of rufous on the tail. Rectrices are broad and rounded in some species, narrower and more pointed in others. All canasteros are quite similar vocally, so voice usually is of limited value in separating the various species.

Cipó Canastero
Asthenes luizae

17 cm (6¾"). Uncommon and local on rocky slopes ("campo rupestre") with scattered bushes and ground bromeliads on serras of interior se. Brazil (cen. Minas Gerais on Serra do Cipó; also recently on Campina do Bananal). 1000–1300 m. Above grayish brown with a narrow whitish superciliary; tail dusky brown, outer feathers rufous-chestnut. Chin patch white with fine black streaks; below grayish. No other canastero occurs anywhere near this species' range; cf. Itatiaia Spinetail (no known overlap). Behavior much as in many other canasteros; a mainly terrestrial bird that hops and runs on rocky slopes, frequently disappearing among boulders. The tail is often partially cocked. Song a rather musical series of 10–15 descending notes.

Rusty-vented Canastero
Asthenes dorbignyi   PLATE 8(2)

15.5–16.5 cm (6–6½"). Fairly common in a variety of habitats with scrub and scattered shrubs, especially in ravines and where columnar cacti are present, in Andes from w. Bolivia (La Paz) to w. Argentina (Mendoza). Mostly 2500–4000 m. The following two species are sometimes considered conspecific, as Creamy-breasted Canastero. Sandy brown above with pale grayish superciliary; wings mainly rufous, and rump rich rufous contrasting with mostly black tail (outer feathers rufous). Chin patch rufous; below creamy whitish. Favors rocky, steep slopes, generally not in areas with grass. Cf. very

similar Steinbach's and Berlepsch's Canasteros; does not overlap with Dark-winged Canastero. Streak-fronted Thornbird (often sympatric) is slightly larger, never shows a chin patch, and lacks the rump-tail contrast. Usually in pairs, often feeding on the ground, not lingering in the open, scampering from beneath one bush to another; typically cocks its tail. Nests are often conspicuous, placed in the open and often well above the ground. Song a series of high-pitched notes that accelerate into a sputtering trill.

Pale-tailed Canastero
Asthenes huancavelicae

15.5–16.5 cm (6–6½"). Not uncommon but very local in arid montane scrub with scattered columnar cacti in Andes of w. Peru. 1800–3700 m. Grayish brown above with whitish superciliary, mainly rufous wings, and entire tail strikingly pale; from north to south, the tail is bright cinnamon-rufous in Ancash, pale cinnamon in Huancavelica and n. Ayacucho, and whitish in s. Ayacucho and Apurímac. Whitish below with a faint pale rufous chin patch (more evident in some individuals). Regardless of race, the rather contrasting pale tail is distinctive. Behavior much as in Rusty-vented Canastero; often perches in and sings from tall cacti. Song of northern birds similar to Rusty-vented, but Ayacucho birds reportedly give a simple high-pitched trill (J. Fjeldså and N. K. Krabbe).

Dark-winged Canastero
Asthenes arequipae   PLATE 8(3)

15.5–16.5 cm (6–6½"). Fairly common in and near Polylepis-dominated woodland and in arid montane scrub in Andes from w. Peru (Lima) to w. Bolivia (sw. La Paz and nw. Oruro) and n. Chile (Tarapacá). Mostly 3500–4800 m, in w. Peru locally to 2500 m. Grayish brown above with pale grayish superciliary, blackish ear-coverts, mainly blackish wings, and rich rufous rump contrasting with mostly black tail (outer feathers rufous). Chin patch rufous; below creamy whitish. Rather striking and readily known in range; cf. Rusty-vented Canastero (no overlap; with rufous in wings, etc.). Behavior and voice much as in Rusty-vented but usually lacking any sharp introductory notes.

Berlepsch's Canastero
Asthenes berlepschi

16.5 cm (6½"). Uncommon and local in semiarid montane scrub and agricultural terrain with hedgerows and scattered trees on east slope of Andes in w. Bolivia (w. La Paz). 2800–3700 m. Closely resembles Rusty-vented Canastero (no overlap). Slightly larger with a somewhat heavier bill; chin patch tiny or absent; and *shows more rufous on lateral tail* (outer two pairs of feathers entirely rufous, not just the outermost web). Behavior much as in Rusty-vented, likewise mainly foraging on or near the ground in shrubbery; their conspicuous nests, however, are sometimes placed much higher, often in trees such as *Eucalyptus*. Song a chippered trill that trails off toward end.

Steinbach's Canastero
Asthenes steinbachi PLATE 8(4)
16 cm (6¼"). Rare to uncommon and apparently local in sparse arid montane scrub, often in ravines, in *Andes of nw. Argentina* (w. Salta to n. Mendoza). Mostly 1500–2500 m. Closely resembles Rusty-vented Canastero, which seems to outnumber it where they occur together. Steinbach's *lacks a chin patch* (lower throat only flecked black) and shows *more rufous on lateral tail* (outer two pairs of feathers all rufous, not just outermost web); duller and more grayish below. Must be identified with care as all characters are hard to confirm in the field. So far as known, behavior similar to Rusty-vented.

Short-billed Canastero
Asthenes baeri PLATE 8(5)
15.5 cm (6"). *Fairly common in chaco scrub and woodland, and in monte, from se. Bolivia* (s. Santa Cruz) *and w. Paraguay to cen. Argentina* (Mendoza and Río Negro). Below 800 m. *A plain canastero with a rather short and stout bill*. Pale grayish brown above with *fairly broad grayish superciliary;* wings slightly more rufescent; tail mainly blackish, outer feathers rufous. *Fairly large chin patch orange-rufous;* below mainly pale grayish. Sharp-billed Canastero has longer tail and noticeably longer and thinner bill; its superciliary is less evident and its chin patch smaller. Little Thornbird (frequently sympatric) lacks the chin patch, has a rufous patch on shoulders. Rather arboreal for a canastero, Short-billed forages in pairs in foliage and on lateral branches, is usually easy to observe (easier than many canasteros); not often on the ground. Song a series of wiry, mechanical trills, usually descending in pitch and slowing.

Sharp-billed Canastero
Asthenes pyrrholeuca PLATE 8(6)
16.5 cm (6½"). Fairly common in low shrubby growth and sparse scrub in *s. Argentina* (mainly from Mendoza and s. Buenos Aires to s. Santa Cruz, a few northward) *and cen. and s. Chile* (locally from Aconcagua to Magallanes); in winter migrates as far north as s. Bolivia, w. Paraguay, and Uruguay. Mostly below 2000 m. A *plain* canastero with a *comparatively long tail* and a *straight, thin bill*. Above pale grayish brown with vague grayish superciliary; wings somewhat more rufescent; tail dusky with outer feathers rufous. Chin patch pale orange-rufous; below pale grayish. A *very dark* form is a local resident around salt lagoons in **Santiago del Estero**. Short-billed Canastero is similar (and sometimes sympatric) but has a markedly heavier bill, shorter tail, and larger and brighter chin patch. Cordilleran Canastero also has shorter tail; it has a streakier effect on sides of head and neck and is buffier below. Cf. also Patagonian Canastero. Usually hops in dense shrubby growth where hard to see well; sometimes drops to the ground, especially to run between patches of cover (seldom flying far). Does not cock tail. Fairly musical song a fast, rollicking "whi-di-di-di-wheediyiu-wheedidyiu-wheedidyiu."

Patagonian Canastero
Asthenes patagonica PLATE 8(7)
15.5 cm (6"). Uncommon in low scrub on *Patagonian steppes of s. Argentina* (Mendoza and s. Buenos Aires to n. Santa Cruz). To 700 m. Above grayish brown with grayish superciliary; wings more rufescent and *tail mainly blackish* (rufous only on outer web of outermost feathers). Below grayish, *throat whiter and finely speckled black* (*no* discrete chin patch). Sharp-billed Canastero has longer tail, more rufous in outer tail, and an orange-rufous chin patch. Feeds in shrubby growth, sometimes hopping on the ground with tail cocked; unless singing, generally hard to see well. Song a rather strident and penetrating trill on an even pitch, distinctively different from Sharp-billed's.

Dusky-tailed Canastero
Asthenes humicola PLATE 8(8)
15.5 cm (6"). Fairly common in dense scrub (matorral) in *cen. Chile* (sw. Antofogasta to Malleco); an old record from w. Argentina (Mendoza). To 2200 m. Brown above with whitish superciliary; *lesser wing-coverts rufous; tail blackish* (essentially *no* rufous). *Throat white with fine*

black speckling, breast pale grayish with fine white streaking, flanks cinnamon to tawny. Patagonian Canastero (not known to overlap with Dusky-tailed, though ranges come close) lacks rufous on wing-coverts and also white streaking on breast; it shows some rufous in its outer tail. Cordilleran Canastero is paler, has much more rufous in tail and more diffuse streaking on foreneck. Behavior much as in Sharp-billed Canastero, but seems even harder to observe. Gives a sharply enunciated ticking, "ts-ts-ts-ts-ts-ts-ts."

Cordilleran Canastero
Asthenes modesta   PLATE 8(9)
14.5–15 cm (5¾–6″). *Often common in open arid grassland, usually where boulder-strewn, in Andes from cen. Peru* (Junín) *to s. Chile* (Magallanes) *and s. Argentina* (s. Santa Cruz), spreading east onto Patagonian plains. To 4500 m. Sandy brown above with whitish superciliary and *plain back;* wings more rufescent; central pair of tail feathers mostly dusky, *all lateral ones mainly rufous.* Chin patch usually orange-rufous, *face and foreneck whitish finely streaked dusky;* below buffy whitish. **Southern birds** are slightly smaller, darker above and whiter below. *Most similar canasteros show streaking on back.* Streak-throated is the most similar, but its foreneck streaking is more pronounced and its tail mainly dusky. Sharp-billed Canastero, also plain-backed, *lacks* foreneck streaking altogether and has narrower bill; it favors scrub, not grassland. A mainly terrestrial canastero that hops and runs rapidly, usually with tail cocked; often seen scampering across little-used roads. Generally easy to observe, sometimes perching atop boulders or on grass clumps for protracted periods. Song a short, semimusical trill that ascends distinctively.

Streak-throated Canastero
Asthenes humilis   PLATE 8(10)
15.5–16 cm (6–6¼″). Fairly common in arid puna grassland (favoring boulder-strewn areas with short grass) in *Andes from n. Peru* (Cajamarca) *to w. Bolivia* (La Paz). 3100–4800 m. Above grayish brown with narrow whitish superciliary and *indistinct dark streaking on back; rather short tail mostly dusky,* outer feathers pale grayish. Chin patch rufous, *face and foreneck whitish finely streaked dusky;* below buffy whitish. Cordilleran Canastero has a *plain back,* less streaking on foreneck (though it shows some), and *much more rufous in tail* (the best mark of all). Found singly or in pairs, feeding mostly as it hops on

the ground, usually with tail cocked; often not shy. Frequently perches atop clumps of grass or on boulders. Song a simple trill that varies in length.

Cactus Canastero
Asthenes cactorum   PLATE 8(11)
14.5 cm (5¾″). *Uncommon and local on open, very arid slopes with scattered columnar cacti and boulders on west slope of Andes in w. Peru* (Lima to Arequipa). Mostly 500–2500 m. *Resembles Cordilleran Canastero, but range and habitat very different. Bill strikingly longer;* chin patch often larger (but more diffused); less streaky effect on sides of head and foreneck; breast whiter. The only canasteros at all likely to occur with the Cactus are the dissimilar Dark-winged and Canyon. Hops among boulders and often perches on the cacti on which are placed its conspicuous big stick nests (easier to see than the birds themselves). Usually cocks tail. Song a short rattling trill.

Canyon Canastero
Asthenes pudibunda   PLATE 8(12)
16.5 cm (6½″). Uncommon and local on rocky slopes and in gorges with scattered bushes and low trees, sometimes in *Polylepis*-dominated woodland, on *west slope of Andes from nw. Peru* (La Libertad) *to extreme n. Chile* (recently found in Tarapacá). 2500–4000 m. Brown above with narrow buffyish superciliary; *wings and tail mainly rufous-chestnut. Grayish below;* chin patch chestnut to cinnamon. **Northern birds** (south to Ancash) are darker generally. Does not occur with either Rusty-fronted or Maquis Canasteros; sometimes found with radically different Rusty-vented Canastero. Ranges in pairs that sometimes hop on the ground (usually with tail cocked high) but are more arboreal than most canasteros, moving on branches and in foliage. Song a loud accelerating trill that descends in pitch.

Rusty-fronted Canastero
Asthenes ottonis   PLATE 8(13)
18 cm (7″). Fairly common in arid montane scrub and low woodland and patches of *Polylepis*-dominated woodland in *Andes of s. Peru* (Huancavelica to Cuzco). 2750–4000 m. Above brown with *rufous forehead* and narrow buffyish superciliary; *wings and long, graduated, quite pointed tail mainly rufous-chestnut.* Chin patch orange-rufous; below grayish, foreneck with fine white streaking. *The only canastero in its limited*

range with a mostly rufous tail. Streak-fronted Thornbird is larger with a shorter, mainly dusky tail (rufous only on sides); it is whiter below with *no* chin patch. Ranges singly or in pairs, rarely leaving cover; sometimes scampers across open places, usually with tail cocked. Song a rapidly descending series of high-pitched notes, e.g., "bzee-bzée-bzee-di-di-di-di-d-d-d."

Maquis Canastero
Asthenes heterura
16.5 cm (6½"). Uncommon in arid montane scrub and low woodland, including *Polylepis* woodland and scrub, in *Andes from w. Bolivia* (La Paz) *to extreme nw. Argentina* (recently found in n. Jujuy and n. Salta). Mostly 2900–4200 m, lower in Argentina (to 2500 m, even lower in winter). Resembles Rusty-fronted Canastero (no overlap), but smaller and with shorter rufous tail; further, Maquis *lacks* the rufous forehead, shows virtually no foreneck streaking, and is more ochraceous below. At southern end of range, Maquis can occur with wintering Sharp-billed Canasteros; Sharp-billed has a mainly blackish tail (rufous only laterally) and less rufous in wings. Behavior much as in Rusty-fronted, though Maquis tends not to cock its tail. Song a short and rather variable series of notes, sometimes ascending (e.g., "trew tri-tri-tri-tri?") but at others dropping slightly or more jumbled.

Streak-backed Canastero
Asthenes wyatti   PLATE 8(14)
15.5–18 cm (6–7"). Locally fairly common in paramo and puna grassland and arid montane scrub in *Andes of w. Venezuela* (Trujillo and Mérida) *and n. Colombia* (Norte de Santander; Santa Marta Mts.), and from *n. Ecuador* (Pichincha) *to s. Peru* (Puno) *and extreme w. Bolivia* (recently in w. La Paz). Mostly 3000–4500 m. In **Peru** (illustrated) *brown above with blackish streaks* except on rump, narrow superciliary buff; wings more rufescent (especially on flight feathers); *rather long tail dusky with outer three pairs of feathers rufous.* Chin patch orange-rufous; below dull tawny-buff. **Northern birds** (cen. Ecuador north) are smaller and more buffy grayish below. Puna Canastero (narrowly overlaps with Streak-backed near Peru-Bolivia border) is very similar aside from having black base to outer tail feathers. Streak-throated Canastero lacks rufous in tail, shows streaking on foreneck, and has dingier, more grayish underparts. Occurs singly or in pairs; mostly terrestrial, scampering among grass tussocks and hopping on rocks, tail

often held partially cocked; except when singing, adept at hiding. Song a fast trill that typically accelerates and slightly rises.

Puna Canastero
Asthenes sclateri
18 cm (7"). Uncommon and local in puna grassland (bunchgrass with scattered rocks and shrubs), and edge of *Polylepis* scrub in *Andes from extreme s. Peru* (Puno) *to nw. Argentina* (La Rioja; also in sierras of w. Córdoba). 1800–4000 m. Resembles Streak-backed Canastero, with which Puna apparently overlaps very locally in Lake Titicaca region. Puna Canastero differs in having *outer tail feathers mainly black,* their terminal third rufous (these feathers all rufous in Streak-backed). Cordilleran Canastero has much more rufous in tail and an *un*streaked back. Streak-throated Canastero lacks rufous in tail, has foreneck streaking and dingier, grayer underparts. Behavior and voice much as in Streak-backed Canastero.

Hudson's Canastero
Asthenes hudsoni   PLATE 8(15)
18 cm (7"). *Locally fairly common in grassy or sedgy areas in and around marshes and seasonally flooded places in extreme se. Brazil* (s. Rio Grande do Sul), *Uruguay, and e. Argentina* (Entre Ríos to Río Negro). To 950 m. Sandy brown above *streaked with blackish and silvery grayish,* with narrow buffyish superciliary; cinnamon patch on flight feathers; *tail long and pointed, dusky prominently edged silvery gray.* Chin patch usually white; below buff, *flanks with black streaking. The only canastero found primarily in the pampas region.* Short-billed Canastero, also found locally in the pampas (but in scrub and monte), is unstreaked above, etc. Hudson's most resembles Austral Canastero, found well to south in Patagonia; Austral is smaller, has shorter tail with less silvery gray. Cf. also Bay-capped Wren-Spinetail. Found singly or in pairs, usually hard to see, as it tends to creep about in dense vegetation. Watch for it on calm early mornings, and when birds are singing, for then it sometimes lingers on exposed perches. The short song is a simple rising trill of semimusical notes.

Austral Canastero
Asthenes anthoides   PLATE 8(16)
16.5 cm (6½"). *Uncommon and local on shrubby Patagonian steppes from s. Argentina* (north to s. Neuquén) *and adjacent Chile to Tierra del Fuego. To 1500 m. Occurs farther south than any*

other canastero, barely overlapping with congeners. Sandy brown above *streaked blackish,* narrow buffyish superciliary; cinnamon patch on flight feathers; *tail rather short, feathers pointed, dusky edged buffy whitish.* Chin patch orange-rufous; below drab grayish buff, some blackish streaking on flanks. Patagonian and Cordilleran Canasteros are *un*streaked above. Found singly or in pairs, sometimes hopping on the ground with partially cocked tail, rarely far from scrubby cover. Song much as in Streak-backed and Hudson's Canasteros, often given from atop a shrub.

Scribble-tailed Canastero
Asthenes maculicauda PLATE 8(17)
17 cm (6¾"). Uncommon and local in puna grassland in *Andes from extreme s. Peru* (s. Cuzco) *to nw. Argentina* (Tucumán); favors relatively lush areas. Mostly 3000–4300 m. *Forecrown rufous,* narrow superciliary buff; *above blackish brown streaked buff;* wings with much rufous in flight feathers; *long and pointed tail rufous with irregular black markings* (the "scribbles," hard to discern in the field). Dull buffyish below *with no chin patch,* a little streaking on breast and flanks. Junín Canastero lacks rufous on crown, has shorter and browner tail with no scribbles, and shows a pale chin patch. Behavior and voice much as in Many-striped Canastero, though Scribble-tailed seems to cock tail less.

Many-striped Canastero
Asthenes flammulata PLATE 8(18)
16 cm (6¼"). Fairly common in paramo and puna grassland with scattered shrubs (e.g., *Espeletia*) in *Andes from Colombia* (Norte de Santander) *to cen. Peru* (locally to Ancash and Junín). Mostly 3000–4500 m. In **Ecuador and Nariño, Colombia** (illustrated), blackish brown above with fine tawny streaking on crown and *ochraceous streaking on mantle,* narrow buffyish superciliary; *wings with much rufous-chestnut in flight feathers;* tail dark brown, feathers pointed and edged rufous. Chin patch orange-buff; *below streaked whitish and dusky-brown.* In **Colombia's E. Andes** has a darker chin patch. In **Peru** has a whitish throat and reduced dark streaking below. Streak-backed Canastero is much less streaked generally. In Peru cf. Junín Canastero (limited or no overlap). This handsome canastero hops on or near the ground and can be rather sneaky; it sometimes cocks its tail. Perches in the open mainly early, or when calm. Song a fast accelerating series of "trree" notes usually ending in a chipper.

Junín Canastero
Asthenes virgata
17 cm (6¾"). Uncommon and local in puna grassland and near patches of *Polylepis*-dominated woodland in *Andes of s. Peru* (Lima to Puno). 3300–4300 m. Resembles Many-striped Canastero (found to north; no known overlap), differing in its larger size, *pale rufous chin patch* (throat all whitish in Peruvian races of Many-striped), *less extensive rufous in wing,* and *more brownish* (not so dusky) *streaking below.* Scribble-tailed Canastero (limited overlap) has rufous forecrown, longer and more rufescent tail with scribbles, *no* chin patch. Behavior and voice as in Many-striped Canastero.

Line-fronted Canastero
Asthenes urubambensis PLATE 8(19)
16 cm (6¼"). Uncommon and local in sparse *Polylepis* scrub and low woodland in *Andes from n. Peru* (s. San Martín) *to w. Bolivia* (Cochabamba). Mostly 3200–4300 m. *Above umber brown with streaking only on forecrown and sides of head* and *no rufous in wings or tail;* fairly long whitish superciliary. Chin patch orange-buff; *below streaked whitish and dusky-brown.* This distinctive canastero is the only one in which uniform upperparts are combined with streaked underparts. It is more arboreal than most, hopping and sidling along branches; sometimes hops and walks on the ground, but does not seem to cock tail. Voice resembles Many-striped Canastero.

Thripophaga

The genus *Thripophaga* is almost surely not a natural unit, though the species now classified in it are united in having broadly rounded, unpointed tail feathers. Some softtails are streaked, others plain; some have a chin patch, others not. They are found *mainly in lowland forests,* though one species (Russet-mantled) is Andean.

Orinoco Softtail
Thripophaga cherriei PLATE 9(1)
14.5 cm (5¾"). *Very local, recorded only from shrubby undergrowth of várzea forest at a single site in s. Venezuela* (Río Capuana in nw. Amazonas); there apparently fairly common. 150 m. Olive brown above with indistinct whitish superciliary; wings more chestnut, tail rufous-chestnut. *Chin patch orange-rufous;* below olive

brown, *foreneck and breast with fine buff streaking*. Speckled Spinetail has a rufous crown, spotted breast, *no* chin patch. Virtually unknown in life.

Striated Softtail

Thripophaga macroura   PLATE 9(2)

18 cm (7"). *Rare and local in lower and middle growth of humid forest and borders in se. Brazil* (s. Bahia to n. Rio de Janeiro). To 1000 m. Above rufous brown streaked buff on head and back and with narrow buff superciliary; wings rufous-chestnut, *rump and tail bright cinnamon*. Chin patch orange-rufous; below brown *streaked pale buffyish*. Pale-browed Treehunter is larger with a heavier bill, wider superciliary, and broader streaking below; it usually forages higher above the ground. The softtail is an inconspicuous bird that skulks in undergrowth and viny tangles; it sometimes accompanies mixed flocks. Most frequent call a repetition of a single strident note, "tch-tch-tch-tch-tch. . . ."

Plain Softtail

Thripophaga fusciceps   PLATE 9(3)

16.5–19 cm (6½–7½"). *Generally rare and local* (locally more numerous, e.g., in n. Bolivia) in vine tangles and thick vegetation at edge of humid forest and woodland, favoring secondary and várzea situations. Locally to 1200 m in Ecuador. Likely more than one species. *Drab.* In **w. Amazonia** (illustrated) *mostly olivaceous brown* with an indistinct buffyish superciliary; wings and tail rufous. **Lower Amazon** birds are darker and browner. **Bolivian birds** are *larger.* The *uniform and unstreaked* plumage distinguishes this well-named, notably plain bird from any vaguely similar foliage-gleaner. It typically does not occur with any thornbird; Rufous-fronted Thornbird is whiter below and has an obvious rufous forehead. Arboreal, clambering about in pairs or small groups; unless vocalizing inconspicuous. Generally not with flocks. Distinctive song, often given as a duet, a sharp loud churring that gradually slows and becomes weaker; it can continue for 20 or more seconds before finally petering out. Call a sharp "chrr" or "t-chrr."

Russet-mantled Softtail

Thripophaga berlepschi

18 cm (7"). *Rare and local in lower growth of montane forest and elfin woodland in Andes of n. Peru* (Amazonas, San Martín, and e. La Libertad). 2800–3300 m. Iris hazel. *Plain rufous above*

with *crown and chin pale grayish buff. Breast also rufous,* belly olivaceous brown. A rufous furnariid with a contrasting ashy crown, this scarce species is unlikely to be confused; cf. Sepia-brown and Peruvian Wrens. Forages singly and in pairs, generally not with mixed flocks. Call a loud, ringing, and fast "chididee, chu-chi-chi-chr," vaguely like a *Cranioleuca* (B. Walker recording).

Phacellodomus

Plain, unstreaked furnariids found primarily in semiopen, nonforested areas, thornbirds are most diverse in s.-cen. South America. Many species have *rufous on forecrown* (with feathers often stiffened and streaky). Though generally inconspicuous birds, thornbirds are *quite vocal,* and their loud vocalizations often draw attention to them. They are best known for—indeed, are named for—their *large and conspicuous, multichambered stick nests.*

Streak-fronted Thornbird

Phacellodomus striaticeps   PLATE 9(4)

17 cm (6½"). Locally fairly common in montane scrub and agricultural areas, *often where cacti are prevalent,* in *Andes from s. Peru* (Apurímac) to nw. Argentina (n. Catamarca). Mostly 2800–4200 m. Brown above with *rufous forecrown,* fine streaking on crown, and narrow white superciliary; *shoulders and patch at base of flight feathers rufous* (showing even on closed wing); *outer tail feathers basally rufous.* Below whitish, buff on flanks. Resembles better-known Rufous-fronted Thornbird of lowlands (no overlap known); Rufous-fronted *lacks* rufous in wings and tail. Cf. also various canasteros, especially Rusty-vented (sympatric); the latter is somewhat smaller and has a chin patch, more rufous in wing, and rufous rump contrasting with blacker tail. Forages both in shrubbery and while hopping on the ground, then usually with tail cocked. Their large stick nests are conspicuous, and the birds often sing while perched nearby; vocalizations, with a distinctive descending effect, resemble Rufous-fronted's.

Rufous-fronted Thornbird

Phacellodomus rufifrons*   PLATE 9(5)

16.5 cm (6½"). *Locally common* in a variety of semiopen and lightly wooded habitats, often in agricultural areas and ranch country, from *n. and e. Bolivia to ne. Brazil,* with an outlying population in *upper Río Marañón valley of nw. Peru and extreme s. Ecuador.* Mostly below 1300 m. Formerly called Common Thornbird (when the Plain Thornbird was included). In **most of range** (illustrated) uniform drab brown above with *rufous forecrown* and pale buffyish superciliary. Whitish below, buff on flanks. In **ne. Brazil** has some rufous on shoulders, in flight feathers, and basally on tail. Little Thornbird (of chaco; minimal overlap at most) is markedly smaller with obvious rufous shoulders and in outer tail. Ranges in pairs or small groups; although usually arboreal, sometimes drops to the ground. Often conspicuous, especially when around their large stick nests (usually placed at the tips of large branches). Vocal, with typical song a loud and abrupt series of forceful "cheh" or "chit" notes that start slowly, then accelerate and drop. Often both members of a pair call in sequence, or ♀ contributes a chatter.

Plain Thornbird
Phacellodomus inornatus*
15.5 cm (6"). *Common* in semiopen country with scattered large trees and in woodland borders in *n. Venezuela and ne. Colombia; especially numerous in llanos.* To 950 m. Formerly considered conspecific with Rufous-fronted Thornbird. Resembles that species (no overlap), differing in *lacking* rufous on forecrown. Among the plainest of birds, this species can be known from its *lack* of field marks; it is vaguely wrenlike. Behavior as in Rufous-fronted Thornbird, though in appropriate habitat the Plain can be more numerous. Plain's conspicuous stick nests are much the same, and are a notable feature of the llanos. They are multichambered, with the lower chambers sometimes usurped by other birds (e.g., Saffron Finches and Venezuelan Troupials). Song as in Rufous-fronted but markedly faster and higher-pitched.

Little Thornbird
Phacellodomus sibilatrix   PLATE 9(6)
14 cm (5½"). *Fairly common in chaco woodland and scrub in n. Argentina* (south to Córdoba and n. Buenos Aires), *w. Paraguay, and adjacent Bolivia and Uruguay.* To 2000 m in nw. Argentina. Resembles Rufous-fronted Thornbird (no known overlap), but *markedly smaller.* Little Thornbird shows less rufous on forecrown, has *rufous shoulders* and *some rufous in outer tail feathers* (both lacking in Rufous-fronted). Short-billed Canastero has a stubbier bill and is more grayish overall (not so brown); it has a distinct

chin patch but *lacks* rufous shoulders. Forages in pairs or small groups, and often quite confiding; though mainly arboreal, like some other thornbirds it also regularly drops to the ground. Song a well-enunciated series of shrill "cheep" notes that descend slightly, somewhat higher-pitched than Rufous-fronted's.

Greater Thornbird
Phacellodomus ruber   PLATE 9(7)
20.5 cm (8"). Fairly common in undergrowth of gallery woodland and shrubby areas, almost invariably near water, from *n. Bolivia* (west to La Paz) *and interior Brazil to n. Argentina* (Santa Fé and Entre Ríos). Locally to 1400 m in Bolivia. *Iris bright yellow. The largest thornbird.* Brown above, *more rufous on crown, wings, and tail;* lores pale, but *shows little or no superciliary.* Whitish below, foreneck sometimes scaled dusky. Frecklebreasted Thornbird can be similar (depending on molt stage, even breast patterns can be alike). Freckle-breasted is smaller, its wings are concolor and tail duskier (both wings and tail show less rufous than in Greater). Usually in pairs and skulking, especially when not vocalizing; fortunately it sings a lot, and then is more often in the open. Song a series of loud, arresting notes that start explosively and accelerate, becoming less forceful, e.g., "kur-cheé-chee-chee-chee-che-che-che-chew-chew-chew-chu-chu-chu-chuchuchu"; some songs are shorter, and pairs sometimes duet.

Freckle-breasted Thornbird
Phacellodomus striaticollis   PLATE 9(8)
18 cm (7"). Uncommon in shrubby borders of gallery and monte woodland, and in thickets in more open marshy terrain (almost always near water), from *se. Brazil* (e. Paraná) *and s. Paraguay to ne. Argentina* (n. Buenos Aires). To 700 m. *Iris yellow.* Brown above, forecrown more rufescent, with indistinct whitish superciliary; outer tail feathers basally rufous. Whitish below, *breast buffier and with minute white freckling* (often hard to see). Does not overlap with Spotbreasted Thornbird of Andean slopes; thus Freckle-breasted is most apt to be confused with larger Greater Thornbird (also yellow-eyed), though that species shows more rufous in wings and tail. Behavior much as in Greater Thornbird, likewise occasionally leaving its usual thickety haunts to forage in more open marshy terrain. Song also similar, though usually includes a series of softer preliminary notes before it bursts into much louder main song.

Spot-breasted Thornbird
Phacellodomus maculipectus   PLATE 9(9)
18 cm (7"). Uncommon in undergrowth and borders of deciduous and semihumid woodland, and in adjacent cleared areas, in *Andes from s. Bolivia* (se. Cochabamaba and w. Santa Cruz) *to nw. Argentina* (La Rioja). 1000–2900 m. Iris gray. Brown above with *rufous crown showing sometimes prominent white shaft streaks* and whitish superciliary; flight feathers edged rufous, outer tail feathers mostly rufous. Below buffy whitish, *sides of throat and breast more orange-rufous with small white chevron markings*. Not likely confused in its limited range; cf. Freckle-breasted Thornbird (no overlap). Generally skulking behavior as in that species, though Spot-breasted shows *no* predilection for vicinity of water. Song a series of loud, well-enunciated notes, e.g., "kip-kíp-ki-kee-kee-kew-kew," higher-pitched than in Rufous-fronted; like that species, sometimes duets.

Chestnut-backed Thornbird
Phacellodomus dorsalis   PLATE 9(10)
19.5 cm (7¾"). *Uncommon and local in dense low scrub and agricultural areas in upper Río Marañón valley in nw. Peru* (s. Cajamarca and La Libertad). 2000–2700 m. Iris gray. Grayish brown above, forecrown more rufescent and with streaked effect, lores whitish; *rufous-chestnut saddle across back;* wings and tail mostly rufous. Whitish below with *rufous spotting across breast* and rufous flanks. Not likely confused in its very limited range. Rufous-fronted Thornbird (which occurs at lower elevations in the Marañón valley; no overlap) is much plainer, lacking the rufous area on back. Behavior much as in other thornbirds; reminiscent of geographically far-removed Greater. Song recalls Greater's, an abrupt loud series of ringing notes that descends and slows, lasting up to 5–10 seconds; also has a shorter song (much like Greater).

Orange-eyed Thornbird
*Phacellodomus erythrophthalmus**   PLATE 9(11)
17 cm (6¾"). *Uncommon in dense lower growth of secondary woodland and humid forest borders, often near rivers, in e. Brazil* (s. Bahia [perhaps only formerly] and s. Minas Gerais to ne. São Paulo). Formerly considered conspecific with Red-eyed Thornbird. Locally to 1600 m. *Iris orange to yellow.* Resembles Red-eyed, differing (apart from eye color) in having *rufous on crown only on forecrown,* an *entirely rufous tail,* and *only throat rufous* (not breast as well; underparts

olivaceous brown). Red-eyed occurs mainly to south. Behavior as in Red-eyed, though less an inveterate skulker. Song like Red-eyed's, but individual notes less doubled, e.g., "ku-ku-ku, kweeé, kweeé, kweeé, kweeé, kweeé, kuh."

Red-eyed Thornbird
*Phacellodomus ferrugineigula**   PLATE 9(12)
17 cm (6¾"). *Uncommon in dense lower growth and borders of marshes and swampy woodland in se. Brazil* (s. Minas Gerais and s. Espírito Santo to Rio Grande do Sul). To at least 700 m. As sympatry has now been established at several sites, this is now treated as a separate species from Orange-eyed Thornbird. *Iris red.* Brown above with *deep rufous crown;* outer tail feathers rufous. *Throat and breast orange-rufous,* midbelly whitish. Orange-eyed Thornbird has an orange iris, rufous only on forecrown and throat; occurs mainly to north. Cf. also various *Philydor* foliage gleaners. An inveterate skulker, hopping singly and in pairs in low, damp vegetation; even when singing, only rarely does it emerge. Song a series of loud ringing notes preceded by a softer one, e.g., "ku-ku-ku, kwee-eé, kwee-eé, kwee-eé, kwee-eé, kwee-keé, kuh."

Canebrake Groundcreeper
Clibanornis dendrocolaptoides   PLATE 9(13)
21.5 cm (8½"). *Rare and local in lower growth of humid forest and woodland, usually associated with bamboo thickets,* in *se. Brazil region* (north to s. São Paulo). To 1300 m. Rufous brown above, brighter on crown and tail, with *bold pale grayish postocular stripe* and dusky auriculars. *Throat white scaled black on sides;* below pale grayish. Superficially like a thornbird, though larger and with a bolder head pattern. Hops in pairs within thick growth; shy and hard to observe. Does not associate with mixed flocks, and despite its English name, drops to the ground only rarely. Song a series of loud staccato notes, at first well enunciated, ending in a stutter of variable length, e.g., "chet, chet, chet, chit-chit-chit-chit-chit."

Lark-like Brushrunner
Coryphistera alaudina   PLATE 9(14)
16.5 cm (6½"). A *unique,* largely terrestrial furnariid, *quite common and conspicuous in chaco woodland and scrub* in w. Paraguay, n. and cen. Argentina (south to Mendoza and La Pampa), and adjacent Bolivia and Uruguay. Mostly below 500 m. *Strongly crested* and *profusely streaked. Bill and legs pinkish to orangy.* Above streaked brownish, blackish, and white with a black-

ish crest; *conspicuous white patches above and below eye* and cinnamon-rufous ear-coverts; tail blackish, outer feathers basally rufous. *Below white streaked rufous to buff.* A social bird, almost always occurring in groups that sometimes associate with other birds. Brushrunners forage mainly on the ground, often in the open but generally near cover, to which they retreat when alarmed. They recall small quail more than they do larks. Has a variety of semimusical chatters and trills, often given by several birds at once. The large stick nest resembles a thornbird's but is placed in a fork or crotch.

Firewood-gatherer
Anumbius annumbi   PLATE 9(15)
19.5 cm (7¾"). Locally fairly common in cerrado, pastures with scattered trees, borders of light woodland, and around ranch and farm buildings from *s. Brazil* (Goiás) *to cen. Argentina* (La Pampa). To 1100 m. Above sandy brown, crown and back streaked blackish and with rufous forehead and whitish superciliary; flight feathers edged rufescent; *tail long and graduated, feathers pointed and broadly tipped white. Throat white,* often outlined with black spots; below pale buffyish. Vaguely recalls a thornbird or the Chotoy Spinetail, though these do not show such obvious white in tail. Long-tailed silhouette also recalls Wedge-tailed Grassfinch. Feeds mainly on the ground or within cover, thus inconspicuous except when near their nests, around which they can linger for protracted periods. These nests are exceptionally large and conspicuous, and are constructed from thorny and often surprisingly long twigs; each year a new nesting chamber is added. Most frequent song, often given while perched on or near nest, a fast gravelly "chit, chit, chit, che-che-che-che-ee-ee-ee-ee-eu."

Orange-fronted Plushcrown
Metopothrix aurantiaca   PLATE 10(1)
11.5 cm (4½"). *Uncommon in clearings and gardens with scattered trees, secondary woodland, and forest borders in w. Amazonia.* Mostly below 650 m, to 1000 m in s. Peru. *Small and warbler-like,* very unlike other furnariids. *Legs orange. Forehead orange* (feathers plushlike, but this usually not evident), *foreface and throat bright yellow,* otherwise grayish olive above. Below pale yellowish. **Immature** has reduced facial orange and yellow, but *legs already orange.* Not likely confused; vaguely recalls Orange-headed Tanager, or ♀ Yellow Warbler. Plushcrowns range in small (family?) groups, generally independent of flocks. They glean actively, even hanging upside

down, in foliage and on twigs, and also feed on fruit and at flowers. Often seen around its large, conspicuous stick nests. Not especially vocal, but gives high-pitched sibilant notes, sometimes in a short series, e.g., "tswit-tsweét" or "tsweet-tsweet," but can be run together.

Xenerpestes

Two small, obscure, *mainly gray* (thus atypical) furnariids that are *rare and local* in canopy of humid forests in *nw. South America.*

Double-banded Graytail
Xenerpestes minlosi   PLATE 10(2)
11 cm (4¼"). *Rare and local in canopy and borders of humid and foothill forest and tall woodland in nw. Colombia and nw. Ecuador* (south to w. Pichincha). To 900 m. *Olive gray above* with *blackish forecrown* and *narrow white superciliary;* wings with *two bold white wing-bars.* Below creamy whitish, some gray mottling on sides. Distinctive in its limited range. Overall pattern reminiscent of certain nonbreeding boreal migrant warblers. Equatorial Graytail ranges only on *east* slope. Behavior similar to Equatorial, favoring mid-level viny tangles. Dry, reeling, trilled song similar to Equatorial (P. Coopmans and M. Lysinger). Also: e. Panama.

Equatorial Graytail
Xenerpestes singularis   PLATE 10(3)
11.5 cm (4½"). *Rare and local in canopy and borders of foothill and lower montane forest on east slope of Andes from n. Ecuador* (Napo) *to n. Peru* (n. San Martín). 1000–1700 m. *Olive gray above* with *streaky rufous forecrown* and *narrow white superciliary. Below creamy whitish with conspicuous gray streaking.* Other vaguely similar furnariids are larger and basically brown above (not gray). Streaking below distinguishes it from Gray-mantled Wren; the two can occur in the same flock. Because of their small size, graytails are actually more apt to be confused with a warbler or greenlet. Seen singly or in pairs, often foraging with mixed flocks; generally remains in canopy and therefore is hard to see well, except when around its large and quite conspicuous stick nest. Gleans from leaves and twigs; occasionally sidles along a branch, much like Gray-mantled Wren. Song a long, dry, almost insectlike trill lasting 5 or more seconds, "tzzzzzzzzzzzzzzzzz". Also gives dry "tsew" calls, often doubled.

Spectacled Prickletail

Siptornis striaticollis   PLATE 10(4)

12 cm (4¾"). *Rare and local in subcanopy and borders of montane forest on east slope of Andes from Colombia* (Cundinamarca) *to extreme n. Peru* (n. Cajamarca). 1300–2300 m. In **Colombia** (illustrated) rufous brown above with chestnut crown and *short bold white postocular stripe and lower eyelid;* wing-coverts and tail rufous-chestnut. Below brownish gray with *fine whitish streaking on throat and breast.* In **Ecuador and n. Peru** eye markings less prominent but *foreneck more boldly streaked.* Streaked Xenops has an obviously upturned lower mandible and a silvery white malar, but no white postocular. Found singly or in pairs, often accompanying mixed flocks. Usually at mid-levels or higher, hitching along moss-covered limbs, probing into crevices or epiphytic plants; sometimes taps into dead wood.

Margarornis

Attractive furnariids found in *Andean forests,* treerunners are more *arboreal* than the *Premnoplex* barbtails. Well-named, they *habitually creep on trunks and branches;* their tail feathers end in stiff projecting spines.

Star-chested Treerunner

Margarornis stellatus   PLATE 10(5)

15 cm (6"). *Rare and local in mid-levels and subcanopy of mossy montane forest on west slope of Andes in w. Colombia and nw. Ecuador* (south to Pichincha); seemingly more numerous in Colombia. 1200–2200 m. *Bright chestnut above* with an indistinct pale superciliary. *Throat contrasting white, chest with small but conspicuous white "stars" edged with black;* below rufous-chestnut. The far more numerous Pearled Treerunner is much more profusely spotted below and has an obvious white superciliary. Behavior not well known but seems to resemble Pearled Treerunner. Voice not known at all but certainly must be very quiet (as is Pearled).

Pearled Treerunner

Margarornis squamiger   PLATE 10(6)

15 cm (6"). *Widespread and often common* in montane forest and woodland in Andes from w. Venezuela (Trujillo) to w. Bolivia (w. Santa Cruz). Mostly 2000–3500 m. In **most of range** (illustrated) *bright rufous-chestnut above,* browner on crown and with *bold white superciliary.* Throat white to creamy white; below brown *profusely marked with large tear-shaped creamy white, black-edged spots.* From **Puno, Peru, southward** has yellower superciliary, throat, and spotting below, and crown rufous. Montane Woodcreeper has somewhat similar overall pattern but is streaked below and has a decurved bill. Found singly or in pairs, this is a frequent and conspicuous member of mixed flocks, especially at higher elevations. Hitches along mossy branches and up trunks, often using tail for support like a woodcreeper; sometimes moves out onto smaller terminal twigs. Not very vocal. Foraging birds occasionally give thin, high-pitched "tsit" contact calls, sometimes in a quick series.

Though still unrecorded, Beautiful Treerunner (*M. bellulus*) should occur in extreme nw. Colombia near the Panama border. It differs from Pearled Treerunner in being browner above and less spotted below.

Rusty-winged Barbtail

Premnornis guttuligera   PLATE 10(7)

14.5 cm (5¾"). Uncommon in lower growth of montane forest in *Andes from sw. Venezuela* (s. Táchira) *to s. Peru* (Puno). Mostly 1600–2300 m. Brown above with indistinct buff superciliary, sides of neck streaked buff; wings and tail rufous. Throat whitish; below brown *with buff scalloped streaking.* Resembles certain foliage-gleaners, though barbtail is considerably smaller. Smaller and darker Spotted Barbtail *lacks* rufous on wings and tail, and its throat is deep buff. Found singly or in pairs, often accompanying understory flocks. Clambers about in dense vegetation, often where viny or tangled, probing or even entering clumps of moss or dead leaf clusters. Usually does not hitch up limbs or trunks. Foraging birds infrequently give a sharp "tseep" or "tsip" call, sometimes run together into an emphatic series.

Premnoplex

Small *dark* furnariids that favor shady undergrowth inside montane forests of the Andes. Their tail feathers end in stiff protruding spines.

Spotted Barbtail

Premnoplex brunnescens   PLATE 10(8)

13.5 cm (5¼"). Fairly common in undergrowth of foothill and montane forest and woodland in *Andes from n. Venezuela to w. Bolivia* (w. Santa Cruz). Mostly 900–2500 m. A *small, dark, incon-*

spicuous furnariid, *dark brown above* with indistinct buff superciliary; tail brownish black. *Throat tawny-buff;* below brown with *profuse large oval buff, black-edged spots.* Less numerous Rusty-winged Barbtail has rufous wings and tail (not concolor) and is more streaked (less spotted) below. Cf. also Wedge-billed Woodcreeper (very different behavior, etc.). Quiet and unobtrusive, this barbtail hops and creeps on mossy branches and trunks, generally not using its tail for support (despite having protruding spines); sometimes accompanies understory flocks, but also regularly forages away from them. Infrequent song a short, descending trill, "pseerrr," sometimes preceded by several emphatic higher-pitched notes. More often heard is a sharp "teep!" or "teeyk!" call. Also: Costa Rica and Panama.

White-throated Barbtail
Premnoplex tatei
14 cm (5½"). *Uncommon in undergrowth of foothill and montane forest in ne. Venezuela.* 800–2400 m. Resembles Spotted Barbtail (no overlap) but with *white superciliary, throat, and more profuse and larger spotting below.* Stripe-breasted Spinetail occurs with this barbtail but differs in its rufous wings and tail, buff-streaked underparts, etc. Behavior similar to Spotted Barbtail, but often even harder to see because of the dense nature of its dank, mossy habitat. Usually not with flocks.

Roraiman Barbtail
Roraimia adusta   PLATE 10(9)
14.5 cm (5¾"). *Uncommon in lower growth of montane forest and woodland on tepui slopes of s. Venezuela region.* 1000–2500 m. Boldly patterned and even, for a furnariid, colorful. *Chestnut above, brightest on neck and broad superciliary;* crown dark brown, *auriculars blackish. Throat snowy white* contrasting with *streaked underparts.* Found singly or in pairs, foraging by hitching or sidling up vertical trunks; an inconspicuous bird that seems usually not to accompany mixed flocks. Favors very wet, mossy forest. Quiet, with rarely heard song a slow series of metallic notes (D. Ascanio recording).

Great Xenops
Megaxenops parnaguae   PLATE 10(10)
16 cm (6¼"). *Uncommon and local in caatinga woodland and scrub in interior ne. Brazil* (south to w. Minas Gerais). To 1100 m. Unmistakable. *Heavy bill with lower mandible sharply upturned, pinkish at base. Bright cinnamon-rufous above,*

somewhat paler below, with some dusky around eye; *throat contrasting white.* Found singly or in pairs, usually independent of the small mixed flocks found in its limited range; often forages like a typical *Xenops,* hitching along branches, pecking or prying off small bark pieces, but also can glean more like a foliage-gleaner. Distinctive song a bubbly series of closely spaced notes that become louder and higher-pitched before trailing off at end.

White-throated Treerunner
Pygarrhichas albogularis   PLATE 10(11)
14.5–15 cm (5¾–6"). *Uncommon in Nothofagus-dominated forest and borders from cen. Chile* (Santiago) *and adjacent Argentina* (north to w. Neuquén) *to Tierra del Fuego.* To 1500 m. *Bill long, slender, and upswept, most of mandible whitish.* Brown above with blackish auriculars; most of wings and *rather short tail* rufous. *Throat and breast pure white,* belly variably scaled with brown (often profuse). Found singly or in pairs, creeping about energetically on trunks and larger branches. Often accompanies flocks of Thorn-tailed Rayaditos and other birds, and like the rayadito, treerunners can be very tame. Most frequent call a loud, metallic "tsi-dik" or "tsik," often repeated rapidly.

Xenops

Distinctive small arboreal furnariids that are found widely in humid and lower montane forests, most xenops (not the Rufous-tailed) have short laterally compressed bills with an *upturned lower mandible,* and sport a *silvery malar streak.* Nests are in small holes excavated in soft, rotten wood.

Rufous-tailed Xenops
Xenops milleri   PLATE 10(12)
11 cm (4¼"). *Rare and apparently local* (perhaps just overlooked) in canopy and borders of humid forest in *Amazonia.* To 1000 m in s. Ecuador. Differs from other xenops in its *essentially straight bill* and *lack* of a white malar streak. Above brown streaked pale buff and with whitish superciliary; wings mainly rufous; rump and *entire tail rufous.* Throat whitish streaked olive; below brownish olive with whitish streaking. As it lacks the white malar, Rufous-tailed has a plainer face than the other xenops; its all-rufous tail can be surprisingly evident. Behavior similar to other xenops (cf. under Streaked). Like the Slender-billed,

Rufous-tailed forages well above the ground and often accompanies mixed flocks. Song a short, rising trill similar to Chestnut-winged Hookbill's short trill.

Streaked Xenops
Xenops rutilans　　　　　　　　PLATE 10(13)

12–12.5 cm (4¾–5″). *Widespread and locally fairly common* in canopy and borders of foothill and montane forest and woodland in Andes from n. Venezuela to nw. Argentina (Tucumán), and in deciduous and humid forest and woodland in lowlands from Bolivia and cen. and e. Brazil to ne. Argentina (n. Corrientes). Mostly below 2400 m. *Lower mandible strongly upturned.* Rufous brown above, *lightly streaked buff on crown and upper back;* superciliary whitish, *prominent silvery white malar streak;* wings mostly rufous (a wing-band shows in flight); rump and tail rufous, inner webs of inner tail feathers with black. Throat whitish; *below olive brown streaked whitish. Streaked is the only montane xenops,* and ranges at elevations well above the others. *It occurs sparingly or not at all in Amazonia.* Slender-billed Xenops is very similar but occurs *only* in Amazonia (with at most limited overlap); cf. under that species. Plain Xenops is much less generally streaked; it *shows no streaking at all above,* and below only a little on chest. Found singly or in pairs, often with mixed flocks, foraging at various levels though usually not in lower growth inside forest. Hitches along or under twigs and in vine tangles, swiveling from side to side and tapping at dead wood or flaking off bark, not using its tail for support. Song a short series, first rising, then dropping, of 4–7 shrill notes, e.g., "swee-swee-swee-swee-swee." Also: Costa Rica and Panama.

Slender-billed Xenops
Xenops tenuirostris

11.5 cm (4½″). Rare and local (perhaps just overlooked) in canopy and borders of humid forest of *Amazonia.* Mostly below 600 m. Closely resembles more numerous Streaked Xenops, which does not occur in Amaz. lowlands (little or no confirmed overlap). Slender-billed differs in having a longer and slightly more slender bill; tail slightly shorter and shows more black (black often visible, whereas in Streaked it generally isn't); and somewhat sparser streaking below. Behavior similar to other xenops (cf. under Streaked). Slender-billed almost always forages well above the ground while accompanying canopy flocks; like the Rufous-tailed Xenops,

may be more overlooked than actually rare. Song a simple series of shrill, evenly pitched notes, "tsip-tsip-tsip-tsip" (Streaked's slightly faster and lower pitched).

Plain Xenops
Xenops minutus　　　　　　　　PLATE 10(14)

11.5–12.5 cm (4½–5″). *Widespread and fairly common to common* in lower and middle growth and borders of humid forest and woodland from Colombia and Venezuela to Amazonia and the Guianas, and in se. Brazil area. Mostly below 900 m. *By far the least streaked xenops. Lower mandible strongly upturned.* In **most of range** (illustrated) above olive brown with pale buff superciliary and *prominent silvery white malar streak;* wings mainly rufous (a wing-band shows in flight); rump and tail rufous, tail with black on lateral feathers. Throat whitish; pale brown below with whitish chest streaking. In **w. Colombia and w. Ecuador** has a whiter throat and more chest streaking. In **e. Brazil area** *smaller* with a slighter bill, less chest streaking. *All other xenops are more streaked, especially below* (but note that their streaking can be hard to see). Cf. Wedge-billed Woodcreeper. Habits similar to other xenops (cf. under Streaked), though Plain more often forages at lower levels. East of Andes song similar to Streaked Xenops, a series of shrill notes, first rising and then dropping, e.g., "swee-swee-swee-swee-swee." West of Andes the song is faster (almost trilled), a mostly ascending series of notes, e.g., "ts-tsi-tsi-tsi-tsi-tsi?" Also: Mexico to Panama.

Sharp-billed Treehunter
Heliobletus contaminatus　　　　PLATE 10(15)

13.5 cm (5¼″). *Uncommon in canopy and borders of humid and montane forest and woodland in se. Brazil region* (north to e. Minas Gerais and Espírito Santo). To 1800 m. An as-yet undescribed form of *Heliobletus* has recently been found farther north, on the Serra das Lontras/Javi in s. Bahia (L. F. Silveira et al.). In **most of range** (illustrated) olive brown above, crown dusky streaked buff, with *long yellowish buff superciliary;* back more broadly streaked buff; tail rufous. *Throat pale yellowish buff extending onto sides of neck as a partial collar;* below streaked olive brown and whitish. From **Rio de Janeiro north,** back has little or no streaking, and belly less. Streaked Xenops has an upturned bill, silvery malar streak, rufous in wing. White-browed Foliage-gleaner has a whiter superciliary and throat, lacks back streaking, and is less streaked below. Found singly or in pairs, often with mixed flocks. Climbs on branches and in vine tangles, and though often hanging upside down, does not seem to use its tail for support; also does not peck or tap into wood. Rather quiet, but gives an accelerating, leaftosserlike chipper that ends in a trill.

Anabacerthia

Arboreal foliage-gleaners found in forest lower growth and borders in both the *Andes and the se. Brazil area*. Aside from their relatively small size, they resemble *Philydor. Anabacerthia* may not form a natural unit.

White-browed Foliage-gleaner
Anabacerthia amaurotis   PLATE 10(16)
15.5 cm (6"). Uncommon in lower and middle growth of humid and montane forest in *se. Brazil region* (north to s. Espírito Santo). To 1500 m. Rufous brown above, darker on crown and ear-coverts with a *broad white superciliary;* tail bright rufous. *Throat whitish;* below brownish olive, breast with blurry whitish streaking. Buff-browed Foliage-gleaner has a narrower superciliary that is rich buff; it also is more olive brown above. Sharp-billed Treehunter is smaller with a buffier superciliary and throat, and shows streaking on back. Pale-browed Treehunter is larger with a longer bill; it is streaked above and more sharply streaked below. Forages singly and in pairs, often accompanying mixed flocks; gleans along limbs and on terminal branches. Song a stuttering chatter followed by several shrieking notes, e.g., "t-t-t-t-t-t-t-t-jreék-jreék-jreék."

Montane Foliage-gleaner
Anabacerthia striaticollis   PLATE 10(17)
16.5 cm (6½"). Fairly common in subcanopy and borders of foothill and lower montane forest *mainly on east slope of Andes from n. Venezuela to w. Bolivia* (w. Santa Cruz). Mostly 900–2100 m. In **most of range** (illustrated) brown above with *conspicuous buffy whitish eye-ring and narrow postocular streak;* tail rufous. Throat yellowish white faintly scaled olivaceous; *below dull brownish with sparse whitish breast streaking.* In **Colombia and Venezuela** shows little or no breast streaking. A drab foliage-gleaner with a distinctly spectacled look. Rufous-rumped Foliage-gleaner overlaps in Andean foothills but has bolder brow, more contrasting throat that *lacks* scaling, and *no* streaking on breast. Scaly-

throated Foliage-gleaner occurs only on *west* slope of Andes. Found singly or in pairs, often with mixed flocks; forages by moving along horizontal branches and in tangled growth, twisting and jerking and flicking tail; often inspects and even enters curled-up dead leaves. For a foliage-gleaner, regularly in the open and easy to observe. Song a fast-paced, evenly pitched series of up to 15–20 piercing and harsh "skee" or "tjik" notes. More frequent call a single "skeeyh" or "skek" note with similar sharp, dry quality.

Scaly-throated Foliage-gleaner
Anabacerthia variegaticeps
16.5 cm (6½"). Fairly common in subcanopy and borders of foothill and lower montane forest and woodland on *west slope of Andes in w. Colombia and w. Ecuador* (south to w. Loja). Mostly 700–1700 m. Crown dusky with faint olivaceous streaking, *contrasting with wide, bright ochraceous postocular stripe and eye-ring,* ear-coverts dusky; *rufous brown above,* tail rufous-chestnut. Throat yellowish white, *feathers edged dusky with a scaly look;* breast blurrily streaked ochraceous and brownish olive, belly olive brown. Boldly marked, this handsome foliage-gleaner is unlikely to be confused. Montane Foliage-gleaner is duller and looks more uniform; it occurs mainly on *east* slope of Andes, and in w. Colombia ranges at higher elevations than Scaly-throated. Behavior and voice much as in Montane. Also: Mexico to Panama.

Pseudocolaptes

Two *large,* handsome furnariids that are *arboreal in Andean forests,* the tuftedcheeks sport *unique conspicuous "tufts" on the sides of the neck.*

Streaked Tuftedcheek
Pseudocolaptes boissonneautii   PLATE 11(1)
21–21.5 cm (8¼–8½"). Uncommon to locally fairly common in montane forest and borders in Andes from n. Venezuela to w. Bolivia (w. Santa Cruz). Mostly 1800–3100 m. Brown above, crown duskier, with narrow buff superciliary, *crown and especially back streaked buff;* rump and tail bright rufous. *Throat white, feathers on sides of neck flaring back to form a conspicuous snowy white tuft;* breast whitish with brown scaling, belly fulvous. **Immature** has blacker crown with little or no streaking, bolder blackish scaling on breast, more rufous belly. Aside from Pacific

Tuftedcheek of west slope (cf.), this striking, *large* furnariid is unmistakable. Found singly or in pairs, often with mixed flocks. Forages mainly by working along larger horizontal limbs, probing into bromeliads and other epiphytes, sometimes propping itself up with tail and hammering or rummaging about. Not especially vocal. Foraging birds give a loud "chink!" or "cheeyk!" Song is a loud and infrequently heard combination of these and more trilled notes.

Pacific Tuftedcheek

Pseudocolaptes johnsoni   PLATE 11(2)
20.5 cm (8"). *Uncommon and local in canopy and borders of foothill and lower montane forest on west slope of Andes from nw. Colombia* (Riseralda) *to sw. Ecuador* (El Oro). 700–1700 m. Occurs *below* the elevational range of the similar and more numerous Streaked Tuftedcheek; *Pacific favors mossy cloud forest conditions.* Differs from Streaked in having an *unstreaked rufous-chestnut back, darker breast with white chevrons* (not Streaked's scaled effect), and *buff-tinged tuft.* Behavior much as in Streaked Tuftedcheek; voice similar but tending to be higher pitched.

Thripadectes

A group of large, *robust* **furnariids with heavy black bills** that range in the *understory of montane forest in the Andes* (some species favoring bamboo), where they generally remain hidden in dense growth. *All are buff-streaked to some degree,* the streaking *prominent in a few.* Nests are placed in holes dug into banks.

Flammulated Treehunter

Thripadectes flammulatus   PLATE 11(3)
24 cm (9½"). *Rare in undergrowth of upper montane forest in Andes from w. Venezuela* (Mérida) *to extreme n. Peru.* Mostly 2200–3500 m. Favors *Chusquea* bamboo stands. *The most boldly patterned treehunter. Above and below blackish with conspicuous buff striping;* wings, rump, and tail rufous-chestnut. Cf. similar Peruvian Treehunter (no overlap). The smaller Striped Treehunter has similar overall pattern but is less contrasty, with a duskier (not so blackish) ground color, and less conspicuous streaking (especially below). Usually forages singly, most often apart from mixed flocks; furtive, remaining in heavy cover. Infrequently heard song a fast staccato trill of harsh, evenly pitched notes that lacks

descending effect of Striped Treehunter. Call a sharp "chek."

Peruvian Treehunter

Thripadectes scrutator
24 cm (9½"). *Rare and seemingly local (overlooked?) in undergrowth of upper montane forest on east slope of Andes from n. Peru* (Amazonas south of Río Marañón) *to w. Bolivia* (Cochabamba). 2450–3300 m. Sometimes called Buffthroated Treehunter. Resembles Flammulated Treehunter. Differs in its *brown (not blackish) upperparts with more diffused buff streaking* that does not extend onto lower back; also more brownish (not so blackish) below with less prominent streaking especially on belly. Striped Treehunter is smaller and more narrowly streaked; its streaking above extends farther down back, and streaking below ends at chest. Behavior and apparently voice much as in Flammulated Treehunter; Peruvian likewise favors extensive stands of *Chusquea* bamboo.

Striped Treehunter

Thripadectes holostictus   PLATE 11(4)
20.5–21.5 cm (8–8½"). Uncommon in undergrowth of montane forest in *Andes from sw. Venezuela* (Táchira) *to w. Bolivia* (w. Santa Cruz). Mostly 1500–2500 m. *Above dusky brown prominently streaked buff;* wings more rufescent, rump and tail rufous-chestnut. *Brown below streaked buff, especially on throat and breast* (**southern birds** show less streaking). This species is intermediate in appearance between the larger and more boldly striped Flammulated and Peruvian Treehunters (Striped mainly occurs at lower elevations) and the more uniform Streak-capped and Black-billed Treehunters (neither of which shows as much streaking below). Cf. also the smaller and less robust Lineated Foliage-gleaner, especially on east slope (where more extensively streaked); Lineated differs in its unmarked pale buff throat. Skulky behavior much as in Flammulated Treehunter, likewise favoring areas with *Chusquea* bamboo. Song much as in Flammulated, but faster and somewhat higher-pitched, descending toward end.

Black-billed Treehunter

Thripadectes melanorhynchus   PLATE 11(5)
20.5–21 cm (8–8¼"). Uncommon in undergrowth of foothill and lower montane forest and woodland on *east slope of Andes from n. Colombia to s. Peru* (Puno). 900–1700 m. Above dark brown, duskier on crown, *crown and back nar-*

rowly streaked buff; wings more rufescent, rump and tail rufous-chestnut. Throat ochraceous, *feathers edged black giving scaly appearance;* below brown *with virtually no streaking.* Streak-capped Treehunter is somewhat larger, more streaked on back, and has a streaky (not scaly) pattern on its less ochraceous throat. Skulky behavior as in other treehunters (cf. Flammulated). Song a short series of sharp, loud "kyip" notes, sometimes paired.

Streak-capped Treehunter
Thripadectes virgaticeps PLATE 11(6)
21.5 cm (8½"). Uncommon in undergrowth of montane forest in *Andes from n. Venezuela to n. Ecuador* (Pichincha and w. Napo). Mostly 1300–2100 m. Above dark brown, *head and nape duskier and with narrow buff streaking;* wings rufescent, rump and tail rufous-chestnut. *Throat and chest ochraceous-buff streaked dusky;* below ochraceous brown with *no* streaking. Much less streaked overall than Striped Treehunter. Most resembles Black-billed Treehunter (they can overlap on Andes' east slope, though Streak-capped usually ranges higher), which differs in having streaking on back and a scalier (less streaky) throat pattern. On west slope most resembles Uniform Treehunter, which is smaller, with a stouter bill, and *plainer overall.* Skulky behavior as in other treehunters (cf. Flammulated). Song a short series of emphatic notes, "chup, cheyp-cheyp-cheyp-cheyp-cheyp." Call a sharp "chidik."

Uniform Treehunter
Thripadectes ignobilis PLATE 11(7)
19 cm (7½"). Uncommon in lower growth of foothill and lower montane forest on *west slope of Andes from nw. Colombia* (Chocó) *to sw. Ecuador* (El Oro). 700–1700 m. *Short, stout bill. Plain.* Above dark rufescent brown with *no streaking aside from an indistinct buff postocular streak;* wings more rufescent, tail rufous-chestnut. *Below dull brown,* throat and sides of neck with vague buff streaking. Streak-capped Treehunter is larger with a longer bill; its crown and nape are streaked. Western Woodhaunter has a longer and more slender bill; its throat is distinctly buff, contrasting with rest of underparts. Behavior as in other treehunters (cf. Flammulated), but somewhat less furtive, more often foraging up into mid-levels and more likely to accompany mixed flocks. Song a series of 6–8 "kyip" or "kik" notes (higher-pitched and faster-paced than in Streak-capped).

Syndactyla

Midsized foliage-gleaners with short straight (or slightly upturned) bills and streaking below (though they have *unmarked, paler throats*). All are united by their *similar voices.* An additional species, Planalto Foliage-gleaner, can be found on p. 308.

Lineated Foliage-gleaner
Syndactyla subalaris PLATE 11(8)
18–18.5 cm (7–7¼"). Fairly common and widespread in lower growth of montane forest in *Andes from w. Venezuela* (Lara) *to s. Peru* (Cuzco). Mostly 1000–2100 m. **East-slope birds** (illustrated) brown above, crown and nape more blackish, with a buff postocular streak and narrow *buff streaking from crown to back;* wings more rufescent, tail rufous. *Throat yellowish buff;* below brown streaked yellowish buff. **West-slope birds** have a browner crown and are less streaked above (*often confined to a nape band*). **Juvenile** more rufescent, with an *orange-ochraceous postocular streak, and back and breast streaking.* Can be confusing. Of the treehunters, Striped and Uniform are the most similar. Striped especially resembles east-slope Lineated, though it is a heftier bird with a heavier bill and streaking on throat. Uniform differs from west-slope Lineated in having a stouter bill and in *lacking streaking above* (which in this Lineated shows mainly on nape); below, the treehunter has streaking *only* on throat. Also resembles the two woodhaunters, though Eastern's buff streaking is blurrier and less extensive than in sympatric Lineateds, and Western is *nearly unstreaked above.* Found singly or in pairs, often accompanying understory flocks; hops and clambers on branches and in tangles, frequently investigating dead-leaf clusters; hard to see well, or for long. Song an accelerating series of harsh, nasal notes, sputtering at first, "anh, anh, anh-anh-anh-anhanhanhanh." Also: Costa Rica and Panama.

Guttulated Foliage-gleaner
Syndactyla guttulata PLATE 11(9)
18.5 cm (7¼"). Uncommon in lower growth of montane forest in *n. Venezuela* (Sucre to n. Anzoátegui, and Distrito Federal to Falcón). 800–2100 m. Resembles Lineated Foliage-gleaner (no overlap), differing in its *more upturned lower mandible, essentially unstreaked crown, more prominent buff superciliary,* and *wider and more extensive buff streaking below* ("guttulated"). Behavior and voice much as in Lineated.

Buff-browed Foliage-gleaner

Syndactyla rufosuperciliata PLATE 11(10)

17.5–18 cm (6¾–7″). Fairly common and widespread in lower growth of montane and humid forest and woodland in Andes from extreme s. Ecuador (Zamora-Chinchipe on Cordillera del Cóndor) to nw. Argentina (La Rioja), and from se. Brazil (Minas Gerais and Espírito Santo) to ne. Argentina (n. Buenos Aires). Mostly 900–2500 m in Andes, to 1600 m elsewhere. In **southeast** (illustrated) above brownish olive (with *no* streaking; **Andean birds** are a richer brown) with a *prominent ochraceous-buff superciliary;* wings more rufescent, tail rufous. *Throat buffy whitish; below brownish olive with yellowish buff streaking.* Lineated Foliage-gleaner shows streaking above and has a less obvious superciliary and a buffier throat. White-browed Foliage-gleaner is more rufescent above and has a creamy whitish superciliary and contrasting dark ear-coverts. Cf. also Sharp-billed Treehunter. Behavior much as in Lineated Foliage-gleaner, though Buff-browed usually is much less furtive. Song a fast series of harsh notes that accelerates a little, e.g., "kuh-kuh-kuh-ki-ki-ki-ki-ki-ku" (less nasal than in Lineated).

Rufous-necked Foliage-gleaner

Syndactyla ruficollis PLATE 11(11)

18 cm (7″). Now uncommon and local in lower growth of *montane forest from sw. Ecuador* (Loja) *to nw. Peru* (Lambayeque and Cajamarca). 600–2600 m. Above rufescent brown with *superciliary and sides of neck contrasting orange-rufous;* tail rufous. *Throat cinnamon-buff;* below olive brown, breast streaked buff. Not likely confused in its limited range, where there is no really similar furnariid. Ranges singly or in pairs, often accompanying small mixed flocks. Forages by hitching along larger limbs and trunks, inspecting moss, epiphytic plants, and tangles; easier to see than other *Syndactyla.* Song much as in Lineated Foliage-gleaner, a fast series of harsh, nasal, ratchety notes that starts slowly and accelerates, ending in a roll.

Pale-browed Treehunter

Cichlocolaptes leucophrus PLATE 11(12)

20.5–22.5 cm (8–8¾″). *Uncommon in montane and humid forest in se. Brazil* (s. Bahia to ne. Rio Grande do Sul). To 1400 m (northward only in highlands). Perhaps more than one species. *Long, straight bill.* Birds from **Rio de Janeiro north** (A) rufous brown above with a pale buff superciliary and streaking on crown and back;

wings more rufescent, *tail bright pale cinnamon.* Throat whitish; *below boldly streaked pale buff and brown.* Birds from **São Paulo south** (B) are *markedly smaller;* they have a *rufous tail,* browner back, and more prominent superciliary. Striated Softtail occurs locally with the large northern form of this treehunter; softtail is smaller with a more slender (less daggerlike) bill, finer streaking below, and a small orange-rufous chin patch. Cf. also Buff-browed and White-browed Foliage-gleaners. Forages singly and in pairs from lower growth up into subcanopy, clambering about mainly on larger limbs and often inspecting bromeliads and other epiphytes. Song a loud arresting "wreeyp! wreeyp! wreeyp-wreeyp-wreeyp" (the number of notes varies, sometimes interspersed with chattering).

Simoxenops

Two scarce furnariids resembling foliage-gleaners, found in *humid forests of s. Amazonia.* Both species are marked by a *heavy, upturned bill.*

Peruvian Recurvebill

Simoxenops ucayalae PLATE 12(1)

19 cm (7½″). Uncommon and local in undergrowth of humid forest in *s. Amazonia, almost always in or near thickets of Guadua bamboo.* To 1300 m. *Massive pale bill* with *lower mandible strongly upturned.* Above rufescent brown with narrow ochraceous superciliary; rump and tail rufous-chestnut. *Below orange-rufous, extending onto sides of neck.* **Juvenile** has a bolder superciliary and obvious black scalloping on underparts. Cf. Bolivian Recurvebill (no known overlap). *Automolus* foliage-gleaners have much more slender bills, and none is so bright below. Forages singly and in pairs, often hitching up bamboo stalks and hammering or probing for food items; usually hard to observe as it tends to remain in heavy cover. Generally not with flocks. Distinctive song a fast series of harsh nasal notes that ascends sharply (recalling a *Syndactyla* foliage-gleaner).

Bolivian Recurvebill

Simoxenops striatus

19 cm (7½″). *Rare in lower growth of foothill forest along base of Andes in Bolivia* (La Paz to w. Santa Cruz). 650–1400 m. Resembles Peruvian Recurvebill (no overlap), but bill less massive and upperparts darker brown with *prominent buff*

streaking on head, neck, and back. Cf. *Thripadectes* treehunters. Behavior of this scarce bird
remains poorly known, but seems basically similar to Peruvian Recurvebill. Its voice is similar.

Hyloctistes

Two *drab* foliage-gleaners found in humid
lowland forests, until recently considered
conspecific though they have very different
voices.

Eastern Woodhaunter

Hyloctistes subulatus*   PLATE 12(2)
17 cm (6¾"). Uncommon and inconspicuous in
lower growth of humid forest and woodland of
w. Amazonia. Mostly below 1300 m. Formerly
called Striped Woodhaunter. Olive brown above,
duskier on crown with *blurry buff streaking on
crown, neck, and mantle;* wings more rufescent,
tail rufous-chestnut. Throat pale buffyish; below
dull brownish, *breast somewhat flammulated
buff.* Western Woodhaunter occurs only *west*
of Andes. Lineated Foliage-gleaners east of the
Andes have a more montane distribution (but
with some overlap); they are more crisply and
extensively streaked both above and below,
and vocalizations differ notably. Buff-throated
Foliage-gleaner is unstreaked above and shows
an eye-ring. Forages singly and in pairs, often
accompanying mixed flocks; feeds much like an
Automolus, hopping and rummaging in tangled
vegetation, epiphytes, and curled-up dead leaves.
Distinctive doubled song a ringing "teeu-teeu,"
when excited followed by a softer and lower-
pitched rattle "tr-r-r-r-r."

Western Woodhaunter

Hyloctistes virgatus*
17 cm (6¾"). Uncommon and inconspicuous
in lower growth of humid forest and woodland
in *w. Colombia and w. Ecuador* (south to El
Oro). Mostly below 1100 m. Resembles Eastern
Woodhaunter (only *east* of Andes), but darker
above with *streaking above restricted to crown;
throat more ochraceous* and underparts slightly
browner (less olivaceous), with *less* flammulation on breast. Uniform Treehunter is darker
generally with a shorter and stouter bill, and
its throat is nearly uniform with rest of underparts (not notably paler, as in the woodhaunter).
Lineated Foliage-gleaner west of the Andes
has a distinct band of streaking on nape. Buff-
throated Foliage-gleaner west of the Andes

is white-throated. Habits similar to Eastern
Woodhaunter. Distinctive song, very different,
a series of sharp nasal notes, "keeu-keeu-keeu-
keeu, . . ." evenly pitched and paced, sometimes
long-continued. Also: Nicaragua to Panama.

Chestnut-winged Hookbill

Ancistrops strigilatus   PLATE 12(3)
19 cm (7½"). Uncommon in mid-levels and
subcanopy of humid forest in *w. and cen. Amazonia.* Mostly below 900 m. Despite its name,
bill not much more hooked than in other
foliage-gleaners. Above olive brown *prominently
streaked yellowish buff* and with buffyish superciliary; *wings and tail contrasting rufous.* Below
yellowish buff *streaked dusky-olive.* The less robust Chestnut-winged Foliage-gleaner is *un-*
streaked and has an orangy throat and lores; the
two sometimes forage in the same flock. Otherwise not likely confused. Found singly or in
pairs, most often while accompanying a mixed
canopy flock. Forages along larger limbs and in
vine tangles, often lingering in the semiopen and
thus for a foliage-gleaner not hard to see. Song a
protracted trill that can continue for 30 seconds
or more, sometimes ascending a bit.

Philydor

Fairly large, long-tailed furnariids found
widely in lowland and lower montane forests;
some species are arboreal and relatively easy
to observe, whereas others remain in lower
growth and thus generally are more furtive.
They show *little or no streaking,* but all have a
superciliary (bold in some). Compared with
the *Automolus* foliage-gleaners, *Philydor*
are slenderer and more strongly patterned.
Note that one species, *dimidiatum,* formerly
placed in the genus *Philydor,* was recently
transferred to the genus *Syndactyla.*

Chestnut-winged Foliage-gleaner

Philydor erythropterum   PLATE 12(4)
18.5 cm (7¼"). Uncommon in mid-levels and
subcanopy of humid forest (mainly terra firme)
in *w. and s. Amazonia.* Mostly below 900 m. *Olive
grayish above* with *lores and throat pale ochraceous orange* and narrow buff superciliary; *wings
and tail contrasting rufous.* Below pale dingy buff.
Readily known by its *lack* of streaking, contrasting wings, and orangy throat. Chestnut-winged
Hookbill is heavier with a stouter bill, and shows
prominent streaking; it *lacks* the orangy throat.

Rufous-rumped and Rufous-tailed Foliage-gleaners have concolor wings, and except in Peru and Bolivia their throats are only slightly ochraceous. Chestnut-winged ranges singly, less often in pairs, and often accompanies mixed flocks. It tends to remain well above the ground, but drops lower in vine tangles or treefall clearings; clambers in foliage, often inspecting curled dead leaves. Infrequently heard song a trill about 5 seconds long that descends slightly.

Buff-fronted Foliage-gleaner
Philydor rufum   PLATE 12(5)
18.5–19 cm (7¼–7½"). Locally fairly common in subcanopy and borders of foothill and lower montane forest and woodland in Andes from n. Venezuela to w. Bolivia (Chuquisaca), and in humid and gallery forest and woodland in se. Brazil region. To 1800 m. In **southeast** (illustrated) has *forehead and broad superciliary buff, gray crown and postocular stripe;* olive brown above with rufous wings and tail. Below uniform buff. In **most of Andean range** duller, with less contrast in head pattern and reduced buff on forehead (especially northward); **west-slope** birds are smaller and darker overall, except on throat, and have a paler bill. In the southeast, confusion is most likely with Ochre-breasted Foliage-gleaner, but note the latter's entirely gray crown (no buff on forehead). In higher mountains of se. Brazil, cf. also the similarly patterned Brown Tanager (with much heavier bill, etc.). In Peru and Bolivia foothills, cf. Rufous-rumped Foliage-gleaner (smaller, with no rufous on wings and no buff on forehead). Russet Antshrike is stockier, with a shorter tail and heavier bill. Forages singly or in pairs, often accompanying mixed flocks; frequently lingers in semiopen, hopping and twisting along horizontal limbs, sometimes in terminal foliage. Song a fast descending series of sharp, metallic notes, "whi-ki-ki-ki-ke-ke-ke-kuh-kuh," recalling a *Veniliornis* woodpecker. Also: Costa Rica and w. Panama.

Ochre-breasted Foliage-gleaner
Philydor lichtensteini   PLATE 12(6)
18 cm (7"). *Fairly common in mid-levels and subcanopy of humid forest and woodland in se. Brazil region* (north to s. Goiás and s. Bahia). To 1000 m. *Crown and nape grayish* with slight scaly effect, and *broad buff superciliary* and gray postocular stripe; above brown; wings and tail rufous. Below ochraceous. Buff-fronted Foliage-gleaner (often with it) is larger and shows a prominent buff forehead. In interior of range, cf.

Planalto Foliage-gleaner. Behavior much as in Buff-fronted Foliage-gleaner, also mainly foraging with mixed flocks but tending to inspect viny tangles and dead leaves more (less often out on terminal branches). Song also similar.

Rufous-rumped Foliage-gleaner
Philydor erythrocercum   PLATE 12(7)
16.5–17 cm (6½–6¾"). Fairly common in lower growth and mid-levels of humid forest (mainly terra firme) in *lowlands and foothills of Amazonia*. To 1600 m in Peru and Bolivia. In **most of range** (illustrated) olive brown above with *pale buff lores and superciliary; rump and tail contrasting rufous.* Throat whitish, below pale buffy olivaceous. From **se. Colombia to ne. Peru** similar but with less rufous on rump. In **foothills of cen. Peru to Bolivia** more strongly ochraceous-tinged below (*especially on throat*) and shows rufous on rump. Cf. rarer Rufous-tailed Foliage-gleaner. Montane Foliage-gleaner is smaller with an even more obvious spectacled look, and it shows fine streaking on breast. This rather dull foliage-gleaner is fairly often seen across much of its range, and it regularly accompanies mixed flocks in understory; favors viny tangles, and usually not too hard to observe. Not very vocal, but gives a querulous "shree?" and an abrupt, shrill "wheeeeyk!"; also other sharp calls.

Rufous-tailed Foliage-gleaner
Philydor ruficaudatum   PLATE 12(8)
17 cm (6¾"). Generally rare to uncommon in mid-levels and subcanopy of terra firme forest in *Amazonia and the Guianas;* seemingly more numerous in s. Venezuela. Mostly below 800 m. Closely resembles usually more numerous Rufous-rumped Foliage-gleaner (which does not occur in Venezuela). Subtle differences are Rufous-tailed's *lack* of rufous on uppertail-coverts (an absence that is hard to discern in the field; further, note that Rufous-rumped in w. Amazonia shows very little), and its *dull olivaceous mottling or flammulation on breast* (Rufous-rumped is relatively uniform below). Rufous-tailed is more arboreal than Rufous-rumped (this often helps to distinguish them) and thus is almost always seen with mixed canopy flocks (Rufous-rumped tends to accompany understory flocks). Song (in se. Peru) a staccato series of 5–10 evenly pitched notes that drop in pitch and accelerate toward end, e.g., "te-te-te-te-te-te-te-t-t-r" (P. Coopmans); in sw. Brazil a loud, evenly pitched repetition of "ke" or "kee" notes is given (K. J. Zimmer recording).

Planalto Foliage-gleaner
Syndactyla dimidiata *   PLATE 12(9)
17–17.5 cm (6¾–7"). *Uncommon and local in lower and middle levels of humid and gallery forest and woodland in interior s. Brazil* (north to Goiás and Tocantins) *and adjacent Paraguay.* To 1200 m. Formerly placed in the genus *Philydor. Above uniform rufescent brown* with long superciliary and sides of neck rich ochraceous; tail brighter rufous. *Below uniform rich ochraceous.* Buff-fronted and Ochre-breasted Foliage-gleaners have gray on crown, and are paler and buffier below; both species are more arboreal. Cf. also Henna-capped Foliage-gleaner. Found singly or in pairs, most often foraging independently of mixed flocks, regularly inspecting epiphytic plants on branches. Song a series of strongly emphasized, harsh metallic notes preceded by a softer accelerating chatter.

Cinnamon-rumped Foliage-gleaner
Philydor pyrrhodes   PLATE 12(10)
16.5–17 cm (6½–6¾"). Uncommon in lower growth of humid forest from *Amazonia to the Guianas.* To 700 m. Rufescent brown above with *cinnamon superciliary; wings contrasting slaty;* rump and tail *bright* cinnamon-rufous. *Below uniform rich orange-ochraceous.* Hard to confuse in its Amazonian range. Slaty-winged Foliage-gleaner occurs only *west* of Andes. Found singly or in pairs, usually foraging independently of mixed flocks. Active but furtive, remaining under cover and hard to see well or for long; inspects tangles and hanging dead leaves. Seems to favor vicinity of forest streams, often where there is an understory of palms. Distinctive but infrequently heard song typically in two parts, starting with a long low reeling trill that becomes louder before breaking into a much louder trill that slides up to a crescendo.

Slaty-winged Foliage-gleaner
Philydor fuscipenne
17 cm (6¾"). Uncommon and local in lower growth and mid-levels of humid forest and woodland in *nw. Colombia* (east to middle Río Magdalena valley) *and w. Ecuador* (s. Pichincha south locally to El Oro). To 1200 m in Colombia. Rufescent brown above, duskier on crown with *bold cinnamon-buff superciliary* and *cinnamon-rufous sides of neck; wings contrasting dusky;* rump and tail rufous. *Below uniform buffy-ochraceous.* Nothing really resembles this boldly patterned, *trans-Andean* foliage-gleaner. Usually found singly or in pairs, often accompanying

mixed flocks; nervous and fast-moving, hard to observe for long. Song a short accelerating chatter; foraging birds give a sharp "chef!" Also: Panama.

Black-capped Foliage-gleaner
Philydor atricapillus   PLATE 12(11)
16.5–17 cm (6½–6¾"). Uncommon in lower growth of humid forest in *se. Brazil region* (north to s. Bahia). To 1050 m. Unmistakable. *Head striping black, contrasting strongly with buff postocular stripe and ear-coverts* and *orange-rufous nape;* above rufescent brown, wings duskier, rump and tail bright cinnamon-rufous. Below bright ochraceous. Ranges singly and in pairs, often with mixed flocks in understory; forages actively, probing into crevices and dead leaves from a variety of sometimes contorted positions. Rather musical song a fast trill that descends in pitch, recalling Long-billed Gnatwren.

Alagoas Foliage-gleaner
Philydor novaesi
18 cm (7"). *Now very rare and local in undergrowth of humid forest and woodland in ne. Brazil* (Alagoas and Pernambuco). 400–550 m. Resembles Black-capped Foliage-gleaner (no overlap), but slightly larger with a *less contrasting head pattern;* crown browner (not so black), and nape much browner (not orange-rufous). The only *Philydor* in its limited range. Not well known, but behavior apparently much as in Black-capped Foliage-gleaner. Approaching extinction.

Automolus

Fairly large, *drab* furnariids with a quite heavy bill that mainly range in the lower growth of *humid lowland forests,* some species favoring bamboo. *Automolus* foliage-gleaners are inconspicuous and hard to see, but *all species have distinctive and oft-given vocalizations.* They are more robust and less arboreal than *Philydor* foliage-gleaners. Nests are placed in holes dug into banks.

Chestnut-crowned Foliage-gleaner
Automolus rufipileatus   PLATE 13(1)
19 cm (7½"). Uncommon in undergrowth and borders of humid forest and woodland in *Amazonia and the Guianas. Favors várzea and riparian areas* (also river islands), often where there is an understory of *Gynerium* cane or bam-

boo. Mostly below 750 m. *Iris yellow-orange. Rufescent brown above* with *slightly contrasting rufous-chestnut crown;* shoulders, rump, and tail rufous-chestnut. Throat pale buff; below ochraceous (illustrated; **most of range**) to drab olivaceous brown (**s. Amaz. Brazil**). Brown-rumped Foliage-gleaner (also orange-eyed) lacks the chestnut crown and has a shorter bill; its throat is brighter (especially to sides). Sympatric Buff-throated Foliage-gleaners (also buff-throated) are dark-eyed, more olivaceous above with a buff eye-ring (but no rufous on crown), and flammulated on breast. Cf. also Ruddy Foliage-gleaner. Even more skulking than most other *Automolus* foliage-gleaners; the very dense nature of its favored habitats doesn't help. Rarely joins mixed flocks. Heard much more often than seen. Song a run-together series of sharp, staccato notes dropping in pitch, "d-r-r-r-r-r-r-r-r," resembles Olive-backed Foliage-gleaner but faster and higher-pitched.

Olive-backed Foliage-gleaner
Automolus infuscatus   PLATE 13(2)
19 cm (7½"). Fairly common in lower growth of humid forest (mainly terra firme) in *Amazonia and the Guianas*. To 700 m. *Dull. Brownish olive above* with *only an obscure whitish eye-ring;* rump and tail rufous-chestnut. *Throat white* (often puffed out); below pale buffy grayish. The scarcer Bamboo Foliage-gleaner is more rufescent above with a more prominent superciliary and duskier ear-coverts; it favors bamboo. Sympatric Buff-throated Foliage-gleaner has buff throat, a bolder eye-ring, and is buffier below with flammulated breast. Of the *Philydor* foliage-gleaners, most apt to be confused with Rufous-rumped, which is more slender, has bolder superciliary and less contrasting throat. Seen singly or in pairs, often accompanying mixed flocks of understory birds. Clambers in dense tangled habitat, often hanging upside down while rummaging in epiphytes and suspended dead leaves. Song a fast, loud, evenly pitched staccato rattle, "ch-r-r-r-r-r-r-r-r." Call, often given while foraging, a sharp "chíkah."

Pará Foliage-gleaner
*Automolus paraensis**
19 cm (7½"). Fairly common in lower growth of humid forest in *e. Amaz. Brazil* (south of Amazon from Rio Madeira eastward). To about 500 m. Because of its distinct voice, recently recognized as a different species from Olive-backed Foliage-gleaner. Similar in appearance and behavior to Olive-backed. Song, however, very

different; a harsh and much slower "jureet-reet-reet-reet-reet" with a grating quality.

White-eyed Foliage-gleaner
Automolus leucophthalmus   PLATE 13(3)
19–19.5 cm (7½–7¾"). Fairly common in undergrowth of humid forest and woodland in *e. Brazil, e. Paraguay, and ne. Argentina.* Mostly below 1000 m. *Iris white.* Above uniform rufescent brown, rump and tail bright cinnamon-rufous. *Throat white* (often puffed out); below ochraceous, whiter on midbreast. The *only Automolus in its range,* and as such should be easily recognized; the white eye and white throat both stand out. Cf. White-collared Foliage-gleaner (which also has a contrasting white throat) and the superficially similar Greater Thornbird (yellow-eyed, in very different habitat, etc.). Behavior much like other *Automolus;* not particularly shy or hard to see, often foraging with mixed understory flocks. Seems relatively tolerant of forest disturbance and fragmentation. Distinctive song a loud and fast "ki-deee, ki-dee, ki-dee, ki-dee, ki-dee, ki-dee" (sometimes varied to "ki-trrr . . .").

Tepui Foliage-gleaner
*Automolus roraimae**   PLATE 13(4)
18 cm (7"). Fairly common in lower growth of humid forest and woodland on *tepuis of s. Venezuela area.* 1100–2500 m. Formerly called White-throated Foliage-gleaner. Above dark rufescent brown with *white superciliary* and *blackish cheeks;* rump and tail rufous-chestnut. *Throat white;* below paler brown. Liable to be confused only with Olive-backed Foliage-gleaner, a larger and duller species with a more obscure facial pattern and minimal contrast on underparts; it ranges at lower elevations. Tepui's behavior much as in other *Automolus,* though it is less skulking than many and often forages higher above the ground, occasionally even hitching along limbs. Song a long series of harsh notes that rise in pitch and accelerate; recalls a *Syndactyla* foliage-gleaner.

Buff-throated Foliage-gleaner
Automolus ochrolaemus   PLATE 13(5)
18.5–19 cm (7¼–7½"). *Widespread* in undergrowth of humid forest and woodland from Colombia to Amazonia and the Guianas, where mainly in várzea and near streams. Mostly below 1000 m. Iris dark. **East of Andes** (A) olive brown above with *buff eye-ring and indistinct superciliary;* rump and tail rufous-chestnut. *Throat pale buff;* below dull brownish, *breast flammu-*

lated buff. In **w. Colombia and w. Ecuador** (B) has a *white throat* and less breast flammulation. Olive-backed Foliage-gleaner differs from eastern Buff-throateds in having a white throat and whitish eye-ring; it lacks breast markings. Chestnut-crowned and Brown-rumped Foliage-gleaners have buff to ochre throats (much like sympatric Buff-throateds), but their eyes are orangy and they *lack* eye-ring and breast flammulation. No similar foliage-gleaner occurs west of Andes. Behavior similar to Olive-backed Foliage-gleaner, though often more furtive; sometimes forages in the same flock. Distinctive, oft-given song (similar west and east of Andes) a short descending series of well-enunciated notes, e.g., "kee-kee-ke-krr" or "ki, ki, ki-ki-ke-ke-krr." Also: Mexico to Panama (likely more than one species).

Brown-rumped Foliage-gleaner
Automolus melanopezus   PLATE 13(6)
18.5 cm (7¼"). *Uncommon and local in undergrowth of humid forest, often near streams or swampy places, in w. Amazonia. Mostly 300–600 m. Iris orange to reddish orange. Dark rufescent brown above; tail rufous-chestnut. Throat ochraceous orange, brightest on sides; below drab olivaceous brown.* Buff-throated Foliage-gleaner has a dark eye, more olivaceous upperparts with buff eye-ring and superciliary, and shows breast flammulation. Chestnut-crowned Foliage-gleaner has a chestnut crown, markedly paler throat. Brown-rumped is a shy and reclusive foliage-gleaner that skulks inside dense viny tangles or (in se. Peru and sw. Amaz. Brazil) *Guadua* bamboo thickets; it thus is only infrequently observed. It sometimes accompanies understory flocks. Song a fast and rhythmic "whit-whit-whididit-wrrrrrr" with distinctive cadence.

Ruddy Foliage-gleaner
Automolus rubiginosus   PLATE 13(7)
18–19 cm (7–7½"). Uncommon and local in dense undergrowth and borders of humid and foothill forest; disjunct distribution in ne. South America, w. Amazonia, and from w. Colombia to extreme nw. Peru (recently in Tumbes). To 1300 m; most numerous in foothills. Variable; perhaps more than one species. **West of Andes** (A) *very dark; dark rufescent brown above* with a *black tail. Throat and upper chest rich rufous,* below olivaceous brown. In **w. Amazonia** (B) slightly larger and not quite so dark, with *throat brighter orange-rufous* and *tail rufous-chestnut.* In **se. Peru and w. Bolivia** similar but crown

more chestnut. In **s. Venezuela, the Guianas, and n. Brazil** like Amaz. birds but smaller. Santa Marta birds are the most "ruddy." This species is so dark that it can be confused with a leaftosser, though the latter's chunky and short-tailed shape is quite different. In w. Amazonia, Brown-rumped is the most similar foliage-gleaner; it differs in its shorter bill, orange eye, and paler more orange-ochraceous throat. Cf. also Chestnut-crowned Foliage-gleaner (also orange-eyed). Ruddy moves about in pairs that remain close to the ground in dense vegetation, generally independent of mixed flocks; skulking and hard to see, especially without the aid of tape playback. Persistent call, apparently similar in most of its range, a querulous and nasal, up-slurred "kweeeeahhhh" that vaguely recalls one vocalization of Smooth-billed Ani (*Crotophaga ani*). Also: Mexico to Panama.

Hylocryptus

Two *distinctively patterned and colored* foliage-gleaners found in widely separated areas (the Tumbesian region and s. Brazil), with similar *deciduous forest habitats* and *semiterrestrial behavior.* Both species have a rather long and somewhat decurved bill.

Henna-hooded Foliage-gleaner
Hylocryptus erythrocephalus   PLATE 13(8)
21 cm (8¼"). *Now uncommon and local on or near ground in deciduous and semihumid forest and woodland from sw. Ecuador* (Manabí) *to nw. Peru* (Lambayeque). *Mostly 400–1800 m. Iris orangy brown to hazel. Head, neck, wings, rump, and tail orange-rufous* ("henna"); *back brownish olive. Throat pale orange-rufous; below mostly pale brownish gray.* Unmistakable in its small range, one of the most distinctive Tumbesian endemics. Occurs singly or in pairs, foraging on or near the ground, sometimes accompanying small mixed flocks. Can be noisy when feeding, flicking aside dry leaves with bill. Heard more often than seen, vocalizing especially during the Jan.–May breeding season. Distinctive, far-carrying song a staccato churring "kree-kruh-kruh-kruh-kruh-kruh-kruh-kurr," with an odd, mechanical quality.

Henna-capped Foliage-gleaner
Hylocryptus rectirostris   PLATE 13(9)
20.5 cm (8"). *Now rare and local on or near ground in gallery and deciduous woodland in interior s. Brazil* (s. Bahia to Mato Grosso do Sul and

n. Paraná) *and adjacent Paraguay.* To 1000 m. Iris brownish yellow. Crown and nape orange-rufous ("henna"), *back golden brown;* wings and tail also orange-rufous. *Below mostly bright pale ochraceous.* Essentially unmistakable in its limited range; Planalto Foliage-gleaner is smaller and shorter-billed, more uniformly rufescent above, etc. Not well known, but appears to forage much like Henna-hooded, mainly in leaf litter on the ground. Distinctive song a loud chattering with similar quality to Henna-hooded's, e.g., "cuk-cuk-cuk-cuk, cuh-cuk, cuk-cuk," at times sounding uncannily like the clucking of a domestic chicken.

Anabazenops

Two *heavy-billed* foliage-gleaners, the drab Bamboo Foliage-gleaner of Amazonia and se. Brazil's striking White-collared Foliage-gleaner, were recently united generically. *Both species favor bamboo.*

White-collared Foliage-gleaner
Anabazenops fuscus   PLATE 14(1)
19–19.5 cm (7½–7¾"). Fairly common in humid and montane forest in *se. Brazil* (s. Bahia to e. Santa Catarina). 500–1200 m. *Striking.* Heavy bill mostly bluish horn. Brown above with *contrasting white superciliary, broad nuchal collar, and throat;* tail rufous. Below buffy whitish. ♀ White-bearded Antshrike has similar pattern, but bill is stouter and less pointed, crown and wings rufous. Found singly and in pairs, often accompanying mixed flocks. Forages, sometimes acrobatically, in tangles and on branches; favors stands of bamboo. Generally not hard to observe. Song distinctive, a loud burry "wrr-jek, wrrjejek, wrrjejek, wrrjejek."

Bamboo Foliage-gleaner
Anabazenops dorsalis*   PLATE 14(2)
18.5 cm (7¼"). Local and uncommon in undergrowth of forest borders and woodland in w. Amazonia, and in foothills on east slope of Andes. *Almost invariably in areas with a bamboo understory,* though in Ecuador also found in *Gynerium* cane. Mostly 200–1300 m. Formerly placed in the genus *Automolus,* and called the Crested (or Dusky-cheeked) Foliage-gleaner. Bill rather stout. Above rufescent brown with *narrow buffyish superciliary* and *dusky cheeks;* rump and tail rufous-chestnut. *Throat creamy whitish* (sometimes puffed out); below pale grayish. The more numerous and widespread Olive-backed Foliage-gleaner is more olivaceous (less rufescent) above; it lacks any obvious superciliary and has concolor (not dusky) cheeks. Olive-backed favors terra firme forest. Found singly or in pairs, keeping to dense cover and usually hard to more than glimpse. Sometimes accompanies understory flocks. Generally found through its vocalizations, with song a measured "tcho-tcho-tcho-tcho-tcho" (the number of notes varies); though lower-pitched, quality and tempo recall Ferruginous Pygmy Owl (*Glaucidium brasilianum*). Agitated birds give a rattling that can continue for 30 seconds or more.

Point-tailed Palmcreeper
Berlepschia rikeri   PLATE 14(3)
21.5 cm (8½"). Found locally in *palm stands* (especially *Mauritia)* in Amazonia and the Guianas. To 650 m. *Boldly patterned* and unmistakable. Bill long and straight. *Head, neck, and underparts black boldly streaked white; otherwise bright rufous-chestnut.* Strictly arboreal and, unless vocalizing, inconspicuous as it rummages about in the bases and deep pleats of large, fan-shaped palm fronds, usually well hidden. Palmcreepers occur in widely dispersed pairs and rarely if ever associate with other birds. Song given infrequently, mainly at dawn; an unmistakable, far-carrying series of fast, ringing notes, "dedede-kee!-kee!-kee!-kee!-kee!-kee!-kee!-kee!" Sometimes vocalizes while perched in the open on a palm's spikelike growing stalk, often (especially after tape playback) remaining motionless for long periods.

MINERS AND LEAFTOSSERS: SCLERURIDAE

The genus *Sclerurus* was recently combined with the genus *Geositta* (miners) to form a separate family; miners are covered on pp. 263–265. Note that the Sharp-tailed Streamcreeper, which follows, remains a Furnariid.

Sclerurus

A uniform group of *cryptic, mainly dark brown* furnariids with *short black tails* that range *inside humid and wet forest*. Their legs are short, bills slender. Identification points are subtle; note especially *throat and chest patterns*. Behavior of all leaftossers is similar and will not be repeated in the species accounts. They are furtive and inconspicuous birds, *mainly terrestrial* and for the most part solitary. Favoring damp places and ravines, leaftossers hop and shuffle on the ground, flicking aside leaves and other debris with their bill and also probing the ground. They are not particularly wary, sometimes permitting a close approach; unseen feeding birds may suddenly flush from close by, giving a sharp "tseeeét." Such startled birds then sometimes perch on a low branch for protracted periods.

Rufous-breasted Leaftosser

Sclerurus scansor   PLATE 14(4)
18–18.5 cm (7–7¼"). Uncommon on or near ground inside humid and lower montane forest and woodland in *e. Brazil, e. Paraguay, and ne. Argentina*. To 1500 m. Above dark brown with rufous-chestnut rump and black tail. *Throat whitish scaled dusky* (the scaling lacking in **ne. Brazil**), *contrasting with rufous chest;* below grayish brown. Overlaps with both Black-tailed and Tawny-throated Leaftossers, though Rufous-breasted tends to be more montane. Black-tailed in e. Brazil is darker and duller, showing *no* rufous on chest or rufous-chestnut on rump. Tawny-throated has throat and chest *entirely* tawny-rufous. Song a sharp descending chippered trill that can end in a chatter, e.g., "chee-ee-ee-ee-ee-ee-ee-ee-eu, cht-cht."

Tawny-throated Leaftosser

Sclerurus mexicanus   PLATE 14(5)
16–16.5 cm (6¼–6½"). Uncommon and somewhat local on or near ground inside humid and lower montane forest from Colombia and Venezuela to Amazonia, and in e. Brazil. Mostly below 1500 m. Bill long and slender, *slightly drooped at tip*. Dark brown above with rufous-chestnut rump and black tail. *Throat and chest rich tawny-rufous* (duller in **w. Colombia and w. Ecuador**); dark brown below. Short-billed Leaftosser has a markedly shorter bill, paler and buffier throat, and vague pale eye-ring and short superciliary. Black-tailed and Scaly-throated Leaftossers both have whitish throat. Song a *descending* series of 4–5 high-pitched wheezy notes, each a bit shorter, e.g., "peéeeee-peéeee-peéee-peee," often ending in a chattered "chrrrr" when excited. Also: Mexico to Panama.

Scaly-throated Leaftosser

Sclerurus guatemalensis   PLATE 14(6)
18 cm (7"). Uncommon and local on or near ground inside humid forest in *nw. Colombia and w. Ecuador* (south to Guayas). To 800 m. Bill straight. Uniform dark brown above (including rump); tail black. *Throat white prominently scaled darker;* chest rufescent brown with some buff streaking; below dark brown. Only sympatric leaftosser is Tawny-throated, which has an obvious tawny-rufous throat and chest, rufous-chestnut on rump. Song a fast series of 10–12 sharp, clear whistled notes, at first dropping in pitch, then ascending and speeding up, the series often rapidly repeated. Also: Mexico to Panama.

Gray-throated Leaftosser

Sclerurus albigularis   PLATE 14(7)
17–18 cm (6¾–7"). *Rare and local* on or near ground inside foothill and lower montane forest from n. Venezuela to w. Bolivia (Chuquisaca),

also very locally in sw. Amazonia. Mostly 1000–2000 m. Above dark brown with rufous-chestnut rump and black tail. *Upper throat white, lower throat pale gray, contrasting with rufous chest;* below grayish brown. Birds in **ne. Santa Cruz, Bolivia,** are paler. Tawny-throated Leaftosser has entire throat and chest tawny-rufous (not a contrasting pale throat). Does not overlap with Rufous-breasted Leaftosser. Song an *ascending* series of 4–6 querulous notes, e.g., "kwu-kwu-kwe-kwe-kwi-kwi?" Tawny-throated song descends. Excited birds add trills and chatters at end. Also: Costa Rica and w. Panama.

Short-billed Leaftosser
Sclerurus rufigularis   PLATE 14(8)
16 cm (6¼"). Uncommon on or near ground inside humid forest from Amazonia to the Guianas. Mostly below 500 m. *Bill relatively short.* Dark brown above with *buffyish lores, partial eye ring, and vague postocular;* rump rufous-chestnut, tail black. *Throat cinnamon-buff;* below dark brown, chest variably mottled buffyish. Tawny-throated Leaftosser differs in its longer and slightly decurved bill, more richly colored throat and chest, and *lack* of buff on face. Song a fast series of shrill high-pitched notes, descends at first, then ascends and speeds up, ultimately slowing again.

Black-tailed Leaftosser
Sclerurus caudacutus   PLATE 14(9)
18.5 cm (7¼"). Uncommon on or near ground inside humid forest from Amazonia to the Guianas, and in e. Brazil. Locally to about 1000 m. Bill straight. In **w. and s. Amazonia** (illustrated) brown above, rump slightly more chestnut; tail black. *Throat white scaled darker;* below dark brown. **In e. Brazil** birds are darker generally. In **ne. South America** throat buffier with no scaling. Black-tailed is the only leaftosser in Amazonia with white on its throat, though this admittedly can be hard to discern in the forest's dim light. Tawny-throated Leaftosser especially resembles Black-tailed of ne. South America but is somewhat smaller, lacks white on throat, and has a more decurved bill. Song a series of loud, emphatic, ringing notes that steadily drop in pitch; sometimes faster, ending with a brief trill.

Sharp-tailed Streamcreeper
Lochmias nematura   PLATE 14(10)
15 cm (6"). Uncommon and local along or near streams in foothill and lower montane forest in Andes from n. Venezuela and Colombia to nw. Argentina, on the tepuis, and in se. Brazil region (where slightly more numerous, and also ranging locally in gallery forest). Mostly below 1700 m. Bill long and slender, slightly decurved. In **the southeast and on tepuis** (A) legs dull grayish pink. Dark brown above with *white-spotted superciliary,* mantle more chestnut; tail black. *Below dark brown profusely spotted white.* **Andean birds** (B) have black legs and *lack* the superciliary; they are *less densely spotted below.* Leaftosserlike in shape, but smaller; should be recognized immediately by its bold white spotting below. Hops on or near the ground, with behavior much like the leaftossers and usually equally hard to see, though sometimes one feeds more in the open, even on rocks out in a stream. Probes into damp soil, and also flicks leaves with its bill. Song a series of dry unmusical notes that starts slowly, often preceded by a single sharp note, and accelerates into a chipper. Also: e. Panama.

WOODCREEPERS: DENDROCOLAPTIDAE

A uniform group of mainly brown and rufous birds, sometimes considered to rank as only a subfamily within the Furnariidae. Their stiff tails have exposed shafts that aid them as they hitch up trunks and branches, somewhat woodpeckerlike. Though relatively easy to observe, identification to species is often difficult. Woodcreepers are arboreal, with nearly all species occurring in forests of varying types; they reach maximum diversity in Amazonia. Nests are usually placed in tree holes or behind pieces of bark.

Dendrocincla

Midsized, plain woodcreepers with straight bills found in humid forest and woodland, all but one (Tyrannine) in the lowlands. Most habitually follow swarms of army ants. They often ruffle their crown feathers, and their wings are often flicked nervously.

Tyrannine Woodcreeper
Dendrocincla tyrannina　　　　PLATE 15(1)
24–26.5 cm (9½–10½"). *Uncommon in montane forest and borders in Andes from sw. Venezuela* (Táchira) *to extreme w. Bolivia* (w. La Paz). Mostly 1500–3000 m. *A large and uniform woodcreeper. Essentially uniform olive brown,* throat slightly paler and with faint buff streaking on crown and throat, sometimes extending over chest; wings and tail more rufescent. ♂ averages larger than ♀. Other *Dendrocincla* woodcreepers (equally plain in appearance) are markedly smaller, and *all occur at lower elevations.* Montane Woodcreeper is smaller with a slender decurved bill and shows extensive streaking. Usually found singly, often while accompanying a mixed flock. Forages by hitching up trunks and along larger lateral branches, at varying heights though usually not very high. Song a stuttered rattle 5–10 seconds long that increases in pitch and volume before trailing off and slowing toward the end.

Plain-brown Woodcreeper
Dendrocincla fuliginosa　　　　PLATE 15(2)
19.5–21.5 cm (7¾–8½"). *A widespread and often common* woodcreeper of lower and middle growth in humid forest and woodland (locally also deciduous forest) from Colombia and Venezuela to Amazonia and the Guianas. Mostly below 1300 m. *Essentially uniform brown* with *paler grayish lores and ear-coverts* and *fairly obvious dusky malar stripe;* flight feathers and tail rufous-chestnut. **Northern birds** (A) generally more rufescent, **western birds** more olivaceous; in **Amazonia** (B) often shows a buff postocular and more whitish throat. *Plain-brown is the most uniformly brown woodcreeper found in the lowlands.* In Amazonia, cf. less numerous White-chinned Woodcreeper (with contrasting white throat, usually a bluish eye). Though routinely foraging singly or in pairs, sometimes while accompanying mixed flocks, most often seen while attending army antswarms; at larger swarms six or more birds may gather. Here they sally in pursuit of fleeing prey and can be bold. Hitches up trunks and branches like other woodcreepers, but sometimes also perches normally across branches. Gives a descending series of rattled notes that slows toward the end, lasting 2–3.5 seconds. Less often heard is a protracted series of "keé" or "keh" notes that can continue for 30 seconds or more. A sharp "peeyk" call is frequent. Also: Honduras to Panama.

Plain-winged Woodcreeper
Dendrocincla turdina
20–21 cm (8–8¼"). Fairly common in lower and middle growth of humid forest and woodland in *se. Brazil region* (north to e. Bahia). To 850 m. *Essentially uniform brown* with faint buff streaking on crown; tail rufous-chestnut, but *wings basically uniform brown* (flight feathers *not* contrasting rufous as in Plain-brown); throat pale buff. Does not overlap with the similar Plain-brown Woodcreeper. Behavior, including predilection for following antswarms, much as in Plain-brown Woodcreeper. Song a monotonous series of "kik" or "keek" notes that may last for a

minute or more and fade and strengthen almost at random.

Ruddy Woodcreeper
Dendrocincla homochroa

19.5–20.5 cm (7¾–8″). Uncommon and local in lower growth of humid forest and woodland in *n. Colombia and w. Venezuela* (east to w. Lara and w. Barinas). Mostly below 450 m. Resembles Plain-brown Woodcreeper, but *essentially uniform reddish brown with rufous crown*, grayish lores, and rufous-chestnut wings and tail. Sympatric Plain-browns are much more olivaceous generally and show grayish on auriculars and a dusky malar stripe. Behavior (including predilection for foraging at antswarms) much as in Plain-brown Woodcreeper, but Ruddy seems more furtive and is much less often encountered. Gives sharp calls when at antswarms; infrequently heard song a leisurely series of rather soft "wheep" notes, slowing at end. Also: Mexico to Panama.

White-chinned Woodcreeper
Dendrocincla merula   PLATE 15(3)

19–20 cm (7½–8″). Uncommon in lower growth of humid forest (terra firme and várzea) from *Amazonia to the Guianas*. To 500 m. Perhaps more than one species. *Iris bluish gray in most of range*, but brown in ne. South America. Rufescent brown above; wings and tail rufous-chestnut. *Small, contrasting white throat patch*; below olivaceous brown. Plain-brown Woodcreeper lacks contrasting white throat, never shows bluish eye, and has a stronger face pattern (White-chinned face is unmarked and plain); Plain-brown's throat is often whitish, but it never forms a discrete white patch as in White-chinned. An inveterate follower of army ants, even more of an obligate than the Plain-brown; sometimes also follows peccary herds. Behavior at swarms is similar to Plain-brown Woodcreeper, though White-chinneds are dominant and tend to remain nearer the ground, often actually sallying to the ground itself in pursuit of fleeing prey. Gives a chattered call when at antswarms; song less often heard, a fast "kew-kew-kew-kew-kew-kew-kew-kup" or shorter "kit-it-it-it."

Deconychura

Dull-plumaged, obscure woodcreepers that range in humid forests. Both species have a *notably long tail* and show marked sexual dimorphism in size.

Long-tailed Woodcreeper
Deconychura longicauda   PLATE 15(4)

19–21 cm (7½–8¼″). Uncommon and local in lower and middle growth inside humid forest (mainly terra firme) from Amazonia to the Guianas; also in n. Colombia, and in foothill and lower montane forest on east slope of Andes in Ecuador and n. Peru. To 1700 m. More than one species probably involved. Bill straight and slender. ♂ larger than ♀. **Lowland birds** (illustrated) brown above with *indistinct buff postocular stripe*; wings, uppertail-coverts, and tail rufous-chestnut, *tail proportionally longer than in other woodcreepers* (except for Spot-throated). Throat buff with faint dusky streaking; below dull olivaceous brown, *chest narrowly buff-streaked*. **Montane birds** (and in **nw. Colombia**) similar but *more spotted or chevroned on breast*. Confusing, but *slim shape, accentuated by long tail, helps*. Spot-throated Woodcreeper averages smaller, has rufous rump (not just uppertail-coverts), more spotted breast pattern, and shorter and more slender bill. No *Xiphorhynchus* woodcreeper shows such an obvious postocular; cf. larger and more olivaceous Olive-backed Woodcreeper (spotted below). Wedge-billed Woodcreeper is markedly smaller with a shorter bill. Unobtrusive and seldom encountered, though sometimes accompanies mixed flocks. Forages mainly on trunks and larger branches. Songs vary dramatically but are only infrequently heard. In Amazonia gives a strongly descending series of 8–12 well-separated, clear, penetrating whistled notes; in ne. South America, an evenly pitched series of 6–8 "chuuueee" notes; foothill birds in Ecuador very different, a series of 9–15 "preeeur" notes (J. Nilsson recording). Also: Honduras to Panama.

Spot-throated Woodcreeper
Deconychura stictolaema   PLATE 15(5)

16.5–17.5 cm (6½–7″). *Rare and local (perhaps just overlooked) in lower growth of terra firme forest in Amazonia and the Guianas.* To 750 m in n. Peru. Bill straight and rather short. ♂ larger than ♀. Brown above with indistinct buff postocular stripe; inner flight feathers (*only*) rufous-chestnut; tail rufous-chestnut, *this color extending up over rump; tail proportionally longer than in other woodcreepers* (except Long-tailed). Olivaceous brown below, *throat and chest with small chevron-shaped spots*. Cf. similar Long-tailed Woodcreeper. Spot-throated is a small, obscure woodcreeper, most likely confused with much more numerous Wedge-billed Woodcreeper; though similar in color and pattern, Wedge-billed is smaller and has a shorter, wedge-shaped bill. Not well known, but unobtrusive behavior seems similar to Long-tailed. Found singly, foraging with mixed flocks; remains closer to the ground than Long-tailed. Infrequently heard song a simple, colorless trill, descending at first, then rising.

Wedge-billed Woodcreeper

Glyphorynchus spirurus   PLATE 15(6)

14–15 cm (5½–6"). *Widespread and common* in lower growth of humid forest and woodland from Colombia and Venezuela to Amazonia and the Guianas, and in e. Brazil (e. Bahia and Espírito Santo). Mostly below 1000 m, a few to 2000 m. Likely more than one species involved. A *small* woodcreeper with *distinctive short, wedge-shaped bill.* Above rufescent brown with indistinct buff postocular stripe; rump and tail rufous, tail with *very long protruding spines* (proportionately the longest of any woodcreeper). Throat buff to whitish; below olivaceous brown, breast with fine buffyish streaking. In Amazonia, cf. much rarer Spot-throated Woodcreeper. Plain Xenops has similarly shaped bill but differs markedly in behavior, etc. Usually found singly, less often in pairs, sometimes accompanying mixed flocks of understory birds but also forages alone. Hitches up trunks of larger trees, generally not continuing onto lateral branches. Song a fast and ascending series of upslurred, semimusical notes, e.g., "tuee-tuee-tuee-tuee-teeé-tueé-tueé?" often shriller at end. Oft-given call an abrupt, sneezing "cheeyf!" (varied to 2 clear penetrating "tue" notes in cen. Amaz. Brazil; A. Whittaker). Also: Mexico to Panama.

Olivaceous Woodcreeper

Sittasomus griseicapillus   PLATE 15(7)

14.5–16 cm (5¾–6¼"). *Widespread and often common* in a variety of forested and wooded habitats (humid, deciduous, and montane) from Colombia and Venezuela to n. Argentina and se. Brazil. Mostly below 1500 m, smaller numbers to 2000 m. *Variable,* with more than one species surely involved. A *small, unstreaked* woodcreeper; bill short and quite slender. In **most of range** (A) has *head, neck, and underparts grayish to olive grayish;* back more olivaceous, and flight feathers and tail bright rufous. In **w. Ecuador and nw. Peru** similar but flight feathers and tail more cinnamon-rufous. In **se. Brazil region** (B) *bright ochraceous olive above* (lacking the gray). In **ne. Brazil** (C) even more different, being *more rufescent above* with wings entirely rufous, and

strongly buff-tinged below. Despite the variation, can be readily recognized by the combination of small size and *lack* of streaking; only the very different Wedge-billed Woodcreeper is as small. Seen singly or in pairs, hitching along open trunks and larger branches at varying levels though most often quite high. Sometimes accompanies mixed flocks, but at least as often forages alone. Songs vary strikingly, but always seem to be given at long intervals. Western birds give a fast, rolling, semimusical trill "tr-r-r-r-r-r-r-r-r-r-r-r-r-eu" lasting about 3 seconds. From Amazonia to nw. Argentina and sw. Brazil gives a very different series of 6–14 successively higher-pitched and gradually louder notes, "pu-pu-pew-pew-peh-peh-peé-peh" with a slight drop at end. In se. Brazil region gives an equally different series of 8–10 enunciated "weep" notes that drop in pitch and end in a stutter. In ne. Brazil most often gives a simple, soft "whit" or "whi-du," occasionally in series. Also: Mexico to Panama.

Long-billed Woodcreeper

Nasica longirostris   PLATE 15(8)

35–36 cm (13¾–14¼"). Uncommon in mid-levels, subcanopy, and borders of humid forest in *Amazonia, generally associated with water, in várzea and riparian habitats,* but sometimes in terra firme. Locally to 500 m. *Spectacular and unmistakable,* with long thin neck, small head, and *very long and nearly straight bill ivory white.* Crown blackish narrowly streaked buff, and narrow white postocular stripe; *above bright rufous-chestnut. Throat snowy white;* below brown with black-edged white lanceolate streaks on sides of neck and breast. Found singly or in pairs, foraging in the semiopen along edge of lakes, streams, and rivers, but except for voice not terribly conspicuous; generally not with flocks. Often probes into bromeliads and other epiphytes. Loud, far-carrying song an easily recognized series of 3–4 eerie, plaintive whistled notes, e.g., "twooooo6oo . . . twooooo6oo . . . twooooo6oo." A faster version (recalling Fasciated Antshrike) is sometimes given. Excited birds also utter various chuckled calls.

Cinnamon-throated Woodcreeper

Dendrexetastes rufigula   PLATE 15(9)

24–25 cm (9½–9¾"). Uncommon in canopy and especially borders of humid forest and woodland in *Amazonia and the Guianas.* Mostly below 500 m. *Rather heavy bill horn-colored to greenish horn;* iris dark red. In **ne. South America** (A) mostly brown, more cinnamon-buff on throat with *conspicuous collar of white, black-edged spots on upper back and across breast;* flight feathers and tail rufous. In **w. and s. Amazonia** (B) less striking; *no* white upper back spotting and *on breast only narrow streaks.* A large and rather plain woodcreeper whose stout bill is obviously pale; the breast streaking of Amaz. birds can be hard to see in field. Found singly, less often in pairs, sometimes accompanying mixed flocks but at least as often alone. Hitches along trunks and on larger branches like other woodcreepers, but also clambers about, like a foliage-gleaner, in leafy vegetation; sometimes even rummages among palm fronds. Heard more often than seen. Far-carrying song (often one of the first to be heard at dawn) a fast series of loud rattled notes, ascending at first and trailing off toward end; it may start with a sputter and always ends with a distinctive lower-pitched "tchew" or "trreew" note.

Xiphorhynchus

A *confusing* group of midsized to fairly large woodcreepers found mainly in humid lowland forests; a few (especially Olive-backed and Spotted) are more montane, and one (Straight-billed) ranges into more open habitats. All are *streaked or spotted to some degree* (less plain than in *Dendrocincla*), and their bills typically are only slightly decurved (less so, and less slender, than is seen in *Lepidocolaptes*). Though some issues have recently been resolved, various species continue to present taxonomic challenges.

Straight-billed Woodcreeper

Xiphorhynchus picus   PLATE 16(1)
20–21 cm (8–8¼"). *Generally common and widespread in a variety of lightly wooded and semiopen habitats* (in Amazonia mainly in várzea and riparian areas), locally also in desert scrub and mangroves, from Colombia and Venezuela to Amazonia and ne. Brazil. Mainly below 1100 m. *Pale ivory-colored to pale dull pinkish bill straight and dagger-shaped.* In **most of range** (illustrated) has dusky head and nape, narrowly buff-streaked and with indistinct whitish superciliary, contrasting with rufous back; wings and tail rufous-chestnut. Throat whitish, *chest with large black-edged whitish squamate spots;* below brown. In **n. Colombia and n. Venezuela** paler with a whiter face and throat. In Amazonia cf. the very similar Zimmer's Woodcreeper. The less

numerous Striped Woodcreeper has a darker and more decurved bill and more streaking on back and underparts. Forages singly or in pairs, sometimes in the open and close to the ground or water. Hitches up smaller trunks and along lateral limbs; often with mixed flocks, but also forages alone. Song a descending trill, usually with an upturn at end; sings more often during midday than most other woodcreepers. Also: Panama.

Zimmer's Woodcreeper

*Xiphorhynchus kienerii**
21–22 cm (8¼–8½"). *Uncommon in várzea and riparian forest and woodland, sometimes on islands, along Amazon River and some of its tributaries in ne. Peru* (lower Río Napo eastward) *and Amaz. Brazil* (downriver to near mouth of Rio Tapajós). Below 200 m. Closely resembles Straight-billed Woodcreeper and regularly occurs with it. Differs in its slimmer bill, slightly longer tail, and slightly more streaked (less spotted) breast pattern. Behavior of the two species is similar, though Zimmer's seems less often to forage in the open. They are best distinguished by voice; song of Zimmer's has a faster tempo and lacks Straight-billed's typical upturn at end.

Striped Woodcreeper

Xiphorhynchus obsoletus   PLATE 16(2)
20–20.5 cm (7¾–8"). *Generally uncommon in lower growth of várzea forest and woodland from Amazonia to the Guianas.* To 500 m. *Slightly decurved bill grayish horn.* Above brown, duskier on crown, with *prominent black-edged buff streaks from crown to back;* wings and tail rufous-chestnut. Throat pale buff, below dull brown *prominently streaked buffy whitish* except on belly. Amaz. forms of Straight-billed Woodcreeper are more rufescent and have a paler and straighter bill, *no* back streaking, and more spotted effect on chest. Lineated Woodcreeper has narrower streaking below, a finer, more decurved bill, and no back streaking; it forages higher, mainly in subcanopy. Behavior much as in Straight-billed Woodcreeper, but tends to keep to cover and is not seen as often. Song a harsh staccato trill that distinctly ascends (Straight-billed's drops).

Ocellated Woodcreeper

*Xiphorhynchus ocellatus**   PLATE 16(3)
21.5–22.5 cm (8½–8¾"). Fairly common but inconspicuous in lower growth of humid for-

est (especially terra firme) in *w. Amazonia.* To 1500 m on east slope of Andes in s. Peru and Bolivia. Taxonomy uncertain. In **most of range** (illustrated) bill blackish above, gray below. Above brown, crown and nape duskier and buff-streaked, back with sparse fine buff streaks (but often looks uniform); wings and tail rufous-chestnut. Throat buff, *lower throat feathers scaled dusky;* below brown, *chest with squamate dusky-edged buff spots.* In **se. Peru and Bolivia** bill shorter and *paler;* throat also *paler,* and *lacking* scaling. Cf. very similar Elegant Woodcreeper. Buff-throated Woodcreeper is larger with a longer and heavier bill; its plain buff throat *lacks* scaling. Striped Woodcreeper has a paler bill and is more streaked; it does not occur in terra firme forest. Ranges singly or in pairs, hitching up trunks and larger branches, probing into crevices and epiphytes. Almost always found *inside* forest (not at edge), usually singly; frequently accompanies understory flocks. Song a fast descending series of nasal notes that ends with several sharply emphasized notes, e.g., "whe-whe-whe-whe-whe-chéchécheow." Sometimes only part of this is given.

Elegant Woodcreeper
Xiphorhynchus elegans *   PLATE 16(4)

21–22 cm (8¼–8½"). Fairly common but inconspicuous in lower growth of humid forest (especially terra firme) in *w. and s. Amazonia.* Ranges locally up to 1500 m on east slope of Andes. Formerly considered conspecific with Spix's Woodcreeper. Bill bluish gray, duskier above. In **nw. Amazonia** (A), and in **Amaz. Brazil between Rios Purus and Tapajós and south to ne. Bolivia,** brown above, crown and nape duskier with buff spotting *becoming rather wide, black-edged buff streaks on back;* rump, wings, and tail rufous-chestnut. Throat buffy whitish; below dull brown with *squamate black-edged buff spots on breast.* In **sw. Amazonia east to Rio Madeira** (B) *back streaking much finer* and *breast spotting much smaller.* Does not occur with Spix's. In most of its range, Elegant differs most prominently from the similar Ocellated Woodcreeper in its obvious back streaking (absent in Ocellated). Where Elegant *lacks* back streaking (sw. Amazonia), note Ocellated's *larger* breast spots; also, in se. Peru and w. Bolivia, its shorter and paler bill. Behavior much as in Ocellated; more work is needed on ecological relationships. Voice also similar, though in some areas Elegant's song is believed to have a clearer quality, e.g., a descending "tchip-tchip-tchip-

tchip-tchup-tchup, tchweu, tchweu." Sometimes this continues as a longer series, or it slides up in pitch at end.

Spix's Woodcreeper
Xiphorhynchus spixii

21–22 cm (8¼–8½"). Uncommon in lower growth in humid forest (terra firme and *várzea)* in *e. Amaz.* Brazil (east of Rio Tapajós). To 500 m. Resembles main "type" of Elegant Woodcreeper, differing in having *back streaking very broad* and *streaking below broad and extensive.* Spix's occurs *east* of Elegant's range; no overlap. Behavior of the two is similar, as is voice (reportedly somewhat faster in Spix's).

Chestnut-rumped Woodcreeper
Xiphorhynchus pardalotus   PLATE 16(5)

21.5–22.5 cm (8½–8¾"). Fairly common in lower growth of humid forest and woodland in **ne. South America.** Mostly below 600 m, locally higher on tepuis. Bill blackish. Brown above, duskier on crown and nape with buff spotting, back with sparse buff streaking; wings and tail rufous-chestnut. *Throat fulvous, slightly streaked dusky;* below dull brown, *breast narrowly streaked fulvous.* Ocellated Woodcreeper overlaps with Chestnut-rumped only in sw. Venezuela, there differing in its more spotted effect on breast, less streaked back, and paler throat. The larger Buff-throated Woodcreeper has a longer bill, which is *not* blackish where it overlaps with Chestnut-rumped; its streaking below is broader and its throat plainer. Behavior similar to Ocellated Woodcreeper; most often seen while accompanying understory flocks. Song (as in many other woodcreepers) given mainly at dawn and dusk, a series of notes, "chup, chup, chup, cheh-cheh-chee-chee-ee-ee."

Buff-throated Woodcreeper
Xiphorhynchus guttatus *   PLATE 16(6)

26–26.5 cm (10¼–10½"). A *large* woodcreeper, *common and widespread* in humid forest and borders, gallery and locally semideciduous woodland, even mangroves from Amazonia to the Guianas, and in e. Brazil. Mostly below 700 m, locally to 1100–1200 m. Taxonomy uncertain. *Bill long,* in **most of range** (illustrated) pale dusky to grayish horn, darkest on ridge, but *blackish* in **e. Amaz. Brazil.** Above brown, duskier on crown and nape, with buff spotting on crown and back; wings and tail rufous-chestnut. *Throat pale buff;* below brown with buff streaking, belly plain. In **e. Amaz. Brazil west to Rio Madeira** crown spotting whiter and *streaking on back and below markedly wider and whiter;* apparent intergrades between the two "types" frequent. Because of its large size, this woodcreeper is most often confused with *Dendrocolaptes* or even *Xiphocolaptes* woodcreepers; other *Xiphorhynchus* are smaller with less heavy bills. Neither Black-banded nor Planalto Woodcreeper has an unstreaked throat, and Black-banded has barring on belly; both usually have a dark bill. Strong-billed Woodcreeper is much larger and even heavier-billed. In ne. South America, cf. the smaller Chestnut-rumped Woodcreeper (also blackish-billed). Buff-throated is a rather conspicuous woodcreeper, foraging with mixed flocks at varying levels but often quite high, regularly ranging higher than many smaller *Xiphorhynchus.* It often rummages in dead leaves and palm fronds. *Very vocal,* more so than most woodcreepers, with a variety of vocalizations. Most frequent song, given through day (but especially at dawn and dusk), a series of evenly paced, loud ringing whistled notes that starts slowly and becomes louder. Also has a shorter fast series of descending laughing notes, and a doubled "wheeyer, wheeyer." Oft-heard call a loud "kyoow."

Cocoa Woodcreeper
Xiphorhynchus susurrans
21.5–22 cm (8½–8¾"). Fairly common in lower and middle growth and borders of humid forest and woodland in *n. Colombia and n. Venezuela* (east to Sucre and Monagas). Mostly below 700 m. Resembles Buff-throated Woodcreeper, but *markedly smaller;* no overlap. On **Trinidad and Tobago** throat whiter and breast pattern more spotted. Streak-headed Woodcreeper has a similar plumage pattern but is smaller with a slimmer and more decurved bill. Behavior much as in Buff-throated, but seems to attend army antswarms more often. Oft-heard song a fast series of loud, clear, whistled notes, fast at first and then slowing and fading, "kuwi, kwee-kwee-kwee-kwee-kwee, kwee, kwu, kwu." Also gives a slower "kwee, kwew, kwu-kwu." Also: Guatemala to Panama.

Olive-backed Woodcreeper
Xiphorhynchus triangularis   PLATE 16(7)
23 cm (9"). *Uncommon in montane forest and borders in Andes from n. Venezuela to w. Bolivia* (w. Santa Cruz), south of s. Colombia only on east slope. Mostly 1000–2400 m. Bill mainly bluish horn. *Above brownish olive,* crown dusky with yellowish buff dots, and with indistinct

yellowish buff eye-ring and postocular; wings and tail rufous-chestnut. *Throat buff scaled dusky; below olivaceous with bold yellowish buff spots.* There are rather few woodcreepers in this species' montane range, none so spotted below. Cf. the rare Long-tailed Woodcreeper. Spotted Woodcreeper occurs *only on west slope of Andes,* typically at lower elevations. Found singly or in pairs, often accompanying mixed flocks, hitching up trunks and along larger branches at various levels. Rather quiet (more so than Spotted); call a sharp, piercing, downslurred "keeeyur," at times mixed with a run-together series of semi-musical notes.

Spotted Woodcreeper
Xiphorhynchus erythropygius   PLATE 16(8)
23 cm (9"). Fairly common in humid and montane forest and borders on west slope of Andes in *w. Colombia and w. Ecuador* (south to w. Loja). To 2000 m. Bill mainly bluish horn. *Above brownish olive,* crown duskier with a little buff spotting on forecrown, and with *buff eye-ring and vague postocular;* wings and tail rufous. Throat buff *spotted dusky; below olivaceous boldly spotted dull buff.* The similar Olive-backed Woodcreeper (mainly on *east* slope; no overlap) has more spotting on crown and a scaled (not spotted) throat. Otherwise not likely confused; cf. Montane Woodcreeper. General behavior as in Olive-backed, but considerably more vocal, often calling even in midday. Most frequent song a far-carrying series of rather high-pitched but descending whinnies with distinctive reedy quality and drawn-out effect, e.g., "d-d-d-r-rreeuw, d-d-d-r-rreeuw, d-d-d-r-rreeuw," sometimes with 1–2 clipped notes at end. Also: Mexico to Panama.

Black-striped Woodcreeper
Xiphorhynchus lachrymosus   PLATE 16(9)
24 cm (9½"). Fairly common in humid forest and borders in *w. Colombia and nw. Ecuador* (mainly Esmeraldas). Mostly below 1000 m. Bill blackish, grayer below. *Boldly patterned. Head and mantle black, head streaked pale buff, mantle and scapulars boldly striped pale buff;* wings rufous, tail rufous-chestnut. Throat streaked pale buff; *below boldly streaked pale buff and blackish,* belly more mottled. Handsome and unlikely to be confused in its limited range; cf. the much duller Spotted Woodcreeper. Forages much like other woodcreepers, though more often well above the ground than most; regularly accompanies mixed flocks. Oft-heard call loud and dis-

tinctive, a fast series of 3–4 notes with laughing quality, "whee-hew-hew." Song given less often, a rapid and descending whinnying series of at least 10 notes. Also: Nicaragua to Panama.

Lesser Woodcreeper
Xiphorhynchus fuscus*   PLATE 16(10)

17–18 cm (6¾–7″). Fairly common in humid and lower montane forest, secondary woodland, and borders from *ne. Brazil to e. Paraguay and ne. Argentina* (Misiones). Mostly below 1200 m. Formerly placed in genus *Lepidocolaptes*. Slender, somewhat decurved bill. In **most of range, north to Bahia** (illustrated), brown above, crown and nape duskier with buffyish spotting and postocular, back with faint buff streaking. *Throat buffy whitish; below dusky-olive with blurry buffyish streaking.* In **ne. Brazil** has a longer bill, buffier throat; streaking below more faded. Scaled and Scalloped Woodcreepers are larger, plain-backed, and their streaking below is black-edged and thus more prominent. Narrow-billed Woodcreeper is even larger and longer-billed, with a much more prominent superciliary. Mainly forages in lower growth, single birds or pairs often accompanying mixed flocks. Song commences with a series of stuttered notes, moves into a faster trill, then ends with more stuttered notes, e.g., "chit, chit, chit, chee-ee-ee-ee-ee-ee-ee, chit, chit-chit."

Lepidocolaptes

A uniform group of slim, fairly small woodcreepers with *distinctive pale, slender, decurved bills;* many are *un*streaked above. *Lepidocolaptes* range widely in forested or more lightly wooded habitats, but one (Narrow-billed) is frequent in more open areas such as the Brazilian cerrado.

Lineated Woodcreeper
Lepidocolaptes albolineatus   PLATE 16(11)

18.5–19 cm (7¼–7½″). Uncommon in midlevels and subcanopy of humid forest (mainly terra firme) and woodland in *Amazonia and the Guianas.* Mainly below 1000 m. A smallish, slim woodcreeper with *slender, decurved bill* and *boldly streaked underparts.* In **most of range** (illustrated) above uniform brown, *including the crown;* wings and tail rufous. Throat whitish; below brown with *crisp black-edged whitish streaking.* In **e. Venezuela, the Guianas, and n. Brazil** crown has faint whitish spots. *The*

only *Lepidocolaptes in the humid forests of Amazonia,* so there bill shape should readily identify it; Streak-headed Woodcreeper (local overlap in ne. South America, though mainly in more deciduous habitats) has a whitish superciliary. Striped is the most similar *Xiphorhynchus,* but its bill is heavier and less decurved, and it shows streaking on head and back (Lineated is unstreaked above); Striped favors várzea, never ranging up into terra firme canopy. Lineated tends to remain well above the ground, where it hitches on trunks and larger branches; is frequently accompanies mixed flocks. Song in w. Amazonia a soft becard-like trill that drops in pitch and accelerates, e.g., "ti, ti, ti-ti-tee-tee-teh-teh-tutututututu"; in ne. South America similar but more accelerating. Differs more in s. Amaz. Brazil (east of Rio Madeira) and in upper Río Orinoco area, where it gives a slower series of about 6–12 clear whistled notes.

Scaled Woodcreeper
Lepidocolaptes squamatus   PLATE 16(12)

19 cm (7½″). Uncommon in humid and montane forest, borders, and woodland in *e. Brazil* (s. Piauí to n. São Paulo). Mostly below 1600 m. *Slender decurved bill mostly pinkish.* In **most of range** (illustrated) bright rufous brown above with buff crown spotting and broken whitish superciliary; wings and tail rufous. Throat white; *below brown with bold black-edged whitish streaks.* **West of Rio São Francisco** even brighter rufous above; this form occurs in more deciduous woodland. Lesser Woodcreeper is buffier and more blurrily streaked below, and its back is lightly streaked. Cf. Scalloped Woodcreeper (replaces Scaled southward). Ranges singly and in pairs, hitching up trunks and along slender branches; often with mixed flocks. Song a "peé-deedir" followed by several softer notes and then a louder "peetu-peetu-peeyr."

Scalloped Woodcreeper
Lepidocolaptes falcinellus*

19 cm (7½″). Locally fairly common in humid and montane forest, borders, and woodland (including *Araucaria*-dominated forest) in *se. Brazil region* (north to n. São Paulo). Mostly below 1600 m. Formerly considered conspecific with Scaled Woodcreeper (no known overlap, replacing it southward). Resembles that species, differing in its *duskier crown with prominent buff spotting,* and buff-tinged underparts. Lesser Woodcreeper is buffier and more blurrily streaked below, and its back is lightly streaked.

Behavior much as in Scaled Woodcreeper. Song a rattled, descending "pree-ee-ee-u."

Montane Woodcreeper
Lepidocolaptes lacrymiger PLATE 16(13)
19.5 cm (7¾"). *Fairly common in montane forest and borders in Andes from n. Venezuela to w. Bolivia* (w. Santa Cruz). Mostly 1500–3000 m. *Bill slender and decurved.* In **Colombia and Venezuela** (illustrated) rufescent brown above, crown duskier *with distinct buff spotting* and whitish superciliary; wings and tail rufous. Throat whitish, below brown with *bold black-edged whitish guttate streaks.* From **Ecuador and s. Colombia southward** duller and streakier below. *Shape of slender decurved bill in its Andean range is normally distinctive;* other sympatric woodcreepers have heavier and straighter bill. Olivebacked Woodcreeper is dull and olivaceous with spotting below; cf. Tyrannine. Pearled Treerunner's short bill is distinctly different; it is brighter rufous above, has a bold white brow. Forages in typical woodcreeper fashion, hitching up trunks and along larger limbs (most often on their underside), regularly probing into clumps of moss. Frequently accompanies mixed flocks. Usually at mid-levels or higher, rarely close to the ground. Song (not given all that often) an accelerating series of downslurred whistled notes, e.g., "tseu-tseu, tsip-tsip, tsee-tsee-tsee-tsee-tsee"; distinctive among the woodcreepers but recalls certain *Cranioleuca* spinetails, vaguely like a fruiteater.

Streak-headed Woodcreeper
Lepidocolaptes souleyetii PLATE 16(14)
19–20 cm (7½–8"). Fairly common in deciduous and semihumid forest, woodland, borders, and locally even arid scrub from *n. Colombia to e. Venezuela and s. Guyana,* and from *sw. Colombia to nw. Peru* (south to Lambayeque). Mostly below 800 m, locally to 1800 m in s. Ecuador. *Bill slender, decurved.* In **most of range** (illustrated) rufescent brown above, crown duskier with *distinct buff streaking* and *broken whitish superciliary;* rump, wings, and tail rufous. *Throat buffy whitish;* below brown with *black-edged buffy whitish streaking.* On **Pacific slope** has a longer bill, more extensively whitish throat, and wider streaking below. Montane Woodcreeper (a highland species that only marginally overlaps with Streak-headed) is spotted, not streaked, on crown, and its streaking below is distinctly crisper. Straight-billed Woodcreeper occurs regularly with Streak-headed in

n. South America; its bill is heavier, straighter, and whiter, and its face and throat are more extensively white. Forages singly or in pairs, mainly on trunks and larger limbs (sometimes even on columnar cacti), ranging more in semiopen than most other woodcreepers. Song a clear musical descending trill. Call a short "trrew, trrew." Also: Mexico to Panama.

Narrow-billed Woodcreeper
Lepidocolaptes angustirostris PLATE 16(15)
19.5–21 cm (7¾–8¼"). *Fairly common and widespread* in lighter woodland and scrub, cerrado, and agricultural areas from n. and e. Bolivia (west to La Paz) and ne. Brazil to cen. Argentina (south to La Pampa). To 2300 m or more in Bolivia. *Long, narrow, decurved bill whitish to pinkish.* Crown blackish with buffy to whitish streaking and a *bold whitish superciliary;* above plain rufous brown (brightest in more northerly birds). *Below white to whitish* (streaked dusky in more southerly birds). Long bill, bold head pattern, and pale underparts should preclude confusion; Narrow-billed favors more open situations than most woodcreepers and thus is more conspicuous. Cf. Lesser Woodcreeper (much more a forest bird). A handsome woodcreeper that ranges singly or in pairs, hitching up trunks and along larger limbs (even feeding on fence posts and *Eucalyptus* trees); probes into crannies and flakes off pieces of bark. Song a loud series of sharp, well-enunciated notes that either accelerate and fade away, "peeé, pee-pee-pee-pee-peepeepeepeepupupu," or simply descend, "peer, peer, peer, peeer, peeeer, pweeeer."

Hylexetastes

Large, heavy-bodied woodcreepers with stout, dark red bills that range locally in Amazonian forests; the three species are allopatric. All are scarce and still poorly known.

Bar-bellied Woodcreeper
Hylexetastes stresemanni PLATE 17(1)
28–29 cm (11–11½"). *Rare and local in humid forest, apparently favoring terra firme, in w. Amazonia.* To 450 m. *Very heavy reddish bill.* Mostly uniform brown, with whitish lores and streaking on throat; wings and tail rufous-chestnut. *Lower underparts pale buff barred blackish.* Congeners (none of them sympatric) *lack* barring below. The even larger Strong-billed Woodcreeper has a longer and horn-colored bill, duskier head

with pale streaking, etc. Amazonian Barred Woodcreeper also has a reddish bill but is much more uniformly and prominently barred. Black-banded Woodcreeper has a blackish bill, streaked foreparts and breast. Behavior not well known, but likely much as in Red-billed. Song also similar, though the individual notes may be shorter and more clipped (T. Parker recording).

Uniform Woodcreeper
Hylexetastes uniformis   PLATE 17(2)
26.5–27.5 cm (10½–10¾″). Rare in humid forest, mainly terra firme, in *s. Amaz. Brazil* (Rio Madeira east to lower Rio Tocantins) *and ne. Bolivia* (ne. Santa Cruz). To 600 m. Resembles Red-billed Woodcreeper (no overlap, Red-billed occurring only *north* of Amazon), but bill is somewhat shorter and *lacks* whitish facial markings. Behavior, including voice, much as in Red-billed.

Red-billed Woodcreeper
Hylexetastes perrotii   PLATE 17(3)
28–29 cm (11–11½″). Rare to uncommon in humid forest (mainly terra firme) in *ne. South America.* To 500 m. *Very heavy reddish bill. Mostly brown,* somewhat paler below; *lores, broad submalar stripe, and throat contrasting whitish.* Amazonian Barred Woodcreeper also has a distinctly reddish bill, but it is smaller and obviously barred. Does not overlap with any of its congeners (all similar). Found singly and in pairs, foraging at all levels; regular at army antswarms, but also moves with mixed flocks. Generally rather inconspicuous and not very vocal. When at an antswarm tends to perch on trunks close to the ground, and is dominant over other species in attendance. Infrequently heard song a series of 4–6 loud, piercing, whistled notes, e.g., "shreee-eét, shreee-eét, shreee-eét, shreee-eét."

Dendrocolaptes

Fairly large woodcreepers with *strong straight bills* found primarily in humid forests; they are frequent attendants at antswarms. *Certain species show more barring than other woodcreepers.*

Hoffmann's Woodcreeper
Dendrocolaptes hoffmannsi   PLATE 17(4)
28 cm (11″). Uncommon in lower growth of terra firme forest in *s. Amaz. Brazil* (Rio Madeira east to Rio Tapajos). To 300 m. Bill blackish. Brown above with *crown more rufescent,* feathers with black scaling; wings and tail rufous-chestnut. Below brown with faint dusky belly barring. The sympatric *unbarred* race of Amazonian Barred Woodcreeper has a more reddish bill and more uniform crown (showing no rusty cap). Hoffmann's seems not to occur with the more boldly patterned Black-banded Woodcreeper. Behavior much as in Amazonian Barred, but song resembles Black-banded's.

Amazonian Barred Woodcreeper
Dendrocolaptes certhia*   PLATE 17(5)
27–28 cm (10½–11″). Uncommon to locally fairly common in lower growth of humid forest and woodland (mainly terra firme) in Amazonia and the Guianas. Mostly below 900 m. The following species was formerly considered conspecific, as Barred Woodcreeper. *Bill reddish brown to reddish,* reddest in ne. South America. *Prominently barred in most of range.* Brown with *even black barring on head, back, and underparts;* wings and tail rufous-chestnut. **Ne. South America** birds show less barring. From **Rio Madeira east to Rio Tocantins in s. Amaz. Brazil** *loses barring altogether* (this is the former Concolor Woodcreeper), and **east of Rio Tocantins** (illustrated) it also shows *little* barring. In most of range the obvious barring should preclude confusion; in areas where there is less, note the usually obvious reddish bill (but less red than in *Hylexetastes*). Cf. Hoffmann's Woodcreeper. Black-banded Woodcreeper has streaking on foreparts and a blackish bill. Often seen foraging at swarms of army ants, but also regular away from them (more so than Northern Barred), at times with mixed flocks. Seems sluggish, sometimes remaining motionless for protracted periods. Song a fast series of ringing, whistled notes, "tewtewtewtewtewtew-tutu-tu-tu," fading toward end; not quite as fast as Black-banded's song. Also gives various whines and chatters.

Northern Barred Woodcreeper
Dendrocolaptes sanctithomae*
27–28 cm (10½–11″). Uncommon in lower growth of humid forest in *w. Colombia and w. Ecuador* (south to n. Guayas). To 800 m. Bill blackish. *Resembles more prominently barred populations of that species; no other woodcreeper found west of Andes is obviously barred.* Behavior much as in Amazonian Barred, but forages almost entirely at antswarms. Song very different, a slow series of clear whistled notes that gradually become

louder, "oowít, oowít, oowít, OOWIT, OOWIT!" Also: Mexico to Panama.

Black-banded Woodcreeper
Dendrocolaptes picumnus   PLATE 17(6)
25.5–28 cm (10–11"). Uncommon and somewhat local in lower growth of humid and montane forest, in Amazonia both in terra firme and várzea, from Colombia to the Guianas and nw. Argentina (Tucumán). To about 2000 m. In most of range (A) bill blackish. Above brown, darker on crown, streaked buff on head and, more sparsely, on back; wings and tail rufous-chestnut. Throat streaked buff and brown, breast prominently buff-streaked, *belly barred buff and blackish*. **Montane birds of Colombia and Venezuela** have less prominent belly barring, little back streaking. Differing more are birds from **e. Bolivia and Mato Grosso, Brazil** (B), whose *bills are paler* and plumage paler and more rufescent, with little or no belly barring. A *large* woodcreeper whose *combination of streaking on foreparts and belly barring* is usually distinctive (though the latter can be hard to see in the field). In cen. Amaz. Brazil, cf. Hoffmann's Woodcreeper. Superficially similar Buff-throated Woodcreeper *lacks* barring below and has a *plain* buff throat. Cf. also the heavier-billed and even larger Strong-billed Woodcreeper. Behavior much as in the barred woodcreepers, likewise often foraging at antswarms. Song a fast, slightly descending series of liquid "winh" notes; similar to Amazonian Barred, and with a laughing quality. Also gives various whines and chatters when agitated. Also: Mexico to w. Panama.

Planalto Woodcreeper
Dendrocolaptes platyrostris   PLATE 17(7)
25–26 cm (9¾–10¼"). Fairly common in lower growth of humid forest, secondary woodland, and borders from *e. Brazil to e. Paraguay and ne. Argentina*. Mostly below 1300 m. *Bill black.* **Southern birds** (north to e. Minas Gerais and s. Bahia; illustrated) olive brown above, *blacker on head with buff streaking;* wings and tail dull rufous. *Throat whitish with dusky streaking* (especially on sides); below brown, breast with buffy whitish streaking, belly vaguely barred blackish. In **ne. and interior Brazil and n. Paraguay** has a less contrasting and browner crown, and paler and brighter generally. White-throated Woodcreeper is larger with a notably longer and heavier bill; its pure white throat is *un*streaked. Nearly sympatric race of Black-banded Woodcreeper is paler and more rufescent generally,

with a distinctly paler bill. Found singly or in pairs, sometimes with mixed flocks; seems to attend antswarms less often than other *Dendrocolaptes*. Song a fast series of sharp "whik" notes, sometimes fading toward end; often longer and usually shriller than Black-banded's.

Xiphocolaptes

Very large woodcreepers found widely in humid and montane forests; as with *Hylexetastes*, all species are allopatric. *Bills are massive, long, and somewhat decurved.*

White-throated Woodcreeper
Xiphocolaptes albicollis   PLATE 17(8)
28–29 cm (11–11½"). Uncommon in humid and montane forest, mature secondary woodland, and borders in *se. Brazil region* (north to Bahia). Mostly below 1500 m. *Long, stout, somewhat decurved bill black.* Above olivaceous brown, head blacker with whitish superciliary, supramalar, and streaking; wings and tail dull chestnut. *Throat pure white* bordered by a *blackish malar stripe;* below pale brownish, breast streaked whitish, belly barred blackish. Birds from **Bahia** paler. Planalto Woodcreeper has a shorter and less decurved bill, streaking on throat, no malar. Found singly and in pairs, most often not with mixed flocks. Regularly forages close to the ground, mainly on trunks but also sometimes on fallen logs. Often stolid and tame. Song, given at dawn and dusk (sometimes in near-darkness), a leisurely series of far-carrying, piercing notes, each slightly lower-pitched than its antecedent and preceded by a soft hiccuping, e.g., "mc-wheer, mc-wheer, mc-wheer, mc-wheer, mc-wheer"; often starts with a snarl. During day gives whining or snarling calls.

Strong-billed Woodcreeper
Xiphocolaptes promeropirhynchus   PLATE 17(9)
28–31.5 cm (11–12½"). Uncommon in montane forest and borders in Andes from n. Venezuela and Colombia to w. Bolivia (w. Santa Cruz), and locally in humid forest in Amazonia and the Guianas. To about 3100 m. Perhaps more than one species. *Massive, somewhat decurved bill,* dusky to horn (in **lowland** birds tending to be straighter, longer, and paler); iris brown to (in **lowland** birds) reddish. **Highland** birds (A) brown above with buffyish streaking on head, and *buffy whitish lores, postocular, and supramalar;* wings and tail rufous-chestnut. Throat

whitish *bordered by dusky malar stripe;* below brown, breast streaked buffyish, sometimes with some blackish barring on belly. **Lowland** (B) birds tend to be larger, have a less obvious postocular and supramalar, and are more rufescent generally. In most of its broad range this woodcreeper can be known on the basis of its *large size and heavy-set appearance.* In Andes, cf. rare Greater Scythebill. In lowlands most apt to be confused with much commoner Buff-throated Woodcreeper (smaller with a slighter bill, no dark submalar, and buffier throat). Cf. also Black-banded Woodcreeper. Forages at all levels though generally not too high; often alone, but also regularly accompanies mixed flocks. Regularly attends antswarms, there dominant over most other birds. Far-carrying song a series of 3–5 paired notes, each pair at a slightly lower pitch than the preceding, "pt-teeu, pt-teeu, pt-teeu, pt-teeu." At a distance the initial "pt" may be inaudible, and it all can be overlaid with soft squealing. Agitated birds give a weird, nasal squeal that can end in what sounds like a sneeze. Also: Mexico to w. Panama.

Moustached Woodcreeper
Xiphocolaptes falcirostris   PLATE 17(10)
28–29 cm (11–11½"). *Rare and local in deciduous and gallery forest and caatinga woodland in ne. Brazil* (e. Maranhão and Ceará to n. Minas Gerais). Mostly below 800 m. *Bill pale dusky to horn.* Uniform olivaceous brown with a *pale buff superciliary, supramalar, and throat* (but pale streaking is rather fine, even absent); wings and tail rufous-chestnut. In its restricted range there really is no similar woodcreeper. White-throated Woodcreeper (no known overlap) differs in its obviously black bill; its head is blacker with more pale streaking. Behavior much as in White-throated, as is voice (though Moustached notes are not so clearly bisyllabic).

Great Rufous Woodcreeper
Xiphocolaptes major   PLATE 18(1)
28–30.5 cm (11–12"). Uncommon in deciduous, gallery, and chaco woodland, sometimes venturing out to trees in adjacent cleared areas, in *n. and e. Bolivia* (west to Beni), *sw. Brazil, w. Paraguay, and n. Argentina* (south to Santiago del Estero and n. Córdoba). To 1500 m. *Impressively large* and *mainly rufous. Long, heavy, somewhat decurved bill grayish to horn-colored. Above mostly bright rufous,* paler and browner on head and with dusky lores. *Below somewhat paler rufous.* A few individuals show faint shaft streaking

on breast and faint dusky barring on belly. On account of its massive size (for a woodcreeper), not likely confused. Black-banded Woodcreeper is smaller with a blackish bill, streaked foreparts, etc. Though rather conspicuous, this species never seems to be numerous, and its territories are obviously large. Forages mainly by hitching up trunks and along larger limbs, but also drops to the ground where it hops clumsily and even rummages in leaf litter. Usually found singly or in pairs, less often in small, presumed family groups. Even more than other *Xiphocolaptes* it can seem quite fearless. Far-carrying song a series of double-stopped whistled notes, each pair dropping a little in pitch and interspersed with soft whining or chattered notes.

Scimitar-billed Woodcreeper
Drymornis bridgesii   PLATE 18(2)
30–31 cm (11¾–12¼"). *Uncommon in chaco woodland and scrub from w. Paraguay and adjacent Bolivia to w. Uruguay, extreme s. Brazil* (sw. Rio Grande do Sul), *and cen. Argentina* (south to n. Río Negro). To 600 m. *Very long and rather slender decurved bill mainly blackish;* iris amber. Head chestnut with *contrasting long white superciliary and malar stripe;* above sandy brown, wings duskier, rump and tail rufous. Throat white; *below pale brown with bold black-edged white streaks.* This spectacular, long-billed woodcreeper is unmistakable (but cf. Red-billed Scythebill). One of the signature birds of the chaco (eastward also in espinilho woodland), Scimitar-billed Woodcreepers forage mostly singly and in pairs, sometimes accompanying other species such as various furnariids. Not only do they feed on trunks and larger limbs, but they also frequently drop to the ground where they hop about with tail feathers splayed, probing into loose soil. They often appear awkward on the ground, but in fact can even run for short distances. Song a fast series of loud, shrieking notes that descends and ends in a jumble, e.g., "wreey! wreey! wreé-wreé-wree-wree-jehjehjeh." Reported sometimes to duet.

Campylorhamphus

A distinctive group, unmistakable and easy to recognize as a genus, though identifying to species can be a challenge. Scythebills are characterized by their unique, *strikingly long, deeply decurved bills,* but in other respects they are typical woodcreepers; note that young birds have shorter bills. Also note that (English names notwithstanding) *bill color cannot be used as a character separating most of them.* Scythebills range widely in humid and montane forests; only very locally are two species found together.

Greater Scythebill

Campylorhamphus pucherani PLATE 18(3)
29 cm (11½"); bill 6.5 cm (2½"). *Very rare and local* in montane forest and borders in *Andes from n. Colombia* (Boyacá) *to s. Peru* (Cuzco). Mostly 2000–2800 m. *The largest scythebill.* Bill mostly dull pinkish horn. *Uniform rufescent brown* with a *white superciliary and broad malar streak,* and faint narrow buff streaking on head and neck; wings and tail rufous. Other scythebills are smaller, have proportionately longer bills, and *lack* the conspicuous malar streak. None occurs at elevations as high as this species. Strong-billed Woodcreeper has a more massive and less curved bill and shows prominent breast streaking. An enigmatic bird, still poorly known. Solitary birds have been seen accompanying large mixed flocks, hitching up trunks of larger trees. Song a rather weak and nasal, ascending "ee-ee-ee-ee-ee-énh" (G. Rosenberg recording), very different from other scythebills.

Brown-billed Scythebill

Campylorhamphus pusillus PLATE 18(4)
24 cm (9½"); bill 6.5 cm (2½"). *Rare in lower and middle growth of foothill and lower montane forest from w. Colombia to n. Peru* (Amazonas). Mostly 600–2100 m, locally to 100 m in sw. Colombia and nw. Ecuador. Bill dull reddish brown to dusky-brown. Dark brown above, crown duskier and head narrowly streaked buff, back sparsely streaked dark buff; wings and tail chestnut. Throat buff; below dark brown, breast with dark buff streaking. Red-billed Scythebill is *very* similar, but differs in its paler plumage overall, bolder and whiter throat and streaking; even their bills are similar, though Brown-billed's tends to be shorter and browner. Brown-billed occurs strictly under humid conditions, whereas Red-billed routinely ranges in more deciduous habitats. Behavior much as in Red-billed; most frequently encountered when with a mixed flock. Sweet but variable song has a tremulous quality, a fast series of "tuwee" and "teeur" notes that either rise or fall in pitch and are intermixed with trills, e.g., "teeurrrrr, teeur-teeur-tutututututu." Also: Costa Rica and Panama.

Curve-billed Scythebill

Campylorhamphus procurvoides PLATE 18(5)
22.5–23 cm (8¾–9"); bill 6 cm (2¼"). Uncommon and local in lower and middle growth of terra firme forest from *se. Colombia to Amaz. Brazil and the Guianas.* To 900 m in Venezuela. More than one species perhaps involved. Closely resembles Red-billed Scythebill, with similar bill length and coloration. **North of Amazon** (illustrated), Curve-billed differs in having an *essentially unstreaked back* (but beware certain Red-billeds on which back streaking is faint or essentially lacking); its streaking below is finer. **South of Amazon** distinguishing them is even more problematic. Curve-billeds there are more boldly streaked below, and they show some back streaking; bill color is slightly darker and head more blackish. Many birds are probably not safely identified, and indeed what appear to be Red-billeds sometimes respond to Curve-billed tape recordings. Behavior as in Red-billed, but Curve-billed occurs primarily in terra firme, sometimes with bamboo understory (Red-billeds in Amazonia favor várzea and riparian habitats). Song (north of Amazon) similar to Red-billed, but tends to be more evenly pitched or ascending (not sliding down) and introduced by a longer note. At least at Alta Floresta, Brazil (and presumably west to Rio Madeira), where largely if not totally confined to bamboo, song very different, a sharp and rising "wreee?" followed by a more trilled "tr-r-r-r-r-r."

Red-billed Scythebill

Campylorhamphus trochilirostris PLATE 18(6)
24–28 cm (9½–11"); bill 6.5–9 cm (2½–3½"). *The most widespread scythebill,* locally fairly common from Colombia and Venezuela to n. Argentina (La Rioja and Santa Fé). Tends to avoid humid lowland forest, favoring more deciduous areas such as chaco and caatinga woodland, and gallery forest; in Amazonia ranges mainly in várzea and riparian habitats. Mostly below 1000 m; to 2000 m at least in Venezuela and w. Ecuador. *Bill reddish or reddish brown, in some birds quite bright.* In **most of range** (A) brown to rufescent brown above, somewhat duskier on crown; *head and back narrowly streaked buff to whitish* (boldness varying); wings and tail rufous-chestnut. Throat white to pale buff; below brown to rufescent brown with dark-edged buff streaking. In **e. Brazil** longer-billed and more olivaceous. Birds from **e. Bolivia and sw. Brazil to n. Argentina** (B) are larger, with even longer bill (culminating in more southern birds), and

paler and more rufescent with less streaking. In Amazonia, cf. *very* similar Curve-billed Scythebill. Brown-billed Scythebill favors more humid (often foothill or lower montane) situations; it is darker generally with less obvious (darker) buff streaking and a buffier (not whitish) throat. Red-billed Scythebills feed much like any other woodcreeper (despite their spectacular bill), hitching up trunks and along larger lateral branches at all levels, probing into bark crevices, moss, and epiphytic plants. They often accompany mixed flocks. Song a series of quite musical notes, variable in phraseology, e.g., a descending and gradually slowing series of upslurred notes, "tuwee-tuwee-toowa-tew-tew," or an ascending "twee-twee-twee-twi?-twi?"; sometimes adds a trill at start. In Venezuela the typical song is faster. Agitated birds give a loud semimusical chipper. Also: Panama.

Black-billed Scythebill

Campylorhamphus falcularius   PLATE 18(7)

25.5 cm (10"); bill 6.5 cm (2½"). Uncommon in lower and middle growth of humid forest and woodland in *se. Brazil region* (north to s. Bahia). To 1500 m, most numerous 500–1000 m. *Bill black.* Olivaceous brown above, head blackish and streaked whitish; wings and tail rufous-chestnut. Throat whitish; below pale olivaceous brown, breast sparsely streaked whitish. *The only scythebill in its range.* Behavior much as in Red-billed Scythebill. Its song, however, differs, a series of 8–12 raspy notes that descend slightly in pitch, e.g. "jreet, jreet, jreet, jreet, jree-jree-jree-jrew."

ANTBIRDS: THAMNOPHILIDAE

A large and diverse group of small to midsized insectivorous birds found widely in forested areas, with highest diversity in Amazonia, only a few species ranging up into the Andes or out into more open habitats. Unlike the antthrushes and antpittas, antbirds usually are sexually dimorphic. As they favor dense undergrowth and tend to be restless and fast-moving birds, many are hard to see clearly; plumage patterns are often distinctive, so if seen well they usually can be identified with confidence. Their vocalizations, often loud and readily recognized, frequently will attract attention. Nests are cup-shaped.

Cymbilaimus

Two *barred* antshrikes found in lower and middle growth of humid forests, larger and heavier-billed than the better-known *Thamnophilus.*

Fasciated Antshrike

Cymbilaimus lineatus   PLATE 19(1)
17–18 cm (6¾–7″). *Widespread and fairly common* in tangled borders and openings in humid forest and woodland from n. and w. Colombia to Amazonia and the Guianas. To about 1000 m. Heavy hooked bill; *iris red. ♂ black narrowly barred white* (crown solid black in some areas). ♀ *blackish above narrowly barred buff,* crown rufous-chestnut. *Below buff narrowly barred black.* Much more a forest bird than any of the barred *Thamnophilus* antshrikes. Cf. scarcer and larger Undulated Antshrike, also the range-restricted Bamboo Antshrike. Pairs forage deliberately at low and mid-levels, generally remaining in dense cover and not easy to see; they sometimes accompany mixed flocks. Oft-heard song a series of 4–8 steadily repeated, soft whistled notes with ventriloquial and melancholy quality, "cü-ü, cü-ü, cü-ü . . ." Calls include a complaining "teeeou," often slowly repeated or interspersed with a scold. Also: Honduras to Panama.

Bamboo Antshrike

Cymbilaimus sanctaemariae
17 cm (6¾″). *Uncommon and local in Guadua bamboo thickets in humid forest and borders in sw. Amazonia.* To 1400 m. Both sexes resemble

Fasciated Antshrike (and are often sympatric with that species), but differ in having a *considerably longer crest* and brown iris. ♂ further differs in having its white barring somewhat broader and sharper, ♀ in its *darker crown with black to rear* and *brighter buff underparts* with barring confined to sides and crissum. Usually in pairs and exceptionally sneaky, favoring dense mid-level tangles, generally in areas where bamboo growth is extensive and very infrequent in areas without it; sometimes accompanies mixed flocks. Far-carrying song very different from Fasciated, a fast series of sharp clear notes, "cheeyt, cheeyt, cheeyt, cheeyt . . ." (up to 12 or more cheeyts).

Frederickena

Two *very large* but *relatively short-tailed,* crested antshrikes with *massive bills* that range in undergrowth of Amazonian and Guianan forests.

Undulated Antshrike

Frederickena unduligera   PLATE 19(2)
23 cm (9″). *Rare in undergrowth of terra firme forest in w. Amazonia.* Mostly below 750 m. *Bill very heavy and hooked;* iris amber to orange-brown. *Somewhat crested.* **Adult ♂ in most of range** black *with narrow wavy grayish white barring;* throat and upper chest solid black. ♀ *above evenly barred rufous and black* (wavy pattern as in ♂); tail black barred gray. *Below rich rufous-buff with narrow wavy black barring.* In **sw. Amazonia,** ♂ has wider barring, ♀ has

narrower barring above and *much less barring below*. **Immature** ♂♂ (illustrated), black with variable amount of rufous-buff to white wavy barring, are seen relatively often. Larger than other sympatric antshrikes; does not occur with Black-throated. Cf. especially the smaller Fasciated Antshrike (not so dark, and with *red eyes* and *more even* and prominent barring). Skulking and shy, found singly or in pairs, favoring dense tangled growth (e.g., treefalls). Usually not with mixed flocks; occasionally attracted to swarms of army ants. Seems less vocal than many antbirds, with song a steadily repeated series of whistled notes, "uué, uué, uué . . ." usually 12–14 notes, higher-pitched and faster than Fasciated's. Singing birds may raise and lower crest as they sing. Call a nasal "squehhh"; also gives a drawn-out "keeeeeeeeyur," high-pitched and descending.

Black-throated Antshrike
Frederickena viridis   PLATE 19(3) PLATE 20(1)
20.5 cm (8″). *Rare in undergrowth of humid forest, mainly at borders and openings, in ne. South America.* Mostly below 500 m. *Bill very heavy and hooked; iris red. Somewhat crested.* ♂ *uniform plumbeous gray,* blacker on head and *blackest on throat and midchest.* ♀ (illustrated on Plate 20) *uniform rufous-chestnut above;* tail black barred gray. *Forehead, sides of head and neck, and underparts evenly barred grayish white and black.* Larger and heavier-billed than other sympatric antshrikes. Skulking behavior as in Undulated Antshrike. Song a steadily repeated series of clear, melancholy notes, e.g., "teeü, teeü, teeü, teeü . . ." (usually 9–11 teeüs), faster-paced than Fasciated Antshrike's, and series longer.

Mackenziaena

Two *spectacular, large and long-tailed* (but relatively small-billed) antshrikes that *skulk in forests of se. Brazil region.*

Tufted Antshrike
Mackenziaena severa   PLATE 19(4)
24 cm (9½″). Fairly common in dense undergrowth of humid forest, woodland, and borders in se. Brazil region (north to s. Bahia); *favors areas with Chusquea bamboo, and hardly ever found away from it.* To 1400 m. Iris rufous. *Prominently crested.* ♂ *uniform dark sooty gray,* blacker on head and throat. ♀ has *rufous crown;* above blackish *boldly banded rufous-buff,* tail dark. *Below uniformly barred buff and blackish.*

Large size combined with the crest (*which always is up*) renders confusion unlikely. ♀ Large-tailed Antshrike is *spotted* (not barred), lacks crest. Very skulking and shy, occurring in pairs that almost never emerge from bamboo thickets. Hardly ever with mixed flocks. Heard much more often than seen, with far-carrying song a series of 6–8 loud, sharp, and piercing whistled notes, "pseuw, pseeee, pseee, pseee, psee, psee." Call a nasal "squeeeyahh."

Large-tailed Antshrike
Mackenziaena leachii   PLATE 19(5)
26.5 cm (10½″). Uncommon in dense undergrowth of humid forest, woodland, and borders in se. Brazil region (north to s. Bahia). To 2100 m, northward mainly in mountains. *Tail very long.* ♂ *black with profuse small white spots on head, neck, and mantle.* ♀ has crown and neck black *spotted rufous;* above black with *obvious but sparse buff spots,* many chevron-shaped; tail blackish. Below black *thickly spotted buffy whitish.* A striking antshrike whose conspicuous spotting is unique. The arboreal Spot-backed Antshrike is also spotted above, but mainly white below. Behavior much as in Tufted Antshrike (can occur with that species), but Large-tailed is not quite as sneaky and is less tied to bamboo. Likewise heard more often than seen, with song a fast series of piercing whistled notes that rise in pitch before falling toward end; Tufted's song is shorter and slower. The nasal "squeeeyahh" call is much the same.

Spot-backed Antshrike
Hypoedaleus guttatus   PLATE 19(6)
20.5 cm (8″). *Uncommon to locally fairly common in subcanopy and borders of humid forest and woodland in se. Brazil region* (north to Minas Gerais and Espírito Santo). To 900 m. In **most of range** (illustrated) ♂ *black above profusely spotted white,* tail boldly banded white. *Below white,* chest feathers outlined black (looks spotted), flanks and crissum ochraceous. ♀ differs in buff-tinged spotting above, and underparts tinged ochraceous. **Northern** ♂♂ lack the ochre below, and ♀♀ have it only on belly. Boldly patterned, this *arboreal* antshrike is unlikely to be confused. It forages singly or in pairs, remaining in leafy cover and usually sluggish, not often seen unless singing. Sometimes accompanies mixed flocks, then occasionally coming to edge or lower. Distinctive song a fast musical trill that builds in strength and recalls a loud Long-billed Gnatwren. Calls include a

piercing "pyeeeeeeeeeyeuw" and an abrupt "chrrrt!"

Great Antshrike
Taraba major   PLATE 19(7) PLATE 20(2)
20 cm (8"). *Widespread and locally common in* thickets, clearings, secondary woodland, and forest borders from Colombia and Venezuela to n. Argentina (Córdoba and Entre Ríos); found in both humid and deciduous situations. Mostly below 1500 m. Heavy hooked bill; *iris bright red.* Slight shaggy crest. *Bicolored.* ♂ *black above with white edging on wing-coverts; tail with white banding in* **east** *and* **south.** *White below.* ♀ (illustrated on Plate 20) has *rufous replacing* ♂'s *black;* wings and tail *lack* white. Nearly unmistakable, no other antshrike is as boldly black (or rufous) and white. Ranges in pairs that hop through thick undergrowth where, though not all that shy, it usually remains hard to see. Generally does not accompany mixed flocks, but this seems more frequent southward. Heard much more often than seen. Song an accelerating series of hoots with a bouncing-ball effect, trogonlike aside from the snarled "nyaah" ending (occasionally left off). Also has various gravelly or rattled calls. Also: Mexico to Panama.

Giant Antshrike
Batara cinerea   PLATE 19(8)
30.5–35.5 cm (12½–14"). *Local and rare to uncommon in humid and montane forest lower growth and mid-levels on east slope of Andes from s. Bolivia* (w. Santa Cruz) *to nw. Argentina* (Tucumán), *and in se. Brazil region* (north to Espírito Santo). *A spectacular large and very long-tailed antshrike with a massive hooked bill.* **Andean birds** smaller. To 2500 m in Bolivia. *Crested.* ♂ *has black crown; above black boldly banded white. Below gray.* ♀ *has chestnut forecrown, black hindcrown* (less in **Santa Cruz, Bolivia**); *above broadly banded black and ochraceous.* Below buff to grayish buff. So much larger than other antbirds that confusion is improbable; it's almost the size of a Squirrel Cuckoo (*Piaya cayana*)! Despite their size, Giant Antshrikes are hard to see as they sneak about in thick growth, only rarely emerging from cover. They range in pairs, often well separated; infrequent with flocks. Prey consists not only of large insects but also small vertebrates such as lizards and frogs. Their resounding song carries far, but is ventriloquial and hard to track down to its source. A fast series of musical notes that starts with more of a trill, e.g., "trede-de-deh!-deh!-deh!-deh!-

deh!-deh!-deh!-deh!-deh!-ch-ch." Call similar to Tufted and Large-tailed Antshrikes.

White-bearded Antshrike
Biatas nigropectus   PLATE 20(3)
18 cm (7"). *Rare and local in lower and mid-levels of humid and lower montane forest in se. Brazil* (s. Minas Gerais to e. Santa Catarina) *and ne. Argentina* (Misiones). Mostly 500–1300 m. Stout bill; short, somewhat shaggy crest often raised. ♂ has *black crown* and *creamy nuchal collar connecting to white cheeks and chin;* above reddish brown, wings and tail rufous. *Large pectoral shield black,* belly brownish. ♀ has rich rufous crown and white superciliary; above otherwise like ♂ (*including nuchal collar*). Brownish below, with *no* black. Virtually unmistakable, but ♀ can be confused with similarly patterned White-collared Foliage-gleaner (which regularly occurs with it). Shows a strong predilection for bamboo, usually *Merostachys* spp.; rarely or never away from it. Seen singly and in pairs, often accompanying understory flocks. Song, given by both sexes, a series of 6–8 soft, querulous and high-pitched notes, "kiu-kiu-kiu-kiu-kiu-kiu-kiu," often accompanied by tail-pumping. Call a more nasal "caw," sometimes doubled.

Sakesphorus

A heterogeneous group, *some species with obvious crests* (among the most prominent of any of the antbirds), though a few species have none. They inhabit either *arid scrub and woodland* (the first four species) *or humid forest and borders* (Band-tailed and Glossy).

Black-crested Antshrike
Sakesphorus canadensis   PLATE 20(4)
16 cm (6¼"). *Locally common in lighter woodland, arid scrub, savannas, and mangroves from n. Colombia to the Guianas and n. Brazil, also very locally in Amazonia west to ne. Peru* (there favoring blackwater areas). To 800 m. *Conspicuous bushy crest.* ♂ in **most of range** (illustrated) has *head, throat, and midbreast black outlined by white;* back rufous brown, wings and tail blackish with conspicuous white markings; flanks grayish. In **n. Colombia and nw. Venezuela** face and throat speckled white; in **far s. Venezuela and n. Brazil** *much blacker generally.* ♀ lacks ♂'s black foreparts, has *rufous crown, sides of head whitish speckled black.* Above as in ♂; below buffy whitish, *throat and breast with blackish streaking*

fine to bold. No overlap with Collared Antshrike. Black-backed Antshrike is much less crested; its ♂ has a solid black head, nape, and back, and ♀ a blackish crown, rufous tail, etc. Usually in pairs and easy to see (for an antshrike), hopping in undergrowth and often in the semiopen; frequently wags its tail, especially when vocalizing. Sometimes with mixed flocks. Song an accelerating series of notes that rise in pitch, e.g., "woh, woh, woh-woh-wehwehwehwehwehweh?" ♀ often echoes.

Collared Antshrike

Sakesphorus bernardi   PLATE 20(5)
16.5–17 cm (6½–6¾"). *Common in lower growth of deciduous woodland and forest, secondary woodland, and desert scrub from sw. Ecuador* (Manabí) *to nw. Peru* (La Libertad). Mostly below 1500 m. *Expressive bushy crest.* In **most of range** (illustrated) ♂ has *head, throat, and midchest black,* some white scaling on face and throat; *nuchal collar, sides, and underparts contrasting white.* Back brown to rufous brown; wings dusky with white markings; tail black tipped white. ♀ *lacks* ♂'s black foreparts; crown rufous with buffyish forehead, *sides of head black speckled white, nuchal collar and underparts ochraceous buff.* Back rufous brown; wings dusky with buffyish markings; *tail rufous.* In **Marañón drainage,** ♂ has a splotchy chest and ♀ is whiter below. Engaging and distinctive in its small range. Cf. ♀ Chapman's Antshrike. Bold and easily observed, ranging in pairs that forage in lower and (less often) middle growth. They sometimes accompany loose mixed flocks. *Wags tail almost incessantly.* Song, given by both sexes (higher-pitched in ♀), a short fast series of well-enunciated notes with accented final note, recalling Western Slaty but more nasal. Frequent call a distinctive fast "ánk, ar-r-r-r-r-r"; also a repeated "anh."

Silvery-cheeked Antshrike

Sakesphorus cristatus   PLATE 20(6)
14.5 cm (5¾"). Fairly common but somewhat local in lower growth and borders of deciduous woodland and arid scrub in ne. *Brazil* (Ceará to n. Minas Gerais). Mostly 500–1200 m. *Crested.* ♂ has *foreface, crown, and bib black* contrasting with *silvery to grayish white cheeks, hindneck, and sides;* back rufous brown, *wings black with white markings, tail barred white.* ♀ pale rufous above, *brightest on crest and tail;* dusky *wings marked as in* ♂. Below buffy whitish. Dapper ♂ readily known in its limited range. ♀ resembles ♀ Rufous-winged Antshrike, though

that species has plain rufous wings. Usually in pairs, often skulking in thick growth and hard to see unless vocalizing. Song a gravelly "chup, chup, chup, chup, chuh-chuh-chuh-ch-ch-ch-chah"; resembles Rufous-winged Antshrike's song. Also has a musical "too" call repeated at intervals of 1–2 seconds.

Black-backed Antshrike

Sakesphorus melanonotus   PLATE 20(7)
15.5–16 cm (6–6¼"). *Uncommon, local, and inconspicuous in dense, viny lower growth of deciduous woodland and arid scrub in n. Colombia and n. Venezuela* (east to e. Miranda). Mostly below 500 m. Much less crested than the previous *Sakesphorus.* ♂ *mainly black above and on throat and breast* (ending in a point), wings and tail with conspicuous white markings. Sides of breast and belly white. ♀ has *blackish crown,* a buff eye-ring, and dull brownish upperparts; wings dusky with buffy whitish wing-bars, *tail rufous.* ♀ of more numerous Black-crested Antshrike has a rufous crown (and crest), mainly blackish tail, scaling on face and streaking on foreneck. Cf. also ♂ Northern White-fringed Antwren. Forages in pairs, generally independent of mixed flocks, moving about lethargically; rather shy and inconspicuous. Tail often lowered, then raised. A rather quiet bird, with song a slowly repeated "krrrrr"; also gives various nasal call notes.

Band-tailed Antshrike

Sakesphorus melanothorax   PLATE 20(8)
17 cm (6¾"). *Rare and apparently local in undergrowth of humid forest, especially around treefalls, in the Guianas and n. Brazil.* To 500 m. ♂ *uniform deep black;* wing-coverts with small white spots, *tail broadly tipped white.* ♀ *uniform bright rufous-chestnut above. Face, throat, and breast contrasting black,* becoming brownish gray on belly. Both sexes distinctive in range; no other lustrous black antbird shares ♂'s obvious white tail-tip, and the black-bibbed rufous ♀ is unique. Not well known. Apparently forages in pairs, usually not accompanying mixed flocks. Song a slow-paced, hollow "kaw, kaw, kaw, kaw, kü, kü," with a distinctive pair of emphasized notes at end.

Glossy Antshrike

Sakesphorus luctuosus   PLATE 20(9)
17.5 cm (7"). Locally fairly common in riparian thickets, lower growth of várzea woodland, and river islands in e. and cen. *Amaz. Brazil.* Below 300 m. *Long, shaggy crest often fully raised,* espe-

cially when singing. ♂ *uniform deep black,* scapulars edged white and outer tail feathers narrowly tipped white. ♀ similar but *sootier black* with contrasting *chestnut crown.* Distinctive in its range and *nonforest* habitat. Castelnau's Antshrike is larger, has no crest. Usually in pairs that hop methodically in viny tangles and bushes, sometimes mounting higher into trees; the tail often slowly wagged. Song a series of slow, measured, nasal notes that speed up toward end, "caw, caw, caw, caw-caw-caw-ca-ca-ca-cacaca."

Speckled Antshrike

Xenornis setifrons   PLATE 20(10)

16 cm (6¼"). *Rare (or overlooked) in undergrowth of humid and foothill forest in extreme nw. Colombia* (nw. Chocó). Mostly 350–800 m. Iris gray. ♂ *dark brown above streaked with tawny-buff;* wings with two buff bars, tail mostly blackish. *Face and underparts dark slaty gray.* ♀ like ♂ above but *streaking narrower. Throat streaked whitish and dusky;* breast and belly brown, *breast flammulated buff.* Uniquely patterned and colored, almost recalling a furnariid, though its behavior is typical of antshrikes. Known primarily from Panama, where it forages in pairs and often accompanies understory flocks (at least locally may even act as a leader for such flocks). Quiet and inconspicuous, perching vertically and sallying out after insect prey. Song a series of 5–6 high-pitched (for an antshrike) notes that gradually rise in pitch. Call a fast "chak-chak-chak." Also: e. Panama.

Thamnophilus

A complex genus whose members are found widely in forested and shrubby areas in both tropical and montane areas, though fewer species inhabit the latter. They have *hooked, often quite stout, bills.* There are two basic groups: *more or less barred species* (these favor scrubby habitats or forest edge), and *more or less gray species* (♀♀ rufescent or brown; most are in actual forest). They are vocal and are generally located by voice; though not particularly skulking, *Thamnophilus* favor densely vegetated habitats where they typically remain hard to see (especially without tape playback).

Blackish-gray Antshrike

Thamnophilus nigrocinereus   PLATE 21(1)

16.5–17.5 cm (6½–7"). Locally fairly common in undergrowth of gallery and riparian woodland (sometimes on islands), deciduous woodland, and humid forest borders from *s. Venezuela and e. Colombia to lower Amaz. Brazil. Below 400 m.* **Eastern** ♂ (A) slaty black above and on throat and breast with *obvious white fringing on wing-coverts* and a semiconcealed dorsal patch; belly grayer. **Northwestern** ♂ (south to n. Brazil) grayer on back and below. ♀ in **most of range** (A) rufescent above with *contrasting slaty head;* wings nearly plain. *Below uniform cinnamon-rufous.* In **cen. Amaz. Brazil south of Amazon** (B) *much darker generally.* ♂'s wing-covert fringing distinctive in range; White-shouldered Antshrike has wing *spots.* Limited or no overlap with Castelnau's Antshrike. ♀'s overall color pattern recalls ♀ Spot-winged and Caura Antbirds, but these show *buff spotting on wing-coverts.* Ranges in pairs, sometimes with small mixed flocks; usually slowly wags its tail. Distinctive song an accelerating, bouncing "kyoh, kyoh, kyoh, kyuh-kuh-kuh"; ♀ often chimes in with a faster and higher-pitched version. Most frequent calls a low-pitched, complaining "caw" and a growling "urr-r-r-r-r-r."

Castelnau's Antshrike

Thamnophilus cryptoleucus   PLATE 21(2)

16.5–17.5 cm (6½–7"). Locally fairly common in lower and middle growth of riparian forest and river islands *along Amazon River and its tributaries from around Manaus upstream to e. Ecuador and ne. Peru. Below 300 m.* ♂ *lustrous black* with semiconcealed white dorsal patch; *wing-coverts boldly fringed white.* ♀ as in ♂ but black duller, and *lacks white on wing.* ♂ not likely confused in its *river-based habitat;* it is much blacker than even the darkest race of Blackish-gray Antshrike (limited if any overlap). The all-black ♀ can be more confusing; cf. ♂ White-shouldered Antbird (with some bare blue skin around eye, white at bend of wing), ♂ Cocha Antshrike (only ne. Ecuador, in blackwater areas; bill smaller), and ♂ White-shouldered Antshrike (only in terra firme). Usually in pairs, foraging deliberately inside older stands of riparian woodland. Infrequently with mixed flocks. Often wags tail slowly. Song a short, fast, accelerating "keoh, keoh, kuh-kuh-kuhkuhkuhkuh" with nasal, bouncing-ball quality. Call a drawn-out "kawh," sometimes repeated; also a "kowah, kr-r-r-r."

Black Antshrike

Thamnophilus nigriceps   PLATE 21(3)

16 cm (6¼"). Fairly common in shrubby clearings and borders of humid woodland and forest, usually in swampy or damp areas, in *n. Colombia*

(south to n. Tolima). To 600 m. ♂ *uniform deep black.* ♀ has *head, neck, and underparts black streaked buffy whitish,* buffier on belly; *above contrasting rufous. No other black antbird in its range lacks white on wing;* ♀ unmistakable in range. Forages mostly as pairs, hopping methodically in thickets and lower growth, occasionally joining small mixed flocks. Song a nasal, slightly accelerating "kuok, kuok, kuok, kuok-ku-ku-ku-ku" (G. Rosenberg recording). Also: e. Panama.

Cocha Antshrike
Thamnophilus praecox   PLATE 21(4)
16 cm (6¼"). *Fairly common but very local in lower growth of várzea forest, mainly in thickets along blackwater streams, in ne. Ecuador.* Below 300 m. ♂ *uniform deep black;* underwing-coverts white. ♀ has *head, throat, and chest black. Above bright rufous; below cinnamon-rufous.* Both sexes resemble the *much commoner* White-shouldered Antbird, almost uncannily so, though that species is larger and has bare blue skin around eye; ♂ White-shouldered differs further in having white at bend of its wing, and their songs are utterly different. Usually in pairs, foraging in dense tangles where hard to see, and rarely noted except when vocalizing. Favors terrain that is flooded much of the year; often hops close to water. Generally not with mixed flocks. Song a hollow, evenly paced "ko-ko-ko-ko-ko-ko-ko-ko-ko-ko," given as it vibrates tail; ♀ sometimes follows with a higher-pitched, shorter version.

White-shouldered Antshrike
Thamnophilus aethiops   PLATE 21(5)
16 cm (6¼"). Uncommon and somewhat local in undergrowth of terra firme and foothill forest in *Amazonia and s. Venezuela,* and in *ne. Brazil* (Pernambuco and Alagoas). Mostly below 1300 m, a few higher on east slope of Andes. *Iris red* (♂) *or reddish brown* (♀). ♂ in **most of range** (A) dark gray, slightly paler below, with *crown blackish;* wing-coverts with small white spots (smallest in w. Amazonia). **Eastward** slightly less dark. In **e. Ecuador and adjacent Colombia** (B) *uniform lustrous black* with little or no wing-spotting. ♀ *uniform rufous-chestnut,* somewhat paler below. Plain-winged Antshrike is smaller with a slighter bill; except in west part of its range, its ♂♂ lack black on crown, and they *always show an unmarked wing;* ♀♀ are much less richly colored. Cf. also Blackish-gray Antshrike. An inconspicuous and rather skulking antshrike, always infrequently encountered; favors dense shady tangled areas. Seems quite sedentary, and rarely follows flocks for long. Distinctive song an

evenly paced, slow series of nasal notes, "anh . . . anh . . . anh . . . anh . . . anh," reminiscent of a Barred Forest Falcon (*Micrastur ruficollis*). Call a slurred "keyurr."

Barred Antshrike
Thamnophilus doliatus   PLATE 21(6)
16–16.5 cm (6¼–6½"). *Widespread and often common* in thickets and dense lower growth of borders, clearings, scrub, and even gardens from Colombia and Venezuela to n. Argentina (Santiago del Estero); occurs in both humid and arid regions. Mostly below 1500 m. Expressive loose crest. Iris yellow. ♂ *above black barred white;* crown black, often with semiconcealed white; sides of head and hindneck more streaked. *Below white barred black* (less barring in **southern birds,** which therefore look whiter). ♀ *bright cinnamon-rufous above; sides of head and hindneck streaked buffy whitish and black.* Below pale to ochraceous buff. Use this familiar antshrike as the basis of comparison with other scarcer or more localized "barred" antshrikes. Cf. especially Chapman's Antshrike (no overlap) and Bar-crested Antshrike (limited overlap). Barred is easily the best-known member of its genus, though even it can be frustratingly hard to see, remaining hidden in dense vegetation. Forages in pairs, hopping and peering about, in search of insects; generally not with mixed flocks. Heard much more often than seen, with song a fast, accelerating series of nasal notes, e.g., "wah-wah-wa-wa-wawawawawawawawa-wánh," with distinctive emphasized final note; singing ♂♂ usually raise their crest and spread their tail, and sometimes bob stiffly. ♀ may echo with her higher-pitched song. Both sexes also give several nasal, snarling calls. Also: Mexico to Panama.

Chapman's Antshrike
Thamnophilus zarumae
15.5 cm (6"). *Fairly common in undergrowth of montane woodland, forest borders, and clearings from sw. Ecuador* (El Oro and Loja) *to nw. Peru* (Lambayeque). Mostly 600–2000 m. *A pallid version of Barred Antshrike* (no overlap). ♂ has back mixed with gray and some buff on rump. *Black barring below faint and restricted to breast; flanks and lower belly buff.* ♀ has grayer sides of head and hindneck; it *shows faint dusky speckling on throat and breast.* The only antshrike sympatric with Chapman's is the Collared; ♂ Collared is very different, and ♀ shows bold wing markings (whereas wings are plain rufous in ♀ Chapman's). Behavior much as in Barred Antshrike. Song a fast series of at least 8–10 "chup" notes,

ending with several higher-pitched and more nasal notes, obviously two parts and *lacking* a final accented note. Calls include a nasal "nah."

Bar-crested Antshrike
Thamnophilus multistriatus   PLATE 21(7)
16.5 cm (6½"). Fairly common in shrubby thickets, clearings, gardens, and forest borders in *w. and n. Colombia* (south to Nariño) *and adjacent Venezuela* (Zulia). Mostly 900–2200 m. ♂ resembles ♂ Barred Antshrike but has *black crown barred with white.* ♀, on the other hand, resembles ♀ Lined Antshrike, though it appears whiter below because the black barring is narrower; Bar-crested and Lined do not overlap. Bar-crested and Barred more or less replace each other altitudinally, with *Bar-crested occurring on Andean slopes above range of Barred.* Behavior, including vocalizations, of the two very similar.

Rufous-winged Antshrike
Thamnophilus torquatus   PLATE 21(8)
14 cm (5½"). Uncommon in scrub, lighter woodland, and cerrado (locally even in sun-coffee plantations) in *e. and cen. Brazil* (south to São Paulo), *ne. Bolivia* (e. Santa Cruz), *and recently in ne. Paraguay.* To 1000 m. Iris orangy. ♂ has a *black crown,* grayish face and neck, brownish back, and *contrasting rufous-chestnut wings;* tail black with white barring. Below whitish with *black barring across breast.* ♀ like ♀ Rufous-capped Antshrike but somewhat buffier below. Rufous-winged is markedly smaller than Rufous-capped (whose crown is never black); the two species barely overlap in range. Behavior, including vocalizations, much as in that species.

Lined Antshrike
Thamnophilus tenuepunctatus   PLATE 21(9)
16–16.5 cm (6¼–6½"). Locally fairly common in undergrowth in shrubby clearings, secondary woodland, and montane forest borders in *foothills and on east slope of Andes from Colombia* (mainly Cundinamarca southward) *to n. Peru* (San Martín). Mostly 400–1400 m. Expressive loose crest. Iris yellow. ♂ *black above with narrow white barring;* crown solid black. *Below barred black and white.* ♀ *bright rufous-chestnut above* except *sides of head and hindneck streaked black and white.* *Below barred black and white;* flanks tinged buff. ♂ resembles ♂ Barred Antshrike, but blacker generally with narrower white barring above; ♀♀ of the two differ markedly. Lined and Barred occur together only marginally, if at all; Lined is more forest-based. Ranges in pairs that tend to skulk in thick vegetation, in some areas

regularly in bamboo. Only infrequently do they accompany mixed flocks. Oft-heard song, given by both sexes (♀ echoing ♂'s louder effort), a fast accelerating series of nasal notes with emphasized and lower-pitched final note, "hah-hah-ha-ha-hahahahahahaha-hánh"; resembles Barred's. Growling calls include a nasal "nah!"

Chestnut-backed Antshrike
Thamnophilus palliatus   PLATE 21(10)
16–16.5 cm (6¼–6½"). Locally fairly common in undergrowth in humid and montane forest borders (sometimes in *Chusquea* bamboo), regenerating clearings, and secondary woodland from *cen. Peru* (Huánuco) *to n. Bolivia and across s. Amaz. Brazil* (east to n. Maranhão), and in *e. Brazil* (Paraíba to Rio de Janeiro). Mostly 500–2300 m on east slope of Andes; in e. Brazil below 800 m. Iris yellow. ♂ has *black crown,* black and white streaks on sides of head and hindneck, and *rufous-chestnut upperparts. Below barred black and white.* ♀ like ♂, but *crown rufous-chestnut,* and whiter below (black barring narrower). No overlap with Lined Antshrike. ♂ Rufous-capped Antshrike has duller grayish or brownish back, lacks streaking on face and sides of neck. Behavior and vocalizations much as in Lined Antshrike; as with that species, more forest-based than Barred.

Rufous-capped Antshrike
Thamnophilus ruficapillus   PLATE 21(11)
16–16.5 cm (6¼–6½"). Locally fairly common in scrub, regenerating clearings, and forest borders in *Andes of n. Peru* (Cajamarca and Amazonas), *from s. Peru* (Cuzco) *to nw. Argentina* (Tucumán), and in *se. Brazil region* (north to Minas Gerais and Espírito Santo). 1500–2200 m in n. Peru; 1000–3100 m in s. Peru and Bolivia; to 2100 m in se. Brazil. Iris reddish. ♂ in **se. Brazil region** (A) reddish brown above, *brightest on crown and wings;* tail dusky, outer feathers barred white. Below whitish, *breast barred black.* In **s. Bolivia and nw. Argentina** similar but back grayer. In **s. Peru** (B) very different; *much darker generally* with *extensive black-and-white barring below.* Birds of **n. Peru** and in **w. Bolivia** intermediate. ♀ in **most of range** olivaceous gray to brown above with *rufous crown, wings,* and *tail;* below dingy whitish. In **Peru and w. Bolivia** (C) darker above and *rather bright fulvous below. Confusingly variable,* but *never shows the striking contrasts of Chestnut-backed and Lined Antshrikes.* Cf. Rufous-winged Antshrike. Usually in pairs, with unobtrusive behavior and thus rarely noticed except when singing; forages

independently of mixed flocks. Song a rather high-pitched and nasal "renh, renh, renh, reh-reh-reh-reh-rénh." Distinctive call a querulous "kwuuri?" (recalling a Smooth-billed Ani, *Crotophaga ani*).

Uniform Antshrike

Thamnophilus unicolor   PLATE 22(1)
15.5–16 cm (6–6¼"). Uncommon in lower growth of montane forest in *Andes from n. Colombia to s. Peru* (Cuzco). Mostly 700–2200 m. *Iris usually gray* (but sometimes brown). ♂ *uniform slaty gray*. ♀ rufous brown above with *contrasting gray face and chin*. Below ochraceous brown. Nothing really similar in its *montane range*. The smaller Plain-winged Antshrike occurs in Amaz. *lowlands,* overlapping only slightly. Note latter's reddish iris; in overlap area ♂ has a fairly obvious black crown. Cf. also White-streaked and Bicolored Antvireos. Ranges mainly in pairs, usually sluggish and inconspicuous; generally does not follow mixed flocks. Rather soft song a simple short series of nasal notes, "anh, anh, anh, anh" (sometimes 3 or 5 notes). Both sexes give a rattled "kar'r'r'r" call.

Upland Antshrike

Thamnophilus aroyae   PLATE 22(2)
14.5–15 cm (5¾–6"). Uncommon in shrubby lower growth at edge of montane forest and woodland on *east slope of Andes from extreme s. Peru* (Puno) *to w. Bolivia* (w. Santa Cruz). 600–1900 m. ♂ *slaty gray* with *white-edged wing-coverts* and *white-tipped tail feathers.* ♀ like ♀ Uniform Antshrike (no overlap, replacing that species southward) but paler generally with *more contrasting rufous crown* and *less contrasting grayish face.* Mainly occurs *above* range of other gray antshrikes. Sympatric ♂ White-shouldered Antshrikes are darker and have less white on wings and tail. ♀ Plain-winged Antshrike is smaller and drabber, lacking the ochraceous tone below. Cf. also Bolivian Slaty Antshrike (though both sexes have a whiter belly and much more white on wings and tail). Behavior as in Uniform Antshrike *though Upland favors edge much more.* Song a fairly fast series of 4–6 well-enunciated nasal notes, "wanh, wanh, wanh, wanh, wánh-ah."

Plain-winged Antshrike

Thamnophilus schistaceus   PLATE 22(3)
14 cm (5½"). Common (especially westward) in lower and middle growth in humid forest (mainly terra firme) of *w. and s. Amazonia.* To 1300 m along base of Andes. *Iris reddish brown to red.* ♂ in **most of range** (illustrated) uniform slaty gray, slightly paler below. In **se. Colombia, e. Ecuador, and ne. Peru** has *fairly contrasting black crown.* ♀ olivaceous brown above with *rufous crown* and grayish face. Below olivaceous buff. Both sexes (especially ♀♀) resemble Mouse-colored Antshrike, though latter's iris is gray to pale hazel; ♂ has browner wings with whitish tipping, ♀ is whiter below (less buffy). ♂ Cinereous Antshrike never shows black on crown. Ranges in pairs that hop in tangled lower and middle growth, somewhat lethargic and often permitting a close approach. They usually forage independently of mixed flocks. Oft-heard and far-carrying song (frequently given even at midday) a fast series of nasal notes, "anh-anh-anh-anh-anh-anh-anh-anhanh" with a distinctive doubled (and lower-pitched) final note; ♀ may chime in with a higher-pitched and briefer version. The number of notes and speed of delivery vary, causing potential confusion with Mouse-colored. Mainly ♂♂ also give a slow "arr . . . arr . . . arr . . ." with barking effect recalling a Barred Forest Falcon (*Micrastur ruficollis*).

Mouse-colored Antshrike

Thamnophilus murinus   PLATE 22(4)
14 cm (5½"). Fairly common (especially eastward) in lower and middle growth of terra firme forest from Amazonia to the Guianas. Mostly below 500 m (to 1300 m on tepui slopes). *Iris gray to pale hazel. Both sexes resemble Plain-winged Antshrike* (locally sympatric), but differ in eye color (reddish in Plain-winged). ♂ further differs in its *narrow white tips on wing-coverts* and whiter midbelly; in **most of range** (illustrated) has *decidedly brownish wings* (but not in **e. Ecuador, e. Peru, and w. Brazil**). ♀ differs slightly in its less rufous crown and *whiter midbelly* (much buffier in Plain-winged). Behavior similar to Plain-winged, and in some areas the two occur in close proximity; Mouse-colored favors better-drained hilly ridges, Plain-winged flatter, damper areas. Oft-heard song a series of nasal notes, "anh-anh-anh-anh-anhánh," with distinctive doubled final note; ♀ sometimes chimes in with a higher-pitched, briefer version. It resembles Plain-winged's but is shorter, higher-pitched, and slower; however, some songs, especially when bird is agitated, can be similar. Also has an abrupt *Micrastur*-like barking call.

Eastern Slaty Antshrike

*Thamnophilus punctatus**   PLATE 22(5)
14.5–15 cm (5¾–6"). *Locally common* in lower growth and borders of deciduous woodland,

forest borders, and scrub (often on sandy soil) from e. Colombia to n. Brazil and the Guianas; also in Marañón drainage of n. Peru and extreme s. Ecuador, where scarce and local. Mostly below 1100 m (to 1500 m on tepui slopes). *T. punctatus* is now split into multiple allospecies, all best distinguished by range and voice. ♂ gray above with black crown and mixed black and gray back; *wings black with bold white markings;* tail and uppertail-coverts black, *feathers tipped white. Gray below.* ♀ brownish above, crown more rufescent, with *wings and tail marked as in* ♂. Below buffy brownish. In **Peru and Ecuador** both sexes have a whiter belly and pale irides. *Eastern does not occur with other slaty antshrikes.* ♂ most likely confused with Amazonian Antshrike (often occur together); Amazonian's back is blacker, but the species are best distinguished through their very different ♀♀ (and voice, also very different). Usually in pairs, sometimes accompanying mixed flocks; *wags tail almost constantly* (not just when singing). Song a series of well-enunciated nasal notes that starts slowly and then accelerates, e.g., "anh-anh-anh-anh-ah-ah-ahahahahah."

Western Slaty Antshrike
Thamnophilus atrinucha
14.5–15 cm (5¾–6"). *Common and widespread* in lower growth of humid and semideciduous forest and woodland from *n. and w. Colombia to w. Ecuador and extreme nw. Peru* (Tumbes). Mostly below 1100 m. ♂ *gray above with black crown,* facial feathers edged black, giving a grizzled look; back mixed black and gray. Wings black *with bold white markings;* tail and uppertail-coverts black, feathers tipped white. *Below gray.* ♀ olive brown above with dull rufous crown, face grizzled as in ♂. Wings blackish *with bold buff markings;* tail brown, feathers tipped white. Below pale buffyish. No other similar *Thamnophilus* occurs *west of Andes.* Cf. ♂ Dusky Antbird. For an antbird, easy to observe, hopping deliberately in lower growth; often accompanies mixed understory flocks. Unlike Eastern Slaty, does *not* perpetually wag its tail. Oft-heard song a fast, rolling "anhanhanhanhanhanhanhánh" with a distinctive emphasized final note. Also: Guatemala to Panama.

Natterer's Slaty Antshrike
Thamnophilus stictocephalus *
14.5–15 cm (5¾–6"). Locally fairly common in lower growth of deciduous woodland and forest borders in *s. Amaz. Brazil and n. Bolivia* (n. Beni and ne. Santa Cruz). To 700 m. Closely re-

sembles Eastern Slaty Antshrike (formerly considered conspecific). Both sexes have a whitish belly. Behavior, including incessant tail-wagging, as in Eastern Slaty. Song a series of nasal notes, leisurely at the start, "anh, anh, anh, anh, anh, anh-anh-ah-ah-ah-ah-ah."

Bolivian Slaty Antshrike
Thamnophilus sticturus *
14.5–15 cm (5¾–6"). Locally fairly common in lower growth of deciduous woodland and forest borders in *n. and e. Bolivia* (Beni to Santa Cruz) *and adjacent sw. Brazil and extreme n. Paraguay.* 200–900 m. *Iris pale grayish.* Closely resembles Eastern Slaty Antshrike (formerly considered conspecific). Both sexes have a whitish belly. Behavior, including incessant tail-wagging, as in Eastern Slaty. Song higher-pitched and faster than Natterer's Slaty Antshrike, and ending in a rather trogonlike rattle.

Planalto Slaty Antshrike
Thamnophilus pelzelni *
14.5–15 cm (5¾–6"). Locally common in undergrowth of caatinga and gallery woodland in *e. Brazil* (south to Mato Grosso do Sul and São Paulo). To 1100 m. Iris grayish. Both sexes have a whitish belly. Behavior, including incessant tail-wagging, similar to Eastern Slaty Antshrike (formerly considered conspecific). Song relatively fast-paced, rising in pitch and ending in a rattle.

Sooretama Slaty Antshrike
Thamnophilus ambiguus *
14.5–15 cm (5¾–6"). Uncommon in undergrowth of humid forest and borders in *se. Brazil* (Bahia to Rio de Janeiro). Below 400 m. Closely resembles Eastern Slaty Antshrike (formerly considered conspecific). Behavior, including incessant tail-wagging, similar. Song resembles Planalto's, but slower at start.

Amazonian Antshrike
Thamnophilus amazonicus   PLATE 22(6)
14–15 cm (5½–6"). Locally fairly common in lower and middle growth in várzea and sandy-belt woodland (often in blackwater regions) from *Amazonia to the Guianas.* Mostly below 400 m. In **most of range** (A) ♂ closely resembles ♂ Eastern Slaty Antshrike but has blacker back. ♀ radically different from ♀ Eastern Slaty; *head, neck and underparts orange-rufous;* back and rump olive brown, wings and tail as in ♂. In **nw. Brazil, adjacent Venezuela and Colombia, and ne. Ecuador** (B) *smaller;* here ♂ has con-

color gray crown and less black on back, ♀ a pale buffyish belly. Cf. Eastern Slaty Antshrike, from which usually distinguished by ♀♀, also by voice; *Amazonian does not habitually wag tail.* Usually in pairs, often with small mixed flocks and regularly foraging higher (e.g., in viny tangles) than many other *Thamnophilus.* South of the Amazon routinely in bamboo thickets. Song a fast accelerating series of nasal trogonlike notes, fading at end, "kuh, kuh, kuh-kuh-kuh-kuhkuhkuh-kunh"; ♀ may echo with her higher-pitched version.

Acre Antshrike

Thamnophilus divisorius *
16.5–17 cm (6½–6¾"). Common but extremely local in undergrowth of stunted forest and woodland on *remote ridges in extreme w. Brazil* (Serra do Divisor in Acre). 500 m. A recently described species. ♂ *dark bluish gray* with somewhat blacker hood, wings, and tail. ♀ *bluish gray above, brownish orange below.* There is no similar antshrike in range. Forages in pairs, independently of mixed flocks, hopping through undergrowth. Song an accelerating series of notes, ending with a slightly louder and longer note, sometimes 2 notes. All information from B. M. Whitney, who discovered the species.

Streak-backed Antshrike

Thamnophilus insignis   PLATE 22(7)
16.5–17 cm (6½–6¾"). Uncommon in lower and middle growth of stunted montane forest and forest borders on *tepuis of s. Venezuela.* Mostly 1200–2000 m. Resembles Eastern Slaty and Amazonian Antshrikes, but *appreciably larger and darker; occurs at higher elevations.* ♂ has *crown black with obvious white to rear; back intermixed gray, black, and white* (with somewhat streaked effect); below uniform dark gray. ♀ *much like* ♂ but with *chestnut on crown* (white showing as in ♂). Ranges in pairs or family groups, often rather bold; sometimes accompanies small mixed flocks. Leisurely song a series of nasal notes, "anh, anh, anh, anh, anh-anh-anh-anh-ánh," recalling Barred Antshrike; wags tail downward with each note.

Variable Antshrike

Thamnophilus caerulescens   PLATE 22(8)
14.5 cm (5¾"). *Widespread and locally common* in lower growth of humid and montane forest and woodland, often at borders, and equally in rather humid or arid areas, from Andes of n. Peru (Amazonas) to nw. Argentina (La

Rioja), and east into e. Brazil and Uruguay. To about 2000 m in Brazil; mostly 1000–2500 m in Andes. *Aptly named; confusingly variable* (perhaps more than one species), but *both sexes can usually be recognized by the tawny color, at least on belly.* In **se. South America** (A) ♂ basically gray with black crown, black wings and tail with white markings, and *tawny on flanks and crissum.* In **ne. Brazil** tawny lacking; in **s. Bolivia and nw. Argentina** *tawny extends up over breast.* In **Peru** (B) ♂ *totally different, all black* except for white wing and tail markings; **w. Bolivia birds** are intermediate. ♀ olivaceous brown above, slatier on crown, wings and tail much as in ♂; throat and chest grayish olive, *lower underparts bright tawny.* In **ne. Brazil** grayer above with rufous crown, less white in wings, and uniform buff below (no tawny). Ne. Brazil birds (lacking tawny below) especially can be confused with Planalto Slaty Antshrike, though latter differs in its faster-paced song and near-constant tail-wagging. ♂'s simple song, basically similar across its vast range, a fairly fast repetition of "kaw" or "kow" notes, usually 5–7 of them; ♀'s version higher-pitched. In ne. Brazil, however, rather different (same species?), slower and more nasal with fewer notes.

Pearly Antshrike

Megastictus margaritatus   PLATE 22(9)
13.5–14 cm (5¼–5½"). *Rare and local (unaccountably so) in lower growth of terra firme forest in w. and cen. Amazonia.* To 400 m. Iris gray. ♂ *pure gray above; wings and tail black, coverts and tertial tips with very large round white spots, uppertail-coverts and tail feathers broadly tipped white.* Below somewhat paler gray. ♀ brown above, *wings and tail marked as in ♂, but spotting bright buff.* Below ochraceous-buff. No other antshrike has wing-covert spotting as large as the Pearly, and the tertial spotting is unique. Typically forages in pairs that most often are not associated with mixed flocks. Unmistakable, distinctly two-part song consists of several querulous notes followed by a fast series of lower-pitched and more raspy notes, e.g., "whee? whee? whee? jrr-jrr-jrr-jrr-jrr-jrr."

Spot-winged Antshrike

Pygiptila stellaris   PLATE 22(10)
13–13.5 cm (5–5¼"). Fairly common (less so eastward) in mid-levels and subcanopy of humid forest and woodland in *Amazonia,* also locally in the Guianas. Mostly below 500 m. *Bull-headed, with heavy bill; very short tail.* ♂ dark

gray above with *black crown;* wing-coverts with *small but conspicuous white spots.* Below somewhat paler gray. ♀ gray above, *wings contrasting rufescent* (but *no* spots). Face and underparts dull ochraceous. *The stocky, short-tailed shape of this arboreal antshrike is distinctive. Myrmotherula* antwrens are much smaller with slighter bills. Favors viny tangles, usually well above the ground; generally not hard to see. Often in pairs that regularly accompany mixed flocks. Distinctive song a sharp and penetrating trill followed by a whistled note, e.g., "t-t-t-t-t-t-treéuw," often given repeatedly. Calls include a sharp "chet!" sometimes followed by a "keeeuw."

Thamnomanes

Rather plain antshrikes found in *Amazonian forests,* both the Dusky-throated/Saturnine and Cinereous/Bluish-slate pairs of species replacing each other allopatrically. *Thamnomanes* often forage with understory flocks and resemble *Dysithamnus* antvireos (*which avoid Amazonia*) but are slightly longer-tailed and less chunky.

Dusky-throated Antshrike
Thamnomanes ardesiacus PLATE 23(1)
14 cm (5½"). Fairly common in lower growth of humid forest (mainly terra firme) from w. Amazonia to the Guianas, primarily *north of Amazon River.* In **n. Amaz. Brazil, s. Venezuela, and the Guianas** (A) ♂ *gray,* somewhat paler below, with *black throat* (can be hard to see); semiconcealed white dorsal patch at most small. ♂ from **se. Colombia to ne. Peru** (B) lacks black on throat (a trace may show). ♀ olive brown above, with dorsal patch small or absent; wings and tail more rufescent. Buffy ochraceous below, throat more whitish and breast mottled olivaceous. Cf. Saturnine Antshrike (only marginal overlap). Both sexes resemble respective sexes of widely sympatric Cinereous Antshrike; Cinereous is slightly larger, with longer tail, and tends to perch more vertically. ♂ Cinereous never shows black on throat and is more uniform below (belly not somewhat paler). Belly of ♀ Cinereous is usually a richer cinnamon-rufous. Dusky-throated occurs in pairs, less often in small groups; accompanies mixed flocks of understory birds, regularly with Cinereous or Bluish-slate Antshrikes. Tends to perch lower and less often in the open than Cinereous, gleaning from foliage and branches rather than sallying. Song a series of raspy but

musical notes that accelerates and rises in pitch before ending in a snarl, "grr, grr, grr-grr-gee-gee-gee-geegeegeegigigi? greeeyr." Calls include a sharp, raspy "greeyr" and a sneezing "tchif!"

Saturnine Antshrike
Thamnomanes saturninus PLATE 23(2)
14 cm (5½"). Fairly common in lower growth of humid forest (mainly terra firme) in *w. and cen. Amazonia, south of Amazon* River. To 600 m in Bolivia. *Closely resembles Dusky-throated Antshrike; distributions of the two do not normally overlap* as they replace each other across the Amazon. ♂ somewhat darker with *large black patch on throat and upper chest* and *large white dorsal patch* (the latter usually concealed except when bird is excited). ♀ very similar to ♀ Dusky-throated, but with whiter throat and *white dorsal patch.* ♂♂ of somewhat longer-tailed Cinereous and Bluish-slate Antshrikes have concolor gray throat. ♀ Bluish-slate distinctive, with contrasting gray and rufous-chestnut underparts. Behavior and voice as in Dusky-throated.

Bluish-slate Antshrike
Thamnomanes schistogynus PLATE 23(3)
14.5 cm (5¾"). Common in lower growth of humid forest and woodland in *sw. Amazonia.* Mostly below 800 m. ♂ *uniform dark bluish gray.* ♀ *bluish gray above.* Throat and chest bluish gray, *lower underparts contrasting rich rufous.* Both sexes have a large white dorsal patch, usually concealed except when excited. ♀ shows by far the most contrast below of any *Thamnomanes.* ♂ Saturnine and ♂ of sympatric Dusky-throated Antshrikes both have black throat. Ranges in pairs or small family groups, around which flocks of understory birds frequently coalesce; often acts as their sentinel. Usually perches erectly on horizontal limbs, scanning nearby foliage for prey, abruptly sallying out or pursuing insects flushed by another bird. Song starts slowly with several shrill whistled notes (almost with quality of a *Pipile* piping guan), then accelerates before ending in a bubbling trill, "whee? whee? whee-whee-whee-wheep-wheep-whipwhipwhip-p-p-p-p-p-p-prrrrr." Both sexes give a distinctive staccato "wer-chicory" or "wu-chidididik" call.

Cinereous Antshrike
Thamnomanes caesius PLATE 23(4)
14.5 cm (5¾"). Common in lower growth of humid forest (mainly terra firme) and woodland in *much of Amazonia* (though *not* in the south-

west) *and the Guianas,* and in *e. Brazil.* Mostly below 600 m. ♂ *uniform slaty gray.* ♀ olivaceous brown above with an indistinct buff eye-ring and lores; wings and tail more rufescent. Throat dull whitish, chest grayish olive; *lower underparts cinnamon-rufous* (brightest in west and north of Amazon; dullest in e. Brazil). ♂ resembles ♂ of western Dusky-throated Antshrike (with no black on throat) but has longer tail; often best recognized by accompanying ♀♀, its less vertical posture, and voice. ♂ Plain-winged Antshrike also superficially similar to ♂ Cinereous, but habits and voice differ markedly, and it has a reddish eye. Flock-leading behavior and voice as in Bluish-slate Antshrike.

Russet Antshrike
Thamnistes anabatinus   PLATE 23(5)
14.5–15 cm (5¾–6"). *An arboreal antshrike of foothill and lower montane forest and borders in Andes from w. Colombia and extreme sw. Venezuela* (s. Táchira) *to w. Bolivia* (Cochabamba). To 1700 m. *Heavy bill.* Sexes alike, aside from ♂'s semiconcealed orange-rufous dorsal patch. In **Peru and Bolivia** (illustrated) brown above, grayer on crown, with wings and tail rufous. *Superciliary, lower face, and underparts rather bright ochraceous,* belly duller. **Northern birds** are smaller with shorter tail; crown more rufous, back more olive, paler superciliary more yellowish, and more olivaceous below. Russet's color pattern is more reminiscent of a *Philydor* foliage-gleaner than most antshrikes; cf. especially Buff-fronted and Rufous-rumped, the two *Philydor* spp. most likely found with it (Russet's bill is heavier and tail shorter). Of the antshrikes, ♀ Spot-winged is the most similar, but it ranges in Amaz. lowlands with at most limited overlap with Russet. Ranges singly or in pairs, foraging higher than most other antshrikes, often accompanying mixed flocks; inspects branches, limbs, and vine tangles, peering at leaves and also sometimes probing clusters of dead leaves. Infrequently heard song a rather loud and penetrating "teeeu, tseu!-tseu!-tseu!-tseu!" Call a much thinner and more sibilant "wee-tsip." Also: Mexico to Panama.

Dysithamnus

Rather small, *chunky,* bull-headed antbirds with *fairly stout bills* that are found widely in undergrowth of forest, *mainly in the foothills or subtropics;* none ranges in Amazonia.

They resemble *Thamnomanes* but are stouter and shorter-tailed; most species are more strongly patterned.

Plain Antvireo
Dysithamnus mentalis   PLATE 23(6)
11.5–12 cm (4½–4¾"). *Widespread and often common* in lower growth of foothill and lower montane forest and woodland from Colombia and Venezuela to se. Brazil region (absent from Amazonia); locally (e.g., in w. Ecuador and Brazil) also in deciduous forest, and southward occurs widely in lowlands. Mostly below 1800 m. ♂ gray to olive grayish above, grayest on head and neck and with *dusky auriculars;* wing-coverts edged whitish. Below paler gray, throat and belly whiter. In **se. Brazil region** and **w. Ecuador** *belly pale yellow.* ♀ olive to olive brown above with *contrasting rufous crown, dusky auriculars,* and white eye-ring. Below mostly pale olive grayish, whiter on throat and midbelly. In **se. Brazil region** belly yellower. *No other similar antbird shows the contrasting dark auriculars;* rufous on crown of ♀ is also usually distinctive. *Myrmotherula* antwrens are smaller and more active, *Thamnophilus* antshrikes larger with longer tail. ♀ vaguely recalls Rufous-crowned and Gray-eyed Greenlets. Most often in pairs, foraging lethargically in lower growth where it peers about and gleans in foliage; regularly accompanies understory flocks, but also sometimes alone. Song, basically unvarying across its broad range, a short series of rapidly repeated semimusical notes that accelerates into a descending clipped roll. Both sexes give a soft "ert" call, sometimes interminably repeated; also has a more abrupt and nasal "nyah." Also: Mexico to Panama.

Spot-breasted Antvireo
Dysithamnus stictothorax   PLATE 23(7)
12.5 cm (5"). Locally fairly common in lower growth of humid and foothill forest and woodland in *se. Brazil region* (north to se. Bahia). To 1100 m. ♂ dusky-olive above, head more blackish with a *postocular stripe of white spots arching behind ear-coverts;* wing-coverts edged whitish. *Pale apricot yellow below with black spotting on breast.* ♀ similar but with *rufous crown.* Plain Antvireo is a bit smaller, *lacks* spotting below and on face. Behavior much like Plain Antvireo; the two sometimes even forage in the same flock. Loud and vigorous song an accelerating series of mellow musical notes, longer and less

run-together at end than Plain Antvireo's. Call a burry "wurr," often steadily repeated.

White-streaked Antvireo
Dysithamnus leucostictus   PLATE 23(8)
12.5 cm (5"). Uncommon and local in lower growth of montane forest on *east slope of Andes from s. Colombia* (s. Cundinamarca) *to extreme n. Peru* (Cordillera del Cóndor). 800–1900 m. ♂ slaty gray, blacker on chest, with semiconcealed white dorsal patch; wing-coverts tipped white. ♀ *rufous brown above, crown more rufescent. Face and underparts gray boldly streaked white.* White-streaked ♀ is more easily recognized than her plain blackish mate. Compared with the latter, ♂ Plain Antvireo is smaller and much less blackish (more gray); it has contrasting auriculars. Cf. rare Bicolored Antvireo (found mainly at higher elevations). ♂ Uniform Antshrike is larger and more uniform gray (showing no black) and has pale eyes. Usually found in pairs, gleaning methodically in lower growth, most often accompanying mixed flocks of understory birds. Song a well-enunciated and descending series of 7–8 soft whistled notes.

Venezuelan Antvireo
*Dysithamnus tucuyensis**
12.5 cm (5"). Uncommon in lower growth of montane forest and borders in *n. Venezuela* (Miranda to s. Lara, and locally in Falcón; n. Monagas). 800–1900 m. Resembles White-streaked Antvireo (with which formerly considered conspecific; no overlap). ♂ has slightly more white on its wing-coverts. ♀ somewhat paler, with wider pale streaking below. Behavior of the two similar. Song a series of whistled notes, longer and faster than White-streaked's.

Plumbeous Antvireo
Dysithamnus plumbeus   PLATE 23(9)
12.5 cm (5"). *Rare and local in undergrowth of humid forest in e. Brazil* (s. Bahia and e. Minas Gerais to n. Rio de Janeiro). Below 200 m. ♂ virtually identical to ♂ of geographically distant White-streaked Antvireo. ♀ very different, olive brown above, *wing-coverts tipped whitish.* Throat whitish, below dull grayish brown, lower belly more ochraceous. In its limited range cf. especially Cinereous Antshrike, both sexes of which *lack* wing markings; ♂ Cinereous lacks black on chest. *Myrmotherula* antwrens are smaller, etc. An inconspicuous bird that forages in pairs close to the ground, sometimes with small mixed flocks. Song a series of about 10 melancholy

whistled notes with an even, slow cadence, at first slightly rising, then fading.

Rufous-backed Antvireo
Dysithamnus xanthopterus   PLATE 23(10)
12.5 cm (5"). Uncommon in mid-levels and subcanopy of *montane forest in se. Brazil* (Rio de Janeiro to e. Paraná). 800–1700 m. ♂ has head and upper back gray, *face dotted white, imparting a grizzled effect; above bright rufous-chestnut.* Pale grayish below. ♀ similar but with *rufous crown;* facial spotting and underparts yellowish buff. Often forages higher above the ground than other antvireos; like them Rufous-backed often accompanies mixed flocks. Song a fast-paced series of 10–12 minor-keyed whistled notes, slightly descending or fading.

Spot-crowned Antvireo
Dysithamnus puncticeps   PLATE 23(11)
12 cm (4¾"). Uncommon in lower growth of humid forest in *w. Colombia and nw. Ecuador* (mainly Esmeraldas). To 1000 m. *Iris pale gray.* In **nw. Colombia** (illustrated) ♂ *gray above, crown black boldly spotted white;* wing-coverts tipped white. Whitish below, *throat and breast with gray streaking.* In **sw. Colombia and Ecuador** crown *streaked gray.* ♀ olive brown above, *crown streaked blackish and rufous;* wing-coverts tipped buff. *Below buffy ochraceous,* with *blurry streaking on throat and chest.* Plain Antvireo differs in its dark eye, dusky auriculars, plain crown that *lacks* spots or streaks, and *un*streaked underparts. Behavior much as in Plain Antvireo. Song a rather long series of soft notes with a faster and more even cadence than Plain Antvireo's. Also: Panama.

Bicolored Antvireo
Dysithamnus occidentalis   PLATE 23(12)
13.5 cm (5½"). *Rare and local* in undergrowth of montane forest and woodland on *west slope of Andes from sw. Colombia* (Cauca) *to extreme nw. Ecuador* (Carchi), *and on east slope in Ecuador and n. Peru* (recently found in Amazonas). 1500–2400 m. ♂ in **e. Ecuador** (illustrated) *uniform slaty,* slightly paler below, with semiconcealed white dorsal patch; wing-coverts with small white spots. ♀ has *chestnut crown, dark chestnut brown upperparts;* wing-coverts with small buffy whitish spots. *Sides of head and underparts dull gray,* lower belly browner. On **west slope,** ♂ somewhat blacker overall, ♀ with faint white shaft streaks below, especially on face. ♂ White-streaked Antvireo is smaller and shows greater contrast between black bib and

gray belly; ♀♀ of the two species are quite different, White-streaked being prominently streaked below. White-streaked tends to occur at lower elevations, though overlap occurs in e. Ecuador. Cf. also ♂ White-shouldered Antshrike (larger, with red iris). Found singly or in pairs, gleaning like other antvireos but usually moving independently of mixed flocks and remaining very low. Most frequent call a fast throaty scold "jeér-deer-dur," recalling a wood wren; also gives clear "peeu" calls, and (M. Lysinger recording) a fast ascending "pu-pu-pooyeh?"

Myrmotherula

A large complex of *small, rather short-tailed* antbirds, likely not a monophyletic group, *Myrmotherula* antwrens occur primarily in *humid lowland forests,* with a few ranging up into foothills and lower subtropics. A large number have very small ranges and are scarce. Many antwrens are hard to come to grips with; they move quickly, favor dense habitats, and often are quite shy. ♀♀ can be especially difficult. Some *Myrmotherula* are more or less arboreal; these species constitute the Pygmy/Streaked group. Most, however, range at lower levels inside forest; many of these form an important component of mixed understory flocks. It has recently been suggested that a suite of "dead-leaf-searching" species be separated in the genus *Epinecrophylla.*

Pygmy Antwren

Myrmotherula brachyura   PLATE 24(1)
8 cm (3¼"). *Fairly common and widespread* in mid-levels and subcanopy of humid forest from Amazonia to the Guianas. Mostly below 800 m. *Tiny,* with *very short* tail. ♂ above black streaked white, with white auriculars and semiconcealed dorsal patch; wings black with two white bars. *Throat white* bordered by *narrow black malar stripe; below pale yellow,* a few black streaks on sides. ♀ like ♂ but with buff streaking on crown and buff tinge to face and chest. Both sexes of Moustached Antwren (often sympatric) are blacker above with a wider, more obvious black malar stripe. Ranges in pairs, favoring viny tangles at forest edge and around treefalls; usually hard to see. Sometimes accompanies mixed flocks, but at least as often forages apart. Generally first located through its vocalizations. Song a fast and accelerating series of slightly husky chippers, "chree-chree-chree-chee-chee-

ee-ee-ee-ee-rrr," rising at first and then descending, ♀ sometimes chiming in with her shorter version. Both sexes give trilled contact calls.

Moustached Antwren

*Myrmotherula ignota**   PLATE 24(2)
8 cm (3¼"). Uncommon in subcanopy and borders of humid forest in *w. Colombia and nw. Ecuador* (primarily Esmeraldas), and mainly in terra firme in *w. Amazonia.* To 800 m. Trans-Andean birds were formerly considered a monotypic species (Griscom's Antwren, *M. ignota*) or a subspecies of Pygmy Antwren. When specifically separated, w. Amazon birds were called *M. obscura* (Short-billed Antwren). **Both sexes** resemble Pygmy Antwren but are *blacker above* (white streaking narrower, hence showing less) with a *wider and more conspicuous black malar stripe.* ♀ further differs in having *throat and chest buff* (but a few Pygmies can be nearly as buff). ♂ Sclater's Antwren is *yellow*-streaked above and does not look so black; ♀ Sclater's is yellower below (with *no* buff) and has black breast streaking. Habits much as in Pygmy Antwren, but even less inclined to accompany mixed flocks. The two species occur together in w. Amazonia, though Moustached is more confined to terra firme forest. Song resembles Pygmy but is slower and less run-together, with a somewhat more musical quality. Also: e. Panama.

Sclater's Antwren

Myrmotherula sclateri   PLATE 24(3)
8.5 cm (3¼"). Fairly common in subcanopy and borders of humid forest (mainly terra firme) in *s. Amazonia, south of Amazon.* To 550 m. ♂ *above black streaked pale yellow;* wings black with two white bars. *Below, including throat, pale yellow.* ♀ like ♂ above. *Below pale yellow* with *black streaking on breast* (usually prominent, but reduced in a few individuals). Pygmy and Moustached Antwrens are *white*-throated; Moustached is much blacker above. Yellow-throated Antwren occurs *north* of Amazon. Generally forages in pairs, like many other arboreal *Myrmotherula* favoring viny tangles; Sclater's differs, however, in regularly accompanying mixed flocks. Song very different from the Pygmy/Moustached pair, a slow series of 4–6 rather soft, melancholy "peeu" notes, recalling Fasciated Antshrike's louder song.

Yellow-throated Antwren

Myrmotherula ambigua
8.5 cm (3¼"). Uncommon in subcanopy and borders of humid forest in *limited area of nw.*

Amazonia (sw. Venezuela, nw. Brazil, and adjacent Colombia). Below 200 m. ♂ much like ♂ Pygmy Antwren but *below entirely pale yellow* (throat *not* white). ♀ *very* similar to ♀ Pygmy, but throat slightly yellower (not whitish) and crown streaking more rufescent. Sclater's Antwren occurs only *south* of Amazon. Both sexes of Moustached Antwren are much blacker above, and ♀ is buffier on foreneck. Behavior much as in Sclater's Antwren, as is its song, though the series of notes is longer (typically 10–15).

Amazonian Streaked Antwren
Myrmotherula multostriata *   PLATE 24(4)
9.5 cm (3¾"). *Fairly common in shrubby growth along margins of lakes and streams in much of Amazonia.* To 600 m in Bolivia, and called Streaked Antwren. Formerly considered conspecific with Guianan Streaked and Pacific Antwrens. ♂ *black above streaked with white,* semiconcealed dorsal patch white; wings black with two white bars. *White below streaked black.* ♀ has *crown and nape orange-rufous streaked black;* semiconcealed dorsal patch white; wings black with two white bars. *Below pale ochraceous with extensive fine black streaking,* belly whiter. Somewhat larger Stripe-chested Antwren occurs along eastern base of Andes, overlapping with Amazonian Streaked only very locally; its ♂ has streaking below only on breast, and ♀ is essentially *unstreaked* below. Usually in pairs or small groups that forage low in bushes and low trees close to water, often where vegetation is sometimes partially submerged. Most often not with flocks, though sometimes joined by a few other small antbirds. Vocalizations include a dry trill, "dr-r-r-r-r-r," lower-pitched than Guianan's, and a distinctive, more musical song, e.g., "pur-pur-peé-peé-peé-pur" with a slower cadence than in Guianan. Also gives a "chee-pu" contact note.

Guianan Streaked Antwren
Myrmotherula surinamensis *   PLATE 24(5)
9.5 cm (3¾"). Uncommon in shrubby lake and river margins from *s. Venezuela and the Guianas to n. Brazil.* To 400 m. Formerly considered conspecific with Amazonian Streaked and Pacific Antwrens. ♂ very similar to ♂ Amazonian Streaked. ♀ has *head and underparts bright orange-rufous,* with black streaking only on hindcrown, paler belly; dorsal patch and wings as in ♂. Does not overlap with Amazonian Streaked; cf. the range-restricted Klages's and Cherrie's Antwrens. Behavior much as in Amazonian Streaked. Song a dry trill, "dr-r-r-r-r-r-r-r"; call a lilting, more musical "pur-pur-pi-pi-pi-pi-pur."

Pacific Antwren
Myrmotherula pacifica *
9.5 cm (3¾"). Fairly common in shrubby humid forest and woodland borders and adjacent clearings and gardens in *w. Colombia and w. Ecuador* (south to Azuay). Mostly below 800 m. Formerly considered conspecific with Amazonian and Guianan Streaked Antwrens (both found *east* of Andes). Somewhat longer bill. ♂ resembles those species. ♀ has *head and neck bright orange-rufous* with blackish streaking on hindcrown, *plain ochraceous underparts;* otherwise as in ♀ Amazonian Streaked. Nothing really similar west of Andes. Compared with Amazonian and Guianan Streaked Antwrens, the Pacific is much more likely to forage higher above the ground and is nowhere near as tied to water. Song a fast, spritely chipper rising slightly in pitch, e.g., "chee-chee-chi-chich-ch-ch-ch-ch-ch-ch." Both sexes give "chee-pu" and "chee-cher" calls. Also: Panama.

Cherrie's Antwren
Myrmotherula cherriei   PLATE 24(6)
10 cm (4"). Locally not uncommon in shrubby gallery forest borders, várzea forest borders, and sandy-belt woodland in *e. Colombia, sw. Venezuela, and nw. Brazil;* also recently found very locally in ne. Peru (Río Tigre). Distribution closely tied to *blackwater regions,* often on white-sand soils. To 500 m. ♂ resembles slightly smaller Guianan and Amazonian Streaked Antwrens but *more coarsely streaked with black below,* and lacks white dorsal patch (latter is hard to ascertain in the field). ♀ has *entire crown black with narrow buffyish streaking* and *ground color of underparts uniform ochraceous* (belly not whiter). ♀ Guianan Streaked Antwren is *un*streaked below; ♀ Amazonian Streaked differs in its unstreaked rufous forecrown, whiter belly. Cf. also Klages's Antwren. Behavior much as in Guianan Streaked Antwren, but less tied to water's edge. Distinctive song a mechanical rattle, "trrrrrrrrrrrrrr"; also gives more musical "cheeyp" and "chee-du" calls.

Klages's Antwren
Myrmotherula klagesi
10 cm (4"). *Locally fairly common in canopy and borders of várzea and riparian forest in Amaz. Brazil along lower Rio Negro* (Anavilhanas Archipelago) *and lower Amazon* (downstream to near mouth of Rio Tapajós). Below 100 m. **Both sexes** closely resemble Cherrie's Antwren (and occur with it on the Anavilhanas). Both sexes of Cherrie's have coarser, more extensive black

streaking below (especially ♀♀), but *the two species are usually distinguished by their very different voices.* ♀ Amazonian Streaked Antwren is also very similar, but it has an *un*streaked rufous forecrown. Song a soft musical "cheedi-cheedi-cheedi..." similar to Stripe-chested Antwren but usually with fewer notes.

Stripe-chested Antwren
Myrmotherula longicauda   PLATE 24(7)
10 cm (4"). Uncommon in subcanopy and mid-levels of woodland and forest borders in *foothills on east slope of Andes from s. Colombia* (Putumayo) *to w. Bolivia* (Cochabamba), also *very* locally in ne. Peru lowlands. Mostly 400–1400 m. ♂ *black above streaked white;* wings black with two white bars. *Below white with black streaking on breast.* ♀ *black above streaked buff;* wings black with two buff bars. *Below ochraceous buff* (*no* streaking), belly white. Likely to be confused only with Amazonian Streaked Antwren, which ranges in w. Amaz. lowlands; both sexes of that species differ in being black-streaked below. Arboreal, remaining higher above the ground than Amazonian Streaked Antwren. Generally forages independently of mixed flocks. Distinctive song a fast repetition of a musical phrase, "chidu-chidu-chidu-chidu..." up to a dozen or so notes.

Plain-throated Antwren
Myrmotherula hauxwelli   PLATE 24(8)
10 cm (4"). Fairly common on or near ground in humid forest (mainly terra firme) in *w. and s. Amazonia.* To 600 m. *Tail short.* ♂ *uniform gray,* slightly paler below, with semiconcealed white dorsal patch. Wings blackish with *two bars and tipping on tertials white;* uppertail-coverts and tail feathers tipped white. ♀ olive brown above, dorsal patch as in ♂; *wings and tail as in ♂, but buff replacing white. Below cinnamon-rufous.* Other *Myrmotherula* do not habitually remain so close to the ground, and none shows the conspicuous tertial tipping. ♂ most resembles ♂ Scale-backed Antbird, but latter is larger, has scaly pattern on back. Most often found in pairs, hopping about near the ground, frequently near streams or swampy spots; usually not with mixed flocks. Foraging behavior reminiscent of *Hylophylax* antbirds, likewise often clinging to slender vertical stems. Song a series of 6–10 high-pitched and penetrating "tueee" notes that start slowly and increase in volume. Contact calls include a sharp "chik!"

Rufous-bellied Antwren
Myrmotherula guttata   PLATE 24(9)
9.5 cm (3¾"). Uncommon on or near ground in humid forest in *ne. South America.* To 700 m. *Tail short.* ♂ mostly gray above with semiconcealed white dorsal patch; wings blackish with *two bold ochraceous-buff bars and tertial tipping,* uppertail-coverts and tail also tipped. Below gray with *contrasting rufous belly.* ♀ olive brown above; *wings and tail as in ♂.* Below olivaceous brown with *rufous belly.* This attractive antwren is easily recognized by its bold wing markings and rufous belly. Behavior as in Plain-throated Antwren, as is song (though often longer, up to 10–15 notes).

Star-throated Antwren
Myrmotherula gularis   PLATE 24(10)
9.5 cm (3¾"). Uncommon on or near ground in humid and foothill forest in *se. Brazil* (s. Bahia to w. Paraná and n. Rio Grande do Sul). Mostly 300–1500 m. ♂ *rufescent brown above,* face grizzled gray; wing-coverts black with two buff bars. *Throat black spotted white;* below mostly gray. ♀ like ♂ but *throat spots larger. Does not range with the many other Myrmotherula that have throat spotting.* Cf. the various *Drymophila* (larger and longer-tailed) and smaller *Myrmeciza* antbirds found in se. Brazil. Ranges in pairs, foraging independently of mixed flocks; favors ravines and vicinity of streams. Song a series of up to about 12 penetrating and sibilant notes.

Checker-throated Antwren
Myrmotherula fulviventris   PLATE 24(11)
10 cm (4"). Fairly common in lower growth of humid forest and woodland in *w. Colombia and w. Ecuador* (south to El Oro). Mainly below 1100 m. *Iris pale.* ♂ olive brown above, wing-coverts black with *two buff-spotted bars,* tail rufescent. Throat checkered black and white, below fulvous brown. ♀ above like ♂. *Uniform fulvous brown below,* throat with a few dusky streaks. *The only Myrmotherula west of Andes with a checkered throat.* Obscure ♀ can be confusing; ♀ White-flanked Antwren is less uniform below, with whitish throat and white flanks, and ♀ Slaty Antwren has plain wings (*no* buff bars). Forages in pairs or small groups, usually with mixed understory flocks. Gleans in foliage and frequently inspects curled-up dead leaves, sometimes even crawling into them. Song a descending series of high-pitched notes, "seee, seee, seeu, seeu." Also: Honduras to Panama.

Stipple-throated Antwren

Myrmotherula haematonota PLATE 24(12)

11 cm (4¼"). Uncommon in undergrowth of humid forest (mainly terra firme) from *s. Venezuela to w. Amazonia.* Mostly below 500 m. Iris variable (can be dark, orangy, or grayish white). ♂ brown above with *rufous-chestnut back and rump;* wing-coverts blackish with two white-spotted bars. *Throat black spotted white;* face and underparts mostly gray. ♀ much like ♂ above, *including rufous-chestnut back* (faint in some birds); wing-coverts tipped buff. *Sides of head and underparts ochraceous, usually with some flammulation on throat.* The combination of checkered throat and rufous back is usually distinctive; White-eyed, Brown-bellied, and Yasuní Antwrens also have checkered throat but their back is brownish (except for White-eyeds in Amaz. Brazil between lower Rios Madeira and Tapajós, where it is rufous; these ♂♂ differ in their buff, not white, wing markings). Foothill Antwren occurs at higher elevations; it likewise lacks rufous on back. Rufous-tailed Antwren has *rufous* (not brown) tail. Ornate Antwren ♂♂, regardless of race, have a solid black throat; ♀♀ in most of range have throat black checkered white. Occurs in pairs or small groups, usually foraging with understory flocks. Gleans in foliage and on stems, also inspects curled-up dead leaves. Song a high-pitched and thin "zee-ee-ee-ee-ee-ee," recalling certain piculets.

Yasuní Antwren

*Myrmotherula fjeldsaai**

11 cm (4¼"). Uncommon and local in undergrowth of humid forest (mainly terra firme) in *e. Ecuador and extreme ne. Peru.* Below 250 m. A recently described species; also called Brown-backed Antwren. Iris grayish brown. ♂ *brown above; wing-coverts blackish tipped buff.* Throat black spotted white; face and underparts mostly gray. ♀ like ♀ Stipple-throated Antwren, differing in *brown back* (with *no* rufous) and *whitish throat with small black streaks.* Both sexes of Stipple-throated are rufous-backed; it and the Yasuní are not known to occur together (and ♀♀ would be hard to distinguish if they did). Cf. also Rufous-tailed Antwren. Habits similar to Stipple-throated, foraging usually below eye-level with mixed flocks, favoring dense tangled vegetation. Tends to forage lower than Rufous-tailed. Voice as in Stipple-throated.

Foothill Antwren

Myrmotherula spodionota PLATE 24(13)

11 cm (4¼"). Uncommon in lower growth of foothill forest on *east slope of Andes from s. Colombia* (e. Cauca) *to s. Peru* (Puno). 600–1425 m. Iris hazel to pale grayish. ♂ olivaceous gray above, browner on crown; wing-coverts dusky tipped whitish. *Throat black spotted white;* face and underparts mostly gray. ♀ olive brown above; wing-coverts dusky *tipped buff forming two spotted wing-bars. Sides of head and underparts ochraceous, usually some flammulation on throat.* Occurs *above* range of most similar *Myrmotherula;* here the only one with a checkered throat. Overlapping Ornate Antwrens have rufous on back and a contrasting black throat (solid in ♂, checkered in ♀). Cf. also ♀ Slaty Antwren. Behavior and voice much as in Stipple-throated Antwren.

Rufous-tailed Antwren

Myrmotherula erythrura PLATE 24(14)

11.5 cm (4½"). Uncommon in lower and middle growth of humid forest in *w. Amazonia.* Mostly below 700 m. Iris reddish to orange. Somewhat longer tail than other *Myrmotherula.* ♂ olive brown above with *rufous back* and *rufous tail;* wing-coverts tipped buffy whitish. *Throat and breast gray* (some have black throat scaling), belly olive brown. ♀ like ♂ above, with *rufous back and tail. Throat and breast bright ochraceous buff,* belly duller. ♂ is only comparable *Myrmotherula without* a contrasting throat patch. White-eyed Antwren in area of overlap has no rufous on back. ♀ Stipple-throated Antwren has *brown* (not rufous) tail. Usually in pairs or small groups, often accompanying understory flocks; regularly investigates curled-up dead leaves and tends to forage higher above the ground than many other *Myrmotherula.* Song a high-pitched "swee, swee-swi-swi-seeseeseer" with squeaky quality.

White-eyed Antwren

Myrmotherula leucophthalma PLATE 24(15)

11.5 cm (4½"). Uncommon in lower growth of humid forest in *s. Amazonia.* Mostly below 800 m. Iris usually (but not always) pale. ♂ in **most of range** (illustrated) olive brown above; wing-coverts black with two buff *bars* (effect *not* spotted), tail rufescent. *Throat checkered black and white; sides of head and breast gray,* belly brownish. ♀ above like ♂; *sides of head, throat, and underparts ochraceous buff.* In **Amaz. Bra-**

zil between lower Rios Madeira and Tapajós, both sexes have *lower back rufous*. ♂ Stipple-throated Antwren, also with a checkered throat, is rufous-backed (sympatric White-eyeds are brown-backed; Stipple-throated apparently does not occur in range of rufous-backed White-eyed). ♂ Foothill Antwren is gray (not brown) above and largely occurs *above* range of White-eyed. ♀ Stipple-throated and Foothill both have streaky throats (not unmarked ochraceous) and are duller below and less rufescent tail. Cf. also Ornate Antwren (especially in Brazil). Behavior as in Stipple-throated Antwren. Song similar, a descending "seee, seee, seeu, seeu."

Brown-bellied Antwren
Myrmotherula gutturalis   PLATE 24(16)
11 cm (4¼"). Fairly common in lower growth of humid forest in *ne. South America.* To 1000 m. ♂ olive brown above, wing-coverts with whitish dots. *Throat checkered black and white; sides of head and breast gray,* belly brownish. ♀ above like ♂ but with *dots on wing-coverts buff.* Below uniform ochraceous. Does not overlap with similar White-eyed Antwren (south of Amazon). ♂ *is only Myrmotherula in range with a checkered throat;* ♀ relatively featureless, brown overall with buff-tipped wing-coverts. ♀ Stipple-throated Antwren (may overlap in Venezuela) has a rufous back. Behavior as in Stipple-throated Antwren. Song a high-pitched chippered trill that slowly descends, "see-ee-ee-ee-ee-ee-eu-eu."

Ornate Antwren
Myrmotherula ornata   PLATE 25(1)
11 cm (4¼"). Locally fairly common in lower growth of humid forest in *much of w. and s. Amazonia, favoring viny tangles in treefalls and bamboo.* To 1200 m. *Variable.* ♂ in **se. Colombia, e. Ecuador, and ne. Peru** (A) gray above with *chestnut saddle;* wing-coverts blackish with two white-spotted bars. *Throat black, with contrasting gray underparts.* ♀ like ♂ above, but olive brown replaces gray. *Throat black checkered white,* below fulvous. In **e. Peru and Bolivia** (B), **both sexes** similar to (A) but *lacking the chestnut saddle.* In **s. Amaz. Brazil** (C), **both sexes** revert to *having a (somewhat smaller) chestnut saddle;* ♀ lacks the checkered throat and wing-spots buffy. Though smartly patterned, the variation can be confusing. The neatly demarcated throat patch in conjunction with the chestnut saddle is usually distinctive; ♂ Gray Antwren, *also* black-throated in Peru and Bolivia (where Ornate *lacks* the chestnut saddle), has white fringing

(not spotting) on wing-coverts. Except in Brazil, the contrasting checkered throat patch of ♀♀ distinctive; there, cf. ♀ Rufous-tailed (with longer, rufous tail) and ♀ White-eyed (which usually lacks rufous on back and, in any case, has fringed, not spotted, wing-coverts). Usually in pairs that often search for prey in hanging dead leaves; sometimes forages with mixed understory flocks. Song a thin, high-pitched chipper that fades away, "tsee-tsee-tsi-tsi-tsitsitsi."

Slaty Antwren
Myrmotherula schisticolor   PLATE 25(2)
11 cm (4¼"). *Fairly common in lower growth of foothill and lower montane forest and woodland in Andes from n. Venezuela to s. Peru* (Puno). Mostly 900–1800 m, lower (to nearly sea level) in w. Ecuador. ♂ *dark gray with a black bib from throat over median breast;* wing-coverts black with two white-spotted bars. ♀ in **most of range** (illustrated) *bluish gray above* with *only faintly marked wing-coverts.* Below rich ochraceous. In **w. Colombia and w. Ecuador** *grayish olive above,* duller buff below. Occurring at higher elevations than most other *Myrmotherula,* the Slaty can often be identified on that basis alone. Long-winged Antwren ♂ is notably paler gray (hence its black bib contrasts more), and it has distinctive whitish grizzling on lower face, but ♀♀ are hard to differentiate (behavioral characters help more). Cf. also Río Suno and Plain-winged Antwrens (both rare). ♀ Checker-throated Antwren has buff wing-bars. Usually in pairs, gleaning from foliage and tangled vegetation; often with mixed understory flocks. Infrequently heard song an upward-inflected "wheeyp," often doubled or tripled. More often gives a nasal complaining scold, e.g., "skeeeur" or "skeeuh-skur." Also: Mexico to Panama.

Río Suno Antwren
Myrmotherula sunensis   PLATE 25(3)
9 cm (3½"). *Rare and apparently local (perhaps just overlooked) in undergrowth of terra firme forest in w. Amazonia.* To 700 m. Resembles much more numerous Long-winged Antwren, but *smaller* and with *shorter tail.* ♂ *darker gray* (much as in ♂ Slaty), and *white tipping on wing-coverts gives a spotted effect* (not fringed or barred). ♀ *notably drab,* olive grayish above and dull ochraceous below. ♀ Long-winged Antwren is similar apart from the size difference. Behavior similar to Long-winged Antwren, though Río Suno mainly forages closer to the ground and often inspects dead leaves. Song a clear, high-

pitched "wi-weedy-weedy-weedy" or "s-weee, s-weee, s-weee."

White-flanked Antwren
Myrmotherula axillaris PLATE 25(4)
10–10.5 cm (4–4¼"). *Common and widespread* in lower and middle growth of humid forest and woodland from Colombia and Venezuela to Amazonia and the Guianas. Mostly below 1000 m. ♂ blackish to dark gray above; wing-coverts with two white-spotted bars, tail also tipped white. *Below blackish, axillars and long silky plumes on flanks white* (often conspicuous, but can be hidden beneath wings). ♀ olive to grayish brown above, wings and tail browner, wings with two faint buff-dotted bars. Ochraceous below with whiter throat and *white plumes on flanks* (sometimes concealed). *No other Myrmotherula shows the white on flanks.* ♀ Long-winged Antwren is more uniform ochraceous below. In e. Brazil, cf. Silvery-flanked and Narrow-billed Antwrens. Ranges in pairs and small groups, a frequent member of understory flocks. Gleans actively in foliage and viny tangles, often flicking its wings as if to expose its white flanks. Song a descending series of well-enunciated whistled notes, e.g., "pyii, pii, pee, pey, peh, puh, pu"; also a faster, run-together descending chipper. Oft-heard call a fast "chee-du" or "chee-doo." Also: Honduras to Panama.

Silvery-flanked Antwren
*Myrmotherula luctuosa** PLATE 25(5)
10–10.5 cm (4–4¼"). Fairly common in lower and middle growth of humid forest and woodland in e. Brazil (Pernambuco to Rio de Janeiro). To 800 m. Formerly considered conspecific with White-flanked Antwren. ♂ is gray-backed and differs from White-flanked in its *shorter flank plumes, which are silvery gray* (not white). ♀ resembles ♀ White-flanked Antwren. Behavior similar to White-flanked Antwren, but ♂'s song quite different, much burrier and not dropping in pitch, e.g., "drew-drew-drew, dree-dree-dree-dree-dree."

Salvadori's Antwren
Myrmotherula minor PLATE 25(6)
9 cm (3½"). *Uncommon and local in lower and middle growth of humid forest and woodland in se. Brazil* (Espírito Santo to e. Santa Catarina); old records from w. Amazonia are erroneous. To 800 m. ♂ rather pale gray with *small black bib* and *blackish subterminal tail-band;* wing-coverts black with two white-spotted bars. ♀ has

ashy gray crown and brownish olive back; wing-coverts dusky tipped buff. Throat whitish, *below olivaceous buff.* ♂ Silvery-flanked Antwren is darker gray with a much larger black bib and sil-very flanks; ♀ Silvery-flanked shows contrasting paler flanks. Both sexes of Band-tailed Antwren show an obvious white tail-tip. ♀ Unicolored Antwren is more uniform and rufescent above, lacking gray on crown. Behavior similar to other forest-interior *Myrmotherula.* Song a repeated clear "peeyr," often with interspersed chattered notes (B. M. Whitney recording).

Band-tailed Antwren
Myrmotherula urosticta PLATE 25(7)
9.5 cm (3¾"). *Uncommon and local in lower growth of humid forest in se. Brazil* (s. Bahia to n. Rio de Janeiro). To 200 m. ♂ gray with black bib on throat and midchest; wing-coverts black with two white-spotted bars, *tail black with white tip* (quite evident in field). ♀ rather pale gray above, wings with two whitish-spotted bars and *tail as in* ♂. Throat whitish, underparts creamy buff. White tail-band is *the* mark, not shared by any other *Myrmotherula* (a few show narrow white on tail-tip, but no more). Behavior much as other forest-interior *Myrmotherula.* Song a series of 3–6 nasal ascending notes, often preceded by several harsh "beer" calls (B. M. Whitney recording).

Long-winged Antwren
Myrmotherula longipennis PLATE 25(8)
11 cm (4¼"). Fairly common in lower and middle growth of terra firme forest from Amazonia to the Guianas. Mostly below 500 m (to over 900 m in Venezuela). ♂ gray, somewhat paler below, with *contrasting black bib on throat and median chest; lower face often shows whitish frosting.* Scapular fringes white; wing-coverts black with two white bars; tail narrowly tipped white. In **most of range,** ♀ *brown to rufescent above* with nearly unmarked wings; ochraceous below, **north of Amazon from the Guianas to e. Colombia and ne. Ecuador** with whitish belly. In **e. Peru and sw. Amaz. Brazil** (illustrated) olive grayish above; in **most of e. Ecuador and adjacent Peru** *bluish gray above.* Cf. much rarer Río Suno Antwren. Slaty Antwren occurs at higher elevations than Long-winged. Otherwise most apt to be confused with Gray Antwren. ♂ Gray differs in having wing-coverts gray with a black subterminal band and a smaller black bib (south of Amazon) or none at all (elsewhere). ♀♀ of the two can be *very* similar, especially in areas where

Gray is gray above, but ♀ Gray is purer blue-gray above. *Long-winged often flicks its wings* (like White-flanked Antwren), whereas *Gray often twitches its tail sideways.* Forages in pairs with mixed understory flocks, often with other antwrens; gleans from foliage, sometimes hovering. Songs vary. In the Guianas gives an evenly paced series of around 10 "chuwee" notes; in e. Ecuador and e. Peru a harsher, woodcreeperlike "chuwey-chuwey-chuwey-chuwee-chuwee-chuwee" increasing in strength and pitch; in s. Amaz. Brazil (B. M. Whitney recording) a faster rising "chwee-chwee-chwee-chwi-chwi?-chwi?"

Ihering's Antwren
Myrmotherula iheringi   PLATE 25(9)
9 cm (3½"). Uncommon in lower growth of humid forest from *se. Peru to s. Amaz. Brazil.* To 650 m. ♂ gray, somewhat paler below, with *contrasting black bib on throat and midbreast;* wing-coverts black with two white-spotted bars, *short tail all black.* ♀ *pale grayish above,* wing-coverts like ♂. Below dingy buff. ♂ Long-winged Antwren is larger and its longer tail is white-tipped; ♀ Long-winged's wings are much plainer and its underparts are less drab. Behavior as in many other understory *Myrmotherula* but has distinctive habit of *twitching tail sideways almost constantly.* In se. Peru largely restricted to stands of bamboo. Song a series of 10–15 fairly musical, penetrating "peeu" notes.

Rio de Janeiro Antwren
Myrmotherula fluminensis
9.5 cm (3¾"). *Known from only a single specimen taken in se. Brazil* (Rio de Janeiro below Serra dos Orgãos foothills). Taxonomic status uncertain. 20 m. ♂ resembles Ihering's Antwren (of Amazonia) but slightly larger with more slender bill and longer, more graduated tail; more bluish gray, and black bib larger. ♀ unknown. ♂ Salvadori's Antwren has a small black bib; ♂ Silvery-flanked Antwren is a little larger and has long gray flank plumes. Unknown in life.

Gray Antwren
Myrmotherula menetriesii   PLATE 25(10)
9.5 cm (3¾"). Fairly common in mid-levels and subcanopy of humid forest (mainly terra firme) from *Amazonia to the Guianas.* Mostly below 900 m. ♂ **north of Amazon** (A) gray, somewhat paler below chest; *wing-coverts gray with black subterminal band and white tips.* **South of Amazon** (B) differs in having black midthroat and upper chest. ♀ *gray to olive grayish above* with

wings nearly unmarked. Below bright ochraceous. ♂'s *fringed wing-coverts* are usually evident in the field. ♀ most apt to be confused with ♀ Long-winged Antwren (both have plain wings), though the latter is always less brightly colored below; northward, ♀ Long-winged differs more, there having a brown back and whiter belly. *Gray often twitches tail from side to side,* providing a useful behavioral clue distinguishing it from Long-winged (which flicks its wings). Behavior similar to other antwrens, though *Gray tends to forage higher above the ground than other non-streaked Myrmotherula,* sometimes even accompanying subcanopy flocks. Thin song a wavering series of 10–12 "ree" or "shree" notes that rise and accelerate, sometimes less shrill and more jacamarlike.

Leaden Antwren
Myrmotherula assimilis   PLATE 25(11)
9.5–10 cm (3¾–4"). *Fairly common in várzea woodland on islands in Amazon River and some major tributaries from ne. Peru to Brazil* (east to near mouth of Rio Tapajós) *and n. Bolivia* (Pando to n. Santa Cruz). Below 200 m. ♂ *gray,* somewhat paler below, with semiconcealed white dorsal patch; wings slaty with two white-fringed bars. ♀ pale olivaceous gray above, *wings with two buffyish bars.* Below mostly pale cinnamon-buff. Normally the *only gray Myrmotherula in its riverine habitat.* Gray Antwren is a bird of terra firme and has a different wing-covert pattern. Forages in pairs at varying levels, sometimes with loose mixed flocks; usually easy to observe. Song a fast musical trill that accelerates and descends slightly in pitch.

Unicolored Antwren
Myrmotherula unicolor   PLATE 25(12)
9.5 cm (3¾"). Uncommon and local in lower growth of humid forest and woodland in *se. Brazil* (Rio de Janeiro to ne. Rio Grande do Sul). Mostly below 200 m. ♂ *uniform gray,* usually with a *small* blackish throat patch. ♀ *uniform fulvous brown above, more rufescent on tail.* Throat whitish, underparts pale olivaceous buff. The only *Myrmotherula* in its range with *plain wing-coverts.* Note that wing markings are faint in ♀ Silvery-flanked (with silvery flank plumes) and ♀ Salvadori's (less rufescent above and with grayer crown). Behavior as in other forest-interior *Myrmotherula;* often accompanies the more numerous Silvery-flanked Antwren. Song a high-pitched "eeeeeu," often repeated and sometimes interspersed with mewing scolds.

Alagoas Antwren

Myrmotherula snowi

9.5 cm (3¾"). *Now very rare and local* in lower growth of humid forest and woodland in ne. Brazil (Alagoas, mainly from Murici). 400–550 m. Both sexes closely resemble Unicolored Antwren (no overlap; perhaps conspecific); bill slightly longer and tail shorter. ♀ is more rufescent below. Behavior much like Unicolored Antwren, as is its song, a clear "eeeu" repeated at a faster pace (recalling call of Blue-naped Chlorophonia).

Yungas Antwren

Myrmotherula grisea   PLATE 25(13)

10 cm (4"). Uncommon and local in lower and middle growth of humid forest and woodland in *foothills of w. Bolivia* (La Paz to w. Santa Cruz). 600–1650 m. ♂ *uniform gray* with *unmarked* wing-coverts. ♀ *olivaceous brown above*, wings and tail more rufescent, *wing-coverts nearly plain.* Below bright ochraceous. Mainly ranges at higher elevations than other *Myrmotherula*; does overlap, however, with Gray Antwren, ♂♂ of which have bold wing markings and a black bib, ♀♀ markedly grayer above. Behavior much like other forest-interior *Myrmotherula*; regularly inspects dead leaves. Song a fast series of 6–8 "peeyr" notes.

Plain-winged Antwren

Myrmotherula behni   PLATE 25(14)

9 cm (3½"). Uncommon and local in lower growth of foothill and lower montane forest on *tepuis of s. Venezuela region;* rare and very local on *east slope of Andes in Colombia* (w. Meta) *and Ecuador* (south to Zamora-Chinchipe). 800–1800 m. Short tail. ♂ *plain gray* with *contrasting black bib on throat and breast;* wing-coverts unmarked. ♀ *olivaceous brown above*, with *plain wing-coverts.* Drab olivaceous buff below, whiter on throat. Occurs above range of most other *Myrmotherula*. ♀ Slaty Antwren (also plain-winged) is less drab overall (grayer above, deeper ochraceous below); tail longer. Behavior much as in Slaty, gleaning in understory and often with mixed flocks. Calls include a soft "keeeur-kerr" (P. Coopmans recording) and a sharp "swee-ík" (N. K. Krabbe recording).

Terenura

Small, warblerlike antwrens that range in *canopy and subcanopy of tall humid or (two species) lower montane forest; ranges mainly* allopatric or parapatric. Though *Terenura* antwrens have long been considered rare birds, recent field work combined with increased awareness of their *frequently given songs* (all similar) has shown that they are more inconspicuous than actually rare.

Streak-capped Antwren

Terenura maculata   PLATE 26(1)

10 cm (4"). Fairly common in canopy and borders of humid forest and woodland in *se. Brazil region* (north to s. Bahia). To 1100 m. ♂ has *head and nape black narrowly streaked white, contrasting with bright rufous back;* wings blackish with two white bars. Below mainly white, sides with some black streaking, belly yellowish. ♀ like ♂ but streaking on head buffier, wing-coverts browner, and throat tinged buff. Nothing really similar in range, but cf. ♀ of larger Rufous-winged Antwren. Does not overlap with Orange-bellied Antwren. Usually seen in pairs, gleaning actively in foliage, showing strong preference for viny tangles; often accompanies mixed flocks. Song a simple dry trill; more distinctive is its rhythmic, syncopated call, a series of rapidly repeated "pichíchu" or "picheéya" phrases, sometimes appended to the song.

Orange-bellied Antwren

Terenura sicki   PLATE 26(2)

10 cm (4"). *Rare and now very local in canopy and borders of humid forest and woodland in ne. Brazil* (ne. Pernambuco and Alagoas). 300–700 m. ♂ *mostly black above*, crown and nape narrowly white-streaked; wings with two white bars. *Below pure white.* ♀ differs in having *back and rump rufous* and *underparts mostly rich orange-rufous.* Not likely confused in its tiny range; no overlap with closely related Streak-capped Antwren. Behavior and voice much as in that species; Orange-bellied gives a dry trill, though not as often as the rollicking phrase.

Ash-winged Antwren

Terenura spodioptila   PLATE 26(3)

10 cm (4"). Uncommon in canopy of humid forest from the *Guianas to ne. Ecuador and ne. Peru.* To 1100 m in Venezuela. ♂ has *black crown,* gray face and neck, and narrow whitish superciliary; *lower back and rump contrasting rufous;* wings and tail blackish, wings with two white bars. *Below grayish white.* ♀ brown above with rufescent crown and buffyish superciliary; *lower back and rump rufous;* wings and tail as in ♂.

Throat and breast buffy whitish, belly whiter. Chestnut-shouldered Antwren (no known overlap) is more olive above, with bolder wing-bars, and has yellow on flanks; *Ash-winged apparently occurs only north of Amazon/Río Napo.* Rufous-rumped Antwren of montane forests (likely no overlap) is much yellower below, has rufous only on rump. Several forest-canopy greenlets are somewhat similarly shaped, but all lack wing-bars. Found in pairs, almost invariably as they accompany a mixed canopy flock, gleaning energetically in foliage, often in outer branches and the semiopen, sometimes even turning upside down to inspect the underside of leaves. Song often heralds the approach of a canopy flock; a fast, high-pitched "tsii-tsii-tsi-tsi-titititititititi" accelerating into a chipper.

Chestnut-shouldered Antwren
Terenura humeralis

11 cm (4¼"). Uncommon in canopy of terra firme forest from *e. Ecuador to nw. Bolivia and sw. Amaz. Brazil.* To 600 m. Resembles Rufous-rumped Antwren (which is *more montane;* no known overlap). ♂ differs in its *chestnut shoulders* (not yellow), darker more rufous-chestnut lower back and rump, and *whitish midbelly* (pale yellow only on flanks and crissum). ♀ differs in slightly browner crown and deeper rufous rump; some individuals show rufous on shoulders. Ash-winged Antwren occurs only north of Río Napo/Amazon. The several greenlets occurring with it all *lack* wing-bars. Behavior and voice as in Rufous-rumped.

Rufous-rumped Antwren
Terenura callinota   PLATE 26(4)

11 cm (4¼"). Uncommon in canopy and borders of lower montane forest in *Andes from w. Venezuela* (w. Barinas) *to s. Peru* (Cuzco); also locally in *s. Guyana and s. Suriname.* Mostly 800–2000 m. ♂ has *black crown,* gray face and neck, and narrow whitish superciliary; back olive *with rufous lower back and rump;* wings dusky with *yellow shoulders,* wing-coverts black with two yellowish bars. Throat and chest pale grayish, *breast and belly pale yellow.* ♀ like ♂ but crown barely contrasting with olive back, superciliary faint, and no yellow on shoulders. The *montane* Rufous-rumped Antwren is not known to occur with any other *Terenura;* Yellow-rumped replaces it southward. Chestnut-shouldered Antwren is especially similar; ♂♂ differ principally in shoulder color (hard to see in the field). Ash-winged Antwren has whiter underparts (both

sexes). Overall shape and posture vaguely recall various small tyrannulets. Behavior and voice much as in Ash-winged Antwren. Also: Costa Rica and Panama.

Yellow-rumped Antwren
Terenura sharpei   PLATE 26(5)

11 cm (4¼"). Rare and local in canopy and borders of lower montane forest on *east slope of Andes from s. Peru* (Cuzco) *to w. Bolivia* (Cochabamba). 1000–1700 m. Resembles Rufous-rumped Antwren, *basically replacing that species southward* (the two overlap along the Manu road in Cuzco). ♂ differs in having *lower back and rump bright yellow;* ♀'s *lower back and rump yellowish olive.* Essentially unmistakable, *no other Terenura has yellow on rump.* Behavior and voice much as in Ash-winged Antwren.

Herpsilochmus

Rather long-tailed antwrens found primarily in the canopy of humid lowland forest, a few species up into lower montane areas or in more deciduous habitats. All are *boldly patterned,* but two groups of gray-and-white species are very similar and are *best distinguished by voice and range.* Singing birds vibrate their tail, a good way to spot them; ♀♀ often echo ♂ with shorter version of his song. All, especially the forest inhabitants, are heard far more often than seen.

Large-billed Antwren
Herpsilochmus longirostris   PLATE 26(6)

12.5 cm (5"). Locally fairly common in mid-levels and subcanopy of gallery and deciduous forest in *n. Bolivia* (west to La Paz) *and interior e. Brazil* (south to n. Paraná). 200–1000 m. Rather long bill. ♂ has black crown, long white superciliary, and black postocular line; back mottled gray, black, and white; wings and tail black, wings with two bold white bars, tail feathers broadly tipped white. Below white, *throat and breast with numerous gray streaky spots.* ♀ has *bright orange-rufous head and neck,* gray back; wings and tail as in ♂. *Below bright cinnamon-buff.* Larger than other sympatric *Herpsilochmus* (e.g., Black-capped). ♂ has distinctive spotting below; pretty ♀ unlikely confused. Forages mostly in pairs, gleaning in foliage and sometimes joining loose mixed flocks. Song a series of about 15 evenly chippered notes, slowing markedly toward end, e.g., "wh-chchchchchchchchchchchch-chu-chu."

Pectoral Antwren
Herpsilochmus pectoralis PLATE 26(7)

11.5 cm (4½"). *Rare and local in mid-levels and subcanopy of caatinga woodland, also locally in restinga scrub, in ne. Brazil* (n. Maranhão to e. Bahia). To 500 m. ♂ resembles ♂ of larger Black-capped Antwren (no overlap) but has an *obvious black crescent across chest.* ♀ has *rufous crown,* brownish olive back; wings and tail as in ♂. *Uniform buff below.* No other *Herpsilochmus* shares the chest crescent. ♀ Large-billed Antwren is much more brightly colored (and larger). Behavior much as in Large-billed Antwren. Song a fast series of 15–20 rising, nasal chippered notes that gradually become louder and more emphatic.

Ancient Antwren
Herpsilochmus gentryi* PLATE 26(8)

11.5 cm (4½"). Local in canopy and borders of terra firme forest in ne. Peru and extreme se. Ecuador. 100–200 m. A recently described species. ♂ has *crown black, long superciliary pale yellow,* black postocular line; back gray with large semiconcealed white dorsal patch; wings black with two bold white bars; tail black, feathers broadly white-tipped. *Below pale yellow,* sides and flanks clouded olive. ♀ like ♂ but *crown spotted with yellowish white* and *more ochraceous tinge to chest.* Both sexes of Dugand's Antwren (sympatric) are whitish below; their voices differ. Yellow-breasted Antwren occurs only on lower Andean slopes. Seems to favor areas with sandy soil. Often with mixed flocks. Song a series of chippered notes, slowing markedly and falling slightly, e.g., "chedidididi-di-di-deh-deh-deh."

Caatinga Antwren
Herpsilochmus sellowi* PLATE 26(9)

11 cm (4¼"). *Uncommon* in caatinga scrub and deciduous woodland borders, locally in restinga scrub, in ne. Brazil (south to n. Minas Gerais). Formerly named *H. pileatus* (that name is now assigned to a species of coastal Bahia). To 1000 m. Resembles Black-capped Antwren but smaller with *shorter tail.* ♂ differs further in having *grayer superciliary* and *reduced* postocular line. ♀'s black crown has faint grayish streaks; forehead and back grayer, and *entire face essentially plain buffy grayish* (overall effect quite different). Behavior of the two similar, though Caatinga tends to be less arboreal, foraging closer to the ground. Song also similar, but more a trill that is faster and more evenly paced, with gradual crescendo peaking in middle, then fading.

Black-capped Antwren
Herpsilochmus atricapillus PLATE 26(10)

12 cm (4¾"). *Fairly common and widespread* in deciduous, gallery, and caatinga woodland, and borders of more humid forest from *e. Bolivia* (north to Cochabamba, locally in La Paz) *and e. Brazil* (south to n. Paraná) *south to nw. Argentina* (Jujuy) *and e. Paraguay.* Locally to 1700 m in Bolivia. ♂ has *black crown and postocular line* and *long white superciliary,* gray back; wings and tail black, wings with two white bars, tail feathers broadly tipped white. Below grayish (**ne. Brazil**) or whitish (**remainder of range,** illustrated). ♀ has *buff forehead, crown black streaked white,* whitish superciliary, and grayish olive back; wings and tail as in ♂. Below whitish, breast tinged buff. Cf. similar but smaller and shorter-tailed Caatinga Antwren (widely sympatric), also very similar Bahia Antwren. Large-billed Antwren can occur with this smaller *Herpsilochmus* (usually not in exactly the same sites); its ♂ has obvious spotting below, and ♀ is very different. Forages in pairs, mainly in foliage and usually easy to observe; comes lower at edge. Song a chippered trill often introduced by a hiccuping note, accelerating into a louder sputter toward end.

Bahia Antwren
Herpsilochmus pileatus*

11 cm (4¼"). *Uncommon and very local in restinga woodland and coastal forest in e. Brazil* (se. Bahia). Below 50 m; had been called Pileated Antwren. Range and taxonomy recently clarified. Both sexes closely resemble Black-capped Antwren (no overlap), but have *notably shorter tail.* Song similar to Black-capped (K. J. Zimmer recording).

Creamy-bellied Antwren
Herpsilochmus motacilloides

12 cm (4¾"). Fairly common but local in canopy and borders of montane forest on *east slope of Andes in s. Peru* (Huánuco to Cuzco). Mostly 1000–2200 m. Resembles Black-capped Antwren (no overlap). Both sexes differ in having *black lores* (not white) and a *creamy yellowish midbelly.* Does not overlap with Ash-throated Antwren of n. Peru. Both sexes of Yellow-breasted Antwren are much yellower below; ♂'s crown is spotted, ♀'s rufous. Usually forages in pairs, often accompanying canopy mixed flocks. Song resembles Ash-throated Antwren but slightly faster and higher-pitched (T. Schulenberg recording).

Ash-throated Antwren
Herpsilochmus parkeri

12 cm (4¾"). Not uncommon but very local in canopy and mid-levels of montane forest and woodland on *east slope of Andes in n. Peru* (northeast of Jerillo and above Afluente in San Martín). 1300–1450 m. Resembles Black-capped Antwren (no overlap), but ♂ has black lores and *somewhat darker grayish underparts;* ♀, also black-lored, has *superciliary and foreneck buff* (not whitish), whiter belly and grayer flanks. Does not overlap with Creamy-bellied Antwren of s. Peru. Behavior as in other *Herpsilochmus.* Found primarily in areas with sandy soil. Song an accelerating, slightly descending and fading chippered trill preceded by several introductory notes.

Roraiman Antwren
Herpsilochmus roraimae   PLATE 26(11)

12.5 cm (5"). Locally fairly common in canopy and borders of montane forest on *tepuis of s. Venezuela region.* 900–2000 m. A *large, long-tailed Herpsilochmus.* ♂ has black crown and postocular line, long white superciliary; back gray *with ample black streaking;* wings and tail black, wings with bold white bars, tail feathers broadly white-tipped and *central feathers with at least five rows of spotlike bars.* Below whitish. ♀ has *black crown dotted white (no* rufous or buff); above otherwise much like ♂. Whitish below with *buff wash on breast.* Cf. other *Herpsilochmus,* all of which are smaller *and occur at lower elevations.* Typically forages in pairs high in canopy, often in outer foliage so not too hard to see; habitually accompanies mixed flocks. Song a fast staccato chipper of 15–20 notes, slowing slightly toward end.

Todd's Antwren
Herpsilochmus stictocephalus   PLATE 26(12)

11.5 cm (4½"). Uncommon in canopy and borders of humid forest in the *Guianas and adjacent Venezuela and Brazil.* To 600 m. ♂ has *black crown* with inconspicuous white streaks on forehead, *long white superciliary,* and black postocular line; back gray with large but usually concealed white dorsal patch; wings black with bold white bars; tail black, feathers broadly white-tipped and *central feathers with white spots on inner webs.* Below grayish white. ♀ has *crown black dotted white;* otherwise like ♂ above. Whitish below with *buff wash on breast.* ♂ *closely resembles* ♂ of slightly smaller Spot-tailed Antwren, and *the two species are often sympatric.* With a good view (infrequent!), note Spot-tailed's black forecrown

(*no* white streaking on forehead) and somewhat darker gray underparts. ♀ Spot-tailed has crown with rufous streaks, no buff wash on breast. They are usually best distinguished by voice. Roraiman Antwren is larger and longer-tailed, may not overlap (occurs at higher elevations). Behavior as in Roraiman, remaining high above the ground and hard to see well. Song a short series of descending chippered notes, higher-pitched and more musical than Spot-tailed's.

Spot-tailed Antwren
Herpsilochmus sticturus   PLATE 26(13)

11 cm (4¼"). Uncommon in canopy and borders of humid forest in *se. Venezuela, the Guianas, and extreme n. Brazil.* To 400 m. ♂ *closely* resembles ♂ Todd's Antwren; Spot-tailed is slightly smaller, has a solid black forecrown (*no* fine white streaks) and somewhat darker gray underparts. ♀ more distinctive, with *crown black with rufous-chestnut streaks* (not white-dotted) and dingy grayish white underparts (*no* buff on breast). Cf. also Spot-backed Antwren. Does not overlap with Dugand's Antwren. Behavior much like Roraiman Antwren; like Todd's, typically forages very high above the ground, sometimes both species in the same flock. Song an accelerating series of fast chippered notes that slightly drop in pitch, e.g., "ch, ch, ch-ch-chchchchchchch" (resembles Pygmy Antwren); Todd's song is higher-pitched.

Dugand's Antwren
Herpsilochmus dugandi

11 cm (4¼"). Uncommon in canopy and borders of terra firme forest in *se. Colombia, e. Ecuador, and ne. Peru.* Mostly below 450 m. ♂ closely resembles ♂ Spot-tailed Antwren (no overlap), but back plainer gray. ♀ resembles ♀ Spot-tailed but has *uniform rufous crown* (little or no black). *The only Herpsilochmus antwren in most of its low-land w. Amaz. range.* Cf. Ancient Antwren (with yellower underparts, etc.). Behavior much as in Roraiman Antwren. Hard to see well from the ground, but at times easier from the canopy observation platforms now at many tourist lodges. Song resembles Spot-tailed's.

Spot-backed Antwren
Herpsilochmus dorsimaculatus   PLATE 26(14)

11.5 cm (4½"). Fairly common in canopy and borders of humid forest in *s. Venezuela, e. Colombia, and nw. Brazil.* To 400 m. **Both sexes** resemble Spot-tailed Antwren (some overlap), but have *back broadly striped and spotted black, gray, and* *white.* ♀ differs further from ♀ Spot-tailed in its *obvious white crown spots* (on forecrown a few ochraceous; Spot-tailed's crown *streaked rufous-chestnut*), and buffier face, throat, and chest. Todd's Antwren is also very similar, but ♂'s back is smoother gray, and all the ♀'s crown spots are white (not ochraceous on forecrown). The larger Roraiman Antwren occurs on the tepuis. Song a fast and evenly paced chippered trill, fading and slightly dropping in pitch toward end.

Rufous-winged Antwren
Herpsilochmus rufimarginatus PLATE 26(15)
11–11.5 cm (4¼–4½"). *Local* (though *can be fairly common*) in canopy and borders of humid lowland and lower montane forest and woodland from Colombia and Venezuela to se. Brazil region. To 1400 m. More than one species perhaps involved. **Both sexes** have *distinctive rufous edging on flight feathers.* ♂ has *black crown*, long white superciliary, and black postocular line; back mixed gray and black; wings black with bold white bars and rufous edging; tail blackish, feathers broadly tipped white. *Below pale creamy yellowish,* throat whiter (except in **se. Brazil region,** where more uniform and brighter yellow below). ♀ like ♂ but *crown rufous-chestnut,* postocular line dusky, and back brownish olive. Cf. somewhat similar Yellow-breasted Antwren, which lacks rufous in wing, etc.; also Rufous-winged Tyrannulet (likewise with rufous in wing). Arboreal behavior similar to many other *Herpsilochmus,* though in many areas most frequent at edge, favoring viny tangles and sometimes even foraging in trees in clearings. Song a fast, descending, accelerating series of nasal, gravelly notes, "chu, chu, chu-chu-ch-ch-chchch-rrr-chúp" *with accented final note;* less gravelly in se. South America. Also: e. Panama.

Yellow-breasted Antwren
Herpsilochmus axillaris PLATE 26(16)
11.5 cm (4½"). Uncommon in canopy and borders of lower montane forest on *east slope of Andes from s. Colombia* (Caquetá) *to s. Peru* (Puno), also on their west slope in Colombia (Caldas to Cauca). 800–1800 m. ♂ has *crown black spotted with white,* long whitish superciliary, white-speckled ear-coverts; back grayish olive; wings black with bold white bars; tail blackish, feathers broadly tipped white. *Below pale yellow,* clouded olive on sides. ♀ like ♂, but *crown rufous* and above slightly browner. Both sexes of Rufous-winged Antwren show obvious rufous in wings. Behavior much as in

other forest-based *Herpsilochmus.* Song a simple chippered trill that descends evenly in pitch, "tree-ee-ee-ee-ee-ee-ew."

Drymophila

Attractive antbirds with *bold, often streaky patterns* and long graduated tails, *most diverse in se. Brazil region.* Many species are strongly tied to bamboo thickets. Drymophila forage in pairs, usually independently of mixed flocks, and have somewhat wrenlike behavior. All species have a semiconcealed white dorsal patch, most evident when the bird is excited. Often vocal, these antbirds are *rather skulking* and are most readily seen after tape playback.

Scaled Antbird
Drymophila squamata PLATE 27(1)
11.5 cm (4¾"). Fairly common in undergrowth of humid forest, borders, and woodland in e. Brazil (Alagoas to ne. Santa Catarina). Mostly below 600 m. ♂ black above with *bold white spotting* and superciliary; wings black with two white bars, *tail black with prominent white bands.* Below white spotted black. ♀ similarly patterned but browner above with *buff spotting, superciliary, and wing and tail markings.* Below whitish spotted dusky. The only Drymophila in its e. Brazil range with a boldly marked tail; *less montane than most.* Hops near the ground where, for a Drymophila, often quite easy to see; unusual among the Drymophila, shows no predilection for bamboo. Distinctive song a raspy "pseey-pseeu-pseeu-pseeu-psew," markedly descending; ♀ often chimes in. Also has a "dee-deét" call.

Ochre-rumped Antbird
Drymophila ochropyga PLATE 27(2)
13.5 cm (5¼"). Locally fairly common in bamboo-dominated undergrowth of montane forest, borders, and openings in se. Brazil (Bahia to e. Santa Catarina). Mostly 600–1500 m. ♂ has black crown and *white superciliary;* above brownish gray with *bright rufous lower back and rump;* wings black with two white bars, *tail blackish tipped white.* Throat and breast white streaked black, *flanks and crissum rufous.* ♀ with similar pattern but crown streaked, back less gray, and anterior underparts buffier. Dusky-tailed Antbird lacks rufous on rump and lower underparts; it shows no superciliary. Rufous-

tailed Antbird has obvious rufous tail and rufous on wings; Ochre-rumped usually occurs at elevations *below* Rufous-tailed. Song a nasal, snarling "jur, jeeeéu"; ♀ may add a series of descending notes.

Ferruginous Antbird
Drymophila ferruginea   PLATE 27(3)

14 cm (5½"). Fairly common in undergrowth of humid forest and secondary woodland in e. *Brazil* (s. Bahia to e. Santa Catarina). Mostly below 1200 m. Handsome ♂ has black crown and postocular stripe, *white superciliary;* above rufescent brown; wings and *tail black,* wings with two white bars, tail feathers tipped white. *Below uniform bright ferruginous.* ♀ similar but paler and less bright below, tail duskier, and forecrown streaked grayish. Cf. paler and less intensely colored Bertoni's Antbird; where they overlap, Ferruginous occurs at *lower* elevations. Behavior much like other *Drymophila,* though seems more apt to accompany mixed flocks. Distinctive song a simple "jee, jeweé?" sometimes followed by a few quick nasal notes.

Bertoni's Antbird
Drymophila rubricollis

14 cm (5½"). Fairly common in undergrowth of humid forest and borders in *se. Brazil region* (north to Rio de Janeiro), northward in Brazil at higher elevations than the similar Ferruginous Antbird (with some overlap). To 1800 m in Rio de Janeiro area; southward mostly below 1000 m. **Both sexes** are paler generally than Ferruginous, with *belly especially distinctly paler and duller* and *tail dusky* (not black). ♀ also has more rufescent forecrown. Behavior much as in Ferruginous. Song a series of 5–8 nasal notes that descend characteristically, "jeep, ji-ji-jee-jee-jew"; ♀ may add a higher-pitched version.

Rufous-tailed Antbird
Drymophila genei   PLATE 27(4)

14 cm (5½"). Fairly common in bamboo-dominated undergrowth of montane forest and woodland in *higher mountains of se. Brazil* (s. Espírito Santo to ne. São Paulo). Mostly 1200–2200 m. ♂ has black crown and *white superciliary;* brown above, back mixed with black, *becoming rufous on rump and entire tail; conspicuous rufous on flight feathers.* Below mainly whitish, *breast feathers scaled black.* ♀ brownish above, crown and neck streaked black and superciliary buffy whitish; *wings and tail as in* ♂. Below pale buffyish. No other *Drymophila* shows

the obvious rufous in wing, or the rufous tail. Ochre-rumped Antbird ranges mainly at lower elevations, lacks rufous in wing, has blackish tail. Behavior much like other *Drymophila,* though somewhat more apt to accompany mixed flocks. Distinctive song a snarling "pi-jzzz-jzzz-jzzz-jzzz-jzzz" on level pitch.

Dusky-tailed Antbird
Drymophila malura   PLATE 27(5)

14.5 cm (5¾"). Uncommon and local in undergrowth of humid forest and woodland in *se. Brazil region* (north to Minas Gerais). Mostly below 1400 m. ♂ has *head and neck black streaked pale gray;* back grayish olive; wings and *tail brownish,* wing-coverts blackish with two white bars. *Throat and breast white streaked black,* flanks and crissum dull brownish. ♀ like ♂ but more olivaceous brown generally, buffier below with breast streaking dusky. Ochre-rumped Antbird has an obvious superciliary, much rufous on rump and flanks, and blackish white-tipped tail. Rufous-tailed Antbird has rufous (not dusky) tail. Behavior much as in other *Drymophila;* usually not with mixed flocks. Song a series of accelerating chippered notes that descend, "chew, chew-chee-chee-chi-chi-chch-chchchch."

Striated Antbird
Drymophila devillei   PLATE 27(6)

13.5–14 cm (5¼–5½"). Locally fairly common, *but strictly confined to stands of Guadua bamboo,* in humid forest of *sw. Amazonia;* rare in ne. Ecuador and se. Colombia. To 1300 m in Peru. Possibly more than one species involved. Long tail. In **most of range,** ♂ has *head, neck, and back streaked black and white* and *rufous rump;* wing-coverts black with two white bars; tail blackish with *large white spots on middle feathers.* White below with lateral black chest streaking, flanks and crissum bright rufous. ♀ like ♂ but streaked buff and black above, and buff-tinged below. In **cen. Amaz. Brazil, both sexes** are deeper buff below. *The only Drymophila in Amazonia,* but could overlap with larger, longer-tailed, and more montane Long-tailed Antbird along eastern base of Andes. The chunkier and much shorter-tailed Warbling Antbird is less streaked above, lacks rufous on rump. Ranges in pairs or small groups, hopping in lower growth (sometimes higher) and gleaning from foliage and bamboo nodes. Oft-heard song a series of 4–5 wheezy "dzzrrip" notes, the last ones so fast as to be almost a trill; ♀ sometimes echoes with a softer, shorter version.

Long-tailed Antbird
Drymophila caudata   PLATE 27(7)

15 cm (6"). Locally fairly common in bamboo-dominated undergrowth and borders of *montane forest in Andes from n. Venezuela to w. Bolivia* (La Paz). Mostly 1500–2600 m, locally lower. A *long-tailed, profusely streaked* antbird, ♂ has *head and back streaked black and white,* with *bright rufous rump;* wing-coverts black with two white-spotted bars; tail dusky, feathers white-tipped. *Throat and breast white streaked black, flanks and crissum bright rufous.* ♀ patterned much the same, but *streaking above black and cinnamon-buff* and tinged buff below. *The only Drymophila in its Andean range;* cf. Striated Antbird of Amaz. lowlands (may overlap). Warbling Antbird (also of lowlands) is markedly chunkier, with shorter tail. Forages in pairs, hopping in dense lower growth where often hard to locate except through their frequent vocalizing. Usually not with mixed flocks. Song a distinctive raspy "cheeyt-cheeyt, wheeyz-wheeyz-wheeyz"; in n. Venezuela the introductory notes are clearer and less wheezy. ♀ may chime in with a few "cheet" calls.

Formicivora

Attractive, fairly long-tailed antwrens found across South America in *semiopen habitats or edge situations.* ♂♂ are unusual in being darker below than they are above. ♂♂ of most species have a *distinctive fringe of white from the brow down onto sides,* with the first and last species in our sequence being atypical. The recently discovered Marsh Antwren was described in the new genus *Stymphalornis,* but this is very close to *Formicivora.*

Narrow-billed Antwren
Formicivora iheringi   PLATE 27(8)

11.5 cm (4½"). Rare to uncommon and very local in mid-levels of deciduous forest and woodland in *interior e. Brazil* (Bahia to ne. Minas Gerais). 500–900 m. ♂ *dark gray above;* wings blackish with two white bars, tail feathers narrowly white-tipped. *Throat and midbreast black, flanks white* (sometimes concealed by wings). ♀ grayish brown above, rufescent on uppertail-coverts; wings and tail browner, wings with two faint buff-dotted bars. Ochraceous below, throat and flanks whiter. Though longer-tailed, both sexes bear an uncanny resemblance to White-flanked and Silvery-flanked Antwrens; Narrow-billed is

not known to overlap with either, though Silvery-flanked comes close. Arboreal, typically in pairs some 3–8 m above the ground; often with small mixed flocks. Foraging birds glean in foliage, sometimes pumping their tail. Song a series of 7–14 fairly musical, syncopated "peer" notes; ♀ may add a softer version.

Southern White-fringed Antwren
*Formicivora grisea**   PLATE 27(9)

12–12.5 cm (4¾–5"). Fairly common in arid scrub, low shrubby woodland and regenerating clearings, and mangroves from the *Guianas and sw. Venezuela (Amazonas) to Amaz. and e. Brazil and ne. Bolivia* (ne. Santa Cruz); favors areas with sandy soil. Mostly below 1000 m. Formerly included the next species. ♂ *grayish brown above* with *white superciliary extending as stripe down neck and sides to flanks* (where especially wide); wings blackish with white bar and spotting on coverts; tail feathers broadly white-tipped. *Below otherwise black.* ♀ like ♂ above but with merely the superciliary white. *Below cinnamon-buff,* throat whiter. Cf. Northern White-fringed Antwren (no overlap, though they come close in Venezuela). ♂ Black-bellied Antwren has a less conspicuous fringe on lower underparts; ♀♀ very different. Generally forages in pairs, hopping methodically and gleaning in foliage; often swivels its partially spread tail from side to side. Usually remains in thick cover and thus, though not shy, often hard to see without tape playback. Song a repeated sharp, penetrating "chup-chup-chup . . ." (up to 20 or more such notes), sometimes varied to "chedep. . . ."

Northern White-fringed Antwren
*Formicivora intermedia**

12–12.5 cm (4¾–5"). Locally common in shrubby arid woodland and forest, gallery woodland, and mangroves in *n. Colombia and n. Venezuela* (mainly north of Río Orinoco). Mostly below 1000 m. Formerly considered conspecific with previous species. ♂ resembles ♂ Southern White-fringed Antwren, though in **Río Orinoco drainage** more rufescent above. ♀♀ vary. In **Colombia** (except Santa Marta area) similar to ♀ Southern White-fringed but *paler creamy buff below.* **Elsewhere** very different below; *whitish with dusky or black streaking or mottling on breast.* Distinctive in range, *occurring with no other Formicivora.* Behavior much as in Southern White-fringed. Song markedly different, a mellow "tu" or "tu-du" in varying patterns and often long continued or becoming a trill. Also: e. Panama (Pearl Islands).

Rusty-backed Antwren
Formicivora rufa PLATE 27(10)
12.5 cm (5"). Locally fairly common in low shrubby areas, cerrado, and gallery woodland mainly in *interior and e. Brazil and n. Bolivia;* local in e. Peru and lower Amaz. Brazil. To 1450 m in s. Peru. ♂ *rufous brown above with white superciliary extending as stripe down neck and sides;* wings blacker with two white-dotted bars, tail feathers broadly tipped white. Below otherwise black, *flanks buff.* ♀ like ♂ above. Below white, *narrowly streaked with black on throat and breast,* flanks buff. ♂ Southern White-fringed and Black-bellied Antwrens are much less rufescent above than ♂ Rusty-backed; the former's white fringe incorporates flanks, while the latter's is narrower and grayer. ♀♀ of all three are very different below. Behavior much as in Southern White-fringed. Song a fast, gravelly "che-de-de, che-de-de, che-de-de, . . ." repeated up to 12–15 times, sometimes run together as almost a trill.

Black-bellied Antwren
Formicivora melanogaster PLATE 27(11)
12.5–13.5 cm (5–5¼"). Uncommon in caatinga scrub and lower growth of deciduous woodland, including north edge of chaco, from *ne. and interior Brazil to e. Bolivia* (Santa Cruz to Tarija) *and extreme n. Paraguay.* To 1100 m in Bolivia. ♂ dark grayish brown above with *broad white superciliary extending as stripe down sides of neck;* wings blackish with a bold white bar, spotting on coverts, and *whitish tertial edging;* tail feathers broadly white-tipped, outers edged white. *Below black.* ♀ like ♂ above, with *blackish cheeks. Below uniform whitish.* ♂ Southern White-fringed Antwren similar but has narrower white superciliary and wider white stripe on flanks; ♀♀ are very different. ♂ Serra Antwren is more rufescent above and has buff tertial edging; ♀ Serra very similar but buffier below. Behavior much like Southern White-fringed. Song a rather slow series of "cha" notes, often long-continued.

Serra Antwren
Formicivora serrana PLATE 27(12)
12.5 cm (5"). Uncommon and local in scrub and shrubby regenerating clearings in *interior se. Brazil* (s. Minas Gerais and adjacent Espírito Santo and Rio de Janeiro). To 1300 m. **Northern** ♂ (illustrated) resembles ♂ Black-bellied Antwren (no overlap) but *crown and back richer and more rufescent* and *tertial edging rufescent* (not white); its flanks show even less white. **Southern** birds darker brown above (more like Black-bellied) with less prominent superciliary and less white on wing-coverts. ♀ like ♀ Black-bellied but slightly buffier below. Cf. also Rusty-backed and Restinga Antwrens. Behavior much as in Southern White-fringed Antwren. Song a fast series of up to 15–20 "cha" notes.

Restinga Antwren
Formicivora littoralis
12.5 cm (5"). **Now rare** *and very local in remnant restinga scrub and woodland in coastal se. Brazil* (Rio de Janeiro). Near sea level. ♂ differs from ♂ Serra Antwren in being *blacker above* and in *lacking white superciliary* and spotting on *inner* wing-coverts; also has narrower white tips on tail feathers. ♀ like ♀ Serra. Behavior much as in other *Formicivora.* Song resembles Serra Antwren's, but shorter and usually softer.

Black-hooded Antwren
Formicivora erythronotos PLATE 27(13)
11.5 cm (4½"). *Uncommon and very local in restinga, overgrown clearings and plantations, and woodland undergrowth in coastal se. Brazil* (s. Rio de Janeiro and extreme e. São Paulo). Below 100 m. ♂ has *head, neck, and underparts black* with *contrasting rufous-chestnut back* and silky white flank plumes (often hidden by wing); wing-coverts fringed white, underwing-coverts also white (exposed when wings are flicked). ♀ has olive brownish and ochraceous replacing ♂'s black, but retains its *rufous-chestnut back* and white on flanks. Striking ♂ can hardly be confused, and even ♀'s duller rufous on back is obvious enough normally to preclude confusion. Most often in pairs, foraging in dense lower growth within 3–4 m of the ground, usually independent of mixed flocks. Song a fast series of fairly musical "tcho" notes; also gives a sharp, nasal "jeer-jeer" call.

Marsh Antwren
*Stymphalornis acutirostris**
13.5 cm (5¼"). *Very local in cattail (Typha) marshes and nearby shrubbery in se. Brazil* (coastal e. Paraná and ne. Santa Catarina). A recently described species, much like *Formicivora* but with longer bill. ♂ *dark brown above;* wing-coverts black with extensive white tipping, tail feathers narrowly tipped whitish. *Below dark gray* with usually hidden white flank plumes.

♀ brown above, speckled pale grayish on face. *Blackish below extensively streaked whitish.* Comportment similar to various *Formicivora,* none of which ranges this far south in Brazil or is so strictly confined to marshes. Occurs in pairs that generally remain within cattail growth. Song a series of 6–8 emphatic "chu-chí" or "piu-pí" phrases.

Cercomacra

Midsized antbirds with *slender bills, fairly long graduated tails,* and *simple plumage patterns* (♂♂ mainly black or gray, wings usually with white fringing; ♀♀ browner or gray, sometimes ochraceous, some species streaked below). They have a semiconcealed white dorsal patch, most evident when excited. *Cercomacra* antbirds are inconspicuous in undergrowth of woodland and forest borders, mainly in the lowlands; they are most often located through their vocalizations, which are often distinctive.

Gray Antbird
Cercomacra cinerascens   PLATE 28(1)
14.5 cm (5¾"). *Often common in viny tangles in subcanopy and borders of humid forest from Amazonia to the Guianas.* To about 1000 m. ♂ *plain gray,* a bit paler below; white spotting on wing-coverts is either inconspicuous, **north of Amazon** (A), or prominent, **south of Amazon** (B); *tail feathers broadly white-tipped.* ♀ olive brown above; wings as ♂; tail duskier, *feathers broadly white-tipped. Dull ochraceous below. Ranges higher above the ground than other Cercomacra* and identifiable on that basis alone; the white tail-tips are usually readily apparent from below. Cf. Spot-winged Antshrike (also in canopy). Usually found in pairs and well above the ground, creeping about in dense viny tangles, only rarely appearing in the open. Though occasionally with mixed flocks, usually they are alone. *Heard far more than seen.* Distinctive gravelly song, given through heat of day, a measured "ch-krr, ch-krr, ch-krr" (up to 7–8 ch-krrs), hiccuplike. Both sexes have a nasal but sharp "keeyr" call, sometimes steadily repeated.

Dusky Antbird
Cercomacra tyrannina   PLATE 28(2)
14–14.5 cm (5½–5¾"). Fairly common in undergrowth of humid and semideciduous forest borders and secondary woodland from Colom-

bia to sw. Ecuador (El Oro) *and n. Amaz. Brazil.* Mostly below 1000–1200 m. ♂ *plain gray,* somewhat paler below; blacker *wing-coverts fringed white; tail feathers narrowly tipped white.* ♀ olive brown above; wing-coverts fringed and tail feathers narrowly tipped ochraceous. *Below quite bright ochraceous tawny.* Blackish Antbird (limited overlap in the Guianas) similar, ♂♂ especially so, but Blackish is slightly darker and lacks pale tipping on tail (often so slight on Dusky as to be marginally visible); ♀ Blackish is brighter orange-rufous below *and on forehead.* Cf. also very similar Parker's and Willis's Antbirds (range-restricted). Forages in pairs, usually in dense undergrowth where hard to see. Sometimes moves with small flocks, but more often alone. Oft-heard song a series of whistled notes that starts slowly but then accelerates and rises in pitch, e.g., "pü, pü, pee-pee-pipipi?" ♀ frequently chimes in with a softer and higher-pitched version. Also: Mexico to Panama.

Willis's Antbird
*Cercomacra laeta**
14–14.5 cm (5½–5¾"). *Uncommon and local* in lower growth at edge of humid forest and woodland, and (westward) in campina woodland near streams and swamps, in *n. and e. Amaz. Brazil and adjacent Guyana,* also ne. *Brazil* (Pernambuco and Alagoas). To 600 m. Formerly considered conspecific with Dusky Antbird. ♂ closely resembles ♂ Dusky. ♀ in **ne. Amaz. Brazil** differs in its *grayish cheeks* (not buffy); in **ne. Brazil** paler, especially below. Behavior as in Dusky. Song, however, differs strikingly, a loud and musical "pur, peéur, peéur, peéur."

Parker's Antbird
*Cercomacra parkeri**
14–14.5 cm (5½–5¾"). *Uncommon in undergrowth at edge of montane forest and secondary woodland in W. and Cen. Andes of Colombia* (Antioquia to Cauca). 1100–1850 m. A recently described species. *Both sexes closely resemble Dusky Antbird; Parker's occurs at higher elevations* and is *best distinguished by its distinctive voice.* Behavior much as in Dusky. Song a forceful "pur, pee-pee-pee-pi-pi-pi-pr" (D. Willis recording), recalling an antvireo and rather different from Dusky's song.

Rio de Janeiro Antbird
Cercomacra brasiliana   PLATE 28(3)
14.5 cm (5¾"). *Rare and local* in undergrowth at edge of humid forest and in secondary wood-

land in *se. Brazil* (s. Bahia to Rio de Janeiro). To 1000 m. **Both sexes** closely resemble Dusky Antbird (geographically distant); tail slightly longer. Behavior as in Dusky, but *unmistakable song very different,* a bizarre, ringing "pr-kárnk" phrase repeated slowly 4–6 times.

Black Antbird
Cercomacra serva   PLATE 28(4)

15 cm (6″). Uncommon in undergrowth of humid forest borders and secondary woodland in *w. Amazonia.* To 1300 m. ♂ *uniform black;* white fringes on wing-coverts (but *no* tailtips). ♀ *olivaceous brown above; lower face and underparts deep orange-rufous.* Blackish Antbird *closely* similar, but ♂ Blackish is slatier (not as black) below, ♀ Blackish has rufous on forehead; often best distinguished by voice. Usually in pairs, foraging in dense undergrowth where hard to observe; as with other *Cercomacra,* generally not with mixed flocks. Often vocal; song a rising series of loud, rather harsh notes, starting deliberately but speeding up, "wor, chur, cheh-cheh-che-che-chi-chi-chi?" Its mate may chime in with a softer and usually shorter version.

Blackish Antbird
Cercomacra nigrescens*   PLATE 28(5)

15 cm (6″). Fairly common in undergrowth of secondary and riparian woodland (regular in bamboo in some areas) in *w. and s. Amazonia,* and locally in the *Guianas;* also in foothill and lower montane forest borders on *east slope of Andes from s. Colombia to w. Bolivia* (w. Santa Cruz). Mostly below 1600 m. Based on voice, likely more than one species. ♂ *slaty gray to blackish* (somewhat paler below); white fringes on wing-coverts. ♀ olivaceous to rufescent brown above; *forehead, sides of head, and underparts deep orange-rufous.* Black Antbird *very* similar; ♂ Black is blacker below, and ♀ Black is more olivaceous (less rufescent) above with little or no rufous on forehead. Dusky Antbird only overlaps in Guianas (where Blackish is rare); ♂ Dusky has narrow white tail-tips (none at all in Blackish); ♀ Dusky is much less richly colored below and on face. Behavior much as in Black, though Blackish seems easier to observe. Two song types. One song, given mainly on Andean slopes, is a fast "wor, chíh-chih-cheh-cheh-cheh-cheh," ♀ often adding 4–5 rising notes, "pur, pu-puh-peh-pih-pi?" In Amazonia, very different song is a loud and drawn-out "wor-cheeéyr"; ♀ often chimes in with a rising series of notes.

Manu Antbird
Cercomacra manu   PLATE 28(6)

15 cm (6″). *Locally not uncommon in Guadua bamboo thickets in humid forest of sw. Amazonia.* To 1350 m in se. Peru. ♂ *jet black* with wing-coverts conspicuously fringed white and narrow white tail-tips. ♀ *olivaceous brown above;* wings and tail duskier, wing-coverts fringed white, tail feathers narrowly tipped white. *Below uniform gray.* ♂ is blacker than ♂ Blackish Antbird (which can also occur in bamboo and is otherwise similar, aside from its lack of white tail-tips); ♀♀ of the two are very different (as are their songs). Found in pairs, foraging in lower and middle growth; often hard to see without tape playback. Song a series of low, guttural phrases, e.g., "ko-chok, ko-chok, chi-di-kok" or "ker-chérrr-chok, ker-chérrr-chok, chi-di-dok."

Jet Antbird
Cercomacra nigricans   PLATE 28(7)

15 cm (6″). Locally fairly common in tangled, viny undergrowth of semihumid and deciduous forest borders and secondary woodland in *n. Venezuela and n. Colombia,* and in *w. Ecuador* (w. Esmeraldas to El Oro). Mostly below 500 m. ♂ *uniform jet black; prominent white fringing on wing-coverts; tail feathers broadly tipped white.* ♀ dark slaty, *throat and breast with fine white streaking; wings and tail as in* ♂. Some (perhaps immatures) resemble ♀♀ but are more extensively streaked and scaled white below. In its northern range, ♂ is much the blackest *Cercomacra* and ♀ is the only one that shows streaking. Ranges in pairs that skulk in dense undergrowth, shy and hard to see except when vocalizing. Song a fairly loud, measured series of 4–5 (occasionally more) harsh paired "tchék-er" phrases, the second note lower-pitched; ♀ often adds a "ka-rump" phrase in syncopation. Also: Panama.

Bananal Antbird
Cercomacra ferdinandi   PLATE 28(8)

16 cm (6¼″). *Uncommon in dense thickets of riparian woodland and islands in Rio Araguaia in e. Amaz. Brazil.* Around 200 m. ♂ closely resembles ♂ of slightly smaller Jet Antbird (no overlap). ♀ gray above and below, *throat and breast with fine white streaking.* Nothing really similar in range; cf. Blackish Antbird, which comes close. ♀ Mato Grosso Antbird (no overlap) is *unstreaked* below. Behavior much like Jet, though more often in the open and easier to observe; also accompanies small mixed flocks more often. Rather nasal song a jumbled "caw-

cuh-didi-cuhdidi-cúh-chuk-chuk" with many variations; also gives single "cawh" and "ch-kúk" phrases.

Mato Grosso Antbird
Cercomacra melanaria   PLATE 28(9)
16.5 cm (6¼"). *Fairly common in thickets of gallery and deciduous woodland, usually near water, in n. Bolivia (Beni to w. Santa Cruz), sw. Amaz. Brazil (pantanal region), and extreme n. Paraguay.* Below 500 m. ♂ *uniform jet black; wingcoverts prominently fringed white, tail feathers tipped white.* ♀ *gray above; wings and tail as in* ♂. *Below pale grayish (unstreaked).* Does not occur with any other *Cercomacra.* Cf. ♀ Bandtailed Antbird (locally with it). Occurs in pairs and generally not too hard to observe; regularly moves with small loose flocks. Frequently heard song a slow, measured, and guttural "ker-cheeeér-chk, ker-cheeeéi-chk, ker cheeeér." Both sexes also have a low "churk" call.

Rio Branco Antbird
Cercomacra carbonaria
15 cm (6"). *Locally fairly common in undergrowth of riparian woodland and on islands, and in humid forest borders, in extreme n. Brazil (Roraima) and adjacent Guyana.* Below 200 m. ♂ closely resembles ♂ Jet Antbird (no overlap). ♀, however, quite different: *throat white streaked gray; breast, sides, and midbelly washed with ochraceous.* Does not occur with any other *Cercomacra.* Behavior much as in Jet, though distribution much more closely tied to proximity of water. Song a fast, repeated "ki-koók, ki-koók, ki-koók . . ." (up to 10–20 phrases).

Dot-winged Antwren
Microrhopias quixensis   PLATE 28(10)
11.5–12.5 cm (4½–5"). *Fairly common to common in lower growth and borders of humid forest and woodland in w. Colombia and w. Ecuador, and from w. and s. Amazonia to Guianas;* most numerous west of Andes. Mostly below 900 m. Likely more than one species. ♂ *uniform glossy black with large semiconcealed white dorsal patch, white spotting on wing-coverts, a single broad white wing-bar, and broad white tipping on tail feathers.* ♀ *in s. Amazonia* (A) like ♂ above, but duller and sootier. *Below uniform rufous-chestnut.* **West of Andes** similar but markedly smaller. ♀ from **se. Colombia to ne. Peru** (B) has *contrasting black throat,* in **e. Peru** also a black belly and especially broad white tail-tips. Differs most **east of Rio Tapajós in s. Amaz. Brazil**

(C): larger, with *throat and chest chestnut, belly black,* narrower tail tipping. The flashy white in the wings and tail should preclude confusion, not being equaled by any other antwren. Cf. ♂ White-flanked Antwren. Favors viny tangles and bamboo stands in Amazonia, but wider-ranging west of Andes. Often cocks and spreads its long tail, showing off the white. Forages actively, gleaning in foliage and, for an antwren, easy to observe. Song variable, typically an accelerating and descending series of 5–10 semimusical whistled notes, e.g., "wee, tsee-tsi-tsi-tsi-tu-tu"), sometimes with rougher "zhait" or "zheeeit" notes mixed in. These rougher notes, sometimes more drawn out, are also given alone. In e. Amaz. Brazil the most frequent call is very different, a sharper "skeeeu." Also: Mexico to Panama.

Pyriglena

Three rather large, long-tailed antbirds **found in forest and woodland undergrowth; unlike most antbird groups, none occurs widely in Amazonia.** ♂♂ *of all species are mainly glossy black;* both sexes always have **bright red irides.**

White-backed Fire-eye
Pyriglena leuconota   PLATE 29(1)
17.5–18 cm (6¾–7"). Fairly common in undergrowth of montane forest and woodland (locally also in adjacent lowlands and more deciduous situations) from *s. Colombia to n. and e. Bolivia, and locally in Brazil* (not in Amazonia or the southeast). Mostly below 600 m, though on Andes' east slope mainly 1000–2000 m. *Iris bright red.* ♂ *glossy black* with semiconcealed white dorsal patch. ♀♀ *vary greatly.* From **s. Andes to sw. Brazil** (A) rufescent brown above with semiconcealed white dorsal patch, *white supraloral,* and *dusky lores;* tail blackish. *Throat and breast ochraceous buff,* belly olivaceous brown. In **ne. Brazil and lower Amazon east of Rio Tapajós** similar but lacking white supraloral. In **lower Amazon west of Tapajós,** and disjunctly in **cen. Peru** (B), very different, a *rich umber brown* with *sooty black head.* On **east slope of Andes from s. Colombia to n. Peru** has *head and underparts sooty black,* mantle chestnut brown; in **w. Ecuador and extreme nw. Peru** (C) much duller; *brown above, grayish buff below. Does not occur with other fire-eyes.* No similar antbird (e.g., large *Myrmeciza* such as Immaculate and Sooty) has such an obvious red eye. Usually in pairs,

though groups of up to 4–6 gather at antswarms. Pounds tail downward when agitated. Song a far-carrying, fast series of ringing notes, "peer-peer-peer-peer-peer-peer-peer-peer-peer," fading toward end; ♀ sometimes echoes with a softer, higher-pitched version. This seems not to vary geographically. Calls include a loud "chik" or "chi-djik."

White-shouldered Fire-eye
Pyriglena leucoptera   PLATE 29(2)

18 cm (7″). Locally common in undergrowth of humid forest and woodland in *se. Brazil region* (north to Bahia). To 1250 m. *Iris bright red. ♂ glossy black* with semiconcealed white dorsal patch, and *white bend of wing and tipping of wing-coverts forming two bars. ♀ rufescent brown above,* tail blackish. Throat whitish, *below dingy buffy brownish. Does not occur with other fire-eyes.* In Bahia, range comes close to (very rare) Fringe-backed Fire-eye; in Mato Grosso do Sul, comes close to White-backed Fire-eye (♂♂ of which *lack* white in wing, ♀♀ of which have white supraloral, etc.). Forages in pairs, independently of mixed flocks though sometimes several gather at swarms of army ants. Frequently given song a loud, penetrating "peer-peer-peer-peer-peer-peer," less run together than in White-backed.

Fringe-backed Fire-eye
Pyriglena atra

17.5 cm (7″). *Now very rare and local in patches of remnant humid forest and woodland in ne. Brazil* (ne. Bahia and Sergipe). Below 100 m. ♂ resembles ♂ White-shouldered Fire-eye (no known overlap, but their ranges come close) but *lacks any white in wing,* and feathers of *large dorsal patch* (*always visible*) extensively white at base and with broad white "fringe." ♀♀ are not distinguishable in the field. Behavior, including voice, much as in White-shouldered Fire-eye.

Slender Antbird
Rhopornis ardesiacus   PLATE 29(3)

19 cm (7½″). *Undergrowth of deciduous woodland in e. Brazil* (interior s. Bahia and ne. Minas Gerais), *where now very local because of deforestation, though in the right habitat it can still be fairly* common. To 1000 m. Tail graduated and rather long. *Iris bright red. ♂ plumbeous gray above;* wings and tail blackish, wing-coverts prominently fringed white. *Throat black, below contrasting pale gray. ♀ has crown russet,* contrasting

with gray back. *Throat white,* below mostly pale grayish. No other similar, semiterrestrial antbird occurs in this species' limited range. Forages in pairs, hopping on or near the ground, and generally not all that shy; favors areas with ground bromeliads. Song a loud and rather shrill "peer, peer-peer pccr-peer-peer-peer-peer-peer" with much the quality of a fire-eye; ♀ often follows with a shorter, less vigorous version. Calling birds slowly wag their long slim tails.

Stripe-backed Antbird
Myrmorchilus strigilatus   PLATE 29(4)

16–16.5 cm (6¼–6½″). *Fairly common on or near ground in caatinga woodland and scrub in ne. Brazil* (south to n. Minas Gerais), *and in chaco woodland and scrub from e. Bolivia* (Santa Cruz) *and adjacent Brazil to n. Argentina* (n. Santiago del Estero and Santa Fé). To 1100 m in Bolivia. ♂ *boldly streaked black and rufous,* narrow superciliary pale buff (in **chaco;** illustrated) or white (in **caatinga**); wing-coverts black with two white bars and white dots; rump and central tail feathers rufous, lateral ones broadly tipped black and edged white. *Throat and breast black,* lower face and belly contrasting whitish. ♀ much like ♂ above. Buffy whitish below (*no* black bib), *breast streaked dusky.* Not likely confused in range and habitat, where there are few other antbirds, none so terrestrial. Found singly or in pairs, hopping on or near the ground, and hard to see without tape playback, tending to remain in dense growth. Distinctive song a loud wheezy "cheem, cheery-gweér" or "chree, chree-cho-weé." ♀ sometimes follows with a descending "pur, cheer-cheer-chur-chur-chr-chr." Both sexes also give a "pee-yeér" call.

Black Bushbird
Neoctantes niger   PLATE 29(5)

16 cm (6¼″). *Rare* and seemingly local in undergrowth of humid forest and woodland, mainly at borders and around treefalls, primarily in *w. Amazonia.* Mostly below 600 m. *Lower mandible upturned;* bill bluish gray below. ♂ *deep black;* large semiconcealed dorsal patch white. ♀ as in ♂ (the black somewhat sootier), but *broad breast shield rufous-chestnut;* dorsal patch as in ♂. No other all-black antbird shares the bushbird's chisel-shaped bill; further, many of these show bare blue skin around eye. ♀'s broad cummerbund unique among vaguely similar antbirds. Skulking and hard to see, in part because of the dense habitat it favors. Found singly

or in pairs, hopping near the ground (sometimes on it); rarely associates with flocks. Feeds by hammering at dead or soft wood, then employing bill as a wedge to open a slit in the substrate, exposing small arthropod prey (B. M. Whitney). Distinctive song a long-continued and quite fast series of "werk" notes that can continue for a minute or more.

Clytoctantes

Two rare and little-known antbirds, likely most closely related to the previous genus. Both species have a *large, compressed, up-swept bill* and very long curved hindclaw.

Recurve-billed Bushbird
Clytoctantes alixii   PLATE 29(6)
16.5 cm (6½"). *Rare and local in dense under-growth of forest borders, secondary woodland, and regenerating clearings in n. Colombia and adjacent Venezuela* (Sierra de Perijá region). To 1200 m. *Bill laterally compressed, lower mandible strongly upturned. ♂ dark gray* with *black fore-face, throat, and chest;* wing-coverts with white dots. ♀ mostly rufous-chestnut, slightly brighter on face and underparts; wing-coverts with small buff dots. Given its unusual bill, unmistakable in range. Poorly known. Has been seen attending an army antswarm, but has also been seen pecking at and ripping into dead stems with bill. Song a pretty, becardlike "teeeu, teeeu, teeeu, teu-ti-ti?" (O. Laverde recording); also a nasal descending snarl.

Rondônia Bushbird
Clytoctantes atrogularis   PLATE 29(7)
17 cm (6¾"). *Very rare and local in undergrowth at edge of terra firme forest, favoring dense viny tangles, in s. Amaz. Brazil* (single localities in Rondônia, n. Mato Grosso, and Amazonas). 300–400 m. Still known from only a single specimen, a ♀ that resembles Recurve-billed Bushbird, thus *rufous-chestnut,* but with a *large black bib on throat and chest,* plain wing-coverts, and dark gray uppertail-coverts and crissum. ♂ (brief sightings only) apparently *black.* Very poorly known, but has been seen foraging in thick undergrowth, singly or in pairs. A loud trilled whistle, "tree-tree-tree" has been heard (S. M. Lanyon et al.), thought to be an alarm call (B. M. Whitney).

Myrmoborus

Four *rather plump, short-tailed,* attractively plumaged antbirds found in undergrowth and borders of humid forest and woodland in Amazonia. The species mainly segregate by habitat and range.

White-browed Antbird
Myrmoborus leucophrys   PLATE 30(1)
13.5 cm (5¼"). *Widespread and usually fairly common* in undergrowth of secondary woodland, regenerating clearings, and terra firme forest borders (locally in bamboo) from Venezuela and the Guianas to n. Bolivia and Amazonia. Mostly below 1100 m. ♂ has a *broad snowy white superciliary extending back from forehead,* black face and throat. Otherwise uniform dark bluish gray, *wing-coverts unmarked.* ♀ has *broad cinnamon-buff superciliary* contrasting with *black mask;* brown above, buff dots on wing-coverts. *Below mainly white.* No other *Myrmoborus* has as bold a brow as this species; both sexes of Black-faced Antbird have obvious wing-bars. Ranges in pairs, less often family groups, that forage close to the ground in dense early-succession growth, often in *Heliconia* along streams; not in extensive unbroken forest. Often perches on slender saplings, hopping and sally-ing for short distances. Song a fast, descending stream of loud, ringing notes that increases in volume, then fades away, "pipipipipipipipipip'p 'p'p'p'p'rr," lasting 3–4 seconds.

Black-faced Antbird
Myrmoborus myotherinus   PLATE 30(2)
13.5 cm (5¼"). *Fairly common to common in undergrowth of terra firme forest and wood-land in Amazonia.* Mostly below 700 m, a few to 1300 m. Iris dark red. ♂ bluish gray above with *contrasting black face and throat,* outlined above by *whitish border,* and a semiconcealed white dorsal patch; *wing-coverts black fringed white forming three obvious bars.* Below pale gray. **Northwestern** birds (illustrated) darker gray below. ♀ olive brown above with *contrast-ing black mask* and semiconcealed white dorsal patch; *wing-coverts black fringed with buff form-ing three bars. Throat white, contrasting with ochraceous-buff underparts;* sparse necklace of black spots on throat's lower margin. In **Brazil east of Rio Madeira** *uniform ochraceous below.* White-browed and Ash-breasted Antbirds have *plain* wings; neither of these normally ranges

inside terra firme. Behavior much as in White-browed Antbird, though Black-faced is easier to observe, in part because it favors forests with a more open understory. Frequently heard song a loud, descending, fairly fast series of raspy notes, e.g., "dree-dree-dree-dree-dree-dree-dree-drew"; sometimes ♀ follows with a briefer and shriller version. In se. Peru and Bolivia, song strikingly different, with a much less raspy quality and strongly recalling White-backed Fire-eye's song.

Ash-breasted Antbird
Myrmoborus lugubris   PLATE 30(3)
13.5 cm (5¼"). Locally fairly common in undergrowth of várzea and riparian forest and woodland along *Amazon River and a few of its tributaries* **upriver to ne. Peru and extreme e. Ecuador.** To 200 m. *Iris red (♂) or more orange (♀). ♂* bluish gray above, paler on forehead, with *contrasting black face and throat; wings plain.* Below pale gray. **Eastern ♀ (west to Santarém region;** illustrated) *all rufous above,* wing-coverts buff dotted; mostly white below. **Western ♀ (east at least to Leticia region)** browner above with *black mask* and virtually plain wings. In **middle part of range** intermediate, rufous above with black mask, dots on wings. Throat white with faint necklace of black spots; *below mostly pale gray.* White-browed Antbird does not occur in Ash-breasted's restricted habitat; other *Myrmoborus* show wing markings. Habits much as in White-browed Antbird, favoring dense undergrowth, often in *Heliconia* thickets. Song like White-browed Antbird's, but slower. Calls include a "peeyr" and a "peeyr-pur."

Black-tailed Antbird
Myrmoborus melanurus   PLATE 30(4)
12.5 cm (5"). *Uncommon and seemingly local in undergrowth of várzea forest and riparian thickets,* apparently only in seasonally flooded areas, in ne. Peru (south bank of Amazon River, and along lower Ríos Marañón and Ucayali) *and extreme w. Brazil* (lower Rio Javarí). Below 150 m. *♂ mostly dark slaty gray,* face and throat blacker; wings blackish, *feathers fringed white forming three bars.* ♀ brown above with *indistinct dusky mask,* wings as in *♂. Whitish below, tinged buff on breast.* Cf. much more numerous Black-faced Antbird (only in terra firme forest), and Black-headed Antbird (not in várzea). Behavior much as in White-browed Antbird. Song a fast series (faster than in Ash-breasted) of 6–8 "peeyr"

notes ending in a chipper; ♀ often chimes in with a higher-pitched version.

Banded Antbird
Dichrozona cincta   PLATE 30(5)
10 cm (4"). *Uncommon on ground in terra firme forest in Amazonia,* favoring areas with an open understory. Mostly below 450 m. *Short tail* and long slender bill. *♂* chestnut brown above with narrow whitish superciliary; lower back and rump black *crossed by conspicuous white band;* wings black with *two conspicuous buff bars,* outer tail feathers white. *Below white with band of black spots across breast.* ♀ similar but rump-band buff, slightly buffier below. Pattern of this unique antbird vaguely recalls Spot-backed Antbird. More terrestrial than most other small antbirds, Banded *habitually walks on the ground,* often wagging and spreading tail as it goes. Usually found singly, less often in pairs; not with mixed flocks. Song a long series of up to 15 loud "pueeeée" notes with an odd ringing and piercing quality, steadily delivered at about a note per second. It recalls Scale-backed Antbird, though Banded's song has more and longer notes.

Hylophylax

Small, short-tailed antbirds with *attractive and relatively ornate plumage patterns* that range in lowland forests, *mainly in Amazonia.* Some species regularly follow antswarms.

Spot-backed Antbird
Hylophylax naevius   PLATE 30(6)
11.5 cm (4½"). Fairly common in undergrowth of humid forest in Amazonia and the Guianas. Mostly below 1200 m. Legs pinkish. *♂* has crown and upper back brownish, *face gray; back black with large buff spots;* wing-coverts black with three whitish-spotted bars, tertials tipped buff; tail olive to rufous brown with blackish subterminal band and white tip. Throat black, below white with *large black breast spots.* ♀ like *♂* above but wing-bars and tail tip buff. Throat white, prominent black malar stripe; *below buff* with *large black breast spots.* Cf. scarcer Dot-backed Antbird. Banded Antbird has a rump *band* (not back *spots*). Usually in pairs, foraging close to the ground and often perching on vertical stems. Frequently spreads tail, and flicks it upward. Less often at army antswarms than

Scale-backed Antbird, seldom lingering long. Has two song types, a fast, high-pitched, wheezy "wur, wheépur-wheépur-wheépur-wheépur-wheépur-wheépur-wheépur-wheépur," and a slightly slower series of 7–10 "wheézee" notes. Call a sharp "beet" or "beet-bit."

Spotted Antbird
Hylophylax naevioides

11.5 cm (4½"). Fairly common in undergrowth of humid forest and secondary woodland in w. Colombia and w. Ecuador (south to e. Guayas). To 900 m. Legs pinkish gray. Recalls Spot-backed Antbird. ♂ has *head ashy gray* with *contrasting rufous-chestnut back;* wings black with *two broad rufous bars and tertial tips.* Throat black, below white with *large black breast spots.* ♀ duller, but *patterned much as in* ♂; head brownish, underparts buff-tinged with white throat and less distinct dusky breast spots. Nothing really similar *west* of Andes; Spot-backed Antbird occurs *east* of them. Behavior much as in Spot-backed Antbird, though Spotted is a much more frequent attendant at army antswarms, sometimes even in small groups. Song a descending series of 7–10 high-pitched wheezy notes that fades away, e.g., "peezee, wheezee, wheezee, wheezee, wheeya." Also has soft churring calls, and in alarm a sharper "pseek." Also: Honduras to Panama.

Dot-backed Antbird
Hylophylax punctulatus   PLATE 30(7)

10.5 cm (4¼"). *Uncommon and local* in *undergrowth of várzea forest and woodland, usually near streams and lakes,* in Amazonia, usually found in *blackwater drainages.* Below 300 m. Resembles more numerous Spot-backed Antbird. Dot-backed differs in its even shorter tail, *gray legs* (not pinkish), *whitish lower face* (not gray), *smaller white* (not buff) *spots on back that extend down over rump,* and black tail (not brown). Sexes alike, aside from ♀ having ♂'s black throat reduced to a *black malar stripe* (more prominent than in ♀ Spot-backed). Usually in pairs that forage close to the ground, generally independent of mixed flocks; does not follow army ants. Distinctive song a leisurely series of emphatic phrases, "whee-beéyr, whee-beéyr, whee-beéyr. . . ."

Scale-backed Antbird
Hylophylax poecilinotus   PLATE 30(8)

13 cm (5"). Fairly common in undergrowth of humid forest in Amazonia and the Guianas. Mostly below 1200 m. ♂ in **w. Amazonia** (A) *gray*

with midback and wing-coverts black, *feathers prominently scaled white;* tail black with large white spots and tipping. In **lower Amaz. Brazil** (mainly between lower Rio Tapajós and Rio Tocantins) and in **ne. Peru and extreme w. Brazil,** has **throat black.** ♀♀ *vary.* In w. **Amazonia** (A) rufous brown above (forecrown and face more rufous); *midback and wing-coverts scaled white as in* ♂; ochraceous-buff below. From s. **Venezuela and the Guianas to n. Brazil** (B) *scaling buff,* and *underparts mostly gray.* In se. **Peru, n. Bolivia, and most of s. Amaz. Brazil** (C) *unscaled;* rufous brown above, *uniform gray below and on face.* No other similar antbird shows such an obvious scaly back pattern, seen in all but the ♀♀ found in s. Amazonia (which are distinctively *bicolored*). Usually in pairs, foraging on or near the ground, hopping from one vertical stem to another and capturing prey by dropping to the ground or sallying to nearby foliage. A frequent attendant at army antswarms. Song a leisurely series of 5–10 piercing upslurred notes, each higher in pitch and a bit louder, "teeuw, tuweeé? tuweeé? tuweeé? tuweeé?" In e. Amaz. Brazil phraseology much the same, but quality burrier (B. M. Whitney recording). Calls include a sneezing "tchef" and nasal scolds.

Hypocnemis

Two *chunky, rather short-tailed* antbirds with *bold streaky patterns* found in Amazonian forests and borders.

Warbling Antbird
*Hypocnemis cantator**   PLATE 30(9)

12 cm (4¾"). *Fairly common to common and widespread* in lower growth of humid forest borders and openings in *Amazonia and the Guianas.* Mostly below 600 m, a few to 1200 m or more. Recent evidence suggests that a complex of species is involved. ♂ in **most of range** (A) has *black head with white streaking and superciliary;* back mixed black, brownish, and white; wing-coverts black with three white-spotted bars. White below, *sides scalloped black, flanks rufous.* In **sw. Venezuela area** tinged yellow below. In se. **Peru area** (B) *distinctly yellow below* with black *streaking* on sides, less rufous on flanks. ♀ much like respective ♂♂ but wing-bars buffyish. Yellow-browed Antbird has superciliary yellow, lacks rufous on flanks. *Herpsilochmus* antwrens inhabit subcanopy; none shows rufous flanks.

Drymophila antbirds have longer, white-tipped tails. Forages in pairs, mainly in lower growth but sometimes higher, favoring dense tangles, light gaps, and (where present) bamboo; accompanies small mixed flocks, but usually moves independently. Raspy song an almost snarling (hardly a "warbling"!), descending "peér, peer-peer-peer-peer-pur-pur-pyur" with some variation (e.g., faster in lower Amazon birds; B. M. Whitney recording); its mate may answer with a shorter higher-pitched version. There is significant geographic variation in calls.

Yellow-browed Antbird
Hypocnemis hypoxantha   PLATE 30(10)
12 cm (4¾"). *Uncommon and local in undergrowth of terra firme forest in Amazonia.* Mostly below 400 m. ♂ in *most of range* (illustrated) has black crown with white streaks, *long bright yellow superciliary and cheeks,* and olive back with sparse black streaking; wing-coverts black with three white-spotted bars. *Below bright yellow,* sides variably streaked black. In **e. Amaz. Brazil** has rufous on flanks. ♀ like ♂ but crown streaks pale yellow. With its *bright yellow,* this pretty antbird is nearly unmistakable. Warbling Antbird is patterned in black *and* white, never has *yellow* brow, and has obvious rufous on flanks. Behavior as in Warbling Antbird, though forages with understory flocks more. Song recalls Warbling Antbird's but somewhat less raspy, with a slower, more evenly paced tempo.

Black-and-white Antbird
Myrmochanes hemileucus   PLATE 30(11)
11.5 cm (4½"). A distinctive *small, black and white* antbird, *locally not uncommon in early-succession growth on islands in Amazon River and some of its tributaries* **upriver to e. Ecuador and ne. Peru.** Below 300 m. *Long slender bill.* ♂ *black above* with semiconcealed white dorsal patch, gray rump; wing-coverts spotted white, tail feathers tipped white. *White below.* ♀ similar, but some white on lores and flanks tinged buff. *Limited range and restricted habitat should preclude confusion.* Favors low growth with *Tessaria* shrubs, young willows, and *Gynerium* cane, also under open canopy of young *Cecropia* trees. Forages in pairs, gleaning in foliage; for an antbird, easy to observe. Distinctive song a fast "tu-tu-u-u-u-u-u" with an odd chortled quality; its mate often replies with a higher-pitched version. Also gives an inflected "toot!" (sometimes doubled or tripled).

Hypocnemoides

Two small, fairly long-billed, *gray and white* antbirds found in *swampy areas, mainly separated by range on either side of Amazon.* Iris pale grayish and legs grayish.

Band-tailed Antbird
Hypocnemoides maculicauda   PLATE 30(12)
12 cm (4¾"). Locally fairly common in undergrowth of várzea and swampy forest, thickets in lake and stream margins, and gallery woodland (but always near water) in *Amazonia south of Amazon River.* To 500 m in se. Peru. ♂ gray, somewhat paler below, with *black throat* and *large semiconcealed white dorsal patch;* wing-coverts black with three white bars, *tail black with wide white tip.* ♀ like ♂ above (including dorsal patch); whitish below *mottled grayish especially on breast.* Cf. Black-chinned Antbird (mainly found *north* of Amazon). Silvered Antbird is larger with pink (not grayish) legs, no white on tail. In the Brazilian pantanal, cf. ♀ Mato Grosso Antbird. Forages in pairs, hopping in thickets usually within a meter of the water, sometimes down to swampy ground. Easy to see, and usually not at all shy. The tail is often held slightly cocked. Song a loud series of notes that accelerate and become raspy, "pee-pee-pi-pipipipipipipi-pe-pe-peh-pez-pez-pzz."

Black-chinned Antbird
Hypocnemoides melanopogon
11.5 cm (4½"). Locally fairly common in undergrowth of várzea and swampy forest, and thickets in lake and stream margins (always near water) in *Amazonia mainly north of Amazon River.* Mostly below 400 m. Resembles slightly larger and longer-tailed Band-tailed Antbird, but both sexes *lack* Band-tailed's white dorsal patch and *white tail-tipping slightly narrower.* The two species generally separate by range. Silvered Antbird is larger, has a dark eye and pink legs, white spots on wing-coverts, *no* white tail-tips; cf. also ♀ of the rare Yapacana Antbird. Song as in Band-tailed Antbird, but shorter.

Silvered Antbird
Sclateria naevia   PLATE 30(13)
14–14.5 cm (5½–5¾"). Fairly common in undergrowth of várzea forest and woodland and along swampy margins of lakes and streams in *Amazonia and the Guianas.* To 600 m. *Long bill; rather long legs pinkish.* **Eastern** ♂ *gray above;*

wings and tail blackish, *wing-coverts with small white spots. Below prominently streaked gray and white.* ♀ patterned much the same, but *brown replaces gray,* and wing-coverts dotted buff. **Western** ♂ (east to sw. Venezuela and Rio Madeira in Brazil) ♂ similar but *mainly white below,* ♀ white below with *sides and flanks orange-rufous.* Compare ♂ Silvered with ♀♀ of smaller Bandtailed and Black-chinned Antbirds (in the same habitat). Cf. also rare Yapacana Antbird. Found in pairs, hopping on or close to wet ground or working through vegetation along edge of lakes and streams; generally not shy. Song a loud and ringing "jyíp, ji-ji-ji-ji-ji-ji-jíjíjíjíjí-ji-ji-jrrr" that reaches a crescendo, then fades; the initial accented note is distinctive.

Percnostola

Three "typical" antbirds with wing-covert fringing (not spotting) found in Amazonian forests. They are of uncertain taxonomic affinity and may not be congeneric.

White-lined Antbird
Percnostola lophotes   PLATE 31(1)
14.5 cm (5¾"). Locally fairly common in lower growth of humid forest borders, often in *Guadua* bamboo, in *sw. Amazonia.* To 1300 m in se. Peru. *Long shaggy crest.* ♂ *dark slaty, blacker on head and foreneck; wing-coverts boldly fringed white.* ♀ *rufous brown above, brighter and more cinnamon on crown and wings,* cheeks dusky; tail rufous-chestnut. *Mostly white below.* The crest, usually conspicuous, should preclude confusion; bicolored ♀ superficially resembles ♀ Great Antshrike (*uncrested,* with heavy bill, red iris, etc.). Ranges in pairs, hopping within a few meters of the ground and usually in dense growth, hence often hard to see (especially without tape playback). Often pounds tail downward and then slowly lifts it; frequently raises crest. Usually not with flocks. Song a loud, accelerating series, "kew, kew-kew-kew-ku-ku-ku-kukukuku"; ♀ often follows with a shorter version. Calls include a frequent loud "chéwf."

Black-headed Antbird
Percnostola rufifrons   PLATE 31(2)
14.5–15 cm (5¾–6"). Locally fairly common in undergrowth of terra firme forest borders and woodland from the *Guianas to n. Amazonia.* To 500 m. *Slightly bushy crest* (especially in east).

♂ dark gray with *black crown and throat; wing-coverts blackish with white fringing;* iris either gray (Guianas to lower Rio Negro and sw. Venezuela, A), or red (more eastern). **Eastern** ♀ (B) dusky above with *blackish crown;* wings and tail blackish, *wing-coverts with obvious tawny fringing. Forehead, face, and underparts rich orange-rufous.* **Western** ♀ similar but *crown dull chestnut* and iris gray. Both sexes of Spot-winged and Caura Antbirds have wing-*spotting* (not fringing). Cf. also White-shouldered and Blackish-gray Antshrikes, and ♂ of smaller Black-chinned Antbird. Found singly or in pairs, hopping in undergrowth and often quite easy to observe; regular at antswarms. Song an even, loud "peer-peer-peer-peer-peer" (up to 8–9 notes); in west (R. H. Wiley recording), faster and with a slight initial hesitation.

Allpahuayo Antbird
Percnostola arenarum*
14.5 cm (5¾"). *Uncommon and very local in undergrowth of swampy forest, usually where soils are sandy (varillal),* in ne. Peru. Below 200 m. A recently described species. Resembles Black-headed Antbird; they are not known to be sympatric. Iris gray. ♂ differs in being uniform dark gray above (*crown not blacker*). ♀ also is uniform dark gray above (crown concolor), and has whitish throat and white midbelly. Behavior as in Black-headed Antbird. Song a loud ringing "chu-du-du-dududududududu," fading slightly toward end.

Schistocichla

A trio of very similar antbirds inhabiting humid forest. ♂♂ *gray with white wing dots,* ♀♀ *orange-rufous below with buff wing dots.*

Spot-winged Antbird
Schistocichla leucostigma*   PLATE 31(3)
15 cm (6"). Uncommon in undergrowth of terra firme forest *in Amazonia and the Guianas.* Recent evidence suggests that a complex of species is involved. Mostly below 1000 m, but to 1500 m on tepuis. *Legs gray* (w. Amazonia and on tepuis) *or pinkish.* ♂ in **w. Amazonia** (illustrated) and on **tepuis** *dark gray,* slightly paler below; wings and tail blacker, *wing-coverts with small white dots.* ♀ *rufous brown above* with *dark gray head;* wing-coverts with buff spots. *Below deep orange-rufous.* **Elsewhere,** ♂♂ are more two-

toned (paler gray above than below) and their wing-spots often larger, ♀♀ paler orange-buff below and only crown gray, or head all brown. Cf. scarcer, range-restricted Slate-colored and Caura Antbirds. Plumbeous Antbird has obvious bare skin around eye; Black-headed Antbird has fringing (not spotting) on wings. Inconspicuous and shy, usually hopping in pairs in thick vegetation close to the ground, often along forested streams; rarely associates with mixed flocks, nor does it attend antswarms. Songs vary. In w. Amazonia gives a fast series of fairly musical, chippered notes that descend and fade; in the Guianas and n. Brazil an even, fairly musical trill; on tepui slopes a very different, much higher-pitched and shriller series of descending notes; in s. Amaz. Brazil also different, a series of strident "chee" notes followed by several chrrs.

Slate-colored Antbird

Schistocichla schistacea PLATE 31(4)

14.5 cm (5¾"). Uncommon in undergrowth of terra firme forest in *w. Amazonia.* To 300 m. ♂'s *bill all black,* lower mandible gray in ♀; *iris grayish;* legs bluish gray. ♂ nearly identical to ♂ of more numerous Spot-winged Antbird, best distinguished by soft-part colors (Spot-winged's iris brown, lower mandible bluish gray). ♀ more distinctive, differing in its rufescent head with blurry shaft streaks (*lacking gray*). Furtive behavior is similar. Song (distinctly different from sympatric Spot-winged) a simple series of penetrating notes, "peeyr-peeyr-peeyr-peeyr-peeyr," recalling Sooty Antbird.

Caura Antbird

Schistocichla caurensis PLATE 31(5)

17.5 cm (7"). Fairly common but local in undergrowth of humid forest on *lower slopes of tepuis in s. Venezuela and adjacent n. Brazil.* Mostly 300–1300 m. Iris reddish; *legs gray.* Resembles Spot-winged Antbird but *larger with longer tail.* ♂ is darker than sympatric Spot-wingeds and more uniform gray (not paler below), with gray (not pinkish) legs; Caura does not occur with Spot-wingeds of the tepuis (which also have gray legs). Aside from its larger size, ♀ Caura very similar to ♀ Spot-winged. ♂ White-shouldered Antshrike has blacker crown, more spots on wing-coverts, and shorter, heavier bill. *Favors areas with boulders and rocky outcrops.* Forages in pairs on or near the ground, frequently tossing leaves. Song a series of 10–12 well-enunciated, loud and shrill "jeeyp" notes that descend and speed up (K. J. Zimmer recording).

Myrmeciza

A diverse genus of forest or forest-based antbirds, almost all found in the lowlands, comprising several distinctly different groups, almost certainly not all congeneric. First we present an assemblage of *smaller Myrmeciza, most with attractive and complex plumage patterns, especially ♂♂.* Two of these species (Gray-headed and Yapacana) likely do not belong in this genus at all. We then continue with five large and robust species whose plumage is relatively plain, and end with a group of smaller species that can be considered typical *Myrmeciza.*

Gray-headed Antbird

Myrmeciza griseiceps PLATE 31(6)

13.5 cm (5¼"). *Now rare and local in undergrowth and borders of montane forest and woodland in sw. Ecuador* (mainly sw. Loja) and *nw. Peru* (Piura and Lambeyeque). 600–2500 m. ♂ has *head and neck gray;* back olive brown with a semiconcealed white dorsal patch; wing-coverts black with white fringing; *graduated tail* dusky, *feathers tipped white.* Throat gray, *midbreast black;* below gray. ♀ like ♂ above but head and neck paler gray. *Throat and breast pale gray with mottled whitish streaking* (a few have some black on breast). In its limited range, no antbird is any more similar than the Plain Antvireo (really quite different). Forages singly or in pairs in dense undergrowth, where hard to see well; *favors bamboo patches,* and has recently declined due to widespread deforestation. Song a short, clearly descending trill, "trrrrrrrrr." Foraging birds give a nasal, somewhat querulous contact call "skrree-squirt," steadily repeated every 2–5 seconds.

Yapacana Antbird

Myrmeciza disjuncta PLATE 31(7)

13.5 cm (5¼"). *Very local (but can be common) on or near ground in dense, seasonally flooded savanna woodland and shrubby campinas in sw. Venezuela, adjacent Colombia, and nw. Amaz. Brazil.* Below 150 m. *Legs pinkish.* ♂ *dark gray above* with semiconcealed white dorsal patch; wings and tail blackish, wing-coverts fringed white. *Below whitish,* flanks gray. ♀ dark gray above, wing-coverts *unmarked. Below pale ochraceous-buff.* Silvered Antbird is quite similar, though larger; the two species occur together, and both have pink legs. ♂ Silvered has white wing spots (not fringes); ♀ Silvered is brown above.

♀ Black-chinned Antbird has tail broadly tipped white, lacks buff below. Forages in pairs, and because of its nearly impenetrable habitat, hard to see; does not associate with flocks. Regularly flicks wings and tail, also wags tail. Weird song, unlike any other antbird, a buzzy "zzzzzzzzzzzip-ke-zzzzzzzzzip" (K. J. Zimmer recording).

Southern Chestnut-tailed Antbird
*Myrmeciza hemimelaena** PLATE 31(8)
12 cm (4¾"). Fairly common in undergrowth of terra firme forest and woodland in *s. Amazonia.* Mostly below 1400 m. Formerly included the next species. *Tail short.* ♂ has *dark gray head and neck* and reddish brown upperparts; wing-coverts blackish tipped buff or white, *tail rufous-chestnut. Throat and breast black,* gray and brown on sides and flanks with white on midbelly. ♀ like ♂ above but paler. *Throat and breast cinnamon-buff to orange-rufous, belly buffy white.* Unlikely to be confused; *similar species lack the rufous-chestnut tail.* Does not occur with the very similar Northern Chestnut-tailed Antbird. Forages singly or in pairs, hopping on or near the ground, often in dense undergrowth near treefalls. Rarely with mixed flocks, and seldom attends antswarms. Oft-heard song a far-carrying series of ringing clear notes that descends, "klee-klee-kli-kli-kli-klu."

Northern Chestnut-tailed Antbird
*Myrmeciza castanea**
12 cm (4¾"). *Rare to uncommon and local in undergrowth of humid forest in n. Peru, e. Ecuador, and s. Colombia* (Putumayo). To 1300 m. Recently split from previous species, which it *closely resembles,* though its pale tertial tips are indistinct (these are obvious in Southern Chestnut-tailed). Has also been called Zimmer's Antbird. *Best identified on the basis of range and voice.* Behavior as in Southern Chestnut-tailed Antbird, but seems to be shyer and more difficult to see. Song very different, a distinctly rising series of clear, high-pitched notes, e.g., "teeee-teee-tee?" or "teeeee-teee-tee-tee-titi?"

Black-throated Antbird
*Myrmeciza atrothorax** PLATE 31(9)
14 cm (5½"). Generally common (less so westward) in undergrowth of humid forest borders, secondary woodland, and riparian growth in *Amazonia and the Guianas.* Mostly below 1200 m. ♂ in **most of range** (illustrated) umber brown above with semiconcealed white dorsal patch; wing-coverts with white dots, *tail black-*ish. *Throat and breast black; face, sides of neck, and belly gray.* In **nw. Amazonia** *essentially uniform blackish* aside from the dorsal patch and dots on wing-coverts. ♀ brown above, dorsal patch as in ♂; wing-coverts with buffyish dots; *tail blackish. Throat white, breast orange-rufous,* flanks olivaceous. Both Chestnut-tailed Antbirds are smaller with a shorter, chestnut tail. ♀ Spot-winged Antbird is more uniform orange-rufous below (*no* white throat). Cf. range-restricted Gray-bellied Antbird. ♂ in nw. Amazonia is so black that it is most likely confused with ♂ of Black or Blackish Antbirds; those show white *fringing* on wing-coverts and have very different songs. Usually in pairs, foraging close to the ground, frequently near water; because of their active, fidgety behavior often hard to observe clearly or for long. Incisive song a fast ascending series of high-pitched notes, "chee-ch-chee, chi-chi-chi-chí-chí" (sounding like the peeping of baby chicks).

Gray-bellied Antbird
Myrmeciza pelzelni
13.5 cm (5¼"). *Rare* on or near ground in humid forest and woodland, *mainly in areas with sandy soil,* in *sw. Venezuela and adjacent Colombia and Brazil.* To 350 m. ♂ resembles ♂ Black-throated Antbird but more rufescent above with *shorter tail rufous-chestnut* (not blackish), *wing-coverts with larger buff spots* (not small white ones), and *face grizzled grayish and whitish.* ♀ like ♂ above (likewise with *grizzled face* and *large buff spots on wing-coverts*); *mostly white below,* breast scaled black. Found in pairs, often walking on the ground, sometimes on logs; favors areas with a relatively open understory, and does not accompany mixed flocks. Song a series of 12–15 high-pitched and shrill "zree" notes that become a little louder and more insistent.

Ferruginous-backed Antbird
Myrmeciza ferruginea PLATE 31(10)
15 cm (6"). Fairly common on or near ground in terra firme forest and woodland in *ne. South America.* To 550 m. Unmistakable. *Large bare orbital area bright blue.* ♂ above bright chestnut, wing-coverts black with *two bold buff bars. Face, throat, and breast black* outlined by *white stripe back from eye and down sides of neck and breast;* belly whitish, flanks rufescent brown. ♀ like ♂ but *throat white.* Generally occurs in pairs that daintily walk and hop on the ground, often bobbing their head; as it favors areas with a relatively open understory, normally this attractive

antbird is not too hard to see. Does not accompany flocks. Oft-heard song a fast-paced series of couplets, e.g., "wheehee-wheehee-wheehee-wheehee-wheehee."

Scalloped Antbird
Myrmeciza ruficauda   PLATE 31(11)

14.5 cm (5¾"). Uncommon and local on or near ground in humid forest and woodland in *e. Brazil* (Paraíba to Alagoas, and se. Bahia to Espírito Santo). Mostly below 500 m. Legs pinkish. ♂ dark olive brown above, *back feathers fringed buff,* rump and tail rufous; wing-coverts blackish with two buff bars. Cheeks, throat, and midbreast black; *sides of neck and breast feathers scalloped grayish,* belly ochraceous. ♀ like ♂ above; throat white, *breast whitish boldly scalloped and spotted black,* belly ochraceous. Squamate and White-bibbed Antbirds have longer tails and bold white superciliaries. Found singly or in pairs, hopping on the ground and often flicking leaves with bill. Rarely accompanies flocks. Song an almost trilled "tree-ee-ee-ee-ee-ee-ee-ee" lasting 2–3 seconds.

Squamate Antbird
Myrmeciza squamosa   PLATE 31(12)

15.5 cm (6"). Uncommon on or near ground in humid forest and woodland in *se. Brazil* (Rio de Janeiro to n. Rio Grande do Sul). To 1000 m. Legs pinkish. ♂ brown above with *white superciliary outlining black face,* back with semiconcealed white dorsal patch; wing-coverts black with bold spotted wing-bars. *Breast black, feathers broadly tipped white producing a bold scaly effect;* belly mainly whitish. ♀ like ♂ above; *throat and breast white* with *faint blackish scaling,* belly mainly whitish. ♂ White-bibbed Antbird has white bib on lower throat, a wider white brow; ♀ has throat buff. Behavior much as in Scalloped Antbird. Song a shrill "wheesee, wheesee, wheesee, wheesee, wheesee," gradually descending.

White-bibbed Antbird
Myrmeciza loricata   PLATE 31(13)

15.5 cm (6"). Uncommon on or near ground in montane forest and woodland in *e. Brazil* (s. Bahia, and from s. Espírito Santo and se. Minas Gerais to ne São Paulo). 700–1300 m. Legs pinkish. ♂ resembles ♂ Squamate Antbird but with *wider and more prominent white superciliary. Sides of head and upper throat black; white below* with *band of black, white-scaled feathers across chest.* ♀ like ♂ above except for its buff wing-spotting. *Throat ochraceous-buff;* below

whitish, sides with dark scaling and mottling. ♂ Squamate Antbird has a solid black foreneck (*no white bib*), narrower white brow. ♀'s buff throat is unique among the three e. Brazilian *Myrmeciza.* Behavior and voice much as in Squamate Antbird, but song not so high-pitched.

Plumbeous Antbird
Myrmeciza hyperythra   PLATE 32(1)

17–18 cm (6¾–7"). Fairly common to common in undergrowth and borders of *várzea and floodplain forest in w. Amazonia.* Mostly below 500 m. *Extensive bare blue skin around eye.* ♂ *uniform slaty gray;* wings and tail blacker, *wing-coverts with small but conspicuous white spots.* ♀ like ♂ above (*including wing-spots*). *Below uniform bright orange-rufous.* ♂ Spot-winged and Slate-colored Antbirds *lack* blue skin around eye, and their wing-spotting is less prominent; ♀ Spot-winged's color pattern resembles that of ♀ of heftier Plumbeous. ♂ White-shouldered and Sooty Antbirds are blacker than ♂ Plumbeous, and they *lack* wing spots. Usually seen in pairs, less often small groups, hopping through swampy lower growth; rather unsuspicious and relatively easy to see. Rarely with mixed flocks, and infrequent at antswarms. Pounds tail downward when disturbed. Distinctive song a fast, slightly rising series of accelerating, rattled notes, "wo-wu-wu-wu-wu-wu-wu-wrrrrrrrrrr," with an odd chortling quality. Calls include a "wo-púr" or "klo-kú," often repeated.

Immaculate Antbird
Myrmeciza immaculata   PLATE 32(2)

18.5 cm (7¼"). Fairly common in undergrowth of humid and lower montane forest and woodland in *w. Colombia and w. Ecuador* (south to w. Loja), *where the only large Myrmeciza.* Mostly below 1400 m. *Extensive bare skin pale blue in front of eye, whitish behind.* ♂ *uniform lustrous black* with white on shoulders (usually hard to see). ♀ *uniform rich dark brown* with *blackish face and upper throat;* tail blackish. Cf. smaller Chestnut-backed Antbird (which also has blue skin around eye). Though they follow antswarms when these are available, pairs of Immaculate Antbirds often are also seen foraging independently. Pounds tail downward, especially when disturbed; often clings to vertical stems. Song a loud series of clear, ringing, whistled notes, "peer-peer-peer-peer-peer-peer-peer-peer," slowing toward end. Distinctive call an explosive "cheek!" Also: Costa Rica and Panama.

Sooty Antbird

Myrmeciza fortis   PLATE 32(3)

18.5 cm (7¼"). *Uncommon in undergrowth in terra firme forest in w. Amazonia.* Mostly below 900 m. *Extensive bare blue skin around eye. ♂ uniform sooty gray,* crown and foreneck slightly blacker; white along bend of wing (hard to see). ♀ has *rufous-chestnut crown;* otherwise brown above, grayer on back and more rufescent on wings and rufous-chestnut on tail. *Face, foreneck, and underparts uniform gray.* ♂ White-shouldered Antbird is blacker with less blue around eye and a bit more white on wing; it inhabits edge, not deep forest. ♀ White-shouldered is very different. Immaculate Antbird occurs only *west* of Andes. Most often seen at antswarms, when sometimes quite bold. Otherwise Sooties forage as pairs, generally not with flocks; they then tend to be shy. Pounds tail downward, especially when nervous. Song a loud penetrating "teeuw-teeuw-teeuw-teeuw-teeuw-teeuw-teeuw-teeuw," slightly ascending and lasting 2–4 seconds. Less vocal than either White-shouldered or Immaculate.

White-shouldered Antbird

Myrmeciza melanoceps   PLATE 32(4)

18–18.5 cm (7–7¼"). *Fairly common in lower growth of várzea and riparian forest and woodland, and terra firme borders, in w. Amazonia.* Mostly below 500 m. *Small area of dull bare blue skin around eye. ♂ uniform lustrous black* with white at bend of wing (hard to see). ♀'s *black head, throat, and chest* contrast with *rufous upperparts* and *cinnamon-rufous underparts.* ♂ Sooty Antbird is duller black and has more extensive and brighter blue around eye. Striking ♀ unmistakable, aside from ♀ of very localized Cocha Antshrike (which is smaller, with *no* bare blue skin around eye); ♂ antshrike *lacks* white on bend of wing. Usually in pairs that hop through lower growth, often where dense and viny, at times ranging up to 5–8 m above the ground. Sometimes accompanies mixed flocks, and occasionally attends antswarms. Pounds tail downward. Heard much more often than seen. Distinctive song a far-carrying "pur, pee-ur pee-ur pee-ur pee-ur" with ringing quality; ♀ sometimes answers with a soft, short version. Agitated birds give an abrupt "cheedo-cheeo-cheeo-cheeo-cheeyo."

Goeldi's Antbird

Myrmeciza goeldii   PLATE 32(5)

18 cm (7"). *Locally fairly common in dense lower growth of transitional and várzea forest in sw. Amazonia.* Mostly below 450 m. ♂ resembles ♂ White-shouldered Antbird (no overlap), but has a *red iris* (not dark) and *virtually no bare skin around eye* or white at bend of wing; Goeldi's does have a semiconcealed white dorsal patch. ♀ very different, rufous above with *dusky gray head;* throat white, below bright ochraceous. ♂ White-backed Fire-eye has a smaller bill, longer tail. Goeldi's favors *Heliconia* thickets and stands of bamboo. Behavior and voice much as in White-shouldered, but song more often stuttered at the start.

White-bellied Antbird

Myrmeciza longipes   PLATE 32(6)

14.5–15 cm (5¾–6"). *Locally common* on or near ground in deciduous and semihumid forest and woodland, locally also at edge of humid forest, from *n. Colombia to lower Amaz. Brazil.* Mostly below 1300 m. Legs pinkish. ♂ from **s. Venezuela south** (illustrated) *bright rufous-chestnut above* with *gray superciliary wrapping around cheeks and down sides;* often has black spots on wing-coverts. *Cheeks and bib black,* breast and sides gray, midbelly white. **Elsewhere** *lacks* wing spots and (usually) the gray on breast; in **Colombia's upper Río Magdalena valley** has gray crown and on breast. ♀ similar but duller, with browner crown, dusky cheeks, and *ochraceous throat and breast.* Of the few antbirds found in this species' deciduous forest habitat, none is uniform rufous above. Found in pairs that hop about quietly, generally within cover, their presence periodically revealed by leaves being flicked aside. Occasionally attends antswarms. Song loud and often heard, a fast, ringing crescendo that trails off at end, e.g., "cheer, cheer, cheer-cheer-cheer-cheercheercheercheer-chew-chew, chew, chew." Also: Panama.

Chestnut-backed Antbird

Myrmeciza exsul   PLATE 32(7)

13.5 cm (5¼"). Fairly common in undergrowth of humid forest and woodland in *w. Colombia and w. Ecuador* (south to El Oro). Mostly below 900 m. *Extensive bare blue skin around eye. ♂* in **most of range** (illustrated) has *head, neck, and underparts slaty black* contrasting with *dark chestnut back, wings, and tail;* wing-coverts with small but conspicuous white spots. In **extreme** nw. Colombia *lacks* wing-spots. ♀ like ♂ above but duller; wing spots buff. Upper throat slaty; *below mostly orange-rufous* (**Ecuador and Pacific Colombia**) to browner with *orange-rufous on chest* (**n. Colombia**). Cf. scarcer Esmeraldas Antbird and (in n. Colombia) Dull-mantled Antbird; both of these have *red* eyes, and neither shows bare skin around eye. Usually in pairs, foraging close to the ground, often perching on vertical saplings; sometimes in areas with an open understory but favors denser growth along streams and around treefalls. Sometimes at antswarms, though not a persistent follower. Pounds tail downward when alarmed. Oft-heard song an easily recognized set of 2–3 whistled notes, "chee, cheeea" or "cheeh, cheeh, cheeéa" (paraphrased as "come . . . here" or "come . . . right . . . here"); ♀'s song higher-pitched. Also: Honduras to Panama.

Esmeraldas Antbird
Myrmeciza nigricauda   PLATE 32(8)

14 cm (5½"). Uncommon in undergrowth of humid and (mainly) foothill forest and woodland from *w. Colombia* (s. Chocó) *to w. Ecuador* (El Oro). 400–1100 m. *Iris bright red. ♂ dark leaden gray* with semiconcealed white dorsal patch; wing-coverts blacker with small but conspicuous white dots. ♀ like ♂ but back, rump, and wings chestnut brown with wing spots buffier; *throat lightly spotted or scaled white.* ♀ Dull-mantled Antbird similar to ♀ Esmeraldas (no known overlap), but brighter and more rufescent above (especially on tail) and throat markings more obvious. ♂ Chestnut-backed Antbird differs from ♀ Esmeraldas in its dark iris, blue skin around eye, and *lack* of throat flecking; ♀ Chestnut-backed, with its orange-rufous below, very different. Cf. also Stub-tailed Antbird. Habits as in more numerous Chestnut-backed, and sometimes found with it. Song a short series of very high-pitched, thin and sharp notes, well-enunciated but does not carry far; "psee-pseé-psi-psi-psi-pseé" with last note higher-pitched and emphasized. ♀ echoes with a short version.

Dull-mantled Antbird
Myrmeciza laemosticta

14 cm (5½"). Uncommon and local in undergrowth of humid forest, *favoring ravines and shady streamsides,* in *n. Colombia and nw. Venezuela* (east to Mérida). Mostly 400–1100 m. *Iris red. ♂* has *head, neck, and most of underparts gray* with *blackish throat.* Back olive brown; wings and tail more rufescent, wing-coverts

with white spots. ♀ like ♂ but *throat scaled black and white* and wing spots buff, thus resembling ♀ Esmeraldas Antbird. Both sexes of commoner Chestnut-backed Antbird have obvious bare blue skin around eye, etc. Dull-mantled does not occur in range of Esmeraldas Antbird (the two species were long confused). Behavior much as in Chestnut-backed Antbird. Song a series of about 6 high-pitched, rather weak notes, e.g., "beet, beet, beet-beet-beet-beet"; ♀ may follow with a softer "beet-beet-chututu." Also: Costa Rica and Panama.

Stub-tailed Antbird
Myrmeciza berlepschi   PLATE 32(9)

13.5 cm (5¼"). Uncommon in undergrowth of humid forest, woodland, and borders in *w. Colombia* (north to s. Chocó) *and nw. Ecuador* (mainly Esmeraldas). Mostly below 400 m. Iris reddish brown. *Tail short. ♂ uniform black;* semiconcealed white dorsal patch. ♀ as in ♂, but wing-coverts with sparse white spotting, and *throat and breast with conspicuous white spotting.* Esmeraldas Antbird has obvious red eye; ♂ Esmeraldas is grayer with white wing-spotting, ♀ is gray and brown with white flecking below only on throat. Usually in pairs that forage close to the ground in dense undergrowth, favoring areas of secondary growth and tangles around treefall gaps. Pounds tail downward. Song a series of downslurred notes that first drops, then rises in pitch, e.g., "chi-chu-chu-chu-chew-chéw-chéw-chéw."

Bare-crowned Antbird
Gymnocichla nudiceps   PLATE 32(10)

16 cm (6¼"). Uncommon in lower growth of humid forest borders and woodland in *n. Colombia.* To 400 m. ♂ unmistakable, *uniform black* with *crown and ocular area bare and bright blue;* semiconcealed white dorsal patch; *wing-coverts fringed white.* ♀ has *only orbital area bare and bright blue.* Above olivaceous to rufescent brown, dorsal patch as in ♂, *wing-coverts more broadly fringed rufous; below uniform rufous.* Chestnut-backed Antbird is smaller, grayer on head, not so bright and uniform below. ♀ Immaculate Antbird is darker brown with *no* wing-covert edging. Usually ranges in pairs, and quite skulking except when at an antswarm (where larger numbers sometimes gather); often in *Heliconia* thickets. Song a series of about 8 loud, ringing, evenly pitched notes, e.g., "chew-chew-chew-chew-cheep-cheep-cheep," recalling Immaculate. Also: Guatemala to Panama.

Wing-banded Antbird
Myrmornis torquata PLATE 32(11)

15.5–16 cm (6–6¼"). *Rather rare and local on or near ground in terra firme forest in n. Colombia, Amazonia, and the Guianas;* perhaps more numerous eastward. Mostly below 400 m, but to 1200 m on tepuis. An *odd-looking* (dumpy) antbird with *short legs, very short tail, and long bill.* Bare orbital skin blue. In **most of range** (illustrated) ♂ brown above mottled with chestnut and dusky; wings blackish, *coverts and outer flight feathers boldly edged buff;* rump and tail rufous-chestnut. *Throat and chest black* bordered by *extensive black and white scaling;* below mostly gray. ♀ differs in having *throat and upper chest rufous.* In **n. Colombia,** ♂ has reduced white scaling, ♀ has rufous only on throat. So oddly shaped that confusion is improbable; though short-tailed like an antpitta, Wing-banded has much shorter legs than they do, and its behavior is much more like that of various typical antbirds. Found mainly as pairs, hopping or shuffling (*not* walking) in leaf litter; often quite tame. Forages by probing into the ground or flicking leaves with bill. Rarely or never with flocks or at antswarms. Infrequently heard song, given from a perch 3–6 m up, a series of emphatic whistled notes that ascend in pitch and increase in intensity, e.g., "tueee-tueee-tueee-tueee-tueee . . . tueee!-tueee!-tueee!" Gives a nasal "churr" call, especially when nervous. Also: Nicaragua to Panama.

Pithys

Two distinctive species, both classic ant-following antbirds found in Amazonian forests, one of them (White-masked) rare, very local, and only recently rediscovered.

White-plumed Antbird
Pithys albifrons PLATE 33(1)

12–12.5 cm (4¾–5"). Fairly common in undergrowth of terra firme forest in the *Guianas and n. and w. Amazonia.* Mostly below 1100 m. Legs yellow-orange. *Conspicuous long white plumes on sides of forehead are held up in a point,* and *shorter white plumes on chin form a beard.* Head and throat black, mantle dark blue-gray. *Nuchal collar, underparts, rump, and tail bright chestnut.* **Juvenile** duller with white plumes reduced or absent, and no rufous collar. Only possible confusion is with rare and range-restricted White-masked Antbird. The attractive White-plumed

is only rarely seen away from antswarms, where a dozen or more individuals may gather; even there they are usually wary, retreating to cover when disturbed, churring in alarm. Typically they cling to slender vertical stems, dropping quickly to the ground in pursuit of prey. A thin listless "tseeeeu" note apparently functions as a song; much more often heard, however, is its descending "chyurrr" call.

White-masked Antbird
Pithys castaneus *

14 cm (5½"). *Recently (2001) rediscovered in undergrowth of humid forest on sandy soil (varillal) in extreme n. Peru* (nw. Loreto). 200–250 m. Legs yellow-orange. Recalls White-plumed Antbird but larger and *lacking white plumes. Mostly chestnut* with *black head and throat, white face and chin.* Evidently an obligate antswarm follower (D. Lane et al.). Distinctive song a whistled and inflected "whoooooeee" repeated at intervals of several seconds (D. Lane recording).

Gymnopithys

Plump antbirds with shortish tail, found widely in humid lowland forest and woodland, *Gymnopithys* are *often the most numerous of the "professional" army ant followers.*

Bicolored Antbird
Gymnopithys leucaspis PLATE 33(2)

14–14.5 cm (5½–5¾"). Fairly common in undergrowth of humid forest and woodland in *w. Colombia and w. Ecuador* (south to Azuay) and *nw. Amazonia.* To 900 m. By some considered two species: *G. leucaspis* (White-cheeked Antbird) east of Andes, *G. bicolor* (Bicolored Antbird) west of them. *Bare ocular area pale bluish east of Andes, dusky* (thus less conspicuous) *west of Andes.* **Eastern birds** (illustrated) *chestnut brown above. Below white,* with black band extending from face onto sides of neck and breast. ♀ differs in its semiconcealed cinnamon-rufous dorsal patch. **Western birds** have a *gray border above black* (not white) *cheeks;* ♀ lacks dorsal patch. This well-named antbird, basically brown above and white below, is hard to confuse. It almost always is found at army antswarms, where it is often the most numerous species present. Like so many other small ant-following antbirds, Bicoloreds habitually perch on slender vertical stems, dropping to the ground in pursuit of prey flushed by the ants. Song a series of whistled notes, at first rising and semimusical, then descending and more nasal, ending with a distinctive snarl or "chrrr." Both sexes often give a "chirr" call. Also: Honduras to Panama.

Rufous-throated Antbird
Gymnopithys rufigula PLATE 33(3)

14.5–15 cm (5¾–6"). Fairly common in undergrowth of humid forest in *ne. South America.* Mostly below 600 m. Large pale bluish ocular area. Brown above with blackish forehead; semiconcealed dorsal patch white in ♂, cinnamonrufous in ♀. *Throat bright rufous;* below dull ochraceous. The wide eye-ring makes this species virtually unmistakable in its range. Behavior and voice as in Bicolored Antbird; often accompanies White-plumed Antbird at antswarms.

White-throated Antbird
Gymnopithys salvini PLATE 33(4)

14.5 cm (5¾"). Uncommon in undergrowth of humid forest in *sw. Amazonia.* To 800 m. ♂ *gray* with *white throat and supraloral stripe;* tail blackish *barred with white.* ♀ has blackish crown and *rufous face, throat, and breast; back brown with blackish and rufous barring, tail rufous barred black.* Belly brownish. Only possible confusion is with Lunulated Antbird; little or no overlap. Behavior and voice (including descending nasal song) much as in Bicolored Antbird.

Lunulated Antbird
Gymnopithys lunulatus

14.5 cm (5¾"). Uncommon and local in undergrowth of *várzea forest* in *e. Ecuador and ne. Peru.* Mostly below 450 m. ♂ resembles ♂ White-throated Antbird but has *plain blackish tail.* ♀ like ♀ White-throated but more olive brown (not so rufous) generally and with *contrasting white supraloral stripe and throat;* tail *dusky* with whitish bars on inner webs. In range the obvious white throat in both sexes distinctive; cf. White-throated (limited or no overlap; ♂ has white barring on tail, ♀ lacks white throat) and Bicolored Antbird. Behavior and voice much as in congeners. Lunulated seems much less numerous than they are, and its song rises less in the middle.

Rhegmatorhina

A quintet of obligate army ant followers, all marked by their *unmistakable round and very wide eye-rings; some are among the fanciest of the antbirds.* They are rather plump

and short-tailed, and *their crown feathers are quite long, sometimes being raised in a loose or spiky crest. Rhegmatorhina occur in Amazonia, where they have entirely allopatric or parapatric ranges, and range primarily in terra firme forest undergrowth.*

White-breasted Antbird
Rhegmatorhina hoffmannsi PLATE 33(5)

15 cm (6"). Uncommon in undergrowth of terra firme forest in *cen. Amaz. Brazil* (east of Rio Madeira and south to Rondônia and w. Mato Grosso). To 300 m. *Wide bare ocular area yellowish green.* ♂ has *black crown,* uniform olive brown upperparts. *Throat and breast white* contrasting with gray belly. ♀ differs in its dark chestnut crown, *mantle with bold black and buff scaling,* and *belly with irregular black and buff banding.* Virtually unmistakable. ♀ Harlequin Antbird (no overlap) is similarly patterned but *lacks* white on foreneck. Like other members of genus, forages principally at army antswarms, usually only a few individuals at a time. They often cling to vertical stems, briefly dropping to the ground in pursuit of prey items. Especially when excited, their long crown feathers are often raised into a loose crest. Flicks tail upward. Song a rather slow, wheezy, "wheeeu, whew-whew-whew-whew-whrr" with descending effect. Sometimes a few snarling notes are appended at end; these and nasal chirrs are also often given independently, especially when at antswarms.

Harlequin Antbird
Rhegmatorhina berlepschi PLATE 33(6)

15 cm (6"). Uncommon in undergrowth of terra firme forest in *small area of e. Amaz. Brazil (west of lower Rio Tapajós).* Below 100 m. *Wide bare ocular area yellowish to glaucous green.* Boldly patterned ♂ unmistakable; crown and nape chestnut with some black intermixed, *black face and throat,* and *rufous chest.* Above olive brown; *sides of neck and underparts gray.* ♀ similar but mantle with black and buff barring, and *lower underparts irregularly banded black and buff.* ♀ White-breasted Antbird (no known overlap, though ranges abut) has striking white throat and chest. Behavior and voice much as in White-breasted Antbird.

Bare-eyed Antbird
Rhegmatorhina gymnops PLATE 33(7)

14.5 cm (5¾"). Uncommon in undergrowth of terra firme forest in *small area of e. Amaz. Brazil (east of lower Rio Tapajós).* Below 200 m. *Wide* ocular area pale glaucous green. ♂ has *head, neck, and breast sooty black;* otherwise brown. ♀ similar but most of breast also brown. Not likely confused in its limited range; ♂ Sooty Antbird is larger and entirely black, has no crest. Behavior and voice much as in White-breasted Antbird.

Chestnut-crested Antbird
Rhegmatorhina cristata PLATE 33(8)
15 cm (6"). Uncommon in undergrowth of terra firme forest in *extreme se. Colombia and nw. Amaz. Brazil.* To 350 m. *Wide bare ocular area pale bluish.* ♂ has *rufous-chestnut crown; sides of neck and underparts rufous,* contrasting black face and throat; otherwise olive brown. ♀ similar, but scattered small black bars on back. Not likely to be confused in its small range. Behavior and voice much as in White-breasted Antbird.

Hairy-crested Antbird
Rhegmatorhina melanosticta PLATE 33(9)
15 cm (6"). Uncommon in undergrowth of terra firme forest in *w. Amazonia.* Mostly below 900 m, but to 1350 m in cen. Peru. *Wide bare ocular area pale bluish to whitish.* ♂ in **most of range** (A) has *pale smoky gray crown* (the feathers filamentous and hairlike; when crest is raised, it looks loose and fluffy, not spiky as in other *Rhegmatorhina*) and *black face and throat;* brown above, wings more rufescent. Below grayish brown. ♀ like ♂ but *mantle with black and buff barring.* **Along Peru's eastern base of Andes** (San Martín to n. Cuzco; B) both sexes differ in their *golden buff crown.* No other antbird in its range has nearly so wide and prominent an eye-ring. Behavior and voice much as in White-breasted Antbird.

Pale-faced Antbird
Skutchia borbae PLATE 33(10)
16.5–17 cm (6½–6¾"). *Rare and local in undergrowth of terra firme forest in small area of cen. Amaz. Brazil* (between lower Rios Madeira and Tapajós). Below 150 m. Small triangle of pale grayish bare skin behind eye. *Large upstanding patch of white feathers on lores and forehead;* upstanding black feathers above eye. Rufescent brown above, back with scattered black bars; tail blackish. *Throat and chest cinnamon-rufous, narrow pectoral band of black and white bars;* dull brown below. Striking and not likely confused. ♀ Reddish-winged Bare-eye has red skin about eye and bold wing-bands, no pectoral band or white on forehead. Behavior much as in various *Gymnopithys* and *Rhegmatorhina* antbirds, likewise most often seen at army antswarms

(on very special occasions together with White-breasteds or Harlequins). Simple, leisurely song a short series of penetrating notes, "peeeeeeeyr, peeeeeyr, peeyur," each note a little shorter (B. M. Whitney recording).

Phlegopsis
Two *boldly patterned, large* antbirds found in Amazonian forests. Both are persistent ant-swarm attendees.

Reddish-winged Bare-eye
Phlegopsis erythroptera PLATE 33(11)
18.5 cm (7¼"). *Uncommon in undergrowth of terra firme forest in nw. Amazonia* (east to lower Rios Negro and Madeira). To 750 m. *Large bare ocular area bright red in ♂, much reduced in ♀.* ♂ unmistakable; *mostly black with feathers of back, wing-coverts, and rump narrowly white-fringed; wings with bold rufous markings.* ♀ dark rufescent brown above with blackish wings and tail, *wings with bold buff bands. Below rich rufous,* belly browner. ♀ can be readily known by combination of large size, rich rufous coloration, and prominent buff on wings. Ranges in pairs that forage in dense undergrowth; typically shy and hard to see well. Often forages at army antswarms (and is dominant over other passerine birds there, except the large woodcreepers), but remains quick to retreat to cover even then. Song a short descending series of 4–6 harsh and piercing notes that drop in strength; Black-spotted's similar song has fewer notes and is slower. Call a snarling, downslurred "skíyarrr," often given at antswarms.

Black-spotted Bare-eye
Phlegopsis nigromaculata PLATE 33(12)
17–18.5 cm (6¾–7¼"). Fairly common in undergrowth of humid forest in *Amazonia;* westward primarily in várzea and floodplain forest, but eastward also in terra firme. Mostly below 600 m. *Unmistakable. Large bare ocular area bright red* (darker in juveniles). **Western birds** (illustrated) have *head, neck, and underparts black,* flanks and crissum brown. Mantle olive brown *with large round or tearlike buff-rimmed black spots;* flight feathers and tail rufous-chestnut. **East of Rio Xingú in e. Amaz. Brazil** smaller, and with *even more extensive bare red eye-ring;* **east of Rio Tocantins,** spots smaller and sparser. Usually found when at antswarms; at large swarms a dozen or more may be in attendance. On rare occasions both bare-eyes can even be at the

same swarm. Song a simple, slow-paced, raspy "zhweé, zhwu" or "zhweé, zhwu, zhwu." Call a rough, drawn-out "zhheeeuw," given especially when at antswarms.

Ocellated Antbird

Phaenostictus mcleannani   PLATE 33(13)

19.5 cm (7¾"). Uncommon in undergrowth of humid forest in *w. Colombia and nw. Ecuador* (mainly Esmeraldas). To 900 m. *Unmistakable. Very large area of bare bright blue skin around eye.* Crown grayish; above olive brown, *mantle with large buff-rimmed black spots;* tail blackish. Ear-coverts, throat, and chest black; *nuchal collar and underparts rufous-chestnut,* with black spots on breast and upper belly. Usually in pairs that forage mainly at antswarms, where dominant over other antbirds. Tail often jerked upward, then slowly lowered. Song a series of high-pitched, penetrating whistled notes that at first rise rapidly, then drop, e.g., "peee-peee-pee-peepee-ee-ee-ee-ee-ee-ee-eer-eer." A nasal "dzurrr" or "dzeerr" call is often given at antswarms. Also: Honduras to Panama.

ANTTHRUSHES: FORMICARIIDAE

Only recently separated from the other antbirds as a distinct family, the Formicariidae has been split apart again and now is considered to include only the genera *Formicarius* and *Chamaeza*. Antthrushes are somberly plumaged terrestrial birds that range in lowland and montane forests where they walk about with tails often partly cocked. Though the birds are hard to see, their far-carrying and beautiful songs are frequently heard. Nests are usually placed atop stumps or on banks.

Formicarius

Dark, rather plain "ground antbirds" that are mainly terrestrial in humid and montane forest and woodland. Shy and much more often heard than seen, these antthrushes are usually seen only after tape playback. *Formicarius* tend to be solitary, walking about with their *short blackish tail jauntily cocked*, resembling nothing so much as a little rail.

Black-faced Antthrush
Formicarius analis PLATE 34(1)
17–18 cm (6¾–7"). Fairly common on or near ground in humid forest and woodland in *Amazonia and the Guianas*. To 1000 m. *The most widespread and numerous Formicarius*. Bare ocular area bluish white, widest behind eye. Brown above with small white loral spot. *Lower cheeks and throat black;* underparts gray, paler on belly; crissum rufous. **Northeastern birds** have some rufous on sides of neck. **Juvenile** has throat flecked whitish or scaled dusky. Cf. Panama Antthrush, until recently considered conspecific. The more boldly marked Rufous-capped Antthrush has contrasting rufous on crown and black on face extending down over breast; in Amazonia, Rufous-capped favors terra firme and Black-faced takes over in second-growth and várzea. Usually seen alone, walking on forest floor. Turns leaves over with bill, or flicks them aside, searching for invertebrate prey in leaf litter. Sometimes attends swarms of army ants. Far-carrying, musical song an emphasized note followed by a pause, then a fast series of shorter notes, first ascending and becoming louder, then slowly descending, e.g., "tüüü, ti-ti-tí-tí-tí-ti-te-

te-tu-tu-tu-tu." Alarm call, given by both sexes, an abrupt "churlew!"

Panama Antthrush
*Formicarius hoffmanni**
18 cm (7"). Uncommon on or near ground in humid forest and woodland in *n. Colombia and n. Venezuela*. Locally to 1600 m. Formerly considered conspecific with Black-faced Antthrush (no overlap), which it resembles in appearance and behavior. However, *song very different*, a much slower "pee, pü, pü, pü . . ." (up to 10–15 püs) with distinctive hesitation after the first note. Also: Honduras to Panama.

Rufous-breasted Antthrush
Formicarius rufipectus PLATE 34(2)
19 cm (7½"). *Uncommon on or near ground in foothill and lower montane forest and woodland in Andes from sw. Venezuela* (Táchira) *to s. Peru* (Cuzco). Mostly 1000–2000 m. Bare ocular area bluish white, broadest in front of and behind eye. **East-slope birds** (illustrated) dark brown above. Face and throat black, *contrasting with rich rufous-chestnut breast;* flanks olivaceous brown, crissum rufous-chestnut. From **w. Venezuela to w. Ecuador** differs in having *contrasting rufous-chestnut crown and nape*. **Juvenile** duller, with whitish throat. Not likely confused in *montane* range; rufous breast unique in genus. Behavior much like Black-faced Antthrush, though generally harder to see. ♂'s simple song a pair of whistled notes, rapidly delivered, "hü-hü," with second note either a semitone above the first (usually) or on the same pitch. Yellow-breasted Antpitta can sound very similar, especially when its first note cannot be heard. Alarm call as in

Black-faced, but can be given in a short series. Also: Costa Rica and w. Panama.

Rufous-capped Antthrush
Formicarius colma PLATE 34(3)

18 cm (7"). Uncommon on or near ground in terra firme forest and woodland from *Amazonia to the Guianas*, and in *e. Brazil.* Mostly below 500 m. **Southern birds** (e. Brazil, and s. Amaz. Brazil east of Rio Madeira; illustrated) have *crown and nape bright rufous,* brown upperparts. *Face, sides of neck, throat, and breast black* becoming grayish on belly. **Elsewhere** has forecrown black. **Juveniles** (perhaps especially ♀♀) have throat white, usually speckled black. Blackfaced Antthrush, which tends *not* to occur in terra firme, differs in its brown crown (showing *no* rufous) and *black on throat only.* Beautiful song a fast series of high-pitched musical notes, which at first falter and drop a little in pitch, then rise; in e. Brazil shorter and somewhat higherpitched. Alarm call a sharp "kyew!" or "tchew!" different from other *Formicarius.*

Black-headed Antthrush
Formicarius nigricapillus PLATE 34(4)

17 cm (6¾"). Fairly common on or near ground in humid lowland and foothill forest in *w. Colombia and w. Ecuador* (south to e. Guayas). Mostly below 900 m. Bare ocular area as in Black-faced Antthrush. *Head, neck, throat, and chest black,* shading into slaty gray on breast; crissum rufous-chestnut. Upperparts rich dark brown. ♀ has belly tinged olivaceous brown. *The only Formicarius in most of its Pacific-lowland range;* overlaps locally with more montane Rufousbreasted Antthrush. Behavior much as in Blackfaced Antthrush. Distinctive and oft-heard song a loud, resonant series of 15–30 short whistled notes, the first few slower, then rising in pitch, the last notes slower again and ending abruptly. Also: Costa Rica and Panama.

Rufous-fronted Antthrush
Formicarius rufifrons PLATE 34(5)

18 cm (7"). *Rare and local on or near ground in swampy floodplain forest in se. Peru and adjacent Brazil and Bolivia.* 300–400 m. Resembles Black-faced Antthrush; occurs with it, but always seems outnumbered. Differs in having less extensive bare skin around eye, an *orange-rufous forecrown,* and entirely sooty gray underparts. Behavior much as in Black-faced Antthrush, but shyer and harder to see. Distinctive song a series of musical notes with even cadence, the

first few lower in pitch, the last sliding off, e.g., "pü-pü-pü-pü-pee-pee-pee-pu-pu-peh-eh."

Chamaeza

Fairly large, plump "ground antbirds" found inside humid or montane forest and woodland. Most are similar and are *best distinguished by their lovely and far-carrying voices;* all are heard much more often than seen. Plumage features include *bold patterning below.*

Short-tailed Antthrush
Chamaeza campanisona PLATE 34(6)

19–20 cm (7½–8"). Locally not uncommon on or near ground in humid forest and woodland, mainly in foothills and subtropics, from n. Venezuela to se. Brazil area (but not in Amazonia). Mostly 500–1800 m, locally higher in Bolivia (exceptionally to 2800 m). *The most widespread Chamaeza;* more than one species likely involved. Lower mandible pale (bill entirely pale in **Ceará, Brazil**). In **most of range** (illustrated) brown above with blackish forehead blotch, *whitish loral spot, postocular streak, and patch on sides of neck* (lores dark in **Ceará, Brazil**); *tail with blackish subterminal band and whitish tip.* Below buffy whitish *coarsely streaked blackish brown,* throat variably speckled. Birds from **e. Brazil southward** are larger. Cf. other, more range-restricted *Chamaeza;* all species are most readily identified by voice. Striated Antthrush (of Amaz. lowlands, limited overlap) is larger, more rufescent above, and much whiter on throat and median lower underparts. Shy and hard to see, found singly or in pairs walking slowly on forest floor, often pumping their somewhat cocked tails (held lower than in *Formicarius*), recalling a bantam hen. Singing birds often take an elevated perch. Beautiful song a series of hollow musical "cow" notes that starts slowly but quickly accelerates and becomes louder, then abruptly shifts into a descending series of 4–6 lower-pitched "wo" or "woop" notes that become weaker and fade away. In Ceará ends with a very different, fast "kuh-kuh-kuh-kuh-kuh," recalling a machine-gun, low-pitched and guttural. Alarm call a "ku-it."

Schwartz's Antthrush
*Chamaeza turdina** PLATE 34(7)

19–19.5 cm (7½–7¾"). Uncommon on or near ground in montane forest in *n. Venezuela* (Yara-

cuy to Miranda), and *very locally in w. Colombia.*
1400–2600 m. Formerly sometimes called Scalloped Antthrush. Bill short, blackish. Rufescent
brown above (including tail, which *lacks* white
tip) with buffyish loral spot and whitish postocular streak. Below white with *well-marked
scalloped pattern, especially across breast.* Shorttailed Antthrush occurs at somewhat lower elevations, has larger and paler bill, more streaked
pattern below, and less uniform tail; most readily
told apart by *voice.* Behavior as in Short-tailed.
Very long song a series of "cu" notes that accelerate and increase in strength, and can go 30 seconds or longer.

Rufous-tailed Antthrush

Chamaeza ruficauda   PLATE 34(8)

19–19.5 cm (7½–7¾"). Common on or near
ground in montane forest and woodland in *se.
Brazil region* (north to Espírito Santo). Mostly
1000–2200 m, lower southward. Bill short, blackish. Resembles geographically distant Schwartz's
Antthrush, but *underparts buffier and with a
coarsely streaked and speckled pattern* (not scalloped). Short-tailed Antthrush occurs at lower
elevations, has a larger bill and less uniform tail.
Short-tailed, Cryptic, and Rufous-tailed Antthrushes occur on the same Brazilian mountains but *segregate by elevation,* with Rufoustailed ranging the highest; *all are best identified
by voice.* Rufous-tailed's song a short, fast series
of bubbling musical notes that rise in pitch, typically lasting 2–3 seconds.

Cryptic Antthrush

Chamaeza meruloides

19–19.5 cm (7½–7¾"). Uncommon and local
on or near ground in montane forest in *se.
Brazil* (se. Bahia to e. Santa Catarina). To 1500
m; *mainly occurs at elevations between those
of Short-tailed and Rufous-tailed Antthrushes.*
Closely resembles Rufous-tailed Antthrush; best
distinguished by voice. Short-tailed Antthrush
has a larger paler bill, blotch on forehead, and
less uniform tail; it too is usually recognized by

voice. Cryptic's distinctive song a *very long* series
(20–30 seconds long) of "cu" notes that gradually
increases in strength.

Striated Antthrush

*Chamaeza nobilis**   PLATE 34(9)

22.5 cm (8¾"). Uncommon on or near ground in
terra firme forest in *w. Amazonia.* Mostly below
700 m. Has been called Noble Antthrush. *Rufescent brown above* with *white loral spot, postocular streak, and patch on sides of neck;* tail with
blackish subterminal band and narrow whitish
tip. *White below* (*no* buff tinge) with *bold blackish scalloping across breast.* More montane Shorttailed Antthrush is smaller; it is less white below
and its pattern is more streaked. Behavior much
as in Short-tailed, but shyer and even harder to see
(often difficult even after tape playback). Beautiful song resembles Short-tailed's but longer and
faster, often with more terminal "woop" notes.
Alarm call a loud, froglike inflected "kowep?"
often given as it paces back and forth. Also gives
a loud ringing "wak-wak-wak-wak-wak . . ." (up
to 20 waks).

Barred Antthrush

Chamaeza mollissima   PLATE 34(10)

20.5 cm (8"). *Rare and local on or near ground
in montane forest in Andes from s. Colombia to
w. Bolivia* (Cochabamba). Mostly 1800–3000 m.
In **most of range** (illustrated) rich chestnut
brown above with buffyish loral spot and *postocular stripe and stripe on sides of neck closely
barred dusky-brown and white. Below densely
barred dusky-brown and white.* In **s. Peru and
Bolivia** throat more streaked, breast with chevron pattern. Other *Chamaeza* are streaked or
scalloped below; none ranges so high. Several
Grallaria antpittas are also barred below, but
these are very differently shaped. Behavior much
as in Short-tailed Antthrush, though Barred is
even more secretive. Beautiful song a long, ascending, gradually louder series of musical "cuh"
notes that ends abruptly (no terminal notes).
Alarm call a fast "whi-whik!"

ANTPITTAS: GRALLARIIDAE

All of the antpitta genera (with the exception of *Pittasoma*, now thought to be most closely related to the gnateaters) were recently placed in their own family. In many ways similar to the antthrushes, antpittas are rounder, plumper birds with short tails and long legs. They too are mainly terrestrial, hopping or scampering on the ground, occasionally mounting into undergrowth but always hard to see. Their loud and distinctive vocalizations will draw attention to these wonderful birds.

Pittasoma

Large, very long-legged and *long-billed, beautifully patterned* antpittas found on or near the ground inside forest in *nw. South America*. Unlike *Grallaria*, they are sexually dimorphic. It has been suggested that they may actually be more closely allied to the gnateaters (Conopophagidae), but we still place them here.

Rufous-crowned Antpitta
Pittasoma rufopileatum   PLATE 34(11)
16–17.5 cm (6¼–7"). *Rare and seemingly local* on or near ground in humid and foothill forest in *w. Colombia and nw. Ecuador* (mainly Esmeraldas). To 1100 m. Unmistakable. Long bill blackish; long legs gray. ♂ in **nw. Ecuador** (A) has *rufous-chestnut crown and nape* and *long broad black superciliary;* olive brown above, back with broad black striping; wing-coverts and tertials dotted whitish. *Face, sides of neck, and throat ochraceous* sparsely dotted black; *below evenly barred black and white.* ♀ has whitish-dotted superciliary and *ochraceous underparts with only sparse spotting and speckling.* In **nw. Colombia** (B) smaller and both sexes plainer, *below unmarked dull buffyish.* In **sw. Colombia** intermediate. Found singly or in pairs, bounding along rapidly, then pausing and freezing for extended periods. Startled birds may flush to low branches. Regularly feeds at army antswarms and then often surprisingly bold. Song a piercing whistled "keeee-yurh," repeated steadily at intervals of several seconds. Calls include a loud and emphatic "tche-tchik!" and a harsh guttural "kuk kuk kuk kuk kuk" (O. Jahn recordings).

Black-crowned Antpitta
Pittasoma michleri
18 cm (7"). *Uncommon on or near ground in humid forest of nw. Colombia* (n. Chocó). To 1000 m. Long bill has lower mandible pale. Unmistakable. ♂ has *crown and nape glossy black* and *chestnut cheeks;* upperparts brown, wing-coverts and tertials dotted buffyish. Throat blackish, *below white boldly scalloped black.* ♀ has throat mainly rufous, buffier underparts with sparser scalloping. Behavior much as in Rufous-crowned Antpitta. Song a long series of clear penetrating "tu" notes that start rapidly and gradually slow, lasting a minute or more. Call is heard more often, a sudden, loud series of 10–16 harsh "wak" notes, fast at start, then slowing. Also: Costa Rica and Panama.

Grallaria

A wonderful group of *plump, round-looking* antbirds with *extremely short tails* and *very long legs* that are found widely in humid and montane forests, reaching their *greatest diversity in the Andes. Grallaria* are patterned in shades of brown, rufous, and gray, and they often show some barring, scaling, or streaking. *Primarily terrestrial* (though ♂♂ often mount to low perches when singing), antpittas can move with surprising agility and speed; most are notoriously shy and secretive, though a few species (notably two found in the high Andes, Stripe-headed and Tawny) range more in the semiopen, and in Ecuador a few others have even been trained to feed on worms, literally coming to your feet! *All antpittas are best known from their simple but attractive songs, generally the best indication of their presence in an area.*

Santa Marta Antpitta
Grallaria bangsi   PLATE 35(1)
18 cm (7"). Common on or near ground in montane forest, secondary woodland, and borders on *Santa Marta Mts. of n. Colombia.* Mostly 1600–2400 m. Olive brown above with whitish lores and eye-ring. *Throat ochraceous buff; below whitish with brownish olive streaking. The only antpitta on the Santa Martas that shows streaking.* Favors dense tangled habitat and so, like the other antpittas, often not easy to see, but in early morning sometimes feeds along the edge of trails and roads. Song a hollow, far-carrying "whow-whoit."

Cundinamarca Antpitta
Grallaria kaestneri
15.5 cm (6"). Uncommon and very local on or near ground in montane forest and woodland on *east slope of E. Andes in ne. Colombia* (e. Cundinamarca). 1800–2300 m. Resembles Santa Marta Antpitta (no overlap), but *smaller* and *darker generally;* throat whitish, *breast grayish olive with white shaft streaking.* Chestnut-crowned Antpitta is larger and has obvious orange-rufous on head. Not well known, but behavior presumably much as in other antpittas. Song (high-pitched for an antpitta) a sharp, shrill "whir, whee-whee" (M. A. Rebolledo recording).

Chestnut-crowned Antpitta
Grallaria ruficapilla   PLATE 35(2)
18.5–19 cm (7¼–7½"). *Common and widespread* on or near ground in montane forest, woodland, and borders in *Andes from n. Venezuela to n. Peru* (Cajamarca and San Martín). Mostly 1900–3100 m. *Legs grayish blue.* In **sw. Ecuador and n. Peru** (illustrated) *head and nape orange-rufous* with whitish lores and streaking on ear-coverts; above olive brown. Throat white; *below white with blackish brown streaking, mainly on sides and flanks.* **Elsewhere** somewhat darker with *entire head orange-rufous* (no white on face), and more streaked below. *In most of range the only antpitta with extensive streaking below.* In sw. Ecuador and far nw. Peru, cf. Watkins's Antpitta; in ne. Colombia, cf. Cundinamarca Antpitta. Though typically shy and secretive like other *Grallaria,* Chestnut-crowneds some-

times hop in the semiopen (especially soon after dawn), though they never stray far from cover. They tolerate disturbed conditions, often favoring bamboo and persisting even in agricultural areas so long as some scrub and thickly vegetated hedgerows remain. Frequently heard and distinctive song a loud whistled "wheee whuuu wheúu" (aptly paraphrased as "com-pra pan" or even "can't-see-me"). Call, also frequent, a loud and abrupt "keeeuw."

Watkins's Antpitta
Grallaria watkinsi   PLATE 35(3)
18 cm (7"). *Common* on or near ground in deciduous and montane forest, woodland, and borders, locally even in regenerating scrub, in *sw. Ecuador* (north to s. Manabí) *and adjacent nw. Peru* (Tumbes and n. Piura). To 1800 m. *Legs pinkish to pale horn.* Watkins's replaces Chestnut-crowned Antpitta at lower elevations, and differs in leg color (Chestnut-crowned's being bluish) and *more pallid and less extensive rufous on crown and nape,* with more white streaking on ear-coverts. The two species are usually distinguished by voice; sometimes they can even be heard from the same spot. Behavior similar, likewise occasionally in the semiopen but usually skulking and hard to see. Distinctive, oft-heard song a series of 4–7 well-enunciated and emphatic whistled notes, the last longer and sharply upslurred, e.g., "keeu, kew-kew-kew k-wheeeei?"

Stripe-headed Antpitta
Grallaria andicolus   PLATE 35(4)
16–16.5 cm (6¼–6½"). *A boldly streaked antpitta of Polylepis groves and scrubby woodland just below treeline in Andes of Peru* (north to Cajamarca and Amazonas) *and extreme w. Bolivia* (La Paz). 3000–4300 m. In **most of range** (illustrated) dark olive brown above, *crown and back with black-edged white streaks.* Below whitish, *feathers edged with black giving scalloped appearance.* In **s. Peru and Bolivia** streaking above restricted to forecrown, and more coarsely marked below. Occurs at higher elevations and in more open terrain than most other antpittas. Hops on the ground inside patches of woodland, sometimes emerging onto adjacent grassy areas. Song weird and utterly unlike other antpittas, with a froglike quality; in Cordillera Blanca a reeling "rrr-rreee?"; in se. Peru a purring "prree-prree-rrréeeeu" (T. Meyer recording).

Ochre-striped Antpitta
Grallaria dignissima   PLATE 35(5)
19 cm (7½"). *Uncommon on or near ground in terra firme and transitional forest in w. Amazonia.* To 450 m. Long legs bluish gray. Above brown, grayer on crown and lores buffyish; long plumes on lower back and rump with white shaft streaks. *Throat and chest rich orange-ochraceous,* chest feathers with white shaft streaks; below white, *sides and flanks broadly striped black and white.* Other than the similar Elusive Antpitta of se. Peru, no other *lowland* antpitta is prominently streaked below. Favors areas near shady streams, there ranging singly or in pairs and always shy and hard to see, hopping and bounding on the ground. Distinctive song a far-carrying and mournful "whü, wheeeow," the second note slurred downward, repeated slowly.

Elusive Antpitta
Grallaria eludens
19 cm (7½"). *Rare and seemingly local on or near ground in terra firme and transitional forest in e. Peru and adjacent w. Brazil.* To 500 m. Resembles Ochre-striped Antpitta (no overlap) but paler and more olivaceous brown above, throat white, and breast tinged buff (*thus lacking orange-ochraceous on foreneck*). Behavior, including voice, similar to Ochre-striped Antpitta. The species lives up to its name!

Great Antpitta
Grallaria excelsa   PLATE 35(6)
24 cm (9½"). *Rare and local on or near ground in montane forest in Andes of n. and w. Venezuela* (Aragua, Lara to Táchira, and on Sierra de Perijá). 1700–2300 m. *Very large.* Olive brown above with gray crown and nape. *Face, sides of neck, and underparts tawny with wavy black barring;* midthroat white. Does not overlap with Giant Antpitta. Undulated Antpitta is smaller with a less contrasting gray crown; it shows a distinct submalar. Great's behavior and voice resemble Giant Antpitta (S. Hilty). Like the Giant, Great apparently is found primarily along forest streams.

Giant Antpitta
Grallaria gigantea   PLATE 35(7)
24 cm (9½"). *Rare and seemingly local on or near ground in montane forest and borders in Andes of s. Colombia and n. Ecuador* (south on west slope to w. Cotopaxi, on east slope to Tungurahua). Mostly 2000–3000 m, but to 1400 m in nw. Ecuador. *Heavy bill. Very large.* In **w. Ecua-**

dor (illustrated) has *rufous forehead* grading into gray crown and nape; above olive brown. *Face, sides of neck, and underparts rich orange-rufous with wavy black barring.* **On east slope and in Colombia** similar but *ground color below a paler ochraceous buff.* Giant is markedly larger than other antpittas except the Great (no overlap). Though still hefty, Undulated Antpitta is noticeably smaller, and further differs in its prominent blackish submalar and lack of rufous on forehead; it ranges at higher elevations than the Giant. Seen singly, hopping with springing bounds through undergrowth and up onto low limbs. Feeds on the ground, probing in muddy soil and leaf litter, often near streams or moving along forest trails; seems to feed primarily on large earthworms. Song on west slope a fast, quavering, hollow trill lasting about 5 seconds; it gradually increases in strength and has an overall owllike effect. East-slope song similar but slightly higher-pitched and typically without an accented ending. It closely resembles Undulated Antpitta's song.

Undulated Antpitta
Grallaria squamigera   PLATE 35(8)
21.5–22.5 cm (8½–8¾"). Uncommon on or near ground in montane forest and woodland in *Andes from w. Venezuela* (Trujillo) *to w. Bolivia* (Cochabamba). 1800–3700 m. Legs grayish. From **s. Ecuador southward** (illustrated) *uniform gray above* with whitish loral spot. *Face, sides of neck, and underparts ochraceous with wavy black barring;* midthroat white bordered by a *prominent black submalar stripe.* **More northern birds** more olivaceous above, with pure gray only on crown and nape; loral area buffyish. A *large* antpitta, usually readily recognizable on that basis alone; Great and Giant Antpittas are even bigger, and have heavier bills, and *no* malar. Shy, retiring, and infrequently seen even in optimal habitat; occasionally seen hopping along forest trails. Feeds mainly on earthworms. Song a fast hollow quavering trill that ascends and lasts 3–4 seconds, e.g., "hohohohohohohohohohohoho," the last few notes more enunciated.

Plain-backed Antpitta
Grallaria haplonota   PLATE 35(9)
16 cm (6¼"). Uncommon to fairly common but rather local on or near ground in *foothill and lower montane forest in Andes from n. Venezuela to n. Peru* (n. San Martín). 700–1800 m. Legs grayish pink. In **most of range** (illustrated) *olive brown above* with pale buffyish lores. *Mid-*

throat whitish bordered by *dusky submalar* and *buff malar; underparts ochraceous,* darker on chest. In **e. Ecuador and ne. Peru** similar but faintly scaled blackish above, and not so richly colored below. Scaled Antpitta has a white chest crescent and is less bright ochraceous below; Plain-backed is never so scaly. An exceptionally secretive antpitta, often judged the hardest to see (though it has stiff competition). Song a series of 10–18 low, hollow, mournful notes that gradually become louder and rise slightly in pitch, then fall at end. Thrush-like Antpitta's song is similar in quality but has fewer notes.

Variegated Antpitta
Grallaria varia   PLATE 35(10)

18–20.5 cm (7–8"). Rare to uncommon on or near ground in humid and lower montane forest and woodland in *the Guianas and lower Amaz. Brazil,* and in *e. Brazil region* (Pernambuco, and s. Bahia southward), where locally more numerous. To 1400 m in Brazil, below 600 m in north. In **e. Brazil region** (illustrated) olive brown above with *gray hindcrown and nape, feathers edged black, giving a scaly look,* and with scattered pale shaft streaks. *Lores and broad malar white,* semiconcealed white patch on chest; *below buff with wavy dusky barring.* **Elsewhere** *markedly smaller* and with *barring below reduced to flank speckling* and pale shaft streaks above reduced. Southern birds are so much larger than other sympatric antpittas that confusion is improbable. Northward it does resemble Scaled Antpitta, but Scaled is a little smaller, never shows shaft streaking on back, and has a wider white crescent across chest and more richly colored belly. Shy and retiring, encountered singly as it hops on forest floor but generally very difficult to see; in early morning one will occasionally forage on damp trails or forest roads. Startled birds may flush to branches up to 4 m above ground. Song in e. Brazil a series of deep, hollow notes that swell in volume, "whoo-doo-doo-doo, WHOO-WHOO-WHOO-WHOO-WHOO-whoo." Northern birds' song similar but shorter and slower.

Scaled Antpitta
Grallaria guatimalensis   PLATE 35(11)

16–16.5 cm (6¼–6½"). Uncommon and local on or near ground in humid forest and woodland on *lower Andean slopes and adjacent lowlands from n. Venezuela to w. Bolivia* (w. Santa Cruz), also *on tepuis.* Mostly 500–1300 m, locally into w. Amaz. lowlands and up to 2000 m. Above olive brown

with grayer crown and nape, *feathers edged black, imparting a scaly look;* lores whitish. Throat and chest brownish olive with *semiconcealed white crescent on upper chest* and *whitish malar; below rufous to tawny-buff* (deepest in **Trinidad** birds, palest in **Peru and Bolivia**). Some birds show white streaking on breast. In s. Colombia and n. Ecuador cf. Moustached Antpitta (replacing Scaled at higher elevations). Plain-backed Antpitta has a whitish throat and shows little or no scaly pattern above. Shy, secretive behavior as in Variegated Antpitta. Song a series of low-pitched, hollow, resonant notes that gradually increases in pitch and volume, slowing in the middle before accelerating again; ♀ may answer with a shorter trill. Giant, Great, and Undulated Antpittas' similar songs are faster. Also: Mexico to Panama.

Moustached Antpitta
Grallaria alleni

16.5 cm (6½"). Rare and local on or near ground in montane forest in *Andes of s. Colombia* (Quindío and Huila) *and n. Ecuador* (w. Pichincha and w. Napo), where somewhat more numerous. 1850–2500 m. Ranges *above* similar Scaled Antpitta. Differs from Scaled in its darker upperparts, uniform dark brown cheeks, and *black scaling in the white malar stripe* (which is often bolder than in Scaled). In **most of range** belly ochraceous, but creamy whitish in **Cen. Andes of Colombia.** Habits as in Scaled and Variegated Antpittas. Song an ascending series of hollow notes that gradually become louder; higher-pitched and slower-paced than song of Scaled.

Táchira Antpitta
Grallaria chthonia

17 cm (6¾"). On or near ground in montane forest in *Andes of sw. Venezuela* (sw. Táchira). 1800–2100 m. Resembles Scaled Antpitta but belly dull whitish, and *breast and flanks barred gray.* Status unknown. The species is not known in life, only from four specimens taken in the 1950s. Behavior presumed to be as in Scaled.

Tawny Antpitta
Grallaria quitensis   PLATE 36(1)

16–18 cm (6–7"). Fairly common to common in shrubby paramo, elfin and scrubby woodland, and hedgerows in *Andes from n. Colombia* (Boyacá) *to n. Peru* (e. La Libertad). *This plain antpitta is relatively easy to see* and is *especially numerous in n. Ecuador.* Mostly 2800–4500 m. *Olive brown above* with *whitish lores and eye-ring. Below dull buffy ochraceous,* whiter on throat and midbelly. In **Colombia's E. Andes** smaller. Rufous Antpitta is much more rufous, and is a forest bird. Usually seen singly, often hopping about in the open (though rarely far from cover), sometimes (especially early morning) on roads or atop low shrubs. Often flicks wings and tail, and bobs up and down on its long legs. Even this antpitta is heard more often than seen; song a loud and far-carrying "took, tu-tu" with hollow ring; unlike most antpittas, sometimes sings from a fairly exposed perch. Also has a loud and penetrating "keeyurr!" call, reminiscent of Great Thrush (which perhaps accounts for the aggression the thrush often shows toward the antpitta).

Rufous-faced Antpitta

Grallaria erythrotis   PLATE 36(2)

18.5 cm (7¼"). *Common on or near ground at borders of montane forest and woodland in Andes of w. Bolivia* (La Paz to w. Santa Cruz). 1700–3300 m. Olive brown above, crown grayer, with *orange-rufous face and sides of neck.* Whitish below, more rufescent on breast and whitest on throat. White-throated Antpitta has entire head rufous and (aside from pure white throat) grayer underparts. Behavior much as in other montane antpittas; occasionally hops at edge of roads passing through forest. Oft-heard song a loud "heeo heu-heu"; also gives a "keeeu" call.

Rufous Antpitta

*Grallaria rufula**   PLATE 36(3)

14.5–15 cm (5¾–6"). *Widespread and locally common* on or near ground in montane forest and woodland in Andes from w. Venezuela (Táchira) to w. Bolivia (Cochabamba). Mostly 2200–3300 m. Multiple species surely involved. In **most of range** (A) *uniform rich rufous,* slightly paler below (especially on belly), with an indistinct eye-ring. In **nw. Peru** (B) much less rufous overall, *more olivaceous brown above* and *paler ochraceous below.* **Sierra de Perijá** birds are olivaceous brown above and pale drab buffy brownish below. In most of range, small size and uniform rufous coloration are sufficient for recognition; in n. Peru, cf. Chestnut Antpitta. Behavior similar to other montane forest-based antpittas, though Rufous seems easier to see than most. Hops singly on forest floor and low in undergrowth, in many areas favoring thickets of *Chusquea* bamboo. In n. Andes has two vocalizations, the more frequent a clear "píh, pipee" or "peé, pipipee," and a series of ringing "tu" notes given so rapidly as to be almost a trill. In Bolivia gives a simple

fast "pee-peu." Song in nw. Peru very different, a piercing "ku-ku kew kew kew," sometimes with an extra "ku" at end. Song also very different in ne. Peru, a repeated "pr-trrrrr" recalling a soft police whistle. Song in ne. Colombia utterly different, a slowly repeated "peeee-trrrr," with an eerie quality unlike any other antpitta.

Chestnut Antpitta

Grallaria blakei

14.5 cm (5¾"). Uncommon and local on or near ground in montane forest and woodland in *Andes of n. Peru* (s. Amazonas and San Martín to Pasco). Mostly 2100–3100 m. Resembles sympatric races of Rufous Antpitta but *darker and more chestnut,* and *shows no eye-ring.* Behavior reportedly much as in Rufous. Song a fast series of evenly pitched ringing notes lasting 3–4 seconds (T. J. Davis).

Gray-naped Antpitta

Grallaria griseonucha   PLATE 36(4)

16 cm (6¼"). Uncommon on or near ground in montane forest in *Andes of w. Venezuela* (s. Trujillo to n. Táchira). 2300–2900 m. Chestnut brown above with *dark gray band extending back from eye to encircle nape.* Below bright rufous. No other similar antpitta in range; Rufous Antpitta does not occur so far north. Behavior much like other montane *Grallaria.* Short song a fast series of hollow notes that become louder and faster, e.g., "ho-ho-ho-hó-hó-hóhóhó"; ♀ sometimes follows with a briefer version.

Bicolored Antpitta

Grallaria rufocinerea   PLATE 36(5)

15.5–16 cm (6–6¼"). Uncommon and local on or near ground in montane forest and woodland in *Cen. Andes of Colombia and on their east slope in extreme n. Ecuador* (Sucumbíos). Mostly 2200–3150 m. *Rufous brown above and on throat; below contrasting gray.* Some birds show gray feathers on face and throat. Chestnut-naped Antpitta is larger, much less rufescent above, and has a black throat. Reclusive behavior similar to other better-known montane *Grallaria* such as the Chestnut-naped. Song a high clear whistled "treeeee" or "treeeeeuh"; ♀ sometimes follows with a "kree-kree-kree-kree-kree-kree" (J. Nilsson recording).

Chestnut-naped Antpitta

Grallaria nuchalis   PLATE 36(6)

19.5–20 cm (7¾–8"). Locally fairly common to common on or near ground in upper montane forest in Andes from n. Colombia (Antioquia) to extreme n. Peru (n. Cajamarca). Mostly 2000–3000 m. *Triangular patch of bare whitish skin behind eye;* legs leaden gray. In **e. Ecuador and Peru** (illustrated) *head dark rufous-chestnut* (brightest on nape); above reddish brown. *Below dark gray,* darker on throat. In **Colombia** slightly brighter on nape and paler below. In **w. Ecuador** darker generally, with *chestnut-rufous only on nape.* Readily recognized by its large size and dark gray underparts. Favors thickets of *Chusquea* bamboo, where usually very hard to see, even with tape playback. In early morning occasionally seen hopping on forest trails. Song on east slope a far-carrying series of musical but somewhat metallic notes that hesitate, then accelerate before ending in a short series of rising tinkling notes, e.g., "tew; tew, tew, tew-tew-tew-teh-te-ti-ti-titititi?" On west slope song similar in quality but lacks initial hesitation and starts with a fast phrase, e.g., "tew-te-te-tew, tew-tew-tew-tew-tew-titititi?" Also gives an unexpectedly different call, essentially a repetition of a much higher-pitched note (almost like a hummingbird), e.g., "tsi-tsi-tsi-tséw-tséw-tsi-tsi-tsi."

Pale-billed Antpitta
Grallaria carrikeri

19 cm (7½"). Uncommon and local on or near ground in montane forest and borders on *east slope of Andes in n. Peru* (s. Amazonas and e. La Libertad, south of Río Marañón). 2350–2900 m. *Bill ivory-colored; iris red.* Resembles Chestnut-naped Antpitta (no overlap, Chestnut-naped only north of Río Marañón), but *crown, face, and throat black.* Like the Chestnut-naped, Pale-billed Antpitta strongly favors bamboo thickets. Distinctive song a rather staccato "kow-kuh, kow kow kow kow kow kow," often slowing and fading toward end; quality recalls a *Glaucidium* pygmy owl.

Yellow-breasted Antpitta
Grallaria flavotincta   PLATE 36(7)

17 cm (6¾"). Uncommon on or near ground in montane forest and borders on *west slope of Andes in w. Colombia and nw. Ecuador* (south to Pichincha). 1300–2350 m. *Above rufous brown,* eye-ring pale grayish. *Below pale yellowish;* sides, flanks, and crissum mottled rufous brown. Not likely confused in its west-slope range, where there is no similar *Grallaria;* the yellow below is unique. Secretive behavior similar to other montane antpittas; seems more confined to actual forest than the White-bellied. Song a fast,

musical, whistled "pu-püüü-puuh," the first note often so quick and soft as to be almost inaudible. Agitated birds can give a shrill and piercing "eeeeeeeeee-yk."

White-bellied Antpitta
Grallaria hypoleuca   PLATE 36(8)

17 cm (6¾"). Fairly common on or near ground in montane forest borders and woodland in Andes from n. Colombia (Antioquia and Santander) *to extreme n. Peru* (n. Cajamarca) 1400–2200 m. *Above rufous brown,* lores pale grayish and slightly darker on crown. Throat white; *below very pale gray,* lower flanks brown. This basically bicolored antpitta (rufescent above, whitish below) should be easily recognized. The larger Chestnut-naped Antpitta is *much* darker gray below and is blackest on throat (instead of having throat white); it occurs at higher elevations. Yellow-breasted Antpitta occurs only on west slope. Secretive behavior similar to other montane forest *Grallaria,* though White-bellied seems to favor second-growth and borders and persists well even in areas with fragmented habitat. Simple, far-carrying song a fast "too, téw-téw," given at rather long intervals (often 10 or more seconds). Also has a vocalization strikingly similar to pygmy owl (*Glaucidium*), "too, too, too, too . . ." (M. Lysinger recording).

Rusty-tinged Antpitta
Grallaria przewalskii   PLATE 36(9)

17 cm (6¾"). Not uncommon on or near ground in montane forest borders and secondary woodland on *east slope of Andes in n. Peru* (Amazonas s. of Río Marañón to e. La Libertad). 2000–2750 m. Rufous brown above with sooty crown and pale grayish lores. *Throat buffyish, deeper rufous on face, sides of neck, and breast;* belly pale gray, lower flanks rufous. White-bellied Antpitta (replaces this species northward) has white throat and pale gray breast. Bay Antpitta replaces this species southward; it is nearly uniform rufous-chestnut. Secretive behavior similar to other montane *Grallaria.* Simple, fast song a whistled "tu teh túu," usually repeated some 5–6 times, then a pause before the sequence is repeated again.

Bay Antpitta
Grallaria capitalis

17 cm (6¾"). Fairly common on or near ground in montane forest, woodland, and borders on *east slope of Andes in cen. Peru* (Huánuco to Junín). Mostly 2000–3000 m. Resembles a saturated

Rusty-tinged Antpitta (the two do not occur together, Bay occurring south of Rusty-tinged), but *throat, breast, and flanks rufous-chestnut* with only midbelly being a paler rufous-buff. Secretive behavior similar to other montane *Grallaria.* Song consists of 4–5 notes with the first higher-pitched, e.g., "tew, too-too-too."

Red-and-white Antpitta
Grallaria erythroleuca   PLATE 36(10)

17.5 cm (7"). Uncommon to locally fairly common on or near ground in montane forest, woodland, and borders on *east slope of Andes in s. Peru* (Cuzco). 2150–2950 m. *Above bright rufous red.* Below white, with *bright rufous red extending down onto sides, flanks, and crissum, some feathers tipped white, giving a spotted effect.* Red-and-white is an exceptionally handsome antpitta that occurs locally with the White-throated; latter is olive brown above, shows no red below. Secretive behavior similar to other montane *Grallaria.* Song a simple, far-carrying "too, teh-too," the second note not as loud.

White-throated Antpitta
Grallaria albigula   PLATE 36(11)

18.5 cm (7¼"). Locally common on or near ground in montane forest, woodland, and borders on *east slope of Andes in s. Peru* (Puna and s. Madre de Dios) *and from w. Bolivia* (Cochabamba) *to extreme nw. Argentina* (Jujuy and Salta). 800 m (in Argentina) to 2700 m (in Bolivia). *Head bright rufous-chestnut* with *prominent white eye-ring* and whitish lores; above olive brown. *Throat pure white;* below grayish white, darkest on sides. Rufous-faced Antpitta (of Bolivia) has a dark crown contrasting with rufous face and is less gray below. Secretive behavior similar to other montane *Grallaria.* Song a pair of mellow whistled notes, "hu-hooo"; excited birds give a short trill.

Jocotoco Antpitta
*Grallaria ridgelyi**   PLATE 36(12)

23 cm (9"). *Rare and very local on or near ground in montane forest with extensive bamboo on east slope of Andes in s. Ecuador* (Zamora-Chinchipe). 2300–2650 m. A recently described species, *unmistakable* and *very different from other antpittas. Crown glossy black, broad snowy white malar stripe starting at lores,* the latter outlined by a *black submalar stripe;* rich olive brown above, back suffused black; flight feathers more rufescent. *Throat snowy white;* below white, suffused and mottled gray. No other antpitta is pat-

terned like this large and striking species. Behavior seems similar to other antpittas, but usually even more difficult to observe, in part because of the steep terrain it favors, in part because it appears to be genuinely wary; however, at Tapichalaca Reserve, the species' stronghold, a few now come in to be fed worms. Ranges in pairs, mainly on steep slopes near streams. Agitated birds run back and forth on branches, bobbing their heads, occasionally singing. Unmistakable song a series, sometimes long-continued (up to a minute or more), of steadily repeated low-pitched hooting "hoo" notes. Other calls include a "hoo-coo" and a more guttural "hoó-krrr."

Brown-banded Antpitta
Grallaria milleri   PLATE 36(13)

16.5 cm (6½"). *Rare and very local on or near ground in montane forest, woodland, and borders in Cen. Andes in Colombia* (on west slope in Caldas and Quindío; also recently found in Ucumarí Park in Riseralda, and on east slope in Río Toche valley of Tolima). 1800–3100 m. *Above dark brown.* Lores, throat, and midbelly grayish white; *breast band and flanks brown.* A dark, unpatterned antpitta. The far more numerous Tawny Antpitta is paler and more ochraceous below, and shows *no* breast band. Behavior not well known, but reportedly similar to other montane antpittas. Most frequent vocalization a loud and slightly rising "wooee," also a soft whistled "puuh, pü-pü" (G. H. Kattan and J. W. Beltrán).

Myrmothera

Two **dull brownish,** forest-inhabiting ant-pittas that recall *Grallaria* but have slenderer bills. Like the other antpittas, heard much more often than seen.

Thrush-like Antpitta
Myrmothera campanisona   PLATE 37(1)

14.5–15 cm (5¾–6"). Fairly common in dense thickets in humid forest and borders of *Amazonia and the Guianas.* Mostly below 1000 m. Possibly more than one species. *Above brown* with grayish lores and whitish postocular spot or triangle. Below white *with extensive blurry grayish brown streaking,* throat and midbelly less marked. Plainer than the various *Hylopezus* ant-pittas found with it in parts of Amazonia. Tepui Antpitta lacks streaking below. Favors areas around treefalls and along streams. Found singly or in pairs, and sedentary, often vocalizing from the same thicket for days on end. Shy and hard to see; usually not responsive to tape playback. Song a fast series of 4–6 hollow mournful notes, "whoh-whoh-whoh-whoh-whoh"; between Rio Madeira and Rio Tapajós in Amaz. Brazil differs in increasing in volume and rising in pitch (K. J. Zimmer and A. Whittaker). Vocalizing birds remain motionless, aside from puffing the throat. Also gives, especially when agitated, a musical trill, e.g., "t-r-r-r-r-r-r-r-r-r-r-r," often while flicking wings.

Tepui Antpitta

Myrmothera simplex PLATE 37(2)
16 cm (6¼"). *Fairly common in humid and montane forest and woodland on tepuis of s. Venezuela region.* Mostly 1200–2400 m. In **most of range** (illustrated) chestnut brown above with *conspicuous white postocular triangle.* Throat white, *breast and flanks plain olivaceous gray.* Birds in **s. Amazonas** have breast and flanks a warmer olivaceous brown. Thrush-like Antpitta is obviously streaked below. Behavior much as in Thrush-like, but seems not as excessively shy. Song a series of 7–10 hollow whistled notes, "wh-wh-wh-whoh-whoh-whoh-whoh-whoh."

Hylopezus

Fairly small antpittas found primarily in humid lowland forests or their borders, all *Hylopezus* have *streaks or spots on breast,* and many have an *obvious eye-ring.* Like other antpittas *Hylopezus* are shy and mainly terrestrial, heard much more often than seen; singing birds often rock from side to side, and also inflate air sacs on sides of neck.

Spotted Antpitta

Hylopezus macularius PLATE 37(3)
14 cm (5½"). Uncommon and rather local on or near ground in humid forest from *the Guianas to Amaz. Brazil, s. Venezuela, and ne. Peru.* To 500 m. *Crown and nape gray* with a *bold ochraceous eye-ring* and buff lores; olive brown above, wing-coverts tipped tawny. White below with black submalar and *conspicuous black spotting across breast,* breast and flanks buff. In n. Bolivia cf. Masked Antpitta (no overlap). Other *Hylopezus* in Amazonia show little or no eye-ring and are *streaked* (not spotted) *on breast.* Behavior much as in Streak-chested Antpitta. Songs vary (more than one species?). In the Guianas and Brazil north of Amazon, gives a modulated

series of hollow whistled notes with unmistakable cadence, "koh, koh, ko-wóh, ko, ko-woh-ko." South of Amazon in Brazil, song a short fast series of hollow notes, "ko-ko-ko-ko-ko." In ne. Peru also different, a more musical "kuhlo-kuhlo-kuhlo, klu, klu."

Masked Antpitta

Hylopezus auricularis *
14 cm (5½"). *Uncommon and very local on or near ground in humid forest borders and secondary woodland in n. Bolivia* (se. Pando and n. Beni). 150–200 m. Recently recognized as a species separate from Spotted Antpitta. Similar to that species aside from Masked's *blackish mask* and more streaked pattern on breast. Song very different, a series of tremulous notes (almost recalling a screech owl) lasting about 4 seconds (S. Mayer recording).

Streak-chested Antpitta

Hylopezus perspicillatus PLATE 37(4)
14 cm (5½"). Uncommon on or near ground in humid forest in *w. Colombia and nw. Ecuador* (mainly Esmeraldas). Mostly below 900 m. Crown and nape gray with *bold ochraceous eye-ring and buff lores;* brown above, wing-coverts tipped buff. White below with black malar streak and *extensive blackish streaking across breast and down flanks.* Thicket Antpitta has a plainer face (no eye-ring), plain wings with no spotting, and buffier underparts with much finer and blurrier streaking. A solitary bird of deep forest that hops or runs for short distances, pausing to flick leaves aside with bill. Sometimes attends antswarms. Surprised birds may flush a short distance to a low perch, pausing there before hopping back to the ground and (usually) scurrying off. Nervous birds often flick wings. Song, often given from a fallen log, a slow series of melancholy whistled notes, first rising but then fading, "poh, po-po-po-po-po-peu-peu-peu." Also: Honduras to Panama.

Amazonian Antpitta

Hylopezus berlepschi PLATE 37(5)
14.5 cm (5¾"). Uncommon in dense thickets at edge of humid forest and woodland from *e. Peru* (Ucayali) *to n. Bolivia and s. Amaz. Brazil.* To 700 m. *Olive brown above* with *buffyish lores and postocular triangle.* Throat white, *partial nuchal collar buff;* below white, *tinged buff on breast and especially on flanks and crissum,* breast streaked dusky. White-lored Antpitta differs in its gray crown, and white lores and nuchal col-

lar; it ranges north of Amazonian. Thrush-like Antpitta lacks buff patterning on face, also lacks buff on flanks. Secretive and hard to see; hops through thick growth, frequently just above the ground in tangles. Song like White-lored, but usually consists of more notes (typically 5–7) and is slower-paced. An inflated pinkish air sac is sometimes exposed when singing. Alarmed birds give a fast "kokokokokokokoko."

White-lored Antpitta
Hylopezus fulviventris   PLATE 37(6)
14.5 cm (5¾"). Uncommon in dense thickets at edge of humid forest and woodland in *s. Colombia, e. Ecuador, and ne. Peru*. To 750 m. Olive above, *darker and slatier on head and nape* with *prominent whitish lores* and a small white postocular triangle. Throat and partial nuchal collar white; below as in Amazonian Antpitta. Amazonian lacks gray on crown; replaces White-lored southward. Thrush-like Antpitta is browner and more uniform above, *lacks* whitish lores and has no buff below. Behavior as in Amazonian Antpitta. Song a short slow series of 3–4 abrupt and hollow notes, e.g., "kwoh-kwoh-kwoh-kwoh," with the first note soft and inaudible at a distance. Also gives a faster, accelerating series of shorter notes, "kow-kow-kow-kow-ko-ko-ko-ko-ko-ko-ko."

Thicket Antpitta
*Hylopezus dives**
14 cm (5½"). Fairly common in dense thickets at edge of humid forest and woodland in *w. Colombia and very recently in extreme nw. Ecuador* (n. Esmeraldas). To 900 m. Formerly called Fulvous-bellied Antpitta. Resembles White-lored Antpitta of w. Amazonia, but has *less conspicuous buffyish lores,* crown and nape not as dark slaty, and *brighter orange-rufous flanks.* Cf. Streak-chested Antpitta, which replaces this species inside more mature forest; it has a bold eye-ring, wider and blacker streaking below, etc. Behavior much as in Amazonian Antpitta, and equally difficult to see. Song very different, a series of 6–8 whistled notes that ends abruptly (not fading away as in Streak-chested), "oh-oh-ou-ou-ou-uu-uu-uu." Also: Honduras to Panama.

White-browed Antpitta
Hylopezus ochroleucus   PLATE 37(7)
13.5 cm (5¼"). *Uncommon and local on or near ground in caatinga woodland and scrub in ne. Brazil* (Piauí to n. Minas Gerais). 500–1000 m. Olive brown above, grayer on crown with *white*

lores, eye-ring, and postocular stripe; ochraceous patch at base of primaries. White below, breast boldly spotted dusky, flanks buff. *The only antpitta in its range and habitat;* Speckle-breasted (of se. Brazil; no overlap) lacks the postocular, and has a very different song and habitat. Hops on or near the ground, and almost always hard to see; even singing birds are normally difficult to locate, remaining within dense thickets. Far-carrying and distinctive song a ringing, two-part "whu-whú, whu-whú-whu-whu-wheú-wheú-wheú-wheú-wheú-wheú-wheú-wheú."

Speckle-breasted Antpitta
Hylopezus nattereri   PLATE 37(8)
13.5 cm (5¼"). Locally fairly common on or near ground in montane and humid forest and woodland in *se. Brazil region* (north to s. Minas Gerais). To 1600 m (northward mainly above 900 m). Olive brown above with *buffy whitish lores and partial eye-ring;* ochraceous patch at base of primaries. Below pale buffyish, whiter on throat, with black submalar and *profuse black spotting and speckling.* Does not overlap with White-browed Antpitta. Only other antpitta in Speckle-breasted's range is the very different and much larger Variegated. Behavior much as in White-browed Antpitta but perhaps even harder to see; favors areas with dense bamboo. Song a fairly fast series of 7–10 whistled notes that slide upscale and become more emphatic, e.g. "teeu-teeu-teeu-teeu-teeu-téw-téw-téw-téw!"

Grallaricula

Very small, often attractively patterned antpittas found inside montane forest and woodland, where they are notably inconspicuous; unlike other antpitta genera, *Grallaricula only rarely descend to the ground.* They sometimes rock from side to side while holding their legs stationary. Many *Grallaricula* have notably small ranges, and some of these also appear to be genuinely rare, even in appropriate habitat. Some species are quite vocal, but others appear to be much less so.

Hooded Antpitta
Grallaricula cucullata   PLATE 37(9)
10 cm (4"). *Seemingly rare and local* (but may just be overlooked) in undergrowth of montane forest in *Andes of extreme sw. Venezuela* (sw. Táchira) *and Colombia* (south to w. Caquetá). Mostly 1800–2550 m. *Bill orange-yellow. Head*

and throat orange-rufous; above olive brown. Below pale gray, with white crescent on lower throat. *No other small antpitta has a completely rufous head.* Color pattern, and indeed shape, reminiscent of Rufous-headed Pygmy-Tyrant. Behavior much as in Slate-crowned Antpitta.

Slate-crowned Antpitta
Grallaricula nana   PLATE 37(10)

11 cm (4¼"). Locally fairly common in undergrowth of montane forest in *Andes from n. Venezuela to extreme n. Peru* (n. Cajamarca), and on *tepuis.* Mostly 2000–2900 m, but lower in Venezuela and w. Colombia. *Crown slaty gray with lores and eye-ring buffy ochraceous; above olive brown. Below rich orange-rufous.* Rusty-breasted Antpitta lacks the gray crown and is less richly colored below. Inconspicuous and difficult to see in its favored *Chusquea* bamboo thickets, but does respond to tape playback. Frequently remains motionless for long periods, occasionally flicking its wings. Does not associate with flocks. Song a pretty, rather high-pitched series of 14–18 notes that fades and descends slightly, e.g., "we-e-e-e-e-e-e-e-ew."

Crescent-faced Antpitta
Grallaricula lineifrons   PLATE 37(11)

11.5 cm (4½"). Uncommon and very local (perhaps just overlooked) in undergrowth of upper montane forest and woodland in *Cen. Andes of s. Colombia* (Quindío; Puracé Nat. Park in Cauca) and on *east slope of Andes in Ecuador* (se. Carchi to n. Loja). 2900–3400 m. *Head dark slaty with conspicuous white crescent in front of eye,* white postocular spot, and *ochraceous patch on sides of neck;* above brownish olive. Midthroat white, submalar black; *below heavily streaked black and buff.* The fancy facial pattern is unique. Behavior much as in Slate-crowned Antpitta, and equally hard to see (or even harder), though when breeding it responds to tape playback. Song an ascending series of high-pitched piping notes, the last few shriller, "pu-pu-pe-pe-pee-pee-pi-pi-pi?"

Ochre-breasted Antpitta
Grallaricula flavirostris   PLATE 37(12)

10 cm (4"). Uncommon and seemingly local (perhaps just overlooked) in undergrowth of montane forest and borders in *Andes from n. Colombia* (Antioquia) *to w. Bolivia* (Cochabamba). Mostly 800–2200 m. *Bill usually bicolored, dark above and yellow below,* but all dark in a few birds from east slope, and entirely yellow in most sw. Ecuador birds. In **most of range** (A) olive

brown above with an *ochraceous eye-ring and lores. Throat and breast ochraceous,* belly whitish, breast and flanks streaked blackish (often extensively); most birds from **sw. Ecuador** are uniform ochraceous on throat and breast *with little or no streaking.* Birds from **Peru and Bolivia** (B) are *much more boldly scalloped with blackish below* and have a blackish malar. Rusty-breasted and Leymebamba Antpittas show no streaking below and have white eye-rings. Cf. Peruvian and Ochre-fronted Antpittas (both rare). Behavior much as in Slate-crowned Antpitta, but even less frequently seen, in part because it isn't very vocal. Only vocalization known for certain is a weak piping "weeeu," repeated at long intervals. Also: Costa Rica and Panama.

Rusty-breasted Antpitta
Grallaricula ferrugineipectus   PLATE 37(13)

10 cm (4"). Fairly common in undergrowth and borders of montane forest in *Andes of n. and w. Venezuela and n. Colombia* (south to Cundinamarca). 600–2200 m. Brownish olive above with buff lores and *bold white eye-ring. Uniform rich ochraceous below.* Rusty-breasted lacks the obvious dark streaking below shown by virtually all Ochre-breasted Antpittas. Behavior much as in Slate-crowned Antpitta. Song a fast series of soft, somewhat nasal notes that accelerates before the last note drops, e.g., "kwi-kwi-kwi-kwi-kwi-kwi-kwi-kwi-kwu."

Leimebamba Antpitta
Grallaricula leymebambae*   PLATE 37(14)

10.5 cm (4¼"). Uncommon in undergrowth of montane forest in *Andes from s. Ecuador* (s. Loja) *to w. Bolivia* (La Paz). 1750–3350 m. Usually considered conspecific with Rusty-breasted Antpitta (occurring far to the north). Brownish olive above with buff lores and *bold white triangular patch behind eye. Rich ochraceous below* with a dusky malar and olive mottling on breast. Sympatric Ochre-breasted Antpittas (which mainly occur at higher elevations) are less ochraceous and much more heavily marked below. Song a fast series of melodic notes, "pi-pee-pee-pee-pee-pee," quite different from Rusty-breasted.

Peruvian Antpitta
Grallaricula peruviana   PLATE 37(15)

10 cm (4"). Rare and local in undergrowth of montane forest on *east slope of Andes from ne. Ecuador* (w. Napo) *to extreme n. Peru* (Cajamarca and Piura). 1650–2100 m. ♂ has *crown and nape rich rufous* with buff lores and bold

partial eye-ring; above brown. *White below* with black submalar and *heavy black scalloping across breast and on flanks.* ♀ has brown crown and blackish forecrown. Cf. the rare Ochre-fronted Antpitta. Ochre-breasted Antpitta shows at least some ochraceous below. Not well known, but behavior seems much as in other *Grallaricula*, though Peruvian is felt to be warier and even harder to see than most (fide M. Lysinger). It favors undisturbed forest and is *not* in bamboo. Not very vocal, the only known vocalization a soft, plaintive "peeeu" given at intervals of 10–15 seconds.

Ochre-fronted Antpitta
Grallaricula ochraceifrons
10.5 cm (4¼"). Rare and local in undergrowth of stunted and montane forest in *Andes of n. Peru* (Amazonas and San Martín, south of Río Marañón). 1900–2400 m. Resembles Peruvian Antpitta. ♂ differs in having an *ochre forecrown,* buff eye-ring, *olive brown crown,* and *coarse streaking below mainly confined to breast.* ♀ lacks the ochre frontal area. Sympatric Ochre-breasted

Antpittas are buffier below with a more scalloped (not so streaked) pattern and buff loral spot. Poorly known, but behavior seemingly similar to other *Grallaricula.* Presumed song a whistled "wheeu" repeated every 5–6 seconds (H. Lloyd recording).

Scallop-breasted Antpitta
Grallaricula loricata   PLATE 37(16)
10 cm (4"). Seemingly rare (but apparently often overlooked, and locally not uncommon) in undergrowth of montane forest in *mountains of n. Venezuela* (Yaracuy to Distrito Federal). 1400–2100 m. Bill yellowish below. *Crown and nape rufous, lores and partial eye-ring buff;* above olive brown. Throat pale buff, malar streak black; *below white with black scalloping.* In its limited range, nothing remotely similar. Inconspicuous behavior as in other *Grallaricula,* hopping in undergrowth and generally solitary. Song a series of 3–5 "shiiiuu" notes repeated at intervals of 3–5 seconds; also gives a much more drawn-out but similar note (C. Verea).

GNATEATERS: CONOPOPHAGIDAE

A small group of small, plump, short-tailed birds that resemble certain smaller antpittas but are sexually dimorphic and almost always sport a distinctive silvery postocular tuft, flared when the bird is agitated. Gnateaters range on or near the ground inside forests and, being not particularly vocal, are hard to see.

Chestnut-crowned Gnateater
Conopophaga castaneiceps   PLATE 38(1)
13–13.5 cm (5–5¼"). Uncommon and local in undergrowth of *montane forest in Andes from n. Colombia* (Chocó and Antioquia) *to s. Peru* (Cuzco). Mostly 1000–2000 m. Lower mandible pale. In **s. Peru** (illustrated) ♂ *chestnut brown above,* more rufous on forecrown, with *long white postocular tuft. Below slaty gray,* paler on belly. In **Colombia and n. Ecuador** has a brighter crown and grayer mantle. In **e. Ecuador and n. Peru** intermediate. ♀ like ♂ above but with brighter forecrown. *Throat and chest orange-rufous,* belly pale grayish. *Limited or no overlap with other gnateaters;* Ash-throated Gnateater (both sexes) has buff spots on wing-coverts and a prominent scaly pattern on back. Found singly or in pairs, favoring dense tangles that spring up around treefalls. Often perches on vertical saplings, remaining low but rarely actually dropping to the ground. Does not follow mixed flocks. Not particularly shy. Infrequently heard song an ascending series of rattled notes, "chrrr, chrr-chrr-chrr-chrr-chrr-chrrít." Call a sharp and abrupt "zhweeík" similar to other gnateaters.

Slaty Gnateater
Conopophaga ardesiaca   PLATE 38(2)
13–13.5 cm (5–5¼"). Locally fairly common in undergrowth of montane forest and woodland on *east slope of Andes from s. Peru* (s. Cuzco) *to s. Bolivia* (Tarija). Mostly 800–1700 m. Lower mandible pale. ♂ olive brown above with *long white postocular tuft. Below plumbeous gray,* belly whiter. ♀ as in ♂ but with *orange-rufous forecrown* and virtually no postocular tuft. ♂ Chestnut-crowned Gnateater (occurring just to north of Slaty) has an orange-rufous forecrown. ♂ Ash-throated Gnateater (of Amaz. lowlands; no known overlap) has grayer back and buff dots on wing-coverts. Behavior as in Chestnut-crowned Gnateater. Calls include a

repeated, sometimes querulous "jereeé" and a sharp "psii."

Rufous Gnateater
Conopophaga lineata   PLATE 38(3)
13 cm (5"). Locally common in undergrowth and borders of humid forest and woodland from *ne. Brazil to e. Paraguay and ne. Argentina.* To 2400 m. Bill pale below. In **most of range** (north to s. Bahia; A) ♂ rufescent brown above with *gray superciliary merging into silvery postocular tuft* (all gray in ♀). *Throat and breast orange-rufous,* midbelly white. In **ne. Brazil** (B, sometimes treated as a separate species, Ceará Gnateater, *C. cearae*) ♂ lacks gray superciliary (but retains the silvery postocular, *cinnamon in* ♀) and is *brighter cinnamon-rufous generally.* Behavior as in other gnateaters, *though Rufous typically is more numerous and easier to see,* and sometimes even moves with mixed flocks. It can persist even in rather degraded or fragmented habitat. Song a series of 8–10 high-pitched whistled notes, hesitating at first, then rising, e.g., "tew; tew; tew, tew, tew-tew-tiw-tiw-ti-ti"; there is little variation across its range. Also frequent is a sharp, sneezing "chiff" or "cheff" call.

Black-cheeked Gnateater
Conopophaga melanops   PLATE 38(4)
11.5 cm (4½"). Uncommon in undergrowth inside humid forest and woodland in *e. Brazil* (Paraiba to e. Santa Catarina). To 1000 m. **Southern** ♂ (north to s. Bahia; illustrated) has *bright orange-rufous crown and nape, black face and sides of neck;* brown above, back feathers scaled black and wing-coverts dotted buff. Throat white; below mainly gray. **Northern** ♂ similar but with a black frontlet, gray upper midback. ♀ rufescent brown above with *long narrow white superciliary, black fringing on back feathers,* and *buff-tipped wing-coverts.* Below mostly orange-rufous. ♀ resembles slightly larger Rufous Gnateater though

that has a pale lower mandible (bill all black in Black-cheeked) and no dots on wing-coverts or back scaling. Behavior as in other gnateaters, though seems more terrestrial. Song a fast trill lasting 5–8 seconds (B. M. Whitney), but much more often heard is a sharp "bzheeyk!" call.

Ash-throated Gnateater
Conopophaga peruviana   PLATE 38(5)
11.5–12 cm (4½–4¾"). Uncommon in undergrowth of humid forest in *w. Amazonia*. Mostly below 600 m, locally to 1000 m in Peru. ♂ has crown dark brown with grayish lores and a *long white postocular tuft;* brownish gray above, *back feathers margined black;* wings chestnut brown, *coverts tipped buff. Below gray,* midbelly whiter. ♀ above much like ♂ but browner generally and with rufous crown. Throat whitish, *sides of neck and breast orange-rufous,* midbelly whitish. ♀ Chestnut-belted Gnateater differs from ♀ Ash-throated in its nearly plain back (little or no black scaling) and wings (no obvious buff dots). Favors tangled habitat around treefalls and viny areas on well-drained ridges. Hard to see, but often unwary once located. Song a loud and inflected "zhweeík" repeated at well-spaced but regular intervals. Also gives a soft, low-pitched call, "shreff."

Chestnut-belted Gnateater
Conopophaga aurita   PLATE 38(6)
11.5–12 cm (4½–4¾"). Uncommon in undergrowth of humid forest from Amazonia to the Guianas. Locally to 700 m. ♂ from **w. Amazonia to the Guianas** (A) has chestnut crown with a *long white postocular tuft;* brown above, back feathers faintly scaled black. *Forehead, face, and throat black* contrasting with rufous sides of neck and breast (the "belt"); midbelly white, flanks pale brownish. In **e. Amaz. Brazil** (B) the black throat extends down over breast, obliterating the rufous. ♀ like ♂ above (including white tuft). *Sides of neck, throat, and breast orange-*

rufous; midbelly white, flanks pale brownish. Dapper ♂ can hardly be confused. ♀ resembles ♀ Ash-throated Gnateater, aside from its plainer upperparts (less black scaling, no buff wing dots). Behavior similar to Ash-throated. Song a loud, harsh rattling trill that ascends slightly, then levels off.

Hooded Gnateater
Conopophaga roberti   PLATE 38(7)
12 cm (4¾"). Uncommon and local in undergrowth of humid forest in *ne. Brazil* (Pará to Ceará). Below 300 m. Bill pale below. ♂ has *head, throat, and breast black* with *contrasting long white postocular tuft.* Above rufous brown; *belly mainly whitish.* ♀ rufous brown above with *white postocular tuft. Below mainly ashy gray.* ♂ Chestnut-belted Gnateater in e. Amaz. Brazil resembles ♂ Hooded but has chestnut crown and buffy belly. ♀ Black-bellied Gnateater is much larger and has dull crown contrasting with much brighter mantle. Not well known, but behavior and voice seem similar to congeners.

Black-bellied Gnateater
Conopophaga melanogaster   PLATE 38(8)
14.5 cm (5¾"). Uncommon and local in undergrowth of humid forest in *s. Amaz. Brazil.* To 700 m. *Large* and long-tailed. Stunning ♂ has *entire head and most of underparts black* with *contrasting long silvery postocular tuft. Upperparts bright rufous-chestnut.* ♀ has dark gray forecrown, dark brown hindcrown and nape, and *white postocular tuft; above bright rufous-chestnut. Mostly pale gray below.* Cf. ♀ of substantially smaller Hooded Gnateater. Behavior much as in other gnateaters, favoring dense tangles, most often near streams or on banks. Infrequently heard song a series of 2–5 short grating notes, e.g., "k-cherr, k-cherr, k-cherr, k-cherr"; calls include a gruff "chuff" or "cheff" and other rattles.

Spotted Bamboowren

Psilorhamphus guttatus PLATE 38(9)

13.5 cm (5¼"). Rare to uncommon and local in lower growth of humid forest, woodland, and borders in *se. Brazil* (Espírito Santo and e. Minas Gerais to ne. Rio Grande do Sul) *and ne. Argentina* (Misiones). To 900 m. Iris yellowish; *rather long slender bill,* pale below. ♂ *above mostly gray with small white dots;* wings and tail rufescent, wing-coverts white-dotted and rather long tail dusky, notched along sides with buff and tipped white. *Below pale grayish with minute black dots,* flanks rufous. ♀ brown above instead of gray, buffier below; *retains ♂'s spotting.* Virtually unmistakable, but cf. Long-billed Gnatwren. Well named, the bamboowren strongly favors bamboo, but it can also occur in thick growth of other types. Found singly or in pairs, gleaning in foliage 2–5 m above the ground; often cocks tail. Usually not with mixed flocks. Unique song a fairly fast series of hollow resonant notes like a ringing bell, lasting 15 seconds or more, e.g., "to-to-to-to-to. . . ." Note that the bamboowren continues to be classified as a tapaculo; accounts for that family commence on p. 392.

CRESCENTCHESTS: MELANOPAREIIDAE

This small genus of attractive, ultradistinctive birds was recently separated as a family distinct from the tapaculos; the odd Sandy Gallito (cf. p. 393) is usually placed with them. Crescentchests favor low grassy scrub and, except when singing, are skulking birds; they range from w. Ecuador to nw. Argentina. Nests are woven grass structures hidden in tall grass on or near the ground.

Olive-crowned Crescentchest

Melanopareia maximiliani　　PLATE 38(10)

15 cm (6"). Uncommon in grassy areas with scattered bushes and chaco scrub in *Andes from w. Bolivia* (La Paz) *to n. and w. Argentina* (n. San Luis and Córdoba) *and east to w. Paraguay.* Mostly below 2200 m, but locally to 3000 m in Bolivia. **Andean and foothill birds** (illustrated) *olivaceous above* with long narrow whitish superciliary, *black sides of head,* and large but semiconcealed white dorsal patch. Throat pale buff, *narrow pectoral band black;* below mostly rufous. **Lowland birds farther east** have a whiter throat and darker chestnut underparts. Collared Crescentchest, found to north and east, has a prominent rufous nuchal collar. Ranges singly or in pairs, creeping and hopping in grass on or near the ground, usually remaining out of sight except when singing, then often mounting into a shrub. Song in most of range a fast series of 15–20 syncopated "tu" notes; however, birds in Argentinian highlands give a faster trill that lasts 3–4 seconds, e.g., "tree-ee-ee-ee-ee-ee-ee-ee-ee." Sings periodically throughout day. Collared's song is much more leisurely.

Collared Crescentchest

Melanopareia torquata　　PLATE 38(11)

14.5 cm (5¾"). Uncommon in grassy cerrado with scattered bushes in *interior cen. Brazil, n. Bolivia, and extreme ne. Paraguay.* To 1000 m. In **most of range** (illustrated) rufescent brown above with long narrow white superciliary, *black sides of head, rufous nuchal collar,* and large but semiconcealed white dorsal patch. Throat buff, *narrow pectoral band black;* below tawny-buff.

In **e. Bolivia** more brownish olive above, deeper ochraceous below. Olive-crowned Crescentchest (no overlap) lacks the nuchal collar. Behavior as in Olive-crowned. Far-carrying song a leisurely, monotonous series of sharp but melodic "tü" notes given at rate of about 1 per second for up to 20–30 seconds.

Elegant Crescentchest

Melanopareia elegans　　PLATE 38(12)

14.5 cm (5¾"). Uncommon to locally fairly common in dense arid scrub and woodland undergrowth from *sw. Ecuador* (Manabí) *to nw. Peru* (La Libertad). To 2300 m in s. Ecuador. ♂ has *head black* with *long buffy white superciliary;* back grayish olive. Wing-coverts and inner flight feathers edged rufous, primary-coverts and outer primaries edged silvery. *Throat buffy white, black pectoral crescent across chest,* bordered below by chestnut blending into cinnamon-buff belly. ♀ duller above, with sooty brown crown and *lacking chestnut* below its narrower black pectoral band. This handsome bird is not likely confused in range; it does not occur with Marañón Crescentchest. Forages low in dense vegetation, sometimes hopping on the ground. Furtive, even when singing rarely in the open for long. Distinctive and far-carrying song a chortling "cho-cho-cho-cho-cho-cho-cho-cho." Sings at intervals throughout day.

Marañón Crescentchest

Melanopareia maranonica

16 cm (6¼"). Uncommon in arid scrub in *Río Marañón drainage of extreme s. Ecuador* (s. Zamora-Chinchipe) *and nw. Peru* (Cajamarca).

200–1050 m. Resembles Elegant Crescentchest (no overlap), but *larger*. Both sexes differ further in having *conspicuous silvery edging on most of wing feathers* (and *no* rufous edging), and more deeply colored underparts; ♀'s black pectoral band is wider. Unmistakable in its restricted range. Habits and voice as in Elegant Crescentchest.

TAPACULOS: RHINOCRYPTIDAE

Small to midsized birds found mainly in the Andes and in s. South America, tapaculos have lax plumage in which gray predominates (though a few species are more boldly barred or spotted); there is little or no sexual dimorphism. Well over half the tapaculos are members of the genus *Scytalopus*, one of the most confusing and difficult Neotropical bird groups (though at least many of its constituent species replace each other geographically). Tapaculos are skulking, weak-flying, and mouselike birds found in forest undergrowth or scrub, best known from their vocalizations. Nests are globular, ball-shaped structures very well hidden on or near the ground.

Pteroptochos

Three splendid, *very large* and *boldly patterned* tapaculos *found mainly in Chile*. *Pteroptochos* tapaculos are characterized by their *long legs and very large, strong feet with long claws*.

Black-throated Huet-huet
Pteroptochos tarnii   PLATE 39(1)
24–25 cm (9½–9¾"). *Locally common on and near ground* in Nothofagus-*dominated forest and woodland in s. Chile* (Arauco and Bío-Bío to n. Magallanes) *and adjacent Argentina. Very large* and *long-tailed.* To 1500 m. Crown rufouschestnut; *head, neck, chest, and upperparts slaty black* with *conspicuous buffy pinkish eye-ring,* rump rufous. Below rufous-chestnut with a variable amount of barring on belly. Cf. Chestnutthroated Huet-huet. Chucao Tapaculo is conspicuously smaller, etc. Usually remains hidden as it walks on forest floor, pausing to scratch, often vigorously, in ground litter; in early morning sometimes emerges to forest edge. Favors areas with extensive bamboo. The long tail is often held cocked. Heard much more often than seen, the most frequent call being a loud and onomatopoeic "whet," sometimes doubled or trebled. Also gives a descending series of hollow notes, e.g., "wok-wok-wok-wok-wok-wu." Low, sonorous, and powerful song a fast series of about 25 "whoo" notes that gradually become louder.

Chestnut-throated Huet-huet
Pteroptochos castaneus
24–25 cm (9½–9¾"). *Uncommon on and near ground in* Nothofagus-*dominated forest and woodland in cen. Chile* (Colchagua to Nuble and Concepción) *and adjacent Argentina* (a recent record in n. Neuquén). To 1500 m. Replaces Black-throated Huet-huet northward, north of the Río Bío-Bío. Resembles that species, and also has a *pinkish eye-ring.* Differs in its *solid chestnut foreneck and throat* contrasting with *gray sides of neck;* chestnut on crown darker and less extensive; and more barring on belly. Moustached Turca occurs in more open, arid habitats and has obvious white on sides of throat. Chestnutthroated's behavior is much as in Black-throated Huet-huet, and it likewise favors bamboo. Song similar but somewhat higher-pitched, softer, and faster-paced, with slightly more notes; call a rather different series of nasal clucking "wehk" notes (S. N. G. Howell and S. Webb).

Moustached Turca
Pteroptochos megapodius   PLATE 39(2)
23–24 cm (9–9½"). *Common on or near ground in matorral and scrub on arid, semiopen slopes in cen. Chile* (Atacama to Concepción). Locally to about 3000 m. *Very large* and *long-tailed.* In **most of range** (illustrated) *pale grayish brown above* with *superciliary and broad moustache white.* Breast rufescent brown, belly whitish with black and brown barring (usually extensive). **Northern birds** are smaller and paler with reduced barring below. The conspicuous moustache

renders this splendid tapaculo unmistakable. White-throated Tapaculo is markedly smaller, more skulking, etc. Turcas often walk and stand in the open early and late in the day, sometimes even on roadsides; they also perch atop boulders and shrubs. The long tail is usually held sharply cocked; large, powerful feet scratch the ground vigorously. Turcas fly infrequently, preferring to hop and run, and at times they can move astonishingly fast. Breeding birds are vocal, giving a fast series of "wok" notes and a much slower series of 10–15 far-carrying "wook" or "wuuk" notes that gradually drop in pitch.

Scelorchilus

Two distinctive, *fairly large,* and *boldly patterned* tapaculos found *primarily in Chilean forests and woodlands.*

Chucao Tapaculo
Scelorchilus rubecula　　　　PLATE 39(3)
18.5–19 cm (7¼–7½"). *Locally common on or near ground in* Nothofagus-*dominated forest and woodland in s. Chile* (north to Colchagua) *and adjacent Argentina.* To 1500 m. Above rufescent brown with *lores and postocular stripe orange-rufous* and gray auriculars and sides of neck. *Throat and chest orange-rufous; below barred black and white,* sides gray. Unlikely to be confused, but cf. the much larger huet-huets. This handsome tapaculo favors the bamboo stands that are so prevalent across its range; Chucaos also can be frequent in patchy, fragmented landscapes. They are mainly terrestrial, walking on the forest floor usually with long tail cocked, only rarely coming to edge. They occur singly and in pairs. During the nesting season heard much more often than seen, its resoundingly loud and abrupt "chuu, chu-chu-chu-caoow" then emanating from all around, though without tape playback the birds themselves usually remain tantalizingly out of sight.

White-throated Tapaculo
Scelorchilus albicollis　　　　PLATE 39(4)
18.5–19.5 cm (7¼–7¾"). *Uncommon on or near ground in dense matorral and scrub in cen. Chile* (Antofogasta to Curicó). Mostly below 1000 m. In **most of range** (illustrated) above pale rufescent brown with *white lores and superciliary. Throat white;* below whitish *variably barred dusky brown* (especially on sides and flanks). **North-**

ern birds are smaller and paler above, more barred below. Moustached Turca is much larger, with white on throat confined to sides, brown breast. White-throated regularly ranges with the turca, but seeing the tapaculo is a much harder proposition, as it seems almost always to remain within cover, sometimes running rapidly from one patch to the next. As with the turca (and the Chucao), long tail usually sharply cocked. Vocalizing birds often perch a bit above the ground, but even after tape playback usually remain hidden. Song a loud and obviously onomatopoeic "tá-pa, tá-pa-ku-lo, tá-pa-ku-lo, tá-pa-ku, tá-pa-ku, tá-pa-ku, tá-ku, tá-ku." Also gives a repeated "whha-poo, whha-poo, whha-poo . . ." and a repeated "poo-poo-poo-poo-poo-pah."

Crested Gallito
Rhinocrypta lanceolata　　　　PLATE 39(5)
21.5 cm (8½"). *Locally fairly common in chaco scrub and Patagonian steppes from se. Bolivia* (s. Santa Cruz) *to cen. Argentina* (n. Río Negro). To 1800 m. *Large and conspicuously bushy-crested.* Short bill. *Head brown narrowly streaked white;* above brownish, long full tail dusky. Below pale grayish, *sides and flanks bright rufous.* Mainly terrestrial and often elusive and hard to see, in part because it favors such thick and often thorny undergrowth. Crested Gallitos run rapidly on the ground, often with tail cocked high; they fly little and only weakly. Singing birds mount into a bush or low tree, usually remaining partially hidden, there giving a steadily repeated "cholloh . . . cholloh . . ." every few seconds.

Sandy Gallito
Teledromas fuscus　　　　PLATE 39(6)
19 cm (7½"). *Uncommon and local on or near ground in sparse arid scrub of w. Argentina* (w. Salta to Río Negro). To 3500 m. Bill stubby. *Above pale sandy brown with whitish eye-ring and supraloral; long slender tail* with pale tip. *Below buffy whitish.* Paler and more uniform than any other sympatric bird; cf. various miners (whose tails and bills are much shorter). Mainly terrestrial, this shy, elusive tapaculo is only infrequently encountered; favoring thick cover, it sometimes is seen sprinting between patches of vegetation, cocking its tail vertically (at times so far forward that it almost touches the back). Song a series of about 10 "cho" or "chu" notes recalling a crescentchest, and now usually classified with them in a separate family (cf. p. 390).

Merulaxis

Two midsized, *long-tailed* tapaculos found in e. Brazil forests, both species with *stiff bristles on forehead.*

Slaty Bristlefront
Merulaxis ater   PLATE 39(7)

18.5 cm (7¼"). Locally fairly common on or near ground in montane and humid forest and woodland in *se. Brazil* (s. Bahia to e. Santa Catarina). Mostly 400–1500 m, locally lower (especially southward). *Stiff pointed plumes spring from forehead in both sexes. ♂ mostly bluish slate;* rump and flanks rufous, tail dusky. ♀ brown above, tail duskier. *Below cinnamon-rufous.* Cf. the very rare Stresemann's Bristlefront. Mouse-colored Tapaculo is much smaller, etc. Found singly or (more often) in pairs, walking and hopping on the ground, usually in thick vegetation or among rocks; shows no affinity for bamboo. Seldom or never cocks tail. Heard much more often than seen, the bristlefront's enchanting and powerful song is a cascading series of rich musical notes that start loudly and tumble downward while becoming softer. Foraging birds remain in contact with an odd "tink" call note.

Stresemann's Bristlefront
Merulaxis stresemanni

19.5 cm (7¾"). *Now very rare and local on or near ground inside humid forest in e. Brazil* (se. Bahia and extreme ne. Minas Gerais). Nearly extinct, but rediscovered in 1995 near Una, and in 2004 a small population was found near the Bahia–Minas Gerais border. To 700 m. Resembles Slaty Bristlefront of *highlands* (no known overlap), but somewhat larger. Apparently has a white iris (fide R. Ribon). ♀ somewhat brighter below than ♀ Slaty. Hardly known in life, but behavior reportedly much as in Slaty Bristlefront. Song similar but lower-pitched and less musical (R. Ribon).

Rusty-belted Tapaculo
Liosceles thoracicus   PLATE 39(8)

19–19.5 cm (7½–7¾"). *Fairly common on or near ground in humid forest of w. and cen. Amazonia.* Mostly below 600 m. Head and neck grayish with *narrow white superciliary;* rufescent brown above, wing-coverts with buff spots. *Throat and breast white,* orange-rufous spot on chest; flanks and belly barred blackish, brown, and white. Not likely confused; *no other tapaculo occurs with it.* Plumage pattern vaguely wrenlike (Coraya

being the most similar), and could conceivably be confused with certain terrestrial antbirds as well. Forages singly, walking or hopping on forest floor, usually in dense vegetation; often hops atop fallen logs. Shy and furtive, even after tape playback hard to see, sneaking in with head held low and tail depressed (the tail is rarely or never cocked). Oft-heard song a series of low, mellow, whistled notes, "pü-pü-pü-pü-pu-pu-pupupu," accelerating slightly and trailing off at the end. Alarm call a nasal, abrupt "squeah!" often given in series of 2–3.

Ocellated Tapaculo
Acropternis orthonyx   PLATE 39(9)

21.5–22 cm (8½–8¾"). *Uncommon in undergrowth in upper montane forest of Andes from w. Venezuela* (Trujillo) *to n. Peru* (s. Amazonas on Cordillera Colán). Mostly 2300–3500 m. *Large and ornately patterned.* Note the exceptionally long hallux. *Mostly black to blackish with profuse white spots,* tail unspotted. *Forehead, face, and throat contrasting cinnamon-rufous;* rump, and lower flanks rich rufous. Ranges singly or in pairs, favoring stands of *Chusquea* bamboo. Walks, runs, and hops through dense undergrowth, dropping to the ground mainly to feed, there scratching, often quite noisily, with both feet at once. Like so many tapaculos, this spectacular species is much more often heard than seen. Song a loud and far-carrying jaylike "keeeuw!" repeated at intervals of roughly 2–4 seconds. Also gives a less penetrating, but still loud, "queeu-queeu-queeu-queeu."

Ochre-flanked Tapaculo
Eugralla paradoxa   PLATE 40(1)

14.5 cm (5¾"). *Uncommon on or near ground in dense undergrowth of* Nothofagus-*dominated forest in cen. Chile* (Maule to Chiloé) *and adjacent Argentina* (sw. Río Negro). To 1000 m. *Legs yellow;* heavy bill with "swollen" culmen. Uniform gray with *rufous flanks and lower belly,* white midbelly. **Immature** browner and more scaled. Magellanic Tapaculo is smaller and proportionately shorter-tailed, lacks bright rufous on flanks. A secretive denizen of damp forests that is rarely seen without aid of tape playback. Creeps and runs mouselike on or near the ground, tail slightly cocked, rarely or never lingering in the open. Forages by scratching the ground with its strong feet. Song a sharp staccato "cheh" or "chek" note, sometimes repeated for long periods but also in shorter bursts of 3–5 notes.

Ash-colored Tapaculo

Myornis senilis   PLATE 40(2)

14–14.5 cm (5½–5¾″). Fairly common in under-growth and borders of upper montane forest in *Andes from n. Colombia* (Norte de Santander) *to cen. Peru* (n. Pasco). Mostly 2300–3500 m. *Comparatively long tail. Ashy gray,* slightly paler below, a little cinnamon on lower flanks. **Juvenile** very different, rufous brown above and ochraceous below, wings and tail faintly barred. Various *Scytalopus* tapaculos occur with the Ash-colored, but all have a markedly shorter tail; their voices differ. Favors dense stands of *Chusquea* bamboo, where it creeps and hops, usually not on the ground. The long tail is often held cocked. As with other tapaculos, noted mainly when singing. Song a mechanical trill or "churr" that can last a minute or more (sometimes a series of such trills), usually introduced by a sharp "chef!" or "chedef!" (this sometimes given in a series at an accelerating pace).

Scytalopus

A complex, very difficult group of small, secretive, almost *mouselike* birds that creep about near ground in forest and woodland and are found *primarily in the Andes; a few outlying species range in the e. Brazil region. All are similar in plumage, many nearly identical,* being *basically some shade of gray* (varying from rather pale gray to quite blackish), often with rufous or brown on flanks (sometimes dusky barring as well). A few sport white facial markings. Juveniles are browner overall, often with considerable dusky barring. Identification to species level is thus generally made on the basis of *range, elevation,* and *primary song.* Note that many tapaculos have quite similar contact notes and scolding calls, and these are usually not described here. *Scytalopus* taxonomy is complex and still in flux, with no less than seven species having recently been described (and more are yet to come) and others only recently raised to species rank. We follow the latest findings of Krabbe and Schulenberg (2003), in which species limits were defined narrowly, along with a few more recent findings.

Large-footed Tapaculo

Scytalopus macropus   PLATE 40(3)

14.5 cm (5¾″). Rare and local in mossy under-growth of montane forest and borders on *east slope of Andes in n. Peru* (s. Amazonas to Junín). 2400–3500 m. *The largest Scytalopus. Uniform blackish gray.* Very dark. Cf. the smaller Rufous-vented and Tschudi's Tapaculos; does not occur with Blackish Tapaculo. Secretive and mainly terrestrial, favoring vicinity of rocky streams. Song a monotonous series of low-pitched notes that can continue for a minute or more.

Blackish Tapaculo

Scytalopus latrans*   PLATE 40(4)

12 cm (4¾″). *Widespread and locally common* in undergrowth of montane forest, woodland, and borders in *Andes from w. Venezuela* (Mérida) *to n. Peru* (Amazonas); locally ranges even in fairly arid areas. Mostly 2000–3500 m. Formerly considered conspecific with Unicolored Tapaculo. *Uniform dark gray to blackish slate,* with *no* rufous or barring. Blacker and more uniform than most *Scytalopus.* Scurries in dense vegetation; more tolerant of habitat disturbance than most tapaculos. Song a series of low-pitched "pir" notes repeated steadily for 15 or more seconds. Frequently given call an often-doubled, rising "huir-huir."

Unicolored Tapaculo

Scytalopus unicolor   PLATE 40(5)

12 cm (4¾″). Locally fairly common in under-growth and borders of montane forest and wood-land in *Andes of nw. Peru* (s. Cajamarca and La Libertad). 2000–3250 m. *Uniform gray,* slightly paler below, with a little rufous on lower flanks. Behavior much as in Blackish Tapaculo; likewise seems catholic in habitat choice. Song a fast and short series of 3–5 notes, rapidly repeated, e.g., "ti-ti-ti-tu," very different from Blackish.

Tschudi's Tapaculo

Scytalopus acutirostris*

11 cm (4½″). Fairly common in undergrowth and borders of upper montane forest on *east slope of Andes in n. Peru* (e. La Libertad to Junín). Mostly 2700–3400 m. Formerly considered part of the Magellanic ("Andean") Tapaculo complex. Closely resembles Blackish Tapaculo, so dark, but slightly smaller. The very similar Trilling Tapaculo replaces this species at lower elevations. Song a short (ca. ½ second) trill repeated about 5–10 times, then a pause.

Trilling Tapaculo
Scytalopus parvirostris *

11.5–12 cm (4½–4¾″). Fairly common in undergrowth of montane forest and woodland on *east slope of Andes from n. Peru* (s. Amazonas) *to w. Bolivia* (w. Santa Cruz). 1800–2500 m in Peru, but to at least 3200 m in Bolivia. Resembles Blackish Tapaculo; paler gray and has rufous on lower flanks. *Voice differs.* Cf. also Tschudi's Tapaculo, ranging at higher elevations. Song a fast trill that lasts about 15 seconds.

The following species constitute the *S. femoralis* group. The last two are allopatric, and were formerly considered conspecific under the name "Rufous-vented Tapaculo." The three "White-crowned Tapaculos" (including the Santa Marta), described first in this set, were also long treated as races of *S. femoralis.*

Bolivian White-crowned Tapaculo
Scytalopus bolivianus *   PLATE 40(6)

12.5 cm (5″). Locally fairly common in undergrowth and borders of montane forest on *east slope of Andes from s. Peru* (n. Puno) *to w. Bolivia* (Chuquisaca). Mostly 1100–2300 m. Sometimes called simply the Bolivian Tapaculo. Distinct among sympatric *Scytalopus* in having a *small white crown patch* (often hard to see in field, however). Does not occur with the other two "white-crowned" tapaculos. Song a fast series of "ch" notes, about 15 seconds long, at first accelerating, then slowing.

Northern White-crowned Tapaculo
Scytalopus atratus *

12.5 cm (5″). Locally fairly common in undergrowth and borders of montane forest on *east slope of Andes from w. Venezuela* (Mérida) *to s. Peru* (Cuzco). 850–1700 m. Sometimes called simply the White-crowned Tapaculo. Resembles Bolivian White-crowned Tapaculo. Slightly darker (more blackish), and *white crown patch* slightly smaller (thus even harder to see). Exceptionally skulking. Song very different from Bolivian's, a fast and *strikingly froglike* "wr-wr-wr-wr-wért."

Santa Marta Tapaculo
Scytalopus sanctaemartae   PLATE 40(7)

12 cm (4¾″). Uncommon in undergrowth and borders of lower montane forest in *Santa Marta Mts. of n. Colombia.* 750–2000 m. Readily iden-

tified as *the only Santa Marta Scytalopus with a white crown patch* (small). Brown-rumped Tapaculo occurs at *higher* elevations. Song a fast trill, lasting about 15 seconds.

Long-tailed Tapaculo
Scytalopus micropterus *   PLATE 40(8)

13.5 cm (5¼″). Fairly common in undergrowth and borders of montane forest on *east slope of Andes from n. Colombia* (Cundinamarca) *to extreme n. Peru* (n. Cajamarca). Mostly 1500–2200 m. Has been called Equatorial Rufous-vented Tapaculo. Identical in plumage to Rufous-vented Tapaculo (no overlap); the tail is indeed slightly longer. Song, however, is distinctly different, a long series of *doubled* notes that starts slowly and then accelerates, e.g., "chu-dok, chu-dok, chudók, chudók, chudók-chudók. . . ."

Rufous-vented Tapaculo
Scytalopus femoralis

12.5 cm (5″). *Fairly common in undergrowth and borders of montane forest on east slope of Andes in e. Peru* (s. Amazonas to Junín). Mostly 1400–2300 m. *Dark gray,* flanks rufous with quite heavy dark barring. Song a sharp note that can be repeated for minutes on end at a rate of about 2 notes per second.

The following eight species constitute what can be termed the *S. latebricola* complex; two were only recently described. Most or all were formerly considered conspecific under the name "Brown-rumped Tapaculo" or were confused with members of that complex. *All are gray with flanks rufous barred dusky.* They are allopatric, and are here arranged essentially from north to south. Note, however, that some species in w. Ecuador replace each other altitudinally.

Mérida Tapaculo
Scytalopus meridanus *   PLATE 40(9)

12 cm (4¾″). Common in undergrowth of montane forest, woodland, and borders in *Andes of w. Venezuela* (s. Lara to Táchira). 1600–3300 m. Unlike many other *Scytalopus, not* especially associated with *Chusquea* bamboo. Song a series of fast short trills lasting 10–15 seconds.

Caracas Tapaculo
Scytalopus caracae

12 cm (4¾″). Common in undergrowth of montane forest and borders in *mountains of n. Vene-*

zuela (Aragua to Miranda, and w. Sucre). Mostly 1200–2000 m. *The only Scytalopus in its range, and here widespread and unusually numerous;* the Caracas Tapaculo even seems easier to see than most other tapaculos. Song a rhythmic "pur-chee, chí, chi-pur," with variations but not including trills.

Brown-rumped Tapaculo
Scytalopus latebricola
12 cm (4¾"). Fairly common in undergrowth and borders of montane forest on *Santa Marta Mts. in n. Colombia.* 2000–3600 m, thus ranging *higher* than the other *Scytalopus* tapaculo, *S. sanctaemartae,* found on the Santa Martas. *Lacks* the small white crown patch of that species. Song a fast trill, much shorter than Santa Marta's, introduced by several sharp notes.

Spillmann's Tapaculo
*Scytalopus spillmanni**
12.5 cm (5"). Fairly common in undergrowth and borders of upper montane forest in *Andes from n. Colombia* (Antioquia) *to n. Ecuador* (south to w. Cotopaxi and ne. Azuay). Mostly 1900–3200 m. Replaced by the very similar Nariño Tapaculo at lower elevations, with slight overlap. Favors areas with extensive *Chusquea* bamboo. Song a long, very fast, high-pitched trill that rises slightly in pitch and lasts 10–15 seconds, often introduced by slower notes.

Chusquea Tapaculo
*Scytalopus parkeri**
12.5 cm (5"). Fairly common in undergrowth and borders of upper montane forest on *east slope of Andes in s. Ecuador* (north to sw. Morona-Santiago) *and extreme n. Peru.* Mostly 2300–3200 m. A recently described species. *Very* similar to Spillmann's Tapaculo, distinguishable by range and (barely) by voice. Song a fast trill, initially descending, similar to but slightly lower-pitched and slower than in Spillmann's.

Nariño Tapaculo
Scytalopus vicinior
12.5 cm (5"). Fairly common in undergrowth and borders of montane forest on *west slope of Andes from sw. Colombia* (Riseralda) *to nw. Ecuador* (w. Cotopaxi). Mostly 1250–2000 m; replaced by the very similar Spillmann's Tapaculo at higher elevations. Distinguishable only by voice. Song rather different from Spillmann's; a fast series of well-enunciated, ringing notes that starts with

a stutter but then can go on for 15–30 seconds, "pididi-ü-ü-ü-ü-ü-ü-ü-ü-ü. . . ."

Stiles's Tapaculo
*Scytalopus stilesi**
11.5 cm (4½"). Fairly common but local in undergrowth and borders of montane forest in *Cen. Andes of n. Colombia* (Antioquia to Riseralda). 1420–2130 m. A recently described species. Essentially identical in plumage to Nariño, Spillmann's, and Upper Magdalena Tapaculos, best identified by voice. Song a fast series of up to 35 or more "churr" notes (A. M. Cuervo et al.).

Upper Magdalena Tapaculo
*Scytalopus rodriguezi**
11.5 cm (4½"). Fairly common but local in undergrowth and borders of montane forest in *Cen. Andes of Colombia* (Huila in the upper Río Magdalena valley). 2000–2300 m. A recently described species. Essentially identical in plumage to Nariño, Spillmann's, and Stiles's Tapaculos, best identified by voice. Song a fast repetition of a single note, 4–5 notes per second, continued for up to a minute or more ("among the simplest [songs] of any *Scytalopus*"; N. K. Krabbe et al.).

Chocó Tapaculo
*Scytalopus chocoensis**
11.5 cm (4½"). Locally fairly common in undergrowth of foothill and lower montane forest on *west slope of Andes in w. Colombia and nw. Ecuador* (Esmeraldas and w. Imbabura). Mostly 350–1100 m. A newly named species (formerly part of the Nariño Tapaculo). *Occurs at lower elevations than other Scytalopus on west slope of Andes.* Song a series of sharp, high-pitched and well-enunciated notes, sometimes introduced by a stutter, e.g., "p-d-d-d-pi-pi-pi-pi-pi-pi-pi-pi. . . ." Also: e. Panama.

El Oro Tapaculo
*Scytalopus robbinsi**
11.5 cm (4½"). *Rare and local in undergrowth and borders of foothill and lower montane forest in sw. Ecuador* (single sites in Azuay and El Oro). 700–1250 m. A newly described species, replacing the virtually identical Chocó Tapaculo southward. Has been called Ecuadorian Tapaculo. Song much as in Chocó Tapaculo, but the notes are given at a faster rate, often seeming doubled.

Tacarcuna Tapaculo
Scytalopus panamensis

12 cm (4¾"). *Common in undergrowth and borders of montane forest on slopes of Cerro Tacarcuna in nw. Colombia* (nw. Chocó). 1100–1500 m. Sometimes called Pale-throated Tapaculo (though its throat is not particularly "pale"). Distinctive, *the only tapaculo in its limited range.* Readily known on that basis alone; note further its *distinctive whitish superciliary.* Call a strident "tuh-tu-tu-tu-t" repeated at intervals of several seconds (M. Pearman). Also: e. Panama.

The next nine species constitute the Andean portion of the *S. magellanicus* complex. All were formerly considered conspecific with that species, now considered a Fuegian endemic, together with the Dusky Tapaculo. In Ridgely and Tudor (1994) most (not the two far southern species) were treated as a single species, *S. griseicollis* (Andean Tapaculo), that name having priority. These tapaculos are mainly found at *high elevations in the Andes,* often near the treeline and typically higher than the *Scytalopus* in other groups. They are somewhat easier to see than the more forest-based *Scytalopus.* They are allopatric and are here *arranged essentially from north to south; most are best distinguished by range,* though their voices also often differ. These tapaculos are basically gray, with most species showing brown or rufous on their flanks and some dusky barring as well. Only significant divergences from this basic description are noted below.

Matorral Tapaculo
Scytalopus griseicollis *   PLATE 40(10)

11.5 cm (4½"). Fairly common in undergrowth of upper montane forest and woodland borders, and in montane scrub, in *Andes of ne. Colombia* (Boyacá and Cundinamarca). 2000–3300 m. *Rather pale gray; contrasting flanks bright rufous.* Notably tolerant of disturbed situations. Song a low-pitched trill, recalling a *Laterallus* crake.

Lara Tapaculo
Scytalopus fuscicauda *

11.5 cm (4½"). Uncommon in undergrowth and borders of upper montane forest and stunted woodland in *Andes of w. Venezuela* (s. Lara and Trujillo). 2500–3200 m. Rather pale gray; *contrasting flanks bright rufous.*

Paramo Tapaculo
Scytalopus canus *

11.5 cm (4½"). Locally fairly common in undergrowth of upper montane forest, woodland, and scrub, *principally at and just above treeline,* in *Andes from n. Colombia* (north to Antioquia, Caldas, and Huila) *to extreme n. Peru* (n. Cajamarca). Mostly 3050–4000 m. ♂ rather dark and gray with little brown or rufous. In **far south,** often shows a small white wing patch. ♀ browner above, flanks rufous-brown with dusky barring. Song a fast dry trill, often introduced by several notes, e.g., "trrrrrrrrrrr."

Ancash Tapaculo
Scytalopus affinis *

11.5 cm (4½"). Locally fairly common in undergrowth of *Polylepis* woodland patches and in adjacent rocky and grassy areas, in *Andes of nw. Peru* (s. Cajamarca to Ancash). Mostly 3000–4200 m. Relatively pale gray. Song a short descending "churr" repeated rapidly for long periods (up to 30 seconds or more).

Neblina Tapaculo
Scytalopus altirostris *

11.5 cm (4½"). Uncommon in undergrowth of upper montane forest *near treeline on east slope of Andes in n. Peru* (s. Amazonas to Huánuco). Mostly 3100–3500 m. Song a descending "churr" repeated rapidly for up to about 20 seconds.

Vilcabamba Tapaculo
Scytalopus urubambae *

11.5 cm (4½"). Fairly common in undergrowth of upper montane forest and borders on *east slope of Andes in s. Peru* (w. Cuzco, including near Machu Picchu). Mostly 3600–4100 m. Darker gray than the previous two species, but with bright rufous flanks. Song a fast "churr" repeated rapidly for a minute or more, sometimes ending with a series of rising notes (N. K. Krabbe).

Puna Tapaculo
Scytalopus simonsi *   PLATE 40(11)

11.5 cm (4½"). Fairly common in undergrowth of upper montane forest, mainly near treeline, and patches of *Polylepis* woodland on *east slope of Andes from s. Peru* (Cuzco) *to w. Bolivia* (Cochabamba). Mostly 3000–4300 m. ♂ has a *short whitish superciliary.* Replaced at somewhat lower elevations by Diademed Tapaculo. Song a rapidly repeated "chyurr" that can continue for several minutes or more.

Zimmer's Tapaculo
*Scytalopus zimmeri**
11.5 cm (4½"). Fairly common in undergrowth and borders of alder-dominated and *Polylepis* woodland and boulder-strewn slopes in *Andes* from **s. Bolivia** (Chuquisaca) **to nw. Argentina** (Salta). 1700–3200 m. Very similar to White-browed Tapaculo (no overlap); *superciliary and throat more pale grayish.* Song a repeated fast phrase "chititi chrr" or "chí ch chr," often continuing for protracted periods (N. K. Krabbe recording).

White-browed Tapaculo
*Scytalopus superciliaris**   PLATE 40(12)
11.5 cm (4½"). Uncommon in undergrowth of alder-dominated woodland and boulder-strewn slopes in *Andes of nw. Argentina* (Tucumán to n. La Rioja). 2000–3000 m. Rather striking, with a *bold white superciliary and throat;* above quite brown. Song a gravelly "tsit-tzeeeu, tzit-tzeeeu, tzit-tzeeeu . . ." repeated for long periods.

Diademed Tapaculo
*Scytalopus schulenbergi**   PLATE 40(13)
11.5 cm (4½"). Fairly common in undergrowth of upper montane forest *near and just below treeline on east slope of Andes from s. Peru* (Cuzco) *to w. Bolivia* (Cochabamba). 2800–3400 m. A recently described species, relatively distinctive for a *Scytalopus*, with a *conspicuous and broad silvery white forehead and supraloral;* throat also whitish. Song a fast series of notes that becomes louder and speeds up into a trill, lasting some 15–20 seconds.

Magellanic Tapaculo
Scytalopus magellanicus   PLATE 40(14)
11 cm (4¼"). Fairly common and widespread in undergrowth of humid forest, borders, shrubby clearings, and grassy or rocky areas from *cen. Chile* (north locally to Aconcagua) *and adjacent Argentina* (north to Neuquén) *to Tierra del Fuego.* Mostly below 1000 m, but to 2500–3000 m in cen. Chile. Legs flesh-colored. ♂ sometimes with silvery scaling on crown (though apparently northern birds do not show this). Cf. Dusky Tapaculo. Favors areas with *Chusquea* bamboo in many regions; northward mainly on rocky scree slopes. Frequently heard song an endlessly repeated, rhythmic "ka-chéw, ka-chéw, ka-chéw . . ." often continuing for several minutes.

Dusky Tapaculo
Scytalopus fuscus   PLATE 40(15)
11.5 cm (4½"). Uncommon in undergrowth of woodland and matorral in *cen. Chile* (s. Atacama to Bío-Bío). To 800 m. *Legs orange-yellow. Uniform blackish slate.* Basically *lacks* rufous brown on flanks; *lacks* white on crown shown by some Magellanics, and tail slightly longer. Easily recognized song a steadily repeated "j-reeén . . . j-reeén . . . j-reeén . . ." often continuing for several minutes.

The next five species are basically Brazilian in distribution.

Mouse-colored Tapaculo
*Scytalopus speluncae**   PLATE 40(16)
11.5 cm (4½"). Fairly common in undergrowth and borders of montane and humid forest and woodland in *se. Brazil region* (north to e. Bahia). To 2500 m. ♂ *uniform dark gray.* **Immature** browner with variable dusky scaling. Most other *Scytalopus* tapaculos in e. Brazil region show some white below (but in Paraná, cf. Marsh Tapaculo). Oft-heard song a fast series of "chit" or "chek" notes that may continue for as long as several minutes, the pace even faster when the singer is agitated.

Marsh Tapaculo
*Scytalopus iraiensis**
11.5 cm (4½"). *Rare and local* in tussocky, seasonally inundated grasslands adjacent to gallery woodland in *se. Brazil* (e. Paraná). 750–950 m. A recently described species. Has been called Tallgrass Wetland Tapaculo. Legs yellowish or pinkish. Closely resembles Mouse-colored Tapaculo, but occurs in a totally different habitat, so no overlap. Song also similar, a repeated "chef," but starts with several low-pitched churring notes and then gradually accelerates.

White-breasted Tapaculo
Scytalopus indigoticus   PLATE 40(17)
11.5 cm (4½"). Uncommon in undergrowth and borders of humid forest and woodland in *se. Brazil* (s. Bahia to n. Rio Grande do Sul). To 1500 m (where they overlap, Mouse-colored Tapaculo is usually at higher elevations). Legs yellowish. Bluish slate above and on sides. *Throat and median underparts white,* flanks rufous barred blackish. Brasília Tapaculo (no known overlap) is slightly less pure white below; in s. Bahia,

cf. Bahia Tapaculo. Song is a froglike, guttural "rrrrrrrrrrrrroowww" with slight upturn at end.

Brasília Tapaculo
Scytalopus novacapitalis   PLATE 40(18)

11.5 cm (4½"). Uncommon and local in undergrowth of gallery forest and woodland, often in areas that are flooded seasonally, in *interior s. Brazil* (s. Goiás and w. Minas Gerais). 800–1000 m. Legs yellowish. Resembles White-breasted Tapaculo but less clean-cut, with *median underparts pale gray to whitish* (not pure white) and less barring on flanks. Dramatically different song a steady repetition of rather high-pitched "chet" notes with an insectlike quality.

Bahia Tapaculo
Scytalopus psychopompus

11.5 cm (4½"). *Very rare and local* in undergrowth of humid forest, apparently in or near seasonally flooded areas, in *e. Brazil* (se. Bahia). Below 50 m. Closely resembles White-breasted Tapaculo (which in Bahia is exclusively montane), but has *less barring on flanks*. Essentially unknown in life.

TYRANT FLYCATCHERS: TYRANNIDAE

Tyrant flycatchers have more species in South America than any other bird family. They have radiated into every conceivable habitat, from tall tropical forest to barren open grassland in the Andes and Patagonia. In many areas flycatchers are among the most numerous and conspicuous birds, though diversity is highest in humid lowland forests. Some are strongly migratory, a few species coming from North America, others moving north during the austral winter. Generalizations are difficult. Most species are relatively drab, though some are boldly patterned or colorful (or even both). Most are small birds, but a few are fairly large. Most glean for insects in foliage, but a substantial number sally for flying insects and others are more or less terrestrial; some consume considerable fruit, especially when not breeding. Most flycatchers are conspicuous, but a few are notorious for remaining hidden in dense growth. Many are very vocal, and voice is often a key identification aid, but some seem essentially mute. For many groups, identification presents a major challenge. Nest shape and placement vary widely.

Phaeomyias

Two *nondescript* tyrannulets found in scrub, both with rather thick bills showing pale at base of lower mandible.

Mouse-colored Tyrannulet
Phaeomyias murina   PLATE 41(1)
12 cm (4¾"). *Widespread and locally common* in scrub, lighter woodland, and well-vegetated gardens from Colombia and Venezuela to n. Argentina; in Amazonia and the Guianas mainly in várzea, riparian areas, and savannas, but spreading with deforestation). Most numerous in arid areas. Mostly below 1000 m. *Brownish olive to dull brown above* (brownest in Venezuela and Colombia) with *weak whitish superciliary,* wings duskier with two buffyish bars. Throat whitish, breast dull olive grayish, belly pale yellow. *Drab and easily confused.* The perkier-looking Southern Beardless Tyrannulet is smaller with an expressive crest, usually cocked tail, *no* superciliary. Slender-billed Inezia is smaller with a narrower, all-black bill; Plain Inezia is notably grayer on head, has whiter wing-bars, etc. The scrub fly-

catchers are larger with stubbier, all-black bills and in most of overlap zone show more contrast below. Tumbesian Tyrannulet occurs only *west* of Andes. Usually inconspicuous, gleaning for insects in dense foliage, usually not long in the open; except for its voice, apt to be overlooked. Distinctive dry, gravelly song a fast chattering or jumbled "jejejejejéjew" or "jejejejejéw," sometimes shortened to just a "ji-jéw." Also: Costa Rica and Panama.

Tumbesian Tyrannulet
*Phaeomyias tumbezana**
12.5 cm (5"). *Fairly common in desert scrub, lighter woodland, and gardens from sw. Ecuador* (Manabí) *to nw. Peru* (Lima). Locally to 2300 m in arid intermontane valleys. Resembles Mouse-colored Tyrannulet (*east* of Andes; formerly conspecific), but with even deeper ochraceous wing-bars; belly whiter than in most Mouse-coloreds. Southern Beardless Tyrannulet is smaller and paler generally with a bushy crest and usually cocked tail. Gray-and-white Tyrannulet has white always showing in its obvious crest. Inconspicuous behavior similar to Mouse-colored

Tyrannulet, but vocalizations very different. Song a sharp and squeaky "squeéky, squeey-kít!" Also gives a weird, mechanical "kit-wrzzzzzzzzzz."

Southern Beardless Tyrannulet
Camptostoma obsoletum   PLATE 41(2)
9.5–10 cm (3¾–4"). *Widespread, ecologically tolerant, and generally common* in semiopen and edge habitats from Colombia and Venezuela to n. Argentina, mainly in lowlands but also in arid interandean valleys; *in Amazonia less numerous,* favoring canopy and borders of várzea and riparian forest. *Commonest in arid regions west of the Andes, and in n. Colombia and n. Venezuela.* To 2800 m. Likely more than one species. *Usually looks bushy-crested,* and *often cocks its rather short tail.* Bill short and pale, at least at base. **Southern birds** (north to w. Ecuador, se. Peru, and cen. Brazil; illustrated) *pale overall, olive grayish above,* grayest on crown; wings duskier with *two well-marked ochraceous bars.* Throat and breast pale grayish, belly yellowish white. **Northern birds** (south to ne. Brazil and much of Amazonia) somewhat smaller and *darker,* with grayish olive upperparts, whiter wing-bars, and yellower belly. In many areas one of the most frequently seen small tyrannids, so learn it well; its jaunty crest and perky mannerisms help more than any specific field mark. East of the Andes cf. especially Mouse-colored and Yellow-crowned Tyrannulets, west of them Tumbesian and Gray-and-white Tyrannulets. An engaging and often confiding bird that forages in foliage at all levels and in just about any situation. Often with mixed flocks, but also moves independently. Very vocal, with calls varying geographically. Most frequent call of southern birds a slightly husky "freee?" or "weeeé?" and a more musical, descending "kleeu, klee-klee-klee." Northern birds give a quick high-pitched "free" followed by several fast chortling notes that drop in pitch. Also: Costa Rica and Panama.

Yellow-crowned Tyrannulet
Tyrannulus elatus   PLATE 41(3)
10.5 cm (4¼"). *Fairly common and widespread* but inconspicuous in canopy and borders of humid forest, woodland, and clearings from *Colombia and Venezuela to Amazonia and the Guianas.* Mostly below 800 m. *Stubby black bill.* Olive above with slaty crown, dusky line through eye, and *gray head;* wings duskier with *two bold whitish bars* and edging. *Throat and chest pale grayish,* below clear yellow. A yellow crown stripe is seen mainly when vocalizing. Forest

Elaenia is slightly larger with longer tail, longer bill, and streaky effect on breast. Slender-footed Tyrannulet lacks wing-bars (its wings show *edging*), and it has a paler iris and a more horizontal posture. Sooty-headed Tyrannulet has plain wings with no bars or edging. All of these have distinctly different voices. Yellow-crowned tends to perch vertically, often remaining quite still; generally in pairs, not accompanying mixed flocks. Heard much more often than seen, with characteristic song a clear whistled "pray-teér," repeated at intervals through day. Also: Costa Rica and Panama.

Ornithion

Two *very small,* heavy-billed tyrannulets that are *inconspicuous* in the canopy and borders of humid lowland forests, and are mainly recorded by voice.

Brown-capped Tyrannulet
Ornithion brunneicapillus   PLATE 41(4)
8 cm (3¼"). Fairly common in humid forest and woodland canopy and borders from *n. Venezuela to sw. Ecuador* (El Oro). To 1200 m in Venezuela. *Tiny and short-tailed.* Olive above with *dark brown to grayish brown crown* and *prominent white superciliary;* wings duskier and *plain. Bright yellow below.* Most sympatric tyrannulets have wing-bars (but cf. Sooty-headed). Found singly or in pairs, usually well above the ground where it gleans in foliage; often with mixed flocks. Mainly recorded through its distinctive song, a fast series of high-pitched piping notes, "pleee, pih-pey-peh-puh"; cadence characteristic, with a pause after first note. Also: Costa Rica and Panama.

White-lored Tyrannulet
Ornithion inerme   PLATE 41(5)
8.5 cm (3½"). Fairly common in humid forest and woodland canopy and borders from *Amazonia to the Guianas,* and in *e. Brazil.* Mostly below 900 m. Olive above with slaty crown and *prominent short superciliary and narrow eye-ring white* (*producing a spectacled look*); wings with *two rows of large white spots.* Throat whitish, breast pale yellowish olive, belly clear yellow. Numerous other tyrannulets have wing-bars, but White-lored is unique in having its bars made up of discrete white *spots.* Behavior as in Brown-capped Tyrannulet, and likewise inconspicuous and usually located by voice. Song a persistently

repeated, high-pitched and wheezy "pee, dee-dee-deet" or "pee, dee-deet."

Zimmerius

A *confusing* group of tyrannulets united by their *wing-pattern, in which the feathers are sharply edged with yellow* but there are *no wing-bars*. *Zimmerius* range in the canopy and borders of humid forest, where they eat considerable fruit (as well as insects); some species, perhaps all, frequently consume mistletoe berries. *Relatively conspicuous* tyrannulets, they frequently perch in the open atop leaves and have distinctive voices.

Golden-faced Tyrannulet
Zimmerius chrysops   PLATE 41(6)
11 cm (4¼"). *Often common* in canopy and borders of humid and montane forest and woodland, and adjacent clearings, from *ne. and w. Venezuela to n. Peru* (San Martín). Mostly below 2000 m. *Distinctive yellow on face.* Likely more than one species. Olive above with *frontlet and supraloral yellow;* wings dusky, *coverts and flight feathers crisply edged yellow* (but *no* wing-bars). Throat whitish, breast pale grayish, becoming whitish on belly. Venezuelan Tyrannulet lacks yellow on face, has a contrasting dark brown or slaty crown. In sw. Ecuador cf. the very similar Loja Tyrannulet, and in w. Amazonia the Slender-footed Tyrannulet. Frequently in the open, tending to perch horizontally, often with tail held half-cocked. Though not inconspicuous, heard more often than seen, with vocalizations varying geographically. In most of range most frequent call a simple clear "cleeuw" or "peuur," sometimes in a quick series, also a more spritely and varied "teeu, te tititi?" In w. Ecuador gives a rather different "treeu, tree-ree-ree-ree?" and a repeated simple "cheli" call.

Loja Tyrannulet
*Zimmerius flavidifrons**
11 cm (4¼"). Fairly common in canopy and borders of montane forest and woodland and adjacent clearings *in Andes from sw. Ecuador* (Chimborazo) *to extreme nw. Peru* (Piura and n. Cajamarca). 900–2400 m. Formerly considered conspecific with Golden-faced Tyrannulet, which it closely resembles; no, or very limited, overlap. Differs in having *less yellow on face;* some individuals have virtually none. Habits similar to Golden-faced Tyrannulet. Loja's voice,

however, is strikingly different, with oft-heard call a loud, drawn-out "truuu-eeé." Song, given mainly around dawn, a fast "ti tuueé!"

Peruvian Tyrannulet
Zimmerius viridiflavus
11.5 cm (4½"). Fairly common in canopy and borders of montane forest and woodland on *east slope of Andes in cen. Peru* (Huánuco to Junín). 1000–2500 m. Resembles Golden-faced Tyrannulet. Differs in its *gray crown, whitish* (not clearly yellow) *frontlet and supraloral,* and *mainly pale yellow underparts.* Red-billed Tyrannulet occurs mainly at lower elevations, has a pale iris, and much plainer facial pattern (lacking supraloral). Behavior much as in Golden-faced Tyrannulet. Oft-repeated song distinctly different, a clear and fast "kleederoweéoo."

Bolivian Tyrannulet
Zimmerius bolivianus   PLATE 41(7)
12 cm (4¾"). Fairly common in canopy and borders of montane forest and woodland, and in adjacent clearings, on *east slope of Andes from s. Peru* (Huánuco, and from Ayacucho south) *to w. Bolivia* (w. Santa Cruz). 1000–2600 m. Iris pale grayish. *Uniform dark olive above* with *no obvious facial pattern;* wings duskier, *coverts and flight feathers edged yellow.* Throat whitish, breast pale olive, belly clear yellow. A *large* and *drab Zimmerius,* recognizable in range by its *lack* of obvious field marks and concolor olive crown. Most other tyrannulets in its range show wing-bars and have a stronger facial pattern. Behavior similar to other *Zimmerius,* and likewise not too hard to observe. Song a fast whistled "whee-whee-whee-wheéoo."

Mishana Tyrannulet
*Zimmerius villarejoi**
10.5 cm (4"). Uncommon and very local in canopy of swampy forest on sandy soil (varillal) *west of Iquitos, and near Rioja and Tarapoto in n. San Martín, in n. Peru.* 150 m. A recently described species. Differs from Slender-footed Tyrannulet in its *reddish lower mandible* and *lack* of contrasting gray crown and whitish supraloral; also has pale eye. Behavior much as in Slender-footed Tyrannulet. Most frequent call a fast pair of thin, rising, whistled notes (J. Alvarez and B. M. Whitney).

Slender-footed Tyrannulet
Zimmerius gracilipes   PLATE 41(8)
10.5 cm (4"). Fairly common in canopy and bor-

ders of humid forest and adjacent clearings from *Amazonia to the Guianas.* Mostly below 1000 m, but recorded to 2000 m in Venezuela. *Iris pale grayish.* Above olive with *gray crown* and *short whitish supraloral;* wings dusky, *coverts and flight feathers edged yellow.* Throat whitish, breast pale grayish olive, belly clear yellow. Often confused Golden-faced Tyrannulet has yellow on face and a dark iris; also cf. Red-billed Tyrannulet of east-slope foothills. Other than *Zimmerius,* most likely confused with Yellow-crowned Tyrannulet (which has obvious whitish wing-bars, a dark iris, etc.), Forest Elaenia (larger, though with a proportionately shorter tail; the elaenia is dark-eyed and has blurry breast streaking), and Sooty-headed Tyrannulet (with basically plain wings). Usually in forest canopy well above the ground, where hard to see well. Often in pairs, perching more or less horizontally and often holding tail half-cocked. Sometimes accompanies mixed flocks. Recorded mostly by voice. Song a soft, rising "peeu, tri-ri-ri" (somewhat like a becard), repeated steadily; Golden-faced's higher-pitched song has a more drawn-out initial note.

Red-billed Tyrannulet
Zimmerius cinereicapilla
11.5 cm (4½"). *Rare and local* (perhaps just over-looked) in canopy and borders of foothill and lower montane forest on *east slope of Andes from n. Ecuador to w. Bolivia* (La Paz). 700–1350 m. *Iris yellow;* bill blackish above, purplish flesh below (hard to see). Above olive with grayer crown and relatively plain face; wings dusky, *coverts and flight feathers boldly edged yellow* (but *no* wing-bars). Throat grayish white, breast grayish olive, belly clear yellow. Much more common Golden-faced Tyrannulet differs in having a dark eye, yellow on face, and whiter underparts. Behavior as in Golden-faced, likewise seen to best advantage when it comes lower at forest edge and in clearings. Song an accelerating and slightly descending series of clear notes, "teeuw tew-tew-te-te-te-te-te-te" (B. Hennessey recording), often given at long intervals (several minutes).

Venezuelan Tyrannulet
Zimmerius improbus   PLATE 41(9)
11.5 cm (4½"). *Common* in canopy and borders of montane forest and woodland in *Andes from n. Venezuela to ne. Colombia* (Norte de Santander). Mostly 1200–2400 m. **N. Venezuela birds** (illustrated) olive above with *slaty crown* and a *conspicuous white frontlet and supraloral;* wings dusky, *coverts and flight feathers edged yellow.* Throat whitish, breast pale grayish, belly pale

yellowish. **In nw. Venezuela and ne. Colombia** has *crown dark brown.* Golden-faced Tyrannulet (limited overlap in Venez. Andes) has yellow on face, concolor olive crown, different voice. Cf. Paltry Tyrannulet. Behavior much as in Golden-faced Tyrannulet. Song a loud series of 3–4 evenly paced notes, "wheeyr, wheeyr, whccyr, wheeyr," then usually with a long pause (often a minute or more) before being given again.

Paltry Tyrannulet
Zimmerius vilissimus
10 cm (4"). Canopy and borders of humid forest and woodland in *extreme nw. Colombia* (nw. Chocó). Recorded below 100 m (but likely ranges higher). Resembles Venezuelan Tyrannulet (no overlap), differing in *smaller size, pale grayish iris, less contrast in facial pattern,* and basically pale grayish underparts. Perky behavior much as in Golden-faced and Venezuelan Tyrannulets. Characteristic call an often interminably given whistle, "peeayik." Also: Mexico to Panama.

Phyllomyias

Obscure, *short-billed* tyrannulets found in humid or montane forests, most species with *bold wing-bars* (duller in a few) and often with *fairly distinct facial patterns.* Their tails are generally not held cocked, though some species do occasionally wing-lift. *Phyllos-cartes* have longer bills and proportionately longer tails; *Mecocerculus* have even bolder wing-bars and superciliaries; *Zimmerius* have obvious wing-edging (but *no bars*). The genus seems likely to be polyphyletic.

Sooty-headed Tyrannulet
Phyllomyias griseiceps   PLATE 41(10)
10 cm (4"). Fairly common but local in humid forest borders and clearings from *Colombia to the Guianas and e. Peru* (Ayacucho). Mostly below 1200 m. *Crown sooty brownish,* grayer on sides of head, with narrow white superciliary; olive above, wings duskier with *narrow whitish edging* (but *no evident wing-bars*). Throat grayish white; below pale yellow, breast clouded olive. This basically *nonforest* tyrannulet has the *plainest wings* of any similar species; Yellow-crowned Tyrannulet is the most alike, but it has *bold wing-bars.* Cf. similarly patterned but notably larger Greenish Elaenia. Generally in pairs that perch upright, usually independent of mixed flocks. Easily overlooked until its distinctive song is recognized, a rather loud rhythmic "whip, whip-

dip-tiríp" or "whit, whit-típ" with rollicking cadence reminiscent of Yellow Tyrannulet. Also: e. Panama.

Gray-capped Tyrannulet
Phyllomyias griseocapilla   PLATE 41(11)
11 cm (4¼"). A *brightly marked* tyrannulet, uncommon in humid and montane forest borders and adjacent clearings in *se. Brazil* (s. Bahia to ne. Santa Catarina). Mostly 500–1600 m. *Head gray contrasting with bright olive back,* whitish surpraloral; wings duskier with *coverts and flight feathers sharply edged yellow* (but wing-bars *weak,* the pattern *Zimmerius*-like). Mainly whitish below, *sides and flanks bright yellowish.* All sympatric tyrannulets have more prominent wing-bars, and none shows such bright color on its sides. Usually found singly, often foraging rather low; sometimes accompanies mixed flocks. Regularly eats mistletoe berries. Rather quiet, but sometimes gives a soft whistled "wheeuw-wheeuw" (up to 4 wheeuws).

Planalto Tyrannulet
Phyllomyias fasciatus   PLATE 41(12)
11–11.5 cm (4¼–4½"). Locally common in canopy and borders of humid and deciduous forest and woodland, *mainly in e. Brazil* (south to Rio Grande do Sul); a w. Bolivia population represents an as-yet undescribed species. To 1800 m. *Brownish olive above,* darker and grayer on crown, with short superciliary and eye-ring whitish; wings duskier with *two dull olive to whitish bars.* Throat whitish; below yellow, breast clouded olive. Dull-plumaged and confusing; like so many other small tyrannids, most readily recognized by voice. Cf. very similar Rough-legged Tyrannulet. Greenish Tyrannulet is brighter olive above with concolor crown, bolder wing-bars, longer tail. Mottle-cheeked Tyrannulet has longer bill, longer tail (often cocked), etc. An arboreal tyrannulet that generally remains well above the ground, often foraging with mixed flocks. Voice very distinctive once learned, a far-carrying clear "pee, puu, puuit?"

Sclater's Tyrannulet
Phyllomyias sclateri   PLATE 41(13)
12 cm (4¾"). Uncommon in canopy and borders of montane forest and woodland on *east slope of Andes from s. Peru (Cuzco) to nw. Argentina* (Tucumán). 1000–2200 m. Olive above with gray crown and short white superciliary, *wings dusky with two bold yellowish white bars and edging.* Throat and breast grayish white, belly whitish. Buff-banded Tyrannulet is smaller with a darker

gray crown, but (despite its name) its wing-bars are only slightly buffier. Plumbeous-crowned Tyrannulet has darker ear-coverts, yellower underparts. Mottle-cheeked Tyrannulet also is yellower below; its bill is longer, and crown more olive. Found singly or in pairs, often foraging with mixed flocks. Often shivers or even briefly lifts its wings. Song a short series of harsh and nasal sputtering notes.

Plumbeous-crowned Tyrannulet
Phyllomyias plumbeiceps   PLATE 41(14)
11.5 cm (4½"). Uncommon and seemingly local (perhaps just overlooked) in mid-levels and subcanopy of montane forest in *Andes from n. Colombia* (Cundinamarca) *to s. Peru* (Cuzco). 1200–2200 m. *Crown gray* with white superciliary and dusky streak through eye; *sides of head whitish with distinct dusky crescent on ear-coverts;* back bright olive; wings dusky with two prominent pale yellowish bars and edging. Throat grayish white; below yellow, breast clouded olive. Ecuadorian Tyrannulet has a longer bill and longer tail; it lacks any paler area behind its dark ear crescent, and has a distinctly different voice. Ashy-headed Tyrannulet has a bluer crown, blacker ear crescent, and streaky effect on breast. Cf. also Marble-faced Bristle Tyrant. Found singly or in pairs, often foraging with mixed canopy flocks. Perches horizontally, frequently lifting a wing up over back. Distinctive (almost like a furnariid), two-part song consists of 4–5 rising, well-enunciated "pik" notes followed by a lower-pitched and more stuttered "didideu."

Ashy-headed Tyrannulet
Phyllomyias cinereiceps   PLATE 41(15)
11 cm (4¼"). Uncommon in mid-levels, subcanopy, and borders of montane forest in *Andes from sw. Venezuela* (s. Táchira) *to s. Peru* (Cuzco). Mostly 1000–2500 m. *Brightly patterned.* Iris dark red. *Crown bluish gray contrasting with bright olive back;* lores and area around eyes white grizzled black; sides of head yellowish white with *obvious black crescent on ear-coverts;* wings blackish with *two yellowish white bars* and edging (but *none on coverts*). Throat whitish; *breast finely streaked yellowish white and olive;* belly bright yellow. Pattern and coloration recall Plumbeous-crowned Tyrannulet, Marble-faced Bristle Tyrant, and even the larger Slaty-capped Flycatcher; however, Ashy-headed differs from any of these in its bluer crown (quite striking in good light) and the breast streaking. Found singly or in pairs, often foraging with mixed flocks, coming lower at borders. Perches some-

what more vertically than its congeners; occasionally lifts a wing up over back. Song a high-pitched, sibilant "sweeeee, see-ee-ee-ee-ee."

Rough-legged Tyrannulet
Phyllomyias burmeisteri PLATE 41(16)
11.5 cm (4½"). Locally fairly common in canopy and borders of humid and foothill forest in *se. Brazil region* (north to se. Bahia), and on *east slope of Andes from w. Bolivia* (La Paz) *to nw. Argentina* (Tucumán). To 1300 m. *Lower mandible mostly yellow-orange.* Olive above with short superciliary and eye-ring yellowish; wings duskier with two blurry yellowish bars and edging. *Throat and breast grayish olive,* belly clear yellow. Planalto Tyrannulet has an all-black bill, grayer crown, and whiter throat. Greenish Tyrannulet has considerably bolder wing-bars, olive-yellow underparts. Cf. also Mottle-cheeked Tyrannulet. Rough-legged is an obscure arboreal tyrannulet, *mainly recorded from its vocalizations.* Its tail is not especially long, and is usually not cocked; occasionally the wings are flicked up. Song, given at rather long intervals (often a minute or more), a high-pitched and rather strident "psee-psee-psee-psee-psee-psee-psee-psee" falling slightly at end. Sometimes the "psee" is given individually.

White-fronted Tyrannulet
Phyllomyias zeledoni
11.5 cm (4½"). Uncommon and local (often overlooked) in canopy and borders of foothill and lower montane forest in *Andes from n. Venezuela and n. Colombia to s. Peru* (Puno). 600–1600 m. *Lower mandible mostly flesh to yellow.* Olive above with *slaty crown* and *white frontlet and short superciliary;* lower face grizzled gray and white; wings dusky with two yellowish bars and edging. Throat whitish; below pale yellow, breast vaguely flammulated olive. *Confusing and obscure.* Sclater's Tyrannulet (limited overlap in s. Peru) lacks white on frontlet, is whiter below. Slender-footed Tyrannulet lacks definite wing-bars, facial grizzling, and has an all-dark bill; it occurs in *lowlands.* White-fronted lacks the cheek patch of Plumbeous-crowned Tyrannulet, which mainly occurs at higher elevations. Ecuadorian Tyrannulet has longer, all-black bill, lacks white on frontlet. Rough-legged Tyrannulet (sometimes considered conspecific, despite distinct plumage differences) is not known to occur with White-fronted, though their ranges come close; differs in olive crown, etc. Behavior and vocalizations much as in Rough-legged. Also: Costa Rica and w. Panama.

Greenish Tyrannulet
Phyllomyias virescens PLATE 41(17)
12 cm (4¾"). Uncommon in canopy and borders of humid and montane forest and woodland in *se. Brazil region* (north to Espírito Santo). To at least 1400 m. Lower mandible yellowish at base; tail quite long. *Uniform and rather bright olive above* with short superciliary and eye-ring yellowish; wings duskier with *two bold pale yellow bars* and edging. *Below quite uniform clear yellow,* some olive clouding on chest. Cf. very similar Reiser's Tyrannulet (limited or no overlap). Rough-legged Tyrannulet is duller above with much less contrast in wing-bars; its bill is bicolored, and tail shorter. Mottle-cheeked Tyrannulet has longer bill and a grizzled facial area. Behavior similar to Planalto and Rough-legged Tyrannulets, gleaning in foliage and often accompanying mixed flocks. Song a series of staccato chattered notes, "ch-ch-ch-ch-ch-ch-ch," last note often a slightly lower "chew."

Reiser's Tyrannulet
Phyllomyias reiseri
11.5 cm (4½"). *Rare and local in deciduous and gallery forest in interior s.-cen. Brazil* (s. Maranhão to nw. Minas Gerais and Mato Grosso do Sul) *and ne. Paraguay* (Concepción). Mostly 500–1000 m. Resembles Greenish Tyrannulet (limited overlap), differing in its even brighter olive upperparts, less olive clouding on breast, and grayer crown. Behavior similar to Greenish Tyrannulet. Song a rough, descending "bzuu, bzi-bzi-bzi-bze-bzu," very different from Greenish.

Urich's Tyrannulet
Phyllomyias urichi*
12 cm (4¾"). *Very rare and local in ne. Venezuela* (sw. Sucre, nw. Monagas, and ne. Anzoátegui). 900–1100 m. Likely found in canopy and borders of lower montane forest and woodland, but not definitely known in life. Formerly considered conspecific with Reiser's Tyrannulet. Resembles Greenish Tyrannulet (geographically distant), differing in its even brighter olive upperparts, *grayer crown,* and *whiter wing-bars.* White-fronted Tyrannulet differs in its white frontlet, dingier (less yellow) foreneck. Behavior presumably much as in Greenish and Reiser's Tyrannulets.

Tawny-rumped Tyrannulet
Phyllomyias uropygialis PLATE 41(18)
11.5 cm (4½"). Uncommon and local in borders of upper montane forest and woodland and adjacent clearings in *Andes from w. Venezuela*

(Mérida) *to extreme nw. Argentina* (n. Salta); *generally more numerous southward.* 1800–3100 m. *Crown dark sepia brown with narrow white superciliary; back olive brown, tawny on rump and uppertail-coverts;* wings blackish with two buff bars. Throat and breast grayish, belly pale yellowish. *The tawny rump is unique.* Black-capped Tyrannulet is much yellower below and more olive above with no tawny on rump. White-banded and White-tailed Tyrannulets lack brown above and have much bolder white superciliaries. Tawny-rumped is less tied to forest than the other montane *Phyllomyias.* Often accompanies mixed flocks, though also forages alone. Gleans actively in foliage, frequently hovering while inspecting leaf surfaces, the distinctive tawny rump then often visible. Infrequently heard call a sharp sibilant "skee, skee-zu" or "pseee-psít," sometimes quickly repeated.

Black-capped Tyrannulet
Phyllomyias nigrocapillus PLATE 41(19)
11 cm (4¼"). Uncommon in borders of upper montane forest and woodland in *Andes from w. Venezuela* (Lara) *to s. Peru* (Junín); *often most numerous near treeline.* Mostly 1800–3300 m. In **most of range** (illustrated) *crown black* with narrow white superciliary; otherwise dark olive above; wings blackish with *two bold yellowish white bars.* Throat grayish; below yellow, breast clouded olive. In **w. Venezuela and Santa Marta Mts.** has *crown sepia brown,* yellower superciliary and underparts. Tawny-rumped Tyrannulet is browner above with buffier wing-bars and extensive tawny on rump, and is much grayer and whiter below. Gleans actively in foliage, often twitching wings. Frequently with mixed flocks. Song a thin, high-pitched "tzi-tzi-tzrrr," often with a double-noted effect.

Gray-and-white Tyrannulet
Pseudelaenia leucospodia PLATE 41(20)
12.5 cm (5"). *Locally fairly common in desert scrub from sw. Ecuador* (Guayas) *to nw. Peru* (La Libertad). To 600 m. *Pale grayish brown above* with *considerable white nearly always exposed in its often-spread crest,* and faint whitish superciliary; wings with weak whitish bars and edging. *Below whitish,* sides tinged gray. *The white in crest is conspicuous,* rendering this otherwise obscure tyrannid easy to identify. Often sympatric Tumbesian and Southern Beardless Tyrannulets have buff wing-bars. Gray Elaenia occurs in a totally different, humid forest habitat. Gray-and-white favors desert washes and dry streambeds. It perches horizontally and gleans actively

in foliage, often cocking tail, which sometimes is even slowly wagged. Distinctive call a sharp and emphatic "chevík" or "chevík-chet."

Stigmatura

The wagtail-tyrants form a distinctive group of attractive, slender flycatchers with *long graduated tails. Stigmatura* range in scrub of varying sorts, with two species of ne. Brazil (Caatinga and Bahia) having recently been split.

Greater Wagtail-Tyrant
Stigmatura budytoides PLATE 42(1)
15 cm (6"). *Locally common in arid scrub and chaco woodland from w. Bolivia* (Cochabamba) *to cen. Argentina* (n. Río Negro). To 2700 m in arid Bolivian valleys, but mostly below 1000 m. In **most of range** (illustrated) grayish olive above with *yellow superciliary;* wings and tail dusky, wings with a *broad whitish longitudinal patch, tail broadly tipped whitish* and with white at base. Below yellow. In **cen. Argentina** less sharply patterned with breast shaded olive. Essentially unique in its range. Lively and often bold, usually ranging in pairs, favoring dense undergrowth but not hard to observe. The tail is often held partially cocked, with feathers fanned exposing their white tips; it is not, however, actually wagged. A common contact call is a gravelly "chirt," sometimes varied to "chirt, wuri-tit, chirt." Pairs give a syncopated duet, swiveling their bodies as they give an animated rollicking "whidididitdeh, whidididitdeh. . . ."

Caatinga Wagtail-Tyrant
Stigmatura gracilis*
14.5 cm (5½"). *Fairly common in caatinga scrub and riparian woodland in ne. Brazil* (w. Pernambuco through Bahia to n. Minas Gerais). To 500 m. Resembles geographically distant Greater Wagtail-Tyrant (formerly considered conspecific) but is smaller, and voice is different. Caatinga overlaps with Bahia Wagtail-Tyrant, though Caatinga tends to occur in somewhat lusher, better vegetated sites; Bahia differs in being duller and buffier below, and is browner above. The two species are best distinguished by voice. Behavior similar to Greater Wagtail-Tyrant. Song an abrupt and very fast jumbled series of phrases and notes lasting 5 seconds or more, with elements given by both members of a pair. Also gives various mewing calls, e.g., "cheuw, chichi-cheuw."

Lesser Wagtail-Tyrant
Stigmatura napensis PLATE 42(2)

13.5 cm (5¼"). *Locally fairly common in early-success growth on river islands from Amaz. Brazil upriver to e. Ecuador and ne. Peru;* also recently found on Río Orinoco islands in s. Venezuela. Below 300 m. Grayish olive above with *yellow supercilary;* wings and tail dusky, *wings with a broad whitish longitudinal patch, tail broadly tipped and edged yellowish white* and with white at base. Below yellow. Unmistakable in its restricted range and habitat. Usually in pairs that move restlessly through dense growth, favoring stands of *Tessaria* trees. Behavior much as in Greater Wagtail-Tyrant. Calls include a querulous "kweeurt?" or "kweeurt? kwee," sometimes ending in a jumble, often with a distinctive rollicking cadence, e.g., "kwi-kwu-kwrr, kwi-kwu-kwrr, . . ." given as a duet.

Bahia Wagtail-Tyrant
*Stigmatura bahiae**

13.5 cm (5¼"). *Uncommon in barren, overgrazed scrub in ne. Brazil* (Bahia and w. Pernambuco). To 600 m. Resembles geographically distant Lesser Wagtail-Tyrant, formerly considered conspecific. Differs in being browner above and *duller and more buffy yellowish below.* Bahia regularly occurs close to Caatinga Wagtail-Tyrant, though Caatinga favors lusher habitats. Caatinga is more grayish above (not so brown), clearer yellow below. The two are usually best distinguished by voice. General behavior as in other wagtail-tyrants, but Bahia's voice is distinctly different. Song a repeated "pur, pee-dir-pur, pee-dir-pur, pee-dir-pur," sometimes the "pee-dir-pur" or a "pee-dir" alone, at more leisurely pace than Caatinga.

Serpophaga

A *diverse* group of tyrannulets, two species (Torrent and Sooty) strongly tied to water (a third, River, to river islands), the others more generalized in semiopen areas in s. South America. Probably not a monophyletic unit, and unresolved species-level taxonomic issues remain.

White-crested Tyrannulet
*Serpophaga subcristata** PLATE 42(3)

10.5–11 cm (4–4¼"). *Widespread and generally fairly common* in forest borders, gallery woodland and monte, shrubbery and groves of trees, and deciduous scrub from *e. Bolivia to cen.*

Argentina (ne. Chubut) *and s. and e. Brazil.* To 2000 m in se. Brazil. Grayish olive above, grayest on head and neck with short white superciliary, long blackish crown feathers, and *semiconcealed white coronal patch;* wings and tail blackish, wings with two bold whitish bars. Throat whitish, breast pale gray, *belly pale yellow.* The best mark is the white and black in crown, *both* colors usually being visible. White-bellied Tyrannulet is grayer above and entirely whitish below; Plain Inezia lacks black and white in its smoothly gray crown. Further confusing the situation is a still unnamed species of tyrannulet closely resembling the White-crested but evidently basically western in distribution, though at least some birds move east during austral winter. Our distribution map includes areas inhabited by this undescribed form, with true White-cresteds occurring mostly east of the Río Paraguay area. White-cresteds forage actively at varying levels, often quite in the open. Song a soft chippering trill introduced by one or more rising notes, e.g., "psee? psee-ee-ee-ee-ee" or "chit-chit-chit-trrrreeeeu." Call a fast, rhythmic "cheedidireép" or "cheedeedit."

White-bellied Tyrannulet
*Serpophaga munda** PLATE 42(4)

11–11.5 cm (4¼–4½"). Fairly common in deciduous scrub and woodland *in highlands from s. Bolivia* (s. La Paz) *to w. Argentina* (n. Río Negro), spreading east and north during austral winter. Locally to 3000 m in Bolivia. Similar to White-crested Tyrannulet but grayer (not so olivaceous) above and *all white below (no pale yellow).* The two species (there still is some dispute as to this point) sometimes occur together during the austral winter, but apparently do not do so when breeding. Behavior and voice similar.

River Tyrannulet
Serpophaga hypoleuca PLATE 42(5)

11 cm (4¼"). Uncommon and local in early-success growth and shrubbery on *river islands from Amaz. Brazil upriver to e. Ecuador and e. Peru,* and *along Río Orinoco in s. Venezuela.* To 600 m. *Uniform grayish brown above, elongated crown feathers blackish* partially concealing a white coronal patch; *plain wings* and rather long tail somewhat duskier. Below whitish. Drab Water Tyrant is markedly larger and grayer overall, with different behavior. Usually in pairs, like most other island birds not foraging in mixed flocks. Gleans in foliage, often in isolated bushes and small trees, but seems restless, seldom remaining long in any one area.

Gives a variety of spritely chippers, often in an excited series. Also has a more rattled, upslurred "d-d-d-r-r-ree-eet?"

Sooty Tyrannulet
Serpophaga nigricans   PLATE 42(6)

12 cm (4¾"). Uncommon in shrubbery and semi-open areas *near water* (either still or flowing) *from s. Brazil* (s. Goiás and Minas Gerais) *and s. Bolivia* (Tarija) *to cen. Argentina* (Río Negro). To 1000 m. *Dark brownish gray above,* paler and purer gray below; *contrasting tail black. So dark and drab as to be nearly unmistakable.* Found in pairs that are conspicuous as they forage on or near the ground near water, hopping at edge and perching on rocks or branches just above the surface. Rarely or never far from water. Tail often partially spread, and jerked upward. Rather quiet, but gives a repeated "ch-víyt, ch-víyt. . . ."

Torrent Tyrannulet
Serpophaga cinerea   PLATE 42(7)

11.5 cm (4½"). *Conspicuous and fairly common along fast-flowing, rocky streams and rivers in Andes from w. Venezuela* (Trujillo) *to w. Bolivia* (w. Santa Cruz), occurring in both forested and semiopen terrain. Mostly 700–2800 m. *Mainly gray,* slightly paler below. *Crown and sides of head black,* with usually concealed white coronal patch; wings and tail also black, wings with two narrow whitish bars. This perky tyrannulet is unique and nearly unmistakable in its restricted habitat. It occurs in sedentary pairs, generally remaining close to water (though sometimes venturing out onto adjacent pastures); often perches on rocks, wagging or elevating tail. Regularly feeds on damp roads. Makes short aerial sallies after insects, also sallying to rocks and banks. Not very vocal, but does give a sharp "seep," sometimes in series.

Inezia

A diverse genus of small tyrannulets found in scrub and woodland borders. The first two species recall the *Stigmatura* wagtail-tyrants, the third (Slender-billed) resembles Southern Beardless Tyrannulet, and the fourth (Plain) is very similar to White-crested Tyrannulet. All were formerly called tyrannulets.

Pale-tipped Inezia
*Inezia caudata**   PLATE 42(8)

11.5 cm (4½"). Fairly common in shrubby woodland borders, scrub, and mangroves from *n. Co-* *lombia to e. Venezuela, the Guianas, and extreme n. Brazil.* To 400 m. Formerly considered conspecific with the next species. Iris pale (Amazonian Inezia's is dark). Above brownish olive with *short white superciliary and "spectacles";* wings and tail duskier, *wings with two prominent white bars, tail feathers tipped and outer web edged whitish.* Below pale yellow, breast washed ochraceous. Cf. Amazonian Inezia (no known overlap). Slender-billed Inezia and Southern Beardless Tyrannulet are smaller, lack the spectacles, have duller wing-bars, no white in tail. Found singly or in pairs, generally low and most often in thickets near water. Tail frequently held partially cocked. Vocalizes a good deal, with most frequent call a clear, soft "teep, ti-ti-tu."

Amazonian Inezia
*Inezia subflava**

11.5 cm (4½"). Uncommon and somewhat local in gallery woodland and shrubby growth at edge of rivers and lakes from *sw. Venezuela* (Amazonas) *and extreme e. Colombia to n. and e. Amaz. Brazil and ne. Bolivia.* To 400 m. Closely resembles Pale-tipped Inezia (formerly considered conspecific). Amazonian is dark-eyed, and its underparts lack ochraceous and are more clouded with olive. Behavior as in Pale-tipped Inezia, but Amazonian rarely seems as numerous. Most frequent call a fast rollicking "pur chirri-kurra, chirri-kurra, chirri-kurra, . . ." often long-continued and given as a duet; very different from the simpler calls of Pale-tipped Inezia.

Slender-billed Inezia
*Inezia tenuirostris**   PLATE 42(9)

9 cm (3½"). *Common in arid scrub and dry woodland in n. Colombia and nw. Venezuela.* To 800 m. *Above dull olive brown* with short whitish superciliary; wings duskier with two pale buff bars. *Mostly whitish below,* belly tinged yellow. Southern Beardless Tyrannulet's bill shows color on lower mandible (*not all black*); it has a bushy crest and more olive upperparts. The inezia regularly occurs with Beardless; note that both species often cock their tail. Characteristic call a fast dry trill that ends abruptly, "bzz-zee-ee-ee-ee-ee-eep."

Plain Inezia
*Inezia inornata**   PLATE 42(10)

10 cm (4"). Uncommon in chaco woodland, scrub, riparian woodland and borders of humid and várzea forest from *sw. Amazonia to nw. Argentina* (Jujuy and Salta) *and w. and n. Paraguay,* occurring as an austral migrant to sw.

Amazonia. To at least 500 m. *Head gray* with short white superciliary; back olive, wings dusky with two white bars. *Below whitish,* belly tinged pale yellow. Closely resembles White-crested Tyrannulet; differs in usually having some yellowish at base of lower mandible (White-crested bill is all black), *lack of a white coronal patch,* and *smoothly gray crown* (showing no black streaking). Gleans in foliage at varying heights, often partially cocking tail. Quite vocal, with most frequent calls a fast, high-pitched trill, "pseee, tee-ee-ee-ee-ee," and a descending "pseeeeu."

Mecocerculus

Attractive tyrannulets that range mainly in *Andean forests* and are united by their *bold superciliaries* and *very contrasting wing-bars.* The genus will almost certainly need to be split apart.

White-tailed Tyrannulet
Mecocerculus poecilocercus   PLATE 42(11)

11 cm (4¼"). Fairly common in canopy and borders of montane forest in *Andes from n. Colombia to s. Peru* (Cuzco). 1500–2600 m. Olive above with gray crown and long white superciliary; *rump and uppertail-coverts pale greenish yellow;* wings blackish with two prominent yellowish bars; *outer two pairs of tail feathers mostly white* (conspicuous from below, and in flight). Throat and breast pale gray, belly yellowish white. White-banded Tyrannulet is larger, with longer tail, a bolder white superciliary, and pure white wing-bars; it *lacks* white in tail and the pale rump. White-banded mainly ranges at higher elevations. Cf. also Rufous-winged Tyrannulet, and migrant warblers such as the Blackburnian. Forages actively, often exposing pale rump and white in tail; often with mixed flocks. Most frequent call a series of 3–4 (occasionally more) high-pitched, minor-keyed notes that drop in pitch, "psi-psee-pseh."

Buff-banded Tyrannulet
Mecocerculus hellmayri

11 cm (4¼"). Uncommon in canopy and borders of montane forest and woodland on *east slope of Andes from extreme se. Peru* (Puno) *to nw. Argentina* (Jujuy). Mostly 1100–2600 m. Resembles White-tailed Tyrannulet (no overlap) but *lacks* white in tail, rump not as pale, and has slightly buffier wing-bars. Of sympatric tyrannulets, Sclater's is the most similar; Sclater's

is larger with whiter wing-bars. White-banded Tyrannulet is also larger and has obviously *white* wing-bars. Behavior much as in White-tailed Tyrannulet. Most frequent call a high-pitched, minor-keyed "psee-pee" or "psee-pee-pee" (sometimes only a single "psee" or with a jumble at end), similar to White-tailed.

Rufous-winged Tyrannulet
Mecocerculus calopterus   PLATE 42(12)

11 cm (4¼"). Uncommon in canopy and borders of foothill and lower montane forest, woodland, and adjacent clearings from *nw. Ecuador* (Imbabura) *to n. Peru* (Lambayeque and e. La Libertad), *mainly on lower Andean slopes.* 600–2200 m. Olive above with slaty crown and blackish ear-coverts, long white superciliary; wings blackish with two prominent whitish bars and *rufous flight-feather edging* (forming an obvious patch); *outer two pairs of tail feathers white.* Throat and breast pale gray, belly whitish. *Rufous in the wings of this pretty tyrannulet unique;* its pattern vaguely resembles ♂ Rufous-winged Antwren. Cf. White-tailed Tyrannulet (which has no rufous). Seen singly or in pairs, foraging mainly high but coming lower at borders and in clearings. Frequently accompanies mixed flocks. Not very vocal, with one reported call a husky, emphatic "pur-cheé, chi-chichu" (B. Walker recording).

White-banded Tyrannulet
Mecocerculus stictopterus   PLATE 42(13)

12.5 cm (5"). Fairly common in canopy and borders of upper montane forest and woodland in *Andes from w. Venezuela* (Trujillo) *to w. Bolivia* (w. Santa Cruz). Mostly 2400–3500 m. Brownish olive above with gray head and a *long broad white superciliary;* wings blackish with *two broad white bars* and buffy yellowish edging. Throat and breast pale gray, belly yellowish white. In **w. Venezuela** has *extensive white in outer tail feathers.* Confusion most likely with White-tailed Tyrannulet (smaller and shorter-tailed, with distinctly yellower wing-bars and less prominent superciliary); White-tailed ranges mainly at lower elevations. White-tailed does not occur in Venezuela, so it cannot be confused with White-bandeds there (with so much white in tail). Behavior much as in White-tailed, though seems less agile. Distinctive call an oft-given, somewhat raspy and inflected "squeeyh?" sometimes repeated 3–5 times or lengthened to a "squeeee-ee-eeeyh? squeh-d'd'd'd'd'd'd," the latter notes slurred into a descending trill.

Sulphur-bellied Tyrannulet
Mecocerculus minor PLATE 42(14)
11.5 cm (4½"). Uncommon in canopy and borders of montane forest and woodland in *Andes, mainly on their east slope, from extreme sw. Venezuela* (s. Táchira) *to cen. Peru* (Huánuco). 1600–2800 m. Dark olive above with gray crown and *long white superciliary;* wings blackish with *two broad buff bars. Mostly yellow below.* Unique among the *Mecocerculus* in having *yellow* underparts. Variegated Bristle Tyrant plumage similar, but it perches vertically and has a prominent dark ear crescent and orange-yellow lower mandible. Cf. also the scarce Plumbeous-crowned Tyrannulet. Forages singly or in pairs, often with mixed flocks; generally remains well above the ground, though comes lower at forest borders. Calls include a sharp, fast "chew-chew-chew" (sometimes more notes), and a squeakier, more nasal "skwi-skwe-skwu-skwu."

White-throated Tyrannulet
Mecocerculus leucophrys PLATE 42(15)
14 cm (5½"). Widespread in borders of upper montane forest and woodland and adjacent shrubby clearings in Andes from n. Venezuela to nw. Argentina (La Rioja), and on tepuis of s. Venezuela area. Mostly 2800–3500 m, but lower (to 1500 m) in Venezuela and Argentina. *Most numerous in Venezuela, Colombia, and Argentina. An upright-perching tyrannulet with a distinctive puffy white throat.* In **most of range** (illustrated) umber brown above with faint whitish superciliary; wings blackish with *two prominent rufous bars. White throat contrasts with olive grayish breast,* belly pale yellow. From **s. Bolivia to Argentina,** and in **n. Venezuela,** more olivaceous above and *wing-bars whiter.* Other *Mecocerculus* perch more horizontally, and none has the contrasting throat. *White-throated looks quite long-tailed* and often perches in the open with tail hanging down. Pairs or small groups frequently associate with mixed flocks. Argentinian birds seem to perch more horizontally. In some areas it occurs up to and above treeline, even in *Polylepis.* Infrequently heard song, given mainly around dawn, an excited "ch'd'dik, ch'd'dik, ch'd'dik, chéw," with variations.

Polystictus

Two *dissimilar* small tyrannids, both distinctive, found locally in *open grassy areas* with at most scattered shrubs.

Bearded Tachuri
Polystictus pectoralis PLATE 43(1)
9.5–10.5 cm (3¾–4¼"). *Uncommon and local in less-disturbed grasslands* from Colombia and Venezuela south very locally to n. Argentina. To 2600 m in E. Andes of Colombia (where perhaps extirpated); otherwise mostly below 1300 m. A *tiny, slender* flycatcher. ♂ *brown above, crown gray and blackish with white coronal patch; lower face and upper throat finely streaked black and white* (forming the "beard"); wings duskier with two cinnamon-buff bars and edging. Below pale yellowish with *cinnamon wash on breast and flanks.* ♀ has a brown crown and lacks the beard. **Northern lowland birds** smaller. Rufous-sided Pygmy-Tyrant differs from ♀ tachuri in its longer and narrower tail and more contrasting white throat. The tachuri is a scarce bird, its overall numbers now much reduced by overgrazing, burning, and outright conversion of most savannas. Usually found singly, less often in pairs, sometimes accompanying other grassland birds; clings to grass stems, flying only weakly. Generally quiet, but displaying ♂♂ have a plaintive "wheee? whidididrrr" song, sometimes given in a brief low display flight.

Gray-backed Tachuri
Polystictus superciliaris PLATE 43(2)
9.5 cm (3¾"). *Rare and very local in shrubby or rocky grasslands on a few serras in interior se. Brazil* (cen. Bahia, and s. Minas Gerais to n. São Paulo). 1000–1600 m. *Brownish gray above,* grayer on head with *short white superciliary* and a semiconcealed white coronal patch; wings duskier with two faint brownish bars and edging. *Below pinkish buff,* midbelly white. Basically bicolored, this small tyrannid is distinctive in its very limited range and habitat. Forages in pairs, clinging to grass stems or perching in low shrubs. Distinctive call a throaty "tchudi"; apparent song (R. Parrini recording) a strange, reeling, buzzy trill, "tzzzzzzzzzzzzzzzz," lasting about 5 seconds.

Euscarthmus

Two small, predominantly brownish tyrannids found in shrubby or semiopen areas, one of them (Rufous-sided Pygmy-Tyrant) scarce and local. We question whether they are congeneric.

Rufous-sided Pygmy-Tyrant
Euscarthmus rufomarginatus   PLATE 43(3)
11 cm (4¼"). *Rare and local in savannas and ce-rrado of e. South America, mainly in s.-cen. Bra-zil.* To 1000 m. Brown above with a short buffy whitish supraloral and rufous coronal patch; wings and *rather long slender tail* duskier, *wings with two ochraceous bars* and edging. *Throat white, below pale yellow with sides and flanks ochraceous.* Resembles ♀ Bearded Tachuri, and the two are sympatric at a few locales, though the pygmy-tyrant favors shrubbier habitats, the tachuri purer grass. Tachuri has a shorter tail and more uniform buffyish underparts (without the contrasting white throat and rufescence on flanks). Found singly or in pairs; generally in-conspicuous except when vocalizing. Overall numbers are much depleted by habitat destruc-tion and disturbance. Song, often given with puffed out throat, a rapidly repeated "cht-cht-cht-chididideét, cht-cht-cht-chididideét. . . ."

Tawny-crowned Pygmy-Tyrant
Euscarthmus meloryphus   PLATE 43(4)
10 cm (4"). *Widespread and often common* in arid scrub, regenerating clearings, and undergrowth and borders of deciduous woodland in three areas: n. Colombia and n. Venezuela, w. Ecua-dor and w. Peru, and n. Bolivia to e. Brazil and n. Argentina. Mostly below 1500 m, but to 2000–2500 m in Ecuador and Peru. In **most of range** (illustrated) *brown above* with rufous coronal patch; wings with faint rufescent bars. Mostly whitish below, belly yellower. In **w. Ecuador and nw. Peru** has a *conspicuous buff facial area* and rufous-tinged forecrown; wing-bars more prominent. A small, plain, brownish tyrannid that really resembles no other in its lowland thicket habitat, but cf. Fuscous Flycatcher. In-conspicuous, remaining in heavy cover and most often recorded from vocalizations. Characteris-tic, often endlessly repeated call a sharp staccato "plee-tirik" or "plee-ti-re-tik." Song a fast "tr-tr-tr-tr-tr-trreétrrt. . . ."

Pseudocolopteryx

The doraditos are rather scarce, *marsh-inhabiting* tyrannids with thin bills and *bright yellow underparts*. They range pri-marily in *s. South America.*

Subtropical Doradito
Pseudocolopteryx acutipennis   PLATE 43(5)
11.5 cm (4½"). *Rare to uncommon and local in reedbeds, sedgy areas, and shrubbery near water in Andean valleys from Colombia to nw. Argen-tina* (La Rioja and Córdoba). Mostly 1000–3500 m, a few moving into adjacent lowlands during austral winter. *Bright olive green above;* cheeks, wings, and tail somewhat duskier. *Bright yellow below.* The only doradito in most of its range, and thus readily recognizable. In Argen-tina, cf. Warbling Doradito, a *lowland* bird that is duller overall, with more brownish olive upper-parts; cf. also the rarer Dinelli's Doradito. ♀ Southern Yellowthroat is quite similar, but has pinkish (not black) legs and shows a vague yel-lowish supraloral lacking in the doradito. Gen-erally inconspicuous, doraditos are likely to be seen only when specifically sought out. On calm early mornings one will sometimes perch atop a shrub or reed, but otherwise they remain within cover. Song a "tzit-tzit-tzit t-konk" followed by a wing-whirr, sometimes given in a brief display flight (B. M. Whitney).

Dinelli's Doradito
Pseudocolopteryx dinelliana   PLATE 43(6)
11.5 cm (4½"). *Rare and local in marshes* (some-times quite small) *and adjacent shrubbery, breed-ing in n. Argentina* (mainly in n. Córdoba and Tucumán), *moving north into Paraguay in winter.* To 500 m. Resembles more numerous Warbling Doradito, differing in *lacking dusky on cheeks* and its more olive upperparts (not so rufescent). Behavior of Dinelli's Doradito (not a well-known bird) is apparently similar to the Warbling; the two species are not known to breed sympatri-cally. Odd song a soft but twangy "redek-redek-redídek" or soft "cht-cht-cht-cht-rederiik."

Warbling Doradito
Pseudocolopteryx flaviventris   PLATE 43(7)
11.5 cm (4½"). *Uncommon in marshes and fring-ing shrubbery in cen. Chile, and from n. and cen. Argentina to extreme se. Brazil* (Rio Grande do Sul), a few migrating north in austral winter. Below 500 m. Dull olive to brownish olive above, *more rufescent on crown* with *dusky cheeks;* wings and tail duskier. Below bright yellow. *Generally the most numerous and widespread doradito;* cf. scarcer, more local Subtropical and Dinelli's Doraditos. ♀ Southern Yellowthroat can occur with this species and is similarly colored, except that it lacks rufous on crown. The yellowthroat

usually behaves quite differently, and its bill is bicolored (pale below), legs flesh, and it shows a vague yellow supraloral (doradito's bill and legs are blackish). Warbling's inconspicuous behavior is much as in Subtropical Doradito. Odd, disjointed song (hardly a warbling!) a series of sharp, squeaky, almost hiccuping notes, distinctive but soft and easy to overlook.

Crested Doradito
Pseudocolopteryx sclateri   PLATE 43(8)
11 cm (4¼"). A *distinctive* doradito of marshes and adjacent shrubbery; *generally rare and local*, mainly in the pantanal of Paraguay and n. Argentina, but also occurs very locally north to Venezuela and Trinidad. Below 300 m. Olive above, mottled dusky on back; *facial area and crest feathers blackish, the latter usually parted enough to reveal pale yellow coronal stripe*. Wings dusky with whitish bars and edging. Below bright yellow. The other doraditos lack blackish on head. Behavior similar, though Crested perches more in the open for extended periods, especially in the early morning and when calm. Its presence in some areas seems erratic, perhaps being dependent on local water levels. Song, often accompanied by short jumps into the air, a high-pitched, weak "tsit-tsit-tsi-tit" (J. Hornbuckle recording).

Sharp-tailed Grass Tyrant
Culicivora caudacuta   PLATE 43(9)
10.5 cm (4¼"). *Uncommon and local in less-disturbed campos and grassy cerrado from n. Bolivia* (west to La Paz) *to interior s. Brazil and ne. Argentina* (n. Santa Fé). To 1100 m. *Tail very long and narrow*, feathers pointed and frayed. *Buffy brown above streaked blackish; long and conspicuous superciliary white*. Whitish below, sides and flanks cinnamon-buff. Distinctive, resembling a spinetail more than any tyrannid. Found singly or in pairs, moving through stands of tall grass; once located often quite tame. Not especially conspicuous and thus likely often overlooked, like the Bearded Tachuri requiring extensive tracts of unburned grassland; overall numbers are much depleted by the conversion of so much of its habitat to intensive agriculture. Not very vocal, with call a weak and somewhat nasal "wree? wree? wree?" (up to a dozen or more "wree" notes).

Many-colored Rush Tyrant
Tachuris rubrigastra   PLATE 43(10)
11–11.5 cm (4¼–4½"). *Locally common in marshes from n. Peru* (Lambayeque) *to s. Chile and s. Argentina;* in winter a few wander to s. Brazil. To 4100 m in Andes. *Unmistakable and colorful. Head black* (face bluer and glossy) with *golden superciliary* and partially concealed red coronal stripe. Back green; wings and tail black, wings with *conspicuous longitudinal white stripe, outer tail feathers also white* (obvious in flight). Below bright yellow with *partial black breast band and reddish crissum.* ♀ duller. **High Andean birds** slightly larger with a wider superciliary; **coastal Peru birds** can be whiter below and have a greener superciliary. The beautiful little "siete colores" (actually there are eight or nine) moves about restlessly within the cover of reedbeds and often is hard to see; on occasion one will emerge to feed at water's edge, and in the early morning they regularly perch more in the open. Quite musical song a rich gurgled "treeutu-tu, treeutu-tu-tu-tu."

Anairetes

A distinctive group of small *Andean and Patagonian* tyrannids that inhabit scrub. *Their prominent crests are usually raised and spread, exposing white.* All but one species (the rare Ash-breasted) have *prominent streaking,* a pattern that is unusual among the smaller tyrant flycatchers.

Tufted Tit-Tyrant
Anairetes parulus   PLATE 43(11)
11 cm (4¼"). Fairly common in shrubby clearings and borders of upper montane forest in Andes from s. Colombia to Tierra del Fuego, in Chile and Argentina also in lowlands. Northward mostly 2500–3500 m (up to treeline, locally in *Polylepis*). *Tiny* and *obviously crested. Iris pale yellow.* Head blackish with a *long, wispy, recurved crest* (usually parted), *supraloral and postocular stripe white.* Above dull grayish brown; wings duskier with two narrow whitish bars (less evident in **southern birds**), outer tail feathers with whitish outer webs. *Throat and breast whitish streaked black,* belly pale yellow. Yellow-billed Tit-Tyrant (Peru south) favors more arid montane scrub, has a dark iris and less recurved crest, and broader black breast streaking. Larger and longer-tailed Agile and Unstreaked Tit-Tyrants

have a flatter crown with *no* long recurved crest. Usually in pairs, foraging restlessly in foliage, sometimes with mixed flocks but usually not. Often flutters wings; gleans in foliage, sometimes hover-gleaning or even making short sallies into air. High-pitched song a fast "chuit-chuit-chuit-chuit-chuit-chidi-didi"; sometimes just the "chu-it" is given in a slower series.

Juan Fernández Tit-Tyrant
Anairetes fernandezianus
12.5 cm (5"). *Common in all wooded habitats on Isla Robinson Crusoe in the Juan Fernández Islands off Chile.* To 900 m. Resembles Tufted Tit-Tyrant, but larger with longer crest, heavier breast streaking, and whiter belly. Unmistakable on its island, where *the only insectivorous bird.* Behavior evidently much as in Tufted Tit-Tyrant.

Yellow-billed Tit-Tyrant
Anairetes flavirostris   PLATE 43(12)
11.5 cm (4½"). Fairly common in montane scrub and low woodland in *Andes from n. Peru* (Piura and Cajamarca) *to w. Argentina* (Mendoza and n. Chubut), in Argentina also in lowlands (especially in austral winter). To 4000 m. *Lower mandible dull yellow-orange* (often inconspicuous); *iris dark.* Crown blackish, feathers elongated into a *short crest* (but *not* recurved); *face, sides of neck, throat, and breast boldly streaked black and white.* Otherwise olive brown above, wings duskier with two white bars. Belly contrasting unstreaked pale yellow. Tufted Tit-Tyrant favors more humid areas, and has an all-dark bill but an obviously pale iris; its crest is longer and much more recurved. Pied-crested Tit-Tyrant has a blacker face and throat, much longer black and white crest, streaked back, white belly. Behavior much as in Tufted Tit-Tyrant. Yellow-billed favors quite sparse and barren habitats. Rather quiet; song a series of high-pitched, wiry notes, e.g. "jzt-jzt-jzt-jeteteteree-tzititititit" or a soft "dzreeeet."

Pied-crested Tit-Tyrant
Anairetes reguloides   PLATE 43(13)
11.5 cm (4½"). Uncommon in shrubby areas, light woodland, and hedgerows in *w. Peru* (north to Ancash) *and extreme n. Chile.* Ranges up in Andean valleys to about 3000 m. Lower mandible yellowish. *Long bifurcated crest mainly black, usually parted to reveal extensive white; otherwise streaked black and white above,* ♂

with *black face and throat.* Wings and tail blackish, wings with two white bars, outer tail feathers edged and tipped white. *Breast boldly streaked black and white,* belly white. Cf. notably larger Black-crested Tit-Tyrant, mainly at higher elevations. Yellow-billed Tit-Tyrant is smaller with less black on face and *no* back streaking. Usually in pairs, with behavior much as in Tufted and Yellow-billed Tit-Tyrants; Pied-crested can occur with the latter. Call a "loud descending series of whistles" (Fjeldså and Krabbe 1989).

Black-crested Tit-Tyrant
Anairetes nigrocristatus
13 cm (5"). Uncommon in shrubby areas and woodland (including patches of *Polylepis*) in *Andes from extreme s. Ecuador* (s. Loja) *to nw. Peru* (Ancash and Huánuco). 2300–3900 m. Resembles Pied-crested Tit-Tyrant, but *notably larger, bill mostly reddish,* and *crest feathers much longer; tail feathers more broadly tipped and edged white.* Black-crested ♂ has white throat streaking (not solidly black as in ♂ Pied-crested), but ♂♂ **in Ecuador** have more extensive black on throat and breast. Behavior of this striking tit-tyrant is much as in its congeners. Call a fast series of harsh chippered notes, e.g., "tree-tr-ri-i-i-i-i-tr-r-reu" trailing off at end.

Ash-breasted Tit-Tyrant
Anairetes alpinus   PLATE 43(14)
13.5 cm (5¼"). *Rare and very local in patches of Polylepis woodland in high Andes from w. Peru* (Ancash) *to w. Bolivia* (La Paz). 3700–4600 m. *Mostly dark ashy gray,* somewhat paler below, with *long bifurcated crest usually parted to reveal extensive white;* wings and tail black, wings with two white bars, outer tail feathers mostly white. Midbelly whitish. This large *unstreaked* tit-tyrant should not be confused in its limited range and habitat. Cf. Unstreaked Tit-Tyrant (uncrested, with superciliary and vague breast streaking, etc.); though montane, it occurs at lower elevations. Behavior similar to other tit-tyrants; seems always to occur at low densities. Call a nasal, burry "breee, dreeu-dreeu-dreeu-dreeu-dreeu."

Uromyias

Two distinctive tyrannids found in high-elevation Andean forests, closely related to *Anairetes.* They have *long, flat recumbent crests,* plain wings, and *long tails.*

Agile Tit-Tyrant

Uromyias agilis   PLATE 43(15)

13.5 cm (5¼"). Uncommon in lower growth and borders of upper montane forest in *Andes from w. Venezuela* (Mérida) *to s. Ecuador* (n. Loja). Mostly 2600–3500 m, most numerous just below treeline. *Long flat crest blackish,* usually protruding slightly, bordered below by a *long, narrow whitish superciliary.* Brown above, streaked whitish on nape and blackish on back; wings dusky. *Below yellowish white narrowly streaked brown,* belly pale yellow. Tufted Tit-Tyrant is markedly smaller and shorter-tailed, and it sports an obviously recurved crest; it has wing-bars (wings *plain* in Agile). Unstreaked Tit-Tyrant occurs south of range of this species. Usually in small groups that accompany mixed flocks, foraging actively in foliage, often in outer branches and not hard to see. Favors stands of *Chusquea* bamboo. Call a brief soft trill. Song an excited, jumbled series of "treerrr" trills and "tseeyk," "tsi-dik," or "tseee" notes.

Unstreaked Tit-Tyrant

Uromyias agraphia   PLATE 43(16)

13 cm (5"). Uncommon and local in lower growth and borders of upper montane forest on *east slope of Andes in Peru* (Amazonas, south of Río Marañón to Cuzco). Mostly 2700–3500 m. *Crown and nape blackish,* bordered below by *long whitish superciliary;* back, wings, and tail plain brown. *Sides of head, throat, and breast pale gray vaguely streaked whitish;* belly pale yellow. Unstreaked is the southern replacement for Agile Tit-Tyrant; the two do not overlap. Tufted Tit-Tyrant is smaller, with shorter tail, and has recurved crest feathers, etc. Behavior much as in Agile Tit-Tyrant, sharing its predilection for *Chusquea* bamboo. Vocalizations similar.

Suiriri

Elaenia-like flycatchers found in semiopen terrain and light woodland of e. and s. South America, *Suiriri* differ from *Elaenia* in their **all-black bills** (not with pale lower mandible of *Elaenia*) and white-spotted juvenal plumage.

Chaco Suiriri

Suiriri suiriri*   PLATE 44(1)

15.5 cm (6"). *Fairly common in chaco woodland, scrub, and monte woodland from w. Bolivia* (Cochabamba) *to n. Argentina* (La Pampa), a few moving to ne. Bolivia in austral winter. To over 2000 m in Bolivia. Sometimes considered conspecific with Campo Suiriri. *Mostly gray above* with white supraloral; wings and tail blacker, *wings with two bold grayish bars,* tail feathers edged and tipped white. *Whitish below.* This *obviously gray and white* flycatcher should be readily recognized. Arboreal, perching quite upright and recalling a small *Myiarchus;* it gleans and sallies to foliage. Suiriris often accompany loose flocks, and when not breeding can occur in small groups. An abrupt harsh scold, "dyyrr," is frequently given, sometimes in fast succession or as a chatter.

Campo Suiriri

Suiriri affinis*   PLATE 44(2)

16 cm (6¼"). Uncommon in cerrado, campos with scattered shrubs and trees, and the edge of gallery woodland from *ne. Brazil to n. Bolivia* (east to Beni) *and ne. Paraguay.* To 1100 m. Sometimes considered conspecific with Chaco Suiriri. Olive above with grayer head and *distinctly paler buffy yellowish rump and base of tail;* wings and tail blacker, wings with two yellowish bars, tail feathers edged yellowish. Throat and chest pale grayish, breast and belly pale yellow. A few supposed intergrades with Chaco Suiriri are recorded from where their ranges come into contact (principally in ne. Paraguay). Cf. Chapada Suiriri. Southern Scrub Flycatcher has a shorter bill and lacks the pale rump. Usually in pairs, foraging low and sometimes dropping to the ground; often hovers, exposing the pale rump and spreading tail. Pairs give a fast jumbled series of notes as a duet (a common phrase is "pichu!"), sometimes vigorously drooping and flapping their wings.

Chapada Suiriri

Suiriri islerorum*

16 cm (6¼"). *Uncommon and local in shrubby cerrado in cen. Brazil and adjacent Bolivia* (ne. Santa Cruz). 250–1000 m. A recently described species that closely resembles Campo Suiriri but which differs in its *shorter bill* and *pale tips to tail feathers.* Behavior of the two species is similar, and locally they even occur together. Chapada's vigorous display is also similar, but it tends to hold its wings above the horizontal (not seen in Campo Suiriri). Its voice has a similar quality, and likewise is often given as a duet; common phrases, each often repeated several times, have

been paraphrased as "where where" and "whooz it" (K. J. Zimmer et al.).

Elaenia

One of the more challenging Neotropical bird genera, *Elaenia* elaenias regularly confound even the most experienced observers, especially when the bird in front of you isn't vocalizing. Focus on the following: *size* (there are a few notably large species); *crest* (its size and shape; some elaenias, lacking a crest, look round-headed); *the presence or absence of white in the crest*; and *belly color* (whether pale yellow or whitish). Arboreal tyrannids found in a variety of wooded or shrubby habitats, none ranges in humid lowland forest. Elaenias perch quite upright and consume both insects and fruit; they generally do not accompany flocks, though sometimes several congregate at fruiting trees. Most species are conspicuous and numerous, so you should have plenty of opportunities to test your knowledge.

Yellow-bellied Elaenia
Elaenia flavogaster   PLATE 44(3)
16–16.5 cm (6¼–6½"). *Widespread and often common* in semiopen shrubby areas, clearings, and gardens from Colombia and Venezuela to n. Argentina, but absent from much of Amazonia. *Non*migratory. Mostly below 1500 m, a few to 2000 m or more. Often shows a *conspicuous upstanding bushy crest that generally is parted; in northern part of range this reveals a white coronal patch* (especially when vocalizing, which it does frequently). Brownish olive above with a faint whitish eye-ring; wings duskier with two whitish bars. Throat whitish, breast grayish olive, belly pale yellow (despite its name, *not* particularly yellow-bellied). Learn this elaenia well, as in many areas it is the most numerous member of its difficult genus. Cf. especially Lesser and Large Elaenias. Though drab in appearance, the Yellow-bellied's demeanor is animated and excitable, and it often perches in the open, attracting attention. Regularly seen at fruiting trees. Noisy, with most frequent calls, all of them exuberant and with a hoarse quality, including a "breeeyr" and a "wreek-kreeeyuup," the latter often doubled. Also: Mexico to Panama, and Lesser Antilles.

Mottle-backed Elaenia
Elaenia gigas   PLATE 44(4)
18 cm (7"). Uncommon in shrubby clearings with scattered trees and on river islands in lowlands and foothills along *eastern base of Andes from s. Colombia* (Meta) *to w. Bolivia* (w. Santa Cruz). Mostly below 1250 m. Unmistakable with *prominent bifurcated crest* that *protrudes straight up from forehead, exposing much white.* Olive brown above with mantle feathers edged paler with a mottled effect; wings duskier with two whitish bars. Throat pale grayish, breast and flanks flammulated and clouded olive, midbelly clear yellow. *No other elaenia has such a crest.* Behavior similar to Yellow-bellied Elaenia, though Mottle-backed is rarely as numerous. Calls include a martinlike "drreet" and a shriller "woreet!" or "wurdít," the latter sometimes doubled.

Highland Elaenia
Elaenia obscura   PLATE 44(5)
18 cm (7"). Uncommon in lower growth and borders of montane forest and woodland in *Andes from s. Ecuador* (Azuay) *to nw. Argentina* (Catamarca), and in *se. Brazil region.* Mostly 1700–3000 m in Andes, lower in Argentina; to 2000 m in se. Brazil. A *large, round-headed* elaenia whose *short bill imparts a snub-nosed effect.* Dark olive above with *yellowish eye-ring* and *no* crest or coronal patch; wings duskier with two yellowish bars; tail rather long. Throat pale yellowish, breast and flanks dull olive, midbelly clear yellow. Sierran Elaenia is markedly smaller and somewhat crested; its white coronal patch is usually evident. Large Elaenia is less olive overall (more grayish) and has a markedly grayer foreneck; it usually shows a vague crest. Highland is a rather inconspicuous elaenia, more forest or woodland-based than many, only infrequently perching in the open. Call a fast "burrr" or "burrreep." Song (in Bolivia) a plaintive first note followed by several shorter, scratchier ones, e.g., "weeeéuw-drrr-deet!" (S. Mayer recording).

Sierran Elaenia
Elaenia pallatangae   PLATE 44(6)
14.5 cm (5¾"). Locally fairly common in borders of montane forest, secondary woodland, and shrubby clearings in *Andes from s. Colombia to w. Bolivia* (w. Santa Cruz), and on *tepuis of s. Venezuela region.* Mostly 1500–3000 m. Olive to brownish olive above with *narrow white coronal stripe* (usually visible, but *does not show much of a crest*) and vague whitish eye-ring;

wings duskier with two whitish bars. Throat and breast dull olive, *belly pale yellow.* **Tepui birds** are browner above, darker and more uniformly olive below. Easily confused with White-crested Elaenia, though that species is whiter on belly. Sierran also closely resembles Lesser Elaenia, though that species typically shows at least some crest, has less white inside crest, and tends to be darker above. In Colombia, cf. also Mountain Elaenia. A *difficult* species; silent birds often cannot be safely identified. Generally less conspicuous than Yellow-bellied Elaenia, and certainly not as noisy. Often perches quietly for long periods, but also accompanies mixed flocks. Several birds may congregate at fruiting trees. Calls include an abrupt burry "breeyp," a "wreee-yr," and a "wree?" These are similar to some of White-crested Elaenia's calls; some individuals, at least in Ecuador, cannot be distinguished vocally. Tepui birds (same species?) give a quite different and sharper "pseeu."

Plain-crested Elaenia
Elaenia cristata   PLATE 44(7)
14.5 cm (5¾"). *Locally not uncommon in savannas and cerrado with scattered bushes and low trees from cen. and e. Venezuela to e. and cen. Brazil.* Locally to 1500 m. Usually appears *crested,* but unlike other crested elaenias, *Plain-crested never shows white in crown. Very dull.* Olive brown above, wings duskier with two whitish bars. Throat and chest pale grayish, breast more olive, belly pale yellow. Lesser Elaenia often occurs with Plain-crested; it differs principally in having white in crown (though this is often inconspicuous), and usually looks less crested. Their calls differ. Behavior similar to various other open-country elaenias; Plain-crested is restricted to natural savannas, so is less wide-ranging than various congeners. It also seems less vocal than many; song a fast gravelly "jer-jéhjeh" or "jer, jujujujuju."

White-crested Elaenia
Elaenia albiceps   PLATE 44(8)
14.5–15 cm (5¾–6"). Locally fairly common in secondary habitats and montane scrub in *Andes from s. Colombia to w. Bolivia, in Pacific lowlands of w. Peru and n. Chile, and very common as a breeder in various wooded habitats in cen. and s. Chile and w. and s. Argentina,* migrating to Amazonia during austral winter. Mostly below 3200 m. **Southern breeders** (illustrated) dark olive above with white coronal stripe and whitish

eye-ring; wings duskier with two prominent whitish bars. Throat and breast pale gray, belly whitish. **Andean birds** are duller and dingier (especially those in w. Peru and n. Chile), browner above and olivaceous on breast. White-crested *closely* resembles Small-billed Elaenia; many individuals cannot be identified, especially as wintering birds vocalize rarely, if at all. In se. Brazil area, cf. Olivaceous Elaenia. In Andes most likely confused with Sierran Elaenia, though Sierran is yellower on belly. Cf. also Lesser Elaenia. White-crested Elaenia is one of the most numerous nesting birds in austral forests, at times seeming to outnumber all other birds combined. Despite being so abundant there, they are rarely noted on their wintering grounds, in part because they spread out across such a vast area but also because they are so hard to identify at that season. Breeding austral birds are very vocal, interminably giving a burry "feeur" or "feeo" (giving rise to their local name "fio-fio"); their dawn song, also burry, is a "breeo-breeyr." Calls of Andean birds, some of them closely similar to Sierran Elaenia, include an abrupt "peeyr," a "wheeo," and a burry "brreeo." Typical dawn song a "breeyr, breeyr-it."

Slaty Elaenia
Elaenia strepera   PLATE 44(9)
15.5 cm (6"). *Locally common breeder in montane woodland and forest borders in Andes from s. Bolivia* (w. Santa Cruz) *to nw. Argentina* (La Rioja); during austral winter migrates to n. Venezuela. Mostly 600–2000 m when breeding. ♂ distinctive for an *Elaenia, mostly slaty gray,* slightly paler below, with white coronal streak and faint eye-ring, two indistinct pale grayish wing-bars, and white midbelly. ♀ similar but tinged olive above; wing-bars more ochraceous. Smoke-colored Pewee is more uniformly gray than ♂ Slaty Elaenia; cf. also Crowned Slaty Flycatcher. Even though ♀ is less pure gray than ♂, it still is much grayer than any other *Elaenia* (none has such ochraceous wing-bars either). Behavior much as in Sierran and Mountain Elaenias, but Slaty is less conspicuous and more tied to forest. Song, given frequently by breeding birds, a dry, gravelly "eh-eh-ehhhhh?" with a mechanical quality unlike any other elaenia.

Brownish Elaenia
Elaenia pelzelni   PLATE 44(10)
18 cm (7"). *Uncommon and local in low riparian woodland and borders on islands of Amazon*

River system from Brazil upriver to ne. Peru and n. Bolivia. Below 200 m. A large, dull brownish *Elaenia. Head rounded* with a small white coronal patch (this often hidden, and may be lacking in ♀♀). *Dull brown above,* wings duskier with two obscure buffyish bars. *Below dingy pale grayish brown,* whitish on midbelly. Unlike other *Elaenia, Brownish shows no olive.* Large and Mottle-backed Elaenias occur with this species, but neither is at all brown. Favors *Cecropia*-dominated woodland where it is inconspicuous, notably so for an *Elaenia.* Most frequent call a repeated clear "cleeu" and a sharper "kéw-ik."

Great Elaenia
Elaenia dayi   PLATE 44(11)
20 cm (8"). *Uncommon in scrub, secondary woodland, and at edge of montane forest on tepuis of s. Venezuela,* most numerous at higher elevations. *Very large* and *dark.* 1300–2600 m. Slightly crested. *Dark sooty brown above* with narrow white eye-ring; wings duskier with two whitish bars. Dull olive grayish below, midbelly pale yellow. The size of a large *Myiarchus* flycatcher, it is so much larger (and also darker) than other *Elaenia* that confusion is improbable. Voice not well known; a fast rollicking duet has been heard, e.g., "wreh che-che-che wreh wreh che-che-che" (D. Ascanio recording).

Rufous-crowned Elaenia
Elaenia ruficeps   PLATE 44(12)
14.5 cm (5¾"). *Found locally in shrubby savannas with scattered trees from e. Colombia to the Guianas and e. Amaz. Brazil.* To 1400 m in s. Venezuela. Distinctive. Dark brownish olive with *rufous patch on rearcrown usually visible* and a whitish eye-ring; wings duskier with two whitish bars. Below pale yellowish, *foreneck whiter with distinct grayish olive streaking.* Occurs with Lesser and Plain-crested Elaenias, neither of which have rufous in crown or show streaking below. Behavior as with other *Elaenia;* often conspicuous. Call a burry "d-rr-rr-rr."

Large Elaenia
Elaenia spectabilis   PLATE 44(13)
18 cm (7"). *Fairly common breeder in forest and woodland borders and in clearings from e. Brazil to n. Argentina;* during austral winter migrates into w. Amazonia, there favoring riparian areas. To about 1000 m. Brownish olive above with a faint whitish eye-ring and short crest; wings duskier with 2–3 whitish bars. *Throat and breast*

pale gray, belly pale yellow. Resembles more numerous Yellow-bellied Elaenia, differing in its somewhat larger size, *reduced crest showing little or no white,* and purer gray foreneck; *voice* is often the best clue. Cf. also Highland Elaenia as well as Short-crested and Swainson's Flycatchers. Less conspicuous and vocal than Yellow-bellied Elaenia, Large is more of a woodland bird. Most frequent call a fairly melodic "p-cheeu" that lacks Yellow-bellied's raucous quality.

Noronha Elaenia
Elaenia ridleyana
17 cm (6¾"). Common in scrub, light woodland, and trees around houses on *Ilha Fernando de Noronha off ne. Brazil.* Resembles Large Elaenia (no overlap) but has a longer bill and a shorter tail. Hardly to be confused; *only other resident passerine bird on Noronha is the very different Noronha Vireo.* Call reminiscent of Large Elaenia (its closest relative), and often with similar quality, "pcheeu" but more often varied with chattered introductory notes and other phrases (M. Allen recording).

Mountain Elaenia
Elaenia frantzii   PLATE 44(14)
14 cm (5½"). Common in shrubby clearings and borders of montane forest and woodland in *Andes of n. and w. Venezuela and Colombia* (south to Nariño). Mostly 1500–2500 m. Above dull brownish olive with a *yellowish eye-ring;* wings duskier with two pale yellowish bars. *Below yellowish olive,* belly yellower. Mountain Elaenia *lacks* any trace of Sierran's white coronal stripe, and Sierran's eye-ring is much less prominent; Mountain has a rounder head shape. Lesser Elaenia also shows white in crown and usually looks slightly crested; it is grayer below than Mountain. Behavior similar to Sierran Elaenia. Calls include a whistled "peee-oo" or "twee-oo," and a more drawn out "peeee-err." Also: Guatemala to w. Panama.

Small-billed Elaenia
Elaenia parvirostris   PLATE 44(15)
14.5 cm (5¾"). *Common breeder in woodland, humid and montane forest borders, and adjacent clearings from e. Bolivia to se. Brazil and n. Argentina;* in austral winter migrates north as far as w. Amazonia, Venezuela, and the Guianas. Mostly below 1200 m. Olive above with *narrow white coronal stripe* (usually visible, but has *no* crest so it looks *round-headed*) and a *distinct*

round white eye-ring; wings duskier with 2–3 whitish bars. *Throat and breast pale gray,* midbelly whitish. The very similar White-crested Elaenia is dingier generally (its foreneck notably so), has a less obvious eye-ring, and never seems to show a third wing-bar. Small-billed's slightly stubbier bill *cannot* be used as a field character. Olivaceous Elaenia lacks the coronal stripe and has more uniform underparts. Cf. also Lesser Elaenia. Behavior as with other elaenias; generally conspicuous and not shy. Distinctive song, given only on its breeding grounds, a "weedablewee" phrase that is repeated steadily at 3-second intervals. Calls include a sharp "chu" or "cheeu."

Olivaceous Elaenia
Elaenia mesoleuca

14 cm (5½"). Generally uncommon in humid and montane forest in *se. Brazil region,* some birds apparently moving north into gallery forest of cen. Brazil (e.g., s. Mato Grosso and s. Goiás) when not breeding (but status there uncertain). To at least 2000 m. Olive above with little or no white in crown; wings duskier with two pale yellowish bars. Throat pale grayish, *breast grayish olive,* midbelly whitish with flanks more greenish yellow. *Closely resembles Small-billed Elaenia;* Olivaceous differs in being drabber and more uniform with a less evident eye-ring (also lacking Small-billed's often evident white in crest) and more olive breast (Small-billed is a purer gray); voice is often the best clue. Behavior much as in White-crested and Small-billed Elaenias, though Olivaceous seems a more forest-based bird. Distinctive song a harsh, fast "whik, whikiur"; also gives a "chirr" call.

Lesser Elaenia
*Elaenia chiriquensis** PLATE 44(16)

13.5–14 cm (5¼–5½"). Fairly common and widespread in savannas, cerrado, shrubby clearings, gardens, and cultivated areas with hedgerows and scattered trees from *Colombia and Venezuela to s. Brazil,* but absent from most of Amazonia. Mostly below 1500 m, locally to 2500 m in n. Ecuador. Usually shows a *slight crest exposing some white.* Grayish olive above with narrow whitish eye-ring; wings duskier with two whitish bars. Throat and breast pale grayish, breast more olive, belly yellowish white. *A difficult Elaenia, easily confused;* nonvocalizing birds often cannot be certainly identified. Sierran Elaenia is slightly brighter yellow on belly, and White-crested Elaenia is whiter on belly; cf. also Small-billed

Elaenia. Plain-crested Elaenia is very similar aside from lacking white in its usually more evident crest (but at times white is not visible in Lesser's either). Yellow-bellied Elaenia is slightly larger with a fuller crest that northward exposes more white; it is much more likely to be found in gardens and other human-modified habitats than the Lesser. Mountain Elaenia is rounderheaded, lacks white in crest, and is more uniform below. Song in most of range a burry, bisyllabic "chíbur" or "jwebu"; in nw. Ecuador and sw. Colombia (likely not same species) gives a very different burry "bweer, wheéb, wher'r'r" (P. Coopmans). Also: Costa Rica and Panama.

Caribbean Elaenia
Elaenia martinica

15 cm (6"). *Uncommon in deciduous woodland, scrub, cultivated land, and mangroves on Netherlands Antilles.* Resembles Lesser Elaenia (which is recorded from there as a vagrant of uncertain status), but Caribbean is somewhat larger and more crested, and also has more white in crest. Behavior similar to other elaenias. Call a whistled "wee-weeu" or "wee-wee-weeu." Also: West Indies.

Myiopagis

Obscure and drab, these elaenias are found in humid or deciduous forest and woodland, mainly in the lowlands. They are less conspicuous and vocal than *Elaenia,* most of which are larger; each species does have a *distinctive vocalization.* Some *Myiopagis* are more apt to join mixed flocks. Their head patterns tend to be more complex, though their coronal patches usually remain concealed.

Yellow-crowned Elaenia
Myiopagis flavivertex PLATE 45(1)

13 cm (5"). Uncommon and local in lower and middle growth of *várzea and swampy forest in Amazonia and the Guianas.* Below 300 m. Olive above, duskier on crown with a *bright yellow coronal stripe* (often concealed) and whitish supraloral; wings duskier with two prominent yellow bars. *Throat and breast grayish olive;* belly pale yellow. Can look disheveled; usually identified by habitat and voice more than appearance. Forest Elaenia (more a canopy bird) has a longer whitish superciliary and streaky effect on breast; their voices are utterly different. Found singly

or in pairs, perching rather upright inside forest. Generally not with mixed flocks. Distinctive song an explosive, sharp and burry "jeeér-jeeer-jeeer-jew" repeated at often long intervals; can be varied to a faster "jéw-jijijijijijijew-jew."

Forest Elaenia
Myiopagis gaimardii   PLATE 45(2)

12.5 cm (5"). *Widespread and fairly common* in canopy and borders of humid forest and woodland from Colombia and Venezuela to s. Brazil (n. São Paulo). Mostly below 1000 m. In **most of range** (illustrated) head brownish gray, crown darker with indistinct whitish superciliary and *white coronal stripe* (often concealed); brownish olive above, wings duskier with two prominent pale yellowish bars. Throat whitish, breast pale yellow *mottled and streaked olive,* belly pale yellow. Birds from **n. Colombia** have a yellow coronal stripe. Obscure, *best known for its distinctive voice.* Yellow-crowned Elaenia has a bright yellow coronal stripe, yellower wing-bars, and lacks the streaky effect on breast; general behavior and voice very different. Except for ♀ Gray Elaenia, most similar flycatchers of the canopy lack Forest Elaenia's coronal stripe (though this can be hard to see). Zimmer's and Gray-crowned Flatbills have wider bills; Slender-footed Tyrannulet has a pale eye and *no* wing-bars; *none of these shows blurry breast streaking.* Usually ranging well above the ground, Forest Elaenias thus are often easier to see in secondary woodland and borders. Often forages with mixed flocks, gleaning in foliage and slightly cocking tail. Song often heard (though usually given at long intervals), a distinctive sharp and emphatic "ch-weét," sometimes varied to "cheewi chi-chi-chi." Also: Panama.

Gray Elaenia
Myiopagis caniceps   PLATE 45(3)

12–12.5 cm (4¾–5"). Uncommon in canopy and borders of humid forest from *w. Colombia and s. Venezuela to n. Argentina and e. Brazil.* Locally to 1100–1200 m. **More northern and western** ♂♂ (illustrated) *blue-gray above* with white coronal stripe (often concealed); *wings black with two bold white bars and edging. Throat and breast pale gray,* belly grayish white. **More southern and eastern** ♂♂ duller gray. ♀ bright olive above, head grayer with pale yellowish coronal streak; *wings black with two bold pale yellow bars and edging.* Throat grayish white; below pale greenish yellow, brightest on belly. **West of Andes, ♀** has

coronal patch white. Forest Elaenia's wing markings are less well defined; it is duller overall, with blurry breast streaking. Cf. also various *Phyllomyias* tyrannulets. Almost always in pairs, regularly with mixed flocks; gleans in foliage, partially cocking tail and sometimes wing-lifting. Rarely comes low, even at edge, and thus *apt to be overlooked until you learn its voice.* Song a fast and shrill chippering that descends and fades toward end, introduced by several sharper notes, e.g., "swee swee swee wee-ee-ee-ee-ee-ee-ee-ee." In w. Amazonia also gives a "tsi-si-tseeuw, tsi-tseeuw." Also: Panama.

Foothill Elaenia
*Myiopagis olallai**

12.5 cm (5"). *Uncommon and very local in canopy and borders of foothill forest along eastern base of Andes in Ecuador* (w. Napo and Zamora-Chinchipe) *and cen. Peru* (Ayacucho); likely overlooked. 900–1300 m. A recently described species. Resembles ♀ Gray Elaenia but *crown gray* (not olive) and *coronal patch white* (and somewhat larger). Differs from Forest Elaenia in its purer olive back, grayer crown with whiter coronal patch, and *more well-defined wing-bars;* Foothill does not seem to occur with Forest. Arboreal behavior similar to those species. Song a very different harsh trill that rises slightly and lasts about 2 seconds, sometimes preceded by several introductory notes; best identified by voice.

Greenish Elaenia
Myiopagis viridicata   PLATE 45(4)

13.5 cm (5¼"). Fairly common in lower growth, mid-levels, and borders of semihumid and deciduous forest and woodland from *Colombia and Venezuela to n. Argentina and s. Brazil;* absent from much of Amazonia, though occurs as an austral migrant in the southwest; vacates southern areas during austral winter. Mostly below 1000 m. Perhaps more than one species. Crown grayish with yellow coronal stripe (often hidden), *short superciliary and eye-ring white;* otherwise olive above; wings duskier with *dull yellowish edging* (but *no* bars). Throat pale grayish, breast grayish olive, belly pale yellow. In Tumbesian region, cf. Pacific Elaenia. In e. South America, Pale-bellied Tyrant-Manakin differs in its plainer face and virtually unmarked wings. Sooty-headed Tyrannulet is markedly smaller, brighter yellow below, and lacks the coronal stripe. A quiet and unobtrusive bird, generally overlooked unless it is vocalizing. Usually perches quite upright. Most frequent call a high-pitched, strident and burry "cheerip" or "cheeyree" or "zrreeeeer." Also: Mexico to Panama.

Pacific Elaenia
Myiopagis subplacens PLATE 45(5)
14 cm (5½"). *Locally not uncommon in lower growth and borders of deciduous and semi-humid forest and woodland from nw. Ecuador (w. Esmeraldas) to nw. Peru (Piura). To 1700 m in s. Ecuador.* Crown grayish brown with yellow coronal stripe (often concealed), *broad superciliary grizzled whitish and arcing around blackish ear-coverts;* above brownish olive, wings duskier with *dull yellowish edging (but no bars).* Throat and breast pale grayish with blurry streaking, belly pale yellow. Greenish Elaenia is slightly smaller, grayer on head with a shorter superciliary and plainer ear-coverts, and more olive breast; calls differ strikingly. Yellow-olive Flatbill has a wider bill and bolder wing markings (including wing-bars). Behavior much as in Greenish Elaenia; in area of overlap, Pacific favors more arid situations, but the two can be together. Oft-heard call a sharply enunciated "cheer! woorr-it" repeated at intervals of 3–4 seconds.

Sublegatus

*Elaenia-*like flycatchers with *short, all-black bills* (shortest in Southern Scrub Flycatcher) found in semiopen areas, where they are *notably quiet and retiring,* which is rather different from the otherwise quite similar *Elaenia.*

Southern Scrub Flycatcher
Sublegatus modestus PLATE 45(6)
14 cm (5½"). *Uncommon in scrub, lighter woodland, and cerrado from n. and e. Bolivia and e. Brazil to n. Argentina* (n. Buenos Aires); in austral winter some birds migrate into s. Amazonia. To 2000 m or even more in Bolivia, but mostly below 1000 m. Olive brown above with *narrow whitish supraloral,* wings duskier with *two bold whitish bars. Throat and breast pale gray, contrasting with pale yellow belly.* Amazonian Scrub Flycatcher has a less short bill, decidedly less conspicuous wing markings, and shows less contrast below. *Elaenia* have longer bills with pale lower mandible (not short and all black) and less contrast below; they show no supraloral.

A quiet and unobtrusive flycatcher that perches upright and remains in or close to cover; it sallies to foliage and hover-gleans. Simple song a weak, high-pitched "pseeu" repeated at intervals of about 1 second.

Northern Scrub Flycatcher
Sublegatus arenarum PLATE 45(7)
14 cm (5½"). *Uncommon in arid scrub, savannas, light deciduous woodland, and mangroves from n. Colombia to the Guianas. To 500 m.* Olive brown above with *narrow whitish supraloral,* wings duskier with two dull brownish bars. *Throat and breast pale gray, contrasting with pale yellow belly.* Cf. Amazonian Scrub Flycatcher (overlapping with Northern in e. Venezuela and the Guianas). *Elaenia* have longer bills with a pale lower mandible (not short and all black), less contrast on underparts, and do not show a supraloral. *Myiarchus* flycatchers are larger with a longer bill, no supraloral. Behavior as in Southern Scrub Flycatcher. Gives a soft plaintive "pee" call, often doubled. Also: Costa Rica and Panama.

Amazonian Scrub Flycatcher
Sublegatus obscurior
14 cm (5½"). Uncommon and perhaps local in borders of humid forest, secondary woodland, and clearings in *Amazonia, s. Venezuela, and the Guianas.* To 1000 m. Resembles Northern Scrub Flycatcher but above more grayish, below dingier with *gray foreneck and pale yellow belly.* Both other scrub flycatchers show a sharper contrast below; usually best distinguished from similar-looking elaenias by its obviously short bill. Behavior much as in Southern Scrub Flycatcher; the even more inconspicuous (and doubtless often overlooked) Amazonian is more arboreal and can occur in forest canopy. Not very vocal, but foraging birds occasionally give a plaintive "pseeeu." Rarely heard song a repeated, rather sweet "chwedeé ... chwedeé ... chwedeé...."

Leptopogon

Slender, long-tailed, and narrow-billed flycatchers found in lower growth of humid or montane forest. All species show *grizzling on face* and *at least a trace of a dark auricular patch,* both recalling the smaller *Pogonotriccus* bristle tyrants. *They characteristically lift a wing up over their back.*

Sepia-capped Flycatcher

Leptopogon amaurocephalus   PLATE 45(8)

13.5–14 cm (5¼–5½″). Uncommon to locally fairly common in lower growth of humid and semihumid forest and woodland from *Colombia and w. and s. Venezuela to n. Argentina and s. Brazil*. Mostly below 1100 m. In **most of range** (illustrated) *crown dark brown, facial area dull buff grizzled dusky,* and *dusky patch on ear-coverts*. Otherwise olive above, tail more brownish; wings dusky *with two broad buff bars* and yellowish edging. Throat pale grayish, breast dull olive, belly pale yellow. **Southern birds** slightly larger with *blacker auricular patch*. The montane Slaty-capped Flycatcher has a gray crown and whitish facial area. Behavior as in Slaty-capped, including the frequent wing-lifting; Sepia-capped is more unobtrusive and only rarely comes to forest edge. Call a fast, sputtering chatter that trails off toward the end, e.g., "skeúw-k'k'k'k'k'k'kew." Also: Mexico to Panama.

Slaty-capped Flycatcher

Leptopogon superciliaris   PLATE 45(9)

13.5 cm (5¼″). *Common in lower growth of foothill and lower montane forest in Andes from n. Venezuela to w. Bolivia* (w. Santa Cruz). Mostly 500–1800 m, lower in w. Colombia and w. Ecuador. *Bill black*. **Venezuela birds** (illustrated) have *crown slaty gray* with *facial area whitish grizzled gray* and *dusky patch on ear-coverts;* olive above, wings dusky with *two yellowish bars*. Throat pale grayish, breast olive, belly clear yellow. In **Colombia south through much of Peru** has *wing-bars ochraceous to buff.* In **s. Peru and Bolivia** reverts to having yellowish wing-bars; also has a grayer breast and whitish belly. Marble-faced Bristle Tyrant is smaller; from Colombia to Peru it differs in having yellowish (not buff) wing-bars, but this distinction breaks down both farther north and farther south, and there size is the main distinguishing point. Variegated Bristle Tyrant (with ochraceous wing-bars) is smaller and has an orangy lower mandible. In Peru cf. Inca Flycatcher. Sepia-capped Flycatcher occurs only in lowlands. Found singly or in pairs, regularly accompanying mixed flocks of understory birds, even out to forest edge. Perches erectly, often on open branches, and easy to observe. Sallies to pick off insects from leaves, less often twigs and branches. Frequently gives a distinctive sharp "skeeéy, deeer," Pacific-slope birds a less nasal "tse-tsrrr." Also: Costa Rica and Panama.

Rufous-breasted Flycatcher

Leptopogon rufipectus   PLATE 45(10)

13 cm (5¼″). Uncommon in lower growth of montane forest in *Andes from sw. Venezuela (s. Táchira) to extreme n. Peru* (n. Cajamarca). Mostly 1600–2500 m. *Crown dark gray; facial area, sides of head, throat, and chest rufous,* ear-coverts with obscure grizzling and a dusky patch. Otherwise olive above, tail brownish; wings dusky with two buff bars. Belly yellow. Handsome Flycatcher is smaller with a buffier throat and chest (not so deep rufous); it shows *no* rufous on its facial area and a pale lower mandible. Behavior as in Slaty-capped Flycatcher; Rufous-breasted never seems as numerous or conspicuous. Often gives a loud and emphatic "skwee!" (like squeezing a child's bath toy), sometimes run together into a fast series of sputtered notes.

Inca Flycatcher

Leptopogon taczanowskii

13 cm (5¼″). Uncommon in lower growth of montane forest on *east slope of Andes in Peru* (Amazonas, south of Río Marañón to Cuzco). 1700–2700 m. Resembles Rufous-breasted Flycatcher, which Inca replaces south of the Río Marañón. *Lacks rufous on face and foreneck;* instead, Inca's *facial area and sides of head are grizzled gray and white,* throat grayish, and *breast dull tawny-olive.* Slaty-capped Flycatcher has a purer olive breast and more tawny-buff (not rufous) wing-bars; it mainly occurs at lower elevations. Behavior as in Slaty-capped and Rufous-breasted Flycatchers. Call an oft-repeated, explosive "tzeet" (B. Walker).

Mionectes

Inconspicuous and plain, Mionectes are slim, slender-billed tyrannids that range in lower growth of humid or montane forests. Like Leptopogon they regularly lift a wing up over back, and are notably frugivorous.

Olive-striped Flycatcher

Mionectes olivaceus   PLATE 45(11)

13–13.5 cm (5–5¼″). Fairly common in lower growth and borders in humid and lower montane forest and woodland from *n. Venezuela and n. Colombia to extreme w. Bolivia* (La Paz). Mostly below 2000 m, along eastern base of Andes not ranging below 400 m. Bill black. Olive above with a *small but prominent white spot behind eye;* wings duskier with faint yellowish edging. *Below pale yellow extensively streaked olive.* Overlaps with more montane Streak-necked Flycatcher at some mid-elevation localities. In most of range Streak-necked differs in its gray (not olive) hood; in addition its postocular spot is slightly less prominent, and its yellow below is brighter with less olive streaking (especially on midbelly, *where unstreaked*). The two species are most similar in w. Ecuador, where the race of Streak-necked shows less gray on its hood. Inconspicuous, usually found alone but occasionally joins flocks (though seemingly less often than Streak-necked). Perches vertically, sometimes leaning forward or nodding its head; occasionally lifts a wing up over back. Regularly seen at fruiting trees. Rather quiet, though ♂♂ at their small leks give a high-pitched sibilant song, e.g., "ts-ts-ts-tsu." Call a descending "seeeu." Also: Costa Rica and Panama.

Streak-necked Flycatcher
Mionectes striaticollis   PLATE 45(12)
13–13.5 cm (5–5¼"). Fairly common in lower growth and borders of montane forest and woodland in *Andes from n. Colombia to w. Bolivia* (w. Santa Cruz). Mostly 1200–2700 m. Base of lower mandible pale. In **most of range** (illustrated) *head and neck gray* with *small but prominent white spot behind eye*; olive above, wings duskier with faint olive edging. Throat and chest olive gray finely streaked white; *breast and belly clear yellow,* breast and flanks finely streaked olive. In **sw. Colombia and w. Ecuador** has hood more grayish olive. Cf. similar Olive-striped Flycatcher (mainly found at *lower* elevations). Streak-necked's inconspicuous and solitary behavior is similar to Olive-striped. It regularly accompanies flocks, and also joins aggregations of various species (often tanagers) at fruiting trees. Rarely vocal away from its small leks; there they give a leisurely series of rhythmic, squeaky notes with a hummingbird-like quality. Singing birds may sway from side to side with bill wide open, exposing their orange gape.

Ochre-bellied Flycatcher
Mionectes oleagineus   PLATE 45(13)
13 cm (5"). *Widespread and often common* in lower growth of humid and deciduous forest and woodland from Colombia and Venezuela to Amazonia and the Guianas, and in e. Brazil. Mostly below 1400 m. *Olive above,* wings dusky with two indistinct ochraceous bars and edging (*more prominent on tertials*). Throat olive grayish, breast ochraceous olive, *belly ochraceous*

(richest in **Amaz. birds**). Cf. McConnell's and Gray-hooded Flycatchers. Ruddy-tailed Flycatcher is smaller and more compact. Unobtrusive and quiet, with quick darting movements; ranges singly inside forest and woodland, occasionally coming to edge. Sometimes accompanies mixed flocks, but more often solitary; also joins aggregations of other small birds at fruiting trees. Sometimes ruffles its crown feathers. Mainly quiet, but displaying ♂♂ can be vocal, giving a variety of chirping notes, some fast and sharp, others nasal, the most distinctive phrase being a twangy "cheeá-cheeá-cheeá." Also: Mexico to Panama.

McConnell's Flycatcher
Mionectes macconnelli
13 cm (5"). Uncommon in lower growth of terra firme and lower montane forest from *s. Venezuela and the Guianas to e. Amaz. Brazil,* and in *se. Peru and w. Bolivia.* To about 2000 m in Bolivia, and on tepuis; in Peru below 1200 m. Resembles more widespread Ochre-bellied Flycatcher; in areas where the two occur together, Ochre-bellied favors second-growth and borders (though elsewhere it ranges equally in terra firme). McConnell's differs in having *plain wings* that show *no bars or edging* (the latter especially evident on Ochre-bellied's *tertials*). Behavior much as in Ochre-bellied. Displaying ♂♂ sing close to the ground, often near buttressed roots of a large tree. Two vocalizations are given, a nasal "wreeunh" interspersed with an occasional more musical "cheewu."

Gray-hooded Flycatcher
Mionectes rufiventris   PLATE 45(14)
13.5 cm (5¼"). Uncommon in lower growth of humid forest, woodland, and borders in *se. Brazil region* (north to s. Minas Gerais). To about 1000 m. *Hood gray;* brownish olive above, with essentially plain wings. Breast brownish olive, *belly rich ochraceous.* Ochre-bellied Flycatcher never shows the gray hood; in area of overlap they largely segregate by elevation, Ochre-bellied in lowlands. Behavior as in Ochre-bellied Flycatcher. Displaying ♂'s song a series of rough nasal notes that starts slowly but accelerates before it abruptly stops.

Yellow Tyrannulet
Capsiempis flaveola   PLATE 46(1)
11.5 cm (4½"). Locally fairly common in lower and middle growth of more humid woodland and forest borders from Colombia and Vene-

zuela to se. Brazil region, but absent from much of Amazonia. To 1500 m. *Slender, long-tailed, and mainly yellow.* In **most of range** (illustrated) yellowish olive above with *bold yellow superciliary,* wings duskier with *two broad yellow bars and edging. Below all yellow.* In **n. Colombia and n. Venezuela** has *white superciliary.* No other tyrannulet imparts such a yellow overall impression. In many areas shows a *predilection for bamboo.* Forages mainly in pairs, gleaning actively; then perches horizontally with tail held partially cocked, but perches more vertically when at rest. Rather vocal, members of a pair staying in contact via a variety of soft calls; also gives a short dry trill "tr-r-r-r-r." Song a pleasant rollicking series of notes that often lacks discernible pattern; it starts slowly but speeds up, and vaguely recalls Sooty-headed Tyrannulet. Also: Nicaragua to Panama.

Phylloscartes

Slender tyrannulets with *long narrow tails* (notably so in some species) and *quite long, slender, usually all-black bills,* mainly found in the *canopy and borders of montane forests,* only a few occurring lower at forest borders or in lowlands. Many have *very restricted ranges,* and no less than four species have been described since the 1980s. *Their posture is quite horizontal,* often with *tail held partially cocked* and wings drooped; wings are also often briefly lifted up over back.

Olive-green Tyrannulet
Phylloscartes virescens *   PLATE 46(2)
12 cm (4¾"). Uncommon (perhaps just overlooked) in canopy and borders of humid forest in the *Guianas and n. Amaz. Brazil.* To 500 m. Olive above with vague yellowish supraloral but *quite distinct yellow eye-ring,* dusky mottling on cheeks; wings dusky with *two distinct yellowish bars* and edging. Throat whitish, breast clouded grayish olive, belly pale yellow. The only *Phylloscartes* in its range, so identifiable on the basis of its slender, long-tailed shape, reminiscent of a gnatcatcher. Slender-footed Tyrannulet has a different wing pattern (no bars); cf. also Forest and ♀ Gray Elaenias. Pairs and singletons often accompany mixed flocks in canopy, almost always remaining well above the ground and thus hard to observe. Wing-lifting is frequent, and the wings are also sometimes shivered. Song a fairly loud and spritely "spee! spee-spee-spee-spee."

Bahia Tyrannulet
Phylloscartes beckeri *
12 cm (4¾"). *Now very rare and local in canopy and borders of montane forest in e. Brazil* (s. Bahia). 700–1000 m. A recently described species. Bright olive above, crown slightly darker, with *yellowish ochre eye-ring and superciliary;* wings blacker with two pale yellow bars and edging. Below yellow, somewhat clouded olive on breast. The only other *Phylloscartes* occurring with this species is the markedly different Ousta-let's. Cf. also the stubbier-billed Planalto Tyrannulet. Behavior as in Mottle-cheeked Tyrannulet. Has declined significantly because of forest destruction in its always limited range. Frequent call a sharp "tik" note (at times uncannily like the call of a *Forpus* parrotlet); apparent song a softer twittering.

Alagoas Tyrannulet
Phylloscartes ceciliae
12 cm (4¾"). *Now very rare and local in canopy and borders of humid forest in hills of ne. Brazil* (Alagoas). 400–550 m. Olive above with *prominent whitish superciliary* and ear-coverts, the latter outlined dusky; wings duskier with *two pale yellowish bars. Below whitish. The only Phylloscartes in its range,* and as such readily recognized by generic characters, especially its long and usually cocked tail. Slender-footed Tyrannulet lacks wing-bars, has a shorter tail, etc. An arboreal tyrannulet with behavior much as in Mottle-cheeked Tyrannulet. Like the Bahia Tyrannulet, has declined significantly because of forest destruction in its always limited range. Infrequent call a fast "sweek! sweek-a-dee-deek."

Ecuadorian Tyrannulet
Phylloscartes gualaquizae   PLATE 46(3)
11.5 cm (4½"). Uncommon in canopy and borders of foothill and lower montane forest on *east slope of Andes from ne. Ecuador* (w. Sucumbíos) *to n. Peru* (San Martín). 700–1500 m. *Crown gray, short superciliary and eye-ring white and ear-coverts whitish indistinctly outlined with blackish.* Olive above; wings dusky with two pale yellow bars and edging. Throat whitish, breast mottled olive, belly clear yellow. Very similar Plumbeous-crowned Tyrannulet is larger and has a stubbier bill and a pale area behind its dark ear crescent. White-fronted Tyrannulet, also similar, has a slightly heavier bill with lower mandible at least basally pale, and white across forehead and a more prominent superciliary. Spectacled Bristle Tyrant perches upright and differs in its pale

lower mandible, bolder eye-ring, and yellower underparts. Forages singly or in pairs, often with mixed flocks, generally remaining well above the ground. Perches horizontally, usually cocking its long tail; sometimes flicks a wing up over back. Calls include a thin "feeee" and a spitting, almost rattled trill, "sp-i-i-i-i-i-i," that at first descends, then ascends, then descends again.

Mottle-cheeked Tyrannulet
Phylloscartes ventralis   PLATE 46(4)
12 cm (4¾"). *Common* (especially southward) in canopy and borders of humid and montane forest and woodland on *east slope of Andes from n. Peru* (San Martín) *to nw. Argentina* (Catamarca), and in *se. Brazil region*. 1000–2400 m in Andes; to 1500 m in se. Brazil region (northward only in highlands). More than one species perhaps involved. Olive above with *whitish supraloral and partial eye-ring*, dusky line through eye and indistinct mottling on ear-coverts; wings duskier with two pale yellow bars and edging. *Mostly pale yellow below*, whiter on throat and more olive on chest. Compare this relatively numerous tyrannulet with various other, scarcer species, e.g., Sclater's (in Andes), Rough-legged, and (in southeast) Planalto and Greenish. Generic characters (long slender all-black bill, horizontal posture, cocked tail) are actually more helpful than any particular field character. Found singly or in pairs, foraging actively, often in the open; regular with mixed flocks. Song in se. Brazil a musical "chididididit," in nw. Argentina a spritely "whík, whík-whi-i-i-i-r, whik-whik," also an oft-repeated "whik" note.

Restinga Tyrannulet
Phylloscartes kronei
12 cm (4¾"). Uncommon and local in scrubby restinga woodland along *coast of se. Brazil* (São Paulo to ne. Rio Grande do Sul). Resembles Mottle-cheeked Tyrannulet, *which in area of overlap occurs only in the highlands*. Restinga differs in its *yellow supraloral* (not whitish) and *yellow cheeks and throat* (with dusky mottling similar to Mottle-cheeked). Behavior much as in Mottle-cheeked, but Restinga seems not to cock its tail as much. Oft-heard call a short "feesee" or "plee"; song fast and twittering, e.g., "sit-it-it-it-it-it-it-it-sitit-sitit."

Rufous-browed Tyrannulet
Phylloscartes superciliaris   PLATE 46(5)
11.5 cm (4½"). Uncommon and very local in canopy of lower montane forest in *n. Colombia*,

and on east slope of Andes in s. Ecuador (Cordillera de Cutucú and Cordillera del Cóndor) *and extreme n. Peru*. 1300–2000 m. Crown and nape slaty with *narrow rufous frontal band and superciliary*; spot at base of bill and *ear-coverts white, the latter narrowly encircled by black*. Olive above, wings duskier with yellowish green edging. *Throat and breast pale grayish*, belly white. Striking facial pattern and *lack* of yellow below should preclude confusion though, as it usually remains so high above the ground, colors can be hard to discern. Behavior as in Ecuadorian Tyrannulet. Song a spritely "spee-ee-ee-ee-ee, spee-didi-dee." Also: Costa Rica and Panama.

Black-fronted Tyrannulet
Phylloscartes nigrifrons   PLATE 46(6)
13 cm (5"). Uncommon in canopy and borders of lower montane forest on *tepuis of s. Venezuela region*. 900–1800 m. *Forehead and lores black with gray crown* and short whitish superciliary; *cheeks mottled whitish and outlined with black*. Olive above, wings duskier with two yellow bars and edging. *Below mostly pale grayish*, whiter on belly. *The only Phylloscartes tyrannulet in its range*, so identifiable on generic characters. Chapman's Bristle Tyrant has very different plumage and posture. Behavior much as in Ecuadorian Tyrannulet, though Black-fronted seems more frequent at edge. Distinctive song a "tsit" note followed by a dry rattled trill.

Rufous-lored Tyrannulet
Phylloscartes flaviventris   PLATE 46(7)
11.5 cm (4½"). Uncommon in canopy and borders of foothill and lower montane forest in *mountains of n. Venezuela* (Yaracuy to Miranda). 750–1100 m. *Lores and eye-ring rufous*, short superciliary yellowish, *ear-coverts mostly black*; olive above, wings dusky with two pale yellow bars and edging. *Below bright yellow*. Not likely confused in its limited range, where the only *Phylloscartes* tyrannulet. Formerly mistakenly considered a bristle tyrant. Active behavior much as in Ecuadorian Tyrannulet. Call a short fast series of high-pitched notes.

Cinnamon-faced Tyrannulet
*Phylloscartes parkeri**
11.5 cm (4½"). Uncommon in canopy and borders of foothill and lower montane forest along *eastern base of Andes from cen. Peru* (Huánuco) *to w. Bolivia* (La Paz and s. Beni). 650–1500 m. A recently described species. Resembles geographically distant Rufous-lored Tyrannulet

(also with *cinnamon-rufous supraloral and eye-ring*), differing in its *gray crown*, buff auricular patch, and *more olive breast and flanks* (not all bright yellow below). Behavior much as in Ecuadorian Tyrannulet. Song a fast, spritely "chit, chit, tr-ree-ee-ee-ee."

Minas Gerais Tyrannulet
Phylloscartes roquettei
11.5 cm (4½"). *Now very rare and local in canopy and borders of gallery forest in interior e. Brazil* (nw. Minas Gerais near upper Rio São Francisco). 400–500 m. Olive above, forecrown with faint brownish tinge and *fairly bold yellowish eye-ring* (but, contra some references, does *not* have rufous in facial area), wings with two bold yellowish bars. Below pale clear yellow. Behavior similar to other arboreal *Phylloscartes*, perching horizontally and often cocking tail; usually not with flocks. Has declined significantly because of forest destruction in its always limited range. Song a fast, twittering "tz-tz-tz-tz-tz-tz-tzit-tzit-tzit."

Bay-ringed Tyrannulet
Phylloscartes sylviolus   PLATE 46(8)
11 cm (4¼"). Uncommon and local in canopy and borders of humid forest in *se. Brazil region* (north to Espírito Santo). To 600 m. Iris whitish. Bright olive above with *lores and eye-ring rufous*; wings duskier with yellowish edging (but *no* bars). Throat and crissum pale buffy yellow; *remaining underparts whitish*. A small, slender *Phylloscartes*, with rufous on face unique in range (though it can be hard to discern). Found singly or in pairs, often with mixed flocks. Forages actively, with long slender tail usually held cocked; its silhouette recalls Creamy-bellied Gnatcatcher, which sometimes is even in the same flock. Song a spritely "swit-swi-swi-swi-swi-sweéseéseéseésee-swi-swi."

Serra do Mar Tyrannulet
Phylloscartes difficilis   PLATE 46(9)
11.5 cm (4½"). Uncommon in lower growth and shrubbery of montane forest in *se. Brazil* (s. Espírito Santo to ne. Rio Grande do Sul). 900–2100 m. *Bright olive above* with *prominent white eye-ring and supraloral* and grayish cheeks bordered behind by black crescent; wings with olive edging (but *no* bars). *Mostly grayish below,* throat and midbelly whiter. Eye-ringed Tody-Tyrant has much yellower underparts, broad pale tertial edging; its shape and behavior differ markedly, as do vocalizations. Cf. also Drab-breasted Bamboo Tyrant. Less arboreal than most other

Phylloscartes, rarely more than 4–5 m above the ground. Usually in pairs, generally not with mixed flocks; cocks tail and droops and shivers wings. Often gives a fast harsh chipper, sometimes also a snapping noise produced either by bill or wings.

Oustalet's Tyrannulet
Phylloscartes oustaleti   PLATE 46(10)
13 cm (5"). Locally fairly common in mid-levels and subcanopy of humid forest in *se. Brazil* (s. Bahia to ne. Santa Catarina). Mostly 400–900 m. *Readily recognized on the basis of its constantly quivered tail.* Olive above with a *conspicuous yellow eye-ring, large blackish auricular patch* with *bright yellow in front and behind;* yellow below, breast duskier with olive edging. Yellow below, breast clouded olive. São Paulo Tyrannulet is markedly smaller; it tends to perch more vertically (rarely cocking its tail and never quivering it). Usually in pairs, often foraging with mixed flocks but sometimes independently. The long tail is almost always cocked, at times acutely. Call a soft "kudut" (D. F. Stotz) or "twededit."

São Paulo Tyrannulet
Phylloscartes paulista   PLATE 46(11)
10.5 cm (4"). Uncommon in lower growth of humid forest and borders in *se. Brazil region* (north to Espírito Santo). Mostly below 600 m. Olive above with *narrow yellow superciliary wrapping around black auricular patch;* wings duskier with olive edging and often two dull bars. Dull yellow below, breast clouded olive. Smaller than other sympatric *Phylloscartes*. Oustalet's Tyrannulet has markedly different behavior (quivering tail, more horizontal posture). Cf. also Yellow Tyrannulet (no auricular patch, etc.). São Paulo tends to perch less horizontally than other Brazilian *Phylloscartes;* foraging birds make quick sallies, gleaning relatively little. Usually in pairs, and often with mixed flocks. Call a soft, whistled "swhee-eet" or "swhee-ee-eet."

Pogonotriccus

Small, *upright-perching* tyrannids found in lower and middle growth *mainly in Andean forests;* there is also a species on the tepuis, another in se. Brazil area. Most have *bold facial patterns* and *obvious wing-bars*. Because of confusion as to the correct allocation of a few species, for a time the genus was subsumed into the more horizontal-perching

Phylloscartes. As in that genus, *bristle tyrants periodically lift a wing up over back.*

Variegated Bristle Tyrant
Pogonotriccus poecilotis   PLATE 46(12)

11.5 cm (4½"). Uncommon in lower and middle growth of montane forest in *Andes from w. Venezuela* (s. Lara) *to s. Peru* (Puno). 1500–2300 m. *Lower mandible yellow to orange-yellow. Crown gray, facial area and indistinct superciliary grizzled gray and white,* with *white-bordered blackish crescent on ear-coverts.* Otherwise olive above, wings duskier with *two broad cinnamon bars* and greenish yellow edging. Upper throat grayish white, lower throat and breast yellowish olive, belly yellow. Marble-faced Bristle Tyrant lacks the strongly bicolored bill and has yellowish wing-bars. Slaty-capped Flycatcher is larger with a longer, all-black bill; in much of their respective ranges, it and Variegated have similar cinnamon wing-bars. Sulphur-bellied Tyrannulet has a distinct superciliary, no ear-covert crescent; its posture and behavior differ. Found singly or in pairs, often with mixed flocks of understory birds, generally foraging a bit higher up than Slaty-capped Flycatcher (sometimes they are in the same flock). Rather active, perching on open branches, sallying out short distances. Calls include a tanagerlike "tsit" often repeated several times, sometimes extended into a "tsit-tsit-tsit-ts-ts-ts-tseweeeét."

Chapman's Bristle Tyrant
Pogonotriccus chapmani   PLATE 46(13)

12 cm (4¾"). Locally common in lower growth inside montane forest on *tepuis of s. Venezuela* (but scarce on the Escalera). 1000–2000 m. Resembles Variegated Bristle Tyrant (of Andes) but *crown olive,* concolor with back (not gray); in addition, lower mandible apparently tipped dark (not entirely pale). *The only bristle tyrant found on the tepuis.* Behavior as in Variegated Bristle Tyrant. Song a high-pitched "tseedidi" (P. Boesman recording).

Marble-faced Bristle Tyrant
Pogonotriccus ophthalmicus   PLATE 46(14)

11.5 cm (4½"). Locally fairly common in lower and middle growth of montane forest and forest borders in *Andes from Colombia to w. Bolivia* (w. Santa Cruz), also in *mountains of n. Venezuela* (Yaracuy to Distrito Federal, and in Falcón). Mostly 800–2200 m. In **most of range** (illustrated) crown gray, *facial area grizzled gray and white,* with *white-bordered blackish crescent on*

ear-coverts. Olive above; wings duskier with *two yellowish bars* and edging. Upper throat grayish white, lower throat and breast yellowish olive, belly yellow. In **s. Peru and Bolivia** has whiter wing-bars, *gray throat and breast, much whiter belly.* Variegated Bristle Tyrant has an obviously bicolored bill, bold cinnamon wing-bars. Ashy-headed Tyrannulet has more bluish gray crown, no edging on wing-coverts, and streaky (not mottled) effect on chest. Plumbeous-crowned Tyrannulet is very similar though it is less grizzled on face and its crescent on ear-coverts is less distinct; it perches more horizontally. Slaty-capped Flycatcher is larger with longer bill, and has ochraceous wing-bars. Behavior much like Variegated Bristle Tyrant; the two species sometimes even range with same flock. Two-part song a fast "psee-ee-ee-ee-u, tsi-tsi-tsi," the first part descending, then ending with several higher-pitched emphatic notes.

Venezuelan Bristle Tyrant
Pogonotriccus venezuelanus   PLATE 46(15)

10.5 cm (4"). Fairly common in lower and middle growth of montane forest and borders in *mountains of n. Venezuela* (Carabobo to Distrito Federal and Miranda). 800–1400 m. Closely resembles somewhat larger Marble-faced Bristle Tyrant, and often seen with that species. Venezuelan has a *pale lower mandible* (flesh to dull yellowish), *blacker greater wing-coverts that lack edging* (thus its wing-bars contrast more), and greenish yellow throat and breast (not whitish). Slaty-capped Flycatcher is markedly larger with a longer, all-black bill. Behavior much as in Variegated Bristle Tyrant. Spritely song a "tree-ee-ee-ew, tee-tee-tee" with a distinctive cadence.

Spectacled Bristle Tyrant
Pogonotriccus orbitalis   PLATE 46(16)

11 cm (4¼"). Uncommon in lower and middle growth of foothill and lower montane forest on *east slope of Andes from s. Colombia* (w. Putumayo) *to w. Bolivia* (Cochabamba). Mostly 700–1400 m. *Crown gray* contrasting with olive back; *prominent eye-ring whitish, facial area mottled yellowish* with indistinct dusky crescent on ear-coverts; wings duskier with two bold pale yellowish bars and edging. *Below yellow,* throat and breast clouded olive. Spectacled's eye-ring is more conspicuous than in other bristle tyrants, its ear crescent less so. It does not overlap with either Venezuelan or Antioquia Bristle Tyrant. Similarly plumaged Ecuadorian Tyrannulet differs in its all-dark bill, horizontal posture with

cocked tail; it mainly forages in canopy. Behavior much as in Variegated Bristle Tyrant. Song a fast high-pitched trill, descending at first, ending with 2–3 emphasized and sharper notes.

Antioquia Bristle Tyrant
Pogonotriccus lanyoni
11 cm (4¼"). Uncommon and local in lower growth and borders in humid forest and woodland in *foothills at north end of Colombia's Cen. Andes, and on west slope of E. Andes* (Boyacá). 450–750 m. Resembles Spectacled Bristle Tyrant (no overlap), differing in its incomplete whitish eye-ring and wider yellow wing-bars. Behavior of this still poorly known species appears to resemble other bristle tyrants.

Southern Bristle Tyrant
Pogonotriccus eximius   PLATE 46(17)
11 cm (4¼"). Uncommon in lower and middle growth of humid forest and borders in *se. Brazil region* (north to Minas Gerais). To 600 m. Crown gray, *broad superciliary white grizzled with gray, lower face yellow with conspicuous black crescent on ear-coverts.* Above bright olive, wings duskier with olive edging. Throat whitish, breast yellowish olive, belly bright yellow. This species' fancy head pattern is unique in range, but cf. the much smaller Eared Pygmy-Tyrant. Found singly or in pairs, perching vertically and remaining motionless for long periods, then sallying out; sometimes follows mixed flocks, but usually not. Call a dry trill that accelerates, then ends abruptly.

Myiornis

Tiny, virtually tailless tyrannids, these pygmy-tyrants rank among the world's smallest birds. They are inconspicuous at the edge of humid and lower montane forests and are usually noticed from their vocalizations.

Short-tailed Pygmy-Tyrant
Myiornis ecaudatus   PLATE 47(1)
6.5 cm (2½"). Locally fairly common in lower and mid-levels of humid forest borders from *e. Colombia and Venezuela to Amazonia and the Guianas.* To 900 m. Head gray with *prominent white supraloral and eye-ring* (giving a spectacled look); bright olive above, wings duskier with bright yellowish edging. *Below essentially white.* Black-capped Pygmy-Tyrant occurs only *west* of the Andes. Otherwise this *minute* flycatcher is unlikely to be confused (in flight it

can look more like a large insect!). Cf. Yellow-browed Tody-Flycatcher (which occurs in same habitat), and Slate-headed Tody-Flycatcher (an undergrowth bird). Seems sedentary; hardly ever with mixed flocks. Favors viny tangles and borders, where it perches motionless, then suddenly darts off to pick an insect from a leaf, sometimes hovering while doing so. The motions are so fast and abrupt, and the bird so tiny, that it can be very hard to follow. Most frequent song, often passed over as an insect sound, a high-pitched "cr-r-reek?" or "tsr-r-reep?" with a rising inflection, sometimes a series of shorter notes.

Black-capped Pygmy-Tyrant
Myiornis atricapillus
6.5 cm (2½"). Locally fairly common at borders of humid forest in lowlands and foothills of *w. Colombia and nw. Ecuador* (mainly Esmeraldas). To 800 m. Resembles Short-tailed Pygmy-Tyrant. ♂ differs in having an *obvious black crown* (gray in ♀); **both sexes** differ in having a pale yellow belly. Short-tailed occurs only *east* of Andes. Otherwise not likely confused; cf. Black-headed Tody-Flycatcher (in same habitat). Behavior and voice much as in Short-tailed Pygmy-Tyrant. Also: Costa Rica and Panama.

Eared Pygmy-Tyrant
Myiornis auricularis   PLATE 47(2)
7.5 cm (3"). Locally fairly common in lower and mid-levels of humid forest and woodland borders in *se. Brazil region* (north to s. Bahia). To 1300 m. Bright olive above, browner on crown with *cinnamon-buff ocular area;* sides of head pale grayish with *large black spots below eye and on ear-coverts.* Wings and short tail duskier, wings with olive-yellow edging. *Throat and upper chest white sharply streaked with black,* below bright yellow. No *Hemitriccus* tody-tyrant shows such a fancy facial pattern, nor is any so boldly streaked on its foreneck. Eared favors dense viny tangles, but often perches in the semiopen, so not too hard to spot. Most frequent call a trill often preceded by several "pic" notes, e.g., "pic, pic, pic, pree-ee-ee-ee."

White-bellied Pygmy-Tyrant
Myiornis albiventris   PLATE 47(3)
7 cm (2¾"). Uncommon and local in lower and middle growth at borders of foothill forest along *eastern base of Andes from n. Peru* (San Martín) *to w. Bolivia* (w. Santa Cruz). 400–1200 m. Olive above with *buff lores and ocular area* and *gray sides of head* with only an indistinct slaty auricu-

lar patch. Wings and short tail duskier, wings with two yellowish bars and edging. *White below with dusky streaking on throat and chest.* Overall plumage pattern resembles Eared Pygmy-Tyrant (no overlap). Short-tailed Pygmy-Tyrant lacks streaking on foreneck, has gray crown, etc. Behavior much as in Eared Pygmy-Tyrant. Simple, brief song a quite musical "tree-ee-ee-ee-u."

Southern Bentbill
Oncostoma olivaceum PLATE 47(4)
9 cm (3½"). *Fairly common in lower growth of secondary woodland and humid forest borders in n. Colombia. To 1000 m. Rather thick bent-downward bill is unique; iris pale yellowish.* Olive above with whitish lores; wings duskier with two yellowish bars and edging. Olive yellow below, throat whitish, and some olive flammulation on breast. No *Hemitriccus* has such an odd bill, and aside from the very different Pearly-vented Tody-Tyrant, no *Hemitriccus* occurs in range of the bentbill. Usually perches in dense cover, where often hard to spot; its abrupt, short flights to the underside of leaves are often hard to follow. Usually not with mixed flocks. Frequently gives a soft guttural trill, e.g., "trrrr" or "pt, trrrr." Also: Panama.

Lophotriccus

Small, obscure flycatchers found in thick lower growth of lowland and lower montane forest, usually at edge; two species favor bamboo thickets. These pygmy-tyrants resemble *Hemitriccus*, **but most have** *crests with lengthened feathers edged rufous, gray, or olive.*

Scale-crested Pygmy-Tyrant
Lophotriccus pileatus PLATE 47(5)
10 cm (4"). Locally common in lower growth and borders of humid and lower montane forest and woodland, mainly on lower Andean slopes, from *n. Venezuela to s. Peru* (Puno); on east slope of Andes only in foothills and lower subtropics. *Often favors bamboo.* Mostly 500–1900 m, lower in sw. Colombia and w. Ecuador. Iris yellow. Forecrown and facial area brownish, *crown feathers black with rufous edging, sometimes erected into a transverse crest* (but often laid flat); olive above, wings duskier with two yellowish bars. Below whitish with *blurry dusky streaking on throat and breast,* flanks tinged yellow. Double-banded Pygmy-Tyrant occurs only

in Amazonian lowlands, with no known overlap; its crest feathers are edged gray. Otherwise not likely confused, but cf. ♀ Rufous-crowned Tody-Tyrant. Found singly, less often in pairs, generally not with mixed flocks. Perches motionless, hard to spot, then darting out to pick an insect off a leaf surface. Often noisy and heard more than seen, ♂♂ calling at intervals throughout the day, giving a variety of strident calls. Western birds give a fast series of short notes, "tree-tree-tree-tree-tree," sometimes varied to a rising "tree-ee-ee?" East-slope birds give a very different, much buzzier "bzeeyt-bzeet-bzeet" and a more drawn-out trill, "trrrrrreét." Also: Honduras to Panama.

Double-banded Pygmy-Tyrant
Lophotriccus vitiosus PLATE 47(6)
10 cm (4"). Locally fairly common in lower growth and borders of humid forest and woodland in *w. and n. Amazonia and the Guianas.* To 800 m. Iris yellow. In **most of range** (illustrated) forecrown and facial area olive, *feathers of crown black with gray edging,* occasionally erected into a transverse crest (but raised less often than in Scale-crested); olive above, wings duskier with two yellowish bars and edging. Below pale yellowish with *blurry dusky-olive streaking on foreneck.* In **e. Peru and w. Amaz. Brazil** (south of Amazon) *crown feathers edged buffy-yellow* and whiter below. The more montane Scale-crested Pygmy-Tyrant has rufous edging on crown feathers. Cf. Helmeted Pygmy-Tyrant and various *Hemitriccus* tody-tyrants. Behavior similar to Scale-crested Pygmy-Tyrant, though not especially associated with bamboo. Like Scale-crested, Double-banded is very vocal and heard much more often than seen; song a distinctive short harsh trill that drops in pitch, "turrrrrrew," not as loud or forceful as in Scale-crested.

Helmeted Pygmy-Tyrant
Lophotriccus galeatus PLATE 47(7)
10 cm (4"). Locally common in lower and middle growth of humid forest borders and secondary woodland from *se. Colombia, ne. Peru, and s. Venezuela to e. Amaz. Brazil.* To 1100 m. Resembles Double-banded Pygmy-Tyrant, differing in having *elongated crown feathers edged grayish olive* (not pure gray) and *wing-bars obscure or lacking.* In area of overlap Helmeted tends to be commoner. *Hemitriccus* tody-tyrants all *lack* elongated crest feathers. Found singly or in pairs, usually not with mixed flocks; usually overlooked unless vocalizing, which fortunately

it does a lot. Most frequent call north of Amazon a series of dry staccato "pik" notes. At Alta Floresta in Mato Grosso, Brazil, gives a series of long, harsh trills punctuated by "tic" notes (K. J. Zimmer et al.).

Long-crested Pygmy-Tyrant
Lophotriccus eulophotes
10 cm (4"). *Rare and local in Guadua bamboo-dominated undergrowth and borders of swampy and transitional forest and woodland in sw. Amazonia.* 250–400 m. Resembles Double-banded Pygmy-Tyrant (no overlap), but *wings plain* (*no wing-bars*) and *underparts whitish.* Usually seen singly, sometimes while accompanying mixed flocks. Frequent call a fast series of 5–8 "tic" notes; also gives a short, descending trill.

Pale-eyed Pygmy-Tyrant
Lophotriccus pilaris *   PLATE 47(8)
9.5 cm (3¾"). Fairly common in arid scrub and lower growth of deciduous woodland from *n. Colombia to s. Guyana and extreme n. Brazil.* Mostly below 800 m. Formerly placed in genus *Atalotriccus.* Pale yellow iris. Olive above with whitish lores; wings duskier with two narrow yellowish bars. Whitish below with *indistinct brownish streaking on throat and breast.* Obscure; note its limited range (and habitat). Pearly-vented Tody-Tyrant is larger with a longer bill, more prominent wing-bars, and streaking below. Pearly-vented has an equally "pale" iris. Cf. also Slate-headed Tody-Flycatcher. Usually in pairs, remaining in cover but quite active. Apt to be overlooked until its vocalizations are recognized. The quality of its loud strident calls is reminiscent of Scale-crested Pygmy-Tyrant; typical phrases include a "kip-kip-trrrr" or "kip-kip-trrrreeép." Also: Panama.

Hemitriccus

A *difficult* group of *obscure, usually drab, small tyrannids,* most found in the lower and middle growth of humid forest and woodland, mainly in the lowlands with only a few species being montane. Their *bills are fairly long, flat, and narrow* (but not as extreme as in *Todirostrum*). Many species, especially those comprising the White-eyed group, present major identification challenges. *Hemitriccus* are generally inconspicuous, sedentary birds that typically do not follow mixed flocks. *Most often attention will be drawn to them through their vocalizations, frequently given and often distinctive* (at least to the practiced ear).

Pearly-vented Tody-Tyrant
Hemitriccus margaritaceiventer   PLATE 47(9)
10–10.5 cm (4–4¼"). *Widespread and locally common* in lower growth of arid scrub, deciduous woodland, and gallery forest from n. Colombia and Venezuela to n. Argentina and e. Brazil, but absent from most of Amazonia. To 2000 m. Iris yellow to whitish. Likely more than one species is involved. **Southern birds** (illustrated) olive above with a grayer crown, whitish lores and eye-ring; wings duskier with two bold yellowish bars and edging. White below, *throat and foreneck streaked grayish.* **Northern birds** are more brownish above, and those of **sw. Venezuela** are dark brown above with buff belly. *The most wide-ranging nonforest Hemitriccus,* so use it for comparison to other scarcer, more range-restricted species. Cf. also Pale-eyed Tody-Tyrant and Slate-headed Tody-Flycatcher (both occurring with Pearly-vented). Found singly or in pairs, sometimes with small mixed flocks but at least as often alone. Perches upright, flitting upward to the underside of leaves. Call a staccato "tik" or "stik," sometimes given in series. Song several notes followed by a descending trill, e.g., "tik, tik, tr-r-r-r-r-r-r-r."

Pelzeln's Tody-Tyrant
Hemitriccus inornatus
9.5 cm (3¾"). *Very local in campina woodland in n. Brazil* (Rio Negro drainage); only recently rediscovered, but in correct habitat apparently can be common. Below 200 m. Resembles Pearly-vented Tody-Tyrant (no overlap), but slightly smaller, darker above, with *wing-bars whitish* (not yellowish). Behavior much as in Pearly-vented, though Pelzeln's seems more often to forage higher above the ground. Song a short series of insectlike notes, e.g., "ti-dip, tip, te-de" sometimes with a trill at end (A. Whittaker and K. J. Zimmer).

Boat-billed Tody-Tyrant
Hemitriccus josephinae   PLATE 47(10)
11 cm (4¼"). *Rare and apparently local* in lower and mid-levels at edge of humid forest in the *Guianas and n. Amaz. Brazil.* Below 200 m. *Iris reddish brown. Plain olive above* (wings with *no* bars or edging) with *pale grayish lores and auricular region. Below yellowish,* throat whiter

and breast clouded olive. White-eyed Tody-Tyrant has pale irides, shows wing-bars and some streaking on foreneck. Cf. also much more numerous Helmeted Pygmy-Tyrant. Not a well-known bird, but apparently favors viny tangles and lianas at forest edge or treefalls; seems very sedentary. Call a dry "pik-pik-pik."

Stripe-necked Tody-Tyrant
Hemitriccus striaticollis   PLATE 47(11)
11 cm (4¼"). Locally fairly common in shrubbery, low woodland, and savannas, mainly across *cen. and s. Amaz. Brazil and n. Bolivia;* also very locally in e. Peru and e. Colombia. To 1000 m. *Iris yellow.* Olive above with *browner crown and white lores and eye-ring; wings plain.* Throat white *sharply streaked blackish;* below bright yellow, some olive streaking on breast. Cf. very similar Johannes's Tody-Tyrant (only limited overlap). Spotted Tody-Flycatcher's grayer crown contrasts more with its olive back, and it *lacks* an eye-ring and has prominent wing-bars and edging. Found singly or in pairs; inconspicuous unless vocalizing, which fortunately it does a lot. Call a simple, inflected "kweep," sometimes doubled. Song a fast "pit-pit-pit-pit, whi-didit."

Johannes's Tody-Tyrant
Hemitriccus iohannis
11 cm (4¼"). Uncommon in borders of riparian woodland and shrubby areas *near water in w. Amazonia.* To 800 m. Resembles Stripe-necked Tody-Tyrant, differing in its *brownish ocular area and lores* (*lacking* Stripe-necked's prominent white lores and eye-ring), *faintly indicated wing-bars* (wings *plain* in Stripe-necked), and reduced foreneck streaking. Spotted Tody-Flycatcher has a grayer crown (not brownish olive), crisper (not blurry) foreneck streaking, and shows wing-bars. Cf. also White-eyed Tody-Tyrant. Behavior much as in Stripe-necked Tody-Tyrant, but often harder to see. Favors viny tangles and thickets, inconspicuous apart from its distinctive voice. Song a simple, fast, upslurred trill introduced by "tk" or "kip" note (or interspersed with them), e.g., "tk-trrrrrrrrrree," vaguely woodcreeperlike.

Black-throated Tody-Tyrant
Hemitriccus granadensis   PLATE 47(12)
10 cm (4"). Uncommon in shrubby borders of montane forest and woodland in Andes from n. Venezuela to w. Bolivia (Cochabamba). 1500–3000 m. Likely more than one species. Birds of **Santa Marta Mts.** (illustrated) and on **east**

slope of Andes from s. Ecuador to w. Bolivia olive above with *prominent buff lores and ocular area. Upper throat contrasting blackish;* below whitish, breast clouded gray. In **n. Venezuela to n. Ecuador** has *lores and ocular area whitish.* The *unmistakable fancy face pattern* unites all forms, regardless of ocular area's color. Found singly or in pairs, and though often quiet, not too difficult to see as it regularly forages in semiopen. Makes short abrupt hops, with a wing-whirr often audible. Sometimes accompanies mixed flocks. Vocalizations vary geographically. Northern birds give a short trilled "tri-triiiiii" (N. K. Krabbe recording). Southern birds give a rather different, well-enunciated, but rather soft "whik-whik-whik-whik" or "whididik"; in Bolivia a hesitating, soft "pu, pu, peh-peh-pe-pe-pe-pe" (S. Mayer recording). Courting ♂♂ give a weird reeling sound, continued for up to a minute or more, while hovering near ♀; apparently produced by wings.

Buff-throated Tody-Tyrant
Hemitriccus rufigularis   PLATE 47(13)
12 cm (4¾"). Rare and local in middle growth and subcanopy of lower montane forest on *east slope of Andes from n. Ecuador* (w. Napo) to w. Bolivia (w. Santa Cruz). 800–1500 m. Iris pale yellow. Olive above, gray on crown; *ocular area, sides of head and neck, and breast pale dull buff; belly whitish. Wings basically plain.* The range-restricted Cinnamon-breasted Tody-Tyrant is smaller, with brighter cinnamon on face and breast, and has a yellow belly. Found singly or in pairs, favoring relatively low stature or open taller forest where the soil is granular and nutrient-deficient. Usually not with flocks. Calling ♂♂ give a fast series of 4–10 (sometimes more) inflected "kwep" or "kwdíp" notes from perches some 5–10 m above the ground.

White-eyed Tody-Tyrant
Hemitriccus zosterops   PLATE 47(14)
11 cm (4¼"). Uncommon in lower and middle growth in humid forest of w. and n. Amazonia and Guianas (*mainly north of Amazon*). Mostly below 1000 m. *Iris pale gray.* Olive above with whitish lores, wings duskier with *two fairly prominent yellowish bars* and edging. Throat and breast streaked grayish and whitish, belly pale yellow. A *drab* small tyrannid of tall forest. Double-banded and Helmeted Pygmy-Tyrants have lengthened, gray-edged crest feathers; Double-banded is more an edge bird. White-bellied Tody-Tyrant occurs only *south* of Amazon. An inconspicuous

bird that perches alone or in pairs at mid-levels; apt to be overlooked until you recognize the ♂'s song, often tirelessly repeated, a simple staccato "pik, pik-pik-pik-pik," sometimes accelerated into "pik-pik-pik-pikpikpikpik."

White-bellied Tody-Tyrant
Hemitriccus griseipectus *
11 cm (4¼"). Uncommon in lower and middle growth in humid forest of s. Amazonia (*south of Amazon*). To 850 m. Formerly considered conspecific with White-eyed Tody-Tyrant. Differs in having a *grayish breast* (not olive) and *whitish belly* (not yellow). Cf. very similar Snethlage's and Zimmer's Tody-Tyrants, both of which can occur with White-bellied. Flammulated Bamboo Tyrant has plain wings (White-bellied has yellowish wing-bars) and a dark iris. Behavior much as in White-eyed Tody-Tyrant. Voice, however, is quite different, merely a staccato "kwidíp" given at intervals of 2–3 seconds, sometimes varied to "kwididíp" or just a "kip."

Snethlage's Tody-Tyrant
Hemitriccus minor
10 cm (4"). Locally fairly common in dense vegetation and viny tangles at edge of humid and várzea forest in *Amaz. Brazil and ne. Bolivia*. To 600 m. Iris pale yellow to whitish. Closely resembles White-bellied Tody-Tyrant, thus with a *grayish breast* and *whitish belly*. Differs subtly in its slightly smaller size and less prominent wing-bars. *Snethlage's is usually found through, and identified by, voice*. Behavior similar to White-bellied and White-eyed Tody-Tyrants. Distinctive call a mechanical, gravelly trill given at quite long intervals (often 10 or more seconds), sometimes accompanied by "pik" notes.

Zimmer's Tody-Tyrant
Hemitriccus minimus
10 cm (4"). *Uncommon and very local in canopy of humid forest in Amaz. Brazil and ne. Bolivia; also found recently in ne. Peru and se. Ecuador*. To 500 m. Closely resembles White-eyed Tody-Tyrant (thus with an olive breast and a yellow belly). Zimmer's differs in its buffyish lores, darker crown and browner cheeks, more finely streaked throat, and *yellow edging only on inner flight feathers*. Resembles broadly sympatric Snethlage's Tody-Tyrant even more closely; Snethlage's is somewhat paler olive above with fainter wing-bars, as well as usually showing yellow edging on *all* its flight feathers (*no two-toned effect*). Zimmer's is rarely detected except by voice, and is hard to see and doubtless much

overlooked; it favors areas with white-sand soils. Ventriloquial call a soft "tinkling" trill, usually slightly rising in pitch, e.g., "tree-ee-ee-ee-ee-ee?," almost recalling song of Long-billed Gnatwren.

Yungas Tody-Tyrant
Hemitriccus spodiops
11 cm (4¼"). Uncommon in lower growth at borders of humid foothill and lower montane forest and secondary woodland on *east slope of Andes in w. Bolivia* (La Paz to w. Santa Cruz) *and extreme s. Peru* (s. Puno). 800–2100 m. *Iris pale yellow*. Olive above with grayish buff lores, wings duskier with two vague yellow-olive bars. Throat and breast grayish olive vaguely streaked whitish, belly yellowish white. Drab, *usually identified by range*. Flammulated Bamboo Tyrant has a dark iris, no wing-bars at all, browner breast. Shy and often very hard to observe. Ranges singly and in pairs, perching low, generally not with mixed flocks, making short upward strikes to the underside of leaves. Most frequent call a harsh, almost buzzy trill, e.g., "dzzeeeeu," usually given several times in a row.

Buff-breasted Tody-Tyrant
Hemitriccus mirandae   PLATE 47(15)
10 cm (4"). Uncommon and local in lower and middle growth of semihumid forest and woodland in *ne. Brazil* (Ceará to s. Bahia). 700–1000 m. Olive above with plain wings aside from *broad creamy edging on tertials. Face and underparts pale creamy buff*, belly paler. Virtually unique in its small range. Cf. White-bellied Tody-Tyrant and the differently shaped Ochre-bellied Flycatcher. Found singly or in pairs, generally not accompanying mixed flocks. Song slowly delivered in a clearly enunciated series of notes, e.g., "pic-pic-píc-pic-píc-pu-pic."

Kaempfer's Tody-Tyrant
Hemitriccus kaempferi
10 cm (4"). *Now rare and local* in lower growth at edge of humid forest and woodland in *se. Brazil* (ne. Santa Catarina and se. Paraná). Below 150 m. Olive above, *more brownish on head and neck*; wings and tail duskier, wings with two narrow buffy-olive bars and *broad yellowish tertial edging*, tail somewhat forked and outer feathers tipped whitish. *Orbital area and cheeks buffyish, becoming dull ochraceous on foreneck*, belly pale yellow. Eye-ringed Tody-Tyrant (mostly at slightly higher elevations, but does occur with Kaempfer's) also shows tertial edging but has a conspicuous white eye-ring and olive on

chest; it lacks any brownish tone on head. Cf. also Brown-breasted Bamboo Tyrant. Behavior similar to Buff-breasted Tody-Tyrant, but shyer and harder to observe. Has declined precipitously because of deforestation across much of its small range. Call a series of high-pitched, strident notes, sometimes given in pairs or triplets, e.g., "kuít" or "kuít-kuít."

Cinnamon-breasted Tody-Tyrant
Hemitriccus cinnamomeipectus
10 cm (4"). Rare and local in undergrowth of montane forest and woodland on east slope of Andes from *extreme s. Ecuador* (Zamora-Chinchipe on Cordillera del Cóndor) *to n. Peru* (n. San Martín), *mainly on outlying ridges.* 1700–2200 m. Olive above, browner on crown, with *pale yellowish edging on tertials. Ocular area, cheeks, throat, and breast cinnamon;* belly pale yellow. Buff-throated Tody-Tyrant is larger with a duller buff face and foreneck, whitish belly; it *lacks* tertial edging. Poorly known; most records are of birds captured in mist-nets. Solitary birds have been seen in dense mossy undergrowth; one accompanied a small understory flock. Call a harsh, sharp "dredredrt."

Fork-tailed Tody-Tyrant
Hemitriccus furcatus   PLATE 47(16)
11 cm (4¼"). *Rare and local* in thick lower growth at edge of humid forest and woodland in *se. Brazil* (s. Bahia to e. São Paulo). To 1200 m. *Head and throat cocoa brown, ocular area paler buff.* Olive above, wings duskier with chestnut edging on inner flight feathers; *tail long and notched* with a *black subterminal band* and *prominent white tip.* White below, breast grayer. With its distinctive head and tail pattern, virtually unmistakable. Usually found in pairs, seemingly sedentary and rarely following flocks; often in areas with extensive bamboo understory. Primary call a fast, sharp, staccato "chídididik" or "kikky-tutu."

Eye-ringed Tody-Tyrant
Hemitriccus orbitatus   PLATE 47(17)
11.5 cm (4½"). Uncommon in lower and middle growth of humid forest and woodland in *se. Brazil* (Espírito Santo to ne. Rio Grande do Sul). Mostly below 600 m. Olive above with a *prominent white eye-ring* and black and white loral area; wings duskier with *broad white tertial edging.* Yellowish below, whiter on throat, and more olive on chest. Kaempfer's Tody-Tyrant *lacks* the eye-ring, etc.; the smaller Hangnest Tody-Tyrant is much whiter below, has pale iris. Serra do Mar Tyrannulet's overall head pattern quite similar,

though its horizontal posture is very different; Serra do Mar also has mostly grayish underparts and *lacks* tertial edging. Behavior much as in other forest-based tody-tyrants. Most frequent call a snappy "tr-r-r-r-r-r" or "te-te-te-tk."

Hangnest Tody-Tyrant
Hemitriccus nidipendulus   PLATE 47(18)
9.5 cm (3¾"). Locally fairly common in lower growth at edge of humid forest and secondary woodland in *e. Brazil* (Sergipe, and Bahia to e. Paraná). To 1400 m. *Iris whitish. Bright olive green above* with pale supraloral spot, wings duskier with yellowish edging. *Essentially whitish below,* some fine dusky throat streaking. A *small,* relatively unpatterned tody-tyrant. Eye-ringed Tody-Tyrant has a dark eye, different facial pattern, yellow underparts. Behavior much as in other forest-based tody-tyrants. Call a fast "weet-weet-weet" often preceded by a few "tic" notes.

Drab-breasted Bamboo Tyrant
Hemitriccus diops   PLATE 47(19)
11 cm (4¼"). Uncommon in undergrowth of humid forest and woodland in *se. Brazil region* (north to s. Bahia). *Favors bamboo throughout its range.* To 1300 m. Plain olive above with *whitish supraloral spot and eye-ring. Throat and breast dull mauve grayish;* belly whitish. Cf. generally scarcer Brown-breasted Bamboo Tyrant. No tody-tyrant is as dull and dark; most have pale tertial edging (lacking in this species). Unobtrusive and seemingly very sedentary in dense tangles. Call a short dry trill, often doubled, e.g., "tr-r-r-r, tr-r-r-r-r." The wings whirr audibly in flight.

Brown-breasted Bamboo Tyrant
Hemitriccus obsoletus   PLATE 47(20)
11 cm (4¼"). Uncommon in undergrowth of humid and montane forest and woodland in *se. Brazil* (Rio de Janeiro to Rio Grande do Sul) *and ne. Argentina* (recently recorded from Misiones). *Favors bamboo throughout.* 500–2300 m, northward only at higher elevations. Resembles Drab-breasted Bamboo Tyrant, differing in its *buffier supraloral spot and eye-ring* and *dingy buff throat and breast.* Where the species overlap, Brown-breasted occurs at higher elevations. Very rare Kaempfer's Tody-Tyrant has obvious pale tertial edging and a clear yellow belly. Inconspicuous behavior much as in Drab-breasted Bamboo Tyrant. Call a short fast series of sharp notes, sometimes syncopated, e.g., "tic-tic-tic-tic, tic-tic, tic," less run-together or trilled than

in Drab-breasted. As with that species, the wings whirr audibly in flight.

Flammulated Bamboo Tyrant
Hemitriccus flammulatus   PLATE 47(21)
11 cm (4¼"). Locally fairly common in dense undergrowth of humid forest in *sw. Amazonia.* Mostly below 750 m. *Plain olive above* with *dull whitish supraloral spot and eye-ring.* Throat whitish streaked grayish, *breast vaguely flammulated brownish,* belly whitish. A plain tyrannid, resembling the other two bamboo tyrants (both of them geographically distant). White-bellied Tody-Tyrant has a pale eye and wing-bars; it is more arboreal. Yungas Tody-Tyrant likewise differs in its pale eye, vague wing-bars. *Strongly favors Guadua bamboo thickets* in most of its range (but not always the case in Bolivia). Usually inconspicuous, occurring as sedentary pairs; most often recorded by voice. Gives a variety of sharp "tik" notes, sometimes in a phrase (e.g., "tidik, tidik, tip-tip"); also a more trilled "trrrrrríp" and others. Wings whirr audibly in flight.

Pseudotriccus

A trio of *very inconspicuous* small tyrannids found in *undergrowth inside Andean forests.*

Bronze-olive Pygmy-Tyrant
Pseudotriccus pelzelni   PLATE 47(22)
11 cm (4¼"). Fairly common but inconspicuous in undergrowth of foothill and montane forest in *Andes from n. Colombia to s. Peru* (Cuzco). Iris reddish. Mostly 600–2000 m. *Dark and uniform.* In **most of range** (illustrated) uniform dark olive above. Throat whitish, breast and flanks olive, midbelly creamy yellow. **West-slope birds** are browner above (especially on wings and tail) and more ochraceous below (especially on breast). Nondescript and potentially confusing. Vaguely recalls a *Myiobius,* though very differently shaped and without the obvious yellow rump; behavior is also markedly different. East-slope birds resemble certain ♀ manakins, though the pygmy-tyrant is less plump and round in shape. Quiet and easy to overlook, solitary birds are sometimes encountered in shady forest undergrowth; they often jump upward to snap insects off underside of leaves. Usually not with flocks. Wings whirr audibly as it flies, and also often makes a sharp rattling sound, apparently with its wings (L. Navarrete). Call infrequently heard, a shrill and high-pitched "psee-ee-ee-ee,"

sometimes hesitating and even higher-pitched at end. Also gives a drier descending trill. Also: e. Panama.

Hazel-fronted Pygmy-Tyrant
Pseudotriccus simplex
11 cm (4¼"). Uncommon and local in undergrowth and borders of montane forest on *east slope of Andes from s. Peru* (north to s. Cuzco) *to w. Bolivia* (w. Santa Cruz). Mostly 1300–2500 m. Resembles Bronze-olive Pygmy-Tyrant (minimal overlap), differing in having *forecrown and sides of head dull rufous;* wing and tail feathers more broadly edged rufous. Rather similar Rufous-headed Pygmy-Tyrant normally occurs at higher elevations (perhaps local overlap); it shows more extensive rufous on head (though this can be reduced in younger Rufous-headeds) and on its wings and tail. Behavior much as in Bronze-olive Pygmy-Tyrant, as are vocalizations (including the shrill "psee-ee-ee-ee?") and the wing-whirring and snaps.

Rufous-headed Pygmy-Tyrant
Pseudotriccus ruficeps   PLATE 47(23)
11 cm (4¼"). Fairly common but inconspicuous in undergrowth of upper montane forest in *Andes from n. Colombia to w. Bolivia* (Cochabamba). Mostly 2000–3300 m. A cute, nearly unmistakable tyrannid, with *contrasting bright rufous head and throat;* dark olive above, with *contrasting chestnut wings and tail.* Breast and flanks olive, midbelly pale yellow. **Young birds** gradually acquire the rufous and chestnut; the youngest may show only a little. Cf. Rufous-crowned Tody-Flycatcher (which despite its similar name looks quite different). Behavior much as in Bronze-olive Pygmy-Tyrant, which Rufous-headed replaces at higher elevations. Call a sharp and drawn-out, rattled "tzrrrrrrrrrrrr" with descending effect. Song a protracted and very high-pitched trill, at first descending, then ascending, "tsi-i-i-i-i-i-e-e-e-u-e-e-e-i-i-i-i?" Also makes wing snaps as in the Bronze-olive.

Poecilotriccus

Small flycatchers with *broad spatulate bills* found primarily in the lowlands and mainly associated with secondary and edge habitats. We follow the 1998 AOU Check-list in expanding the genus *Poecilotriccus* to include the following six species, all formerly classified in the genus *Todirostrum.* All *Poeci-*

lotriccus range in lower growth, where they usually remain hard to see, though their frequent vocalizations often draw attention to them. After a break, coverage of the genus continues on p. 437.

Ruddy Tody-Flycatcher
Poecilotriccus russatus PLATE 48(1)
9.5–10 cm (3¾–4″). Uncommon in undergrowth and borders of montane forest and woodland on *tepuis of s. Venezuela region.* 1100–2500 m. *Unique in its limited range;* a dark, richly colored relative of the Ochre-faced Tody-Flycatcher. *Forehead and sides of head cinnamon-rufous, extending down over throat and breast;* crown slaty; wing-bars rufous. Behavior and voice much as in Ochre-faced Tody-Flycatcher, though Ruddy never seems as numerous.

Ochre-faced Tody-Flycatcher
Poecilotriccus plumbeiceps PLATE 48(2)
9.5–10 cm (3¾–4″). Fairly common in undergrowth and borders of humid and lower montane forest and woodland on *east slope of Andes from s. Peru* (Cuzco) *to nw. Argentina* (Salta), and in *e. Brazil* region. Mostly below 2500 m. Crown gray outlining *cinnamon-buff sides of head,* auriculars dusky; olive above, wings duskier with two ochraceous bars. Whitish below; **Andean birds** are grayer. *No comparable small tyrannid shows the contrasting bright face.* Ranges singly or in pairs, generally not with mixed flocks; sometimes not as difficult to observe as many small tyrannids inhabiting undergrowth. Frequent call a sharp rattle, "trrrrr," often repeated several times and sometimes preceded by 1–2 "tic" notes.

Rusty-fronted Tody-Flycatcher
Poecilotriccus latirostris PLATE 48(3)
9.5 cm (3¾″). Locally fairly common in dense undergrowth of shrubby clearings, forest and woodland borders, and river islands in *w. and s. Amazonia.* To 1000 m. Crown and neck gray with *prominent buff lores and facial area;* olive above, wings dusky with *two ochraceous bars* and olive edging. *Below dull grayish white.* Smoky-fronted Tody-Flycatcher (limited overlap) shows less buff on face, yellower wing-bars, and mainly pale yellow underparts. Inconspicuous behavior much as in Ochre-faced Tody-Flycatcher, and likewise mostly recorded by voice. Call a sharp, low-pitched, rattled "tik, trrrr" or "tik, trrrr, trrrr," sometimes the "tik" alone.

Smoky-fronted Tody-Flycatcher
Poecilotriccus fumifrons PLATE 48(4)
9 cm (3½″). Uncommon in dense shrubbery in clearings, secondary woodland, and at edge of humid forest from the *Guianas to ne. Brazil;* one recent record from sw. Venezuela (s. Amazonas). To 500 m. *Lores buff;* olive above, forecrown grayer, wings duskier with two yellowish buff bars and olive edging. Throat whitish, *below pale yellowish,* brightest on belly. Rusty-fronted Tody-Flycatcher has more buff on face and all whitish underparts. Slate-headed Tody-Flycatcher *lacks* buff on face and is whitish below. Behavior and voice similar to Ochre-faced Tody-Flycatcher, though seems scarcer and is harder to observe.

Buff-cheeked Tody-Flycatcher
Poecilotriccus senex
9 cm (3½″). *Uncommon and very local* in dense stunted campina forest and at edge of várzea forest along edge of blackwater rivers in *s. Amaz. Brazil.* Only recently rediscovered (B. M. Whitney and M. Cohn-Haft; A. Whittaker). Below 100 m. Resembles Smoky-fronted Tody-Flycatcher, differing in its *pinkish cinnamon ocular area* and *yellowish white wing-bars.* Behavior much as in the previous four species of tody-flycatchers. Voice a "rather loud, dry metallic trill" (A. Whittaker).

Slate-headed Tody-Flycatcher
Poecilotriccus sylvia PLATE 48(5)
9.5 cm (3¾″). Fairly common in dense thickets of regenerating clearings and borders of woodland and forest (both deciduous and humid) from *n. Colombia to lower Amaz. Brazil.* To 1000 m. Iris color varies (can be either pale or dark). In **most of range** (illustrated) *crown slaty gray* with *contrasting white supraloral and eyering;* above bright olive, wings blackish with two bold yellow bars. *Below grayish white,* grayest across breast. In **ne. Brazil** darker generally with a grayer breast, ochraceous wing-bars. Pale-eyed Pygmy-Tyrant is duller overall, lacking gray on crown and showing vague streaking on foreneck; it is always pale-eyed. Smoky-fronted Tody-Flycatcher has buff lores and supraloral, yellowish underparts. Cf. also Pearly-vented Tody-Tyrant. Behavior and voice much as in previous tody-flycatchers. Also: Mexico to Panama.

Todirostrum

Small flycatchers characterized by their *spatulate bill, Todirostrum* differ from *Poecilotriccus* in being *markedly more arboreal,* hence they tend to be easier to see. *Todirostrum* likewise mainly range in the lowlands and are primarily associated with secondary habitats (though three species, the "Painted complex," inhabit humid forest canopy). As with *Poecilotriccus, Todirostrum* have a more horizontal posture than the *Hemitriccus* tody-tyrants, and they likewise forage mostly with upward strikes to the underside of leaves.

Spotted Tody-Flycatcher
Todirostrum maculatum   PLATE 48(6)
10 cm (4"). *Locally common in riparian woodland and shrubby areas (often on river islands), shade trees, and mangroves from Amazonia to the Guianas and e. Venezuela.* To 500 m. Iris orange-yellow. *Head gray* with whitish supraloral spot; above olive, wings dusky with yellow bars and edging. Throat white; below yellow, belly brighter, *foreneck with narrow blackish streaking.* Often sympatric with either Johannes's or Stripe-necked Tody-Tyrant; their streaking below is blurrier, and they are duller overall with less gray on head and less evident or no wing-bars. Common Tody-Flycatcher shows *no* streaking below. Spotted is an arboreal tody-flycatcher that gleans at varying heights and is usually inconspicuous (though its vocalizations often draw attention); much less apt to forage close to the ground than Common Tody-Flycatcher. Most frequent song a short series of sharp, loud "peek" notes that can be given as a syncopated duet by a pair, thus "pik-peek, pik-peek, pik-peek. . . ."

Yellow-lored Tody-Flycatcher
Todirostrum poliocephalum   PLATE 48(7)
9.5–10 cm (3¾–4"). Fairly common in borders of humid forest and woodland and adjacent clearings and gardens in *se. Brazil* (s. Bahia to e. Santa Catarina). To 1350 m. Iris orange-yellow. Resembles much more wide-ranging Common Tody-Flycatcher, and occurs with that species locally. Yellow-lored differs in its *conspicuous yellow lores,* more olive (not so gray) back, and olive tail that *lacks* white edging. Common Tody-Flycatchers in se. Brazil show at most a minute spot of yellow at the base of the bill. Yellow-lored behavior is much the same, though it tends to be more forest-based. Its song, though typically shorter and less run-together, has a similar quality, e.g., a sharp "cheep, chip-chip."

Common Tody-Flycatcher
Todirostrum cinereum   PLATE 48(8)
9–9.5 cm (3¾–4"). *Widespread and often common* in trees in a variety of secondary and semi-open habitats from Colombia and Venezuela to s. Brazil, but largely absent from Amazonia and scarce in mainly forested regions. Mostly below 1200 m, but reaches 2000 m in some Andean valleys of s. Peru and Bolivia. *Iris whitish to pale straw.* In **most of range** (illustrated) *forecrown and face black, shading to slaty on nape and gray on back;* wings blackish conspicuously edged yellow; rather long and graduated tail black with outer feathers whitish. Below bright yellow. **Southern birds (Bolivia to s. Brazil)** have a paler gray nape, more olive back, and usually a small yellow loral spot; **west of Andes** has a white throat. Cf. Yellow-lored and Maracaibo Tody-Flycatchers (both with very small ranges), and in w. Amazonia the more colorful Golden-winged Tody-Flycatcher. *Common is generally the most frequently encountered tody-flycatcher;* further, it often forages in the open so is easy to see. Basically an arboreal bird, it also sometimes moves quite low; its mannerisms are animated, with tail often cocked and flipped around, sometimes even standing high on its legs. Usually in pairs, and generally not with mixed flocks. Quite vocal, both sexes giving quick, rather cricketlike trills and also various "tik" notes. Also: Mexico to Panama.

Maracaibo Tody-Flycatcher
Todirostrum viridanum
9 cm (3½"). Fairly common in arid woodland and thickets in *nw. Venezuela* (n. Zulia and Falcón). Below 200 m. Resembles a pale Common Tody-Flycatcher. Differs in its *shorter and ungraduated tail,* dark iris, *whitish forehead and supraloral,* and *generally paler plumage* (paler gray nape, more olive back, paler and buffier wing-edging and underparts). Apparently the two species have not been found together; Maracaibo seems especially to favor trees along dry washes. Behavior much as in Common Tody-Flycatcher, as is its voice, typically consisting of several "pik" or "chip" notes, sometimes in a short series.

Black-headed Tody-Flycatcher
Todirostrum nigriceps   PLATE 48(9)
8.5 cm (3¼"). Uncommon and inconspicuous in canopy and borders of humid forest and wood-

land from *nw. Venezuela to sw. Ecuador* (El Oro). To 900 m. Iris dark. *Head glossy black, contrasting with bright olive-yellow back;* wings black with two yellow bars and edging. *Throat white; below bright yellow.* Along eastern base of Andes in sw. Venezuela and ne. Colombia nearly overlaps with Yellow-browed Tody-Flycatcher, which there differs in its yellow postocular and black breast streaking. Common Tody-Flycatcher favors more open habitats, is larger and longer-tailed with a pale iris; it shows much less contrast on head. An attractively patterned but tiny bird that remains high in forest canopy and thus usually is hard to see; only rarely does one come lower, at forest borders. Found singly or in pairs, usually not joining mixed flocks. Heard much more often than seen. Song a slightly accelerating series of high-pitched, emphatic "tsip" notes, generally 5–8 per series. Also: Costa Rica and Panama.

Painted Tody-Flycatcher
Todirostrum pictum   PLATE 48(10)
9 cm (3½"). Uncommon and inconspicuous in canopy and borders of humid forest and woodland and in adjacent clearings in *ne. South America.* To 400 m. Iris dark. *Head glossy black with white supraloral spot; bright olive above,* wings blackish with two yellow bars and edging. Lower face and throat white; below bright yellow with *black streaks on malar area and across chest.* Replaces the similar Yellow-browed Tody-Flycatcher *north of Amazon and east of Rio Negro;* the two species do not range together. Behavior much as in Black-headed Tody-Flycatcher, as is its voice, a repeated "cheevik" or (sometimes at a faster pace and long-continued) "cheeyt."

Yellow-browed Tody-Flycatcher
Todirostrum chrysocrotaphum   PLATE 48(11)
9 cm (3½"). Uncommon and inconspicuous in canopy and borders of humid forest and woodland and in adjacent clearings from *w. Amazonia to e. Amaz. Brazil* (in latter only *south* of Amazon). Mostly below 600 m, a few to 1000 m. Iris dark. Varies, but *all races are united by their bold golden yellow postocular stripe.* In **sw. Amazonia** (A) *head glossy black* with yellow postocular stripe; bright olive above, wings blackish with two yellow bars and edging. *Below bright yellow.* In **e. Amaz. Brazil** similar but with a white loral spot; **farther east** birds lack this, instead having a black malar. In **nw. Amazonia north of Amazon and east to lower Rio Negro** (B) differs in having *prominent black streaking on throat and*

breast; also has a white loral spot. Painted Tody-Flycatcher (no overlap) *lacks* the golden brow; Black-headed Tody-Flycatcher does likewise, and ranges primarily *west* of Andes. Behavior and voice much as in Black-headed Tody-Flycatcher, though Yellow-browed's series of notes is often longer (ca. 8–12 notes).

Poecilotriccus

These represent the true *Poecilotriccus* tody-flycatchers. Several species are *attractively colored and patterned,* and most are *quite rare or have small ranges;* a few are even *sexually dimorphic* (rare among tyrannids).

Golden-winged Tody-Flycatcher
Poecilotriccus calopterus   PLATE 48(12)
9.5 cm (3¾"). Uncommon in undergrowth at borders of humid lowland and foothill forest, secondary woodland, and regenerating clearings in foothills and adjacent lowlands along *eastern base of Andes in se. Colombia, e. Ecuador, and ne. Peru.* To 1300 m. *Head and neck black, back bright olive;* wings black with *conspicuous golden yellow band on greater-coverts,* maroon-chestnut shoulders; outer tail feathers edged whitish. Throat white; below bright yellow. Common Tody-Flycatcher is pale-eyed, gray-backed, and lacks the striking wing pattern. Found in pairs that remain in dense growth where, despite their bright colors, they remain hard to see. Does not join mixed flocks. Distinctive call a dry, gravelly, sputtering "dre'd'd'd'deu" or "p-drrrew," often repeated several times; sometimes given as a duet.

Black-backed Tody-Flycatcher
Poecilotriccus pulchellus   PLATE 48(13)
9.5 cm (3¾"). Uncommon in undergrowth at borders of humid lowland and foothill forest, secondary woodland, and regenerating clearings along *eastern base of Andes in se. Peru* (Cuzco and Puno). 500–1500 m. ♂ *black above* with a small whitish postocular spot; wings with *conspicuous golden yellow band across greater-coverts;* outer tail feather edged whitish. Throat and *malar stripe white,* separated by *black submalar streak;* below bright yellow. ♀ differs in its sooty-olive back, adding a whitish loral spot. Behavior and voice much as in geographically distant Golden-winged Tody-Flycatcher.

Black-and-white Tody-Flycatcher
Poecilotriccus capitalis   PLATE 48(14)
9.5 cm (3¾"). *Uncommon and very local* in tangled viny thickets in lower growth and borders of humid forest in *w. and s. Amazonia;* also in *bamboo-dominated understory and borders* of foothill and lower montane forest on *east slope of Andes from s. Colombia to cen. Peru* (Pasco). To 1350 m. Bill mostly orange-yellow. ♂ *glossy black above* with a small white loral spot; *tertials broadly edged pale yellow,* bend of wing also yellow. *White below,* a little black on sides of throat and chest. ♀ olive above with gray head and neck, *chestnut crown,* and buff supraloral spot; wings and tail dusky-olive, *tertials broadly edged yellow.* Throat whitish, breast grayish, belly mainly whitish. Striking and unlikely to be confused. Forages singly and in pairs, appearing quite sedentary; does not move with mixed flocks. Often confiding but, because of the dense nature of its habitat, hard to observe. Call a fast sharp "tik, t-r-r-r-r-r-ew." Agitated birds give a more explosive "tk, tk, tk, whey-whey-whey-whuh."

White-cheeked Tody-Flycatcher
Poecilotriccus albifacies   PLATE 48(15)
9.5 cm (3¾"). *Uncommon and local in Guadua bamboo thickets in humid forest of se.* Peru (Cuzco and Madre de Dios). Locally to 900 m. Lower mandible orange-yellow. ♂ has *crown bright rufous-chestnut* contrasting with *white sides of head* and *black nuchal collar;* back bright yellowish olive; wings and tail black, tertials edged white. White below with black malar stripe and on sides of chest. ♀ duller, with cheeks and neck grayer and flight feathers broadly edged olive. Not known to occur with Black-and-white Tody-Flycatcher. White-cheeked favors very dense bamboo stands, there occurring in sedentary pairs and hard to see; associates only rarely with mixed flocks. Call a fast series of sharp "pik" notes, often hesitating at first; less trilled than comparable call of Flammulated Bamboo Tyrant (often with it and usually more numerous).

Rufous-crowned Tody-Flycatcher
Poecilotriccus ruficeps   PLATE 48(16)
9.5 cm (3¾"). Uncommon in lower growth and borders of montane forest and in adjacent clearings in *Andes from w. Venezuela* (Trujillo) *to extreme n. Peru* (n. Cajamarca). Mostly 1500–2500 m. In **most of range** (A) *crown bright rufous* bordered behind by a black line and gray nape, *cheeks buff;* bright olive above, wings black with two pale yellowish bars. *Throat and upper chest white to buffy whitish,* usually some black in malar area, and separated from bright yellow of underparts by a diffuse blackish breast band. In **s. Ecuador and adjacent Peru** has a *conspicuous black malar stripe* and *variable amount of black around eye;* in **w. Colombia** (B) *whitish cheeks broadly encircled by black.* Despite its similar name, Rufous-headed Pygmy-Tyrant is really quite different; it inhabits actual forest. A colorful but inconspicuous little tyrannid that forages close to the ground, often in bamboo understory; ranges singly or in pairs, only rarely with mixed flocks. Inconspicuous, most apt to be found by tracking down a vocalizing bird. Soft calls include a gravelly stuttered "tttrew," "pít-tttrew," or "tttrew-pít," sometimes delivered as a duet.

Lulu's Tody-Flycatcher
*Poecilotriccus luluae**
9.5 cm (3¾"). Uncommon and local in shrubbery clearings and montane forest borders on *east slope of Andes in n. Peru* (s. Amazonas and San Martín). 1800–2200 m. A recently described species; also has been called Johnson's Tody-Flycatcher. Resembles Rufous-crowned Tody-Flycatcher, replacing that species south of Río Marañón and differing in its *mainly rufous head and throat.* Behavior and voice very similar.

Black-chested Tyrant
Taeniotriccus andrei   PLATE 48(17)
11.5 cm (4½"). *Rare and apparently local in dense bamboo- and vine-dominated lower growth of humid forest and woodland (often várzea) from s. Venezuela to e. Amaz. Brazil.* To 350 m. Unmistakable and, for a small flycatcher, spectacular. ♂ *black above* (including median crown) with *contrasting rufous-chestnut face and frontlet;* wings with a *broad pale yellow band across flight feathers and tertials.* Broad breast band sooty black, belly grayish. Though the crown feathers are long, they usually are recumbent and *not* raised in a crest. ♀ similar (*including facial and wing pattern*) but face paler, forehead blackish like midcrown, back more olive, breast grayer. Sedentary, foraging singly or in pairs, perching on open branches or vines but generally remaining within dense tangled habitat, so hard to see (especially without tape playback). Most frequent call a single, reedy "chewp," given at intervals of several seconds, sometimes lengthened into a "chewp, ch-dewp, ch-dewp."

Corythopis

A distinct genus of two similar, long-legged and *basically terrestrial* flycatchers that range in lowland forests. Nest a moss-covered, oven-shaped ball placed on the ground.

Ringed Antpipit
Corythopis torquatus PLATE 48(18)
14 cm (5½"). *Uncommon on or near ground in terra firme forest from Amazonia to the Guianas.* Mostly below 1000 m. *Distinctive pipitlike shape; walks* on the ground. Dark olive brown above, often with a little whitish around eye. Throat white, *breast with broad band of bold black streaks, which may coalesce and become almost solid*), belly whitish, grayer on flanks and crissum. **Immature** has browner breast streaking. Essentially unmistakable, but cf. Spot-backed and Banded Antbirds. Along southern periphery of range, cf. similar Southern Antpipit (minimal or no overlap). Antpipits walk on the ground with a mincing gait, often nodding head and pumping tail. They regularly perch on fallen logs, sometimes flying up to low branches, and make short sallies up from the ground, snatching insects from the underside of leaves. Generally solitary, less often in pairs, not associating with mixed flocks. Often first noticed from its frequent and emphatic bill snapping. Distinctive whistled song a shrill "peur, peur-peépit" or "preeur-preeyúr," with variations.

Southern Antpipit
Corythopis delalandi
14 cm (5½"). Fairly common on or near ground in humid forest and woodland from *e. Bolivia* (Santa Cruz) *to cen. and s. Brazil* (north to Mato Grosso and s. Maranhão), *e. Paraguay, and ne. Argentina. Replaces the similar Ringed Antpipit southward.* Mostly below 800 m. Differs in being *more olive* (not so brown) *above* and creamier on throat (not so white); underwing-coverts whitish (not grayish). Behavior and bill snapping much as in Ringed Antpipit. Fortunately, given the deforestation that has swept so much of its range, Southern seems more tolerant of disturbed conditions and even survives in relatively young second-growth. Its whistled song has the same distinctive shrill quality, but the phrase is longer, e.g., "peee, peur-pi-pi-peépit" ("three cheers for the pípit!").

Platyrinchus

Small, *stub-tailed* flycatchers with *exceptionally wide flat bills* found in undergrowth inside humid forest (not at borders), principally in the lowlands, though two species are montane. Spadebills are *inconspicuous* birds that tend to perch quietly, then all too often dart off. Sexes alike, but their semiconcealed coronal patches are smaller or absent in ♀♀.

White-crested Spadebill
Platyrinchus platyrhynchos PLATE 49(1)
11 cm (4¼"). *Rare and local in undergrowth of terra firme forest in Amazonia and the Guianas.* Mostly below 500 m. *Very wide flat bill. Crown and head gray* with white coronal patch (usually concealed) and buffy loral spot; above ochraceous brown, wings and tail duskier. Throat white, *below bright ochraceous. The largest spadebill in Amazonia.* Cinnamon-crested Spadebill is smaller, lacks gray on head, is more whitish below. Cf. also smaller and narrow-billed Ruddy-tailed Flycatcher and Cinnamon Neopipo. Perches quietly in understory, often in semiopen situations and somewhat higher above the ground than other spadebills. Like other spadebills does not join mixed flocks. Most frequent call a loud and explosive "skeep!" or "skeeuw!" Song, heard much less often, a sharp and burry trill that rises and becomes louder before falling toward the end. In a flight display the singing bird angles downward before recovering and flying to another perch with a manakinlike wing-whirr.

Cinnamon-crested Spadebill
Platyrinchus saturatus PLATE 49(2)
9.5 cm (3¾"). *Uncommon in undergrowth of terra firme forest from the Guianas, s. Venezuela, and n. Amaz. Brazil* (where most numerous) *west very locally into w. and s. Amazonia.* To 900 m. *Very wide flat bill. Dark rufous brown above* with whitish lores and an inconspicuous eye-ring, and an orange-rufous coronal streak (usually mostly concealed). Midthroat silky white; below whitish, sides washed brown, belly pale yellow. *A rather plain spadebill,* showing less facial pattern than either White-throated or Golden-crowned; Cinnamon-crested occurs only with Golden-crowned (though White-throated occurs just above it on tepui slopes). White-crested Spadebill is larger, with gray on head, white in crest, and brighter underparts. Behavior much as in White-crested, though seems to join mixed

flocks more often. Calls include a simple sharp "kwip," sometimes doubled to a "kwi-dip" or lengthened to a "kwip, kwi-di-dip"; south of Amazon seemingly quite different, a series of "ka-nee" notes.

Yellow-throated Spadebill
Platyrinchus flavigularis   PLATE 49(3)
9.5 cm (3¾"). *Rare in lower growth of montane forest in Andes (mainly on east slope) from w. Venezuela* (Lara) *to s. Peru* (Cuzco). Mostly 1250–2100 m. *Very wide flat bill. Head rufous with a large white coronal patch* (usually concealed); olive above, duskier on wings and tail. *Below pale yellow, brightest on throat,* with olive across breast. *A distinctive "yellow" spadebill.* The more numerous and widespread White-throated Spadebill has an obviously white throat; its facial pattern is much more complex and it lacks rufous on head. Favors areas with a relatively open understory, especially on ridges. Often perches in the open, regularly higher above ground than other spadebills; remains motionless for long periods, so not easy to spot. Call a sharp "peeeyr!" repeated at long intervals, typically 4–5 seconds.

Golden-crowned Spadebill
Platyrinchus coronatus   PLATE 49(4)
9 cm (3½"). Uncommon in undergrowth of terra firme forest from *Colombia to Amazonia and the Guianas.* Mostly below 700 m, but to 1500 m on tepui slopes. *Very wide flat bill.* Brownish olive above with *black-bordered rufous crown* (♂ also has yellow coronal streak, usually concealed) and *complex facial pattern of buffy yellowish and black.* Dull yellowish below, washed olive on breast and flanks. White-throated Spadebill has similar facial pattern but lacks the black-bordered crown and has an obviously contrasting white throat. Cf. Cinnamon-crested Spadebill. Behavior similar to other spadebills, though Golden-crowned favors areas with a more open understory. Song a rather weak, colorless, and high-pitched (but rising and falling) trill, easily passed over as an insect. Also: Honduras to Panama.

White-throated Spadebill
Platyrinchus mystaceus   PLATE 49(5)
9.5–10 cm (3¾–4"). *Widespread and fairly common* in undergrowth of montane forest and woodland (locally also in lowlands) from Colombia and Venezuela to Bolivia and se. Brazil area (where most numerous); absent from Amazonia. Mostly 600–2000 m, locally lower.

Very wide flat bill. **Eastern birds** (A) have a *pale lower mandible* and are olive brown above with a yellow coronal patch (usually concealed) and *complex buffy yellowish and black facial pattern. Throat white,* breast and belly buffyish. **Andean birds** (B) have *bill mostly dark,* brownish on sides of breast, and pale yellow belly. The only other montane spadebill is the very different Yellow-throated. In se. Brazil region cf. the larger and much rarer Russet-winged Spadebill. Behavior much as in White-crested Spadebill, though tending to remain lower, in dense growth, and thus often harder to see; mist-netting can reveal it to be numerous, and it can persist even in small forest fragments. Most frequent call a sharp "squeep!" or "squik!" sometimes doubled. Distinctive song a fairly musical trilling, at first descending, then rising; in the southeast ends with a "whik." Also: Costa Rica and Panama.

Russet-winged Spadebill
Platyrinchus leucoryphus   PLATE 49(6)
12.5 cm (5"). *Now rare and local in undergrowth of humid forest in se. Brazil region* (north to Espírito Santo). To 900 m. *A large, relatively long-tailed spadebill. Very wide flat bill* mostly bright yellow. Above olive brown with white coronal patch (usually concealed) and complex buffy yellowish and blackish facial pattern; *wing-coverts and flight feathers broadly edged rufous.* Throat white, breast olive brown, belly dull yellowish white. White-throated Spadebill has a similar facial pattern but is much smaller and *lacks* rufous on wings. Solitary behavior much as in other spadebills. Overall numbers much reduced because of deforestation. Vocalizations resemble White-crested Spadebill.

Tolmomyias

A *difficult* group of flycatchers with *wide flat bills* (though not as extreme as in the *Rhynchocyclus* flatbills), hence the reversion to the "flatbill" group name. *All species are usually best recognized by voice.* Their taxonomy is in flux, with several species having recently been recognized and the prospect of more to come. Mainly ranging in humid forest, *Tolmomyias* tend to forage well above the ground and regularly join mixed flocks. Unless otherwise indicated, wings and tail are dusky, wings with two yellowish bars and edging. Their nests, often placed near a wasp's nest, are bag-shaped with a tubular entrance near bottom and pointing downward.

Yellow-olive Flatbill
Tolmomyias sulphurescens*   PLATE 50(1)
13.5–14 cm (5¼–5½"). *Widespread and locally common* in lower and middle growth and borders of deciduous and semihumid forest and woodland, and in foothill and lower montane forest, from Colombia and Venezuela to n. Argentina; in Amazonia primarily in riparian habitats. To over 2000 m. More than one species almost certainly involved. *Iris typically pale* (grayish to brownish). Olive above (brightness varies) with *gray crown and nape,* whitish supraloral, and dark patch on ear-coverts. Throat pale grayish, breast and flanks pale olive, belly pale yellow. **Southeastern birds** (A) have *ear-covert patch quite blackish;* patch is more obscure **elsewhere** (B). Cf. very similar Yellow-margined and Zimmer's Flatbills, though these species (*mainly in humid lowland forest canopy*) tend not to occur with Yellow-olive. Found singly or in pairs, usually perching quite upright; makes short sallies to leaves for insects. Generally not hard to observe, and often with mixed flocks. Song west of Andes a thin, well-enunciated series of quick notes, "psee-pset-pset-pset." East of Andes the notes are a little longer, e.g. "swit-swit-swit-swit" or "dzeeyp, dzeeyp, dzeeyp." There is additional geographic variation. Also: Mexico to Panama.

Orange-eyed Flatbill
Tolmomyias traylori*
13.5 cm (5¼"). Rare to locally uncommon in canopy and borders of várzea and riparian forest and woodland in *ne. Peru, e. Ecuador, and se. Colombia.* Below 300 m. A recently described species. *Iris pale orange.* Olive above, crown somewhat grayer. *Loral area, ear-coverts, throat, and chest dull buff;* below pale yellow. No other *Tolmomyias* has either the orangy eye or the buff on foreneck. Found singly or in pairs, usually not with mixed flocks; more arboreal than Yellow-olive, recalling Olive-faced Flatbill (and sometimes with that species). Most frequent call a distinctive buzzy "wheeeeezzz-birrt," sometimes with a few other buzzy notes appended. Song up to 5–7 well-enunciated "zhree" notes (longer and wheezier than Olive-faced).

Zimmer's Flatbill
Tolmomyias assimilis*   PLATE 50(2)
13.5 cm (5¼"). Fairly common in mid-levels and subcanopy of humid forest from *Amazonia to the Guianas.* To 1000 m. Formerly considered conspecific with Yellow-margined Flatbill; very different voice. *Closely* resembles Yellow-olive

Flatbill, but typically differs in its darker iris, reduced gray on crown, and *pale speculum at base of outer primaries* (wing-bars *not* very evident). Gray-crowned Flatbill (regularly with Zimmer's, sometimes even in the same flock) shows less prominent wing-bars and lacks the primary speculum; also has a nearly all-dark bill (lower mandible not paler) and paler irides. Forages singly or in pairs, often accompanying mixed flocks; rather horizontal posture, sometimes with cocked tail. Distinctive song a leisurely series of three or so whistled notes, each slightly higher-pitched and shriller, e.g., "weeeuw . . . weeeu . . . weeé!"; paraphrased as "one . . . two . . . three!" (J. Moore).

Yellow-margined Flatbill
Tolmomyias flavotectus*
13.5 cm (5¼"). Fairly common in mid-levels and subcanopy of humid forest and woodland in *w. Colombia and nw. Ecuador* (mainly from Pichincha north). Below 500 m. Formerly considered conspecific with what we consider Zimmer's Flatbill (found *east* of Andes; voice very different). *Closely* resembles Yellow-olive Flatbill, but differs in its darker iris, reduced gray on crown, *pale speculum at base of outer primaries,* and *broad yellow edging on greater wing-coverts.* Yellow-olives found in lowland w. Ecuador favor more deciduous habitats, with Yellow-margined taking over in humid forest; nonetheless, voice is often the best way to distinguish these two very similar species. Yellow-margined's wing pattern vaguely recalls that of the much smaller Golden-faced Tyrannulet. Behavior much as in Zimmer's Flatbill. Distinctive song a series of harsh and emphatic notes, "zhweyk, zhwek-zhwek-zhwek-zhwek," with pause after the first. Also: Costa Rica and Panama.

Gray-crowned Flatbill
Tolmomyias poliocephalus*   PLATE 50(3)
12 cm (4¾"). Fairly common in mid-levels and subcanopy of humid forest and woodland from *Amazonia to the Guianas,* and in e. Brazil. Mostly below 1000 m. Iris pale, typically brownish; *bill mainly black.* Olive above with gray crown and whitish supraloral. Throat pale grayish, breast and flanks grayish olive, belly pale yellow. Zimmer's Flatbill is very similar but somewhat larger, dark-eyed, and has a mainly pale lower mandible; its wing-bars are more prominent and it shows a pale primary speculum (faint or lacking in Gray-crowned); voice differs dramatically. Frequently accompanies mixed flocks; as with Zimmer's,

Gray-crowned Flatbill has a rather horizontal posture, sometimes cocking its tail. Song an inflected, somewhat wheezy "fiwee?" given either at intervals of 1–2 seconds or in a short series.

Olive-faced Flatbill
Tolmomyias viridiceps *   PLATE 50(4)

12 cm (4¾"). Common in lighter and riparian woodland, clearings, and borders in *w. Amazonia*. Mostly below 1100 m. Sometimes considered conspecific with Ochre-lored Flatbill. Olive above. Yellow below, clouded olive on breast and flanks. *Very plain, showing no facial pattern or gray on crown.* Ochre-lored (no known overlap) is brighter, especially about face, and voice differs markedly. Behavior much as in Ochre-lored Flatbill. Song a series of 2–5 sharp, shrill notes that gradually become louder, faster-paced than in Ochre-lored.

Ochre-lored Flatbill
Tolmomyias flaviventris *   PLATE 50(5)

12 cm (4¾"). Common in lighter and gallery woodland, gardens, and mangroves from *n. Colombia and Venezuela to cen. Amaz. and e. Brazil.* Sometimes considered conspecific with Olive-faced Flatbill, under the name Yellow-breasted Flatbill (or Flycatcher). To 900 m. In **most of range** (illustrated) uniform yellowish olive above. Yellow below. From **n. Colombia to Amapá, Brazil,** brighter above with *lores and eye-ring ochraceous,* foreneck tinged ochre. Other than Olive-faced, other *Tolmomyias* show more facial pattern and gray on crown. Aside from its vocalizations, Ochre-lored is inconspicuous, found singly or in pairs and rather less active than many of its congeners; usually not with flocks. Song a loud, shrill "shreeeép" given at intervals of several seconds or more.

Rhynchocyclus

Large-headed, *mainly dull olive* flycatchers that range inside humid forest, these flatbills are most notable for their *very wide flat bills;* they are larger than *Tolmomyias.* Their bulky, pear-shaped nests also have an entrance that points down.

Olivaceous Flatbill
Rhynchocyclus olivaceus   PLATE 50(6)

15 cm (6"). Uncommon to locally fairly common in lower growth of humid forest and woodland from *Colombia and Venezuela to Amazonia and the Guianas,* and in *e. Brazil.* Locally to 1100 m.

A stolid, heavy-bodied flycatcher. Very wide flat bill, lower mandible pale. Dark olive above with an indistinct whitish eye-ring; wings duskier with two dull wing-bars and edging yellowish to ochraceous olive. Throat pale grayish, breast and flanks flammulated grayish olive, belly pale yellow. Not known to occur with any other *Rhynchocyclus. Ramphotrigon* flatbills are smaller and more slender, have bold wing-bars, etc. *Tolmomyias* flatbills also have wide bills but are smaller, more active, and much more arboreal. Forages singly or in pairs, often accompanying understory flocks; perches upright, often on open branches, slowly looking around with what seems like a dazed expression, but then abruptly sallying out to foliage or a branch in pursuit of prey. Quiet and inconspicuous, though one occasionally will give a harsh and abrupt "tshreet." Also: Panama.

Eye-ringed Flatbill
Rhynchocyclus brevirostris

15 cm (6"). Lower growth of montane forest on *slopes of Cerro Tacarcuna in nw. Colombia.* 700–1500 m. Resembles Olivaceous Flatbill, which in area of overlap occurs at *lower* elevations. Eye-ringed has a *much bolder white eye-ring* and more yellowish olive wing-bars. Pacific Flatbill (no overlap) has only a very indistinct grayish eye-ring, and more prominent fulvous wing-bars and edging. Hardly known in Colombia, but in Middle America behavior as in Olivaceous Flatbill. Also: Mexico to Panama.

Fulvous-breasted Flatbill
Rhynchocyclus fulvipectus   PLATE 50(7)

15 cm (6"). Uncommon in lower growth of montane forest in *Andes from extreme sw. Venezuela* (s. Táchira) *to w. Bolivia* (w. Santa Cruz). Mostly 800–2000 m. *Very wide flat bill,* lower mandible pale. Dark olive above with indistinct grayish eye-ring, wings duskier with *prominent tawny-fulvous edging. Throat and breast tawny-fulvous,* belly pale yellow with vague olive flank streaking. Pacific Flatbill shows *no* tawny on underparts (but is otherwise quite similar); it mainly occurs at lower elevations, with possible overlap in the foothills. Behavior and voice of this inconspicuous flatbill much as in Olivaceous Flatbill.

Pacific Flatbill
Rhynchocyclus pacificus

15 cm (6"). Uncommon in lower growth of humid and foothill forest in *w. Colombia and nw. Ecuador* (south to Pichincha). Mostly below 1000 m. Resembles Fulvous-breasted Flatbill

(which replaces it at slightly higher elevations, with limited or no overlap), but *lacks* tawny-fulvous on throat and breast. Note, however, that verifying this absence can be hard in the dim light of the shady forests that this species favors. Broad-billed Sapayoa's wings are plain (lacking flatbill's tawny-fulvous edging), and its bill is not nearly as wide. Behavior much as in Olivaceous Flatbill. Song a fast descending series of burry notes.

Ramphotrigon

A trio of inconspicuous, forest-interior fly-catchers found primarily in Amazonia. Despite their *fairly wide bills, Ramphotrigon* flatbills are not all that closely related to the other flatbills, and apparently are closer to *Myiarchus.* They have quite bold wing-bars. Their nests are placed in holes or tree cavities, very unlike the other flatbills.

Large-headed Flatbill
Ramphotrigon megacephalum　　　PLATE 50(8)

13 cm (5"). *Fairly common but local in bamboo-dominated undergrowth of humid forest and woodland,* and in *se. Brazil region.* To 1400 m in Brazil. Sometimes called Bamboo Flatbill. Dull olive above with a *prominent yellowish supraloral and eye-ring* contrasting with dusky lores; wings duskier with *two prominent ochraceous wing-bars.* Throat yellowish, breast ochraceous olive, belly pale yellow. The scarce Dusky-tailed Flatbill (also often found in bamboo) is larger and darker; it lacks the supraloral, and differs markedly in voice. Large-headed is a retiring bird that perches upright in dense cover and is rarely seen except by tracking down vocalizations. Infrequent with mixed flocks. Characteristic call, typically given at long intervals, a mournful "whoo-whou" or (in se. Brazil area) a burrier "wheeu . . . whoo," the second note lower in pitch; this can be paraphrased as "bam-bü." Dawn song, a slow "tee-tu-twit," heard less often.

Dusky-tailed Flatbill
Ramphotrigon fuscicauda

15.5 cm (6"). *Rare and very local in tangled lower growth, in most areas favoring bamboo, in humid forest and woodland in w. and cen. Amazonia; most numerous in se. Peru region* (an area where bamboo is especially prevalent). Mostly below 600 m. Brownish olive above, crown somewhat darker, with broken whitish eye-ring; wings and *tail dusky, wings with two bold cinnamon wing-*

bars and buffier edging. *Below dark olive coarsely streaked yellow,* midbelly yellow. Large-headed Flatbill is smaller and has a prominent pale supraloral as well as an eye-ring; it lacks streaking below. Olivaceous Flatbill is more uniform olive overall and has no obvious wing-bars. Very inconspicuous; occurs singly and in pairs, generally not with flocks. Recorded mainly by voice, and most often seen after tape playback (though often hard to see even then). Distinctive song a mellow "peeeeu, tr'r'r, treer-treer-treer-treer."

Rufous-tailed Flatbill
Ramphotrigon ruficauda　　　PLATE 50(9)

16 cm (6¼"). Uncommon in lower and middle growth in humid forest of *Amazonia and the Guianas.* Mostly below 600 m. Above dull olive with narrow yellowish supraloral and eye-ring; wings dusky with *two broad rufous wing-bars and wide edging; tail bright rufous.* Throat streaked olive and yellowish, breast and flanks olive with blurry yellowish streaking, midbelly yellow. No other similar tyrannid shares the contrasting rufous tail and extensive rufous in wings. Found singly or in pairs, favoring areas with an open understory; often perches quietly on unobstructed branches or lianas. Generally not with mixed flocks. Distinctive call a mournful "preeyeé-yoú," the first note drawn out and mournful, the second shorter and more abrupt, almost as if in reply. Often vocalizes through the day.

Brownish Twistwing
Cnipodectes subbrunneus　　　PLATE 50(10)

♂ 18 cm (7"), ♀ 15.5 cm (6"). Uncommon in tangled, often viny lower growth of humid and semihumid forest and woodland from *w. Colombia to w. and cen. Amazonia.* Mostly below 600 m. Fairly wide bill, pale below; *orangy eye. Mostly dull brown, rufescent on rump and rather long tail;* wings duskier with rufous edging. *Throat and breast brown,* belly dingy yellowish white. ♂'s outer primaries are stiff and twisted, often evident in the field, making the wing look "messy." Royal flycatchers have differently shaped heads, spots on wing-coverts, etc. Twistwings are usually found singly, rarely or never with flocks. They often slowly stretch a wing up over back. Displaying ♂♂ are heard more often than seen, and tend to be very sedentary. Song a sharp "keeéuw," often doubled and sometimes accompanied by bill snapping. Call an arresting and more nasal "kuuuwit!"; also often doubled. Also: Panama.

Onychorhynchus

Spectacularly crested, the otherwise rather drab royal flycatchers are *surprisingly inconspicuous* midsized tyrannids that range in the understory of lowland forest and woodland. Though basically similar in plumage, they are now generally treated as four allospecies. Their very long pendulous nests are usually suspended over a shady stream.

Amazonian Royal Flycatcher
*Onychorhynchus coronatus** PLATE 50(11)
16 cm (6″). Uncommon in lower growth of humid and deciduous forest and woodland in *Amazonia and the Guianas; favors várzea forest and swampy areas near streams.* Mostly below 1000 m. *The spectacular crest is only rarely seen. Long flat bill;* legs yellowish flesh. Dull brown above with buff spots on wing-coverts; *rump cinnamon-rufous, tail rufous.* Throat whitish, below ochraceous-buff, breast with narrow dark barring. **Immature** shows irregular barring above. *Expanded crest is a large, semicircular fan of shiny scarlet feathers (orangy in ♀) with a few black spots and broad steel-blue tips; it is held perpendicular to body's axis.* Even when closed the crest protrudes to the rear, imparting a distinct *hammerhead effect;* usually a bit of color also shows. Not likely confused, but cf. the other royal flycatchers (all allopatric) and Brownish Twistwing. Generally forages quietly in undergrowth, most often alone. Makes quick sallies to foliage in pursuit of insects. Preening birds occasionally open their crest (its primary function remains uncertain), as may birds perched near their nest. Mist-netted birds invariably reveal it, and they also twist their head rhythmically from side to side while also slowly opening and closing the bill. Not especially vocal, but gives a whistled "preeé-o" or "keee-you," sometimes in series, recalling a *Manacus* manakin or *Galbula* jacamar.

Northern Royal Flycatcher
*Onychorhynchus mexicanus**
16.5 cm (6½″). Uncommon and rather local in lower growth of humid and deciduous forest and woodland, especially near streams, in *n. Colombia and nw. Venezuela.* Mostly below 1400 m. Resembles Amazonian Royal Flycatcher, with similar spectacular crest and long flat bill, but has a more mottled breast and a *paler bright cinnamon tail.* Other royal flycatchers are allopatric; otherwise not likely confused. Behavior and voice much as in Amazonian Royal Flycatcher. Also: Mexico to Panama.

Pacific Royal Flycatcher
*Onychorhynchus occidentalis** PLATE 50(12)
16.5 cm (6½″). Rare to uncommon and local in lower growth of deciduous and semihumid forest and woodland in *w. Ecuador* (north to w. Esmeraldas) *and extreme nw. Peru* (Tumbes). Mostly below 600 m. Resembles Amazonian Royal Flycatcher, with same *spectacular crest, hammerhead effect,* and *long flat bill;* larger and brighter generally. *Above cinnamon-brown* with buff wing-covert dots, *rump and tail cinnamon; orange-ochraceous below* (*no* breast barring). Other royal flycatchers are allopatric; otherwise not likely confused. Behavior and voice much as in Amazonian Royal Flycatcher.

Atlantic Royal Flycatcher
*Onychorhynchus swainsoni** PLATE 50(13)
16.5 cm (6½″). Rare and local in lower growth of humid forest in *se. Brazil* (e. Minas Gerais to n. Paraná). To 900 m. Resembles Amazonian Royal Flycatcher, and with the same *spectacular crest, hammerhead effect,* and *long flat bill,* but larger and in plumage more like the geographically distant Pacific Royal Flycatcher. *Below ochraceous-buff* (*no* breast barring). The other royal flycatchers are allopatric, and otherwise this species is of course not likely to be confused. Behavior and voice much as in Amazonian Royal Flycatcher.

Cinnamon Flycatcher
Pyrrhomyias cinnamomeus PLATE 51(1)
13 cm (5″). *Generally common and conspicuous* at shrubby borders of foothill and montane forest and woodland in Andes from n. Venezuela to nw. Argentina (Tucumán). 1200–3000 m. In **most of range** (A) olive brown above with a semiconcealed yellow coronal patch and cinnamon rump-band; wings blackish with *two broad cinnamon-rufous bars and broad secondary edging.* Below rich cinnamon-rufous. In **Venezuela and Santa Marta Mts.** (B) *rufous-chestnut above. No other small, montane tyrannid is so rufescent overall.* Found in rather sedentary pairs that perch erectly, frequently along roads or trailsides; at times remarkably confiding. Does not follow mixed flocks. Makes short sallies into air after flying insects, often repeatedly returning to same perch. Distinctive, oft-heard call a low-pitched dry rattle, "tr-r-r-r-r-r" or "dr-r-r-r-r-r."

Myiophobus

Small tyrannids that typically *perch upright,* *Myiophobus* flycatchers are found in a variety of habitats and situations (most favoring lower growth); most have *Andean distributions,* with only one species (Bran-colored) being more wide-ranging. Rather variable in form, they most resemble *Empidonax* flycatchers, but all *Myiophobus* have a coronal patch; wing-bars, if present, are usually buff rather than pale. The genus likely will need to be split apart.

Orange-crested Flycatcher
Myiophobus phoenicomitra   PLATE 51(2)
11.5 cm (4½"). Uncommon and inconspicuous in lower growth of foothill and lower montane forest in *Andes from w. Colombia to n. Peru* (San Martín). 500–1550 m. Bill black above, *fleshy yellow below.* Dark olive above with a *narrow yellow eye-ring* and semiconcealed orange-rufous coronal patch (absent in ♀♀; yellow in a few ♂♂); wings blackish with two ochraceous bars but *only a little edging.* Below pale yellow, brightest on belly, breast washed olive. Flavescent Flycatcher has an all-black bill, yellow supraloral, a more prominent (though broken) eye-ring, and more extensive edging on flight feathers; it tends to occur at *higher* elevations than Orange-crested. Color of crown patch is of little or no use in distinguishing them. Behavior as in Flavescent, but shyer and even less often out to edge. Song a weak, thin, high-pitched "tsut-tseép-tsu."

Flavescent Flycatcher
Myiophobus flavicans   PLATE 51(3)
12 cm (4¾"). Fairly common but inconspicuous in lower and mid-levels of montane forest in *Andes from n. Venezuela to s. Peru* (n. Cuzco). 1300–2500 m. *Bill all black.* Olive above with *prominent yellow supraloral and partial eye-ring* and semiconcealed yellow coronal patch (absent in ♀♀; orange in a few ♂♂); *dusky wings virtually plain other than flight feather edging* (in **Peru south of Río Marañón;** illustrated) or with *two ochraceous bars* (**northward**). Below yellow, brightest on belly, breast washed olive. Orange-crested Flycatcher is slightly smaller and darker above with an obvious pale lower mandible; it has a narrow but *complete* eye-ring (but *no* supraloral) and shows only a little edging on flight feathers. Orange-crested occurs at *lower* elevations than Flavescent. Cf. also Roraiman Flycatcher. Found singly or in pairs, perching

quietly inside forest, generally not with mixed flocks. Makes short sallies to foliage and into air. Not very vocal, with infrequently heard song a fast rhythmic series of about 5–8 "kawhik" notes.

Unadorned Flycatcher
Myiophobus inornatus
11.5 cm (4½"). Uncommon in lower and middle growth in montane forest and borders on *east slope of Andes from s. Peru* (Cuzco) *to w. Bolivia* (Cochabamba). 1000–2100 m. Resembles southern form of Flavescent Flycatcher (overlap at most marginal), differing in its slightly smaller size, *pale lower mandible* (bill all dark in Flavescent), *more prominent and complete yellow eye-ring* (accentuated by its dark lores), and *broader cinnamon-rufous wing-bars and edging.* Behavior much as in Flavescent Flycatcher. Call a sharp "tziit!," sometimes steadily repeated.

Roraiman Flycatcher
Myiophobus roraimae   PLATE 51(4)
13.5 cm (5¼"). *Rare and local* in lower and mid-levels of montane forest on *tepuis of s. Venezuela area,* and on *east slope of Andes from s. Ecuador* (Morona-Santiago) *to extreme w. Bolivia* (La Paz), *mainly on outlying ridges.* 1100–1700 m in Andes, but to 2000 m on tepuis. *Lower mandible yellow-orange.* Brown above with a pale yellowish eye-ring and semiconcealed orange-rufous coronal patch (small or lacking in ♀♀); blackish wings with *two bold cinnamon-rufous wing-bars and extensive flight feather edging.* Throat yellowish white, breast and flanks grayish olive, midbelly pale yellow. Larger than Flavescent Flycatcher and much browner above (not so olive) with more extensive rufous in wing. Euler's Flycatcher has no coronal patch and never shows extensive rufous in wings. Not well known, but quiet behavior seems much like Flavescent. Song in Ecuador a sharp, high-pitched "chit-tit, tsee-ee-ee-ee-ee-ee" (T. S. Schulenberg recording).

Orange-banded Flycatcher
Myiophobus lintoni   PLATE 51(5)
13 cm (5"). Locally not uncommon in canopy and borders of montane forest and woodland on *east slope of Andes in s. Ecuador* (north to nw. Morona-Santiago) *and extreme n. Peru* (n. Cajamarca). 2250–3200 m. *Fairly long tail.* Lower mandible orange. Dark brownish olive above with semiconcealed orange coronal patch (reduced or lacking in ♀♀); wings with *two bold pale cinnamon wing-bars* and narrow edging.

Mostly yellow below, throat whitish and chest tinged olive. Distinctive in its limited range. Handsome Flycatcher (not known to overlap) is smaller with a notably shorter tail, ochraceous on breast. Behavior as in Handsome, also at times in small groups. Characteristically perches atop large leaves, from there making short sallies, both to foliage and into air. Call a sharp and arresting "peeyk," given repeatedly as it forages.

Handsome Flycatcher
Myiophobus pulcher   PLATE 51(6)
10.5–11 cm (4–4¼"). Uncommon and local in canopy and borders of montane forest in *Andes from Colombia to extreme n. Peru, and in s. Peru* (Cuzco and Puno) *and w. Bolivia* (Cochabamba), where rare. Mostly 1500–2500 m. Lower mandible flesh-yellow. **West-slope birds** (illustrated) have crown grayish with white loral spot and narrow eye-ring, and semiconcealed orange-rufous coronal patch (reduced in ♀); above olive, wings dusky with *two bold pale ochraceous bars and prominent edging. Throat and breast dull ochraceous,* belly clear yellow. **East-slope birds** slightly larger, and with *deeper ochraceous wing-bars and breast.* Orange-banded Flycatcher (little or no overlap) is larger and longer-tailed; lacks buff below. Rufous-breasted Flycatcher (a bird of lower growth) is larger with longer tail, and rufous extends up onto face. An arboreal tyrannid that often forages with mixed flocks. It tends to perch more horizontally and to forage actively, making short sallies to foliage. Song a rather sharp and clear "tsi-tsi-tsi."

Ochraceous-breasted Flycatcher
Myiophobus ochraceiventris   PLATE 51(7)
14 cm (5½"). Uncommon in canopy and borders of montane forest and woodland on *east slope of Andes from n. Peru* (s. Amazonas) *to w. Bolivia* (La Paz), most numerous *near treeline.* Mostly 2500–3400 m. Bill all black. Above dark brownish olive with narrow ochraceous supraloral and semiconcealed coronal patch (duller and darker in ♀♀); wings dusky with *two bold buffy whitish bars and edging. Throat and breast orange-ochraceous, extending onto sides of neck;* belly bright yellow. Orange-banded Flycatcher replaces this species north of the Río Marañón. Handsome Flycatcher is markedly smaller and shorter-tailed, not as dark above, etc. Behavior much as in Orange-banded Flycatcher. Habitually accompanies mixed flocks, often perching conspicuously atop large leaves. Call a sharp

"tchew-it," often accompanied by more twittering notes.

Bran-colored Flycatcher
Myiophobus fasciatus   PLATE 51(8)
12–12.5 cm (4¾–5"). *Often common* in shrubby clearings and pastures, lighter woodland, and borders from Colombia and Venezuela to n. Argentina (Buenos Aires). *The most widespread Myiophobus,* but absent from much of Amazonia. Mostly below 1500 m, locally to 2700 m in Andean valleys. In **most of range** (A) *reddish brown above* with a weak whitish supraloral and semiconcealed yellow coronal patch (faint or absent in ♀♀); wings dusky with two broad buff bars. Whitish below, *breast and sides with brown streaking,* belly sometimes yellowish. From **sw. Colombia** to **nw. Peru** (south to Lambayeque) *duller, more grayish brown above* and streaking below also more grayish. From **La Libertad in w. Peru to extreme n. Chile** (B) very different (same species?), with *plain cinnamon underparts.* In w. Amazonia cf. similar Olive-chested Flycatcher. Neither Euler's nor Fuscous shows streaking below, and neither is as rufescent above as most Bran-coloreds. Gray-breasted Flycatcher lacks streaking below (it has more of a gray wash). Found singly or in pairs, perching low and upright; though sometimes in the open, generally not a conspicuous bird. Makes short sallies in pursuit of insects, both into air and to foliage. Song a "wee-ub" or "wee-eb" note, sometimes given in a protracted series. Frequent call a fast "whee-deedeedeedee." Calls of northwestern birds include a wheezy "whis? whee-yee" and a fast "whee-yee-yee-yee-yee-yee." In n. Chile a 1-second slow trilling has been reported (A. Jaramillo). Also: Costa Rica and Panama.

Olive-chested Flycatcher
Myiophobus cryptoxanthus   PLATE 51(9)
12 cm (4¾"). Fairly common to common in shrubby clearings, pastures, and light secondary woodland and borders in foothills, lower subtropics, and adjacent lowlands along *eastern base of Andes in Ecuador and n. Peru* (San Martín). Increasing because of deforestation. Mostly 300–1600 m. *Above dull grayish olive-brown* with faint whitish supraloral and a semiconcealed yellow coronal patch (smaller in ♀♀); wings dusky with two pale buff bars. Throat whitish, *breast and sides with blurry grayish olive streaking, belly pale yellow.* Sometimes occurs with Bran-colored Flycatcher (where they overlap, Olive-chested is more numerous); these Bran-coloreds are mark-

edly more rufescent above and have browner breast streaking and a whiter belly. Not known to occur with duller west-slope Bran-coloreds. Cf. also Euler's Flycatcher. Behavior much as in Bran-colored. Song a repeated "chwee . . . chwee . . . chwee. . . . ." Calls include a spritely "weee d'd'd'd'd'd'd?"

Ornate Flycatcher
Myiotriccus ornatus   PLATE 51(10)
12 cm (4¾"). *Common and conspicuous at borders of foothill and montane forest in Andes from n. Colombia to s. Peru* (Puno). Mostly 600–2000 m, lower in nw. Ecuador. Unmistakable. *Head and throat gray*, blacker on face and crown, with *obvious white preocular patch* and semiconcealed yellow coronal stripe; back dark olive, *rump bright yellow; tail dusky with rufous at base* (**west slope;** A), or *tail all rufous* (**east slope;** B). Breast olive, belly bright yellow. A cute, perky little flycatcher found in pairs that often sit close together, perching upright at low to middle heights, making short sallies into the air. They seem sedentary and do not accompany flocks. Call a sharp, high-pitched and emphatic "wheep!" or "peeyp!" often with a short chipper appended.

Myiobius

Acrobatic, small flycatchers of lowland forests and woodlands that have a *characteristic yellow rump* and black tail. The genus is easy to recognize, though identification of the various species (usually called "flycatchers") can present difficulties. They have notably long rictal bristles. None is particularly vocal.

Whiskered Myiobius
*Myiobius barbatus**   PLATE 51(11)
12.5 cm (5"). Uncommon to fairly common in lower growth of humid forest in *Amazonia and the Guianas*. Mostly below 900 m. Sometimes considered conspecific with Yellow-rumped and Sulphur-rumped Myiobius. Above olive, ♂ with yellow coronal patch (usually concealed); *conspicuous sulphur yellow rump* and rather rounded *black tail*. *Throat and breast grayish olive;* belly pale yellow. Black-tailed Myiobius is dull buff on throat and breast, tends to occur in younger, more secondary habitats. Whiskered is a forest-interior bird that often accompanies understory flocks; forages actively and often pirouettes, fan-

ning its tail and drooping its wings. Quiet, but occasionally gives a sharp "psik."

Yellow-rumped Myiobius
*Myiobius mastacalis**   PLATE 51(12)
12.5 cm (5"). Uncommon and local in lower growth of humid forest and woodland in *e. Brazil* (Paraíba to ne. Santa Catarina, and in s. Goiás). To about 1000 m. Above olive, ♂ with yellow coronal patch (usually concealed); *conspicuous sulphur yellow rump* and rather rounded *black tail*. Throat whitish, *breast tawny,* belly yellow. Potentially sympatric Black-tailed Myiobius is similar, but uniform yellowish buff below, lacking the tawny seen in this species. Behavior much as in Whiskered Myiobius.

Sulphur-rumped Myiobius
*Myiobius sulphureipygius**
12.5 cm (5"). Uncommon to fairly common in lower growth of humid forest and woodland in *w. Colombia and w. Ecuador* (south to w. Loja). Mostly below 1000 m. Above olive, ♂ with yellow coronal patch (usually concealed); *conspicuous sulphur yellow rump* and rather rounded *black tail*. Throat whitish, *breast and flanks bright tawny,* midbelly bright yellow. Black-tailed Myiobius is dull buff on throat and breast; favors secondary habitats. Tawny-breasted Myiobius, found in more montane areas, is larger and more uniformly tawny-brown below, showing much less yellow on belly. Behavior much as in Whiskered Myiobius. Also: Mexico to Panama.

Black-tailed Myiobius
*Myiobius atricaudus**   PLATE 51(13)
12.5 cm (5"). Locally fairly common in lower growth of secondary woodland and humid forest borders, usually near water, from n. Colombia to se. Brazil. To 1400 m in w. Colombia. Resembles Whiskered, Yellow-rumped, and Sulphur-rumped, with equally *conspicuous sulphur yellow rump*. **West of Andes** and in **Amazonia** *throat, breast, and flanks drab buff to olive buff,* belly yellow. In **e. Brazil** more uniform below, *plain yellow* in **northeast,** *plain yellowish buff* in **southeast.** Sulphur-rumped Myiobius (west of Andes) readily distinguished from Black-tailed there on the basis of its bright tawny breast. Whiskered Myiobius in w. Amazonia is more similar to Black-tailed but drabber and more olive on breast (not so buff); in e. Amazonia the two species are especially similar (both being buffy on breast) but Whiskered *lacks* buff on flanks (present in Black-tailed). Yellow-rumped

Myiobius of e. Brazil again shows tawny on breast. Behavior much as in those three species, but not as spritely or acrobatic. Also: Costa Rica and Panama.

Tawny-breasted Myiobius
*Myiobius villosus** PLATE 51(14)
14 cm (5½"). Uncommon in lower and middle growth of foothill and lower montane forest and woodland in *Andes from w. Venezuela* (Mérida) *to w. Bolivia* (La Paz). Mostly 1000–1800 m. Occurs at *higher elevations* than its congeners. *Dark* brownish olive above, brownest on head, ♂'s yellow coronal patch usually concealed (cinnamon or lacking in ♀); *conspicuous sulphur yellow rump* and rather rounded black tail. Throat whitish; *breast tawny-brown extending broadly down flanks and onto crissum,* only midbelly is pale yellow. Sulphur-rumped Myiobius is smaller and paler and brighter below, with a bright tawny breast. Behavior as in its congeners, though less active and agile, and more often forages higher above the ground. Also: e. Panama.

Ruddy-tailed Flycatcher
Terenotriccus erythrurus PLATE 51(15)
10 cm (4"). *Fairly common and widespread* in lower and middle growth of humid forest and woodland from Colombia and Venezuela to Amazonia and the Guianas. Mostly below 1100 m. Legs yellowish. Head and neck olive gray, back browner, *cinnamon on rump,* and *rufous on tail;* wings dusky with *broadly edged cinnamon-rufous.* Below cinnamon-buff, throat whiter. Cf. the similar *but much rarer* Cinnamon Neopipo. Otherwise this cute, large-eyed flycatcher with its very long rictal bristles is not apt to be confused, but cf. Ochre-bellied Flycatcher. Found singly, perching erectly on open branches, sallying to capture small insects. Sometimes accompanies understory flocks, but also moves about on its own. Occasionally twitches a wing up over back. Frequent call a weak thin "pseeoo-pseé," the second note sharper. Also: Mexico to Panama.

Mitrephanes

Two small, peweelike tyrannids found at edge of Andean forests, both recognizable from their *obvious crests.*

Northern Tufted Flycatcher
*Mitrephanes phaeocercus** PLATE 52(1)
12.5 cm (5"). Uncommon in borders of humid lowland and foothill forest in *w. Colombia*

and nw. Ecuador (mainly Esmeraldas). Mostly 100–600 m. Has been called Common Tufted Flycatcher. *Pointed crest.* Lower mandible yellow. Olive above with whitish loral spot and inconspicuous eye-ring; wings dusky with two narrow grayish bars. *Throat and breast olive-buff, belly yellow.* Though vaguely like a pewee, *no similar flycatcher with yellow on underparts shows such a prominent crest.* Found singly and in pairs, this perky flycatcher perches upright on open branches, generally not too high above the ground; does not follow flocks. Sallies into air in pursuit of insects, often returning to the same perch, sometimes making several short sallies in quick succession. Usually quivers tail upon alighting. Oft-heard call a fast series of "pee" or "pik" notes. Song a repeated fast phrase of high, thin notes, e.g. "tsu-tsu-tseét." Also: Mexico to Panama.

Olive Tufted Flycatcher
Mitrephanes olivaceus PLATE 52(2)
13 cm (5¼"). Uncommon in lower and middle growth of montane forest and borders on *east slope of Andes from n. Peru* (Amazonas, south of Río Marañón) *to w. Bolivia* (w. Santa Cruz). 1200–2100 m. Resembles Northern Tufted Flycatcher (no overlap), and *equally crested,* but slightly larger; *below more or less uniform buffy-olive.* Behavior much as in Northern Tufted. Calls include a sharp "psii" or "psii-ptii" (S. Herzog recording) or "psi-ii, tutututu" (T. S. Schulenberg recording).

Lathrotriccus

Two *drab, Empidonax*-like flycatchers that range in forest and woodland undergrowth, where they are inconspicuous aside from their vocalizations.

Euler's Flycatcher
Lathrotriccus euleri PLATE 52(3)
13–13.5 cm (5–5¼"). *Widespread and locally common* (most so southward) in lower growth of humid forest, secondary woodland, and borders from e. Colombia and Venezuela to n. Argentina. To at least 1500 m. **Northern birds** (illustrated) *brownish olive above* with obscure whitish supraloral and obvious eye-ring; wings dusky with *two dull buff wing-bars* and edging; tail olive brown. Throat grayish white, becoming brownish olive on breast and pale yellow on belly. **Southern birds** are slightly larger and browner above and whiter on belly. Willow and

Alder Flycatchers are never as brown above and their wing-bars are not so buff; Euler's is more of a forest bird. Fuscous Flycatcher differs in its all-black bill and well-marked whitish superciliary. Inconspicuous, tending to remain in forest and woodland undergrowth, there perching upright and sallying to foliage; usually not with mixed flocks. Song a series of burry notes, "zhweé, zhwee-zhwee-zhwee" recalling Gray-breasted Flycatcher; also gives a simpler "zhwee-buu." Dawn song a less burry "beeu . . . beeu-wheéu," recalling an *Elaenia*. Also: Grenada.

Gray-breasted Flycatcher
Lathrotriccus griseipectus   PLATE 52(4)
13 cm (5"). *Now uncommon and local in lower growth of humid and deciduous forest and woodland from w. Ecuador* (w. Esmeraldas) *to nw. Peru* (Lambayeque). To 1700 m in s. Ecuador. Grayish olive above with *supraloral and eye-ring white,* wings dusky with *two bold white bars.* Throat pale grayish, *breast gray,* belly yellowish white. **Juvenile** has buffier wing-bars and yellower belly. Looks rather gray in the field, which combined with the eye-ring and supraloral should preclude confusion. Tumbes Pewee is somewhat larger and lacks spectacles and prominent wing-bars; behavior differs, the pewee taking prominent perches at borders (not remaining inside). Behavior much as in Euler's Flycatcher. Tolerates drier areas and favors viny tangles. Like Euler's, most apt to be noted when vocalizing. Song a burry "zhweéur zhweer-zhwer-zhwer." Most vocal during rainy season (Jan.–May).

Black-billed Flycatcher
Aphanotriccus audax
13.5 cm (5¼"). Uncommon in lower growth of humid forest and woodland in *n. Colombia* (east locally to Cesar and Santander). To 700 m. *Short black bill.* Olive above with *white supraloral and broken eye-ring;* wings duskier with two pale buff bars. Throat whitish, breast clouded olive, belly pale yellow. Size and plumage recall Acadian Flycatcher (which winters with it), but note the (well-named) Black-billed's all-black bill (lower mandible *not* pale) and pale supraloral (not just an eye-ring). Sepia-capped Flycatcher has very different facial pattern. Fuscous Flycatcher is browner above with longer superciliary, bolder wing-bars. Black-billed is an inconspicuous small tyrannid of shady places, favoring areas near streams and swamps. Found singly or in pairs, generally not with mixed flocks. Distinctive call a sharp, burry "jee-jee-jew." Also: e. Panama.

Empidonax

Three drab *boreal migrant* flycatchers, difficult to distinguish from each other except by *voice.* Fortunately their vocalizations are reasonably distinctive and are given quite often on their wintering grounds.

Acadian Flycatcher
Empidonax virescens
14 cm (5½"). *Uncommon boreal migrant* (Oct.–Mar.) to lower growth of humid and semihumid forest, woodland, and plantations from *w. Colombia and nw. Venezuela to sw. Ecuador* (El Oro). Mostly below 1500 m. *Olive above* with whitish lores and *yellowish white eye-ring;* wings dusky with two bold whitish bars. Throat whitish, breast pale olive gray, flanks and crissum yellowish olive, midbelly whitish. **Juvenile** has buffier wing-bars and is yellower below, especially on belly. Acadian closely resembles the Willow and Alder Flycatcher pair, but note that for the most part Willows and Alders occur *east* of the Andes, Acadians *west* of them. Acadians tend to be more olive above and yellowish below, and to have a more prominent eye-ring. Found singly in shady lower growth, perching upright and sallying to foliage (Willows and Alders favor more open habitats). Distinctive call a sharp inflected "wheeyk," often repeated endlessly. Breeds in e. North America.

Willow Flycatcher
Empidonax traillii

Alder Flycatcher
Empidonax alnorum
14 cm (5½"). *Two very similar boreal migrants* (Sep.–Apr.), uncommon to fairly common in shrubby clearings, lighter woodland, river islands, and borders, *mainly in w. Amazonia.* Mostly below 1000 m, transients higher. Brownish to grayish olive with an inconspicuous whitish eye-ring (often lacking); wings dusky with two bold whitish bars. Throat whitish, breast pale grayish to brownish olive, belly yellowish white. **Juvenile** browner above with buffier wing-bars, belly yellower. It is nearly impossible to distinguish the two species by plumage, though Alders tend to be more olive (less grayish) above and can show more of an eye-ring (even extending to lores). Wood pewees can also look similar, though they are more crested, have weaker wing-bars, and never show an eye-ring; perched pewees do not flick their tail, a frequent *Empidonax* mannerism. Alders and Willows are usually

seen singly, often perching atop bushes, usually near water; they sally both to foliage and into the air. *Willows winter in Middle America and nw. South America, Alders mainly in w. Amazonia.* Alder's call is a sharp flat "peep" or "tip," not always easy to tell from Willow's more liquid "whit." Alder's song, heard rather often, is a burry "free-breéo," with accent on *second* syllable. Willow's is a snappy "wítz-bew," with accent on *first* syllable. Both species breed in North America.

Fuscous Flycatcher
Cnemotriccus fuscatus *　　　　　PLATE 52(5)
14.5 cm (5¾"). Widespread and fairly common in undergrowth of gallery and secondary woodland, forest borders, and (in Amazonia) on river islands from Colombia and Venezuela to n. Argentina (Santa Fé); withdraws from southern areas during austral winter. Mostly below 900 m, but to at least 2200 m in w. Bolivia (perhaps not same species). *Drab* and *inconspicuous;* rather long tail. In **most of range** (illustrated) grayish to rufescent brown above with *whitish superciliary;* wings dusky with *two broad buff bars* and edging. Throat whitish, breast olive brownish, belly pale yellow. In **Amazonia** has a less distinct superciliary and duller wing-bars. Euler's Flycatcher (often with Fuscous) similar but lacks the superciliary. Mouse-colored Tyrannulet has a shorter bill and very different behavior and voice. Favors shady undergrowth, rarely coming to edge and avoiding open places; in some areas usually near water. Vocalizations vary. In most of range gives a fast, gravelly "wor, jeér-jeér-jeér-jeér-jeér-jeér-jew" and a more piercing "wheéeeu" at rather long intervals. In Bolivian highlands gives a much higher-pitched and more piercing, jumbled "weeyk-weeyk-weeyk-weeyk-cheedidi?" (S. Herzog recording).

Contopus

Drab, small to midsized tyrannids that *perch erectly at forest edge, sallying into the air* in pursuit of insects. All pewees are some shade of grayish to blackish, and they show a slight crest. Identification to species level can be difficult, with silent birds posing a particular challenge.

Blackish Pewee
Contopus nigrescens 　　　　　PLATE 52(6)
13 cm (5"). *Rare to uncommon and very local in canopy and borders of humid forest in foothills* and adjacent lowlands on east slope of Andes in Ecuador and Peru, also *very locally in e. Amazonia.* Mostly 400–1000 m. *Uniform dark gray,* blackest on crown, wings, and tail. Nearly identical in color to the much more numerous Smoke-colored Pewee, *which ranges mainly at higher elevations.* Aside from being larger, Smoke-colored can be known by its bushy crest, much more noticeable than in Blackish. Blackish usually perches very high in tall trees, where it doubtless often goes unnoticed; it favors forest edge and openings, often near streams. Pairs are sedentary and often found in the same area (even in the same tree) day after day. They make long sallies into the air, usually shivering tail upon alighting. Song a snappy but somewhat burry "chí-bew" repeated at intervals of 3–4 seconds. Both sexes give a repeated sharp "pip" or "peep" call, sometimes in an irregular series.

White-throated Pewee
Contopus albogularis
13 cm (5"). Rare and local in canopy and borders of humid forest in *Suriname, French Guiana, and extreme n. Brazil* (Amapá). Mostly 400–500 m. Lower mandible yellow-orange. *Dark gray* with *large throat patch white.* Aside from the throat patch, resembles Blackish Pewee (no overlap). Tropical Pewee is never as dark, and in any case lacks the contrasting white throat. Behavior much as in Blackish Pewee, likewise very sedentary; tends not to perch as high (more frequently 8–12 m up), repeatedly returning to the same branches. Soft "pik" call can be given interminably. Dawn song a repeated "free-bit, wheeyr, wheeyr."

Tropical Pewee
Contopus cinereus 　　　　　PLATE 52(7)
14 cm (5½"). Widespread and fairly common in forest borders, secondary and lighter woodland, clearings, plantations, and locally even in mangroves from Colombia and Venezuela to n. Argentina, but absent from much of Amazonia. Mostly below 1500 m. Lower mandible yellowish. In **most of range** (A) grayish olive above with *whitish lores* and usually a darker crown; wings dusky with two whitish to pale grayish bars. Throat whitish, breast and flanks olive grayish, midbelly whitish to pale yellowish. In **se. Brazil area** (B) *darker and grayer generally,* lores less pale and with weak wing-bars. The *very* similar wood pewees are slightly larger, lack pale lores, and have different calls. Cf. also Tumbes Pewee (no overlap), and the Alder and

Willow Flycatcher pair. Usually found singly, often perching on exposed branches; quivers tail upon alighting after a sally. Vocalizations vary across its broad range (all same species?), with northern birds giving a fast dry "sree-ip," those in nw. Argentina a clear "pe-wheer" (J. M. Barnett recording), those in se. Brazil a frequent "pip-pip-pip."

Tumbes Pewee
*Contopus punensis**
14 cm (5½"). Uncommon in borders of deciduous and semihumid woodland and forest and adjacent clearings from *sw. Ecuador* (Manabí) *to w. Peru* (Ica), also in *upper Río Marañón valley of Peru.* Locally to over 2000 m in Peru. Formerly considered conspecific with Tropical Pewee. Closely resembles that species (no overlap), differing mainly in *voice.* Gray-breasted Flycatcher (sympatric) is smaller and shows an obvious eyering and supraloral, as well as bolder wing-bars, it inhabits forest and woodland *undergrowth.* Behavior much as in Tropical Pewee, also shivering its tail upon alighting. Call a clear "peee pir" or "peee, pidit," with quality reminiscent of Southern Beardless Tyrannulet, markedly different from Tropical.

Eastern Wood Pewee
Contopus virens

Western Wood Pewee
Contopus sordidulus
14.5 cm (5¾"). *Two very similar boreal migrants* (Sep.–Apr.) to forest borders and shrubby clearings in w. South America, both of them locally common, *Eastern mainly in lowlands of w. Amazonia, Western primarily on Andean slopes.* Eastern ranges mostly below 600 m (migrants higher), Western mostly 400–1700 m. Lower mandible yellowish in Eastern, bill usually all dark in Western. Both species closely resemble typical Tropical Pewee, though they do not show such pale lores; Westerns tend to be darker and more uniform below. These pewees are so similar that they usually cannot be distinguished by appearance alone; fortunately, even when not breeding, they often sing their name. Eastern's most frequent call is a sweet plaintive "pee-wee?" sometimes interspersed with a burrier downslurred "pee-ur." The full song, "pee-a-wee," is given much less often. Western's most frequent call is a melancholy and burry "preeer" or "freeer," typically a single note. Full song is a burry "preé-ur," sometimes with a "pur-

didi" interspersed. Both species breed in North America.

Smoke-colored Pewee
Contopus fumigatus   PLATE 52(8)
17–17.5 cm (6¾–7"). Fairly common and conspicuous in borders of montane forest and adjacent clearings in *Andes from n. Venezuela to nw. Argentina* (Tucumán), and on *tepuis of s. Venezuela area.* Mostly 800–2600 m. *Bushy crest usually prominent.* Color varies clinally; **southern birds** (north to s. Bolivia; A) are paler olivaceous gray; **northern birds** (south to s. Peru; B) *uniform dark gray.* Juvenile less crested and somewhat paler, especially below. Much rarer Blackish Pewee has coloration similar to northern races but is far smaller (smaller than even the wood pewees). Olive-sided Flycatcher has similar behavior but is less crested, shorter-tailed, and does not look so uniform. The other pewees are markedly smaller, less gray, and show much less of a crest. Usually perches in the open, frequently on tall snags; sallies into air, often flying out great distances and repeatedly returning to the same perch. Oft-heard call a loud "pip-pip-pip," typically tripled (but sometimes 2 or 4 notes). Song of northern birds (e.g., Ecuador and Peru), given mainly at dawn, a series of "wu-didit, weeu" or "weeeuw, wu-didit!" or "weu, weedit" phrases; southern birds (e.g., in Argentina) give a subdued "per-wheer."

Olive-sided Flycatcher
*Contopus cooperi**   PLATE 52(9)
18 cm (7"). *Uncommon boreal migrant* (mostly Sep.–May) to borders of foothill and montane forest and adjacent clearings to w. South America, smaller numbers scattering farther east and in lowlands. Mostly 400–2000 m, transients lower. Formerly called *Contopus borealis. Rather bull-headed* and *distinctly short-tailed.* Dark grayish olive above; wings dusky with two pale grayish bars. Throat and median underparts whitish, with *olive grayish sides and flanks almost extending across breast* (suggesting a dark, unbuttoned vest); *a tuft of white sometimes protrudes from behind wing onto sides of rump.* Pewees are smaller with proportionately longer tails; they never have such a vested look, nor do they show the white tuft. The longer-tailed and more crested Smoke-colored Pewee is much more evenly gray below. Olive-sideds habitually perch on high snags or branches, launching out for long distances after insects, often returning to the same branch. Call a loud, typically tripled

"pip-pip-pip" (similar to Smoke-colored). The true song is heard less often in South America, a far-carrying "hic, three-beers." Breeds in North America.

Black Phoebe
Sayornis nigricans   PLATE 52(10)
17.5 cm (7"). *Fairly common along Andean streams and rivers from n. Venezuela to nw. Argentina* (Catamarca). Mostly 500–2800 m. *Favors semiopen areas, but also occurs in forested regions.* Unmistakable. **Northern birds** (illustrated) *sooty black with lower midbelly white. Wings with two indistinct white bars, feathers narrowly edged white;* outer web of outer pair of tail feathers also white. **Southern birds** (north to Bolivia) have broader white wing-edging. Only possible confusion is with the much smaller (and really quite different) Torrent Tyrannulet. Usually in pairs, confiding and often seen around buildings and bridges. Black Phoebes perch in the open, generally not far above the ground, sometimes on rocks out in the water; the tail is periodically jerked upward. Feeds by sallying short distances into the air after insects. Infrequently heard song a rather shrill "zhrreeee, pseekiyu," recalling Tropical Kingbird. Also: sw. United States to Panama (same species?).

Vermilion Flycatcher
Pyrocephalus rubinus   PLATE 52(11)
14.5–15 cm (5¾–6"). *Widespread, conspicuous, and often common* in semiopen areas with scattered bushes and trees, regularly around houses and farm buildings, from Colombia and Venezuela to n. Chile and cen. Argentina; southern breeders move into Amazonia during austral winter. To about 3000 m. *Dazzling ♂* unmistakable; *crown and underparts brilliant scarlet,* contrasting with sooty blackish upperparts and narrow mask through eyes. **Southern-breeding ♀** (A) *ashy brown above,* paler on forehead and brow, and sootier on wings and tail; wings virtually plain. Whitish below with *extensive dusky streaking.* **Melanistic morph** of w. Peru and n. Chile (B) *uniform sooty;* this occurs in both sexes (up to 50 percent of birds around Lima are sooty). **West-slope ♀** (C) has less streaking below, and *belly and crissum extensively pink to reddish pink.* A few ♀♀ have yellow (not red) on underparts. Bran-colored Flycatcher and various ♀ *Knipolegus* are browner above and have wingbars; they never show any red, of course, and unlike Vermilions rarely perch in the open. Sallies for insects, most often dropping to the ground,

but also flying into the air. Breeding ♂♂ have a spectacular display in which they mount into the air and hover, all the while repeating a musical phrase, e.g., "pi-d'd'd'reeít." Displaying ♂♂ perform both in predawn and during the day. Austral migrants are silent or nearly so. Also: sw. United States to Nicaragua; Galápagos Islands (same species?).

Tumbes Tyrant
Tumbezia salvini   PLATE 53(1)
13.5 cm (5¼"). *Now rare to uncommon and local in arid scrub and woodland in nw. Peru* (Tumbes to La Libertad). To 800 m. Grayish olive above, blacker on cheeks, with *forehead and broad superciliary bright yellow;* wings blackish with *two white bars and edging,* outer tail feather edged white. *Below bright yellow.* This pretty flycatcher is unmistakable in its limited range. It favors dry washes where native vegetation has not been too heavily affected by grazing and cutting for firewood (sadly, not the case in very many areas). Forages within a few meters of the ground, usually perching horizontally, making short upward strikes to vegetation, sometimes raising or wagging its tail. Most often in dispersed pairs and not with flocks. Most frequent call a soft trill, "tr-rr-rr-rr," varied to "tr-rr-ree," given as it forages.

Patagonian Tyrant
Colorhamphus parvirostris   PLATE 53(2)
12 cm (4¾"). *Uncommon at borders of humid forest and in shrubby clearings in Chile* (breeding north to Valdivia, wintering north to Coquimbo) *and adjacent s. Argentina to Tierra del Fuego* (where rare). To 1000 m. Short bill. *Head and neck gray,* browner on crown and nape, with narrow white eye-ring and *prominent blackish patch on ear-coverts;* above olive brown, dusky wings with *two broad cinnamon-rufous bars.* Throat and breast gray, belly whitish. Not likely confused in its far southern range. An inconspicuous bird that perches erectly at varying heights, when nesting mainly remaining quite high. Often first noted from its distinctive call, a high-pitched and drawn-out "pseeeuwww."

Ochthoeca

Attractively patterned, midsized flycatchers found *in the Andes,* primarily at higher elevations; most chat-tyrants are quiet unobtrusive birds of forest undergrowth, though a few are more conspicuous. All species show a *bold superciliary,* and most have *prominent wing-bars.* Some species were recently placed in the genus *Silvicultrix,* but recent evidence has not supported this generic division. Nests are neat cups placed on or near the ground.

Blackish Chat-Tyrant
Ochthoeca nigrita *   PLATE 53(3)
12 cm (4¾"). Uncommon in lower growth and borders of montane forest and woodland in *Andes of w. Venezuela* (Mérida and Barinas to n. Táchira). 1500–2900 m. Formerly considered conspecific with Slaty-backed and Maroon-belted Chat-Tyrants. *All slaty blackish* except for *a bold white supraloral.* No other flycatcher in its range is similarly colored; Slaty-backed Chat-Tyrant (ranging to the south) is mostly chestnut below. Found in pairs, perching rather low and making short looping sallies into the air and to foliage, often returning to the same branch; generally not with mixed flocks. Favors areas near streams. Infrequent call a rather loud buzzy whistle, slightly descending (S. Hilty).

Slaty-backed Chat-Tyrant
Ochthoeca cinnamomeiventris   PLATE 53(4)
12 cm (4¾"). Fairly common in lower growth and borders of montane forest and woodland, *almost always near streams, in Andes from extreme sw. Venezuela* (s. Táchira) *to extreme n. Peru* (n. Cajamarca). Mostly 1700–2800 m. Slaty blackish above with *bold white supraloral.* Throat blackish; *breast and belly chestnut.* A small, short-tailed, *very dark* chat-tyrant; not likely confused. Behavior much like Blackish Chat-Tyrant, but Slaty-backed's presence seems even more tied to the vicinity of rushing water. Quite sedentary, not following mixed flocks. High-pitched call a drawn-out, sharp, "dzweeéyeeuw," surprisingly loud (presumably so as to carry over the sound of rushing water).

Maroon-belted Chat-Tyrant
Ochthoeca thoracica *   PLATE 53(5)
12.5 cm (5"). Uncommon in lower growth and borders of montane forest and woodland on *east slope of Andes from n. Peru* (Amazonas south of Río Marañón) *to w. Bolivia* (w. Santa Cruz). 1700–3200 m. In **most of range** (illustrated) slaty blackish with bold white supraloral and *wide maroon-chestnut chest band.* In **n. Peru** the chest band is slightly narrower. Not likely con-

fused; Slaty-backed Chat-Tyrant ranges only *north* of the Río Marañón. Behavior much as in Blackish and Slaty-backed Chat-Tyrants, likewise favoring areas near streams. Call a high-pitched "tseeeeeyeeee" recalling a *Pipreola* fruit-eater, sometimes followed by a sputter.

Yellow-bellied Chat-Tyrant
Ochthoeca diadema   PLATE 53(6)
12.5 cm (5"). Fairly common but inconspicuous in undergrowth of montane forest in *Andes from n. Venezuela to n. Peru* (Cajamarca). Mostly 2000–3100 m. In **most of range** (illustrated) brownish olive above, blacker on crown, with *yellow forehead and long broad superciliary;* wings duskier with two rufescent bars. *Yellowish below,* clouded olive on breast and flanks. In **Venezuela and n. Colombia** wing-bars obscure or lacking. *Yellow-bellied is much more extensively yellow than any other chat-tyrant.* Cf. Flavescent Flycatcher (with no superciliary, etc.). Color pattern recalls Citrine Warbler, though behavior very different. Found singly or in pairs, low in dense undergrowth where often hard to see, though once located can be quite tame. Does not seem to follow mixed flocks. Most frequent song a very dry trill, slightly inflected at the start, e.g., "tsueéurrrrr." Dawn song a shorter "psi-uw" repeated at intervals of several seconds.

Golden-browed Chat-Tyrant
Ochthoeca pulchella   PLATE 53(7)
12.5 cm (5"). Uncommon in undergrowth of montane forest on *east slope of Andes from n. Peru* (Amazonas south of Río Marañón) *to w. Bolivia* (w. Santa Cruz). Mostly 2000–3000 m. Dark brown above, grayer on head and neck, with *forehead and superciliary yellow;* wings dusky with *two broad and bright rufous bars.* Below gray, lower flanks and crissum buff. Kalinowski's Chat-Tyrant differs in having a white superciliary (yellow only on its frontal area) and somewhat less prominent rufous wing-bars. Unobtrusive and not often seen, though as with other chat-tyrants dependent on forest, mist-netting can reveal it to be not uncommon. Calls include an inflected "pweet?" and a burrier "pee pr-eeee?".

Jelski's Chat-Tyrant
Ochthoeca jelskii   PLATE 53(8)
12.5 cm (5"). Now uncommon and local in undergrowth of montane forest and woodland in *Andes from s. Ecuador* (Loja) *to nw. Peru* (w. Huánuco and Lima). 2200–2800 m. Brown

above, blackish on crown and gray on nape, with *superciliary bright yellow in front of eye but white behind;* wings dusky with *two bold rufous bars.* Below gray with dull buff crissum (more extensive in ♀). Crowned Chat-Tyrant, which has a similar superciliary, differs principally in having *plain* wings. Golden-browed Chat-Tyrant has entirely yellow superciliary. Behavior much as in Golden-browed, though Jelski's seems more tolerant of disturbed, fragmented habitat (a good thing, given that so much of its range is mainly deforested). Song a high-pitched and sharp "tseeeee!" lasting about a second. Excited birds can vary this to a "tseee-krrrr."

Crowned Chat-Tyrant
Ochthoeca frontalis   PLATE 53(9)

12.5 cm (5"). Uncommon in undergrowth of montane forest and woodland in *Andes from n. Colombia to n. Peru* (e. La Libertad). Mostly 2600–3800 m. In **most of range** (illustrated) dark brown above, blackish on crown and grayer on nape, with *superciliary bright yellow in front of eye but white behind;* wings dusky and *unmarked.* Below gray with a dull buff crissum. In **Colombia's E. Andes** *entire superciliary white.* Jelski's Chat-Tyrant has prominent rufous wing-bars; in the area of overlap, Crowned occurs only on Andes' east slope (Jelski's westward). Behavior much as in Yellow-bellied Chat-Tyrant. Song a drawn-out, rather high-pitched but descending trill, "ssrrrrrrrrrrr."

Kalinowski's Chat-Tyrant
*Ochthoeca spodionota**

12.5 cm (5"). Uncommon in undergrowth of montane forest on *east slope of Andes from cen. Peru* (Huánuco) *to w. Bolivia* (w. Santa Cruz). Mostly 2000–3100 m. Formerly considered conspecific with Crowned Chat-Tyrant. Resembles Crowned and replaces it southward. Kalinowski's differs in usually showing *fairly prominent rufous wing-bars* (though sometimes they are faint) but has little or no buff on crissum. Golden-browed Chat-Tyrant differs in its fully yellow superciliary (not white with a yellow front); it tends to occur at somewhat lower elevations. Behavior much as in Yellow-bellied Chat-Tyrant. Song a leisurely series of rising "pseee?" notes, sometimes followed or interspersed with a sputter.

Rufous-breasted Chat-Tyrant
Ochthoeca rufipectoralis   PLATE 53(10)

13.5 cm (5¼"). Fairly common in borders of upper montane forest and woodland in *Andes*

from *n. Colombia to w. Bolivia* (w. Santa Cruz). Mostly 2500–3600 m. In **most of range** (south to Junín, Peru; illustrated) brown above, blacker on head with *long white superciliary;* wings blackish with *a single broad rufous bar,* outer web of outer pair of tail feathers white. Throat grayish, *chest orange-rufous,* underparts white. In **s. Peru and Bolivia** *wings are plain.* No other chat-tyrant has the obvious rufous across chest. More arboreal and conspicuous than most forest-based chat-tyrants (which favor undergrowth), usually perching in pairs from mid-levels up into subcanopy, often in the semiopen. Makes short sallies into air and to foliage. Sometimes active around mixed flocks but does not seem to follow them, and pairs are often seen on their own. Frequently gives a loud and harsh chatter, "ch-brrr, ch-brrr, ch-brrr."

White-browed Chat-Tyrant
Ochthoeca leucophrys   PLATE 53(11)

14.5–15 cm (5¾–6"). Rare and local in montane scrub, patches of woodland, and hedgerows in agricultural regions in *Andes of s. Ecuador* (s. Azuay and n. Loja), and fairly common from *n. Peru to extreme n. Chile and nw. Argentina* (San Juan). Mostly 2000–3500 m, in Peru locally to near sea level and up to over 4000 m. *Found in more arid terrain than most chat-tyrants; overall the grayest.* From **Ecuador to Chile** (A) brownish gray above with *long white forehead patch and superciliary;* wings dusky with at most faint rufescent wing-bars, outer web of outer pair of tail feathers white. *Below pale gray,* lower belly whiter. In **Bolivia and Argentina** (B) has two broad rufous wing-bars. D'Orbigny's Chat-Tyrant is mostly rufous below, etc. In nw. Peru cf. the scarce Piura Chat-Tyrant. Found singly or in pairs, perching upright and usually in the open, on fences or phone wires or atop shrubs or low trees, sallying short distances into the air or dropping to the ground. Often flicks wings and tail. Most frequent call a sharp "queeuw."

Piura Chat-Tyrant
Ochthoeca piurae

12.5 cm (5"). *Rare and local in montane scrub and borders of woodland patches in Andes of nw. Peru* (Piura to Ancash). 1500–2800 m. Resembles White-browed Chat-Tyrant, but *much smaller.* In area of overlap, White-browed's wings are *plain; Piura Chat-Tyrant has broad rufous wing-bars.* Jelski's Chat-Tyrant also shows rufous wing-bars but has a yellow frontal area and much darker gray underparts; it favors woodland interior and is rarely in the open. Behavior much as in White-browed.

D'Orbigny's Chat-Tyrant

Ochthoeca oenanthoides PLATE 53(12)

14.5–15 cm (5¾–6″). Uncommon to locally fairly common in shrubby areas and patches of woodland near and above treeline, including *Polylepis* groves, in *Andes from n. Peru (La Libertad) to extreme n. Chile and nw. Argentina (La Rioja).* Mostly 3200–4200 m. In **most of Peruvian range** (illustrated) grayish brown above with *broad frontal band and superciliary white;* wings plain, tail with outer web of outer feather white. Throat and chest pale gray, *below cinnamon-rufous.* Birds from **Puno, Peru, south** are slightly smaller and paler with vague rufous wing-bars. Brown-backed Chat-Tyrant (all races) is browner above with a buffier brow and more prominent rufous wing-bars. Behavior much like White-browed Chat-Tyrant, but less conspicuous and presence more tied to woodland. Not very vocal, but gives a fast rollicking "weeteekera, weeteekera, weeteekera" (N. K. Krabbe recording).

Brown-backed Chat-Tyrant

Ochthoeca fumicolor PLATE 53(13)

14.5–15 cm (5¾–6″). *Widespread and often common* (especially northward) in shrubby areas (including paramo), borders of montane woodland (including *Polylepis* woodland), and pasture edges in *Andes from w. Venezuela (Trujillo) to w. Bolivia (Cochabamba). Most numerous near and just above treeline,* though spreading downward with forest clearing. 2600–4400 m. In **most of range** (A) brown above with *long broad buffyish forehead and superciliary;* wings black with *two rufous bars,* tail with outer web of outer feather white. Throat and lower face grayish; *below cinnamon-rufous* (slightly duller in ♀). In **s. Peru and Bolivia** (B) superciliary narrower and paler; in **w. Venezuela** (C) has a *broader, rufous superciliary.* D'Orbigny's Chat-Tyrant differs in having a white brow, virtually plain wings, and grayer upperparts; it and Brown-backed can be locally sympatric near treeline on Andes' east slope. Otherwise Brown-backed is the only chat-tyrant combining a long brow and rufescent underparts. Found singly or in pairs, often perching prominently, sallying short distances into the air or (more often) to the ground. Generally confiding; flicks its tail in alarm. Rather quiet, but gives a soft "pseeu" call.

Agriornis

Large, heavy-bodied flycatchers that range in *open areas in the Andes, mostly at high elevations, and Patagonia.* Shrike-tyrants are characterized by their *prominently hooked bills,* used to capture relatively large prey. They are relatively uncommon and, unlike the ground tyrants, are never gregarious.

Lesser Shrike-Tyrant

Agriornis murinus* PLATE 54(1)

18.5 cm (7¼″). *Uncommon breeder on shrubby Patagonian steppes with scattered grassy areas in s. and w. Argentina,* during austral winter some migrating north to e. Bolivia. Mostly below 1500 m, but to 2500 m in winter. *Black bill rather slender and slightly hooked.* Above pale grayish brown with vague whitish supraloral; wings and tail dusky, tail with outer web of outermost feather white. *Throat white with dusky streaking,* breast pale grayish brown, belly creamy whitish. Other shrike-tyrants are markedly larger with heavier bills; cf. especially Gray-bellied, which also shows much bolder throat streaking. Found singly or in pairs, often perching atop shrubs or on fence posts; frequently drops to the ground where it may run about for protracted periods.

Black-billed Shrike-Tyrant

Agriornis montanus PLATE 54(2)

24 cm (9½″). Wide-ranging but never especially numerous in paramo and puna grasslands and agricultural terrain with scattered bushes and trees in Andes from s. Colombia to s. Argentina, where also in Patagonia. Mostly 2500–4200 m, but near sea level southward. *Hooked bill black* (some pale at base in **immatures**); *iris yellowish to ivory.* Grayish brown above with indistinct whitish supraloral, duskier wings. *Tail mostly white* (conspicuous in flight), central pair of feathers blackish. *Throat white streaked brown;* breast and flanks ashy brown, midbelly whitish. **Southern birds** (north to s. Bolivia) have *less white in tail,* and their iris may be dark. Cf. rarer and larger White-tailed Shrike-Tyrant. Ground tyrants show much less white in tail, etc.; White-fronted is the most similar. Looks vaguely thrushlike at rest. Usually solitary, often perching atop a rock, bush, or low tree, dropping to the ground to capture prey, sometimes hovering briefly before pouncing. Foraging birds move restlessly and also run on the ground. At times unwary, but when flushed may fly off for a long

distance. Not very vocal, but does give a loud, ringing "wheee, wheeeu" or just a "wheeeu."

White-tailed Shrike-Tyrant
Agriornis andicola PLATE 54(3)

27–28 cm (10¾–11"). *Rare and local* in open, sparsely vegetated shrubby areas at higher elevations in Andes from n. Ecuador to n. Chile and nw. Argentina (Catamarca). Mostly 2500–4000 m. Often confused with much more numerous Black-billed Shrike-Tyrant; *despite its name, White-tailed's tail pattern is virtually identical* (though a little extra white shows in Chile and Argentina, compared with Black-billed southern race). White-tailed differs in its *larger size* and bulkier shape, *heavier bill* whose *lower mandible may be yellowish* (but is always paler; bill never all black as in Black-billed), *dark iris* (pale in Black-billed), and *bolder and sharper blackish throat streaking*. White-tailed is somewhat paler overall, and its belly can be buff-tinged. Behavior of the two differs little if at all; occasionally (perhaps mainly in n. Peru) the two species are even seen together. Infrequently heard song a loud and surprisingly melodic "teeu, tcheeu-tcheeu-tcheeu"; also gives various jumbled or squeaky notes.

Great Shrike-Tyrant
Agriornis lividus PLATE 54(4)

28–28.5 cm (11–11¼"). Rare to uncommon in semiopen shrubby and agricultural areas from *cen. Chile* (Atacama) *and adjacent Argentina south to Tierra del Fuego*. To 1500 m. *The largest shrike-tyrant*, with *heavy, strongly hooked bill* showing some yellowish at base of lower mandible. Dull grayish brown above with *whitish lores;* wings and tail dusky, outer web of outermost rectrix whitish. *Throat white sharply streaked black;* below pale brownish gray with *lower belly and especially crissum washed cinnamon.* Gray-bellied Shrike-Tyrant is somewhat smaller, and has a markedly more prominent supraloral and only crissum tinged buff. Behavior as in other shrike-tyrants, like them occurring at low densities.

Gray-bellied Shrike-Tyrant
Agriornis micropterus PLATE 54(5)

25–25.5 cm (9¾–10"). Uncommon in puna grassland with widely scattered shrubs and boulders in *Andes from s. Peru* (Cuzco) *and w. Bolivia to nw. Argentina* (Catamarca), and on *shrubby Patagonian steppes of s. Argentina;* during austral winter some migrate north to n. Argentina

and w. Paraguay. In Andes mostly 2000–4000 m, but to sea level in Argentina. Hooked bill, *lower mandible with yellowish base.* Dull brownish gray above with *prominent white supraloral;* wings and tail dusky, outer web of outermost rectrix white. *Throat white sharply streaked black,* below pale brownish gray with *crissum tinged buff.* Great Shrike-Tyrant is larger (though *both* species are heavy, bull-headed birds), has whitish only on lores (not extending back as a supraloral), and has more buff on belly. White-tailed Shrike-Tyrant shows much more white in tail. Cf. also Lesser Shrike-Tyrant. Behavior as in other shrike-tyrants, though Gray-bellied seems even warier.

Myiotheretes

Large flycatchers that range at higher elevations in the Andes, the bush tyrants are more or less forest-based, though the most numerous and widespread species (Streak-throated) favors more semiopen terrain. They are quiet, and none is ever particularly numerous. *All species show rufous or cinnamon in wings, flashing conspicuously in flight.*

Rufous-bellied Bush Tyrant
Myiotheretes fuscorufus PLATE 54(6)

19 cm (7½"). Uncommon at borders of montane forest and woodland on *east slope of Andes from cen. Peru* (Pasco) *to w. Bolivia* (w. Santa Cruz). Mostly 2000–3400 m. Above brown with a short whitish superciliary; *wings blackish with two rufous bars and prominent edging,* and cinnamon underwing-coverts and band along base of flight feathers. Throat whitish, *below cinnamon-rufous,* breast with a little obscure streaking. Though many bush tyrants have a rufous belly, this species is unique in *also showing much rufous in its closed wing.* Streak-throated is larger, shows sharp throat streaking, rufous in tail, etc. Found singly or in pairs, perching primarily in midlevels and sallying into air and to foliage. Sometimes joins mixed flocks. Call a peweelike "puh, pe-pe-pe-pe-pe-pe" (S. Mayer recording).

Smoky Bush Tyrant
Myiotheretes fumigatus PLATE 54(7)

20.5 cm (8"). A *nondescript,* vaguely thrushlike flycatcher, *uncommon in mid-levels and subcanopy of montane forest and woodland in Andes from w. Venezuela* (Trujillo) *to s. Peru* (Cuzco).

Mostly 2000–3400 m. In **most of range** (illustrated) *uniform sooty brown* with vague whitish supraloral; wings and tail blackish, wing-coverts narrowly edged buffyish and with *cinnamon underwing-coverts and broad band along base of flight feathers.* In **w. Venezuela** only lores are whitish. Found singly or in pairs, generally staying inside forest; sometimes tags along with mixed flocks, but often seen alone. Sallies into air for insects, also hover-gleaning at foliage; on rare occasions even drops to the ground. Often quiet, but gives a soft "pü-pü-pü" (sometimes more "pü" notes).

Streak-throated Bush Tyrant
Myiotheretes striaticollis PLATE 54(8)
23 cm (9"). Widespread but uncommon in semiopen shrubby or grassy areas and borders of forest and woodland in *Andes from w. Venezuela* (Mérida) *to nw. Argentina* (Tucumán). Mostly 2300–3200 m, locally lower southward and in w. Peru. Brown above with whitish supraloral; wings blackish with cinnamon-rufous edging, *cinnamon underwing-coverts* and *wide cinnamon-rufous band along base of flight feathers;* tail dusky above, but *below cinnamon with outer third blackish. Throat and upper chest white boldly streaked blackish,* below cinnamon-rufous. Cliff Flycatcher has somewhat similar wing and tail pattern but is markedly smaller and has darker rufous-chestnut underparts with *no* streaking; it mostly occurs at *lower* elevations. Forages singly or in pairs, usually perching in the open (sometimes high above ground) and sallying after aerial insects; often occurs in disturbed terrain, even in *Eucalyptus* woodland. Rather quiet, but gives a loud, clear, rising whistled note with a human quality, e.g., "weeeeeuw" or a more inflected "weeeí."

Santa Marta Bush Tyrant
Myiotheretes pernix
19 cm (7½"). Rare to uncommon at borders of montane forest and woodland and in adjacent clearings on *Santa Marta Mts. of n. Colombia.* 2100–2900 m. Dark brown above with whitish lores; wings duskier, coverts and flight feathers edged rufous, and with *cinnamon underwing-coverts and broad band along base of flight feathers.* Throat whitish obscurely streaked black; *below deep rich rufous.* Streak-throated Bush Tyrant is markedly larger, paler below with more obvious throat streaking, and its tail shows much more rufous. Streak-throated occurs at higher elevations on the Santa Martas than does

this more forest-based species. Behavior much as in Smoky Bush Tyrant.

Rufous-webbed Bush Tyrant
Polioxolmis rufipennis PLATE 54(9)
21–21.5 cm (8¼–8½"). Uncommon and local in semiopen terrain with scattered shrubs and in woodland patches (including *Polylepis*) in *Andes from n. Peru* (Cajamarca) *to extreme n. Chile and nw. Argentina* (Jujuy and n. Salta). Mostly 3000–4400 m. Ashy gray above with a whitish supraloral; *underwing-coverts and wide band along base of flight feathers cinnamon;* tail dusky with cinnamon basal half. *Below slightly paler ashy gray,* lower belly and crissum white. Found singly or in pairs, and conspicuous, though always seeming to occur at very low densities. Primarily drops to the ground after prey, but also sometimes sallies into air. Also frequently hovers. Usually quiet, it does give a soft "treeeu."

Red-rumped Bush Tyrant
Cnemarchus erythropygius PLATE 54(10)
23 cm (9"). *Uncommon in paramo and semiopen areas with scattered shrubs and woodland patches in Andes from n. Colombia to w. Bolivia* (Cochabamba). Mostly 2900–4100 m. Unmistakable. *Forecrown frosty whitish becoming pale gray on hindcrown;* above dark brownish gray with *contrasting rufous rump.* Wings have a *white patch on tertials* (especially conspicuous in flight) and cinnamon underwing-coverts; central tail feathers blackish, *others rufous with terminal third black.* Throat streaked gray and white, breast gray, *belly contrasting rufous.* Found singly or in pairs, generally in the open, perching on boulders, bushes, wires, or fences; usually drops to the ground after prey, less often sallying into air. Generally wary, not allowing a close approach. Usually quiet; gives a shrill "kyeee" and a "skyeik" (N. K. Krabbe recordings).

Cliff Flycatcher
Hirundinea ferruginea PLATE 54(11)
18.5 cm (7¼"). Locally fairly common *around roadcuts, natural cliffs, and (southward) buildings* in Andes from w. Venezuela (Barinas) to w. Argentina, on tepuis of s. Venezuela area, and widely from ne. Brazil to ne. Argentina. *More numerous southward.* Mostly below 2000 m, locally to 3500 m in nw. Argentina. **From Bolivia and Brazil south** (A) brown above with *conspicuous cinnamon-rufous rump and basal tail;* wings dusky with *most of flight feathers rufous* (obvious even at rest). *Below mostly cinnamon-rufous.*

Andean birds (B) are darker, more blackish above with *whitish grizzling on face and crown; rump and tail from above mostly dark* (tail mainly cinnamon from below). **Tepui and Guianan** birds resemble Andean birds but have grizzling only on face, tail all dark. Not likely confused given its *close ties to roadcut and cliff habitat.* Streak-throated Bush Tyrant has prominent streaking on throat, etc. Found in sedentary pairs or small family groups, usually perching on rockfaces and buildings (austral migrants can occur in atypical situations, however); sometimes seems oblivious to the roar of traffic or the close presence of people. Inconspicuous until they fly, the rufous in wings then flashing out and catching your eye; flight fast and acrobatic. Often keeps up a chatter of distinctive high-pitched calls, including a "wheeeyp!" and a "whee, dee-dee-ee-ee-ee" or "wheeuw-d'd'd'r!" Also a continued "wha-deép, wha-deép. . . ."

Drab Water Tyrant
Ochthornis littoralis   PLATE 55(1)
13.5 cm (5¼"). *Locally fairly common to common along riverbanks in Amazonia.* To 600 m in Venezuela. *Mostly pale sandy brown,* paler on rump and below, and with *short white superciliary;* wings and tail plain dusky brown. Nondescript. Little Ground Tyrant has a more slender bill with pale area at base, obscure superciliary, vague wing-bars, and white on outer tail. The water tyrant is invariably found near water and favors areas where strong currents have undercut banks, exposing roots where it often perches. Water tyrants also occur on river islands, there favoring piles of accumulated driftwood. Most often in pairs that perch close to the water, often flushing repeatedly (like a kingfisher) in front of passing boats. Rather quiet, but gives an occasional soft "free." Displaying birds posture with wings outstretched while giving a fast, excited "weet-weedidee, weet-weedidee . . ." repeated several times.

Muscisaxicola

Slim, *terrestrial* flycatchers found primarily in *open puna or paramo grasslands in the Andes,* many species favoring areas near water or rockfaces; some southern breeders are migratory. They have slender dark bills, long pointed wings, and long legs. Ground tyrants are *basically gray or brownish gray, whiter below,* with *some color or pattern on*

head (an important identification aid). Unless otherwise indicated, wings are dusky or brownish, and tail black with whitish outer web of outermost rectrix. Often rather wary, foraging birds run and hop on the ground, sometimes fluttering a short distance into air in pursuit of insects; the tail is often flicked open and shut. Flight is fast and direct. Displaying ♂♂ hover in place, stall and drop a bit, then recover; the sequence can be repeated many times. Ground tyrants are generally quiet.

Little Ground Tyrant
Muscisaxicola fluviatilis   PLATE 55(2)
13.5 cm (5¼"). *Uncommon on sparsely vegetated sandbars and river islands in w. Amazonia, where the only ground tyrant. To 800 m,* wanderers higher. *Base of lower mandible yellowish. Sandy brown above* with *vague* whitish supraloral; wing feathers edged cinnamon-buff; *tail black with outer web of outermost rectrix whitish.* Below buffy whitish, belly whiter. Cf. very similar Spot-billed Ground Tyrant (possible overlap along base of Andes). Drab Water Tyrant has a shorter black bill, more prominent supraloral, whitish rump, no white on tail. Found singly or in pairs, running on the ground, usually fully in the open but nonetheless often inconspicuous, its dorsal coloration matching the color of its muddy or sandy habitat.

Spot-billed Ground Tyrant
Muscisaxicola maculirostris   PLATE 55(3)
14 cm (5½"). Uncommon in barren open places, gullies, and sparsely vegetated agricultural areas in Andes from n. Colombia to s. Chile (Magallanes) and s. Argentina (w. Santa Cruz); favors arid regions. Mostly 2400–4000 m, lower from s. Peru south. *The smallest ground tyrant in the Andes,* with *browner (less gray) upperparts than most. Base of lower mandible yellowish,* forming the minute "spot," not visible in the field. *Sandy brown above* with *short white supraloral; wing feathers edged cinnamon-buff.* Below buffy whitish (**Peru south;** illustrated), or breast and belly washed dull cinnamon-buff (**Colombia and Ecuador**). Little Ground Tyrant, found in w. Amazonia (at most limited overlap with Spot-billed), lacks the supraloral and has a distinctly whiter belly. Other similar ground tyrants are grayer above, lack buff wing-edging and the buff tinge below. Found singly or in pairs, sometimes a few together when not breeding; often near

stone walls. Rarely associates with other ground tyrants.

White-fronted Ground Tyrant
Muscisaxicola albifrons   PLATE 55(4)
21.5 cm (8½″). *Uncommon and local around cushion bogs in high Andes from w. Peru* (Ancash) *to extreme n. Chile and w. Bolivia* (Oruro and Cochabamba). Mostly 4100–5200 m. *Large.* Pale brownish gray above with *broad white forecrown and short superciliary,* crown tinged brown; *wing-coverts and inner flight feathers prominently edged whitish.* Pale grayish below. Aside from Ochre-naped Ground Tyrant, White-fronted is *markedly larger than its congeners;* Ochre-naped differs most notably in having an ochre-yellow occipital patch. Less gregarious and more sedentary than other ground tyrants, and more restricted to higher elevations. Has a notably upright stance.

White-browed Ground Tyrant
Muscisaxicola albilora   PLATE 55(5)
17 cm (6¾″). *Fairly common breeder on rocky, sparsely vegetated slopes in Andes of cen. and s. Chile and adjacent Argentina,* in austral winter a few ranging north in Andes as far as n. Ecuador. Breeds mainly 1200–2600 m, otherwise mostly 2500–4000 m. Brownish gray above, *browner on crown, which blends into more rufous hindcrown,* and with *long narrow white superciliary* (not very conspicuous); wings with some pale edging on coverts. Below grayish white. Paramo Ground Tyrant is somewhat larger and has a bolder white supraloral; it shows *no* rufous on crown, though its forecrown is dark brown. Cf. the very similar Puna Ground Tyrant. Migrating and wintering birds often occur in loose flocks, sometimes associating with other ground tyrants, and they then frequent grasslands and pastures, often near water.

Paramo Ground Tyrant
*Muscisaxicola alpinus**   PLATE 55(6)
19 cm (7½″). Fairly common in paramo grassland, sometimes where rocky, in *high Andes from n. Colombia to extreme n. Peru.* Mostly 3600–4600 m. Formerly considered conspecific with Plain-capped Ground Tyrant (found farther south). Brownish gray above, crown tinged sepia, with a *prominent white supraloral;* some pale edging on wing-coverts. Below grayish white. White-browed Ground Tyrant has a longer but narrower white superciliary (despite its name, usually *less* prominent in the field than

Paramo's supraloral), and some rufous shows on crown (but this often is not very evident; remember that Paramo's crown can itself look quite brown). Spot-billed Ground Tyrant is smaller, buffier below, etc. Found in pairs or (when not nesting) small loose groups; often perches on slightly elevated sites such as rocks or walls, drooping wings and flicking tail.

Plain-capped Ground Tyrant
*Muscisaxicola griseus**   PLATE 55(7)
19 cm (7½″). Uncommon in puna grasslands, often where rocky, in *high Andes from n. Peru* (Cajamarca and Piura) *to w. Bolivia* (Cochabamba). 3300–4700 m. Formerly considered conspecific with Paramo Ground Tyrant (found to north); has been called Taczanowski's Ground Tyrant. Gray above with a *prominent short white superciliary;* wings with some pale edging on coverts. Below grayish white, grayest on breast. Cinereous Ground Tyrant is similarly colored but markedly smaller, with only an inconspicuous white supraloral (extending back only to above eye, and not as wide as in Plain-capped). When not breeding, often ranges in small flocks, sometimes associating with other ground tyrants.

Cinereous Ground Tyrant
Muscisaxicola cinereus
16.5 cm (6½″). Locally common in puna grassland, often where rocky or around lakes, in *high Andes from extreme s. Peru* (Puno) *and w. Bolivia to cen. Chile and adjacent Argentina;* in austral winter some migrate north to cen. Peru. 2500–4500 m. Resembles Plain-capped Ground Tyrant; often found with it, usually outnumbering it. Cinereous is markedly smaller. Though their plumage is much the same, Cinereous has *only an inconspicuous short, narrow white supraloral* and a paler gray breast (such that the white throat contrasts little). *Thus the Cinereous shows the weakest head pattern of any ground tyrant in its range.* Spot-billed Ground Tyrant, also with a weak head pattern, is smaller still, much browner overall, etc. Puna Ground Tyrant's head pattern is almost equally subdued, but is less pure gray above, has a brown tinge on crown and a slightly longer superciliary.

Puna Ground Tyrant
Muscisaxicola juninensis   PLATE 55(8)
16.5 cm (6½″). Locally common in puna grassland, usually near rocky outcroppings or cliffs, or around bogs and marshes, in *high Andes from cen. Peru* (Ancash) *to nw. Argentina* (Tucumán,

where rare). Mostly 4000–5000 m. *Non*migratory. Above brownish gray, *tinged brown on crown* with a short narrow white superciliary. Below grayish white, belly whiter. The very similar White-browed Ground Tyrant breeds south of this species' range but then migrates through it; has more rufous on crown and a longer and somewhat more prominent superciliary. Cinereous Ground Tyrant is grayer above (lacking Puna's brown tinge). Rufous-naped Ground Tyrant is paler and purer gray above with a more conspicuous and discrete rufous occipital patch. Behavior as in other Andean ground tyrants.

Rufous-naped Ground Tyrant
Muscisaxicola rufivertex   PLATE 55(9)
16.5–18 cm (6½–7″). Locally fairly common in puna grassland, rocky slopes, and near lakes and streams in *high Andes from n. Peru* (Cajamarca) *to cen. Chile* (Colchagua) *and adjacent Argentina. Mostly 2200–4500 m; locally to 600–1000 m in lomas of sw. Peru and n. Chile. Always has an obvious and discrete rufous patch on hindcrown* (actually not the nape). **Southernmost birds** (A) *pale pure gray above* with *orange-rufous occipital patch* and short narrow white superciliary. Below grayish white, belly whiter. In **sw. Peru, sw. Bolivia, n. Chile,** and **nw. Argentina** similar but even paler. From **Peru to w. Bolivia** (B) larger with *occipital patch more rufous-chestnut* and a longer superciliary. White-browed and Puna Ground Tyrants are browner above and their entire crown is brownish. Plain-capped and Cinereous Ground Tyrants *lack any rufous on crown at all.* Rufous-naped has an especially upright posture; it favors flat barren areas, usually near water. Often ranges in small monospecific groups when not breeding.

Ochre-naped Ground Tyrant
Muscisaxicola flavinucha   PLATE 55(10)
20 cm (8″). Uncommon in areas with short grass, especially near water, and on adjacent barren slopes with scattered rocks, in *high Andes from n. Peru* (Cajamarca) *to Tierra del Fuego;* most numerous on its Chilean breeding grounds, northward only (or primarily) as an austral migrant. Mostly 3000–4500 m, southward lower (nesting at 500–1000 m on Isla Grande). *Large* and long-winged. Pale brownish gray above with *broad forecrown and short superciliary white* and *ochre-yellow occipital patch* (not always prominent); wing-coverts and inner flight feathers pale-edged. Below grayish white, belly whiter.

White-fronted Ground Tyrant is even bigger, lacks the yellow, and its pale edging on wings is more conspicuous. Regularly seen in small groups, when not breeding sometimes in association with other ground tyrants.

Black-fronted Ground Tyrant
Muscisaxicola frontalis   PLATE 55(11)
18 cm (7″). Uncommon, breeding in puna grassland of *high Andes of Chile and w. Argentina,* in austral winter a few migrating north in Andes to s. Peru (Puno). Breeds 2500–4500 m, on its winter quarters up to 4300 m. Ashy gray above with *conspicuous white lores* and *black forehead extending back on midcrown* (where it turns chestnut). Below grayish white. The striking head pattern of this dapper ground tyrant is unique. Cinereous Ground Tyrant lacks any black on head; Dark-faced has entire foreface black (showing no white on lores).

Cinnamon-bellied Ground Tyrant
Muscisaxicola capistratus   PLATE 55(12)
17.5 cm (7″). *Uncommon, breeding locally in s. Argentina and adjacent Chile, favoring open grassy areas adjacent to rocky slopes or cliffs,* in austral winter migrating north in Andes to s. Peru (Puno). Breeds mostly below 500 m, but in winter at 2000–4000 m. Brownish gray above with *black face and forehead* and *chestnut crown.* Throat whitish, breast dull grayish buff, *lower belly and flanks cinnamon-rufous.* The attractive head pattern is usually obvious, though the belly color often is not. Dark-faced Ground Tyrant lacks chestnut on crown and is much grayer below.

Dark-faced Ground Tyrant
Muscisaxicola maclovianus   PLATE 55(13)
16.5 cm (6½″). Common breeder in grassy areas at edge of woodland and forest, and above treeline, in *Andes of s. Chile and s. Argentina, and on Falkland Islands; in austral winter migrates north, especially along either coast, as far as Uruguay and w. Peru.* To 2500 m. Brownish gray above with *black foreface. Pale grayish below,* lower belly and crissum whiter. The scarcer Cinnamon-bellied Ground Tyrant has bright chestnut on crown and a cinnamon-rufous lower belly. Cf. also Black-fronted Ground Tyrant (with bright white lores, etc.). When breeding this species is more arboreal than other ground tyrants, perching freely in low trees at woodland edge.

Short-tailed Field Tyrant
Muscigralla brevicauda   PLATE 55(14)

11 cm (4¼"). Locally fairly common in *open barren areas with scattered bushes and low trees from sw. Ecuador* (Manabí) *to extreme n. Chile.* To 1500 m in arid interior valleys. Unmistakable; a *small, mainly terrestrial* tyrannid with *long legs and very short tail.* Legs yellowish flesh; tibia bare. Pale brownish gray above with white supraloral and semiconcealed yellow coronal patch; *rump band pinkish buff, uppertail-coverts rufous-chestnut.* Wings dusky with two whitish bars; tail black narrowly tipped buff. Creamy whitish below. Found singly, less often in pairs; hops on the ground, and also runs in fast bursts, flicking its short tail like a ground tyrant. Pursues insects on the ground and in short fluttering sallies. Song a weak, sibilant "tizztízzz," sometimes preceded by a few "tik" notes; usually given from a low perch, but sometimes mounting 10–20 m up.

Chocolate-vented Tyrant
Neoxolmis rufiventris   PLATE 55(15)

23 cm (9"). *Uncommon breeder on shrubby Patagonian steppes with short grass in s. Argentina and adjacent Chile;* in austral winter migrates north to e. Argentina and Uruguay, there favoring large fields. Mostly below 500 m. *Ashy gray above* with black foreface and ocular area; *shoulders pale sandy* (can look silvery), *inner flight feathers bright cinnamon broadly tipped whitish,* long outer flight feathers black; tail blackish tipped and edged white. *Throat and breast gray, contrasting with rufous belly.* A large, handsome tyrannid of windswept plains, unlikely to be confused; cf. various ground tyrants, none of which shows Chocolate-vented's *flashy wing pattern.* Vaguely thrushlike in appearance, though in behavior Chocolate-vented more resembles a ground tyrant. Primarily terrestrial, though nesting birds perch on bushes. Flight is swift on pointed, almost falconlike wings. During winter it ranges in small monospecific flocks.

Xolmis

Attractive, fairly large flycatchers found in *open and semiopen terrain in s. and e. South America,* the monjitas are *patterned in white, gray, and black.* Taxonomic relationships remain unresolved, with two species (Rusty-backed and Salinas) sometimes placed in *Neoxolmis,* and another (Black-and-white)

variously retained in *Xolmis* or (as here) separated in the monotypic *Heteroxolmis.*

Rusty-backed Monjita
Xolmis rubetra   PLATE 56(1)

19 cm (7½"). *Locally not uncommon in shrubby steppe vegetation and grasslands with scattered low bushes in cen. and s. Argentina* (Mendoza to n. Santa Cruz), in austral winter some migrating to n. and e. Argentina. To 1000 m. *Rusty brown above* with *long white superciliary;* wings black with buffyish edging, tail blackish with outer web of outer feathers white. Sides of neck and underparts white, with *sides of neck and foreneck streaked black.* ♀ duller. This handsome tyrannid of the Patagonian plains is unlikely to be confused; other vaguely similar flycatchers are nowhere near so rufous. In nw. Argentina cf. Salinas Monjita (no overlap). Found singly and in pairs (small flocks in winter), foraging by dropping to the ground from a low perch. Sometimes runs rapidly on the ground.

Salinas Monjita
Xolmis salinarum

16.5 cm (6½"). Uncommon and very local in halophytic scrub around *salt lakes in nw. Argentina* (mainly nw. Córdoba and sw. Santiago del Estero). Below 200 m. Resembles Rusty-backed Monjita. *Smaller and much whiter* with *virtually no streaking on foreneck,* a white nuchal collar, and *mostly white scapulars and wing-coverts.* Behavior much as in Rusty-backed Monjita.

Fire-eyed Diucon
Xolmis pyrope   PLATE 56(2)

21–21.5 cm (8¼–8½"). Fairly common in borders of humid forest and woodland, regenerating clearings, and orchards in *cen. and s. Chile and adjacent Argentina south to Tierra del Fuego.* To 2000 m. *Iris red. Dark gray above;* wings blacker and virtually plain, tail gray, outer feathers slightly paler. *Below paler ashy gray,* throat and midbelly whiter. Size and overall gray appearance should be distinctive in **austral** range; cf. smaller Common Diuca Finch. Usually perches in the open, dropping to the ground after prey, less often sallying into air. Also eats fruit, probably mainly in winter. Rather quiet, but occasionally gives a soft "pit" or "whit" call.

Gray Monjita

Xolmis cinereus PLATE 56(3)

23 cm (9"). Fairly common and widespread in cerrado and other semiopen areas with scattered trees, sometimes also around airports and buildings in agricultural regions, *mainly from extreme se. Peru* (s. Madre de Dios), *n. Bolivia, and ne. Brazil to n. Argentina* (Buenos Aires). To 1200 m. Iris red. *Ashy gray above* with *broad white supraloral;* wings black with a *white speculum* at base of primaries (forming *conspicuous square patch in flight*), tail black tipped whitish. Throat white with a *black malar streak,* breast gray, belly white. Black-crowned Monjita has a black crown encircled by white, a white wing *stripe* (not a patch), and entirely white underparts. Cf. various mockingbirds (different shape and behavior). Conspicuous, remaining active through heat of day, perching atop bushes and low trees or on fences and wires, dropping to the ground in pursuit of prey. Occasionally sallies into air or even runs on the ground. Its flight is fast, direct, and graceful. Quiet, but breeding ♂♂ give a soft "peee, preeu."

White Monjita

Xolmis irupero PLATE 56(4)

17–18 cm (6¾–7"). *Always conspicuous* and *often common* in open and semiopen terrain (both natural and agricultural) with scattered bushes and trees from *n. Bolivia to cen. Argentina,* and in *ne. Brazil.* To 1300 m in Bolivia. *Ethereally white* relieved only by black primaries and primary-coverts, and on tip of tail. ♀ tinged gray on back. In **ne. Brazil** slightly smaller with a wider black tail-band. Unmistakable; cf. only the much rarer Black-and-white Monjita (with black tail, etc.). Perches in the open, even during midday heat, often atop a shrub or low tree or on a wire, from those vantage points dropping to the ground in pursuit of prey, sometimes after hovering. Quiet, but breeding ♂♂ occasionally give a soft "preeeyp . . . tooit . . . preeeyp . . . tooit. . . ."

Black-crowned Monjita

Xolmis coronatus PLATE 56(5)

21–21.5 cm (8¼–8½"). Uncommon breeder in open and semiopen areas with scattered shrubs and low trees in *w. and cen. Argentina* (south to Río Negro), in austral winter some migrating north to se. Bolivia, w. Paraguay, and extreme s. Brazil. *Crown black surrounded by a white diadem;* otherwise gray above, ear-coverts blackish. Wings and tail blackish, wing-coverts and flight feathers edged whitish with *white stripe along*

base of flight feathers (obvious in flight). Below white. Gray Monjita lacks the black crown, is grayer (e.g., on breast), and in flight shows a square white *patch* in wings (not a *stripe*). Behavior much as in Gray Monjita, though Black-crowned tends to be warier. Usually quiet, but breeding ♂♂ give a soft, melodic "whut-whut, wheeeyr? whut" (R. Straneck recording).

White-rumped Monjita

Xolmis velatus PLATE 56(6)

19.5 cm (7¾"). Fairly common in semiopen areas with scattered bushes and small trees, often around buildings, in *cen. and e. Brazil, n. and e. Bolivia, and ne. Paraguay.* To about 1000 m. *Head white with pearly gray hindneck;* back gray with *contrasting white rump and basal half of tail,* outer half of tail black. Wings blackish with white edging, *white stripe along inner flight feathers* (obvious in flight). Below white. Gray Monjita is larger and heftier, grayer on head and breast, lacks white on rump, has a black malar, etc. ♀ Black-and-white Monjita's wings and tail are mainly black, and its back browner; it and the White-rumped are not known to overlap in range. Found in pairs, perching conspicuously on fence posts, wires, and bushes, often spreading its tail; quite approachable. The species is colonizing some recently deforested areas.

Black-and-white Monjita

Heteroxolmis dominicanus PLATE 56(7)

21 cm (8¼"). *Now rare and very local in open grassy areas around marshes and boggy swales in s. Brazil* (north to s. Santa Catarina) *and ne. Argentina* (south to e. Buenos Aires). To 1000 m. ♂ mostly white with *contrasting black wings and rather long tail,* outer third of primaries white (visible mainly in flight); head and back sometimes smudged pale gray. ♀ similar but with crown and back pale brownish gray and with white scapular stripe. The much commoner White Monjita is smaller (shorter-tailed) and purer white; it shows less black on wings and has black only on tip of tail. Cf. also White-rumped Monjita. Behavior similar to White Monjita, dropping to the ground from low perches in pursuit of prey, but seems more restless; has declined greatly because of agricultural intensification and exotic tree plantations. Occurs in wide-ranging and very conspicuous pairs. At least in s. Brazil associates with and often seems to lead small flocks of the equally rare Saffron-cowled Blackbird. Quiet; has a soft "weeyrt" call.

Yellow-browed Tyrant
Satrapa icterophrys   PLATE 56(8)
16.5 cm (6½"). Widespread but generally uncommon among scattered trees and groves and
in gallery woodland and monte from *n. and
e. Bolivia and e. Brazil to n. Argentina;* in austral winter some migrate north into w. Amazonia; *an isolated population in Venezuela* is resident there. Mostly below 2000 m (to 2500 m
in Bolivia). Olive above, grayer on crown, with
prominent bright yellow superciliary and *blackish
cheeks;* wings blackish with two pale gray bars,
tail with outer web of outermost rectrix whitish.
Below bright yellow. ♀ slightly duller, with olive
breast mottling. Social and Rusty-margined Flycatchers have obviously white brows, etc.; also
cf. Lemon-browed Flycatcher (an Andean bird).
Usually seen singly, less often in pairs, perching erectly and often in the semiopen; not with
flocks. Mainly feeds by making short sallies to
foliage. Seems singularly quiet.

Cattle Tyrant
Machetornis rixosa   PLATE 56(9)
19.5 cm (7¾"). *Widespread and generally common* in semiopen areas, agricultural regions,
and open ground around buildings in Venezuela and n. Colombia, and from n. and e. Bolivia and e. Brazil to n. Argentina. Spreading
into some deforested areas. Mostly below 800 m,
locally much higher in E. Andes of Colombia.
Long legs; *mainly terrestrial,* but also perches on
rooftops, etc. Red iris. In **most of range** (illustrated) *plain olive brown above,* grayer on crown
and nape, with usually concealed orange coronal patch; *tail narrowly tipped whitish.* Throat
whitish, below bright yellow. In **Venezuela and
Colombia** throat pale yellow. Superficially like a
kingbird, but much more often on the ground.
Found in pairs or small loose groups, running
with an erect stance. They often attend grazing
domestic animals, even Capybaras and Marsh
Deer where these occur, sometimes hitching
rides on their backs. Calls include a rising series
of squeaky notes, recalling Tropical Kingbird.
Also: Panama (recent immigrant).

Streamer-tailed Tyrant
Gubernetes yetapa   PLATE 56(10)
38–40 cm (15–16"). Uncommon and rather
local in damp shrubby grasslands and marshy
terrain near streams in *n. Bolivia,* and from *interior s. Brazil to ne. Argentina.* To 1100 m. *Spectacular tail very long, graduated, and very deeply
forked;* bill stout. *Above pale gray,* somewhat

streaked forecrown and superciliary whitish;
wings blackish with rufous at base of primaries
(*showing as conspicuous stripe in flight*). *Throat
white, outlined by chestnut pectoral collar;* breast
and sides pale gray. ♀ slightly smaller with
shorter tail. Essentially unmistakable; one of
the finest flycatchers (RSR's favorite). Occurs in
pairs that perch conspicuously atop bushes and
trees, sallying out often for long distances after
insects, their long tails whipping around. Their
loud calling often attracts attention, even from
long distances; the most notable vocalization is a
"whee-irt!" or "wiirt!" Displaying birds flair and
flap their wings exuberantly while they call.

Shear-tailed Gray Tyrant
Muscipipra vetula   PLATE 56(11)
22.5 cm (8¾"). Uncommon at borders of humid and montane forest and woodland in *se.
Brazil region* (north to s. Bahia); in Paraguay
and Argentina seems to occur mainly or only
during austral winter. To 2200 m. *Mostly gray
with dusky auriculars and white throat; wings
contrasting black,* as is its *long and rather deeply
forked tail.* Virtually unmistakable in its limited range. Cf. Crowned Slaty Flycatcher. Often
perches in the open on high snags, usually in
pairs but occasionally small loose groups. Sallies
into air, often for considerable distances, pursuing aerial insects. Usually quiet but does give a
peweelike "pup-pup-pup."

Knipolegus

Midsized flycatchers found primarily in
wooded or forested terrain, mainly in
s. South America, with a few species northward. Well-named, ♂♂ *of all species except
the Rufous-tailed Tyrant are mainly black or
gray,* ♀♀ *browner and often streaked below.
Bills are often blue or bluish gray,* irides often
red. *Knipolegus* are notably quiet tyrannids;
some are very inconspicuous as well.

Cinereous Tyrant
Knipolegus striaticeps   PLATE 57(1)
13–13.5 cm (5–5¼"). *Locally common in chaco
woodland, borders, and openings from e. Bolivia*
(Santa Cruz) *to n. Argentina* (San Luis); perhaps only an austral migrant at north edge of
range. Mostly below 1000 m. ♂ has *red iris* and
is *dark gray, face and foreneck blacker;* wings
blackish with two grayish bars, and outer web of
outermost tail feather whitish. *Belly paler gray.*

♀ brownish above, *rufous on crown and nape,* and cinnamon on uppertail-coverts; wings dusky with two white bars; tail blackish with considerable rufous on inner webs (visible mainly from below). Whitish below with *fine dusky streaking.* ♂♂ of other sympatric *Knipolegus* are actually black; many have white in wing. ♀ Hudson's Black Tyrant is larger, lacks rufous on crown and nape but is more rufous (not just cinnamon) at base of tail. Bran-colored Flycatcher is more rufescent above with buff (not white) wing-bars. Found singly or in pairs, generally in the open, perching erectly and often twitching its tail. Displaying ♂♂ mount into the air, then drop quickly while giving a sneezing "skidi-ik."

Rufous-tailed Tyrant
Knipolegus poecilurus   PLATE 57(2)
14.5 cm (5¾"). Uncommon and local at borders of montane forest and in shrubby clearings in *Andes from n. Venezuela to w. Bolivia* (where rare) and on *tepuis of s. Venezuela area.* Mostly 900–2200 m. *Iris red.* In **Andes** (illustrated) grayish above, wings duskier with two dull buffyish bars; tail dusky *with inner webs mostly rufous. Mostly cinnamon-buff below,* washed gray on breast. **Tepui** birds have more gray on breast, a paler belly, and little rufous in tail. Superficially like a pewee but much buffier below; no pewee has the red eye. ♀ Andean Tyrant is more streaked below and has brown eyes; ♀ Whitewinged Black Tyrants have, depending on race, whitish or rufous on rump, etc. Found singly or in pairs, most often perching erectly in the semi-open, sallying into air in pursuit of insects. Does not associate with mixed flocks. Often raises tail, then slowly lowers it. Quiet, but sometimes gives high-pitched, faint but raspy "tzreeet" notes followed by some jumbles, sometimes accompanied by an aerial display in which the bird mounts up some 10–15 m.

Andean Tyrant
Knipolegus signatus   PLATE 57(3)
16–16.5 cm (6¼–6½"). Rare (northward) to uncommon in lower growth inside montane forest and woodland on *east slope of Andes from extreme s. Ecuador* (recently found in Zamora-Chinchipe on Cordillera del Cóndor) *to nw. Argentina* (Catamarca). 700–2600 m (southward), 1900–3000 m (northward). Likely two separate species. **Southern** ♂ (north to se. Peru; illustrated) has a dark red iris, blue-gray bill; ♀'s iris brown and bill blackish. ♂ *uniform plumbe-*

ous gray, wings and tail blackish. ♀ dull brown above, *bright rufous on rump;* wings dusky with two pale buff bars, tail feathers edged rufous. Pale grayish below with *blurry grayish olive streaking,* belly whiter. **Northern** ♂ is larger with a longer bill and reddish brown iris; *uniform dull black.* ♀ darker above and with *darker mottled streaking below; tail has less rufous, so it too looks darker.* The dull, uniform ♂♂ are distinctive in their *Andean ranges* (where there are few other *Knipolegus*); cf. Smoke-colored Pewee and ♂ of differently shaped Jet Manakin. ♀ White-winged Black Tyrant is typically more ochraceous below (or, in n. Peru, whiter below) with little or no streaking; it also shows more color on rump. An inconspicuous tyrannid that tends to remain within cover. Typically found singly, not joining mixed flocks. Perched birds shiver the tail sideways. In flight display southern breeding ♂♂ mount up and emit a soft "tic" on re-alighting.

Hudson's Black Tyrant
Knipolegus hudsoni   PLATE 57(4)
15 cm (6"). Uncommon breeder in lower growth of woodland and dense scrub in *cen. Argentina,* in austral winter migrating north as far as *n. Bolivia,* then favoring more open situations. Mostly below 500 m. Bill mostly bluish gray. ♂ shiny black with *small whitish area on flanks* and a *white band across primaries* (hidden at rest but obvious in flight). ♀ grayish brown above, rump and basal tail rufous, remainder of tail blackish; wings dusky with two buff bars. Below buffyish with *mottled dusky-olive breast streaking.* ♂ White-winged Black Tyrant is larger and lacks the flank patch; sympatric ♀ White-wingeds are buffier and more uniform below. ♀ Cinereous Tyrant is smaller and has much more rufous on crown and tail. ♀ Blue-billed Black Tyrant more coarsely streaked below with a more rufescent crown. Inconspicuous when nesting, but more in evidence during winter. Breeding ♂♂ display from dead snags, launching into air and giving soft hiccuping or snapping sounds.

White-winged Black Tyrant
Knipolegus aterrimus   PLATE 57(5)
16.5–18 cm (6½–7"). Often common in montane scrub and woodland and forest borders in *Andes from n. Peru* (Cajamarca) *to s. Argentina* (w. Santa Cruz; spreads east in winter). Mostly 1500–3000 m northward, but down to nearly sea level in Argentina. Bill mostly bluish gray. ♂ *shiny black* with *white band across primaries* (hidden

at rest but conspicuous in flight). **Southern** ♀ (Argentina and most of Bolivia; A) brown above, grayer on head, with *rump and most of tail bright cinnamon-rufous;* wings blackish with two broad cinnamon-buff bars. *Below buffy ochraceous, unstreaked.* **Northern** ♀ (south to Ancash and Huánuco, Peru; B) smaller and mainly whitish below (some dusky mottling, but no buff), with *whitish rump* and wing-bars. Intermediates have mottled streaking on breast, less rufous on tail than southern birds. ♀ variation is striking, but in most of range it is the only *Knipolegus* combining buff below and a rufous rump and basal tail; n. Peru birds' whitish rump unique. Larger than Hudson's Black Tyrant, which ranges primarily in lowlands. Mainly perches in the open, erect and usually not much above the ground; sallies to air and foliage, when white wing band or rufous rump are conspicuous. Mainly quiet, but in display breeding ♂♂ repeatedly fly up a short distance and emit a faint "chit-tzzzr."

São Francisco Black Tyrant
Knipolegus franciscanus*
16.5 cm (6½"). *Rare and local in deciduous woodland, primarily near larger rock outcroppings, in interior e. Brazil* (sw. Bahia, nw. Minas Gerais, and Distrito Federal). Mostly 400–700 m. Formerly often considered conspecific with geographically distant White-winged Black Tyrant. Sometimes called Caatinga Black Tyrant. ♂ like White-winged ♂; given its limited range, *unmistakable* (no other black tyrant occurs with it). ♀ quite different from White-winged: brownish gray above with indistinct whitish wing-bars, *whitish below with dusky streaking on breast.* Forages mainly in woodland subcanopy and canopy, generally in pairs (sometimes loosely associated), at times accompanying mixed flocks. Occasionally sallies into air, but seems mainly to stay within canopy.

Blue-billed Black Tyrant
Knipolegus cyanirostris   PLATE 57(6)
14.5–15 cm (5¾–6"). Locally common at borders of humid forest and woodland, also gallery woodland, in *se. Brazil region* (north to Minas Gerais); apparently only an austral migrant to Paraguay and Mato Grosso do Sul. To 2200 m. ♂'s bill pale blue, *iris bright red;* ♀'s bill dusky, iris orangy. ♂ *uniform glossy black with no white in wing* (a little shows in the hand). ♀ rufescent brown above, *most rufous on crown and especially rump;* wings blackish with two buff bars,

tail feathers edged cinnamon-rufous. Whitish below *streaked dark olive brown,* crissum cinnamon. *In its range ♂ is only ♂ black tyrant lacking white in wing;* note too its obvious red eye. ♀ is so dark and heavily streaked below that confusion is unlikely; cf. Bran-colored Flycatcher and ♀ Hudson's Black Tyrant. Found singly or in pairs, generally not much above the ground; usually inconspicuous and often confiding. ♂ in display mounts into air some 5–10 m, then drops like a stone, seeming to remain silent.

Amazonian Black Tyrant
Knipolegus poecilocercus   PLATE 57(7)
14 cm (5½"). *Uncommon and local in undergrowth of seasonally flooded várzea woodland from s. Venezuela and Guyana to Amazonia.* Below 300 m. ♂'s bill blue, ♀'s dusky. ♂ *glossy blue-black.* ♀ olive brown above, *lores and narrow eye-ring whitish,* and rufescent on uppertail-coverts; wings dusky with *two pale buff bars, tail feathers broadly edged cinnamon-rufous.* Whitish below with *heavy olive brown breast streaking.* Riverside Tyrant inhabits more open areas on river islands, is larger and never as black. Other black tyrants do not occur in Amazonian's range or restricted habitat. The similar Black Manakin is not associated with water. A quiet and inconspicuous bird that strongly favors seasonally inundated areas. Found singly or in pairs, perching near the ground or (more usually) water, making short sallies to foliage or water's surface. ♂ in presumed display jumps a few feet up and quickly returns, sometimes accompanied by a soft snapping (perhaps mechanical).

Riverside Tyrant
Knipolegus orenocensis   PLATE 57(8)
15 cm (6"). Uncommon and local in early-succession shrubby growth on *river islands in Amazon and Orinoco River drainages upriver to e. Ecuador and ne. Peru.* Below 300 m. Bill mostly blue-gray. ♂ **along Río Orinoco** and in **e.-cen. Brazil** (illustrated) *uniform dark slaty.* ♂ **along Amazon River** *dull black.* ♀ *dull olive-grayish above* (darker and less olivaceous along **Amazon**), wings and tail duskier. Below whitish with blurry olive-gray breast and flank streaking. The smaller Amazonian Black Tyrant inhabits woodland lower growth (not river islands); ♂ is a glossier blue-black, ♀ browner (less gray) above with white on lores, definite wing-bars (*wings essentially plain* in Riverside), and rufous in tail. Ranges in pairs that generally remain

within cover, but early in the day are more likely to perch in the open. Often sallies to the ground for prey. Displaying ♂♂ mount a few meters into air, then return to the perch, accompanied by a snap. Quiet, though both sexes give a soft "tuk" note.

Crested Black Tyrant
Knipolegus lophotes   PLATE 57(9)
20.5–21 cm (8–8¼"). Uncommon in open grassy and shrubby areas in *interior e. and s. Brazil and Uruguay.* To 1400 m. ♀ slightly smaller. *A large black tyrant with prominent crest. Bill black.* Glossy black with a white band along base of primaries (obvious in flight but hidden when perched). Velvety Black Tyrant is smaller, with a much smaller crest and a bluish bill. Occurs in well-dispersed pairs; conspicuous, regularly perching atop shrubs and low trees (sometimes even wires), but in most areas not often encountered. Sallies into the air for insects and also eats some fruit. N. Am. observers will be struck by its uncanny resemblance to the Phainopepla (*Phainopepla nitens*).

Velvety Black Tyrant
Knipolegus nigerrimus   PLATE 57(10)
18 cm (7"). Local and generally uncommon in semiopen areas and woodland borders, often where rocky, in *highlands of e. Brazil* (Bahia and Goiás to n. Rio Grande do Sul). 700–2700 m. Bill bluish gray; iris dark red. *Slight bushy crest.* ♂ *glossy blue-black with white band along base of primaries* (conspicuous in flight). ♀ similar but *throat chestnut with black streaks.* ♂ Blue-billed Black Tyrant is smaller with a brighter red eye and *no* white in wing. Crested Black Tyrant is larger and obviously crested, and has a black bill. ♂ São Francisco Black Tyrant lacks the blue gloss; ♀♀ of the two very different. Usually in pairs, generally foraging close to the ground. Quiet.

Long-tailed Tyrant
Colonia colonus   PLATE 58(1)
♂ 23–25 cm (9–10"), ♀ 18–20 cm (7–8"). *Conspicuous and often common* in canopy and borders of humid forest, secondary woodland, and adjacent clearings from Colombia to se. Brazil region, but largely absent from n. Amazonia. To about 1500 m, locally higher in Andes. Unmistakable. Stubby bill. *Black with white forecrown and superciliary;* crown and nape silvery in **southern birds** (A), ashy in **northern birds** (B); rump patch white; *central tail feathers*

greatly elongated. ♀ paler and grayer on belly. **Immatures** may *lack* lengthened tail feathers and the pale crown, and thus can be confusing (note their short bill; cf. certain black tyrants). Usually in pairs (sometimes family groups) and highly sedentary, not joining mixed flocks. Often perches on dead snags and branches, flicking the long tail and sallying into the air after insects. The most frequent call is a distinctive soft, rising "sweee?" Also: Honduras to Panama.

Lessonia

Two small, plump, nearly terrestrial tyrannids of open terrain found in the Andes and s. South America, *almost always found near water. The unmistakable ♂♂ are black and rufous.*

Austral Negrito
Lessonia rufa   PLATE 58(2)
12 cm (4¾"). *Common and conspicuous breeder in open grassy or barren areas, usually near water, in cen. and s. Chile and s. Argentina;* in austral winter migrates north, especially along either coast, a few reaching Bolivia and Paraguay. Mostly below 1000 m. ♂ *black* with *contrasting rufous back.* ♀ has head and nape brownish gray, *back rufous brown;* wings and tail contrasting black. Below dull grayish, belly whiter. Cf. Andean Negrito. ♀ might be confused with Spot-billed Ground Tyrant (though that lacks even a tinge of rufous on back). Basically a terrestrial bird, though perching freely on fences and shrubs; runs about actively, often fluttering into the air in pursuit of insects. When breeding can be locally abundant, especially in the far south; at other times often occurs in small loose groups.

Andean Negrito
Lessonia oreas   PLATE 58(3)
12.5 cm (5"). Uncommon in open areas, almost invariably near water, in *high Andes from cen. Peru* (Ancash) *to n. Chile and nw. Argentina* (Catamarca). Mostly 3000–4300 m. ♂ resembles ♂ Austral Negrito but slightly larger with a paler rufous back and *whitish inner webs of flight feathers* (these visible mainly in flight). ♀ differs from Austral in having white in wing; it is more rufous on back and *much sootier below.* A few Australs may migrate north into or near Andean's range; Andean seems to be more or less resident, but a few occasionally descend to the Peruvian coast. Behavior much as in Austral,

though Andean rarely or never is as numerous and seems not to gather in groups.

Spectacled Tyrant
Hymenops perspicillatus   PLATE 58(4)
15.5–16 cm (6–6¼"). *Conspicuous and often common in and around marshes and damp grassy or shrubby areas;* breeds mainly in Argentina and cen. Chile, in austral winter a few migrating north to Bolivia. To 2000 m. *Both sexes have prominent yellow wattle around eye* (the spectacles) *and a yellow iris;* nonbreeding birds have wattle reduced or even lacking. ♂'s bill pale yellow, ♀'s duskier. Unmistakable ♂ *black* with *mainly white primaries* (tips black), the white *very* conspicuous on flying birds (usually visible even when perched). ♀ streaked brown and dusky above with a buffyish superciliary; wings with two buff bars and *mainly rufous primaries* (visible on perched birds, obvious in flight). Below whitish to pale buff, chest streaked dusky. Usually solitary, perching low and in the open, dropping down to mud or grass in pursuit of insect prey; sometimes runs on the ground. Breeding ♂♂ are especially obvious and perform a spectacular looping aerial display. More gregarious when not breeding, ♀-plumaged birds (some doubtless immatures) then more numerous than ♂♂.

White-headed Marsh Tyrant
Arundinicola leucocephala   PLATE 58(5)
13 cm (5"). *Widespread and fairly common in marshes, damp shrubby grasslands, and river islands from Colombia and Venezuela to n. Argentina.* Mostly below 500 m. Lower mandible yellow basally. Slightly bushy-crested ♂ unmistakable, *black* with *contrasting white head and throat.* ♀ *ashy grayish brown above* with white forecrown and blackish tail. Whitish below, *sides and flanks washed ashy brown.* Pied and Black-backed Water Tyrants vaguely resemble ♀ but are more sharply black and white. Conspicuous, perching erectly on grass stems or on a shrub or low tree, sallying short distances into air. Unlike the *Fluvicola* water tyrants, White-headeds infrequently drop to the ground; they never fan or cock their tail. Usually quiet.

Fluvicola
An attractive trio of boldly patterned, *essentially black and white* flycatchers that are *conspicuous near water,* where they often occur together with the White-headed Marsh Tyrant.

Pied Water Tyrant
Fluvicola pica   PLATE 58(6)
13 cm (5"). Common in and around marshes, ponds, and lakes, foraging in adjacent open areas, from *n. Colombia to the Guianas.* To 1000 m. *Head and underparts white, contrasting with black hindcrown, back, wings, and tail;* scapulars, rump, and narrow tail-tip also white; some white mottling on back. ♀ White-headed Marsh Tyrant not nearly as sharply black and white, being ashy brown above. Usually in pairs, foraging on or near the ground and often quite bold; regularly hops out onto floating vegetation, flicking and fanning its slightly cocked tail. Frequent call a nasal "zhweeoo" or "zhreeo." Also: Panama.

Black-backed Water Tyrant
Fluvicola albiventer   PLATE 58(7)
14 cm (5½"). Fairly common around marshes and in adjacent shrubby vegetation from *e. Brazil to n. Argentina* (n. Buenos Aires), in austral winter a few migrating north to w. Amazonia. Mostly below 1000 m. *Replaces slightly smaller Pied Water Tyrant southward.* Differs in its *entirely black back* with narrow white rump band and *wing-bars* (variable in extent). Pied Water Tyrant has broad white scapulars and plain black wings (*no bars*). ♀ White-headed Marsh Tyrant is ashy brown (not black) above, has no white on rump and wings. Behavior as in Pied Water Tyrant. Black-backed seems quieter but does give a nasal "zree-zri-zri-zri" and a sharper "treeu!" (J. M. Barnett recording).

Masked Water Tyrant
Fluvicola nengeta   PLATE 58(8)
14.5 cm (5¾"). *Remarkably disjunct range. Fairly common around marshes, ponds, and in nearby semiopen shrubby areas in w. Ecuador (north to Esmeraldas) and extreme nw. Peru (Tumbes), and in e. Brazil* (Maranhão to São Paulo). To 1000 m in Brazil, where it continues to spread and increase, even colonizing many city parks. *Mostly white with black stripe through eye and black wings and tail,* with broad white tips on tail; back pale brownish gray. Pied and Black-backed Water Tyrants are mainly black above, aside from their white heads that *lack* the Masked's black eye-stripe. This dapper bird, conspicuous and charmingly tame, forages singly or in pairs,

mainly on or near the ground and while hopping on floating vegetation. More often around houses than Pied or Black-backed Water Tyrants. Usually holds tail slightly cocked. Distinctive call a sharp "kirt!" or "kirt-kirt," often given in flight; pairs sometimes chatter together.

Alectrurus

Two amazing tyrannids found locally in *southern grasslands, ♂♂ with unique tail forms.* Populations of both species are now sadly *much reduced* because of agricultural expansion and intensification. Both species seem nearly if not in fact mute.

Strange-tailed Tyrant

Alectrurus risora   PLATE 58(9)

20 cm (8"), long-tailed breeding ♂♂ up to 31 cm (12"). *Now very local, but given good conditions can be numerous, in damp grassland and marshy areas from s. Paraguay to ne. Argentina* (mainly Corrientes). To 500 m. Bill pinkish (♂) or yellow (♀). Unmistakable ♂ *black above* with gray on rump, scapulars and wing edges whitish. Throat white, but *feathers lost while breeding, exposing salmon red skin; breast black,* belly white. *Tail bizarre* with *outer pair of feathers much lengthened, basally reduced to the shaft but with rest of inner web very broad, springing from crissum and twisted* (thus *perpendicular to and below rest of tail*). Molting birds have reduced tail plumes and more mottled plumage. ♀ mottled brown above, buffier on superciliary, scapulars, and rump. Whitish below with *narrow buff pectoral band. Outer pair of tail feathers (structurally like ♂'s) elongated and reduced to their shafts but ending in small rackets.* ♀ Cock-tailed Tyrant (not known to occur with Strange-tailed, favoring drier habitats) is similar but smaller; it *lacks* elongated rackets and has only a *partial* chest-band. The spectacular Strange-tailed Tyrant is conspicuous in the few areas where it persists, there perching on grass stems and fences and sallying short distances into the air and down into tall grass. Nonbreeders sometimes gather into loose groups. ♂'s flight is slow and labored, the plumes held below rest of tail and whipped up and down.

Cock-tailed Tyrant

Alectrurus tricolor   PLATE 58(10)

12 cm (4¾"), long-tailed breeding ♂♂ up to 18 cm (7"). *Now very local in less-disturbed grasslands* (grass must be *tall,* having gone unburned

for several years), but given good conditions can be common, from *s. Brazil to n. Bolivia and e. Paraguay.* To 1100 m. Unmistakable ♂ *black above* with gray on rump, white shoulders and secondary edging. *Face and underparts white,* with *black patch on either side of chest. Bizarre tail usually held cocked,* with *inner pairs of feathers lengthened and very broad, held perpendicular to body;* tail usually looks frayed. ♀ mottled brown above, buffier on superciliary, shoulders, and scapulars; short tail has normal shape. Whitish below with *brown smudge on sides of chest.* Full-plumaged ♂♂ are typically a minority; ♀♀ are plump, short-tailed, brown and buff, not likely confused. Bearded Tachuri and ♀ seedeaters have very different shape. Cf. also ♀ Strange-tailed Tyrant (with small tail rackets). Cock-tailed perches in tall grass, gleaning and sallying for insects; sometimes accompanies seedeater flocks. Breeding ♂♂ engage in a fantastic display in which they launch into the air on fast fluttery wingbeats with the tail held so far forward over back that it almost touches head.

Attila

Fairly large, *bull-headed* tyrannids with *heavy hooked bills,* attilas are retiring birds of humid forest and woodland in the lowlands. Vocal, they are *heard much more often than seen.* Most are *primarily some shade of rufous,* the wide-ranging Bright-rumped (in most of its morphs) being the exception. Nests are placed in holes, often in epiphytic vegetation.

Rufous-tailed Attila

Attila phoenicurus   PLATE 59(1)

18 cm (7"). *Rare* to uncommon in canopy and subcanopy of humid forest and woodland; *breeds locally in se. Brazil region* (north to Espírito Santo), in austral winter migrating to cen. Amazonia (where it does not sing and therefore is rarely recorded). To 1500 m. Bill blackish. *Head and nape dark gray contrasting with deep rufous upperparts,* primaries blackish. *Below orange-ochraceous.* Gray-hooded Attila is larger and has throat whitish streaked gray. Citron-bellied Attila has a less contrasting gray head, yellower rump, more pale on bill. ♀ Crested Becard is less bright overall with stouter bill, gray on crown only (not nape). Found singly or in pairs, usually not associated with mixed flocks. Most in evidence when it is singing on its breed-

ing grounds, with far-carrying song a fast "whee? whee? whee-bit," repeated over and over. Softer call a repeated "peeur."

Gray-hooded Attila
Attila rufus PLATE 59(2)

21 cm (8¼"). Fairly common in subcanopy and mid-levels of humid and montane forest and forest borders in *se. Brazil* (e. Bahia to Rio Grande do Sul). To 1500 m. *Large*. Bill basally pinkish. In **most of range** (illustrated) *head and nape gray;* otherwise rufous above, palest on rump; primaries blackish. *Throat white streaked gray, contrasting with orange-ochraceous breast and flanks,* midbelly yellow. In **Bahia** has a mostly rufous throat. Rufous-tailed Attila is smaller and is entirely rufous below (including throat). Rufous-morph Bright-rumped Attila shows wing-bars, breast streaking, whitish belly. Ranges singly or in pairs, and for an attila often conspicuous, more often at forest edge than the others. Nonetheless, when breeding, heard far more often than seen, with song a far-carrying series of 6–9 slowly delivered "whee" notes that rise in pitch and strength before fading on the last note; also gives a shorter, softer "wee, tee-tee-pu."

Citron-bellied Attila
Attila citriniventris

18.5 cm (7¼"). *Rare and local in subcanopy of humid forest in w. Amazonia;* seems to favor areas with sandy soil. Below 500 m. Bill basally pinkish. *Head gray,* back rufous brown, *rump paler cinnamon-rufous* and tail rufous. Upper throat pale grayish; *below bright ochraceous,* belly yellower and chest with obscure dusky streaking. Rufous morph (rare) of Bright-rumped Attila lacks gray on head, has a brighter rump and whitish belly. Cf. also Rufous-tailed Attila (a rare migrant into Citron-bellied's range). An infrequently encountered attila, with inactive behavior much as in the Bright-rumped. Song, often repeated tirelessly, a fast and rising "whee? whee? whee? whee? wheé? bu" that ascends until the final lower-pitched note; recalls Bright-rumped Attila, though most notes in the Bright-rumped song are doubled and the last note is higher, not lower.

Cinnamon Attila
Attila cinnamomeus PLATE 59(3)

19.5 cm (7¾"). Fairly common in várzea forest and woodland, swampy places, and lake and stream margins from *Amazonia to the Guianas*. To 500 m. *Bill black. Mostly cinnamon-rufous,*

paler on rump and yellower below; primaries and greater wing-coverts mainly blackish. The similarly colored Várzea Schiffornis differs markedly in shape and behavior. Citron-bellied Attila has a gray head, pale lower mandible, etc.; it inhabits terra firme canopy. White-eyed Attila has a staring white iris, pale lower mandible, less rufous upperparts. Found singly or in pairs, regularly foraging at forest (or water's) edge; often not hard to see. Often raises its tail, then jerks it back. Has two vocalizations, both with a loud ringing quality, the more distinctive a slurred "tuu-eeeeur," almost like a hawk-eagle. Full song a leisurely series reminiscent of other attilas but shorter, e.g., "whoor, wheer wheeér-wher."

Ochraceous Attila
Attila torridus

20.5 cm (8"). Now rare to uncommon and local in mid-levels and subcanopy of humid and semihumid forest, woodland, and adjacent plantations from *extreme sw. Colombia* (w. Nariño) *to extreme nw. Peru* (Tumbes). Mostly below 1500 m. Bill black. *Mostly cinnamon above,* yellower on rump, with contrasting blackish wings. *Below ochraceous yellow,* yellowest on belly. Nothing similar in range; *nearly an Ecuador endemic.* West of Andes the only other attila is the very different Bright-rumped. Rufous Mourner and Rufous Piha are truly rufous. Like other attilas, seen singly and in pairs and generally inconspicuous; like Cinnamon Attila, often raises its tail before pounding it downward. Presence made known by its far-carrying calls, the most frequent a "whoeeeer," like a hawk-eagle, sometimes extended into a "whoeeeer, wheéu, whit-whit." Also gives a sharp "wheek!" or "keek." Song a rising series of whistled notes, "wuuu-wuuu-weee-weee-weeé-weeé-wuyeép!"

White-eyed Attila
Attila bolivianus PLATE 59(4)

19 cm (7½"). Uncommon in várzea and gallery forest and their borders from *s. Amazonia to e. Bolivia and pantanal of sw. Brazil*. Below 300 m. Often called Dull-capped Attila. *Staring yellowish white eye*. Bill mainly horn. *Rufous brown above* with grayish crown, bright cinnamon-rufous on rump and tail; primaries and greater wing-coverts blackish. Below cinnamon-rufous, belly paler. The pale eye, always obvious, should preclude confusion, though a few Bright-rumped Attilas also have pale irides. The more uniform Cinnamon Attila is dark-eyed and has a black bill. Found singly or in pairs, usually not with flocks.

Song an ascending series of whistled notes, halting at first, e.g., "whup; whup, wheep, wheep, wheep, wheeyp, wheeyp, wheebit, wheeeur," the last note distinctly lower and slurred.

Bright-rumped Attila
Attila spadiceus PLATE 59(5)
18.5–19 cm (7¼–7½"). *Widespread but generally uncommon* in subcanopy and borders of humid forest from Colombia and Venezuela to Amazonia, and in e. Brazil; in Amazonia confined to terra firme. Mostly below 1500 m, locally to 2000 m in nw. Ecuador. Iris reddish brown, rarely whitish; bill basally pinkish. *Polymorphic, especially in Amazonia; intermediates occur.* **Olive morph** (the most frequent; illustrated) olive above with a vague yellowish brow and *contrasting yellow rump* (can be tinged buff); wings duskier *with pale grayish to rufescent wing-bars. Throat and breast olive streaked yellow,* belly whiter and unstreaked. **Gray morph** has *solid gray head and neck,* gray throat and breast vaguely streaked whitish. **Rufous morph** *rufous above* with ochraceous yellow rump; *throat and breast rufous* vaguely streaked whitish. *No other attila is ever predominantly olive and none has such prominent wing-bars, nor any streaking below.* Stolid and inconspicuous, perching erectly at various levels, though mainly remains well above the ground. Sallies for insects and some fruit; usually solitary and not with flocks. Often wags or jerks tail downward. Far-carrying song an ascending series of spirited notes, whistled and doubled, e.g., "whup, whip, wheédip, wheédip, wheédip, wheédip, wheeeyr?" with a distinctive final higher-pitched note. Frequent call a fast laughing "weer-weer-weer-weer-weer-wheerpo." Also: Mexico to Panama.

Casiornis

Two *predominantly rufous* tyrannids of *lighter woodland in e. and s.-cen. South America,* similar to *Myiarchus* but smaller and more slender.

Rufous Casiornis
Casiornis rufus PLATE 59(6)
18 cm (7"). *Fairly common in deciduous and gallery woodland and chaco scrub mainly from n. Bolivia to s. Amaz. and sw. Brazil and n. Argentina;* in austral winter some migrate into sw. Amazonia, then in riparian woodland and thickets.

Mostly below 1500 m. Bill basally pinkish. *Uniform rufous above. Throat and breast cinnamon,* belly pale buffy-yellow. More slender and longer-tailed than any becard. Cf. rarer Ash-throated Casiornis. Arboreal, usually in pairs, perching erectly and often elevating its crest feathers and nodding head like a *Myiarchus.* Regularly accompanies mixed flocks. Quiet, but does give a weak "pseee," sometimes in a quick series.

Ash-throated Casiornis
Casiornis fuscus PLATE 59(7)
18 cm (7"). *Uncommon and local in caatinga woodland, scrub, and campinas of ne. Brazil* (west locally to south of lower Amazon, and south to nw. Minas Gerais). Bill basally pinkish. To 500 m. Crown rufous, *back dull sandy brown;* tail rufous, *wings dusky broadly edged rufous and buff.* Throat whitish, *breast grayish fawn,* belly creamy yellowish. Overlaps marginally with more numerous and wide-ranging Rufous Casiornis (more uniform rufous above and brighter cinnamon below). Ash-throated's behavior is similar. Call a vigorous "cheeyp, chew-chew"; song (less often heard) a series of about a dozen strong "chew" notes, hesitating at end.

Rhytipterna

Three dissimilar, *Myiarchus*-like tyrannids. Two species are found in humid lowland forest on either side of the Andes (Rufous and Grayish Mourners), one very locally in sandy-belt woodland (Pale-bellied).

Rufous Mourner
Rhytipterna holerythra PLATE 59(8)
20.5 cm (8"). Uncommon in mid-levels and subcanopy of humid forest in lowlands and foothills of w. *Colombia and nw. Ecuador* (mainly Esmeraldas). To 1000 m. *Rich rufous,* somewhat paler below; wings slightly duskier. Easily confused with Rufous Piha (a cotinga), a larger but proportionately shorter-tailed bird that differs, subtly, in its stouter bill, paler throat, and vague pale eye-ring; the piha looks "softer," more dove-like. Voices differ strikingly. Speckled Mourner (also a cotinga) has dusky wing-coverts with rufous tips. Cf. also ♀ One-colored Becard. Found singly or in pairs, perching erectly and quietly on open branches, peering around in search of its mainly insect prey; also eats fruit. Regular with mixed flocks. Distinctive wolf-whistle call

a drawled "wheeeip, wheeeur" that recalls song of Barred Puffbird (*Nystalus radiolatus*). Song a snappier series, e.g., "wheee-per, wheeéur." Also: Mexico to Panama.

Grayish Mourner

Rhytipterna simplex   PLATE 59(9)

20.5 cm (8"). Fairly common in mid-levels and subcanopy of humid forest from *Amazonia to the Guianas,* and in e. Brazil. Mostly below 800 m. Iris reddish. *Uniform plain gray,* slightly paler below with a slight yellowish cast. **Juvenile** has fulvous edging on wings and tail. The similarly colored but larger Screaming Piha has a stouter bill, more grayish eye, purer gray plumage (without the yellowish tone below), and a rounder head. Their voices, of course, differ markedly; further, the piha rarely or never accompanies flocks. Cinereous Mourner has prominent rufous wing-spots. Behavior as in Rufous Mourner. Distinctive call a fast "r-t-t-t-t-t-tchéw!"; explosive at end (like a sneeze), sometimes with rising preliminary notes. The "tchéw!" can be given in series.

Pale-bellied Mourner

Rhytipterna immunda   PLATE 59(10)

18.5 cm (7¼"). *Very local in light woodland and scrub in sandy-soil areas from the Guianas and s. Venezuela to cen. Amazonia.* To 300 m. *A Myiarchus-like mourner, with* lower mandible pinkish at base. *Grayish olive brown above,* tail browner; wings duskier with two pale grayish bars and rufous primary edging. Throat and breast grayish, belly pale yellowish with *flanks tinged rusty or buff. This obscure bird is often best identified by a combination of range, habitat, and voice.* It looks like a faded, dingy *Myiarchus,* though no *Myiarchus* shows color on flanks; the mourner's head is rounder and its eye looks larger. Short-crested and the potentially sympatric race of Swainson's Flycatcher both have all-black bills. Inconspicuous, perching quietly in trees and shrubs with a less upright posture than *Myiarchus;* sometimes with small mixed flocks. Most frequent call a distinctive "pur-treeép, cheeeuu" or "puu-puu-treeép, cheeeu" with loud ringing quality of a schiffornis. Also gives a plaintive "pueeer" call recalling Dusky-capped Flycatcher.

Myiarchus

Fairly large flycatchers found widely in semiopen and forest edge situations, *most Myiarchus are very similar to each other in plumage* and *thus are often best identified by range and through their (usually) distinctive voices.* Unless otherwise indicated, wings are dusky with two pale grayish bars and edging. Nests are generally placed in tree cavities.

Rufous Flycatcher

Myiarchus semirufus   PLATE 59(11)

18 cm (7"). *Now rare and local in patches of arid woodland and scrub in nw. Peru* (Tumbes to Lima). To 500 m. Above dull dark grayish brown, tail mostly rufous; *wing-coverts and broad flight feather edging rufous.* Uniform cinnamon below. *Easily the most rufescent Myiarchus and thus unmistakable;* occurs only with Sooty-crowned. Inconspicuous, but with general behavior much as in other better-known *Myiarchus.* This distinctive flycatcher is declining because of widespread habitat destruction and degradation, and also because of direct persecution (it is often killed by beekeepers). Most frequent call a simple "huit"; dawn song a series of "huit" notes interspersed with whistled and sharper notes.

Brown-crested Flycatcher

Myiarchus tyrannulus   PLATE 59(12)

19.5 cm (7¾"). *Widespread and often common in a variety of semiopen habitats* (savanna, cerrado, caatinga and chaco scrub, gallery woodland), from n. Colombia and Venezuela to n. Argentina; *primarily occurs in arid regions,* and absent from much of Amazonia. To 1700 m. Bill pinkish at base. Crown dull brown, otherwise dull grayish brown above; wings with *rufous primary edging* (less evident when worn); tail feathers with *inner webs broadly edged rufous* (most evident from below, and in flight). Throat and breast pale gray, belly pale yellow. Great Crested Flycatcher shows even more rufous in tail and more contrast on underparts. *Otherwise no other Myiarchus shows so much rufous in wings and tail* (juveniles of the others may show a little). Conspicuous and noisy, often perching in the open, peering about and vigorously nodding head. Most frequent call a sharp "peert!" or "weerp!"; and a "hurrip," sometimes repeated. Has no whistled calls. Also: sw. United States to Costa Rica.

Great Crested Flycatcher
Myiarchus crinitus
20 cm (8"). *Uncommon boreal migrant to borders and canopy of humid forest and woodland in nw. South America* (Oct.–Mar.). To 1200 m. Resembles Brown-crested Flycatcher but more olivaceous above, throat and breast darker gray and belly deeper yellow (*hence underparts contrast more*), and inner webs of tail feathers all rufous (*thus underside of tail is almost solid rufous*). More arboreal and less conspicuous than Brown-crested, favoring wooded habitats. Presence sometimes revealed by its inflected "whreeep" call. Breeds in e. North America.

Swainson's Flycatcher
Myiarchus swainsoni   PLATE 59(13)
18–18.5 cm (7–7¼"). *Widespread and generally fairly common* in a variety of forested and wooded habitats and borders, and in savannas, from s. Venezuela and Guianas to cen. Argentina; in austral winter migrates to w. Amazonia, there favoring riparian growth and clearings. Mostly below 1200 m. *Lower mandible pinkish at least at base* (but all black in birds of **s. Venezuela region**). Variation complex; more than one species probably involved. Resident birds in **most of range** (illustrated) *rather pale grayish olive above;* tail blackish with white outer web. Throat and breast pale gray, belly pale yellow. **Argentina and se. Bolivia breeders** (migrating mainly to w. Amazonia) have *distinctly darker ear-coverts.* **Se. Brazil and Uruguay breeders** (migrating to Venezuela) are darker above and brighter on belly. Most divergent are birds resident in **s. Venezuela area:** *markedly darker above* (blackish on crown) and *belly duller creamy yellowish.* Similarly plumaged (but less pallid) Short-crested Flycatcher has an all-black bill; Swainson's in s. Venezuela area (where also black-billed) differ only in their pale belly (also voice). Behavior much as in other forest-based *Myiarchus.* Song of southern breeders a loud "pút-it-here"; also gives a soft "whoo." In s. Venezuela area gives a whistled "wheeyr" interspersed with "hic" notes.

Short-crested Flycatcher
Myiarchus ferox   PLATE 59(14)
18–18.5 cm (7–7¼"). *Widespread and generally common* at borders of humid forest and woodland and in clearings from e. Colombia and s. Venezuela to ne. Argentina and s. Brazil. Mostly below 1000 m. *Bill black.* In **most of range** (illustrated) dark olivaceous brown above, sootiest on head; tail uniform dusky. Throat and breast gray, belly clear yellow. In **llanos of Venezuela and ne. Colombia,** and from **e. Bolivia and s. Brazil to Argentina,** paler above and tail browner. Cf. Venezuelan and Panama Flycatchers (both very similar). Swainson's Flycatcher is paler generally, and its pale lower mandible is normally evident (except in s. Venezuela area, where bill also black; there you must rely on voice, though Short-crested's yellow on belly is brighter). Found singly or in pairs, usually foraging in semiopen close to the ground, *most often near water.* Oft-heard and distinctive call a soft rolling "prrrt" or "dr'r'r'ru."

Panama Flycatcher
Myiarchus panamensis
18 cm (7"). Uncommon in secondary woodland, clearings, forest borders, and mangroves in *n. and w. Colombia* (south to w. Nariño) *and nw. Venezuela.* To 600 m. *Closely* resembles Short-crested Flycatcher (no overlap). Also nearly identical to Venezuelan Flycatcher, which *does* overlap and *is best identified by voice.* Behavior much as in Short-crested Flycatcher, though Panama is less tied to water. Most frequent call a short whistled note given in pairs or short series; dawn song a fast "tseeédew" or "tee, deedeedeedeedeedee." Also: Costa Rica and Panama.

Venezuelan Flycatcher
Myiarchus venezuelensis
18 cm (7"). Uncommon in deciduous woodland, borders, and plantations in *n. Colombia and n. Venezuela.* To 500 m. *Closely* resembles Short-crested Flycatcher; *best identified by range and voice.* Short-crested race found in the zone of overlap (e. Venezuela) is darker above than the Venezuelan. Cf. also Panama Flycatcher (limited overlap), also best separated by voice. Behavior much as in Short-crested Flycatcher, though shows no particular affinity for water. Most frequent call a sharp "wheeyr," often repeated steadily.

Sooty-crowned Flycatcher
Myiarchus phaeocephalus   PLATE 59(15)
18 cm (7"). Uncommon in deciduous woodland, arid scrub, and clearings from *nw. Ecuador* (w. Esmeraldas) *to nw. Peru* (Lambayeque), and *locally in upper Río Marañón valley.* To 1100 m. Bill black. *Forecrown grayish, hindcrown blackish,* back grayish olive; *tail blackish with pale*

tip and outer web of outermost pair of feathers. Throat and breast pale gray, belly pale yellow. Dusky-capped Flycatcher is smaller and in area of sympatry has a fully blackish crown, brighter yellow belly, and some rufous primary edging. Cf. also Brown-crested Flycatcher. Behavior similar to other *Myiarchus.* Most frequent call a simple querulous "freeee?" or "whreee?" Song, less often heard, more complex and variable, e.g., "freee-free-dee-di-di," ending with shorter slurred notes; recalls Red-billed Scythebill.

Pale-edged Flycatcher
Myiarchus cephalotes
18 cm (7"). Uncommon in canopy and borders of montane forest and woodland and adjacent clearings on *east slope of Andes from n. Venezuela to w. Bolivia* (w. Santa Cruz). Mostly 1100–2400 m. Bill black. Above uniform brownish olive; tail blackish *with pale outer web on outermost pair of feathers.* Throat and breast pale gray, belly clear yellow. Short-crested Flycatcher (marginal overlap) *lacks* the pale edge to tail but otherwise is similar. Cf. also Sierran Elaenia. Behavior as in other *Myiarchus;* often forages quite low in clearings. Song a sharp "piyp!" followed by several descending "wheeyr" notes; call a loud repeated clear "pip" or "piup."

Apical Flycatcher
Myiarchus apicalis
18 cm (7"). Uncommon in gallery woodland, arid scrub, and agricultural areas in *w. Colombia* (Santander to Nariño); *favors arid regions.* Mostly below 1700 m. Resembles Sooty-crowned Flycatcher (no overlap), but *tail with feathers broadly tipped whitish,* outer web of outer pair also whitish. Pale-edged Flycatcher lacks pale tip to tail. Behavior much like other *Myiarchus.* Gives a variety of calls, including a "huit" often in series.

Dusky-capped Flycatcher
Myiarchus tuberculifer   PLATE 59(16)
16–17 cm (6¼–6¾"). *A widespread, small Myiarchus, often common,* found in canopy and borders of a wide variety of humid and montane forests and woodlands, also in adjacent clearings, from Colombia and Venezuela to nw. Argentina (Tucumán), a few also in *se. Brazil.* To 2500 m in Andes, occasionally higher. Perhaps more than one species. In **most of range** (illustrated) has *crown sepia brown* and back dark olive; tail dusky. Throat and breast gray, belly

clear yellow. In **w. Ecuador** *crown contrasting blackish;* on **east slope of Andes from s. Ecuador south** has an *equally blackish crown* but also *larger.* Most Dusky-capped races are so much smaller than other *Myiarchus* that confusion is unlikely; the large Andean race is best known by its dark crown, all-dark tail, and voice. Behavior as in other *Myiarchus,* though Dusky-capped is more arboreal and more likely to join mixed flocks. Frequent call a distinctive clear whistled "wheeeuw." Also: sw. United States to Panama.

Sirystes

Two distinctive *black, gray, and white* tyrannids that range in the canopy and borders of humid forests on either side of the Andes. They were formerly considered conspecific and called simply the Sirystes.

Eastern Sirystes
Sirystes sibilator *   PLATE 59(17)
18.5 cm (7¼"). Locally fairly common in canopy and borders of humid forest (in Amazonia especially in várzea) from *s. Venezuela and the Guianas to ne. Argentina and s. Brazil.* To 1000 m in se. Brazil. In **ne. South America** (illustrated) *crown black,* shading to slaty on sides of head, and with *mottled gray back* and *whitish rump;* wings and tail blackish, coverts and inner flight feathers edged grayish. *Throat and breast pale gray, belly white.* In **most of range** *lacks* the whitish rump; in **w. Amazonia** white on rump *more extensive,* wing-edging narrow, and whiter below. Like a *Myiarchus* in aspect and comportment, but with very different black, gray, and white plumage. Found singly or in pairs, frequently accompanying (even leading) mixed flocks. They often lean forward, nodding head and ruffling crown feathers. Very vocal, with calls including a loud "wheeer-péw" or "wheeer-péwpu," sometimes extended into an excited series "wheeer-pe-pe-pew-pew-péw" or "wheeer-péw-péw-péw."

Western Sirystes
Sirystes albogriseus *
18.5 cm (7¼"). Uncommon and local in canopy and borders of humid forest in *w. Colombia and nw. Ecuador* (mainly Esmeraldas). To 500 m. Resembles Eastern Sirystes (its illustrated northeast race), but with a *purer gray back, whiter rump and underparts, broader white wing-bars and edging,* and *white tip to tail.* Like Eastern Sirystes, this

species recalls a *Myiarchus*, though it is colored very differently. Behavior much as in Eastern Sirystes. Vocalizations differ sharply, with Western's most frequent call a husky "chup-chip-chip," or "prup-prip-prip-prip." Also: Panama.

Boat-billed Flycatcher
Megarynchus pitangua   PLATE 60(1)
23 cm (9"). *Widespread and fairly common in canopy and borders of forest and woodland and clearings from Colombia and Venezuela to ne. Argentina and s. Brazil. Mostly below 1500 m. Bill heavy and broad with obvious arch on culmen.* Black crown and face with semiconcealed yellow coronal patch and long white superciliary; above brownish olive, wings and tail dusky *with little or no rufous edging.* Throat white, below bright yellow. **Western birds** have coronal patch tawny-orange. Great Kiskadee has a differently shaped bill (less wide, with straight culmen) and is browner above with more rufous wing and tail edging. Though noisy, Boat-billed is less conspicuous than Great Kiskadee; it is more arboreal and less apt to perch low or in the open. Pairs sometimes range with mixed flocks but most often are alone. Eats mainly large insects, also fruit. Most frequent call a strident, nasal "kryeeeh-nyeh-nyeh-nyeh," sometimes given as it pumps head. West of Andes gives a fast "kreh-kreh-kreh-kreh-kreh-kreeeenh" and a series of "kirrr-wick" calls. Also: Mexico to Panama.

Great Kiskadee
Pitangus sulphuratus   PLATE 60(2)
20.5–23.5 cm (8–9¼"). *Common, conspicuous, and widespread* in a variety of semiopen areas (though less numerous in forested regions, where more or less confined to the margins of lakes and rivers) from Colombia and Venezuela to cen. Argentina. Mostly below 1500 m, a few higher locally in Andean valleys. *Bill quite heavy and straight,* often with pink at gape. Crown and face black with semiconcealed yellow coronal patch and long white superciliary; above olive brown, *wing and tail feathers often with prominent rufous margins* (though birds from **south of Amazonia** show little or none; they also are larger). Throat white, below bright yellow. In **n. Colombia and n. Venezuela** smaller and more rufescent above. Boat-billed Flycatcher has a more massive bill with arched culmen, is more olive above with less rufous in wings and tail. The less robust and slender-billed Lesser Kiskadee is closely tied to water. Noisy and familiar, regularly found even in urban parks, often perching

low and in the open; unwary, at times even brazen and pugnacious. Kiskadees consume mostly insects and fruit but also plunge into water after fish and pursue lizards and even snakes; they are known to rob nests of small birds and sometimes even eat scraps of garbage. Gives a variety of loud calls, the best known and most frequent being the boisterous "kis-ka-dee!" reflected in its English name. This can be varied to a "geép geép gareér" or simply a shrill raptorlike "keeeer." Also: Texas and Mexico to Panama.

Lesser Kiskadee
Philohydor lictor   PLATE 60(3)
17 cm (6¾"). *Fairly common around margins of lakes and sluggish streams and rivers, also in marshy pastures, from Colombia and Venezuela to Bolivia and s. Brazil. Mostly below 500 m. Bill long and slender.* Resembles Great Kiskadee's plumage, differs in *markedly smaller size, less robust shape, proportionately longer, narrower bill,* and *very different voice.* Also resembles Rusty-margined Flycatcher, which differs in its stubby bill and more rufescent upperparts (also voice). Ranges in pairs that perch on branches near water's surface, sallying to foliage and water's surface for insects. Its nasal, raspy calls are distinctive, but subdued compared with Great Kiskadee's. Most frequent is a "dzreeéy, dzwee" or "dzreeéy, dzwee-dzwee-dzwee." Also: Panama.

White-bearded Flycatcher
Phelpsia inornata   PLATE 60(4)
16.5 cm (6½"). *Local and uncommon in gallery woodland and groves, often around ranch buildings, in llanos of n. Venezuela and extreme ne. Colombia. To 450 m. Short black bill.* Olive brown above with black crown and face and long white superciliary; *wings plain (no rufous edging).* Throat white, below bright yellow. Rusty-margined Flycatcher shows prominent rufous wing edging, Social Flycatcher a duskier crown and face and usually pale wing-bars; both species have very different voices. Lesser Kiskadee has a longer and narrower bill, shows rufous wing-edging. White-bearded is usually in pairs, and even in the heart of its limited range is usually inconspicuous, infrequently encountered. Sallies for insects, mainly to the ground and low vegetation. Most easily found through its distinctive calls, often given by a pair as their wings quiver, mostly near dawn; a burst of loud excited calls, e.g., "cheé-dur, cheé-dur, cheé-dur, . . ." varied to "cheedurit, cheedurit, cheedurit. . . ."

Myiozetetes

Midsized flycatchers with stubby bills, two species with bold black-and-white head patterns, two of them duller. All but the Dusky-chested are noisy, common, conspicuous birds that favor secondary habitats.

Dusky-chested Flycatcher
Myiozetetes luteiventris   PLATE 60(5)
14.5 cm (5¾"). Uncommon in canopy and borders of terra firme forest from *Amazonia to the Guianas; much more forest-based than other Myiozetetes*. Mostly below 800 m. *Uniform dark olive brown above* with semiconcealed yellow-orange coronal patch but *no brow*. Throat whitish vaguely streaked dusky; below bright yellow, *breast flammulated olive*. Smaller than the other *Myiozetetes*, also differing in its *unmarked head* and breast streaking; Gray-capped is the most similar. The larger Sulphury Flycatcher has similar plumage but a grayer head, more extensively white foreneck; it favors palms. Dusky-chested is less numerous than other *Myiozetetes*, and as it tends to remain high in forest canopy, is often less conspicuous too. Though rarely with mixed flocks, it does join other birds at fruiting trees, and then sometimes comes lower. Calls recall Gray-capped Flycatcher and include a fast nasal mewing "nyeeuw-nyeeuw-keep-kít," sometimes given as a jumbled duet.

Social Flycatcher
Myiozetetes similis   PLATE 60(6)
17 cm (6¾"). *Common and widespread* in shrubby clearings, plantations, and humid forest and woodland borders from Colombia and Venezuela to e. Paraguay (where scarce) and s. Brazil. Mostly below 1400 m. *Crown dark gray* with *semiconcealed orange-red coronal patch, long white superciliary,* and blackish face; otherwise olive above, *wing-coverts edged pale grayish or buffyish* (wider in **n. Colombia, Venezuela, and w. Ecuador area**). Throat white, below bright yellow. **Juveniles** often show rufous wing-edging. Cf. similar Rusty-margined Flycatcher; Gray-capped Flycatcher lacks the Social's long white brow; Lesser Kiskadee has a longer and more slender bill. Social Flycatchers can be omnipresent in semiopen, cutover terrain. They perch, often in the open and sometimes partially cocking their tail, anywhere from the ground to the canopy of tall trees (though they are infrequent or lacking in canopy of more continuous forest); always especially numerous

near water. Socials sally to foliage for insects (less often into air) and also eat much fruit. They have a variety of mostly harsh calls, including a frequent "kreeoouw." East of Andes gives a chattered "ti-ti-ti-tíchew, chew" (also single "chew" calls); west of Andes a chattered "kree-kree-kree." Also: Mexico to Panama.

Rusty-margined Flycatcher
Myiozetetes cayanensis   PLATE 60(7)
17 cm (6¾"). Fairly common to common (especially near water) in shrubby clearings and plantations, and humid forest and woodland borders from Colombia and Venezuela to Bolivia and se. Brazil; absent from w. Amazonia. Mostly below 1000 m. In **most of range** olive brown above with black crown and face, semiconcealed *yellow coronal patch,* and long white superciliary; *wing feathers edged rufous*. Throat white, below bright yellow. In **Venezuela and ne. Colombia** (illustrated) similar but with broader rufous wing-edging, also some on tail; *se.* **Brazil** birds also show much rufous. Resembles Social Flycatcher and *often best separated by voice.* Social's coronal patch is orange-red (but color often hidden); it differs further in its duskier (less black) crown and sides of head, pale edging on wing-coverts, and *lack* of rufous primary edging (juvenile Socials may show some rufous too, but they also would show it on coverts). Cf. Lesser Kiskadee and (in Venezuela) White-bearded Flycatcher. Behavior much as in Social Flycatcher, though the Rusty-margin tends to be more retiring and is more tied to water. Frequent call a distinctive whining, plaintive "freeeea" or "wheeeeea," recalling Dusky-capped Flycatcher. Also gives faster, excited calls similar to Social's. Also: Panama.

Gray-capped Flycatcher
Myiozetetes granadensis   PLATE 60(8)
17 cm (6¾"). *Common* in borders of humid forest and woodland and in shrubby clearings, often near water, from *Colombia and s. Venezuela to n. Bolivia* (Santa Cruz). Mostly below 1200 m. Iris brownish gray. *Head gray* with semiconcealed orange-red coronal patch and *only a short white superciliary;* olive above, wings with narrow pale edging. Throat white, below bright yellow. ♀ has crown patch reduced or lacking. Social and Rusty-margined Flycatchers have bolder facial patterns with an obvious long white brow. Cf. the scarcer Dusky-chested Flycatcher. Behavior much as in Social Flycatcher, though Gray-capped is more tied to forest and

more often ranges in the canopy. Most calls are sharper than Social's (some rival Great Kiskadee's in strength) and include a "kip!" often repeated in series, and a "kip, keer, k-beer" or "kip, keer, kew-kew." Also: Honduras to Panama.

Conopias

Midsized flycatchers that recall the more numerous *Myiozetetes* flycatchers, *Conopias* have *proportionately longer bills* and are *much more forest-based*. Most have *yellow throats* (not white). All species have characteristic and frequently given *vocalizations*.

Three-striped Flycatcher
Conopias trivirgatus   PLATE 60(9)
14–14.5 cm (5½–5¾"). Uncommon and local in canopy and borders of humid forest from *Amazonia to se. Brazil region*. Mostly below 400 m, but to 950 m in Venezuela. In **se. Brazil region** (illustrated), where somewhat more numerous, has a blackish head with long white superciliary (*no* coronal patch); *above rather pale olive, wings and tail contrasting duskier*. Below bright yellow, *breast clouded olive*. **Amazonian** birds are smaller with no olive on breast. The larger Social Flycatcher has a stubbier bill, white throat, and pale edging on wing feathers (Three-striped's wings are plain and dark, and thus contrast more with back). Cf. also Yellow-throated Flycatcher. Ranges in pairs and small family groups, sometimes with mixed flocks, but remaining in forest canopy and easy to overlook unless vocalizing. Distinctive call a harsh, grating "jew" or "jeeuw," often repeated rapidly.

Lemon-browed Flycatcher
Conopias cinchoneti   PLATE 60(10)
16 cm (6¼"). *Uncommon and local in borders of montane forest and adjacent clearings in Andes from w. Venezuela (Trujillo) to s. Peru (Cuzco).* Mostly 900–2000 m. Above olive with a *long yellow superciliary extending from forehead nearly to nape;* wings and tail dusky. Mostly bright yellow below. No other comparable flycatcher shows the *yellow brow;* the brows of the others are *white.* Yellow-browed Tyrant has an entirely different distribution and behavior. Found in well-separated pairs or family groups, restless and rarely remaining long in one place; sometimes with mixed flocks. Often perches in the open, even atop leaves, looking around alertly. Distinctive, far-carrying call a series of shrill notes, e.g.,

"pi-dee!" or "di-d'reeee," often rapidly repeated; calling bird often vigorously pumps its head.

Yellow-throated Flycatcher
Conopias parvus   PLATE 60(11)
16.5 cm (6½"). Fairly common in canopy and borders of humid forest from s. *Venezuela and n. Brazil to the Guianas;* less numerous and more local in w. and s. Amazonia. To 1300 m. *Dark olive above* with black crown and face, semiconcealed yellow coronal patch, and *long white superciliary that encircles nape. Below all bright yellow.* Myiozetetes flycatchers have stubbier bills, white throats, etc.; they are not true forest birds, and their voices differ. Three-striped Flycatcher is smaller and paler olive above and not so black on head; voice also differs. Ranges in pairs or family groups that remain well above the ground, only rarely coming lower; often with mixed flocks. Regularly perches atop leaves, scanning nearby foliage for insects. Distinctive call a loud, ringing, rhythmic "kleeyuyu kleeyuyu kleeyuyu, . . ." often long-continued.

White-ringed Flycatcher
Conopias albovittatus
16.5 cm (6½"). Uncommon in canopy and borders of humid forest in w. *Colombia and nw. Ecuador* (mainly Esmeraldas). To 900 m. Resembles Yellow-throated Flycatcher (only east of Andes) but *throat white.* Social and Rusty-margined Flycatchers have stubbier bills and a white superciliary that does not encircle nape (sometimes it looks like it does, so beware); they differ vocally, and neither is a true forest bird. Behavior much as in Yellow-throated Flycatcher, though White-ringed's distinctive call is very different, a dry fast, whirring or rattling trill, "tree-r-r-r-r, tree-r-r-r-r. . . ." Also: Honduras to Panama.

Myiodynastes

Large, robust flycatchers with *stout bills* that are noisy and conspicuous in wooded areas. Two species are *prominently streaked*.

Baird's Flycatcher
Myiodynastes bairdii   PLATE 60(12)
23 cm (9"). Uncommon in deciduous woodland, arid scrub, and towns from sw. *Ecuador* (Manabí) to nw. *Peru* (Lima). Mostly below 1000 m. *Broad black mask* surmounted by sandy brown crown (palest above mask) with semiconcealed yellow coronal patch; back olive brown. Wings dusky,

feathers broadly edged rufous; rump and tail mostly rufous. Throat whitish and breast more ochraceous, obscurely streaked; belly pale yellow. Nothing really resembles this handsome and *large* flycatcher. Found in pairs, and often bold and conspicuous. Mainly forages for large insects. Call, given especially in early morning, a steadily repeated and grating "wrrr-yeeít . . . wrrr-yeeít. . . ."

Golden-crowned Flycatcher
Myiodynastes chrysocephalus   PLATE 60(13)
20.5–21.5 cm (8–8½"). *Locally fairly common* in borders of montane forest and woodland and adjacent clearings in *Andes from n. Venezuela to extreme nw. Argentina* (n. Salta). Mostly 1000–2200 m, lower on Pacific slope. From **Ecuador north** (illustrated) crown brownish gray with semiconcealed yellow coronal patch, long white superciliary, and dusky mask; *lower cheeks and throat pale buff, separated by dusky malar stripe.* Above olive, wings and tail dusky with rufous edging. Below yellow, *breast flammulated olive.* In **Peru and Bolivia** larger with less rufous edging on wings and tail. In general aspect recalls Great Kiskadee and Boat-billed Flycatcher (of *lowlands*), neither of which shows a malar stripe or breast flammulation. Streaked Flycatcher is also basically a lowland bird and is much more generally streaked. Found singly or in pairs, perching at varying levels; favors vicinity of streams. Sometimes joins mixed flocks, but usually solitary. Eats both insects and fruit. Loud vigorous calls include a squealing "skweé-ah!" or "squeeé-yu," both often repeated insistently.

Streaked Flycatcher
Myiodynastes maculatus   PLATE 60(14)
19.5–21 cm (7¾–8¼"). *Widespread and fairly common* in borders of forest, secondary woodland, and clearings from Colombia and Venezuela to n. Argentina; in austral winter southern breeders migrate to Amazonia and the Guianas, there favoring várzea and riparian habitats. Mostly below 1500 m. *A large, boldly streaked flycatcher.* In **most of range** (illustrated) *brown above streaked with dusky* with semiconcealed yellow coronal patch, *whitish superciliary*, blackish mask, whitish lower cheeks, and dusky malar streak. Wings with narrow rufous to buff edging; *rump and tail mainly rufous.* Throat white; below whitish to pale yellowish *streaked dusky*. **Migrants from Middle America** are more olivaceous above and yellowish on superciliary. **Southern breeders** (north to s. Peru and s. Brazil) *notably darker above with broad black-*

ish streaking and *more boldly and extensively streaked below; tail mainly blackish.* Cf. similar but less numerous Sulphur-bellied Flycatcher. Variegated Flycatcher is smaller with a stubbier bill and blackish crown; it is less obviously streaked. Found singly or in pairs, usually noisy and conspicuous (though austral migrants are less vocal); sometimes with mixed flocks. Consumes a variety of insects, mostly large, and also eats considerable fruit. Has a variety of loud and harsh calls, the most frequent a repeated "kip!"; also a "chup" or "eechup." More musical song, given at dawn and dusk, a repeated fast, rhythmic "wheeé-cheederee-wheé" (sometimes without the final "wheé"). Also: Mexico to Panama.

Sulphur-bellied Flycatcher
Myiodynastes luteiventris
20.5 cm (8"). *Uncommon boreal migrant* (mostly Oct.–Apr.) to canopy and borders of humid forest and woodland, riparian areas, and shrubby clearings of *w. Amazonia*. Mostly below 1000 m, transients higher. Resembles Streaked Flycatcher, differing from northern races of that species in its *broad dusky malar stripe that extends under the chin* (forming a "chinstrap"), little or no rufous primary edging, and *usually yellower lower underparts.* Behavior much as in Streaked Flycatcher. Generally quiet in South America, only rarely giving the forceful "squeez!-ya" or "squeez!" calls that are heard so often on its breeding grounds. Breeds from sw. United States to Costa Rica.

Piratic Flycatcher
Legatus leucophaius   PLATE 60(15)
14.5 cm (5¾"). *Fairly common and widespread* in borders of humid forest and woodland and in tall trees of adjacent clearings from Colombia and Venezuela to n. Argentina; an austral migrant in the far south, and seems to undertake local movements elsewhere. Mostly below 1200 m. *Stubby black bill. Dark olive brown above* with semiconcealed yellow coronal patch, *long whitish superciliary*, blackish face, whitish malar area, and *dusky submalar streak.* Below whitish, breast streaked dusky-brown, belly pale yellow. Variegated Flycatcher is larger with a longer bill, more mottled back, pale edging on wings, and rufous on uppertail-coverts and tail. *Piratics are persistently vocal when breeding* and most likely to be noticed then; otherwise they are inconspicuous, remaining high in trees, and often hard to detect. They eat mostly small fruit. Pairs usurp the pendant nests of various other birds, pestering their rightful owners until they give it

up; oropendolas and caciques are favored targets, and many of their colonies have a Piratic pair. Singing ♂ gives a whining querulous "wheé-yee," sometimes followed by a fast "pi-ri-ri-ri," repeated tirelessly, pausing only to fly off quickly for food. Also: Mexico to Panama.

Variegated Flycatcher
Empidonomus varius   PLATE 60(16)

18–18.5 cm (7–7¼"). *Widespread and often fairly common* in secondary and gallery woodland and borders, clearings, and savannas from Venezuela to n. Argentina; an austral migrant to w. Amazonia, there favoring riparian growth and shrubby clearings. Mostly below 1900 m. In **most of range** (illustrated) head blackish with semiconcealed yellow crown patch, *whitish superciliary that widens behind eye*, whitish malar area, and dusky submalar streak; *back olive brown mottled and streaked dusky. Wing feathers edged whitish; rump and tail feathers broadly edged rufous.* Throat whitish; below pale yellowish, breast with dusky-brown streaking. Resident birds of **ne. South America** have blurrier streaking below. Intermediate in size between Piratic (smaller) and Streaked (larger) Flycatchers. Piratic's facial pattern is similar, but it has a stubbier bill, narrower superciliary, *plain brown back*, and *lacks* pale wing-edging and rufous on rump and tail; Streaked has a heavier bill, coarser streaking below, etc. Variegateds are generally in the open and (unlike the more arboreal Piratic) are usually easy to see; they sometimes join other tyrannids in fruiting trees, but also frequently sally for insects. A quiet bird; occasionally gives a high-pitched thin "pseee," mainly when breeding.

Crowned Slaty Flycatcher
Griseotyrannus aurantioatrocristatus PLATE 60(17)

18 cm (7"). *Common in lighter woodland, scrub, and savannas with scattered trees from n. Bolivia and e. Amaz. Brazil to cen. Argentina;* an austral migrant to Amazonia, there favoring forest canopy and borders, regularly high above the ground. To 2000 m in Bolivia. *Brownish gray above* with *contrasting black crown,* semiconcealed yellow coronal patch, gray superciliary, and dusky ear-coverts. *Smoky gray below,* paler on belly. This *uniform-looking* flycatcher often appears *flat-crowned.* Cf. various *Knipolegus* black tyrants and Smoke-colored Pewee. Usually solitary, perching in the open, frequently in the crown of trees. Often sallies repeatedly into the air like a pewee or kingbird; wintering birds in

Amazonia often behave much like Olive-sided Flycatcher. Also eats some fruit, though less than Variegated. Breeders give a weak "pseee" (rather like Variegated), sometimes in series, but overall demeanor quiet.

Sulphury Flycatcher
Tyrannopsis sulphurea   PLATE 61(1)

19 cm (7½"). *Uncommon and local, mainly around Mauritia palms, from Amazonia to the Guianas.* Mostly below 500 m, locally to 900 m in Venezuela. *Recalls a stocky, short-billed, short-tailed Tropical Kingbird.* Head gray, darker on face, with semiconcealed yellow coronal patch; back brownish olive, wings and tail brownish dusky. *Foreneck white with a little gray streaking, sides of throat grayer and olive on sides of chest;* below bright yellow. Tropical Kingbird (a much commoner bird) is larger and has a longer and distinctly notched tail, shows *no* streaking, and its throat is not contrasting white. Dusky-chested Flycatcher is much smaller with a stubbier bill, browner upperparts, less white on foreneck. Found in pairs; usually inconspicuous when perching high on palm fronds but periodically bursts into frenzied activity with much calling. Calls high-pitched and piercing, some harsh, some squeaky, e.g., a fast "jee-peet! jee-peeteet, jeepeet!" and a "squeezrr-squeezrr-prrr."

Tyrannus

Conspicuous and often numerous, these flycatchers are *large* tyrannids that range in *open terrain* where they hawk flying insects; several species are long-distance migrants. Typical kingbirds have quite stout bills, dusky ear-coverts (the "mask"), and notched tails; the Eastern Kingbird and Fork-tailed Flycatcher have smaller bills and a more capped appearance. They all have a semiconcealed yellow or orange coronal patch.

Tropical Kingbird
Tyrannus melancholicus   PLATE 61(2)

21.5 cm (8½"). *Common, conspicuous, and nearly omnipresent* in open, agricultural, and urban areas from Colombia and Venezuela to cen. Argentina; less numerous in extensively forested regions, and vacates south during austral winter. Mostly below 1800 m, some higher (to 2200 m or more), especially in arid areas; locally (or wanderers) even higher. *Head gray* with darker mask; grayish olive above. Wings and tail brownish dusky, *tail notched.* Throat pale grayish, *chest grayish olive,* below yellow. Use the familiar Tropical Kingbird as a basis for comparison with various scarcer flycatchers; cf. especially White-throated and Snowy-throated Kingbirds, and Gray-capped and Sulphury Flycatchers. Seen singly or in pairs (flocks are occasional, perhaps austral migrants) that perch in the open, often on wires and usually high; remains active through day. Eats mainly insects captured in aerial sallies, but also consumes considerable fruit. Pugnacious; especially when breeding, chases off even larger birds such as raptors and toucans. Gives a variety of high-pitched twittering calls, e.g., "pee, ee-ee-ee-ee," often accompanied by quivering wings. Dawn song a short series of "pip" or "pee" notes followed by a rising twitter, "piriree?" one of the first bird sounds to greet the dawn. Also: sw. United States to Panama.

White-throated Kingbird

Tyrannus albogularis   PLATE 61(3)
21 cm (8¼"). *Local and generally uncommon in shrubby areas and gallery woodland, mostly near water, favoring stands of Mauritia palms, from s. Venezuela and the Guianas to s. Brazil;* some austral migrants reach w. Amazonia, where it favors semiopen riparian areas, even towns and cities. To 1000 m. Resembles *much* more numerous Tropical Kingbird. Has *paler gray head that contrasts more with blackish mask;* paler and brighter olive back; *pure white throat* that contrasts with bright yellow underparts (*chest with only a tinge of olive*). In strong light Tropical can look deceptively pale-headed and white-throated, but it never is as obviously masked as this species. Snowy-throated Kingbird occurs only *west* of Andes. Behavior similar to Tropical, with which White-throated sometimes consorts; seems somewhat less aggressive. Vocalizations resemble Tropical but average thinner and higher-pitched.

Snowy-throated Kingbird

Tyrannus niveigularis   PLATE 61(4)
19 cm (7½"). Locally fairly common from *extreme sw. Colombia* (w. Nariño) *to nw. Peru* (Ancash); breeds north to cen. Ecuador (Manabí) in desert scrub and shrubby and agricultural areas, moving into more humid terrain during local dry season (Jun.–Nov.). Mostly below 600 m. Crown gray with a blackish mask; *back pale olivaceous gray. Blackish tail nearly square.* Throat white, breast pale gray, belly pale yellow. Tropical Kingbird larger, darker and more olive on back, and not as pale on foreneck; tail more distinctly notched. Behavior much as in Tropical; it and the attractive Snowy-throated sometimes breed together, though Snowy-throated favors more arid terrain. Snowy-throated vocalizations are shorter and drier, include a sharp "kip!" that can be extended into "kip! kip! kip! kr-r-ee-ee-ee."

Gray Kingbird

Tyrannus dominicensis
21.5 cm (8½"). *Locally fairly common nonbreeding visitant* (mostly Sep.–Apr.) to open and semiopen areas, most numerous *near coast, from n. Colombia to the Guianas;* breeds on offshore islands, and a few in the llanos. *Rather heavy bill. Gray above* with a *dusky mask;* dusky tail *slightly forked. Whitish below.* Eastern Kingbird smaller and blacker above with white-tipped tail. Behavior much as in Tropical Kingbird. Wintering birds mainly quiet, though they can give the distinctive loud "pe-cheer-ry" or "pi-tir-re" heard so often from breeding birds. Also: se. United States and West Indies, its primary breeding area.

Eastern Kingbird

Tyrannus tyrannus   PLATE 61(5)
20–20.5 cm (7¾–8"). *Locally common boreal migrant (Oct.–Apr.) to humid forest borders and clearings mainly in w. Amazonia,* smaller numbers as far south as n. Argentina. Mostly below 500 m, transients routinely higher. Bill relatively small. *Slaty above, blackest on head;* squared tail black with *white tip. Whitish below.* Birds in worn plumage look faded, can show little or no white on tail-tip. Juvenile and worn adult Fork-tailed Flycatchers lack tail streamers and can resemble this kingbird, though a tail cleft is almost invariably apparent. Fork-tailed is more distinctly black-capped, has a paler gray back and purer white underparts, and never shows white tail-tip. Eastern Kingbirds often occur in flocks, sometimes large, and are frequently seen migrating by day in compact groups over the forest canopy, pausing at forest edge and along lakes and rivers. They sometimes consort with Fork-tailed Flycatchers. Though primarily frugivorous here, on northward passage they also sally after insects like other kingbirds. Mainly silent in South America, in stark contrast to its boisterous behavior when nesting. Breeds in North America.

Fork-tailed Flycatcher

Tyrannus savana PLATE 61(6)

♂ 38–40 cm (15–16"), ♀ 28–30 cm (11–12"), including *very long, deeply forked tail* (shorter in ♀♀, immatures, and birds in molt). *Widespread and locally common in savannas and pastures with scattered trees from Colombia and Venezuela to cen. Argentina* (Río Negro); local in Amazonia as a breeder. Southern populations are strongly migratory, with austral migrants (Mar.–Sep.) moving into Amazonia and n. South America, sometimes occurring in forest borders and clearings. Mostly below 1000 m, transients and vagrants higher. Virtually unmistakable. *Head black; back pearly gray* (paler in **more northern** breeding birds). Wings dusky, tail black with outer web of outer pair of long feathers basally white (usually prominent). *Below white.* **Juvenile** has more brownish cap and lacks tail streamers, but outer tail feathers are still longer than the others. Short-tailed individuals can vaguely recall Eastern Kingbird. Conspicuous and lovely, Fork-taileds often perch low and make frequent long and graceful sallies in pursuit of flying insects. Pairs separate out when breeding but at other times can be very gregarious, migrating in loose flocks and at times gathering in huge roosting aggregations. Nonbreeders consume much fruit. Rather quiet, even when breeding, but gives weak "tic" notes. Also: Mexico to Panama, vagrants to United States and even Canada.

TITYRAS, BECARDS, AND ALLIES: TITYRIDAE

A long-debated group, its members having variously been placed with the flycatchers, the manakins, and the cotingas. Most recently they have usually been treated as a family, which is done here. Some genera (including *Laniocera, Iodopleura, Calyptura,* and *Laniisoma*) are still often considered "incertae sedis" (taxonomic position uncertain) or as cotingas; we treat them as the latter. As currently constituted, members of this group are primarily arboreal birds found in lowland forests; *Schiffornis* is the exception.

Tityra

Distinctive *chunky short-tailed* birds whose *black and white plumage* renders them easily recognizable. Tityras are conspicuous at the edge of lowland forests and in adjacent clearings. Nests are placed in holes in snags.

Black-crowned Tityra
Tityra inquisitor   PLATE 61(7)
18.5 cm (7¼"). Uncommon to fairly common in canopy and borders of humid and deciduous forest and woodland from *Colombia and Venezuela to ne. Argentina and se. Brazil.* To 1100 m. Bill blackish (*no* red). ♂ in **most of range** (A) has *crown and face black;* above pale pearly gray, white below. Wings (except tertials) and tail black. In **w. Colombia, w. Ecuador, and e. Peru to w. Amaz. Brazil** (B) has white cheeks and tail white with black subterminal band. In **e. Ecuador and se. Colombia** has white cheeks, black tail. ♀ like respective ♂♂, but with *buff frontlet and rufous-chestnut sides of head;* back duller gray, sometimes with brown streaking. Other tityras have conspicuous rosy red on bill and face, but beware southeastern Black-taileds in which red is replaced by less obvious purplish. Calls similar to other tityras, likewise often doubled, but in Black-crowned tends to be drier (less grunty) and weaker, e.g., "zik-zik" or "chet-chet." Also: Mexico to Panama.

Masked Tityra
Tityra semifasciata   PLATE 61(8)
21 cm (8¼"). Fairly common in canopy and borders of humid forest and woodland from *Colombia and w. Venezuela to s. Amazonia.* Mostly

below 1500 m. *Wide orbital area and most of bill rosy red,* bill tipped black. ♂ has *forecrown and face black, pale pearly gray upperparts* and *white underparts.* Wings (except for tertials) black, *tail grayish white* with wide black subterminal band. ♀ like ♂ but head dusky brownish, back gray; below pale gray. Black-tailed Tityra has *all-black* tail; ♂ has more black on head than ♂ Masked; ♀ shows streaking on back and breast. Black-crowned Tityra *lacks* red on bill and face. Often in pairs, regularly perching on high exposed branches; especially fond of snags, where they can perch for long periods (and often nest). Flight strong and direct, often sweeping for long distances in the open. Eats much fruit, also large insects. Unusual call, frequently uttered in flight, a nasal croak or grunt, "urt," sometimes given in series. Also: Mexico to Panama.

Black-tailed Tityra
Tityra cayana   PLATE 61(9)
21.5 cm (8½"). Widespread and often common in canopy and borders of humid forest and woodland from *e. Colombia and Venezuela to ne. Argentina and s. Brazil.* Mostly below 500 m, but to 1100 m in Venezuela. In **most of range** (illustrated) *wide orbital area and most of bill rosy red,* bill tipped black. ♂ has *head black, pearly gray upperparts,* and *white underparts;* wings (except for tertials) and tail also black. ♀ grayer above with *variable amount of coarse black streaking* (often prominent), *especially on back; breast has (narrower) black streaking.* From **e. Bolivia and e. Brazil south** *orbital area reddish purple* (hence less conspicuous), bill mostly black. ♂ similar but whiter. ♀ very different, *lacking black cap,* above grayish brown *with coarse black streaking,*

below *more profusely* streaked black. ♀ is *the only tityra with obvious streaking.* Black-crowned Tityra lacks red on bill and face; southern ♂ Black-tailed differs from sympatric ♂ Black-crowned in being larger and whiter with *no reddish purple on face and bill.* ♂ Masked Tityra has white on back extending to hindcrown and a mainly whitish tail (not all black). Behavior and voice much as in Masked Tityra.

White-naped Xenopsaris
Xenopsaris albinucha*   PLATE 62(1)
13 cm (5″). *Uncommon and local in riparian growth and lighter woodland in Venezuela and recently in s. Guyana,* and from *n. Bolivia* (west to Beni) *and ne. Brazil to n. Argentina* (n. Córdoba and n. Buenos Aires). Mostly below 500 m, but to 1100 m in s. Bolivia. Sometimes called simply the Xenopsaris. ♂ has *crown black* with white lores and pale gray nape; above brownish gray, *brownest on wings;* tail blackish, outer web of outer feathers white. *Below white.* ♀ has browner crown, browner upperparts, and buff-tinged belly; **juvenile**'s crown scaled whitish. ♂ of chunkier and shorter-tailed Cinereous Becard is grayer above and below, and has vaguely pale-*tipped* tail feathers (not sharply white on outermost rectrix). Found singly or in pairs, usually apart from mixed flocks. Generally quiet; ♂'s thin, high-pitched song a whistled "tsip, tsiweeé, tseee-ti-ti-ti-ti?"

Pachyramphus

Attractive, *large-headed,* and broad-billed birds with rather sluggish and inconspicuous behavior, the becards are arboreal in forest and borders and occur mainly in the lowlands, though a few species are montane. Nests are large, messy globular structures with an entrance on the bottom or a side. Sexually dimorphic, ♂♂ *tend to gray and black with white accents (rufous or buff in* ♀♀*)*; two *rufous* species *lack* dimorphism. The last three becard species (One-colored, Crested, Pink-throated) were formerly often separated in the genus *Platypsaris,* now subsumed into *Pachyramphus.*

Green-backed Becard
Pachyramphus viridis   PLATE 62(2)
14.5 cm (5¾″). *Uncommon in lighter and gallery woodland and forest, mainly from ne. Brazil to e. Bolivia and n. Argentina* (Tucumán and Entre

Ríos), also locally in se. Venezuela and lower Amaz. Brazil. Mostly below 1000 m. ♂ in **most of range** (illustrated) has *glossy black crown* with white lores and *gray sides of head and nuchal collar;* bright olive above, blacker on outer flight feathers. Throat whitish, *pectoral band bright yellow,* belly whitish. **Northern birds** have nuchal collar and pectoral band *diffused.* ♀ like ♂ but duller, with olive crown and rufous lesser wing-coverts. *The only becard in its lowland range with olive upperparts;* no overlap with Yellow-cheeked Becard. Forages in pairs, gleaning in foliage at varying heights; usually not with mixed flocks. Attractive, simple song a series of musical notes with slight crescendo, "tridídideédeédeédeé?"

Yellow-cheeked Becard
Pachyramphus xanthogenys   PLATE 62(3)
14.5 cm (5¾″). Uncommon in borders of humid forest and woodland, and in clearings, along *eastern base of Andes from n. Ecuador* (w. Sucumbíos) *to s. Peru* (Cuzco). 650–1700 m. ♂ has *crown glossy black* with white lores; *above bright olive; wings mostly black. Cheeks, sides of neck, and throat bright yellow,* breast yellowish olive, belly whitish. ♀ has forecrown blackish with *sides of head, nape, and throat gray;* olive above, wings as in ♂ but *lesser wing-coverts rufous.* Chest yellowish olive, belly whitish. Barred Becard is smaller, and both sexes show barring below; it occurs at higher elevations. Behavior as in Green-backed, but Yellow-cheeked more often forages well above the ground. Pretty song, often given at long intervals, a subdued series of soft whistled notes, "du, du-de-de-de-dididididídí?" sometimes preceded by one or more upslurred "te-wik?" notes.

Barred Becard
Pachyramphus versicolor   PLATE 62(4)
13 cm (5″). Uncommon in canopy and borders of montane forest and woodland in *Andes from w. Venezuela* (Trujillo) *to w. Bolivia* (w. Santa Cruz). Mostly 1500–2600 m. ♂ *glossy black above* with gray rump; *scapulars and wing feathers boldly edged white. Lores, sides of head and neck, and throat greenish yellow;* below whitish, *sides of head and underparts with light dusky barring.* ♀ has *slaty crown,* yellow eye-ring, and olive upperparts. *Wing-coverts rufous-chestnut,* rufous to buff edging on flight feathers. Below pale yellow, fading on belly; *light dusky barring throughout.* Recognizable in its montane habitat from chunky, round-headed shape and lethargic behavior. ♂'s white in wing is prominent, as

is ♀'s rufous, though their barring often is not. Ranges singly or in pairs, regularly with mixed flocks. Song a fast, clear, musical "tree, tree-dee-dee-dee-dee?" with a distinctive pause after the first note. Also: Costa Rica and w. Panama.

Glossy-backed Becard
Pachyramphus surinamus   PLATE 62(5)
13.5 cm (5¼"). *Rare in canopy and borders of humid forest from the Guianas to n. Amaz. Brazil.* Below 300 m. ♂ *glossy black above and pure white below.* ♀ has *black-speckled dark chestnut crown, pale gray upper back, white lower back and rump; wings and tail blackish,* feathers margined rufous. Below white. Both sexes are striking and unlikely to be confused, though ♀'s pattern somewhat recalls Eastern Sirystes. Usually seen in pairs, generally well above the ground and most often while accompanying a canopy flock. Its distinctive whistled song, e.g., "puweee, pweet-pweet-pweet-pweet?" regularly announces the approach of just such a flock.

White-winged Becard
Pachyramphus polychopterus   PLATE 62(6)
14.5–15 cm (5¾–6"). *Widespread and fairly common* in secondary and riparian woodland, and in humid and montane forest borders, from Colombia and Venezuela to n. Argentina; perhaps withdraws from austral part of range during austral winter. Mostly below 900 m but locally to 2000 m or more in the Andes. ♂ **in w. Amazonia** (A) *black to blackish above,* crown glossier; wings with two bold white bars, outer tail feathers tipped white. *Below sooty black.* ♂ **elsewhere** (B) has *gray nuchal collar, rump, and underparts;* in addition to wing-bars, has *white edging on scapulars and flight feathers.* ♀ olive brown above, *more grayish on crown,* supraloral and partial eye-ring whitish; wings dusky with *prominent cinnamon-buff on scapulars, wing-bars, and edging;* outer tail feathers tipped cinnamon-buff. Below dull yellowish, breast clouded olive. ♂ is only *Pachyramphus without white or pale gray on lores;* the black races of w. Amazonia are especially distinctive. Cf. ♂ Black-and-white and Black-capped Becards. ♀ Black-capped has obviously rufous crown, favors true forest. Bright chestnut crown of ♀ Black-and-white is boldly outlined in black. Forages lethargically in pairs in leafy canopy and outer branches of trees, sometimes with mixed flocks; never very numerous or conspicuous. ♂'s song a series of pretty and melodic notes, e.g., "teu, teu, tu-tu-tu-tu-tu-tú," always with the slow first

notes. Western ♂'s song slower, e.g., "teu, teu, teu, teu, ti-teu, teu." Also: Guatemala to Panama.

Black-capped Becard
Pachyramphus marginatus   PLATE 62(7)
14 cm (5½"). Uncommon in canopy and borders of humid forest (mainly terra firme) *from Amazonia to the Guianas,* and in e. Brazil. To 1000 m. ♂ has crown glossy black with pale gray lores, *back mixed black and gray,* rump pure gray. Wings black with *white scapulars, two wing-bars, and edging;* tail black, outer feathers broadly tipped white. *Below pale gray.* ♀ like ♀ of larger White-winged Becard, but *crown rufous-chestnut.* In Amazonia, ♂ White-winged is *much blacker;* further, it favors second-growth, rarely entering forest canopy. Elsewhere they are more similar, but note the smaller Black-capped's pale lores. Cf. also Black-and-white Becard, though for the most part these do not overlap, as Black-and-white does not occur in Amazonia. Black-capped is an arboreal becard that often accompanies mixed canopy flocks, generally remaining well above the ground in tall forest. ♂'s pretty song a short series of clear, musical notes with varying pattern, e.g., "teeu, whee-do-weét" (often repeated several times in fast succession); one phrase can be transcribed as "fleur-de-lis."

Black-and-white Becard
Pachyramphus albogriseus   PLATE 62(8)
14.5 cm (5¾"). Uncommon in canopy and borders of montane forest in *Andes from n. Venezuela to s. Peru (Ayacucho); in w. Ecuador and nw. Peru also near sea level,* there also inhabiting deciduous habitats and second-growth. Mostly 1000–2200 m. ♂ has crown glossy black with *white or pale gray supraloral, plain gray back and rump;* wings black with *two white bars and edging (none* on scapulars); tail black, outer feathers tipped white. *Below pale gray.* ♀ much as in slightly larger White-winged Becard, but *rufous-chestnut crown has black margin.* ♂ of west-slope (*non*-Amazonian) White-winged *lacks* pale lores and shows black on back; ♀ White-winged has a plainer head pattern. Black-capped Becard ranges in *Amaz. lowlands only.* Behavior as in Black-capped, but often a more conspicuous bird (especially in deciduous biomes); voices also similar. Western ♂ has a pleasant "tu-tu-dwít" song, repeated several times, then a pause. East-slope ♂ gives a more leisurely and longer phrase, "twe, twe, tweu, tu-wít?" Also: Costa Rica and w. Panama.

Chestnut-crowned Becard
Pachyramphus castaneus PLATE 62(9)
14 cm (5½"). Locally fairly common in borders of humid forest and adjacent clearings in *Venezuela and Amazonia,* and in *se. Brazil region.* Mostly below 1200 m. *Cinnamon-rufous above,* darker on crown, with dusky lores and buffy supraloral becoming a *gray band that encircles nape;* blackish greater primary-coverts and inner webs to primaries. *Cinnamon-buff below,* throat and midbelly paler. ♀ Cinereous Becard lacks the nape band, is whiter below. Cinnamon Becard occurs *west* of Andes. Usually in pairs, generally not with flocks; unless vocalizing often easy to overlook as it tends to remain well above the ground in leafy canopy. Soft musical song typically a melancholy whistled "teeeuw-teeu-teeu-teeu"; also "titititi?"

Slaty Becard
Pachyramphus spodiurus PLATE 62(10)
14 cm (5½"). *Uncommon and local in semihumid and deciduous woodland and plantations from nw. Ecuador* (w. Esmeraldas) *to nw. Peru* (n. Piura and n. Cajamarca). Mostly below 750 m. ♂ has crown black with *pale grayish lores;* above slaty gray, back mixed black. Wings and tail blackish, *wing feathers with whitish edging.* Below gray. ♀ bright cinnamon-rufous above with grayish lores; black greater primary-coverts and inner primary webs. *Pale buff below.* More numerous One-colored Becard is very similar but larger (admittedly often hard to judge). ♂ One-colored *lacks* Slaty's pale lores and wing-feather edging, so it looks *plainer.* ♀♀ closely similar (some One-coloreds even have black on greater wing-coverts), but ♀ One-colored has grayer lores and most show a dusky eye-smudge (never present in Slaty). Cinnamon Becard's buffy whitish supraloral is *absent* in ♀ Slaty; Cinnamon favors more humid habitats. Often in pairs, usually not too far above the ground; generally not with flocks. Song a fast series of musical notes that starts slowly, then accelerates and rises in pitch, "tru, tru, tee-tee-titititititi."

Cinereous Becard
Pachyramphus rufus PLATE 62(11)
13.5–14 cm (5¼–5½"). *Uncommon and somewhat local in lighter woodland, forest borders, and clearings with scattered tall trees from n. Colombia to the Guianas and Amazonia.* Mostly below 1000 m. ♂ *gray above* with *contrasting black crown* and *prominent white supraloral and frontlet.* Wings blackish, feathers narrowly edged

white. Below grayish white. ♀ very like ♀ Slaty (*west* of Andes), *bright cinnamon-rufous above* with whitish lores; black greater primary-coverts. *Below whitish,* breast tinged buff. ♂ Black-and-white Becard is larger and shows more white in wings and tail. Chestnut-crowned Becard has a distinctive (though often inconspicuous) gray nape band. Arboreal behavior of this *nonforest becard* as in its congeners; generally not with mixed flocks. Voice resembles Slaty Becard. Also: e. Panama.

Cinnamon Becard
Pachyramphus cinnamomeus PLATE 62(12)
14 cm (5½"). Common in borders of humid forest, secondary woodland, and plantations in *w. Colombia and w. Ecuador* (south to El Oro). To 1500 m. *Cinnamon-rufous above* with *distinct dusky lores and buffy whitish supraloral; lacks* black on greater primary-coverts. *Pale cinnamon-buff below,* throat and midbelly whiter. ♀ Slaty Becard *lacks* Cinnamon's pale supraloral and *has* black greater primary-coverts (often obvious). ♀ One-colored Becard distinctly larger; it too lacks a pale supraloral; usually shows dusky around eye, lacking in Cinnamon (except on lores). Chestnut-crowned Becard occurs *east* of Andes. Habits as in Chestnut-crowned, though Cinnamon tends to occur more at edge and in clearings. ♂'s song resembles Chestnut-crowned but is usually spritelier and contains more terminal "teeu" notes. Also: Mexico to Panama.

One-colored Becard
Pachyramphus homochrous * PLATE 62(13)
16.5–17 cm (6½–6¾"). Locally fairly common in canopy and borders of deciduous and humid forest and woodland from *nw. Venezuela to nw. Peru* (n. Piura). To 1500 m. Rather stout bill. ♂ *slaty black above,* blackest on crown, wings, and tail. *Below gray.* A few (perhaps older) ♂♂ show a little pink on throat. ♀ *rufous above* with *dusky lores* and *often some dusky around eye;* primaries dusky, usually some blackish on greater wing-coverts. *Cinnamon-buff below,* throat paler. **Young** ♂♂ at first resemble ♀, gradually acquiring adult's black and gray starting on crown and then back, ending with wings and tail. Neither sex is really "one-colored," both being paler below. ♂ of smaller and scarcer Slaty Becard has prominent edging on wing feathers. ♀ One-colored is plainer than other rufous becards, and it *lacks* any pale loral area; note too the unique dusky coloring around eyes. Often in pairs, foraging much like other becards. Frequently ruffles

crown feathers and also pumps head alertly (like a *Myiarchus*). Sometimes with flocks, but at least as often alone. Song a loud, sharp, sputtering "stet-ee-ee-teet-tsit-tsitts-tsít," less melodic than in most other becards. Oft-given call a high-pitched squeaky "tweíuuw." Also: e. Panama.

Crested Becard
Pachyramphus validus *   PLATE 62(14)
18.5 cm (7¼"). Uncommon in montane woodland and forest borders in *Andes from s. Peru* (Ayacucho) *to nw. Argentina* (n. Córdoba), *and east in lighter woodland and borders into e. Brazil;* also recently in extreme s. Ecuador (s. Zamora-Chinchipa). To 2500 m. Rather stout bill. ♂ in **most of range** (illustrated) *black above* and *olivaceous gray below.* ♀ *rufous above* with *contrasting sooty crown* and buffyish lores; primaries blackish. Below cinnamon-buff. ♂ on **Andean slopes** purer gray below. The Crested is the *largest* becard, but it is not especially "crested." Seen singly and in pairs, sometimes accompanying mixed flocks. In montane se. Brazil favors stands of *Araucaria* trees, regularly nesting in them. Not very vocal, but gives various squeaky or twittery notes, e.g., "tsee-eéyk," also up to about 6 clearer notes, "sui-sui-sui. . . ."

Pink-throated Becard
Pachyramphus minor *   PLATE 62(15)
17–17.5 cm (6¾–7"). *Uncommon in canopy and borders of terra firme forest from Amazonia to the Guianas.* To 600 m. Rather stout bill. ♂ *mainly black above.* Blackish gray below with *patch of rosy pink on lower throat* (often inconspicuous). ♀ has *slaty gray crown and back, contrasting rufous wings and tail.* Below cinnamon-buff. Some (perhaps younger) ♀♀ have crown and back more olivaceous gray. ♂ distinctive in range; ♂ of sympatric White-winged Becard (also basically black) has obvious white in wings and tail. The simply patterned ♀, with its contrasting dark crown and back, is dissimilar from other becards. Usually in pairs, regularly accompanying mixed flocks; often overlooked, tending to stay well above the ground. Relatively quiet; song a clear, melodic "teeuuuweeet" often followed by twittering notes.

Schiffornis

A group of *plain* birds found in the understory of humid and montane forests, the three members of this genus (one species,

the Thrush-like, will probably need to be split) are best known from their loud whistled vocalizations. They used to be considered manakins, and were sometimes called mourners.

Greenish Schiffornis
Schiffornis virescens   PLATE 63(2)
16 cm (6¼"). Fairly common in undergrowth of humid forest, secondary woodland, and gallery forest in *se. Brazil region* (north to Bahia). To 1200 m. Mostly olivaceous, with narrow but distinct pale eye-ring; *wings and tail contrasting rufescent.* Does not seem to occur with Thrush-like Schiffornis; in area of overlap, Greenish ranges at higher elevations. Thrush-like there is larger, grayer below. etc. Actually more apt to be confused with ♀ Blue Manakin, which is greener generally, lacks rufous in wings, has reddish legs and slightly elongated central tail feathers. An inconspicuous bird that forages alone, hopping in undergrowth and often clinging to vertical stems; only rarely with mixed flocks. Heard much more often than seen. Simple but musical song a clear "teeeo, toweé?" or "teeeo, to, toweé?"

Thrush-like Schiffornis
Schiffornis turdina   PLATE 63(3)
15.5–16.5 cm (6–6½"). Fairly common in undergrowth of humid and lower montane forest and secondary woodland from *Colombia and Venezuela to Amazonia,* and in *e. Brazil.* To about 1500 m. *Dull-plumaged,* with *round-headed* shape and *prominent large dark eyes* and indistinct paler eye-ring. **Typical birds** (illustrated) are brownish olive above, olive grayish below. **Northern birds** are more rufescent above and on foreneck; **western birds** are especially dark below. Infrequently seen, and readily confused when it is; the near absence of actual field marks is often the best clue. Cf. Brownish Twistwing, Várzea Schiffornis, Broad-billed Sapayoa. Behavior is as in Greenish Schiffornis. Heard much more often than seen, though songs may be given at long intervals and are therefore hard to track down except through tape playback. Songs vary geographically, though all have an attractive clear, whistled quality. Examples include a slow "teeeeuuu . . . wheee-tú" (w. Ecuador), a more rhythmic "teeu, wheeu, wheé-tu-tu" (w. Amazonia), and a slower "teeuu, youuweé, tu tu-wee?" (ne. Brazil). Also: Mexico to Panama.

Várzea Schiffornis

Schiffornis major PLATE 63(4)

15.5 cm (6"). *Uncommon in undergrowth of várzea forest and woodland in w. Amazonia.* Mostly below 300 m, but recorded to 1000 m in se. Peru. *More or less uniform bright cinnamon-rufous, paler on rump and below, especially on belly.* Shows variable amount of gray on face, in some birds extensive (reaching crown), in others entirely lacking. Thrush-like Schiffornis is much duller and inhabits forests in uplands. Cinnamon Attila similarly colored (and also frequents várzea), but its larger size, upright posture, and behavior are very different. Behavior similar to Greenish, though seems more often to come to edge (such as along streams). Song, a slow "tee, towee-tee, towee?" or "teeoo, teewee? . . . teeoo . . . teeoo, teewee," has same clear quality as Thrush-like.

SAPAYOA: SAPAYAOIDAE

The sole member of this family was long considered an aberrant manakin, but now based on various characters it has been judged to be in a family of its own, perhaps with an affinity to the broadbills (Eurylaimidae) of the Old World.

Broad-billed Sapayoa
Sapayoa aenigma   PLATE 63(1)

15 cm (6"). Uncommon and inconspicuous in lower growth of humid forest in *w. Colombia and nw. Ecuador* (mainly Esmeraldas). To 1100 m. Sometimes called simply the Sapayoa. Rather broad flat bill. *Uniform olive,* duskier on wings and tail, somewhat yellower on throat and mid-belly. ♂ has semiconcealed yellow coronal patch. Larger and longer-tailed than several ♀ manakins that occur with it (Red-capped, Blue-crowned), and with different behavior. Green Manakin is most similar in size and shape, though it too is smaller; Green shows a vague yellowish eye-ring as well as more yellow on belly. *Rhynchocyclus* flatbills have even wider bills and prominent yellowish wing edges and bars (sapayoa's wings are *plain*). Usually seen singly, less often in pairs, regularly joining understory flocks with *Myrmotherula* antwrens. Tends to perch upright, scanning nearby foliage like a *Rhynchocyclus,* sallying abruptly. Quiet, but gives a soft trill, also a louder "chipp, ch-ch-ch." Also: Panama.

MANAKINS: PIPRIDAE

Typical manakins are small, chunky birds with short bills and short tails that range mainly in tropical forests; they are strongly dimorphic, males often very colorful. Other genera, usually duller plumaged, here retained with the manakins may better be classified as tyrant flycatchers; these genera include *Tyranneutes, Neopelma, Piprites,* and *Neopipo*). Males of most "true" manakins engage in a stereotyped display, either alone or in leks, to attract females; in most species females alone care for the young, with their nests being simple cup-shaped structures. Manakins are mainly or entirely frugivorous.

Tyranneutes

These *very small* manakins of Amazonian and Guianan forests are *obscure and inconspicuous* birds that are *best known from vocalizations of* ♂♂. Both species also have an amazing (but only rarely seen) *aerial display*.

Dwarf Tyrant-Manakin
Tyranneutes stolzmanni   PLATE 63(5)
8 cm (3¼"). Fairly common in lower and middle growth of humid forest (mainly terra firme) in *Amazonia*. Mostly below 600 m. *Iris pale*. Plain olive above. Throat and breast pale grayish, belly pale yellow. ♀♀ of several *Pipra* manakins are not quite as small as this species. Almost always noted from vocalizing ♂♂, which are solitary; also occasionally seen coming to fruiting trees, sometimes with other manakins. Song a well-enunciated "jew-pit" or "ur-jit," typically delivered as the motionless bird perches on a branch 5–10 m up, hard to see. Birds in the canopy also give a very different and more melodic "tuee-tuee-tuee-tuee," the number of notes varying.

Tiny Tyrant-Manakin
Tyranneutes virescens   PLATE 63(6)
7.5 cm (3"). Locally fairly common in lower and middle growth of humid forest in *ne. South America*. To 500 m. Plain olive above, ♂ with small yellow coronal patch. Throat and breast pale grayish, belly pale yellow. Does not overlap with the slightly larger (and dark-eyed) Dwarf Tyrant-Manakin. ♀ Golden-headed Manakin is slightly larger and plumper, has a pale bill.

Behavior much like the more wide-ranging Dwarf Tyrant-Manakin, likewise almost always recorded through solitary calling ♂♂. Distinctive song a fast "whippy-jebree" (or "Jimmy the Greek"), given interminably at intervals of 3–6 seconds.

Neopelma

A group of *very dull*, obscure, inconspicuous olive birds that range in woodland and forest lower growth; the five species are essentially allopatric. ♂♂ gather in *small leks* to display.

Saffron-crested Tyrant-Manakin
Neopelma chrysocephalum   PLATE 63(7)
13 cm (5"). Uncommon and local in lower and middle growth of woodland and forest on sandy soils (e.g., campinas in Brazil, muri scrub in Guyana, and varillal in ne. Peru), *mainly in ne. South America*. To 700 m. *Iris pale yellow*. Plain olive above with *large coronal patch golden yellow* (darker border) and gray sides of head. Throat and chest pale grayish, *belly clear pale yellow*. The only *Neopelma* in range. Tiny Tyrant-Manakin is much smaller with shorter tail; it inhabits taller, more humid forest. Greenish Elaenia (limited overlap in s. Venezuela) shows prominent wing-edging and a stronger facial pattern. Apt to be overlooked unless vocalizing; otherwise found singly and not associated with mixed flocks (though occasionally gathering at a fruiting tree, sometimes with other manakins). Displaying ♂♂ perch 6–8 m up, usually within earshot of

each other; certain branches are used regularly. Most frequent call is a nasal "skeenh!" interminably repeated every few seconds. Bizarre song a twangy "wrraaaaang, wrang-wrang-wrang" often given as it jumps off perch and flares crest.

Wied's Tyrant-Manakin
Neopelma aurifrons   PLATE 63(8)

13 cm (5"). *Rare and local in lower and middle growth of humid forest in se. Brazil* (s. Bahia to Espírito Santo, formerly also Rio de Janeiro). Locally to 1000 m. Iris mauve. Plain olive above with small yellow coronal patch. Throat whitish, breast clouded grayish, *belly clear pale yellow.* Cf. very similar Serra do Mar Tyrant-Manakin; the two generally segregate by range and elevation, Serra do Mar occurring higher. Pale-bellied Tyrant-Manakin (no known overlap) has a whitish belly. Inconspicuous behavior much like other *Neopelma.* Song differs from Serra do Mar, a burry, quite musical phrase, e.g., "choy-choy-cheeró" (reminiscent of a schiffornis) or "chir-pit chee-poreé."

Serra do Mar Tyrant-Manakin
*Neopelma chrysolophum**

13 cm (5"). Uncommon in lower and middle growth of montane forest, borders, and secondary woodland in *se. Brazil* (s. Minas Gerais and Rio de Janeiro to e. Paraná). Mostly 900–1750 m. Closely resembles Wied's Tyrant-Manakin (formerly considered conspecific), differing in having a longer tail and a larger orange-yellow coronal patch in ♂♂. The two species mainly segregate by range, Wied's occurring north of the Serra do Mar and at lower elevations. Behavior similar, but Serra do Mar's song is distinctly different, fast and spritely with notes well enunciated, e.g., "chip, chip, dree-zee-zee-zéw" or "chip, chip, dree-dree-dreuw," with many variations.

Pale-bellied Tyrant-Manakin
Neopelma pallescens   PLATE 63(9)

14 cm (5½"). Uncommon and local in lower and middle growth of deciduous and gallery woodland, mainly in *e. Brazil.* To 900 m. Iris grayish mauve. Plain olive above with large coronal patch bright yellow. Throat whitish, breast clouded olivaceous gray, *belly creamy whitish. The plainest of a plain genus,* and the only one with whitish (not yellow) belly; not known to overlap with any. Pale-bellied does occur with similar Greenish Elaenia, which has yellower belly, white eye-ring and short superciliary. Like the other tyrant-manakins, inconspicuous and most apt to be noticed when you find a displaying ♂. These perch on open low branches and periodically give a soft nasal "wraah, wra-wra," sometimes simultaneously jumping off perch, often landing facing the other way.

Sulphur-bellied Tyrant-Manakin
Neopelma sulphureiventer   PLATE 63(10)

13.5 cm (5¼"). *Uncommon and local in lower growth of várzea and riparian forest and woodland in sw. Amazonia.* Locally to 1000 m. Iris pale grayish to creamy brown. Plain olive above with pale yellow coronal patch. Throat whitish, breast clouded grayish, *belly clear pale yellow.* Greenish Elaenia has a dark iris, prominent yellowish wing-edging, and more facial pattern. Cf. also ♀♀ of various manakins; their plumage is equally dull, but they are plumper with shorter tail. Inconspicuous behavior much as in other *Neopelma.* Song a nasal "wraanh-wraanh" (J. Hornbuckle recording), with quality similar to Pale-bellied though lower-pitched.

Piprites

Two attractively patterned, arboreal birds found in forest subcanopy; the taxonomic affinities of *Piprites* are still debated, though it seems certain that they are not true manakins. Only two nests are known, one having been placed in a cavity (Wing-barred), the other (Black-capped) a spherical nest with a side entrance, composed of moss; both are utterly unlike the nests of any "true" manakin.

Wing-barred Piprites
Piprites chloris   PLATE 63(11)

12.5 cm (5"). Uncommon and local in mid-levels and subcanopy of humid and foothill forest and woodland, mainly in Amazonia and the Guianas, and in se. Brazil region. Mostly below 1300 m. **Western birds** (A) bright olive above with *yellow lores and eye-ring, gray nape and sides of neck; wings with yellowish bars and tertial tipping; short tail tipped whitish. Below mostly pale yellow.* In **se. Brazil area** has little gray on nape. In **e. Amazonia** (B) *mainly pale grayish below.* More resembles a flycatcher or a ♀ becard than any true manakin; note its plump proportions with large round head, short tail. Seen singly or in pairs, gleaning for insects and often with mixed flocks. Heard much more often than seen; far-carrying song has a distinctive hesitant cadence, e.g., "whip, pip-pip, pididip, whip, whip?"

Black-capped Piprites
Piprites pileata PLATE 63(12)

12 cm (4¾"). *Rare in subcanopy and borders of montane forest and woodland in se. Brazil* (s. Minas Gerais to n. Rio Grande do Sul) *and ne. Argentina* (Misiones). To 1800 m. *Bill and legs yellow. Striking pattern*, not likely confused. ♂ has *black crown and nape* contrasting with *rich chestnut back, rump and wing-coverts;* wings dusky with whitish speculum; outer tail rufous. *Face and underparts cinnamon-buff,* midbelly paler. ♀ similar but with olive back, whitish wing-bars. Behavior much as in Wing-barred Piprites, also most often recorded through ♂'s distinctive chortling song, a fast rollicking "chik, chik, cheeút, chee-unh."

Cinnamon Neopipo
Neopipo cinnamomea* PLATE 63(13)

9.5 cm (3¾"). *Rare and local (perhaps overlooked) in lower growth of terra firme forest in Amazonia and the Guianas.* Locally to 1000 m. Formerly considered a manikin; has been called Cinnamon Tyrant-Manakin, or Cinnamon Tyrant. *Legs bluish gray.* Head and back gray with usually concealed yellow coronal patch (smaller and more orange-rufous in ♀); *rump and tail cinnamon-rufous;* wings dusky with *rufous edging. Mostly cinnamon below.* Easily passed over as the much more numerous and similarly plumaged Ruddy-tailed Flycatcher, which has shorter and pinkish legs, prominent rictal bristles, and no coronal patch. Not well known, but apparently mainly solitary or in pairs inside forest. Most frequent call a thin, high-pitched "pseeeu" repeated steadily at intervals of 5–8 seconds. Song a series of notes of similar quality, at first going upscale, then fading away, e.g., "psee-psii-psii-psii-psii-pse-pse-psu."

Heterocercus

A trio of rather large, *boldly patterned* manakins with graduated tails. The species are similar, and their ranges allopatric in Amazonian forests, *mainly in várzea or near water.* ♂♂ have *white throats that flare to sides.*

Flame-crested Manakin
Heterocercus linteatus PLATE 63(14)

14 cm (5½"). Uncommon in lower growth of várzea and riparian forest and woodland, *mainly in s. Amaz. Brazil.* To 500 m. ♂ has *black head*

with *flame red coronal stripe* (usually hidden); dark olive above. *Throat silky white, lengthened at sides;* chest sooty olive, breast chestnut becoming rufous on belly. ♀ dark olive above with no coronal stripe. *Throat gray; below dull cinnamon-buff,* duller on breast and sides. Not known to occur with any congener; contrasting throat distinctive in both sexes. Like other *Heterocercus* usually seen singly, sometimes joining small mixed flocks; also occasionally seen at fruiting trees. Displaying ♂♂ have been reported to flare their gorgets and chase each other. The singing birds we have seen, however, have perched singly on low open branches for protracted periods, remaining quiet and nearly motionless, only at long intervals emitting an explosive "skeeeeéeeuw, skeeeu" with a curassow quality (sometimes preceded by a "ts-ik" note).

Yellow-crested Manakin
Heterocercus flavivertex PLATE 63(15)

14 cm (5½"). Uncommon in lower growth of várzea, riparian, and gallery woodland and forest in *drainages of Rios Negro and Orinoco;* favors blackwater drainages with sandy soil. To 300 m. ♂ olive above with *golden yellow coronal stripe* (usually hidden) and slaty cheeks. *Throat silky white, lengthened at sides;* chest sooty olive, breast chestnut becoming rufous on belly. ♀ like ♀ Flame-crested Manakin (no overlap) but less dark above and darker ear-coverts more contrasting. Both sexes easily recognized by their contrasting throat color; Yellow-crested does not occur with any congener. Behavior much as in Flame-crested. ♂♂ have regularly used display perches 2–5 m up, sitting there quietly for long periods, occasionally emitting an explosive and high-pitched "weeeeeee? whitcheeeeu." ♂♂ in full display bow forward while flaring their gorget.

Orange-crested Manakin
Heterocercus aurantiivertex PLATE 63(16)

14 cm (5½"). Uncommon and local in lower growth of várzea forest and woodland in *e. Ecuador and ne. Peru,* mainly in *blackwater drainages.* Below 300 m. *Duller* than other *Heterocercus* (♂ more "hen-plumaged"). ♂ has *grayish cheeks* with an *orange coronal stripe* (usually hidden); otherwise dull olive above. *Throat grayish white; below uniform dull cinnamon-buff,* chest and sides more olive. ♀ similar, but lacking crown stripe. Overall shape and posture vaguely thrushlike; cf. also White-crested Spadebill. Behavior much like other *Heterocercus;* an amazing

flight display in which ♂ flies well above canopy has been observed (J. Alvarez) and likely occurs in other *Heterocercus* as well. At long intervals while on its display perch ♂ gives a penetrating, high-pitched trill.

Manacus

The classic bearded manakins, ♂♂ with lengthened throat feathers flared during noisy displays at their leks. Ranges are allopatric, with limited hybridization where they meet.

White-bearded Manakin
Manacus manacus   PLATE 64(1)
11 cm (4¼"). *Widespread and often common in dense undergrowth of woodland and humid forest borders from Colombia and Venezuela to Amazonia, and in se. Brazil region*. Mostly below 1000 m. *Legs orange.* ♂ essentially *black and white: black above* with gray rump. *Throat— which displaying birds often puff out into a "beard"—and nuchal collar white,* grayish below. Nuchal collar width and belly color (gray to white) vary geographically. ♀ olive above, paler and more grayish olive below, belly yellower. In w. Colombia cf. Golden-collared Manakin. Most other small ♀ manakins have dark legs; most similar is ♀ of larger Blue-backed Manakin, which has longer tail and yellower legs. White-beardeds are inconspicuous away from their leks and are usually encountered singly, often at fruiting trees (where several may gather). Both sexes utter an occasional "chee-pu" call. At leks each ♂ has a small court cleared of leaves; they display on certain low branches, flying back and forth and flaring throat feathers. A great variety of sounds, including whistled "peeur" calls, is given, but most notable is a loud snap like a firecracker, apparently produced by the wings.

Golden-collared Manakin
Manacus vitellinus   PLATE 64(2)
11 cm (4¼"). Common in dense undergrowth of woodland and humid forest borders in *w. Colombia* (south to w. Cauca). Mostly below 1000 m. *Legs orange.* Unmistakable ♂ resembles White-bearded Manakin, but *bright golden yellow replaces the white,* and olive replaces the gray. ♀ closely resembles ♀ White-bearded but is brighter and more yellowish below. Behavior and voice as in White-bearded. Also: Panama.

Corapipo

Small manakins, ♂♂ with characteristic white bibs, found in n. South America, where they range mainly in undergrowth of foothill forests.

White-throated Manakin
Corapipo gutturalis   PLATE 64(3)
9 cm (3½"). Locally fairly common in lower growth of humid and foothill forest in *ne. South America.* To 1300 m, favoring hilly regions and absent or less numerous in more level terrain. ♂ *glossy blue-black above;* some white in flight feathers. *Snowy white bib on throat ends in a point on chest;* black below. ♀ bright olive above, *mostly grayish white below.* ♂ essentially unmistakable in range (White-ruffed Manakin occurs in nw. South America). ♀ *whiter below* than other sympatric manakins. Forages singly, less often in small groups; sometimes joins mixed flocks. Distinctive call a thin, high-pitched "seeu." Display of ♂♂ focuses on a mossy log on forest floor; they perch nearby, calling with neck stretched upward and wings drooped. In full display one flaps furiously while slowly flying toward the log, bouncing up upon landing. In another display ♂ rises steeply above the canopy, then plummets back, landing on the log.

White-ruffed Manakin
Corapipo leucorrhoa   PLATE 64(4)
9.5 cm (3¾"). Uncommon and local in lower growth of humid forest, mainly in foothills, in *n. Colombia and w. Venezuela* (east to Mérida). To 1200 m. ♂ *glossy blue-black above. Snowy white throat lengthened at sides to form a ruff;* black below. ♀ olive, somewhat paler below, with *throat and sides of head contrasting grayish.* ♂ essentially unmistakable in range (White-throated Manakin occurs only in *ne.* South America). ♀ White-crowned Manakin has gray on crown (and none on throat), a reddish iris. Behavior and voice as in White-throated Manakin. Also: Honduras to Panama.

Pin-tailed Manakin
Ilicura militaris   PLATE 64(5)
♂ 12.5 cm (5"), with *elongated central tail feathers;* ♀ 11 cm (4¼"), with shorter and *more wedge-shaped tail.* Uncommon to locally fairly common in lower growth of humid and foothill forest and woodland in *se. Brazil* (s. Bahia to e. Santa Catarina). 600–1200 m northward, to sea level southward. *Iris orange.* Unmistakable ♂

black above with *red forehead patch, lower back and rump* and olive flight feathers. Sides of head pale gray, grayish white below. ♀ bright olive above, *sides of head and throat contrasting gray;* whitish below. ♀ Blue and White-bearded Manakins lack ♀ Pin-tailed's gray on face. Usually seen singly; Pin-tailed seems to follow mixed flocks more than most other manakins. Distinctive and oft-heard call a simple, descending series of 3–4 high-pitched notes. Displaying ♂♂ give a longer version of this call from certain regularly used branches, often with rump feathers raised.

Golden-winged Manakin
Masius chrysopterus   PLATE 64(6)
11 cm (4¼"). *Fairly common in lower growth of montane forest in Andes from w. Venezuela* (Lara) *to n. Peru* (n. San Martín). Mostly 1000–2000 m, lower on west slope; locally lower in sw. Colombia and nw. Ecuador. *Bill pinkish; legs purplish.* **East-slope** ♂ (illustrated) *black* with *yellow crown* (*curling forward over bill*) becoming *orange on nape,* feathers on sides of crown forming "horns." Small throat patch yellow; *inner webs of flight feathers golden* (flashing in flight). **West-slope** ♂ similar but *scalelike nape feathers reddish brown.* ♀ olive, paler below, with *pale yellow patch on midthroat and upper chest.* ♂ unmistakable; yellow on ♀'s throat not shared by any other ♀ manakin. Not very vocal, so often overlooked; sometimes seen at fruiting trees. ♂♂ display in small groups around a mossy log or buttress. They approach slowly, then crouch with crest raised and horns flared, bowing from side to side. A distinctive froglike "nurrt" call is given then and occasionally elsewhere.

Xenopipo

Very inconspicuous manakins with rather long tails, found in undergrowth montane or foothill forests. Most species are *very quiet,* and displays are minimal (if they prove to have any at all). The first four species (Green, Yellow-headed, Jet, and Olive Manakins) were formerly separated in the genus *Chloropipo,* now subsumed into Xenopipo.

Green Manakin
Xenopipo holochlora*   PLATE 64(7)
12 cm (4¾"). Uncommon in undergrowth in humid and (where most numerous) foothill forest from *w. Colombia to se. Peru* (Puno). Mostly below 1300 m. Legs grayish. **East of Andes** (illustrated) *moss green above* with indistinct pale

eye-ring; olive below, belly pale yellow. **West of Andes** duller and darker generally (more olive), *so the yellow belly contrasts more.* A confusing bird, but larger and longer-tailed than ♀♀ of various similar manakins that occur with it (east of Andes, ♀ Blue-crowned is most similar). ♀ Blue-backed Manakin is about the same size and shape but has dull orange legs. West of Andes cf. Broad-billed Sapayoa. Only infrequently seen, typically hopping quietly in undergrowth, sometimes with a mixed flock or joining other birds at a fruiting tree. Quiet, rarely giving a growling "arrn" (R. O. Prum) or a soft sputter (O. Jahn). Also: e. Panama.

Yellow-headed Manakin
Xenopipo flavicapilla   PLATE 64(8)
12 cm (4¾"). Rare and local in undergrowth and mid-levels of montane forest in *Andes of w. Colombia and ne. Ecuador* (south to Tungurahua). 1200–2400 m. *Iris orange.* ♂ has *crown and hindneck bright golden yellow;* bright olive above; underwing-coverts white. Cheeks and throat yellowish olive; *mostly bright yellow below.* ♀'s pattern similar though not as brightly colored; *crown and nape still much yellower than back.* Both sexes of this lovely manakin are so yellow as normally to preclude confusion; Green Manakin occurs at lower elevations and is substantially darker and greener. Behavior not well known, but seems more arboreal than other *Chloropipo* and more likely to join mixed flocks of tanagers and other birds. Voice (if any) unknown.

Jet Manakin
Xenopipo unicolor*   PLATE 64(9)
12 cm (4¾"). Uncommon and local in undergrowth of montane forest on *east slope of Andes from n. Ecuador* (w. Napo) *to s. Peru* (Puno). 950–1900 m. ♂ *glossy blue-black above, duller black below;* underwing-coverts white. ♀ *uniform dark olive* with vague paler eye-ring, grayer on throat and belly; underwing-coverts white. ♂ distinctive in its limited range and habitat. Green Manakin mainly occurs at lower elevations (minimal overlap at best), is brighter green above than ♀ Jet, and has a yellowish belly and dark (not white) underwing-coverts. Behavior much as in Green. Jet likewise vocalizes very little, but has been heard to give a nasal, rising "dreee-ee-ee?" (J. Nilsson recording).

Olive Manakin
Xenopipo uniformis*   PLATE 64(10)
14 cm (5½"). Uncommon in undergrowth of montane forest and stunted woodland on *tepuis*

of s. *Venezuela region*. 800–2100 m. *Bill and legs dusky*. Rather long wings and tail. *Uniform dark olive*, slightly paler on belly; underwing-coverts whitish. ♀ Scarlet-horned Manakin is slightly smaller with shorter tail, probably is best told by its pinkish bill and legs. ♀ Black Manakin is virtually identical to Olive, but they would not be expected to occur together, as Black is found at lower elevations in scrubbier woodland. Behavior much as in Green Manakin. Infrequently heard call a drawn-out "tk-wheeeyp."

Black Manakin
Xenopipo atronitens   PLATE 64(11)
12 cm (4¾"). Locally fairly common in woodland and scrub with sandy soil, mainly in *ne. South America and e. Amazonia*. Mostly below 700 m. ♂'s bill mainly bluish gray; ♀'s maxilla black, mandible gray. ♂ *glossy blue-black*. ♀ mostly *dark* olive green, paler yellowish olive on belly. ♂ very similar to ♂ Amazonian Black Tyrant, though that has a larger bill; they differ in habitat, the black tyrant favoring seasonally flooded areas. Cf. also ♂ Red-shouldered Tanager. Found singly or (less often) in small groups, sometimes accompanying mixed flocks; inconspicuous and hard to see, seeming restless and flying quickly between perches. Has a variety of loud and sharp calls, including a "skee! kip-kip-kip-krrr" and a "trrrrrrrup" rattle.

Chiroxiphia

Quite large manakins that are inconspicuous in forest or woodland lower growth, the *beautiful ♂♂ have intense blue at least on the back. The complex cooperative displays of ♂♂ are unique.*

Lance-tailed Manakin
Chiroxiphia lanceolata   PLATE 64(12)
♂ 13.5 cm (5¼"), ♀ 13 cm (5"). Fairly common in lower growth of deciduous and semihumid forest and woodland in *n. Colombia and n. Venezuela*. Mostly below 1200 m. Legs orange (♂) or orange-yellow (♀). Both sexes resemble Blue-backed Manakin, but have *projecting and pointed central tail feathers*, longer in ♂. ♂ is brighter blue on back and sootier below. ♀ White-bearded Manakin is smaller with brighter orange legs; it lacks projecting tail spikes. Behavior much as in Blue-backed, and can be equally shy and hard to see. Displaying ♂♂ simply jump up and down on their perches (with no cartwheeling). Vocalizations rather different, the most frequent being

a mellow "doh" or "dee-o," sometimes a rolling "dowee-oh." Both sexes give a more nasal snarl. Also: Costa Rica and Panama.

Yungas Manakin
Chiroxiphia boliviana   PLATE 64(13)
13 cm (5"). Fairly common in lower growth of montane forest and woodland on *east slope of Andes from s. Peru* (Cuzco) *to w. Bolivia* (Chuquisaca). 650–2150 m. *Legs purplish*. Both sexes resemble Blue-backed Manakin (*found in lowlands; no overlap*), but legs darker and tail longer; ♂'s coronal patch darker red. *Usually identified by range, or from its distinctive voice.* Cf. also Green Manakin (limited overlap in s. Peru). General behavior similar to Blue-backed. Calls are distinctly different, including a higher-pitched, less husky "chereeo." Displaying ♂♂ give a fast "wheeyr-wheeyr-wheeyr-wheeyr" with variations.

Blue-backed Manakin
Chiroxiphia pareola   PLATE 64(14)
12–12.5 cm (4¾–5"). Locally fairly common in lower growth of humid forest and woodland from *Amazonia to the Guianas*, and in *e. Brazil*; in Amazonia mainly in terra firme. Mostly below 500 m. *Legs orange (♂) or orange-yellow (♀)*. In **most of range** (illustrated) ♂ black with *deep red crown patch* and *pale azure blue mantle*. In **s. Amazonia (east to Rio Tapajós)** *crown patch yellow*. ♀ olive above with indistinct paler eyering. Paler olive below, belly more yellowish. ♂ nearly unmistakable, but cf. range-restricted Yungas and Lance-tailed Manakins; *none of these manakins co-occur*. ♀ can be confusing. Cf. especially ♀ of darker Black Manakin (with grayish legs, different scrubbier habitat), ♀ White-bearded Manakin (smaller with shorter tail, brighter orange legs), and Green Manakin (brighter green above with dark legs). Shy and unobtrusive, most often seen at fruiting trees or around their leks. Leks are spectacular, with ♂♂ (usually two) performing together, cartwheeling around each other in the presence of a ♀. Most frequent call a rich throaty "che-wurrr" or "te-turrr," but displaying ♂♂ give a more nasal "wr-r-r-aang, wr-r-r-aang. . . ." Both sexes also give a clear "tooo-eee," sometimes doubled.

Blue Manakin
Chiroxiphia caudata   PLATE 64(15)
♂ 15 cm (6"), with *elongated central tail feathers*; ♀ 14.5 cm (5¾"), with slightly shorter central tail feathers. *Common in lower growth of humid forest, woodland, and borders in se. Brazil region*

(north to s. Bahia). Mostly below 1500 m. Legs dull reddish. ♂ *mostly rich cerulean blue* with *scarlet crown* and black head, wings, and outer tail feathers. ♀ olive, slightly paler below; a few have orange on crown. *Beautiful ♂ is by far the bluest manakin.* ♀ resembles Greenish Schiffornis, though that species has dark legs, a normal tail, rufescent wings. Cf. also ♀ Blue-backed Manakin (smaller and lacking elongated tail feathers). Behavior much like Blue-backed, but Blue is easier to see and often ranges to edge and into clearings. Cartwheeling display also similar, though usually three ♂♂ perform together. Throaty "qua-a-a-a-a" calls are given during display. Both sexes frequently emit a "chorreeo, cho-cho-cho."

Antilophia

Two large, *beautiful* manakins with *expressive, forward-curling frontal crests* and long tails.

Helmeted Manakin
Antilophia galeata   PLATE 64(16)
14.5 cm (5¾"). *Locally fairly common in lower and middle growth of gallery forest and woodland, mainly in interior s. Brazil.* Mostly 400–1000 m. Unmistakable ♂ *black* with *red frontal crest, crown, nape, and midback.* ♀ has *miniature frontal crest;* olive, somewhat paler and grayer below. Ranges higher above the ground than many manakins, thus often easier to observe; not particularly shy. ♂'s distinctive and rollicking song a fast, rich, musical phrase, e.g., "whip-dip, whih-deh-deh-dédidip," sometimes given as they chase each other through the trees. Seems to have no organized display. Both sexes give a throaty "wreee? pur."

Araripe Manakin
*Antilophia bokermanni**   PLATE 64(17)
14.5 cm (5¾"). *Rare and very local in lower growth of semihumid deciduous forest in ne. Brazil* (Chapada do Araripe in s. Ceará). 800 m. A recently described species. Stunning ♂ similar to ♂ Helmeted Manakin (no overlap), with *same red on head and frontal crest,* but *body plumage snowy white;* only the flight feathers and tail are black. ♀ similar to ♀ Helmeted Manakin. Behavior, including voice, much as in that species. One of the more spectacular new species to be discovered in recent decades, this manakin is acutely threatened by deforestation.

Machaeropterus

Small manakins, ♂♂ *strikingly patterned and with unusual songs,* that are found in humid and montane forests. *The only manakins with streaking.*

Western Striped Manakin
*Machaeropterus striolatus**   PLATE 65(1)
9 cm (3½"). Locally fairly common in lower growth of terra firme forest and woodland *mainly in w. Amazonia, also on Andean slopes in n. Colombia and w. Venezuela.* To 1300 m. Here considered a separate species from the geographically distant Eastern Striped Manakin. ♂ in **most of range** (illustrated) olive above with *red crown and nape. Below mainly streaked reddish and white.* In **s. Venezuela, nw. Brazil, and very locally in n. Peru** has yellow chest band. ♀ olive above; whitish below with a *vague brownish chest band* and *indistinct reddish streaking on flanks.* ♂ unmistakable. ♀ Fiery-capped Manakin has blurry olive streaking below (not reddish); range overlap only marginal. Inconspicuous, mainly noted from calling ♂♂ (though even these are hard to locate). Distinctive song a soft, clear, whistled "who-cheéuw" or "whoo-cheet" repeated at intervals of 10–15 seconds. Yellow-chested males give a very different rising "chiwee?" (T. S. Schulenberg et al.).

Eastern Striped Manakin
Machaeropterus regulus
9.5 cm (3¾"). Uncommon and local in lower growth of humid forest borders and secondary woodland in e. Brazil (s. Bahia to Rio de Janeiro). Below 200 m. Here considered a separate species from Western Striped Manakin. Slightly larger. ♂ lacks the red chest stain, and *its streaking below is broader but sparser.* ♀ similar to ♀ Western aside from its larger size. General behavior similar, though jumping and rotating on its display perches has been reported (H. Sick). ♂'s song is, however, utterly different, a buzzy, mechanical "eeeuw" given at intervals of 4–6 seconds (A. Whittaker recording).

Fiery-capped Manakin
Machaeropterus pyrocephalus   PLATE 65(2)
9 cm (3½"). Uncommon in lower growth of humid forest and woodland, *mainly in s. Amazonia.* To 1200 m in Peru. ♂ in most of range (illustrated) has *crown and nape golden with a red median stripe; back and rump rosy rufous,* wings olive with whitish inner flight feathers. *Below*

whitish streaked rosy rufous. In **far north** has less red in crown. ♀ olive above; *pale yellowish below with blurry olive breast and belly streaking.* Cf. ♀ Western Striped Manakin (the two overlap only in n. Peru). Behavior similar to Western Striped. ♂'s song distinctive (though easily passed over as a frog or insect and hard to track to its source), a high-pitched bell-like "pling" or "cling," given at intervals of 10 seconds or more.

Club-winged Manakin
Machaeropterus deliciosus   PLATE 65(3)
9.5 cm (3¾"). Locally fairly common in lower growth of foothill and lower montane forest and secondary woodland on *west slope of Andes in w. Colombia and w. Ecuador* (south to El Oro). 400–1600 m, locally lower when not breeding. Unmistakable ♂ with *scarlet crown* but otherwise *mostly rufous-chestnut;* wings and tail black, *inner flight feathers partially white, the shafts of inner primaries peculiarly thickened and twisted,* underwing-coverts white. ♀ olive above with *cinnamon-rufous on face (mainly malar area); inner secondaries white on their inner webs,* underwing as in ♂. Dingy olive below, midbelly pale yellow. ♂ easily recognized, even in flight when wings flash much white. No other ♀ manakin shows rufous on face or white on wings. Behavior much as in the Striped Manakins, though Club-winged seems more frequent at forest edge, at least when feeding. Displaying ♂♂ give a very odd, ringing "kip, kip, buuuuww," sometimes only one "kip." With each "kip" the wings are fluttered, and with each clear "buuuuww" they are held upward (almost meeting over back) and shaken, extremely rapidly, as the bird leans forward, with one of the club-shaped feathers rubbing against an adjacent one.

Lepidothrix and *Pipra*

Small, short-tailed manakins found inside humid forests, mainly in the lowlands. ♂♂ of these genera are well known for their colorful plumage (*most often mainly black with contrasting white or some bright color*) and their stereotyped displays performed at leks. ♀♀ are *notably drab and dumpy* and often hard to identify except by range. The first eight species were formerly placed in the genus *Pipra* but are now usually separated in the genus *Lepidothrix* on the basis of anatomical characters.

Blue-crowned Manakin
Lepidothrix coronata   PLATE 65(4)
8.5 cm (3¼"). Often common in lower growth of humid and foothill forest and secondary woodland in *w. Colombia and nw. Ecuador,* and in *w. Amazonia.* Mostly below 1000 m. ♂ in **most of range** (A) *black* with *bright blue crown.* In **most of e. Peru, Bolivia, and sw. Amaz. Brazil** (B) *viridian green* with a *paler bright blue crown,* yellow belly. The two types intergrade south of the Amazon in Peru and w. Brazil. ♀♀ *viridian to bluish green above;* duller on breast, *belly pale yellow.* In se. Peru, cf. Cerulean-capped Manakin (montane); *otherwise ♂ Blue-crowned is the only manakin with a blue crown.* ♀ Blue-crowneds are brighter green (less olive) above than most other ♀ manakins, and belly not as yellow. They rarely or never occur with other comparably colored species; cf. especially ♀ Cerulean-capped and ♀ Orange-bellied. Inconspicuous and more or less solitary in shady forest and woodland, perching quietly and motionless, then darting off; they come to edge mainly to feed at fruiting trees. ♂'s song, delivered from a persistently used low branch, a soft "chi-werr" given every few seconds; often preceded by a high-pitched "sweee?" Several are usually within earshot, though only infrequently do they interact. Both sexes give a soft trill. Also: Costa Rica and Panama.

Cerulean-capped Manakin
Lepidothrix coeruleocapilla   PLATE 65(5)
8.5 cm (3¼"). Uncommon and local in lower growth of foothill and lower montane forest on *east slope of Andes in s. Peru* (Huánuco to Puno). Mostly 700–1600 m. Unmistakable ♂ has *crown and nape bright cerulean blue, rump and uppertail-coverts a slightly deeper blue;* otherwise black. ♀ like ♀ Blue-crowned Manakin, but duller below; Cerulean-capped is found at elevations *above* Blue-crowned. Blue-rumped Manakin occurs northward on east slope (no overlap). Behavior apparently much like Blue-crowned. Call a sharp "tee-zeek" (B. Walker).

Blue-rumped Manakin
Lepidothrix isidorei   PLATE 65(6)
7.5 cm (3"). Uncommon and local in lower growth of foothill and lower montane forest on *east slope of Andes from s. Colombia* (Meta) to *cen. Peru* (Huánuco). 900–1700 m. In **Colombia and Ecuador** (illustrated) ♂ black with *white crown and nape* and *azure blue rump and uppertail-coverts.* In **n. Peru** (south of Río Marañón) has *milky white rump and uppertail-*

coverts. ♀ viridian green above, *more yellow-ish on crown* and *paler on rump and uppertail-coverts* (contrasting with dusky tail). Below paler and duller green, midbelly yellowish. ♂ virtually unmistakable; ♂ White-crowned Manakin lacks the blue rump and is larger. ♀ Blue-crowned Manakin is more uniform green above, lacking Blue-rumped's yellowish crown and paler rump. Behavior much as in Blue-crowned, but seems less numerous. ♂'s song an upslurred "koooit" repeated at intervals of 2–5 seconds.

White-fronted Manakin
Lepidothrix serena   PLATE 65(7)
9 cm (3½"). Fairly common in lower growth of humid forest from the *Guianas to n. Amaz. Brazil.* Below 500 m. ♂ black with *white forehead and azure blue uppertail-coverts; spot on chest and entire belly yellow.* ♀ *bright green above, bluer on crown;* throat and breast olive green, belly pale yellow. Cf. Orange-bellied Manakin (found at higher elevations; no known overlap). ♀ greener above (less olive) than other sympatric manakins, and unlike ♀ White-throated has *no gray.* Behavior much as in Blue-crowned Manakin. ♂'s song a burry "prreee" or "prreee-prrur," sometimes in series; typically a few ♂♂ are fairly close by.

Orange-bellied Manakin
Lepidothrix suavissima
9 cm (3½"). Fairly common in lower growth of foothill and lower montane forest on *tepuis of s. Venezuela and n. Guyana.* 500–1400 m. ♂ resembles ♂ White-fronted Manakin (no overlap) but *lacks the chest spot,* and *belly orange-yellow.* ♀ closely resembles ♀ White-fronted. Blue-crowned Manakin overlaps marginally (in s. Venezuela); ♀ Blue-crowned lacks bluish on crown and is greener on chest. ♀ Scarlet-horned Manakin is larger and more olive. Behavior similar to Blue-crowned and White-fronted. ♂'s song a nasal, froglike "yeyp" repeated irregularly; several may sing around a mossy log, flying between adjacent saplings.

Opal-crowned Manakin
Lepidothrix iris   PLATE 65(8)
9 cm (3½"). Uncommon and local in lower growth of terra firme forest and secondary woodland in *e. Amaz. Brazil.* To 400 m. *Rather heavy bill pale bluish; iris creamy white.* ♂ *bright grass green above* with *crown and nape bright silvery opalescent;* throat and breast pale green, belly yellow. ♀ like ♂ but crown bright green, tinged

blue **near Rio Tapajós** (illustrated). Stunning ♂ unmistakable. ♀ is the only small, pale-eyed, bright green manakin in range (aside from possible limited overlap with smaller-billed Snow-capped). Behavior, including vocalizations and ♂'s display, similar to Blue-crowned and Snow-capped Manakins.

Golden-crowned Manakin
Lepidothrix vilasboasi
8.5 cm (3¼"). Known from lower growth of humid forest at two sites between Rio Jamanxim and Rio Teles Peres. 200 m. ♂ resembles ♂ Snow-capped Manakin but *crown and nape glittering greenish gold.* ♀ indistinguishable. ♀ Opal-crowned Manakin (no known overlap) has a heavier bill and is slightly larger overall. Behavior of this gorgeous manakin, still virtually unknown in life, seems likely to be similar to Snow-capped and Blue-crowned Manakins.

Snow-capped Manakin
Lepidothrix nattereri   PLATE 65(9)
8.5 cm (3¼"). Uncommon in lower growth of terra firme forest in *cen. Amaz. Brazil, south of Amazon.* To 500 m. Iris pale yellowish; bill pale bluish. ♂ has *crown, nape, rump and uppertail-coverts shiny white* contrasting with grass green upperparts. Throat and chest pale olive, *belly yellow.* ♀ resembles ♂ but white *replaced by grass green;* crown tinged blue **northward.** Cf. Opal-crowned Manakin, which mainly or entirely occurs *east* of Snow-capped's range; also the very range-restricted Golden-crowned. Other sympatric small manakins have dark irides, are more olive above, etc. Behavior, including vocalizations, similar to Blue-crowned Manakin.

White-crowned Manakin
Pipra pipra *   PLATE 65(10)
9–10 cm (3½–4"). *Widespread and fairly common* in lower growth of humid forest and woodland, locally also in *lower montane forest in n. Andes;* ranges from *Colombia and s. and e. Venezuela to Amazonia* (more numerous eastward), and in se. Brazil (where rare). To 2000 m. More than one species likely involved. *Iris red.* ♂ black with *snowy white crown and nape.* ♀ in **most of range** (illustrated) has *crown and sides of head gray;* dark olive above. Below grayish, sides tinged olive. **More eastern** ♀♀ tend to have less gray on head, **Andean** ♀♀ to be more olive below. **Immature** ♂♂ in **e. Brazil and e. Amaz. Brazil** have grayish white crown, dark olive back, dark gray underparts. No other ♀ manakin shares the red

iris and gray on head; most similar are ♀ White-ruffed and White-throated (dark-eyed). An inconspicuous bird and generally solitary, though several will sometimes gather at fruiting trees. Usually recorded from displaying ♂♂, which make stereotyped slow flights between branches with their crown feathers spread outward. Songs differ markedly, lowland birds giving a slightly buzzy spadebill-like "dzee-ee-ee-ew," Andean birds a louder and sharper "dzzzzeew-weúw." Also: Costa Rica and w. Panama.

Round-tailed Manakin

Pipra chloromeros PLATE 65(11)

11 cm (4¼"). Locally fairly common in lower and middle growth of humid and foothill forest and woodland from *ne. Peru (Amazonas) to w. Bolivia* (w. Santa Cruz). To 1400 m. Iris whitish. ♂ black with *scarlet head and nape, nape feathers often protruding somewhat; thighs mostly yellow.* ♀ olive above, paler and more grayish olive below, belly pale yellowish. Closely resembles Red-headed Manakin (locally occurring with it); cf. under that species. Red-headed's tail is indeed more squared. Inconspicuous and generally quiet, tending to perch motionless, hunched up, then abruptly darting off. Most likely to be seen at fruiting trees, or when ♂♂ are displaying. Groups of up to 10 birds gather at leks (which may be used for many years), flying rapidly back and forth between favored perches, sidling along branches, and quickly turning back and forth. ♂'s calls include a sharp "ti-zeeeeek!" and a softer "peeeuw, pew-pew-pew."

Red-capped Manakin

Pipra mentalis

10 cm (4"). Locally common in lower and middle growth of humid forest and woodland in *w. Colombia and w. Ecuador* (south mainly to Azuay). Mostly below 500 m. Iris white (♂) or brown (♀); bill whitish below. ♂ similar to ♂ Round-tailed Manakin, black with *scarlet head;* thighs and underwing-coverts yellow (thighs seen mainly in display). ♀ dull olive above; paler and more grayish olive below, pale yellowish on belly. ♂ unmistakable in range. ♀ Blue-crowned Manakin is brighter green above with an all-dark bill. Behavior similar to Round-tailed. Displaying ♂♂ at leks are noisy; gives variety of loud and sharp calls including a "tzik-tzik-tzeeeeeeeeuw-tzík!" as it flies between display branches, the sharp "tzík!" as it lands. Some other calls may be mechanical. Also: Mexico to Panama.

Scarlet-horned Manakin

Pipra cornuta PLATE 65(12)

12.5 cm (5"). Uncommon in lower growth of lower montane forest and woodland on *tepuis of s. Venezuela region.* Mostly 900–1600 m. Iris white (♂) or (♀) pale brown; *bill pale pinkish.* Rather large and long-tailed. Unique ♂ black with *scarlet head, hindcrown feathers elongated and projecting back;* thighs scarlet. ♀ olive above with *slight tufted effect on nape;* paler and more grayish olive below, belly pale yellowish. ♀ most likely confused with Olive Manakin; Olive is larger with longer tail, has no tuft on nape, and soft parts are dark. Behavior similar to Round-tailed Manakin; lek size smaller. Calls include a hoarse "sweeénk-aank" and a loud mechanical "brrrt" (R. O. Prum).

Golden-headed Manakin

Pipra erythrocephala PLATE 65(13)

9 cm (3½"). Common in lower and middle growth of humid forest and woodland from *Colombia and Venezuela to w. and n. Amazonia* (where only *north* of Amazon). Iris white (♂) or pale grayish (♀); *mandible pinkish white;* legs dull flesh. Unmistakable ♂ black with *golden yellow head;* thighs red and white. ♀ dull olive above; paler and more grayish olive below, belly pale yellowish. ♀♀ are dumpy and featureless; ♀ Blue-crowned and White-fronted Manakins are brighter green above, have dark bills and irides. Behavior much as in Round-tailed Manakin. Displaying ♂♂ give a variety of sharp chips, buzzes, and trills, some perhaps mechanical; these include a "jeet-jeet jeje-e-e-e-e-e jeet" and a "whir-whír-whíyt! tzeeét," sometimes given while approaching the display branch. Common call a clear "pu." Also: e. Panama.

Red-headed Manakin

Pipra rubrocapilla PLATE 65(14)

10 cm (4"). Locally common in lower and middle growth of terra firme forest and woodland in *Amazonia south of Amazon and in e. Brazil.* To 500 m. Bill pinkish; iris pale hazel. ♂ black with *flame-scarlet head; thighs red and white.* ♀ olive above, paler and more grayish olive below, belly pale yellowish. Golden-headed Manakin only occurs *north* of Amazon River. Both sexes closely resemble slightly larger Round-tailed Manakin, which does indeed have a rounder tail (Red-headed's tail is square, but this is hard to see in the field). ♂ Round-tailed has whiter iris, yellow thighs, and slightly more extensive red on nape; thigh color can be seen on displaying ♂♂.

♀ Blue-crowned and Snow-capped Manakins are smaller and brighter green above. Behavior, including displays, similar to Round-tailed. ♂'s calls include a sharp "dzeek, dzeeuw" and "drree-dit, dree-dee-dew."

Wire-tailed Manakin
Pipra filicauda   PLATE 65(15)

11.5 cm (4½"); ♂'s tail filaments add 4 cm (1½"), ♀'s 2 cm (¾"). Fairly common in undergrowth of várzea forest, and near streams in terra firme forest from *w. Venezuela to w. Amazonia;* in Venezuela also near water in deciduous and gallery forest and woodland. Mostly below 500 m. *Iris white.* Beautiful ♂ has *crown and nape bright red,* otherwise black above; white on inner flight feathers shows mainly in flight; *shafts of tail feathers project as unique long wiry filaments that curve down and inward. Forehead, face, and underparts golden yellow.* ♀ olive above, somewhat paler olive below, belly pale yellow; *tail as in ♂* but filaments not as long. ♂ unmistakable; does not overlap with Band-tailed or Crimson-hooded Manakins. Even ♀'s relatively short tail filaments are long enough to be readily visible. Like other manakins, Wire-tailed is inconspicuous and most apt to be seen at fruiting trees or where ♂♂ are displaying at their small leks. ♂♂ perform either alone or with a partner, sometimes even tickling the face or throat of the partner or a ♀ with their tail filaments. Most frequent call a drawn-out, nasal, descending "eeeeuw."

Band-tailed Manakin
Pipra fasciicauda   PLATE 65(16)

11 cm (4¼"). Fairly common in undergrowth of várzea, riparian, and gallery forest and woodland from *s. Amazonia to e. Paraguay and ne. Argentina.* Mostly below 600 m. *Iris white.* ♂ has *crown and nape bright red,* otherwise black above; *basal tail yellowish white* and *white on inner wing obvious in flight.* Bright yellow below, *variably stained scarlet on breast* (most in **ne. Peru**). ♀ olive, brighter above and somewhat paler below, belly yellow. Cf. Crimson-hooded Manakin; otherwise ♂ is unmistakable. ♀ best known by her staring white eye and bright olive and yellow coloration; cannot be distinguished from Crimson-hooded (limited overlap). Behavior much as in Wire-tailed Manakin, though of course there is no tickling; ♂'s white in wing and tail figure in display.

Crimson-hooded Manakin
Pipra aureola   PLATE 65(17)

11 cm (4¼"). Uncommon in undergrowth of várzea and swampy forest and woodland from *e. Venezuela to e. Amaz. Brazil.* Below 300 m. ♂ in **most of range** (illustrated) has *head, nape, and most of underparts crimson red* with *mainly black belly;* wings as in Band-tailed Manakin, but *tail all black* (no white at base). In **Amaz. Brazil west of Rio Xingú** has yellow throat. ♀ indistinguishable from ♀ Band-tailed. Behavior of the two species is similar.

SHARPBILL: OXYRUNCIDAE

Often considered a cotinga, more recently the consensus seems to be that the Sharpbill deserves recognition in its own monotypic family.

Sharpbill

Oxyruncus cristatus   PLATE 66(1)

17 cm (6¾"). Uncommon to fairly common but quite local in canopy and borders of humid and foothill forest; *most numerous on the tepuis, and in se. Brazil region.* To 1600 m, especially 500–1000 m. *Pointed bill;* iris reddish to orange. Mainly olive above with *black crown concealing an orange to red crest,* and *head and neck whitish with blackish scaling. Throat white scaled blackish, below pale yellowish to whitish spotted black* (yellowest in **se. South America;** illustrated). Scaled and spotted plumage in conjunction with pointed bill distinctive. On tepuis cf. ♀ Red-banded Fruiteater. The distinctive Sharp- bill gleans along branches and among leaves, sometimes even hanging upside down, probing into moss and curled-up leaves; also eats fruit, often with tanagers. It can be stolid, perching quietly for long periods, but also accompanies mixed flocks. Easily overlooked except for ♂'s unmistakable, far-carrying song, a drawn-out, shrill, buzzy trill that drops in pitch and fades away, "zheeeeeeeeu-uuu'u'u'u'u'u'ur," in some areas more nasal and attenuated, especially in se. Brazil region sounding uncannily like a falling bomb; in se. Ecuador a similar "zheeeeeeu, dzzzzzz" (N. K. Krabbe and J. Nilsson recordings). Also: Costa Rica and Panama.

COTINGAS: COTINGIDAE

A heterogeneous group, several of the genera here considered to comprise the cotinga family have been placed in families of their own, others in the Tyrannidae (into which the whole family has sometimes been subsumed). For the most part cotingas are arboreal birds found in lowland forests; a few genera are more montane or occur in more arid regions. Included within the family are some of the most colorful, spectacular, and even bizarre of all Neotropical birds. Mating systems are diverse, the males of some species engaging in elaborate courtship displays in leks. Vocalizations also run the gamut, some genera being quiet or even mute, others extraordinarily vocal. Most cotingas are primarily frugivorous.

Phibalura

Two ultra-distinctive cotingas with *long, deeply cleft tails* and *barred plumage*. The very isolated Bolivian form has recently been recognized as a separate species from the mainly Brazilian one.

Swallow-tailed Cotinga
Phibalura flavirostris   PLATE 66(2)
21.5–22 cm (8½–8¾"). Uncommon and local in forest and woodland borders and adjacent clearings and gardens in *se. Brazil region*. Mostly below 1400 m. *Bill yellow*. Unmistakable, with a *unique long, slender, deeply forked tail*. ♂ has mostly black crown, yellowish olive upperparts *barred black;* wings and tail mainly bluish black. Throat bright yellow, breast white barred black, belly pale yellow with sparse black streaking. ♀ with grayer crown, wings and tail more olive, and below duller yellowish with denser black spotting and scaling. In flight, tail held closed in a point; slim overall shape recalls a *Pyrrhura* parakeet. Perches at varying heights in clearings and at edge, *not a true forest bird.* Often quite conspicuous, as are its nests, usually placed on a lichen-encrusted limb in the semiopen. Apparently feeds primarily on mistletoe berries. In nonbreeding season sometimes gathers in small groups. Very quiet.

Palkachupa Cotinga
Phibalura boliviana*
21.5–22 cm (8½–8¾"). *Rare and very local in semihumid montane forest borders and adjacent clearings in Andes of w. Bolivia* (recently around Apolo in w. La Paz, in quite disturbed terrain). 1400–2000 m. Similar to Swallow-tailed Cotinga, but ♂ has *more white on sides of neck and throat* and less belly streaking. Not well known, but behavior apparently similar to Swallow-tailed. A "harsh and weak" call has been recorded (G. Bromfield et al.).

Iodopleura

Three distinctive, *small* cotingas with *short tails* and *notably long wings* that range in the canopy and borders of lowland forests.

Dusky Purpletuft
Iodopleura fusca   PLATE 66(3)
11 cm (4¼"). *Rare* in canopy and borders of humid forest from the *Guianas and se. Venezuela to n. Amaz. Brazil*. To 600 m. *Mostly dark sooty brown* (blacker above) with *white restricted to rump band, median belly, and crissum.* ♂ has purple flank tufts (white in ♀), usually hidden beneath wings. Not likely confused in its small range, where no other purpletuft occurs; White-browed Purpletuft ranges the closest, in sw. Venezuela. Swallow-winged Puffbird (*Chelidoptera tenebrosa*) is larger with rufous belly, much

more white on rump, etc. Behavior, including voice, much as in the better known White-browed Purpletuft.

White-browed Purpletuft
Iodopleura isabellae   PLATE 66(4)
11.5 cm (4½"). Uncommon in canopy and borders of humid forest and secondary woodland in *w. and s. Amazonia.* Mostly below 700 m. Brownish black above with *bold white facial markings;* rump band also white. *Throat and median underparts white,* sides and flanks mottled and barred brown. ♂ has purple flank tufts (white in ♀), usually hidden beneath wings but flared in display. Cf. Dusky Purpletuft of ne. South America (no overlap). Usually perches high above the ground where easily overlooked, though often on dead branches. Frequently in pairs; does not associate with other birds. Purpletufts make long flycatcherlike sallies in pursuit of aerial insects, and also eat some fruit (e.g., mistletoe). Usually quiet, but sometimes gives a soft plaintive "wheee," occasionally doubled or tripled.

Buff-throated Purpletuft
Iodopleura pipra   PLATE 66(5)
9.5 cm (3¾"). *Rare and local* in canopy and borders of humid and foothill forest, woodland, and adjacent plantations in *e. Brazil* (Paraíba to e. São Paulo). To 1000 m. *Very small,* even tinier than the other purpletufts. In *most of range* (illustrated) *ashy gray above,* blacker crown feathers sometimes raised in a short crest. *Throat and chest buff, underparts white barred with dusky.* ♂ has pale purple flank tufts (lacking in ♀), usually hidden beneath wings. In *ne. Brazil* has a white rump band. Unique in its limited range. Behavior much as in other purpletufts. Occasionally gives a high-pitched "swee-yee" call (R. Parrini recording).

Kinglet Calyptura
Calyptura cristata   PLATE 66(6)
8 cm (3¼"). *Recently rediscovered* (by R. Parrini)—after going unrecorded for almost 150 years—in *canopy of montane forest of se. Brazil* (Rio de Janeiro). *Exceedingly rare,* with a pair being seen several times in Oct. 1996 on lower slopes of the Serra dos Orgãos, but sadly, none has been found here since; also a 2006 sighting from se. São Paulo near Ubatuba. 400–900 m. *Extremely small. Bright olive above* with *orange-red crest bordered by wide black stripe;* forehead and uppertail-coverts yellow; wings and *short*

tail dusky, wings with *two bold white bars. Mostly bright yellow below.* A tiny, ultra-distinctive bird that cannot be confused. Hardly known in life. Recent sightings were of birds that perched on certain branches high in forest canopy, with overall comportment reminiscent of Buff-throated Purpletuft (R. Parrini).

Laniisoma

Recently split as species (formerly called Elegant Mourner, or Shrike-like Cotinga), the two laniiosmas are infrequently seen cotingas found in widely disjunct areas of humid foothill forest.

Brazilian Laniisoma
*Laniisoma elegans**   PLATE 66(7)
17.5 cm (6¾"). *Rare and local in humid forest and woodland of se. Brazil* (Espírito Santo to Paraná). Mostly 400–1200 m. ♂ has *black crown* with yellow eye-ring, olive green upperparts. *Bright yellow below* with *black scaling across breast, down flanks, and on crissum.* ♀ similar but crown dusky and *entire underparts scaled black.* **Immature** like ♀ but with *large rufous spots on tips of wing-coverts.* Not likely confused. Sharpbill has very different bill shape and is more spotted below, scaly on face. Usually seen singly, ranging at all levels in forest but most often not very high. Singing ♂ gives a series of 8–10 forceful, piercing, high-pitched "psee-yeé" notes (often starting with several simple "psii" notes) from a low but usually unobstructed branch, opening bill wide and puffing throat and depressing tail with each call.

Andean Laniisoma
*Laniisoma buckleyi**   PLATE 66(8)
17.5 cm (6¾"). *Rare and local in foothill and lower montane forest on east slope of Andes from w. Venezuela* (Barinas) *to w. Bolivia* (La Paz). 400–1350 m. ♂ resembles ♂ Brazilian Laniisoma but with *only a limited amount of black scaling below, mainly on flanks.* ♀ also like ♀ Brazilian Laniisoma, and *equally boldly scaled with black below;* its crown is concolor olive (not dusky). **Immatures** similar. The chunkier and shorter-tailed Scaled Fruiteater has scaly-patterned *upper*parts, a white throat, less bright yellow underparts. Cf. also Sharpbill. Usually found singly inside tall forest, often near streams, ranging at varying levels above the ground;

sometimes with mixed flocks. ♂'s song a thin and high-pitched "psiiiiiiiueeeé," given at long intervals and recalling Black-streaked Puffbird (*Malacoptila fulvogularis*).

Carpornis

Two fine large cotingas endemic to the *forests of e. Brazil*, where they replace each other altitudinally.

Hooded Berryeater
Carpornis cucullata   PLATE 66(9)
23 cm (9"). *Locally fairly common in mid-levels and subcanopy of humid and lower montane forest in se.* Brazil (Espírito Santo to Rio Grande do Sul). Mostly 500–1500 m, lower southward. ♂ has *head, neck, and breast black* contrasting with *yellow nuchal collar and belly; back rich chestnut brown,* rump olive; wings and tail blackish, wings with narrow yellow bars. ♀ duller, with more olive head and foreneck, back only suffused chestnut, flanks faintly scaled. This handsome cotinga is not likely to be confused, but cf. Black-headed Berryeater (lower elevations). Seen singly or in pairs, perching quite upright, like a thrush or trogon; sometimes with mixed flocks. Eats fruit, and captures larger insects. Heard much more often than seen; its powerful, far-carrying song is a characteristic sound of se. Brazil's wetter montane forests, an abrupt, whistled "weeok, wee-kow!" given at long intervals and hard to track to its source.

Black-headed Berryeater
Carpornis melanocephala   PLATE 66(10)
21 cm (8¼"). *Uncommon and local in mid-levels and subcanopy of humid forest in e. Brazil* (Alagoas, and e. Bahia to ne. Paraná). To 500 m. *Iris red.* ♂ has *head and upper throat black* contrasting with olive upperparts and *yellowish underparts, the latter faintly scaled blackish.* ♀ has some olive on head. Behavior much as in Hooded Berryeater but less vocal and therefore less often encountered. Does not seem to accompany mixed flocks. Loud whistled song an abrupt and loud "tuhweéo."

Ampelion

Two cotingas found at *higher elevations in the Andes,* both species with *striking nuchal crests.*

Red-crested Cotinga
Ampelion rubrocristata   PLATE 67(1)
21 cm (8¼"). *Widespread and locally fairly common* at borders of upper montane forest and woodland up to treeline, and in agricultural areas with hedgerows and scattered trees, in Andes from w. Venezuela (Trujillo) *to w. Bolivia* (w. Santa Cruz). Mostly 2500–3700 m. *Bill chalky white with black tip;* iris red. *Mostly dark gray,* blacker on head, wings, and tail; *semiconcealed maroon nuchal crest,* usually laid flat with little color evident but sometimes flared. Some white streaking on rump and belly, crissum white streaked black; a *broad white band across tail* is visible in flight and from below. **Juvenile** browner with no nuchal crest, whitish streaking on rump, and *whitish underparts with coarse dark streaking.* In a quick view can look vaguely thrushlike. Usually seen singly or in pairs, often perching motionless and upright atop a shrub or low tree. Seems sluggish, usually quite tame. Does not accompany mixed flocks. Eats much fruit, especially mistletoe, but also sallies for insects. Displaying birds fan crest and bow with tail spread. Usually quiet, but gives a low, guttural "rrreh"; in song extended into a froglike stuttered "k-k-k-k-k-rrrréh."

Chestnut-crested Cotinga
Ampelion rufaxilla   PLATE 67(2)
20.5 cm (8"). *Rare to uncommon and seemingly local in canopy and borders of montane forest in Andes from n. Colombia to w. Bolivia* (w. Santa Cruz). Scarcer and more forest-based than Red-crested Cotinga, and occurring at *lower elevations.* 1750–2700 m. Unmistakable. Bill grayish blue with black tip; iris red. Crown blackish with *nuchal crest of long bright chestnut feathers* (sometimes flared widely); *sides of head and neck, and throat, cinnamon-rufous;* above olivaceous gray. Wings and tail blackish with bright chestnut shoulders. Chest gray, *breast and belly pale yellow boldly streaked blackish.* Behavior much like more numerous Red-crested, though much more dependent on actual forest. Usually perches well above the ground, often on open branches. Most frequent call a dry, raspy, and nasal stuttered "reh, r-r-r-r-réh," longer than comparable Red-crested call; often vibrates tail while vocalizing.

White-cheeked Cotinga
Zaratornis stresemanni   PLATE 67(3)
21 cm (8¼"). *Rare and local in forest and woodland, mainly near treeline and including Polylepis*

woodland, in Andes of w. Peru (La Libertad to Ayacucho). Mostly 3700–4300 m. Bill bluish gray; iris red. *Crown black contrasting with white face; above buff broadly streaked dusky. Throat and chest brownish gray; below buff broadly streaked blackish.* Juvenile Red-crested Cotinga also is streaked below but always has white in tail (lacking in White-cheeked) and never shows white cheeks. Behavior similar to the more numerous Red-crested, with which White-cheeked can occur. Apparently feeds largely on orange-flowered mistletoe berries, and can sometimes be found simply by looking for areas where the mistletoe itself is frequent. Usually quiet, but has a nasal song similar to Red-crested.

Doliornis

Two cotingas with subdued coloration that are restricted to *woodland near treeline in the n. Andes.*

Bay-vented Cotinga
Doliornis sclateri   PLATE 67(4)

21.5 cm (8½"). *Rare and local in woodland near treeline on east slope of Andes in cen. Peru* (s. San Martín to Junín). 2600–3600 m. ♂ has *crown and nape black* with semiconcealed maroon nuchal crest; above mostly dark grayish brown. *Throat and sides of head and neck gray; below brown, with rufous-chestnut crissum.* ♀ lacks black crown. Distinctive in its limited range; cf. more numerous Red-crested Cotinga (with conspicuous whitish bill, etc.). Chestnut-bellied Cotinga occurs to the north. Usually seen singly or in pairs, perching atop shrubs and low trees in the early morning but remaining within cover for the rest of the day or if it is windy. Frequently feeds on fruits of *Escallonia* trees. Usually silent; a raspy "shhh" call has been heard.

Chestnut-bellied Cotinga
*Doliornis remseni**

21 cm (8¼"). *Rare and local in woodland near treeline on east slope of Andes in Ecuador,* also in *Colombia's Cen. Andes* (Quindío). A recently described species. 2900–3500 m. Iris dark red. Resembles Bay-vented Cotinga (of Peru), but has *entire belly and crissum rufous-chestnut.* Behavior as in Bay-vented.

Scaled Fruiteater
Ampelioides tschudii   PLATE 67(5)

19 cm (7½"). *Uncommon in mid-levels and sub-canopy of foothill and lower montane forest in Andes from w. Venezuela* (Lara) *to w. Bolivia* (w. Beni). Mostly 900–2000 m. A *plump, arboreal* fruiteater with heavy bill, *short tail.* Iris yellow. ♂ has black head, *whitish lores and moustachial stripe,* and *pale yellow nuchal collar; above bright olive; feathers black-centered imparting a scaly look.* Wings mostly black, greater-coverts olive forming a wide band. Throat whitish; below yellow, *feathers with broad olive edges imparting a scalloped effect.* ♀ has olive head (no black) and *feathers of underparts broadly scaled black* (thus even more striking). Nearly unmistakable, but cf. other fruiteaters and Andean Laniisoma. Inconspicuous and often stolid; seen singly or in pairs, most often when accompanying mixed flocks. Hops along larger horizontal limbs looking for insects; also eats fruit and has been reported to eat snails. Distinctive raptorlike song a loud whistled "wheeeeééééeeur," fading and dropping toward end, repeated at intervals of 3–6 seconds.

Phytotoma

A distinct group of cotingas found in *semi-open areas of s. and w. South America.* Their bills are rounded with serrations along the cutting edge, and they have *short, expressive crests.*

White-tipped Plantcutter
Phytotoma rutila   PLATE 67(6)

19.5 cm (7¾"). *Locally fairly common in scrub, groves, and low woodland, always favoring arid regions, from w. Bolivia* (La Paz) *to cen. Argentina* (ne. Chubut); in austral winter a few migrate to Paraguay and Uruguay. To 3500 m in Bolivian Andes. Iris hazel to yellow. ♂ has *forecrown and most of underparts cinnamon-rufous; gray above* with black back streaking; *broad white wing-bars and tail-tips.* ♀ brownish above *boldly streaked black;* wings and tail dusky, wings with white bars and *tail with white corners.* Below buffy whitish to ochraceous *conspicuously streaked blackish.* The only plantcutter in its range. ♀'s streaky pattern recalls certain ♀ finches. Usually in small groups, often perching calmly in the open atop bushes and small trees; regularly around houses. Eats mainly fruit, also buds and leaves. Frequent call a weird, dry, gravelly, mechanical "wree-ee-ee-eh" or "wraaaaaah."

Peruvian Plantcutter
Phytotoma raimondii   PLATE 67(7)
18.5 cm (7¼"). *Now very local in patches of woodland in nw. Peru* (mainly Piura to Ancash); can be faii ly common in the few places where it (and its habitat) survives. To 550 m. Iris yellow. ♂ resembles ♂ White-tipped Plantcutter (no overlap), but *crown all gray* (rufous only on lores) and *throat, chest, and sides gray* (not all-rufous underparts). Its *streaky* ♀ is similar. Behavior, including voice, as in White-tipped, but this species is *much* rarer, now endangered as a result of severe habitat loss.

Rufous-tailed Plantcutter
Phytotoma rara   PLATE 67(8)
19 cm (7½"). *Fairly common in shrubby areas, low woodland, and agricultural areas with orchards and hedgerows in cen. and s. Chile and adjacent s. Argentina.* To 2300 m. Iris red. ♂ has *chestnut crown, face black* with whitish patches, back brownish heavily streaked black; wings black with *large white patch on lesser coverts; undertail rufous with broad black terminal band.* Below cinnamon-rufous. Streaky ♀ like ♀ White-tipped Plantcutter but browner above and *tail with rufous on inner webs* (but *no white*). The only plantcutter in its range. ♀'s pattern vaguely finchlike. Usually occurs in pairs (not groups) and often inconspicuous, though it also sometimes calmly perches in the open. Presence often tied to barberries, a nonnative shrub that is spreading rapidly and apparently causing an increase in the plantcutter's numbers. Distinctive call a nasal and guttural "r-r-r-ra-ra-raah" (onomatopoeic for the species name "rara"—the plantcutter is not rare) that starts slowly and is more stuttered than in its congeners.

Pipreola

Attractive, plump birds of *Andean forests,* with an outlying species on the tepuis. Andean species are *predominantly green, ♂♂ often with either black on head or orange-red on chest; bills and legs are often some shade of red.* Found singly or in pairs, most species regularly accompany mixed flocks. Fruiteaters are lethargic, and despite their bright coloration, all too often they remain hard to see. Vocalizations help but are high-pitched and usually hard to track to their source. Appropriately enough, the birds mainly eat fruit, generally plucked during a quick hover, sometimes while perched.

Barred Fruiteater
Pipreola arcuata   PLATE 68(1)
23 cm (9"). Uncommon to locally fairly common in lower and mid-levels of *upper montane forest in Andes from w. Venezuela* (Trujillo) *to w. Bolivia* (w. Santa Cruz). Mostly 2250–3300 m; *ranges at higher elevations than other fruiteaters.* Iris varies from orange-red (**northward;** A) to grayish olive or even whitish (**southward;** B); bill and legs coral red. ♂ has *head, throat, and chest glossy black;* otherwise olive above. Wings with large pale yellowish spots on wing-coverts and tertials; tail with black terminal band. *Below evenly barred black and pale yellow.* ♀ lacks black on head and bib; *below evenly barred blackish and pale yellow.* The largest fruiteater, and the only one with barring on underparts. Often even more sluggish and unsuspicious than the others. Sometimes accompanies mixed flocks, but more often solitary; several may gather at an especially productive fruiting tree. Song a thin and very high-pitched "seeeeeeeeeeh."

Green-and-black Fruiteater
Pipreola riefferii   PLATE 68(2)
17.5–18.5 cm (6¾–7¼"). Fairly common in lower and mid-levels of montane forest and borders in *Andes from n. Venezuela to cen. Peru* (Huánuco). Mostly 1500–2700 m. *Bill and legs coral red.* ♂ *head, throat, and chest black suffused with green,* and *yellow border on neck and bib;* otherwise moss green above, *tertials tipped whitish.* Below yellow mottled or streaked green, as illustrated (but **south to w. Ecuador** midbelly unmarked yellow). ♀ has black replaced by green, and no yellow border; lower underparts streaked and mottled green. In **Huánuco, Peru,** smaller with midbelly again an unmarked yellow. In Peru cf. Band-tailed Fruiteater. Black-chested Fruiteater (east slope) has whitish iris, grayish legs, and lacks tertial tipping; ♂ lacks yellow margin to bib. On west slope cf. ♀ Orange-breasted Fruiteater. Seems to range in small groups more often than other fruiteaters; in many areas generally the most frequently seen species. Song a very high-pitched and sibilant "ts-s-s-s-s-s-s-s-s," slowing a little toward end and lasting 2–3 seconds, sometimes fading as it ends.

Band-tailed Fruiteater
Pipreola intermedia   PLATE 68(3)
19 cm (7½"). Uncommon in lower and mid-
levels of upper montane forest on *east slope of
Andes from cen. Peru* (e. La Libertad) *to w. Bolivia* (w. Santa Cruz). 2300–3000 m, but lower
(to 1500 m) southward. Resembles sympatric (in
cen. Peru) Green-and-black Fruiteater but *larger*,
with an *olive-yellow iris. In zone of overlap, Band-
tailed mostly occurs at higher elevations.* ♂ differs
in having a brighter yellow margin to bib and
black chevrons on flanks; it lacks any green suffusion to bib. Both sexes also have a *black subterminal tail-band* and *whitish tail-tip* (black may
be faint in ♀). Behavior and voice much as in
Green-and-black.

Black-chested Fruiteater
Pipreola lubomirskii   PLATE 68(4)
18 cm (7"). Uncommon in mid-levels of montane
forest on *east slope of Andes from s. Colombia to
n. Peru* (s. Amazonas). 1500–2300 m. *Iris yellow;*
bill coral red; *legs olive-gray.* ♂ has *head, throat,
and midchest glossy black;* bright green above,
extending to sides of chest. Below yellow, green
mottling on flanks. ♀ bright green above and on
throat and chest; *below streaked green and pale
yellow.* Both sexes of Green-and-black Fruiteater
differ in their dark eye and red legs, and they
have tertial tipping; ♂ also has obvious yellow
border to bib. Behavior more arboreal than in
many other fruiteaters. Thin, very high-pitched
song a drawn-out and ascending "pseeeeeeeét,"
easy to pass over.

Masked Fruiteater
Pipreola pulchra   PLATE 68(5)
18 cm (7"). Uncommon in lower and mid-
levels of montane forest on *east slope of Andes
in Peru* (s. Amazonas to Cuzco). 1500–2200 m.
Iris yellowish; bill coral red; *legs olive-gray.* ♂
bright green above with *blackish face and upper
throat* (the "mask"); *lower throat and midchest
orange, arcing up onto sides of neck.* Below yellow, sides mottled green. ♀ bright green above;
entire underparts streaked green and yellow. Both
sexes of Scarlet-breasted Fruiteater have tertial
tipping (none in Masked); ♂ also has a scarlet
chest patch, lacks the partial collar, and ♀ has a
yellow upper throat and solid green chest (lacking Masked's streaked effect). Behavior and song
much as in Black-chested Fruiteater.

Orange-breasted Fruiteater
Pipreola jucunda
18 cm (7"). Uncommon in lower and mid-levels
of foothill and lower montane forest on *west
slope of Andes from sw. Colombia* (s. Chocó) *to
sw. Ecuador* (e. Guayas). Mostly 600–1900 m. *Iris
yellow;* bill coral red; *legs olive-gray.* Resembles
Masked Fruiteater (no overlap), but ♂ has *entire
head and throat glossy black* (no green on crown)
and *chest more fiery orange.* ♀ indistinguishable
from ♀ Masked. ♂ Golden-breasted Fruiteater
lacks black on head; ♀ Golden-breasted has pale
tertial tipping (lacking in Orange-breasted) and
shows more yellow throat streaking. Orange-
breasted occurs at lower elevations than other
sympatric fruiteaters; cf. Green-and-black (both
sexes with coral red bill and legs, etc.). Behavior
similar but seems less apt to follow mixed flocks.
Song a thin, high-pitched "pseeeeeeeeét," drawn
out and ascending as in Black-chested.

Golden-breasted Fruiteater
Pipreola aureopectus   PLATE 68(6)
17 cm (6¾"). Fairly common in lower and mid-
levels of montane forest in *Andes of n. Venezuela
and ne. Colombia;* also on *west slope of Andes in
w. Colombia*, where apparently rare and local.
Mostly 1000–2300 m. Iris yellow; bill coral red;
legs olive-gray. ♂ in **n. Venezuela** (illustrated)
bright green above; tertials tipped whitish.
Throat and midchest bright golden yellow; below
paler lemon yellow, green streaking on sides.
Santa Marta birds have yellow arcing up onto
sides of neck; in **Andean range** shows more belly
streaking. ♀ resembles ♀ Masked Fruiteater (no
overlap). ♂ Orange-breasted and Handsome
Fruiteaters both have black heads; ♀ Orange-
breasted is closely similar to Golden-breasted
♀ but *lacks* tertial tipping. Song resembles
Orange-breasted.

Handsome Fruiteater
Pipreola formosa   PLATE 68(7)
16.5 cm (6½"). Uncommon in lower and mid-
levels of montane forest and borders in *mountains of n. Venezuela* (Yaracuy to Paria Peninsula). 800–2200 m. Iris yellow; bill coral red;
legs olive-gray. ♂ has *head and throat glossy
black;* above bright green, tertial spots whitish.
Patch on chest fiery orange, below bright yellow.
♀ bright green above with pale tertial tipping;
throat also green, *small patch on chest golden;
below narrowly barred or scaled green and yellow.* Beautiful ♂ is unmistakable; no other Venezuelan fruiteater has orange on chest. ♀ Golden-

breasted Fruiteater has a streaked (not barred) pattern below, and no chest patch; it generally occurs at higher elevations. Song a high-pitched "pseeéé-eeee-ee."

Scarlet-breasted Fruiteater
Pipreola frontalis   PLATE 68(8)

15.5–16.5 cm (6–6½"). Uncommon in mid-levels and subcanopy of montane forest on *east slope of Andes from n. Ecuador* (w. Napo) *to w. Bolivia* (w. Santa Cruz). Mostly 1100–2000 m. Iris yellow; ♂'s bill and legs orange-pink, duskier in ♀. Two species likely involved. In **Ecuador and n. Peru in San Martín** (A) ♂ has *crown and cheeks shiny bluish green;* bright green above, tertials tipped whitish. Upper throat yellow, *lower throat and chest fiery red; below bright yellow,* green on flanks. ♀ bright green above with tertial tipping as in ♂. Throat yellowish *scaled green;* below yellow, *breast and flanks densely scaled green.* **Southward from Junín, Peru** (B) *larger;* ♂ differs in having head concolor green (no bluish) and more extensive red on chest, ♀ in its *yellow frontlet and throat,* solid green breast. Fiery-throated Fruiteater is notably smaller and both sexes are greener below, ♂ especially showing little or no yellow. More arboreal than many fruiteaters. Song of northern birds infrequently given a sharp and piercing "psii"; that of southern birds a much longer "pseeeeeu-iii."

Fiery-throated Fruiteater
Pipreola chlorolepidota   PLATE 68(9)

13 cm (5"). Uncommon in lower and mid-levels of *foothill forest on east slope of Andes, locally out into adjacent lowlands, from se. Colombia to cen. Peru* (Pasco; also an isolated Puno record); seemingly rarer southward. Mostly 600–1250 m. *The smallest fruiteater. Iris pale grayish;* bill salmon with dusky tip; legs orange. ♂ bright green above with tertials tipped whitish. *Throat and chest scarlet, contrasting with green of underparts,* midbelly somewhat yellowish. ♀ like ♂ above; *below barred green and yellowish,* most densely green on breast. Cf. larger Scarlet-breasted Fruiteater. Infrequently encountered, everywhere occurring at low densities. Song rarely heard, a very short and high-pitched "tsi" (P. Coopmans).

Red-banded Fruiteater
Pipreola whitelyi   PLATE 68(10)

16.5 cm (6½"). Uncommon in lower and mid-levels of montane forest and stunted woodland on *tepuis of se. Venezuela and adjacent Guyana.* 1200–2100 m. Iris orange (♂) to ochre (♀); bill

and legs salmon red (duller in ♀). Unmistakable ♂ grayish green above with *long tawny-gold superciliary that arcs around ear-coverts; wings and tail tawny-brown. Below gray* with *orange-red chest band,* ochraceous crissum. ♀ moss green above with *pale greenish yellow echoing ♂ head pattern. Below whitish boldly streaked black.* Cf. Sharpbill. Sluggish behavior, like fruiteaters of the Andes, and like them sometimes accompanies mixed flocks; comes to forest edge when feeding at fruiting trees. Infrequently heard, high-pitched song a thin hissing trill, "tseeeeeeeeeeee," lasting 2–3 seconds.

Purple-throated Cotinga
Porphyrolaema porphyrolaema   PLATE 69(1)

18.5 cm (7¼"). *Uncommon in canopy and borders of humid forest in w. and cen. Amazonia.* Mostly below 400 m. Rather heavy bill. Unmistakable ♂ black above, feathers of upperparts fringed white, also a *single broad white wing-stripe* and tertial edging. Throat deep purple; *below essentially white.* ♀ brown above, *feathers fringed buffy whitish, crown irregularly barred buff and blackish. Throat cinnamon-buff; below evenly barred black and buff,* crissum cinnamon-buff. No ♀ *Cotinga* has barring below, nor does any have a rufous throat; ♀ Purple-throateds can look vaguely thrushlike. More often noted in pairs than *Cotinga* species. Unlike the virtually silent *Cotinga,* Purple-throated does vocalize, though not often. ♂'s song, a loud "wheeeeeeeur," lasts 1–2 seconds and recalls Dusky-capped Flycatcher's call, despite being longer and dropping more in pitch.

Cotinga

Well-known birds of the tropical forest canopy, the *vivid blue Cotinga* ♂♂ are among the most gorgeous of Neotropical birds. Seeing one is always a treat, though birds in much duller ♀ plumage (some of them juvenile ♂♂) are generally noted more often. They have mainly allopatric ranges, though the Spangled Cotinga overlaps with several others. *Cotinga* cotingas have a distinctive *round-headed shape* with a wide-eyed dovelike expression. They are usually seen perching high, especially in early morning, often open branches, and they come to fruiting trees, sometimes with other cotingas; they are entirely frugivorous. Flight swooping, fast, and direct; flying ♂♂ sometimes produce a twitter or rattle, apparently with their wings.

Banded Cotinga
Cotinga maculata PLATE 69(2)

20 cm (7¾"). *Now very rare and local in canopy and borders of humid forest in e. Brazil* (s. Bahia to n. Espírito Santo, formerly Rio de Janeiro). Below 200 m. Beautiful ♂ *bright cobalt blue above*, black bases of feathers showing through irregularly; most of wings and tail black. *Below mostly bright deep purple;* breast band and lower belly cobalt blue. ♀ dusky brown above, feathers scaled whitish and with whitish eye-ring. Grayish buff below, *feathers dark-centered giving a bold spotted effect.* Banded has always been less numerous than the sympatric White-winged Cotinga; ♀ White-wingeds are grayer, less scaled and spotted, with bold white on wing. Seriously endangered, this gorgeous cotinga seems to have disappeared from most of the forested areas where they could still be found a few decades ago. At times it comes—or came—to fruiting trees with White-winged Cotingas, a spectacular sight indeed.

Blue Cotinga
Cotinga nattererii

18.5 cm (7¼"). Uncommon and local in canopy and borders of humid forest from *nw. Venezuela to nw. Ecuador* (where rare, mainly in nw. Esmeraldas). To 1000 m. ♂ *mostly bright shining blue*, with black around eye; wings (except lesser-coverts) and tail also black. *Contrasting patch on throat and upper chest purplish black* and *band down median lower underparts dark purple.* ♀ dusky brown above, feathers scaled whitish and often showing a vague pale eye-ring. Below dull buff, more cinnamon-buff on belly, *dark centers of feathers on breast (especially) and belly create a scaly effect. The only Cotinga in its trans-Andean range,* and as such virtually unmistakable. ♀ Black-tipped Cotinga is grayer, not scaly, and has obvious white in wing. Also: Panama.

Purple-breasted Cotinga
Cotinga cotinga PLATE 69(3)

18 cm (7"). Uncommon in canopy and borders of humid forest in *ne. South America,* also very locally in sw. Brazil and ne. Peru; in some areas favors sandy-belt forest. Mostly below 600 m. Both sexes resemble Banded Cotinga (no overlap); Purple-breasted *markedly smaller.* ♂ differs further in having *entire throat and breast rich*

purple. ♂ of often sympatric Spangled Cotinga is a paler, more turquoise blue and has purple only on throat. Apart from its larger size, ♀ Spangled differs in being more uniform brownish below with *less scaling.*

Plum-throated Cotinga
Cotinga maynana PLATE 69(4)

19.5 cm (7¾"). Fairly common in canopy and borders of humid forest and adjacent clearings in *w. and cen. Amazonia.* Mostly below 700 m. Iris yellow, more grayish in juveniles (and perhaps some ♀♀). ♂ *bright shining turquoise blue* with a few scattered pink feather bases showing through; *small throat patch plum purple;* flight feathers and tail mainly black. ♀ grayish brown above, narrowly scaled whitish or pale buff; *underwing-coverts cinnamon-buff* (evident in flight). Below slightly paler grayish brown, *more ochraceous on belly;* dark centers of breast feathers impart a somewhat scaly look. ♂ of slightly larger Spangled Cotinga is a paler blue, and more black from its feather bases shows (looks more dappled); Spangled also has more extensive black on wings and a larger purple throat patch. ♀♀ *can be hard to distinguish,* but ♀ Spangled is slightly darker and more ashy grayish, and more uniformly scaly below (instead of mainly on breast, with belly plainer and more ochraceous). On infrequent but memorable occasions Plum-throated and Spangled Cotingas can be seen feeding in the same tree.

Spangled Cotinga
Cotinga cayana PLATE 69(5)

20 cm (8"). *Widespread and fairly common in* canopy and borders of humid forest (mainly terra firme) in *Amazonia and the Guianas.* Mostly below 600 m. ♂ *bright, pale, shining turquoise blue* with black bases of many feathers showing through, resulting in a *dappled (or "spangled") effect; large patch on throat and upper chest bright magenta purple; wings and tail mostly black,* wing-coverts edged pale blue. ♀ *rather dark grayish brown above and on throat and breast,* darkest on wings, feathers narrowly scaled whitish; underwing-coverts dull pale buff. Below dull pale buff, flank feathers dark-centered. Cf. Plum-throated Cotinga (especially ♀♀). Behavior much as in other *Cotinga,* but very infrequently ♂ gives a soft, low "boo" call (A. Whittaker recording).

Xipholena

A trio of fine, canopy-dwelling cotingas found in humid lowland forests (ranges almost entirely allopatric). Spectacular ♂♂ have *body plumage ranging from bright deep purple to purplish black,* and their feathers are hard and glossy; wings (at least) *highly contrasting white.* Behavior much as in *Cotinga;* likewise most often seen early and late, perching high on exposed branches or snags. ♂♂ of at least some species differ in having spectacular aerial displays. Both sexes of all species occasionally give an abrupt "purp!" note, sometimes repeated for several minutes (B. M. Whitney). ♂♂ also sometimes produce a rattling sound in flight.

Pompadour Cotinga

Xipholena punicea   PLATE 69(6)
19.5 cm (7¾"). Fairly common in canopy of terra firme forest, *mainly from the Guianas to cen. Amaz. Brazil,* very local westward (mainly in areas with poor soils). Mostly below 800 m. Iris creamy white to pale yellow. Stunning ♂ *shining crimson purple with mainly white wings,* black primary tips. Some purple scapular feathers are stiff, pointed, and elongated, and extend down over white wings. ♀ *ashy gray,* darker above and palest on belly, a few birds with pink on crissum; *wing-coverts and inner flight feathers prominently edged white.* ♂ unmistakable; the snowy white wings flash out even at tremendous distances. ♀'s pale eye, overall gray plumage, and white wing edging distinctive in range; ♀♀ of other *Xipholena* (none known to be sympatric) are more mottled below. Small groups of displaying ♂♂ sometimes approach each other from treecrown to treecrown, the flying bird displacing a perched bird, repeated over and over.

White-winged Cotinga

Xipholena atropurpurea   PLATE 69(7)
19 cm (7½"). Now uncommon and local in canopy and borders of humid forest and secondary woodland in *e. Brazil* (Paraíba to Espírito Santo, formerly to Rio de Janeiro). To 900 m. Iris pale yellow. ♂ *mostly blackish purple,* scapular feathers elongated but not as long as in Pompadour Cotinga; more purplish on tail, but *wings contrasting white* (primaries also black-tipped). ♀ like ♀ Pompadour (no overlap) but breast more mottled whitish. ♂ not likely confused in range. ♀ Banded Cotinga is much scalier below, lacks white wing edging, and has a dark iris. Be-

havior much as in Pompadour, though no flight display has (yet) been documented.

White-tailed Cotinga

Xipholena lamellipennis   PLATE 69(8)
20.5 cm (8"). Uncommon in canopy and borders of terra firme forest in *e. Amaz. Brazil south of Amazon.* To 400 m. Iris pale yellow. ♂ *mostly shining purplish black,* feathers stiff and pointed; *wings and tail white,* scapular feathers elongated as in Pompadour Cotinga. ♀ like ♀ Pompadour (limited overlap in w. Pará) but *more mottled grayish and whitish on breast.* ♂ Pompadour Cotinga is much more purple and has a *dark tail;* ♀ Pompadour is smoother gray below. Displaying ♂♂ have been seen fluttering into the air.

Black-tipped Cotinga

Carpodectes hopkei   PLATE 69(9)
♂ 25 cm (9¾"), ♀ 24 cm (9½"). *Locally not uncommon in canopy and borders of humid forest in w. Colombia and nw. Ecuador* (south to Pichincha). Mostly below 900 m. Iris orange. Unmistakable ♂ *pure snowy white,* with outer primaries and central tail feathers minutely tipped black (hard to see in field). Slightly smaller ♀ recalls a ♀ *Xipholena, ashy gray above,* blacker on wings and tail with *wing-coverts and inner flight feathers conspicuously edged with white.* Throat and breast paler gray, belly white. Snowy white ♂♂, which almost resemble a white pigeon, can hardly be confused; flying ♂ tityras can also look mainly white, but they have black on head, wings, and tail. Cf. also ♀ Blue Cotinga. ♂♂ are very conspicuous, regularly perching on high dead snags where they can be spotted from far off. ♀♀ are noted less often, usually at fruiting trees, where several may gather. In display flight ♂♂ fly slowly with exaggerated deep wingbeats from tree to tree; at other times flight is faster and more direct. Also: e. Panama.

Black-faced Cotinga

Conioptilon mcilhennyi   PLATE 69(10)
23 cm (9"). *Uncommon and local in mid-levels and subcanopy of humid forest and woodland, usually where swampy or seasonally flooded, in se. Peru and adjacent Brazil and Bolivia.* 200–350 m. *Crown, face, and throat black,* face and throat bordered white. *Otherwise dark gray above,* blacker on wings and tail; *below much paler gray,* somewhat flammulated on breast. Nearly unmistakable, but cf. Screaming Piha. Ranges in pairs, mostly independent of mixed flocks, though sometimes with other birds at

fruiting trees. Rarely or never perches high or in the open in forest canopy. Swooping flight and some other aspects of behavior are reminiscent of Purple-throated Fruitcrow. Rather loud call a distinctive ascending "o-o-o-e-e-eeé" that recalls a frequent Smooth-billed Ani (*Crotophaga ani*) vocalization.

Laniocera

Two infrequently encountered birds that range inside humid lowland forests, one on either side of the Andes, both of these mourners are *round-headed,* imparting a soft dovelike expression, and have narrow golden eye-rings. Their taxonomic affinities remain unresolved. Most recent evidence points to their being cotingas, but *Laniocera* has also been considered a tyrannid genus.

Cinereous Mourner

Laniocera hypopyrra PLATE 70(1)
20 cm (8″). Uncommon in lower and mid-levels of terra firme forest in *Amazonia and the Guianas,* and locally in *e. Brazil.* To 900 m. *Ashy gray,* somewhat paler below; wings duskier with *two rows of large cinnamon-rufous spots,* tertials and tail tipped cinnamon-rufous; *pectoral tuft (sometimes hidden) can be either pale yellow or orangerufous.* **Immatures** have some rufous on breast, and scattered black spots on underparts. Grayish Mourner (a flycatcher) lacks wing-spots and shows no pectoral tuft; its crown is flatter, resulting in a "fiercer" expression. Cf. also Screaming Piha. Inconspicuous and only rarely seen. A solitary bird, occasionally seen while accompanying an understory flock. Mainly recorded from its far-carrying but ventriloquial voice, a plaintive, high-pitched, and ringing "teeyr, teeoweeét, teeoweeét, teeoweeét . . ." (up to 10 teeoweeéts in succession), given from certain regularly used perches; sometimes repeated tirelessly (even during heat of day), though often there is a long pause between song bouts.

Speckled Mourner

Laniocera rufescens PLATE 70(2)
20 cm (8″). Uncommon in lower and mid-levels of humid forest and woodland in *w. Colombia and nw. Ecuador* (mainly Esmeraldas). To 1000 m. *Mostly rufous brown,* breast feathers often scaled dusky (especially in **immatures**); *wing-coverts dusky* with *large rufous tips.* ♂ has a pale yellow pectoral tuft (usually lacking

in ♀), often hidden. Rufous Mourner (a flycatcher) is more uniform rufous, showing none of Speckled's wing pattern, and has flatter crown. Cf. also Rufous Piha. Inconspicuous habits as in Cinereous Mourner. ♂♂ tirelessly repeat, from a low perch, a ringing and ventriloquial "tleeyr, tlee-yeeí, tlee-yeeí, tlee-yeeí . . ." with up to 12–15 tlee-yeeís, then a pause; pattern and quality recall Cinereous Mourner. Several ♂♂ sometimes sing within earshot of each other. Also: Mexico to Panama.

Snowornis

Two scarce pihas that range locally in wet *foothill and subtropical forests in the Andes. Mainly or entirely olive green. The genus was recently separated from Lipaugus.*

Gray-tailed Piha

Snowornis subalaris * PLATE 70(3)
23.5 cm (9¼″). *Rare and local* in lower and mid-levels of foothill and montane forest on *east slope of Andes from s. Colombia* (w. Cauca) *to s. Peru* (Madre de Dios). 500–1400 m. Narrow eyering whitish. ♂ *olive above* with semiconcealed black coronal patch and more grayish rump, *tail pale gray;* bend of wing and underwing-coverts yellow. Throat and breast paler olive, *belly and crissum pale gray.* ♀ has smaller coronal patch (or it may be lacking). Olivaceous Piha lacks any gray, has yellow belly. Inconspicuous habits as in Olivaceous, except that voice is strikingly loud. ♂'s far-carrying song is given at long intervals (often a minute or more, thus very hard to track down), a clear ringing "cheeeer-yeeéng!" with second syllable higher-pitched than first. A softer and shorter "chureeee?" is also given (perhaps by ♀).

Olivaceous Piha

Snowornis cryptolophus * PLATE 70(4)
23.5 cm (9¼″). Uncommon and local in lower and mid-levels of montane forest in *Andes from w. and s. Colombia* (Antioquia) *to cen. Peru* (Huánuco). Mostly 1200–2200 m. Narrow yellow eye-ring. ♂ *olive green above,* duskier on wings and tail and with semiconcealed black coronal patch; bend of wing and underwing-coverts yellow. *Throat and breast olive, becoming yellower on belly.* ♀ lacks the coronal patch. Gray-tailed Piha (mainly at *lower* elevations) is gray on tail and belly. Cf. also Olive and Ochre-breasted Tanagers (both much more active birds). Occasion-

ally accompanies mixed flocks and has been seen feeding on fruit and large insects. Seems solitary, and always lethargic and inconspicuous. Amazingly, no vocalization seems to be on record.

Lipaugus

Plain, fairly large cotingas found inside humid or montane forests, where they perch erectly and (except when displaying) are usually solitary. Aside from their *frequent and strikingly loud vocalizations,* all are inconspicuous. Except for the Rose-collared Piha, they show little or no sexual dimorphism.

Rufous Piha
Lipaugus unirufus　　　　　PLATE 70(5)
23.5 cm (9¼"). *Fairly common in lower and mid-levels of humid forest in w. Colombia and nw. Ecuador* (mainly Esmeraldas). Mostly below 700 m. Bill flesh or brownish at base. *Uniform cinnamon-rufous,* slightly paler below, palest on throat. Some show a vague eye-ring. Easily confused with Rufous Mourner (a tyrannid); often best separated by voice. The mourner is smaller and more slender, with proportionately longer tail and a less stout bill; more uniform below (not paler on throat). The piha's head is rounder, resulting in a "softer," more dovelike expression (mourner has flatter crown). Rufous Pihas perch lethargically for long periods, then abruptly sally after a large insect or to pluck fruit. They sometimes are in small, loose groups but rarely join mixed flocks. Unlike the Screaming Piha, Rufous seems not to form true leks. ♂♂ give loud and explosive whistled calls, e.g., "peeeéuw," a "wheeeéo," and a "chow-eeéo," sometimes in a short series. They call sporadically, sometimes right after a sudden loud noise. Also: Mexico to Panama.

Screaming Piha
Lipaugus vociferans　　　　　PLATE 70(6)
24.5-25.5 cm (9½-10"). *Often common in lower and mid-levels of humid forest in Amazonia and the Guianas,* and locally in *e. Brazil. Very vocal,* but *surprisingly inconspicuous.* Mostly below 500 m, but to 1400 m in s. Venezuela. *Plain gray,* a bit duskier on wings and tail, belly somewhat paler. **Juvenile** browner on wings. Dusky Piha is exclusively montane (so no overlap). More apt to be confused with Grayish Mourner (sympatric),

though the mourner differs in its smaller size, browner and paler iris, more slender bill, and yellowish cast to belly. Though proportionately longer-tailed, the piha's shape is vaguely thrush-like; no thrush in Amazonia is uniform gray. Perches erectly, periodically sallying out in pursuit of a large insect or for fruit; sometimes with mixed flocks but more often alone. With one of the most powerful and best-known voices of any Amazonian bird, the Screaming Piha is well named, but trying to see the bird itself is often frustrating. ♂♂ gather in loose leks inside humid forest, perching 5-8 m above the ground and remaining nearly motionless; calling birds hardly even open their bill. The classic call is a loud and ringing "weee weee-ah" (sometimes 2 initial "weee" notes), often warming up with softer and more guttural notes. Also gives a querulous "kwceeah" and a series of loud "kweeeo" notes.

Rose-collared Piha
Lipaugus streptophorus　　　　　PLATE 70(7)
22.5 cm (8¾"). Uncommon in mid-levels and subcanopy of montane forest, woodland, and borders on *tepuis of se. Venezuela region.* 1000-1800 m. Unmistakable ♂ gray, paler below (especially on belly), with *conspicuous magenta-pink collar and crissum.* ♀ *lacks* the pink collar, and has a *rufous crissum.* Screaming Piha is entirely gray (unlike ♀ Rose-collared, showing *no* rufous on crissum) and occurs at lower elevations. ♀ is actually more apt to be confused with a thrush (similar in size and shape), though no thrush on the tepuis is so gray. Rose-collared seems to range more often at edge than other pihas and is more likely to forage as pairs. ♂'s call, given at long intervals, a loud and sharp "skeeyr!" (T. Meyer recording).

Chestnut-capped Piha
*Lipaugus weberi**　　　　　PLATE 70(8)
22.5 cm (8¾"). Rare and very local in mid-levels and subcanopy of montane forest in a *limited area at n. end of Colombia's Cen. Andes* (Antioquia). Mostly 1500-1800 m. A recently described species. Resembles Dusky Piha, but notably smaller. Darker gray with *chestnut-brown crown* and cinnamon-brown crissum; orbital ring yellow. Dusky is not known to occur in or near the limited area where Chestnut-capped has been found. Behavior seems similar to other pihas; occasionally accompanies mixed flocks. Usually noted through its distinctive call, a loud and piercing "sreeck" (A. M. Cuervo et al.).

Scimitar-winged Piha

Lipaugus uropygialis   PLATE 70(9)

30 cm (11¾"). Rare and local in mid-levels and borders of montane forest on *east slope of Andes in w. Bolivia* (La Paz and Cochabamba) *and extreme s. Peru* (recently recorded in Puno). Seems to be declining, for reasons unknown. 1800–2600 m. *Tail very long. Mostly gray,* darker above, with *rump, flanks, and crissum rufous-chestnut.* ♂ has narrow recurved primaries (the "scimitar" wings). Nearly unmistakable in its limited range, *where the only piha,* but cf. Great Thrush. Poorly known, usually seen singly, but sometimes several are together, and they occasionally accompany mixed flocks. Call a loud shriek that has been compared to the call of an *Aratinga* parakeet; sometimes several birds burst into vocalizing more or less together (R. Bryce et al.). The vocalization provisionally ascribed to it (Ridgely and Tudor 1994) has proven to be the song of the form of Blue-winged Mountain Tanager found in Bolivia.

Dusky Piha

Lipaugus fuscocinereus

32.5 cm (12¾"). Uncommon in canopy and borders of montane forest and woodland in *Andes from n. Colombia* (Antioquia and Norte de Santander) *to extreme n. Peru* (n. Cajamarca). 1700–3000 m. *Large* and *long-tailed. Gray above,* duskier on wings and tail. *Olivaceous-tinged gray below,* somewhat paler on throat. Occurs with no other *Lipaugus;* the similar (though smaller and shorter-tailed) Screaming Piha ranges only in the lowlands. *Snowornis* pihas are much more olive, etc. In a quick view this piha can be taken for the far commoner Great Thrush (which has an orange bill and legs). Inconspicuous and rather solitary, though sometimes seen in small groups while foraging in flocks with other largish birds such as caciques, jays, and mountain tanagers. Not very vocal, much less so than Screaming Piha. ♂♂ give, perhaps in loose leks, a loud "wheeeo-wheeeeyr" or "whee-a-whee," repeated at intervals of 5–10 seconds (can be much longer) with mouth wide open; often just the "wheeeo" or "whee" is given. At even less frequent intervals a flying bird will burst into a loud wing-whirring reminiscent of the wing-whirrs of certain guans (*Penelope, Pipile*).

Cinnamon-vented Piha

Lipaugus lanioides   PLATE 70(10)

28 cm (11"). Uncommon and local in mid-levels and subcanopy of humid and montane forest in *se. Brazil* (s. Bahia to ne. Santa Catarina). To 1400 m. *Mostly dull brownish gray,* grayest on head and brownest on wings and tail, and somewhat paler below with vaguely streaked throat; crissum buff-tinged. In area of overlap with Cinnamon-vented, Screaming Piha occurs at *lower* elevations; Screaming is not quite so large, and is more uniformly gray, lacking Cinnamon-vented's brown tinge. Cinnamon-vented Piha seems not to form such large noisy leks (though its vocalizations *are* loud), and it joins mixed flocks and occurs at edge more often. ♂'s arresting call a far-carrying "skeeo-skeeo, skeeo-skeeo, skeeo-skeét!"

Tijuca

Two fairly large, pihalike cotingas restricted to the *high mountains of se. Brazil.* One species, the spectacular Black-and gold, shows striking sexual dimorphism, but the other exhibits none at all.

Black-and-gold Cotinga

Tijuca atra   PLATE 70(11)

26.5–27.5 cm (10½–11"). Fairly common in mid-levels and subcanopy of *montane forest in se. Brazil* (se. São Paulo, Rio de Janeiro, and s. Minas Gerais). 1100–1700 m. *Bill orange* (♂) or orangebrown (♀). ♂ *deep black* except for a *large patch of golden yellow in flight feathers* (conspicuous even when perched). Slightly smaller ♀ *mainly olive,* brighter and yellower on belly and flight feathers. ♂ virtually unmistakable, though cf. Golden-winged Cacique and ♂ Yellow-legged Thrush. ♀, though much less flashy, is also not likely to be confused as there are no other uniform olive birds of its size in its limited range. Olive-green Tanager is substantially smaller; cf. also ♀ Bare-throated Bellbird (limited overlap). Inconspicuous and seemingly shy, often hard to see; even singing ♂♂ can be hard to locate on their typically hidden perches. Their strange, memorable song is one of the great sounds of the mountains of se. Brazil; its eerie, high-pitched, ringing "eeeeeeeeee-yeeeé" carries amazingly far and almost seems to float on the air.

Gray-winged Cotinga

Tijuca condita

24 cm (9½"). *Rare and very local in elfin forest at high elevations in mountains of se. Brazil* (Rio de Janeiro on Serra dos Orgãos and Serra do Tingua). Mostly 1600–2000 m. Both sexes

resemble ♀ Black-and-gold Cotinga, but Gray-winged is *smaller* with a yellow wash on rump, yellower underparts, *markedly grayer wings,* and *gray tail.* Behavior as in Black-and-gold, replacing it at higher elevations, but Gray-winged seems markedly scarcer and warier. Song a shorter and more explosive "so-ee-wheé," given at much longer intervals (often 5–10 minutes) so singing birds are much harder to locate.

Bare-necked Fruitcrow
Gymnoderus foetidus   PLATE 71(1)
♂ 38 cm (15"), ♀ 33 cm (13"). Fairly common and conspicuous at borders of humid forest in *Amazonia and the Guianas* (much more local in the latter); favors várzea and water's edge, but also ranges in the canopy of terra firme. To 500 m. Bill pale bluish, black at tip. ♂ *mainly black* with *contrasting silvery gray wings* (obvious, both on perched birds and in flight); head feathers short and plush; *sides of neck and throat unfeathered and pale blue, the skin wrinkled and folded.* Smaller ♀ is slatier, wings concolor with back, paler on belly and undertail; bare skin on neck less extensive. **Juvenile** like ♀ but scaled whitish below. ♀ vaguely recalls ♀ Amazonian Umbrellabird, especially in distant flight, and the two can be found together; the fruitcrow's silhouette of small head and slender neck is, however, very different. Often seen flying high above the forest canopy with distinctive deep, rowing wingstrokes, the ♂'s wings flashing silver; perhaps engages in local movements. Perched birds hop from branch to branch like toucans. Eats both fruit and large insects. Usually silent, but displaying males do give an umbrellabird-like boom. Despite its scientific name, does not smell.

Purple-throated Fruitcrow
Querula purpurata   PLATE 71(2)
♂ 28 cm (11"), ♀ 25.5 cm (10"). Uncommon to fairly common and widespread in mid-levels and subcanopy of humid forest, less often at borders, from *w. and n. Colombia to Amazonia and the Guianas.* Mostly below 700 m. Bill leaden blue. *Entirely black,* ♂ with *large throat patch shiny reddish purple.* No other similar bird shares ♂'s purple throat patch (in poor light the color can be hard to discern). Can be confused with various mainly black caciques, or even a ♀ umbrellabird; note the fruitcrow's chunky, short-tailed shape and bill. In flight shows broad rounded wings; flight swooping, often punctuated by glides. Ranges through forest in noisy bands

of 3–6 birds in which purple-throated (adult) ♂♂ are a minority; they sometimes accompany flocks of other birds such as caciques or nunbirds. Eats both fruit and large insects. Variety of loud and mellow calls includes a drawn-out "ooo-waáh" or a "kwih-oo, ooo-waáh," in flight often a "wah-wah-wheéawoo." Calling birds often flick or spread tail. Imitating their calls can often lure them in, the ♂♂ flaring their gorgets. Also: Nicaragua to Panama.

Red-ruffed Fruitcrow
Pyroderus scutatus   PLATE 71(3)
♂ 38–43 cm (15–17"), ♀ 35.5–39.5 cm (14–15½"). *Rare to uncommon and local* in mid-levels and subcanopy of montane forest in *Andes from n. Venezuela to e. Peru* (Pasco) in deciduous and gallery forest), and in se. Brazil region. To 850 m in east; to 2200 m on Andean slopes. Bill bluish gray (♂) or dusky (♀). In se. **South America** and **n. Venezuela to E. Andes of Colombia** (illustrated) *black* with *large shiny flame-red bib on throat and chest* that has a somewhat crinkled effect. **Elsewhere** *lower underparts mainly rufous-chestnut.* This large fruitcrow can hardly be confused; umbrellabirds show no red. Mostly solitary and inconspicuous, remaining inside forest and infrequently perching in the open. At times can almost seem curious. ♂♂ gather in small leks where they display on branches close to the ground, leaning forward and extending their red foreneck feathers, which hang away from body like a ruff; they emit a very deep booming call, "ooom-ooom-ooom." Mainly silent away from their leks, but a single "ooom" is occasionally given.

Crimson Fruitcrow
Haematoderus militaris   PLATE 71(4)
33–35 cm (13–14"). *Rare and local* in subcanopy and canopy of humid forest in the *Guianas and n. Amaz. Brazil.* Below 300 m. Heavy bill dull reddish. Spectacular **adult** ♂ *mostly shiny crimson,* the feathers long, glossy and stiff; wings and tail blackish. ♀ and **immature** ♂ has *rosy crimson head, neck, and underparts* (feathers less stiff than in ♂); mantle, wings, and tail dusky brown. Cf. Guianan Red Cotinga (much smaller, etc.). Rather sluggish, perching in the open primarily during early morning. Mainly solitary. Flight undulating, reminiscent of an umbrellabird or large woodpecker. Generally quiet, though a short low-pitched hooting has been heard, and also a sharp loud "bok" (A. Whittaker).

Capuchinbird
Perissocephalus tricolor   PLATE 71(5)
34.5–35.5 cm (13½–14″). Uncommon in mid-levels and subcanopy of humid forest in *ne. South America*. Mostly below 600 m. An unmistakable, *strange-looking* cotinga. *Bare crown and face pale gray*, extending to lower part of heavy bill. *Cinnamon-brown*, brighter and paler below; underwing-coverts white, tail black. The featherless head looks disproportionately small, resulting in a unique silhouette. Generally inconspicuous and solitary, ranging inside forest, Capuchinbirds come into their own at their leks, where ♂♂ posture and emit one of the strangest sounds made by any bird, a far-carrying "grrrrrrr, aaaaa-ooo" reminiscent of a distant outboard engine (has also been likened to a calf). Displaying ♂♂ lean forward, then stand high with plumage fluffed out, neck feathers forming a ruff around the bare head; lengthened undertail-coverts are then curled above the tail, like two fluffy balls.

Cephalopterus

Two *large* and *bizarrely ornamented* cotingas with *black plumage* found in more remote montane and lowland forests. Both have *modified crests* and *long, pendent feathered wattles.*

Amazonian Umbrellabird
Cephalopterus ornatus   PLATE 71(6)
♂ 48–49.5 cm (19–19½″), ♀ 41–42 cm (16–16½″). Generally uncommon and local in canopy and borders of várzea and riparian forest in *Amazonia*, and in foothill and montane forest on *east slope of Andes from e. Colombia to n. Bolivia* (w. Santa Cruz). To 1500 m. *Iris whitish. ♂ glossy black* with unmistakable large umbrella-shaped crest (sometimes recurved forward over bill, but more often held upright, spikelike) with *white shafts of frontal feathers* prominent. A *wide, pendent wattle* 8–10 cm (3–4″) long hangs from lower throat but often is partially retracted. ♀ smaller and less glossy, with crest smaller (*still very evident;* shows *no* white feather shafts), and *short* wattle. Long-wattled Umbrellabird occurs only *west* of Andes. Regularly seen in flight when can look vaguely like a large woodpecker. Usually seen singly, less often in small groups, perching stolidly in trees, hopping from branch to branch, toucanlike; seems wary, especially so in the lowlands. Eats both large insects and

fruit. Umbrellabirds in the lowlands favor stands of *Cecropia* and other trees, particularly on river islands. Small groups of displaying ♂♂ gather in traditionally used leks, usually quite high in trees. At intervals they lean forward with crest expanded and wattle enlarged and emit a low-pitched moaning "boom" that has been likened to a bellowing bull. Otherwise essentially silent.

Long-wattled Umbrellabird
Cephalopterus penduliger   PLATE 71(7)
♂ 40–42 cm (15¾–16½″), ♀ 35.5–37 cm (14–14½″). Rare and local in canopy and borders of foothill and montane forest on *west slope of Andes from sw. Colombia* (Valle) *to sw. Ecuador* (El Oro). Mostly 200–1100 m. Resembles respective sexes of Amazonian Umbrellabird (only *east* of Andes). Long-wattled is smaller with a proportionately shorter tail, and both sexes have a *dark brown iris. ♂* has shafts of crest feathers black (*not white*), and *its wattle is much longer,* 20–30 cm (8–10″). Behavior similar to that of montane population of Amazonian. Though usually wary, at times these umbrellabirds can be much bolder, seeming indifferent to the observer's presence, indeed even curious. Up to 5–6 ♂♂ gather at traditionally used leks inside montane forest, where they periodically emit very low-pitched and far-carrying "boooh" or "wooom" calls. Before calling, the bird leans forward and greatly lengthens and expands the wattle and flares the crest—a truly spectacular performance.

Procnias

A trio of *large* and *spectacular* cotingas; ♂ bellbirds are *predominantly or entirely white* and sport *some type of ornamentation on head.* The much more obscure ♀♀ are *boldly streaked below.* Bellbirds are best known from ♂♂'s *resoundingly loud calls* and are otherwise very inconspicuous. They are entirely frugivorous.

White Bellbird
Procnias albus   PLATE 72(1)
♂ 28.5 cm (11¼″), ♀ 27 cm (10½″). *Uncommon and local in canopy and borders of humid and (especially) foothill forest in ne. South America;* wanders when not breeding. Mainly below 1250 m. Obviously unmistakable ♂ *pure white* with a *single large fleshy wattle springing from base of bill and hanging downward* (usually to right of bill). ♀ olive above, *yellowish below*

coarsely streaked with olive. ♀ Bearded Bellbird is similar, but crown is dusky-olive and throat streaked blackish; *the whole head looks darker.* Occasionally seen at fruiting trees, but it and other bellbirds most likely seen when ♂♂ vocalize from branches high in the canopy. Calling ♂ Whites are in the open more often so are a little easier to see, but any vocalizing bellbird is usually a challenge to spot. White's calls are more musical, the only ones that can remotely be described as bell-like. Most frequent is a very loud "kóng-kay!" given as it leans right, then swings quickly to the left, briefly flipping the wattle. Usually the wattle is limp and fairly short, but it has been observed to lengthen during calling sessions, reaching astonishing lengths of 10–12 cm (4–5").

Bare-throated Bellbird

Procnias nudicollis   PLATE 72(2)

♂ 28 cm (11"), ♀ 26.5 cm (10½"). Now rare to locally fairly common in canopy and borders of humid forest from *ne. Brazil* (Alagoas) *to e. Paraguay and ne. Argentina.* Only seasonal in some areas, with overall numbers depleted by trapping for the cagebird market as well as by deforestation. To 1000 m. Unmistakable ♂ *pure white* with *ocular area and throat patch bare bright greenish blue.* ♀ closely resembles ♀ Bearded Bellbird but crown and sides of head are darker; pale throat streaking can be more prominent than in Bearded. **Subadult** ♂♂ require several years to acquire white plumage; they look like ♀♀ but may already have acquired blue on throat, and sometimes sing. Inconspicuous, though occasionally seen at fruiting trees. Even singing ♂♂ are hard to spot; they tend to remain in dense foliage, and their calls are notably ventriloquial. Has two main vocalizations, the very loud "bock" or "bonk" call, given with gape wide open (as illustrated), and a series of 6–8 less loud metallic "clink" or "tonk" calls, given with bill closed (though the throat visibly pulsates).

Bearded Bellbird

Procnias averano   PLATE 72(3)

♂ 28 cm (11"), ♀ 26.5 cm (10½"). Uncommon and local in canopy and borders of humid and (especially) montane forest in *n. Venezuela, Trinidad, the tepui region, and ne. Brazil.* To 1900 m. **Northern** ♂ (illustrated) is *grayish white* with contrasting coffee brown head, *black wings,* and *bare black throat covered with clusters of long stringy wattles.* In **ne. Brazil** body plumage

whiter, and throat wattles apparently sparser. ♀ olive above with *dusky-olive crown and sides of head. Throat blackish* with fine pale streaking; below coarsely streaked olive and pale yellow. ♂ unmistakable. ♀ White Bellbird (overlaps on s. Venezuelan tepuis, sometimes to be heard simultaneously) is more olive generally than ♀ Bearded, and shows *no* dusky on head or throat. Bearded is known to overlap with Bare-throated Bellbird only in ne. Brazil (Alagoas), where it occurs mainly in lowlands (Bare-throated in remnant montane forests); both are now very rare there. Behavior much as in Bare-throated, likewise mainly known from the far-carrying calls of ♂♂. Those calls are quite similar to Bare-throated, but in most areas (seemingly not in ne. Brazil) Bearded also gives a bisyllabic vocalization, in n. Venezuela a more musical "kay-kong," in s. Venezuela a repeated "bisset, bisset. . . ."

Phoenicircus

Two *beautiful, mainly red* cotingas found *inside humid forests of Amazonia.* They are unusual in that ♂♂ are smaller than ♀♀; outer primaries of ♂♂ are narrowed and curved. Red Cotingas are frugivorous.

Black-necked Red Cotinga

Phoenicircus nigricollis   PLATE 72(4)

♂ 23 cm (9"), ♀ 24 cm (9½"). Uncommon and local on lower and mid-levels of humid forest (mainly terra firme) in *w. and cen. Amazonia.* To 400 m. Bill pale reddish brown. Stunning ♂ has *brilliant scarlet crown* contrasting with *deep black nape and back; rump and most of tail scarlet,* tail tipped black. Throat deep black, *contrasting with scarlet underparts.* ♀ resembles ♀ Guianan Red Cotinga but brighter reddish on crown and tail, more bronzy olive above, and *distinctly brighter red below* with *more contrasting dark throat* (thus echoing ♂'s pattern). ♂ is one of Amazonia's most beautiful birds, not likely confused. ♀ has enough of ♂'s pattern that it too should be readily recognized; cf. Guianan (no overlap). An elusive and shy denizen of remote forests, now eliminated from most areas near human settlement. Usually seen singly, but ♂♂ gather at leks where they perch on branches with their red rump feathers fluffed, periodically uttering an explosive "skeéyh!" sometimes in series. Other ♂♂ may follow suit, producing a burst of calling that may continue for a minute or two before they gradually fall silent. Foraging birds (of both sexes) occasionally give the same call, sometimes in flight.

Guianan Red Cotinga
Phoenicircus carnifex   PLATE 72(5)
♂ 22 cm (8½"), ♀ 23 cm (9"). Uncommon in lower and mid-levels of humid forest in *ne. South America*. To 600 m. ♂ has *bright scarlet crown*, blackish brown back becoming rufous brown on wing-coverts and inner flight feathers; *rump and tail bright red*, tail-tip brown. *Throat and breast brownish maroon, belly rosy red.* ♀ has *crown and tail dull reddish*; brownish olive above and on throat and chest, *merging into rosy red lower underparts*. Not known to overlap with Black-necked Red Cotinga, though their ranges come close. Crimson Fruitcrow is *much* larger, etc. Behavior and most vocalizations much as in Black-necked. ♂♂ at leks reported to give a "pee-chew-eet" (P. Trail), different from anything known from Black-necked.

Rupicola

Large and chunky cotingas, cocks-of-the-rock are renowned for their *bright plumage, unique fan-shaped crests,* and elaborate displays, which provide one of the world's great bird spectacles.

Guianan Cock-of-the-rock
Rupicola rupicola   PLATE 72(6)
26–27.5 cm (10¼–10¾"). Locally uncommon to fairly common in lower and mid-levels of humid forest, *principally near rocky areas and gorges*, in *ne. South America*. Mostly below 1200 m. *Laterally compressed frontal crest* (smaller in ♀) obscures bill. Unmistakable ♂ *mostly intense orange* with narrow maroon border to crest. Wings blackish with a large white speculum, *tertials very wide* with white border, *lower scapulars and inner edge of tertials ending in orange filaments*; tail short, mainly black. ♀ *uniform dark dusky-brown*. Distinctive crest shape of the dull ♀

makes confusion improbable; Guianan does not overlap with Andean Cock-of-the-rock. Foraging birds move solitarily through forest, and several often gather at fruiting trees. Comes into its own at leks, where several dozen ♂♂ may gather (typically only 5–10). They hold court on several display branches over a patch of bare ground, engaging in stereotyped movements, bill snaps, and ritualized chases, frequently interrupted by loud raucous calls (e.g., an explosive "kakrrow!"). When a ♀ appears, the ♂♂ drop to the ground and freeze, trembling, as she proceeds to select her partner.

Andean Cock-of-the-rock
Rupicola peruvianus   PLATE 72(7)
30–30.5 cm (11¾–12"). Locally not uncommon in montane forest, *principally around gorges and ravines*, in *Andes from w. Venezuela* (nw. Barinas) *to w. Bolivia* (w. Santa Cruz). 500–2400 m. *Laterally compressed frontal crest* (smaller in ♀) obscures bill. Spectacular ♂ on **east slope** (illustrated) *mostly bright reddish orange to orange*; wings and tail black, *innermost flight feathers wide and contrasting pearly gray*. On **west slope** *mostly intense blood-red*. ♀ on **east slope** *mostly orangy brown*, wings and tail browner. On **west slope** redder, *mostly brownish carmine*. Even the comparatively dull ♀♀ are easily known by their distinctive shape and orangy or reddish plumage. Ranges mainly inside forest, favoring the vicinity of streams but often seen flying across clearings or gorges. Except when at fruiting trees, foraging birds are mainly solitary; in most areas they are shy, though where not persecuted they can be surprisingly bold. Seen to best advantage at leks, where a dozen or more ♂♂ may gather to display on branches and lianas 2–6 m above the ground (♀♀ often nest nearby on wet ledges and hollows). Here ♂♂ bow, strut, and jump about, wings flapping and bills snapping. The variety of loud squawking and grunting calls rises to cacophony when a ♀ approaches; unlike the Guianan, however, ♂♂ do not drop to the ground. Both sexes give a loud querulous "uaankk?" or "kwaannk?" especially in flight.

CROWS AND JAYS: CORVIDAE

Only jays are found in South America where, though they occur widely, they are not a particularly numerous or conspicuous element of the avifauna. Blue predominates in most species. Jays are omnivorous birds that typically range in small groups composed of related individuals. They construct large shallow nests of twigs, usually well hidden.

Cyanolyca

Sleek, elegant jays found in *Andean forests*. Smaller and more slender than *Cyanocorax* jays, *Cyanolyca* are *essentially blue* and *lack white on their underparts and tail*. They range in small groups, sometimes joining mixed flocks of fairly large birds such as caciques and mountain tanagers. They can be vocal, but at other times slip noiselessly through the forest.

White-collared Jay
Cyanolyca viridicyanus   PLATE 73(1)
34 cm (13¼"). Uncommon in montane forest on *east slope of Andes of Peru* (Amazonas south of Río Marañón) *to w. Bolivia* (w. Santa Cruz). Mostly 2200–3300 m. In **s. Peru and Bolivia** (illustrated) *all blue* with a *contrasting white forecrown, narrow brow, and narrow pectoral collar*; throat very dark (almost black, especially in Bolivia). Birds from **n. and cen. Peru** are more violet-blue generally (including the throat, which contrasts with the mask). Does not overlap with other *Cyanolyca* jays. Little variation in its vocal repertoire, some calls being nasal, others more ringing; repeated phrases like "jeet-jeet-jeet" or "jho-jho-jho-jho" are most frequent.

Black-collared Jay
Cyanolyca armillata   PLATE 73(2)
33 cm (13"). Uncommon in montane forest of *Andes from w. Venezuela* (Trujillo) *to n. Ecuador* (Napo); most numerous in Venezuela. Mostly 1800–3000 m. *Rich dark blue to greenish blue*, deeper and more violet in **Venezuela and ne. Colombia** (as illustrated), greener southward; somewhat paler on crown, with a *prominent black pectoral collar*. Confusion likely only at south end of range where Black-collared overlaps

with similarly patterned Turquoise Jay, which has a *markedly brighter and paler blue crown and throat*. In the overlap zone, *Black-collared is much rarer*. Vocal repertoire substantial, includes variety of short calls, most frequently a rising "shrwee?"

Turquoise Jay
Cyanolyca turcosa   PLATE 73(3)
32 cm (12½"). Fairly common in montane forest, woodland, and borders in *Andes, mainly in Ecuador, where widespread and numerous* (for a *Cyanolyca*); also in adjacent Colombia (Nariño) and extreme n. Peru (Piura, north and west of Río Marañón). Mostly 2000–3200 m. Greenish blue with *black collar outlining a pale turquoise blue throat*; crown also pale blue. Cf. the much less numerous Black-collared Jay; otherwise this beautiful jay should not be confused. Gives a variety of calls, most frequent a loud, arresting "sheeyr!" often given repeatedly; calls are sometimes more clipped and nasal, sometimes more guttural, are sometimes burrier ("cheeuyr"). Less frequent is a whistled call like a tinamou.

Beautiful Jay
Cyanolyca pulchra   PLATE 73(4)
27 cm (10½"). Uncommon in montane forest on *west slope of Andes from nw. Colombia* (s. Chocó) *to nw. Ecuador* (Pichincha). 900–2200 m. A *dark* jay, mostly violet-blue with *crown contrasting milky bluish white* deepening to violet-blue on upper back; mantle and breast variably (but often strongly) suffused with dusky brown. *Lacks the black pectoral collar* of Turquoise Jay (which is markedly paler and brighter blue overall). Scarce and infrequently encountered, mostly remaining inside forest and closer to the ground than other *Cyanolyca*. Usually ranges in pairs, not the small flocks typical of the Turquoise. Quite

vocal, giving a repeated "chee" or more emphatic "chewp," also various clicking calls.

Cyanocorax

Found widely in the *lowlands* (in the genus, only the Inca Jay is really montane), *Cyanocorax* jays are large birds (among South American passerines rivaled in size only by certain oropendolas and cotingas), with heavier bodies than *Cyanolyca* jays. Most *Cyanocorax* show at least a short, plush *frontal crest* (reaching an extreme in the Curl-crested). They divide readily into two groups, the first larger, dark-eyed, and usually more uniformly colored, the second pale-eyed and more boldly patterned (often with white below and on tail-tips). Two species, Curl-crested and Azure-naped Jays, appear to bridge the two groups. All *Cyanocorax* are bold, vocal, and often inquisitive birds that forage in groups of up to 6–8 (likely related) individuals.

Purplish Jay

Cyanocorax cyanomelas PLATE 73(5)
37 cm (14½"). *Widespread and often common in deciduous woodland, humid forest borders, and even scrub and adjacent clearings from se. Peru (Cuzco) and sw. Brazil (s. Mato Grosso) to ne. Argentina (Santa Fé). To 2000 m in Bolivia. Large and drab, mostly dull purplish mauve,* blackish on head and foreneck, violet only on upperside of tail. Cf. the much scarcer and more range-restricted Azure Jay. Conspicuous and often noisy, giving loud raucous "raa-raa-raa . . ." calls (less often a shorter "crah-crah . . .") as they perch in trees or during their rather labored flight. They sometimes drop to the ground, and often come for food around buildings in the Brazilian pantanal.

Azure Jay

Cyanocorax caeruleus PLATE 73(6)
38 cm (15"). Uncommon to fairly common but local in *s. Brazil* (São Paulo to Rio Grande do Sul), *especially numerous in Araucaria-dominated forest and coastal restinga woodland;* small numbers in *ne. Argentina* (s. Misiones and ne. Corrientes). To 1400 m. In recent decades range has contracted inexplicably, and it no longer appears to occur in Paraguay. *A large* jay, *frontal crest* often quite prominent. *Mainly purplish blue* with con-

trasting blackish foreparts. A scarce morph is more greenish blue. More common Purplish Jay is much drabber generally, showing no blue on body. Voice and behavior much as in Purplish; most frequent call an excited "creeyr! creeyr! creeyr! . . ." often long-repeated.

Violaceous Jay

Cyanocorax violaceus PLATE 73(7)
37 cm (14½"). Fairly common in forest and woodland canopy and borders and adjacent clearings from *Venezuela to w. Amazonia. In most of its range the only jay.* To about 1000 m. *Mostly dull blue,* brightest on wings and tail, with *head, throat, and chest black* and *upper nape milky bluish white.* Often shows a slightly squared-off crest. Purplish Jay (overlaps only in s. Peru) is drabber, with a *concolor* nape; in upper Río Orinoco area, cf. also range-restricted and scarce Azure-naped Jay. Always noisy and conspicuous, Violaceous Jays troop about in groups of up to 10–12 individuals, seeming to wander over large areas. Though sometimes consorting with other large birds, usually they move on their own. Most common call an arresting "jeeyur!" sometimes repeated interminably; also a variety of other sounds.

Azure-naped Jay

Cyanocorax heilprini PLATE 74(1)
33.5 cm (13¼"). *Rare and local in a limited area of sw. Venezuela* (Amazonas) *and adjacent e. Colombia and nw. Brazil;* favors woodland growing on sandy soil. Below 200 m. *Yellowish iris.* Mostly dull brownish violet with *bluish white crown, nape, and moustachial streak;* upstanding forecrown, face, and foreneck black; *tail narrowly tipped white.* Larger but often-confused Violaceous Jay is routinely sympatric with Azure-naped, and even in its range Violaceous is the more numerous; Violaceous is dark-eyed, bluer generally, and has *no* white on tail and *less* on crown. Recent recordings (D. Delaney) confirm that this scarce jay's voice is *not* like Violaceous (contra several references) but rather resembles many pale-eyed *Cyanocorax.* Calls include a ringing "chyoh" (often doubled), a softer "che-che-che," a nasal "renk-renk," and others.

Plush-crested Jay

Cyanocorax chrysops PLATE 74(2)
35.5 cm (14"). *Fairly common in woodland and forest mainly from Bolivia and s. Brazil to n. Argentina, extending locally north in deciduous habi-*

tats into s. *Amazonia*. Mostly below 1500 m. Iris yellow. An attractive jay with *stiff and plushlike crown feathers*, imparting a flat-topped look and a *somewhat crested effect on rearcrown*. Otherwise violet-blue above, tail broadly tipped white. Throat and chest black; *below creamy yellowish*. An isolated form in **Amaz. Brazil** has longer and more upright crest feathers, reduced facial markings, and a bluer hindneck. White-naped Jay of ne. Brazil (range nearly meets Plush-crested; sympatric?) has obvious and extensive white on hindneck, browner (not so blue) upperparts, and lacks the rearcrown bulge. Occurs in flocks up to about 12 individuals, sometimes together with Purplish Jays; they forage at all levels and though sometimes bold, usually do not range far into the open. Most frequent of its wide repertoire of calls is a loud ringing "cho-cho-cho."

Black-chested Jay
Cyanocorax affinis

35.5 cm (14"). Locally fairly common in forest borders and woodland, both humid and deciduous, and adjacent plantations in *n. Colombia and nw. Venezuela* (east to Falcón). Here Black-chested is the *only* jay present in the lowlands and thus is essentially unmistakable. Mostly below 1500 m. Iris yellow. Head, throat, and chest black with blue facial markings and plush forecrown feathers; above violet-brown, wings and tail bluer, *tail broadly tipped white. Below mainly creamy white*. Behavior much as in Plush-crested Jay, though usually shyer, with stealthy movements; sometimes attends swarms of army ants. Most frequent of a wide variety of calls is a loud "chowng! chowng!" Also: Costa Rica and Panama.

Curl-crested Jay
Cyanocorax cristatellus   PLATE 74(3)

34.5 cm (13½"). *Fairly common in cerrado, gallery woodland, and trees in agricultural areas of s.-cen. Brazil and adjacent Bolivia and Paraguay*. To about 1100 m. *Conspicuous upstanding and curled frontal crest* (never laid flat). Head and foreneck sooty black; above dull blue. Tail rather short, with *terminal half white. Lower underparts white. The only dark-eyed jay that is white below*. Both Plush-crested and White-naped Jays can be sympatric with Curl-crested, though both favor woodland and rarely venture much into the open; neither species has a crest, and both are pale-eyed and have facial markings. Bold and conspicuous, Curl-cresteds range in small groups often seen flying laboriously from one

tree or wooded area to the next. Vocalizations similar to other dark-eyed jays, with a repeated and raucous "kyaar!" being most frequent.

Inca Jay
Cyanocorax yncas   PLATE 74(4)

29.5–30.5 cm (11½–12"). Widespread and locally common in montane forest, borders, and clearings in *Andes from n. Venezuela to w. Bolivia* (w. Santa Cruz); from Ecuador south occurs only on the east slope, and in upper Río Marañón valley of n. Peru ranges out into arid scrub. Mostly 1300–2600 m, locally to 500 m in n. Peru and to near sea level in n. Venezuela. *The only montane Cyanocorax jay*. Formerly considered conspecific with the true Green Jay of n. Middle America. Beautiful and unique. Iris yellow. Stiff frontal crest of blue feathers; *mostly bright green above*, and *mostly bright yellow below*. Face and bib black with blue markings, and in **most of range** (illustrated) crown and nape bluish white (blue in **Venezuela and ne. Colombia**). *Outer tail feathers bright yellow*, very obvious in flight. Conspicuous though often shy, Inca Jays troop about in flocks of up to 10 birds, foraging at all levels, regularly with other fairly large birds such as caciques. Vocalizations are notably variable, including a usually trebled "nyaa-nyaa-nyaa" or "kwin-kwin-kwin," and various distinctive metallic notes.

White-tailed Jay
Cyanocorax mystacalis   PLATE 74(5)

32.5 cm (12¾"). Uncommon and local in deciduous woodland and scrub from *sw. Ecuador* (Guayas) *to nw. Peru* (La Libertad). *The only jay in this area and thus unmistakable*. Mostly below 1200 m, locally to 1900 m in Ecuador. Iris pale yellow. Handsome and boldly marked, with *mainly white tail* (only the central feathers are blue). Face and bib black accented by *white facial markings and hindneck*; dark blue above. Below white. Behavior much as in Plush-crested Jay, though White-tailed groups are typically smaller (rarely more than 3–5 birds), and they tend to forage more on or near the ground. Usually quite conspicuous, but overall numbers have been reduced by habitat degradation. Has a relatively limited vocal repertoire, the most frequent call a fast dry "cho-cho-cho."

White-naped Jay
Cyanocorax cyanopogon   PLATE 74(6)

34.5 cm (13½"). Uncommon and local in deciduous and gallery woodland in *e. Brazil* (south to

Minas Gerais). To about 1100 m. Iris yellow. Head black with stiff forecrown feathers and blue facial markings and a short moustache; *broad area of white on hindneck. Mantle essentially dull brownish;* tail broadly tipped white. Throat and chest black, below white. Plush-crested Jay's hindneck band is considerably smaller and bluer, and its mantle much bluer (not so brown); White-naped *lacks* Plush-crested's bulge on rearcrown. The two species seem never to have been found together, though their ranges come close. Behavior and vocalizations much as in Plush-crested.

Cayenne Jay

Cyanocorax cayanus   PLATE 74(7)
33 cm (13″). Uncommon and local in forest borders and woodland in *ne. South America,* where basically *the only jay present.* To 1100 m. Iris bluish white. Face, throat, and chest black with white facial markings and a *broad area of white on hindneck. Above dull brownish with a violet gloss; tail broadly tipped white.* Below white. Only possible confusion is with the dark-eyed Violaceous Jay (limited overlap), which is mainly bluish with no white on tail or underparts, etc. Cf. also Azure-naped Jay (no overlap at all). Behavior and vocalizations much like Plush-crested, though Cayenne tends to remain higher above the ground and usually seems sneakier and less bold.

SWALLOWS AND MARTINS: HIRUNDINIDAE

Well-known and nearly cosmopolitan birds, swallows and martins are highly aerial birds with long pointed wings and wide gapes; flight is swift, buoyant, and graceful, perfectly suited to the capture of their predominant prey, flying insects. Blue and/or white predominate in most species. Often gregarious, they frequently nest close to humans, usually in holes or crevices. Many species are migratory.

Progne

Large swallows with *broad, triangular wings* and *fairly long, forked tails,* easy to recognize as a genus though it is often not so easy to identify to species level. Martins are generally numerous, tame, and conspicuous swallows that favor open, often agricultural country and built-up areas; they frequently perch on wires. During the nonbreeding season the blue-backed species often roost in very large aggregations. Their flight is slow and languid; all species except the Brown-chested often circle high overhead. All give a pretty, liquid chortling or gurgling, especially when nesting.

Brown-chested Martin
Progne tapera*   PLATE 75(1)
18 cm (7"). Fairly common and widespread in semiopen areas, especially near water, from Colombia and Venezuela to n. Argentina, in austral winter vacating south part of range and migrating north. Mostly below 600 m, migrants higher. *A distinctive, brown-backed martin.* Dull *grayish brown above.* White below with a *prominent brownish breast band,* in **southern birds** (A) extending down as spots on median breast. Southern birds migrate north into range of **resident birds of tropical latitudes** (B). Sand Martin has similar color and pattern but is markedly smaller and has a different flight style. Cf. other martins, none of which is ever so brown-backed, even when young. Swoops around mainly at low heights, often on characteristically bowed wings, exposing the silky white on sides of tail. Nests in old hornero nests or in burrows dug into banks, occasionally in snags. Though gregarious, Brown-chested is less so than other martins and

is not colonial when breeding. Also: Panama and Costa Rica (as an austral migrant).

Gray-breasted Martin
Progne chalybea   PLATE 75(2)
18–19 cm (7–7½"), southern birds larger. *Widespread and common* in open areas from Colombia and Venezuela to n. Argentina, vacating southern areas during austral winter. To about 2000 m in s. Ecuador, migrants occasionally higher. *Steely blue above* (♂ glossier); throat and breast grayish brown, *belly whitish* sometimes with some dark streaking. Cf. other blue-backed martins, none nearly as numerous as this species. Brown-chested Martin has *brown* back and a chest band. Very gregarious, especially in human-dominated landscapes, where it can be very familiar indeed; much less numerous in extensively forested areas. Gray-breasted often flies high above the ground and has a leisurely, languid flight style. Nests are usually placed under the eaves of buildings or other structures, but in forested areas can be in holes in dead snags. Also: Mexico to Panama.

Purple Martin
Progne subis   PLATE 75(3)
18–19 cm (7–7½"). *Locally common boreal migrant* (Sep.–Mar.) in semiopen terrain, often near water, *south to s. Brazil and n. Argentina.* Mostly below 1000 m, transients in Andes up to 3000–3400 m. ♂ closely resembles ♂ Southern Martin, usually not distinguishable in the field; it differs only in its slightly shorter and less deeply forked tail (recent evidence suggests even this is not invariably reliable). ♀ brown above with a blue gloss (often faint) and a *whitish or pale grayish forecrown* and *fairly obvious whitish nuchal collar.* Below grayish brown with some dark

scaling, *paler on belly* (sometimes with dark streaking). Underparts of ♀ Purple Martin are not as uniformly dusky as in ♀ Southern; between that and the collar, distinguishing ♀♀ is relatively straightforward. Behavior much as in Southern; likewise sometimes occurs in large flocks, and roosting aggregations, sometimes on high-tension wires, can be immense. Breeds in North America.

Southern Martin
Progne elegans   PLATE 75(4)
19–19.5 cm (7½–7¾"). *Fairly common breeder in Argentina and s. Bolivia* (north to Cochabamba), in austral winter migrating to w. Amazonia. To about 2000 m in Bolivia. ♂ *glossy blue-black; tail quite deeply forked.* ♀ resembles ♂ but slightly duller above, sometimes with a pale forecrown; *dusky brown below* with *pale mottling or feather edging*, palest on belly. Cf. very similar Purple Martin; ♀ Southern never shows a pale collar and is darker below. Southern and Purple normally do not occur together, both more often flocking with Gray-breasteds. Wintering Southerns in Amazonia can occur in large flocks, and their roosts can be tremendous. Nests under the eaves of buildings, usually in small colonies. Also: Panama (vagrants), once even to Florida.

Peruvian Martin
*Progne murphyi**
18 cm (7"). *Rare and local resident near coast of w. Peru* (north to Tumbes) *and extreme n. Chile.* Smaller than Southern Martin (no overlap; formerly considered conspecific). Plumage of ♂ virtually identical to ♂ Southern Martin, but slightly less glossy. ♀ differs only in its smaller size. Behavior similar to Southern, but Peruvian is decidedly scarcer, never occurring in the large flocks for which nonbreeding Southerns are noted. Nesting recently reported in stone walls on islands just off the coast of La Libertad, Peru (K. B. Abadie et al.). Feeds over the water and sometimes over mainland fields.

Caribbean Martin
Progne dominicensis
18 cm (7"). *Breeds on Tobago,* there favoring coastal cliffs and ridges. Nonbreeders apparently migrate to n. South America, but status on the mainland remains uncertain; there are records from the Netherlands Antilles and sightings from Trinidad and Guyana. Below 500 m. ♂ resembles ♂ Southern Martin but has a *narrow but*

contrasting white median breast, belly, and crissum. ♀ most resembles ♀ Gray-breasted Martin, but *brownish color extends down over flanks.* Also: West Indies.

It is possible that both the Cuban Martin (*P. cryptoleuca*) and the Sinaloa Martin (*P. sinaloae*) occur in South America during the boreal winter. Cuban has been collected as a transient on Curaçao, and Sinaloa is known to vacate its Mexican breeding grounds. Their status remains obscured by identification difficulties. ♂ Cuban's white belly feathers are normally concealed by dark feathers, and ♂ Sinaloa's white on belly typically is broader than in Caribbean.

Sand Martin
Riparia riparia   PLATE 75(5)
12 cm (4¾"). *Uncommon to fairly common boreal migrant* (Sep.–Apr.) *south to cen. Argentina,* favoring open areas and near water; rarer southward, and in extensively forested regions. Often called Bank Swallow. Mostly below 1000 m, transients higher. A *small* swallow, *uniform brown above,* somewhat darker on wings. White below with *distinct brown chest band* (sometimes hard to pick out on flying birds), usually extending downward as a spike in middle. Brown-chested Martin has similar coloration and pattern but is considerably larger. Cf. also Southern Rough-winged Swallow. Often in groups, and frequently associates with Barn and American Cliff Swallows; usually feeds over water or grasslands. Distinctive flight style fast, erratic, and fluttery. Call, often given in flight, a short gravelly "chirt." Breeds in North America; also in Old World.

American Cliff Swallow
*Petrochelidon pyrrhonota**   PLATE 75(6)
13–13.5 cm (5–5¼"). *Uncommon to fairly common boreal migrant* (Sep.–Apr.) to open and semiopen areas *across much of South America,* but rare in far south. Often called simply Cliff Swallow. Mostly below 1000 m, transients higher. Tail essentially square. Mostly steely blue-black above with a *prominent buffy whitish forehead* (chestnut in at least one race), grayish nape, and *cinnamon-rufous rump. Sides of head and throat mostly chestnut;* below grayish white. With its obvious pale rump, likely to be confused only with Chestnut-collared Swallow (found only in w. Ecuador and nw. Peru). Favors semiopen terrain, especially near water, and often associates with larger numbers of Barn Swallows. Voice similar to Chestnut-collared, though tends not

to call often while in South America. Breeds in North America.

Cave Swallow (*P. fulva*), which breeds in sw. United States, Mexico, and West Indies, has been recorded as a boreal migrant on the Netherlands Antilles. It should be watched for on the S. Am. mainland, especially as it is increasing on its breeding grounds. A specimen was identified as the form *pallida*.

Barn Swallow
Hirundo rustica   PLATE 75(7)
14–16.5 cm (5½–6½"), depending on length of tail streamers. *Boreal migrant* (Aug.–May) to open areas almost throughout South America; *often common*, though less numerous in far south. In the 1980s began to breed in e. Buenos Aires province, Argentina, and now increasing. Mostly below 1000 m, though transients regularly occur higher in the Andes. *Tail long and deeply forked* (streamers shorter in juveniles and southward-passage adults, but *some fork always evident*), with *white spots on inner webs*. Steely blue above with chestnut forehead. Throat chestnut to buff; *below cinnamon-buff to buffy whitish*. **Juveniles** and **worn-plumaged adults** (A) are duller above and paler below than **breeding plumage birds** (B). The former are the birds most likely confused with other swallows (cf. especially American Cliff Swallow). Feeds in open country, especially around and over water, with graceful swooping flight; often roosts, sometimes in huge aggregations, in sugarcane fields. Quiet on its winter quarters, but sometimes gives a rising "veeet?" Breeds in North America; also in Old World.

Tachycineta

Attractive swallows with glossy blue or green upperparts, white or whitish underparts, and notched tails; all but one species (Tree Swallow) has a *white rump*. Immatures are browner above. These swallows are found in open and semiopen country, often near water (especially White-winged). Most are numerous and familiar birds.

White-winged Swallow
Tachycineta albiventer   PLATE 76(1)
13.5 cm (5¼"). *Common and widespread* in open areas around rivers, lakes, and ponds from Colombia and Venezuela to extreme n. Argentina. Below 500 m. *Large and usually conspicuous*

patch of white on inner flight feathers and upper wing-coverts is unique among Tachycineta swallows (though when plumage is worn the white can be abraded and then is not so obvious); *rump also white*. Otherwise glossy bluish green above and pure white below. Conspicuous and often confiding; perches on snags or rocks just above water, flying out gracefully to skim the surface. Rarely strays far from water and seems to be resident throughout its range; never in large flocks. Frequent call a rising "tree-eet?" given both in flight and when perched. Also: recently found in e. Panama.

Tumbes Swallow
*Tachycineta stolzmanni**   PLATE 76(2)
12 cm (4¾"). *Rare and local in arid semiopen scrub, including severely overgrazed areas, in extreme sw. Ecuador* (s. Loja) *and nw. Peru* (south to La Libertad). Usually *not* associated with water. Below about 150 m. *Glossy bluish green above*. Below *grayish* white with *narrow dusky shaft streaking; rump whitish*, also with *shaft streaking*. Perches on wires and dead trees, when not breeding occasionally in small groups; seems not to associate with other swallows. Its "dree-eet" call is similar to White-winged Swallow.

Mangrove Swallow (*T. albilinea*) has perhaps been seen along Caribbean coast of Colombia. Tumbes was formerly often considered a race of the Mangrove.

White-rumped Swallow
Tachycineta leucorrhoa   PLATE 76(3)
13.5 cm (5¼"). Fairly common in semiopen areas and woodland edges from *cen. Brazil to n. Argentina* (La Pampa and Buenos Aires), favoring areas near water; in austral winter a few vacate southern portion of range. To about 1000 m. *Adult* (A) dark glossy blue above (greener in fresh plumage) with *white rump* and a *narrow but distinct white supraloral streak*. Pure white below. **Immature** (B) more grayish brown above. Chilean Swallow is *very* similar, though it lacks the white frontlet and never seems to be as green above; other purported differences (e.g., color of underwing-coverts) are not valid. In breeding season separates out in pairs, nesting in holes; at other seasons more gregarious, sometimes associating with other swallows.

Chilean Swallow
*Tachycineta meyeni**   PLATE 76(4)
13 cm (5"). *Common breeder in forest borders and clearings in s. Chile and s. Argentina*; in aus-

tral winter moves north into n. Argentina and Paraguay, a few reaching Bolivia; thus much more strongly migratory than White-rumped Swallow. To about 1000 m. Slightly smaller than the closely similar White-rumped; can occur together during austral winter. Never as green as the White-rumped can be at that season, and *never shows White-rumped's white supraloral streak* (always evident, given a decent view, in White-rumped). The two species separate out when nesting, Chilean being more forest-based and more southern. Behavior and voice similar.

Tree Swallow
Tachycineta bicolor

13.5 cm (5¼"). *Rare boreal migrant* (Jan.–Apr.) to semiopen terrain, most often near water, in *nw. South America.* Recorded mostly near sea level, but to 2800 m in Colombia. Glossy dark greenish blue above; pure white below. ♀ duller. **Immature** dusky brown above, usually with a smudgy brownish breast band. *The only Tachycineta that does not have a white rump.* It thus superficially recalls Blue-and-white Swallow, though the Blue-and-white is smaller and has a black crissum. Immatures (brown-backed) somewhat resemble the smaller Sand Martin, which is paler brown above and has a more defined breast band that projects downward like a spike in the middle. Though only an irregular vagrant to South America, when it does occur it can be in fair-sized flocks. Breeds in North America.

Violet-green Swallow (*T. thalassina*) has been seen once in n. Colombia.

Bahama Swallow (*T. cyaneoviridis*) also has been seen once recently in n. Colombia.

Notiochelidon

Fairly small swallows found *mainly in highlands* (two species only in the Andes), these swallows are marked by their *forked tails* (deepest in Brown-bellied) and *dark crissums.*

Brown-bellied Swallow
Notiochelidon murina   PLATE 76(5)

13.5 cm (5¼"). *Locally common in semiopen areas in Andes from w. Venezuela* (Trujillo) *to w. Bolivia* (w. Santa Cruz). Mostly 2500–4000 m. A *slim, dark swallow.* Dark steely bluish green above, with a *quite deeply forked tail. Entirely smoky*

grayish brown below. The chunkier Andean Swallow (not north of Peru) is also dark overall, but its lower underparts are white and its tail only notched. Brown-bellied favors areas adjacent to cliffs or roadcuts, especially when near shrubbery or woodland; there small groups swoop about gracefully, usually not too high. Where their elevation ranges overlap, they often accompany Blue-and-white Swallows. Not very vocal, but occasionally gives "tsweet" calls and gurgles.

Blue-and-white Swallow
Notiochelidon cyanoleuca   PLATE 76(6)

12–12.5 cm (4¾–5"). *Widespread and locally common in semiopen areas, mainly in Andes and other highland areas, from Colombia and Venezuela to Tierra del Fuego;* in tropical lowlands occurs primarily during austral winter, when it vacates austral portion of range. Mostly 500–3000 m, down to sea level in south and in winter. In **most of range** (illustrated) *glossy steely blue above.* White below with a *prominent black crissum.* **Immature** browner above. Highly migratory **southern breeders** (nesting mainly in Patagonia) are slightly larger with a paler and grayer underwing, and have black on crissum more restricted to sides. Cf. much scarcer Pale-footed Swallow (of Andean forests) and Tree Swallow (a rare boreal migrant). Blue-and-white is a familiar swallow, often confiding, especially in the Andes; it favors built-up regions and agricultural terrain, and groups are often seen resting on wires. Nests in holes in roadside banks or buildings. Frequent call a long, thin, rising "treeeeeelee" or buzzier "tz-tz-tz-z-z-z-zee?" often repeated over and over; frequent flight call a clipped "tzee." Also: Costa Rica and Panama.

Pale-footed Swallow
Notiochelidon flavipes   PLATE 76(7)

11.5 cm (4½"). *Uncommon and seemingly local at edge of montane forest and in adjacent clearings in Andes from w. Venezuela* (Trujillo) *to w. Bolivia* (w. Santa Cruz). Mostly 2400–3200 m. Resembles much more numerous and slightly larger Blue-and-white Swallow. Differs in its *pinkish buff throat and upper chest* and *more extensive sooty brown on sides and flanks;* in decent light both (especially the foreneck) can be discerned on flying birds. Pale-footed and Blue-and-white have equally "pale" (pinkish) feet. Pale-footed is most often in small flocks that fly above montane forest and nearby clearings, sometimes accompanying Blue-and-whites but usually not; they avoid settled, cleared areas. Unlike Blue-and-whites, Pale-footed Swallows are infrequently seen perched, then usually on dead snags. Until recently it was often overlooked. Call a gravelly "d-d-d-dreet," similar to Blue-and-white's but drier and more broken.

White-thighed Swallow
Neochelidon tibialis   PLATE 76(8)
10.5–11.5 cm (4¼–4½"). *Uncommon to locally fairly common in humid forest borders and adjacent clearings from w. Colombia to Amazonia, and in se. Brazil; most numerous west of Andes.* To 1100 m. A *small, uniform, dark brown* swallow with a vaguely paler rump. Below slightly paler, more markedly so in **se. Brazil.** The white thighs are always hard to see. On **Pacific slope** slightly smaller with a shorter tail, and *darker generally* with a nearly concolor rump. Southern Rough-winged Swallow is larger and paler below, and has a cinnamon throat. Often in small groups, usually not associating with other swallows and more forest-based; perches mostly on snags, less often on wires. Flight fast, swooping, and erratic. Call a soft "zeet-zeet," often given in flight; also has various chittered notes. Also: Panama.

Atticora

Attractive, boldly patterned swallows, *both species with long, deeply forked tails,* and both found *along rivers* in lowlands east of the Andes.

White-banded Swallow
Atticora fasciata   PLATE 76(9)
14.5 cm (5¾"). *Widespread and often common along forest-bordered rivers and larger streams in Amazonia and the Guianas.* To about 1100 m, following rivers up into Andean foothills. Unmistakable. *Entirely dark steel blue with a conspicuous white band across breast.* This beautiful swallow is almost always found in small groups; it often perches on rocks or dead snags that protrude from the water, flying off abruptly and en masse when approached too closely. Their graceful flight is typically low over the water's surface; only infrequently do they fly high. Rarely wanders far from water. Call a "bzzreet" often given in flight, also tinkling notes.

Black-collared Swallow
Atticora melanoleuca   PLATE 76(10)
14.5 cm (5¾"). *Local near rapids in larger rivers from s. Venezuela and the Guianas to s. Amaz. Brazil,* also very locally south to se. Paraguay and ne. Argentina (Misiones). Can be numerous, but strictly confined to the vicinity of rapids. Below about 300 m. Steely blue-black above. White below with *blue-black band across breast* and a blue-black crissum. Blue-and-white Swallow lacks the breast band (though its absence can be hard to discern when the birds are flying against the sky), and its tail is *only notched* (not deeply forked). Usually in small groups, often seen resting on jumbled piles of rocks out in the water; there they nest when water levels drop. Black-collareds feed mainly while swooping and fluttering low over the water's surface (sometimes looking like so many storm petrels), but sometimes they circle above the canopy of adjacent forest, accompanying other swallows or (occasionally) swifts.

Southern Rough-winged Swallow
Stelgidopteryx ruficollis   PLATE 76(11)
13 cm (5"). *Widespread and locally common* in semiopen areas, *especially near water* and often in mainly forested regions, from Colombia and Venezuela to n. Argentina; vacates austral portion of range during austral winter. Mostly below 1000 m, a few to 2000 m. Tail notched. Above grayish brown, darkest on forecrown, wings, and tail; birds **west of Andes** and in **n. South America** (A) have *rump conspicuously whitish,* but rump concolor in birds from **Amazonia south** (B). *Throat cinnamon-buff;* below pale grayish brown, midbelly pale yellowish. The smaller White-thighed Swallow is darker and more uniform below, never has a pale rump or buff throat. Cf. also the smaller Tawny-headed Swallow. Found in pairs or small groups that often rest on dead branches or wires; they sometimes fly with other swallows but usually are on their own. Rough-wingeds are especially numerous along forested or wooded rivers and streams, there nesting in holes in banks, and usually solitary but sometimes in small groups. Most frequent call a rough, upslurred "djreeet." Also: Honduras to Panama.

Northern Rough-winged Swallow (*S. serripennis*) has been reported as a rare boreal migrant on Bonaire and should be watched for along the northern periphery of South America.

Tawny-headed Swallow
Alopochelidon fucata *   PLATE 76(12)
12 cm (4¾"). *Widespread but never very numerous in semiopen areas* (especially savannas and cerrado, and not particularly tied to vicinity of water) mainly from *n. Bolivia* (Beni) *and s. Brazil to cen. Argentina* (Mendoza and n. La Pampa); much more local northward, some perhaps austral migrants, though known to breed on the Venezuelan tepuis (RSR and D. Ascanio). To 1600 m. *Small. Bright cinnamon superciliary, face, and nuchal collar merges into buff throat and upper chest;* otherwise grayish brown above, white below. The distinctive head colors are often hard to pick out in flight. Cf. Southern Rough-winged Swallow (larger) and Sand Martin. Usually in small groups, generally not associating with other swallows; typically seen in low flight over grassland. Nests in holes in banks, sometimes in isolated buildings.

Andean Swallow
Haplochelidon andecola *   PLATE 76(13)
13.5 cm (5¼"). Uncommon to locally fairly common in *puna grasslands in high Andes from cen. Peru* (Ancash) *to extreme nw. Argentina* (n. Jujuy and nw. Salta) *and n. Chile.* 3000–4500 m. *Dull* blue-black above with *paler dusky brown rump;* tail notched. *Throat and chest ashy brown,* becoming *white on lower underparts.* **Juvenile** is drab, with dull cinnamon-buff forehead, throat, and rump. Brown-bellied Swallow is uniformly dark below with more deeply forked tail. The smaller Blue-and-white Swallow is bluer above and pure white below. Found in open country, often near water, roadcuts, or houses; ranges in small groups, sometimes associating with other swallows such as Blue-and-whites, but usually not. Nests and roosts in holes dug into banks. Call a rich gurgling, e.g., "ddrreeúp."

Chestnut-collared Swallow
Petrochelidon rufocollaris *   PLATE 76(14)
12 cm (4¾"). *Found locally—though it seems to be increasing—in semiopen areas and around towns from sw. Ecuador* (Manabí) *to nw. Peru* (Lima). To 2000 m in Ecuador. A *handsome* swallow. Tail essentially square. Crown glossy black with *conspicuous rufous nuchal collar connecting with rufous breast band and contrasting with white cheeks and throat;* back black streaked grayish, *rump rufous. Chest and sides rufous-chestnut,* below buffy whitish. **Ecuadorian birds** have face and throat buffier (so less contrasting) than **Peruvian birds** (illustrated). Slightly larger American Cliff Swallow has dark cheeks and throat, almost always shows a pale forehead. At least in Ecuador this attractive swallow is usually seen around towns and cities, where it nests in colonies (sometimes large) under eaves of buildings, constructing a ball or retort-shaped nest of mud. Feeds over agricultural terrain, especially near water. Call, often given in flight, a soft "drrt."

DONACOBIUS: DONACOBIIDAE

With a checkered taxonomic history, the distinctive donacobius has recently been considered an aberrant wren, but the latest evidence points to its being distinct enough to warrant placement in a monotypic family.

Black-capped Donacobius
Donacobius atricapilla   PLATE 77(1)
22 cm (8½"). *Widespread and often common in marshes, lake margins, and wet pastures with tall grass from Colombia and Venezuela to ne. Argentina and se. Brazil.* Mostly below 600 m, but locally to 1400 m on east slope of Andes. *Sleek,* with a *bold yellow iris* and rather long tail. Chocolate brown above with black head; small white wing patch and tail with broad white tips obvious in flight. *Below rich buff.* In **Bolivia** has a narrow white postocular streak, as do **juveniles** throughout range. Usually conspicuous, perching in grass and on top of shrubs, generally in pairs. Flight low and direct, and despite fast wingbeats, seems rather slow. The delightful donacobius gives a variety of loud whistled or churring calls, often repeated in series, e.g., a liquid "whoit, whoit, whoit. . . ." Pairs regularly duet, perching side by side, bobbing their heads and swiveling their fanned tails, also inflating an odd orange pouch on sides of neck—a charming performance. Recent genetic evidence suggests that it is not an aberrant wren after all but rather an isolated relative of the "sylvoid assemblage" of Old World warblers. Also: e. Panama.

WRENS: TROGLODYTIDAE

Basically an American group of birds (only one occurs in the Old World), wrens are most numerous and diverse in Middle America and n. South America, only a few reaching austral regions. Wrens typically are found in undergrowth of forest and woodland, where they can be hard to see; a few species occur in grassy areas, and others frequent the vicinity of habitations. They are rather dull plumaged, brown and rufous predominating, and often have dark wing and tail barring; tails are often cocked. Wrens are best known for their often marvelous songs, in some given as fast and very precise duets. Most build domed nests with a side entrance (dummy nests are also often constructed); in some species helpers assist with the care of young.

Campylorhynchus

Large and boldly patterned wrens. The Bicolored and Thrush-like Wrens are distinctive and easy to identify. The others have basically *allopatric distributions,* except in n. Colombia, where two of them segregate by habitat. *Campylorhynchus* are *noisy, social wrens;* loud duets are frequent.

Bicolored Wren
Campylorhynchus griseus   PLATE 77(2)
22 cm (8½"). Locally common in light woodland and scrub, favoring *palm groves and vicinity of houses,* from *n. Colombia across much of Venezuela to n. Guyana. Most numerous in arid zones.* Mostly below 1600 m. *Very large.* In **most of range** (illustrated) rufescent to grayish brown above with black crown and *bold white superciliary; tail feathers broadly tipped white* (most obvious in flight). *Immaculate white below.* In **n. Colombia and nw. Venezuela** the black of crown extends to nape; in **Colombia's Río Magdalena valley** sootier above. Nearly unmistakable, but cf. Black-capped Donacobius and Tropical Mockingbird. Bold and inquisitive, hopping deliberately and peering into crannies for food items; regularly forages on the ground. Often noisy, giving a variety of guttural calls, e.g., "owk-cha-chok, owk-cha-chok. . . ."

Thrush-like Wren
Campylorhynchus turdinus   PLATE 77(3)
20.5 cm (8"). *Widespread and often common*

in borders of humid forest and adjacent clearings of *w. and s. Amazonia;* also locally south to sw. Brazil and Paraguay, where it favors gallery woodland and edge. To 1400 m along eastern base of Andes. Very *large.* In **most of range** (A) brownish above with dark scaling and whitish superciliary. *Below white boldly spotted grayish brown.* In **pantanal and n. Bolivia** (B) grayer above and *essentially unspotted* below. Essentially unmistakable, and certainly not very "thrush-like." Usually found in family groups of up to 6–8 birds that hop and clamber on larger limbs and among epiphytes, sometimes recalling a furnariid; in Amazonia not seen all that often, considering how frequently it is heard. Its explosive, far-carrying song, regularly given as a duet, is more musical than in other *Campylorhynchus;* often includes the phrases "chookadadoh, choh, choh" or "chooka-chook-chook."

Fasciated Wren
Campylorhynchus fasciatus   PLATE 77(4)
19 cm (7½"). *Common in arid scrub, agricultural regions, and trees around houses from sw. Ecuador* (s. Manabí) *to nw. Peru* (Ancash). Mostly below 2000 m, locally up to 2500 m. *Above boldly banded blackish and pale grayish to whitish.* Below whitish *boldly spotted grayish brown.* The similar Band-backed Wren occurs just to the north in Ecuador, occupying *more humid* habitats; its belly is more ochraceous. Conspicuous, often in small groups that clamber about at all levels in trees and shrubbery; though basically arboreal, it often drops to the ground.

Loud rhythmic song, sometimes given as a duet, a repetition of a harsh scratchy phrase; also gives several "chak" calls or variants.

Band-backed Wren
Campylorhynchus zonatus
18.5 cm (7¼"). Fairly common in canopy and borders of humid forest and adjacent clearings with tall trees in *n. Colombia* (south in Río Magdalena valley to Cundinamarca), and *disjunctly in nw. Ecuador* (Esmeraldas to n. Manabí). Mostly below 800 m. Resembles Fasciated Wren (which replaces it southward) but browner overall (not so grayish), and with an *ochraceous belly*. Band-backed favors *more humid terrain* than Thrushlike and Fasciated Wrens; not known to overlap with either. Like them it occurs in noisy groups that clamber about in dense growth, often in palms and well above the ground. Voice much as in Fasciated. Also: Mexico to w. Panama.

White-headed Wren
Campylorhynchus albobrunneus   PLATE 77(5)
18.5 cm (7¼"). Uncommon and seemingly local in tangled borders of humid forest in *w. Colombia* (south to w. Nariño). Mostly below 1000 m. Unmistakable, with *entirely white head and underparts* (the white sometimes soiled from dustbathing); back, wings, and tail dark brown. Apparent intermediates with Band-backed Wren are found near the Colombia-Ecuador border; their head and underparts are more mottled and indicate that despite their dissimilar appearance, Band-backed and White-headed may be conspecific. Behavior and voice as in Band-backed. Also: Panama.

Stripe-backed Wren
Campylorhynchus nuchalis   PLATE 77(6)
17 cm (6¾"). Fairly common in dry and gallery woodland, semiopen areas, and trees around houses in *n. Colombia and n. Venezuela* (east to Delta Amacuro; in east also in more humid regions). To about 800 m. *Iris yellow.* Grayish brown above with *white superciliary* and *bold white striping and banding. Below whitish boldly spotted grayish brown.* Does not occur with either Fasciated or Band-backed Wrens; its *back is striped* and its iris is not brownish. Sometimes occurs with the larger Bicolored Wren but is generally not as bold and familiar. Behavior and voice much as in Fasciated.

Cinnycerthia
Rather short-billed, *uniform-looking* wrens that range in *undergrowth of Andean forests.* Some individuals show a *variable amount of white on face*, most frequent and extensive in the Peruvian Wren. In Sepia-brown and Rufous Wrens, the white is mainly or entirely restricted to forehead.

Rufous Wren
Cinnycerthia unirufa   PLATE 77(7)
16.5 (6½"). Often common in undergrowth of *upper montane forest in Andes from extreme sw. Venezuela* (Táchira) *to extreme n. Peru.* Mostly 2200-3400 m. Birds of **Ecuador and most of Colombia** (illustrated) are *uniform deep rufous brown* with *only faint blackish barring on wings and tail* (hard to see in the field); *lores blackish.* In **ne. Colombia and Venezuela** *brighter and paler rufous* (especially on forecrown). Sepia-brown Wren occurs at lower elevations, is duller brown (less rufous) with more prominent wing and tail barring. Rufous Spinetail has more pointed tailtips, no wing and tail barring at all, very different voice and behavior. Rufous Wrens keep to dense cover and are hard to see well or for long; movements are quick and nervous. They troop about in groups, sometimes large and fast-moving, at times with mixed flocks, though sometimes independently. In many areas favors thickets of *Chusquea* bamboo. The fine musical song is complex, and often delivered by several birds as a chorus; it typically consists of repeated single notes or short phrases overlaying a trill.

Peruvian Wren
*Cinnycerthia peruana**   PLATE 77(8)
15 cm (6"). Uncommon in undergrowth of montane forest on *east slope of Andes in Peru* (Amazonas, south of Río Marañón, to Ayacucho). Mostly 2400-3200 m. Now considered a separate species from Sepia-brown (and Fulvous) Wrens. Uniform dull rufous brown with dull ashy gray brow and often a *variable amount of white on face; distinct black barring on wings and tail.* Usually ranges in smaller groups than Rufous Wren (sometimes only pairs), and regularly accompanies understory flocks. The fine loud song consists of a variable series of rich musical trills and warbles; also often gives a chattered call.

Sepia-brown Wren
*Cinnycerthia olivascens**
16 cm (6¼"). Uncommon in undergrowth of montane forest in *Andes from n. Colombia to n. Peru* (Piura and n. Amazonas). Mostly 1500–2500 m, down to 900 m in w. Colombia. Sometimes called Sharpe's Wren. Resembles Peruvian Wren but darker and somewhat less rufescent, with *no grayish brow* and *little or no facial white* (when present, only on forehead). Also resembles Rufous Wren, but usually segregates by elevation (Rufous ranging *higher*), and the more rufescent Rufous shows only *faint* wing and tail barring. In nw. Ecuador, cf. also Western Hemispingus. Behavior and voice much as in Peruvian.

Fulvous Wren
*Cinnycerthia fulva**   PLATE 77(9)
14–14.5 cm (5½–5¾"). Uncommon in undergrowth of montane forest on *east slope of Andes from s. Peru* (Cuzco) *to w. Bolivia* (Cochabamba). Mostly 2000–3000 m. Resembles Peruvian Wren (no known overlap, Fulvous replacing it south of the Río Apurímac), but *smaller* and with a dark eye-stripe. On **Cordillera Vilcabamba** has a dark crown and buffy whitish superciliary; **southward** (illustrated) superciliary more ochraceous. Facial pattern recalls smaller Mountain Wren, but that species cocks its short tail, etc. Behavior much as in Peruvian. Song similar, a series of phrases usually consisting of simple repetitions of musical notes.

Thryothorus

The midsized wrens of this large genus are *found primarily in n. and w. South America;* none extends to Argentina or Chile. Rufous and various shades of brown predominate; *barred tails* characterize most species. Virtually all have *streaked cheeks* and a *white superciliary;* many are boldly patterned below. *Thryothorus* wrens occur in pairs and tend to *skulk* in thickets or dense forest and woodland undergrowth; most do not often forage with mixed flocks. Most have *wonderful rich musical songs,* frequently delivered as a duet by a pair. They are heard much more often than seen.

Whiskered Wren
Thryothorus mystacalis   PLATE 78(1)
16 cm (6¼"). Uncommon in thickets and tangles at forest edge and secondary woodland in *foothills and Andes from n. Venezuela to sw. Ecuador* (w. Loja). Mostly 600 to 2400 m, lower in w. Ecuador. A *large* wren with gray crown and upper back *contrasting with rufous-chestnut mantle; cheeks boldly streaked,* and *conspicuous white malar and black "whisker."* Dull buffy grayish below. In **most of range** (illustrated) tail has black barring, but in **n. Venezuela** *tail plain rufous.* Moustached Wren (no overlap) has a narrower black whisker, very different song. Plain-tailed Wren has an *unbarred tail, spotted breast;* occurs only at higher elevations in the Andes. Whiskered tends to be a skulker, though it also ranges higher above the ground than many *Thryothorus,* often creeping about in tangled growth and suspended dead leaves. Rarely joins mixed flocks. Song rich and musical, a series of slowly repeated gurgling phrases, overall reminiscent of Black-bellied Wren.

Plain-tailed Wren
Thryothorus euophrys   PLATE 78(2)
16–16.5 cm (6¼–6½"). Fairly common in undergrowth of *upper montane forest in Andes from s. Colombia* (Nariño) *to n. Peru* (e. La Libertad). *Strongly favors Chusquea bamboo thickets.* Mostly 2200–3300 m. A *large* wren with an *unbarred tail* (nearly unique in this respect); wings also unbarred. Crown brownish gray with *back, wings, and tail bright rufous;* white superciliary and malar streak, black submalar. Mostly white below; **east-slope birds** (A) are relatively to entirely *unspotted,* and **west-slope birds** (B) are *spotted with black on breast.* Whiskered Wren never shows any spotting below and has a barred tail; it occurs at lower elevations. Cf. Inca Wren of s. Peru (no overlap). Usually in pairs, generally not with mixed flocks, skulking in dense bamboo thickets. Frequently heard song carries far, a fast, rollicking duet given by a mated pair, but in its nearly impenetrable habitat usually hard to see without tape playback. Call a distinctive "ter-chérk, ter-chérk, ter-chérk."

Inca Wren
*Thryothorus eisenmanni**
15 cm (6"). Fairly common in dense undergrowth of montane forest borders, woodland, and regenerating areas on *east slope of Andes in s. Peru* (Cuzco). 1800–3300 m. Resembles slightly larger Plain-tailed Wren, found northward in the Andes (no overlap). Inca likewise has a *plain tail. Bolder and more extensive black spotting below,* reaching upper belly. Behavior much as in Plain-

tailed, but seems less hard to see; like that species it favors dense stands of *Chusquea* bamboo.

Sooty-headed Wren
Thryothorus spadix   PLATE 78(3)

14.5 cm (5¾"). Uncommon in dense viny tangles in humid and montane forest on *lower Andean slopes of w. Colombia* (south to w. Nariño). Mostly 800–1800 m. Crown sooty, becoming *black on face and throat; mainly rufous brown* above, tail barred black. The larger Bay Wren has a white throat, white ear patch, and barred wings. Sooty-headed is more of a *forest-interior* wren than most other *Thryothorus*. Ranges in pairs, foraging independently of mixed flocks, and often probes into curled dead leaves. Song a series of fast loud phrases. Also: e. Panama.

Black-bellied Wren
Thryothorus fasciatoventris   PLATE 78(4)

15 cm (6"). Locally fairly common in dense undergrowth of humid and foothill forest borders and woodland, often thickets near water, in *n. and w. Colombia* (south to Valle). To about 1000 m. A fairly large wren with *distinctive contrasting white bib.* Chestnut brown above with black ear-coverts and wing and tail barring. *Throat and breast white, belly mainly black* (with faint whitish barring). Bay Wren has a black crown and nape, and in area of overlap with Black-bellied is boldly barred below. Behavior much as in other *Thryothorus* wrens, equally hard to see and heard much more often. Distinctive song a series of rich throaty gurgling phrases, many ending with a distinctive upslurred "wheeo-weeét." Also: Costa Rica and Panama.

Bay Wren
Thryothorus nigricapillus   PLATE 78(5)

14.5 (5¾"). *Locally common* in dense lower growth of forest and woodland borders, especially near water, in *w. Colombia and w. Ecuador* (south to El Oro). Mostly below 1300 m. In **w. Colombia south to Valle** (illustrated) has *head and neck black* with *white cheek-patch,* and *underparts boldly barred black and white.* Extent of barring decreases southward, **Ecuadorian** birds showing a *white throat and midchest* with barring only on sides and belly. All are rufous-chestnut above, wings and tail barred black. For a *Thryothorus* wren, Bay is bold and relatively easy to observe. Very vocal, with vigorous loud song a series of complex musical phrases repeated several times before switching to the next; also gives various

chirrs and calls (a "heetowíp" being frequent). Also: Nicaragua to Panama.

Moustached Wren
Thryothorus genibarbis   PLATE 78(6)

15.5 cm (6"). Fairly common in dense lower growth of woodland and forest borders from *s. Amazonia to e. Brazil* (south to Rio de Janeiro). To 1500 m. Crown grayish brown, gray on nape; rufous-brown above; *sides of head boldly streaked black and white* with a *well-defined* (though thin) *black moustachial streak;* tail boldly barred black. Pale grayish below, buffier on flanks. Coraya Wren, regardless of race, always looks comparatively black-faced. Buff-breasted Wren is much more buffy and rufous. Usually ranges in pairs, skulking and heard much more often than seen. Like most *Thryothorus* it tends not to follow flocks. Song a series of fast rollicking phrases, some ending with a distinctive "chochocho." Also querulous "jeeyr" calls interspersed with scolds.

Coraya Wren
Thryothorus coraya   PLATE 78(7)

14.5 (5¾"). Fairly common in forest and woodland undergrowth from *w. and n. Amazonia to the Guianas.* Ranges up to 2400 m on the tepuis, and to 1500 m or more on Andean slopes. In **most of range** (illustrated) crown dusky brown becoming rufous-brown on mantle; *sides of head mainly black* (with white streaking in some races), *extending over malar area;* tail barred black and buff. Below dingy grayish buff, throat white. **Tepui birds** much more rufescent on belly. *Black-faced look* is distinctive; never shows the well-defined moustachial streak so obvious in Moustached Wren. Forages more often with flocks and higher above the ground than other *Thryothorus,* and is less tied to the vicinity of water than the often sympatric Buff-breasted Wren. Variable but always spirited song is similar to many other *Thryothorus,* though less rich; phrases often start with a longer note and then a shorter note is repeated several times. Frequently gives a "jeeyr-jeeyr" or "choh-choh-choh."

Stripe-throated Wren
Thryothorus leucopogon   PLATE 78(8)

12 cm (4¾"). Uncommon in viny tangles and undergrowth of humid woodland and forest borders in *w. Colombia and w. Ecuador* (south to Azuay). To 900 m. A *rather small,* dull wren with *sides of head and throat narrowly streaked*

black and white. Above brown, *wings and tail barred black. Below pale cinnamon brown.* The slightly larger Speckle-breasted Wren can look similar (its spotting below can be faint), but note its *unbarred wings;* range overlap minimal at best. Unlike most *Thryothorus,* Stripe-throated routinely accompanies understory flocks. Call a distinctive "chu, ch-chu," with song a lengthened series. Also has a series of whistled notes, "teeee ... teee ... teee. ..." Also: e. Panama.

Speckle-breasted Wren
Thryothorus sclateri   PLATE 78(9)
13.5–14 cm (5¼–5½"). *Common* in undergrowth and borders of deciduous and semihumid woodland and scrub in *w. Colombia* (where very local) and from *sw. Ecuador* (Manabí) *to nw. Peru* (Cajamarca). Mostly below 1600 m, but 1300–2000 m in Colombia. In **sw. Ecuador and adjacent Peru** (illustrated) brown above with black barring on tail but *none on wings; sides of head speckled black and white.* Below white, *breast speckled black,* flanks more rufous. In **Río Marañón drainage** and **Colombia** breast speckling even denser. Stripe-throated Wren favors more humid habitats (with no known overlap) and is never spotted below. Cf. Rufous-breasted Wren. Usually in pairs and often inquisitive. Rollicking phrased song is typical of genus, but slightly higher-pitched. Call distinctive, resembling the rising sound made by rubbing one's finger against a comb's tines.

Rufous-breasted Wren
Thryothorus rutilus   PLATE 78(10)
14 cm (5½). Fairly common in lower growth of woodland and forest borders in *n. Colombia and n. Venezuela.* To 1900 m, but most numerous in foothills. Basically similar to Speckle-breasted Wren (no overlap) but has a *bright orange-rufous breast* (with *no* spots) that contrasts with its *black-and-white speckled face and throat.* **Santa Marta and Perijá** birds vaguely spotted below. Habitat, behavior and vocalizations much as in Specklebreasted. Also: Costa Rica and Panama.

Buff-breasted Wren
Thryothorus leucotis   PLATE 78(11)
14–14.5 cm (5½–5¾"). *A widespread, basically rufescent wren of thickets, usually near water, locally common from Colombia and Venezuela to s. Brazil.* Locally to 950 m. Rufescent to grayish brown above with white superciliary and streaked cheeks; wings and tail barred black.

Throat white, *below buff deepening to rufous on belly.* **Cen. Brazil** birds are more rufous below, **Caribbean-slope** birds whiter below. Coraya, Moustached, and Whiskered Wrens all show much more black on face and have *un*barred wings. Cf. Long-billed and Fawn-breasted Wrens (both with limited ranges). Usually in pairs that hop in thickets near water, rummaging in dense growth and occasionally dropping to the ground; even when singing, hard to see well. Loud vigorous song a series of fast staccato phrases, each repeated rapidly before the bird switches to another. Oft-heard call a "cheet cho-cho," sometimes just the "cho-cho." Also: Panama.

Fawn-breasted Wren
Thryothorus guarayanus
13.5 cm (5¼"). Fairly common in thickets and woodland undergrowth near water in *n. Bolivia* (west to Beni) *and adjacent Brazil* (w. Mato Grosso do Sul) *and n. Paraguay.* To 600 m. Resembles Buff-breasted Wren. Slightly smaller, duller, and paler generally than the Buff-breasted race found with it in sw. Brazil, and slightly grayer above than the Buff-breasted race found to the northwest in se. Peru. *In the field usually best simply to go by range.* Behavior and voice much as in Buff-breasted, but also often delivers a distinctive shorter song, e.g., a slow and melodic "sweeyr, cheer-chowee, chowee." In the southern pantanal of Brazil, also frequently gives a notably slow "chee! cheeu, cheeu" or "cheeíp, chee-u, chee-uu," different from anything given by Buff-breasted.

Long-billed Wren
Thryothorus longirostris   PLATE 78(12)
15 cm (6"). Uncommon to fairly common in dense thickets at woodland and forest borders and in shrubby clearings, often near water, in *e. Brazil* (south to e. Santa Catarina). To 900 m. Resembles Buff-breasted Wren, but *bill obviously longer.* Also more rufescent (less grayish) above than adjacent race of Buff-breasted. Behavior and voice much as in Buff-breasted; a frequent call in the southeast is a ringing "cho-cho-cho."

Superciliated Wren
Thryothorus superciliaris   PLATE 78(13)
14.5 cm (5¾"). Uncommon to fairly common in arid scrub, woodland thickets, and agricultural terrain from *sw. Ecuador* (Manabí) *to nw. Peru* (Ancash); most numerous in Peru. To 1500 m in s. Ecuador. *Bright rufous above with a bold*

white superciliary and face, wings and tail barred black. *Pure white below,* some rufous on flanks. In its limited range this striking wren is unlikely to be confused; no overlap with any similar *Thryothorus* (occurs only with quite different Speckle-breasted). Behavior much as in Buff-breasted Wren, though without the affinity for water. Song similar to Buff-breasted, but not as fast or rollicking, and usually has longer pauses between phrases.

Rufous-and-white Wren
Thryothorus rufalbus   PLATE 78(14)

14.5–15 cm (5¾–6″). Locally fairly common in undergrowth of deciduous woodland and forest in *n. Colombia* and *n. Venezuela* (east to Sucre and Monagas); in ne. Venezuela also in várzea forest. To 1500 m. *Bright rufous above, sides of head extensively streaked black and white,* wings and tail barred black. *White below,* brownish on sides and flanks. Buff-breasted Wren is less two-toned, browner above and buffier below. In n. Colombia cf. Niceforo's Wren (*very* local). Notably skulking and hard to see; forages closer to the ground than most *Thryothorus,* often actually hopping on it. Song unmistakable, a lovely slow series of low-pitched hooting whistled notes on differing pitches, usually ending with a high note. Also: Mexico to Panama.

Niceforo's Wren
Thryothorus nicefori

14.5 cm (5¾″). *Rare and very local in thick acacia scrub and coffee plantations on east slope of E. Andes in ne. Colombia* (Santander near San Gil, and Boyacá at Soatá). 1100–1900 m. Resembles Rufous-and-white Wren; recent evidence suggests they could be conspecific. *Browner above* (not so rufous) and *grayer on sides and flanks* (not brown). Hardly known in life, but behavior and voice reportedly very similar to Rufous-and-white (P. G. W. Salaman).

Gray Wren
Thryothorus griseus   PLATE 78(15)

11.5 cm (4½″). Locally common in tangled lower growth and mid-levels at edge of várzea forest and woodland in *limited area of w. Amaz. Brazil.* About 200 m. A distinctive, *small Thryothorus* with *notably short tail. Dull gray above* with indistinct whitish superciliary, tail barred dusky. *Pale grayish below. No other Thryothorus is nearly so gray.* Not well known, but pairs have been seen foraging in tangles at varying levels. Rhythmic

song a series of melodic phrases repeated several times before switching to another (S. Hilty).

Odontorchilus

A distinctive pair of arboreal, somewhat gnatcatcherlike wrens with *long, narrow, often cocked tails.* They range locally in *forest subcanopy;* both species are relatively scarce.

Gray-mantled Wren
Odontorchilus branickii   PLATE 79(1)

12 cm (4¾″). *Uncommon in montane and foothill forest in Andes from s. Colombia* (Valle) *to w. Bolivia* (La Paz). On east slope mostly 1300–2200 m, on west slope lower, mostly 250–1100 m. *Bluish gray above,* browner on crown with some dusky streaking; *tail boldly barred blackish.* Whitish below. Pairs regularly accompany canopy flocks; they *characteristically hop along larger lateral branches, inspecting the underside.* Song a dry, high-pitched trill, not that often heard; the notes are sometimes better-separated and shriller.

Tooth-billed Wren
Odontorchilus cinereus   PLATE 79(2)

12 cm (4¾″). *Uncommon and local in canopy and borders of humid forest in s. Amaz. Brazil and adjacent Bolivia* (ne. Santa Cruz). To 600 m. Resembles Gray-mantled Wren (no overlap), but duller and more brownish gray above, throat and breast tinged with buff. Behavior much as in Gray-mantled. Song a rather melodic repetition, "tree-ree-ree-ree-ree-ree-ree-ree," becoming shriller and faster in response to playback, e.g., "sree-sree-sree-sree-sree-sree-sree."

Cistothorus

Small, buffyish wrens with *prominently black-and-white streaked backs,* found in marshy areas or tall grass. All are *inconspicuous unless singing.*

Grass Wren
Cistothorus platensis   PLATE 79(3)

9.5–11 cm (3¾–4¼″). *The most wide-ranging member of the genus,* locally fairly common in *lowland savannas and Andean grasslands* from Colombia and Venezuela to Tierra del Fuego. To 4000 m in Andes. A *small* wren, variable but always *mainly buffy* with a *streaked back* and barred wings; *tail coarsely barred.* **Southern birds** (A) have crown blacker and more prominently streaked than in **Andean birds** (B), which have browner crown and buffier underparts. Southern House Wren is plainer, with only indistinct barring on wings and tail, a less prominent brow, and no back streaking. Usually hard to see, creeping about mouselike on or near the ground in tall vegetation (either dry or moist, the requirement being a relatively tall, dense grass cover). When breeding, however, the ♂'s complex and musical songs often reveal its presence, and they often perch in a somewhat exposed situation, much easier to see. Songs vary geographically and basically consist of repetitions of gurgles and trills. Frequent call a repeated "jer-jer-jer" or "ju-ju-ju." Also: Mexico to w. Panama. North American birds are here considered a separate species, *C. stellaris* (Sedge Wren); the Grass Wren itself may consist of more than one species.

Mérida Wren
Cistothorus meridae
10 cm (4″). *Uncommon and local in paramo (especially in wet areas near water, but also large boulder fields) in Andes of w. Venezuela* (mainly Mérida). 2900–4100 m. Resembles Grass Wren (which in area of overlap apparently occurs only at lower elevations) but has *bolder and whiter superciliary* and *conspicuous blackish barring on flanks* (both lacking in Grass Wren). Behavior much as in Grass Wren. Song less complex, a simple phrase of high trilled musical notes repeated over and over, e.g., "tk-tk-tseeee-tsweew-tseeuwww."

Apolinar's Wren
Cistothorus apolinari
12.5 cm (5″). *Now uncommon and local in marshes in E. Andes of ne. Colombia* (Boyacá and Cundinamarca). 2000–3000 m. Resembles the smaller Grass Wren (evidently not strictly sympatric), but Apolinar's has *grayish superciliary* and *dingier and grayer underparts;* its crown is brown. Rarely leaves its marshy habitat and thus generally hard to see. Typically located through its fast, rhythmic, chirring song, usually given from a partially exposed perch. Threatened by drainage of the last remnants of its marshy habitat, always limited in extent.

Troglodytes

Small wrens, *basically brown* and *relatively unpatterned.* The Southern House Wren is widespread in semiopen terrain (well named, it is often a commensal of humans), but most of its congeners are less familiar, more arboreal, and usually forest-based.

Mountain Wren
Troglodytes solstitialis   PLATE 79(4)
11 cm (4¼″). Fairly common to common in montane forest and forest borders in *Andes from w. Venezuela* (Lara) *to nw. Argentina* (Tucumán). Mostly 1500–3500 m, lower (to 700 m) in w. Ecuador and Argentina. Small and *short-tailed. Quite rufescent above,* buffyish below; rather bold superciliary is *buff* **northward,** *whitish* and more evident **southward** (illustrated bird is intermediate). Liable to be confused only with Southern House Wren, the Mountain Wren is markedly more rufescent, with a more obvious brow, and much more arboreal and forest-based. Single birds or pairs regularly accompany mixed flocks, hopping on mossy trunks and larger limbs at varying levels, frequently quite high. Tinkling, musical song delivered at intervals while foraging.

Santa Marta Wren
Troglodytes monticola
11.5 cm (4½″). *Now rare in undergrowth of remnant forest near and above treeline on Santa Marta Mts. of n. Colombia.* 3200–4600 m. Recalls slightly smaller Mountain Wren (*no overlap*), but *flanks and crissum boldly barred blackish.* Voice seems unknown, as indeed is its status and basic natural history. Threatened by excessive burning and overgrazing of paramo.

Tepui Wren
Troglodytes rufulus
12 cm (4¾″). Locally common in forest borders and shrubbery at *higher elevations on tepuis of s. Venezuela region.* 1000–2800 m, but most numerous 1500–2400 m. Somewhat larger with longer tail than Mountain Wren (*no overlap*), and more richly colored and rufous brown; some races are more grayish or whitish below, particularly on median underparts. Usually in pairs and less arboreal than Mountain, foraging in undergrowth, sometimes even on the ground itself. Song a series of high-pitched thin notes delivered in a choppy manner (D. Ascanio recording).

Southern House Wren
Troglodytes musculus *   PLATE 79(5)
11.5 cm (4½"). *Very common and widespread* in
open or semiopen habitats from Colombia and
Venezuela to Tierra del Fuego; avoids mostly forested regions, but quickly colonizes such areas
subsequent to deforestation. At least locally to
over 4000 m in the Andes; formerly just called
House Wren. Here considered a species distinct
from birds of North America. *Nearly uniform
brown and buffyish*, more whitish below and
more rufescent on rump, with a weak whitish
superciliary and *indistinct dusky barring on
wings and tail*. **Altiplano race of Peru and nw.
Bolivia** is more rufescent below. Familiar, easy to
watch and frequently around houses, numerous
even in urban areas. They occur in pairs and are
confiding, hopping in shrubbery, along walls, on
buildings, etc. *Gurgling, warbled song*, often ending with an accented note, repeated at intervals
almost constantly, generally from a prominent
perch. Also gives a nasal "jeeyah" scold. Also:
s. Mexico to Panama; Lesser Antilles.

Cobb's Wren
Troglodytes cobbi *
12 cm (4¾"). Endemic to *Falkland Islands*, where
now restricted to rat-free outlying islets; *favors
tussock grass and rocky shorelines, often foraging
in stranded kelp*. Formerly considered a race of
Southern House Wren, but larger, with longer
bill, relatively uniform dark appearance, no
superciliary, and different habitat. Cf. also Grass
Wren (streaked back, etc.), a much more skulking bird. Cobb's typically does not occur around
houses and is very tame.

Henicorhina

Distinctive, small wrens with *very stubby,
cocked tails* and *boldly streaked cheeks*. *Henicorhina* range *near the ground inside forest*,
creeping about on logs and in dense undergrowth, flying but little. Most are montane.
They are often heard but, unfortunately, are
hard to observe for long.

White-breasted Wood Wren
Henicorhina leucosticta   PLATE 79(6)
11 cm (4¼"). Locally common in undergrowth of
humid forest, *mainly in lowlands* (also foothills),
from *Colombia to e. Peru and the Guianas*. To
about 1300 m. *Throat and breast obviously white*.
In **Amazonia and nw. Colombia** (illustrated)

has *black crown*; rufous-brown above, wings and
tail barred black. *Throat and breast white*, flanks
rufescent. In **remainder w. of Colombian range
and nw. Ecuador**, crown brown and white breast
dingier. The latter in particular can be confused
with Gray-breasted Wood Wren, which, however,
is still distinctly grayer on breast. Gray-breasted
ranges at higher elevations, though there is local
overlap. This pert, attractive wren normally remains *inside* forest. Though heard far more often
than seen, not particularly shy. Song somewhat
variable, but always rich and melodic, with comparatively short phrases repeated more often
than in Gray-breasted; a frequent one is "churry-
churry-cheer." Also: Mexico to Panama.

Gray-breasted Wood Wren
Henicorhina leucophrys   PLATE 79(7)
11 cm (4¼"). *Common and widespread* in undergrowth and borders of montane forest in *Andes
from n. Venezuela to w. Bolivia* (w. Santa Cruz).
Mostly 1500–3000 m, but locally down to near
sea level in sw. Ecuador. Perhaps more than one
species. Resembles White-breasted Wood Wren
(of lowlands) but *throat and breast gray*, its deep-
ness varying geographically (palest in birds of
sw. Ecuador and the lower-ranging form on the
Santa Marta Mts., but never as white as White-
breasted). Cf. also Bar-winged and Munchique
Wood Wrens (both range-restricted). Behavior
similar to White-breasted, though Gray-breasted
is more often at edge. Very vocal, and heard more
than seen; typical song a series of rather long
phrases, each repeated a few times, with geographic variation. Also: Mexico to Panama.

Munchique Wood Wren
Henicorhina negreti *
11 cm (4¼"). *Locally not uncommon in dense
undergrowth of stunted cloud forest and woodland
on west slope of Andes in sw. Colombia* (Munchique Natl. Park in w. Cauca). 2250–2650 m.
A recently described species. Resembles Gray-
breasted Wood Wren (which on Cerro Munchique is found at slightly lower elevations) but
darker brown above and darker gray on breast,
with a more barred belly. Best distinguished
through its distinctive song, typically a series of
repetitions of 6–12 pure notes, less slurred than
in Gray-breasted (P. G. W. Salaman et al.).

Bar-winged Wood Wren
Henicorhina leucoptera   PLATE 79(8)
11 cm (4¼"). Locally fairly common in undergrowth of montane forest and woodland on

montane ridges on and near east slope of Andes from extreme s. Ecuador (Zamora-Chinchipe on Cordillera del Cóndor) to n. Peru (e. La Libertad). Mostly 1700–2400 m, in its range usually replacing Gray-breasted Wood Wren at higher elevations. Differs from Gray-breasted in its *conspicuous bold white wing-bars;* somewhat whiter below than sympatric Gray-breasteds. Favors areas where the forest is stunted; most numerous near ridgetops. Voice and behavior so similar that Gray-breasteds sometimes respond to Bar-winged tapes, and vice versa.

Cyphorhinus

Relatively chunky wrens with *orange-rufous foreparts, distinctive thick bills with a high ridged culmen,* and at least some bare skin around eye. *Cyphorhinus* are found inside humid or montane forest, and all have *truly enchanting songs.*

Musician Wren
Cyphorhinus arada*   PLATE 79(9)
13 cm (5"). Uncommon on or near ground in humid forest (mainly terra firme) from Amazonia to the Guianas. To about 1000 m. In **most of range** (A) *forehead, throat, and breast orange-rufous,* short superciliary rufous or whitish; otherwise dull brown, wings and tail barred black. Birds from **the Guianas to n. Amazonian Brazil** (B) have a *conspicuous partial nuchal collar of white streaks.* Chestnut-breasted Wren of the Andes (limited overlap) is larger with darker crown and *no* barring on wings or tail. Hops on the ground in pairs or small family groups, rummaging in leaf litter; they usually move on their own and do not accompany mixed flocks. Beautiful song consists of a variety of often complex and musical phrases accompanied by low guttural churring notes, each phrase repeated many times before going on to the next. The most renowned Amazonian bird in Brazil, where it is called "guira puru."

Song Wren
Cyphorhinus phaeocephalus   PLATE 79(10)
13 cm (5"). Fairly common on or near ground in humid forest and woodland in *w. Colombia and w. Ecuador* (south to El Oro). To about 900 m. Resembles the larger Chestnut-breasted Wren of the Andes (limited or no overlap) but has a *conspicuous pale blue, bare ocular area* and *blackish barring on wings and tail.* **Pacific**

birds (illustrated) are darker on crown and have a more deeply colored rufous bib than birds of **n. Colombia.** Habitat, behavior, and voice much as in Musician Wren, but song typically not quite so complex. Also: Honduras to Panama.

Chestnut-breasted Wren
Cyphorhinus thoracicus   PLATE 79(11)
15 cm (6"). Rare to uncommon on or near ground in montane forest in Andes from n. Colombia to w. Bolivia (La Paz); perhaps most numerous in sw. Colombia. Mostly 1300–2300 m, thus at *higher elevations* than its congeners. Dark brown above (including entire crown) with wings and tail *unbarred. Throat and breast orange-rufous.* Musician Wren (east of Andes) has an orange-rufous forecrown, barred wings and tail. Song Wren (west of Andes) has obvious pale bare skin around eyes and likewise has barred wings and tail. Behavior much as in Musician. Song simple but lovely, a repetition of a minor-key note or pair of notes, sometimes continuing for several minutes without a pause.

Microcerculus

Small wrens, very short-tailed, long-billed, and long-legged, that *skulk on or near the ground inside humid forest* and are *hard to see.* Their presence is frequently revealed, however, by their marvelous songs.

Southern Nightingale-Wren
Microcerculus marginatus   PLATE 79(12)
11 cm (4¼"). Fairly common on or near ground in humid forest from *Colombia and w. Venezuela to s. Amazonia. The most numerous and widespread Microcerculus;* more than a single species is almost surely involved. Mostly below 1000 m, locally to 1800 m in Venezuela. Also called Scaly-breasted Wren. Striking geographic variation. In **most of range** (A) dark brown above; *below mostly white* with a brown belly and a variable amount of dark scaling, more in young birds. In **most of w. Ecuador** and from **n. Colombia and nw. Venezuela** (B) *conspicuously scaled dusky below,* except for white throat. Forages singly, furtively walking and hopping on or near the ground, seeming to favor ravines and to linger around fallen logs. Regularly teeters its rear end. Heard far more often than seen, with *two very different song types.* West of Andes and in w. Amazonia, after a fast irregular opening, gives an extended series of sibilant notes that gradu-

ally drop in pitch and are delivered at increasingly long intervals (toward the end, the pauses may last 10 seconds or more). In sw. Amazonia, song a series of randomly paced and pitched notes with a pure clear quality (even the loudness changes). Also: Costa Rica and Panama.

Wing-banded Wren

Microcerculus bambla   PLATE 79(13)

11.5 cm (4½"). Uncommon on or near ground in humid forest (principally terra firme) in *ne. South America,* and *locally along eastern base of Andes in e. Ecuador and e. Peru.* Mostly below 1300 m. Dark brown above, wings blacker and crossed by a *single conspicuous white band.* Throat and breast gray, belly browner and faintly scaled. The white wing-band stands out so much that the species is essentially unmistakable. Habitat and furtive behavior much as in Southern Nightingale-Wren (locally sympatric, though in such situations

Wing-banded is either rarer or occurs mainly at higher elevations). Heard much more often than seen. Song a beautiful series of clear notes on the same pitch, gradually accelerating into a crescendo, then a pause (sometimes long) before another series; this resembles Southern Nightingale-Wren's song in sw. Amazonia.

Flutist Wren

Microcerculus ustulatus   PLATE 79(14)

11.5 cm (4½"). Fairly common on or near ground in montane forest on *tepuis of s. Venezuela region.* Mostly 900–1500 m. *Essentially uniform rufescent brown* with a variable amount of dusky scaling. Tepui Wren has a similar uniform brownish coloration, but it *lacks scaling,* its long tail gives it a very different shape, and it has a buff superciliary. Behavior much as in Southern Nightingale-Wren. Beautiful song a series of musical notes that gradually slide upscale.

THRUSHES: TURDIDAE

The thrushes form a cosmopolitan group of birds, most numerous and diverse in the Old World. In South America members of the well-known genus *Turdus* predominate, with other genera more montane and considerably shyer. Neotropical thrushes are not especially colorful birds, though many are handsomely patterned in shades of black, gray, rufous, and brown. Some are among the world's finest songsters, this extending to mimicry in a few. Some species are long-distance migrants. Nests are almost always cup-shaped.

Myadestes

Mainly arboreal thrushes with rather short, wide bills found primarily in Andean forests, where they are heard more often than seen. *Myadestes* perch more vertically than most other thrushes. Nests are placed on or near the ground on steep banks, on rotten stumps, etc.

Andean Solitaire
Myadestes ralloides   PLATE 80(1)
18 cm (7″). Locally common in montane forest and woodland in *Andes from n. Venezuela to w. Bolivia* (Chuquisaca). Mostly 1000–2500 m, locally lower on Pacific slope. Perhaps more than one species. Basal bill and legs yellow (bill dusky in **Peru and Bolivia**). *Warm rufescent brown above,* forecrown grayer; wings with *silvery gray band at base of inner web of primaries,* and *outer tail feathers silvery gray,* both flashing conspicuously in flight. *Below leaden gray.* Buff-spotted **immatures** are frequently seen. Shy and unobtrusive, often perching quietly and motionless for long periods; regularly seen feeding in fruiting trees, often with various tanagers. Best known from its loud and beautiful, but ventriloquial, song. On west slope a leisurely series of clear liquid notes often intermixed with more guttural or gurgling ones, e.g., "tleee . . . leedlelee . . . lulee . . . turdelee . . . treelee . . . teeulteeul. . . ." On east slope in Ecuador shriller and less flutelike, with more jumbled phrases and longer intervals.

Varied Solitaire
Myadestes coloratus
18 cm (7″). *Fairly common in montane forest in nw. Colombia* (nw. Chocó on Cerro Tacarcuna). 1100–1500 m. Resembles Andean Solitaire (no overlap) but *bill entirely orange-yellow* and *forehead and face black* (contrasting with gray head). Behavior, including voice, much like west-slope Andeans. Also: e. Panama.

Entomodestes

A stunning and unmistakable pair of *large* and long-tailed, *mainly black* thrushes. *Entomodestes* solitaires range locally in Andean forests, where they are heard more often than seen. Both species have *conspicuous white in wings and tail,* a white pectoral patch (often hidden), and an orange lower mandible.

White-eared Solitaire
Entomodestes leucotis   PLATE 80(2)
24 cm (9½″). Uncommon in montane forest on *east slope of Andes from n. Peru* (n. San Martín, south of Río Marañón) *to w. Bolivia* (w. Santa Cruz). Mostly 1500–2800 m. *Head and underparts jet black* with *broad white patch below eye; mantle bright rufous-chestnut; white band at base of inner web of primaries* and *white outer tail feathers,* both especially obvious in flight. Despite the bold and flashy plumage pattern, an inconspicuous and mainly solitary bird, most often noted at fruiting trees, in flight, or when singing. Weird song a weak but surprisingly far-carrying "wreeeeenh," given at long intervals of 9–15 seconds, with a ringing but almost nasal

or buzzy quality (recalls odd final note of Club-winged Manakin).

Black Solitaire
Entomodestes coracinus   PLATE 80(3)
23 cm (9"). *Rare to uncommon and local in montane forest on west slope of Andes in sw. Colombia and nw. Ecuador* (south to Pichincha); in recent years seems to have declined in Ecuador. 600–2250 m. Iris red. *Jet black aside from white slash on face, white band at base of primaries,* and *lateral tail feathers* (conspicuous in flight). Behavior much as in White-eared Solitaire. Infrequently heard song a single note given at long intervals (typically 6–8 seconds), clearer and lower-pitched than White-eared's with a much less buzzy or ringing quality.

Rufous-brown Solitaire
Cichlopsis leucogenys   PLATE 80(4)
20.5 cm (8"). *Uncommon and very local in foothill and lower montane forest in sw. Colombia and nw. Ecuador, e. Peru, tepuis of se. Venezuela region, and in se. Brazil.* 550–1400 m. Bill *longer* than in *Myadestes, yellow-orange below;* inconspicuous eye-ring yellow. *Mainly rufous brown.* **Tepui** and **Brazil** birds (A) have an *ochraceous tawny median throat stripe;* **Chocó** birds (B) have *entire throat and supraloral rich reddish chestnut* and also a *bright orange ochraceous crissum* (**Peru** birds are similar). Various *Turdus* thrushes are also rufescent, but none has the bicolored bill or tawny on throat (rather, they show throat *streaking*). Andean Solitaire is smaller, gray below, with silvery in wings and tail. Inconspicuous in lower and mid-levels inside forest. Singing birds often flutter their wings as they deliver a musical and notably variable series of complex, fast phrases interspersed with chattering or twittering notes, e.g., "tleeowít-tsiii-trrrr—tr-tr-teeo-teeo, . . ." very different from other solitaires.

Catharus

Rather shy and inconspicuous thrushes found primarily *on or near the ground inside forest and shady woodland.* The three boreal migrants are dull and brown, relieved only by *some breast spotting,* while the three resident species (all found in the Andes) are more strongly patterned and have *bright orange bills and legs.*

Swainson's Thrush
Catharus ustulatus   PLATE 80(5)
18 cm (7"). *Locally common boreal migrant* (Oct.–Apr.), *mostly to lower Andean slopes and adjacent lowlands, in w. South America south to nw. Argentina;* a scatter of records from lowlands to the east. Mostly below 2000 m, higher (to 3000 m or more) as a transient. *Buff lores and eye-ring* impart an *obvious spectacled look* not seen in other migrant *Catharus. Above olivaceous brown* with *buffyish cheeks.* Below whitish, *spotted blackish on buff-washed breast.* Cf. less numerous Gray-cheeked Thrush and Veery. Swainson's favors humid and montane forest borders, also secondary woodland; it also often feeds at fruiting trees in clearings. Usually solitary (though concentrations occur when migrating), less terrestrial than the other *Catharus,* and not as shy. A liquid "whit" call is frequently heard, less often "wrenh"; the song, a pretty series of upslurred phrases, is also sometimes given, especially on northward migration. Breeds in n. North America.

Wood Thrush (*Hylocichla mustelina*) has been recorded as a boreal migrant on a few occasions in n. Colombia and on the Netherlands Antilles.

Northern Wheatear (*Oenanthe oenanthe*) has been recorded as a vagrant in the Netherlands Antilles and on Trinidad; it ranges primarily in the Old World.

Gray-cheeked Thrush
Catharus minimus
18 cm (7"). *Uncommon boreal migrant* (Sep.–May) to undergrowth of humid forest and borders in *nw. Amazonia.* Mostly below 1500 m. Resembles Swainson's Thrush but *lores and vague eye-ring grayish* (not buff, and *not* contrasting), *cheeks usually grayish* (not buffyish as in Swainson's), and usually not so buffy across breast. Favors forest floor inside humid forest and borders, tending to remain within cover; shy and not often seen on its winter quarters (where it is much more inconspicuous than Swainson's). A "veer" call note is sometimes heard, but (unlike Swainson's) its jumbled, nasal, descending song is only rarely given here. Breeds in n. North America.

Veery
Catharus fuscescens
18 cm (7"). *Uncommon boreal migrant* (Sep.–Apr.) to undergrowth of humid forest and bor-

ders in Amazonia and northward; *apparently overwinters primarily in s. Brazil.* Mostly below 1500 m. Resembles Swainson's Thrush, but has *warmer and more rufescent upperparts, lacks* distinct eye-ring (instead face looks plain, with large-eyed expression), and has *fewer and smaller spots on breast.* Shy and easily overlooked, not much is known about the Veery on its winter quarters, where it is usually seen singly, hopping on or near the ground inside cover. Regularly gives a distinctive downslurred "pheeuw" call, as well as a more nasal "waaa-a-a-a," but does not seem to sing in South America. Breeds in North America.

Orange-billed Nightingale-Thrush
Catharus aurantiirostris   PLATE 80(6)
16.5 (6½"). Locally fairly common in lower growth of montane forest borders, secondary woodland, and coffee plantations in *Andes from n. Venezuela to s. Colombia* (Nariño). 600–2200 m. *Bill and legs bright orange; narrow orange eye-ring.* In **most of range** (illustrated) essentially *two-toned,* with *olivaceous to russet brown upperparts* and *mainly pale grayish underparts.* In **s. Colombia** head grayer. The differently shaped Andean Solitaire is darker generally, with silvery in wings and tail. Inconspicuous, hopping on or near the ground, usually in dense vegetation at forest edge. For a nightingale-thrush, the song is relatively poor and unmusical, a series of short jumbled phrases, almost squeaky. Distinctive call a nasal "waaa-a-a-a." Also: Mexico to Panama.

Spotted Nightingale-Thrush
Catharus dryas   PLATE 80(7)
17 cm (6¾"). Locally fairly common in undergrowth of foothill and montane forest and woodland in *Andes from w. Venezuela* (Lara) *to nw. Argentina* (Salta). Mostly 750–1800 m (but locally much higher in Bolivia, to 2500–2600 m). *Bill and legs orange; narrow orange eye-ring. Head black,* otherwise olive above; *below apricot yellow with conspicuous dusky spotting.* Slaty-backed Nightingale-Thrush mainly occurs at higher elevations; it has a pale eye and adults never show spotting below. None of the migrant *Catharus* has bright soft-part colors or a black head. Inconspicuous, hopping on or near the ground inside forest (sometimes at edge in early morning), often nervously flicking its wings; picks at the ground and tosses leaves. Heard much more often than seen; song a series of

lovely short musical phrases with brief intervals and interspersed with occasional guttural notes, e.g., "tru-lee? . . . cheelolee . . . troloweé . . . cheetrelelee . . . troloweé. . . ." Call a thin high-pitched "tseeu," very different from Slaty-backed. Also: Mexico to Honduras.

Slaty-backed Nightingale-Thrush
Catharus fuscater   PLATE 80(8)
18 cm (7"). Locally fairly common in undergrowth of montane forest and woodland in *Andes from w. Venezuela* (Lara) *to w. Bolivia* (w. Santa Cruz). Mostly 1200–2600 m, locally higher in Bolivia. *Bill, legs, and narrow eye-ring orange; iris white to pale grayish* (but brown in Colombia's Cen. Andes). In **most of range** (illustrated) *dark slaty gray above* (sometimes more grayish or olive brown) with slightly blacker head. *Below dark olivaceous gray,* whitish on midbelly. Birds from **Santa Marta Mts.** and **s. Peru and Bolivia** are grayer below. Never shows the spotting of Spotted Nightingale-Thrush, which also is *dark*-eyed and has a *contrasting* black head. Behavior as in Spotted, and equally hard to see; usually occurs at higher elevations (but ranges lower in Spotted's absence). Sometimes attends antswarms. Song similar to Spotted but simpler, delivered with longer pauses between phrases, often just a repetition of a "too-tee?" phrase but regularly varied to "toh-toh-tee . . . tee-toh" or "tlee-to-tleedelee . . . to-wee-tlee?" Call a querulous "wrrenh?" Also: Costa Rica and Panama.

Turdus

These thrushes are often *familiar* and common birds; found in a variety of habitats, they occur virtually throughout the world. Though many range in the semiopen, a few are more reclusive and are found in forest. Color and plumage patterns vary, but almost all show *throat streaking,* sometimes bold. Identification of most species is relatively straightforward, though ♀♀ of certain montane species can present a challenge, as does the Great-Chiguanco Thrush pair in some parts of their ranges. Many are renowned for their attractive, lilting songs. All build substantial cup nests, often lined with mud. The genus *Platycichla* (formerly comprising two species, Pale-eyed and Yellow-legged) has recently been subsumed into *Turdus.*

Plumbeous-backed Thrush

Turdus reevei   PLATE 80(9)

23 cm (9"). Locally fairly common (but in most areas seasonal and often erratic) in montane and deciduous forests, woodland, and adjacent clearings from *sw. Ecuador* (Manabí and Los Ríos) *to nw. Peru* (Lambayeque). Mostly below 1500 m. *Iris bluish white;* bill and legs yellow. *Blue-gray above,* head duller. *Mostly pale grayish white below,* sides and flanks broadly tinged buff. Immatures with buff spotting above and dark spotting below are frequently seen. A mostly arboreal thrush, often gathering in fruiting trees. Call an abrupt, descending "pseeeeu" that recalls a Scrub Blackbird. Song a typical *Turdus* caroling, apparently given only briefly when nesting, during the rainy season.

Marañón Thrush

Turdus maranonicus   PLATE 80(10)

21.5 cm (8½"). Locally fairly common in woodland and adjacent clearings as well as more arid scrub in *upper Río Marañón drainage of extreme s. Ecuador* (s. Zamora-Chinchipe) *to n. Peru* (e. La Libertad). 400–2000 m. *Dark brown above;* white below with *profuse and bold brown spotting and scaling.* No other *Turdus* is so heavily spotted below, but note that immatures of *all* species do show spotting (though none is also essentially plain above). A fairly conspicuous thrush, often seen hopping on the ground in clearings and (especially in early morning) at roadsides. Song a pleasant, typical *Turdus* caroling, slower than the Black-billed Thrush and with more slurred notes.

Pale-eyed Thrush

*Turdus leucops**   PLATE 81(1)

21.5 cm (8½"). Uncommon and local in montane forest and borders in *Andes from n. Venezuela to w. Bolivia* (w. Santa Cruz), also on *tepuis of s. Venezuela region.* Mostly 900–2100 m. Distinctive ♂ *lustrous black* with a *bluish white iris* (conspicuous) but *no eye-ring;* bill and legs bright yellow. ♀ mostly dark brown, *paler and more mottled fulvous or grayish on belly;* iris pale brown or gray (also with *no eye-ring*), bill blackish, and legs duller than ♂'s. Several similar ♀ thrushes can occur with Pale-eyed. ♀ Yellow-legged Thrush has yellow eye-ring and shows some throat streaking, ♀ Glossy-black is *more uniform brown below,* and ♀ Black-hooded has echo of ♂'s hooded pattern. Mainly arboreal, most often noted when ♂♂ are singing, as they then mount to tall treetops, often for long

periods. Song a series of variable (sometimes musical, more often squeaky) but usually short phrases with intervening pauses; mimicry is frequent, at least in some populations.

Yellow-legged Thrush

*Turdus flavipes**   PLATE 81(2)

22 cm (8½"). Locally common in montane forest, woodland, and adjacent clearings and plantations in *Andes of n. Venezuela and ne. Colombia,* on *tepuis of se. Venezuela,* and in *se. Brazil region.* Mostly 500–1500 m. *Yellow eye-ring;* ♂ with *bright yellow bill* (sometimes with some dusky) *and legs;* ♀ with *yellowish legs* and mainly dusky bill. In **most of range** (illustrated) ♂'s pied pattern of black *contrasting with gray back, rump, and belly* is unique. In **ne. Venezuela and Trinidad** has gray restricted to *flanks and crissum;* on **Tobago** *all black.* ♀ *dingy* and best known from its yellow eye-ring, *dusky throat streaking,* and *rather pale belly.* It especially resembles (and often occurs with) ♀ Black-hooded Thrush, which has yellower bill, a shadow of ♂'s dark hood, and more uniform tawny-buff below. ♀ Glossy-black Thrush is darker overall and has brownish legs. Mainly arboreal and often shy, though less tied to actual forest than Pale-eyed Thrush. Variable song, usually delivered from a perch at mid-levels, a series of phrases (some musical, others squeaky or metallic), each repeated several times before a pause and then on to a new one; at least in e. Brazil sometimes mimics other species.

Glossy-black Thrush

Turdus serranus   PLATE 81(3)

25 cm (9¾"). Often common in montane forest and borders in Andes from *n. Venezuela to nw. Argentina* (Salta). Mostly 1500–2800 m, lower in w. Colombia, w. Ecuador, and Argentina. ♂ *lustrous black* with yellow-orange bill and legs, orange eye-ring. ♀ *uniform rufescent brown (not* appreciably paler on belly except in Venezuela) with a yellowish brown bill, dull brownish legs, and orange-yellow eye-ring. In **ne. Venezuela,** ♀ *uniform sooty* with yellow bill. ♂ most likely confused with Great Thrush, especially where that species is very dark, but Great is obviously larger, never as deep black, and less forest-based. ♀ is more uniform, especially below, than the several similar thrushes that occur with it. Basically arboreal, rarely leaving forest cover, though sometimes at edge (even hopping on the ground) in the early morning. Song distinctive (though, for a *Turdus,* not very inspired), typically delivered

from a hidden perch, a tirelessly repeated fast phrase that usually rises, e.g., "tee-do-do-eét?"

Great Thrush
Turdus fuscater   PLATE 81(4)

33 cm (13″). *Widespread and often common, especially northward, in semiopen areas,* gardens, and borders of montane woodland and forest in *Andes from w. Venezuela* (s. Lara) *to w. Bolivia* (w. Santa Cruz). *Favors more open areas than many other montane thrushes,* and *considerably larger.* Mostly 1800–4000 m. Bill orange, legs orange-yellow, and *eye-ring bright yellow;* eyering *lacking* in ♀, but aside from this *not* sexually dimorphic. Marked geographic variation in color causes potential confusion with several other thrushes, especially the Chiguanco; **se. Peru** birds are the *blackest,* **Santa Marta Mts.** birds the palest (*olivaceous brown,* somewhat paler below). From **Colombia to cen. Peru** (illustrated) *essentially sooty;* in **Bolivia** olivaceous brown with a darker head (blackish on foreface), and ♂♂ have obvious blackish throat streaking. The smaller and shorter-tailed Chiguanco Thrush potentially overlaps from Ecuador south to w. Bolivia, though throughout this area it favors more arid terrain; *here Chiguanco never shows an orange or yellow eye-ring,* and in most of this range *Chiguanco is substantially paler* (but in Bolivia about the same overall color). Especially conspicuous and familiar in the n. Andes (where it doubtless has increased because of deforestation), the Great Thrush here often hops about on the ground in the open and is numerous even in many urban areas. Call notes (including a "keeyert!" and a "kurt!-kurt!") are loud and arresting, though its lilting song (given mostly in predawn darkness) is attractive but surprisingly weak.

Chiguanco Thrush
*Turdus chiguanco**   PLATE 81(5)

27–28 cm (10½–11″). Fairly common, mainly in more arid regions, in *Andes from n. Ecuador* (Cotopaxi) *to cen. Argentina* (La Pampa); favors semiopen and agricultural terrain, gardens. Mostly 1500–3500 m, a few down locally to coast in cen. and s. Peru; also in lowlands in cen. Argentina. Bill and legs yellow. Two very different types perhaps represent separate species. In **Ecuador to w. Bolivia and extreme n. Chile** (A) essentially *pale ashy brown.* From **Cochabamba, Bolivia, south into w. Argentina and adjacent Chile** (B) has *yellow eye-ring* (absent or barely evident in ♀) and is essentially *uni-*

form sooty (slightly browner in ♀, which also has duller bill). Cf. larger and longer-tailed Great Thrush, which favors more humid regions; ♂ has a prominent eye-ring, *lacking* in overlapping Chiguancos. In area of overlap Great is also substantially *darker.* The situation is more complex in w. Bolivia, where, aside from size, some birds cannot be safely differentiated. Generally familiar and conspicuous, often hopping on open ground. Song in Argentina a relatively brief and simple phrase repeated over and over, e.g., "teeo-weetee, cherrowee." Northward it is more mimidlike, a series of short phrases, each often repeated several times.

Austral Thrush
Turdus falcklandii   PLATE 81(6)

26 cm (10¼″). *Often common* in woodland and forest borders, clearings, and gardens from *cen. Chile* (Atacama) *and s. Argentina* (Río Negro) *to Tierra del Fuego.* Bill, legs, and eye-ring yellow. Olive brown above with *contrasting blackish head; throat sharply streaked blackish;* pale buffy brownish below. *Occurs farther south than any other Turdus.* Creamy-bellied Thrush overlaps along northern edge of range but lacks any blackish on head. Generally conspicuous and tame, often hopping on the ground in the open. Song a series of rich and musical phrases, the individual phrases often repeated several times.

Black-hooded Thrush
Turdus olivater   PLATE 81(7)

23.5 cm (9¼″). Uncommon and quite local in canopy and borders of montane forest and woodland and adjacent clearings in *Andes of n. Venezuela and adjacent Colombia,* and on *tepuis of s. Venezuela region.* Bill, legs, and eye-ring yellow (duller in ♀). ♂ has *distinctive contrasting black hood and chest;* above olive brown, below ochraceous. On **tepuis** has black on foreneck reduced to mottled streaking and a more rufescent belly. An isolated population in **Andes of sw. Colombia** (where *rare*) has *black only on head,* black streaking on throat, and *sandy buff underparts.* Much duller ♀ has hood dull brown (faint, but usually evident), *uniform dull ochraceous underparts.* The tricky ♀ resembles ♀ Yellow-legged Thrush, which has a paler median belly. Also resembles ♀ Glossy-black Thrush, though that is darker (especially below). Behavior much like many other montane and arboreal thrushes, though seems less shy. Song typical of the genus, a series of loud musical phrases usually delivered at a distinctively *slow pace.*

Chestnut-bellied Thrush

Turdus fulviventris   PLATE 81(8)

24 cm (9½"). Uncommon and local in borders and canopy of montane forest and woodland in *Andes from w. Venezuela* (Trujillo) *to n. Peru* (n. Cajamarca). 1400–2600 m. Bill yellow; eye-ring orange. *Black head contrasts with dark gray upperparts.* Breast gray, *belly bright orange-rufous.* ♀ slightly duskier on head. This handsome thrush is *the only Turdus in the n. Andes with a rufous belly.* Mainly arboreal, though it sometimes drops to the ground along roads and on trails. Song rather poor (and not often heard), a series of clipped phrases interspersed with a few short trills.

Rufous-bellied Thrush

Turdus rufiventris   PLATE 82(1)

24.5 cm (9¾"). *Widespread and often common in semiopen terrain, lighter woodland, and gardens from s. Bolivia* (Santa Cruz) *and ne. Brazil to n. Argentina* (n. Buenos Aires). Mostly below 1500 m, locally to 2500 m in Bolivia. A mostly brown thrush with contrasting *orange-rufous belly and crissum* (somewhat paler in ♀); throat white with dusky streaking. Though it regularly hops on the ground and often occurs around houses, only rarely emerges far from cover. Attractive and melodic song a fast rich caroling, usually given from a hidden perch and often early in the day, even before first light. Despite its rather ordinary appearance, this is the national bird of Brazil.

American Bare-eyed Thrush

Turdus nudigenis*   PLATE 82(2)

23 cm (9"). Widespread and generally common in lighter woodland, semiopen areas, and gardens from *ne. Colombia to the Guianas and e. Amaz. Brazil.* Mostly below 1000 m, locally to 1800 m in Venezuela. Formerly called Bare-eyed Thrush. *Wide yellow to dull orange ocular ring* unique among the American *Turdus* (many of which have *much narrower* eye-rings). Dull olivaceous brown, throat lightly streaked dusky and midbelly and crissum more whitish. Mainly arboreal, but also hops about on lawns and other open ground. Song a musical caroling similar to many of its congeners; call more distinctive, a nasal querulous "queeoww." Also: s. Lesser Antilles. The English name of Spectacled Thrush has recently been proposed for this species, but unfortunately too late to be used here.

Ecuadorian Thrush

Turdus maculirostris

23 cm (9"). Fairly common in forest, woodland, and clearings from *nw. Ecuador* (Esmeraldas) *to extreme nw. Peru* (Tumbes), mainly in more humid regions. Locally to 2200 m. Bill olive yellow; narrow yellow eye-ring. *Very dull and unpatterned,* with coloration much as in American Bare-eyed Thrush. Ecuadorian does not occur with any similar thrush; Pale-vented and ♀ Glossy-black and Pale-eyed Thrushes are all considerably darker brown. Mainly arboreal and relatively shy, in general not a familiar *Turdus.* Song and querulous call much as in American Bare-eyed.

Clay-colored Thrush

Turdus grayi

23 cm (9"). Fairly common in lighter woodland, clearings, and gardens in more humid lowlands of *n. Colombia.* Below 300 m. Bill olive yellow; no evident eye-ring. Dull olivaceous brown above, *uniform dull sandy to fulvous brown below* with throat only faintly streaked. No similar thrush occurs with it; Pale-breasted Thrush has a contrasting grayish head. Behavior and voice much as in American Bare-eyed Thrush. Also: Mexico to Panama.

Pale-breasted Thrush

Turdus leucomelas   PLATE 82(3)

23 cm (9"). *Widespread and often common* in forest borders, secondary woodland, and clearings and gardens (though avoiding humid forest) from n. and e. Colombia and Venezuela to e. Brazil and ne. Argentina. Mostly below 1500 m. Bill olive yellowish. Usually shows *distinctly contrasting gray head and nape,* but the gray is more washed out in some populations and individuals. Otherwise rufescent brown above and mostly pale grayish buff below. Most apt to be confused with Creamy-bellied Thrush (regularly with that species), though Pale-breasted lacks the dark lores and sharp throat streaking; Creamy-bellied head does *not* contrast. Behavior is typical of genus, regularly feeding on the ground in semiopen (especially early in the day); often anything but shy. Song a series of melodic phrases, usually delivered from a hidden perch and often hard to distinguish from its congeners; more distinctive is its guttural, usually trebled call, a fast "wert-wert-wert."

Creamy-bellied Thrush
Turdus amaurochalinus   PLATE 82(4)

23 cm (9"). *Common and widespread in lighter woodland and clearings from s. Bolivia* (Santa Cruz) *and s. Brazil to cen. Argentina* (Río Negro), in austral winter migrating north to s. Amazonia and ne. Brazil. To 2100 m in Bolivia, but mostly below 1500 m. ♂'s *bill bright yellow,* sometimes with dusky tip; mostly dusky in ♀. Olive brown above; below pale brownish gray, midbelly whiter. Can be known from the combination of *contrasting blackish lores* and *sharp black throat streaking. No similar thrush has the black on its lores;* Pale-breasted also has a grayer head and less bold throat streaking; Black-billed has dark bill, only vague throat streaking. *Habitually quivers its tail upon alighting* (some other thrushes do this occasionally, but not so often). Behavior otherwise similar to other nonforest *Turdus.* Song a typical *Turdus* caroling, but less forceful; call a sharp "pok."

Black-billed Thrush
Turdus ignobilis   PLATE 82(5)

22.5 cm (8¾"). *Locally common in w. and cen. Amazonia* (up to 1200 m); *also on lower Andean slopes of w. Colombia and w. Venezuela* (mostly 1000–2000 m), *and from s. Venezuela* (on tepuis to 2000 m) *to Suriname. Dingy overall, with blackish bill.* **W. Amazonian** birds have more prominent throat streaking, a white patch on upper chest, and more grayish breast. **Andean** birds have less distinct throat streaking, no white chest patch, and browner breast. Illustrated bird (from **Venezuela-Guianas**) is intermediate. Cf. other potentially sympatric dark-billed thrushes (e.g., White-necked, Hauxwell's, and ♀ Black-hooded). Favors semiopen areas and clearings, forest and woodland borders; especially numerous and conspicuous in w. Colombia. Song a series of pleasant musical phrases, often delivered rather softly.

Unicolored Thrush
Turdus haplochrous

23 cm (9"). *Apparently rare in a very limited range in n. Bolivia* (s. Beni and n. Santa Cruz). Little known, with uncertain status; a few recent reports from semideciduous woodland and várzea forest. 200–400 m. *Dull and patternless.* Bill olive-yellow; narrow eye-ring dull orange. Olivaceous brown above; uniform sandy brown below, throat lightly streaked brown. The sympatric Hauxwell's Thrush is more rufescent brown

above and less sandy below; it usually shows at least some white on its lower underparts and has a dark bill and no noticeable eye-ring. Leisurely melodic song reportedly resembles Hauxwell's (C. G. Schmitt).

White-necked Thrush
Turdus albicollis   PLATE 82(6)

21.5–23 cm (8½–9"). *Fairly common and widespread in undergrowth of humid forest and secondary woodland from Colombia and Venezuela to Amazonia, and in se. Brazil region.* Below 1500 m. *Yellow eye-ring. Above deep brown; conspicuous white crescent below the thick dusky streaking on throat; breast and sides pale gray.* Bill blackish in **most of range** (A), but mostly yellow in birds of **se. Brazil region** (B), which also are larger and have *extensive rufous on flanks.* The more arboreal Eastern Slaty Thrush also shows a prominent white crescent on chest, but it is much grayer on flanks, and ♂ is also grayer above. This reclusive thrush, though often numerous, is heard much more often than seen; in some areas can be seen hopping at edge or on shady roads. Song varies little across its wide range, a melodic but rather monotonous series of short musical phrases, often given through heat of day but most frequent in late afternoon, always hard to track to its source.

Dagua Thrush
*Turdus daguae**

21.5 cm (8½"). Locally fairly common in humid forest and borders in w. Colombia and w. Ecuador (south locally to Guayas). To 900 m. *Bill mostly black;* eye-ring yellow. Formerly considered conspecific with White-throated Thrush (*T. assimilis*) of Middle America, but more resembles typical White-necked Thrush (found *east* of the Andes; no overlap). Differs in its *dull brown breast and flanks* (no gray tone). *No other thrush in its limited range shows such a conspicuous white crescent across upper chest.* Behavior much as in White-necked, but seems more arboreal. Song a long-continued musical caroling with monotonous effect similar to White-necked. A common call is an excited, repeated "queeyrp." Also: e. Panama.

Hauxwell's Thrush
Turdus hauxwelli   PLATE 82(7)

23 cm (9"). Uncommon in lower and middle levels of humid forest *(especially várzea)* in w. Amazonia. *Occurs west of Cocoa Thrush's range, with*

544   THRUSHES

at most limited overlap. Below 800 m. Bill dark gray to brown. *Mostly warm brown* with *midbelly and crissum white* (usually contrasting, but this area is sometimes washed with buff). Very similar Cocoa is slightly more rufescent overall and usually much buffier on belly and crissum. ♀ Lawrence's Thrush has narrow yellow eye-ring and is darker and more grayish brown above and somewhat dingier brown below. Black-billed Thrush is more olivaceous brown generally, shows more streaking on throat, and (in area of overlap) a whitish chest patch. Inconspicuous, shy, and infrequently seen. Song a leisurely, protracted series of simple but melodic phrases; at least some individuals incorporate imitations of other birds but not with the frequency or fidelity of Lawrence's.

Pale-vented Thrush
Turdus obsoletus
23 cm (9"). *Uncommon and local in lower and middle levels of montane forest in foothills of w. Colombia, w. Ecuador, and extreme nw. Peru* (recently found in Tumbes). Mostly 500–1500 m. Closely resembles Hauxwell's Thrush (only *east of Andes*) but slightly duller and darker brown above, and *crissum pure white*. Black-billed Thrush is more olivaceous brown, shows more throat streaking, is not found in forest. Ecuadorian Thrush likewise is usually in semiopen areas, and is considerably paler and more olivaceous brown. Essentially arboreal, usually shy and hard to see. Song a fairly fast and melodic caroling usually delivered from a hidden perch in the subcanopy. Also: Costa Rica and Panama.

Lawrence's Thrush
Turdus lawrencii   PLATE 82(8)
23 cm (9"). *Uncommon in canopy and borders of humid forest in w. and cen. Amazonia.* Below 400 m. ♂ has *bright orange-yellow bill and eye-ring*, bill blackish and yellow eye-ring narrower in ♀. Dark brown above; below somewhat warmer brown, with whitish throat streaked blackish. Hauxwell's Thrush has dark bill, is a warmer and more rufescent brown, never shows an eye-ring. Though occasionally dropping to moist ground when feeding, usually remains well above the ground, where hard to see; even singing ♂♂ are frustratingly difficult to locate. Song a long-continued series of near-perfect imitations of usually short portions of the songs and calls of other birds, ranging from tinamous, parrots, and toucans to antbirds and grosbeaks; a few phrases of its own are often also included,

and it sometimes starts by repeating a phrase that sounds like an Andean Solitaire.

Cocoa Thrush
Turdus fumigatus   PLATE 82(9)
23 cm (9"). Uncommon in lower and middle levels of humid forest, borders, and adjacent clearings from *e. Colombia and Venezuela to e. Amazonia,* and in *e. Brazil.* Mostly below 1000 m. Closely resembles Hauxwell's Thrush (some birds are hard to distinguish) but *warmer and more rufescent brown generally* (especially across breast), and typically with *hardly contrasting buff median belly and crissum* (but sometimes more whitish, then very hard to separate). *Favors areas near water.* Generally shy and not often seen, though seems tamer and more conspicuous on Trinidad. Song a rich and loud series of musical phrases and notes, not too different from many congeners. Also: s. Lesser Antilles.

Andean Slaty Thrush
Turdus nigriceps   PLATE 82(10)
21.5 cm (8½"). *Fairly common breeder in montane forest and woodland on east slope of Andes from w. Bolivia* (Cochabamba and s. Beni) *to nw. Argentina* (La Rioja and n. Córdoba), in austral winter migrating north to e. Peru; also breeds locally in montane woodland and even scrub from *sw. Ecuador* (mainly Loja) *to nw. Peru* (n. Cajamarca and Lambayeque). Mostly 500–2000 m. ♂ has bill, legs, and eye-ring yellow; ♀'s bill blackish and legs more brownish. ♂ *mostly dark gray above,* blacker on crown. Somewhat *paler gray below,* white throat sharply streaked blackish. ♀ basically brown where ♂ is gray, though some gray shows on sides and flanks. The gray ♂ is distinctive in range (no overlap with Eastern Slaty), but ♀ can be confusing. It lacks the white crescent on foreneck of White-necked Thrush and is browner across breast; potentially sympatric Black-billed Thrush lacks the eye-ring and its throat streaking is less sharp. Arboreal, shy and often difficult to see even when singing. Song a series of rather high, jumbled phrases, some notes high-pitched and even shrill.

Eastern Slaty Thrush
Turdus subalaris   PLATE 82(11)
21.5 cm (8½"). Uncommon breeder in humid forest and woodland (often in *Araucaria*), also in parklike areas and plantations, in *se. Brazil region* (north to Paraná), in austral winter migrating north to woodland in cen. Brazil. To 1000 m. Both sexes resemble Andean Slaty Thrush. ♂

paler gray above, sometimes washed with olive and with concolor crown; as with Andean Slaty, shows a *prominent white crescent across upper chest*. ♀ bill yellowish brown (not blackish); also shows the *white chest crescent*. Sympatric White-necked Thrush also has a white chest crescent, but its flanks are obviously rufous. Behavior much as in Andean Slaty, but in general not quite so wary. Song rather weak, a series of brief bursts of high-pitched notes, somewhat squeaky.

Cedar Waxwing (*Bombycilla cedrorum,* in the Wax-wing family, Bombycillidae) has been recorded as a vagrant in w. Colombia and w. Venezuela.

DIPPERS: CINCLIDAE

The dippers form a distinctive group of uniquely aquatic passerine birds found along swiftly flowing streams and rivers in the Andes. They are chunky birds whose large feet, dense plumage, and well-developed nictitating membrane are clearly adaptations to this habitat. Their domed nests are large and mossy, placed in rock crevices or under bridges.

Cinclus

Unmistakable, *chunky* birds, dippers *range strictly along rocky streams and rivers.* Our two species range in the Andes where they perch on boulders along or out in the rushing torrent, often bobbing up and down. Flight is fast and low over the water, the wings flapping furiously. The two South American dippers feed by picking at insects along the water's edge; unlike dippers elsewhere, neither seems to walk or swim underwater. Both species often flick their wings.

birds are less contrastingly patterned, the dark areas being paler. From **Venezuela to Ecuador and in adjacent Peru** rather different, with *underparts mainly whitish* and a *large white patch on midback.* Call a sharp "dzeet," often given in flight, loud enough to be heard over the sound of rushing water. Song a "prolonged loud trill" (S. Hilty), rarely heard.

Not known to occur south of w. Panama, sightings of what appeared to be American Dipper (*C. mexicanus*) in the n. Venezuela mountains have yet to be confirmed.

White-capped Dipper
Cinclus leucocephalus   PLATE 83(1)

15.5 cm (6"). Widespread and locally not uncommon along rocky streams and rivers in Andes from w. *Venezuela* (Trujillo) *to w. Bolivia* (w. Santa Cruz). Mostly 1000–3400 m, locally lower (to 500–700 m) where suitable habitat extends down the mountains. In **Peru and Bolivia** (illustrated) sooty black with *contrasting white crown and large white bib;* **Santa Marta Mts.**

Rufous-throated Dipper
Cinclus schulzi   PLATE 83(2)

15.5 cm (6"). Uncommon and local on *east slope of Andes from extreme s. Bolivia* (Tarija) *to nw. Argentina* (Tucumán). Mostly 1000–2500 m. *Uniform dark leaden gray* with a *pale rufous throat patch;* a *white patch on primaries* is conspicuous in flight and also can be seen as the bird flicks its wings.

MOCKINGBIRDS AND THRASHERS: MIMIDAE

Slender, somewhat thrushlike birds with long tails that range in semiopen habitats, mainly in s. South America (where no thrashers occur); a few are austral migrants. Some mockingbirds are well known for their complex songs, songs that can include near-perfect mimicry. Nests are open cups placed in shrubbery.

Mimus

Slender and *long-tailed,* mockingbirds usually have a *bold white pattern on wings and tail.* They are conspicuous in the semiopen areas where they occur, reaching their highest diversity in s. South America. All species have yellow to orange irides.

Tropical Mockingbird
Mimus gilvus   PLATE 83(3)
24 cm (9½"). *Locally common in semiopen terrain, gardens, and coastal scrub from Colombia, Venezuela, and the Guianas south mainly near coast to se. Brazil* (Rio de Janeiro); *especially numerous in arid regions.* Mostly below 1500 m, but to 2500 m in Andes of Colombia and n. Ecuador. *The only mockingbird in n. South America. Pale gray above;* wings blackish with white feather edges and two narrow bars; tail blackish, *outer feathers broadly tipped white. Superciliary and underparts white.* Chalk-browed Mockingbird is browner and more mottled above, and has a wider superciliary; the two species overlap locally in e. Brazil. Conspicuous, perching atop shrubs and cactus (also often on wires) and hopping on the ground with tail raised, often lifting and partially spreading wings. Song a series of phrases, most of them musical, each often repeated a few times and interspersed with various clucking or wheezy notes; usually does not mimic other birds. Also: Mexico to Panama; Lesser Antilles.

Chalk-browed Mockingbird
Mimus saturninus   PLATE 83(4)
26 cm (10¼"). *Widespread and common* in semiopen areas and around buildings from n. and e. Bolivia (west to Beni) and lower Amaz. and e. Brazil to cen. Argentina (Río Negro). Mostly below 1500 m, locally higher in open areas. Grayish brown above with *darker mottling,* a broad *chalky white superciliary,* and blackish eyestripe; broad white tail corners. Mostly whitish below. Dust-bathing can make some birds look more rufescent, especially on underparts. Tropical Mockingbird is grayer and looks "smoother" above. Cf. Patagonian Mockingbird, which replaces Chalk-browed southward. White-banded Mockingbird has more white in wings, all-white outer tail feathers. Bold and conspicuous, often seen hopping about on the ground with tail raised; the tail is characteristically thrown forward as the bird alights. Song, usually delivered from a prominent perch, varies in form and content and has little pattern; it engages in only limited mimicry. A sharp "chert" call is heard frequently.

Long-tailed Mockingbird
Mimus longicaudatus   PLATE 83(5)
29.5 cm (11½"). *Common in desert scrub, low woodland, and agricultural areas from arid sw. Ecuador* (Manabí) *to sw. Peru* (Arequipa). *The only mockingbird found in this area, making recognition easy. Avoids* humid regions. Up to 2000 m or more in arid intermontane valleys. Brownish gray above with a *complex blackish and white facial pattern; very long tail* shows *large white corners in flight.* White below with dusky scaling on breast. Conspicuous, often perching on top of shrubs, low trees, and cacti, and hopping on the ground with its long tail held high; remains active even during midday heat. Flight slow and labored, interspersed with long glides, seeming to hold tail loosely (like an ani, *Crotophaga* spp.). Frequently heard song an often lengthy series of chuckling or gurgling notes with little discernible pattern; limited or no mimicry.

White-banded Mockingbird
Mimus triurus PLATE 83(6)
23.5 cm (9¼"). Fairly common and conspicuous in scrub and shrubby areas, low chaco woodland, and (especially during winter) semiopen and agricultural areas from cen. *Argentina (Río Negro) north into n. Bolivia*. Now known to breed in Bolivia and perhaps w. Paraguay, but numbers definitely increase there during austral winter. Mostly below 500 m, a few higher in Bolivia during winter. The handsomest mockingbird, with *bold white on inner flight feathers* (prominent in flight, showing as a block on rearwing; evident even at rest). Above grayish brown with long white superciliary and *rufescent rump*; tail black, *outer feathers white* (most obvious in flight). Mostly whitish below. Cf. Brown-backed Mockingbird (only on Andean slopes). Chalk-browed and Patagonian Mockingbirds have *much less white on wings and tail*. Behavior much like other mockingbirds. Song a lengthy but rather leisurely stream of pure melodic notes intermixed with imitations of the songs of other birds.

Brown-backed Mockingbird
Mimus dorsalis PLATE 83(7)
25.5 cm (10"). Fairly common in montane scrub (often where tall cacti are prevalent) and agricultural areas in *Andes from w. Bolivia* (La Paz) *to nw. Argentina* (Salta). Mostly 2300–3500 m. A high-elevation replacement for the smaller White-banded Mockingbird, which it resembles. *More uniformly rufescent brown above* (lacking White-banded's gray tone on crown and back), with *white on wings restricted to primary coverts and base of primaries* (showing in flight only as a white patch on front of wing); *outer tail feathers all-white* (as in White-banded). Chalk-browed and Patagonian Mockingbirds *lack any solid white patch on wing* and *show much less white in tail* (restricted to corners). Behavior much as in White-banded, but song not as strong or varied.

Patagonian Mockingbird
Mimus patagonicus PLATE 83(8)
25 cm (9¾"). Locally common in shrubby areas and Patagonian scrub in *w. and s. Argentina* (Jujuy to Santa Cruz) *and adjacent s. Chile*; during austral winter some migrate north and a few straggle to cen. Chile. To 3000 m in arid intermontane valleys of nw. Argentina. Resembles somewhat larger and longer-tailed Chalk-browed Mockingbird but has a *less prominent superciliary, more uniform grayish mantle* (little or no mottling), *distinct grayish wash across breast,* and *buffier belly.* Chilean Mockingbird is larger and has a longer tail, with a prominent blackish malar streak and flank streaking. Though conspicuous, often perching in the open atop bushes, it is less familiar than Chalk-browed and generally shuns the vicinity of habitations. Song as in Chalk-browed but not as loud or forceful; there is some mimicry.

Chilean Mockingbird
Mimus thenca PLATE 83(9)
27 cm (10½"). *Matorral scrub (especially) and agricultural areas in cen. Chile* (Atacama to Valdivia), where *common and the only mockingbird normally present* (Patagonian and White-banded Mockingbirds occur only as vagrants in Chile). To 2200 m. A *coarse-looking* mockingbird, dull brown above with a *fairly prominent but mottled blackish malar stripe* and a white brow; tail blackish, feathers narrowly tipped white. *Dull buffyish below* with *distinct blackish streaking on flanks.* The smaller and shorter-tailed Patagonian is grayer above, lacks the obvious malar, and has more prominent white wing markings. Conspicuous behavior much as in other mockingbirds. Long-continued song consists of many phrases, each of them repeated multiple times and interspersed with chuckles and gurgles; limited mimicry.

Pearly-eyed Thrasher
Margarops fuscatus
27 cm (10½"). *Occurs only on Bonaire, where uncommon in arid scrub and low woodland;* a vagrant to Curaçao. Apparently now extinct on La Horquilla Island off ne. Venezuela, an inexplicable disappearance. A coarse-looking, long-tailed mimid with a *milky white iris* and *heavy bill mostly yellowish flesh. Brown above;* whitish below *streaked and mottled with brown;* outer tail feathers *tipped white.* Rather skulking, but at least elsewhere also aggressive and omnivorous. A variety of harsh calls, and a more pleasant thrushlike song. Also: Lesser Antilles to Puerto Rico and s. Bahamas.

Brown Thrasher (*Toxostoma rufum*) has been recorded as a vagrant on Curaçao.

Gray Catbird (*Dumetella carolinensis*) has been recorded as a boreal migrant on a few occasions in the lowlands of n. Colombia.

GNATCATCHERS AND GNATWRENS: POLIOPTILIDAE

Small, spritely birds found in forest and woodland, formerly the gnatcatchers and gnatwrens were usually considered to be part of a very large, mainly Old World–inhabiting family, the Sylviidae. They are now classified in their own family. Nests are open cups.

Microbates and *Ramphocaenus*

Distinctive small, wrenlike birds of woodland and forest undergrowth, sometimes with understory flocks. Gnatwren bills are *long and slender. Tails are usually cocked, constantly flipped about animatedly, and often held at odd angles.*

Tawny-faced Gnatwren
Microbates cinereiventris　　　　PLATE 84(1)
10.5 cm (4″). Uncommon and somewhat local in undergrowth of humid forest from *Colombia to nw. Bolivia* (La Paz). Mostly below 1000 m. *Short tail.* Dark brown above with *bright tawny sides of head and neck.* Throat white bordered by a black malar streak; *partial collar of black streaks across chest; below mostly gray.* **West of Andes** (illustrated) has a blackish postocular streak lacking in birds **east of Andes.** Long-billed Gnatwren has both a longer bill and a longer tail, also notably paler underparts with *no* streaking. Forages mostly in pairs, hopping restlessly in dark and often heavy undergrowth; regularly accompanies understory flocks. Foraging birds keep up a nasal "nyaar" and various scolding notes; heard less often is a clearer "peeu" given at intervals of 2–4-seconds, recalling Tawny-crowned Greenlet. Also: Nicaragua to Panama.

Collared Gnatwren
Microbates collaris　　　　PLATE 84(2)
10.5 cm (4″). Rare to uncommon in undergrowth of humid forest in *n. Amazonia from se. Colombia to the Guianas,* somewhat more numerous eastward. To 900 m in Venezuela. *Short tail.* Distinctive; complex facial pattern with *white superciliary and face crossed by black postocular line, bordered below by a black malar stripe;* brown above. *White below with a broad black pectoral band* (the "collar"), flanks grayish. Behavior much as in Tawny-faced Gnatwren. In addition to scolding notes, infrequently heard song consists of a series of soft thin notes repeated steadily at intervals of 3–4 seconds, similar to Tawny-faced (and likewise recalling Tawny-crowned Greenlet).

Long-billed Gnatwren
Ramphocaenus melanurus　　　　PLATE 84(3)
12 cm (4¾″). *Fairly common and widespread* in lower growth of humid and deciduous forest and woodland from Colombia and Venezuela to Amazonia, and in e. Brazil. To about 1500 m. Perhaps more than one species. *Very long, slender bill; long, slim tail.* **East of Andes** (illustrated) brown above, face more rufescent; tail black, all but central feathers tipped white. Whitish to pale grayish below. **West of Andes** has grayer back, more cinnamon-buff underparts and cheeks, and broader tail-tipping. On **eastern tepuis** lacks tail-tipping. Tawny-faced and Collared Gnatwrens have stubbier tails and shorter bills, and differ markedly in plumage pattern. Cf. also Long-billed Wren. Favors the vine tangles often found at borders and around openings such as treefalls. Usually in pairs, hopping actively through dense growth, flipping and wriggling its tail around; sometimes accompanies mixed flocks but at least as often forages apart from them. Typically ranges higher above the ground than *Microbates.* Song a distinctive, clear musical trill, often preceded by a few "cht" notes; west of Andes tends to be markedly faster and to rise in pitch. Also: Mexico to Panama.

Polioptila

An attractive group of very small, slender, *mainly gray* birds with hyperactive behavior. Their *long narrow tails are often held cocked.*

550 GNATCATCHERS AND GNATWRENS

Gnatcatchers range in a variety of forested and wooded habitats, with three species (Tropical, Marañón, and Masked) wholly or in part in scrubbier situations; Slate-throated and members of the Guianan complex are less numerous and entirely restricted to humid forest canopy.

Tropical Gnatcatcher
Polioptila plumbea   PLATE 84(4)

10.5 (4″). *Widespread and often common* in a variety of habitats, ranging from canopy of humid forest to arid scrub and mangroves, from Colombia and Venezuela to Amazonia and ne. Brazil. Mostly below 1500 m. Even after the Marañón Gnatcatcher has been split off, more than one species is almost certainly involved. **East of Andes** (illustrated) *bluish gray above,* ♂ with *contrasting glossy black crown;* wings and tail black, inner flight feathers edged white, outer tail feathers white. White to very pale gray below. From **n. and w. Colombia to nw. Peru** (Lima) both sexes have *white extending up onto face, encompassing the eyes.* ♀ in **ne. Brazil** has a black streak on ear-coverts. Cf. other scarcer and more range-restricted gnatcatchers. Usually ranges in pairs and forages at varying heights, gleaning actively and often twitching usually cocked tail; regularly with mixed flocks. Song west of Andes a simple series of high thin "weet" notes, dropping in pitch toward end or ending in a twitter; in much of Venezuela a whistled "swee-swee-swee-swee-swee-swee"; in w. Amazonia very different, a stronger and faster "chichichichichichichi." Throughout often gives a nasal "nyeeah" call. Also: Mexico to Panama.

Marañón Gnatcatcher
Polioptila maior*

11.5 cm (4½″). Fairly common in arid scrub and woodland borders in *upper Río Marañón valley in nw. Peru* (Cajamarca to Ancash). About 500–2500 m. Formerly considered conspecific with Tropical Gnatcatcher, but appreciably *larger.* ♂ has more white edging on inner flight feathers than ♂ Tropical, as well as an additional outer pair of white feathers in tail. ♀ is *black-crowned* like ♂, but has a small white supraloral and broken eye-ring. Does not occur with Tropical. Behavior much as in Tropical, often equally bold. Song, very different, seems to consist merely of various scolding and mewing notes.

Creamy-bellied Gnatcatcher
Polioptila lactea   PLATE 84(5)

11 cm (4¼″). Rare to uncommon and local in canopy and borders of humid forest in *se. Brazil region; now apparently mainly or entirely confined to e. Paraguay and adjacent Brazil and Argentina.* Below 400 m. Resembles geographically distant Tropical Gnatcatcher of the trans-Andean *white-faced* type, but both sexes are *distinctly creamy yellowish below* (not grayish white). As in Tropical, ♂ has a *black crown.* Behavior much as in Tropical, though more arboreal, rarely leaving forest canopy. Song a simple, fast repetition of a high thin "weet" note, similar to trans-Andean Tropicals.

Guianan Gnatcatcher
Polioptila guianensis   PLATE 84(6)

11 cm (4¼″). Uncommon and seemingly local in canopy and borders of terra firme forest from the *Guianas to n. Amaz. Brazil.* To 300 m. Recently split; cf. the following three species. ♂ *bluish gray* with narrow white eye-ring, whitish throat, and white belly; wings and tail black, outer tail feathers white. ♀ facial area slightly paler. ♀ Tropical Gnatcatcher (limited overlap at most) is whiter below (not so gray on breast), shows more contrast between gray crown and white face, and has white (not gray) edging to inner flight feathers. Cf. also the other gnatcatchers in the "Guianan complex," none of them sympatric with this species. Infrequently seen as it tends to remain well above the ground in forest canopy; pairs often move with mixed flocks of tanagers and other insectivorous birds. The rather weak song is a fast repetition of 5–8 high-pitched "see" notes.

Pará Gnatcatcher
Polioptila paraensis*

11 cm (4¼″). Rare and local in canopy and borders of humid forest in *s. Amaz. Brazil.* To about 400 m. Only recently recognized as a full species. Closely resembles Guianan Gnatcatcher but overall color a paler bluish gray. Behavior and voice similar.

Rio Negro Gnatcatcher
Polioptila facilis*

11 cm (4¼″). Uncommon in canopy and borders of humid forest in *sw. Venezuela* (s. Amazonas) *and extreme nw. Brazil.* To about 200 m. Only recently recognized as a full species. Closely resembles Guianan Gnatcatcher but *lacks* narrow

white eye-ring and has less white in tail. Behavior and voice much as in Guianan, though song typically has more notes (10–15) and slightly higher pitch.

Iquitos Gnatcatcher
*Polioptila clementsi**

11 cm (4¼"). *Rare and very local in canopy of varillal forest growing on white-sand soil in ne. Peru* (known only from Loreto in Allpahuayo-Mishana Natl. Reserve west of Iquitos). 150 m. A recently described species. Closely resembles geographically distant Guianan Gnatcatcher, but has uniform pale gray throat and breast (throat not whiter). General behavior similar to Guianan. Song faster paced, starts with 3 slower and sharper notes.

Slate-throated Gnatcatcher
Polioptila schistaceigula

11 cm (4¼"). Uncommon and local in canopy and borders of humid forest in *w. Colombia and nw. Ecuador* (south to w. Pichincha). To 1000 m. *Slaty* with a narrow but bold white eyering and *contrasting white belly;* tail with outer feathers *only very narrowly fringed and tipped white* (not all white, as in other gnatcatchers). ♀ slightly paler, especially on foreneck. Tropical Gnatcatcher, which can occur with it, is much paler gray. Behavior as in Guianan Gnatcatcher, likewise seen singly or in pairs, usually as it accompanies a mixed flock well above the ground. A canopy inhabitant, may not be rare so much as it is inconspicuous. Call a faint, short, ascending trill, "trrrrrrt?" Infrequently heard song an emphatic "tsee-tsee-tsee-tsee-tsee-tsee-tsee-tsee." Also: e. Panama.

Masked Gnatcatcher
Polioptila dumicola   PLATE 84(7)

12.5 cm (5"). Locally fairly common in lighter woodland and scrub, including chaco and gallery woodland and monte, from *nw. Bolivia* (Beni) *and interior cen. Brazil to n. Argentina* (n. Buenos Aires). To 2800 m in Bolivia. ♂ from **southern part of range** (north to Cochabamba, Bolivia, and sw. Mato Grosso do Sul, Brazil; A) *bluish gray above* with *wide black mask* bordered below by a white line; wings and tail black, inner flight feathers edged white, outer tail feathers white. ♀ has *black on face reduced to a narrow black stripe on ear-coverts.* Below slightly paler gray, belly whitish. In **northern part of range** (B) **both sexes** paler gray above and *whiter below;* ♂ has *narrower black mask.* A natty little bird that usually forages in lower growth and often accompanies small mixed flocks; general behavior much like other gnatcatchers, though less arboreal than many and never in actual forest. Song sweet and musical, typically a few short notes, sometimes several repetitions of the same lilting phrase, then on to another.

PIPITS AND WAGTAILS: MOTACILLIDAE

A handful of pipits are found in South America, mainly in the southern part of the continent; the family is far more diverse in the Old World, where all the wagtails are found. Pipits range in grasslands and are terrestrial and usually inconspicuous (though males engage in flight songs); they are slender, brownish, and streaky. Identification, particularly of nonsinging birds, can be difficult. Nests are hidden on the ground.

Anthus

Slim, brown, and streaked, pipits are *terrestrial in grasslands,* occurring in *both the lowlands (mainly southward) and in the Andes.* Often cryptic, crouching motionless before flushing, they are also often seen *walking* (not hopping) on their long pinkish legs; they have a notably long claw on the hindtoe (the hallux). Pipits have *slender bills* and *notched tails* with *pale outer feathers* (whiter in fresh plumage, duller when worn). Unlike pipits elsewhere, Neotropical species seem rarely or never to gather in flocks, even during their nonbreeding season. Identification to species level often presents a challenge, though singing birds are easier.

Yellowish Pipit
Anthus lutescens   PLATE 84(8)
13 cm (5″). *Widespread and locally fairly common in lowland grasslands* from Colombia and Venezuela to n. Argentina (Mendoza and Buenos Aires), but absent from most of Amazonia. To 1300 m in s. Venezuela. *Small.* Above brown streaked buff and blackish; tail dusky, outer feathers white. *Buffy yellowish below* (whiter in worn plumage) with dark streaking on chest. *The only pipit in most of its range.* Except for the range-restricted Campo Pipit, it also is markedly the smallest. Cf. the rare Ochre-breasted Pipit. Favors areas with short grass. Singing ♂♂ give a series of "tzit" or "tizit" notes as they gradually ascend some 10–20 m up, then a long slurred "dzeeeeeeeeeeeu" as they glide back to the ground; a shorter version is sometimes given when perched. Also: Panama.

White Wagtail (*Motacilla alba*) has been seen once recently on Trinidad.

Campo Pipit
Anthus chacoensis*
13 cm (5″). Uncommon and local in pastures with taller grass, also wheat fields, in *e. Argentina* (south to s. Buenos Aires) *and s. Paraguay.* Perhaps more overlooked than actually scarce; may have somewhat larger range. Below 300 m. Formerly called Chaco Pipit (though does not occur in the chaco!). *Very* similar to Yellowish Pipit, probably not safely distinguished by plumage in the field. *Best identified by ♂'s characteristic song* (utterly different from Yellowish but somewhat like Short-billed), a series of pretty canarylike warbled notes, "tritritritretretretretretrutrutru-tru" given as the bird flies high above its territory, sometimes so high as to be invisible from the ground. Singing birds may remain "on station" for over an hour (R. Straneck).

Ochre-breasted Pipit
Anthus nattereri   PLATE 84(9)
14.5 cm (5¾″). *Now rare and local in less-disturbed campos in se. Brazil* (north to s. Minas Gerais), *se. Paraguay, and ne. Argentina* (mainly Corrientes). To at least 1300 m. *Above boldly streaked blackish and golden ochre;* tail dusky with outer feathers white. Throat whitish, *breast rich golden ochre with quite heavy black streaking,* belly whitish. An attractive pipit, most apt to be confused with the far commoner Yellowish, which is smaller and much less richly colored. Most often noted when singing. In a relatively brief display, ♂ mounts some 20–25 m up into the air while giving a complex and musical song that terminates with a slurred "eeeeeeeur" as it drops back to the ground.

Short-billed Pipit
Anthus furcatus   PLATE 84(10)
14.5 cm (5¾″). Locally fairly common in well-

drained pastures and fields with relatively short grass from *s. Paraguay and extreme se. Brazil* (Rio Grande do Sul) *to cen. Argentina* (n. Chubut); also uncommon in puna grassland in *Andes from cen. Peru* (Huánuco) *to nw. Argentina* (Tucumán). To 4000 m in Andes. Bill slightly shorter than in other pipits (but this is of marginal value as a field character). Best distinguished by its *relatively unstreaked pattern across back* (which often looks mottled or even scaly) and *usually bold and coarse breast streaking* that does not extend down flanks (which are whitish, like belly). Also shows a *fairly prominent black malar streak.* Hellmayr's is the most similar pipit, but it has a more streaked back, finer breast streaking, usually some streaking down flanks, and no malar streak. Displaying ♂ repeats a musical phrase (e.g., "cheep, chip-chip-cheeeeyr, chir-chir-chir-chir-chir") as it flies high over its territory, hovering and briefly gliding; the display can continue for an hour or more.

Hellmayr's Pipit
Anthus hellmayri   PLATE 84(11)

14.5 cm (5¾"). Uncommon to fairly common but local in grassland, especially on well-drained and often rocky slopes, in *Andes from s. Peru* (Puno) *to s. Argentina* (w. Santa Cruz); also from *se. Brazil* (Espírito Santo) *to e. Argentina* (Buenos Aires). To 2200 m in se. Brazil, to 3700 m in Andes. Note *band of quite fine blackish streaking (sometimes sparse) across breast, with a little streaking extending down flanks as well.* Fairly prominent back streaking. Cf. similar Short-billed Pipit. Paramo Pipit shows less breast streaking than even a worn-plumaged Hellmayr's, and Paramo never shows *any* on its flanks. Correndera Pipit is more coarsely streaked on breast and flanks and more boldly streaked above, with a distinctive pair of wide pale stripes down either side of back. ♂ song a usually *short,* "tsee-ee-ee-chu-ti-ti-chuduwee," given both in a display flight (generally not very high) and from perches such as fence posts.

Correndera Pipit
Anthus correndera   PLATE 84(12)

15 cm (6"). *Locally common in lusher grasslands from extreme se. Brazil* (Rio Grande do Sul) *and*

n. Argentina to Tierra del Fuego; also in *Andes north to cen. Peru* (Lima and Junín), where scarcer and more local. To 4400 m in Andes. *The most coarsely and boldly marked South American pipit. Above boldly streaked blackish and buff,* with an *often prominent pair of whitish stripes down either side of back.* Has bold black spotting across breast, *extending down flanks as obvious coarse streaking;* a blackish submalar streak is also usually prominent. Singing ♂♂ are conspicuous during breeding season when they mount into the air, hovering into the wind, and repeat a pleasant, musical "glishawa-glishawa, gleweeeer . . . glishawa-glishawa, gleweeeer, . . ." with some variation but usually a distinctive drawled final note (Short-billed's drawled note is in the *middle* of its song phrase). When singing, their abundance on the Buenos Aires pampas is apparent; also common in cen. Chile.

The similar though larger (16.5 cm, 6½") and even more heavily streaked South Georgia Pipit (*A. antarcticus*) is endemic to tussock grasslands of South Georgia Island, where it now ranges only on less disturbed (rat-free) islets off the main island itself.

Paramo Pipit
Anthus bogotensis   PLATE 84(13)

15 cm (6"). Uncommon in paramo and puna grasslands and pastures in *Andes from w. Venezuela* (Trujillo) *to nw. Argentina* (Tucumán). *The only pipit in the Andes north of cen. Peru;* rarer and more local southward, especially in nw. Argentina. 2500–4500 m. Above boldly streaked ochraceous and blackish; tail dusky with outer feathers whitish to dull buff. *Below dull buff* (paler and grayer in worn plumage) with *only a little dusky streaking or spotting across chest. Paramo is the least marked pipit below;* some Hellmayr's are almost as plain, but they also show at least some streaking on flanks. Displaying ♂♂ often sing while perched, sometimes also in a low display flight; song reminiscent of Correndera Pipit, though the slurred note typically comes first.

LARKS: ALAUDIDAE

The sole member of this family in South America is the Horned Lark, which has an outpost from its mainly Holarctic range in the Andes of n. Colombia.

Horned Lark

Eremophila alpestris   PLATE 84(14)

15 cm (6″). Mainly *terrestrial* in pastures with *short, sparse grass* and fields in *Andes of ne. Colombia* (Boyacá and Cundinamarca). This isolated population of a species widespread elsewhere is *now quite small* (F. G. Stiles); it continues to decline. 2500–3000 m. *Unmistakable and complex facial pattern of black and pale yellowish* (more obscure in ♀♀ and immatures); *prominent black chest band; outer web on outer pair of tail feathers white.* Otherwise basically brown above and whitish below. Feeds on the ground, in nonbreeding season sometimes gathering in small groups. Has a weak but distinctive tinkling song, often given by ♂ in a display flight. Also: North America to Mexico; Eurasia.

VIREOS: VIREONIDAE

The vireos form a group of dull-plumaged birds that superficially resemble warblers but in fact are only rather distantly related to them. They are found in forested and wooded habitats throughout South America; some species are highly migratory. A few can be quite difficult to identify. Nests are deep cups suspended in the forks of branches.

Cyclarhis

Thick-set, bull-headed vireos with *massive hooked bills*. Both peppershrikes are arboreal birds found in forest and woodland canopy. Very vocal, their far-carrying songs are heard much more often than the birds are seen.

Rufous-browed Peppershrike
Cyclarhis gujanensis   PLATE 85(1)
15 cm (6"). *Widespread and often common in* woodland, clearings, and forest borders (usually not in humid lowland forest) from Colombia and Venezuela to n. Argentina. Mostly below 2000 m, locally to 2500–3000 m in Andes. *Heavy bill pale horn;* legs pinkish. **Typical birds** (A) olive above with gray neck and *obvious rufous superciliary.* Whitish below with *broad olive-yellow chest band.* In **w. Ecuador and nw. Peru** (B) has olive crown and chestnut brow; in **upper Río Marañón valley of nw. Peru and adjacent se. Ecuador** crown is olive mixed with or entirely chestnut and underparts grayer. In **se. Brazil** crown either gray or brownish, with rufous restricted to lores. Confusion most likely with the similar Black-billed Peppershrike of n. Andes; cf. also Green-backed and Yelllow-cheeked Becards. Gleans sluggishly in foliage at varying heights; generally not often seen except in arid regions where it comes lower and vegetation is sparser. Joins mixed flocks but also forages alone or in pairs. Heard far more often than seen. Song tirelessly repeated even at midday, a series of brief and melodious phrases, each repeated many times before switching to a new phrase. Also gives a slurred call, "dreeu, dreeu . . ." repeated up to 7–8 times, each note progressively lower-pitched, recalls a woodcreeper. Also: Mexico to Panama.

Black-billed Peppershrike
Cyclarhis nigrirostris   PLATE 85(2)
15 cm (6"). Uncommon in canopy and borders of montane forest in *Andes from n. Colombia to n. Ecuador* (Pichincha and w. Napo). Mostly 1200 2300 m. *Bill mainly black* (some pink shows at base of lower mandible, at least in some birds); *legs bluish gray.* Above olive (*including crown*) with *forehead and short superciliary chestnut. Below mostly gray.* Typical Rufous-browed Peppershrikes show a more contrasting rufous brow and a yellowish pectoral band, but aside from color difference in soft parts, the Marañón form of Rufous-browed is quite similar (equally gray below); it shows at least some chestnut on crown. Behavior, including song and call, much like Rufous-browed.

Vireolanius

Chunky and large-headed vireos with *heavy hooked bills* similar to the peppershrikes; they differ in their brighter coloration. Both species range in *canopy of humid lowland and foothill forest* and, like peppershrikes, are *heard much more often than seen.*

Slaty-capped Shrike-Vireo
Vireolanius leucotis   PLATE 85(3)
14 cm (5½"). Uncommon and somewhat local in canopy of humid and foothill forest, *mainly from Amazonia to the Guianas,* also in w. Colombia and w. Ecuador. Mostly below 1400 m, rarely to 2100 m. Iris lime green. In **most of range** (A) *head gray* with *broad superciliary, spot below eye, and underparts bright yellow,* greener on sides. Above olive green. In **s. Venezuela, the Guianas, n. Brazil, ne. Peru, and e. Ecuador** (B) has a *white cheek stripe;* in addition, birds from **west**

of Andes have pink (not grayish) legs. Yellow-browed Shrike-Vireo is much brighter green above with a blue crown. Forages well above the ground, regularly joining mixed flocks (and usually seen when doing so). Sings almost as tirelessly as a peppershrike. Distinctive and far-carrying song repeats a single penetrating note, "tyeer ... tyeer ... tyeer, ..." about one note per second.

Yellow-browed Shrike-Vireo
Vireolanius eximius   PLATE 85(4)
13.5 cm (5¼"). Uncommon and local in canopy of humid forest in *n. Colombia and extreme nw. Venezuela.* To 1250 m. *Bright emerald green above* with *blue crown and nape* and *bright yellow superciliary, lower eye-crescent, throat, and chest.* Slaty-capped Shrike-Vireo has gray on head and is duller, more olive green above. Cf. also Blue-naped Chlorophonia and ♀ Green Honeycreeper. Forages lethargically in foliage, usually well above the ground, where its green coloration blends in well; sometimes accompanies mixed flocks, and then somewhat easier to see. Song a tirelessly repeated phrase of 3–4 notes, e.g., "peeyr-peeyr-peeyr." Also: e. Panama.

Vireo

Arboreal birds with *dull plumage,* their upperparts olive and underparts whitish or yellow, the vireos are generally best distinguished by *differences* (sometimes subtle) *in their facial patterns.* They are rather sluggish and, except when singing, tend to be inconspicuous. Their fairly stout bills are hooked at tip.

Yellow-throated Vireo
Vireo flavifrons
14 cm (5½"). *Uncommon boreal migrant* (Nov.–Apr.) to forest and woodland canopy and borders in Colombia and n. Venezuela. To 1800 m. *Brightly patterned for a vireo. Conspicuous yellow lores and eye-ring* (forming "spectacles"); olive above, wings with *two bold white wing-bars. Throat and breast bright yellow,* contrasting with white belly. Arboreal, mainly in *montane* forest and woodland; regularly joins mixed flocks, often with migrant warblers. Sometimes gives snatches of its burry phrased song, but more often heard is its distinctive call, 3–5 hoarse descending notes, "ship-shep-shep-shep." Breeds in e. North America.

Red-eyed Vireo
Vireo olivaceus   PLATE 85(5)
14.5 cm (5¾"). *Widespread and often common in a variety of wooded and forested habitats,* long-distance migrants often occurring in canopy and borders of Amaz. forests. Includes resident forms (some of which migrate within South America; "Chivi Vireo complex") and boreal migrants (which winter in Amazonia). Mostly below 1500 m, transients higher; nests up to at least 2000 m in Andean valleys of s. Peru and Bolivia. Perhaps more than one species. *Iris red* in boreal migrant adults; otherwise brown. *Crown gray* with *prominent white superciliary bordered above and below by blackish lines;* olive above. Whitish below; amount of greenish yellow on sides, flanks, and crissum varies both individually (young birds having more) and racially (most in *w. Ecuador and nw. Peru* birds). Cf. Yellow-green and Black-whiskered Vireos. The more montane Brown-capped Vireo is smaller with a distinctly brown crown, less prominent superciliary, and yellower belly. Gleans for insects at varying levels, also eats much fruit (such as *Cecropia* catkins), especially when not breeding. Often accompanies mixed flocks of arboreal insectivores, and nonbreeding birds are regularly in small loose groups. Song in much of South America a series of short, somewhat musical phrases with distinct intervening pauses; at least some resident forms in Amazonia repeat only a simpler, greenletlike phrase. Also breeds in North America.

Black-whiskered Vireo
Vireo altiloquus
15 cm (6"). *Uncommon boreal migrant to n. Amazonia* (Sep.–Apr.); also *resident on some islands off Venezuela, including the Netherlands Antilles.* Below 1000 m. Resembles Red-eyed Vireo, but has slightly heavier and longer bill, duller and more grayish olive upperparts with crown more or less concolor, and *narrow blackish malar streak.* Certain molting (or even wet) Red-eyed Vireos can appear to show a similar "whisker," so beware. Wintering birds favor the canopy and borders of humid forest and secondary woodland; breeding birds are numerous in scrub and mangroves. Behavior much as in Red-eyed, as is its somewhat hoarser and more clipped song. Also breeds in Florida and West Indies.

Noronha Vireo
Vireo gracilirostris*

14 cm (5½"). *Restricted to Ilha Fernando de Noronha off ne. Brazil, where common in woodland and scrub.* Resembles Red-eyed Vireo but duller, with *bill longer and much more slender;* crown more brownish (not gray) with *no* blackish line separating it from the whitish superciliary. Only one other passerine bird occurs on Noronha, the dissimilar Noronha Elaenia. Behavior much like Red-eyed, foraging mainly by gleaning from the underside of leaves, sometimes even dropping to the ground; very tame. Song a leisurely, almost disjointed series of short musical phrases (M. Allen recording).

Yellow-green Vireo
Vireo flavoviridis   PLATE 85(6)

14.5 (5¾"). *Locally fairly common boreal migrant to Colombia and w. Amazonia* (Sep.–Apr.). Mostly below 1500 m. Resembles Red-eyed Vireo, regularly occurring with it. Has duller facial pattern (*crown more olive grayish, head striping more obscure*) and *rather bright yellow sides, flanks, and crissum.* Note that immature Red-eyed can also show considerable yellow on flanks and crissum, and that Red-eyed race resident in w. Ecuador and nw. Peru has extensive yellow on lower underparts (equal to that seen in Yellow-green). Behavior much as in Red-eyed, though seems to favor edge situations more and is notably frugivorous. Gives short snatches of song much more often than boreal migrant Red-eyeds. Breeds from Mexico to Panama.

Brown-capped Vireo
Vireo leucophrys   PLATE 85(7)

12.5 cm (5"). *Common in canopy and borders of montane forest and woodland in Andes from n. Venezuela to w. Bolivia* (w. Santa Cruz). 1300–2500 m, locally to 600 m in w. Ecuador. Plain overall, but with a distinctive *brownish crown* and whitish superciliary; olive above. Whitish below, belly becoming yellowish. *No other Vireo has brown on crown;* the greenlets that do have brown on crown are all markedly smaller, more active birds that *lack* an eye-stripe. Forages deliberately in foliage, where usually easy to see; often joins mixed flocks. Distinctive song frequently heard, a short, fast musical warbling that rises at end. Equally distinctive call a rising burry "zhree," often doubled. Also: Mexico to Panama.

Philadelphia Vireo (*V. philadelphicus*) has been recorded in n. Colombia.

Chocó Vireo
Vireo masteri*

11 cm (4¼"). Rare and local in canopy and borders of montane forest on *west slope of Colombia's* W. Andes (Riseralda and w. Nariño) *and extreme nw. Ecuador* (recently found in n. Esmeraldas near Alto Tambo). 850–1600 m. A recently described species. Olive above, crown more grayish and contrasting with *prominent yellowish superciliary* and dark postocular stripe; *two broad creamy wing-bars.* Throat whitish, *breast ochraceous yellow,* belly clear yellow. Not likely confused, there being no really similar vireo in range (but cf. Yellow-throated). Forages with mixed flocks, gleaning the underside of leaves in outer branches. Song rather variable, consisting of very fast, high-pitched warbled phrases.

Hylophilus

An *often confusing* group of *small,* warbler-like vireos with olive upperparts, the greenlets are smaller than typical *Vireo* vireos and have more pointed, often pale brownish or pinkish bills; greenlets also tend to forage more actively. There are three main groups: the usually *pale-eyed* species with simple repetitive songs, found primarily in secondary habitats (a few also in forest canopy); the *dark-eyed* species usually found in humid forest canopy, which frequently give a single more complex phrase; and the distinctive Tawny-crowned Greenlet.

Rufous-crowned Greenlet
Hylophilus poicilotis   PLATE 85(8)

12.5 cm (5"). Fairly common in lower and middle growth of humid and montane forest in *se. Brazil region* (north to Espírito Santo). To 1800 m. Tail often held partially cocked. *Crown bright rufous* with *mottled blackish patch on ear-coverts;* bright olive above. Below buffy yellowish. Cf. Gray-eyed Greenlet (recently split). ♀ of Plain Antvireo (also rufous-crowned, and broadly sympatric) is chunkier and shorter-tailed with a heavier and more hooked (not so pointed) bill. Often forages in pairs, regularly with mixed flocks. Fast song a fairly loud, emphatic "sweee-sweee-sweee-sweee."

Gray-eyed Greenlet
*Hylophilus amaurocephalus**
12.5 cm (5"). *Uncommon in caatinga woodland and scrub in e. Brazil* (Ceará to n. São Paulo); also locally in *sw. Brazil* (sw. Mato Grosso do Sul) and *n. Bolivia* (Beni). To 800 m. Resembles Rufous-crowned Greenlet (from which Gray-eyed was recently split), but iris usually gray (not dark brown), auricular patch obscure or lacking, and belly buffier (not so yellow). They co-occur only very locally, in interior se. Brazil. Gray-eyed is otherwise unlikely to be confused in its habitat and range. Behavior much as in Rufous-crowned, though usually forages lower and is more often in open. Song similar but more complex, a series of 3–5 "chwee-erter" or "chee-wee" phrases, often with interspersed complaining scolds and chatters.

Scrub Greenlet
Hylophilus flavipes   PLATE 85(9)
11.5 cm (4½"). Fairly common in scrub, lighter woodland, and gallery forest, in *n. Colombia and n. Venezuela* (east to ne. Bolívar). To 1200 m. Iris whitish in Colombia and w. Venezuela (as illustrated), but usually dark in remainder of Venezuela and on Tobago; *bill and legs pinkish. Very dull.* Olive to brownish olive above. Throat whitish, below pale buffy yellowish. Golden-fronted Greenlet has brownish crown with yellower forehead, brighter yellow underparts; its iris is always dark. Usually inconspicuous, foraging in foliage and sometimes clinging upside down to leaves as it searches for insects. Sometimes with small mixed flocks. Presence often made known by song, a fast series of musical whistled "tuwee" or "peer" notes. Also: Panama (same species?).

Olivaceous Greenlet
Hylophilus olivaceus
12 cm (4¾"). Locally fairly common in second-growth and lower montane forest borders in foothills on *east slope of Andes from n. Ecuador* (Sucumbíos) *to cen. Peru* (Junín). 600–1600 m. Resembles Scrub Greenlet (no overlap) and also has *pale iris. Underparts more uniformly yellowish olive.* Behavior, including voice, similar to Scrub.

Lemon-chested Greenlet
*Hylophilus thoracicus**   PLATE 85(10)
12 cm (4¾"). Uncommon and somewhat local in canopy and borders of humid forest from *w. Amazonia to the Guianas;* also in *se. Brazil*

(same species?), in secondary and low woodland as well as restinga. To about 1000 m. *Iris whitish;* bill dull pinkish. Bright olive above with *gray hindcrown.* Grayish white below with *olive-yellow band across breast.* Ashy-headed Greenlet has a similar pattern below but is *dark*-eyed, with entirely gray head and nape (not merely rear-crown) and a broader area of yellow on breast; it is much less of a forest bird. Gray-chested Greenlet is much more uniformly gray below. In se. Brazil, the Lemon-chested Greenlet is unique. Usually in pairs, foraging fairly actively in foliage (regularly clinging upside down to leaves); often joins mixed canopy flocks. Song a simple, fast repetition of 6–8 "tweee" or "peedit" notes.

Tepui Greenlet
Hylophilus sclateri   PLATE 85(11)
12 cm (4 3.4"). Fairly common to common in canopy and borders of montane forest and woodland on *tepuis of s. Venezuela and Guyana.* 600–2000 m. Bill pinkish; iris whitish. *Head and nape gray;* olive above with *contrasting gray wings and tail.* Mostly whitish below with *yellow band across chest.* No other greenlet occurs on the tepuis with this species. Behavior much as in Lemon-chested Greenlet. Song a simple but musical "suweé seeu."

Gray-chested Greenlet
Hylophilus semicinereus   PLATE 85(12)
12 cm (4¾"). *Fairly common in canopy* and borders of humid forest and woodland from *s. Venezuela to cen. and e. Amazonia.* To 400 m. *Iris whitish;* bill pinkish below. Olive above, somewhat yellower on forecrown and with *gray midcrown and nape. Below mostly dull gray.* The similar Lemon-chested Greenlet has broad greenish yellow chest band. Usually ranges in dense foliage and viny tangles, where hard to see well; regularly accompanies mixed canopy flocks. Song a fast repetition of clear whistled "seeur" notes.

Ashy-headed Greenlet
Hylophilus pectoralis   PLATE 85(13)
12 cm (4¾"). Fairly common in deciduous and gallery woodland, mangroves, and shrubby clearings from *n. Bolivia* (west to Pando and Beni) *to e. Amaz. Brazil and the Guianas.* Below 400 m. *Iris dark reddish brown;* bill pinkish. *Entire head and nape gray;* olive above. Whitish below with *contrasting yellow breast.* Lemon-chested Greenlet has a pale eye, gray on head restricted to nape, narrower yellow chest band. Behavior similar to

the preceding greenlets; *not* a humid forest bird, so Ashy-headed is easier to see, more often foraging lower and in the open. Song a fast musical "peeer-peeer-peeer-pri-i-i-i-i-i," always with the distinctive terminal trill.

Dusky-capped Greenlet
Hylophilus hypoxanthus   PLATE 85(14)

11.5 cm (4½"). *Common* in canopy, subcanopy, and borders of humid forest in *w. and s. Amazonia.* Mostly below 600 m. *The only Amaz. greenlet with underparts basically yellow.* Iris dark. In **most of range** (illustrated) *crown brown;* olive above, back brownish to dusky-olive. *Below mostly pale yellow,* whitish on throat. **East of Rio Tapajós** paler below with a buffy whitish breast. Cf. Buff-cheeked and the much more local Brown-headed Greenlet, both of which are whitish below. An inveterate member of mixed canopy flocks of tanagers and other birds; it usually remains well above the ground and thus is not often seen well. Quite vocal; the fast phrase "itsochuwéet" is typical and most frequent, often the first clue a flock is approaching.

Brown-headed Greenlet
Hylophilus brunneiceps

11.5 cm (4½"). Uncommon and local in várzea scrub and woodland on sandy soil in *upper Rio Negro drainage of sw. Venezuela, far e. Colombia, and extreme nw. Brazil.* Below 200 m. *Crown brown;* olive above. *Below mostly grayish white.* Dusky-capped Greenlet in limited area of sympatry is more dusky-olive on back and distinctly yellower below, and ranges in a different habitat, the canopy of humid forest. Cf. also Buff-cheeked Greenlet. This dull greenlet is found singly or in pairs, and sometimes joins mixed flocks. Distinctive song a leisurely series of 4–7 ringing, penetrating "teeeeu" notes (with quality of Slaty-capped Shrike-Vireo).

Buff-cheeked Greenlet
Hylophilus muscicapinus   PLATE 85(15)

11.5 cm (4½"). Fairly common to common in canopy, subcanopy, and borders of humid forest from the *Guianas and s. Venezuela to cen. Amaz. Brazil* (south to s. Mato Grosso and Goiás). To 1100 m. Iris dark. *Face bright buff,* continuing as a *buff wash on breast;* olive above with a gray crown; whitish below. *No other greenlet shows buff on face or breast.* ♀ Rose-breasted Chat has a vaguely similar face pattern, though its behavior is quite different. Behavior, including voice,

similar to Dusky-capped Greenlet, which in general the Buff-cheeked seems to replace.

Golden-fronted Greenlet
Hylophilus aurantiifrons   PLATE 85(16)

11.5 cm (4½"). Fairly common in deciduous woodland, dry scrub, and shrubby clearings in *n. Colombia and n. Venezuela* (east to Delta Amacuro). Mostly below 700 m. Iris dark. *Forehead dull tawny-gold,* becoming *pale brown on crown;* olive above. Below mostly pale yellowish. Scrub Greenlet (often sympatric) is duller, lacks brown on crown, and has very different voice. Tawny-crowned Greenlet occurs in a totally different habitat, humid forest understory. Often forages relatively low, a regular member of small mixed flocks. Oft-heard song a fast "cheetsacheéyou"; also has a nasal scolding note. Also: Panama.

Rufous-naped Greenlet
Hylophilus semibrunneus   PLATE 85(17)

12.5 cm (5"). Local and uncommon in canopy, subcanopy, and borders of montane forest in *Andes from extreme w. Venezuela* (Sierra de Perijá) *and n. Colombia to n. Ecuador* (w. Napo). Mostly 900–2000 m. *Crown and nape rich rufous;* bright olive above. Below whitish with *some rufous on sides of chest.* Occurs at *higher elevations* than any other canopy-inhabiting greenlet, though it is locally sympatric with the Tawny-crowned (which ranges in understory). Behavior and voice much as in Dusky-capped Greenlet, but song slightly longer and even faster, e.g., "deedidoreét," characteristically doubled.

Lesser Greenlet
Hylophilus decurtatus   PLATE 85(18)

10 cm (4"). *Common* in canopy, subcanopy, and borders of humid and deciduous forest and secondary woodland, from *w. Colombia to extreme nw. Peru* (Tumbes). To 1100 m. *A plump, puffy-headed, short-tailed greenlet; very plain.* Iris dark. Yellowish olive above, darker on head with a narrow white eye-ring. *Mainly whitish below. The only arboreal greenlet in its trans-Andean range.* Tennessee Warbler has a finer bill, narrow whitish eye-stripe, etc. Behavior, including voice, much as in Dusky-capped Greenlet, though more likely to occur in small groups (not just in pairs) and closer to the ground. Typical song phrase shorter (e.g., "wichee-cheeu"). Also: Mexico to Panama.

Tawny-crowned Greenlet

Hylophilus ochraceiceps   PLATE 85(19)

11.5 cm (4½"). *Uncommon in lower growth of humid forest from Colombia and Venezuela to Amazonia and the Guianas.* To 1600 m in s. Venezuela, but mostly below 1000 m. *Crown tawny, brightest on forecrown,* but reduced or lacking in birds from **ne. South America** (B), which have a dark iris; *iris is obviously pale* in **most of range** (A). Olive above, wings and tail browner. Below pale grayish, more olive on breast. Cf. ♀

Plain Antvireo. Birds of ne. South America resemble several ♀ *Myrmotherula* antwrens, especially Long-winged and Gray. The only greenlet normally found inside forest, Tawny-crowned forages mostly in pairs, gleaning in foliage and regularly accompanying understory flocks of antwrens and other birds. Song a distinctive clear penetrating "teee-yeeé" or a more descending and slurred "teeeeuw"; also gives a "nyah-nyah-nyah" scolding call. Also: Mexico to Panama.

NEW WORLD WARBLERS: PARULIDAE

These birds form a significant part of what has been termed the 9-primaried Emberizine assemblage, formerly often only with subfamily rank but now considered to constitute a full family. A large number of migratory species from North America occur in n. South America, where most are arboreal in forest and woodland; these can be tricky to identify. The numerous resident warblers, mainly in the genus *Basileuterus,* favor lower growth, and most are more distinctive. All warblers glean for insects in foliage; the resident species, a majority of which occur in the Andes, are quite vocal. Residents construct open cup nests, typically placed near the ground.

Rose-breasted Chat

Granatellus pelzelni   PLATE 86(1)
12.5 cm (5"). Uncommon in subcanopy and borders of humid forest, deciduous and secondary woodland, and shrubbery near water from *s. Venezuela and the Guianas to s. Amaz. Brazil and n. Bolivia.* To 850 m. The genus *Granatellus* is apparently most closely allied to the Cardinalid finches. Pretty ♂ unmistakable. Head black with a *prominent white postocular stripe;* blue-gray above, tail black. *Below rosy red, with white throat and on flanks.* In **lower Amaz. Brazil,** only forecrown black and no white on flanks. ♀ *blue-gray above* with *cinnamon-buff forehead, face, and underparts; crissum pink.* Cf. lowland conebills, none of which has ♀ chat's buff on face or its pink crissum. Usually in pairs, gleaning in foliage and often joining mixed flocks; *strong preference for vine tangles.* Perches horizontally, cocking and fanning tail and drooping wings. Song a series of 5–6 clear sweet notes, e.g., "sweet-sweet-tuwee-tuwee-tuwee-tuwee," recalling a greenlet. Both sexes have a sharp "jrrt" call, sometimes given in series.

Myioborus

An attractive group of *animated, conspicuous* warblers found *primarily in Andean forest and woodland;* additional species occur on the tepuis. *All whitestarts have a black tail with prominent white outer feathers that are* frequently exposed by fanning; we thus employ the group name "whitestart" in place of the long used, but inaccurate, "redstart." No more than two species of whitestarts occur in any one area, the Slate-throated generally ranging at elevations below that of a member of the Spectacled or Brown-capped complexes.

Slate-throated Whitestart

Myioborus miniatus   PLATE 86(2)
13.5 cm (5¼"). *Common and widespread* in lower montane forest, woodland, and borders in *Andes from n. Venezuela to s. Bolivia* (Chuquisaca); also on *tepuis of s. Venezuela region.* Mostly 700–2500 m, on tepuis 600–1800 m. *Above slaty gray, extending down over throat.* Below mostly bright yellow. All other whitestarts have yellow of underparts extending up to include the throat. Numerous (less so on the tepuis) and relatively tolerant of habitat disturbance. Forages actively with much posturing, generally not too high above the ground, and frequently accompanies mixed flocks. Often droops its wings, and also flicks and spreads tail, almost as if to expose the white (its actual function is to startle prey items). Song a series of relatively weak and accelerating "chi" notes on one pitch or slightly rising. Also: Mexico to Panama.

Golden-fronted Whitestart

Myioborus ornatus   PLATE 86(3)
13.5 cm (5¼"). Common in montane forest, woodland, and borders in *Andes of extreme sw. Venezuela* (s. Táchira) *and Colombia* (south to Cauca). Mostly 2400–3400 m. In **most of range**

(illustrated) has *foreface and most of under-parts bright golden yellow.* Rear of head black-ish; olivaceous gray above. Birds from **Colombia's E. Andes and adjacent Venezuela** have *more white on face.* Does not overlap with other whitestarts of the Spectacled complex, though birds showing characters seemingly intermediate toward the Spectacled Whitestart are known from Nariño, Colombia, and extreme n. Ecuador; these show reduced yellow on face (resulting in a more "spectacled" look) and varying amounts of rufous on forecrown. Conspicuous, with behavior much as in Slate-throated Whitestart, though does not droop wings and fan tail as often. Song a variable and jumbled series of high-pitched "tsit" and "tsee" notes.

Spectacled Whitestart
Myioborus melanocephalus   PLATE 86(4)
13.5 (5¼"). Common in montane forest, woodland, and borders in *Andes from s. Colombia* (Nariño) *to w. Bolivia* (w. Santa Cruz). 2000–4000 m. Head pattern variable but *always has yellow lores and ocular area, forming the "spectacles."* **Southern birds** (north to cen. Peru; A) have crown entirely black; **northern birds** (south to n. Peru; B) have a rufous crown patch. Otherwise gray above; mostly bright yellow below. At northern end of range, cf. Golden-fronted Whitestart; in Bolivia, cf. Brown-capped Whitestart. Behavior and song as in Golden-fronted.

White-fronted Whitestart
Myioborus albifrons   PLATE 86(5)
13.5 cm (5¼"). Common in montane forest, woodland, and borders in *Andes of w. Venezuela* (Trujillo to n. Táchira). 2200–3200 m. *White forehead, lores, and ocular area forming conspicuous "spectacles"; patch on crown cinnamon-rufous* (but yellow in at least some ♀♀ in Táchira). Otherwise gray above, mostly bright yellow below. Golden-fronted Whitestart (which replaces this species southward) has yellow forecrown; recall that this form of Golden-fronted is white-faced. Behavior as in Golden-fronted. Song an attractive but rambling series of sweet and melodic notes that gradually becomes louder and more forceful.

Yellow-crowned Whitestart
Myioborus flavivertex   PLATE 86(6)
13.5 cm (5¼"). Common in montane forest, woodland, and borders on *Santa Marta Mts. of n. Colombia.* Mostly 2000–3000 m. *Crown patch yellow;* loral spot and upper eye-crescent

buffyish; above otherwise olive (not gray as in other whitestarts). Below mostly bright yellow. Cf. Slate-throated Whitestart, the only other whitestart on the Santa Martas and occurring at *lower* elevations. Behavior and song much as in Golden-fronted Whitestart.

Tepui Whitestart
Myioborus castaneocapillus   PLATE 86(7)
13 cm (5"). Common in montane forest borders, woodland, and shrubby clearings on *tepuis of s. Venezuela region. Crown rufous-chestnut* with narrow white supraloral stripe and broken eye-ring (indistinct in some races); dull olive-gray above. Below mostly yellow to deep orange-yellow (**Gran Sabana race** is illustrated). Does not occur with either of the other tepui-endemic whitestarts. The only other whitestart in its range is the very different Slate-throated, which occurs at lower elevations. Behavior and song as in Golden-fronted Whitestart.

Paria Whitestart
Myioborus pariae
13 cm (5"). *Restricted to Paria Peninsula in ne. Venezuela, where now uncommon and very local in and near what little montane forest remains.* 700–1150 m. Resembles Tepui Whitestart, with rufous-chestnut crown and mostly bright yellow underparts, but *lores and orbital area bright yellow, forming prominent "spectacles."* The only other whitestart in range is the very different Slate-throated. Behavior, so far as known, much like that of other whitestarts, though seems more often to forage alone or in pairs apart from flocks.

White-faced Whitestart
Myioborus albifacies
13 cm (5"). *Restricted to several remote tepuis in n. Amazonas, Venezuela,* where probably fairly common (but seems unknown in life). 900–2250 m. *Crown black, contrasting sharply with pure white sides of face;* olivaceous gray above. Below mostly deep orange-yellow. The only other whitestart occurring on these tepuis is the very different Slate-throated. Behavior unknown, but likely as in other whitestarts.

Guaiquinima Whitestart
Myioborus cardonai
13 cm (5"). *Restricted to remote Cerro Guaiquinima in cen. Bolívar, Venezuela,* where probably fairly common (but seems unknown in life). 1200–1600 m. *Crown black* with an incon-

spicuous broken white eye-ring; olivaceous gray above. Below mostly deep orange-yellow. The only other whitestart occurring on this tepui is the very different Slate-throated. Behavior unknown, but likely as in other whitestarts.

Brown-capped Whitestart
Myioborus brunniceps   PLATE 86(8)
13 cm (5"). Common in montane forest, woodland, borders, and shrubby clearings in *Andes from s. Bolivia* (s. La Paz) *to nw. Argentina* (San Luis and n. Córdoba). 500–3000 m. *Crown rufous-chestnut with a narrow white supraloral stripe and eye-ring; olive area on gray back.* Below mostly bright yellow. The similar Tepui Whitestart is geographically very far removed. Cf. also Spectacled Whitestart (which has a black crown in area of possible contact) and Slate-throated Whitestart. Behavior much as in other whitestarts. Song markedly different, however, an even, fast, sibilant trill with slight crescendo.

Geothlypis

Yellowthroats are found in *rank shrubbery and tall grass* in much of the lowlands; except when breeding and ♂♂ are singing, they are rather *skulking*. Both sexes of all species are *bright yellow below; ♂♂ have black on face, giving the effect of a mask*. The legs and base of mandible are pinkish.

Southern Yellowthroat
*Geothlypis velata**   PLATE 86(9)
14 cm (5½"). Widespread and often common in shrubby areas, grassy clearings, and marshes from *se. Peru, n. Bolivia, and cen. Brazil to n. Argentina* (Buenos Aires). Mostly below 1500 m, a few to 2000 m or more in Bolivia. Often considered conspecific with Masked and Black-lored Yellowthroats, then called Masked Yellowthroat. ♂ has *black mask broadly outlined above with gray;* above olive green. Below bright yellow. ♀ has *yellow supraloral and narrow eye-ring,* with *crown and ear-coverts at least tinged gray.* No overlap with other yellowthroats. Subtropical and Warbling Doraditos can be confused with ♀ yellowthroat (and even can occur with it in the same marshes), but doraditos have more slender *black* legs, *no* supraloral, etc. Usually in pairs that skulk in thickets or tall grass, most often near water; more conspicuous when ♂♂ are giving their sweet, warbled song, which recalls a seed-

finch or seedeater. Call a fast chatter that distinctively drops in pitch and strength.

Masked Yellowthroat
*Geothlypis aequinoctialis**
14 cm (5½"). Fairly common in shrubby areas, grassy fields, and marshes from *n. Colombia and Venezuela to lower Amaz. Brazil.* To 900 m. Formerly considered conspecific with Southern Yellowthroat. ♂ closely resembles that species, but with somewhat less gray on sides of head behind the black mask. ♀ very like ♀ Southern. Behavior as in Southern; even their songs are not dissimilar.

Black-lored Yellowthroat
*Geothlypis auricularis**
13–14 cm (5–5½"). Fairly common in shrubby clearings and woodland borders, not necessarily near water, from *w. Ecuador* (Manabí) *to w. Peru* (Ica), and in *upper Río Marañón valley of n. Peru and adjacent Ecuador.* To 1500 m. *Smaller* than similar Masked and Southern Yellowthroats (formerly considered conspecific), though the larger Marañón birds are about the same. In ♂ *black mask reduced to a small area from frontlet to around eyes.* ♀ similar to ♀ Southern Yellowthroat. Behavior as in Southern. ♂'s song a short vigorous series of clear notes ending in a warble, "swee-swee-swee-swee-chuchuchu," with quality recalling Southern House Wren.

Olive-crowned Yellowthroat
Geothlypis semiflava   PLATE 86(10)
13.5 cm (5¼"). Locally fairly common in tall grass and shrubbery from *nw. Colombia* (s. Chocó) *to sw. Ecuador* (El Oro). To 1500 m. ♂ has *broad black mask from forecrown over cheeks to sides of neck,* the mask *not* bordered by grayish; olive green above. Mostly bright yellow below. ♀ much like ♀ Black-lored Yellowthroat but lacks gray on crown and ear-coverts, with at most an indistinct yellowish eye-ring and supraloral stripe. Behavior much like other yellowthroats; *more confined to humid areas.* Song a rich and musical series of phrases ending in a jumbled twittering, longer and more complex than Black-lored. Call a nasal "chee-uw." Also: Honduras to w. Panama.

Common Yellowthroat
Geothlypis trichas
12.5 cm (5"). *Rare boreal migrant* (Oct.–Apr.) to grassy and shrubby areas in *n. Colombia.* Mostly below 1500 m. Resembles the larger Masked

Yellowthroat. ♂ has *larger black mask bordered above by distinct but narrow whitish or pale gray band,* yellow underparts that *fade to dingy whitish on belly* (not uniform yellow). ♀ and immature differ from ♀ Masked in lacking gray on crown and ear-coverts; *yellow of underparts restricted to throat and chest.* Skulking behavior same as other yellowthroats. Call a distinctive husky "tchek." Breeds in North America and Mexico.

Tropical Parula
Parula pitiayumi   PLATE 86(11)

11 cm (4¼"). *Widespread and locally common in a variety of habitats,* ranging from canopy and borders of montane forest, deciduous and gallery woodland, to chaco scrub and monte, from Colombia and Venezuela to n. Argentina; absent from more humid forested lowlands such as Amazonia. To 2500 m. ♂ *dull blue above* with *black foreface, olive patch on midback,* and *two bold white wing-bars.* Below bright yellow, *throat and breast washed with ochraceous or orange* (intensity varying racially). ♀ slightly duller. A *small,* pretty warbler, not likely to be confused, but cf. various boreal migrants (perhaps especially Cerulean Warbler). Arboreal, foraging in pairs; often accompanies mixed flocks, usually remaining rather high when in forest but coming lower at edge and in clearings. ♂'s frequently heard song a distinctive (though variable) accelerating and rising buzzy trill preceded by several thin notes, "tzip-tzip-tzip-tzip-tzrrrrrrrrip." Also: Mexico to Panama.

Northern Parula (*P. americana*) has been recorded from Caribbean islands off north coast of South America (Curaçao, Bonaire, and Tobago), and once in n. Venezuela (Falcón).

Migrant Wood Warblers (mainly *Vermivora* and *Dendroica*)

Attractive small birds with *slender bills,* these warblers *breed in North America* but pass the boreal winter in the Neotropics. In South America they occur primarily in forests and woodlands of the northwest, especially in the Andes; migrants can occur almost anywhere. Most species glean in foliage (a few are nectarivorous) and accompany mixed flocks, but a few (mainly those that remain near the ground) establish wintering territories here. Most rarely or never sing in South America. Most species are sexually dimor-

phic, with additional nonbreeding and immature plumages in a few; in the accounts that follow, the additional plumages are discussed first, then the breeding plumages (usually assumed in Feb.–Mar.).

Vermivora

Small, arboreal warblers with *fine, sharply pointed bills* and relatively simple plumage patterns.

Golden-winged Warbler
Vermivora chrysoptera

12 cm (4¾"). Uncommon boreal migrant to canopy and borders of montane forest and woodland in *Colombia and Venezuela* (Sep.–Mar.). Mostly 500–2400 m. Beautiful ♂ unmistakable, with *conspicuous black patches on ear-coverts and throat,* and *bright golden yellow forecrown and large patch on wing-coverts.* Otherwise olive above and white below. ♀ echoes ♂'s pattern, *dark gray replacing the black.* Usually seen singly, often while accompanying mixed flocks. In addition to gleaning from foliage, often inspects dead leaves for insects, sometimes while hanging upside down. Has declined markedly in recent decades. Breeds in e. North America, also wintering in s. Central America.

Blue-winged Warbler (*V. pinus*) is known from one record in the Santa Marta area of n. Colombia and another in n. Venezuela.

Tennessee Warbler
Vermivora peregrina

12 cm (4¾"). Locally fairly common boreal migrant to humid and (especially) montane forest and woodland borders, and clearings and gardens with scattered trees in *w. and n. Colombia, n. Venezuela, and n. Ecuador* (Sep.–Apr.). Mostly 500–2200 m. *Plain overall,* with *narrow white to pale yellowish superciliary* and *mainly pale yellowish underparts* but for a *white crissum;* olive above, usually showing *just a single whitish wing-bar.* Breeding ♂ gray on crown and nape, white below; ♀ duller, tinged yellow on chest and sides. Gleans for insects in foliage, but also has a special predilection for flowering trees (e.g., *Erythrina* spp.), where a dozen or more may gather with birds such as orioles, hummingbirds, and honeycreepers. In some areas also comes to feeding trays for fruit. Breeds in n. North America, wintering mostly in Central America.

Dendroica

Active, spritely warblers that usually have more complex plumage patterns than do *Vermivora;* many *Dendroica* show a white flash in the tail. The vast majority are migratory to South America, with only one species (the Mangrove Warbler) being resident here.

Mangrove Warbler
Dendroica petechia*   PLATE 86(12)
12.5 cm (5"). *Locally fairly common to common resident along the Pacific south to extreme nw. Peru* (Tumbes) and *along the Caribbean to ne. Venezuela* (also on offshore islands) and in French Guiana. *Strictly coastal, with distribution for the most part closely tied to the presence of mangroves,* but on some islands also in scrub. Has been considered conspecific with Yellow Warbler. *♂ bright yellow,* more olive above and with *chestnut streaking on breast and sides; tail spots yellow.* **Caribbean coast** birds have *entire hood rufous-chestnut,* but **Pacific coast** birds (and also those on Caribbean islands) have *rufous-chestnut more or less restricted to crown* (as illustrated). ♀ duller, with chestnut streaking faint or absent; often more grayish above and whitish below. Cf. Tennessee Warbler and Bicolored Conebill. An active and conspicuous bird, mainly arboreal but also often dropping to the ground, feeding among mangrove roots and on mud exposed at low tide. An excited chipping is often given; ♂'s lively song a short series of "swee" notes followed by an emphasized note or warble. Also: coasts of Middle America, West Indies, and Galápagos Islands.

Yellow Warbler
Dendroica aestiva*
12.5 cm (5"). Boreal migrant, northward often common, to trees and shrubbery in semiopen areas and clearings in *n. South America* (mainly Sep.–Apr.). Mostly below about 1000 m, but higher as a transient. ♂ resembles ♂ Mangrove Warbler, but *lacks rufous on head or crown* (only streaks on breast). ♀ resembles ♀ Mangrove but brighter and paler yellow (never so grayish), especially below. Mainly arboreal, most often not with other birds; sometimes occurs in mangroves with Mangrove Warbler, though usually they do not actually forage together. Very active, gleaning and hover-gleaning in foliage, often in the semiopen and easy to observe. Frequently gives

an excited chipping. Breeds in North America, wintering mostly in Central America.

Blackpoll Warbler
Dendroica striata   PLATE 86(13)
13 cm (5"). Fairly common boreal migrant to canopy and borders of humid forest and woodland, and in adjacent clearings *mainly in nw. Amazonia,* scattered records elsewhere (Sep.–May). Mostly below 1000 m (transients higher). Legs pale. Nonbreeding birds (illustrated) olive above with back streaked blackish; *two bold white wing-bars.* Whitish to pale yellowish below with *fine dusky streaking on breast and flanks* and *white crissum.* Breeding ♂ very different, with *striking black crown and white cheeks, black malar stripe continuing down as streaking on sides.* Breeding ♀ like nonbreeding birds but grayer (not so olive) above and whiter below. Nonbreeding Bay-breasted Warbler has plainer underparts *with no streaking,* a trace of chestnut on flanks (usually), a pale buffyish (not white) crissum, and blacker legs. Bay-breasted generally occurs *west* of the Andes, Blackpoll *east* of them. Gleans in foliage and often accompanies mixed flocks. Breeds in n. North America, with extraordinarily long migration route over the open Atlantic Ocean.

Bay-breasted Warbler
Dendroica castanea
13 cm (5"). Uncommon boreal migrant to canopy and borders of humid forest and woodland, and adjacent clearings to *Colombia and nw. Venezuela* (Oct.–Apr.). Mostly below 800 m (transients higher). Resembles Blackpoll Warbler above. *Below pale buffyish with little or no streaking* but usually shows at least a *trace of chestnut on flanks.* Breeding ♂ very different, with *crown, throat, chest, and sides chestnut* and a *large pale buff patch on sides of neck.* Breeding ♀ echoes pattern of ♂ but much duller. Behavior as in Blackpoll. Breeds in n. North America, wintering mainly in s. Central America.

Cerulean Warbler
Dendroica cerulea
12 cm (4¾"). Uncommon boreal migrant to canopy and borders of humid and montane forest and woodland, and in plantations, from *n. Colombia and n. and w. Venezuela to se. Ecuador* (Sep.–Mar.), a few reaching e. Peru and w. Bolivia (La Paz). Mostly 500–1500 m, sometimes lower as a transient. *♂ mainly azure blue*

above; two bold white wing-bars; white below with *narrow black band across chest* (sometimes incomplete) and black streaking down flanks. ♀ *more bluish green above* with *narrow pale yellowish superciliary;* more yellowish below, with no chest band and little or no streaking. Immature ♀ more olive above and even yellower below. Nonbreeding Blackpoll and Bay-breasted Warblers are larger, have back streaking but no superciliary, etc. Behavior much as in Blackpoll, generally remaining well above the ground. Has declined markedly in recent decades. Breeds in e. North America.

Chestnut-sided Warbler
Dendroica pensylvanica
12.5 cm (5"). Rare boreal migrant to humid forest borders, woodland, and clearings in *Colombia and nw. Venezuela* (mainly Oct.–Apr.). Mostly below 1000 m. *Bright yellowish olive above* with *narrow white eye-ring; face and underparts grayish white,* usually with at least some *chestnut on sides.* Breeding ♂ very different, with *bright yellow crown,* black eye-stripe and malar, black-streaked back, and *extensive chestnut on sides.* Breeding ♀ similar but duller. Bay-breasted Warbler is larger with a streaked back, no eye-ring, buffier underparts (not so gray). An arboreal warbler that gleans in foliage; *often cocks its tail.* Breeds in e. North America, wintering mainly in Central America.

Black-throated Green Warbler
Dendroica virens
12.5 cm (5"). Rare boreal migrant to canopy and borders of montane forest and woodland and adjacent clearings in *n. Colombia and n. Venezuela* (Oct.–Apr.). Mostly 500–2000 m. *Distinctive contrasting yellow face in all plumages.* Above bright olive; wings with two white bars. *Throat and chest black,* extending down as streaking on sides. ♀ duller than ♂, showing less black on throat and chest; immatures even more so. Immature Blackburnian Warbler has dark ear-coverts (thus does not look yellow-faced) and streaked back (not plain olive). Behavior much as in Blackburnian. Breeds in n. North America, wintering mostly in Middle America.

Townsend's Warbler (*D. townsendi*) is known from a single record from n. Colombia.

Blackburnian Warbler
Dendroica fusca   PLATE 86(14)
12.5 cm (5"). *Common* boreal migrant to canopy and borders of montane forest and woodland,

and in adjacent clearings, *primarily on Andean slopes south to e. Peru* (mostly Oct.–Apr.). Mostly 500–2800 m, sometimes lower as a transient. ♂ *mostly black above* with *two very bold white wing-bars* (in some forming a patch) and *fiery orange throat and chest.* ♀ and immature (illustrated) *patterned like ♂* but duller, more grayish olive above and with *yellow replacing the orange.* Cf. much rarer Black-throated Green and Cape May Warblers. Often in small groups, especially when migrating; regularly associates with mixed flocks of tanagers and other birds. Breeds in n. North America.

Yellow-throated Warbler (*D. dominica*) is known from a few sightings in n. Colombia.

Cape May Warbler
Dendroica tigrina
12.5 cm (5"). Very rare boreal migrant to clearings, gardens, mangroves, and deciduous woodland borders, *mainly near Caribbean coast* (Oct.–Apr.). To 1500 m. *Distinctive yellow patch on sides of neck* in all plumages (but duller in immature ♀♀), and *variably but usually heavily streaked with dusky below.* Older ♂♂ are brighter and yellower below, with *contrasting rufous-chestnut cheek patch.* Duller ♀♀ can be very drab and grayish, best known by their yellowish cheek patch and the streaking below. Yellow-rumped Warbler can look similar but always has a much bolder yellow rump. ♀ Blackburnian Warbler has a more prominent superciliary, streaking only on sides. Usually seen singly; here a *non*forest warbler, often attracted to flowering trees. Breeds in n. North America, wintering mainly in West Indies.

Palm Warbler (*D. palmarum*) has been recorded a few times on Netherlands Antilles; a recent sighting from nw. Colombia and one also from w. Venezuela.

Prairie Warbler (*D. discolor*) is known from a few records from coastal n. South America.

Yellow-rumped Warbler
Dendroica coronata
13 cm (5"). Very rare boreal migrant to low woodland, scrub, and gardens to *n. Colombia and n. Venezuela* (Dec.–Apr.). To 3000 m, but mainly near coast. Plumage variable, *usually brownish above* with *distinctive bright yellow rump; whitish below* with *yellow patch on sides* (sometimes hidden by wings). Breeding birds grayer above, ♂ with black on chest. Cf. Cape May Warbler. A *non*forest warbler, usually seen

singly in South America and more numerous on offshore islands. Frequent call a distinctive loud "tchek." Breeds in n. and w. North America, wintering mainly in United States and Middle America.

Magnolia Warbler (*D. magnolia*) is known from a few records in n. Colombia and n. Venezuela, and on Trinidad-Tobago.

Black-throated Blue Warbler
Dendroica caerulescens
13 cm (5"). Very rare boreal migrant to lower growth of woodland and humid forest borders in *n. Colombia and n. Venezuela, mainly near Caribbean coast* (Sep.–Mar.). Below 1000 m. Dapper ♂ unmistakable, *mainly dark blue above with a small but bold white speculum at base of primaries; lower face, throat, chest, and sides contrasting black,* midbreast and belly white. ♀ much duller, brownish olive above and buffyish below, but with narrow whitish superciliary and *distinctive wing speculum as in ♂.* No similar bird shares the wing speculum (especially helpful in the drab ♀). Found singly, often accompanying understory flocks. Breeds in e. North America, wintering mainly in West Indies.

Black-and-white Warbler
Mniotilta varia
12.5 cm (5"). Fairly common boreal migrant to humid forest, woodland, and borders mainly in *Colombia and n. Venezuela* (Sep.–Mar.), smaller numbers reaching Ecuador and a few n. Peru. Mostly 500–2200 m, sometimes lower as a transient. Unmistakable, with *bold black and white striping on head, mantle, and underparts;* median belly white. ♀ and immature whiter and less streaked below (whitest on throat), older ♂♂ with black throat. Found singly, usually while accompanying mixed flocks; *habitually forages by creeping on trunks and larger tree limbs.* Breeds in e. North America, wintering mainly in Middle America.

Oporornis

Fairly large migrant warblers with *plain olive and yellow plumage,* two species sporting a bib and with an eye-ring.

Mourning Warbler
Oporornis philadelphia   PLATE 86(15)
13 cm (5"). Uncommon boreal migrant to dense undergrowth in thickets at edge of humid and montane forest and woodland, and shrubby clearings, *often near water, south to Ecuador* (mainly Oct.–Apr.). Mostly below 2000 m. ♂ with *gray hood, becoming black on chest* (often scaled paler); plain olive above. Lower underparts yellow. ♀ (illustrated) duller, with no black on bib and *often a partial white eye-ring.* Immature even duller, with *hood more brownish and most pronounced on sides of chest.* ♀ resident yellowthroats are more uniform and brighter yellow below. Cf. the scarce Connecticut Warbler. Rather skulking, usually occurring alone. Breeds in n. North America, wintering primarily in s. Central America.

Connecticut Warbler
Oporornis agilis
14 cm (5½"). Uncommon and very inconspicuous boreal migrant on or near the ground in undergrowth of humid forest, woodland, and borders *south to n. Bolivia and Amaz. Brazil* (mainly Oct.–Apr.); north of s. Amazonia mainly or entirely a transient. Mostly below 1000 m (higher as a transient). *In all plumages shows a conspicuous and complete white or buffy whitish eye-ring* (not incomplete as in a few yellowthroats and Mourning Warbler). ♂ has *gray hood,* slightly paler on throat. Olive above, bright yellow below. ♀ *hood more brownish gray;* immature hood and even upperparts browner. ♀ and immature Mourning eye-ring, if present at all, is incomplete or less conspicuous; Mourning is smaller and never as brownish as Connecticut can be. *Very skulking,* doubtless under-recorded. Sometimes *walks* on the ground; when Mourning is on the ground (infrequent), it hops. Breeds in n. North America.

Kentucky Warbler
Oporornis formosus
13.5 cm (5¼"). Rare boreal migrant to undergrowth of humid forest and woodland in *n. Colombia and nw. Venezuela* (Sep.–Mar.). To 1200 m. ♂ with *black forecrown and sides of head and neck* (forming "sideburns"), and *prominent yellow supraloral and incomplete eye-ring* (forming "spectacles"). Above olive, below bright yellow. ♀ has less black on face, immature sometimes none (though spectacled pattern remains). Immature Canada Warbler (which may virtually lack a necklace) is grayer above; its behavior is much less skulking than the Kentucky. Breeds in se. North America, wintering mainly in Middle America.

Prothonotary Warbler
Protonotaria citrea
13.5 cm (5¼"). Fairly common boreal migrant to lower and mid-levels of deciduous woodland and scrub, *almost invariably near water, and in mangroves (where most numerous) from w. and n. Colombia to the Guianas, especially near coast* (Sep.–Mar.). Mostly below 500 m. Rather short tail. Lovely ♂ unmistakable; *head and underparts bright golden yellow; wings and tail blue-gray*, extensive white in outer tail feathers. ♀ duller, with head and underparts clouded olive. ♀ Yellow Warbler is smaller, has dusky-olive wings, etc. Breeds in e. North America, wintering mainly in Middle America.

Worm-eating Warbler (*Helmitheros vermivorum*) is known from a few recent records in n. Venezuela.

Swainson's Warbler (*Limnothlypis swainsonii*) is known from one recent record from nw. Venezuela.

American Redstart
Setophaga ruticilla   PLATE 86(16)
12.5 cm (5"). Uncommon to fairly common boreal migrant to borders of humid and deciduous forest, woodland, and mangroves (where often numerous) in nw. South America (Sep.–Apr.), more numerous northward. Mostly below 2000 m (higher as transient). Adult ♂ unmistakable, *mostly black* with *large orange patches on wings, base of tail, and sides;* white belly. ♀ (illustrated) and immature have *yellow replacing the orange;* they are grayish olive above (grayest on head) and white below. An arboreal warbler that forages actively, even acrobatically, *posturing with a fanned tail and drooped wings.* Breeds in North America, wintering mainly in Middle America.

Wilsonia

Two attractive migrant warblers found in the understory of forest and woodland; only rarely do they actually descend to the ground.

Canada Warbler
Wilsonia canadensis   PLATE 86(17)
13 cm (5"). *Common* boreal migrant to lower growth of montane forest and woodland and borders, *especially in foothills, in Andes as far south as se. Peru* (mostly Oct.–Apr.). Mostly 500–2000 m, sometimes lower as a transient. Best known from its *necklace of streaks across chest,* black

and well-marked in ♂, fainter (though usually still evident) in ♀ and immature. ♂ *bluish gray above* with *yellow supraloral and eye-ring forming spectacles* and a *black foreface.* Bright yellow below. ♀ (illustrated) and especially immature duller, and less bluish above. Forages actively, often with tail partially cocked. Snatches of its jumbled, warbled song are given during northward passage. *Breeds* in n. North America.

Hooded Warbler
Wilsonia citrina
14 cm (5½"). Rare boreal migrant to lower growth of humid forest and woodland in *n. Colombia and n. Venezuela,* at least so far only near coast (Oct.–Apr.). ♂ unmistakable, with *striking black hood enclosing bright yellow forehead and face; extensive white in outer tail feathers.* Otherwise olive above, bright yellow below. ♀ lacks the black hood (or it is faint), and its *bright yellow underparts extend to face and forehead;* white in tail as in ♂. ♀ Prothonotary Warbler has blue-gray wings, white lower underparts. ♀ Canada Warbler is smaller, grayer above, lacks white in tail and facial yellow restricted to supraloral (not extending over forehead). ♀ yellowthroats lack white in tail and yellow on face and forecrown. Seen singly, sometimes with understory flocks. Tail often flicked open, exposing the white. Breeds in e. North America, wintering mainly in Middle America.

Wilson's Warbler (*W. pusilla*) is known from a few recent records from w. Colombia and one from nw. Ecuador.

Seiurus

Aberrant migrant warblers with fairly long legs and *more or less terrestrial habits.* All three species are olive brown above and *streaked below.*

Northern Waterthrush
Seiurus noveboracensis   PLATE 86(18)
14 cm (5½"). Fairly common boreal migrant on or near ground inside humid and deciduous woodland near water, often most numerous in mangroves, mainly from *Colombia to the Guianas* (Sep.–May); a few reach Ecuador and ne. Peru. To 2000 m. *Olive brown above with narrow but prominent yellowish buff superciliary.* Buffy whitish below with *dark brown streaking.* Cf. rarer Louisiana Waterthrush and Ovenbird. Buff-rumped Warbler has somewhat similar

behavior but lacks streaking below, has buff basal tail, etc. Found singly, walking sedately on the ground, *almost constantly bobbing its rearparts up and down*. Its distinctive loud metallic "tchink" call is often heard. Breeds in n. North America, wintering mainly in Middle America and West Indies.

Louisiana Waterthrush
Seiurus motacilla

14.5 cm (5¾"). Rare boreal migrant on or near ground along streams, mostly in montane forest and woodland, to *n. Colombia and nw. Venezuela* (Oct.–Feb.). Mostly 500–1800 m. Resembles much more numerous and slightly smaller Northern Waterthrush, differing in its *wider and whiter superciliary* (flaring behind eye) and *usually contrasting buff flanks and crissum* (underparts of Northern are relatively uniform). Behavior similar to Northern, though more confined to running fresh water; bear in mind that Northern can occur in a wide variety of habitats near water (*including streams*). "Tchink" call note also similar, but somewhat louder and more emphatic. Breeds in e. North America, wintering mainly in Middle America.

Ovenbird
Seiurus aurocapilla

14.5 cm (5¾"). Rare boreal migrant on or near ground in humid and deciduous woodland and forest in *n. Colombia and n. Venezuela* (mostly Oct.–Apr.); transients can be numerous on *Netherlands Antilles*, but Ovenbird is seemingly only a vagrant farther south (overlooked?). To 1200 m. Recalls Northern Waterthrush, but *not* tied to water. *Olive above* with *white eye-ring* (no superciliary) and *dull orange coronal stripe bordered with black*. White below with *black streaking on breast and flanks*. Shy and unobtrusive; walks sedately on the ground, often slowly bobbing rearparts up and down. Breeds in e. North America, wintering mainly in Middle America.

Basileuterus

A large group of *dull-plumaged* warblers found in forest and woodland undergrowth. The genus reaches its *highest diversity in the Andes*, where a number of species have very limited ranges. Most are olive above and yellow below, often with *quite distinct head patterns*, usually including crown striping. Some of the duller species resemble certain *Hemispingus* tanagers, though the warblers

are more vocal, frequently giving spritely, sometimes quite musical songs. Unlike most resident Neotropical passerines, they often respond to pishing.

Gray-throated Warbler
Basileuterus cinereicollis   PLATE 87(1)

14 cm (5½"). *Now rare and local* in undergrowth of montane forest and borders in *Andes from w. Venezuela* (Mérida) *to ne. Colombia* (Cundinamarca). 800–2100 m. *Head and neck gray*, crown darker with *narrow coronal stripe yellow;* olive above. *Throat and breast pale gray*, midthroat whitish; belly yellow. Unlike Russetcrowned Warbler, looks *plain-faced*, with *no* black postocular stripe and no distinct border to its *yellow* (not orange-rufous) coronal stripe. Not well known, usually occurs at lower elevations than the more numerous Russet-crowned. Favors second-growth on steep slopes and re generating landslides. Song very high-pitched, often in two parts (given apparently by the members of a pair), e.g., "twzee-zee-zee-zee" followed by a more jumbled, often ascending "tzweet-tzitzitzitititi."

Gray-and-gold Warbler
Basileuterus fraseri   PLATE 87(2)

14 cm (5½"). Locally common in undergrowth of deciduous and humid woodland and scrub from *nw. Ecuador* (n. Manabí) *to nw. Peru* (Lambayeque). Mostly below 1700 m. Handsome and distinctive in range, with *mainly bluish gray upperparts*, black crown, *obvious white supraloral*, and *bright yellow underparts*. Birds from **nw. Peru and sw. Ecuador** (illustrated) have coronal stripe yellow, but this ochraceous orange in birds found **northward in Ecuador**. Other *Basileuterus* are more olive above. Usually in pairs, often with understory flocks; generally not hard to observe. Possibly engages in local movements, breeding in deciduous habitats during the rainy season, moving into more humid montane areas. Song hesitates at first, then moves into a fairly short, rising series of musical notes "titu, titu, titututeeteechee?" reminiscent of Russetcrowned Warbler.

Gray-headed Warbler
Basileuterus griseiceps   PLATE 87(3)

14 cm (5½"). *Now very rare and local* in undergrowth of montane forest and borders in ne. Venezuela (near Sucra-Monagas border). Gravely threatened by deforestation in its always limited range. 1100–2100 m. *Head dark gray* with

conspicuous white supraloral streak; olive above. Below bright yellow. *The only mainly gray-headed Basileuterus in its limited range.* Cf. Golden-crowned and Three-striped Warblers, both with prominent crown striping. Behavior poorly known; single birds and pairs have been seen foraging with small understory flocks. Song a fairly melodic "hu-wee-che-tseew" or "wee-tsee, tchew," often accompanied by the constant chipping of its mate.

Three-banded Warbler
Basileuterus trifasciatus PLATE 87(4)
12.5 cm (5"). Locally not uncommon in lower growth of montane forest, woodland, and borders in *Andes from sw. Ecuador* (El Oro and Loja) *to nw. Peru* (La Libertad). Mostly 800–3000 m. *Coronal streak and superciliary pale ashy gray,* separated by *black lateral crown stripe;* olive above. *Throat and chest pale grayish;* below yellow. Not likely confused in its limited range; cf. Three-striped Warbler (lacks gray on head and throat, etc.). Forages actively, usually in pairs and not hard to see, often at edge. As in Golden-crowned Warbler, the tail is often held cocked. Song a very high-pitched, fast series of squeaky and twittering notes.

Chocó Warbler
Basileuterus chlorophrys* PLATE 87(5)
13 cm (5"). Locally common in lower and middle growth of foothill and lower montane forest and woodland on *west slope of Andes from sw. Colombia* (w. Valle) *to sw. Ecuador* (e. Guayas). 300–1400 m. Formerly considered conspecific with *B. chrysogaster,* and then called Golden-bellied Warbler. *Head pattern relatively dull* with *superciliary mainly olive and yellow only on supraloral;* olive above. Yellow below, sides and flanks olive. Three-striped Warbler has a much bolder face pattern and is mainly buffyish below. Cf. Golden-crowned Warbler (no known actual overlap). Forages in pairs or small groups, often with understory flocks, more routinely ranging higher above the ground than congeners. Song a very thin, wiry, buzzy "t-t-t-t-tzzzzzzzzz."

Cuzco Warbler
Basileuterus chrysogaster*
13 cm (5"). *Uncommon in lower growth of foothill forest and woodland on east slope of Andes from cen. Peru* (Huánuco) *to w. Bolivia* (La Paz). 700–1200 m. Resembles geographically distant Chocó Warbler (long considered conspecific, as Golden-bellied Warbler). *Superciliary is longer*

and brighter yellow; otherwise plumage similar to Chocó. Must be distinguished with care from Two-banded Warbler, which occurs mostly at higher elevations and has brighter yellow eye-crescents, yellower underparts (less olive on sides), and more olive superciliary. Behavior much as in Chocó, though seems mainly to remain lower. Song a series of ringing "tew" notes that rise into a crescendo, very different from Chocó (vaguely recalls Buff-rumped Warbler).

Citrine Warbler
Basileuterus luteoviridis PLATE 87(6)
14 cm (5½"). Locally common in lower growth of upper montane forest and woodland in *Andes from w. Venezuela* (Mérida) *to w. Bolivia* (w. Santa Cruz). Mostly 2300–3200 m. In **most of range** (A) olive above with a *short yellow superciliary.* Mostly yellow below. Superciliary slightly longer in birds from **most of Peru. Puno, Peru, and w. Bolivia** birds (B) are rather different, with an *even longer yellow superciliary* margined above and below with black. In **W. Andes of Colombia** duller and much less yellow generally, with *throat and short superciliary whitish.* Cf. very similar Pale-legged Warbler. Superciliaried Hemispingus has a longer and narrower *white* superciliary (yellow only in w. Venezuela). Oleaginous Hemispingus is duller and more uniform (less yellow below), shows only a faint superciliary. In Cuzco, Peru, cf. also Parodi's Hemispingus. Ranges in pairs or small groups, foraging actively and often accompanying mixed flocks; not especially skulking. Song a long series of fast, high-pitched notes that rises and falls erratically and often accelerates into a trill.

Pale-legged Warbler
Basileuterus signatus
13.5 cm (5¼"). Locally common in lower growth of montane forest and woodland on *east slope of Andes from cen. Peru* (Junín) *to nw. Argentina* (Salta). Mostly 2000–2800 m. Resembles Citrine Warbler, especially in s.-cen. Peru. *Leg color doesn't help;* both have the same yellowish pink. Pale-legged differs from sympatric Citrine in its *slightly shorter yellow superciliary* and *distinct yellow lower eye-crescent.* Generally occurs at *lower* elevations than Citrine, but there is some overlap. Race of Citrine in s. Peru and Bolivia has striking black margins to its yellow superciliary. Behavior as in Citrine. Song is also similar, though not as high-pitched and more musical; some phrases also recall Black-crested Warbler.

Black-crested Warbler
Basileuterus nigrocristatus PLATE 87(7)
13.5 cm (5¼"). *Common* in shrubby lower
growth (including bamboo) at edge of upper
montane forest and woodland, locally in low
secondary scrub and even hedgerows, in *Andes
from n. Venezuela to n. Peru* (Ancash and e. La
Libertad). Mostly 2500–3500 m. *Conspicuous
black crown stripe and broad bright yellow superciliary; lores black; bright olive above. Bright yellow below.* Citrine Warblers sympatric with the
snappier-looking Black-crested *lack* black on
crown and are duller overall. Usually in pairs,
sometimes joining mixed flocks; not particularly skulking, though its fast movements make
it hard to see well for long. Oft-heard song starts
slowly with several "chit" notes, then accelerates
into a more musical phrase that usually ends
with a crescendo of "chew" notes

Russet-crowned Warbler
Basileuterus coronatus PLATE 87(8)
14 cm (5½"). Locally common in undergrowth
of montane forest and woodland in *Andes from
w. Venezuela* (Trujillo) *to w. Bolivia* (w. Santa
Cruz). Mostly 1500–2500 m, locally to 3000 m.
*Prominent black-bordered stripe down center of
crown orange-rufous; gray face crossed by black
stripe through eye; olive above. Throat grayish
white;* in **most of range** (A) yellow below, but
in **sw. Ecuador and nw. Peru** (B) grayish white
below. Golden-crowned Warbler is smaller,
has a whitish (not gray) superciliary, all yellow
underparts. Cf. Gray-throated Warbler. Usually
in pairs, regularly joining understory flocks; inquisitive and normally not hard to see. Attractive
musical song often given as a duet, sometimes
even just before dawn, a series of fast notes that
rise and seem to end with a query, followed by
a similar (but less ascending) reply from the
mate; in w. Venezuela shriller with final note
lengthened.

White-lored Warbler
Basileuterus conspicillatus
13.5 cm (5¼"). Common in undergrowth of lower
montane forest and woodland on *Santa Marta
Mts. of n. Colombia.* Mostly 1000–1800 m. *Conspicuous white supraloral and eye-crescents,* face
otherwise gray with *no* black stripe through eye;
olive above. Throat whitish, yellow below. Recalls the yellow-bellied group of Russet-crowned
Warbler (not found on the Santa Martas). The
smaller Golden-crowned Warbler has an obvious
broad whitish superciliary, no gray on face, en-

tirely yellow underparts, duller olive upperparts.
Santa Marta Warbler has a more complex and
very different face pattern. Behavior as in Russet-
crowned, but song higher-pitched, squeakier,
and less musical, the first half rising, the second
half evenly pitched (P. Boesman recording).

Three-striped Warbler
Basileuterus tristriatus PLATE 87(9)
13 cm (5"). Locally common in lower growth of
foothill and montane forest in *Andes from n. Venezuela to w. Bolivia* (w. Santa Cruz). Mostly 1000–
2000 m. *Bold facial pattern throughout, with
coronal streak and superciliary yellowish buff, and
lateral crown stripe and cheeks black* (**Venezuelan birds** have cheeks mainly dark olive). Above
olive. Color below varies from yellowish buff in
most of range (as illustrated) to yellow on **east
slope of Andes** (brightest in Peru). The complex face pattern is shared only by Santa Marta
Warbler (no overlap). In Venezuela, cf. Golden-
crowned Warbler (with orange-rufous coronal
stripe, yellow underparts, etc.). Forages actively,
often flipping its tail upward, in pairs or small
groups and regularly with understory flocks.
Song a very fast series of high-pitched notes that
rise and accelerate into a jumbled crescendo.
Also: Costa Rica and Panama.

Santa Marta Warbler
Basileuterus basilicus
14 cm (5½"). Uncommon in undergrowth of
upper montane forest and woodland on *Santa
Marta Mts. of n. Colombia.* Mostly 2300–3000 m.
Resembles the duller Three-striped Warbler (not
present on the Santa Martas), but larger and with
*a similar but even bolder black and white head
pattern.* Throat white, below bright yellow. Virtually unmistakable; only other *Basileuterus* on the
Santa Martas is the very different White-lored.
Behavior much as in Three-striped. Favors areas
with extensive *Chusquea* bamboo.

Two-banded Warbler
Basileuterus bivittatus PLATE 87(10)
13.5 cm (5¼"). Often common in lower growth
of montane forest and woodland on *east slope
of Andes from s. Peru* (Cuzco) *to nw. Argentina*
(n. Salta). 750–2200 m. *Coronal streak yellow
or orange-rufous mixed with yellow, superciliary
olive with yellow only on supraloral,* fairly prominent yellow eye-crescents; olive above. Mostly
bright yellow below. Cuzco Warbler is very similar (overlaps locally, though usually at *lower* elevations) but has longer, entirely yellow super-

ciliary and more extensive olive on sides and flanks. Golden-crowned Warbler has a whitish superciliary, duller olive upperparts, etc. Behavior much as in Three-striped Warbler. Song a complex, jumbled, warbled phrase with a rich musical quality; pairs often duet, ♂♂ giving the first, rising phrase and ♀♀ answering.

Roraiman Warbler
Basileuterus roraimae
13.5 cm (5¼"). Fairly common in lower growth of montane forest and woodland on *tepuis of s. Venezuela region.* 800–1800 m. Closely resembles Two-banded Warbler of the distant s. Andes, formerly considered conspecific. Really nothing very similar in its tepui range; cf. Golden-crowned Warbler. Behavior as in Two-banded, but song completely different, a very fast buzzy "tuh-te-te-te-tzzeeeeeeeeééé."

Golden-crowned Warbler
*Basileuterus culicivorus**   PLATE 87(11)
12.5 cm (5"). *Widespread and often common in lower growth of a variety of montane and deciduous forest and woodland types in Colombia and Venezuela, and from n. Bolivia to e. Brazil and n. Argentina.* Mostly below 1800 m. Likely more than one species involved. Birds from **most of range (north to ne. Venezuela;** illustrated) have *coronal streak orange-rufous, superciliary whitish to pale gray,* olive upperparts, and *all yellow underparts.* Birds from **w. Venezuela and Colombia** have *coronal streak yellow* and *mantle gray.* Chocó, Cuzco, and Two-banded Warblers have superciliary olive or yellowish (not whitish). White-bellied Warbler has whitish (not yellow) underparts. Forages actively, moving constantly, flicking wings and jerking its often partially cocked tail; frequently with mixed understory flocks and easy to see. Song a spritely series of 6–8 semimusical "swee" notes, the next to last usually higher and accented; little or no geographic variation. Also: Mexico to w. Panama (different song; same species?).

White-bellied Warbler
*Basileuterus hypoleucus**   PLATE 87(12)
˙ 12.5 cm (5"). Fairly common in lower growth of deciduous woodland, gallery forest, and borders in *interior s. Brazil and adjacent e. Bolivia and n. Paraguay. Coronal streak orange-rufous; superciliary and underparts whitish;* olive above. Resembles Golden-crowned Warbler and occurs with it locally, sometimes even in the same understory flock. Favors drier regions and differs

markedly in its whitish (not yellow) underparts. White-striped Warbler is larger with *no* rufous in crown, a bolder white eye-stripe, etc. Behavior and song much as in Golden-crowned; despite their apparent sympatry, the two have been considered conspecific.

Chestnut-capped Warbler
*Basileuterus delatrii**   PLATE 87(13)
13 cm (5"). Fairly common in undergrowth of deciduous and secondary woodland and shrubby clearings in *n. Colombia* (south to Río Magdalena valley) *and adjacent Venezuela* (Sierra de Perijá region). Mostly below 1300 m. A perky, brightly colored warbler. *Brick-red crown and ear-coverts separated by a long white superciliary;* bright olive above. *All bright yellow below.* Attractive and unlikely to be confused in its limited range; *no other Basileuterus has reddish ear-coverts.* Forages in pairs close to the ground, usually not hard to see. Tail usually held partially cocked. Song a sweet, fast jumble of notes typically ending with an accented last note. Also: Guatemala to Panama.

Pirre Warbler
Basileuterus ignotus
13 cm (5"). Uncommon in lower growth of lower montane forest and woodland in *extreme nw. Colombia* (nw. Chocó on Cerro Tacarcuna). 1200–1400 m. *Crown rufous-chestnut with black margins; long superciliary pale greenish yellow;* olive above. Mainly creamy yellowish below. Three-striped Warbler lacks rufous on crown, has a more complex facial pattern. Behavior much like Three-striped; Pirre more restricted to higher elevations. Apparent song a simple, high-pitched and sputtering "tssi-i-i-tit." Also: e. Panama.

Flavescent Warbler
Basileuterus flaveolus   PLATE 87(14)
14.5 cm (5¾"). *Fairly common on or near ground in deciduous and gallery woodland from n. Bolivia* (Beni) *to e. Brazil;* isolated populations north of Amazon. Locally to 1300 m. *Simply patterned,* with *bright olive upperparts* and *bright yellow short superciliary and underparts; legs orange-yellow.* Citrine and Pale-legged Warblers have similar plumage but entirely different Andean distributions; also differ in behavior (they are not semiterrestrial). ♀ Masked and Southern Yellowthroats can occur with it, but they too are less terrestrial and have gray on crown, no yellow superciliary. Ranges singly or in pairs,

walking or hopping on the ground on its long legs, often swiveling fanned tail sideways. Heard much more often than seen. Song a loud, ringing, musical series of fast notes, "titi, teetee, teetee, chéw-chéw-chéw-chéw."

White-striped Warbler
Basileuterus leucophrys   PLATE 87(15)

14.5 cm (5¾"). *Uncommon and local on or near ground in gallery forest of interior s.-cen. Brazil* (s. Mato Grosso to w. Bahia and São Paulo). To about 1000 m. Crown slaty with a *striking broad white superciliary* and *black stripe through eye; bronzy olive above.* Below white, breast mottled gray. White-bellied Warbler is smaller with a less stout bill, orange-rufous coronal stripe, and different behavior. Occurs in pairs that walk and hop through thick undergrowth and are hard to see well without tape playback; generally not with flocks. The tail is often raised, spread, and swiveled sideways. Song a beautiful loud, ringing cascade of pure melodic notes; other shorter versions (e.g., "t-r-r-r-r, ti-i-i-i, tr-r-r") may be repeated several times in succession.

White-rimmed Warbler
Basileuterus leucoblepharus   PLATE 87(16)

14.5 cm (5¾"). Fairly common on or near ground in humid forest and woodland, usually near water (locally also in gallery and monte woodland), in *se. Brazil region* (north to Rio de Janeiro and adjacent Minas Gerais). To 1600 m. *Head mainly gray* with *white supraloral and prominent partial eye-ring;* olive above. Below white, *breast mottled gray.* White-striped Warbler has a prominent long white superciliary, etc.; exclusive to interior Brazil, it is not known to occur with White-rimmed. More closely resembles sympatric race of Riverbank Warbler (and they can occur together, though Riverbank is even more closely tied to water); Riverbank has buff on sides and flanks and shows no gray below. Usually

ranges in pairs that walk and hop through thick undergrowth, frequently fanning tail, which is sometimes wagged or swiveled sideways. Oft-heard song a series of separated tinkling notes, at first high-pitched but then gradually dropping; the overall effect is enchanting.

Buff-rumped Warbler
Basileuterus fulvicauda   PLATE 87(17)

13.5 cm (5¼"). *Fairly common on or near ground along forested and wooded streams and rivers, and in swampy areas, from Colombia to sw. Ecuador* (w. Loja) *and extreme nw. Bolivia* (Pando and La Paz) *and w. Brazil.* Mostly below 1000 m. Easily identified by its *obvious buff rump and basal half of tail.* Brownish olive above, grayer on crown and with buff superciliary. Below buffy whitish. Riverbank Warbler *lacks* buff rump and tail. Occurs singly or in pairs, hopping near water's edge and on banks, frequently sweeping its often fanned tail sideways. Vigorous song a rising, accelerating crescendo of loud "tew" notes that ends with a series of strongly emphasized "tchéw" notes. Also: Honduras to Panama.

Riverbank Warbler
*Basileuterus rivularis**   PLATE 87(18)

13.5 cm (5¼"). *Replaces Buff-rumped Warbler eastward, south to se. Brazil region,* and also *along base of Andes in w. Bolivia* (La Paz to w. Santa Cruz). To 1400 m. Formerly called River (sometimes Riverside) Warbler. *Lacks* Buff-rumped's buff rump and basal tail, those areas being concolor with olive of upperparts. **Se. Brazil** birds (illustrated) have blackish lateral crown striping and are buffier below. In **Bolivia** they lack the crown striping and are quite white below. **Northeastern** birds are also buffy below and have a buff superciliary and face. Behavior and voice much as in Buff-rumped, but song tends not to accelerate as much.

TANAGERS: THRAUPIDAE

A diverse group of mainly arboreal birds, like the warblers part of the large 9-primaried assemblage formerly united in the family Emberizidae, tanagers are found widely in South America, with most species favoring forested and wooded environments. It has recently been suggested that a few genera (*Piranga, Habia, Chlorothraupis, Mitrospingus, Rhodinocichla,* and *Chlorospingus*) are better placed in the family Cardinalidae, and that the euphonias and chlorophonias are better placed in the family Fringillidae, but all here had to be retained in their traditional position. Some tanagers are among the most colorful of our birds, but others are notably drab. Most tanagers eat both insects and fruit, the latter especially when feeding young, but some species are more warblerlike and exclusively insectivorous. A few are good songsters, though on the whole the family is not known for its vocal prowess. Nests are open cups.

Diglossa

A distinctive group of small tanagers with *obviously upturned and hooked bills* used to pierce the corolla of flowers; the bills of *Diglossopis* show this to a lesser degree. They are found in montane woodland and scrub *in the Andes* (only a few range in taller forest), mostly at higher elevations, with two species on the tepuis. The first four form a cohesive group of more forest-based and insectivorous species, sometimes separated in the genus *Diglossopis*. After the two tepui endemics come two Andean superspecies, the "Black Flowerpiercer complex" and the "Glossy Flowerpiercer complex"; these exhibit essentially parallel geographic interspecific variation. Last come three small, simply patterned, and sexually dimorphic species.

Bluish Flowerpiercer
Diglossa caerulescens   PLATE 88(1)
13.5 cm (5¼"). Locally fairly common in canopy and borders of montane forest in *Andes from n. Venezuela to w. Bolivia* (Cochabamba). Mostly 1600–2700 m. *Uniform-looking; bill has relatively normal shape. Iris reddish to orange. Grayish blue*, somewhat paler on belly; *foreface blackish*. **Southern birds** (north to Ecuador)

whitish on midbelly (as illustrated); **northern birds** darker and bluer. Masked Flowerpiercer is larger and bluer with a brighter red eye and a more contrasting black mask. Usually in or close to montane forest, but also comes into shrubby clearings; can be particularly numerous in elfin woodland on windswept ridges. Often accompanies mixed flocks. Frequently eats small fruits, also gleans for insects more often than many flowerpiercers. Song a series of high-pitched notes that trails away and is interspersed with squeaky twittering; call a metallic "tsii!"

Masked Flowerpiercer
Diglossa cyanea   PLATE 88(2)
14.5 cm (5¾"). *Widespread and often common, especially from Ecuador north,* in montane forest, shrubby woodland, and borders in *Andes from n. Venezuela to w. Bolivia* (w. Santa Cruz). *Iris red,* contrasting with an *obvious black mask;* otherwise *rich ultramarine blue.* ♀ somewhat duller. Cf. Bluish Flowerpiercer and Blue-and-black Tanager. This striking flowerpiercer regularly forages in groups as part of mixed flocks, often gleaning for insects and eating small fruits but also probing into flowers. Song a series of thin notes followed by a twitter (northward), or a jumbled series of high-pitched notes ending with several drawn-out "tseeeee" notes (southward).

Indigo Flowerpiercer

Diglossa indigotica PLATE 88(3)

11.5 cm (4½"). *Rare to locally uncommon in canopy and borders of mossy cloud forest in w. Colombia and nw. Ecuador* (south to Pichincha, and perhaps in El Oro). Mostly 1000–1600 m. *Iris fiery red,* contrasting with *uniform bright deep ultramarine plumage.* The larger Masked Flowerpiercer occurs at higher elevations and has an obvious black mask. Forages singly or in pairs, often with mixed flocks, generally remaining well above the ground; general behavior much like Golden-eyed Flowerpiercer (found on *east* slope).

Golden-eyed Flowerpiercer

Diglossa glauca* PLATE 88(4)

12 cm (4¾"). Fairly common in canopy and borders of foothill and montane forest on *east slope of Andes from s. Colombia* (w. Caquetá) *to w. Bolivia* (Cochabamba). Mostly 1000–1900 m, thus at *lower* elevations than most other flowerpiercers. Usually called Deep-blue Flowerpiercer. *Conspicuous bright golden yellow eye* contrasts with dark blue plumage. ♀ somewhat duller. *No other flowerpiercer has a yellow iris.* Forages singly or in pairs, usually well above the ground, often joining mixed flocks. Gleans for insects, especially along mossy branches and among bromeliads, and also eats small fruits; very infrequent at flowers. Rarely heard song a high-pitched series of thin squeaky notes, jumbled toward end.

Greater Flowerpiercer

Diglossa major PLATE 88(5)

16.5 cm (6½"). Locally fairly common in montane forest and borders, shrubby clearings, and stunted low woodland on *tepuis of se. Venezuela and adjacent Brazil.* 1300–2800 m, most numerous above 1800 m. Easily the *largest flowerpiercer;* does not occur with any other species. Mostly bluish slate with *black mask* and silvery moustache, *fine silvery bluish shaft streaks on crown and mantle,* and *chestnut crissum.* Found singly or in pairs, sometimes accompanying small mixed flocks. Gleans for insects and probes and pierces flowers. Apparent song (quite different from other *Diglossa*) a scratchy rattling, often introduced by tinkling notes.

Scaled Flowerpiercer

Diglossa duidae

14 cm (5½"). *Found only on remote tepuis in Amazonas, Venezuela, and adjacent n. Brazil.* 1400–2600 m. Judging from the large number of specimens taken, this is a common bird, especially above 1800 m. *A dull, unpatterned flowerpiercer,* mostly bluish slate with blacker head (though *no* mask); whitish centers of breast feathers create a vague scaly effect; *no* chestnut on crissum. Does not occur with any congener. Favors montane scrub, smaller numbers also in actual forest. Behavior probably much as in Greater Flowerpiercer.

Black Flowerpiercer

Diglossa humeralis PLATE 88(6)

13.5 cm (5¼"). *Generally common* in shrubby areas, gardens, and forest borders in Andes from sw. Venezuela (s. Táchira) and n. Colombia to extreme n. Peru (n. Cajamarca). Mostly 2500–4000 m, locally to 4500 m in Ecuador. *Uniform dull black.* In **Colombia's E. Andes** has a gray shoulder patch (illustrated), *lacking* elsewhere. Easily confused with Glossy Flowerpiercer (sometimes sympatric), though Glossy is more forest-based and favors more humid regions. Glossy *always* has a blue-gray shoulder patch (in most of its range Black does *not*); where Black does have a shoulder patch (Colombia's E. Andes), go by Glossy's somewhat larger size and proportionally bigger bill, the bluer tone of shoulder patch, and glossier black plumage. Found singly or in pairs, foraging actively at varying heights (most often low), usually independent of mixed flocks. Nectar is obtained both by piercing flower corollas and by direct probing; also gleans from leaves and branches. Song a jumbled and fast twittering.

Glossy Flowerpiercer

Diglossa lafresnayii PLATE 88(7)

14.5 cm (5¾"). Fairly common in shrubby areas and low humid woodland, *most numerous near treeline,* in Andes from w. Venezuela (Trujillo) *to extreme n. Peru* (n. Cajamarca). Mostly 2700–3700 m. *Glossy black with obvious bluish gray shoulders.* Cf. Black Flowerpiercer (which does *not* have shoulder patch in most of range). Found singly or in pairs, most often independent of mixed flocks; seems shy and restless, feeding mainly inside cover and thus hard to see well except when singing. Regularly pierces corollas of flowers; in Ecuador comes to hummingbird feeders at some sites. Also gleans for insects. Song a fast series of semimusical twittery notes, sometimes long-continued.

Moustached Flowerpiercer

Diglossa mystacalis PLATE 88(8)

14.5 cm (5¾"). Uncommon in low woodland, borders of montane forest, and shrubby areas on east slope of Andes, mainly just below treeline, from n. Peru (Amazonas, south of Río Marañón) to w. Bolivia (w. Santa Cruz). 2500–4000 m. Marked geographic variation. Mainly black with contrasting rufous crissum. Birds from **n. and cen. Peru** have a conspicuous *white malar streak* and a *rufous* (**northward;** A) *or rufous and white pectoral band.* Birds from **farther south** have blue-gray shoulder patch and are all black below with *no* pectoral band; in **Bolivia** (B) *malar streak rufous,* in **s. Peru** *buffy white.* Behavior similar to Glossy Flowerpiercer. Musical but rather patternless song a series of sweet notes that rise and fall irregularly.

Gray-bellied Flowerpiercer
Diglossa carbonaria   PLATE 88(9)
14 cm (5½″). Common in scrub, gardens, and montane woodland, in both arid and humid regions, in *Andes of w. Bolivia* (s. La Paz to n. Chuquisaca), nearly meeting Black-throated's range in La Paz; a recent sighting from nw. Argentina (Jujuy). Mostly 2500–4000 m. Mostly black with *lower breast and belly gray,* shoulders and rump also gray; crissum rufous. Sympatric Moustached Flowerpiercers are all black below with a rufous malar streak. Behavior as in Black Flowerpiercer.

Black-throated Flowerpiercer
Diglossa brunneiventris   PLATE 88(10)
14 cm (5½″). Fairly common in scrub, gardens, and montane woodland in *Andes of Peru* (north to s. Cajamarca and Amazonas), *w. Bolivia* (La Paz), *and extreme n. Chile;* an isolated population (same species?) at *n. end of W. and Cen. Andes in Colombia. More often in arid regions than most other flowerpiercers* (except Rusty). Mostly 2500–4200 m. Black above with gray shoulders and rump. *Midthroat black, below rufous-chestnut* (extending up as a malar streak), flanks gray. Moustached Flowerpiercer is somewhat larger and all or mostly black below. Chestnut-bellied Flowerpiercer (*very* local in w. Colombia) also is somewhat larger, and has throat and chest black (rufous-chestnut only on belly). Behavior as in Black Flowerpiercer.

Mérida Flowerpiercer
Diglossa gloriosa   PLATE 88(11)
13.5 (5¼″). *Fairly common in scrub and montane woodland in Andes of w. Venezuela* (n. Trujillo to n. Táchira). Mostly 2700–4000 m. Mostly black with *contrasting chestnut lower breast and belly,* flanks dark gray; shoulders, rump, and in-

conspicuous superciliary gray. Glossy Flowerpiercer is all black below; ♂ Rusty Flowerpiercer is uniform cinnamon below and more bluish gray above. Cf. also Blue-backed Conebill (with a different bill, blue back). Behavior as in Black Flowerpiercer.

Chestnut-bellied Flowerpiercer
Diglossa gloriossisima
14.5 cm (5¾″). *Very local at higher elevations in W. Andes of Colombia* (Antioquia and Cauca). 3100–3800 m. Mostly glossy black with *contrasting rufous-chestnut lower breast and belly and blue-gray shoulders.* In color pattern not unlike Mérida Flowerpiercer (no overlap). The slightly smaller Black-throated Flowerpiercer is almost entirely rufous-chestnut below, with black reduced to a small patch on midthroat. Cf. also Blue-backed Conebill (with different bill, blue back). Not well known, and perhaps scarce (certainly very local); habitat and behavior as in Glossy Flowerpiercer.

White-sided Flowerpiercer
Diglossa albilatera   PLATE 88(12)
12 cm (4¾″). Fairly common and widespread in montane forest borders and shrubby clearings in *Andes from n. Venezuela to s. Peru* (Cuzco); apparently scarcer in Peru. Mostly 1800–2800 m. ♂ *dark slaty* with *partially concealed (but usually visible) white tuft on sides and under wing linings.* ♀ has *white tuft similar to* ♂ but slightly smaller; olive brown above, pale buffy brown below. **Immature** like ♀ but vaguely streaked below. The white on the sides usually shows; if it doesn't, ♂ can be confused with Black Flowerpiercer (which, as the name implies, is black and not slaty). Cf. also ♂ Slaty Finch (with different bill, but otherwise rather similar). Found singly and in pairs, foraging actively and often nervously twitching its wings exposing the white; regularly joins mixed flocks. Punctures flowers and also gleans for insects; in Ecuador comes to hummingbird feeders at some sites. Song a short, dry, and unmusical trill.

Venezuelan Flowerpiercer
Diglossa venezuelensis   PLATE 88(13)
12.5 cm (5″). *Now rare and local* in montane forest, secondary woodland, and borders in mountains of *ne. Venezuela* (mainly near Sucre-Monagas border; also seen on Paria Peninsula). At serious risk due to deforestation. Mostly 1500–2400 m, rarely down to 850 m. Resembles smaller White-sided Flowerpiercer (no overlap),

but Venezuelan's white tuft on sides is somewhat smaller. ♂ *notably blacker* (not just slaty gray). ♀ has *head yellowish olive.* The only flowerpiercer sympatric with this species is the Rusty, ♂ of which is very different; ♀ Rusty is smaller with some streaking below, lacks any white on sides. Not well known, but behavior seems much as in other flowerpiercers. Song a rambling and run-together series of jumbled, semimusical notes, very different from White-sided.

Rusty Flowerpiercer
Diglossa sittoides   PLATE 88(14)
11.5 cm (4½"). Uncommon and rather local in shrubby areas, gardens, and lighter montane woodland in *Andes from n. Venezuela* (east to Sucre) *to nw. Argentina* (Tucumán); found in both humid and arid regions, but basically a nonforest flowerpiercer. Mostly 1500–3000 m, a few locally to treeline and occasionally wandering as low as the Peruvian coast. Distinctive ♂ *bicolored, essentially bluish gray above and cinnamon below.* Much duller ♀ brownish olive above and dingy yellowish buff below with *obscure dusky streaking on throat and chest.* ♀ lacks the white on sides shown by ♀♀ of White-sided and Venezuelan Flowerpiercers. Cf. various montane conebills. Found singly or in pairs, often piercing flowers, sometimes while hanging upside down. Gives a thin trill and a twittering, but neither is heard all that often.

Plushcap
Catamblyrhynchus diadema   PLATE 89(1)
14 cm (5½"). Uncommon in lower growth of upper montane forest, woodland, and borders, almost invariably in stands of *Chusquea* bamboo, in *Andes from n. Venezuela to extreme nw. Argentina* (Jujuy). Mostly 2300–3500 m. *Thick stubby bill. Forecrown bright golden yellow* (feathers short and plushlike); *gray above. Face and underparts rich chestnut.* From **n. Peru southward** somewhat paler. **Immature** duller, more olive and buff. Might carelessly be confused with Golden-crowned Tanager (at least they share yellow on crown), but the tanager is mainly blue, etc. Usually inconspicuous (in part because it favors such dense growth), foraging actively, usually in pairs and regularly with mixed flocks. Often feeds on bamboo stalks, searching for insects by pushing its bill into stems and leaf nodes. Generally quiet; song a long series of almost random chips and twitters, somewhat like a hummingbird.

Pardusco
Nephelornis oneilli   PLATE 89(2)
13 cm (5"). Very local, but common where it occurs, in elfin woodland near treeline on *east slope of Andes in cen. Peru* (e. La Libertad to Huánuco). 3000–3800 m. *Very drab. Dull olive brown above and ochraceous buff below. Slender pointed bill* distinguishes it from any flowerpiercer, but cf. ♀ Tit-like Dacnis and certain finches (e.g., ♀ Slaty). Occurs in groups of up to 15 birds, which often move rapidly, sometimes joining mixed flocks, and are not at all shy. Sometimes jerks tail sideways. Forages by gleaning for insects on leaves and moss. Contact call a frequent "seep."

Tit-like Dacnis
Xenodacnis parina   PLATE 89(3)
13–14 cm (5–5½"). Locally common in shrubbery and patches of low woodland (often in *Polylepis*) in *high Andes of s. Ecuador* (Azuay) and in *Peru* (s. Amazonas to Cuzco and Arequipa). Mostly 3100–4500 m. *Stubby pointed bill.* In **western part of range** (south to Lima, Huánuco, and Arequipa in Peru; A) ♂ *deep blue streaked with glistening paler blue, especially above.* ♀ has *blue forecrown and ocular area* and edging on wing-coverts, rump, and tail; *mostly cinnamon-buff below.* In **se. Peru** (Junín to Cuzco; B) usually smaller; ♂ paler and more grayish blue with little or no streaking; ♀ has *entire crown and nape blue* and slightly brighter underparts. There really are no similar birds in its high-elevation woodlands. Occurs in pairs or small groups, feeding primarily by gleaning from underside of leaves, especially those of *Gynoxys* shrubs, from which they obtain aphids and their sugary secretions. Song a *surprisingly loud,* fast series of penetrating whistled notes (sometimes sounding like the repeated cracking of a whip), e.g., "zwit-zwit-zwit-zhweet-zhweet-zhweet," interspersed with lower-pitched scratchy notes.

Giant Conebill
Oreomanes fraseri   PLATE 89(4)
15–16 cm (6–6¼"). Uncommon and local in groves of *Polylepis* woodland near and above treeline in *high Andes of extreme s. Colombia and Ecuador* (south to Azuay and n. Loja), and from *n.-cen. Peru to extreme n. Chile* (recently found in n. Tarapacá) *and w. Bolivia* (s. Potosí). Mostly 3500–4200 m, rarely (or locally) as low as 2700 m and up to 4800 m. *Bill long and sharply pointed. Mostly gray above* with short chestnut superciliary and *conspicuous white cheeks; below chestnut* (intensity variable). **Ecuadorian**

birds (A) have crown concolor gray; **birds from farther south** (B) have a variable amount of whitish frosting on forecrown. Nearly unmistakable, with very distinctive behavior. Found singly or in pairs, sometimes accompanying small mixed flocks. Usually unobtrusive, but can be located by listening for a bird scaling off pieces of the *Polylepis* tree's flaky bark; they also often simply probe beneath pieces of bark. Hitches along trunks and larger limbs much like a *Sitta* nuthatch, sometimes hanging upside down, less often continuing out onto smaller branches. Not particularly vocal, but occasionally one will break into its fairly musical jumbled song, e.g., "cheet, cheeveét, cheeveét."

Conirostrum

Small, warblerlike tanagers with *slender, sharply pointed bills* found primarily in or near montane forest and woodland in the *Andes;* Cinereous and Tamarugo Conebills range down to the coast in Peru and Chile, and occur more often in semiopen scrub and even gardens. Plumage patterns vary, but *blue or gray and rufous predominate in most species.* Lowland *Conirostrum* follow on pp. 584–585.

Blue-backed Conebill
Conirostrum sitticolor PLATE 89(5)
13 cm (5″). Uncommon to fairly common in montane forest, woodland, and borders in *Andes from w. Venezuela* (Trujillo) *to w. Bolivia* (w. Santa Cruz); more numerous northward. Mostly 2500–3500 m. Head, throat, and chest black contrasting with *mainly blue mantle* and *rich rufous underparts.* Birds from **w. Venezuela** (A) have a blue postocular, lacking in birds of **Colombia, Ecuador, and n. Peru** (B). **Farther south in Peru and Bolivia** the eye-stripe is again present, and *throat and chest are dusky-blue.* Not likely confused, though Blue-backed's pattern somewhat recalls various flowerpiercers (with very different hooked bills, etc.). Occurs in pairs or small groups, often accompanying mixed flocks. Actively gleans and probes in foliage, often hopping about in the open atop leaves; sometimes wags tail (not as persistently as Capped Conebill). Song a jumbled twittering, long-continued.

Cinereous Conebill
*Conirostrum cinereum** PLATE 89(6)
12–12.5 cm (4¾–5″). *Often common* in shrubby and semiopen areas, gardens, and low montane woodland in arid (especially) and humid regions in *Andes from s. Colombia* (Cauca) *to n. Chile and w. Bolivia* (Cochabamba). Mostly 2500–4000 m, but in Peru and Chile found down to sea level. *Distinctive* L-shaped white wing-patch and *bold superciliary.* In **montane s. Peru and Bolivia** (A) leaden gray above with *superciliary white.* Paler gray below, buffier on belly and especially crissum. Birds of **Ecuador and s. Colombia** (B) are brownish above with *superciliary buff;* ochraceous buff below. Birds of **w. Peru and Chile** resemble (gray-backed) highland birds but are slightly paler overall with a shorter superciliary and have drab buffyish underparts. Found singly or in pairs, foraging nervously in foliage at varying heights; sometimes also feeds at flowers. Most often not with flocks. Song a jumbled twittering.

Tamarugo Conebill
Conirostrum tamarugense PLATE 89(7)
12.5 cm (5″). Very local and uncommon in scrub and low woodland with scattered trees (nonbreeding) and (breeding) in groves of *Prosopis* trees, locally called "tamarugos," from *sw. Peru* (Arequipa) *to n. Chile* (n. Antofagasta). Occurs from sea level to 4050 m; now known to breed (Oct.–Mar.) at about 1000 m near Iquique in n. Chile (C. F. Estades), after nesting apparently moving to higher elevations and north into Peru. Resembles western lowland race of Cinereous Conebill (with which Tamarugo is locally sympatric; the two sometimes even forage together), but has *superciliary, throat, and midchest cinnamon-rufous,* a cinnamon crissum, and is somewhat darker gray above. **Juvenile** lacks the cinnamon-rufous. Behavior much as in Cinereous.

White-browed Conebill
Conirostrum ferrugineiventre PLATE 89(8)
12 cm (4¾″). Uncommon in montane forest, woodland, and adjacent shrubby areas on *east slope of Andes from n. Peru* (s. San Martín) *to w. Bolivia* (w. Santa Cruz). Mostly 2500–3800 m, most numerous near treeline. Bluish gray above with *black crown* and *long white superciliary and whitish malar streak. Mainly bright rufous below.* Black-eared Hemispingus differs in its larger size, black upper throat, etc. Cf. also ♀ of larger Slaty Tanager and ♂ Rusty Flowerpiercer. Found singly or in pairs, often accompanying mixed flocks. Forages at all levels, usually in foliage and among smaller branches.

Rufous-browed Conebill

Conirostrum rufum   PLATE 89(9)

12.5 cm (5"). Uncommon in shrubby areas, low montane woodland, borders of montane forest, and gardens in *Andes from sw. Venezuela (s. Táchira) to ne. Colombia* (Cundinamarca), and in *Santa Marta Mts. of n. Colombia.* Mostly 2700–3300 m. Forehead, superciliary, sides of head, and underparts rufous. Otherwise bluish gray above. Distinctive in its limited range; cf. ♂ Rusty Flowerpiercer (which lacks the superciliary, has a hooked bill, etc.). Behavior as in White-browed Conebill.

Capped Conebill

Conirostrum albifrons   PLATE 89(10)

13 cm (5"). Locally fairly common in montane forest and borders in *Andes from n. and w. Venezuela* (northern coastal mountains and s. Táchira) *to w. Bolivia* (w. Santa Cruz). Mostly 1800–2800 m. In **most of range** (A) ♂ black with *dark glossy blue crown* and dark blue suffusion on lesser wing-coverts, scapulars, lower back and rump, and crissum (less blue suffusion in **Peru and Bolivia**). In **Colombia's Cen. and E. Andes, far sw. Venezuela, and far ne. Ecuador** (B) ♂ very different, with a *striking snowy white crown.* ♂ in **n. Venezuela mountains** reverts to having a blue crown. ♀ has *crown grayish blue to blue* (brighter southward); above bright olive. *Throat and breast bluish gray,* belly yellowish olive. White-crowned ♂♂ are unmistakable, but the blue of crown in birds found elsewhere can be hard to see, so these can look essentially all dark. ♀ most resembles Gray-hooded Bush Tanager, but the tanager has a stubbier bill (pink northward), brighter yellow underparts, no bluish on crown. In poor light the conebill's *near-constant tail-wagging* is often a helpful point (but note that the Gray-hooded does this as well). Arboreal, often in tall forest, occurring in pairs or small groups and regularly with mixed flocks. Infrequently heard song a sweet jumbled twittering with a repeated "seesaw" phrase (N. K. Krabbe) often dominating.

Dacnis

Small, active, warblerlike tanagers with *short but sharply pointed bills* found mainly in humid lowland or montane forests. They show *striking sexual dimorphism,* and ♂♂ are *often predominantly blue.* Their voices are insignificant at best.

Scarlet-thighed Dacnis

Dacnis venusta   PLATE 90(1)

12 cm (4¾"). Uncommon in canopy and borders of humid forest and adjacent clearings in *w. Colombia and nw. Ecuador* (south mainly to Pichincha). Mostly 200–700 m. ♂ has *bright turquoise blue crown, sides of head,* back, and rump; *below black,* with scarlet thighs often hidden. ♀ much duller, with *dull greenish blue upperparts* and *dingy buffy grayish underparts.* Beautiful ♂ nearly unmistakable, the only dacnis with black underparts, but cf. Blue-necked Tanager. ♀ Yellow-tufted Dacnis has a yellow eye and bright yellow midbelly. Often forages in small groups, sometimes with mixed flocks; feeds mainly on small fruits. Also: Costa Rica and Panama.

Blue Dacnis

Dacnis cayana   PLATE 90(2)

12.5 cm (5"). *Widespread and often common* in forested and wooded habitats, also in clearings and gardens, from Colombia and Venezuela to s. Brazil area. Mostly below 1000 m, a few to 1600–2000 m in n. Andes. Rather long and pointed bill with pinkish base; legs pinkish. ♂ in **most of range** (A) *mostly turquoise blue; throat patch and back black;* wings and tail black edged blue. In **w. Colombia and w. Ecuador** (B) *darker and more ultramarine blue.* ♀ *bright green,* paler below, with a *bluish head.* In Colombia cf. Viridian Dacnis and Turquoise Dacnis; in se. Brazil, Black-legged Dacnis; all three species are much rarer than Blue. ♀ most likely confused with certain green immature *Tangara* tanagers and ♀ Green Honeycreeper, though none have blue on head. Found in pairs or small groups that often move with mixed flocks, foraging at all levels and mainly gleaning for insects; to a lesser extent congregates with other birds to eat small fruits, and also comes to flowering trees. Also: Honduras to Panama.

Black-legged Dacnis

Dacnis nigripes   PLATE 90(3)

11 cm (4¼"). *Rare in canopy and borders of humid forest in se. Brazil* (Espírito Santo to ne. Santa Catarina). Mostly below 850 m. ♂ resembles ♂ of more common Blue Dacnis (the two species can co-occur) but is smaller with a shorter tail and *blackish* (not pinkish) *legs,* and has less extensive areas of black on back and throat; its black primaries are *not* edged blue (unlike ♂ Blue). ♀ very different from ♀ Blue, brownish olive above with *blue tinge on face, uniform pale dull buffyish below.* ♀ recalls ♀ of geographically

far-removed Scarlet-thighed Dacnis. Behavior much as in Blue Dacnis; sometimes the two even feed together.

Viridian Dacnis
Dacnis viguieri

11.5 cm (4½"). Rare to uncommon in canopy and borders of humid forest and secondary woodland in *nw. Colombia* (n. Chocó, nw. Antioquia, and sw. Bolívar). To 600 m. *Iris yellow. ♂ mainly bluish green, with midback and tail black; wings green with contrasting black primaries.* Much duller ♀ olive green above and mostly pale greenish yellow below. ♂ Blue Dacnis is dark-eyed, has a black throat patch (*lacking in ♂ Viridian*), and is a much purer blue (in poor light the color difference can be hard to discern). ♀ Yellow-tufted Dacnis differs in its bright yellow midbelly; both species have yellow eyes. Behavior much as in Blue Dacnis. Also: e. Panama.

Turquoise Dacnis
Dacnis hartlaubi PLATE 90(4)

11 cm (4¼"). *Rare and local* in montane forest borders and adjacent plantations and clearings in *Andes of w. Colombia* (w. Boyacá to w. Cundinamarca; e. Quindío; Antioquia and Valle). Mostly 1350–2200 m. *Bill stubby. Iris yellow. ♂ turquoise blue and black;* overall pattern recalls ♂ Yellow-tufted Dacnis but with a *black throat patch* and *no yellow below.* Dull ♀ resembles ♀ Yellow-tufted but has a heavier bill and *browner upperparts* (not so olive) with buff wing-edging and buffier underparts. Arboreal, with behavior much as in Blue Dacnis. Sometimes feeds in isolated trees in clearings, and also apparently occurs regularly in shade coffee plantations (though perhaps only where patches of forest or woodland are nearby).

Black-faced Dacnis
Dacnis lineata PLATE 90(5)

11.5 cm (4½"). *Widespread and often common* in canopy and borders of humid forest and woodland from *Amazonia to the Guianas.* Mostly below 1200 m. *Iris yellow.* Beautiful ♂ *bright turquoise blue below and on crown* with contrasting *white midbelly* and underwing-coverts; mostly black above. Much drabber ♀ brownish olive above and dull pale grayish below. ♀ Yellow-bellied Dacnis is slightly larger, red-eyed, and somewhat mottled on breast. Cf. similar (but much rarer) ♀ White-bellied Dacnis. Yellow-tufted Dacnis occurs only *west* of Andes. Behav-

ior much as in Blue Dacnis, but more often in small groups, occasionally up to 10–20 or even more together.

Yellow-tufted Dacnis
*Dacnis egregia** PLATE 90(6)

11.5 cm (4½"). Locally fairly common in canopy and borders of humid and deciduous forest, woodland, and adjacent clearings in *w. Colombia* (Córdoba to Huila) *and w. Ecuador* (w. Esmeraldas to El Oro). To 900 m. *Yellow iris. ♂ resembles ♂ Black-faced Dacnis (found east of Andes; formerly conspecific) but tuft at bend of wing larger, protruding more, and bright yellow; median belly also bright yellow. ♀ differs from ♀* Black-faced in much the same way. **Ecuadorian** ♂♂ are slightly greener, less pure turquoise, ♀♀ grayer on head than Colombian birds (more uniform olive). In Colombia cf. ♀ of heavier-billed Turquoise Dacnis. Behavior much as in Blue Dacnis; not in as large groups as Black-faced.

Scarlet-breasted Dacnis
Dacnis berlepschi PLATE 90(7)

12 cm (4¾"). Rare to locally uncommon in canopy and borders of humid forest from *sw. Colombia* (w. Nariño) *to nw. Ecuador* (mainly Esmeraldas). To at least 1200 m. *Iris yellow.* Unmistakable ♂ *blue above and on throat and chest* with *opalescent streaking on mantle. Wide breast band flame scarlet,* belly pale buff. Much duller ♀ *brown above* and mainly buffyish below with a *red band across breast* (obvious enough, though not as bright as in ♂). ♀ is browner than other vaguely similar *Dacnis* or tanagers and actually looks more like a finch or grassquit (e.g., ♀ Crimson-breasted Finch), though none has red on breast or pale irides. Arboreal behavior much as in other dacnis, though seems to come to borders and second-growth less often; usually in pairs and often with mixed flocks, almost always remaining high above the ground.

White-bellied Dacnis
Dacnis albiventris PLATE 90(8)

11.5 cm (4½"). *Unaccountably rare and local in canopy and borders of humid forest in w. Amazonia.* Below 400 m. *Yellow iris. ♂ mostly bright cobalt blue* with *small black mask* and black scapulars. *Lower underparts white.* Obscure ♀ green above and greenish yellow below, yellower on midbelly. ♂ is darker and less turquoise blue than other ♂ *Dacnis,* closer in color to certain *Tangara,* especially Masked Tanager. ♀

resembles ♀ of much commoner Black-faced Dacnis but is greener above and yellower below. Not well known; seems genuinely scarce, not just overlooked. Has been seen with mixed flocks of other *Dacnis* and tanagers, sometimes at fruiting melastomaceous trees.

Yellow-bellied Dacnis
Dacnis flaviventer　　　　PLATE 90(9)
12.5 cm (5"). Locally fairly common in canopy and borders of humid forest (especially vár-zea) in *Amazonia*. Mostly below 800 m. *Red iris.* Distinctive ♂ has *contrasting olive green crown,* mainly black upperparts with *yellow scapulars and rump. Mainly yellow below* with *black midthroat.* ♀ olive brown above, pale brownish buff below with *obscure brownish mottling on throat, breast, and flanks.* ♀ Black-faced Dacnis is yellow-eyed, more olive (not so brown) overall, lacks mottling below. Behavior much as in other *Dacnis,* though seems to favor areas near water.

Cyanerpes

Attractive small tanagers with *slender de-curved bills* and *brightly colored legs,* especially in the beautiful ♂♂. Most honey-creepers are notably *short-tailed,* the Red-legged less markedly so. ♂♂ are *some shade of blue,* ♀♀ green and *streaked below. Cyanerpes* are forest-based birds and usually range in the canopy (coming lower at edge); they are strongly nectarivorous, and regularly congregate in flowering trees. None seems to have a true song.

Purple Honeycreeper
Cyanerpes caeruleus　　　　PLATE 90(10)
11 cm (4¼"). *Widespread and often* common in canopy and borders of humid and foothill forest, woodland, and adjacent clearings from Colombia and Venezuela to Amazonia and the Guianas. Mostly below 1200 m. *Bill long and decurved; legs bright yellow in* ♂, dusky yellowish in ♀. ♂ *mostly purplish blue;* lores, throat, wings, and tail black. ♀ green above with *buff lores, throat, and face* (latter streaked) and *blue malar streak.* Mostly streaked green and yellowish below. Short-billed Honeycreeper has a shorter bill, and both sexes have pinkish legs. In nw. Colombia cf. Shining Honeycreeper. Often in groups (sometimes quite large, up to a dozen or more birds) that accompany other tanagers and regularly congregate

at fruiting and flowering trees; they sometimes come quite low at borders. Also forages for small insects, especially on branches and twigs. Call a high thin "zree." Also: e. Panama.

Shining Honeycreeper
Cyanerpes lucidus
11 cm (4¼"). Canopy and borders of humid and foothill forest in *extreme nw. Colombia.* To 800 m. ♂ resembles ♂ Purple Honeycreeper (can be sympatric), but Shining's black throat patch is slightly larger and rounded below, bill slightly shorter, and overall blue color slightly paler. ♀ differs more, with *dusky lores* and *grayish crown and face, pronounced blue streaking on breast.* Behavior as in Purple, though never seems to be as numerous. Also: Mexico to Panama.

Short-billed Honeycreeper
Cyanerpes nitidus　　　　PLATE 90(11)
9.5 cm (3¾"). Generally uncommon and local in canopy and borders of humid forest in *Amazonia and s. Venezuela.* To 400 m, locally to 1000 m in Peru. *Short decurved bill; legs pale pink to orange flesh.* ♂ *mostly bright deep blue; black throat patch large.* ♀ green above with *dusky lores;* below much like ♀ Purple Honeycreeper. Purple's bill is markedly longer, ♂ has bright yellow legs and is more purple (less blue), and ♀ has dusky yellowish legs and buff lores. Red-legged Honeycreeper has markedly longer bill and longer tail, etc. Behavior much as in Purple; usually ranges well above the ground, but sometimes comes lower at edge and in clearings, especially when at fruiting trees.

Red-legged Honeycreeper
Cyanerpes cyaneus　　　　PLATE 90(12)
11.5–12 cm (4½–4¾"). *Widespread and locally fairly common* in canopy and borders of humid and deciduous forest and woodland, and in adjacent clearings, from Colombia and Venezuela south to Amazonia, and in e. Brazil. Mostly below 1000 m. *Bill long and decurved; legs bright red in* ♂, duller pink in ♀. Beautiful ♂ *mostly bright purplish blue* with back, wings, and tail black, *contrasting pale turquoise crown.* ♀ olive green above with *vague whitish superciliary.* Dull yellowish below with *blurry olive streaking on breast. Yellow underwing-coverts* (both sexes) flash in flight. **Nonbreeding** ♂'s eclipse plumage resembles ♀, except that it retains the black on wings and tail; legs remain bright. The smaller, shorter-tailed Purple Honeycreeper has yellow

or yellowish legs; ♀ Purple has buff throat and a blue malar streak. Cf. also Short-billed Honeycreeper (with markedly shorter bill, etc.). Behavior much as in Purple; often forage in the same flock, though Red-leggeds are more frequent in the semiopen. Regularly perches on high exposed branches. In some places comes to feeding trays with fruit. Calls include an oft-uttered "tsip" note (sometimes in series) and an ascending "zhreee." Also: Mexico to Panama; Cuba.

Green Honeycreeper
Chlorophanes spiza   PLATE 90(13)

14 cm (5½"). *Widespread and often common* in canopy and borders of humid forest, secondary woodland, and adjacent clearings from Colombia and Venezuela south to Amazonia, and in e. Brazil. Mostly below 1200 m, but to 2300 m in Colombian Andes. *Bill yellow with black ridge* (duller in ♀), *stouter and less decurved* than in *Cyanerpes* honeycreepers. Distinctive ♂ *glistening green to bluish green* with a *contrasting black head.* ♀ *bright green,* paler below and yellower on head. The comparatively plain ♀ *often best known by bill shape.* Cf. various immature and ♀ *Tangara* tanagers (some of which can also be mainly green), and ♀ Blue Dacnis. Found in pairs or small groups, frequently with mixed flocks of other tanagers. Eats much fruit, and in some places comes to hummingbird feeders and to feeding trays where fruit has been set out. Also: Mexico to Panama.

BANANAQUIT: COEREBIDAE

In recent years this widespread bird has usually been considered to warrant recognition as a monotypic family; in the past it was often treated as a tanager, and it has recently been proposed that it might best be considered a cardinalid finch, though others think it closer to the tanagers. The nest is ball-shaped with a side entrance; like wrens, Bananaquits often build dummy nests.

Bananaquit

Coereba flaveola　　　　　PLATE 90(14)

10.5-11 cm (4-4¼"). *Widespread and often common* in a variety of semiopen and disturbed habitats in both humid and fairly arid regions from Colombia and Venezuela south to the s. Brazil region. Less numerous in extensively forested areas (absent from much of w. Amazonia) and most abundant and familiar in coastal n. South America. Mostly below 1500 m, a few to 1800–2400 m in Andean valleys. *Thin, short, distinctly decurved bill,* sometimes with pink at base. **Typical birds** (illustrated) are dusky to black above with a *striking long white superciliary* and white wing speculum (latter lacking in some races), yellow rump. *Throat gray,* contrasting with *yellow underparts.* Considerable geographic variation, **northern birds** being blacker above, this extending to throat on **Netherlands Antilles.** On **some other islands off Venezuela** *all sooty blackish.* A conspicuous bird, active and seemingly nervous, foraging at all levels and often congregating in flowering trees, where they probe for nectar in flowers. Bananaquits also eat small fruits; especially on islands, they can become very tame, even hopping on tables in search of untended sugar bowls and fruit. The short song is frequently given and consists of a fast series of shrill, buzzy notes; there is marked geographic and individual variation. Also: Mexico to Panama; most of West Indies.

On the next page we continue with our coverage of the Tanager family.

Thlypopsis

Small, warblerlike tanagers with short bills and *contrasting rufous to orange-rufous heads,* most species found in Andean woodlands and shrubby areas, with only one (Orange-headed) in the lowlands.

Orange-headed Tanager
Thlypopsis sordida PLATE 91(1)
13.5 cm (5¼"). Fairly common in lighter and gallery woodland, cerrado, riparian growth, and adjacent clearings from *w. Amazonia to e. Brazil and n. Argentina.* Mostly below 800 m, but to 1500 m in Bolivia. *The only Thlypopsis in the lowlands. Crown and sides of head orange-rufous,* becoming *bright yellow on face and throat; above gray.* Below dingy grayish or buffyish. ♀ duller, with face and foreneck yellowish. Occurs in pairs that glean actively in foliage and dead leaves at varying heights but usually not too high; they sometimes accompany mixed flocks but also move about independently. Song a high-pitched stuttering series usually preceded by several longer and even higher-pitched notes.

Buff-bellied Tanager
Thlypopsis inornata PLATE 91(2)
12.5 cm (5"). Uncommon and local in deciduous woodland, shrubby clearings, and forest borders in *Río Marañón drainage of extreme s. Ecuador* (s. Zamora-Chinchipe) *and nw. Peru* (Cajamarca and w. Amazonas). 450–1800 m. ♂ with *crown and nape orange-rufous,* becoming *uniform buff on face and underparts.* Above olivaceous gray. ♀ has crown and nape more olivaceous, barely contrasting with back. Below paler. Buff-bellied does not overlap with any other *Thlypopsis;* Rufous-chested Tanager occurs at higher elevations. Forages in pairs or small groups, most often low in woodland borders, sometimes even in tall grass and small shrubs, gleaning in foliage and also probing flowers. Song a series of high-pitched "seer" and "seek" notes given in various combinations.

Rufous-chested Tanager
Thlypopsis ornata PLATE 91(3)
12.5 cm (5"). Uncommon to locally fairly common in secondary montane woodland, borders of forest, and adjacent shrubby clearings in *Andes from s. Colombia* (Cauca) *to s. Peru* (Cuzco). Mostly 1800–3200 m. *Entire head and underparts orange-rufous,* contrasting with *white*

median belly. Gray above. Cf. range-restricted Buff-bellied and (especially) Brown-flanked Tanagers. Generally in pairs, less often small groups, that forage actively in foliage at all levels though mainly not too high; they sometimes join mixed flocks but also move about alone. Seems to be nomadic, occurring only seasonally in some areas. Song a fast, jumbled series of high-pitched "seer" and "seek" notes.

Brown-flanked Tanager
Thlypopsis pectoralis
12.5 cm (5"). Uncommon and local in borders of montane forest, secondary woodland, and shrubby growth on *slopes of intermontane valleys in Andes of cen. Peru* (Huánuco to Junín). Mostly 2500–3100 m. Resembles Rufous-chested Tanager (locally sympatric), except that *flanks are pale grayish brown* (not orange-rufous). Behavior as in Rufous-chested and Buff-bellied Tanagers.

Fulvous-headed Tanager
Thlypopsis fulviceps PLATE 91(4)
12.5 cm (5"). Locally fairly common in deciduous woodland, borders of montane forest, shrubby clearings, and gardens in *Andes of n. and w. Venezuela and ne. Colombia* (south to Norte de Santander). 800–2000 m. Distinctive in range; *the grayest Thlypopsis tanager. Hood rufous to deep rufous,* contrasting with *dark gray upperparts and paler gray underparts.* ♀ has buffy whitish throat. Behavior much like other *Thlypopsis,* though seems more arboreal and forest-based.

Rust-and-yellow Tanager
Thlypopsis ruficeps PLATE 91(5)
12.5 cm (5"). Fairly common in montane woodland and forest, especially at borders *(favoring alders, but also in Polylepis woodland),* in *Andes from cen. Peru* (Huánuco) *to nw. Argentina* (Tucumán); some southern breeders move north during austral winter. Mostly 1200–3500 m. *Head orange-rufous;* bright olive above and *bright yellow below.* Cf. Fulvous-headed Brushfinch, which is sympatric and has a similar color pattern, though its shape and behavior are very different. Occurs in pairs, less often small groups, often foraging with flocks consisting of various warbling finches and other small birds.

Conirostrum

Small, warblerlike birds found in woodland and forest borders in the *lowlands.* They have *predominantly blue-gray plumage.* The species in this group may constitute a genus (*Ateleodacnis*) distinct from the mainly Andean true *Conirostrum* species. Montane *Conirostrum* are on pp. 578–579.

White-eared Conebill
Conirostrum leucogenys   PLATE 91(6)
9.5 cm (3¾"). Locally fairly common in canopy and borders of deciduous forest and woodland and adjacent clearings in *n. Colombia and nw. Venezuela.* Mostly below 800 m. Very small, with *short tail.* Bill sharply pointed. Distinctive ♂ dark bluish gray above with *black crown and nape* and *conspicuous white ear patch;* rump also white. Below paler bluish gray, with chestnut crissum. More obscure ♀ mostly bluish gray above, *pale yellowish buff on face and below.* Cf. the larger Bicolored Conebill (rarely or never with White-eared; more grayish below, etc.). Almost always occurs in pairs (which helps in identifying ♀♀), less often small groups, generally remaining well above the ground; sometimes with mixed flocks. Gleans actively in foliage, also often congregating at flowering trees. Also: e. Panama.

Chestnut-vented Conebill
Conirostrum speciosum   PLATE 91(7)
11 cm (4¼"). *Widespread and often common (especially southward)* in canopy and borders of woodland and forest, gallery woodland, adjacent clearings and gardens from Venezuela to n. Argentina; in Amazonia favors várzea and riparian forest. To at least 1300 m in e. Brazil. Bill sharply pointed. **Northern** ♂ (Amazonia northward; A) *rather dark and uniform bluish gray* (only slightly paler below) with *chestnut crissum.* **Southern and eastern** ♂ (B) *paler and more grayish blue,* and distinctly paler below; often with a small white wing speculum. ♀♀ throughout have *crown and nape bluish gray* contrasting with *fairly bright olive upperparts;* below grayish white. ♂ distinctive, but comparatively dull ♀ can be tricky. ♀ Blue Dacnis is greener, especially below; cf. also Tennessee Warbler and Scrub Greenlet. Arboreal, foraging energetically in foliage at varying heights, sometimes while hanging upside down. Sometimes with mixed flocks, and also comes regularly to flowering trees. Song a variable, jumbled series of sweet notes, often with little evident pattern; not heard all that often.

Pearly-breasted Conebill
Conirostrum margaritae   PLATE 91(8)
11.5 cm (4½"). Uncommon and local in *Cecropia*-dominated woodland on *islands in Ama-*zon River and some of its tributaries upriver to ne. Peru. Below 100 m. Iris reddish orange; legs dusky pink. *Above pale bluish gray; face and underparts pale pearly gray.* The similar Bicolored Conebill (which can occur with Pearly-breasted) differs especially in its dingy buff tone below; Bicolored favors more open, less wooded, habitats. ♂ Chestnut-vented Conebill is darker with a chestnut crissum. Occurs singly or in pairs, gleaning for insects in foliage. Song a jumbled series of musical notes.

Bicolored Conebill
Conirostrum bicolor   PLATE 91(9)
11.5 cm (4½"). *Locally common in mangroves on Atlantic coast south to s. Brazil,* and in riparian woodland and adjacent clearings on *islands in Amazon River and some of its tributaries upriver to ne. Peru.* Mainly below 150 m. *Iris reddish orange; legs dusky pink. Above pale grayish blue; below dingy grayish buff.* ♀ slightly duller, **immature** variably tinged yellow below. Nondescript; in mangroves likely confused with Mangrove Warbler, especially immatures, which can also look grayish above and yellowish below but always have *dark-colored* soft parts. The conebill and the warbler generally do not occur in the same area of mangroves. On Amazon islands, cf. the similar (and rarer) Pearly-breasted Conebill and slightly larger ♀ Hooded Tanager (Hooded has prominent white lores and an obviously yellow eye). Occurs in pairs or small groups that forage actively in foliage and along branches at varying levels but often quite low (especially in mangroves). Generally not with mixed flocks, and unlike most Neotropical birds, easily attracted by pishing. Song a high-pitched jumble.

Scarlet-and-white Tanager
*Erythrothlypis salmoni**   PLATE 91(10)
13 cm (5"). Uncommon in canopy and borders of humid and foothill forest and secondary woodland in *w. Colombia* (north to Antioquia) *and nw. Ecuador* (mainly Esmeraldas). Mostly 300–800 m. Gorgeous ♂ *vibrant scarlet above and on throat, chest, and stripe down median underparts;* otherwise white below. ♀ much duller, olive above with a bronzy sheen, yellowish buff below with *sides and flanks broadly whitish* (pattern reminiscent of ♂). ♂ obviously unmistakable; ♀♀ of several similar tanagers (e.g., Guira and Yellow-backed) are more uniformly yellow below. Occurs in pairs or small groups that glean actively at varying heights; also eats small fruits. Often joins mixed flocks composed mainly of other tanagers.

Hemithraupis

Small tanagers with *pointed bills* that range in lowland forest and woodland. The attractive ♂♂ are strongly patterned and easily identified, but ♀♀ of the three species are similar and often tricky to separate.

Yellow-backed Tanager
Hemithraupis flavicollis   PLATE 91(11)

13 cm (5"). Fairly common in canopy and borders of humid forest (mainly terra firme) from *Amazonia to the Guianas,* and in *n. Colombia and e. Brazil.* Bill mostly yellowish. To 900 m. ♂ *black above* with *bright yellow lower back and rump, throat, and crissum.* Mostly whitish below. In **n. Colombia** yellow on throat is restricted to sides. ♀ *dark* olive above with *wings edged yellowish; entirely yellow below* (but in **n. Colombia** has *breast and belly whitish*). ♀ Guira Tanager shows a vague yellowish superciliary (lacking in ♀ Yellow-backed) and is more uniformly olive above; below it differs in its grayish belly. Though they can occur together, Guira is less often found in terra firme forest. Occurs singly and in pairs, gleaning in foliage much like Guira; generally remains well above the ground and often with mixed flocks. Also: e. Panama.

Guira Tanager
Hemithraupis guira   PLATE 91(12)

13 cm (5"). *Widespread and often common* in canopy and borders of humid and (especially) deciduous forest and woodland, gallery woodland, and adjacent clearings from w. Colombia and n. Venezuela to n. Argentina. Mostly below 1400 m. Bill mostly yellowish. ♂ has *black face and throat outlined by yellow* and *bordered below by orange-rufous breast;* mainly olive above, lower back orange-rufous and rump yellow. Below grayish. In **w. Colombia and w. Ecuador** superciliary more ochraceous. ♀ much duller, olive above with a *vague yellow superciliary and eye-ring.* Pale yellowish below, tinged olive on breast and gray on flanks. In se. Brazil cf. Rufous-headed Tanager. ♀ Yellow-backed Tanager is darker above and brighter below, and it lacks the yellow brow and eye-ring. Many ♀ euphonias have similar coloration, but all have thicker bills and different, less active behavior. Occurs in pairs, less often small groups, that glean actively, warblerlike, in foliage at varying heights above the ground. Often with mixed flocks. Song an unmusical series of high squeaky notes and phrases.

Rufous-headed Tanager
Hemithraupis ruficapilla   PLATE 91(13)

13 cm (5"). Locally fairly common in canopy and borders of humid forest and woodland, clearings, and gardens in *se. Brazil* (s. Bahia to e. Santa Catarina). To 1500 m. ♂ with *deep rufous head, large yellow patch on sides of neck,* and *orange-rufous throat and breast.* Bright olive above, rump orange-rufous; below pale grayish. ♀ probably not distinguishable in the field from ♀ Guira; they overlap marginally (e.g., in São Paulo), but even here Rufous-headed favors wetter and more forested terrain, Guira deciduous woodland. Cf. also ♀ Yellow-backed Tanager. Behavior as in Guira.

Nemosia

Two rather dissimilar, mainly *gray and white* tanagers; perhaps *not* congeneric.

Hooded Tanager
Nemosia pileata   PLATE 91(14)

13 cm (5"). *Fairly common and widespread* in semiopen situations, forest borders, gallery forest, clearings with scattered trees, cerrado, and mangroves from n. Colombia and n. Venezuela to n. Argentina; in Amazonia mainly in riparian woodland, avoiding humid forest. Locally to 1300 m. *Iris and legs yellow.* ♂ *grayish blue* above with *contrasting black head and sides of neck* and *white frontlet.* White below. ♀ lacks black cap and is tinged buff below. A distinctive tanager, not apt to be confused, but in the south cf. Black-capped Warbling Finch. Bicolored Conebill (sympatric along Amazon) is smaller, with differently shaped dark bill, dark eyes, dingier grayish buff underparts, and *no* frontlet. Hoodeds range in small groups, most often on their own but sometimes loosely associated with mixed flocks. They mainly perch and hop on quite large branches, occasionally peering at bark and gleaning in foliage; on the whole quite sluggish, almost recalling a vireo. They eat relatively little fruit but sometimes visit flowering trees. Foraging birds give rather undistinctive "tsip" notes; the song, not often heard, is a short series of "ti-chew" phrases.

Cherry-throated Tanager
Nemosia rourei   PLATE 91(15)

14 cm (5½"). *Now very rare and local in canopy and borders of montane forest in se. Brazil* (s. Espírito Santo; formerly in se. Minas Gerais). 900–

1100 m. *Critically endangered by deforestation in its always small range;* only recently (1998) rediscovered. Somewhat resembles Hooded Tanager, also with a yellow iris, but larger and with *bright red throat and chest, black mask extending from forehead across face,* and purer gray (less blue) upperparts extending to crown. This stunning bird occurs in wide-ranging pairs and small (family?) groups up to about five individuals; sometimes joins canopy flocks led by the Eastern Sirystes. Gleans in foliage and hops along lateral branches, hitching from side to side. Distinctive call a sharp and piercing "peéyr" or "peéyr-peéyr," sometimes a "peéyr-pit-pit."

Chlorochrysa

Small tanagers with thin bills and *brilliant plumage,* green usually predominating. They have mainly allopatric distributions in *Andean forests.* Each species has a small patch of distinctive (though inconspicuous) club-shaped feathers on ear-coverts.

Multicolored Tanager
Chlorochrysa nitidissima   PLATE 92(1)
12.5 cm (5"). Uncommon and local in montane forest, woodland, and adjacent clearings in *W. and Cen. Andes of Colombia* (Antioquia to Cauca). Mostly 1400–2000 m. Gaudy ♂ has *head and throat bright golden yellow* with green nape and *black and chestnut patch on sides of neck; saddle on midback lemon yellow; rump and most of underparts glistening blue.* ♀ has similar pattern but *much duller;* note its *contrasting yellow face* and *neck patch.* Found singly or in pairs, often accompanying mixed flocks of other tanagers, especially *Tangara.* Gleans actively, usually well above the ground; eats relatively little fruit.

Glistening-green Tanager
Chlorochrysa phoenicotis   PLATE 92(2)
12.5 cm (5"). Locally fairly common in mossy forest, woodland, and adjacent clearings on *west slope of Andes from nw. Colombia,* also at north end of *Cen. Andes* (Antioquia), *to sw. Ecuador* (El Oro). Mostly 1000–2000 m. Beautiful ♂ *bright glistening emerald green* with small glistening gray patches behind and below eye, also on shoulders. ♀ slightly duller. Cf. ♀ Green Honeycreeper (not nearly so vivid a green, with yellowish bill). Behavior much as in Multicolored Tanager.

Orange-eared Tanager
Chlorochrysa calliparaea   PLATE 92(3)
12.5 cm (5"). Often common in montane forest, woodland, and borders on *east slope of Andes from w. Venezuela* (Barinas) *and ne. Colombia* (Cundinamarca) *to w. Bolivia* (Cochabamba). Mostly 1000–1700 m. In **northern part of range** (A) lovely ♂ *mostly bright shining emerald green* with *orange rump, orange-red patch on sides of neck* connecting to *black throat,* and extensive blue on midbreast and belly (less blue in **n. and cen. Peru,** south of Río Marañón to Huánuco). In **s. Peru and Bolivia** (B) rather different, with *yellow crown patch, bright red neck patch,* and *deep violet throat and median lower underparts.* ♀ less patterned than respective ♂♂, essentially green but retaining orange rump; especially dull in **n. and cen. Peru** (C). Behavior much as in Multicolored Tanager.

Tangara

A *widespread and numerous* group of tanagers (no other Neotropical avian genus includes as many species), *Tangara* tanagers are well known for their *colorful and often complex plumage patterns,* though a few species (found mainly in the lowlands) are duller. The genus is most diverse in Andean forests, where upwards of six or more species may be seen foraging in the same flock, but montane forests elsewhere, as well as humid lowland forests and even semiopen areas, also support at least a few. Though all *Tangara* forage for fruit in much the same way, they frequently differ in the way they search for insects. Certain species have distinctive calls, and some are mentioned in the accounts that follow, but on the whole *Tangara* are not noted for their vocal prowess.

We commence with various primarily Andean species, especially those of higher elevations, then present species found mainly on lower Andean slopes, and conclude with those found principally in the lowlands and in the se. Brazil region.

Golden-hooded Tanager
Tangara larvata   PLATE 92(4)
13 cm (5"). Often common in humid forest borders, secondary woodland, clearings and gardens in *w. Colombia and w. Ecuador* (south to n. Los Ríos). Mainly below 800 m. *Hood mostly golden-buff* (with small black mask surrounded

by violet-blue), *contrasting with black back and broad pectoral band; belly white*, rump opalescent blue. Nearly unique in range. Blue-necked Tanager has a bright blue hood, all-dark underparts, etc. Often in small groups and in the semiopen, sometimes joining mixed flocks but at least as often alone. Eats much fruit (e.g., *Cecropia* catkins). Also: Mexico to Panama.

Blue-necked Tanager
Tangara cyanicollis   PLATE 92(5)

13 cm (5"). *Locally common in a variety of semiopen and edge habitats in Andes from n. Venezuela to w.* Bolivia (Santa Cruz); *also locally along the south edge of Amaz.* Brazil. Mostly 500–2000 m, locally to near sea level in w. Ecuador. *Nearly unmistakable. Hood mostly bright turquoise blue contrasting with black back and breast, becoming violet-blue on belly in some races.* In **most of range** (A) wing-coverts and rump glistening straw to yellowish green; in **w. Ecuador** (B) rump turquoise blue and wing-coverts greener. Cf. Golden-hooded Tanager; Masked Tanager occurs only in Amaz. lowlands, has white belly, etc. This beautiful tanager generally does not occur in continuous forest, and is rather frequent in gardens. It forages mainly for fruit, usually not too high above the ground, and often ranges in small groups.

Golden Tanager
Tangara arthus   PLATE 92(6)

13.5–14 cm (5¼–5½"). *Often common* in montane forest, woodland, and borders in *Andes from n. Venezuela to w.* Bolivia (w. Santa Cruz). Mostly 900–2000 m, most numerous below 1500 m. Unmistakable. In **most of range** (A) predominantly *bright golden to ochraceous yellow* with *large black patch on ear-coverts;* back streaked black, wings and tail mainly black. In **Peru and Bolivia** has throat and chest rufous-chestnut; in **ne. Colombia** uniform brownish below; in **Venezuela** (B) has *pectoral band as well as sides and flanks broadly chestnut.* Almost invariably in pairs or small groups, usually accompanying mixed flocks. Though it eats much fruit, also searches a good deal for insects, typically hopping along mossy branches and peering beneath them.

Saffron-crowned Tanager
Tangara xanthocephala   PLATE 92(7)

13.5 cm (5¼"). *Locally common* in montane forest, woodland, and borders in *Andes from w. Venezuela* (Lara) *to w.* Bolivia (w. Santa Cruz); less

numerous on west slope. Mostly 1200–2400 m. *Crown saffron yellow* (**south to n. Peru**) *to orange* (**s. Peru and Bolivia**, as illustrated; in **cen. Peru** intermediate) and *lower face yellow; small mask, throat patch, and nuchal band black;* otherwise opalescent bluish green with *black back streaking.* Flame-faced Tanager has a solid black back (no streaking) and large opalescent patch on wing-coverts, both lacking in Saffron-crowned. Golden-eared Tanager has mainly black midcrown and nape as well as malar stripe, but *no* black on throat. Cf. also ♀ Multicolored Tanager. Behavior as in Golden Tanager, but forages for insects more in outer foliage and on smaller branches.

Beryl-spangled Tanager
Tangara nigroviridis   PLATE 92(8)

13.5 cm (5¼"). Common in montane forest, woodland, and borders in *Andes from n. Venezuela to w.* Bolivia (w. Santa Cruz). Mostly 1500–2500 m. *Below boldly spangled with opalescent green or blue* (bluer in **Venezuela, w. Colombia, and w. Ecuador;** greener on **east slope of Andes,** as illustrated). *Crown, nape, and rump opalescent green with some black showing through;* back black. ♂ Black-capped Tanager lacks the spangled effect and has a solid black crown. Cf. Metallic-green Tanager, which also lacks the spangled effect, etc. Behavior much as in Golden Tanager, but when foraging for insects typically searches among smaller branches and in foliage.

Green-naped Tanager
Tangara fucosa

13 cm (5"). *Montane forest and borders in extreme nw. Colombia* (nw. Chocó on Cerro Tacarcuna). About 1200 m. *Mostly black above and on throat* with *pale green patch on nape* and *blue spangling on chest; below cinnamon.* Distinctive in its limited range; only recently recorded. Colombian status unknown (uncommon in adjacent Panama); behavior much as in Beryl-spangled Tanager. Also: e. Panama.

Golden-eared Tanager
Tangara chrysotis   PLATE 92(9)

14 cm (5½"). Uncommon in montane forest and borders on *east slope of Andes from s. Colombia* (Huila) *to w.* Bolivia (Cochabamba). Mostly 900–2300 m. *Midcrown and malar streak black, opalescent green forehead and superciliary,* and *coppery gold ear-coverts;* otherwise mainly opalescent green, but *median breast and belly*

cinnamon-rufous. Saffron-crowned Tanager has yellow or orange crown and nape, paler median lower underparts, etc. Metallic-green Tanager is duller generally, lacking gold on face. Occurs singly or in pairs, almost always accompanying mixed tanager flocks; feeds for insects by hopping along mossy branches, not often peering underneath.

Golden-naped Tanager
Tangara ruficervix   PLATE 92(10)
13 cm (5″). Fairly common in montane forest, borders, and woodland in *Andes from n. Colombia* (Antioquia and Cundinamarca) *to w. Bolivia* (w. Santa Cruz). Mostly 1400–2400 m. *Band across hindcrown golden buff.* **Northern birds** (south to Huánuco, Peru; illustrated) *mainly turquoise blue,* with hindcrown band bordered by black and violet-blue. **Southern birds** (north to Junín, Peru) *notably darker and more cobalt blue generally,* and lack the bordering colors to the hindneck band. In northern part of range this is the most generally *turquoise*-colored *Tangara.* In south part of range resembles the similarly colored Blue-and-black Tanager (which there also has a nape patch), though that species is solid black on back and has black spotting below. Behavior as in Beryl-spangled Tanager, though more often occurs only in pairs.

Blue-and-black Tanager
Tangara vassorii   PLATE 92(11)
13 cm (5″). *Often common* in higher-elevation montane forest, woodland, and adjacent shrubby areas in *Andes from w. Venezuela* (Trujillo) *to w. Bolivia* (w. Santa Cruz). Mostly 2000–3400 m northward, somewhat lower southward. *No other Tangara occurs so high. Mostly deep shining blue.* **South to nw. Peru** (A) has lores, most of wing, and tail black. From **Huánuco, Peru, southward** (B) rather different, with a *diffuse patch of opalescent straw on nape, solid black back,* and *black spotting below.* **Ne. Peru** birds (Amazonas to Huánuco) resemble northern birds but have *head and neck somewhat paler and more opalescent bluish green.* Not likely confused. Masked Flowerpiercer has the same blue color but different bill, red iris, and not as much black; in southern part of range, cf. Golden-naped Tanager. Found in pairs and small groups, often joining flocks of mountain tanagers, conebills, and furnariids; less often with other *Tangara* than other members of the genus. Forages actively and seems restless, rarely lingering for long in one area.

Metallic-green Tanager
Tangara labradorides   PLATE 92(12)
13 cm (5″). *Locally common* in borders of montane forest, woodland, and clearings in *Andes from n. Colombia* (Antioquia and Cundinamarca) *to n. Peru* (San Martín); most numerous in Colombia. Mostly 1300–2300 m. Compared with many of its congeners, *rather dull. Mostly opalescent bluish green; midcrown and nape, small mask, and scapulars black.* In **s. Ecuador and n. Peru** markedly less bluish on foreneck than **northern birds** (illustrated), and lesser wing-coverts green (not blue). Cf. Black-capped, Golden-naped, and Blue-browed Tanagers. Behavior much like Beryl-spangled Tanager, though less forest-based.

Flame-faced Tanager
Tangara parzudakii   PLATE 92(13)
11–11.5 cm (5½–5¾″). *Fairly common* in montane forest, woodland, and borders in *Andes from extreme sw. Venezuela* (s. Táchira) *to s. Peru* (Cuzco). Mostly 1500–2500 m, locally down to 800 m on west slope. *A spectacular, large Tangara.* On **east slope** (illustrated) has *forecrown and cheeks scarlet,* becoming *bright golden yellow on hindcrown and sides of neck;* this *contrasts with black back, throat, and bar beneath cheeks. Rump and wing-coverts opalescent silvery green.* On **west slope** slightly smaller with *orange* replacing red on face, lower cheeks yellow, and black extending up onto nape. Saffron-crowned Tanager is somewhat similar (especially on west slope) but has a streaked back and lacks opalescent wing-covert patch. Behavior much as in Golden Tanager.

Blue-browed Tanager
Tangara cyanotis   PLATE 92(14)
12 cm (4¾″). Rare to uncommon in montane forest and borders on *east slope of Andes from s. Colombia* (Huila) *to w. Bolivia* (Cochabamba). 1400–2200 m. A relatively *small Tangara.* In **most of range** (illustrated) *mostly black above* with *turquoise blue superciliary, rump, and lesser wing-coverts; mostly turquoise blue below.* In **Bolivia** has lower cheeks and back dusky blue. Metallic-green Tanager is smaller, has bluish green forecrown and back. Generally seen in pairs with mixed tanager flocks. Forages for insects primarily by searching smaller branches and outer leafy areas.

Gray-and-gold Tanager
Tangara palmeri PLATE 93(1)
14.5 cm (5¾"). Uncommon in canopy and borders of foothill forest in *w. Colombia and nw. Ecuador* (south to Pichincha). 300–1100 m. *Mainly pale gray above,* and *white below* with a *sprinkling of black spots on sides of neck and chest;* also a small black mask. Back opalescent green, and tinged opalescent gold across chest, but the opalescence is often hard to see in the field. Occurs in pairs or small groups, tending to perch high and sometimes fly a long distance before re-alighting. At least as often apart from flocks as with them. Calls include a far-carrying sharp "chi-chup sweee?" Also: e. Panama.

Rufous-throated Tanager
Tangara rufigula PLATE 93(2)
12 cm (4¾"). Locally fairly common in borders and canopy of montane forest and woodland on *west slope of Andes in w. Colombia* (north to s. Chocó) *and w. Ecuador* (south to El Oro). Mostly 600–1200 m, but up to 1800 m in Colombia. Distinctive, with *black head* and upperparts, *rufous throat; back looks scaly,* underparts are opalescent with *black spots on breast and sides.* Usually in small groups, often foraging with mixed flocks of other tanagers, feeding on both insects (mostly gleaned from leaves) and various small fruits. Favors mossy forest.

Plain-colored Tanager
Tangara inornata PLATE 93(3)
12 cm (4¾"). Uncommon in borders of humid forest and woodland and in clearings in *nw. Colombia.* Mostly below 1200 m. *Dull* plumage. *Mostly leaden gray,* somewhat paler below and white on median breast and belly; *wings contrastingly blackish* with (often hidden) blue lesser wing-coverts. Not likely confused with any other *Tangara,* but cf. larger Blue-gray and Palm Tanagers (both can look gray in poor light). Basically a *nonforest Tangara;* typically moves in small groups of 3–6 birds, most often independent of mixed flocks. Often feeds on *Cecropia* catkins. Also: Costa Rica and Panama.

Silver-throated Tanager
Tangara icterocephala PLATE 93(4)
13.5 cm (5¼"). *Locally common* in canopy and borders of montane forest, woodland, and adjacent clearings, *in foothills on west slope of Andes from w. Colombia to extreme nw. Peru* (Tumbes). Mostly 500–1300 m, locally lower in sw. Ecuador. *Mainly bright golden yellow* with *large sil-*

very throat patch bordered above by a narrow black malar streak; back boldly streaked black. ♀ duller. Golden Tanager never shows silvery on throat and has a conspicuous black ear patch. Often occurs in quite large groups and is regularly with mixed flocks. Feeds mainly on fruit, foraging for insects mostly by inspecting smaller moss-covered branches. Call a characteristic harsh "bzeet," given especially in flight. Also: Costa Rica and Panama.

Rufous-cheeked Tanager
Tangara rufigenis PLATE 93(5)
13 cm (5"). *Uncommon* in canopy and borders of montane forest and woodland in *mountains of n. Venezuela* (Lara to Distrito Federal). Mostly 900–2000 m. *Mainly opalescent bluish green* with a *rufous mask from lores and chin to cheeks;* lower underparts buff. ♀ of sympatric Black-capped Tanager has duskier crown, streaked effect on breast. Behavior much as in many other montane *Tangara.*

Scrub Tanager
Tangara vitriolina PLATE 93(6)
14 cm (5½"). *Locally common* in scrub, low woodland, gardens, and agricultural areas in *arid, semiopen terrain of w. Colombia* (north to Antioquia and Santander) *and interandean valleys of n. Ecuador* (south to n. Pichincha). *Not a forest bird,* and now spreading into deforested regions. Mostly 500–2500 m. *Rufous crown* and *black mask;* otherwise mostly dull silvery greenish above, paler silvery grayish below. ♀ duller and more greenish. Distinctive in most of range, but almost meets range of Burnished-buff Tanager in ne. Colombia; ♂ Burnished-buff is more golden on crown and straw-colored on back, and has a shiny violet suffusion at least on throat (sometimes more extensive). ♀ Burnished-buff very similar but generally paler (notably so on crown). Occurs in pairs and small groups; except at fruiting trees, most often not with other tanagers.

Green-capped Tanager
Tangara meyerdeschauenseei
14 cm (5½"). *Fairly common* in scrub, gardens, and forest borders on east slope of Andes in extreme s. Peru (Puno in Sandia region) *and extreme w. Bolivia* (recently found in Madidi Natl. Park in w. La Paz). 1750–2200 m. Resembles geographically distant Scrub Tanager, but has *greenish straw crown* (no rufous), *greenish turquoise ear-coverts* (black restricted to lores and

area around eye), and greener mantle. ♀ slightly duller. Burnished-buff Tanager (found in savannas of adjacent lowlands) has shiny straw-colored back, more golden crown, etc. Behavior as in Scrub.

Burnished-buff Tanager
Tangara cayana*   PLATE 93(7)
13.5 cm (5¼"). *Widespread and generally common and conspicuous in open and semiopen terrain* such as savanna, cerrado, scrub, gallery woodland, and forest borders from ne. Colombia and Venezuela south through interior and e. Brazil to n. Bolivia and ne. Argentina. Mostly below 1200 m, locally higher in Venezuela. *Two very different types.* ♂ of **southern group** (mainly e. Brazil; A) *mostly shiny ochraceous buff above,* wings and tail mainly bluish. *Wide area from face and throat to median belly black,* contrasting with *ochraceous sides.* ♂ of **northern group** (ne. Colombia and Venezuela to the Guianas, also locally in Amazonia; B) *lacks the black stripe below,* though does have *black mask; crown golden rufous, back shiny straw, violet suffusion on throat and median underparts.* **Marajó Islands** birds are apparently intermediate. ♀♀ are duller than respective ♂♂, in **south and east** lacking black below (blackish only on mask). Cf. Scrub Tanager (in Colombia) and Chestnut-backed and Black-backed Tanagers (in e. Brazil). More an open-country tanager than most *Tangara,* ranging in pairs (less often small groups) that sometimes fly long distances to reach isolated trees or shrubs. Frequently seen at fruiting trees, but even there generally not with other tanagers.

Chestnut-backed Tanager
Tangara preciosa   PLATE 93(8)
14.5 cm (5¾"). *Uncommon in forest, woodland, and borders from s. Brazil* (north to s. São Paulo) *to ne. Argentina and Uruguay.* To about 1000 m. Handsome ♂ has *shiny coppery rufous head, nape, and back* contrasting with *shining ochraceous yellow wing-coverts; below mainly shining bluish green.* ♀ has *head and nape duller coppery rufous;* back green. Whereas ♀ has dusky only on its lores, ♀ Burnished-buff Tanager (locally sympatric) has a full black mask. ♀ indistinguishable from ♀ Black-backed Tanager, which also is potentially sympatric (you must go by ♂♂). Occurs in pairs and small groups, often conspicuous and perching in the open. Especially numerous in forest where *Araucaria* trees predominate.

Black-backed Tanager
Tangara peruviana*   PLATE 93(9)
14.5 cm (5¾"). *Rare and local in restinga and humid forest and borders near coast of se. Brazil* (Rio de Janeiro to e. Santa Catarina; north of se. São Paulo apparently occurs only during austral winter). To 700 m. Beautiful ♂ has *shiny coppery rufous head and neck* contrasting with *black back* and *shiny opalescent straw wing-coverts and rump.* Below mainly shining turquoise green. ♀ very like ♀ Chestnut-backed Tanager, so one must identify by accompanying ♂♂. Behavior much as in Chestnut-backed, but is much scarcer and at least when breeding is more strictly an inhabitant of coastal regions.

Black-capped Tanager
Tangara heinei*   PLATE 93(10)
13 cm (5"). Fairly common in borders of montane forest and woodland and adjacent clearings in *Andes from n. Venezuela to n. Ecuador* (south to Pichincha and Tungurahua). Mostly 1100–2200 m. ♂ has *crown black* contrasting with shining silvery bluish gray upperparts. *Cheeks, throat, and chest opalescent green with a streaky effect (especially on chest);* below blue-gray. ♀ duller, with *dusky, green-scaled crown* contrasting with bright shining green back; *streaky opalescent effect on throat, sides of neck, and breast; midbelly gray.* Occurs *north* of its allies (Sira, Silver-backed, and Straw-backed Tanagers). ♀ Black-headed Tanager (regularly sympatric) is paler and grayer on head and throat, and its belly is pale yellow (*with no gray*). Behavior as in many other montane *Tangara.*

Sira Tanager
Tangara phillipsi*
13 cm (5"). Fairly common but very local in *montane forest in e. Peru* (remote Cerros del Sira in e. Huánuco). 1300–1600 m. Resembles geographically distant Black-capped Tanager. ♂ differs in *black breast, median belly, and sides of neck,* and more restricted green on throat. ♀ is darker gray on median breast and belly and less streaked on throat. Silver-backed Tanager's throat is coppery (not green); it is not known to occur on the Sira. Behavior much as in other montane *Tangara.*

Silver-backed Tanager
Tangara viridicollis   PLATE 93(11)
13 cm (5"). Locally fairly common in montane forest, woodland, and shrubby clearings in *Andes from s. Ecuador* (s. Azuay) *to extreme*

w. Bolivia (recently recorded in w. La Paz). Mostly 1000–2300 m. ♂ in **most of Peru** (illustrated) has *crown, nape, and most of underparts black,* contrasting with *shining greenish coppery throat and cheeks* and *shining gun-metal gray mantle and flanks.* In **s. Ecuador and nw. Peru** mantle more opalescent and throat purer coppery. Much duller ♀ shining green above except for dusky-brown crown; *throat and cheeks dull greenish coppery,* greener on chest, breast and belly mostly gray. Cf. rare Straw-backed Tanager; both sexes of the *very* local Sira Tanager have a green throat. Behavior much like other montane *Tangara*; often in partially cutover terrain (certainly easiest to see there), but at least locally it also occurs in more continuous forest.

Straw-backed Tanager
Tangara argyrofenges   PLATE 93(12)
13 cm (5"). *Rare and local in canopy and borders of montane forest on east slope of Andes from extreme s. Ecuador* (s. Zamora-Chinchipe) *to w. Bolivia* (w. Santa Cruz). 1100–2100 m. Sometimes called Green-throated Tanager. Pattern recalls commoner Silver-backed Tanager (locally sympatric). Striking ♂ differs in its *shining opalescent straw mantle and flanks* and *opalescent green throat and cheeks.* ♀ has *mantle shining yellowish green* and *throat, cheeks, and chest shining silvery green with streaky effect.* ♀ Silver-backed has greener (not so yellow) mantle and coppery throat. Behavior as in Silver-backed, though rarely or never in extensive secondary habitats.

Black-headed Tanager
Tangara cyanoptera   PLATE 93(13)
13.5 cm (5¼"). Locally common in borders of foothill and montane forest, woodland, and clearings in *Andes of n. Venezuela and extreme ne. Colombia,* and on *tepuis of s. Venezuela region.* Mostly 800–2000 m. In **most of range** (illustrated) ♂ has *black hood* contrasting with *shining opalescent straw of remaining body plumage;* wings and tail black, with *flight feathers broadly edged ultramarine blue.* ♀ looks faded, with *pale grayish head and throat* (throat vaguely streaked); mantle *pale* shining green, *belly pale yellow.* ♂ on **tepuis** notably *duller* with less opalescence generally, some mottling below, and no blue on wings; ♀ there dingy with a pronounced flammulated effect below. ♂ unmistakable (does not overlap with vaguely similar Golden-collared Honeycreeper). ♀ Black-capped Tanager (regularly sympatric) looks more dark-capped and is gray on median breast

and belly (no yellow there). Behavior similar to many other montane *Tangara.*

Golden-collared Honeycreeper
Iridophanes pulcherrimus   PLATE 93(14)
12 cm (4¾"). Uncommon in canopy and borders of foothill and montane forest in *Andes from s. Colombia* (Valle) *to s. Peru* (Cuzco). Mostly 900–1700 m. *Bill fairly long and slender* (differing from any *Tangara*) with *mandible mostly yellow;* iris dark red. On **east slope** (illustrated) ♂ has *head, upper back, and scapulars black* with *prominent orange-yellow nuchal collar;* lower back and rump opalescent blue; *wings mostly ultramarine blue.* Below pale greenish yellow. ♀ much duller (often best identified by an accompanying ♂) but *usually shows at least an echo of ♂'s golden collar;* wing feathers edged bluish green. **Pacific-slope** birds have longer bill, and ♂ has sootier head. Usually in pairs; regularly accompanies mixed flocks of other tanagers. Apparently eats mainly fruit (fewer insects than most *Tangara*), frequently feeding on *Cecropia* catkins.

Bay-headed Tanager
Tangara gyrola   PLATE 94(1)
13.5 cm (5¼"). *Widespread and locally common* in canopy and borders of humid lowland and foothill forest, woodland, and adjacent clearings from Colombia and Venezuela to Amazonia and the Guianas. Mostly below 1500 m. *Head brick red.* ♂ grass green above, **most races** with a *golden yellow nuchal band* (broad in some) and many with yellow on shoulders (shoulders brick red in **Brazil south of Amazon**). In **most of range** *turquoise blue below* with green on sides (as illustrated), but **more northern birds** *all bright green below.* ♀♀ duller than respective ♂♂; **juveniles** can look quite uniform green, *showing little or no rufous on head.* In w. Colombia and nw. Ecuador cf. Rufous-winged Tanager. Young, all-green birds can be confused with ♀ Green Honeycreeper, but note the tanager's heavier bill. Often in pairs or small groups, frequently with mixed flocks; searches for insects mainly by hopping along larger limbs, peering underneath. Also eats much fruit. Also: Nicaragua to Panama.

Rufous-winged Tanager
Tangara lavinia   PLATE 94(2)
13 cm (5"). Fairly common but local in canopy and borders of humid forest and woodland in *w. Colombia and nw. Ecuador* (mainly Esmeral-

das). Mostly below 500 m, a few to 1000 m. Stunning ♂ has *head and most of wing bright brick red*; otherwise mostly bright green, but *nape and back golden yellow* and blue on midthroat and midbelly. ♀ much duller, with no yellow on back, and often, especially in immatures, showing little rufous on wings (*though a patch on flight feathers almost always shows*) and little or none on head. ♀ and immature Bay-headed Tanagers never show *any* rufous on wing; on west slope of Andes they are mainly *blue* below. For the most part, Bay-headed is absent from the wet Chocó forests where Rufous-winged is most numerous. Behavior as in Bay-headed. Also: Honduras to Panama.

Blue-whiskered Tanager
Tangara johannae PLATE 94(3)
13.5 cm (5¼"). Uncommon in canopy and borders of humid forest and woodland from *nw. Colombia* (Antioquia) *to nw. Ecuador* (mainly Esmeraldas). Mostly below 600 m. Mostly bright emerald green with *black face and throat* and a *small but conspicuous blue malar streak* (the "whisker"); back prominently streaked black, rump yellow. Cf. Emerald Tanager (also bright green, but with a black ear patch, no black on throat or black back streaking). Behavior much as in Bay-headed Tanager, but seems everywhere *scarce.*

Green-and-gold Tanager
Tangara schrankii PLATE 94(4)
13.5 cm (5¼"). Fairly common to common in humid forest and borders in *w. Amazonia,* most numerous westward. Mostly below 1400 m. *Bright green* with *yellow crown, median underparts, and rump* and *conspicuous black forehead and broad mask; mantle boldly streaked black.* ♀ duller with a green crown. Yellow-bellied Tanager (regularly sympatric) is smaller and distinctly spotted, especially on breast. No overlap with somewhat similar Emerald Tanager. Behavior much as in other lowland *Tangara,* often occurring with various congeners (e.g., Paradise, Yellow-bellied, Masked). Forages at all levels, regularly coming low at edge, also sometimes accompanying understory flocks.

Emerald Tanager
Tangara florida
13 cm (5"). Locally fairly common in canopy and borders of montane forest and woodland in *foothills of w. Colombia and nw. Ecuador* (south to w. Pichincha). Mostly 400–1200 m.

Bright emerald green with a *bold black patch on ear-coverts; crown bright yellow;* back streaked black. ♀ somewhat duller, with no yellow on crown. Nearly unmistakable. Pattern resembles Golden Tanager, though colors are very different. Behavior similar to many other *Tangara,* often flocking with congeners such as Silver-throated and Rufous-throated. Forages for insects mainly by searching mossy limbs. Also: Costa Rica and Panama.

Spotted Tanager
Tangara punctata PLATE 94(5)
13 cm (5"). Fairly common to locally common in canopy and borders of humid and foothill forest and woodland in *ne. South America,* and in foothill and montane forest and borders on *east slope of Andes from n. Ecuador* (Sucumbíos) *to w. Bolivia* (Cochabamba). Mostly below 1700 m. *Overall spotted or scaly appearance.* Bright green above, *black centers of feathers giving a scaly effect; face, throat, and breast bluish white* with *profuse black spotting; wing and tail feathers edged yellowish green.* Speckled Tanager has a yellower face and bluer wing-edging; it and Spotted overlap only locally, on tepui slopes, with Speckled replacing Spotted upslope. Yellow-bellied Tanager is greener below and has a bright yellow (not white) belly. Behavior as in many other *Tangara;* searches for insects mainly in foliage.

Speckled Tanager
Tangara guttata
13.5 cm (5¼"). Locally common in canopy and borders of montane forest and woodland and adjacent clearings, mainly in *Venezuela and n. Colombia.* Mostly 500–1500 m, a few up to 2000 m. Patterned like the slightly smaller Spotted Tanager, but *forehead and face at least tinged yellow* (brightest in **Trinidad** birds) and *wing feathers edged greenish turquoise* (not yellowish green). The two overlap principally in s. Venezuela, where Spotted occurs mainly in lowlands, Speckled on tepui slopes. Behavior much as in Spotted Tanager. Also: Costa Rica and Panama.

Yellow-bellied Tanager
Tangara xanthogastra PLATE 94(6)
12 cm (4¾"). Fairly common in canopy and borders of humid forest and woodland in *w. Amazonia,* and in montane forest on *tepuis* (where often numerous, generally at higher elevations than Speckled Tanager). Mostly below 1400 m, to 1800 m in s. Venezuela. *Mostly bright emerald*

green; feathers on head, back, throat, and breast black-centered imparting a spotted effect; median belly bright yellow, unspotted. Neither Spotted nor Speckled Tanagers show any yellow on belly. Green-and-gold Tanager does show comparable yellow on belly but lacks spotting below and has a contrasting broad black mask. Behavior similar to other *Tangara* in Amazonia; forages for insects mainly in outer foliage.

Dotted Tanager
Tangara varia   PLATE 94(7)
11.5 cm (4½"). A small, *rare* tanager found locally in canopy and borders of humid forest and woodland *mainly in ne. South America;* recently found very locally in ne. Peru. *Essentially uniform bright grass green;* black bases of feathers on crown, back, and underparts show through, creating a "dotted" effect (not always easy to see in the field); *wing and tail feathers broadly edged bluish.* ♀ lacks ♂'s dotted effect, and its wing-edging is green (so less contrasting). When young, various other *Tangara* (e.g., Bay-headed) can look mainly green, so caution is urged when identifying this rarity. The smallest and plainest green of the genus; *shows no yellow below.* Cf. also ♀ Blue Dacnis (blue head, different bill). Seen singly or in pairs, generally with mixed flocks.

Masked Tanager
Tangara nigrocincta   PLATE 94(8)
13 cm (5"). Uncommon to locally fairly common in canopy and borders of humid forest and adjacent clearings in *much of Amazonia* (but not the far east). Mostly below 1000 m. *Head mostly pale lavender blue* with small black mask and greenish cheeks, contrasting with *black back and broad pectoral band; median belly white,* shoulders blue. ♀ duller, with breast band dusky. Golden-hooded Tanager has similar pattern but is found only west of the Andes. Blue-necked Tanager (mainly at higher elevations, with some overlap) has much more intense blue on head, coppery wing-coverts, and all-dark underparts (no white). Cf. also ♂ of much rarer White-bellied Dacnis, which has similar head color and a white belly but is smaller with no black on chest, yellow iris, etc. Behavior similar to other lowland *Tangara* (regularly with them), but usually in pairs or at most small groups; often perches on open branches for protracted periods. Eats mainly small fruits.

Paradise Tanager
Tangara chilensis   PLATE 94(9)
14 cm (5½"). Fairly common to common in canopy and borders of humid forest and woodland from *Amazonia to the Guianas.* Mostly below 1400 m. *Unmistakably colorful. Head bright apple green* contrasting with *black nape and back; throat violet, below mainly bright turquoise blue.* In **northern races** (Meta, Colombia, east to the Guianas, and in upper Río Huallaga valley of e. Peru) *lower back red and rump bright yellow* (as illustrated); elsewhere *rump all red.* Often in rather large groups of a dozen or more, trooping about actively, mostly remaining high but sometimes coming lower at edge. This gaudy tanager always seems restless, rarely staying in one tree for very long. Forages for insects mainly by peering under smaller branches and investigating bromeliads.

Opal-crowned Tanager
Tangara callophrys   PLATE 94(10)
14.5 cm (5¾"). Uncommon to fairly common in canopy and borders of humid forest and woodland in *w. Amazonia.* Mostly below 700 m. *Forecrown and broad superciliary opalescent straw* contrasting with black nape and back; lower back and rump also opalescent straw. *Below mostly shining deep blue.* Often confused with Opal-rumped Tanager, though in their extensive area of overlap (where they regularly flock together), Opal-rumped *lacks* opalescence on head and has *chestnut* on lower underparts. Behavior much as in other lowland *Tangara;* forages for insects mainly by peering under larger limbs and on trunks.

Opal-rumped Tanager
*Tangara velia**   PLATE 94(11)
14 cm (5½"). Fairly common in canopy and borders of humid forest and woodland from *Amazonia to the Guianas,* and in *e. Brazil.* Mostly below 600 m. In **most of range** (A) mainly black above with *contrasting opalescent straw on lower back and rump;* forehead, face, and throat deep blue. Below mainly purplish blue with *rufous-chestnut midbelly and crissum.* In **e. Amazonia,** entire forehead and sides of head paler greenish blue (Guianas and Brazil north of Amazon) or with a narrow opalescent band on forecrown (south of lower Amazon). Markedly different in **coastal e. Brazil** (B), with a broad opalescent forecrown band, *silvery grayish blue breast, sides, and flanks,* and black chest spotting.

Opal-crowned Tanager has an obvious opalescent crown and brow and no rufous on belly. In e. Brazil, cf. White-bellied Tanager. Generally in small groups, with behavior like many other lowland *Tangara*; forages for insects by searching under larger limbs and inspecting epiphytes.

Turquoise Tanager
Tangara mexicana   PLATE 94(12)
13.5 cm (5¼"). Fairly common in canopy and borders of humid forest and woodland and adjacent clearings from *Amazonia to the Guianas*. To 1000 m. Does not include White-bellied Tanager of e. Brazil. *Mostly black above* with *mainly cobalt blue rump, face, and underparts* (black bases of feathers show through, especially on flanks). Birds from **the Guianas west to far e. Colombia** (illustrated) have *median breast and belly creamy yellow;* elsewhere *median lower underparts richer and brighter yellow.* Cf. especially Opal-rumped and Opal-crowned Tanagers. Usually in groups of 3–6 birds, sometimes with mixed flocks (especially at fruiting trees) but more often moving independently. Eats primarily fruit; forages for insects by inspecting limbs, often dead branches.

White-bellied Tanager
*Tangara brasiliensis**
14 cm (5½"). Uncommon in borders of humid forest, secondary woodland, and adjacent clearings in *se. Brazil* (s. Bahia to Rio de Janeiro). Below 500 m. Similar in pattern to Turquoise Tanager (often considered conspecific); somewhat larger. *Substantially paler and more silvery blue overall,* with *median underparts white* (not yellow). Behavior generally similar, though seems more inclined to move about in pairs.

Green-headed Tanager
Tangara seledon   PLATE 94(13)
13.5 cm (5¼"). Fairly common in canopy and borders of humid forest, woodland, and adjacent clearings and gardens in *se. Brazil region* (north to s. Bahia). To about 1300 m. *Head and chin greenish turquoise* becoming *shining yellowish green* on upper back, contrasting with *black back* and *bright yellow-orange rump; breast and midbelly turquoise blue.* ♀ slightly duller. Not likely confused; Seven-colored Tanager occurs well to the north. Behavior similar to many other *Tangara*, though the beautiful Green-headed can occur in larger groups (10–15 or more birds), sometimes with mixed flocks but at least as often on their own. Forages for insects by hop-

ping along branches, investigating bark crevices and peering into epiphytes. Sometimes comes for fruit on feeding trays.

Seven-colored Tanager
Tangara fastuosa   PLATE 94(14)
13.5 cm (5¼"). *Now rare and local* in canopy and borders of humid forest, woodland, and adjacent clearings in *ne. Brazil* (Rio Grande do Norte and Alagoas). To about 1000 m. Numbers much reduced by massive deforestation, to a lesser extent by trapping for the cagebird market. *Head, chin, and upper back greenish turquoise* contrasting with *black back* and then with *bright yellow-orange rump. Breast and shoulders turquoise blue,* becoming *dark ultramarine blue on belly.* This gaudy *Tangara* does not occur with any similar congener; Green-headed Tanager occurs well to the south. Found in pairs or small groups, often with mixed flocks and foraging at all heights, lowest at borders and in smaller trees in clearings. Forages for insects by hopping along horizontal branches, peering underneath.

Red-necked Tanager
Tangara cyanocephala   PLATE 94(15)
13 cm (5"). Locally fairly common in canopy and borders of humid forest and woodland, especially in wet foothills, in *se. Brazil region,* also locally in *ne. Brazil.* To at least 1000 m. Gaudy ♂ has *crown and throat violet blue* with *cheeks and broad nuchal collar vivid scarlet; back black.* Below bright green. ♀ slightly duller. Not likely confused. Behavior much like other *Tangara,* usually in pairs or small groups that regularly join mixed flocks, generally remaining well above the ground but coming lower when visiting fruiting trees at edge.

Gilt-edged Tanager
Tangara cyanoventris   PLATE 94(16)
13.5–14 cm (5¼–5½"). Fairly common in canopy and borders of lower montane forest and woodland in *se. Brazil* (cen. Bahia to São Paulo). Mostly 500–1200 m. *Above golden yellow, brightest on head and especially around eyes,* streaked black except on face. Throat black, *below bright turquoise blue.* Brassy-breasted Tanager has blue (not yellow) on face and a brassy ochre breast shield. Though they are sometimes together, Gilt-edged tends to occur at lower elevations than Brassy-breasted. Behavior similar to many other *Tangara;* forages for insects by searching smaller branches and foliage.

Brassy-breasted Tanager
Tangara desmaresti   PLATE 94(17)
13.5–14 cm (5¼–5½"). Locally common in canopy and borders of montane forest and woodland in *se. Brazil* (s. Minas Gerais to e. Santa Catarina). Mostly 800–1800 m. *Above bright emerald green* streaked black except on face and rump; *forecrown and ocular area turquoise blue; broad shield on throat and breast brassy ochre* with black spot on lower throat; belly mainly green. A striking bird liable to be confused only with Gilt-edged Tanager; the two overlap locally, but Brassy-breasted usually occurs at higher elevations. Gilt-edged mainly blue below and mainly yellow on head. Behavior much as in Gilt-edged, but seems more numerous and can occur in large monospecific groups.

Euphonia

Distinctive *small* tanagers with *short tails and stubby bills*. Typical ♂♂ are *steely blue above with a yellow forecrown of varying size*, and *some shade of yellow below, usually with a contrasting dark throat*. ♀♀ are duller, mainly olive and yellow, and often have gray or rufous below. Euphonias are arboreal, with most species ranging in humid forests, a few in savannas; some occur in montane areas, but most are lowland birds. Most are relatively conspicuous, often perching on dead branches, especially to vocalize. All are frugivorous and consume large quantities of berries, especially mistletoe, mashing them in their bills before swallowing. Most species have jumbled, twittery songs that are not terribly distinctive; their calls can be more so, and usually only these will be described. Euphonias build dome-shaped fibrous nests with a side entrance. They are likely not "true" tanagers, and recently it has been suggested that they are better placed in the Fringillidae family.

Thick-billed Euphonia
Euphonia laniirostris   PLATE 95(1)
11.5 cm (4½"). Fairly common to common in forest borders, woodland, clearings, and gardens from *Colombia and w. Venezuela to n. Bolivia and w. and s. Amaz. Brazil*. Mostly below 1500 m. Bill *slightly* thicker than in other euphonias, but hard to see in the field. *In most of range ♂ is the only euphonia with all-yellow underparts;* it also has a *relatively large yellow forecrown patch*. Birds from

w. Amazonia have a black undertail (lacking the white tail spots found in other races; illustrated). ♀ olive above, *olive-clouded yellow below*. Immature ♂♂ are frequently seen; they resemble ♀ but early on acquire the yellow forecrown and blue-black on face. Cf. very similar Violaceous Euphonia, which replaces Thick-billed eastward (only limited overlap). ♀ Thick-billed is *larger* than most other similar euphonias with which it often occurs. Ranges in pairs or small groups, foraging for small fruits, sometimes with other euphonias or in mixed flocks. Rather vocal, both sexes often giving a variety of calls including a musical "chweet"; song a variable and often long-continued series of phrases that sometimes includes brief imitations of other bird species. Also: Costa Rica and Panama.

Violaceous Euphonia
Euphonia violacea   PLATE 95(2)
11.5 cm (4½"). *Replaces Thick-billed Euphonia in e. South America (e. Venezuela to se. Brazil region)*, where equally numerous and ranging in borders of humid forest and woodland, gallery woodland, clearings, and plantations. To about 1000 m. ♂ has a *smaller yellow forecrown patch* (reaching only to above eye) and *richer, more ochraceous yellow underparts* than Thick-billed; always has white in tail (sometimes useful for distinguishing black-tailed Thick-billeds in the overlap zone in Amazonia). ♀ not distinguishable from Thick-billed in the field, but in most of its range is the only ♀ euphonia with *yellow and olive underparts* (though in the Guianan area cf. ♀ Finsch's). In se. South America cf. the scarce Green-chinned Euphonia. Behavior much as in Thick-billed, though song includes even better mimicry, with a repertoire encompassing a wide variety of bird species.

Green-chinned Euphonia
Euphonia chalybea   PLATE 95(3)
11.5 cm (4½"). Rare to uncommon in borders of humid forest and woodland and in adjacent clearings in *se. Brazil region* (north to Rio de Janeiro). *Bill notably thick*. To 900 m. ♂ *steely greenish blue above, extending to chin;* only a *small* yellow patch on forehead. Below yellow. ♀ olive above and *mostly gray below* with *chin, sides, flanks, and crissum olive yellowish*. ♂ Violaceous Euphonia has more violet upperparts, white tail spots, no "chinstrap," and more ochraceous underparts (not so pure a yellow). ♀ Violaceous has no gray below. ♀ Green-chinned's pattern below more resembles ♀ Chestnut-

bellied Euphonia, though that has an obvious chestnut crissum. Usually in pairs; sometimes with Violaceous, and with similar behavior (though Green-chinned is never as numerous). Song a short but rather musical gurgling.

Fulvous-vented Euphonia
Euphonia fulvicrissa   PLATE 95(4)
10 cm (4"). Fairly common in humid forest and secondary woodland, mainly in understory and borders, in *w. Colombia and nw. Ecuador* (mainly Esmeraldas). To 800 m. ♂ steely blue above and on throat with a yellow forecrown patch. Yellow below with *median belly and crissum tawny-fulvous.* ♀ olive above with *chestnut forecrown.* Olive yellowish below with *median belly and crissum tawny-fulvous.* In **most of w. Colombia** has small white tail spots, but spots *lacking in* **sw. Colombia and Ecuador;** in **far nw. Colombia** they are larger. No other sympatric euphonia shows the fulvous below. Behavior similar to other euphonias, though less likely to be in forest canopy. Distinctive call a gravelly "treeah-treeah." Also: Panama.

Finsch's Euphonia
Euphonia finschi   PLATE 95(5)
10 cm (4"). Uncommon and local in swampy forest borders and gallery woodland in the *Guianas and adjacent Venezuela and Brazil.* To at least 900 m in Venezuela. ♂ has *yellow forecrown,* steely violet upperparts and throat, yellow breast, and *rich ochraceous lower underparts.* ♀ olive above, yellowish olive below. ♂ Purple-throated Euphonia has a similar pattern, but its forecrown and underparts are purer yellow, and it has white tail spots (no spots in Finsch's). ♀ Violaceous Euphonia is very like ♀ Finsch's but slightly larger with a heavier bill (often best to go by accompanying ♂). Behavior much as in other euphonias, sometimes congregating with them to feed at fruiting trees. Has a "pee-peem" call.

White-vented Euphonia
Euphonia minuta   PLATE 95(6)
9.5 cm (3¾"). Widespread but uncommon in canopy and borders of humid forest and woodland from *Colombia and s. Venezuela to Amazonia and the Guianas;* in w. Amazonia seems to favor swampy or riparian forest-woodland, not terra firme. Mostly below 1000 m. Both sexes have *distinctive white or whitish median lower belly and crissum.* ♂ is a typical dark-throated euphonia, with *only a small yellow patch on forehead.* ♀ has pale grayish throat and a *yellow-*

ish breast band that extends down onto flanks (in other similarly patterned ♀ euphonias, the yellowish doesn't extend across breast). Behavior similar to other euphonias but more forest-based than many; generally remains well above the ground. Call a simple "beem" or "seeu." Also: Guatemala and Belize to Panama.

Purple-throated Euphonia
Euphonia chlorotica   PLATE 95(7)
10 cm (4"). *Widespread and fairly common* in forest and woodland borders, gallery woodland, caatinga, and chaco scrub from ne. Colombia and s. Venezuela to n. Argentina. Mostly below 1200 m. ♂ is a classic *dark-throated* euphonia with typical pattern including white tail spots. ♀ in **most of range** (illustrated) *grayish white below* with *yellowish confined to sides and crissum,* but in **ne. Colombia and Venezuela** *entirely greenish yellow below.* Cf. the very similar Trinidad Euphonia (overlaps very little, fortunately). ♂ White-vented Euphonia has a smaller yellow forecrown patch and a white lower belly and crissum; ♀ White-vented differs in its yellowish breast. ♂♂ of slightly larger Orange-bellied Euphonia are usually more ochraceous below and on forecrown (not so pure a yellow), and ♀♀ typically have gray on nape and are buffyish below. Behavior much like other euphonias; often with Violaceous Euphonia, especially at fruiting trees. Both sexes frequently give a far-carrying clear "bee-beem" call.

Trinidad Euphonia
Euphonia trinitatis
9.5 cm (3¾"). Fairly common in deciduous and gallery woodland, forest borders, gardens, and plantations in *n. Colombia and n. Venezuela.* Mostly below 800 m. Both sexes resemble slightly larger Purple-throated Euphonia; though *they can usually be separated by range,* they do overlap in s. Venezuela, just south of Río Orinoco. Yellow forecrown patch slightly larger in ♂ Trinidad. ♀ resembles Purple-throated from most of that species' range, thus with mainly grayish white underparts, yellowish confined to sides and crissum. Recall that in s. Venezuela the Purple-throated is all greenish yellow below, facilitating their separation. Behavior (including calls) as in Purple-throated.

Velvet-fronted Euphonia
Euphonia concinna
10 cm (4"). Uncommon and local in woodland, plantations, and agricultural areas with scattered

trees in *w. Colombia* (upper Río Magdalena valley, mainly in Huila). Mostly 200–1000 m, locally to 1800 m. ♂ resembles ♂ Purple-throated Euphonia (no overlap), but has a *very narrow black frontlet* and *no white tail spots* (both hard to see in the field). ♀ has *yellowish forecrown* and *all olive yellowish underparts*. Most likely confused with Orange-bellied Euphonia, though that species is more forest-based (whereas Velvet-fronted favors semiopen, often arid terrain). Orange-bellied ♂ has white tail spots; ♀ has mainly buffy grayish underparts. ♀ Thick-billed Euphonia lacks the yellowish forecrown and is larger. Behavior much as in Purple-throated.

Orange-bellied Euphonia
Euphonia xanthogaster   PLATE 95(8)

11 cm (4¼"). *Widespread and common* in montane and humid forest, secondary woodland, and clearings in the Andes from n. Venezuela to w. Bolivia and in w. Amazonia; local and less common in cen. Amazonia and se. Brazil. *Generally the most numerous euphonia in the Andes and many montane areas.* Mostly below 2300 m. ♂ in **most of range** (A) has forehead and underparts yellow *tinged ochraceous* (intensity varies). ♀ has *tawny yellowish forehead, gray nape,* and *mostly buffy grayish underparts.* ♂♂ in **n. and w. Venezuela, ne. Colombia, and w. Bolivia** (B) have *forecrown rufous* and underparts rich ochraceous; ♀♀ there have forehead rufous. ♂ Purple-throated and Trinidad Euphonias (less forest-based) are brighter and purer yellow below and on forecrown. In sw. Colombia and w. Ecuador cf. ♂ Orange-crowned Euphonia. ♀ Rufous-bellied Euphonia has a tawny crissum and yellowish forehead. Occurs in pairs or small groups, foraging at all levels, frequently with understory flocks inside forest. Calls include a clear "dee-dee-deét" and a more gravelly "cheeur-cheeur." Also: e. Panama.

Tawny-capped Euphonia
Euphonia anneae

11 cm (4¼"). *Foothill forest of extreme nw. Colombia* (nw. Chocó on Cerro Tacarcuna). To 1300 m. ♂ has standard euphonia pattern, but *crown is entirely rufous,* crissum white. ♀ dark and dingy, with *forecrown dull brownish to rufous.* Both sexes of Fulvous-vented Euphonia have fulvous on lower underparts, lacking in Tawny-capped. Behavior as in Orange-bellied Euphonia, which the Tawny-capped replaces. Status in Colombia unknown; fairly common in Panama. Also: Costa Rica and Panama.

Orange-crowned Euphonia
Euphonia saturata   PLATE 95(9)

10 cm (4"). Uncommon in semihumid and deciduous woodland, forest borders, and clearings with scattered trees from *sw. Colombia* (Valle) *to extreme nw. Peru* (Tumbes). To 1400 m in s. Ecuador. ♂ has standard euphonia pattern, but *entire crown is deep yellow-orange, underparts deep orange-ochraceous.* Very plain ♀ essentially olive above and yellowish olive below. ♂ Orange-bellied Euphonia has a smaller and yellower crown patch, less ochraceous underparts (only a tinge of ochre), and white tail spots. ♀ of very similar Thick-billed Euphonia is somewhat larger with heavier bill (they often occur together). Behavior much as in other euphonias, as is its "bee-beem" call.

Golden-rumped Euphonia
Euphonia cyanocephala   PLATE 95(10)

11 cm (4¼"). *Local and generally uncommon in borders of montane woodland, adjacent clearings, plantations, and gardens in Andes from n. Venezuela to nw. Argentina* (Tucumán) *and in se. Brazil region. Avoids continuous forest.* Mostly 500 to 2000 m, lower locally and in se. South America. **Both sexes** have a *bright turquoise blue crown and nape* that renders them nearly unmistakable. ♂ has black frontlet (yellow in **s. Ecuador**), *bright yellow rump,* orange-yellow lower underparts. ♀ olive above and yellowish below with the distinctive *blue crown* and a *tawny frontlet.* Cf. ♀ Chestnut-breasted Chlorophonia (also with blue crown). Most often in small groups, perching high but usually quiet and not very conspicuous. Generally does not associate with other euphonias and seems even more addicted to mistletoe than the others. Song a fast stream of twittering notes intermixed with low-pitched "tueer" and "chuk" notes.

White-lored Euphonia
Euphonia chrysopasta   PLATE 95(11)

11.5 cm (4½"). Fairly common in canopy and borders of humid forest and adjacent clearings, from *Amazonia to the Guianas.* To 1000 m. Sometimes called Golden-bellied Euphonia. *Distinctive white loral area in both sexes* (unique among the euphonias), *extending to chin in* ♂. ♂ glossy olive above; *bright golden yellow below,* with extensive but vague olive mottling. ♀ olive above; *mostly pale gray below,* with *flanks and crissum greenish yellow.* ♀ Rufous-bellied and Golden-sided Euphonias are also gray below, but they lack white on lores; Rufous-bellied has a tawny crissum, Golden-sided more extensive olive-yellow on sides. Arboreal, often hard to observe well because it usually remains well above the ground. Often twitches tail. Calls include an almost explosive "pitz-week!" and a "wheet." Song a short, variable series of staccato whistled notes.

Rufous-bellied Euphonia
Euphonia rufiventris   PLATE 95(12)
11.5 cm (4½"). Fairly common in canopy and borders of humid forest in *w. and cen. Amazonia.* To about 1000 m. ♂ glossy steel-blue above (*no crown patch*) and on throat and chest; *below rich tawny.* A golden patch at bend of wing sometimes protrudes but is usually hidden. ♀ olive above with a yellowish forehead and gray-tinged nape. *Breast and midbelly pale gray* with *olive yellow sides and flanks, tawny crissum.* Other similar ♂ euphonias in range have yellow crown patches. ♀ Golden-sided Euphonia (no known overlap) is very similar to ♀ but has a gray crissum. ♀ White-lored Euphonia has yellow (not tawny) crissum and white loral area. An arboreal euphonia that usually occurs in pairs and often joins mixed flocks. Regularly twitches tail sideways. Frequently heard call a harsh, gravelly "drrt-drrt-drrt-drrt."

Chestnut-bellied Euphonia
Euphonia pectoralis   PLATE 95(13)
11.5 cm (4½"). Fairly common in canopy and borders of humid forest and woodland in *e. Brazil, e. Paraguay, and ne. Argentina.* To 1300 m. ♂ glossy steel-blue above (*no crown patch*) and on throat and chest. *Below chestnut* with a *golden patch showing near bend of wing.* ♀ olive above with gray-tinged nape. *Gray below* with *sides and flanks olive-yellow* and a *rufous crissum.* Nothing really similar in range. Behavior (including distinctive call) much as in Rufous-bellied Euphonia.

Golden-sided Euphonia
Euphonia cayennensis   PLATE 95(14)
11.5 cm (4½"). Fairly common in canopy and borders of humid forest and woodland of *ne. South America.* Mostly below 600 m. Striking ♂ *glossy steel-blue* with a *contrasting golden patch at bend of wing* (larger and more protruding than in Rufous-bellied and Chestnut-bellied Euphonias). *Gray below, including crissum,* aside from *olive-yellow sides and flanks.* ♀ White-lored Euphonia resembles ♀ except for its yellow (not gray)

crissum and white on face. Behavior (including distinctive call) much as in Rufous-bellied.

Plumbeous Euphonia
Euphonia plumbea   PLATE 95(15)
9.5 cm (3¾"). Uncommon and rather local in scrubby woodland, shrubby savannas and clearings, and humid forest borders of *ne. South America. Favors areas with sandy soil.* Mostly below 300 m, but to 1000 m in Venezuela. A *small* euphonia. ♂ *glossy steel-gray* with contrasting rich yellow breast and belly, flanks mottled. Dull ♀ dark olive above with *gray crown and nape; throat and chest pale gray,* below greenish yellow. Cf. White-lored Euphonia. Usually occurs in pairs, foraging at all levels for small fruits, generally on its own. Call a high clear "peee" or "weee, peee-peee."

Bronze-green Euphonia
Euphonia mesochrysa   PLATE 95(16)
10 cm (4"). Uncommon in canopy and borders of montane forest on *east slope of Andes from e. Colombia* (w. Meta) *to w. Bolivia* (w. Santa Cruz). Mostly 1000–2000 m. ♂ has a *prominent yellow forehead,* grayish nape, and *dark bronzy olive upperparts.* Below olive, *belly rich ochraceous yellow* (brightest in **southern birds,** as illustrated). ♀ like ♂ but lacks yellow forehead and has *pale gray median breast and belly.* Occurs at higher elevations than other euphonias, except for the Orange-bellied and the very different Golden-rumped. ♀ Orange-bellied is buffyish on its lower underparts and has a dull yellowish forecrown (♂ very different). Cf. also White-lored Euphonia (of lowlands). More arboreal than Orange-bellied; regularly with mixed flocks. Song a simple "treeuu, pit-treu-sit." Distinctive calls include a gravelly "treeuh, treeuh" and a chlorophonia-like (but slightly lower-pitched) "peu."

Chlorophonia

Three *gorgeous, predominantly green* tanagers, essentially large and plump relatives of the euphonias, chlorophonias range primarily in montane forest and woodland, especially in the Andes. Though often in groups, they are less conspicuous than euphonias, remaining in leafy cover and rarely perching on open branches. Chlorophonias also eat much mistletoe. ♂♂ in full adult plumage are infrequently noted in two species (Yellow-collared and Blue-naped). Like the euphonias, chlorophonias are now believed not to be true tanagers; it has been suggested that they too are better placed in the family Fringillidae.

Yellow-collared Chlorophonia
Chlorophonia flavirostris   PLATE 96(1)
10 cm (4"). Uncommon (and perhaps seasonally erratic) in canopy and borders of foothill and montane forest and clearings with scattered trees on *west slope of Andes in sw. Colombia* (perhaps northward) *and nw. Ecuador* (south to Pichincha). Mostly 400–1800 m. *Bill and legs salmon; iris white, wide eye-ring yellow.* Stunning ♂ unmistakable, *bright emerald green* with *broad nuchal collar, rump, border to green bib, and median lower underparts bright yellow.* ♀ *mostly grass green* with yellow only around eye and on median lower underparts. ♀'s soft-part colors should be distinctive; cf. larger Blue-naped Chlorophonia (minimal or no overlap). Often in small groups, but despite their bright colors usually inconspicuous, perching like so many *Forpus* parrotlets in dense foliage, then bursting out and often flying off for long distances. A distinctive, plaintive "peeeeee" call, often given in flight, sometimes draws attention to them; also has a more chattered call. Also: e. Panama (perhaps only a vagrant).

Blue-naped Chlorophonia
Chlorophonia cyanea   PLATE 96(2)
11.5 cm (4½"). Local and usually uncommon in canopy and borders of montane forest and in adjacent clearings from Colombia and Venezuela to Bolivia and in se. Brazil region (but not in Amazonia). Mostly 500–2200 m, but lower in se. Brazil region. Pale blue eye-ring. Beautiful ♂ of **Andes from Venezuela south** and in **se. South America** (A) has *head, throat, and chest bright grass green* contrasting with *bright blue nape, back, and rump;* below bright yellow. In **n. Venezuela mountains** and **Santa Marta mountains** (B) has a yellow frontlet, with blue only on nape and rump (back green); **tepui** ♂ has blue back like Andean and southern birds but also the yellow frontlet of northern birds. ♀♀ are all more or less alike, somewhat duller green than ♂♂ with *blue eye-ring and on nape* (also on rump in **Santa Martas**); yellow underparts somewhat clouded green. *Lacks* the obvious blue crown shown by both sexes of Chestnut-breasted Chlorophonia (found mainly at higher

elevations). Behavior much as in Yellow-collared Chlorophonia and generally equally scarce and hard to see. Distinctive call a plaintive "peeeu," often the first indication that this elusive bird is about.

Chestnut-breasted Chlorophonia
Chlorophonia pyrrhophrys   PLATE 96(3)
11.5 cm (4½"). Uncommon and local in canopy and borders of montane forest in *Andes from w. Venezuela* (Trujillo) *to cen. Peru* (Pasco). Mostly 1500–2700 m. Gaudy ♂ has *crown deep cobalt blue outlined black; bright green sides of head, neck, and throat* separated from *bright yellow underparts by a black line; chestnut stripe down median belly.* ♀ echoes ♂ pattern and *retains its blue crown;* duller (especially the yellow below), and has a *chestnut* border to crown. Overall pattern of ♀ of smaller Golden-rumped Euphonia is vaguely similar; the duller euphonia's blue crown is paler and more extensive (thus more noticeable), and it *lacks* contrast between throat and underparts. Behavior as in other chlorophonias, though typically ranges in pairs (only rarely in small groups). Call a rather different clear "teeeu," dropping at end.

Swallow Tanager
Tersina viridis   PLATE 96(4)
14.5–15 cm (5¾–6"). Widespread and conspicuous, usually in the semiopen, at borders of humid forest and woodland, in clearings with scattered trees, and gallery woodland from Colombia and Venezuela to Bolivia and se. Brazil. *Nomadic; can be seasonally or locally common.* To 1800 m. Bill broad and flat; wings rather long, somewhat swallowlike. ♂ *bright turquoise blue* with *contrasting black face and throat;* midbelly white, black barring on flanks. ♀ *bright green* with *contrasting pale yellow median breast and belly, prominent dusky-olive barring on flanks.* **Immature** ♂ resembles ♀, but irregular patches of blue are often present. ♂ essentially unmistakable (though cf. ♂ Spangled Cotinga). ♀'s flank barring is unique among vaguely similar, greenish tanagers. Gregarious, sometimes even when nesting, though it usually does not associate with other species. Frequently perches on high bare branches (sometimes even wires) and often sallies into the air after insects. Also consumes much fruit. Unique among the tanagers or their close relatives, nests in holes dug into banks, or sometimes buildings. Call a sharp unmusical "tzeep," distinctive and often given in flight. Also: e. Panama.

Black-backed Bush Tanager
Urothraupis stolzmanni PLATE 96(5)
15 cm (6"). Uncommon and local in woodland and shrubbery (including *Polylepis*) *near treeline in Cen. Andes of Colombia and on east slope of Andes in Ecuador* (south to Morona-Santiago). Mostly 3200–4000 m. *Entirely black above* with a *contrasting white throat; below flecked and mottled gray and white.* This distinctive tanager is more likely taken for a brushfinch than a tanager; Slaty Brushfinch is especially similar and does occur with it, but the finch has a chestnut crown, white wing speculum, etc. Most often occurs in small groups of 4–6 birds that glean actively in foliage; they regularly consort with small mixed flocks of various other tanagers, brushfinches, furnariids, and others. Often tame and easy to observe.

Chlorospingus

Small, chunky tanagers found *mainly in the Andes* where they range at varying levels in forest and woodland. Foraging bush tanagers are often quite noisy, with various sharp and fussy calls, but their often long-continued, chippered songs are only infrequently heard and are given mainly at dawn and dusk. *Chlorospingus* are *dull* tanagers in which *olive predominates; the head is often gray* (sometimes brown or black). In some species *iris color* is important for identification. Recent evidence indicates that the genus may belong in the Emberizidae.

Common Bush Tanager
Chlorospingus ophthalmicus PLATE 96(6)
14–14.5 cm (5½–5¾"). *Widespread and often common* in canopy and borders of montane forest and woodland, sometimes out into adjacent clearings with scattered trees in *Andes from n. Venezuela to nw. Argentina* (Tucumán). Mostly 1000–2500 m, locally lower. *Variable* (perhaps more than one species), but almost all races have a *pale iris* (e.g., A and B) or a *white postocular spot* (e.g., C) that contrasts with *gray to brown head, white throat variably speckled with dusky,* and *greenish yellow to yellow pectoral band.* In **Colombia's Cen. Andes** (B) *head black.* Those from **Ecuador and far n. Peru** are the dingiest overall; **cen. Peru** birds lack the pectoral band, having only a buff wash across breast. **Juveniles** can look very dull and unpatterned. Ashy-throated Bush Tanager always has a dark iris, gray head, and an unspeckled white throat. Forages actively and

often noisily at all heights, sometimes in groups of 10 or more; gleans for insects mainly in foliage and also consumes much fruit. Gives a variety of undistinctive "chip" or "tsit" call notes; song (somewhat variable geographically) a series of such notes, sometimes accelerated into a trill. Also: Mexico to Panama.

Tacarcuna Bush Tanager
Chlorospingus tacarcunae
14 cm (5½"). *Montane forest and woodland in extreme nw. Colombia* (nw. Chocó on Cerro Tacarcuna). 900–1400 m. *Iris whitish. Olive above. Throat and breast yellow,* belly duller yellow. No other bush tanager occurs in its very limited range. Mainly arboreal, but at least in Panama (where it can be locally fairly common) also ranges in low elfin forest. Also: Panama.

Pirre Bush Tanager
Chlorospingus inornatus
14.5 cm (5¾"). *Montane forest in extreme nw. Colombia* (nw. Chocó on Cerro Nique). About 900–1200 m; in adjacent Panama, where locally fairly common, ranges as high as 1550 m. *Iris creamy white to orange-hazel,* staring and very obvious. *Head dark gray,* with olive upperparts. *Mainly yellow below,* brightest on throat. As with the Tacarcuna Bush Tanager (no overlap), no other bush tanager occurs in the Pirre's very limited range. Arboreal. Also: e. Panama.

Ashy-throated Bush Tanager
Chlorospingus canigularis PLATE 96(7)
13.5–14 cm (5¼–5½"). Fairly common in canopy and borders of montane forest and woodland of *Andes from extreme sw. Venezuela* (s. Táchira) *to s. Peru* (Cuzco). Mostly 600–2000 m, lower in sw. Ecuador and n. Peru. *Head gray;* above olive. Below grayish white, *chest crossed by bright yellow pectoral band* extending down sides. Birds from **e. Ecuador and e. Peru** also have a *white postocular stripe* (as illustrated). Cf. slightly larger and chunkier Common Bush Tanager, which almost always has dusky throat spotting (never shown by Ashy-throated); most similar in ne. Colombia, but even there they differ in iris color (yellowish in Common, dark in Ashy-throated). Behavior much as in Common, but tends to be more arboreal and rarely or never occurs in the large groups so typical of Common. The two do sometimes forage together. Also: Costa Rica and w. Panama (same species?).

Yellow-green Bush Tanager
Chlorospingus flavovirens   PLATE 96(8)
14.5 cm (5¾"). *Rare and local* in mossy forest and borders in foothills on *west slope of Andes from sw. Colombia* (Valle) *to nw. Ecuador* (w. Pichincha). Mostly 500–1050 m. *Uniform. Olive green above, somewhat duskier on lores and auriculars. Below olive.* Not especially distinctive, but in its limited range the only other bush tanagers present are the rather different Yellow-throated and Dusky. The similar though larger Olive Tanager occurs only on *east* slope of Andes. Cf. also various ♀ *Piranga* tanagers (e.g., the larger Summer) and ♀ Tawny-crested Tanager (darker and much browner). Ranges in pairs and small groups, hopping on mossy epiphyte-laden branches and trunks, generally foraging higher above the ground than the Yellow-throated; occasionally in the same flock as Yellow-throated and Dusky Bush Tanagers. Call a loud husky "chek."

Dusky Bush Tanager
Chlorospingus semifuscus   PLATE 96(9)
14.5 cm (5¾"). Locally common in montane forest and borders on *west slope of Andes from sw. Colombia* (s. Chocó) *to nw. Ecuador* (w. Cotopaxi). 700–2200 m. **Northern birds** (A) have *iris yellowish white* and sometimes a small white postocular spot; from **Nariño south** (B) iris reddish brown to orange. *Notably drab and dark; head and neck dark gray,* otherwise *olive above. Mainly brownish gray to gray below,* olive only on sides and flanks. Yellow-throated Bush Tanager has obvious yellow on throat. Cf. the markedly larger Ochre-breasted Tanager. Behavior much as in Common Bush Tanager, but generally remains in lower strata; sometimes forages in large groups, and though often with mixed flocks, they sometimes move alone. At times they gather in singing assemblies comprising 4–6 birds.

Yellow-whiskered Bush Tanager
Chlorospingus parvirostris   PLATE 96(10)
14.5 cm (5¾"). Uncommon and local in lower and middle growth of montane forest and borders on *east slope of Andes from s. Colombia* (Cundinamarca) *to w. Bolivia* (Cochabamba). Mostly 1300–2400 m. Sometimes called Short-billed Bush Tanager. *Iris whitish to pale gray.* Above olive. *Sides of throat (the "whiskers") mustard to canary yellow;* below dingy brownish to pure gray (grayest southward). Yellow-throated Bush Tanager usually occurs at lower elevations, though some overlap occurs (locally they forage

together in the same flock). Yellow-throated's yellow on throat cuts more or less evenly across lower border (and is not restricted to sides), and it has brownish eyes and distinctly gray lores. Usually in pairs or small groups, foraging actively in lower growth, often accompanying mixed flocks. A sharp "tseep" contact note is often given.

Yellow-throated Bush Tanager
Chlorospingus flavigularis   PLATE 96(11)
15 cm (6"). Fairly common to common in lower and middle growth of montane forest and borders in *Andes from n. Colombia to s. Peru* (Cuzco and Puno, where apparently rarer). Mostly 700–1800 m. *Iris hazel to brownish orange.* Above olive. *Throat bright yellow* contrasting with *gray to brownish gray underparts; lores also gray.* **East-slope** birds (illustrated) are purer gray below than those on **west slope;** in addition, yellow on throat of west-slope birds is more pronounced on the sides (though it doesn't flare as in Yellow-whiskered). Yellow-whiskered Bush Tanager occurs only on *east* slope of Andes, where it mainly ranges at *higher* elevations, and typically is scarcer; its yellow on throat flares to the sides, and it shows concolor olivaceous lores and pale grayish irides. Behavior much as in Yellow-whiskered, though tends to occur in larger and often noisier groups and is most frequent near streams. Also: Panama (same species?).

Gray-hooded Bush Tanager
Cnemoscopus rubrirostris   PLATE 97(1)
15 cm (6"). Fairly common in canopy and borders of montane forest and woodland in *Andes from extreme sw. Venezuela* (s. Táchira) *to s. Peru* (Cuzco) *and extreme w. Bolivia* (recently recorded in Madidi Natl. Park in w. La Paz). Mostly 2100–3000 m. Perhaps more than one species involved. *Bill and legs pinkish* in birds **south to extreme n. Peru** (illustrated); dark grayish in birds from **most of Peru.** *Entire head, throat, and chest gray* (head slightly darker); olive above, *bright yellow below.* **Southern birds** have paler throat and chest and an especially bright yellow belly. Often recognized by its *near-constant tail-wagging;* the movement sometimes incorporates the entire rear half of the bird. *Chlorospingus* are more heavily built, and none is so bright on belly. Cf. ♀ Capped Conebill (which also wags tail). Often forages in small groups, frequently accompanying mixed flocks of other tanagers; gleans for insects along branches and in foliage.

Hemispingus

Plain tanagers found in *Andean forests and woodlands,* especially at higher elevations; their *head patterns* often provide the best identification clues. Somewhat warblerlike (especially to certain *Basileuterus* warblers), they forage by gleaning for insects, consuming little or no fruit. Many species often move in groups, and they often are an important component of mixed flocks. Contact calls are given frequently, their sputtering songs less often.

Black-capped Hemispingus
Hemispingus atropileus   PLATE 97(2)
18 cm (7"). Fairly common in undergrowth of montane forest and borders in *Andes from extreme sw. Venezuela* (sw. Táchira) *to extreme n. Peru.* Mostly 2300–3200 m. *Head sooty blackish with long buffy whitish superciliary;* olive above. Olive yellowish below, throat more ochraceous. Superciliaried Hemispingus is notably smaller, etc. Forages in groups of up to 6–8 or even more birds, regularly with mixed flocks, gleaning in foliage and sometimes eating fruit; favors *Chusquea* bamboo. Often quite tame. Song a high-pitched sputtering.

White-browed Hemispingus
*Hemispingus auricularis**   PLATE 97(3)
16.5 cm (6½"). Fairly common in undergrowth of montane forest on *east slope of Andes in Peru* (Amazonas south of Río Marañón to Cuzco). 2300–3300 m. Formerly considered conspecific with Black-capped Hemispingus. Smaller than Black-capped, with blacker face, *whiter superciliary,* and *ochraceous-yellow underparts.* Black-capped occurs only *north* of the Río Marañón. Parodi's Hemispingus has a yellow superciliary and little or no ochraceous tone below. Cf. Orange-browed Hemispingus (no known overlap). Behavior and voice much as in Black-capped, likewise favoring *Chusquea* bamboo thickets. Song a high-pitched sputtering jumble.

Orange-browed Hemispingus
Hemispingus calophrys   PLATE 97(4)
16 cm (6¼"). Fairly common in undergrowth of upper montane forest, woodland, and borders on *east slope of Andes from extreme s. Peru* (Puno) *to w. Bolivia* (Cochabamba). Mostly 2900–3500 m. Resembles White-browed Hemispingus, but has

markedly wider orange-ochraceous superciliary and *blacker crown and cheeks* (hence more contrast). Attractive and unlikely to be confused in its limited range. Behavior much as in Black-capped Hemispingus, likewise favoring *Chusquea* bamboo.

Parodi's Hemispingus
Hemispingus parodii   PLATE 97(5)
16 cm (6¼"). Uncommon in undergrowth of upper montane forest and woodland just below treeline on *east slope of Andes in s. Peru* (Cuzco). Mostly 2750–3500 m. Distinctive head pattern with *crown showing at least some blackish, long golden-yellow superciliary,* and *dusky-olive auricular region.* Otherwise resembles sympatric White-browed Hemispingus (which replaces Parodi's at somewhat lower elevations); Parodi's lacks White-browed's discrete blackish mask. The similar sympatric race of Citrine Warbler has an olive crown (no black); colors of soft parts also differ, the warbler's bill being solidly black (no horn color) and legs flesh (not gray). Behavior much as in Black-capped Hemispingus. Song a chittering "p-p-p-p-psit-zit-zit" (B. Walker).

Superciliaried Hemispingus
Hemispingus superciliaris   PLATE 97(6)
14 cm (5½"). Fairly common to common in canopy and especially borders of upper montane forest and woodland in *Andes from w. Venezuela* (Trujillo) *to w. Bolivia* (Cochabamba). Mostly 2200–3200 m, locally higher (up to treeline). *Variable* (perhaps more than one species). In **most of range** (A) mainly olive above and *bright yellow below,* with *crown and cheeks gray to blackish* and a *narrow white superciliary.* In **w. Venezuela** (B) *lacks* gray on face and superciliary is *yellow.* In **n. Peru (Amazonas south of Río Marañón to Junín;** C) very different: *gray above* with a *white superciliary, whitish below* with dusky scaling on sides of throat. Yellow-bellied races most resemble Citrine Warbler, though superciliary of hemispingus usually is white (not yellow) and crown entirely olive (not partially gray). The two species are most similar in w. Venezuela, where the hemispingus is *also* olive-crowned and yellow-browed, but the warbler's superciliary is markedly *wider* and its legs are *flesh-colored* (not dark). Cf. also Oleaginous Hemispingus. White-bellied races are most likely confused with Drab Hemispingus (though that lacks a superciliary and has a pale eye). Cf. also Cinereous Conebill. Occurs in pairs or more

often small groups, regularly with mixed flocks, gleaning actively in foliage. Song, apparently similar throughout range, an accelerating and rather loud jumble of notes, often given by several birds at once.

Oleaginous Hemispingus
Hemispingus frontalis   PLATE 97(7)

14–14.5 cm (5½–5¾″). Uncommon in lower growth of montane forest in *Andes from n. Venezuela to s. Peru* (Cuzco); somewhat local, more numerous northward. Mostly 1500–2500 m. *Very drab.* In **most of range** (illustrated) dull olive above with an *indistinct dull yellowish superciliary. Dingy olive yellowish below.* **Venezuelan** birds are more ochraceous below (especially in the northeast), as too is the more prominent superciliary. *This species is essentially devoid of obvious field marks.* It is more likely found *inside* forest than many other *Hemispingus.* Cf., especially in Venezuela, Superciliaried Hemispingus (with a more obvious and yellower superciliary) and Citrine Warbler. Usually found in pairs, often foraging with understory flocks. Song a jumbled, accelerating series of squeaky notes.

Black-headed Hemispingus
Hemispingus verticalis   PLATE 97(8)

14 cm (5½″). Uncommon in canopy and borders of upper montane forest and woodland in *Andes from extreme sw. Venezuela* (sw. Táchira) *to extreme n. Peru.* Mostly 2700–3400 m; *most numerous near treeline. Pale iris contrasts with black head and throat; narrow median crown stripe buffyish. Otherwise mostly gray,* paler below. Distinctive, not overlapping with Drab Hemispingus (found to south). Cf. Black-backed Bush Tanager and various brushfinches with pale grayish underparts (e.g., Slaty). Found in pairs or small groups that usually forage as part of a mixed flock; gleans in foliage, often in open and hopping (sometimes even walking) on top of stiff leaves. Song a fast, sputtering series of twittering high-pitched notes, sometimes given by two birds at once.

Drab Hemispingus
Hemispingus xanthophthalmus   PLATE 97(9)

13.5 cm (5¼″). Uncommon in canopy and borders of upper montane forest and woodland in *Andes from n. Peru* (Amazonas south of Río Marañón) *to w. Bolivia* (La Paz). Mostly 2500–3200 m. *Iris pale. Well-named,* essentially *brownish gray above* and *dingy grayish white below.* Superciliaried Hemispingus, regardless of race,

always has a prominent superciliary. In northern part of Drab's range (south to Junín), Superciliaried is *whitish* below. Behavior and voice as in Black-headed Hemispingus.

Three-striped Hemispingus
Hemispingus trifasciatus   PLATE 97(10)

14 cm (5½″). Fairly common in montane forest borders and woodland, *mainly near treeline, on east slope of Andes from cen. Peru* (Huánuco) *to w. Bolivia* (Cochabamba). Mostly 2900–3500 m. Above brownish olive, with *sides of crown and face blackish* and *long buffy whitish superciliary. Below tawny-ochraceous.* No *Basileuterus* warbler (some of which have a comparable head pattern) is as ochraceous below. Black-eared Hemispingus (regardless of race) never has such a bold superciliary, and is more rufescent below with black at least on chin; it occurs at lower elevations. Cf. also Orange-browed Hemispingus. Usually in small groups that often accompany mixed flocks; actively gleans insects from foliage. Song an endless repetition of a simple "tzit" note.

Gray-capped Hemispingus
Hemispingus reyi   PLATE 97(11)

14 cm (5½″). Fairly common in lower growth of upper montane forest and woodland in *Andes of w. Venezuela* (Trujillo to Táchira). Mostly 2200–3000 m. *Usually associated with Chusquea* bamboo. Simply patterned, with distinctive *gray crown* contrasting with otherwise olive upperparts; *no* superciliary. Below olive yellowish. Superciliaried Hemispingus in Venezuela has an obvious yellow superciliary and an olive crown. Oleaginous Hemispingus in Venezuela has an ochraceous superciliary and olive crown. Often in small groups of about 6 birds that regularly accompany mixed flocks but also sometimes move independently. Song a fast series of sharp, sputtering notes, often given by several birds at once.

Black-eared Hemispingus
Hemispingus melanotis   PLATE 97(12)

14–14.5 cm (5½–5¾″). Uncommon in lower growth and borders of montane forest and woodland, often in *Chusquea* bamboo, mainly on *east slope of Andes from extreme sw. Venezuela* (sw. Táchira) *to w. Bolivia* (w. Santa Cruz). Mostly 1400–2500 m. In **most of range** (illustrated) has *gray crown and nape* and *black face separated by a pale grayish line;* otherwise brownish gray above. *Below cinnamon-buff.*

In **s. Peru and Bolivia** similar, but with *black upper throat* and *long white superciliary* (often reduced). Cf. Western and Piura Hemispingus (no overlap). Rufous-crested Tanager lacks any black or white on head; Fawn-breasted Tanager has blue on crown, etc. Usually in pairs, less often small groups, regularly with mixed flocks, generally foraging inside cover. Sputtering song a fast and accelerating chatter.

Western Hemispingus
*Hemispingus ochraceus**
14–14.5 cm (5½–5¾"). Uncommon and local in undergrowth of montane forest on *west slope of Andes in sw. Colombia and w. Ecuador.* 1700–2300 m. Generally similar to Black-eared Hemispingus (*of east slope*), formerly considered conspecific. *Much duller overall,* with *face only dusky* (hence showing little contrast with head). *Below drab buffy olivaceous,* crissum buffier. Behavior similar to Black-eared, but does not seem especially to favor bamboo.

Piura Hemispingus
*Hemispingus piurae**   PLATE 97(13)
14–14.5 cm (5½–5¾"). Rare and local in undergrowth of montane woodland and forest borders in *Andes of extreme s. Ecuador* (s. Loja) *and nw. Peru* (south to Cajamarca). Mostly 1500–2500 m. Formerly considered conspecific with Black-eared Hemispingus. *Head and throat entirely black* with *bold white superciliary;* above brownish gray. *Below uniform rich cinnamon-rufous.* Black-eared occurs only on east slope. Behavior similar. Song a fast and accelerating chatter, "ch, ch, chi-chi-chi-chi-chi-chí."

Rufous-browed Hemispingus
Hemispingus rufosuperciliaris   PLATE 97(14)
15 cm (6"). Rare and local in dense undergrowth of upper montane forest and woodland on *east slope of Andes in n. and cen. Peru* (Amazonas south of Río Marañón to Huánuco). *Favors stands of Chusquea bamboo.* 2600–3400 m. Striking; *very broad cinnamon-rufous superciliary and underparts,* brownish flanks. Head otherwise black and upperparts slaty. Occurs in pairs or small groups that hop lethargically in thick growth near the ground, often remaining hidden; sometimes joins mixed flocks but also moves about independently. Song a rhythmic series of loud squeaky notes intermixed with slurred squeals (perhaps a duet), often continued for several minutes.

Slaty-backed Hemispingus
Hemispingus goeringi   PLATE 97(15)
14.5 cm (5¾"). Rare in lower growth of montane forest, woodland, and borders in *Andes of w. Venezuela* (Mérida and n. Táchira). 2600–3200 m. *Usually associated with Chusquea bamboo. Black head* with *long white superciliary;* otherwise slaty-gray above. *Mostly rufous below* with a faint white malar streak. Not likely confused in its limited range (Black-eared Hemispingus only occurs just to south). Ranges singly or in pairs in thick undergrowth, at least sometimes accompanying mixed flocks. Song an interminable stream of both high-pitched and more musical notes given simultaneously by the members of a pair.

Iridosornis

These *strikingly beautiful, mainly blue tanagers* all show contrasting yellow. They are found in the Andes, most of them at *high elevations.* They are notably quiet in demeanor.

Purplish-mantled Tanager
Iridosornis porphyrocephalus   PLATE 98(1)
16 cm (6¼"). Uncommon in lower growth of montane forest, usually where mossy, on *west slope of Andes from nw. Colombia* (Antioquia) *to nw. Ecuador* (Pichincha, where very rare). Mostly 1500–2200 m. *Mostly rich purplish blue,* somewhat paler on rump and flanks, contrasting with *large bright yellow patch on throat;* median belly buff, crissum dull chestnut. Golden-chested Tanager (*of lower elevations*) has a yellow *chest* patch. Cf. similarly patterned Yellow-throated Tanager (found only on *east* slope). Sluggish and inconspicuous, hopping through dense undergrowth and foraging quietly; usually in pairs, sometimes joining mixed flocks but also moving alone.

Yellow-throated Tanager
Iridosornis analis   PLATE 98(2)
16 cm (6¼"). Uncommon and local in lower growth of montane forest, woodland, and borders on *east slope of Andes from s. Colombia* (w. Putumayo) *to s. Peru* (Puno). 1200–2300 m. *Mainly dull blue above,* with mask blackish. *Large throat patch bright yellow,* contrasting with *dull buff underparts,* crissum dull chestnut. Purplish-mantled Tanager (no overlap) is similarly patterned but *mainly blue below* (not buff). Sluggish behavior much as in Purplish-mantled Tanager,

though Yellow-throated seems to emerge more often to edge situations. Infrequently gives a downslurred "tseeeur."

Golden-collared Tanager
Iridosornis jelskii   PLATE 98(3)
15 cm (6"). Uncommon in upper montane woodland and shrubbery near treeline on *east slope of Andes from n. Peru* (e. La Libertad) *to w. Bolivia* (La Paz). Mostly 2900–3600 m. *Golden yellow collar extends up from sides of neck onto crown,* outlining black face and throat (crown has black streaks); *otherwise blue above. Below dull rufous.* Yellow-scarfed Tanager is blue below, with yellow on head placed differently. Cf. also Saffron-crowned Tanager. Most often forages in pairs, frequently accompanying mixed flocks; lingers in the open more than other *Iridosornis,* sometimes inspecting moss-covered limbs and trunks.

Yellow-scarfed Tanager
Iridosornis reinhardti   PLATE 98(4)
16.5 cm (6½"). Uncommon in lower growth and borders of upper montane forest and woodland up to treeline on *east slope of Andes in Peru* (Amazonas south of Río Marañón to Cuzco). Mostly 2100–3400 m. Unmistakable. *Bright golden yellow band from sides of neck around rear of crown* (looking like earmuffs) contrasts with black hood; *back and breast rich blue,* becoming duller blue on belly (with *no* chestnut on crissum). Golden-collared Tanager has rufous (not blue) underparts and yellow extending up onto entire crown. Golden-crowned Tanager occurs only *north* of the Río Marañón. Forages in pairs, frequently with mixed flocks; inconspicuous, skulking in cover and rarely remaining in the open for long.

Golden-crowned Tanager
Iridosornis rufivertex   PLATE 98(5)
16.5 cm (6½"). Fairly common in lower growth and borders of upper montane forest and woodland up to treeline in *Andes from extreme sw. Venezuela* (sw. Táchira) *to extreme n. Peru. Mostly bright deep purplish blue* with black hood surmounted by a *rich golden yellow crown patch;* lower belly and crissum chestnut (crissum blue at **north end of Colombia's Cen. and W. Andes**). A lovely tanager, though in poor light it can look dark aside from the golden crown; cf. the often sympatric Plushcap (with chestnut underparts, etc.). Yellow-scarfed Tanager occurs only *south* of the Río Marañón. Behavior much as in Yellow-scarfed.

Anisognathus

Beautiful, boldly patterned tanagers of *Andean forests;* bill shape varies, with the Blue-winged and Black-chinned having more conical bills. Larger and considerably more conspicuous and gregarious than *Iridosornis.*

Blue-winged Mountain Tanager
*Anisognathus somptuosus**   PLATE 98(6)
18 cm (7"). *Generally common* in montane forest, woodland, and borders in *Andes from n. Venezuela to w. Bolivia* (w. Santa Cruz). Mostly 1200–2500 m. Somewhat variable, but in **most of range** (A) black above with *broad yellow crown stripe,* wings with cobalt blue shoulders and *bright turquoise blue flight feather edging.* Bright yellow below. On **west slope of Andes in sw. Colombia and nw. Ecuador** flight feather edging the same cobalt blue as shoulders. In **Andes of Bolivia and southernmost Peru,** black-backed with a contrasting *bright cobalt blue rump.* In **E. Andes of Colombia and ne. Ecuador** (B) *back dark moss green.* In w. Colombia and w. Ecuador cf. Black-chinned Mountain Tanager. This colorful tanager is rather active and conspicuous, often foraging in the open and regularly in groups of 6–10 birds; it frequently joins mixed flocks. In most of range song an unimpressive series of high-pitched phrases and notes (on rare occasions more strident; N. K. Krabbe recording), heard only infrequently. In Bolivia and s. Peru (north to s. Cuzco) dramatically different, consisting of an explosive series of notes that starts off low and weak but quickly becomes louder, culminating in a crescendo of forceful notes (recalling a *Lipaugus* piha!). It therefore seems likely that two species are involved.

Lacrimose Mountain Tanager
Anisognathus lacrymosus   PLATE 98(7)
18–18.5 cm (7–7¼"). *Common* in upper montane forest, woodland, and borders in *Andes of w. Venezuela* (Trujillo) *to s. Peru* (Cuzco, where rare). Mostly 2200–3300 m. *Unique small yellow spot below eye* (the teardrop) *and larger spot behind ear-coverts.* Dusky bluish slate above, wings and tail edged blue. *Deep ochraceous yellow below.* In **Peru south of Río Marañón** lacks the larger post-auricular spot and is bluer above; **Sierra de Perijá birds** dull, with paler bluish gray upperparts and more yellowish olive sides of head and neck. Forages at all levels, generally in small groups and often with mixed flocks; usually not

inside forest. Song an infrequently heard series of high-pitched sputtering and squeaky notes.

Santa Marta Mountain Tanager
Anisognathus melanogenys   PLATE 98(8)
18 cm (7"). Common in montane forest borders, secondary woodland, and shrubby clearings on *Santa Marta Mts. of n. Colombia.* 1600–3200 m. *Crown and nape blue, sides of head black* with small yellow spot below eye; grayish blue above. Golden yellow below. Buff-breasted Mountain Tanager has blue streaking on its dark crown and buff on throat and chest. Cf. also Santa Marta Brushfinch. Behavior as in Lacrimose Mountain Tanager.

Scarlet-bellied Mountain Tanager
Anisognathus igniventris   PLATE 98(9)
18.5 cm (7¼"). Fairly common in upper montane forest, woodland, borders, and shrubbery near treeline in *Andes from extreme sw. Venezuela* (sw. Táchira) *to w. Bolivia* (w. Santa Cruz). Mostly 2600–3600 m. In **most of range** (illustrated) black above with *scarlet post-auricular patch* and *bright blue rump and shoulders* (the rump conspicuous in flight). Throat and breast black; *belly scarlet.* In **s. Peru and Bolivia** slatier above and more orange-red below. This showy tanager moves about in pairs or small groups (sometimes joining mixed flocks), usually remaining within cover and, despite its bright colors, often frustratingly difficult to see well, only glimpsed as they fly from one patch of dense cover to another. Northward it can occur even in hedgerows in agricultural regions, but southward more of a forest bird. Song an attractive jumbled series of bell-like tinkling notes that cascades downward, usually given from concealment; markedly squeakier and less musical southward.

Black-chinned Mountain Tanager
Anisognathus notabilis   PLATE 98(10)
18 cm (7"). Uncommon and local in montane forest and borders on *west slope of Andes in w. Colombia and w. Ecuador* (south to El Oro). 800–2200 m. Head and nape mostly black with *only a small yellow stripe on midcrown; back rather shiny yellow-olive. Below rich orange-yellow.* Sympatric Blue-winged Mountain Tanagers are black-backed, have more lemon yellow underparts, and show much more blue on wing; Black-chinned usually occurs at lower elevations, though occasionally the two range together in the same flock. Behavior much as in Blue-winged, though the equally beautiful

Black-chinned is never as numerous and usually ranges in smaller groups. Seems notably quiet.

Orange-throated Tanager
Wetmorethraupis sterrhopteron   PLATE 98(11)
18 cm (7"). Uncommon and very local in canopy and borders of montane forest near *eastern base of Andes in extreme s. Ecuador* (Cordillera del Cóndor) *and n. Peru* (north of the Río Marañón in extreme n. Cajamarca and n. Amazonas). 600–1000 m. Unmistakable. *Black above* with wing-coverts and edging on inner flight feathers intense blue. *Throat and chest bright orange* contrasting with *yellowish buff lower underparts.* Usually found in small groups (up to about 6 birds), which often move independently of mixed flocks; this spectacular tanager is conspicuous in the few places where it occurs. Hops along larger limbs and probes into moss and epiphytes; also eats fruit. Dawn song a steadily repeated, deliberate 3-noted phrase delivered from a high perch, e.g. "we-tsí-tsoo . . ." (P. Coopmans recording); after playback a long-continued series of strident but still quite musical notes.

Bangsia

Chunky, rather short-tailed tanagers of wet forests in *w. Colombia and nw. Ecuador.* Despite their often bold and colorful patterns, all are rather unobtrusive.

Moss-backed Tanager
Bangsia edwardsi   PLATE 98(12)
16 cm (6¼"). Locally common in mossy foothill and montane forest, borders, and nearby clearings on *west slope of Andes from sw. Colombia* (Valle) *to nw. Ecuador* (Pichincha). Mostly 600–1700 m. Lower mandible flesh-yellow. Virtually unmistakable, with *large, round, dull blue area on sides of head* enclosed by black foreface, crown, nape, and chin; *back and underparts moss green; patch on midchest yellow.* Rather sluggish, often resting quietly for long periods on an open limb, peering about stolidly, sometimes allowing a very close approach. Generally in pairs, often accompanying mixed flocks. Song, given mainly soon after dawn from a prominent perch, an unmusical series of chippered notes.

Golden-chested Tanager
Bangsia rothschildi   PLATE 98(13)
16 cm (6¼"). Uncommon in lower growth of humid forest in foothills at base of *Andes in*

w. Colombia and nw. Ecuador (Esmeraldas). Mostly 200–1000 m. Bill black. *Mostly dark navy blue with a contrasting large yellow patch on chest, crissum also yellow.* Black-and-gold Tanager is blacker and has much more yellow on underparts; Moss-backed Tanager has green upperparts, etc.; both occur at somewhat higher elevations. Purplish-mantled Tanager, also predominantly blue, has a yellow *throat*. Rather stolid in behavior, often perching quietly for protracted periods, then hopping slowly along larger limbs, perhaps briefly fluttering while snatching fruit. Regularly joins mixed flocks when foraging for insects. Infrequently heard song a buzzy, insectlike "tiz-ez-ez-ez-ez-ez-ez."

Black-and-gold Tanager
Bangsia melanochlamys
16 cm (6¼"). Fairly common but very local in mid-levels of mossy montane forest in *Andes of nw. Colombia* (west slope of W. Andes in s. Chocó and nw. Riseralda; n. end of Cen. Andes in e. Antioquia, where likely extirpated because of deforestation). 1400–2200 m. Bill black. *Mostly black above* and on throat and flanks, with blue shoulders. *Large patch on chest ochraceous yellow, extending down median underparts* (where more golden yellow). Golden-chested Tanager is blue above and also across its entire belly (no yellow in middle). Long unknown in life, but behavior recently described by F. G. Stiles. Ranges singly and in pairs, often foraging with mixed flocks searching for insects in moss, epiphytes, and along larger branches; also regularly comes to fruiting trees such as *Miconia* and *Cavendishia*. Song a very high-pitched and penetrating "pit-pseéyee" repeated rapidly 3–5 times; contact note a sharp staccato "tst."

Gold-ringed Tanager
Bangsia aureocincta   PLATE 98(14)
16 cm (6¼"). *Fairly common but extremely local in lower and mid-levels of mossy montane forest on west slope of W. Andes in nw. Colombia* (s. Chocó to n. Valle); seems to favor ridges. In recent years recorded only from Alto de Pisones area, where Black-and-gold Tanager also occurs (mainly a little lower). 1600–2200 m. Lower mandible yellowish. Unmistakable, with *head, throat, and sides of breast glossy black* and a *conspicuous bright yellow ring encircling cheeks and ear-coverts;* otherwise much as in Moss-backed Tanager. In ♀, black on crown duller, yellow ring narrower and not as bright, cheeks

and ear-coverts dark green. As poorly known as the Black-and-gold until recently; behavior (also described by F. G. Stiles) similar, though mainly forages in lower strata. Song a sharp, high-pitched "tseeuurr" repeated 3–6 times; contact call a sharp "chit."

Buff-breasted Mountain Tanager
Dubusia taeniata   PLATE 99(1)
18.5–19.5 cm (7¼–7¾"). Uncommon in understory and borders of montane forest and woodland in *Andes from w. Venezuela* (Trujillo) *to s. Peru* (Cuzco). Mostly 2500–3500 m. Often in *Chusquea* bamboo. In **most of range** (A) *head, neck, and throat black* with *long superciliary of frosted blue streaks;* dark blue above. *Chest band buff,* belly yellow. In **Santa Marta** birds, *buff extends up over midthroat.* In **Peru south of Río Marañón** (B) *entire crown and (especially) nape streaked blue,* so effect of superciliary is lost; buff chest band narrower. Buff on chest is inconspicuous at best, but among the mountain tanagers, Buff-breasted can be known by its frosted superciliary (northward) or entire crown (southward). In Santa Marta Mts., cf. Santa Marta Mountain Tanager (much more numerous than Buff-breasted). Sluggish and notably inconspicuous, foraging singly or in pairs in understory, often independent of flocks. Most often noted from its loud far-carrying song, a simple sweet "feeeu-ba," sometimes lengthened into a "feeeu-feeeu-bay" (paraphrased as "three blind mice") or shortened to just a single forceful "feeeu."

Chestnut-bellied Mountain Tanager
Delothraupis castaneoventris   PLATE 99(2)
17 cm (6¾"). Uncommon in canopy and borders of upper montane forest and woodland up to treeline on *east slope of Andes from n. Peru* (e. La Libertad) *to w. Bolivia* (w. Santa Cruz). Mostly 2200–3400 m. *Above dark blue, crown frosted silvery* and with *black mask and conspicuous submalar streak. Below rufous.* Fawn-breasted Tanager is smaller, paler below (merely buff), lacks the submalar streak; it is much less a forest bird. Found singly or in pairs, sometimes with mixed flocks; generally more conspicuous than Buff-breasted Mountain Tanager, less often in understory. Searches deliberately for insects, working along mossy limbs and inspecting leaves; also eats fruit. Song a simple, sweet "tseee, tee-u-ay" (similar to but not as loud or forceful as Buff-breasted).

Grass-green Tanager

Chlorornis riefferii   PLATE 99(3)

20.5 cm (8″). Fairly common in montane forest and borders in *Andes from n. Colombia to w. Bolivia* (Cochabamba). Mostly 2000–3000 m. Unmistakable. *Bill and legs salmon red. Mostly bright green* with *mask and crissum chestnut-red.* Forages at all heights, often seeming sluggish; regularly accompanies mixed flocks of other tanagers, and sometimes quite tame. Contact call a distinctive, dry and nasal "enk" or "eck" sometimes given in series; heard less often is a fast, complex song consisting of a series of nasal notes, sometimes repeated over and over.

Buthraupis

Spectacular, large tanagers found in forest and treeline shrubbery at high elevations in the Andes; behaviorally rather a diverse group.

Hooded Mountain Tanager

Buthraupis montana   PLATE 99(4)

22–23 cm (8½–9″). Fairly common in montane forests and borders in *Andes from extreme sw. Venezuela* (sw. Táchira) *to w. Bolivia* (w. Santa Cruz). Mostly 1900–3200 m. *Large and unmistakable. Iris bright red.* In **most of range** (illustrated) head and throat black contrasting with *vibrant blue upperparts.* Mostly *bright yellow below* with blue on lower flanks and *surprisingly conspicuous black thighs.* In **Bolivia** has a *pale azure blue nape band.* Showy, noisy, and often remarkably unwary, Hoodeds troop about in groups of 4–8 and often fly long distances in the open, their distinctive far-carrying "tee-tee-tee-tee" call drawing attention to them. They regularly accompany other larger arboreal birds such as mountain caciques and jays. Groups join in loud choruses given at dawn, less often later in the day (then especially in response to sudden noises), consisting of "weeek!" or "too-weeék!" calls.

Black-chested Mountain Tanager

Buthraupis eximia   PLATE 99(5)

20.5–21.5 cm (8–8½″). Uncommon and local in upper montane forest and woodland, generally near treeline, in *Andes from extreme sw. Venezuela* (sw. Táchira) *to extreme n. Peru.* 2800–3700 m. In **most of range** (illustrated) *crown and nape deep blue, otherwise moss green above.*

Sides of head, throat, and chest black; belly yellow. In **Venezuela and ne. Colombia** has *blue rump.* Large size and color pattern should preclude confusion of this generally scarce and inconspicuous mountain tanager; nowhere near as bold as the Hooded. Usually forages as pairs, less often small groups, generally independent of flocks. Rarely perches in the open and is usually quiet, though a long and complex, musical song is occasionally given, mostly at dawn.

Golden-backed Mountain Tanager

Buthraupis aureodorsalis   PLATE 99(6)

22 cm (8½″). Uncommon and very local in upper montane forest and shrubbery near treeline on *east slope of Andes in cen. Peru* (e. La Libertad and Huánuco). 3000–3500 m. *Spectacular.* Crown and nape deep blue with *entire face and foreneck black; back, rump, and most of underparts bright orange-yellow,* with *chestnut streaking on breast;* wings and tail black. Hardly to be confused. Found in pairs and small groups, only occasionally joining mixed flocks; forages deliberately, eating fruit and searching for insects in moss and on branches. Calls include various sharp or thin notes. Song (given around dawn) a fast rhythmic series of staccato, squealing, or churring notes, each repeated several times before going on to the next.

Masked Mountain Tanager

Buthraupis wetmorei   PLATE 99(7)

20.5 cm (8″). Rare and local in treeline shrubbery on *east slope of Andes from s. Colombia* (Cauca) *to extreme n. Peru.* 2950–3600 m. *Crown and nape yellowish olive,* becoming olive on back but then *rump bright yellow* (conspicuous in flight); wing-coverts broadly tipped blue. Face and upper throat black (the "mask"), *outlined with bright yellow;* mainly yellow below. Not likely confused in its limited range. Found singly or in pairs, often while foraging in low shrubbery; regularly accompanies mixed flocks of other tanagers, finches, etc. Very quiet; infrequently heard song a long-continued series of high-pitched "tsee" notes of variable intensity, almost hummingbirdlike, and surprisingly weak given the size of the bird.

White-capped Tanager

Sericossypha albocristata   PLATE 99(8)

23–24 cm (9–9½″). Uncommon and local in canopy and borders of montane forest in *Andes from extreme sw. Venezuela* (sw. Táchira) *to cen.*

Peru (Junín). Mostly 1700–3000 m. Unmistakable, a *large tanager with stunning and very conspicuous white crown. Mostly black, with snowy white crown* and *crimson throat and chest* (color often not very apparent). Throat color bright in ♂, darker and less extensive in ♀. Throat of **juvenile** black, though it already has the white crown. Ranges in flocks of up to 10 or so birds that cover long distances as they move through forest canopy, often perching in the open and flying quite high, blackbirdlike. Generally not with mixed flocks, rather tending to move on their own or sometimes in association with larger birds such as jays (which they resemble in comportment) and mountain caciques. Far-carrying calls often herald the approach of a group, and are regularly given in flight; most frequent is an arresting "cheeeyáp!" sometimes followed by one or several shrieking "cheeeyp!" notes given by another individual; these can be confused with Turquoise Jay.

Fawn-breasted Tanager
Pipraeidea melanonota   PLATE 100(1)
14 cm (5½"). Uncommon to fairly common in borders of montane forest and woodland, clearings and gardens, sometimes even in cultivated areas, mainly in *Andes from n. Venezuela to nw. Argentina* (Catamarca) and *se. Brazil region.* Mostly 1000–2800 m, locally (or seasonally?) lower; in se. South America up to only about 1200 m. Iris red in **Andes and Venezuela** (A), browner in **southeast** (B). ♂ has *crown and nape bright pale blue* contrasting with *black mask.* Otherwise dusky-blue above, *uniform fawn-buff below.* ♀ with same pattern but duller. Similar but larger Chestnut-bellied Mountain Tanager (only Peru and Bolivia) has deeper rufous underparts, more silvery crown, and black submalar streak. Cf. also ♂ of smaller Golden-rumped Euphonia. Usually found in pairs, foraging quietly at varying levels, often hopping on larger limbs; generally not with mixed flocks. Rather quiet, occasionally giving a series of simple, high-pitched "tsee" notes, sometimes rapidly delivered, sometimes more slowly.

Creurgops

Two *rather heavy-billed, simply patterned* tanagers found in small numbers in Andean forests. Both are quiet birds.

Slaty Tanager
Creurgops dentatus   PLATE 100(2)
15.5 cm (6"). Uncommon in canopy and borders of montane forest on *east slope of Andes from s. Peru* (Cuzco) *to w. Bolivia* (Cochabamba). Mostly 1400–2300 m. Unique ♂ *all slaty gray* with a *wide chestnut crown* bordered narrowly with black. ♀ *slaty gray above* with *narrow white superciliary. Sides of head and neck, breast, and flanks rufous,* white on throat and midbelly. Among several other basically gray and rufous tanagers, ♀'s white eye-stripe is distinctive. Forages in pairs, often accompanying mixed flocks dominated by other tanagers, methodically searching for insects in foliage and moss and usually remaining well above the ground. Eats relatively little fruit.

Rufous-crested Tanager
Creurgops verticalis   PLATE 100(3)
16 cm (6¼"). Uncommon and local in canopy and borders of montane forest in *Andes from extreme sw. Venezuela* (sw. Táchira) *to s. Peru* (n. Ayacucho). Mostly 1400–2700 m, locally to 1150 m. *Gray above and cinnamon-rufous below;* inconspicuous coronal patch cinnamon-rufous outlined with black. ♀ lacks rufous in crown and is paler below. Black-eared Hemispingus is found in lower growth (not arboreal), always shows black on head (at least a mask), and is more olive above. ♂ Rusty Flowerpiercer similarly patterned, but is much smaller with a hooked bill, different behavior. Behavior much as in Slaty Tanager.

Thraupis

A *widespread* group of *familiar and numerous* tanagers, most species favoring semiopen situations; the exception is the scarce Azure-shouldered Tanager of se. Brazil. *Thraupis* tanagers have *rather subdued coloration,* grayish blue predominating in all species except the Palm (olive) and sexually dimorphic Blue-and-yellow.

Blue-and-yellow Tanager
Thraupis bonariensis   PLATE 100(4)
16.5–18 cm (6½–7"). Fairly common in lighter woodland, scrub, gardens, and agricultural areas in *Andes from n. Ecuador* (Carchi) *to w. Argentina* (sparingly to Neuquen) and *across n. Argentina to far s. Brazil* (mainly Rio Grande do Sul); some northward migration in austral winter. *In*

Andes favors arid regions. In Andes mostly 1500–3000 m, but locally down to sea level in Peru. ♂ has *blue head and throat* and *bright orange-yellow rump and breast* (the former prominent in flight). In **southern part of range** (north to Cochabamba, Bolivia; A) larger, and *back black.* In **Andes south to n. Chile and La Paz, Bolivia** (B) *back olive.* Much duller ♀ *mostly grayish brown above* and *dingy buff below, head with at least some bluish tinge* (stronger in **Andean birds**). ♀ can be confusing if seen alone (usually it is not); compare to ♀♀ of "hooded" sierra finches. Generally in pairs and easy to see; frequents semiopen areas, where it is often the only tanager present. Song a series of 4–6 sweet notes, sometimes doubled, e.g., "tseé-sur, tseé-sur, tseé-sur, tsee," lacking the squeaky quality of its congeners; stronger and more emphatic southward.

Blue-capped Tanager
Thraupis cyanocephala   PLATE 100(5)
18 cm (7"). Locally common in montane forest borders and secondary woodland in *Andes from n. Venezuela to w. Bolivia* (w. Santa Cruz). Mostly 1800–3000 m. A distinctive tanager, in **most of range** (A) with *shiny bright blue crown* and *yellow lower belly and crissum.* Otherwise olive above and gray to bluish gray below; most races have a black mask, in **ne. Venezuela and Trinidad** bordered below by a speckled whitish malar streak. In **Aragua and Miranda in n. Venezuela** (B) strikingly different, with *entirely bright blue underparts* aside from yellow crissum. Usually in pairs, sometimes small groups that move both independently and with mixed flocks. Often forages in the open. Infrequently heard song a series of high-pitched, squeaky phrases or notes.

Palm Tanager
Thraupis palmarum   PLATE 100(6)
17–18 cm (6¾–7"). *Widespread and generally common* in semiopen terrain as well as in woodland and forest borders and even semiurban areas, mainly in humid regions, from Colombia and Venezuela to s. Brazil. Mostly below 1300 m, a few higher in Andean valleys. *Primarily grayish olive,* often with a *glossy sheen* on back and underparts; forecrown a paler yellowish olive. *Mainly black flight feathers contrast with olive wing-coverts, so that the closed wing looks bicolored;* in poor light this is often the best mark for this dull-plumaged tanager. Blue-gray and Sayaca Tanagers often occur with it, and though their coloring is very different, in poor light they can be confused. In se. Brazil cf. also Golden-

chevroned Tanager. Conspicuous, though generally not as familiar as the Blue-gray or Sayaca; sometimes in small groups, often with mixed flocks. True to its name, does show an affinity for palms and often seen foraging along their fronds, even hanging upside down from the tips. The lengthy squeaky song and calls are similar to Blue-gray. Also: Honduras to Panama.

Golden-chevroned Tanager
Thraupis ornata   PLATE 100(7)
17–18 cm (6¾–7"). Locally fairly common, especially in montane areas, in canopy and borders of humid forest, woodland, and nearby clearings and gardens in *se. Brazil* (s. Bahia to e. Santa Catarina). To 1750 m, apparently descending from higher elevations in winter. ♂ has *head and underparts dark shiny violet-blue,* back duller and blacker; *conspicuous patch on shoulders bright brassy yellow.* ♀ duller and grayer, especially below; *shoulder patch as in ♂.* Most resembles geographically distant Blue-capped Tanager of the Andes. Palm Tanager is mainly olive with a differently patterned, bicolored wing. Like its congeners, generally conspicuous and, except when breeding, regularly occurring in groups. Forages mostly well above the ground, primarily for fruit; comes regularly to feeders. Song a series of squeaky notes.

Blue-gray Tanager
Thraupis episcopus   PLATE 100(8)
16.5–17 cm (6½–6¾"). *Widespread and generally common* in semiopen and settled areas as well as in a variety of forested and wooded habitats from *Colombia and Venezuela to Amazonia and the Guianas;* ranges in both humid and arid regions. Mostly below 1500 m, small numbers to 2000 m. *Mostly pale grayish blue,* darkest on back; *flight feathers edged bright blue. Color of wing-coverts varies,* usually a *solid bright to milky blue,* but in **w. and cen. Amazonia and the upper Río Orinoco valley** *shoulders conspicuously white to bluish white,* often with another wingbar of same color. Cf. Sayaca Tanager, which basically replaces Blue-gray *southward,* and also Glaucous Tanager of n. Colombia and Venezuela. A well-known tanager, active and conspicuous in many areas, and frequently tame around houses; more surprisingly, small numbers also range in the canopy of terra firme. Forages in a variety of situations, feeding mostly on fruit; frequently with mixed flocks. Song a jumbled, fast series of squeaky notes; calls are of a similar quality. Also: Mexico to Panama.

Sayaca Tanager

Thraupis sayaca   PLATE 100(9)

16.5 cm (6½″). Resembles Blue-gray Tanager, replacing it from *w. Bolivia and ne. Brazil to n. Argentina;* overlap limited, but they have been recorded together in La Paz, Bolivia. *Sayaca is equally numerous and wide-ranging.* Mostly below 2000 m, but locally to over 3000 m in nw. Argentina. *Mostly dull bluish gray* (not as bright a blue as Blue-gray), with crown and back the *same* color (crown not paler as in Blue-gray); *wings uniform,* with *flight feathers edged greenish turquoise blue.* In zone of actual or potential sympatry (se. Peru and n. Bolivia), Blue-gray has white on shoulders and is much more numerous (Sayaca occurs primarily or only as an austral migrant); beware immature Blue-grays, duller with greener wing-feather edging. Complicating this is the apparent presence in Beni, n. Bolivia, of a population with variably pale shoulders. In se. Brazil cf. also Azure-shouldered Tanager. Behavior much as in Blue-gray Tanager, though song somewhat more melodic and less squeaky.

Glaucous Tanager

Thraupis glaucocolpa

16.5 cm (6½″). Uncommon in gallery and deciduous woodland, scrub, and gardens in *n. Colombia and n. Venezuela, primarily in arid regions.* Mostly below 500 m. Resembles geographically distant Sayaca Tanager but has a *large dark blue patch on primary-coverts* that contrasts with greenish blue wing-edging on flight feathers; breast and flanks pale turquoise blue contrasting with grayish throat and whitish midbelly. Most likely confused with often sympatric Blue-gray Tanager (which always seems to outnumber it), though Blue-gray has head paler than back and a uniform wing with *no* dark blue patch. Behavior much as in Blue-gray Tanager.

Azure-shouldered Tanager

Thraupis cyanoptera   PLATE 100(10)

18 cm (7″). Uncommon and local in canopy and borders of humid and montane forest and secondary woodland, less often in adjacent clearings, in *se. Brazil* (s. Bahia to ne. Rio Grande do Sul). To 1600 m. Resembles more numerous Sayaca Tanager, and often found with that species, but *larger* with a *notably heavier bill.* Generally bluer above (less gray), especially on crown of ♂, with *dark area on lores* (Sayaca looks plain-faced), *bright deep cobalt blue shoulders* (often not easy to see), and bluer (not so green) edging on flight feathers; some greenish shows on flanks

(lacking in Sayaca). Behavior much as in Sayaca, but much more forest-based; most frequent on slopes of Serra do Mar. Song rather different, a fast phrase starting with a soft jumble and ending with several clear melodic notes, e.g., "jittle-jittle-jittle, jeeeyr-jurr," repeated 2–4 times.

Piranga

Stocky tanagers found in canopy and borders of humid forest and woodland, some species montane. All are sexually dimorphic, most strikingly so, with *most ♂♂ some shade of red,* ♀♀ olive and yellow. The *Piranga* that breed in North America are the only tanagers that have managed to extend that far north. Recent evidence, however, indicates they may not be tanagers at all, but rather are allied to the cardinaline finches.

Lowland Hepatic Tanager

*Piranga flava**   PLATE 101(1)

18.5–19 cm (7¼–7½″). *Widespread and locally fairly common* in various semiopen habitats including savanna with scattered trees, cerrado, chaco woodland, gallery and deciduous woodland, and *Araucaria*-dominated forest from the Guianas to n. Argentina. Generally below 1000 m. Formerly considered conspecific with the Highland Hepatic Tanager. Bill dusky above, horn below. ♂ *red,* paler and brighter below and on forecrown; *lores dusky* and wings and tail somewhat duskier. ♀ *yellowish olive above with dusky lores; rather bright yellow below and on forecrown.* Cf. the similar Highland Hepatic. Arboreal, found principally in pairs that forage in foliage and often seem sluggish. They sometimes accompany loose mixed flocks but at least as often move independently of them. Song a fast series of rich and melodic phrases. Call a soft "chef," sometimes doubled.

Highland Hepatic Tanager

*Piranga lutea**   PLATE 101(2)

18–18.5 cm (7–7¼″). Uncommon in lighter woodland, clearings, and plantations in *highlands of n. and w. South America south to w. Bolivia; also in borders and canopy of more humid montane forest and woodland along eastern base of Andes, on the tepuis, and in the Guianas.* Mostly 900–2000 m, a few higher; ranges down to sea level in Ecuador and nw. Peru. Formerly considered conspecific with Lowland Hepatic Tanager. Bill dusky above, horn below.

♂ *carmine red* with *dusky lores* and somewhat duskier wings and tail. ♀ dark yellowish olive above with *dusky lores; yellow below,* tinged olive on sides and flanks. Known to overlap with the similar Lowland Hepatic only in Guyana and e. Bolivia; here Highland tends to occur in more forested, montane areas, Lowland in more open, savanna areas. Highland is slightly smaller, and both sexes *lack* Lowland's contrasting forecrown (red in ♂, yellow in ♀). ♂ Lowland is a paler and rosier red; ♀ Lowland is a brighter yellow below. Also cf. Summer Tanager. Forages at all levels, though often quite high, gleaning methodically in foliage; also eats much fruit. Usually in pairs, sometimes joining mixed flocks. Call a distinctive, abrupt "chúp-chitup," often shortened to just a "chup." Song a series of rich burry phrases, recalling a *Turdus* thrush; huskier and typically slower than in Lowland Hepatic. Also: Costa Rica and Panama.

Summer Tanager
Piranga rubra   PLATE 101(3)
17.5–18.5 cm (6¾–7¼"). *Fairly common boreal migrant to n. and w. South America* (mostly Oct.–Apr.), smaller numbers to Amazonia. Generally not found in continuous forest, instead favoring secondary woodland, clearings, and borders; most numerous 500–2000 m. *Bill pale to dusky horn.* ♂ *rosy red,* somewhat paler below, wings and tail slightly duskier. **Immature** ♂ develops patches of pale red as it molts. ♀ resembles ♀ Highland Hepatic Tanager but is never so clear yellow on midbelly, and it often shows an *orangy wash* never seen in Hepatics. ♂ Highland Hepatic is a darker, more carmine red overall (Summer is notably rosier, especially below). Neither sex of Summer ever shows dusky lores, and they often have a paler bill; bill lacks Hepatic's notch on upper mandible (a character visible only at close range). *Calls differ.* Cf. also ♀ Scarlet Tanager. Usually found singly, peering around sluggishly, often perching in the open. Oft-heard staccato call a distinctive "pi-ti-chuk" or "pi-tuk." Breeds in North America.

Western Tanager (*P. ludoviciana*) has been recorded as a vagrant on Bonaire.

Scarlet Tanager
Piranga olivacea
16.5–17 cm (6½–6¾"). *Fairly common boreal migrant* (mostly Oct.–Apr.) to canopy and borders of humid forest and secondary woodland in *nw. South America, especially in w. Amazonia.*

Mostly below 1500 m, transients rarely higher. Bill yellowish horn. **Nonbreeding** ♂ olive above with *contrasting blackish wings and tail;* olive-yellow below. Molts into **breeding plumage** well before departing South America, becoming an unmistakable *vivid scarlet* with *jet black wings and tail;* **younger** ♂♂ are paler and more orangy red and may show indistinct wing-bars. ♀ resembles nonbreeding ♂ but has wings duskier, not so black. Wings of ♀ Summer Tanager are never as dusky or as black, and ♀ Summer tends to be more orangy (less lemon) yellow below. Bill colors are similar and variable. Less conspicuous than Summer, and forages mainly in foliage, often well above the ground. Distinctive call a throaty, well-enunciated "chip-burr." Breeds in North America.

White-winged Tanager
Piranga leucoptera   PLATE 101(1)
14 cm (5½"). Uncommon in canopy and borders of montane forest and woodland in *Andes from n. Venezuela to s. Bolivia* (Chuquisaca); also on *tepuis of se. Venezuela.* Mostly 700–2000 m. ♂ *scarlet* with *black lores, wings, and tail,* wings with *two prominent white bars.* ♀ has similar pattern (*including the wing-bars*), but olive above and yellow below. The bold wing-bars are unique among similar tanagers in South America. Usually in pairs that forage lethargically in foliage and outer branches, often accompanying mixed flocks and generally remaining well above the ground. Song a high-pitched and surprisingly loud "tsu-tsu-tsu-tsee" with variations. Both sexes periodically give a "tsupeét" or "wheet, tsupeét" contact call. Also: Mexico to Panama.

Red-hooded Tanager
Piranga rubriceps   PLATE 101(5)
18–18.5 cm (7–7¼"). Uncommon in montane forest and borders in *Andes from n. Colombia to cen. Peru* (Huánuco). 1700–3000 m. ♂ has *bright scarlet head, throat, and breast* contrasting with olive upperparts and bright yellow underparts; wings mainly black with yellow shoulders. ♀ has scarlet below extending only over throat. This stunning tanager is essentially unmistakable, but cf. certain molting ♂ Summer and Scarlet Tanagers. Occurs at low densities, but usually conspicuous once located; forages in pairs or small groups, hopping rather sluggishly and regularly perching high in the canopy, fully in the open. Sometimes with mixed flocks, but at least as often apart from them. Song consists of thin

trills, e.g., "titititiiti," interspersed with sweeter, more musical phrases such as "truh-treetree."

Ramphocelus

A distinct genus, all members showing *obvious silvery on the mandible, especially prominent and swollen in ♂♂*. Most species are *predominantly red* (brighter in ♂♂), and most are *numerous and conspicuous* in their favored shrubby, *nonforest* habitats.

Masked Crimson Tanager

Ramphocelus nigrogularis   PLATE 101(6)

18.5 cm (7¼"). Fairly common in shrubbery and várzea forest borders in *w. and cen. Amazonia.* To 600 m. *A beautiful red and black tanager. Most of head, neck, and breast intense crimson* encircling a *black foreface*, rump also crimson; otherwise black. ♀ somewhat duller, **juvenile** markedly so, though already showing adult pattern. This stunning tanager is unmistakable in its *lowland* range. Troops about in groups of up to 10–12 birds, sometimes joining other tanagers, including Silver-beaked, but just as often on their own. They favor shrubby borders but also range into clearings, *rarely straying far from water.* Most distinctive call a metallic "tchlink"; song a series of simple melodic phrases, often repeated (especially at dawn).

Silver-beaked Tanager

Ramphocelus carbo   PLATE 101(7)

18 cm (7"). *Widespread and generally common* in shrubby, nonforested habitats south to s. Brazil, in Amazonia especially near water. Mainly below 1200 m, locally to 2000 m in Andean valleys. **Trinidad** birds have a large bill. ♂ with *a beautiful velvety sheen, mainly blackish maroon* (**southern** birds blacker) with *dark crimson throat and chest.* ♀ dark reddish brown above *and on throat;* rump and underparts paler dull reddish. ♀ in **much of Bolivia** almost all blackish. ♂ easily recognized. ♀ duller and more easily confused, but the dark throat distinguishes it from other predominantly reddish tanagers. *Does not overlap* with Brazilian, Huallaga, or Crimson-backed Tanagers. Conspicuous and familiar in many areas, moving through its favored semiopen terrain in small groups of up to 6–8 birds (occasionally even more), usually with only one adult ♂ per group. Forages at all levels, mainly for fruit, but generally remains low. Loud "chink" call notes frequently announce its presence; heard

less often is the monotonous song, a repetitive series of short simple musical phrases.

Brazilian Tanager

Ramphocelus bresilius   PLATE 101(8)

18.5 cm (7¼"). Uncommon in shrubby clearings and secondary woodland, especially near water, in *e. Brazil* (Paraiba to e. Santa Catarina). Mostly below 400 m. Beautiful ♂ *intense bright crimson* with contrasting black wings and tail. ♀ resembles ♀ Silver-beaked Tanager (limited or no overlap) but *paler and grayer generally,* especially on crown and throat. Behavior much as in Silver-beaked, but usually in pairs and never seems as numerous.

Huallaga Tanager

Ramphocelus melanogaster   PLATE 101(9)

18 cm (7"). Fairly common in shrubby clearings, secondary woodland, and forest borders in the *Río Huallaga drainage of ne. Peru* (mostly s. Amazonas, San Martín, and Huánuco). 500–2000 m. Sometimes called Black-bellied Tanager. ♂ velvety maroon with *bright crimson lower back, rump, and lower underparts,* latter with a *wide black median stripe.* ♀ dark reddish brown with a *paler and rosier foreface;* breast and belly paler and reddish. Replaces Silver-beaked Tanager, with no known overlap; behavior alike.

Crimson-backed Tanager

Ramphocelus dimidiatus

18 cm (7"). Fairly common in shrubby clearings, gardens, and woodland in *n. and w. Colombia and nw. Venezuela* (Maracaibo basin). To 1300 m. *Swollen lower mandible gleaming silvery white in ♂,* duller in ♀. ♂ virtually identical to ♂ Huallaga Tanager (no overlap), but back slightly redder. ♀ also similar but lacks the paler foreface. The only member of its group found *west* of the Andes. Behavior much as in Silver-beaked Tanager. Also: Panama.

Flame-rumped Tanager

Ramphocelus flammigerus*   PLATE 101(10)

18.5 cm (7¼"). Fairly common in shrubby clearings, gardens, and forest borders in *Río Cauca valley of w. Colombia* (south to Valle and Cauca). Mostly 800–2000 m. Sometimes considered conspecific with Lemon-rumped Tanager. *Bill mostly silvery bluish.* ♂ *velvety black* with *lower back and rump bright orange-red* (often puffed up). ♀ has *lower back and rump as in ♂;* otherwise blackish brown above and yellow below with *orange-red band across breast.* Unlikely to be confused; Lemon-rumped is yellow on rump. Usually in small, noisy groups that troop about in the semiopen, often flying low across roads. Regularly seen perched on open branches, often with wings drooped as if to show off the rump color. Has a variety of harsh call notes; ♂'s simple repetitious dawn song is more musical.

Lemon-rumped Tanager
Ramphocelus icteronotus*   PLATE 101(11)
18.5 cm (7¼"). *Common and conspicuous* in shrubby clearings, gardens, and borders in humid lowlands from *w. Colombia to extreme nw. Peru* (recently recorded in Tumbes). Mostly below 1500 m. Has been considered conspecific with Flame-rumped Tanager and called Yellow-rumped Tanager. *Bill mostly silvery bluish. ♂ velvety black* with *lower back and rump bright lemon yellow* (often puffed up). ♀ has *lower back and rump yellow much as in ♂;* otherwise grayish brown above and *mostly pale yellow below,* throat whitish. Behavior and vocalizations much as in Flame-rumped. They are not known to occur together (Lemon-rumped ranging exclusively on the Pacific slope), though their ranges come close and very limited hybridization is known. Also: Panama.

Vermilion Tanager
Calochaetes coccineus   PLATE 101(12)
18 cm (7"). Uncommon in canopy and borders of montane forest on *east slope of Andes from s. Colombia to s. Peru* (n. Cuzco). Mostly 1100–1900 m. *Shiny scarlet* with *black bib from ocular area down over throat* and *black wings and tail.* Masked Crimson Tanager occurs in Amaz. lowlands, has a black back, etc. Breeding ♂ Scarlet Tanager lacks the black bib. This spectacular tanager is most often seen in small groups of 3–5 birds as they accompany mixed flocks of other tanagers, especially *Tangara* spp. Usually forages well above the ground, hopping along horizontal branches, inspecting moss and leaves. Rather quiet, only some weak "tsit" notes having been heard.

Chlorothraupis

Stocky, nondescript, and mainly olive, the *heavy-billed Chlorothraupis* tanagers are found in humid forest understory on lower Andean slopes. Recent evidence indicates that the genus may belong in the Cardinalidae.

Ochre-breasted Tanager
Chlorothraupis stolzmanni   PLATE 102(1)
18 cm (7"). Uncommon to locally fairly common in lower growth of foothill and lower montane forest and borders on *west slope of Andes in w. Colombia and w. Ecuador* (south to El Oro). Mostly 400–1500 m. *Bill heavy,* often showing pinkish gape; *iris bluish gray.* Dull olive above and *mainly dull ochraceous buff below.* Husky and nondescript, often best recognized by *lack* of obvious field marks. Forages in noisy groups of up to 12–15 birds that move through forest, less often at edge. Gives rough chattering calls almost continually, but its true song is delivered primarily around dawn and consists of an endless series of loud harsh notes, sometimes given simultaneously by several birds, resulting in a cacophonous medley.

Olive Tanager
Chlorothraupis frenata*   PLATE 102(2)
17 cm (6¾"). *Local* (but can be fairly common) in lower growth of foothill and lower montane forest along *eastern base of Andes from s. Colombia* (w. Caquetá) *to w. Bolivia* (w. Santa Cruz). Mostly 500–1200 m. Often considered conspecific with Carmiol's Tanager. *Bill heavy, black. Olive,* somewhat paler below, yellower on throat. ♂ has some faint olive streaking on throat; ♀ has yellowish lores and *clearer yellow throat,* which is not streaked. Cf. various *Chlorospingus* bush tanagers, all smaller with none in Olive's range so uniformly olive. Forages actively in pairs or small groups, sometimes accompanying mixed understory flocks. Lovely but infrequently heard song a distinctive series of loud ringing melodic notes, each note repeated several times before going on to the next, with initial phrasing similar to start of Buff-rumped Warbler song.

Carmiol's Tanager
Chlorothraupis carmioli
17 cm (6¾"). *Lower growth and borders of foothill forest in extreme nw. Colombia* (nw. Chocó on Cerro Tacarcuna). In Panama mostly 300–1200 m. Resembles Olive Tanager (sometimes considered conspecific) but even more uniformly olive. ♂'s yellowish throat lacks olive streaking; ♀'s throat is not so bright and pale, and lacks Olive's yellow lores. Lemon-spectacled Tanager, though a darker olive, is also similar, but it has obvious yellow spectacles; it and Carmiol's are not known to occur together. Not well known in Colombia. In Panama occurs in noisy monospecific groups, occasionally up to 20 or

so together, sometimes with Tawny-crested Tanagers. They utter, at times incessantly, harsh chattering calls, typically a thrushlike "zhwek-zhwek-zhwek." Infrequently heard song a long series of harsh "pseeeuh" notes that start softly but gradually become louder and more penetrating before ending with a jumbled "tew-twe-tii-tii-tii-tii-teeu-teeu." The series lasts 15 or more seconds, and the jumble is often given in flight as the bird moves to another perch and sings again. Also: Nicaragua to Panama.

Lemon-spectacled Tanager
Chlorothraupis olivacea   PLATE 102(3)
17 cm (6¾"). Uncommon in lower growth of humid forest and borders in *w. Colombia and nw. Ecuador* (Esmeraldas). Mostly below 400 m. Heavy bill. Mostly *dark* olive with *contrasting bright yellow lores and eye-ring* (forming the "spectacles") and yellow throat. ♀ slightly less dark than ♂. Ochre-breasted Tanager, which seems to replace it at slightly higher elevations, is considerably more ochraceous below. No overlap with Carmiol's Tanager. Behavior much like Olive Tanager of *east* slope of Andes, also usually in pairs or at most small groups, and regularly with mixed understory flocks. Has loud, excited calls given in a fast series, "treu-treu-treu-treu." Song, less often heard, a distinctive series of musical whistled notes that starts softly but quickly builds to a crescendo, sometimes very loud, e.g., "who, who, who, who, wo-wo-wo-cho-cho-cho-cheú-cheú-cheú-cheú." Also: e. Panama.

Gray-headed Tanager
Eucometis penicillata   PLATE 102(4)
17–18 cm (6¾–7"). Uncommon in lower growth of forest and woodland from Colombia and Venezuela to w. and s. Amazonia and interior s. Brazil. Mostly below 600 m, but to 1200 m in n. Venezuela. From **the Guianas and Amazonia southward** (illustrated) has *head gray with short bushy crest* (feathers showing white bases); olive above. *Throat grayish white, below rich yellow.* In **w. Colombia and n. Venezuela** head darker gray and crest shorter; in **Bolivia and s. Brazil** paler with a pinkish bill, longer crest, buffier throat. ♀ White-shouldered Tanager has similar pattern but is much smaller, more arboreal, etc. Active and excitable with an expressive crest, raised when nervous or agitated. Generally forages in pairs, sometimes accompanying mixed flocks. West of the Andes often follows army ant

swarms. Chatters are frequent; song heard less often, a jumbled series of high-pitched sputtered notes. Also: Mexico to Panama.

Mitrospingus

Two *olive and gray* tanagers that look similar but differ strikingly in their behavior and vocalizations. They occur in far-separated ranges.

Olive-backed Tanager
Mitrospingus oleagineus   PLATE 102(5)
18.5 cm (7¼"). Fairly common in montane forest and woodland on tepuis of *se. Venezuela region*. 900–1800 m. Dull olive above; *gray throat extending up over face and forehead*. Below olive-yellow. Unmistakable in its small range. Moves about in groups of up to 10 or more birds, sometimes joining mixed flocks. Forages at all levels, mainly by moving slowly along lateral branches; eats primarily insects. Harsh call a loud unpleasant "zhhweee," often repeated or given by several birds at once.

Dusky-faced Tanager
Mitrospingus cassinii   PLATE 102(6)
18 cm (7"). Locally common in dense undergrowth at edge of humid forest and woodland in *w. Colombia and w. Ecuador* (south to nw. Azuay). Below 800 m. *Iris grayish white*, obvious against the *blackish face and throat;* above slaty gray, hindcrown and remaining underparts an oily yellowish olive. *Dark overall*, unlikely to be confused in its limited range. Its nervous quick mannerisms, jerking tail and twitching wings, are also distinctive. Usually in small noisy monospecific groups that remain inside cover and rarely linger in the open. Incessant calls, a repeated gravelly "cht-cht-cht, . . ." often herald their approach. Also: Costa Rica and Panama.

Blue-backed Tanager
Cyanicterus cyanicterus   PLATE 102(7)
17 cm (6¾"). Uncommon and local in canopy of humid forest in the *Guianas, se. Venezuela, and cen. Amaz. Brazil*. Below 500 m. Unmistakable. Bill long and heavy; iris red, legs yellow-orange. Striking ♂ has *upperparts, throat, and upper chest bright cobalt blue. Below bright yellow.* Paler ♀ *cerulean blue above*, wings and tail more cobalt. *Face, throat, and chest bright ochraceous yellow*, below bright yellow. Usually in pairs that forage

with mixed flocks of tanagers and other birds, generally remaining high above the ground. Call a loud, arresting, high-pitched "tsee-tsew" or "tsee-tsew-tsew," sometimes given in flight.

Habia

Rather dull tanagers found in lower growth of humid forest and woodland, mainly in the lowlands. *Only one species, the Red-crowned, is widespread in South America; three others occur only in Colombia, one of them montane.* ♂♂ *are reddish* (gray in one), with ♀♀ browner. Despite their name, most ant tanagers do not regularly follow army ants, at least not in South America. Recent evidence indicates that the genus may belong in the Cardinalidae.

Crested Ant Tanager
Habia cristata   PLATE 102(8)
19 cm (7½"). Uncommon and local in lower growth of montane forest and borders in *W. Andes of Colombia; favors vicinity of streams and landslides. 700–1800 m. Prominent long scarlet crest* (slightly shorter in ♀) usually laid flat and projecting behind; raised and flared in excitement and alarm. Dark carmine above; *throat and breast scarlet,* belly gray tinged reddish. The expressive crest renders this most striking of the ant tanagers nearly unmistakable; no cardinal (*Cardinalis* spp.) occurs anywhere near it. Ranges in small groups that move through lower growth, regularly accompanying, even leading, mixed understory flocks. Tends to forage higher above the ground than its congeners. Call a loud "chi-veék," often repeated several times as it flares crest.

Sooty Ant Tanager
Habia gutturalis   PLATE 102(9)
19 cm (7½"). Fairly common but now very local in lower growth of humid forest borders and secondary woodland in *n. Colombia* (upper Río Sinú valley east to middle Río Magdalena valley). To 1100 m. ♂ *dark gray with scarlet coronal patch* (often spread and flared as a *bushy crest*) and *contrasting rosy red throat patch.* ♀ duller and sootier, with less contrasting throat patch; crest shorter. Behavior (including voice) much as in Red-crowned Ant Tanager; marked decline due to deforestation.

Red-crowned Ant Tanager
Habia rubica   PLATE 102(10)
17–19 cm (6¾–7½"). Locally common in undergrowth of humid forest and woodland, mainly in *w. and s. Amazonia and se. Brazil region. Mostly below 900 m. The only ant tanager in most of South America.* In **most of range** (illustrated), ♂ *mainly dull brownish red,* paler and redder (often rosier) below, especially on throat, with flanks gray; *crown patch red* bordered by a thin black line. ♀ olive brown above with *tawny-yellow crown patch.* Dull buff to ochraceous below, brightest on throat. ♀♀ in **most of Amazonia** (not the southwest) paler below, with throat almost whitish. **Southeastern** birds are notably larger and darker, with throat and crown barely contrasting. Cf. other (range-restricted) ant tanagers. ♀ Silver-beaked and Brazilian Tanagers have pale lower mandibles, no crown patch or pale bright throat. ♀ Ruby-crowned Tanager is more rufescent above and deeper ochraceous below and has a mottled breast. Cf. also various *Automolus* foliage-gleaners. Found in pairs or small groups that accompany mixed understory flocks but are usually quite shy and hard to see well. Follows antswarms on Trinidad. Both sexes give a distinctive, grating scold, "chirt" or "chak," often repeated in a series. Sweet, melodic song heard less often, mainly around dawn, and consists of a leisurely series of short, clear phrases, a frequent one being "tee-pur, tee-pur." Also: Mexico to Panama (all same species?).

Red-throated Ant Tanager
Habia fuscicauda
19 cm (7½"). Local in lower growth of humid forest borders and secondary woodland in *n. Colombia* (Córdoba to n. Bolívar). Below 200 m. Resembles Red-crowned Ant Tanager (no known overlap in Colombia). Darker and more carmine ♂ *lacks* black line bordering red coronal patch and has a *notably brighter and paler red throat* that contrasts with underparts. ♀ more olivaceous (not so brown) above with *no crown patch,* and with *contrasting pale yellow or yellowish ochre throat.* Not well known in Colombia. In Panama forages in small active groups, often with mixed understory flocks, which appear briefly but usually soon drop out of sight, all the while giving nasal scolding calls, "ahrr" (like paper being torn). ♂'s simple but pretty, melodic song is heard much less often. Also: Mexico to Panama.

Rosy Thrush-Tanager

Rhodinocichla rosea   PLATE 102(11)

20 cm (7¾"). Uncommon and local in thickets and dense undergrowth of deciduous and semi-humid forest and secondary woodland in *n. Colombia and n. Venezuela*. To 1500 m. Unmistakable. *Long, slender bill*. Beautiful ♂ slaty above and *mostly bright rosy magenta below*, flanks gray; *superciliary rosy in front, white to rear*. ♀ has *rosy magenta replaced by rich ochraceous*. **Sierra de Perijá** birds have a faint superciliary. Shy and furtive, often hard even to glimpse. Pairs forage mainly on the ground where they flick leaves with their bill; they do not accompany flocks. Rich melodic song, delivered from a low perch and reminiscent of certain *Thryothorus* wrens, is loud and attracts attention, but even singing birds are hard to see (especially without the use of tape playback). Typical phrases are a ringing "cho-oh, chowee" or "wheeo, chee-oh, chweeoh." This is the only tanager that sings antiphonally. Also: Mexico; Costa Rica and Panama.

Scarlet-browed Tanager

Heterospingus xanthopygius   PLATE 103(1)

18 cm (7"). Uncommon in canopy and borders of humid forest in *w. Colombia and w. Ecuador* (south mainly to w. Pichincha). To 800 m. Heavy bill. Unmistakable ♂ *mostly black* with a *conspicuous scarlet postocular tuft, bright yellow rump*, and *white pectoral tuft usually protruding from under wing*. ♀ grayer (slaty above, more ashy below) with no head markings but retaining the *bright yellow rump* and *white pectoral tuft*. Even ♀ unlikely to be confused, but in Colombia cf. Plain-colored Tanager. Forages in pairs, generally well above the ground and often with mixed flocks. At times seems sluggish, perching on high bare branches for protracted periods. Call a far-carrying "dzeet" or "dzip." Song an unpatterned and very fast series of squeaky and chattered notes. Also: e. Panama.

Lanio

Two forest-inhabiting tanagers found in Amazonia, where they range *on either side of the Amazon*. ♂♂ are *boldly patterned*. In behavior and general appearance, shrike-tanagers are similar to the arboreal *Tachyphonus* tanagers; their fairly long hooked bills are slightly heavier. *They are frequent flock leaders.*

Fulvous Shrike-Tanager

Lanio fulvus   PLATE 103(2)

18 cm (7"). Fairly common in subcanopy and borders of humid forest in the *Guianas and Amazonia north of Amazon River*. Mainly below 1300 m. Handsome ♂ has *black hood, wings, and tail* contrasting with ochraceous yellow back and *chestnut patch on midchest*; below rich ochraceous. ♀ much duller: ochraceous olive above, more rufescent on rump; ochraceous below, yellowest on midbelly and crissum. Some ♀♀ are more olive above and yellower below. ♂ distinctive in range; does not overlap with White-winged Shrike-Tanager (found *south* of Amazon). ♀ of similar but larger Flame-crested Tanager (regularly together) is more deeply colored and uniform below. Usually in pairs, almost always with mixed flocks, often acting as their sentinel, watching for and calling in response to danger. Shrike-tanagers habitually observe other birds as they forage and then chase down prey items that they flush but cannot catch. Most common call a sharp "tchew!" often doubled.

White-winged Shrike-Tanager

Lanio versicolor   PLATE 103(3)

16 cm (6¼"). Fairly common in humid forest in *Amazonia south of Amazon River*. To 1200 m. Striking ♂ has *blackish head* with olive forecrown and throat; back and rump mottled ochraceous; *large area on wing-coverts white*, contrasting with black wings. Below ochraceous yellow. ♀ *uniform*, essentially *ochraceous brown above* and mainly ochraceous below, *yellower on midbelly*. Larger Fulvous Shrike-Tanager is found only *north* of Amazon, lacks obvious white on wing. ♀ Flame-crested Tanager has ochraceous underparts with *no* yellow on belly. Cf. also Yellow-crested Tanager. Usually in pairs, less often small groups, generally remaining higher than Fulvous but with similar specialized foraging behavior. Has a loud, forceful "tchew!" call, often used in its role as flock leader and sentinel.

Tachyphonus

A widespread, rather diverse (polyphyletic?) genus of tanagers found primarily in lowland forest and woodland. ♂♂ *are usually black*, often relieved by color on the crest, wing-coverts, rump, or flanks; ♀♀ are duller, browner or more olive. *All Tachyphonus show pale bluish on the lower mandible or on the base of the entire bill.*

White-shouldered Tanager
Tachyphonus luctuosus   PLATE 103(4)
13–13.5 cm (5–5¼"). *Widespread and locally common* in canopy, subcanopy, and borders of humid forest and woodland from Colombia and Venezuela to Amazonia and the Guianas. Mostly below 800 m. ♂ *black* with *large white patch on wing-coverts*. ♀ olive above with *contrasting gray head;* throat grayish white, *below bright yellow*. ♂ of larger White-lined Tanager shows little or no white on closed wing. ♀ recalls a miniature Gray-headed Tanager in color but lacks that species' bushy-crested effect and is arboreal (not an undergrowth bird). Cf. also ♀ Fulvous-crested and Yellow-crested Tanagers. Forages actively in foliage and vine tangles and easy to see, feeding in the open and often quite low in second-growth and clearings. Eats mainly insects, relatively little fruit. Often occurs in pairs, and regularly with mixed flocks. Also: Honduras to Panama.

Fulvous-crested Tanager
Tachyphonus surinamus   PLATE 103(5)
16.5 cm (6½"). Fairly common in lower growth and borders of humid forest and woodland from *Amazonia to the Guianas.* Mostly below 700 m. ♂ glossy black; *pectoral tuft whitish,* usually protruding from behind wing; *small patch on lower flanks rufous.* In **eastern part of range** (A) *crown and rump tawny-buff;* in **western part of range** (B) *crown and rump rufous* and crown patches often mostly concealed. ♀ olive above with *gray head* and *broken but conspicuous yellowish eye-ring.* Below dingy grayish buff (**eastward**) to yellowish buff (**westward;** deepest on belly). Flame-crested Tanager is more a bird of forest canopy; its ♂♂ never show a pectoral patch or rufous on flanks, though they do have a buff throat patch, and ♀♀ are much browner above with no eye-ring. Most often occurs in pairs, foraging nervously in lower and middle growth, often flicking wings (exposing, in ♂, the white and rufous). They regularly accompany understory flocks.

Flame-crested Tanager
Tachyphonus cristatus   PLATE 103(6)
15–16.5 cm (6–6½"). *Widespread and often common* in canopy, subcanopy, and borders of humid forest from Amazonia to the Guianas, and in e. Brazil. Mostly below 900 m. ♂ black with *broad flat crest flame orange to scarlet, golden buff rump,* and *ochraceous buff midthroat* (often not too conspicuous). A poorly known taxon of **Mato Grosso** apparently is somewhat smaller

with no throat patch and a smaller rump patch. ♀ brown above (olivaceous to rufescent). *Throat whitish, below ochraceous.* ♂'s crest is always evident (unlike Fulvous-crested's). ♀ resembles shrike-tanager ♀♀, though they are more uniform below, *without* the more whitish throat; Fulvous (especially) is larger. Ranges in pairs that generally forage well above the ground, gleaning actively in foliage; typically accompanies mixed flocks of other tanagers and furnariids. Not very vocal.

Yellow-crested Tanager
Tachyphonus rufiventer   PLATE 103(7)
15 cm (6"). Fairly common in canopy and subcanopy of humid forest in *sw. Amazonia.* Mostly below 1200 m. ♂ black above with *yellow crown patch* and golden buff rump. *Mainly tawny below* with a *narrow black pectoral band* (sometimes incomplete) outlining the throat ♀ olive above, rearcrown tinged gray. Throat whitish, *below ochraceous yellow, deepest on crissum.* ♂'s pattern and color below unlike any other *Tachyphonus;* cf. ♂ White-winged Shrike-Tanager (with white wing-coverts, dark throat). ♀ Flame-crested Tanager (very limited overlap) is browner generally; ♀ Fulvous-crested is more similar but with an eye-ring and buffier (less yellowish) underparts; ♀ White-shouldered Tanager is smaller and purer yellow below. Behavior much as in Flame-crested.

Tawny-crested Tanager
Tachyphonus delatrii   PLATE 103(8)
14.5 cm (5¾"). Locally common in lower growth and shrubby borders of humid forest and woodland in *w. Colombia and nw. Ecuador* (south mainly to w. Pichincha). Below 800 m. ♂ *all black* with *conspicuous golden tawny crest.* ♀ *uniform dark olive brown.* Immature ♂ brown but may already show tawny crest of adult. ♀ is darker brown than any sympatric tanager, superficially resembling a finch or even a suboscine; almost invariably moves in groups, so some of the unmistakable ♂♂ will be there to help. Sweeps through forest understory and borders in fast-moving flocks of 10 or more, usually independent of mixed flocks; only rarely do they pause for long in the open. Their loud "chit" calls almost invariably herald their approach. Also: Honduras to Panama.

Red-shouldered Tanager
Tachyphonus phoenicius   PLATE 103(9)
16 cm (6¼"). Fairly common but local in savan-

nas and gallery woodland from the *Guianas to Amazonia*. To 1900 m on Venezuelan tepuis, but mainly below 400 m. ♂ glossy black (deepest on head) with *small area on inner shoulders red and white* (hard to see, though colors sometimes exposed as bird flicks its wings). Dingy ♀ *brownish gray above, grayest on head, with vague blackish mask. Grayish white below.* ♂ White-lined Tanager is notably larger and more uniformly black (never showing Red-shouldered's vaguely black-hooded effect); ♀♀ are very different. ♀ is much grayer overall than ♀ of locally sympatric Burnished-buff Tanager. Occurs in pairs, often perching in the open and gleaning with quick nervous movements.

Ruby-crowned Tanager

Tachyphonus coronatus   PLATE 103(10)

18 cm (7"). *Common* in lower growth and borders of humid forest and woodland in *se. Brazil region* (north to s. Bahia). To about 1300 m. ♂ *lustrous blue-black* with a *narrow scarlet streak on rearcrown* (usually hidden); white underwing-coverts flash in flight, also has some white on scapulars (often hidden). ♀ rufous brown above, *head grayer. Ochraceous below* with *dusky flammulation across breast.* ♂ resembles ♂ White-lined Tanager, which is more matte black and has no red in crown. Often best distinguished by ♀♀, White-lined ♀ being a very different *uniform rufous.* They nearly segregate by range, and White-lined is much less of a forest bird. Cf. also ♂ Shiny and Screaming Cowbirds. ♀ Red-crowned Ant Tanager is less rufescent, lacks breast mottling. Forages in pairs, mainly in lower and middle growth and generally apart from mixed flocks. The variable song is usually rather monotonous, a series of unmusical notes, e.g., "ch-chweek . . . ch-chweek. . . ." Call a steadily repeated "chef."

White-lined Tanager

Tachyphonus rufus   PLATE 103(11)

18–19 cm (7–7½"). *Widespread and locally fairly common* in shrubby clearings, gardens, and woodland borders, mainly in n. and e. South America south to ne. Argentina; most numerous on Trinidad and Tobago, where it also occurs inside forest. Mostly below 1500 m, in some Andean valleys to 2000 m. ♂ *all glossy black;* white underwing-coverts flash in flight, and a little white on scapulars sometimes shows (but can be hidden). ♀ *uniform rufous, slightly paler below.* ♂ Ruby-crowned Tanager is similar though slightly bluer overall, with a red crown

streak (often hard to see); ♀ Ruby-crowned is much less uniformly rufous, with a grayer head and breast flammulation. Cf. also ♂ Red-shouldered Tanager (markedly smaller). ♀ resembles Rufous Mourner and several becards in color, though these all lack the bluish on bill and behave very differently. Forages in pairs, usually within cover and most often seen as they fly across roads or other openings. Insects and fruit are consumed about equally. Generally not with mixed flocks. Not especially vocal; song a series of repetitions of a simple, somewhat musical phrase, e.g., "cheép-chooi . . . cheép-chooi. . . ." Also: Costa Rica and Panama.

Brown Tanager

Orchesticus abeillei   PLATE 104(1)

18 cm (7"). Uncommon to locally fairly common in montane forest and borders in *se. Brazil* (s. Bahia to ne. Santa Catarina). Mostly 800–1600 m. *Bill very stout. Brown above,* more rufescent on wings and tail and duskier on crown; *forehead, broad superciliary, and face cinnamon* with a thin blackish eyeline. *Below dull cinnamon-buff.* The resemblance to the Buff-fronted Foliage-gleaner is uncanny, and the two sometimes even forage together in the same flock; foliage-gleaner's bill is obviously longer and more slender, with a hooked tip, and the tail is notched. Chestnut-crowned Becard is also vaguely similar. Found in pairs or small groups that often accompany mixed flocks; forages mostly by clambering along larger branches, inspecting epiphytes and dead leaves; at rest often perches quite upright. Infrequently heard song a high-pitched "deh-d-d-d-seeee" with an upward inflection.

Diademed Tanager

Stephanophorus diadematus   PLATE 104(2)

19 cm (7½"). Locally common in montane forest borders (including *Araucaria*), monte, gardens, and shrubbery in semiopen terrain in *se. Brazil region* (north to Rio de Janeiro). To at least 2100 m, montane from São Paulo northward. Bill stubby. *Mostly shining dark purplish blue* with black foreface and a *snowy white midcrown* (the "diadem") with *small red patch on top.* **Immature** duller and duskier with little or no crown pattern. Though very attractive in good light, often looks quite blackish aside from the contrasting white in crown. Forages at all heights, often in the open; sometimes accompanies mixed flocks, but usually on its own, in pairs or small groups. Eats mainly fruit. Attractive song a rich, loud

series of whistled phrases recalling a *Pheucticus* grosbeak, often with a distinctive upslurred ending.

Olive-green Tanager
Orthogonys chloricterus   PLATE 104(3)
20 cm (7¾″). Uncommon in canopy and borders of humid forest, mainly in foothills, in *se. Brazil* (Espírito Santo to e. Santa Catarina). To 1300 m. Bill rather long and slender; legs pinkish. *Uniform olive above; yellow below, sides and flanks tinged olive.* Distinctive in its limited range but cf. ♀ Lowland Hepatic Tanager (little or no overlap); Hepatic has a stouter bill, more yellow in forehead, different habitat and behavior. Troops about in rather large and noisy groups (up to 10 or more birds) that generally remain independent of other birds and well above the ground, though they sometimes drop down to feeders for fruit. The tail is frequently raised, then quickly lowered. Loud chattering calls often herald the approach of a flock; most frequent is a "wheek!" and a "cht-tzeeee."

Black-goggled Tanager
Trichothraupis melanops   PLATE 104(4)
16.5 cm (6½″). Fairly common in lower growth of humid and montane forest, secondary woodland, and gallery forest on *east slope of Andes from n. Peru (San Martín) to extreme nw. Argentina* (n. Salta) and in *se. Brazil region.* In Andes 500–2400 m, in se. Brazil area up to 1550 m. ♂ has *forehead and ocular area black* (the "goggles") and a *golden yellow coronal patch* (often mostly hidden); dusky olive above with *contrasting black wings and tail.* Buff below. A white pectoral patch sometimes protrudes from behind wing, and in flight shows *conspicuous white stripe along base of primaries.* ♀ lacks black on face and yellow in crest; wings and tail duskier. ♂ distinctive; duller ♀ might be confused with ♀ Red-crowned Ant Tanager, which is more uniform and does not show contrasting darker wings. Forages in pairs or small groups that often accompany mixed understory flocks; in some areas is a regular at antswarms. Generally bold and easy to observe. Song a variable series of phrases with a mixture of sweet and sharper notes, often repeated several times.

Chestnut-headed Tanager
Pyrrhocoma ruficeps   PLATE 104(5)
14 cm (5½″). Uncommon in undergrowth and borders of humid and (northward) montane forest and woodland in *se. Brazil region* (north to

Espírito Santo), evidently moving inland in Brazil during austral winter. Mostly below 1000 m, but from São Paulo north only at 1100–1400 m. ♂ *mostly dark gray* with a *contrasting chestnut hood;* foreface black. ♀ much duller; brownish olive above with *dull cinnamon-rufous head* and buff lores and throat. Dull yellowish buff below. **Immature** ♂ like ♀, only gradually attaining adult plumage. Dapper ♂ easy to recognize, but duller ♀ can be difficult; as the species mainly ranges in pairs, the presence of a ♂ normally helps. Generally inconspicuous, skulking near the ground in dense lower growth, often remaining hidden in bamboo thickets; comportment reminiscent of a *Buarremon* brushfinch. Presence often revealed by ♂'s sibilant song, typically 3–4 very high-pitched notes followed by 2–3 that are slightly lower-pitched.

Schistochlamys

Two distinctive, *simply patterned and stout-billed* tanagers found in *shrubby semiopen areas.* Unusual among the tanagers, the Black-faced Tanager has a distinct immature plumage.

Cinnamon Tanager
Schistochlamys ruficapillus   PLATE 104(6)
18–18.5 cm (7–7¼″). Uncommon to fairly common but local in semiopen terrain with scattered trees and bushes, patches of secondary woodland, and clearings and gardens *mainly in e. Brazil.* Mostly below 1200 m, but locally as high as 2050 m. Rather heavy bill bluish gray tipped black. *Foreface black* contrasting with *cinnamon-buff sides of head, throat, and breast; otherwise bluish gray above.* Belly grayish and white, crissum cinnamon. Immature duller, with dusky lores and paler foreneck. A svelte, attractive tanager, unlikely to be confused. Found singly or in pairs, often perching in the open atop shrubs or low trees. Does not associate with flocks; seems to eat mainly fruit. Though not often heard, its short musical song can be repeated over and over, typically as the singer perches in the open.

Black-faced Tanager
Schistochlamys melanopis   PLATE 104(7)
18–18.5 cm (7–7¼″). *Widespread and fairly common* in semiopen areas and savannas with patches of scrub and woodland, cerrado, and shrubby cleared areas from Colombia and

Venezuela to s. Brazil, but absent from most of Amazonia. Mainly below 1600 m. Rather heavy bill bluish gray tipped black. *Mostly gray, somewhat paler below, becoming whitish on midbelly; forehead, face, throat, and midchest contrasting black to brownish black.* Immature entirely different, olive above with *yellow eye-ring;* yellowish olive below. Subadults begin to show the black face and bib when they are still mostly olive. Adult unmistakable, but the olive immatures are potentially confusing, somewhat resembling ♀ hepatic tanager (though they lack the eye-ring). Cf. also ♀ Black-and-white Tanager (could occur together in Black-and-white's nonbreeding range in sw. Amazonia). Behavior as in Cinnamon Tanager, though its song, a rich and melodic grosbeaklike phrase, seems to be given more often.

Shrike-like Tanager
Neothraupis fasciata *   PLATE 104(8)
16 cm (6¼"). *Uncommon to locally fairly common on the cerrado, mainly in interior e. and s. Brazil* (also recently found in Amapá) *and adjacent Bolivia and Paraguay.* Mostly 500–1100 m. Also called White-banded Tanager. *Above gray with prominent black mask extending from lores back over ear-coverts;* wing-coverts mostly black with white band on lesser coverts. Throat whitish; below pale gray. ♀ slightly duller. Immature browner with reduced mask and a yellowish tinge below. Unmistakable in its limited habitat; northern observers will at once be struck by its resemblance to a shrike (*Lanius* spp.). Forages in small groups, with pairs noted when breeding. Basically arboreal, though also sometimes dropping to the ground; eats mainly insects, also some fruit. Call a frequent chipping note; heard less often is the song, delivered mainly around dawn, a loud complex whistled phrase sometimes given as a duet by a pair.

White-rumped Tanager
Cypsnagra hirundinacea   PLATE 104(9)
16–16.5 cm (6¼–6½"). *Locally fairly common In cerrado and savannas in interior e. and s. Brazil and n. Bolivia* (west to Beni), also very locally in savannas and campinas of ne. South America. To about 1100 m. In **most of range** (illustrated) *mostly black above* with a *conspicuous white rump,* band across primaries, and patch in primaries. *Throat rufous, paling to buff on chest;* below mostly creamy whitish. **Southern birds** have *throat and chest paler, only washed with*

ochraceous buff. Immature browner above, uniform creamy buff below. This handsome tanager is unmistakable in range. Though often with Shrike-like Tanagers, White-rumped favors more open terrain, with fewer trees. Most often found in small groups of 4–6 birds, foraging in foliage and along gnarled branches, only occasionally dropping to the ground. Periodically (most often soon after dawn) pairs burst into a loud, rollicking duet that carries for long distances; ♂ gives a continued low churring while the ♀ joins in with a vigorous, melodic phrase, e.g. "cheedoocheechoo, cheedeereeyou-chee-choo," repeated a number of times.

Conothraupis and *Rhynchothraupis*

A pair of little-known tanagers with heavy bills; the *black and white* ♂♂ are similar looking, though recent evidence points to their not being closely related. The Black-and-white Tanager undertakes a nearly unique trans-Andean migration; the Cone-billed Tanager was only recently rediscovered.

Black-and-white Tanager
Conothraupis speculigera   PLATE 104(10)
16.5 cm (6½"). *Generally uncommon; breeds in deciduous woodland and shrubby clearings in sw. Ecuador* (mainly Loja and El Oro) *and nw. Peru* (south to La Libertad) during first half of the year, then migrates across Andes into sw. Amazonia. This trans-Andean migration may be unique. When breeding up to 1700 m. Iris dark red; bill bluish below. Unmistakable ♂ *mostly glossy blue-black* with semiconcealed white patch in crown and *contrasting white belly; conspicuous white patch at base of primaries.* ♀ much duller, essentially olive above and pale yellowish below, *flammulated olive across breast.* Streaked Saltator is superficially similar but always shows a prominent white superciliary. Immature Black-faced Tanager also similar but lacks breast streaking and has a yellowish eye-ring. Cf. ♂ Black-and-white Seedeater (much smaller, etc.). Found singly or in pairs, generally inconspicuous except when breeding, and even then often not easy to see (not even singing birds). ♂'s distinctive icteridlike song carries far, a ringing "chree-yong, chree-yong," repeated up to 3–6 times, sometimes recalls Scrub Blackbird.

Cone-billed Tanager
Rhynchothraupis mesoleuca*
16 cm (6¼). Long known only from a ♂ collected in 1938 in sw. Brazil (Mato Grosso at Juruena), *in 2004 rediscovered in se. Goiás at Emas Natl. Park, a pair found in an area of seasonally flooded gallery forest* (B. Carlos et al.). *Heavy bill whitish in ♂, blackish in ♀. ♂ black above* with a small white wing speculum. *Black below* with *median breast and belly white*. ♀ *mostly dull brown* with a *whitish midbelly*. Still poorly known, but has been observed foraging in woodland undergrowth, sometimes accompanying pairs of White-striped Warblers. ♂'s canarylike song has three parts, "jew-jew-jew-jew, trrrrrrr, triiiii" (the final trill quite high-pitched).

Red-billed Pied Tanager
Lamprospiza melanoleuca   PLATE 104(11)
17 cm (6¾"). Uncommon to fairly common in canopy and borders of terra firme forest in the *Guianas and s. Amazonia*. To 900 m. *Boldly pied. Bill scarlet* (blackish in young birds). ♂ *glossy blue-black above and on throat and upper chest*. White below, with *two blue-black bands angling to either side from midchest* (like a pair of crossed bandoliers). ♀ similar but with *contrasting blue-gray nape, back, and rump*. Generally forages well above the ground, in groups of up to 4–6 birds; sometimes congregates with other species at fruiting trees and regularly with mixed flocks, but also moves about alone. Rather noisy, with a variety of loud calls that often attract attention, the most characteristic being a fairly clear "pur-cheecheéchur."

Magpie Tanager
Cissopis leverianus   PLATE 104(12)
25.5–29 cm (10–11¼"). Conspicuous and locally fairly common in canopy and (especially) borders of humid and montane forest and adjacent clearings with large trees from *Amazonia to the Guianas* and in *se. Brazil region*. Mostly below 1200 m, a few to 1800–2000 m on east slope of Andes. Unmistakable, *large* with *very long tail* and a *golden yellow iris*. In **most of range** (illustrated) *glossy blue-black hood* extends to a point on breast; *otherwise white* with wings and strongly graduated tail mostly black, tail feathers broadly tipped white. In **se. Brazil region** even larger and more extensively black on back. Rather jaylike, ranging in pairs or small groups and generally not with mixed flocks. Often perches in the open, easy to observe. Gives a variety of arresting metallic calls, the most frequent a distinctive loud "tchenk," sometimes in series. A soft, disjointed song is heard less often.

Scarlet-throated Tanager
Compsothraupis loricata   PLATE 104(13)
21.5 cm (8½"). Uncommon in caatinga and gallery woodland, often near water, in ne. Brazil (south to Goiás and n. Minas Gerais). To about 1000 m. A *large* tanager (icterid?). *Mostly glossy blue-black,* ♂ with *scarlet throat and midchest* and bare black skin around and behind eye. Adult ♂ unmistakable, but ♀ and young ♂ resemble various icterids (especially Chopi Blackbird), though Scarlet-throated's bill is heavier and less conical. *General behavior very icterid-like*. Ranges in small flocks of up to 6–8 birds, red-throated ♂♂ a minority though at least one is invariably present; sometimes accompanied by blackbirds (e.g., Chestnut-capped) and Shiny Cowbirds. Conspicuous, often sluggish or even tame, sometimes perching on exposed branches and snags for extended periods. Has a loud, blackbirdlike "chirt" or "kyuh" call, often repeated and regularly given in flight. Dawn song a more ringing version of this note, often repeated interminably.

GROSBEAKS, SALTATORS, AND ALLIES: CARDINALIDAE

A small group of "finches," most with large bills, found in wooded and forested areas across much of South America. Many have exceptionally attractive songs. Cardinalid finches are closely related to the tanagers and emberizid finches, and indeed the placement of several genera is still much debated; for instance, *Saltator* and *Paroaria* may belong with the Thraupidae and *Gubernatrix* with the Emberizidae. Nests are cup-shaped.

Saltator

Large, arboreal cardinalid finches with *heavy swollen bills*, saltators range in a variety of forested or wooded environments, in both lowland and montane areas. Two species, Black-throated and Masked, are decidedly aberrant and may not belong in the genus. Note that two species formerly separated in the genus *Pitylus* (Slate-colored and Black-throated Grosbeaks) are now usually placed in *Saltator*; these are described on page 629. Bills in several species are *brightly colored*. Coloration and pattern are subdued in most saltators, with a *bold superciliary* a feature of many.

Buff-throated Saltator

Saltator maximus   PLATE 105(1)

20.5–21 cm (8–8¼"). *Generally common and widespread* in canopy and borders of humid forest and woodland and in adjacent clearings from Colombia and Venezuela to Amazonia and cen. Brazil and in e. Brazil. Mostly below 1200 m, small numbers to 1600 m or more. *Bright olive above* with gray sides of head and *short* white superciliary. *Lower throat buff* bordered by *black malar stripe*; grayish below with cinnamon-buff crissum. Grayish Saltator is gray above with an entirely white throat; it favors nonforested areas. Basically arboreal, foraging at all levels (though rarely actually inside forest), coming lower at edge; frequently accompanies mixed flocks. Consumes a variety of fruits, flowers, and other vegetative items. Oft-heard song a sometimes subdued series of short sweet and warbled phrases, the individual phrases repeated several times.

Green-winged Saltator

Saltator similis   PLATE 105(2)

20.5–21 cm (8–8¼"). Uncommon to fairly common in canopy and borders of humid woodland and forest and adjacent clearings from *s. Brazil* (north to Mato Grosso, Goiás, and Bahia) *to ne. Argentina* (south to Entre Ríos) *and Uruguay.* To 1200 m. Mostly gray above with a *long white superciliary*; back tinged olive and *much of wings rather bright olive green. Throat white* bordered by black malar stripe; below dingy buffy grayish, buffiest on midbelly and crissum. In area of overlap, Grayish Saltator has a *shorter* eye-stripe and a buff-tinged throat. Usually the green on wings is a good mark, but note that Grayish immatures can also show green wing-edging. Thick-billed Saltator has an obviously buff throat. Behavior much as in Buff-throated Saltator, though more likely to occur inside forest. Its numbers in many areas (especially Brazil?) are now being reduced because of trapping for the cagebird market. Loud song, heard frequently, a short phrase of clear whistled notes, e.g., "chew, chew, cho, chewee."

Orinocan Saltator

Saltator orenocensis   PLATE 105(3)

18.5 cm (7¼"). Uncommon in arid scrub and gallery and deciduous woodland in *n. Venezuela and adjacent Colombia;* widespread in the llanos. To 600 m. Above gray with *extensive black on sides of head and neck* and *long white superciliary. Throat white, breast and flanks ochraceous-buff* with whitish midbelly. This handsome saltator is distinctive in range, where no other saltator shows such bright buff below. Behavior much like other saltators, though tends to be inconspicuous except when singing. That song, often given from a perch out in the open, is a simple repetitive "cheeyir-cheeyir-cheeyir . . ." ending in a musical jumble.

Streaked Saltator

*Saltator striatipectus** PLATE 105(4)
19–20.5 cm (7½–8"). Common in arid scrub, shrubby clearings, gardens, and lighter woodland from *n. Venezuela to w. Peru* (south to Ica). Mostly below 1600 m, but to 2500 m in intermontane valleys. Now considered a separate species from West Indian birds (*S. albicollis*). Bill blackish usually with yellowish tip. Olive to grayish olive above with short white superciliary (*long* in **w. Ecuador and nw. Peru**). In **most of range** (A) whitish below *profusely streaked dusky or olive*, except on midbelly; in **sw. Ecuador and nw. Peru** (B) *unstreaked yellowish white below*, becoming whiter below and grayer above further south in **w. Peru. Immatures from w. Ecuador and w. Peru** are streaked below and have a short eyebrow (thus resembling birds found elsewhere). *Streaked is the only saltator showing streaking below.* Cf. ♀ of the scarce Black-and-white Tanager. Conspicuous and usually familiar, often found in fruiting trees around houses and in gardens; also eats flowers. Song a loud melodic "tchew-tchew-tchew-tcheeér" with distinctive long final note. Also: Costa Rica and Panama.

Grayish Saltator

Saltator coerulescens PLATE 105(5)
20.5–21 cm (8–8¼"). *Widespread and locally common* in scrub, lighter and gallery woodland, and clearings from Colombia and Venezuela to n. Argentina; *avoids extensive forest.* To about 1200 m. *Gray above* (palest in **n. Colombia and n. Venezuela**) with a *short white superciliary.* Throat white (**northward**) to pale buff (**southward**) bordered by a black malar stripe; below grayish, becoming buff on lower belly and crissum. **Amaz. birds** (illustrated) are relatively dark, both above and below. **Immature** more olivaceous generally with flight feathers edged green. Buff-throated Saltator is olive (not gray) above and has an obviously buff throat. In se. South America, cf. Green-winged Saltator. Generally quite conspicuous, often perching in the open, especially when singing. Feeds mainly on fruit and flowers. Usually not with mixed flocks. Song loud and variable, but typically consists of a simple phrase of well-enunciated musical notes, often with a chortling quality, e.g. "chew-chew-

chew, chu-chu, cheéuw" or "chu-chu-cheéu." Call a ringing metallic "tchink." Also: Mexico to Costa Rica (probably not the same species).

Thick-billed Saltator

*Saltator maxillosus** PLATE 105(6)
21 cm (8¼"). Uncommon in canopy and borders of humid forest and woodland in *se. Brazil* (north to Espírito Santo) *and ne. Argentina* (Misiones); especially northward mainly montane. To 2200 m. *Bill heavy and short, with at least some orange at base.* Gray above (olive in ♀; illustrated) with a long white superciliary. *Throat buff* bordered by black malar stripe; buffy grayish below. Green-winged Saltator has a white (not buff) throat and a smaller bill. Buff-throated Saltator (limited or no actual overlap) has a less heavy bill, olive upperparts, etc. An arboreal, forest-based saltator, occurring in some areas with the more widespread Green-winged. Not very vocal, with song a simple series of 4 loud notes, "teeu-teeu-tew-tcheéuw."

Black-winged Saltator

Saltator atripennis PLATE 105(7)
20.5 cm (8"). Uncommon to locally fairly common in canopy and borders of lower montane forest and woodland in *Andes of w. Colombia and w. Ecuador* (south to w. Loja). Mostly 500–1700 m, in Ecuador locally into lowlands. *Boldly patterned. Head mostly black* with *conspicuous white superciliary and patch on ear-coverts;* bright olive above with *contrasting black wings and tail.* Throat white, below pale grayish. Behavior much like other arboreal saltators (such as Buff-throated, sometimes with it); regularly accompanies mixed flocks. The song is given at a distinctly leisurely pace, with long pauses between phrases or notes, e.g., "teeyr, teé-yr" followed by a sputtered jumble, or "twee, twaa, too-u, tower, tweeeear."

Black-cowled Saltator

*Saltator nigriceps** PLATE 105(8)
22 cm (8½"). Uncommon in montane woodland and scrub from *sw. Ecuador* (mainly Loja) *to nw. Peru* (Lambayeque). Mostly 1500–2900 m. *Heavy bill salmon red. Mostly gray* with *contrasting black hood extending down over chest;* lower belly and crissum buff. ♀ duller with more buff below. Nearly unmistakable in its limited range; does not overlap with Golden-billed Saltator. Behavior similar to the more wide-ranging Golden-billed, but less conspicuous, tending to be more

forest-based. Its simple song is quite different, an explosive but shorter "kurt, sweeee-eee!" with variants.

Golden-billed Saltator
Saltator aurantiirostris   PLATE 105(9)
19–20.5 cm (7½–8″). *Widespread and often common and conspicuous* in montane scrub and woodland, chaco woodland and scrub, and clearings in *Andes from n. Peru* (Cajamarca) to *cen. Argentina, and east into adjacent Brazil and Uruguay.* Mostly 1500–3800 m in Andes, eastward down to sea level. ♂ has *bill mainly or entirely orange*, orange duller in ♀♀ and immatures. Handsome ♂ gray above with *broad white superciliary extending back from eye* (buff in birds from *Entre Ríos, Argentina*) and *black forehead and face extending down as a pectoral band* (wider in Andes, narrower elsewhere) enclosing a white or whitish throat. Buffy grayish below. **Andean birds** have outer tail feathers tipped white (as illustrated), but in lowlands this is less evident or absent. ♀ more olive above with pectoral band narrower or absent. Immatures have yellowish brow. *Regardless of plumage or race, this is the only saltator whose superciliary does not start at lores.* Usually in pairs, sometimes moving with mixed flocks. Song carries far, an almost explosive phrase, e.g., "switch-it, tchweet-a-sweéu" or "ch-ch-chew-chwueeé," variable but with last note always emphasized.

Black-throated Saltator
*Saltator atricollis**   PLATE 105(10)
20.5 cm (8″). Fairly common in open terrain, favoring cerrado and shrubby campos, in *interior Brazil, ne. Bolivia, and ne. Paraguay.* Mostly 500–1300 m, locally to 1800 m in e. Brazil. *Bill mostly reddish orange.* Mainly brown above with *obvious black foreface and throat* and gray sides of head. Buffyish below. **Immature**'s foreface and throat ashy brown; its bill is dark. Not likely confused. Rather conspicuous, often perching atop low trees and shrubs and sometimes dropping to the ground to feed. Song differs notably from other saltators, a fast and musical jumbled warbling, sometimes given by several birds more or less at once. Call a sharply inflected "wheék . . . wheék. . . ."

Rufous-bellied Saltator
Saltator rufiventris   PLATE 105(11)
22 cm (8½″). *A distinctive but rare saltator found in montane scrub and woodland in Andes from w. Bolivia (La Paz) to extreme nw. Argentina* (Ju-

juy and Salta). Mostly 2600–3500 m. Iris red (♂) or amber (♀). *Upperparts and throat and chest bluish gray*, contrasting with *rufous lower underparts*; long white superciliary. ♀ more faded and less bluish than ♂. Generally conspicuous, usually ranging in pairs and often perching in the open. Mainly forages on berries. In Bolivia seems largely confined to *Polylepis* scrub. Call a single, rather loud, thrushlike "kreeu"; short fast song a subdued "cheree-cheree-cheree-chew."

Masked Saltator
Saltator cinctus   PLATE 105(12)
21.5 cm (8½″). *Rare and local in montane forest in Cen. Andes of Colombia*, and on *east slope of Andes from n. Ecuador* (w. Napo) *to cen. Peru* (Huánuco). 1700–3000 m. Bill black with at least some reddish (entirely reddish in some birds); iris color also variable, usually yellowish orange. *Above bluish gray* with *black face and throat* (forming the "mask"); *tail strongly graduated, outer feathers broadly tipped white.* Below mostly white, *chest crossed by conspicuous black band*; flanks broadly gray. Inconspicuous and rarely encountered; sometimes accompanies mixed flocks of montane tanagers and other birds. An apparent association with *Chusquea* bamboo has been reported, at least in Peru, but northward an association with *Podocarpus* trees has sometimes been noted. Song rarely heard, a fast "chu-chu-chu-chuwit?"

Paroaria

A distinctive group of attractive and generally numerous birds found in semiopen terrain. The first three (smaller) species are usually near water. *All have red on head.*

Red-capped Cardinal
Paroaria gularis   PLATE 106(1)
16.5 cm (6½″). *The only* Paroaria *cardinal in n. South America*, where locally common in shrubbery and semiopen areas along shores of lakes and rivers (locally also in mangroves) from Venezuela to Amazonia. To 600 m. Bill pinkish below; iris orange. *Head and chin bright red* with black around eye. Otherwise glossy blue-black above, white below. In **most of range** (as illustrated) a small area on lower throat and upper chest is black. In the **Río Orinoco drainage** this area is red, but a narrow black mask across the face is present. In **n. Bolivia and adjacent Brazil** there is no black on face, but it is present on

throat. Regardless of this variation, in range this lovely cardinal is not likely to be confused, as it is the only *Paroaria* cardinal present. Immature less striking, with crown and upperparts brown and *face and bib buff*, and therefore can be confused. Conspicuous, usually seen hopping in pairs or small groups close to water's edge, often on open muddy ground and sometimes out onto floating vegetation. Occasionally mounts into trees, searching for insects on larger limbs. Song a repetitious but variable series of clear sweet notes, e.g., "chit-tweet-tu . . ." or "suwee-chu. . . ."

Crimson-fronted Cardinal
Paroaria baeri   PLATE 106(2)
16.5 cm (6½"). *Rare and local in shrubby riparian growth along the middle and upper Rio Araguaia and upper Rio Xingú in cen. Brazil.* 100–300 m. Resembles the much wider ranging Red-capped Cardinal (not known to overlap, replacing Crimson-fronted downriver), but *head much less bright red, blackish with crimson only on forecrown and throat.* **Rio Xingú** birds have more black on throat, leaving *only a red malar streak* (as illustrated). Behavior much as in Red-capped, though never seems to be as numerous.

Yellow-billed Cardinal
Paroaria capitata   PLATE 106(3)
16.5 cm (6½"). *Common around marshes and along shores of lakes and rivers in drainage of the Río Paraguay in sw. Brazil, Paraguay, and n. Argentina* (south mainly to Santa Fé). *Locally abundant in the pantanal.* To 500 m. *Bill bright pinkish yellow. Head bright red* with a *black bib. Above black* with partial white nuchal collar. *Below white.* Immature has head brown, bib buff, and upperparts duskier. To be confused only with Red-crested Cardinal, which is larger with a *crest* and *gray* upperparts; does not occur with other *Paroaria.* Behavior much as in Red-capped Cardinal, but locally can be much more numerous, occurring in large flocks and regularly congregating around houses to feed on grain and food scraps. Musical song a simple repeated "tsit-whit-tu-cheu."

Red-crested Cardinal
Paroaria coronata   PLATE 106(4)
19 cm (7½"). Uncommon to locally common in semiopen areas, lighter woodland, and monte from *e. Bolivia* (west to Beni) *to cen. Argentina* (La Pampa). *Especially numerous in parts of the chaco;* populations derived from escaped cagebirds are found in the parks of cities such as São Paulo. Below 500 m. Bill mostly whitish. *Head, long crest, and pointed bib bright scarlet. Above mostly gray,* with nuchal collar and underparts white. Immature has brown head and bib, duskier upperparts. Nearly unmistakable; cf. Red-cowled Cardinal (no overlap, but beware escaped captives of either species, which can occur well outside natural range). Yellow-billed Cardinal is smaller, *not* crested, black above. Usually in pairs or small groups, though flocks can gather during the nonbreeding season. This beautiful cardinal's numbers have been reduced in many areas because of its popularity as a cagebird. Feeds mainly on the ground, often with other species. Song a rhythmic series of melodic notes, e.g. "weerit, churit, weer, churit."

Red-cowled Cardinal
Paroaria dominicana   PLATE 106(5)
18.5 cm (7¼"). Fairly common in semiopen areas, scrub, and lighter caatinga woodland in *ne. Brazil* (south to n. Minas Gerais); populations derived from escaped cagebirds are found in the parks of cities such as São Paulo. To 1200 m. Lower mandible whitish. *Head and pointed bib bright scarlet. Above gray with considerable black on nape and upper back, giving a mottled effect; wingcoverts extensively black,* and conspicuous white edging on flight feathers. White below. Nothing really similar in range. Behavior much like other *Paroaria* cardinals, but like Red-crested, less tied to water. Often kept as a cagebird; numbers in the wild have been reduced in many areas. Song a leisurely series of clear melodic notes, e.g. "weerip-weerup-weerip-chúp."

Vermilion Cardinal
Cardinalis phoeniceus   PLATE 106(6)
18.5 cm (7¼"). Uncommon and local in desert scrub and low woodland near *Caribbean coast of ne. Colombia* (Guajira area) *and n. Venezuela* (east to Paria Peninsula); strictly confined to arid regions. To at least 700 m in n. Lara. *Unmistakable, with very long, pointed crest.* Thick bill pale grayish with blackish tip. ♂ *bright rosy red,* wings and tail edged dusky-brown. ♀ pale brown to grayish brown above with reddish tail and *crest as in* ♂. *Mostly ochraceous buff below.* The crest is usually held straight up, spikelike. Usually in pairs, and generally inconspicuous for most of the day, hopping in thickets and on the ground, remaining inside cover. In the early morning ♂♂ especially often linger on prominent lookouts, perching erectly. Song an attractive loud

series of whistled notes, e.g., "cheer, cheer, to-weet, to-weet, cheer, cheer." Both sexes have a loud smacking call.

Yellow Cardinal
Gubernatrix cristata   PLATE 106(7)
20 cm (7¾"). *Now sadly rare and very local in semiopen scrub and low woodland in n. and cen. Argentina* (s. Salta and Corrientes to n. Río Negro), *Uruguay, and extreme se. Brazil* (Rio Grande do Sul). To 500 m. Attractive ♂ olive above with a *long black crest* and *bright yellow superciliary and malar streak (the malar outlines a black throat patch); outer tail feathers yellow* (conspicuous on flushed birds). Bright olive yellow below. ♀ *patterned much like* ♂, also with *long crest;* brow and malar *white,* and cheeks, sides, and flanks gray. No vaguely similar bird shows the obvious *crest.* Numbers in the wild of this elegant bird are now *much reduced,* having been depleted for the cagebird market; it remains numerous only very locally (especially in e. Río Negro and extreme s. Buenos Aires, Argentina; also locally in Corrientes). Ranges in pairs or small family groups (sometimes larger flocks during nonbreeding season, at least formerly); feeds mainly on the ground, sometimes with Red-crested Cardinals and other birds. Song a loud and musical "wert, wrée-cheeu, sweét? wrée-cheeu, sweét? . . ." recalling certain warbling finches in pattern but quality richer.

Pheucticus

Large, robust finches with *very heavy bills,* found primarily in montane regions, where they prefer forest and woodland borders and scrub.

Black-backed Grosbeak
Pheucticus aureoventris   PLATE 106(8)
21.5–22 cm (8¼–8½"). Uncommon to fairly common and local (more numerous southward) in semiopen areas, scrub, deciduous woodland, and borders of montane forest in *Andes from w. Venezuela* (Mérida) *and n. Colombia to w. Argentina* (n. San Luis), *thence east into w. Paraguay and sw. Brazil* (apparently only as an austral migrant). Favors arid regions, especially in Andes, but also found locally in humid montane forest. Mostly 500–3200 m. *Massive bill.* In **most of range** ♂ *mostly black above and on throat and chest,* with bold white markings on wings and white tips on outer tail feathers. Belly bright yel-

low. **Northern races** (illustrated) have rump at least mottled with yellow; in **s. Colombia and Ecuador** entirely yellow below (up to chin). ♀♀ resemble respective ♂♂ but are browner and more or less speckled with yellow above; below yellow with black speckling. Southern Yellow Grosbeak always has head and neck entirely (♂) or mainly (♀) yellow. Found singly or in pairs, often perching in the open, sometimes allowing a close approach; generally not with flocks. Consumes much fruit, also some insects. ♂'s song a bright and rich caroling, very melodic. Both sexes often give a metallic "pink" call.

Southern Yellow Grosbeak
Pheucticus chrysogaster   PLATE 106(9)
21–21.5 cm (8¼–8½"). Locally fairly common in arid scrub, deciduous woodland, and montane forest borders in *mountains of n. Venezuela and n. Colombia and in Andes from extreme s. Colombia* (Nariño) *to sw. Peru* (Moquegua). To 3500 m in Ecuador; in Peru and Ecuador locally down to coast. Sometimes called Golden-bellied Grosbeak. *Massive bill.* ♂ from **s. Colombia southward** (illustrated) has *head, neck, rump, and underparts golden yellow.* Back, wings, and tail mainly black, wings with bold white markings (including tertial tips), and tail with white corners. **Northern** birds have the yellow more mottled. ♀ duller, streakier, and browner above but still with *head and underparts essentially yellow.* Black-backed Grosbeak *always has a dark head,* but some individuals can be confusing (and the two species do occur together, e.g., in the Ecuadorian highlands). Vaguely oriolelike in flight. Behavior and voice much as in Black-backed. Though mainly found in arid regions, also ranges locally into more humid zones.

Rose-breasted Grosbeak
Pheucticus ludovicianus
18.5 cm (7¼"). *Boreal migrant* to borders of montane and humid forest, woodland, and clearings from *n. Venezuela to Ecuador;* fairly common northward, less so to south, with a scatter of records in Amazonia (mainly Nov.–Apr.). Mostly 500–2000 m. *Heavy whitish bill.* **Breeding** ♂ (Feb. onward) has *head, throat, and upperparts black* with *unmistakable rosy red patch on chest,* bold white wing markings. Rump and underparts white. ♀ and **nonbreeding** ♂ more dusky-brown above with *buff to whitish superciliary and coronal stripe.* Below whitish with *narrow dusky streaking,* often tinged buff on throat and breast. Nonbreeding ♂ can be confusing, resembling

an overgrown sparrow or other finch, but heavy bill and head striping should be distinctive. Arboreal, sometimes in small groups of its own species. Call a metallic "pink." Does not sing in South America. Breeds in North America.

Black-headed Grosbeak (*P. melanocephalus*) has been recorded as a vagrant on Curaçao.

Red-and-black Grosbeak
Periporphyrus erythromelas   PLATE 106(10)
20.5 cm (8"). Rare to uncommon and inconspicuous in lower and middle growth of humid forest from e. *Venezuela to e. Amaz. Brazil.* To 500 m. *Very heavy blackish bill.* Unmistakable ♂ *carmine above* and *rosy red below* with a *contrasting black hood.* ♀ *has pattern of ♂,* with *the same black hood,* but is olive above and yellow below. Yellow-green Grosbeak is smaller with only foreface black. Forages singly or in pairs, most often not accompanying mixed flocks; eats mainly fruit. Sweet song resembles Slate-colored Grosbeak, though delivery notably more leisurely, often with long pauses between phrases. Its "spink" call note also recalls Slate-colored.

Saltator

Formerly separated in the genus *Pitylus,* these two distinctive grosbeaks are *mainly bluish gray* and have *red bills;* they range in **humid lowland forests. Despite the generic merger, we retain the long-used English group name "grosbeak."**

Slate-colored Grosbeak
*Saltator grossus**   PLATE 106(11)
20 cm (7¾"). *Fairly common and widespread* in subcanopy and middle levels of humid forest from Colombia and s. Venezuela to Amazonia and the Guianas. Mostly below 1200 m. *Heavy bill coral red.* ♂ *mostly dark bluish gray;* upper throat white, with black foreface and broad margin around the throat patch. ♀ slightly duller; it lacks the black. Easily recognized, especially on account of its bright bill color. Generally ranges in pairs, sometimes with mixed flocks; eats mostly fruit, also some insects. Often not very conspicuous, though frequently heard. Song fine and rich, variably phrased (though usually short), recalling a peppershrike, e.g., "cheewee, chweer, chiwee-chiwer." Oft-heard calls include

a distinctive cardinallike "peek" and a descending, nasal "wrenh." Also: Honduras to Panama.

Black-throated Grosbeak
Saltator fuliginosus   PLATE 106(12)
22 cm (8½"). *Replaces Slate-colored Grosbeak in se. Brazil region* (north to s. Bahia), likewise inhabiting humid and montane forest and woodland. To 1200 m; northward basically montane. *Heavy bill coral red.* ♂ *dark bluish slate* with *blackish throat and chest.* ♀ similar but throat and chest dusky. Behavior much like Slate-colored, as is its melodic voice.

Yellow-shouldered Grosbeak
*Parkerthraustes humeralis**   PLATE 106(13)
16 cm (6¼"). Uncommon and seemingly local (perhaps mostly just overlooked) in canopy and borders of terra firme forest in *w. and s. Amazonia.* To 800 m. *Stout dusky bill, mandible pale* basally. *Crown and nape gray, facial mask black, malar stripe white,* and *white throat scaled with black.* Otherwise yellowish olive above and gray below with yellow crissum. Liable to be confused only with certain arboreal saltators, though none has such a fancy head pattern. Found singly or in pairs, most often accompanying mixed flocks in the canopy. Sometimes perches motionless on a high exposed branch for an extended period. Call a sharp, high-pitched "cheét-swit" or inflected "suweet." Apparent song, heard much less frequently, a jumbled series of similar notes and twitters.

Yellow-green Grosbeak
Caryothraustes canadensis   PLATE 106(14)
17.5–18.5 cm (7–7¼"). Fairly common in humid forest subcanopy and borders from *s. Venezuela to se. Brazil* (south to Rio de Janeiro). To 1000 m. *Bright yellow and olive.* Heavy bill pale at base. In **most of range** (as illustrated) olive above and yellow below with *contrasting black foreface and upper throat.* **Ne. Brazil** birds also have a black frontal band; in **se. Brazil** larger with a yellower forecrown. Nearly unmistakable; cf. other grosbeaks, especially ♀ of the rare Red-and-black. Troops about in groups of up to 10–15 individuals, sometimes moving independently but at other times appearing to form the nucleus of mixed canopy flocks. Frequently heard and distinctive call a loud, buzzy "dzzeet" or "dzreet," sometimes followed by a repeated "chew-chew-chew-chew." Also: e. Panama.

EMBERIZINE FINCHES: EMBERIZIDAE

A widespread and numerous family composed mostly of small birds that range in open and semiopen habitats, a few groups (e.g., the brushfinches) in forest and woodland undergrowth. The family remains poorly defined taxonomically and is closely related to the tanagers and the cardueline finches; some genera will end up being reassigned to different families. Many species have rather thick or conical bills used in crushing seeds; quite a few (notably the *Oryzoborus* seedfinches) are fine songsters. Nests of most species are cup-shaped, but a few build dome-shaped nests with a side entrance.

Blue-black Grassquit

Volatinia jacarina PLATE 107(1)

10 cm (4"). *Widespread and common (locally abundant)* in grassy areas in open and settled regions from Colombia and Venezuela to n. Argentina; scarcer where forest dominates. Mostly below 1000 m, smaller numbers to 2000–2500 m. *Bill relatively slender and pointed. ♂ glossy blue-black* with white axillars. On **Pacific slope from Ecuador south** browner, especially on wings. ♀ dull brown above; whitish to pale buff below, *breast and flanks streaked dusky.* Immature ♂ mottled blackish and brown; breeds when still in this plumage. *Sporophila* seedeaters have thicker, stubbier bills; none is so uniformly black as the ♂ grassquit or as streaked below as the ♀. Cf. more local Sooty Grassquit and ♀ Slaty and Uniform Finches. A familiar roadside bird, often in flocks when not breeding; frequently associates with seedeaters. Feeds on seeds, mostly on the ground. Breeding ♂♂ tirelessly give a buzzy, explosive "dzee-u" from a low perch, often accompanied by a short flutter and jump into the air. Also: Mexico to Panama; Grenada.

Tiaris

Relatively *featureless* small finches of open and shrubby areas, *Tiaris* have a bill shape intermediate between that of *Volatinia* and the *Sporophila* seedeaters. Nests are globular structures with a side entrance, very unlike *Sporophila* seedeaters. The genus likely is allied to the tanagers.

Sooty Grassquit

Tiaris fuliginosus PLATE 107(2)

11.5 cm (4½"). Uncommon, irregular (seasonal?), and local in shrubby clearings, grassy scrub, and woodland borders, from ne. Colombia and n. Venezuela to se. Brazil (south to Paraná) and e. Paraguay. Mostly below 1500 m. *Bill blackish with pink gape in ♂; gape yellowish in ♀. ♂ sooty blackish,* grayer and often paler below. ♀ dull olive brown above, somewhat brighter olive brown below, whiter on midbelly. ♂ Blue-black Grassquit is much glossier blue-black and shows white under wing (obvious in flight). ♂ Uniform Finch is notably grayer. ♀ Sooty is hard to identify on its own, but fortunately it usually occurs in small groups with some ♂♂ around. ♀ of slightly smaller Black-faced Grassquit is most similar; cf. also Dull-colored Grassquit (with bicolored bill, etc.). Infrequently encountered, seems most numerous on Trinidad and in e. Brazil. Usually in pairs or small groups, foraging mainly on or near the ground; often accompanies *Sporophila* seedeaters. High-pitched song ringing but rather unmusical, e.g., "screez-screedelelee."

Black-faced Grassquit

Tiaris bicolor

10 cm (4"). Locally fairly common in arid scrub, grassy areas, and woodland borders in w. *Colombia and n. Venezuela.* To 1000 m. Bill blackish with pink gape in ♂, duskier in ♀. Resembles Sooty Grassquit, but slightly smaller with shorter tail, resulting in a stubbier look. ♂ *decidedly more olive above* (not so uniformly sooty). ♀ virtually indistinguishable in plumage, but slightly

more grayish (not so brown); normally best to go by accompanying ♂♂. Found in pairs or small groups, hopping on or near ground, frequently on lawns; tame, and often around houses. Song a weak buzzy "tz-tzeeteeeteeeeee" sometimes given in a fluttery display flight. Also: West Indies except Cuba.

Dull-colored Grassquit
Tiaris obscurus   PLATE 107(3)
11 cm (4¼"). Uncommon to locally fairly common in shrubby clearings and gardens and woodland borders from *n. Venezuela and w. Colombia to n. Argentina* (Salta and Chaco); a few spread east into Paraguay and sw. Brazil during austral winter. Mostly below 1500–2000 m, favoring lower mountain slopes. *Bicolored bill dusky above and yellowish below. Very dull.* Grayish olive brown above, paler brownish gray below, whitish on midbelly. **Northern birds** darker; **coastal Peruvian birds** grayer. This *nondescript, hen-colored* grassquit resembles many ♀ seedeaters, and sometimes is found in association with them; its *bicolored bill* separates it from most. When breeding readily recognized from ♂'s song, an explosive buzzy "zeetig, zeezeezig" with variations, much more resembling songs of other *Tiaris* than the more musical songs of most *Sporophila*.

Yellow-faced Grassquit
Tiaris olivaceus   PLATE 107(4)
10 cm (4"). Common in semiopen and grassy areas, mainly on *Andean slopes, in sw. Venezuela, w. Colombia, and nw. Ecuador* (spreading south to Pichincha). Mostly 500–2300 m. ♂ olive above with a *unique face pattern in which black crown, face, and breast contrast with bright yellow superciliary and throat patch;* belly grayish olive. ♀ duller, with no black and *showing only a faint facial pattern.* Occurs in scattered pairs or loose groups, sometimes associating with various seedeaters; forages mostly on grass seeds, often clinging to and bending down their stems. Song a colorless thin trill "tee-ee-ee-ee." Also: Mexico to Panama.

White-naped Seedeater
Dolospingus fringilloides   PLATE 107(5)
13.5 cm (5¼"). Uncommon and local in scrubby woodland and savanna patches in *sw. Venezuela and nw. Brazil, extreme e. Colombia, and s. Guyana.* Below 300 m. Seedeater-like but *larger* with longer tail; *bill stout but sharply pointed, whitish in* ♂. ♂ basically black above and white below

with *black chin* and on sides; *nuchal collar and broad wing-bar white.* ♀ *mostly warm brown,* throat and median underparts whitish. ♂ Wing-barred Seedeater is smaller with a stubbier black bill, less obvious white in wing, no black chin. ♀ Lesser Seedfinch has similar color but a heavier squared-off bill and no whitish below; it also shows white under wing. Found singly or in pairs, often in campina vegetation where water is close to the surface; does not associate with other seedeaters. Pretty, canarylike song a loud series of clear, musical notes, often in short series, e.g., "je-je, jree-jree-jree, jreu-jreu-jreu-jreu, jr-jr-jr-jr."

Crimson-breasted Finch
*Rhodospingus cruentus**   PLATE 107(6)
11 cm (4¼"). Locally (and seasonally) common in low scrub and woodland, especially where tall grass is prevalent, from *nw. Ecuador* (w. Esmeraldas) *to nw. Peru* (Piura). To 900 m. Formerly called Crimson Finch (or Crimson Finch-Tanager). Bill rather slender and sharply pointed. Breeding ♂ unmistakable: *black above and scarlet below,* with a crown stripe also scarlet. Fresh-plumaged ♂ has black feathers fringed paler. Much duller ♀ pale brown above and *yellowish buff below,* browner on sides. Immature ♂ like ♀ but often with *orange wash across breast.* ♀ resembles ♀ *Sporophila,* especially ♀ Variable (also quite buffy), but seedeater bills are shorter and stubbier. Breeds during Jan.–May rainy season, then scatters out in pairs and becomes conspicuous, especially ♂♂, whose sibilant "tsee-tzztzz" song is heard often. At other times gathers in groups, sometimes large, that may flock with and feed like seedeaters. Like some seedeaters, can be arboreal, and has even been seen feeding in flowering trees.

Cyanocompsa

These two grosbeaks inhabit undergrowth in forest, woodland, or shrubbery. Their *bills are very heavy,* ♂♂ *dark blue* and ♀♀ *rich brown.*

Blue-black Grosbeak
Cyanocompsa cyanoides   PLATE 107(7)
16 cm (6¼"). *Widespread and fairly common* in lower growth of humid forest and woodland from Colombia and Venezuela to Amazonia and the Guianas. Mostly below 1400 m. *Very heavy bill mostly blackish.* ♂ *mostly dark blue;* in **most**

of range (as illustrated) forehead, brow, malar area, and shoulders paler and brighter blue, but **west of Andes** pale areas less well marked. ♀ *uniform deep rich chocolate brown.* Ultramarine Grosbeak is very similar, but *they tend to segregate by range and habitat,* with Ultramarine (more widespread southward) favoring *lighter woodland and scrub.* Ultramarine's bill is not quite so heavy, and ♀ is always markedly paler below (not so uniform and dark). Usually in pairs that range *inside* forest, independent of mixed flocks; tends to be shy and furtive, an elusive voice in the forest, heard much more often than seen. Song a series of rich musical notes that initially rise and are slow and hesitant, then fade and become more jumbled; ♀'s softer song often echoes ♂. Call a frequently heard metallic "chink." Also: Mexico to Panama.

Ultramarine Grosbeak

Cyanocompsa brissonii   PLATE 107(8)

15–15.5 cm (6–6¼"). Uncommon to fairly common in lower growth of lighter woodland, arid scrub (including chaco and caatinga), and thickets near water, *mainly from n. Bolivia to e. Brazil and n. Argentina;* isolated populations in n. Venezuela and sw. Colombia. Mostly below 900 m, a few to 1500 m. *Very heavy bill blackish.* ♂ *uniform dark blue* with same brighter areas as Blueblack. ♀ uniform cocoa brown above, *paler and brighter fulvous brown below.* **Northern birds** are smaller than in **rest of range** (illustrated). Cf. similar Blue-black Grosbeak (*not* south of Amazonia). Glaucous-blue Grosbeak is smaller with a stubbier bill, and ♂ shows a grayish suffusion on the blue. ♀ Ultramarine resembles ♀ Great-billed and Large-billed Seedfinches, but their brown is somewhat less rich and more olivaceous, and their bills are proportionately more massive. Usually occurs in pairs; reclusive, tending to remain inside heavy cover. Singing ♂♂ do, however, often perch in the open. Song fairly loud and musical, typically starting slowly and ending in a warble.

Glaucous-blue Grosbeak

Cyanoloxia glaucocaerulea   PLATE 107(9)

14 cm (5½"). Rare to uncommon and seemingly local in lower growth in humid forest and woodland borders in *s. Brazil* (north to s. Paraná), *ne. Argentina* (south to n. Buenos Aires), *and Uruguay; spreads north in winter.* Locally to 1700 m in s. Brazil when breeding. *Bill shorter and stubbier than in Cyanocompsa,* with *curved*

culmen more as in *Sporophila.* ♂ *uniform glaucous blue,* slightly brighter on brow. ♀ resembles ♀ Ultramarine Grosbeak in color, though somewhat paler. Ultramarine is considerably larger with a *much more massive bill;* ♂ is also *notably darker blue.* Behavior much as in Ultramarine, tending to be equally shy and not often seen except when nesting. Singing ♂♂ can be bolder; song a fast, jumbled warbling, higher-pitched than Ultramarine and with a more even tempo (lacking Ultramarine's slow start).

Indigo Bunting

Passerina cyanea

12 cm (4¾"). Rare boreal migrant (Nov.–May) to scrub and woodland borders in *n. Colombia, nw. Venezuela, and Caribbean islands.* To 1000 m. Short conical bill. Breeding ♂ *bright rich blue,* often more violet on head and breast. ♀ *tawny brown above* with indistinct buff wing-bars; buffy whitish below with vague dusky breast streaking. Nonbreeding and immature ♂♂ like ♀ but *generally with some blue showing.* Cf. larger Ultramarine Grosbeak and smaller Blue-black Grassquit (♀ Blue-black duller, not so tawny). *Breeds* in North America.

Blue Grosbeak (*P. caerulea*) has been recorded as an accidental boreal migrant in w. Colombia and ne. Ecuador.

Blue Finch

Porphyrospiza caerulescens   PLATE 107(10)

12.5 cm (5"). *Uncommon and local in grassy cerrado with scattered bushes and low trees (apparently favoring rocky terrain) in ne. and cen. Brazil* (e. Maranhão to n. São Paulo and Mato Grosso), and very locally in e. Bolivia. Mostly 500–1100 m. *Slender bill bright yellow* (with blackish culmen in ♀); legs dull reddish. Unmistakable ♂ *uniform bright cobalt blue.* ♀ *rufous brown above;* buffy whitish below with *considerable dusky streaking.* **Molting** ♂♂ have brown tips on feathers, some so broad as to obscure the blue. Even the obscure ♀ and molting ♂ can be readily identified by the unique yellow bill. A distinctive finch that feeds mainly on the ground in or near grassy cover and hence usually inconspicuous; during nonbreeding season it gathers in small groups that do not seem to associate with other small finches. Pairs separate out when breeding; they then are often most easily found by tracking down ♂'s easily recognized song, a series of pretty but high-pitched "swee-sweeu" phrases that resembles the song of several warbling finches. The song is given as the bird perches atop a shrub, low tree, or rock.

Haplospiza

Two small finches with *sharply pointed bills* found inside primarily montane forest and woodland. Both species *strongly favor bamboo.*

Slaty Finch
Haplospiza rustica   PLATE 107(11)
12.5 cm (5″). Uncommon and seemingly local (though perhaps more just erratic) in lower growth of montane forest and woodland in *Andes from n. Venezuela to w. Bolivia* (w. Santa Cruz); also very locally on *tepuis*. Mostly 1500–3000 m. *Bill slender and sharply pointed. ♂ uniform dark gray,* slightly paler below. ♀ olive brown above, wing feathers edged rufescent. Dull whitish below with *blurry dusky streaking on throat and (especially) breast.* Does not occur anywhere near range of the similar Uniform Finch. ♂ resembles ♂ Plumbeous Sierra Finch in color, but the sierra finch is found strictly in paramo and puna grasslands. ♀ Blue-black Grassquit is notably smaller, occurs in open grassy terrain, and has an *unstreaked* throat. Though generally scarce and encountered infrequently, can become temporarily numerous when *Chusquea* bamboo is seeding; this is when they breed. Otherwise it feeds mainly on the ground. Song, given only when bamboo is seeding, a complex fast series of chips, buzzes, and trills, variable but often ending with a buzzy trill; also has a flight song. Also: Mexico to w. Panama.

Uniform Finch
Haplospiza unicolor   PLATE 107(12)
12.5 cm (5″). Locally fairly common (can be temporarily more numerous) in lower growth of humid and montane forest and woodland in *se. Brazil region* (north to s. Minas Gerais and Espírito Santo). To 2000 m. *Bill conical and sharply pointed. ♂ uniform gray.* ♀ dull olive brown above, wing feathers edged rufescent. Below creamy whitish with *blurry dusky streaking especially across breast but also extending down flanks.* ♂ is the only uniform gray finch in its range. ♂ Sooty Grassquit is blacker and its bill has a different shape. Cf. ♂ Blackish-blue Seedeater (sometimes with it). ♀ resembles ♀ of smaller Blue-

black Grassquit, which ranges in open terrain and lacks throat streaking. Usually inconspicuous, generally occurring at low densities, but when bamboo is seeding can temporarily become much more numerous and obvious. Song an explosive series of buzzy notes that varies in length and complexity, e.g., "gl-zhwee-ee-ee-ee-ee-ee."

Amaurospiza

A trio of seedeaters with widely disjunct distributions, the uncommon and local *Amaurospiza* seedeaters range *primarily inside forest* (unlike most *Sporophila*). They *often favor bamboo.* The genus is apparently allied to the Cardinalids.

Blackish-blue Seedeater
Amaurospiza moesta   PLATE 107(13)
12.5 cm (5″). Uncommon in undergrowth of humid forest and secondary woodland, especially in extensive bamboo, *mainly in se. Brazil region* (north to ne. Minas Gerais). To 1200 m. ♂ *uniform slaty blue;* face, throat, and breast more blackish. ♀ *rather bright tawny-brown,* slightly paler below. Both sexes have *white underwing-coverts* (visible mainly in flight). ♂ Blue-black Grassquit is glossier with a more slender, pointed bill. ♀ resembles ♀ Lesser Seedfinch in color, but the seedfinch has a much larger squared-off bill. ♀ Glaucous-blue Grosbeak is larger and not so rich a tawny. Cf. also ♀♀ of various *Sporophila* seedeaters, most of which are smaller and not so bright a brown. Inconspicuous, usually found singly or in pairs feeding within cover, generally not far above the ground. ♂'s somewhat variable song a bright and spirited warbling "swee-swee-swi-sweeseeseeu."

Blue Seedeater
Amaurospiza concolor
12.5 cm (5″). Uncommon and local in undergrowth of montane forest and woodland in *Andes of sw. Colombia, w. Ecuador, and nw. Peru* (Cajamarca). 800–2400 m. Resembles geographically distant Blackish-blue Seedeater. ♂ is a *slightly brighter, more indigo blue,* only foreface more blackish; underwing-coverts brown. ♀ probably indistinguishable in field, but in the hand note its brown (not white) underwing-coverts. Cf. ♂ Blue-black Grassquit and ♀ Lesser Seedfinch. Behavior as in Blackish-blue, except that association with bamboo, though frequent, seems less

strict. Song a brief, fast, and somewhat jumbled warbling, "sweet-sweet-sweet-saweet." Also: Mexico to Panama (all one species?).

Carrizal Seedeater
*Amaurospiza carrizalensis**
12.5 cm (5"). *Rare and very local in undergrowth of Guadua bamboo-dominated deciduous forest in se.* Venezuela (Isla Carrizal, along lower Río Caroni in Bolívar). 100 m. A recently described species. *Both sexes resemble geographically distant Blackish-blue Seedeater;* bill slightly heavier, shoulders bright blue. Behavior apparently unknown; the site where the species was found has since been deforested and flooded, but it is presumed that it still exists nearby.

Oryzoborus

Small to midsized finches with *massive, squared-off bills;* culmens are nearly straight. ♂♂ are mainly or entirely black, ♀♀ brown. They favor shrubby areas, often in or adjacent to marshy terrain. Identification, especially of ♀♀, can be tricky.

Lesser Seedfinch
Oryzoborus angolensis   PLATE 107(14)
12.5 cm (5"). *Widespread and generally fairly common* in shrubby clearings and woodland and forest borders from Colombia and Venezuela to ne. Argentina and s. Brazil. Mostly below 1000 m, a few to 1500 m. Perhaps two species, on west (Thick-billed) and east (Chestnut-bellied) side of Andes. *Very heavy, squared-off black bill.* In **most of range** (illustrated) ♂ glossy black with *contrasting chestnut breast and belly.* **West of Andes,** ♂ *entirely black.* Small wing speculum and underwing-coverts white. A few intermediates occur in n. Colombia. ♀ brown above and *fulvous brown below;* underwing-coverts white, but shows no speculum. All its congeners are larger and have proportionately even more massive bills; ♀♀ especially can be confused. Cf. also ♀ *Sporophila* and *Amaurospiza* seedeaters, all of which have considerably stubbier and rounder bills. Found singly or in pairs, sometimes associating with a group of seedeaters but in general less tied to grassy areas and much less prone to flock. Numbers depleted by cagebird trapping in some areas, especially in Brazil. Song a prolonged series of musical whistled notes gradually becoming more jumbled and twittery; despite

some individual variation, there seems to be no consistent geographic variation. Also: Mexico to Panama.

Great-billed Seedfinch
Oryzoborus maximiliani   PLATE 107(15)
16 cm (6¼"). *Now very rare and local* in marshy areas with luxuriant grass, shrubby clearings, and forest and woodland borders (mainly near water) from e. Venezuela to se. Brazil. To about 800 m. *Bill enormously thick, chalky whitish in ♂,* blackish in ♀. ♂ *glossy black* with conspicuous wing speculum and underwing-coverts white. ♀ brown above, fulvous brown below; underwing-coverts white. Cf. very similar Large-billed Seedfinch. ♂ Black-billed Seedfinch has distinctively *black bill,* but ♀ very similar (they do not occur together). Continues to be in great demand as a cagebird, and its numbers have been so depleted by trappers that the species remains poorly known in the wild. Apparently still relatively numerous in Delta Amacuro, e. Venezuela. Found singly or in pairs, not associating with other finches. Canarylike song individually variable but always complex and highly melodic, a series of notes, trills, and rattles.

Black-billed Seedfinch
*Oryzoborus atrirostris**
16.5 cm (6½"). *Rare and local in damp grassy areas, shrubbery around lakes, and regenerating clearings in lowlands and foothills of w. Amazonia.* 200–1100 m. Formerly considered conspecific with Great-billed Seedfinch. *Bill enormously thick, black in both sexes.* Both sexes are identical in plumage to Great-billed. Does not occur with Great-billed, which ranges much farther east, but apparently does occur locally with Large-billed Seedfinch. ♂ Large-billed has *white bill;* ♀, however, is closely similar, aside from Large-billed's smaller overall size, slightly less massive bill, and slightly paler overall color. Occurs as scattered pairs and does not seem to associate with other finches. Song a rich and quite leisurely warbling, often delivered from a prominent perch.

Large-billed Seedfinch
*Oryzoborus crassirostris**
14–14.5 cm (5½–5¾"). Uncommon and local in damp grassy areas and shrubby clearings from *n. and e. Colombia to ne. Peru and the Guianas,* and from *w. Colombia to sw. Ecuador.* To at least 700 m in Ecuador. *Bill very heavy, whitish in* ♂, blackish in ♀. Both sexes nearly identical to

Great-billed Seedfinch (♀ is slightly paler); hard to separate where sympatric, *only in ne. South America, so far as known.* Great-billed is larger, with proportionately longer tail (61–70 mm versus 53–59 mm). Cf. also Black-billed Seedfinch. Behavior much as in Black-billed. Song a rich and melodic warbling that commences slowly, then speeds up.

Sporophila

These small finches constitute one of South America's most species-rich genera; the genus may be polyphyletic. *Usually only ♂♂ are dealt with here; most of them are attractively, if simply, colored and patterned. Many ♀♀, however, cannot be distinguished to species;* most are olive brown to brown above, paler buffy brownish below, more yellowish on midbelly, some with a wing speculum. Exceptions are noted. Seedeaters feed mainly by gleaning seeds from grass stems; when not breeding, some species occur in mixed flocks that concentrate where feeding conditions are favorable, then move on. The flocks are occasionally large. Nesting usually occurs in the rainy season. Though some species are common and familiar, excessive trapping for the local cagebird market (especially in Trinidad, the Guianas, e. Brazil, and Argentina) has depleted many populations, especially among the smaller species (collectively called "caboclinhos" in Brazil, "capuchinos" in Argentina).

Black-and-white Seedeater
Sporophila luctuosa   PLATE 108(1)
11 cm (4¼"). Uncommon and local in shrubby and grassy areas on *Andean slopes from w. Venezuela* (Trujillo) *to w. Bolivia* (w. Santa Cruz); at least some descend to *w. Amazonia* when not breeding. To about 2500 m. Bill bluish gray (♂) or dusky (♀). *♂ black above and on throat and chest,* with *conspicuous white wing speculum; belly white.* Immature ♂ and nonbreeders brown instead of black. ♂ Yellow-bellied Seedeater's pattern is similar, but more olive above and yellower on belly (though belly can be quite pale); shows little or no wing speculum. Other "black and white" seedeaters do not have the hooded effect. Usually in groups (sometimes large) when not breeding, often with other seedeaters, then favoring areas with tall seeding grass.

Breeding birds scatter out in pairs in shrubbier areas. Song an unusual, unmelodic series of 6–8 rapidly uttered and harsh notes, blackbirdlike and very different from other *Sporophila*.

Yellow-bellied Seedeater
Sporophila nigricollis*   PLATE 108(2)
11 cm (4¼"). *Widespread and often common* in shrubby and grassy clearings and agricultural regions from Colombia and Venezuela to s. Brazil; mainly absent, however, from Bolivia and Amazonia. Locally to 2400 m in Andean valleys. Bill pale bluish gray (♂) or dusky (♀). ♂ has *crown, face, throat, and chest black* contrasting with (in **most of range,** as illustrated) *pale yellow belly;* above olive, with wing speculum small or absent. Some (older?) ♂♂ are blacker above; **trans-Andean** ♂♂ are deeper yellow below. Some ♂♂ in **se. Brazil** have a *white belly* and more or less *gray back; these were formerly called Dubois's Seedeater (S. ardesiaca).* ♂ is the only hooded seedeater with a pale yellow belly; beware, however, faded and pale birds. Short and musical song usually ends with 2 buzzier and emphasized notes, e.g., "tsee-tsee-tsee-bseeooo, bzee-bzee." Song of the white-bellied se. Brazil birds is similar. Also: Costa Rica and Panama.

Hooded Seedeater
Sporophila melanops
11 cm (4¼"). *Still known from only a single ♂ specimen taken in the early 19th century in the upper Rio Araguaia drainage of Goiás, Brazil.* Resembles Yellow-bellied Seedeater, but *hood smaller, extending down only over throat and contrasting* with olive upperparts; wing speculum white. Bill larger, reportedly "yellowish" (H. Sick). The sole specimen was apparently collected from a flock of other *Sporophila* along the edge of a lake. Perhaps not a valid species.

Drab Seedeater
Sporophila simplex   PLATE 108(3)
11 cm (4¼"). Uncommon to fairly common and local in arid scrub, shrubby clearings, and agricultural areas on lower Andean slopes (principally intermontane valleys) in *highlands from s. Ecuador* (Azuay) *to w. Peru* (Ica). Mostly 600–1900 m. Well-named, and *notably drab.* Bill yellowish (especially ♂). Pale grayish brown above with *two prominent whitish wing-bars and speculum* (buffyish in ♀). Drab pale grayish below. ♀ Parrot-billed Seedeater may also show wing-bars, but it has a much larger bill with strikingly

curved culmen. Dull-colored Grassquit similar in color but *lacks* wing-bars. Behavior much as in other *Sporophila*, in nonbreeding season regularly in groups that mix with other seedeaters and grassquits. Song a series of short, harsh phrases, e.g., "tche-tzjee-tzjee-tche-tzjeee-tzjeee-tzjit."

Rusty-collared Seedeater
Sporophila collaris   PLATE 108(4)
12 cm (4¾"). *Fairly common in tall grass and shrubbery near marshes from n. Bolivia* (west to Beni) *and cen. Brazil to n. Argentina* (n. Córdoba and n. Buenos Aires). Below 500 m. *Boldly patterned and fairly large.* Rather heavy blackish bill. In **most of range** (illustrated) ♂ black above with *prominent white patches around eye* and a *tawny-buff nuchal collar.* Throat white, *pectoral band black; cinnamon-buff below.* In **Brazil aside from w. Mato Grosso** has same pattern but is *whiter* instead of buff to cinnamon, especially on collar. ♀ *distinctive for a* ♀ *Sporophila*, echoing ♂'s pattern, brown above with *tawny-buff wing-bars,* a buff speculum and at least a trace of the nuchal collar. *Throat white; buff below.* No other seedeater in its range combines the pectoral band and the buff nuchal collar (♂), or the wing-bars and two-toned underparts (♀). Found in pairs or small groups, often *not* associating with congeners. Song an attractive but patternless jumble of musical notes.

Caquetá Seedeater
Sporophila murallae*   PLATE 108(5)
11.5 cm (4½"). Uncommon in grassy and shrubby areas, often near water, in *w. Amazonia.* Mostly below 400 m. Formerly considered conspecific with Wing-barred and Variable Seedeaters (as the Variable Seedeater, *S. americana*). ♂ black above with rump whitish to gray; white wing speculum and *vague whitish wing-bars.* Whitish below, *extending up on sides of neck to form a partial nuchal collar,* and with *mottled blackish chest band.* Cf. Lined and Lesson's Seedeaters. Generally solitary or in pairs, not joining flocks of other *Sporophila.* Song a variable but usually quite long and fast series of musical, jumbled notes.

Wing-barred Seedeater
Sporophila americana*
11.5 cm (4½"). Uncommon in grassy and shrubby areas, often in agricultural regions, from *e. Venezuela to lower Amaz. Brazil.* Below 400 m. Resembles Caquetá Seedeater (of w. Amazonia),

but ♂ has *more prominent wing-bars.* Cf. the smaller Lined and Lesson's Seedeaters (both with a prominent white malar mark and lacking nuchal collar). Most ♀ *Sporophila* occurring with it have paler bills (though not the Yellowbellied). Behavior as in Caquetá, but tends to be more numerous.

Variable Seedeater
Sporophila corvina*
11 cm (4¼"). *Common and widespread* in grassy and shrubby areas, agricultural regions, and built-up regions from w. Colombia to nw. Peru (Lambayeque). Mostly below 1300 m. ♂ *black above* with whitish rump and white wing speculum. White below, *extending up sides of neck to form partial nuchal collar; neat but narrow black pectoral band.* ♀ yellowish olive brown above, *paler buffy brownish below, even paler and yellower on midbelly.* Dapper ♂ easily recognized in range as the only seedeater with primarily black upperparts. ♀ more yellowish below than other ♀ seedeaters with which it occurs. Cf. also ♀ Crimson-breasted Finch. Behavior much like other *Sporophila*, but seems more arboreal and often feeds in flowering trees high above the ground. Song a variable but always musical twittering; call heard frequently, a clear "cheeu." Also: Mexico to Panama.

Lined Seedeater
Sporophila lineola   PLATE 108(6)
11 cm (4¼"). Locally fairly common in grassy and shrubby areas; *breeds in the caatinga of ne. Brazil* (where apparently resident), and in *n. Argentina* (south to Tucumán and Santa Fé), *Paraguay, and se. Brazil;* migrates north from southern areas during the austral winter. To 1200 m. Bill blackish (♂) or *mostly yellowish* (♀). ♂ black above with *white coronal stripe* (often not obvious) and *prominent broad malar stripe. Throat black* (outlining malar area); white below. Cf. similar Lesson's Seedeater; ♀♀ indistinguishable. Wing-barred Seedeater lacks white head markings, has a black pectoral band and partial white collar. Locally numerous and conspicuous when nesting, but at other times encountered less often, though sometimes mixes with other seedeaters; status in many areas still unclear. Song of southern-breeding ♂♂ a pretty trilled "titititiiti-teé," even heard regularly during migration and when not breeding. Ne. Brazil breeders give a rather different "didididi dr-r-r-r-r dee" (J. Veilliard recording).

Lesson's Seedeater

Sporophila bouvronides

11 cm (4¼"). Locally fairly common in shrubby and grassy areas and woodland borders, especially near water, *breeding from n. Colombia to the Guianas;* then (mainly Dec.–June) migrates to w. Amazonia, where it favors river islands. To 800 m. Resembles Lined Seedeater, but ♂ *crown entirely black* (*no* white coronal stripe); sides and chest mottled with black. ♀ identical. Behavior similar to Lined, with which it sometimes consorts when not breeding. Song a fast, almost trilled "dri-di-di-di-di-di-di."

White-throated Seedeater

Sporophila albogularis   PLATE 108(7)

11 cm (4¼"). Uncommon to locally fairly common in grassy areas of caatinga scrub and woodland in *ne. Brazil* (south to Bahia). To 1200 m. *Bill yellow-orange* (♂) or dusky (♀). ♂ *clear gray above* with blackish head, wings, and tail; prominent white wing speculum. *Entire throat white* extending up sides of neck to form a *partial nuchal collar; sharp black pectoral band;* below white. ♀ grayer above than many other ♀ seedeaters. ♂ virtually unmistakable, but cf. Double-collared (not as snappy-looking, with duller bill and a black throat); ♀♀ very similar, aside from Double-collared's paler lower mandible. One of only two *Sporophila* in its limited range, the other being the very different Capped. Often in small groups. Song a high-pitched warbling.

Double-collared Seedeater

Sporophila caerulescens   PLATE 108(8)

11 cm (4¼"). *Widespread and generally common* in semiopen and shrubby areas and agricultural regions from *n. Bolivia and s. Brazil to cen. Argentina* (La Pampa), spreading into s. Amazonia during austral winter. The *southernmost-ranging seedeater.* Mostly below 1500 m. Bill greenish yellow (♂), or *dusky above and yellowish below* (♀). ♂ gray above, mantle often tinged brownish (especially in first-year birds), sometimes with a white wing speculum. *Upper throat black, outlined by a wide white malar stripe and white lower throat,* bordered in turn by *black pectoral band* (forming the "double collar"). ♂ face and chest pattern distinctive; cf. White-throated Seedeater (at most very limited overlap in e. Brazil). An *ecologically unspecialized* seedeater that occurs primarily in disturbed habitats, often found together with Blue-black Grassquits. Variable song a fast jumbled series of musical notes.

Parrot-billed Seedeater

Sporophila peruviana   PLATE 108(9)

11.5 cm (4½"). Uncommon to locally and seasonally common in arid scrub and agricultural regions from *sw. Ecuador* (Manabí) *to sw. Peru* (n. Arequipa). To 1400 m in s. Ecuador. *Bill extremely large with very curved culmen.* ♂ brownish gray above with white wing speculum and wing-bars. *Throat and chest black,* usually separated from gray head by a *wide white malar stripe;* white below. **Younger and nonbreeding** ♂♂ have a more diffused foreneck pattern, showing little or no black. ♀ pale brownish above, usually with buffier wing-bars; buffy whitish below. Bill so much heavier than other seedeaters' that confusion is unlikely; compare especially to Chestnut-throated (overall pattern similar, but *streaked above*) and Drab. When not breeding, occurs in flocks, sometimes quite large, sometimes associating with other seed eaters and grassquits. Persistent song, given only when breeding, a short harsh phrase, e.g., "jew-jee-jew"; singing birds often remain hidden and change perches frequently.

Chestnut-throated Seedeater

*Sporophila telasco**   PLATE 108(10)

10 cm (4"). Common in grassy and shrubby areas and agricultural regions from *extreme sw. Colombia* (sw. Cauca) *to extreme n. Chile* (Tarapacá). To 1400 m in s. Ecuador. Bill black (♂) or pale brownish (♀). In **most of range** (illustrated) ♂ *gray above, with vague dusky streaking on crown and mantle and whitish on rump and base of tail* (a good field mark in flight). *Upper throat chestnut;* below pure white. In **sw. Colombia** similar but most birds have *more rufous below,* extending down over breast; long considered a separate species (Tumaco Seedeater, *S. insulata*), these were recently shown to be either a race or color morph. ♀ readily known (for a ♀ seedeater) by its *dusky streaking* on brown upperparts. ♀ Parrot-billed Seedeater is larger with a much heavier bill, lacks streaking above, shows wing-bars. Generally the most numerous *Sporophila* in its range; occurs in both humid and arid regions (where irrigated). Song a pretty, short warbling usually delivered from an exposed perch.

White-bellied Seedeater

Sporophila leucoptera   PLATE 108(11)

12 cm (4¾"). Uncommon and local in grassy areas with scattered shrubs in marshy areas or near water from *ne. Brazil to ne. Argentina*

(n. Santa Fé and n. Corrientes), and in *n. Bolivia.* To 800 m. *Bill dull to pinkish yellow.* In **most of range** (illustrated) *bicolored ♂ gray above and white below,* wings with an obvious white speculum. **E. Brazil** birds have more gray on sides. In **n. Bolivia** *glossy black above. Relatively large size* and *wholly pale bill* help to distinguish ♀. Found singly or in scattered pairs, rarely or never in flocks and generally not associating with other seedeaters. Distinctive song of gray-backed birds a repetition of a single clear ringing note, "cleeu, cleeu, cleeu . . ."; that of black-backed birds is similar, but seems more variable.

Buffy-fronted Seedeater
Sporophila frontalis   PLATE 108(12)

13 cm (5"). *Now rare and local in humid and montane forest and borders in se. Brazil region* (north rarely to s. Bahia). Mostly 800–1500 m, formerly (perhaps still) lower. *The largest Sporophila. Thick bill dull yellowish.* Olivaceous brown above, some (older?) birds distinctly grayer on head; *broad frontal band and narrow postocular streak buffy whitish* (frontal band lacking in many, presumably younger, individuals); wings with *two buffyish bars* and a speculum. *Throat and sometimes a malar streak buffy whitish;* below olive brownish, midbelly whiter. ♀ lacks facial markings and is browner, retains the buffyish wing-bars. Variable but because of its large size and *wooded habitat* not likely confused; cf. much smaller Temminck's Seedeater. Numbers have been much depleted by cagebird trapping, despite its notably *un*melodic song. Presence of this arboreal seedeater seems to be governed by bamboo seeding. Birds in immature plumage predominate, hold territories, and sing. Far-carrying song a loud and explosive (astonishingly so) "je-je-jét!" or "cheh-cheh-chéw!"

Slate-colored Seedeater
Sporophila schistacea   PLATE 108(13)

11 cm (4¼"). *Rare to uncommon and local* in humid and montane forest borders and secondary woodland, sometimes in adjacent clearings, from Colombia and Venezuela to n. Bolivia and sw. Amaz. Brazil. Mostly below 1500 m. *Bill rich yellow* (♂) or dusky (♀); claws pale (actually sometimes evident in the field). *♂ mostly slaty gray,* usually with *small whitish patch on sides of neck;* wings blackish with a white speculum and often (older birds?) *a single upper wing-bar.* Cf. closely similar ♂ Gray Seedeater (a bird of more open terrain). Does not overlap with very similar Temminck's Seedeater. Most often arboreal in

woodland and forest; presence sometimes tied to the seeding of bamboo, when it can be temporarily more numerous. Unlike Gray, it rarely or never occurs with other *Sporophila.* Loud, variable song a mostly unmusical "tzee, tsuwee, tí-tí-tí-tí-tí tsi-tsi" or "zit-zit-zee-zee-zee-ze-ze-z-z z z"; somewhat recalls Bananaquit. Sings with bill held wide open. Also: Belize to Panama.

Temminck's Seedeater
Sporophila falcirostris

11 cm (4¼"). *Rare to uncommon and apparently nomadic* in lower growth and borders of humid and montane forest in *se. Brazil region* (north to se. Bahia). *Presence usually tied to seeding bamboo,* can be temporarily more numerous. To 1200 m. Resembles geographically distant Slate-colored Seedeater; *best identified by range.* ♂ somewhat paler gray with white wing speculum slightly larger, but usually *no* patch on sides of neck; can also show white around eye and on throat. Cf. the larger Buffy-fronted Seedeater (sometimes with it). Arboreal behavior much as in Slate-colored. Song a simple, fairly sibilant trill that lasts for several seconds.

Gray Seedeater
Sporophila intermedia

11 cm (4¼"). Common in semiopen and grassy terrain from *w. and n. Colombia to Guyana.* To 2000 m. Resembles Slate-colored Seedeater, but *not* forest-based and *much more numerous.* ♂ has *yellowish flesh bill* (not butter yellow); tarsus entirely dark. In **most of range** ♂ *paler gray below* than ♂ Slate-colored (such that its white midbelly contrasts less), and *lacks* a white submalar mark and upper wing-bar. Especially similar to Slate-colored in w. Colombia (where Gray is darker), but the upper wing-bar is still *never* present. Behavior typical of most other seedeaters, favoring grassy areas, often in disturbed or agricultural regions, and regularly consorting with other seedeaters. Song a varied series of trills, chirps, and twitters, much richer and more musical than Slate-colored.

Plumbeous Seedeater
Sporophila plumbea   PLATE 108(14)

11 cm (4¼"). Uncommon to locally fairly common in *less-disturbed savannas, grassy cerrado, and adjacent scrub* from n. Colombia east locally to the Guianas and lower Amaz. Brazil, and from n. Bolivia to interior e. and s. Brazil and adjacent Paraguay. Avoids agricultural areas. To 1400 m. ♂ *is only gray seedeater with a blackish bill* (but

bill is yellow in some ♂♂ of s. Brazil). ♂ *mostly gray*, paler below, usually with a white subocular crescent and whitish upper throat; wings and tail blackish, wings with white speculum. *Lacks the white neck patch and upper wing-bar of the other "gray" seedeaters.* ♀ *dull*, basically olive brownish above and pale grayish buff below (not as buffy as many other ♀ seedeaters), but usually best identified by accompanying ♂♂. Often in small groups, sometimes with other seedeaters, but more often on its own. Song a long series of loud clear phrases, each often repeated several times, e.g., "deet, di-deet, pi-pi-pi." Sometimes incorporates imitations of other birds (e.g., Pale-breasted Spinetail).

Capped Seedeater

Sporophila bouvreuil   PLATE 108(15)
10 cm (4"). Locally fairly common to common in savannas, campos, and grassy cerrado from *ne. Brazil to ne. Argentina* (Corrientes); *not* in agricultural terrain. Nomadic, but apparently not truly migratory. To 1100 m. Bill black (breeding ♂) or yellowish (♀ and nonbreeding ♂). *Variable.* In **ne. Brazil** (south at least to n. Goiás and Espírito Santo; A) ♂ *mostly cinnamon-rufous* with *crown contrasting black;* wings and tail black, wings with a white speculum and buffy edging. In **most of rest of range** (B) has the same pattern but *lacks* the rufescence: mantle brownish gray and *underparts white or whitish* (at most tinged buff), but still with *striking black crown.* In **Rio de Janeiro** ♂ remains hen-colored, breeding in a ♀-like plumage (olive brownish above with a white wing speculum; mostly ochraceous buff below). ♂♂ **around city of São Paulo** (only formerly?) have *chestnut* replacing the cinnamon-rufous. Occurs in groups when not breeding, then often with other *Sporophila* in large swirling flocks and usually the most numerous species present. Feeds on grass seeds, mainly while clinging to tall stems, sometimes reaching up for them while on the ground. Variable and pretty song a series of melodic phrases and whistled notes, often long continued.

Tawny-bellied Seedeater

Sporophila hypoxantha   PLATE 108(16)
10 cm (4"). Locally fairly common to common in campos, grassy cerrado, lightly grazed pastures, and roadsides from *n. Bolivia* (west to Beni) *and s. Brazil to ne. Argentina* (e. Córdoba and Entre Ríos). Migratory status uncertain. To 1100 m. Bill blackish (♂) or yellowish horn (♀). ♂ brownish gray above; wings and tail duskier, wings with

white speculum. *Rump and underparts tawny-rufous*, extending up onto cheeks, where often paler. Presumed younger ♂♂ are paler below, more cinnamon-tawny. Cf. similarly patterned but much rarer Rufous-rumped Seedeater. The similar Ruddy-breasted Seedeater occurs far to the north. Behavior much as in Capped Seedeater. Song a simple, clear, whistled "cheeu, cheeu, cheweé, chu" with variations (not as fast or warbled as in Ruddy-breasted).

Ruddy-breasted Seedeater

Sporophila minuta   PLATE 108(17)
10 cm (4"). Locally common in savannas and less-disturbed grassland and pastures from *Colombia and nw. Ecuador east to lower Amaz. Brazil.* To 1600 m. Resembles Tawny-bellied Seedeater (found only *south of Amazonia*), but *gray of ♂ crown extends down over cheeks,* and the wing speculum is smaller (occasionally absent); rump and underparts usually a deeper rufous. Nonbreeding ♂ browner above and buffier below. ♀ like ♀ Capped Seedeater, but *speculum lacking or indistinct.* Behavior much as in Capped and Tawny-bellied. Song a fast, pleasant, and musical series of notes, usually commencing with several couplets. Also: Mexico to Panama.

Rufous-rumped Seedeater

Sporophila hypochroma   PLATE 108(18)
10 cm (4"). *Rare and local* breeder in less-disturbed damp grassland (often where seasonally flooded) in *ne. Argentina* (south to Entre Ríos) *and s. Paraguay;* migrates to n. and e. Bolivia and sw. Brazil during austral winter, there favoring moist areas in cerrado and campos where the grass is tall and luxuriant; also breeds locally in n. Bolivia (at least w. Santa Cruz and Beni). To 1100 m. ♂ *gray above,* wings and tail blackish with a white wing speculum and gray edging. *Rump and underparts chestnut,* extending up over cheeks. Has same pattern as the more numerous Tawny-bellied Seedeater, but more richly colored, being more bluish gray above and considerably more deeply colored below. Chestnut Seedeater colors are much the same, but pattern differs notably. Mainly seen as the odd individual or small group accompanying a mixed flock of other (presumably wintering) seedeaters. Its attractive song has a leisurely pace, e.g., "chut, teeu, tsee-tu, cheeu" (S. Davis recording).

Black-and-tawny Seedeater

Sporophila nigrorufa

10 cm (4"). *Rare to uncommon and very local* in less-disturbed seasonally flooded grassland in e. *Bolivia* (Santa Cruz) *and sw. Brazil* (w. Mato Grosso). Apparently not a long-distance migrant. To 500 m. ♂ has *black crown, hindneck, and back;* wings and tail blackish, wings with white speculum and edging. *Rump and entire underparts bright cinnamon-rufous.* ♂'s bold pattern, *with black extending down over back,* differs from other seedeaters that have rufous or chestnut underparts. Behavior as in numerous other small seedeaters, occurring in mixed flocks with certain other species when not breeding. Pretty song a series of melodic phrases and notes, e.g., "tseeeu, chu-tsee-tee?-tee?" (S. Davis recording).

Black-bellied Seedeater

Sporophila melanogaster   PLATE 108(19)

10 cm (4"). *Generally uncommon and local in moist grasslands and adjacent shrubby areas in se. Brazil* (north to Goiás and Minas Gerais in austral winter; breeds in Santa Catarina and Rio Grande do Sul). To 1200 m. Dapper ♂ mostly gray with *striking black throat and median underparts;* wings and tail blackish, wings with gray edging and a white speculum. Behavior much like other small seedeaters; on its wintering grounds flocks with some of them. Song a high-pitched simple whistle followed by a lower trill and a complex series of warbled notes (W. Belton recording).

Chestnut-bellied Seedeater

Sporophila castaneiventris   PLATE 108(20)

10 cm (4"). Common in grassy clearings, along the edges of lakes and rivers, and around towns in *Amazonia and the Guianas, where often the most numerous seedeater.* Mostly below 1000 m, a few up to 1500 m or even higher on east slope of Andes. Handsome ♂ *bluish gray* with *chestnut throat and median underparts;* wings and tail blackish, wings with gray edging but little or no speculum. ♂ Ruddy-breasted Seedeater is less pure gray above, has a rufous rump, and is more extensively rufous below (no gray on sides); ♀♀ very similar. A familiar bird in many areas, most often in small monospecific groups, though at times with other seedeaters (e.g., Lined and Lesson's) when not breeding. Song a pleasant warbling, often given from an exposed perch.

Marsh Seedeater

Sporophila palustris   PLATE 108(21)

10 cm (4"). *Rare and local* (though concentrations occur where conditions are favorable) breeder in seasonally flooded grassland of ne. *Argentina, Uruguay, and extreme se. Brazil* (Rio Grande do Sul); during austral winter migrates to cerrado and campos of s. Brazil (north to s. Goiás and w. Minas Gerais), there favoring moist campos with tall grass. No more tied to marshes than are several other small, southern seedeaters. To 1100 m. ♂ gray above with a rufous-chestnut rump; wings and tail blackish with whitish edging and speculum. *Throat and chest white* contrasting with *rufous-chestnut lower underparts.* With its striking white bib, ♂ unlikely to be confused; cf. range-restricted Entre Ríos Seedeater. Behavior much like other small seedeaters of southern grasslands.

Entre Ríos Seedeater

*Sporophila zelichi**

10 cm (4"). *Very rare and local* breeder in seasonally inundated grassland near patches of woodland in *ne. Argentina* (Corrientes and Entre Ríos); a few recent sightings northward during austral winter (in n. Paraguay and s. Goiás, Brazil) indicate that it likely is an austral migrant like several other seedeaters. Formerly called Narosky's Seedeater. ♂ has *gray crown* and *broad white nuchal collar, throat, and chest; back and rump rufous-chestnut,* as are lower underparts. Marsh Seedeater lacks the white collar and has a gray (not rufous-chestnut) back. Behavior much like other small seedeaters. It has been suggested that this could be just a color morph or hybrid.

Chestnut Seedeater

Sporophila cinnamomea   PLATE 108(22)

10 cm (4"). *Rare and local* breeder (though concentrations occur where conditions are favorable) in seasonally inundated grassland of a *limited area of ne. Argentina* (Corrientes and Entre Ríos) *and Uruguay;* during austral winter migrates to campos and grassy cerrado of sw. Brazil (north to Goiás), there favoring moister areas with tall grass. To 1100 m. Handsome ♂ *mostly chestnut* with a *contrasting gray crown;* wings and tail slaty, wings with a white speculum. ♂ Rufous-rumped Seedeater is similarly colored, but the gray of its crown extends down over the back. Behavior much like the other small seedeaters, and it consorts with some of them when not breeding.

Dark-throated Seedeater

Sporophila ruficollis PLATE 108(23)

10 cm (4"). Uncommon and local breeder in less-disturbed grassland, usually where moist or seasonally flooded, in s.-cen. South America; migrates north into Bolivia and s. Brazil during austral winter, then favoring moist areas with tall grass. Mostly below 1100 m. ♂ gray above, often browner on back and with cinnamon-rufous rump; wings and tail dusky, wings with white speculum. *Throat and upper chest blackish to dark brown* contrasting with *cinnamon-rufous underparts.* Behavior similar to numerous other small seedeaters, though seems to be more widespread and ecologically tolerant than many. Like the others, however, it is undoubtedly declining because of trapping for the cagebird market, especially in Argentina.

Arremon

Handsome but inconspicuous sparrows, mainly terrestrial in lowland forest and woodland. Arremon are olive or gray above with a black head and usually a bold white superciliary; many also have a black pectoral band. The bill in many species is brightly colored.

Pectoral Sparrow

Arremon taciturnus PLATE 109(1)

15 cm (6"). Fairly common in undergrowth of humid forest and woodland from e. Colombia and Venezuela to n. Bolivia and s. Brazil (south to Mato Grosso do Sul and Espírito Santo). *The only Arremon in much of Amazonia.* Mostly below 1000 m, to 1500 m on tepuis. Bill usually black, but has *yellow mandible* in w. **Venezuela and adjacent Colombia. In most of range** (illustrated) head black with gray coronal streak and long white superciliary; *olive above,* shoulders usually yellow. White below with *black pectoral band.* In w. **Venezuela and adjacent Colombia,** and in se. **Peru and n. Bolivia,** pectoral band restricted to sides. ♀ similarly patterned but duller, *buffier below* with pectoral band restricted to sides. In se. Brazil cf. Half-collared Sparrow (with yellow lower mandible, interrupted pectoral band). Saffron-billed Sparrow, regardless of race, *always has a mostly yellow bill* (overlaps only marginally). Hops on or near the ground, usually remaining in dense cover and hard to see; often in pairs, generally not joining

mixed flocks. Song a high-pitched, almost hissing "zitip, tzeee-tzeee-tzeee," given from a low perch such as a log, sometimes the ground.

Half-collared Sparrow

Arremon semitorquatus * PLATE 109(2)

15 cm (6"). Uncommon in undergrowth of humid forest, woodland, and shrubby plantations in se. *Brazil* (Espírito Santo, where it overlaps with Pectoral Sparrow, to n. Rio Grande do Sul). To 900 m. Resembles Pectoral (formerly considered conspecific), but has *lemon yellow lower mandible,* an *interrupted black pectoral collar in both sexes* (complete in ♂ Pectoral), and little or no yellow on bend of wing. Behavior as in Pectoral. Song a very high-pitched "tsi, tsi, tseeu."

São Francisco Sparrow

Arremon franciscanus *

15 cm (6"). Uncommon and very local in undergrowth of deciduous woodland in s.-cen. *Brazil* (n. Minas Gerais and sw. Bahia). To 700 m. A recently described species. Resembles Half-collared Sparrow (no overlap) so with *partial black pectoral collar,* but has *orange-yellow maxilla with black culmen* (maxilla entirely blackish in Half-collared) and paler gray sides. Saffron-billed Sparrow (not known to overlap) has a full black pectoral band. Behavior much as in Pectoral Sparrow. Song a faint, high-pitched "ts-ts-tseú" or "tseeú, tsi-tsi-tsi-tsi-tsi."

Saffron-billed Sparrow

Arremon flavirostris PLATE 109(3)

15.5–16 cm (6–6¼"). Locally fairly common in undergrowth of deciduous woodland and forest from w. Bolivia and s. Brazil to n. Argentina. To 2400 m in Bolivia. *Bill mostly orange-yellow.* From **Mato Grosso, Brazil, and e. Bolivia to ne. Argentina** (A) *mantle mostly gray* with yellow bend of wing; head black with white postocular stripe. Mostly white below with *black pectoral band.* On **Andean slopes from Bolivia to nw. Argentina** (B) *mantle mostly olive* (only upper back is gray) and superciliary white (starting at lores); pectoral band *narrower.* Birds of **s. interior Brazil** (s. Goiás and w. Minas Gerais to Paraná) revert to having an *olive back* (like western birds) but only a *white postocular* (back from eye). ♀♀ like respective ♂♂ but duller and washed buff below. Where range approaches Pectoral Sparrow in w. Bolivia, Pectoral has *incomplete pectoral band.* Where their ranges approach in interior s. Brazil, superciliary is long in

Pectoral, shorter in Saffron-billed. Throughout this area Pectoral has an *all-dark bill*. Unobtrusive behavior much as in Pectoral. Song a similar spitting "tsit, tsee-tsi-tsi, tseép-seép-tseép."

Golden-winged Sparrow
Arremon schlegeli   PLATE 109(4)
16 cm (6¼"). Uncommon and local in undergrowth of deciduous and semihumid woodland and forest in *n. Colombia and nw. Venezuela* (east to Miranda). To 1400 m. *Bill golden yellow. Head entirely black (no eye-stripe) extending down to form a partial collar on sides of chest. Above mostly gray* with *band on wing-coverts across midback golden olive*, shoulders bright yellow. Below mostly white, with *no* pectoral band. Birds from **ne. Colombia** have golden olive only on wing-coverts; their back is gray. *The beautiful Golden-winged is the only Arremon lacking head stripes.* Behavior much as in congeners, but often even more unobtrusive. Song a high-pitched thin "zoot-zoot-zoot-zee."

Orange-billed Sparrow
Arremon aurantiirostris   PLATE 109(5)
15 cm (6"). Fairly common in undergrowth of humid forest and woodland from *w. Colombia to ne. Peru* (Huánuco). Mostly below 1200 m. Perhaps more than one species. *Bill bright orange.* In **w. Colombia and w. Ecuador** (illustrated) *head black* with a *long white superciliary*; bright olive above with yellow on shoulders (flame-orange in **Amaz. birds**). White below with a *black pectoral band* (wider in birds of **far nw. Colombia**). ♀ similar but tinged buff below. Pectoral Sparrows found along the base of the Colombian Andes (farther north than Orange-billed) have an *incomplete* pectoral band and a black maxilla. Behavior as in Pectoral. Song of western birds a fast series of jumbled and sibilant notes, e.g., "tsu-t-t-ti-tu-ti-t-tsee"; in Amazonia a quite different series of buzzy notes, e.g., "tzeeeee-zee-zee-zeeeeeet" (more like Pectoral). Also: Mexico to Panama.

Black-capped Sparrow
Arremon abeillei   PLATE 109(6)
15 cm (6"). Locally fairly common in undergrowth in deciduous woodland, forest, and dense scrub from *sw. Ecuador* (Manabí) *to nw. Peru* (Cajamarca). Mostly below 1000 m, locally to 1600 m in Ecuador. *Bill black.* **Pacific-slope birds** (illustrated) have *head and neck black* with white superciliary starting above eye; *bluish gray above*. Below white with black pectoral band. In

Río Marañón drainage, a longer superciliary starts at the lores, and has back and rump olive. ♀♀ have buff on sides. Overlaps locally with Orange-billed Sparrow, which favors more humid areas; bill color is the most straightforward way to tell them apart. Behavior much as in Pectoral Sparrow. Song on Pacific slope very high-pitched, fast, and jumbled, e.g., "tsu-t-t-ti-tu-ti-t-t"; in the Marañón, a series of buzzy notes, e.g., "tzeeeee-zee-zee-zeeeeeet."

Atlapetes and *Buarremon*

A large, complex group of midsized finches found mainly in undergrowth at borders of montane forest and woodland (both humid and quite arid); the three *Buarremon* species (recently re-separated from *Atlapetes*) are more terrestrial. *Virtually all species are found in the Andes.* The vocalizations of most brushfinches are similar and difficult to distinguish. Their song (given mainly at dawn, often from an exposed perch) consists of a series of pretty, clear notes (e.g., some variation of "tsi-tseee-tseee-tsi-tsi"); a cascading call is often given by members of a pair. They also give various contact notes. After two inserted genera, *Oreothraupis* and *Lysurus* (pp. 644–645), coverage of the genus *Atlapetes* re-commences.

Bay-crowned Brushfinch
Atlapetes seebohmi   PLATE 109(7)
16.5 cm (6½"). Uncommon in lower growth of montane woodland and scrub in *Andes of sw. Ecuador* (Loja) *and nw. Peru* (south to Ancash). Mostly 1300–2600 m. In **w. Peru north to La Libertad** (illustrated) has *crown and nape rich rufous* and forehead, face, and sides of neck black; gray above with *no white wing speculum*. White below with a prominent black submalar streak, sides and flanks broadly gray. In **Ecuador and nw. Peru** (south to Lambayeque) shows little or no black on forehead. White-winged Brushfinch is smaller, has an obvious wing speculum, and usually shows some white on face (with less clean-cut facial pattern). Mostly occurs in pairs (sometimes small groups when not nesting), hopping on or near the ground, generally remaining within cover.

Slaty Brushfinch
Atlapetes schistaceus   PLATE 109(8)
18 cm (7"). Fairly common in shrubby bor-

ders of montane forest and woodland in *Andes from w. Venezuela* (Trujillo) *to e. Ecuador* (nw. Morona-Santiago); also on *east slope of Andes in cen. Peru* (s. San Martín to Junín). Mostly 2500–3400 m. In **Colombia and Ecuador** (A) has *crown and nape chestnut* with *face and submalar streak black,* malar streak white; gray above, wings with *conspicuous white wing speculum.* Below gray, throat and midbelly white. In **w. Venezuela** similar but *without* wing speculum. In **cen. Peru** (B) has a paler crown and *also lacks the wing speculum.* White-winged Brushfinches in Ecuador occur on west and interandean slopes (no overlap); they are smaller and whiter below with a paler crown. Cf. also Cuzco Brushfinch of Cuzco, Peru (no overlap). Occurs singly or in pairs, often joining mixed flocks, sometimes with other brushfinches; more arboreal than many of its congeners.

Cuzco Brushfinch
Atlapetes canigenis*
18 cm (7″). Uncommon in shrubby borders of montane forest and woodland on *east slope of Andes in se. Peru* (Cuzco, including the Machu Picchu area). About 2000–3000 m. Resembles Slaty Brushfinch (formerly considered conspecific; occurs to north), but *looks very dark:* face and throat smoky gray (with *no* white malar streak); has *no* white wing speculum. Behavior as in Slaty.

White-winged Brushfinch
Atlapetes leucopterus   PLATE 109(9)
14.5–15.5 cm (5¾–6″). Locally fairly common in lower growth of montane woodland and shrubby clearings in *Andes from n. Ecuador* (Imbabura) *to nw. Peru* (Lambayeque), *mainly occurring in arid regions.* Mostly 1000–2600 m, locally lower southward. *Variable,* but *always has a large white wing speculum;* essentially gray above and whitish below. In **most of Ecuador** (A) has *entire crown and nape cinnamon-rufous* and sides of head black. In **sw. Ecuador and nw. Peru** (B) the black protrudes onto forecrown and has a *variable amount of white on face* (sometimes extensive). In a **limited and remote area of n. Peru** (east of the preceding area) forecrown and sides of head black, *hindcrown and nape whitish.* Bay-crowned Brushfinch has *no* wing speculum; White-headed shows no rufous on crown (head is black and white). Behavior much as in Bay-crowned, though (at least in nw. Peru) when not breeding it can range in considerably larger groups.

White-headed Brushfinch
Atlapetes albiceps   PLATE 109(10)
16 cm (6¼″). Locally fairly common in undergrowth of deciduous woodland and arid scrub at *relatively low elevations in sw. Ecuador* (s. Loja) *and nw. Peru* (south to Lambayeque). 300–1300 m. A boldly patterned gray and white *Atlapetes* with *wholly white face and throat* and *black hindcrown* (shows *no rufous on crown*); has a *large white wing speculum.* Sympatric White-winged Brushfinches may show almost as much white on face, but they also have rufous on hindcrown. Bay-crowned Brushfinch has extensive rufous on crown and *no* white wing speculum. Behavior as in Bay-crowned, though like the White-winged it can occur in fairly large nonbreeding groups.

Pale-headed Brushfinch
Atlapetes pallidiceps
16 cm (6¼″). Very rare and local in woodland and scrub in arid intermontane valleys of *sw. Ecuador* (Azuay in the Girón area); *recently (1998) rediscovered near Girón.* 1500–2200 m. Resembles a *faded* White-headed Brushfinch (no overlap), but has *entire head whitish* (with *no* black on hindcrown) with ill-defined brownish stripes on sides of crown and behind eye. Behavior differs little from other *Atlapetes* but seems to remain within cover more, and thus is hard to see except when breeding and singing. Population remains perilously small (ca. 70 pairs as of 2006), brought low by massive habitat modification for agriculture and more recently by heavy Shiny Cowbird parasitism. Under intensive management by Fundación Jocotoco, it has recovered from a low of some 15 pairs and continues to increase.

Rusty-bellied Brushfinch
Atlapetes nationi   PLATE 109(11)
17 cm (6¾″). Locally fairly common in *Andes in sw. Peru* (Lima to Arequipa), *where the only Atlapetes present.* 2000–4000 m. In **Lima** (illustrated) has a *blackish foreface* merging into *brownish gray upperparts.* Throat white with *conspicuous black submalar streak;* breast and sides gray, *belly and crissum cinnamon-buff.* From **Ica south** paler with browner head grizzled whitish on face. Behavior as in Bay-crowned Brushfinch, likewise occurring in montane woodland and shrubby areas.

Rufous-eared Brushfinch
Atlapetes rufigenis   PLATE 109(12)
18.5–19 cm (7¼–7½″). Uncommon and local in

dense shrubbery and montane woodland undergrowth (including *Polylepis*) in *Andes of nw. Peru* (Cajamarca, Ancash, and nw. Huánuco). 2750–4300 m. A *large* brushfinch. *Head rufous* contrasting with *gray upperparts;* large loral spot and malar streak white. Mostly whitish below. No other *Atlapetes* in Peru has an entirely rufous head (not just on the crown); also lacks black on face. Behavior much as in other *Atlapetes* brushfinches, foraging in pairs on or near the ground.

Apurímac Brushfinch
*Atlapetes forbesi**
18.5 cm (7¼"). Very local in dense shrubbery and montane woodland undergrowth in *Andes of s. Peru* (mainly Apurímac). About 2750–3400 m. Resembles Rufous-eared Brushfinch (formerly considered conspecific; no overlap) but has darker gray upperparts, richer rufous head, and *black ocular area.* Cf. also the much darker Black-spectacled Brushfinch (also no known overlap). Behavior as in Rufous-eared.

Black-spectacled Brushfinch
*Atlapetes melanopsis**
18 cm (7"). Uncommon and very local in undergrowth and borders of montane woodland in *Andes of cen. Peru* (Huancavelica and s. Junín). A recently described species, initially named *A. melanops.* 2500–3400 m. *Dark,* with a tawny *head, black facial patch,* and weak black malar stripe. Below gray with some yellow flammulation, whitish throat. Apurímac Brushfinch (no overlap) is whiter below, has extensive rufous on head, etc. Behavior much the same.

Stripe-headed Brushfinch
*Buarremon torquatus**   PLATE 109(13)
19–20 cm (7½–7¾"). *Widespread and often common* in undergrowth of montane forest borders and woodland in *Andes from n. Venezuela to nw. Argentina* (Salta). Mostly 1500–3000 m, but occurs lower in Venezuela (900–1800 m), sw. Ecuador and nw. Peru (where locally to below 500 m), and in Bolivia and Argentina. Where they overlap, generally occurs at *higher* elevations than Chestnut-capped Brushfinch, except in Venezuela, where the reverse occurs. *Variable.* Basically olive above and white below with gray or olive on flanks; *head black* with *white or gray coronal stripe and superciliary.* Some races (A) have a *black chest band,* but not (B) birds from **w. Venezuela to n. Peru** and in **s. Bolivia and Argentina.** In w. Colombia cf. Black-headed

Brushfinch, which ranges at *lower* elevations. In Bolivia overlaps locally with similar but smaller Pectoral Sparrow. Occurs in pairs, more terrestrial than *Atlapetes* and less often with flocks. Hops on or near the ground, flicking leaves and debris with bill (not scratching with feet). Often puffs out throat. Song a short, thin, high-pitched phrase (e.g., "tsee-o-tseé"); frequent call a penetrating "tseeep."

Black-headed Brushfinch
*Buarremon atricapillus**
19 cm (7½"). Uncommon and very local in undergrowth of mossy foothill and lower montane forest in *Andes of w. Colombia* (south to Valle). Mostly 500–1300 m. Resembles Stripe-headed Brushfinch. *Occurs at lower elevations* (Chestnut-capped is sometimes between the two). *Head entirely black* (showing *no* gray or white striping; on **Cerro Tacarcuna in the extreme northwest** it sometimes shows a trace). Behavior as in Stripe-headed. Also: Costa Rica and Panama.

Chestnut-capped Brushfinch
*Buarremon brunneinuchus**   PLATE 109(14)
19 cm (7½"). *Widespread and fairly common* in undergrowth of montane forest and woodland in *Andes from n. Venezuela to s. Peru* (Puno). Mostly 800–2500 m. *The only brushfinch with both a chestnut crown and a black chest band* (though chest band is absent in parts of **nw. Venezuela and sw. Ecuador**). Otherwise dark olive above, forehead and face mostly black. *Throat white* (often puffed out); whitish below, sides broadly olive grayish. Stripe-headed Brushfinch shows *no* chestnut on crown. Behavior resembles Stripe-headed, as do its vocalizations. Also: Mexico to Panama.

Tanager Finch
Oreothraupis arremonops   PLATE 109(15)
20.5 (8"). Rare to locally uncommon in undergrowth of montane forest and borders on *west slope of Andes from w. Colombia* (n. Antioquia) *to nw. Ecuador* (Pichincha). 1300–2500 m. Unmistakable. *Mostly rufous* (browner above, with a dusky tail; more orangy below); *head contrasting black* with a *bold whitish coronal stripe and long broad superciliary.* Forages in pairs or small groups, hopping slowly through thick growth and sometimes dropping to the ground; usually does not accompany mixed flocks. Song a series of high-pitched buzzy notes interspersed with more musical ones, e.g., "zzeee-zéee-zzeee-

zi-zi-zéee." Call a distinctive froglike "wert" (S. Hilty).

Lysurus

Two *dark* finches that skulk in heavy undergrowth of Andean ravines.

Olive Finch
Lysurus castaneiceps   PLATE 110(1)
15 cm (6"). Uncommon and local in undergrowth of montane forest in *Andes from w. Colombia to s. Peru* (Cuzco). 700–2200 m. *Mostly dark olive green* with *crown and nape chestnut* and *face and throat dark gray.* Like a brushfinch in shape and comportment, but darker and more uniform (closest to White-rimmed). Usually in pairs that hop through dense undergrowth, *almost always near water in ravines.* Though hard to see (mainly because of its thick habitat), really does not seem all that shy. Rarely accompanies mixed flocks. Song a very high-pitched series of sibilant notes, e.g., "tsee-tsi-tsi-tititi-tsi-tsi-tsü-tsii," hard to hear over the sound of rushing water.

Sooty-faced Finch
Lysurus crassirostris
15 cm (6"). Lower montane forest undergrowth in *extreme nw. Colombia* (nw. Chocó on Cerro Tacarcuna), where it replaces Olive Finch. 800–1300 m (in Panama). Resembles Olive, but has a *conspicuous white malar streak* and *considerable yellow on median belly.* Behavior much as in Olive, as apparently is its song (F. G. Stiles); in addition, it frequently gives a sharp penetrating call "psew-pseeét." Also: Costa Rica and Panama.

Yellow-throated Brushfinch
Atlapetes gutturalis   PLATE 110(2)
18 cm (7"). Fairly common in shrubby borders of montane forest, regenerating woodland, and partially cleared areas in *Andes of Colombia* (south to Nariño). Mostly 1500–2200 m. Dusky-gray above with *black head* and *white median crown stripe.* Throat bright yellow; below whitish. *The only brushfinch with a yellow throat.* More tolerant of deforested conditions than most of its congeners. Nervous and excitable; constantly moves expressive tail and pumps it in flight; often hops on the ground, flicking litter aside with bill. Also: Mexico to w. Panama.

Moustached Brushfinch
Atlapetes albofrenatus   PLATE 110(3)
18 cm (7"). Locally common at borders of montane forest and woodland in *Andes from w. Venezuela* (Mérida) *to ne. Colombia* (Cundinamarca). Mostly 1500–2500 m. *Crown rufous* and face black; otherwise *olive above.* In **Venezuela** (illustrated) *yellow below* with a *broad white malar* and thin black submalar streak; in **Colombia** midthroat (as well as malar) white, and has black forehead. In Venezuela not likely confused, but in Colombia could overlap with Rufous-naped Brushfinch (which Moustached seems to replace northward), though that has a gray (not olive) mantle, white wing speculum, and *no* white malar. Behavior as in other *Atlapetes*, typically in pairs or small groups that forage at forest edge and usually are easy to observe.

Santa Marta Brushfinch
Atlapetes melanocephalus   PLATE 110(4)
17 cm (6¾"). *Common in borders of montane forest and woodland in Santa Marta Mts. of n. Colombia.* 1500–3200 m. *Head and chin black* with conspicuous silvery gray patch on ear-coverts; gray above. *Below yellow.* The only other brushfinch on the Santa Martas is the very different Stripe-headed. Behavior much as in other *Atlapetes.* Among the most numerous of Santa Martas' endemic birds.

Rufous-naped Brushfinch
*Atlapetes latinuchus**   PLATE 110(5)
16.5–17 cm (6½–6¾"). *Generally common* in shrubby borders of montane forest, secondary woodland, and even overgrown clearings and hedgerows in agricultural areas in *Andes from n. Colombia to n. Peru* (south to Ancash). Mostly 1500–3000 m, but to 3700 m in nw. Ecuador. *Variation complex;* three more southern forms (Vilcabamba, Gray-eared, Bolivian) were recently separated as species. *Gray above* with *rufous crown* (palest in **nw. Peru**); *yellow below.* A white wing speculum is prominent in **Colombia's Cen. and W. Andes** and on **east slope in s. Ecuador and n. Peru** (illustrated). A *black malar streak,* faint to (often) obvious, is also evident. Cf. Chocó (with a yellower crown) and Pale-naped (with white rearcrown) Brushfinches. Rather bold, more familiar and arboreal than many brushfinches. Pairs or small groups often forage in the open (especially early in day), often accompanying mixed flocks.

Vilcabamba Brushfinch

Atlapetes terborghi*

16.5–17 cm (6½–6¾"). Found only on remote *Cordillera Vilcabamba in Cuzco, Peru.* 2600–3500 m. Resembles Gray-eared Brushfinch (ranging just to south), but has *yellow-green throat and malar area* (there is no black, and no malar stripe) and more olive-tinged underparts. Behavior doubtless much as in Rufous-naped Brushfinch (formerly considered conspecific).

Gray-eared Brushfinch

Atlapetes melanolaemus*   PLATE 110(6)

16.5–17 cm (6½–6¾"). *Common* at borders of montane forest and in secondary woodland on *east slope of Andes from se. Peru* (Cuzco and Puno) *to w. Bolivia* (w. La Paz). 1500–3000 m. Has been called Black-faced Brushfinch. A *dark* brushfinch: *blackish above and (variably) on throat,* with *rufous crown* and *gray cheeks.* Yellow below, sides clouded olive. Replaced southward by Bolivian Brushfinch (no known overlap). Behavior as in Rufous-naped Brushfinch (formerly considered conspecific).

Bolivian Brushfinch

Atlapetes rufinucha*

16.5–17 cm (6½–6¾"). *Common* in borders of montane forest and secondary woodland on *east slope of Andes in w. Bolivia* (e. La Paz to w. Santa Cruz). About 1600–3200 m. Above blackish to sooty-olive with *rufous crown and nape, gray cheeks,* and *black malar streak.* Below yellow, clouded olive on sides. Replaced northward by similar Gray-eared Brushfinch (with blackish throat). Behavior as in Rufous-naped Brushfinch (formerly considered conspecific).

White-rimmed Brushfinch

Atlapetes leucopis   PLATE 110(7)

18 cm (7"). *Rare and local in undergrowth of upper montane forest on east slope of Andes in s. Colombia and n. Ecuador* (in Ecuador also on west slope in Imbabura). 2100–3100 m. *Very dark.* Blackish above with *chestnut crown and nape* and *conspicuous white eye-ring and short postocular streak.* Below dark olive green. Hops on or near the ground in pairs, usually remaining within cover of forest. Rarely accompanies mixed flocks. Song a forceful series of pretty and melodic notes and phrases, often including repetitions.

Chocó Brushfinch

Atlapetes crassus*   PLATE 110(8)

18 cm (7"). Locally fairly common in undergrowth of lower montane forest borders and woodland on *west slope of Andes from sw. Colombia* (Caldas) *to sw. Ecuador* (El Oro). 600–1800 m. Formerly considered conspecific with Tricolored Brushfinch. Crown rich *brownish gold* and face black; dark olive above. Below yellow, sides and flanks olive. Rufous-naped Brushfinch has a truly rufous crown and occurs at higher elevations. Arboreal, hopping as much as 5–10 m above the ground; generally not hard to observe.

Tricolored Brushfinch

Atlapetes tricolor

17 cm (6¾"). Locally fairly common in lower growth of montane forest borders and woodland on *east slope of Andes in cen. and s. Peru* (e. La Libertad to Cuzco). 1750–2600 m. Resembles Chocó Brushfinch (formerly conspecific), but brighter and slightly smaller. Its pattern recalls Gray-eared Brushfinch, which is rufous on crown (not yellow) and has gray on its cheeks. Behavior as in many other *Atlapetes.*

Pale-naped Brushfinch

Atlapetes pallidinucha   PLATE 110(9)

18 cm (7"). Fairly common in upper montane forest borders and woodland in *Andes from extreme sw. Venezuela* (sw. Táchira) *to extreme n. Peru* (n. Cajamarca); *most numerous near treeline.* 2700–3700 m. Forecrown cinnamon, *white on midcrown and nape;* otherwise gray above. In **ne. Colombia and Venezuela** (illustrated) yellow below; **southward,** heavily suffused with olive below. Rufous-naped Brushfinch (regularly found with this species) has an *entirely* rufous crown. Behavior similar to Rufous-naped, but somewhat more secretive.

Ochre-breasted Brushfinch

Atlapetes semirufus   PLATE 110(10)

17 cm (6¾"). Fairly common in undergrowth at borders of montane forest and woodland and in shrubby clearings in *Andes of n. Venezuela and ne. Colombia* (south to Cundinamarca). In n. Venezuela 1000–2500 m, in w. Venezuela and Colombia 2000–3500 m. *Entire head, neck, and breast cinnamon-rufous,* belly mostly yellow. Above olive green. *The only brushfinch in its range with a wholly rufous head.* Behavior similar to other *Atlapetes;* usually in pairs, tending to remain within tangled cover.

Fulvous-headed Brushfinch
Atlapetes fulviceps   PLATE 110(11)
17 cm (6¾"). Locally fairly common in under-growth in montane woodland (including *Poly-lepis* and alders) and forest borders in *Andes from w. Bolivia* (La Paz) *to nw. Argentina* (Salta). Mostly 1500–3200 m, lower in winter. *Head and submalar streak rufous*, contrasting with olive upperparts. Malar area and entire underparts yellow. *The only brushfinch in its southern range with a wholly rufous head.* Rust-and-yellow Tanager has similar color pattern but very different shape, and is arboreal. Behavior similar to other *Atlapetes.*

Tepui Brushfinch
Atlapetes personatus   PLATE 110(12)
17 cm (6¾"). *Common in shrubby forest borders and regenerating clearings on tepuis of s. Vene-zuela region.* 1000–2500 m. *Head and neck rufous-chestnut*, contrasting with dark gray to black upperparts. *Extent of chestnut on under-parts varies*, from just the chin in **e. Bolívar** (as illustrated), to all of throat in **n. Amazonas,** to down over chest in **s. Amazonas and sw. Bolívar.** Otherwise mainly yellow below. *The only brushfinch on the tepuis.* Behavior much as in other *Atlapetes;* not at all shy, excitable and relatively easy to observe.

Dusky-headed Brushfinch
Atlapetes fuscoolivaceus   PLATE 110(13)
17 cm (6¾"). Locally common at borders of montane forest, secondary woodland, and re-generating clearings around *head of Colombia's upper Río Magdalena valley.* 1600–2400 m. *Head sooty blackish*, with indistinct and narrow black-ish submalar streak. Dark olive above; malar area and underparts yellow, sides and flanks shaded olive. Simply patterned, and not likely confused in range; the rare Yellow-headed Brushfinch is found just to the north. Behavior much as in numerous other *Atlapetes;* relatively active and arboreal.

Yellow-headed Brushfinch
*Atlapetes flaviceps**   PLATE 110(14)
17 cm (6¾"). Now rare and local in shrubby mon-tane forest borders and regenerating clearings on east slope of Colombia's Cen. Andes (Tolima and Huila). 1300–2250 m. Has been called Olive-headed Brushfinch. *Head olive-yellow* with crown more olive and *lores and eye-ring bright yellow;* above dark olive. Below yellow, sides and flanks shaded olive. Young birds have head

blotched olive and dusky. Dusky-headed Brush-finch has a solidly sooty head, occurs south of range (no overlap known). Poorly known, and apparently threatened by deforestation, but a sizable population was recently discovered near Toche, where it seems to be surviving in quite young secondary habitat. Behavior apparently as in Dusky-headed.

Yellow-striped Brushfinch
Atlapetes citrinellus   PLATE 110(15)
17 cm (6¾"). Locally fairly common in under-growth of humid montane forest and wood-land on *Andean slopes of nw. Argentina* (Jujuy to Tucumán; most numerous in Tucumán). 700–2000 m. *Striking head pattern* with *bold yellow superciliary, malar, and midthroat* and *blackish ear-coverts and black submalar streak.* Otherwise olive above. Below yellow clouded olive. The only other brushfinch in its range is the very different Fulvous-headed. Often in pairs, foraging actively in lower growth; generally bold and easy to ob-serve, and readily attracted by squeaking.

Slender-billed Finch
Xenospingus concolor   PLATE 111(1)
15 cm (6"). *Uncommon and local in shrubby areas and patches of low woodland in desert areas from sw. Peru* (s. Lima) *to n. Chile* (Tarapacá). To 2500 m in Chile. *Long slender bill bright yellow;* legs orange-yellow. *Nearly uniform bluish gray* (slightly paler below), loral area black. **Imma-ture** browner above with vague buffyish wing-bars, buffier below with brownish breast streak-ing. *Slender and rather long-tailed;* not likely confused in its limited range and habitat. Usually found in pairs, tending to remain hidden in foli-age; more in the open during early morning. Feeds mostly by gleaning for insects. The tail is often held slightly cocked. Spritely but hesitating song a variable series of clear notes, e.g., "chit-weeyt-chit, chi? ts-ts-tsew, chit-weeyt-chit."

Cinereous Finch
Piezorhina cinerea   PLATE 111(2)
16.5 cm (6½"). *Conspicuous and locally common in open desert terrain with scattered shrubs in nw. Peru* (Tumbes to La Libertad). Mostly below 300 m. *Robust and pallid. Massive yellow bill;* legs yellow. *Pale gray above* with blackish lores and malar spot; *even paler gray below,* throat and midbelly whitish. Band-tailed Sierra Finch is darker gray below and browner above, shows white in tail. Cf. also Sulphur-throated Finch. Found in pairs and small groups, foraging

mainly on the ground, in early morning often seen perching stolidly along roads. Song a pleasant series of loud notes and phrases, e.g., "chew, che-wét-chú, chee, che-wi-cher-chu-wít, cheweé, . . ." but sharp and scratchy calls are more frequent, e.g., "chit, chi-di-dit."

Incaspiza

Five *handsome* but *inconspicuous and uncommon* finches found locally on *arid montane slopes of w. Peru*. All inca finches are marked by their *yellow to orange bills and legs* and *extensive white in outer tail feathers (conspicuous in flight)*. Tails are often held *slightly cocked*.

Great Inca Finch

Incaspiza pulchra   PLATE 111(3)

16.5 cm (6½"). *Uncommon and local on hot, arid slopes and ravines on west slope of Andes in w. Peru* (Ancash and Lima). Mostly 1000–2500 m. Brown above with *contrasting rufous on scapulars and inner flight feathers*, shoulders gray. Face, sides of neck, and breast gray surrounding black ocular area and *fairly large throat patch*; belly whitish. The only inca finch that shows extensive rufous on wings. Rufous-backed Inca Finch has rufous across its back and a smaller black throat patch. Usually in pairs, often quite conspicuous in very early morning when they perch in the open atop shrubbery and on cacti, also on boulders; during the rest of day, however, they become much less easy to observe, hopping on the ground or resting in shade within cover. Favors areas with ground bromeliads and large cacti. High-pitched whistled song a simple repeated "tic sweee-eee?"; call a thin "seet."

Rufous-backed Inca Finch

Incaspiza personata   PLATE 111(4)

16.5 cm (6½"). Uncommon and local in arid montane scrub in *nw. Peru, mainly in drainage of upper Río Marañón* (s. Cajamarca to Ancash and w. Huánuco), *locally onto Pacific slope of Cordillera Blanca*. 2700–4000 m. *Entire back and scapulars rufous*, otherwise brown above. Face and sides of neck gray surrounding *black foreface* (frontal band, loral area, and *small* throat patch); breast gray, belly whitish. Cf. Great Inca Finch (usually at lower elevations, only on Pacific slope). Behavior similar to Great. Song a simple repeated "tic sweee-eee?" similar to Great.

Gray-winged Inca Finch

Incaspiza ortizi

16.5 cm (6½"). Uncommon and local in arid montane scrub with *terrestrial bromeliads and large cacti in nw. Peru* (ne. Piura to upper Río Marañón valley in s. Cajamarca). 1800–2300 m. Above grayish brown with *faint dusky streaking on back and scapulars*. Sides of head, neck, and breast gray with *belly whitish;* forehead, ocular area, and *small* throat patch black. Unlike Great and Rufous-backed Inca Finches, the relatively dull Gray-winged *lacks any rufous on either back or wings*. Inconspicuous behavior similar to that of other inca finches, as is song.

Buff-bridled Inca Finch

Incaspiza laeta   PLATE 111(5)

14.5 cm (5¾"). Fairly common in open dry woodland and thorny montane scrub with columnar cacti and boulders in *upper Río Marañón valley of nw. Peru* (s. Cajamarca and s. Amazonas to e. La Libertad and n. Ancash). 1100–2750 m. Head and neck brownish gray contrasting with *prominent rufous saddle across back and scapulars*. Forehead, loral area, and throat patch black; throat *bordered by a conspicuous pale buff malar streak*. Breast pale gray, belly ochraceous buff. Beautifully marked; malar streak unique among the inca finches. Behavior much as in its congeners, foraging on the ground and in lower growth; often raises tail quickly, then slowly lowers it. Song a repeated "tsueet, tsu-tsee" (E. Barnes recording).

Little Inca Finch

Incaspiza watkinsi   PLATE 111(6)

13 cm (5"). Local and uncommon in desert scrub, especially where boulders and Cereus cactus or ground bromeliads are numerous, in *upper Río Marañón drainage of nw. Peru* (n. Cajamarca and adjacent Amazonas). 600–900 m. Head and neck gray surrounding *black foreface* (frontal band, loral area, and *small* throat patch), lower throat whitish. *Back brownish with some blackish streaking* contrasting with rich rufous scapulars, but wing-coverts mainly gray. Breast pale gray, *belly buff. Considerably smaller* and *occurs at lower elevations than other inca finches*. Resembles a *small* Rufous-backed Inca Finch (no overlap), but back streaked. Gray-winged Inca Finch has less rufescent back and whitish (not buff) belly; it lacks whitish lower throat. Behavior much as in the other inca finches. Song a weak "pseeu."

Catamenia

Small finches found in *open and semiopen areas in the Andes,* in Peru and Argentina also in the adjacent lowlands. ♂♂ are mainly gray, ♀♀ brownish and streaked, with *distinctive chestnut crissums. Bills are pale pinkish to yellow.*

Plain-colored Seedeater
Catamenia inornata   PLATE 111(7)

13.5–14.5 cm (5¼–5¾"). *Locally common* on open grassy areas (including paramo and puna), sometimes with scattered shrubs, in *Andes from w. Venezuela* (Mérida) *to w. Argentina* (Mendoza). Mostly 2500–4000 m, lower in Argentina. *Bill brownish pink.* ♂ *mostly rather pale gray,* with *blackish-streaked back;* belly tinged buff, and crissum chestnut. ♀ grayish brown above with blackish streaks. Yellowish buff below, *streaked dusky on throat and breast;* crissum buff. Extent of streaking in ♀-plumaged birds varies, immatures having the most. **Southern birds** (north to s. Peru; illustrated) are larger. Both sexes of Paramo Seedeater are darker generally but have a paler bill; it favors more humid, wooded terrain. Ash-breasted Sierra Finch (often with Plain-colored) has a heavier dusky bill. Forages mostly on the ground, sometimes in sizable flocks when not breeding, then at times associating with other Andean finches, such as Ash-breasted. Song a brief buzzy to musical trill often introduced by several musical notes.

Paramo Seedeater
Catamenia homochroa   PLATE 111(8)

13.5 cm (5¼"). *Rare to uncommon* in shrubbery at edge of montane forest, often most frequent at treeline (usually not in more open grassy areas) in *Andes from w. Venezuela* (Mérida) *to w. Bolivia* (Cochabamba); also on tepuis. Mostly 2400–3600 m. *Bill pale yellowish to pinkish (can look white;* duller in ♀), somewhat more pointed than other *Catamenia.* ♂ *uniform dark slaty gray* with *blackish foreface* and chestnut crissum. **Tepui birds** are somewhat browner, especially below. ♀ dark olive brown above with blackish streaks. Olive brown below, becoming more fulvous on belly with crissum chestnut. Young birds are browner and more coarsely streaked, gradually becoming grayer. Plain-colored Seedeater (both sexes) is paler generally but has a *darker* pinkish bill; ♂ Plain-colored lacks blackish foreface, and ♀ is more streaked below. Encountered infre-

quently, though sometimes a few will be located as they move with a mixed flock of montane tanagers and other birds. Like other *Catamenia,* they usually feed on the ground. Song a drawn-out clear whistle, sometimes given alone but more often followed by a higher-pitched, shorter and burrier note, e.g., "teeeeeeeee-tjeeeee?"

Band-tailed Seedeater
Catamenia analis   PLATE 111(9)

12.5 cm (5"). *Common and widespread* in a variety of shrubby and agricultural areas, mainly in arid regions, in *Andes from n. Colombia to w. Argentina* (Mendoza, locally or sporadically farther south). Mostly 1000–3300 m, lower in w. Peru and Argentina. *Stubby bill butter yellow in ♂,* duller in ♀. ♂ *plain gray* with blackish foreface and chestnut crissum; tail blackish with *white band across middle,* visible mainly in flight and from below. From s. **Peru south** (illustrated) has wing speculum and belly white. Younger birds are streaked blackish on back. ♀ grayish brown above with blackish streaks. Buffy whitish below with blackish streaks, except on white belly; *tail as in ♂.* Other *Catamenia* lack white in tail (but usually you have to flush birds to see it); ♀ is paler overall than other *Catamenia.* Band-tailed Sierra Finch is larger with a longer and more pointed bill. Occurs in pairs or small groups; conspicuous and often quite tame. Feeds mostly on the ground but regularly perches in shrubs and low trees. Usual song a buzzy trill introduced by a faint but more musical note.

Andean Boulder Finch
*Idiopsar brachyurus**   PLATE 111(10)

18 cm (7"). *Uncommon and local in puna grassland, mainly on steep rocky slopes with loose talus or large boulders,* in *Andes from extreme s. Peru* (Puno) *to nw. Argentina* (Catamarca). 3200–4600 m. Often called Short-tailed Finch. *Bill heavy, quite long and thick at its base;* iris dark red to reddish, legs flesh-colored. *Leaden gray,* somewhat paler below, with *lower face inconspicuously grizzled whitish.* Wings and rather short tail dusky, primaries edged pale gray. Likely confused only with ♂ of considerably smaller Plumbeous Sierra Finch; bill of Plumbeous has a more normal shape, the tail is proportionately longer, and it lacks the grizzled effect under the eye. Found in pairs or small groups, feeding on the ground and sometimes probing into it. Often perches on rocks or boulders, and rarely or never far from them. Gives a sharp, high-pitched "zhit"

call similar to White-winged Diuca Finch; evident song a long series of whistled notes, e.g., "shree su su, shree su su . . ." (H. Lloyd and B. Walker).

Phrygilus

Small to midsized finches (perhaps more closely related to the tanagers) found *mainly in grassy and shrubby terrain in s. South America;* some species extend north in the Andes. They forage mostly on the ground. ♂♂ of most are *predominantly some shade of gray,* and ♀♀ tend to be browner and more streaked; a "hooded" group, wherein ♂♂ are more boldly patterned, is quite different.

Plumbeous Sierra Finch
Phrygilus unicolor PLATE 111(11)
15 cm (6"). *Widespread and often common in paramo and puna grassland in high Andes from w. Venezuela (Trujillo) and n. Colombia to Tierra del Fuego;* more numerous northward. Mostly 3000–4600 m, but lower in Argentina (especially during winter, when sometimes descends to near sea level). ♂ *uniform leaden gray.* **Northern** ♀ (south to n. Peru) brown above and whitish below, *coarsely streaked with dusky throughout;* wings with indistinct whitish bars. **Further south,** ♀ virtually identical to ♂, thus all *gray;* back and crown can be dusky-streaked. Ash-breasted Sierra Finch is smaller, its ♂ paler generally with a whitish belly, and it has streaking on back; ♀ less prominently streaked below than ♀ Plumbeous and also with whitish belly. Cf. also the scarce Andean Boulder Finch. Usually in small groups, often tame, feeding as they shuffle along, sometimes hopping up to perch on rocks or shrubs. Regularly with other birds, especially various finches. Not very vocal (notably less so than Ash-breasted); song rarely heard, a simple brief "zhree."

Ash-breasted Sierra Finch
Phrygilus plebejus PLATE 111(12)
12–12.5 cm (4¾–5"). *Generally common in open grassy and shrubby areas (sometimes where nearly barren) in Andes from n. Ecuador* (Carchi) *to w. Argentina* (Mendoza). Mostly 1500–4500 m, locally down to sea level in sw. Ecuador and nw. Peru. A *small, nondescript finch.* ♂ brownish gray above, grayer on face with vague whitish superciliary; *dusky streaking on back,* gray rump. *Below paler gray,* becoming *whiter on*

belly (especially in **Ecuador and n. Peru;** this also is the smallest race). ♀ brown above with dusky streaking; whitish below streaked dusky. Plain-colored Seedeater has a proportionately longer tail and stubbier pinkish bill; ♂♂ have chestnut crissum, ♀♀ are buffier below. Plumbeous Sierra Finch ♂ is larger, more uniform and darker gray, with no back streaking. In some areas (especially Peru?) occurs in large flocks when not breeding, often with other montane finches. Song a simple buzzy trill, "tzzzzzzzzzi," sometimes with a more musical "tseu-tse-tseu" at end.

Band-tailed Sierra Finch
Phrygilus alaudinus PLATE 111(13) PLATE 112(1)
14–14.5 cm (5½–5¾"). Uncommon to locally fairly common in barren, arid areas with sparse vegetation in *Andes from n. Ecuador* (Carchi) *to w. Argentina* (Córdoba), and in cen. *Chile* (Atacama to Valdivia). Mostly 1500–3500 m; also locally near coast in sw. Ecuador and nw. Peru, and in Chile. *Rather long and slender bill bright yellow;* legs yellow. In **Ecuador and most of Peru** (Plate 111) ♂ *gray,* back browner and broadly streaked blackish; *lower breast and belly contrasting white;* tail black with *white band across center* visible mainly in flight. **Coastal birds** are smaller and paler. From **extreme sw. Peru south** (Plate 112) larger and *paler gray* with *less contrast between breast and belly.* ♀ brown above streaked blackish; whitish below streaked dusky on lower throat and chest; *tail as in* ♂. Superficially resembles smaller Band-tailed Seedeater (tail patterns are similar), but seedeater has a much stubbier bill and a chestnut crissum (♂) or buffier lower underparts (♀). Found singly or in pairs, not in the flocks seen in most sierra finches. Breeding ♂ sings during an undulating display flight, giving a fairly musical series of gurgling phrases that ends with a long buzzy "zzhhhhhh" as it glides back to the ground; also sings from perches.

Carbonated Sierra Finch
Phrygilus carbonarius PLATE 112(2)
14.5 cm (5¾"). *Uncommon breeder in semiopen shrub steppes of s. and cen. Argentina* (Mendoza to Río Negro and e. Chubut, a few in w. Córdoba), during austral winter migrating into n. Argentina. To about 800 m. *Bill bright yellow,* legs yellowish. ♂ has *forecrown, face, and most of underparts black,* flanks gray. Above gray, streaked black on nape and back. In fresh plumage grayer below, becoming blacker with wear. ♀ brownish gray above with black streaks. Whitish below

narrowly streaked dusky across breast and down sides. Mourning Sierra Finch is notably larger, and both sexes have *prominent wing-bars;* black on ♂ Mourning does not extend over belly, and ♀ has distinctive fulvous cheeks. Breeding Carbonateds favor dense shrubby areas; in winter they can gather in groups, sometimes with other finches, and are then more often found in open terrain. ♂ in flight display flutters into the air and then glides to another bush, at its apex bursting into a musical "treeyee-treeyee-treeyee . . ." (up to 9–12 treeyees); also sings while perched.

Mourning Sierra Finch
Phrygilus fruticeti PLATE 112(3)
18–18.5 cm (7–7¼"). *Widespread and generally common* in shrubby areas and cultivated regions with trees and bushes in *Andes from n. Peru* (Cajamarca) *to cen. Chile and s. Argentina* (Santa Cruz). Mostly 2000–3600 m, locally down to sea level in Chile and Patagonia, and up to 4300 m in Bolivia. *Rather heavy bill yellow in breeding ♂,* duller at other seasons and in ♀; legs pinkish to dull yellow. ♂ gray above broadly streaked black, *wings with two bold white bars. Throat and breast black* (often scaled gray), flanks gray, midbelly white. Black is more extensive when plumage is worn; in fresh plumage scalier, with gray and brown predominating. At **high elevations in w. Bolivia** (Oruro and w. Potosí) *almost entirely black* with some whitish on lower belly and crissum. ♀ grayish brown above streaked blackish but *rump gray* (obvious in flight) and *ear-coverts fulvous; wing-bars as in* ♂. Variable below, grayish to whitish with at least some dusky streaking on sides of throat and breast; some show black on bib. Easily recognized among the sierra finches by its large size and prominent wing-bars; ♀'s cheek patch is unique. In Argentina, cf. scarcer Carbonated Sierra Finch. Found in pairs or loose groups; conspicuous and often confiding. Oft-heard song a loud and wheezy "shushglaoww" introduced or ending with gurgling notes, sometimes given in a display flight. Call a distinctive nasal "reeanh."

Patagonian Sierra Finch
Phrygilus patagonicus PLATE 112(4)
14.5 cm (5¾"). Fairly common in forest borders (often in *Nothofagus* forest) and shrubby clearings from *cen. Chile* (Ñuble) *and adjacent w. Argentina to Tierra del Fuego.* Mostly below 1200 m. Bill pale gray. ♂ has *entire hood gray* (darkest on lores) *contrasting with rich ochraceous to russet back,* yellower on upper rump. Below bright yel-

low, sides and flanks often washed ochre; *crissum whitish with gray edging.* ♀ similarly patterned but *back pure olive, lacking* any ochraceous. ♀ resembles ♂ of slightly larger Gray-hooded Sierra Finch, aside from Gray-hooded's more extensive and purer white on underparts (extending to lower belly) and lack of gray edging on crissum; breeding Gray-hooded favors scrubbier terrain (being less forest-based than Patagonian), though the two can be together during winter. Arboreal and usually near water when breeding, though often dropping to the ground to feed; at other seasons in flocks and more wide-ranging. Clear, rhythmic song a short series of well-enunciated spritely notes, e.g., "cleet-clwett, cleet-weet, clweet," sometimes delivered from a high exposed perch.

Gray-hooded Sierra Finch
Phrygilus gayi PLATE 112(5)
15.5–16.5 cm (6–6½"). Fairly common in semi-open shrubby and scrubby terrain and lighter woodland from *cen. Chile* (Atacama) *and w. Argentina* (w. Salta) *to Tierra del Fuego,* in austral winter some moving east. To 3500 m. **Southern birds** have bicolored bill (darker above). ♂ has *entire hood gray* (darkest on lores) contrasting with *bright olive back* and olive-yellow underparts; *lower belly and crissum white.* ♀ much duller, hood paler and brownish with blackish and white streaks in malar area, *breast usually washed ochraceous.* Cf. Patagonian Sierra Finch; these overlap broadly though breeding birds typically segregate by habitat, Patagonian preferring forest edge. ♀ Black-hooded Sierra Finch (which has a gray hood) has an ochraceous (not olive) back. Behavior as in Patagonian, though *less forest-based when nesting.* Song similar but slower, a series of clear notes and simple phrases, e.g., "sweét, sweét, treelili, treeli, treelili" or just "sweét, sweét, sweét. . . ."

Peruvian Sierra Finch
Phrygilus punensis
15.5–16 cm (6–6¼"). Locally common on rocky shrubby slopes and agricultural areas with scattered bushes and low trees, often around houses and towns, in *Andes from n. Peru* (Cajamarca) *to w. Bolivia* (w. La Paz). 2500–4500 m. Resembles ♂ Gray-hooded Sierra Finch (no overlap), but back brighter and more yellowish olive, and *breast and belly washed ochraceous.* ♂♂ from **s. Peru and Bolivia** have an ochraceous tinge on back as well, and thus are difficult to distinguish from ♀ Black-hooded Sierra Finches

(thus watch for ♂ Black-hoodeds, ♀ Peruvians). ♀ similar but hood slightly duller. **Immature** much duller and buffier below. Behavior much as in the other hooded sierra finches. Song resembles Black-hooded but less ringing and with a more varied phraseology.

Black-hooded Sierra Finch
Phrygilus atriceps   PLATE 112(6)
15.5–16 cm (6–6¼"). Fairly common in shrubby slopes and valleys, often where columnar cacti are prevalent, in *Andes from sw. Peru* (Arequipa) *to n. Chile and nw. Argentina* (Catamarca). 2400–4000 m, mostly above 3000 m. Striking ♂ has *shiny black hood* in contrast to *deep ochraceous back* and *rich yellow underparts and rump;* wings and tail dusky, wings broadly edged gray. ♀ similar but duller, with hood slaty gray. Younger ♀ has more brownish hood, often some streaking on malar area, and tends to be buffier below. *♀ is the only ♀ hooded sierra finch with an ochraceous back,* but it does resemble ♂ of possibly sympatric Peruvian Sierra Finch. Usually in pairs or small groups, often with other montane finches and conspicuous; regularly around houses and in villages. Loud, musical song a repetition of a simple clear phrase, e.g., "trileé, trileé, trileé. . . ."

Red-backed Sierra Finch
Phrygilus dorsalis   PLATE 112(7)
18 cm (7"). Local and apparently rare in puna grassland and on rocky slopes in *high Andes of n. Chile, sw. Bolivia, and nw. Argentina* (south to Catamarca). 3300–4500 m. Gray above with *back and scapulars contrasting pale rufous,* freckled whitish below eye; wings and tail blackish. Midthroat white, sides of neck and breast gray, belly whitish. The contrasting rufous back is unique among high Andean finches, but beware immatures of other gray finches as these may show brown on the back. This stocky finch is often tame, foraging on the ground, regularly perching on rocks or stone walls; it favors the vicinity of cushion bogs. Occurs in pairs or small flocks, sometimes with other montane finches (locally even with White-throated Sierra Finches).

White-throated Sierra Finch
Phrygilus erythronotus
18 cm (7"). Locally fairly common in puna grassland and on rocky slopes in *high Andes from sw. Peru* (Arequipa) *to extreme n. Chile* (Arica) *and sw. Bolivia.* 3600–4700 m. Resembles Red-backed Sierra Finch (limited overlap in n. Chile, perhaps elsewhere), but *above entirely gray*

(with *no* rufous). White-winged Diuca Finch is somewhat larger and more clean-cut, with a large white patch on wing and a white crescent below eye. Cf. also Common Diuca Finch (found at lower elevations). Behavior as in Red-backed; likewise favors the vicinity of cushion bogs.

Diuca

A pair of fairly large, *gray and white* finches, quite similar to *Phrygilus.* The two species seem likely not to be congeneric.

White-winged Diuca Finch
Diuca speculifera   PLATE 112(8)
19 cm (7½"). Locally common in puna grassland, especially around cushion bogs, in *high Andes from w. Peru* (Ancash) *to n. Chile and w. Bolivia* (Cochabamba). Mostly 4000–5300 m. *Mostly gray* with *large white crescent below eye;* throat and median breast and belly also white. Wings and tail blackish with *conspicuous white in primaries* (obvious even on perched birds), *tail with outer webs white* (visible mainly in flight). The scarcer White-throated Sierra Finch *lacks* white in wings and tail. Common Diuca Finch occurs at *much* lower elevations. This robust finch is usually in small tame groups that scatter out to feed on the ground, often crouching and remaining unseen until they flush. Probably nests at higher elevations than any other passerine bird in South America; has even been known to roost in glacier crevasses. Not very vocal; flight call a sharp "wheet."

Common Diuca Finch
Diuca diuca   PLATE 112(9)
16–17 cm (6¼–6¾"). *Generally common,* in shrubby areas, gardens and cultivated regions, and steppes *mainly in Chile and Argentina;* in austral winter a few extend to ne. Argentina. Mostly below 2000 m, locally to 3600 m in nw. Argentina. *Gray above,* wings and tail more blackish, *inner webs of outer tail feathers white* (flashing in flight). *Large white throat patch* contrasts with gray breast and sides; midbelly white, *lower flanks rufous.* ♀ slightly brown-tinged, as are both sexes in **Patagonia** (which also are small). Not likely confused in its *austral range;* White-winged Diuca Finch and White-throated Sierra Finch are both high-elevation birds of the Andes. Familiar and conspicuous, this gray and white finch feeds mostly while pottering about on the ground, but also perches freely in shrubs and low trees. During the winter it ranges in

small flocks. Loud and musical song, frequently heard, is delivered quite slowly, e.g., "chit, chuwit, chuwit-chew, chuwit."

Melanodera

Two *scarce* finches found in semiopen terrain of *far southern Patagonia and Tierra del Fuego.* ♂♂ have similar attractive facial patterns and black throats.

White-bridled Finch
Melanodera melanodera* PLATE 112(10)
15 cm (6"). *Rare and local in open tussocky grassland of extreme s. Argentina* (Santa Cruz) *and s. Chile* (Magallanes); at least formerly also on Isla Grande; also on *Falkland Islands,* where *more numerous.* To 500 m. Also called Black-throated Finch or Canary-winged Finch. **Mainland** ♂ (illustrated) with gray crown and hindneck, *conspicuous white superciliary and malar streak outlining black lores and throat patch;* above grayish olive. *Wing-coverts and flight feather edging pale yellow (even the closed wing looks mostly yellow);* outer tail feathers pale yellow. Below grayish, midbreast and belly yellow. Much duller ♀ buffy brown above with blackish streaks, whitish below with brownish streaks and *buff wash across breast; wings and tail as in* ♂ *but yellow less extensive and not as bright.* On **Falklands** *less extensive yellow in wing.* Cf. Yellow-bridled Finch (no overlap when breeding) and ♀ Plumbeous Sierra Finch (no yellow in tail, etc.). Overgrazing by sheep has reduced grass cover across much of range, apparently causing a substantial decline in numbers. Often ranges in small groups, foraging on the ground amid grass tussocks. Song a repetitious series of clear whistled notes with a somewhat hesitant cadence, e.g., "cheet-cheet-wheérip, cheet-cheet-wheerip."

Yellow-bridled Finch
Melanodera xanthogramma PLATE 112(11)
16–16.5 cm (6¼–6½"). *Rare breeder in scrub near treeline in Andes from s. Chile and s. Argentina to Tierra del Fuego,* descending to sea level during austral winter. Breeds mostly 800–2500 m, locally lower in Tierra del Fuego. *Pattern much like the smaller White-bridled Finch, but* ♂ *has superciliary and malar streak bright yellow* and *considerably less yellow on wing* (reduced to olive primary edging). Above mostly bluish gray (more olive in worn plumage); breast and sides also gray, midbelly yellow; outer tail feathers yellow or white. ♀ like ♀ White-bridled but *even*

more heavily streaked (especially below) and with *virtually no yellow on wing* (only narrow edging) and *no buff on breast.* Behavior much as in White-bridled; seems even less numerous. Song a leisurely series of simple notes, e.g., "tuwee . . . chu . . . cheee . . . tuwee . . . chu. . . ."

Poospiza

Small finches found in woodland and thickets *primarily in the Andes and s.-cen. South America.* Warbling finches are handsome but simply patterned, with gray, white, and rufous predominating. Though many species have attractive songs, it must be admitted that few or none actually warble.

Ringed Warbling Finch
Poospiza torquata PLATE 113(1)
13–14 cm (5–5½"). Fairly common in deciduous scrub and woodland in *s. Bolivia, Argentina* (south to Río Negro), *and w. Paraguay.* To 2800 m in Bolivia. *Gray above with long white superciliary* and *black cheeks;* wings with *conspicuous white bars;* outer tail feathers mostly white (flashing in flight). Below white with a *black pectoral band* and *rufous crissum.* ♀ slightly duller. Black-capped Warbling Finch has an all-black head, no pectoral band. Rather active, gleaning in foliage, less often dropping to the ground; especially in winter often joins mixed flocks. Song a loud series of whistled notes and phrases, a frequent one being "wee-tsee, whee-cheeu, tsi."

Collared Warbling Finch
Poospiza hispaniolensis PLATE 113(2)
13.5 cm (5¼"). Locally common in arid scrub and woodland, and shrubbery in agricultural areas from *sw. Ecuador* (sw. Manabí) *to sw. Peru* (Arequipa). Mostly below 1400 m (locally to 2900 m in Peru). Some birds have pink or orange at least at base of bill. ♂ *gray above,* back often browner, with *long white superciliary* and *blackish cheeks;* wings with whitish edges on flight feathers and vague bars; *outer tail feathers with much white* (obvious in flight). Below white with *black patch on midchest,* gray sides and flanks. ♀ drabber; browner above with *head pattern less contrasting but still evident.* Whitish below with *dusky-brown chest streaking enclosing white throat.* The more terrestrial Black-capped Sparrow has an all-black head, except for its white superciliary, and *lacks* white in tail. In pairs when breeding, otherwise small loose groups, sometimes joining mixed flocks of other finches. Mainly arboreal,

but also feeds on the ground. Especially abundant on Isla de La Plata off Ecuador. Vigorous song a ringing "swik-swik-sweéu."

Cinereous Warbling Finch
Poospiza cinerea PLATE 113(3)
13 cm (5"). *Rather rare and local in cerrado and scrub in interior s. Brazil* (s. Mato Grosso to n. São Paulo and Minas Gerais). 600–1200 m. Iris reddish. A *dull* and *simply patterned* warbling finch, *gray above* and *white below,* lores and cheeks blacker, and throat tinged buff; outer tail feathers white (flashing in flight). Black-capped Warbling Finch has a contrasting black cap and occurs south of range of Cinereous, with no overlap. Remains relatively poorly known, never seeming to be as numerous as Black-capped. Mainly arboreal; occurs as scattered pairs, sometimes with loose mixed flocks.

Black-capped Warbling Finch
Poospiza melanoleuca PLATE 113(4)
13 cm (5"). Common in scrub and low woodland from *s. and e. Bolivia* (Cochabamba and Santa Cruz) *to n. Argentina* (n. Córdoba and n. Buenos Aires) *and w. Uruguay.* To 2800 m in Bolivia. Iris orange-red. *Head glossy black* contrasting with *uniform gray upperparts* and *snowy white underparts;* outer tail feathers white (flashing in flight). Ringed Warbling Finch has a bold white superciliary, white in wing, black pectoral band, etc. Cf. Cinereous Warbling Finch (no overlap). Color pattern vaguely recalls ♂ of the very differently shaped Masked Gnatcatcher. Mainly arboreal; when not breeding often in groups of 4–8 birds and accompanying mixed flocks. Gleans in foliage; often bold and excitable, easy to observe. Song, not heard all that often, a series of well-enunciated "ch-veet" notes.

Black-and-rufous Warbling Finch
Poospiza nigrorufa PLATE 113(5)
15 cm (6"). Fairly common in shrubbery and groves of trees from *s. Brazil* (north to s. Paraná) *to e. Argentina* (s. Buenos Aires) *and s. Paraguay.* To 900 m. Brownish gray above with *bold white superciliary and malar streak* and black cheeks; white tips on outer tail feathers. *Below cinnamon-rufous,* white on midbelly. The smaller Cinnamon Warbling Finch has a cinnamon brow and malar, rufous on back, obvious white wing-bars. Red-rumped Warbling Finch has rufous below confined to flanks, browner back with a bright rufous rump. Black-and-chestnut Warbling Finch ranges only well to the *west* of this species. Found singly or in pairs, foraging

near (sometimes even on) the ground. Usually not very conspicuous. Song a rapidly repeated "swit-swit-cheeu, swit-swit-cheeu, . . ." usually 3–4 phrases and ending with a "swee?"

Red-rumped Warbling Finch
Poospiza lateralis PLATE 113(6)
15 cm (6"). Fairly common in shrubbery at forest edge and in woodland from *se. Brazil* (Espírito Santo) *to ne. Argentina* (n. Buenos Aires). To 1800 m in Brazil (montane northward). **Northern birds** (n. São Paulo north; A) have gray upperparts with *long narrow yellowish white superciliary and malar* and *contrasting rufous rump;* wings with whitish edging on coverts and flight feathers; tail with white corners. *Throat and chest yellowish buff, sides and flanks broadly rufous.* **most of range** (s. São Paulo south; B) has a whiter superciliary, olive brown back, and *grayish throat and breast* with less rufous on sides. The smaller Bay-chested Warbling Finch has a chestnut band across entire chest and *no* eye-stripe or malar. Cf. Black-and-rufous Warbling Finch. Active and mainly arboreal (though generally not ranging much above the ground), occurring in pairs when breeding, in small groups otherwise; sometimes with mixed flocks. Song of southern birds a repeated metallic "tzip . . . tzip . . ." (or "tzap"), recalling certain hummingbirds; sometimes considerably more jumbled.

Cinnamon Warbling Finch
Poospiza ornata PLATE 113(7)
13 cm (5"). Uncommon and local in scrub and low woodland of *Argentina* (breeds from San Juan to La Rioja, migrating north and east in austral winter; a few reach sw. Uruguay). To 1000 m. ♂ gray above with *long superciliary and malar cinnamon; lower back and rump chestnut;* wings with two pronounced white wing-bars, outer tail feathers white. *Mostly cinnamon-rufous below, breast more chestnut* (extent of chestnut varies individually). ♀ paler generally, with buffier wing-bars and underparts. Likely confused only with larger and darker Black-and-rufous Warbling Finch. Occurs in pairs when breeding, gathering in small flocks during winter, when it may join with other species to feed in more open terrain. Song an emphatic series of sharp notes, e.g., "cheyp-cheyp-cheeu-cheeu."

Bay-chested Warbling Finch
Poospiza thoracica PLATE 113(8)
13.5 cm (5¼"). Locally fairly common in forest and woodland borders in *mountains of se. Brazil* (e. Minas Gerais to n. Rio Grande do Sul). 800–

1500 m. Gray above with *white crescent below eye* and some primary edging. White below with *prominent chest band and flanks chestnut.* The larger and usually more numerous Red-rumped Warbling Finch has a prominent superciliary, obvious rufous rump, and white in tail; lacks pectoral band. Mainly arboreal, though generally not very high, occurring in pairs or small groups; regularly with mixed flocks. Gleans actively in foliage, seeming rarely to remain long in the open. Very quiet; only sharp call notes have been heard.

Rusty-browed Warbling Finch
Poospiza erythrophrys   PLATE 113(9)
14 cm (5½″). Uncommon in montane woodland and borders in *Andes from s. Bolivia* (Cochabamba) *to nw. Argentina* (Catamarca). 1200–2800 m. Head and neck gray with *rufous superciliary,* back olivaceous brown; wings dusky with greater coverts and primaries edged white, and outer tail feathers mostly white. *Below rufous.* The larger Cochabamba Mountain Finch has rufous on forehead as well as its brow, etc. In pairs or small groups and quite arboreal, foraging actively and favoring stands of alders. Regularly accompanies mixed flocks. Song a rhythmic series of single notes and simple phrases, e.g., "swee-swee-cheeu, swee-swee-cheeu."

Rufous-breasted Warbling Finch
Poospiza rubecula
16.5 cm (6½″). *Rare and local in montane scrub and low woodland in Andes of w. Peru* (Cajamarca to Ica). 2500–3600 m. Slaty gray above with *black facial area and chin. Forehead, superciliary, and underparts orange-rufous,* midbelly whitish. Essentially unique in range, but cf. certain gray and rufous tanagers. Infrequently encountered, and declining; found singly or in pairs, sometimes accompanying mixed flocks.

Black-and-chestnut Warbling Finch
Poospiza whitii   PLATE 113(10)
15 cm (6″). Uncommon in woodland borders, shrubbery, and hedgerows and copses in agricultural areas on *Andean slopes from w. Bolivia* (s. La Paz) *to w. Argentina* (Córdoba and San Luis). Mostly 600–2500 m. *Slaty gray above* with *bold white superciliary and malar streak* and black cheeks; tail blackish, outer feathers broadly tipped white. *Deep chestnut below,* midbelly white. No other Andean warbling finch has such dark underparts (can look maroon or even blackish). Black-and-rufous Warbling Finch ranges only in lowlands *east* of this

species. Found singly or in pairs, generally not with mixed flocks; on the whole, not very conspicuous. Song (quite different from Black-and-rufous) a spirited series of melodic phrases, recalling a *Pheucticus* grosbeak.

Rufous-sided Warbling Finch
Poospiza hypochondria   PLATE 113(11)
16–16.5 cm (6¼–6½″). *Common* in shrubbery and low woodland in *Andes from w. Bolivia* (s. La Paz) *to nw. Argentina* (Mendoza). Mostly 2500–4200 m. **Argentina** birds (illustrated) *brownish gray above* with *white superciliary* and malar, and a *black submalar;* wing-coverts and flight feathers edged buff, terminal half of outer tail feathers white. Throat white, breast pale grayish, with *contrasting rufous flanks.* **Bolivia** birds slightly smaller, with grayer rump and outer tail feathers all white. Bolivian Warbling Finch has a rufous pectoral band as well as rufous flanks; it shows *no* submalar streak. Forages actively in foliage, only infrequently dropping to the ground; often in small groups, sometimes joining mixed flocks.

Plain-tailed Warbling Finch
Poospiza alticola   PLATE 113(12)
16 cm (6¼″). Local and uncommon in shrubbery and low woodland, including *Polylepis* groves, in *Andes of nw. Peru* (Cajamarca to Ancash). Mostly 2900–4300 m. Grayish brown above, darkest on crown, with white superciliary and malar, black submalar; *wings and tail essentially plain.* Below whitish, *sides rufous* and *flanks cinnamon-buff.* Nothing really similar in range. Occurs in pairs and small family groups, sometimes accompanying mixed flocks. Often feeds on aphids and their sugary secretions on the underside of *Gynoxys* leaves.

Bolivian Warbling Finch
Poospiza boliviana   PLATE 113(13)
16 cm (6¼″). Fairly common in arid montane scrub and low woodland in *Andes from w. Bolivia* (s. La Paz) *to extreme nw. Argentina* (Jujuy). 1700–3000 m. Brownish above, grayer on sides of head with long white superciliary; inner flight feathers edged cinnamon, outer tail feathers mostly white. *Throat white,* contrasting with *bright rufous chest band, extending down flanks. Lacks* the submalar streak shown by Rufous-sided Warbling Finch (sometimes together, though Rufous-sided is typically at higher elevations); Rufous-sided *lacks* rufous chest band. Behavior much as in Rufous-sided.

Compsospiza

Two *simply patterned,* montane finches with *limited ranges in the Bolivian and Argentinian Andes.* They resemble the smaller warbling finches, and have been considered congeneric, but the two *Compsospiza* are notably less active and *much less vocal* (a true song seems never to have been described for either species).

Tucumán Mountain Finch
Compsospiza baeri* PLATE 113(14)
18 cm (7"). Uncommon and local in patches of low woodland and shrubbery, and in montane scrub in *Andes of nw. Argentina* (Salta and Jujuy to Tucumán and adjacent Catamarca). 2000–3000 m. *Gray, with orange-rufous forehead, superciliary, lower eyelid, and throat;* tinged olivaceous above and lower belly paler, with crissum also orange-rufous. Cf. the smaller and more patterned Rusty-browed Warbling Finch, which ranges mainly in better-developed woodland at lower elevations. Usually in pairs; inconspicuous and quite inactive, perching upright and often remaining within cover. Favors areas where alders and *Polylepis* are prevalent.

Cochabamba Mountain Finch
Compsospiza garleppi* PLATE 113(15)
18 cm (7"). *Rare and local in patches of low woodland and shrubbery (often Polylepis) in Andes of w. Bolivia* (Cochabamba). Mostly 2900–3650 m. *Gray above,* with *orange-rufous forehead, superciliary, lower eyelid, and underparts;* lower belly somewhat paler. Tucumán Mountain Finch (no overlap) has mainly gray underparts. Rusty-browed Warbling Finch is smaller with white in wings and tail, gray crown (no rufous on forehead). Behavior similar to Tucumán, but seems to join small mixed flocks more often.

Chestnut-breasted Mountain Finch
Poospizopis caesar* PLATE 113(16)
18.5 cm (7¼"). Locally fairly common in scrub, low woodland, and gardens in *highlands of s. Peru* (Apurímac and Cuzco). 2500–3900 m. *Uniform gray above* with black foreface and long white superciliary. *White throat* and *broad rufous-chestnut breast band;* flanks gray, crissum also rufous-chestnut. Nothing really similar in its limited range; notably *larger* than any warbling finch, and more terrestrial. Usually in pairs, foraging mainly on the ground, recalling a *Buarremon* brushfinch, sometimes at edge of fields but never far from cover. Vigorous song

a rich, grosbeaklike warbling, sometimes delivered from a prominent perch.

Sicalis

Predominantly yellow finches that are conspicuous in open country, with *diversity greatest in the Andes* (several species do occur in the lowlands); recent genetic evidence indicates that they are actually most closely related to the tanagers. Most species are *gregarious* when not breeding; they nest in holes, sometimes semicolonially. Variation due mainly to age and wear can make individual yellowfinches hard to identify, especially in the Andes, but they typically range in *monospecific groups* and some of the more distinctive adult ♂♂ are almost always present. Most of the dull juvenal plumages are not described here.

Sulphur-throated Finch
Sicalis taczanowskii PLATE 114(1)
12 cm (4¾"). *Uncommon in open barren areas with at most scattered bushes from sw. Ecuador* (mainly w. Guayas) *to nw. Peru* (La Libertad). To 400 m. *Nondescript; bull-headed and short-tailed. Very heavy horn-colored bill.* Pale grayish brown above, streaked blackish on back. *Lores, malar streak, and upper throat pale yellow* (color often hard to see); below dull whitish. Best recognized by its drab appearance and stout bill. Can occur in large compact flocks of dozens or even hundreds of birds, feeding mainly on open ground. Erratic, and in some areas (e.g., Ecuador) it appears to have declined steeply.

Saffron Finch
Sicalis flaveola* PLATE 114(2)
13.5–14 cm (5¼–5½"). *Common and widespread* in semiopen areas, agricultural regions, and many towns and cities from Colombia and Venezuela to n. Argentina; absent from Amazonia. *Most numerous in the north* (n. Colombia and n. Venezuela) *and northwest* (sw. Ecuador and nw. Peru), *where easily the most numerous and familiar yellowfinch, favoring arid regions.* Mostly below 2000 m, locally higher in the Andes. To 2000 m in Ecuador and Bolivia. More than one species is perhaps involved. ♂ of **northern forms** (A) *mostly bright yellow, more orange on forecrown* and slightly more olive above. ♀ similar but slightly duller. Immature pale grayish brown above with dusky streaking; paler and more or less unstreaked below, with

yellow pectoral band extending up around nape as a nuchal collar. ♂ of **southern forms** *duller; more olive and streaked above with less orange on crown, breast washed olive.* ♀ of **southern forms** (B) brownish with dusky streaking above; below whitish with finer streaking. Cf. smaller Orange-fronted Yellowfinch. Grassland Yellowfinch especially resembles southern form, though even more olive overall; Grassland usually occurs in agricultural regions, and rarely is around towns and buildings like Saffron. Mainly forages on the ground (often on lawns), sometimes gathering in large flocks and then often associating with other birds. Regularly kept as a cagebird. Vigorous song a variable series of lively, well-enunciated notes and short phrases, e.g., "tsip, tsee-tit, tsee, tseeti, tsee, tsee, tseeti"; appears not to vary geographically. Also: introduced to Panama and various islands in West Indies, etc.

Orange-fronted Yellowfinch
Sicalis columbiana   PLATE 114(3)
11.5 cm (4½"). Local and usually uncommon in semiopen areas, riparian growth, and around ranch buildings in *s. Venezuela and ne. Colombia,* along the *lower Amazon River,* and in *interior ne. Brazil. Generally near water,* but unlike the better-known Saffron Finch *does not usually occur in towns.* Below 300 m. *Smaller than Saffron.* ♂ resembles northern forms of Saffron but has a *contrasting orange forecrown* that does *not* extend back over the crown, *dusky lores* (not yellow), and a more olive face and upperparts. Some show an orange breast tinge. ♀ olive brown above; below whitish, sides tinged grayish buff; unlike young Saffron, shows essentially *no* streaking. Ranges in pairs or small flocks; in Venezuela sometimes together with Saffrons. Forages mainly on open ground, but perches freely in trees and on fences and buildings.

Stripe-tailed Yellowfinch
Sicalis citrina   PLATE 114(4)
12 cm (4¾"). *Uncommon and local in savanna, cerrado, and locally in agricultural land in w. Colombia, Venezuela, and the Guianas,* and from *ne. Brazil to Bolivia and nw. Argentina.* Mostly 800–2800 m, thus *mostly not in lowlands* (unlike Grassland Yellowfinch). ♂ olive above with *forecrown contrasting citrine* and back streaking dusky; *inner web of outer two tail feathers mostly white on terminal half* (distinctive, but hard to see in the field). Yellow below, breast clouded olive. ♀ above more brownish and *conspicuously streaked dusky.* Below pale yellow *extensively*

streaked dusky; tail much as in ♂. Grassland has yellow on face and a streaked crown. ♂ *is the only yellowfinch with extensive streaking on a yellowish ground color.* Behavior as in Grassland, though less numerous and much more local; flock size never seems to be as large. Musical song a fast sputtering, e.g., "switchity, switch-you, switch-you," usually given from a perch but sometimes during a display flight. In s. Bolivia perched birds give a quite different series of drawn-out notes, e.g., "teeeeey? tcheeeuuuuuu-whit," though their twittery flight songs are more similar.

Grassland Yellowfinch
*Sicalis luteola**   PLATE 114(5)
11.5–12.5 cm (4½–5"). *Widespread and locally common* in tall grasslands, fields, and edge of marshes in Venezuela and Colombia, and south in Andes to Chile and cen. Argentina; in *Argentina and s. Brazil also occurs widely in the lowlands. Most numerous in Argentina, Uruguay, and Chile;* migrates north during austral winter. Mostly below 3000 m, but to 4100 m in Bolivia. Perhaps more than one species. ♂ of **southern birds** (illustrated) olive brownish above with dusky streaking on crown and back and *lores and ocular area bright yellow,* rump plain olive; wings and tail brownish. Below yellow, breast washed grayish olive. ♂ of **northern birds** similar but brighter yellow below. ♂ of **Andean population** (Colombia to Bolivia) like northern birds but with less yellow in ocular area. ♀♀ similar to respective ♂♂ but browner above and buffier below. Cf. the much more localized Raimondi's and Stripe-tailed Yellowfinches and also the southern form of Saffron Finch. Can occur in large flocks, especially when not breeding, but is also loosely colonial when nesting; presumed migrants sometimes fly in compact groups, often well above the ground. Feeds on the ground, but frequently perches in shrubbery and on fences. Song a series of buzzy and more musical trilled notes, often given in a hovering flight display but also from a low perch. Flight call a "tzi-tzit" or "tsip-tseep."

Raimondi's Yellowfinch
Sicalis raimondii
11.5 cm (4½"). Local, erratic, and generally uncommon on rocky slopes and in loma vegetation on *west slope of Andes in w. Peru* (Ancash to Tacna). Mostly 500–2000 m, occasionally down to sea level. Resembles Grassland Yellowfinch, but has *no yellow on lores or ocular area* (though note that sympatric Grasslands also have relatively little yellow there); also has *center of crown*

and ear-coverts gray and grayer flanks. Greenish Yellowfinch is larger and more uniformly colored. Can occur in quite large flocks and (unlike Grassland) rarely or never enters agricultural terrain. Song similar to Grassland, though apparently does not engage in a display flight.

Bright-rumped Yellowfinch
Sicalis uropygialis   PLATE 114(6)
14 cm (5½"). *Locally common in puna grassland and around buildings in Andes from n. Peru* (s. Cajamarca) *to n. Chile and nw. Argentina* (Tucumán); *generally the most numerous yellowfinch in this range and habitat.* Mostly 3500–4800 m, but to 2500 m in Chile. In **most of range** (illustrated) ♂ olive yellow above with *contrasting brownish gray mantle* and *distinctly gray cheeks;* bright yellow below with *sides and flanks gray.* ♀ duller, browner above and paler below. In **n. and cen. Peru** the gray cheeks are less well-defined, and gray on flanks is lacking altogether. Cf. the local Citron-headed Yellowfinch. Usually found in groups, sometimes large flocks when not breeding; forages on the ground, often loosely associating with other finches and furnariids. Roosts and nests in holes in banks, walls, and even buildings. Song a musical, sometimes gravelly gurgling, often with a descending effect.

Citron-headed Yellowfinch
Sicalis luteocephala   PLATE 114(7)
14 cm (5½"). Local and generally uncommon on shrubby slopes and in rocky quebradas in *Andes from w. Bolivia* (Cochabamba) *to extreme nw. Argentina* (recently found in n. Jujuy). Mostly 2800–3500 m. Attractive ♂ recalls Bright-rumped Yellowfinch (which occurs in puna grasslands at higher elevations) but has *entire face citron yellow* (no gray on cheeks), and *brownish gray of back extends up onto nape and down over rump; primaries edged bright citron,* forming a patch. Sides and flanks also broadly gray. ♀ a bit duller and browner. Ranges in small groups, with overall behavior as in Bright-rumped; likewise sometimes occurs around habitations, often feeding on small fields. Roosts and nests semicolonially on open rock faces and in crumbling walls. Pleasant, canarylike song a series of rich and musical gurgles, trills, and twitters.

Puna Yellowfinch
Sicalis lutea   PLATE 114(8)
13.5 cm (5¼"). Fairly common on arid puna grassland and adjacent shrubby slopes in *high Andes from s. Peru* (Cuzco and Arequipa) *to*

nw. Argentina (Salta). Mostly 3500–4500 m. *The most uniformly bright and yellow of the high Andean yellowfinches. Above bright yellowish olive,* yellow on rump but duskier on wings and tail. *Below bright yellow.* ♂ Greenish Yellowfinch is similar but duller olive above, especially on rump. Unlike Greenish and Bright-rumped, rarely or never found in towns. Other than that, behavior is similar.

Greenish Yellowfinch
Sicalis olivascens   PLATE 114(9)
14 cm (5½"). *Locally common* on shrubby slopes (sometimes with cactus), adjacent cultivated areas, and in towns in *Andes from n. Peru* (Ancash) *to n. Chile and w. Argentina* (Mendoza). Mostly 2000–3600 m. ♂ *dull olive above,* slightly yellower on rump. *Olive-yellow below,* midbelly yellower. ♀ like ♂ (*likewise relatively unpatterned*) but browner above (fresh plumage often streakier) and more drab grayish buff below, with only throat and midbelly yellow. Puna Yellowfinch is much brighter yellow overall and ranges higher, on altiplano. Greater Yellowfinch (overlaps some in Chile) has richer yellow on head and underparts and much more gray edging on wings. Behavior much as in other Andean yellowfinches, usually occurring in restless, wide-ranging flocks (when not breeding, sometimes large). Song a fast descending gurgling "zhree-zhree-zhree-zhree-zhree-zhree-zhreh."

Greater Yellowfinch
Sicalis auriventris   PLATE 114(10)
14.5–15 cm (5¾–6"). Fairly common in open shrubby and grassy areas and around habitations in *Andes of Chile* (Antofogasta to Talca, and south locally to Magallanes) *and adjacent w. Argentina* (Mendoza south locally to w. Santa Cruz). Mostly 1800–3000 m, lower southward and in winter. Despite its name, *not that much larger than other yellowfinches.* ♂ *head and underparts rather rich and brassy yellow;* back grayish olive, usually with some dusky mottling; wings and tail dusky, *coverts and flight feathers broadly edged gray.* ♀ duller and browner, with little yellow. *The only yellowfinch in most of its s. Andean range,* though it overlaps with Greenish at its north end; Greenish is more olive, *lacking* the gray on wings so prominent in Greater. Behavior similar to other Andean yellowfinches.

Patagonian Yellowfinch
Sicalis lebruni   PLATE 114(11)
14 cm (5½"). Uncommon on open shrubby hillsides and in gorges in *s. Argentina* (north to Río

Negro) *and far s. Chile, where the only yellow-finch present.* Mostly below 800 m. ♂ *olive above, strongly suffused with gray; wings with extensive pale grayish or whitish edging on flight feathers.* Below yellow, *sides and flanks washed pale gray.* ♀ duller, often browner above. ♂ *Melanodera* finches have much stronger patterns, while ♀♀ are much streakier. Occurs in pairs or small flocks, foraging on open ground. Favors areas with some relief, less often on open, level plains; roosts and nests in holes burrowed into banks, sometimes in groups. Pleasant song a jumbled and musical warbling, most often given near its small colonies.

Dickcissel
Spiza americana   PLATE 114(12)
15–16 cm (6–6¼"). *Boreal migrant (mostly Oct.–Apr) to open country and agricultural areas in n. Colombia and n. Venezuela; can be locally abundant on Venezuelan llanos, there favoring rice cultivation.* Mainly below 500 m. Taxonomic affinity still debated; likely allied to cardinalid "finches." **Breeding** ♂ (Mar. onward) has *gray head* with *yellow superciliary and malar;* brown above, back streaked blackish, with *rufous shoulders.* Throat white with V-shaped black bib on lower throat and chest; *breast yellow.* **Nonbreeding** ♂ less sharply patterned. ♀ duller still, with less rufous on shoulders, some streaking below; *it retains the face pattern and some yellow on chest.* Immature Saffron Finch lacks facial pattern and rufous on shoulders; ♀ Bobolink has a boldly striped head pattern, spikier tail, no yellow on chest. Cf. also ♀ House Sparrow. Gregarious, at times congregating in gigantic roosts; often flies in dense flocks. Feeds mainly on the ground. Frequent call a raspy "drrt," often given in flight; also other twitters, but rarely gives full song here. *Breeds* in United States.

Ammodramus

A trio of small, *plain* sparrows with *streaked backs* that are found in open grassy areas.

Yellow-browed Sparrow
Ammodramus aurifrons   PLATE 114(13)
13 cm (5"). *Common and widespread in grassy areas of Amazonia, extending north to along the Río Orinoco in Venezuela.* Ranges to 1300 m or more along east slope of Andes. Above brownish gray streaked dusky, with *conspicuous yellow on foreface* (especially on lores and brow); bend of wing also yellow. Below pale grayish. Grassland Sparrow lacks such prominent yellow on its face, has rufous on wing, and occurs mainly on natural savannas. This familiar bird occurs around towns, along roads, and in agricultural areas; its original habitat was apparently along rivers and on islands. It hops and feeds on the ground, also frequently perching in the open on fences and atop shrubs; usually does not associate with other birds. Song, given throughout day, a distinctive buzzy "tic, tzzzz-tzzzz," markedly different from Grassland. Also has a fast "tseew tseew tsee tsee tsee."

Grassland Sparrow
Ammodramus humeralis   PLATE 114(14)
13 cm (5"). *Widespread and locally common in savannas and grasslands from n. Colombia and Venezuela to cen. Argentina (n. Río Negro), but essentially absent from Amazonia.* Locally to 1750 m. Brownish gray above, *grayest on face and neck,* with blackish and chestnut streaking; lores (*only*) yellow, bend of wing also yellow, and with *rufous edging on inner flight feathers.* Whitish below (sometimes stained buff by soil). Yellow-browed Sparrow has more yellow on face, and voice and habitat differ dramatically. Other streaky sparrows or finches are larger; cf. also Grass Wren. Usually secretive except when singing, creeping about on the ground out of sight, flushing only a short distance and then usually disappearing again, rarely flushing a second time. Early and late in the day sometimes perches atop a shrub or on a fence; singing birds almost always do this. The high-pitched song carries far, a quite musical "eee telee, teeeee" with numerous variations.

Grasshopper Sparrow
Ammodramus savannarum
11 cm (4½"). *Now very rare and local in native grasslands of sw. Colombia (Valle) and nw. Ecuador (Pichincha). Near extirpation in South America because of conversion of most grasslands to more intensive agriculture.* To 3000 m. Recalls Grassland Sparrow (no overlap) but smaller with *tail narrower, shorter, and more pointed. Narrow coronal streak pale buff* and *prominent superciliary yellowish buff; below buff.* Behavior similar to Grassland but much more skulking. Song a high-pitched "pi-tup tzzzzzzzzz." Though weak, in calm conditions it carries far. Also: North America to Panama; Greater Antilles.

Aimophila

Two heavy-billed sparrows, both larger than *Ammodramus,* found locally in scrubby habitats.

Stripe-capped Sparrow
Aimophila strigiceps   PLATE 115(1)
16–17 cm (6¼–6¾"). Uncommon and local in arid scrub and woodland interspersed with grassy areas in *n. Argentina* (south to Córdoba), *w. Paraguay, and extreme se. Bolivia.* **Chaco birds** (illustrated) have *head and nape gray with obvious brown striping;* above brown with blackish streaking. Throat white with a *black submalar streak;* breast pale gray, belly whitish. **Western birds** similar but larger, rustier dorsally with distinct blackish preocular area. Distinctive in its limited range; cf. Rufous-collared Sparrow (with an obvious rufous collar, etc.). Found singly or in pairs (not in flocks), feeding mainly on the ground. Loud melodious song typically a repetition of a single note followed by a trilled note, e.g., "chee-chee-chee-chee, trrr."

Tumbes Sparrow
Aimophila stolzmanni   PLATE 115(2)
14.5 cm (5¾"). Fairly common but inconspicuous in arid scrub and shrubby areas from *sw. Ecuador* (Loja) *to nw. Peru* (La Libertad). To 1400 m. *Heavy bill. Head gray with brown stripes on crown and through eye;* above brown with blackish streaking, *shoulders chestnut* (often prominent) and bend of wing yellow. Throat white with a *dusky submalar streak;* below grayish white. Distinctive in its small range; cf. Rufous-collared Sparrow (with an obvious rufous collar, etc.). Found singly or in pairs, usually not with flocks; though not especially shy, tends to stay within cover and can be hard to see. Song an attractive series of 3–5 ringing metallic notes, e.g., "chew-chew-chew-chew," heard mainly in the rainy season, when it breeds.

Arremonops

Plain sparrows with *obvious dark head striping, Arremonops* range in *nw. South America,* where they favor scrub and shrubby areas.

Black-striped Sparrow
Arremonops conirostris   PLATE 115(3)
15–17 cm (6–6¾"). Fairly common in scrub, low woodland, and shrubby woodland in *n. Colom-* bia and Venezuela, and from *sw. Colombia to extreme nw. Peru* (Tumbes); also very locally in n. Brazil and se. Ecuador. To 1400 m. More than one species perhaps involved. *Head gray with black stripes on lateral crown and through eye;* otherwise olive above (brighter in **western birds,** browner in **northern birds;** much grayer in **se. Ecuador**), with yellow on bend of wing. Below whitish, grayish on sides and flanks. In nw. Venezuela cf. the much scarcer Tocuyo Sparrow. Otherwise not likely confused, but compare to certain *Buarremon* brushfinches and *Arremon* sparrows. Found singly or in pairs, hopping in low vegetation, often feeding on the ground; shy but not too hard to see. Does not join mixed flocks. Songs vary. In Colombia and Panama gives an accelerating series of notes, e.g., "cho; cho; cho, chocho-cho-cho-chochochochch"; also a series of inflected "ho-wheet" notes. In Venezuela song much more melodic, e.g., "cheeo, cheeu, cheeo-chuchuchuchuchu." In w. Ecuador usually gives a much slower "wheep? . . . chorr. . . ." In se. Ecuador very different, a more piercing "wheep-wheep-wheep-wheep" and a "whee-goree" (N. K. Krabbe recordings). Also: Honduras to Panama.

Tocuyo Sparrow
Arremonops tocuyensis
14 cm (5½"). Uncommon and local in arid scrub and low woodland in *nw. Venezuela and extreme n. Colombia.* To 1100 m, but usually below 500 m. Resembles Black-striped Sparrow (can occur with it, though Tocuyo favors drier areas). *Notably smaller,* and plumage is paler and more washed-out (especially on its more clay-colored, not so gray, head). Behavior as in better-known Black-striped. Song a short and sweet "tit, tit, ti-ti, tsuee-tsuee" (S. Hilty).

Rufous-collared Sparrow
Zonotrichia capensis   PLATE 115(4)
14–15 cm (5½–6"). *Widespread, familiar, and often very common* in a variety of open and semiopen shrubby habitats through much of South America, ranging south to Tierra del Fuego; withdraws from far south during austral winter. To 4000 m or more in the Andes, though largely avoids tropical lowlands (e.g., Amazonia). Slightly bushy crest. *Head gray with black striping,* with *contrasting rufous hindneck collar.* Above rufescent brown with black striping on back; wings with two whitish bars. Below whitish with *black patch on sides of breast.* **Southern birds** have much less bold head-striping and

thus look gray-headed; **tepui races** are dark and dingy. **Juvenile** duller and streakier, especially below, but at least a trace of the rufous collar usually shows. The unique rufous collar readily distinguishes this often ubiquitous sparrow. Frequent around habitations, even in many towns and cities; often tame, hopping and feeding on the ground, but singing from prominent perches. In some areas (especially in parts of the Andes and the far south) ranges in large flocks when not breeding. Songs vary regionally, but typically consist of 1–2 pretty, slurred whistles followed by a trill, e.g., "tee-teeoo, treeeee"; some dialects, especially in the south, lack the final trill. Calls also vary geographically, e.g., a "chip" or "chink." Also: Mexico to Panama; Hispaniola.

Whito throated Sparrow (*Z. albicollis*) is known from a vagrant collected on Aruba (possibly a ship assist).

Lincoln's Sparrow (*Melospiza lincolnii*) is known from a vagrant individual mist-netted in n. Venezuela (Aragua).

Coal-crested Finch
Charitospiza eucosma PLATE 115(5)
11.5 cm (4½"). *Uncommon and local (perhaps erratic) in cerrado of interior Brazil and extreme ne. Bolivia. To 1200 m.* Pretty ♂ has *crown and crest black* (crest usually laid flat) and *white face.* Back pale gray, wing-coverts whitish, *basal tail white* (most evident in flight). *Bib on chest black, below cinnamon-buff* (deeper on midbreast). ♀ duller and browner (lacking ♂'s black *but retaining the crest and white in tail*) with weak buff eye-stripe; below dull buff. ♂ unique, but ♀ can be confused with various ♀ seedeaters (none of which has white in tail or shows any crest). Found in pairs or small monospecific groups, mainly feeding on open ground near grassy cover. Perhaps favors recently burned areas. Usually quiet; song an infrequently heard, leisurely and sweet "cheeree-chewee, cheeree-cheewu, cheeree-chewee . . ." (N. Athanas recording).

Black-masked Finch
Coryphaspiza melanotis PLATE 115(6)
13.5 cm (5¼"). *Very local, though still common in a few places, in less-disturbed tall grassy cerrado from interior s. Brazil to ne. Argentina, and in n. Bolivia. To 1000 m. Bill bicolored, with a yellow mandible.* Handsome ♂ has a *black head* with *long white superciliary;* back brown with chestnut streaking; shoulders yellow, wing-edging yellow-olive. *Long graduated tail has*

outer feathers broadly tipped white (conspicuous in flight). *Below white,* patch on sides black. Dingier ♀ has head grayish (lacking ♂ pattern), more prominent wing-edging, less white in tail. ♂ nearly unmistakable; ♀ best recognized by the company she keeps (the obvious white in its tail helps in flushed birds). Feeds on or near the ground, but regularly perches in the open, especially early in morning and when singing. When not breeding, occurs in small groups, associating with other grassland birds. Song a weak "tsee-slee," easily passed over as an insect and hard to locate.

Embernagra

Two *large, predominantly olive* finches with *orangy bills* found in southern grasslands and scrub.

Pale-throated Serra Finch
Embernagra longicauda PLATE 115(7)
21.5 cm (8½"). *Uncommon and local in grassy scrub with palms and ground bromeliads on serras of e. Brazil* (Bahia and Minas Gerais). 700–1300 m. Bill mostly yellowish orange. *Head gray* with *white supraloral streak and lower eyelid;* olive above, flight feathers and long tail edged brighter olive. *Throat white* outlined by a gray malar streak; below pale grayish. Potentially sympatric form of Great Pampa Finch has a shorter and less graduated tail, more olive head with no white facial markings, and *lacks* white on throat. Rather shy, occurring in pairs and usually staying within cover, though ♂♂ typically sing from exposed perches. Song a loud and penetrating "tsi, tsoweeé," repeated steadily at intervals of 4–5 seconds.

Great Pampa Finch
Embernagra platensis PLATE 115(8)
20.5–23 cm (8–9"). Locally common in (usually) damp areas with tall grass, often also a scattering of shrubs, from *n. Bolivia* (Beni) *to se. Brazil* (north to s. Minas Gerais) *and cen. Argentina* (Río Negro). Mostly below 2500 m, locally to 3500 m in Andes. *Bill mostly yellowish orange* (*more orange in western birds*). In **most of range** (illustrated) *head olive gray, duskier on face; above olive* with back streaked blackish and yellowish olive wing-edging. *Mostly pale grayish below.* **Andean birds** (Cochabamba, Bolivia, to Mendoza, Argentina; possibly a separate species) *lack* back streaking. Wedge-tailed

Grassfinch has a longer and more pointed tail, is not as gray on face and underparts. In e. Brazil, cf. the very local Pale-throated Serra Finch. Found in pairs or small family groups, not associating with other birds. More conspicuous than Wedge-tailed, regularly perching atop grass clumps or on fences or shrubs, even during midday. Flight weak and jerky, often with feet dangling. Song a gurgling, musical phrase, e.g., "gledit, gledit, gleeu" or "glee glo-weét," sometimes ending in a sputter; in highlands sharper and more emphatic.

Emberizoides

A trio of fairly large finches with *very long pointed tails* found in *grassy open country,* mainly in lowlands.

Wedge-tailed Grassfinch

Emberizoides herbicola   PLATE 115(9)

18–20 cm (7–8"). *Widespread and locally common* in less-disturbed, taller grasslands, often with scattered bushes, from Colombia and Venezuela to ne. Argentina, but absent from Amazonia. To 1500 m. *Tail very long, graduated and pointed.* Bill mostly yellow. *Above brownish olive with prominent black streaking,* lores and eyering whitish; wings more olive with yellow bend of wing. Whitish below, sides and flanks tinged buff. **Northern birds** (illustrated) are slightly smaller than those from south of Amazon. Great Pampa Finch is larger with a less spiky tail, grayer head and breast, and shows less streaking above. Generally inconspicuous, feeding mostly on the ground and remaining within cover, though especially in early morning it often perches on fences or atop shrubs or grass clumps. Song variable and quite musical, that of northern birds a "tee, teedelee," that of southern birds a "jew-lee, jew-lu" or "jew jew-leéu, ju-leéu." Also gives buzzier or more chattered songs, sometimes in a flight display. Also: Costa Rica and Panama.

Duida Grassfinch

Emberizoides duidae

21 cm (8¼"). *Recorded only from remote Cerro Duida in s. Amazonas, Venezuela.* 1300–2100 m. Resembles much more widespread Wedge-tailed Grassfinch (which does not occur at high elevations on Cerro Duida), but *larger* with a *proportionately longer tail;* darker above, especially on crown and tail, with duskier forecrown and lores. Apparently still unknown in life.

Lesser Grassfinch

Emberizoides ypiranganus   PLATE 115(10)

17–18 cm (6¾–7"). *Uncommon and local in marshes and damp grassy areas in se. Brazil* (mainly north to São Paulo), e. Paraguay, and ne. Argentina (mainly Corrientes). To 900 m. Resembles much more numerous Wedge-tailed Grassfinch (which favors better-drained grasslands, though the two can occur together), but slimmer and *smaller.* Shows more contrast above, with *heavier and blacker streaking on a paler ground color; cheeks and especially loral area darker and grayer, contrasting with white throat;* lower flanks and crissum darker, with blackish streaks. Behavior much as in Wedge-tailed, but song very different and less musical, a fast nasal chattering "ch, ch, ch-ch-ch-ch-ch-ch-ch-ch," somewhat recalling a Grass Wren.

Long-tailed Reedfinch

Donacospiza albifrons   PLATE 115(11)

15 cm (6"). *Uncommon in reedbeds, damp grasslands, and shrubbery near water from se. Brazil* to ne. Argentina (Buenos Aires), also locally in n. Bolivia (Beni). To at least 1300 m. *Rather long slender tail.* Brown above with *superciliary and crescent under eye white,* and *dark grayish cheeks;* back streaked dusky, and shoulders bluish gray. *Below uniform buff.* ♀ has more streaking above. Wedge-tailed and Lesser Grassfinches have more obvious streaking on back, yellow-olive edging on wings and tail. Recalls warbling finch, except that its habitat is mainly grassy and the long tail differs radically. Cf. various warbling finches and ♀ Black-masked Finch (limited overlap). Usually in pairs; though often inconspicuous, does sometimes perch atop grass clumps or on bushes. Fast, spritely song a series of paired notes repeated in an almost random fashion; closely resembles Black-and-rufous Warbling Finch (indeed, they can even respond to each other's songs).

Many-colored Chaco Finch

Saltatricula multicolor   PLATE 115(12)

18 cm (7"). *Common in grassy borders of chaco scrub and woodland from se. Bolivia* (s. Santa Cruz) to n. Argentina (San Luis and Entre Ríos) and w. Uruguay. Mostly below 500 m. This species is apparently most closely allied to the tanagers. Bill mostly yellow. Sandy brown above with *prominent white postocular stripe* and *black mask extending from foreface down over sides of neck; tail rather long and graduated, outer feathers broadly tipped white.* Midthroat white, *gray on sides of neck and chest, sides and flanks broadly*

pinkish buff. This handsome and unmistakable chaco endemic is found in pairs or (especially when not breeding) small groups, and often associates with Red Pileated Finches. Feeds mostly on the ground, when disturbed flushing up into low bushes with a flash of white. Spiritless song a fast "weea-weea-weea," often repeated monotonously through the heat of the day, when few other birds are singing.

Lophospingus

Two distinctive, *mostly gray* finches that sport *unmistakable upstanding crests, Lophospingus* range in open, scrubby habitats of interior s. South America.

Black-crested Finch
Lophospingus pusillus   PLATE 115(13)
14 cm (5½"). *Uncommon and local in chaco scrub and low woodland in se. Bolivia* (north to s. Santa Cruz), *w. Paraguay, and nw. Argentina* (south to n. San Luis and w. Córdoba). Mostly below 1000 m. Bill mostly yellowish flesh. *Conspicuous upstanding black crest.* Dapper ♂ has *head and midthroat black,* with *broad white superciliary and malar area.* Above otherwise gray; wing-coverts tipped whitish, *tail with large white corners* (conspicuous in flight). Mostly pale gray below. ♀'s head pattern less crisp (*though it retains the crest*), and upperparts tinged brownish. Usually in small flocks (especially when not breeding), sometimes associating with other chaco birds; feeds on the ground or at roadsides. Seems to favor areas with sandy soil.

Gray-crested Finch
Lophospingus griseocristatus   PLATE 115(14)
14 cm (5½"). *Locally common in arid scrub and adjacent fields in highlands of w. Bolivia* (north to s. La Paz) *and nw. Argentina* (Salta and Jujuy, where it is rarer). 1500–3100 m. Bill mostly yellowish flesh. *Conspicuous upstanding gray crest. Mainly gray,* slightly paler below with white midbelly; wings and tail duskier, *with large white tail corners* (conspicuous in flight). Other finches may be gray, but this is the only one sporting a spikelike crest. Behavior much as in Black-crested Finch, likewise foraging mainly on the ground, often in the open. Usually quiet; monotonous song heard infrequently, and a simple series of melodious phrases, recalling a warbling finch.

Coryphospingus

Two small finches found in scrub and open woodland, ♂♂ *with distinctive flat, black-bordered crests.* Otherwise they are very similar, one basically gray, the other reddish.

Gray Pileated Finch
Coryphospingus pileatus   PLATE 115(15)
13 cm (5"). Uncommon to fairly common in arid scrub and low woodland, and shrubby borders of deciduous and semihumid woodland in *n. Venezuela and w. and n. Colombia,* and in *e. Brazil* (west to s. Mato Grosso). To 1000 m. ♂ has *black crown partially concealing a scarlet coronal stripe* (can be exposed as a crest, with black flaring to sides). *Above pale gray* with white eye-ring; whitish below, tinged gray on breast and sides. ♀ lacks black and red in crown, but otherwise like ♂ (*including eye-ring*); has some grayish streaking below. ♀ seedeaters are browner and have thicker bills. Often in small groups, especially when not breeding; usually forages on the ground, at edge or inside cover. Simple leisurely song a fairly melodic phrase repeated several times, quite similar to Red Pileated.

Red Pileated Finch
Coryphospingus cucullatus   PLATE 115(16)
13.5 cm (5¼"). *Common* (especially in the chaco region) in scrub and woodland and agricultural areas from *s. Brazil to n. Argentina* (n. San Luis and n. Buenos Aires), with outlying populations in arid intermontane valleys north to extreme s. Ecuador and lower Amaz. Brazil. Mostly below 1500 m, but to 2000 m locally in Cuzco, Peru. Sometimes called Red-crested Finch. ♂ has *crown and crest as in Gray Pileated Finch. Dark vinous red above,* rump more crimson; eyering white. *Below dull crimson.* ♀ like ♂ but lacks black and red on crown and is browner above; *retains the narrow eye-ring. Below rosy pink,* throat whitish. This small finch is the most uniformly reddish of any in its wide range; the eye-ring helps to identify duller ♀♀. When not breeding it gathers in large loose flocks, sometimes joining other species. Forages mostly on the ground. Song a simple phrase repeated 3–6 times, usually with short initial and final notes, e.g., "chewit, weet-chewit, weet-chewit, weet-chewit. . . ."

NEW WORLD BLACKBIRDS: ICTERIDAE

A varied family of midsized to quite large passerines found widely across South America, some species in forest and woodland, others in open grassy areas or even marshes. Often colorful, icterids are characterized by their strong feet and many by their long and pointed bills; some are sexually dimorphic in plumage, and in others ♂♂ are much larger than ♀♀. Many weave pouch-shaped nests, large and conspicuous in the oropendolas and caciques. Some of the latter are colonial breeders, as too are certain other icterids.

Sturnella

Attractive chunky blackbirds, *often conspicuous in grasslands and open shrubby areas.* ♂♂ are usually more colorful, with *bright red or yellow on underparts;* ♀♀ duller and browner. Bills range from rather long and pointed to more conical. They feed mainly on the ground, consuming both seeds and insects.

Eastern Meadowlark
Sturnella magna   PLATE 116(1)
21.5–23 cm (8½–9"). Fairly common in grasslands and pastures from *Colombia to the Guianas and lower Amaz. Brazil.* To 3000–3500 m in Andes. *Chunky, with long pointed bill and short tail. Crown with bold blackish striping,* face grayish; above brown with buff and blackish streaking. *Lores and underparts bright yellow, breast crossed by a broad black V. Outer tail feathers mostly white,* flashing in flight. *The only meadowlark with yellow below.* Feeds on the ground, often flicking tail; crouches when alarmed. Generally not gregarious. Flushes abruptly, with typical flight a series of shallow flaps on bowed wings. Most conspicuous when singing, then often atop a shrub, low tree, or fence post. Variable song typically a simple series of 3–5 whistled slurred notes (resembles Western Meadowlark, *S. neglecta,* more than Eastern Meadowlark in North America). Call a burry "drrt." Also: North and Middle America (all same species?).

Long-tailed Meadowlark
Sturnella loyca   PLATE 116(2)
24–25.5 cm (9½–10"). Common in grasslands,

pastures, and Patagonian steppes in *Argentina and Chile.* To at least 2500 m in nw. Argentina. *The largest and longest-tailed meadowlark, with a long bill.* ♂ above brown streaked blackish, blackest on sides of head and neck, lores red and superciliary white; *underwing-coverts whitish. Below red;* sides, flanks and lower belly blackish. ♀ paler generally with no red on lores. *Throat white;* below grayish streaked dusky, midbreast and belly variably tinged pinkish. Not likely confused in its bleak, often sparsely vegetated surroundings, where it is one of the few really colorful birds. Cf. much rarer Pampas Meadowlark. General behavior much as in Eastern Meadowlark, though more gregarious when not breeding, then sometimes gathering in flocks of 50 or more; flight stronger and more direct. Perches freely in shrubs and low trees. Singing ♂♂ take to an elevated perch; song consists of several short melodic notes followed by a longer wheezier one, e.g., "tshwit, tshwit, tshu-tshee? zheeeuww." Has no display flight.

Pampas Meadowlark
Sturnella defilippii   PLATE 116(3)
21 cm (8¼"). *Now very rare and local in natural grasslands of e. Argentina* (believed to breed only in s. Buenos Aires province) *and Uruguay* (known to breed only at one site in the northwest); possible migratory status unclear. Numbers much reduced because of the conversion of most native grassland to more intensive agricultural pursuits. To 600 m. Resembles much more numerous Long-tailed Meadowlark, which *ranges mostly to the south and west. Smaller, with a finer bill and shorter tail.* ♂ has *blacker upperparts, sides, flanks, and lower belly,* and *black*

underwing-coverts (white in Long-tailed); *on perched birds more red shows at bend of wing.* ♀♀ are closely similar, but ♀ Pampas is blacker generally (beware fresh-plumaged birds in which brown is more prominent), especially on belly, and has a buffier throat; *underwing-coverts black.* Somewhat gregarious even when nesting, forming loose colonies in less-disturbed grasslands. Less likely than Long-tailed to perch conspicuously. ♂♂ often sing while partially hidden in grass, also in a display flight when they ascend 5– 10 m, then glide back; unlike Long-tailed, rarely or never sings from an exposed perch. Song itself is more melodic and less wheezy, with flight song often ending in a pretty trill.

Peruvian Meadowlark
Sturnella bellicosa
20.5 cm (8"). Locally common in cultivated re gions and grassy or shrubby areas from *w. Ecuador* (north to w. Esmeraldas and Cotopaxi) *and extreme sw. Colombia* (recently confirmed to occur in sw. Nariño) *to n. Chile; the only meadowlark in this region.* Locally to 3000 m in Ecuador. Resembles larger Long-tailed Meadowlark (no overlap) but has shorter bill and shorter tail. ♂ has whitish (not black) thighs. ♀♀ similar in plumage, but Peruvian's throat buffier. Behavior similar to Long-tailed, but ♂♂ often engage in a flight display (though they mainly sing while perched). Song a simple "tee tuu tzzzzzz," with variations; call a sharp "chak."

White-browed Blackbird
Sturnella superciliaris   PLATE 116(4)
18 cm (7"). Locally common in grasslands and lusher pastures (often where damp) *mainly from n. Bolivia and e. Brazil to n. Argentina.* To 2500 m in Andean valleys. ♂ black above with *prominent white postocular stripe;* bend of wing red (obvious in flight). *Throat and breast bright red,* belly black. Fresh-plumaged birds have feathers edged brownish, obscuring the black and red, though *the postocular is always obvious.* ♀ streaked blackish and buff above with *long pale buff superciliary and coronal stripe.* Buff below, streaked dusky across chest and on belly, *suffused pink on breast.* Cf. similar Red-breasted Blackbird (known to overlap only in se. Peru). Compared with other meadowlarks, smaller with shorter bill. Gregarious; even when nesting occurs in loose colonies where conditions are favorable, though ♂♂ do defend a territory. Regularly perches on fences and forages around cattle. Frequent in agricultural regions, having

adapted to lush fertilized pastures better than most birds. ♂'s song is given in flight, a buzzy trill followed by a series of "chuk" notes, the buzz as it ascends, the terminal notes as it descends. Both sexes give a "chuk" call.

Red-breasted Blackbird
Sturnella militaris
18.5 cm (7¼"). Locally common in grasslands and lusher pastures from *Colombia and Venezuela to Amazonia,* replacing the similar White-browed Blackbird northward. To 1600 m. ♂ *lacks white brow,* but ♀ cannot be distinguished from White-browed in the field. Behavior as in White-browed. ♂'s song, likewise usually given in flight, is similar, but the series of "chuk" notes typically *precedes* the buzzy trill (rather than following it). Also: Costa Rica and Panama.

Bobolink
Dolichonyx oryzivorus   PLATE 116(5)
18 cm (7"). *Boreal winter resident* (mostly Sep.– Apr.) in marshes, rice fields, and damp pastures with tall grass, *mainly from n. and e. Bolivia to n. Argentina;* a transient northward. Mostly below 500 m, transients higher. *Pointed tail feathers.* ♀ and nonbreeding ♂ streaked buffy brown and blackish above with *bold buff and dusky head striping.* *Yellowish buff below* with sparse blackish flank streaking. Breeding plumage ♂ (seen on northward passage, attained as buff feather tips wear off) *black with a golden buff nuchal collar, broad white scapulars,* and *large white rump patch.* ♀ White-browed and Red-breasted Blackbirds lack the spiky tail feathers, have longer bills, and generally show a pink tinge below. Gregarious, occurring in groups when migrating; on wintering grounds at times in large flocks. Feeding birds associate with *Sporophila* and other seed-eating birds; on wintering grounds eats considerable rice and locally considered a pest. Call a distinctive metallic "pink," often given in flight; during northward passage ♂♂ can erupt into snatches of their exuberant bubbling song. Breeds in North America.

Oriole Blackbird
Gymnomystax mexicanus   PLATE 116(6)
♂ 30.5 cm (12"); ♀ 26.5 cm (10½"). Fairly common in open grassy areas, generally near water, in *Venezuela and ne. Colombia, and along Amazon River and its major tributaries upriver to e. Ecuador and ne. Peru.* Mostly below 1000 m. A *large, black and yellow* blackbird. Bare ocular area and short malar streak black. *Mainly*

rich yellow with *contrasting black back, wings, and tail.* Juvenile less golden, with a black cap, browner back. Venezuelan and Orange-backed Troupials are both much more orange, etc. Cf. also ♂ Yellow-hooded Blackbird. Conspicuous, ranging in pairs or small flocks; forages primarily on the ground, but sometimes perches on snags. Generally does not associate with other birds. Unmusical song, not heard too often, a series of strange wheezy notes, e.g., "zzhhrreéo, zhreo-zhréw." Call a sharp ringing "kring!"

Scarlet-headed Blackbird
Amblyramphus holosericeus   PLATE 116(7)
24 cm (9½"). *Uncommon and local in extensive marshes from s. Brazil* (Mato Grosso do Sul and Rio Grande do Sul) *to ne. Argentina* (Buenos Aires) and in *n. Bolivia* (Beni to n. Santa Cruz). To 600 m in Bolivia. Unmistakable. Bill long, slender, and sharply pointed. *Black* with *brilliant scarlet head, neck, and breast;* thighs also scarlet. Juvenile all black, but it soon acquires red on throat and breast, which gradually spreads onto head. Strictly confined to reedbeds, and even there thinly spread, with pairs holding large territories; gathers in small groups when not breeding, sometimes associating with other icterids. Breeding ♂♂ are conspicuous, perching atop reeds or on adjacent shrubs. Loud, ringing song a clear and melodic "cleer-cleer-clur, clululu."

Pseudoleistes

A distinctive pair of rather large *brown and yellow* icterids with fairly long pointed bills, usually found near water, in *s. South America.*

Yellow-rumped Marshbird
Pseudoleistes guirahuro   PLATE 116(8)
23.5 cm (9¼"). Uncommon to fairly common in grassy areas near water, marshes, and adjacent agricultural fields from *s. Brazil* (Goiás) *to ne. Argentina* (Santa Fé and Corrientes) *and Uruguay.* To 1300 m in s. Brazil. *Brown above* with *yellow patch on rump* and on lesser wing-coverts (visible especially in flight). Throat and chest dark brown, *below bright yellow.* Brown-and-yellow Marshbird (limited overlap) lacks yellow on rump and has extensively dark flanks. Cf. also ♀ of rare Saffron-cowled Blackbird. Forages principally on the ground adjacent to the marshes where it nests and roosts. Frequently in small flocks, sometimes associating with other

blackbirds such as Chopis. Often noisy, with a loud and rich gurgling song that will draw attention to a flock flying past, or to birds that may be hidden in tall grass.

Brown-and-yellow Marshbird
Pseudoleistes virescens   PLATE 116(9)
23.5 cm (9¼"). Fairly common to common in and around marshes, mainly in *ne. Argentina and Uruguay.* Below 300 m. *Brown above and on throat and chest,* with yellow on lesser wing-coverts. *Below bright yellow,* with *dark brown flanks.* Yellow-rumped Marshbird has a yellow rump patch and lacks the dark flanks; it replaces Brown-and-yellow northward, with some overlap. Behavior like Yellow-rumped, and like it always conspicuous. In zone of overlap sometimes forages with it, though Brown-and-yellow rarely ventures as far from water. Quite vocal, giving a variety of chattering calls and songs, sometimes en masse as a flock; most frequent is a "chirr-wii," with chatters and whistles intermixed to compose the song.

Lampropsar, Gnorimposar, Curaeus, Agelaioides, and *Dives*

Six species of *all-black* icterids, most of them allopatric, are classified, on the basis of structural characters, in no fewer than five genera. Despite their external dissimilarity, the Bolivian Blackbird and the Baywing (formerly considered a cowbird) are now classified in the same genus, *Agelaioides;* the Baywing account follows the true cowbirds (*Molothrus*).

Velvet-fronted Grackle
Lampropsar tanagrinus   PLATE 117(1)
♂ 21.5–23.5 cm (8½–9¼"); ♀ 19–21 cm (7½–8¼"). *Local and generally uncommon in várzea forest, along rivers, and around forested lakes from e. Venezuela to n. Bolivia and w. Amaz. Brazil.* To 400 m. A *slender* blackbird with a *long tail* and fairly short bill. *Entirely black,* some races glossed with blue or violet; *forecrown feathers plushlike* ("velvet" hard to see in the field). Pale-eyed Blackbird (even more local) has a straw-colored eye. Solitary Cacique is larger with whitish bill. Can also be confused with chestnut-shouldered Epaulet Oriole; the oriole's tail is equally long, and its epaulets are so dark as to often not be obvious. Ranges in flocks of 10–20 birds, foraging in foliage and even coming down

to water; can be acrobatic. Sometimes accompanies birds such as caciques. Flock members give chuckling calls; the variable song is a fast, rich gurgling, e.g., "chuh-duh-duhree, chá-chá" or "gluk-gluk-glí-gluk."

Chopi Blackbird
Gnorimopsar chopi   PLATE 117(2)
23–24 cm (9–9½"). *A familiar and usually common blackbird of semiopen and agricultural terrain from n. Bolivia and ne. Brazil to ne. Argentina.* Mostly below 1000 m. Fairly short bill has an *inconspicuous but diagnostic diagonal groove on lower mandible.* Glossy black; *feathers of crown and nape narrow and pointed,* often imparting a hackled effect. In e. Brazil cf. the much rarer Forbes's Blackbird; in Bolivia cf. Bolivian Blackbird (ranges at higher elevations). ♂ Shiny Cowbird is much glossier; Screaming Cowbird has less pointed bill, etc. Often tame and conspicuous, parading about on the ground or lawns, or perching in shade trees around buildings. Regularly in small noisy flocks that often roost in palms. Does not associate with cattle. A variety of loud and musical calls, sometimes given as a medley by a flock, even during heat of day (also often in the predawn). Calls include a repeated single "peer," "pur-peer" (or "chopi"), or "chup," sometimes preceding its breaking into a rich gurgled song.

Forbes's Blackbird
Curaeus forbesi
♂ 24 cm (9½"); ♀ 21.5 cm (8½"). *Now very rare and local around forest-fringed lakes and marshes in e. Brazil* (only in Minas Gerais and Alagoas). To 600 m. Closely resembles Chopi Blackbird and can occur with it. Sootier black (not as glossy), more slender, and *the longer and more pointed bill lacks Chopi's diagonal groove on lower mandible. Mouth lining red* (black in Chopi); surprisingly, this can often be seen in singing birds. Occurs in small groups, especially when not breeding; forages mainly on the ground. Noisy, with vocalizations very different from Chopi. Song a repeated "tit-tit-ti-ti-lit," sometimes ending with a buzzy note 1 or 2 seconds long, given as ♂ throws its head back and opens the bill wide (A. Whittaker recording).

Austral Blackbird
Curaeus curaeus   PLATE 117(3)
♂ 26.5 cm (10½"); ♀ 24 cm (9½"). Fairly common in forest and woodland borders and agricultural areas with shrubbery and trees from

cen. and s. Chile (mostly from Coquimbo south) *and adjacent Argentina to Tierra del Fuego.* To about 1500 m. Bill long and pointed. *Glossy black;* crown and nape feathers narrow and pointed (less evident than in the Chopi). *The only true blackbird in its range.* Gregarious and usually seen in small flocks, except when pairs separate out while nesting. Mainly arboreal, but also drops to the ground to feed, even inside forest. Vocalizations are varied and musical; song a series of Chopi Blackbird–like phrases, often slowly delivered with long intervals, though this can be masked when several birds sing at once.

Molothrus

Fairly small, short-billed blackbirds that are gregarious in open country. One, the Giant, is much larger; it was formerly separated in the monotypic genus *Scaphidura*. Most are **brood parasites** on other birds. One species (*badius*) formerly placed in this genus has recently been shown not to be a true cowbird; rather, it is allied to the Bolivian Blackbird.

Screaming Cowbird
Molothrus rufoaxillaris   PLATE 117(4)
19 cm (7½"). Uncommon in open areas and light woodland from *Bolivia and s. Brazil to cen. Argentina* (Rio Negro); *spreading northward.* Mostly below 500 m, wandering higher. *Lustrous black with slight greenish blue sheen;* rufous axillars visible only in the hand. Juvenile resembles Baywing, but quickly shows some dark feathers of adult plumage. Closely resembles ♂ Shiny Cowbird, but *bill shorter and stouter* (looks snub-nosed) and lacks Shiny's violet gloss. Behavior similar to Shiny, during non-breeding season sometimes associating with it. Rarely in large flocks, and though it feeds mainly on the ground, it assembles around cattle only infrequently. An obligate brood parasite on the Baywing in most of its range, though in Brazil it also parasitizes the Chopi Blackbird, a behavioral shift that has permitted it to expand into heretofore unoccupied areas. ♂'s distinctive song a brief, explosive "zhhleeee," often given as it fluffs neck feathers. ♀ gives a harsh buzzy rattle (A. Jaramillo).

Shiny Cowbird
Molothrus bonariensis   PLATE 117(5)
18–21.5 cm (7–8½"), northeastern birds smallest. *Widespread and often common* in semi-

open and agricultural terrain from Colombia
and Venezuela to cen. Chile and cen. Argentina
(Chubut); scarcer and more local in Amazonia.
Mostly below 2000 m. ♂ *glossy purplish black,*
gloss strongest on head and foreneck. ♀ *dingy
gray to brownish gray,* paler below, palest in **sw.
Ecuador and w. Peru;** many birds show a vague
pale postocular streak. Juvenile resembles ♀ but
is more yellowish below with blurry streaking.
Various blackbirds are larger and less glossy than
♂ Shiny; their bills are longer and more pointed.
Cf. Screaming Cowbird. *Usually occurs in flocks,
where the sexual dimorphism is a helpful identification clue;* other similar blackbirds show *no*
dimorphism. Forages mainly on the ground,
often holding tail angled upward; in many areas
frequent among cattle. Roosts can be large, and
are often in rice fields. A brood parasite on various passerine birds. Song a musical twittering,
often given by several ♂♂ together, heads arched
and neck feathers ruffled. Also: Panama, West
Indies, and extreme se. United States; spreading
northward.

Bronze-brown Cowbird

Molothrus armenti*
18.5–19 cm (7¼–7½"). *Uncommon and very local
in arid scrub and semiopen areas along Caribbean
coast of n. Colombia* (Salamanca Natl. Park area).
Iris orange. Mostly lustrous dark bronzy brown
with obvious neck ruff, ♀ slightly smaller and
duller. ♂ Shiny Cowbird is obviously black (not
brown) and has a dark eye; it occurs with (and
outnumbers) the Bronze-brown. Their behavior is much the same. Song a "eez-eez-dzlee"
(A. Jaramillo).

Giant Cowbird

Molothrus oryzivorus*   PLATE 117(6)
♂ 37 cm (14½"); ♀ 32 cm (12½"). *Widespread
and locally not uncommon* in forest borders and
adjacent open areas from Colombia and Venezuela to extreme n. Argentina and s. Brazil.
Mostly below 1000 m, in w. Ecuador to 2000 m.
Iris usually orange. ♂ glossy purplish black with
a *conspicuous ruff on neck, imparting a small-
headed effect.* ♀ sootier, with ruff less evident.
Even the ♀ is *much larger than other cowbirds.*
Frequently seen flying high in the sky, and can
be recognized by the *distinctly undulating flight*
(several quick flaps alternating with the wings
closed on the body). Feeds mainly on the ground
in open terrain (in Amazonia often on riverbanks), sometimes in small groups; occasionally
accompanies cattle. Also sometimes feeds in the

forest canopy. ♀♀ linger around nesting colonies
of oropendolas and caciques, on which Giant is
an obligate brood parasite. Notably quiet. Also:
Mexico to Panama.

Baywing

Agelaioides badius*   PLATE 117(7)
18.5 cm (7¼"). *Locally common* in semiopen
areas, agricultural terrain, and light woodland
from *n. Bolivia to cen. Argentina* (e. Río Negro
and ne. Chubut), and in *ne. Brazil.* Mostly below
1000 m, but locally to 3500 m or more in nw.
Argentina. Formerly called Bay-winged Cowbird and placed in genus *Molothrus.* In **main
part of range** (illustrated) *ashy brownish gray*
with *ocular area blackish* and *contrasting rufous
wings.* In **ne. Brazil** *notably paler,* browner above
and buffier below, with wings cinnamon-rufous.
No similar bird shows such contrasting rufous
wings; cf. juvenile Screaming Cowbird (a brood
parasite on Baywing), which when very young
resembles it. Almost always in small flocks,
sometimes feeding with Shiny Cowbirds, like
them mainly on the ground. Unlike the true
cowbirds, Baywings are *not* brood parasites;
rather, pairs construct their own nests or they
appropriate nests of other species (most often
covered nests). Helpers are often present, de-
fending against (parasitic) Screaming Cowbirds.
Song, given in concert by flock members, a series
of whistled notes on varying pitches, sounding
off-key. Call a simple "chuk."

Bolivian Blackbird

Agelaioides oreopsar*   PLATE 117(8)
23 cm (9"). Uncommon in arid intermontane
valleys in *Andes of Bolivia* (Cochabamba to
w. Chuquisaca). Mostly 1500–3000 m. Formerly
named *Oreopsar bolivianus.* Sooty black, *flight
feathers browner.* Resembles Chopi Blackbird
but *lacks hackles,* and slightly shorter bill *lacks*
groove on lower mandible; note that *Chopi
ranges only at lower elevations.* Forages in pairs
and small flocks, mainly on the ground but also
at cactus flowers and in *Tillandsia* moss. Sometimes roosts in trees, but apparently nests only
on cliffs. Gives various loud calls, notably a clear
"chu-pee" in flight and a series of sharp "chip"
and "chu-pit" notes that serve as a song.

Scrub Blackbird

Dives warszewiczi   PLATE 117(9)
♂ 24–28 cm (9½–11"); ♀ 23–26.5 cm (9–10½"),
northern birds smaller (illustrated; south to
Lambayeque, Peru). Conspicuous and locally

common in scrub, woodland borders, agricultural terrain, and settled areas from *nw. Ecuador* (Esmeraldas) *to sw. Peru* (Ica). Mostly below 1000 m, locally higher. *Glossy black,* ♀ slightly duller. *The only true blackbird in its range;* in Ecuador spreading and increasing because of deforestation. Forages mostly on the ground but perches freely in trees; seen in pairs or at most small flocks. Frequent song is loud and ringing, a series of melodious notes, e.g., "wr-tzzzeeét! worgleeo, wor-gleeo-glezeé." Singing birds bob up and down on their long legs. Oft-heard call a siskinlike "clee."

Saffron-cowled Blackbird
Xanthopsar flavus *　　　　　　PLATE 117(10)
18.5 cm (7¼"). *Now rare and local in open rolling, grassy terrain with marshy swales from ne. Argentina* (mainly ne. Corrientes and se. Entre Ríos) *to extreme se. Brazil* (s. Santa Catarina and Rio Grande do Sul). Declining because of the conversion of much of its habitat to more intensive agriculture, including exotic tree plantations. To 1000 m. ♂ has *head, rump, and underparts a rich golden yellow; lores, nape, mantle, and tail glossy black;* lesser wing-coverts also yellow. ♀ olive brown above streaked dusky, rump and lesser wing-coverts yellowish; *superciliary and underparts yellow.* Usually in flocks, where the presence of the unmistakable ♂♂ will serve to identify their somewhat drabber consorts. Cf. ♀ Unicolored Blackbird. Flocks often contain 10–20 birds (formerly they were larger) that forage while walking on open ground, sometimes with other icterids such as *Pseudoleistes* marshbirds. At least in Rio Grande do Sul, Brazil, flocks habitually associate with pairs of Black-and-white Monjitas, which appear to lead the blackbirds. Short, high-pitched song consists of squeaky notes followed by a buzz.

Chrysomus and *Agelasticus*

Rather small, *mainly black* icterids, with straight, sharply pointed bills, that *favor marshes.* Their black plumage is *usually relieved by some bright color, most often yellow.* Both genera were recently separated from *Agelaius,* whose members are now considered to range only in North America. *Agelasticus* species have thin bills and are more colonial, with ♂♂ attracting ♀♀ through nest building.

Yellow-hooded Blackbird
Chrysomus icterocephalus *　　　　PLATE 117(11)
18–18.5 cm (7–7¼"). Locally common in freshwater marshes, adjacent wet grasslands, and rice fields from *n. Colombia and Venezuela to Amazonia.* Mostly below 500 m, but in Colombia's E. Andes at 2200–2600 m. Unmistakable ♂ black with *bright yellow hood;* lores also black. ♀ olive brown above streaked dusky, superciliary yellowish. *Throat yellow,* breast olive, belly duskier. **Andean** ♀ is darker overall. Does not occur with any other *Chrysomus* blackbird. Rather gregarious, occurring in small flocks (larger at roosts); nests semicolonially. Rarely strays far from water; often hops on floating vegetation. Song a wheezy, unmusical "gleeo, gleeeeyr."

Red-winged Blackbird (*Agelaius phoeniceus*) has occurred as a vagrant on Trinidad.

Chestnut-capped Blackbird
Chrysomus ruficapillus *　　　　PLATE 117(12)
18.5 cm (7¼"). Locally common in freshwater marshes and other wet situations as well as in and around rice fields from *e. Amaz. Brazil to n. Argentina* (n. Buenos Aires). Mostly below 500 m. ♂ glossy black, with *crown and throat chestnut* (darker from **s. Brazil and Bolivia southward,** as illustrated). *Nondescript* ♀ dark olivaceous brown above with obscure blackish streaking; *foreneck buffy fawn,* below dull olivaceous. ♂'s chestnut is so dark that it can be hard to discern. Dull, dark ♀ lacks the prominent streaking shown by most other *Chrysomus.* Gregarious, occurring in flocks year-round; nests colonially. Rarely far from water, though it does forage in adjacent open and agricultural areas; locally considered a pest on rice. Song a drawn-out, descending "chree-chree-chrrrr." Also gives sweet, canarylike whistles and trills.

Yellow-winged Blackbird
Agelasticus thilius *　　　　　　PLATE 117(13)
18–18.5 cm (7–7¼"). Locally common in marshes and adjacent grassland in *Andes from s. Peru* (Cuzco) *to cen. Chile and s. Argentina* (Santa Cruz); in Chile and Argentina mainly in *lowlands;* vacates the extreme south during austral winter. To 4000 m. ♂ black with *yellow lesser wing-coverts* (also underwing-coverts), often hidden at rest but obvious in flight. ♀ streaked brown and blackish above with *prominent pale superciliary* (reduced in **altiplano birds**) and yellow bend of wing and underwing-coverts. Below pale grayish brown *prominently streaked*

blackish. ♀ more streaked than other ♀ blackbirds; cf. especially ♀ Chestnut-capped. Behavior much as in Yellow-hooded Blackbird. Song a drawn-out, descending "chree-layyy" (rhymes with "Chile" in Spanish).

Unicolored Blackbird
*Agelasticus cyanopus**   PLATE 117(14)
19 cm (7½"). Locally fairly common to common in freshwater marshes and the margins of shallow ponds and lakes from *n. Bolivia and s. Brazil to n. Argentina* (n. Buenos Aires) and in *lower Amaz. Brazil.* To 500 m. Especially numerous in Brazilian pantanal. ♂ *uniform glossy black.* ♀ in **most of range** (illustrated) streaked blackish and brown above, with a yellowish superciliary and *blackish lores and cheeks; wings blackish edged rufous-chestnut. Below oily yellow* streaked dusky. ♀♀ from **se. Brazil and in lower Amaz. region** less distinctive and darker, with little yellow below and less rufous on wings. Cf. Chopi Blackbird and Velvet-fronted Grackle. Much less gregarious than Chestnut-capped Blackbird, in pairs or at most small groups. Strictly tied to vicinity of water, walking on floating vegetation and clambering about in reeds or nearby grass. Song a loud and ringing "tchew-tchew-tchew-tchew."

Pale-eyed Blackbird
*Agelasticus xanthophthalmus**   PLATE 117(15)
20.5 cm (8"). Rare and very local in grassy margins and marshy vegetation around a few oxbow lakes in *e. Ecuador and e. Peru.* To 650 m. *Iris straw yellow. Entirely black.* Juvenile browner above and somewhat streaked below. No other all-black blackbird has this conspicuous pale iris. Usually in pairs, foraging mainly inside cover, in the open mainly during the early morning, when it sings. Song a loud, ringing "tew-tew-tew-tew," recalling a Black-capped Donacobius, usually given as it perches atop a shrub.

Quiscalus

Two *large, long-tailed* icterids found in open country in n. South America. Both are commensals of man.

Carib Grackle
Quiscalus lugubris   PLATE 118(1)
♂ 24.5–27.5 cm (9¾–10¼"); ♀ 20.5–23 cm (8–9"). *Common in semiopen and urban areas along and near coast of ne. South America, also inland in llanos of Venezuela and ne. Colombia.*

To 850 m in Venezuela. *Iris yellow;* bill rather long and slender. ♂ glossy purplish black with *somewhat creased, wedge-shaped tail.* ♀ blackish brown above; grayish below, palest on throat and darkest on belly (seems darkest on **Trinidad**). Great-tailed Grackle nearly overlaps along coast of nw. Venezuela; both sexes of Great-tailed are larger, ♂ also has longer, more keel-shaped tail, and ♀ has buffier underparts. Conspicuous and familiar, parading about on the ground and beaches, and hanging around restaurants waiting for scraps. Gathers in large numbers at roosts. Song consists of various loud and harsh notes, sometimes given as ♂ struts with head held high. Also: Lesser Antilles.

Great-tailed Grackle
Quiscalus mexicanus   PLATE 118(2)
♂ 43–46 cm (17–18"); ♀ 32–34 cm (12½–13½"). *Locally common along coast from nw. Venezuela* (Zulia) *to nw. Peru* (Tumbes), *favoring mangroves* but also locally around houses and in urban areas. Unlike North American birds, *does not occur any distance inland. Very large* and *long-tailed.* Iris yellow (♂), or dingy yellowish (♀). ♂ glossy blue-black; *tail very long and noticeably creased, often looking keel-shaped.* Much smaller ♀ dusky brown above with *buff superciliary and throat;* blackish tail shorter and virtually uncreased. *Below pale buffy brownish.* Cf. markedly smaller Carib Grackle (range nearly abuts in nw. Venezuela). Feeds mostly in the open, often on muddy shorelines, striding about boldly and scavenging anything vaguely edible; even robbing bird nests. Roosts in mangroves and in trees in urban areas, sometimes in large aggregations. Noisy, both sexes giving a fast "trit-trit-trit" and a harsh guttural "chak" or "chuk," often in flight. Displaying ♂♂ have a wide repertoire of strident calls, including a prolonged rising whistled "wh-eeék." Also: sw. United States and Middle America.

Macroagelaius

Two *slim, long-tailed* forest grackles with *limited distributions* in n. South America.

Golden-tufted Mountain Grackle
*Macroagelaius imthurni**   PLATE 118(3)
♂ 28 cm (11"); ♀ 25.5 cm (10"). *Fairly common in canopy and borders of montane forest on tepuis of s. Venezuela region.* 500–2000 m. Has been called Tepui Mountain Grackle. Long slender bill; very

long tail. *Glossy blue-black; pectoral tufts yellow* (often barely visible). In its small range the only black icterid. Occurs in monospecific groups that forage in forest canopy, probing into epiphytes and other vegetation, only rarely dropping to the ground. Vocalizations include "chirt," "chuk," or "scree" notes, often given in flight; presumed song a jumbled mixture of whistled and squeaky notes, often given by several birds at once.

Colombian Mountain Grackle
Macroagelaius subalaris

♂ 29.5 cm (11½"); ♀ 27 cm (10½"). *Now very rare and local in canopy and borders of montane forest, mainly where oak predominates, in ne. Colombia* (Norte de Santander to Cundinamarca). 1950–3100 m. Has suffered a major decline because of massive deforestation. Resembles Golden-tufted Mountain Grackle of tepuis but with *proportionately even longer tail*, and *axillars and underwing-coverts dark chestnut*. This slim, montane grackle is not likely to be confused in its very limited range; cf. Red-bellied Grackle (no known overlap). Behavior apparently as in Golden-tufted, and equally easy to observe in the few areas where it persists. Occasionally with mixed flocks. Calls include a loud and rollicking "chududit, chududit, . . ." rather like a mockingbird, and a "chididik chicheéo, chididik chicheéo . . ." (M. A. Rebolledo recording).

Red-bellied Grackle
Hypopyrrhus pyrohypogaster   PLATE 118(4)

♂ 31.5 cm (12¼"); ♀ 27 cm (10½"). *Now rare and local in canopy and borders of montane forest in Andes of Colombia* (Antioquia to Caquetá). 800–2400 m. *Unmistakable. Iris pale yellow.* Glossy black with *bright red belly and crissum,* thighs also black; feathers of crown and nape pointed with shiny shafts. Moves about in noisy groups of 6–10 birds, often with other icterids and Inca Jays; forages in subcanopy, hopping on larger branches and gleaning in epiphytes. Has a variety of calls, including a repeated loud shriek "peeyk!" that recalls White-capped Tanager, and others that are more liquid and gurgling, e.g., "glok-glok, shleee-o, schleee."

Icterus

Bright yellow or orange predominate among these *colorful* midsized icterids. They have *long tails* and *sharply pointed bills* (in some slightly decurved; many species have a sil-

very gray base to the lower mandible). They favor wooded areas and forest borders (not continuous forest) in the lowlands. Most occur in n. South America. Most construct beautifully woven pouched nests.

Moriche Oriole
Icterus chrysocephalus   PLATE 118(5)

21 cm (8¼"). Uncommon in canopy and borders of humid forest from *nw. Amazonia to the Guianas,* in some (*but by no means all*) areas associating with *Mauritia* palms. Mostly below 500 m, to 1200 m in Venezuela. Black with *bright yellow crown, shoulders, rump, and thighs.* Epaulet Orioles, regardless of race, never show any yellow on crown or rump. Handsome and slender, this oriole is found singly or in pairs, tending to remain well above the ground; it sometimes joins mixed flocks. Forages actively and at times acrobatically, inspecting palm fronds and even hanging upside down; also feeds at flowering trees. The long tail is often jerked or held sideways. Song a leisurely series of sweet whistled notes and phrases with intervening pauses, e.g., "sweet . . . peeyr . . . pyur . . . peeyr . . . pyur . . . kreer . . . wrrrt . . ." or "purit . . . skeeyr . . . tyipur-twee-twee. . . ."

Epaulet Oriole
Icterus cayanensis   PLATE 118(6) PLATE 119(1)

20.5–21 cm (8–8¼"). *Widespread and locally common (more numerous southward)* in woodland, humid forest borders, and savannas with scattered trees from *s. Amazonia and ne. Brazil to n. Argentina.* To 1000 m in Bolivia. **Southern birds** (Plate 118) are all black, with *epaulet chestnut to tawny.* **Amaz. birds** (Plate 119) also are all black, but the *epaulet is yellow.* In **e. Brazil** has ochraceous yellow epaulet and yellow thighs. Moriche Oriole shows yellow on crown and rump (never seen in Epaulet). The two species are closely related, with apparent hybrids and mixed pairs known from the Guianas, but they are possibly sympatric at certain sites in n. Bolivia. Behavior much like Moriche, though Epaulet shows no association with *Mauritia* palms. Nonbreeders sometimes range in groups that can be quite large, especially in the south; seems less inclined to join mixed flocks than Moriche. Equally agile and apt to twitch its tail. Song similar to Moriche, though harsher and less musical. Frequent call a sharp "kip." In southern part of range mimics other birds.

Yellow-backed Oriole
Icterus chrysater   PLATE 118(7)

21.5 cm (8½"). Fairly common in borders of forest and woodland and clearings, *mainly in foothills and on lower Andean slopes, in nw. Venezuela and Colombia* (south to Nariño). To 2500 m, thus *higher* than other orioles. *Bright golden yellow (including back)* with *black face and bib, wings, and tail;* some birds have an ochre tinge around bib. Yellow Oriole is smaller, has white in wing and a smaller black bib. Arboreal, foraging mainly in pairs and small (family?) groups. Loud clear song a deliberate series of whistled notes changing pitch up and down randomly, often sounding somewhat off-key. Also: Mexico to Nicaragua; Panama.

Venezuelan Troupial
*Icterus icterus**   PLATE 118(8)

23–23.5 cm (9–9¼"). *Now local (numbers reduced by cagebird trapping) in arid scrub and deciduous woodland and savannas in n. Venezuela and n. Colombia.* Mostly below 500 m. Formerly considered conspecific with next two species, and called simply the Troupial. *Iris yellow,* with *large bare blue ocular area.* In **most of range** (illustrated) *bright orange* with *black hood and bib (bib with shaggy lower margin),* back and wings *(wings with broad white stripe from coverts to secondaries),* and tail. In **ne. Colombia** has orange on nape, black greater wing-coverts. Yellow Oriole is smaller and much yellower. Cf. Campo Troupial and ♂ Baltimore Oriole. Found in pairs, foraging at all levels, often in the open; consumes both insects and fruit. Does not construct its own nest, instead pirating those of Plain Thornbird and Great Kiskadee. Loud clear song a series of two-part phrases, e.g., "tree-trur" or "cheer-tu."

Campo Troupial
*Icterus jamacaii**

23–23.5 cm (9–9¼"). Fairly common in arid scrub and deciduous woodland in *ne. Brazil* (south to Minas Gerais, and now apparently spreading into Espírito Santo). To at least 700 m. Resembles Venezuelan Troupial (formerly considered conspecific; no overlap), but has almost no bare ocular patch, white in wing reduced to a patch in secondaries, and an orange epaulet. Orange-backed Troupial (also no overlap) has a mainly orange head (black only on foreface), smooth lower border to bib, and more extensive orange on back. *In its range the only bright orange*

bird of its size. Behavior and voice much as in Venezuelan.

Orange-backed Troupial
*Icterus croconotus**   PLATE 118(9)

23–23.5 cm (9–9¼"). Uncommon to locally fairly common in riparian growth, clearings, and forest borders from *w. and s. Amazonia to n. Argentina;* from e. Bolivia and sw. Brazil south favors scrub and gallery woodland. To 750 m. Formerly considered conspecific with Venezuelan Troupial (no overlap); bare blue ocular area markedly smaller. *Bright orange* with *black face and bib* (bib with a smooth lower margin), wings (aside from orange epaulet and white patch on secondaries), and tail. Nearly unmistakable; in far north of range cf. much yellower Yellow Oriole. Other troupials have fully black hoods and mainly black backs. Behavior much as in Venezuelan, though mainly in more humid regions; especially in Amazonia remains within cover more. Often pirates Yellow-rumped Cacique nests. Song a series of loud, rich musical phrases, each most often two-part, e.g., "tree-tur" or "cheer-to," often with a softer introductory note; this is repeated slowly, sometimes with long pauses.

Baltimore Oriole
*Icterus galbula**   PLATE 118(10)

19 cm (7½"). Rare to uncommon *boreal migrant* (Oct.–Apr.) to woodland and forest borders and clearings in *w. Colombia and n. Venezuela.* To 1500 m. Formerly called Northern Oriole. ♂ *bright orange* with *black hood and back;* wings black with white wing-bar and edging, and orange epaulet; tail black with *orange in outer feathers.* ♀ and **immatures** variable, some (older birds) resembling ♂, but most much duller; brownish olive above, grayer and sometimes mottled on back, wings dusky with two white wing-bars. Yellow below, *often more orange on breast and whiter on belly.* Smaller than any oriole resident in South America. ♀ Orchard Oriole never shows any orange or white below. Arboreal, regularly in small loose groups; often feeds in flowering trees. Breeds in e. North America.

Orchard Oriole
Icterus spurius

17 cm (6¾"). Rare to uncommon boreal migrant (Sep.–Mar.) to clearings and agricultural areas with scattered trees in *w. Colombia and nw. Venezuela.* To 500 m. *The smallest oriole.* ♂

mostly deep chestnut with a *black hood and back;* wings black with white wing-bar and edging and chestnut epaulet, rather long tail black. ♀ olive above, wings duskier with two whitish wing-bars; *uniform greenish yellow below.* **First year** ♂ like ♀ but with *black throat patch* and often some chestnut on breast. Yellow Oriole is larger and much yellower than immature ♂ Orchard. Quite nectarivorous on its wintering grounds, where frequently in flowering *Erythrina* trees. Often in small groups. Regularly gives snatches of its song. Breeds in e. North America.

White-edged Oriole
Icterus graceannae　　　　　PLATE 118(11)

20.5 cm (8"). *Uncommon in arid scrub and deciduous woodland and forest from sw. Ecuador* (Manabí) *to nw. Peru* (La Libertad). To 1400 m in Peru. *Orange-yellow* with *black face and bib,* back, wings, and tail; wings with yellow epaulet and a *white patch on tertials,* tail with *white edge on outer feathers.* Yellow-tailed Oriole is yellower overall and has prominent yellow in tail (none in White-edged); *both* species have white on inner wing, though more shows in White-edged. Yellow-tailed favors more humid situations, though the two can occur together. Behavior much as in Yellow-backed Oriole. Song a series of rich musical phrases, each repeated several times, e.g., "chiro-chowee . . . weeeenh-weh . . . chiro-chowee . . . piro, chiro-chowee . . . weeeenh-weh, . . ." less musical than Yellow-tailed, with interspersed nasal notes. Call a throaty "jori-jori," distinctively doubled.

Yellow-tailed Oriole
Icterus mesomelas　　　　　PLATE 118(12)

21.5 cm (8½"). Fairly common in borders of fairly humid woodland and forest, clearings, and plantations from *nw. Venezuela to nw. Peru* (La Libertad). Mostly below 900 m, but to 1500 m in s. Ecuador and Peru. **Southern birds** (north to nw. Ecuador; illustrated) golden yellow with black face and bib, wings, and tail; wings with *yellow stripe on wing-coverts* and white edging on tertials; *outer tail feathers yellow.* **Northern birds** similar but lack white in wing. White-edged Oriole has a mainly black tail showing *no* yellow, wings with solid large white patch. Yellow-backed Oriole has entirely black wings and tail. Behavior much as in Yellow-backed. Song a series of repeated rich musical phrases, similar to White-edged but more melodious and often with a crescendo effect. Call a mellow "chup-cheet" or "kip-chur." Also: Mexico to Panama.

Orange-crowned Oriole
Icterus auricapillus　　　　　PLATE 118(13)

20.5 cm (8"). Uncommon in canopy and borders of deciduous woodland, humid forest borders, and clearings in *n. Colombia and n. Venezuela.* *Crown, nape, and sides of head and neck fiery orange;* ocular area and large bib black; wings (aside from yellow epaulet) and *tail black;* rump and underparts golden yellow. A beautiful oriole, not likely confused; Yellow-tailed has obvious yellow in its tail. Behavior similar to Yellow backed Oriole. Song a brief series of whistled notes, often repeated interminably. Also: e. Panama.

Yellow Oriole
Icterus nigrogularis　　　　　PLATE 118(14)

20.5 cm (8"). *Common in* arid scrub, deciduous and gallery woodland, and gardens from *n. Colombia east to near mouth of Amazon River in n. Brazil.* Mostly below 500 m. *Golden yellow* with ocular area and *small bib black;* wings and tail black, *wings with single white wing-bar and narrow white edging.* ♀ slightly duller. **Juvenile** lacks black. *The yellowest of the orioles,* and the one showing the least black. Yellow-backed has wings solidly black. Behavior similar to Yellow-backed Oriole, though more conspicuous, in part because it favors more open habitats. Whistled song a series of rich phrases interspersed with harsher notes, usually introduced by a separate, higher-pitched note.

Yellow-billed Cacique
Amblycercus holosericeus　　　　　PLATE 119(2)

♂ 23 cm (9"); ♀ 22 cm (8½"). Uncommon in undergrowth of woodland and forest borders from *w. Colombia to nw. Peru* (Tumbes); also in *montane forest undergrowth from n. Venezuela to w. Bolivia* (w. Santa Cruz). Western birds to 1500 m; montane birds 1500–3500 m. Perhaps more than one species. *Iris and bill pale yellow. All black.* Resembles the larger, *dark*-eyed Solitary Cacique, which *ranges only in lowlands.* A great skulker, ranging mainly in pairs, rummaging and probing into curled leaves and stems; sometimes joins understory flocks, and also occasionally ascends up into flowering trees. Montane birds are often in *Chusquea* bamboo. Nest is cup-shaped (very different from other caciques). Song in western lowlands a series of loud ringing whistles, e.g., "pee!-pee!-peeo-peeo-peeo . . ."; also a "whew-whew, whew-whew, . . ." sometimes echoed by ♀'s "wheee? chrrrr." In Andes song higher-pitched and shriller, "teeeee teeuw teeeee, teeeee teeuw teeeee," with ♀ chiming in the same way. Calls a harsh "waah" and a guttural "kuhkuhkuhkuhkuh." Also: Mexico to Panama.

Cacicus

Mainly black icterids, *many sporting a yellow or red rump, or yellow on wings.* Pale bills are long and pointed; irides are usually blue, browner in immatures. Usually conspicuous and noisy, and often gregarious; the best-known species are colonial nesters. Nests are pouches or purse-shaped.

Ecuadorian Cacique
Cacicus sclateri   PLATE 119(3)

♂ 23 cm (9"); ♀ 20 cm (8"). *Rare and local* in the canopy and borders of várzea and riparian forest and woodland in *e. Ecuador and ne. Peru.* To 400 m. *Iris blue; bill ivory. All black.* The smaller Solitary Cacique has a dark iris and is much less arboreal. The red rump of perched Red-rumped Caciques is often hidden, so until they fly that species can resemble Ecuadorian; their calls differ markedly. An arboreal cacique, often in pairs but sometimes in small family groups, usually on their own; sometimes at flowering or fruiting trees, and often probes *Cecropia* petioles. Most frequent of a variety of arresting calls is a "peách-yo" (sometimes "peách-yo-yo") that may be repeated many times while raising its tail; also a jaylike "k-cheeyow?," a mournful "kleeéur" preceded by soft "wop" notes, and a penetrating "kweeyh-kweeyh-kweeyh-kweeyh-wonhh?"

Selva Cacique
Cacicus koepckeae

23 cm (9"). *Rare and very local* in humid forest borders, primarily in secondary growth along streams in hilly terrain, in *se. Peru* (Madre de Dios and n. Cuzco). 300–800 m. Iris bluish white; bill bluish ivory. Black with *large yellow rump.* Until recently poorly known, but behavior now known to be much as in Ecuadorian Cacique. Loud and distinctive call a series of explosive paired notes, "chick-pouw" (N. Gerhart).

Solitary Cacique
Cacicus solitarius   PLATE 119(4)

♂ 27 cm (10½"); ♀ 23 cm (9"). Uncommon to fairly common in *dense undergrowth in clearings and riparian woodland, mainly from s. Amazonia to n. Argentina;* most numerous southward. To 800 m. *Bill greenish ivory; iris dark. All black.*

Yellow-billed Cacique does not occur east of Andes, and in any case has a yellow eye. Cf. much scarcer and more range-restricted Ecuadorian Cacique. Red-rumped Cacique's red rump can be hidden on perched birds (note its blue eye). Usually skulks in tangled undergrowth, often in pairs, probing into dead leaves and other suspended debris, sometimes hanging upside down; also sometimes ascends to feed at flowering trees. Not colonial. Has a varied repertoire of loud and strident calls, most frequent a penetrating "keeyoh keeyoh keeyoh" or "kyoong kyoong kyoong," a fast "chochochochochocho," and a repeated "kway." Also gives a nasal "wheeeah-ah" (recalling donacobius) and a loud "popp!"

Red-rumped Cacique
Cacicus haemorrhous   PLATE 119(5)

♂ 28 cm (11"); ♀ 23 cm (9"). *Widespread and locally common* in canopy and borders of humid forest and woodland from Amazonia to the Guianas, and from e. Brazil to ne. Argentina. Less numerous in w. Amazonia, more so in Guianas and se. South America. To 1100 m. Iris blue; bill ivory to pale yellow. In **most of range** (illustrated) *glossy blue-black* with *scarlet lower back and rump* (though extensive, the red is often hidden until the bird flies). **Southeastern birds** (especially ♀♀) have less gloss and an orange-tinged rump. Subtropical Cacique (only limited overlap) has longer tail and is less glossy, has smaller red area on rump; calls notably different. Cf. other all-black caciques. Behavior much like other forest-based caciques, noisy and (where numerous) conspicuous. Nesting colonies are often large. Has a variety of harsh or guttural calls interspersed with more melodic notes, including a drawn-out "zhweeeeeo." Foraging and flying birds give a harsh "zhap! zhap! zhap!"

Subtropical Cacique
*Cacicus uropygialis**   PLATE 119(6)

♂ 29.5 cm (11½"); ♀ 23.5 cm (9¼"). Fairly common in canopy and borders of montane forest in *Andes from w. Venezuela* (Barinas) *to s. Peru* (Cuzco) *and w. Bolivia* (recently found in w. La Paz). 1000–2300 m. Formerly considered conspecific with Scarlet-rumped Cacique. Iris blue; bill ivory. *Black with scarlet rump* (usually hidden except in flight). Scarlet-rumped occurs only in Pacific lowlands (minimal or no overlap in Colombia's W. Andes). Red-rumped Cacique has more extensive red on rump (more often visible on perched birds) and a shorter tail; it inhabits Amaz. *lowlands* (little or no overlap) and has a very different voice. Conspicuous and noisy, ranging in small flocks through canopy, sometimes accompanying jays and mountain caciques. Hops along larger limbs, peering into foliage and inspecting epiphytes. Has a variety of calls, the most frequent a repeated jaylike "greer" or "wheep," a "wee-de-rit!" and a liquid "wurt-wurt-wurt-wurt."

Scarlet-rumped Cacique
Cacicus microrhynchus*

♂ 23.5 cm (9¼"); ♀ 20 cm (8¼"). Fairly common in canopy and borders of humid forest in *w. Colombia and w. Ecuador* (south to El Oro). Mostly below 900 m. Formerly considered conspecific with Subtropical Cacique. Iris blue; bill greenish ivory. Resembles Subtropical (minimal or no overlap) but *markedly smaller* with a proportionately shorter tail and slighter bill. Nothing really similar in range; Yellow-billed Cacique has a yellow iris, different nonarboreal behavior, no red on rump. Behavior much as in Subtropical; often accompanies other icterids or Purple-throated Fruitcrows. Nests in small inconspicuous colonies. Voice very different from Subtropical; most frequent call a loud, ringing "treeo, trew!-trew!-trew!-trew!" but also gives various whistled notes and a liquid "wheeo." Also: Honduras to Panama.

Yellow-rumped Cacique
Cacicus cela*   PLATE 119(7)

♂ 28 cm (11"); ♀ 24.5 cm (9½"). *Common and widespread* in canopy and borders of humid forest (especially várzea), secondary woodland, and trees in clearings from Colombia and Venezuela to Amazonia and in ne. Brazil. To 1000 m. Perhaps more than one species. Iris blue; bill ivory yellow to pale grayish. In **most of range** (illustrated) glossy black with a *large yellow patch on wing-coverts; rump, crissum, and base of tail also yellow.* ♀ sootier. **West of Andes** has less yellow on tail; in **n. Colombia** also has less yellow on its wings, and yellow is richer. Aside from the very rare Selva Cacique, *the only cacique in tropical lowlands showing any yellow.* Oropendolas have yellow only on lateral tail feathers. A flamboyant and noisy bird that attracts attention, especially in Amazonia. Nests in small colonies, sometimes with oropendolas. Feeds mainly on fruit, also on insects and at flowering trees. Has a wide repertoire of loud calls, some harsh and slashing, others more melodic. ♂♂ sing mainly around nesting colonies, leaning forward and ruffling rump feathers. Eastern birds incorpo-

rate mimicry of other species, but western birds (whose songs are more musical) do not. Also: Panama.

Golden-winged Cacique
Cacicus chrysopterus   PLATE 119(8)

♂ 20.5 cm (8"); ♀ 18 cm (7"). Uncommon to locally fairly common in deciduous and gallery woodland, and in borders of humid and montane forest, in *Andes from s. Bolivia* (Cochabamba) *to nw. Argentina* (Catamarca), and in *se. Brazil region.* Mostly below 2100 m. Bill bluish horn; iris color variable, either blue or yellow. Black with *yellow wing-coverts and rump.* Can look shaggy-crested. Yellow-rumped Cacique (minimal if any overlap) is larger and has yellow extending to its basal tail and crissum. Southern Mountain Cacique (also no known overlap) *lacks yellow on wing.* Sympatric Epaulet Orioles have chestnut on wing-coverts. Ranges in pairs and small groups; quieter and less conspicuous than Yellow-rumped. A solitary nester. Song a ringing "gloo-gloo-gleéyu-gleéyu," sometimes given as a duet by members of a pair. Call a more nasal "wreyur."

Northern Mountain Cacique
Cacicus leucoramphus*   PLATE 119(9)

♂ 30.5 cm (12"); ♀ 25.5 cm (10"). Fairly common to uncommon in canopy and borders of montane forest in *Andes from extreme sw. Venezuela* (sw. Táchira) *to cen. Peru* (Junín). 1800–3000 m. Has been considered conspecific with Southern Mountain Cacique. Iris blue; bill ivory yellow. Black with *yellow band on wing-coverts, lower back, and rump.* ♀ sootier. Yellow-rumped Cacique normally ranges much lower, in lowlands, and has yellow on crissum and basal part of its shorter tail. Cf. also Subtropical Cacique. Replaced southward by Southern Mountain (no overlap). Forages in pairs or small groups, often accompanying flocks of jays or large tanagers. Gives a variety of loud, raucous calls, including a "wree-wree-wree-wreeuh," sometimes a single "wree!" or a repeated nasal "skeeuh."

Southern Mountain Cacique
Cacicus chrysonotus*   PLATE 119(10)

♂ 30.5–31.5 cm (12–12½"); ♀ 25.5–26 cm (10–10¼"). Fairly common to uncommon in canopy and borders of montane forest on *east slope of Andes from s. Peru* (Cuzco) *to w. Bolivia* (w. Santa Cruz). 2000–3100 m. Resembles Northern Mountain Cacique (sometimes considered conspecific) but *lacks yellow on wing-*

coverts. Behavior similar, though often more numerous. Vocalizations differ markedly; Southern is higher-pitched and more musical (less raucous, with very different effect), including a "pidiree," a "pidiree, pree-pree-pree" or "piree-piree-piree," and a piercing "peeeyr" (sometimes repeated).

Band-tailed Oropendola
Ocyalus latirostris   PLATE 119(11)

♂ 33 cm (13″); ♀ 25.5 cm (10″). Rare to locally uncommon in várzea and riparian woodland on *islands in w. Amazonia.* Below 300 m. *A small, caciquelike oropendola.* Iris blue; bill yellowish white, small frontal shield and maxilla basally dark. *Velvety black,* wings glossier; *dark chestnut on crown, nape, and upper back* (hard to discern in the field). Tail pattern distinctive but hard to see except in flight; *outer feathers yellow with black tip,* also black along its outer edge. Yellow-rumped Cacique has obvious yellow on wings, rump, and crissum. Solitary and Ecuadorian Caciques lack any yellow at all. Usually in small groups, sometimes (especially at roosts on river islands) associating with Yellow-rumped Caciques and Russet-backed Oropendolas. Foraging calls include liquid chortles, a "chewop," a "ke-cho!" and a "skeedelop-chop."

Psarocolius, Zarhynchus, and Clypicterus

Large to very large icterids with sharply pointed bills, oropendolas are found mainly in the canopy and borders of humid lowland forest. Their basic color can be either olive, chestnut, or black, but *tails are always bright yellow with central feathers blackish* (less yellow in Dusky-green Oropendola). All species are arboreal, often very gregarious birds; breeding is colonial, with conspicuous long pendulous nests suspended from the branches of a tree situated at edge or out in the open. Most if not all species are parasitized by Giant Cowbirds. *Zarhynchus* and *Clypicterus* are sometimes merged into *Psarocolius* but here are maintained as distinct genera; the genus *Gymnostinops* (for the last four species) is also sometimes recognized.

Chestnut-headed Oropendola
*Zarhynchus wagleri**   PLATE 120(1)

♂ 34.5 cm (13½″); ♀ 27.5 cm (10¾″). Fairly common in canopy and borders of humid forest, secondary woodland, and clearings with tall trees in *w. Colombia and nw. Ecuador* (where uncommon, and mainly in Esmeraldas). Mostly below 400 m. Iris blue; *prominent frontal shield and bill mostly ivory.* ♂ with an inconspicuous hairlike crest. *Head and neck rich chestnut* merging into black back, wings, and breast, then back to chestnut on rump and crissum. A handsome oropendola, not likely confused in its limited range. Cf. Russet-backed Oropendola, and in w. Colombia also Crested Oropendola. Gregarious and arboreal, clambering about in canopy as it forages mainly on larger insects; also consumes fruit and feeds at flowering trees. Calls of both sexes include a deep "chok" or "kok," also a startling "chak chak." Displaying ♂'s loud gurgling song is preceded by several harsh slashing notes; unlike other oropendolas it does *not* bow forward but merely ruffles its feathers and rises up on its perch. Also: Mexico to Panama.

Casqued Oropendola
*Clypicterus oseryi**   PLATE 120(2)

♂ 37 cm (14½″); ♀ 29 cm (11¼″). Uncommon in canopy and borders of humid forest in *w. Amazonia.* To 900 m. Iris blue; *conspicuous frontal shield, swollen in* ♂, *and rather short bill yellow. Mainly rufous-chestnut* with *olive-yellow throat and breast.* Sympatric Russet-backed Oropendolas have a *black* bill and *no* casque. Green and Olive Oropendolas have entirely green heads, brightly colored soft parts. All have markedly longer tails than this quite *short-tailed* species. Forest-based, ranging in terra firme but often nesting along streams; generally *not* with other oropendolas. Flight undulating on rather broad wings. Displaying ♂♂ give a startling "squa-a-a-a-a-oóók!" and a ringing "ko-kooó-glee!" Flight call a frequent harsh "shrak!"

Green Oropendola
Psarocolius viridis   PLATE 120(3)

♂ 47 cm (18½″); ♀ 39.5 cm (15½″). Uncommon to fairly common in canopy and borders of terra firme forest from *Amazonia to the Guianas,* less numerous westward. To 1100 m, but mostly below 600 m. Iris blue; *frontal shield and bill pale greenish yellow to ivory, tipped orange-red;* small area of pinkish skin around eye. *Bright olive, darker above;* rump, lower belly, and crissum chestnut. ♂ has inconspicuous hairlike crest. Sympatric Russet-backed Oropendolas have black bills. Olive Oropendola is *brighter* generally, with *chestnut rearparts including wings,* black on bill, and bare pink cheeks. Behavior much as in Crested Oropendola, though more forest-based and less frequent in clearings or along rivers. ♂'s song more liquid and less harsh, with a rolling quality.

Crested Oropendola
Psarocolius decumanus   PLATE 119(12)
PLATE 120(4)

♂ 46.5 cm (18¼"); ♀ 37 cm (14½"). *Widespread and often common* in borders of humid and deciduous forest, secondary woodland, clearings with scattered tall trees, locally even in agricultural and built-up areas, from Colombia and Venezuela to n. Argentina and s. Brazil. Mostly below 1300 m, locally higher. Iris blue; *bill ivory to pale greenish yellow.* In **most of range** glossy black with dark chestnut rump and crissum. Some **southern birds** have a sparse scattering of yellow or white feathers. *The only large, mostly black oropendola in its range;* in nw. Colombia cf. Black and Baudó Oropendolas. Conspicuous and gregarious, often ranges with other icterids but usually nests apart, in an isolated tree. Less forest-based than many oropendolas. Roosts can be very large. In flight looks stretched out, with steady rowing wingbeats. Displaying ♂ leans forward with fluttering wings and raised tail (appearing about ready to fall), uttering a loud gurgling, slashing song that accelerates. Both sexes give a loud "chak" call. Also: Costa Rica and Panama.

Russet-backed Oropendola
*Psarocolius angustifrons**   PLATE 120(5)
♂ 46–47 cm (18–18½"); ♀ 35.5–37 cm (14–14½"). *Common* in riparian and várzea forest and adjacent clearings in *w. Amazonia,* foraging birds ranging into terra firme forest canopy and edge; also in montane forest and borders in *Andes from n. Venezuela to w. Bolivia* (w. Santa Cruz). To 2500 m in n. Andes. Perhaps more than one species involved. Iris can be brown or blue. In **Amazonia** (A) has *black bill.* Dull brownish olive washed with rufous, most rufous on rump. In **Andes** varies, but almost always with *bill orange-yellow to yellowish.* These tend to be more rufescent generally (especially in **w. Colombia and w. Ecuador**) and often show a *yellow frontal area* (B); **n. Venezuela** birds are the smallest and most olive. In Ecuador black-billed (lowland) birds range up onto east Andean slopes; yellow-billed (montane) birds range down into the s. Peru and Bolivia lowlands. *In Amazonia the only oropendola with an all-dark bill. In the Andes usually*

the only oropendola present, but in se. Peru and Bolivia cf. Dusky-green Oropendola. Behavior much as in Crested Oropendola. In Amazonia roosts in sometimes immense flocks on river islands, often with Yellow-rumped Caciques and other icterids, dispersing soon after dawn to feed in large streaming flocks. Usually less numerous in the Andes, there ranging in smaller flocks and accompanying jays and caciques. Songs of displaying ♂♂ are generally similar, in the lowlands a loud and accelerating, slashing "g-g-guh-guh-gágok!" and in the Andes typically a loud "g-kyoooyk!" Both calls are given as the bird leans forward with flapping wings and raised tail. Flying and foraging birds of both sexes give a loud "chak" call.

Dusky-green Oropendola
Psarocolius atrovirens   PLATE 120(6)
♂ 42 cm (16½"); ♀ 33 cm (13"). Fairly common in canopy and borders of montane forest on *east slope of Andes from cen. Peru* (Huánuco) *to w. Bolivia* (w. Santa Cruz). 800–2600 m. Iris brown or (in older birds?) blue; bill greenish ivory. *Rather uniform dusky-green,* rufous on rump and crissum. Sympatric Russet-backed Oropendolas are more rufescent above with a contrasting paler olive head and yellow frontal band (Dusky-green has at most scattered yellow feathers). Behavior and voice much as in montane Russet-backed. Ranges at higher elevations than that species, but some overlap occurs (perhaps especially in Peru). Colony size tends to be small.

Olive Oropendola
*Psarocolius yuracares**   PLATE 120(7)
♂ 49.5 cm (19½"); ♀ 44 cm (17¼"). Uncommon to locally fairly common in canopy and borders of humid forest (mainly terra firme) in *w. and s. Amazonia.* Mostly below 700 m. *Bill black with red-orange tip; conspicuous bare cheek patch bright pink.* In **most of range** (illustrated) *foreparts bright yellow-olive; rearparts (including all of wing) bright chestnut.* ♂ has an inconspicuous wispy crest. **Between Rio Tapajós and Rio Xingú in e. Amaz. Brazil** has *dusky-olive foreparts.* Even farther east cf. Pará Oropendola. Green Oropendola is smaller and not as bright; it shows *no bicolored effect.* Behavior similar to Crested and Russet-backed Oropendolas, though typically scarcer and less gregarious. ♂'s bowing display similar to other *Psarocolius,* with song a loud gurgling "tek-tk-tk-k-k-goo-guhloóp!"

Pará Oropendola

*Psarocolius bifasciatus**   PLATE 120(8)

♂ 49.5 cm (19½"); ♀ 42 cm (16½"). Canopy and borders of humid forest in limited area of *lower Amaz. Brazil.* Below 200 m. In most respects (including soft-part coloration) resembles Olive Oropendola but *foreparts blackish,* resulting in a very different effect. Behavior much like Olive (has been considered conspecific).

Black Oropendola

Psarocolius guatimozinus   PLATE 120(9)

♂ 46 cm (18"); ♀ 39.5 cm (15½"). Locally fairly common in borders of humid forest and partially cleared areas with tall trees in *nw. Colombia* (east to e. Antioquia in Río Magdalena valley). To 800 m. *Bill black with orange tip; bare cheek patch mostly blue,* narrowly pink along lower edge. *Mostly black* with back, rump, crissum, and part of wing-coverts dark chestnut. Cf. the rare Baudó Oropendola. Behavior similar to Olive

and other oropendolas, though in Panama seems actually to avoid extensively forested areas, and regularly noted along rivers. ♂'s song a loud "skol-l-l-l-wool!" (S. Hilty). Also: e. Panama.

Baudó Oropendola

Psarocolius cassini

♂ 46.5 cm (18¼"); ♀ 40 cm (15¾"). Apparently rare at borders of humid forest and partially cleared areas with scattered tall trees in *nw. Colombia* (nw. Chocó). To 350 m. Resembles Black Oropendola, but *bare cheek patch entirely pink, entire mantle (including wings) rich chestnut,* and more chestnut on flanks. Occurs *south* of Black's range. Cf. much more numerous Chestnut-headed Oropendola (smaller, with whitish bill, etc.). Hardly known in life, but behavior likely much as in Black; the two species have not been found together, though their ranges come close.

CARDUELINE FINCHES: FRINGILLIDAE

Mainly an Old World family, the only fringillids that occur in South America are members of the genus *Carduelis* (siskins); it has recently been proposed that the genera *Euphonia* and *Chlorophonia,* traditionally considered tanagers, be transferred to this family. Members of this family differ from all the emberizid assemblage in having 10 rather than 9 primaries. Siskins are small finches with short conical bills and notched tails.

Carduelis

♂ *siskins are attractively patterned in black, yellow, and olive.* ♀♀ *are generally much duller. Except as noted, siskins have black wings with a conspicuous yellow band on the coverts and another across the base of the flight feathers; the tail is black with yellow at its base.* Siskins occur *mainly in semiopen areas in the Andes;* they are notably gregarious and have a *distinctive undulating flight.*

Hooded Siskin
Carduelis magellanica   PLATE 121(1)
11 cm (4¼"). *Common and widespread* in semiopen and cultivated areas with scattered trees, gardens, and forest borders in *Andes from w. Colombia to n. Chile,* on *tepuis of s. Venezuela,* and from *interior cen. Brazil to cen. Argentina* (La Pampa). Locally to 4000 m in the Andes. ♂ has *black hood* contrasting with yellow-olive back (often with some blackish streaking, especially in **s. Andes**) and bright yellow underparts; rump usually contrasting yellow, less so in **n. Andes.** ♀ much duller, lacking black on head; grayish olive with some dusky back streaking and yellowish on rump; olive yellowish below, yellower on belly (as illustrated; but belly dingy pale grayish in **n. Andes**). Cf. other scarcer or range-restricted siskins (especially Olivaceous, Saffron, and Andean). Most often in small groups, foraging at all levels from high in trees to the ground; often quite tame. Pretty song a lengthy and irregular twittering, sometimes given by several ♂♂ at once. A "tseeu" call is often given in flight by both sexes.

Olivaceous Siskin
Carduelis olivacea
10–11 cm (4–4¼"). Fairly common in canopy and borders of montane forest on *east slope of Andes from n. Ecuador* (Sucumbíos) *to w. Bolivia* (Cochabamba). Mostly 900–2500 m. ♂ closely resembles ♂ Hooded Siskin but slightly darker above and more olive-tinged below. ♀ easier in **northern part of range,** where it has *olivaceous underparts* (Hoodeds here are pale grayish below). Farther south, however, ♀♀ are very similar and best identified by habitat and range. Behavior as in Hooded, though seems to come to the ground less often.

Saffron Siskin
Carduelis siemiradzkii
10–10.5 cm (4–4¼"). *Rare to uncommon and local at borders of deciduous woodland and scrub in sw. Ecuador* (sw. Manabí to w. Loja) *and extreme nw. Peru* (Tumbes). Mostly below 600 m. ♂ like ♂ Hooded Siskin but brighter generally with a *more golden olive back,* showing *no* streaking, and *brighter yellow underparts.* ♀ *yellower generally, especially below* (not pale grayish, as in potentially sympatric ♀ Hoodeds). Mainly occurs at lower elevations than Hooded. Behavior similar.

Thick-billed Siskin
Carduelis crassirostris   PLATE 121(2)
13.5–14 cm (5¼–5½"). *Rare to uncommon and local* in patches of *Polylepis* woodland and montane scrub in *Andes from w. Peru* (Ancash) *to nw. Argentina* (Mendoza) and in *cen. Chile* (Aconcagua to Santiago). 3000–4000 m northward, down to 2100 m in south. *Bill thicker than in other siskins* (also often silvery at base); usually identifiable on this basis alone. *Larger* than Hooded Siskin. ♂ similar but with *midbelly whitish.* **Im-**

mature ♂ has similar pattern (including hood) but more grayish olive above and pale grayish below. ♀ very dingy and grayish overall (paler below). Occurs in pairs or small groups, with overall behavior similar to Hooded. Song a prolonged musical twitter; call a "treh-treh-treu-treu," sometimes lengthened into a more nasal "treeeeuw" (S. Herzog recording).

Yellow-faced Siskin
Carduelis yarrellii   PLATE 121(3)

11 cm (4¼"). *Now rare and local in borders of humid forest and woodland in ne. Brazil,* where the *only* siskin present; *numbers much reduced by cagebird trapping.* Old records from Venezuela seem dubious and probably refer to cagebirds. To 900 m. ♂ has *black crown contrasting with bright yellow face and underparts;* back olive with some blackish spotting, rump bright yellow. ♀ yellowish olive above with bright yellow rump; yellow below. Behavior not well known, but in all likelihood similar to Hooded Siskin.

Black-chinned Siskin
Carduelis barbata   PLATE 121(4)

13 cm (5"). *Common* in forest borders, wooded areas, gardens, and around towns from *cen. and s. Chile* (Atacama) *and s. Argentina* (Neuquén and La Pampa) *to Tierra del Fuego.* To 1500 m. ♂ has *crown and midthroat black;* above olive with blackish streaking, rump yellower; wings black with two yellowish bars and patch on primaries. ♀ like ♂ but lacking black on head, duller and more grayish above with vague yellowish superciliary. Dull yellowish olive below, midbelly whitish. *No other siskin occurs so far south.* Hooded Siskin comes fairly close; its ♂♂ are distinctly different, and ♀♀ differ in their yellow rump and base of tail. Behavior much as in Hooded.

Andean Siskin
Carduelis spinescens   PLATE 121(5)

11 cm (4¼"). Fairly common in borders of montane forest and woodland, clearings and agricultural areas with scattered trees, and paramo (often with *Espeletia*) in *Andes from n. Venezuela to n. Ecuador* (Pichincha). Mostly 1800–3700 m. ♂ in **Venezuela and ne. Colombia** (illustrated) has *black crown contrasting with olive face;* above dark olive, rump yellower and with some dusky back streaking. Below yellowish olive. ♀ lacks black crown and is duller, with midbelly whitish. In **Colombia's W. and Cen. Andes and n. Ecuador,** lacks yellow at base of tail; ♀ dif-

fers further by resembling ♂ (*retaining the black crown,* though it is browner in Colombia). ♂ Hooded Siskin has *entire hood black* (not just the crown); in area of overlap, ♀ Hooded lacks black crown and has grayish underparts. Behavior as in Hooded; the two flock together in Ecuador. Vocalizations are typical of genus.

Red Siskin
Carduelis cucullata   PLATE 121(6)

11 cm (4¼"). *Now very rare and local in borders of semihumid forest and woodland in n. Venezuela and ne. Colombia;* recently found at *a single site in s. Guyana. Numbers greatly reduced by trapping for the cagebird market.* 300–1700 m. ♂ mostly *bright vermilion,* darker and more carmine on back; hood, wings and tail black, *wings patterned like other siskins but with red instead of yellow.* ♀ grayish brown above, redder on rump; *wings marked as in ♂ but paler.* Below grayish white with *salmon red on sides.* The only other siskin in range is the very different Andean. Behavior similar to Hooded Siskin.

Yellow-rumped Siskin
Carduelis uropygialis   PLATE 121(7)

13 cm (5"). Rare to uncommon (less numerous northward) on open shrubby slopes and ravines in *Andes from w. Peru* (Ancash) *to cen. Chile* (Santiago) *and adjacent Argentina;* northern records may refer at least in part to austral migrants. *Most numerous in Chile.* Mostly 2000–3500 m, lower in winter. *Mostly sooty black,* with *rump, lower breast, and belly yellow;* base of tail yellow. ♀ slightly more brownish and duller yellow. Black Siskin lacks yellow on rump, and black on underparts extends lower (only the lower belly is yellow); usually occurs at higher elevations. Yellow-bellied Siskin occurs in a very different, montane forest habitat. Generally in small groups, feeding in bushes or on the ground.

Black Siskin
Carduelis atrata   PLATE 121(8)

13 cm (5"). Fairly common in puna grassland, rocky slopes, and ravines in *high Andes from cen. Peru* (Huánuco) *to n. Chile and w. Argentina* (Mendoza). Mostly 3500–4500 m, lower southward. *Mostly glossy black* with *bright yellow only on lower belly;* base of tail yellow. ♀ similar but somewhat sootier. Cf. Yellow-rumped Siskin, a generally scarcer bird usually at somewhat lower elevations. Ranges in pairs and small flocks, feeding both on the ground and in low shrubs, sometimes with yellowfinches or other birds.

Frequently around buildings. Has a twittering and trilled song much as in other siskins.

Yellow-bellied Siskin

Carduelis xanthogastra   PLATE 121(9)

11.5 cm (4½"). *Uncommon and rather local in canopy and borders of montane forest and adjacent clearings in Andes from n. Venezuela to w. Bolivia* (w. Santa Cruz); nearly absent from Peru. Mostly 1200–2200 m, lower in w. Ecuador. ♂ black with *contrasting yellow lower breast and belly.* ♀ *has ♂ pattern but olive replaces the black.* ♂ distinctive in its forest-based range; ♀'s two-toned underparts (olive foreneck, yellow belly) distinctive (other ♀ siskins are uniform below). Ranges in pairs or small groups; more arboreal than other siskins, rarely coming to the ground. Musical song an often lengthy jumble of thin twittering notes; call a high "pee." Also: Costa Rica and w. Panama.

Lesser Goldfinch

Carduelis psaltria   PLATE 121(10)

10 cm (4"). Fairly common but rather local in montane scrub, borders of woodland, and gardens in *Andes from n. Venezuela to nw. Peru* (La Libertad); *favors drier areas.* Mostly 500–2500 m. *Bill paler* than in the siskins. ♂ *glossy black above* and *yellow below;* wings with a *white patch in primaries* and tertial edging, tail with *white at base.* ♀ olive above; wings dusky, *marked as in ♂,* tail without white. Below olive-yellow. Siskins have *yellow* (not white) wing markings. ♂ Yellow-bellied Siskin is as black above as the goldfinch,

but it also is black on throat and chest. Cf. also ♂ Thick-billed Euphonia. Found in pairs or small groups, foraging at varying levels, though usually quite low and often in the semiopen. Like the siskins, rarely associates with other birds. Pretty song a disjointed, often lengthy twittering; call a clear "kleeu." Also: w. United States to Panama.

European Goldfinch

Carduelis carduelis

12 cm (4¾"). *Mainly in Uruguay,* where found in gardens and cultivated areas with shrubbery and scattered trees. Colorful and unmistakable. *Foreface and chin bright red* contrasting with *black hindcrown* and *white cheeks and sides of neck;* buffy brown above and on sides, rump gray. Wings and tail black, *wings with wide yellow band,* tail with white at base. **Juvenile** lacks the red. Ranges in small flocks with behavior similar to that of native siskins; sympatric with Hooded Siskin. Natural range: Eurasia.

European Greenfinch

Carduelis chloris

15 cm (6"). *Mainly in Uruguay and e. Argentina* (Buenos Aires), where locally common in gardens and agricultural areas with scattered trees; appears to be spreading. Rather heavy pale bill. ♂ essentially *olive above, yellowish olive below;* wings dusky with *prominent yellow flash in primaries, tail with extensive yellow at base.* ♀ duller and grayer. ♀ Hooded Siskin is much smaller. Occurs in pairs and small groups, mainly in settled areas. Natural range: Europe.

WAXBILLS, MUNIAS, AND ALLIES: ESTRILDIDAE

Three members of this Old World family have been introduced into South America; only one, the Common Waxbill, is widespread

Common Waxbill
Estrilda astrild   PLATE 121(11)
11.5 cm (4½"). *Introduced and now locally fairly common around various towns and cities in e. and s. Brazil, also very locally in Amazonia.* Still spreading, though not as quickly as the House Sparrow. To at least 1100 m. An unmistakable small finch with a *long tail* and *vivid red bill.* Brown above, vermiculated darker, with *red streak through eye.* Below pale buff vermiculated with dusky on sides and breast; red stain on midbelly. Feeds on the ground in small monospecific groups, often on lawns. Natural range: tropical Africa.

Black-headed Munia
Lonchura malacca
12 cm (4¾"). *Established locally in llanos of n. Venezuela.* Below 300 m. Also called Tricol-ored or Chestnut Munia. Heavy bluish bill. *Head and foreneck black,* contrasting with *chestnut upperparts* and *white underparts;* midbelly and crissum also black. Other races have brown replacing the white on underparts. Its pattern is unlike that of any *Sporophila* seedeater. Occurs in small flocks in grassy areas. Natural range: s. Asia.

Java Sparrow
Padda oryzivora
17 cm (6¾"). *Established locally in n. Venezuela;* apparently increasing, *especially around rice cultivation.* To 400 m. *Very heavy pink bill* and pointed tail. *Mostly soft bluish gray* with *black crown and throat outlining white face; belly pale pink.* A popular cagebird. Natural range: Indonesia (Java and Bali), where now rare because of trapping.

OLD WORLD SPARROWS AND SNOWFINCHES: PASSERIDAE

One member of this Old World family has been introduced into South America, the still-spreading House Sparrow.

House Sparrow
Passer domesticus
15 cm (6"). *Introduced and now locally common in and around towns and cities in many parts of South America, especially in the south and east.* Though still favoring cooler regions, the familiar House Sparrow continues to increase and to spread, even in tropical areas. To at least 3000 m. ♂ *has a gray crown, chestnut nape, white cheeks and sides of neck,* and *black bib;* back brown streaked black, rump plain gray. Below whitish.

The pattern is soiled in many birds. More nondescript ♀ has *yellow on bill.* Grayish brown above with blackish streaking and *pale superciliary;* below dingy whitish. A strict commensal of humans, most numerous in urban and suburban areas; noisy, aggressive, and social. Forages mainly on the ground, often in flocks. In many areas seems to be dispersing along highways, and often nests under the shade awnings of gas stations. Natural range: Eurasia.

WEAVERS AND WIDOWBIRDS: PLOCEIDAE

One member of this Old World family has been introduced into South America, the very local Village Weaver. Apparently an additional species may now be present in Venezuela, African Masked Weaver (*P. velatus*).

Village Weaver
Ploceus cucullatus
14 cm (5½"). *Recently established locally in n. Venezuela* (Carabobo). Also called Blackheaded Weaver. 200–300 m. Thick bill; iris red.

♂ *mostly bright yellow* with *black face and bib;* wings blackish, feathers edged yellow. ♀ much duller: brownish above with *dull yellow superciliary, wing feathers edged yellow. Dull yellow below.* Natural range: east Africa.

STARLINGS: STURNIDAE

One member of this Old World family has been introduced into South America, the much-maligned Common Starling, unfortunately now beginning to spread in Argentina.

Common Starling
Sturnus vulgaris
22 cm (8½"). Introduced and now becoming established in urban and suburban areas of *ne. Argentina, especially around Buenos Aires;* vagrants (perhaps ship-assists) have also been recorded on the Netherlands Antilles. Chunky and short-tailed. *Bill yellow,* duskier when not

breeding. *Black,* with some buff spotting above. Fresh plumage has *white and buff feather tips,* the spots gradually wearing off. **Juvenile** dull grayish. Abundant in North America (where also introduced), unfortunately this aggressive starling appears to be increasing and spreading in Argentina. Natural range: Eurasia.

NOTES ON TAXONOMY AND ENGLISH NAMES

Presented here are taxonomic and nomenclatural changes at the species and genus level where these differ from those employed in *The Birds of South America* Volumes I and II (Ridgely and Tudor 1989, 1994). They are listed in the same sequence as the species accounts in this volume. Also included are comments on English name alterations, which are few; however, note that spelling and group name changes (most of them minor in nature) that were based on the recommendations of the IOC Standing Committee on English Names (recently published as Gill and Wright 2006) are not specified here. Full citations for works cited more than once are given in the Bibliography following these notes. Citations for all newly described species (a surprisingly large number) have also been given.

We follow Remsen (2003) and most recent authors in subsuming the monotypic genus *Geobates* into the genus *Geositta*.

Furnarius cinnamomeus (Pacific Hornero) of w. Ecuador and nw. Peru and *F. longirostris* (Caribbean Hornero) of n. Colombia and nw. Venezuela are recognized as separate species from *F. leucopus* (Pale-legged Hornero), found east of the Andes. This split is based on their differing morphology, voices, and disjunct distributions.

The genus *Ochetorhynchus* was recognized by Ridgely and Tudor (1994) for the earthcreeper species *certhioides* and *harterti* (Chaco and Bolivian Earthcreepers), mainly on account of their divergent voices and nests (constructed of sticks, and often *not* placed in a burrow) from the earthcreeper genus *Upucerthia*. The authors overlooked, however, that the genus *Ochetorhynchus* had been erected for the species *ruficaudus* (Straight-billed Earthcreeper), so either one has to include *ruficaudus* in the separated genus *Ochetorhynchus*, or one has to place all the earthcreepers in the genus *Upucerthia*, or a new genus could be erected for the *certhioides/harterti* pair. Although we remain convinced that the *certhioides/harterti* pair do form a natural unit, likely at the generic level, for now we place all earthcreeper species in the genus *Upucerthia*, in agreement with Barnett and Pearman (2001) and Remsen (2003).

The monotypic genus *Eremobius* remains something of an enigma. Though superficially resembling several typical earthcreepers, and hence long called the Band-tailed Earthcreeper, its nest is entirely different (a mass of thorny twigs with a side entrance), and it has been suggested that the species may actually be more closely related to *Asthenes*. We follow Barnett and Pearman (2001) in drawing attention to its unique attributes by using its generic name as a group name.

We follow K. J. Zimmer and A. Whittaker (*Condor* 102[2]: 4409–4422, 2000) in recognizing *Pseudoseisura unirufa* (Gray-crested Cacholote) of n. Bolivia and the Brazilian pantanal as a species distinct from *P. cristata* (Caatinga Cacholote) of ne. Brazil, based on plumage and vocal characters.

J. R. Navas and N. A. Bó (*Rev. MACN, Zool.* 14: 55–86, 1987) suggested considering *Cinclodes olrogi* (Olrog's Cinclodes) of the sierras of Córdoba and San Luis, Argentina, as conspecific with *C. oustaleti* (Gray-flanked Cinclodes). *Olrogi* was, however, treated as a full species by Fjeldså and Krabbe (1990), Ridgely and Tudor (1994), and Remsen (2003), and we continue to do so, while recognizing that these birds are doubtless very closely related.

J. F. Pacheco and L. P. Gonzaga (*Ararajuba* 3: 3–11, 1995) described *Synallaxis whitneyi* (Bahia Spinetail) as a new species, found in e. Brazil. B. M. Whitney and J. F. Pacheco (*Nattereria* 2: 34–35, 2001) then proposed that the species name *cinerea* was in fact applicable to this taxon, but R. Stopiglia and M. A. Raposo (*Zootaxa* 1166: 49–55, 2006) reinstated the species name *whitneyi*.

We follow the Comite Brasileiro de Registros Ornitológicos (2006) in recognizing *Synallaxis simoni* (Araguaia Spinetail) as a species distinct from *S. albilora* (White-lored Spinetail), based primarily on its different voice.

We follow most recent authors (including Remsen 2003) in transferring three spinetail species formerly usually (including Ridgely and Tudor 1994) placed in the genus *Poecilurus* (*scutata*, *candei*, and *kollari*) to the genus *Synallaxis*.

J. F. Pacheco, B. M. Whitney, and L. P. Gonzaga (*Wilson Bull.* 108[3]: 397–433, 1996) described

Acrobatornis fonsecai (Pink-legged Graveteiro) as a new genus and species, found only in a limited area of s. Bahia in e. Brazil.

S. Maijer and J. Fjeldså (*Ibis* 139: 606–616, 1997) described *Cranioleuca henricae* (Inquisivi Spinetail) as a new species, restricted to a limited area in the Andes of La Paz, Bolivia. Those authors suggested the English name "Bolivian Spinetail," but given the large number of other spinetails found in Bolivia, we consider it preferable to highlight the new species' extremely restricted range in its name.

K. J. Zimmer (*Studies in Neotropical Ornithology Honoring Ted Parker*, Ornithol. Monogr. 48: 849–864, 1997) is followed in recognizing *Cranioleuca vulpecula* (Parker's Spinetail) of Amazon River islands as a species separate from *C. vulpina* (Rusty-backed Spinetail).

Ridgely and Tudor (1994) treated all forms in the *Phacellodomus rufifrons* complex as conspecific, calling it the Common Thornbird. Recent evidence points, however, to regarding *P. inornatus* of Venezuela and ne. Colombia as a separate species (Plain Thornbird); it is distinct in plumage (being very drab and plain), has a different voice, and is widely disjunct. This is the course followed by Hilty (2003). *Peruvianus* of the upper Río Marañón valley in s. Ecuador and nw. Peru is almost equally disjunct from southern *P. rufifrons*, but it is more similar in plumage and voice, so we continue to regard them as conspecific; the English name "Rufous-fronted Thornbird" is appropriate.

Recent evidence (fide R. Parrini) indicates that *Phacellodomus ferrugineigula* (Red-eyed Thornbird) and *P. erythrophthalmus* (Orange-eyed Thornbird) occur sympatrically at several sites in s. Brazil (e.g., in s. Minas Gerais). As the two forms also differ vocally, we treat them as separate species here, in accord with Comite Brasileiro de Registros Ornitológicos (2006).

Trans-Andean *Hyloctistes virgatus* (Western Woodhaunter) is recognized as a separate species from *H. subulatus* (Eastern Woodhaunter) of Amazonia, based mainly on its strikingly different voice.

We follow M. B. Robbins and K. J. Zimmer (*Bull. B.O.C.* 125[3]: 212–228, 2005) in transferring the species *Philydor dimidiatum* (Planalto Foliage-gleaner) to the genus *Syndactyla*.

We follow K. J. Zimmer (*Wilson Bull.* 114[1]: 20–37, 2002) in recognizing *Automolus paraensis* (Pará Foliage-gleaner) of e. Amazonian Brazil as a species separate from *A. infuscatus* (Olive-backed Foliage-gleaner).

As its range is so neatly described by the tepuis, and as several other foliage-gleaners have throats that are white or whitish, the English name of *Automolus roraimae* is changed from "White-throated Foliage-gleaner" to "Tepui Foliage-gleaner." This change was first suggested by Hilty (2003).

A. Kratter and T. A. Parker III (*Studies in Neotropical Ornithology Honoring Ted Parker*, Ornithol. Monogr. no. 48: 383–397, 1997) present evidence that the species formerly called *Automolus dorsalis* was better placed in the genus *Anabazenops*. English names for the species have been vexing. It long (e.g., Meyer de Schauensee 1966, 1970) went by the totally inappropriate name "Crested Foliage-gleaner" (despite showing no crest!). Ridgely and Tudor (1994) suggested that "Dusky-cheeked" would be an improvement, which it was. Then in the late 1990s, S. Hilty suggested that an even better name would be "Bamboo Foliage-gleaner," on account of its predilection for bamboo thickets, and this was employed by Ridgely and Greenfield (2001) and Gill and Wright (2006).

A. Aleixo and B. M. Whitney (*Auk* 119[2]: 520–523, 2002) demonstrated that what was long named *Xiphorhynchus necopinus* (Zimmer's Woodcreeper) should actually be called *X. kienerii*; they also provided the first published information on the species' natural history.

Aleixo (2002) suggested that the Ocellated Woodcreeper (*Xiphorhynchus ocellatus*) likely comprised more than one species, with birds from sw. Amazonia being separated as Tschudi's Woodcreeper (*X. chunchotambo*, with *brevirostris*). *Ocellatus* and *chunchotambo* are very similar morphologically and vocally, and as even the ranges of their constituent taxa remain uncertain, we continue to regard all taxa as conspecific.

J. Haffer (*Studies in Neotropical Ornithology Honoring Ted Parker*, Ornithol. Monogr. 48: 281–305, 1997) is followed in separating *Xiphorhynchus spixii* (Spix's Woodcreeper) of e. Amazonia from the more wide-ranging and polytypic *X. elegans* (Elegant Woodcreeper) of w. and s. Amazonia. This was also the course followed by Marantz et al. (2003).

Aleixo (2002) suggested that the Buff-throated Woodcreeper (*Xiphorhynchus guttatus*) should be split into two species, with *X. guttatoides* of w. Amazonia being considered separate from *X. guttatus* of e. Amazonia and e. Brazil. Though perhaps correct, because of uncertainties in the placement of certain taxa (as well as other complications), this was not followed by Marantz et al. (2003). We likewise do not do so here.

Based primarily on molecular data, Aleixo (2002) concluded that *Lepidocolaptes fuscus* (Lesser Woodcreeper), long assigned to that genus, was better assigned to the genus *Xiphorhynchus*. Morphological and behavioral considerations support this, and the transfer was followed by Marantz et al. (2003).

We follow J. M. C. da Silva and F. C. Straube (*Stud. Neotrop. Fauna Environm.* 31[1]: 3–10, 1996) in recognizing *Lepidocolaptes falcinellus* (Scalloped Woodcreeper) of se. Brazil and adjacent Paraguay and Argentina as a separate species from *L. squamatus* (Scaled Woodcreeper) of e. Brazil. These authors also proposed recognizing *L. wagleri* (Wagler's Woodcreeper) as a species, but we agree with Marantz et al. (2003) that based on presently available evidence, this taxon is better considered as only a race of *L. squamatus*.

We follow C. F. Marantz (*Studies in Neotropical Ornithology Honoring Ted Parker,* Ornithol. Monogr. no. 48: 399–429, 1997) in recognizing *Dendrocolaptes sanctithomae* (Northern Barred Woodcreeper) as a separate species from *D. certhia* (Amazonian Barred Woodcreeper), based in particular on their strikingly different voices.

We follow Marantz et al. (2003) in not recognizing as full species two taxa recently described as such from the Serra do Carajás in e. Amazonian Brazil, *Hylexetastes brigidai* (da Silva, J. M. C., F. C. Novaes, and D. C. Oren, *Bull. B.O.C.* 115[4]: 200–206, 1995; here considered a race of *H. uniformis*) and *Xiphocolaptes carajensis* (da Silva, J. M. C., F. C. Novaes, and D. C. Oren, *Bull. B.O.C.* 122[3]: 185–196, 2002; here considered a race of *X. promeropirhynchus*).

M. L. Isler, P. R. Isler, and B. M. Whitney (*Studies in Neotropical Ornithology Honoring Ted Parker,* Ornithol. Monogr. 48: 355–381, 1997) are followed in recognizing a complex of allospecies in what formerly was treated as a single species, *Thamnophilus punctatus* (Slaty Antshrike): *T. punctatus* (Eastern Slaty Antshrike), *T. stictocephalus* (Natterer's Slaty Antshrike), *T. sticturus* (Bolivian Slaty Antshrike), *T. pelzelni* (Planalto Slaty Antshrike), *T. ambiguus* (Sooretama Slaty Antshrike), and the trans-Andean *T. atrinucha* (Western Slaty Antshrike). The last-named had been previously separated by Ridgely and Tudor (1994) and others; we would note that *stictocephalus, pelzelni,* and *ambiguus* are exceedingly close to each other morphologically and behaviorally. M. L. Isler, P. R. Isler, and B. M. Whitney

(*Condor* 103: 278–286, 2001) concluded that two taxa found in extreme s. Ecuador and nw. Peru, *leucogaster* and *huallagae,* earlier considered of uncertain status (and tentatively recognized as a full species by Ridgely and Greenfield 2001), are better treated as conspecific with *T. punctatus;* we concur.

B. M. Whitney, D. C. Oren, and R. T. Brumfield (*Auk* 121[4]: 1031–1039, 2004) described *Thamnophilus divisorius* (Acre Antshrike) as a new species, found only on remote ridges of extreme w. Brazil.

We follow Hilty (2003) in recognizing *Dysithamnus tucuyensis* (Venezuelan Antvireo) of the n. Venezuela mountains as a species distinct from *D. leucostictus* (White-streaked Antvireo) of the n. Andes.

M. L. Isler and P. R. Isler (*Proc. Biol. Soc. Wash.* 116: 23–28, 2003) suggested treating two taxa formerly considered distinct species, *Myrmotherula obscura* (Short-billed Antwren) of w. Amazonia and trans-Andean *M. ignota* (Griscom's Antwren), as a single species under the name *M. ignota* (Moustached Antwren), with *obscura* as a subspecies. Previously, *ignota* was usually considered a trans-Andean subspecies of *M. brachyura* (Pygmy Antwren). The voices of *ignota* and *obscura* are virtually if not in fact identical.

M. L. Isler, P. R. Isler, and B. M. Whitney (*Auk* 116[1]: 83–96, 1999) are followed in separating *Myrmotherula surinamensis* (Streaked Antwren) into three species: *M. surinamensis* (Guianan Streaked Antwren), *M. multostriata* (Amazonian Streaked Antwren), and the less closely related trans-Andean *M. pacifica* (Pacific Antwren).

M. L. Isler, D. R. Lacerda, P. R. Isler, S. J. Hackett, K. V. Rosenberg, and R. T. Brumfield (*Proc. Biol. Soc. Wash.* 119: 522–527, 2006) suggest that a group of "dead-leaf-searching" specialists long classified in the genus *Myrmotherula* might be better separated in the new genus *Epinecrophylla*. These species are *M. fulviventris, M. gutturalis, M. leucophthalma, M. haematonota, M. fjeldsaii, M. spodionota, M. erythrura,* and *M. ornata.*

N. K. Krabbe, M. L. Isler, P. R. Isler, B. M. Whitney, J. Alvarez A., and P. J. Greenfield (*Wilson Bull.* 111[2]: 157–165, 1999) described *Myrmotherula fjeldsaai* (Yasuní Antwren) as a new species, found in e. Ecuador and ne. Peru. It was originally named the Brown-backed Antwren, but as so many antwrens have brown backs, we follow Ridgely and Greenfield (2001) in employing the modifier "Yasuní" for the species, after the imperiled national park where it was first recognized.

Myrmotherula luctuosa (Silvery-flanked Antwren) of e. Brazil is recognized as a separate species from the wide-ranging *M. axillaris* (White-flanked Antwren) on the basis of its very different song, widely disjunct range, and plumage characters.

B. M. Whitney and J. Alvarez A. (*Auk* 115[3]: 559–576, 1998) described *Herpsilochmus gentryi* (Ancient Antwren) as a new species, found in ne. Peru and extreme se. Ecuador.

B. M. Whitney, J. F. Pacheco, D. R. C. Buzetti, and R. Parrini (*Auk* 117[4]: 869–891, 2000) described *Herpsilochmus sellowi* (Caatinga Antwren) as a new species, with a range in ne. Brazil that closely corresponds to the species called *H. pileatus* (Pileated Antwren) by Ridgely and Tudor (1994). *H. pileatus* was shown by Whitney et al. (op. cit.) to range only in coastal s. Bahia, Brazil; they suggested changing its English name to "Bahia Antwren," employed here.

Formicivora intermedia (Northern White-fringed Antwren) of Colombia and Venezuela is treated as a species distinct from *F. grisea* (Southern White-fringed Antwren), based primarily on its very different song. The ranges of *F. intermedia orenocensis* and *F. grisea rufiventris* approach each other closely in s. Venezuela, with no indication of intergradation.

M. R. Bornschein, B. L. Reinert, and D. M. Teixera (Instituto Iguaçu de Pesquisa e Preservação Ambiental, Rio de Janeiro, 1995) described *Stymphalornis acutirostris* (Marsh, or Paraná, Antwren) as a new species, found in se. Brazil in e. Paraná and ne. Santa Catarina. The genus is very close to *Formicivora*, and it may prove to be preferable to consider the two as congeneric. In 2005 it was reported to RSR that another, as yet undescribed, species of *Stymphalornis* had been discovered in marshes near the city of São Paulo.

R. Bierregaard, M. Cohn-Haft, and D. F. Stotz (*Studies in Neotropical Ornithology Honoring Ted Parker*, Ornithol. Monogr. 48: 111–128, 1997) are followed in recognizing *Cercomacra laeta* (Willis's Antbird) of n. Brazil and s. Guyana as a species separate from *C. tyrannina* (Dusky Antbird).

G. R. Graves (*Studies in Neotropical Ornithology Honoring Ted Parker*, Ornithol. Monogr. 48: 21–35, 1997) described *Cercomacra parkeri* (Parker's Antbird) as a new species, found locally in the Colombian Andes.

Krabbe and Nilsson (2003) suggest recognizing *Cercomacra fuscicauda* of the w. Amazonian lowlands as a species separate from *C. nigrescens* (Blackish Antbird), based primarily on its strikingly different vocalizations. We agree that this is likely the best course, but the situation is complex and we feel that a more thorough analysis is still required, so we follow Zimmer and Isler (2003) in continuing to regard them as conspecific. Krabbe and Nilsson (2003) suggest the English name "Riparian Antbird" for *C. fuscicauda*.

M. L. Isler, P. R. Isler, and B. M. Whitney (*Auk* 124[1]: 11–28, 2007) suggest that *Hypocnemis cantator* (Warbling Antbird) actually comprises six mainly parapatric species.

M. L. Isler, J. Alvarez A., P. R. Isler, and B. M. Whitney (*Wilson Bull.* 113[2]: 164–176, 2001) described *Percnostola arenarum* (Allpahuayo Antbird) as a new species, found in a limited area of ne. Peru.

M. L. Isler, P. R. Isler, B. M. Whitney, and K. J. Zimmer (*Wilson Bull.* 119[1]: 53–70, 2007) suggest that what we call *Schistocichla leucostigma* (Spot-winged Antbird; they place it in the genus *Percnostola*) actually comprises a complex of five mainly parapatric species.

M. L. Isler, J. Alvarez A., P. R. Isler, T. Valqui H., A. Begazo, and B. M. Whitney (*Auk* 119[2]: 362–378, 2002) are followed in separating *Myrmeciza castanea* (Northern Chestnut-tailed Antbird) of nw. Amazonia as a species distinct from *M. hemimelaena* (Southern Chestnut-tailed Antbird).

The exciting rediscovery of *Pithys castaneus* (White-masked Antbird) in ne. Peru is recounted by D. F. Lane, T. Valqui H., J. Alvarez A., J. Armenta, and K. Eckardt (*Wilson Bull.* 118[1]: 13–22, 2006).

M. Irestedt, J. Fjeldså, U. S. Johansson, and P. G. P. Ericson (*Molec. Phylogen. and Evol.* 23: 499–512, 2002) are followed in considering the antpittas (genera *Grallaria, Hylopezus, Myrmothera,* and *Grallaricula*) as a separate family, Grallariidae.

We recognize *Formicarius hoffmanni* (Panama Antthrush) of s. Middle America to n. Colombia and n. Honduras as a species separate from *F. analis* (Black-faced Antthrush), primarily on the basis of its strikingly different song. *F. moniliger* (Mayan, or Mexican, Antthrush) of n. Middle America is also now generally considered a distinct species (cf. S. N. G. Howell, *Cotinga* 1: 20–25, 1994).

The English name of *Chamaeza turdina* is changed to "Schwartz's Antthrush," in preference to "Scalloped Antthrush" (the name employed by Ridgely and Tudor 1994), to accord with most recent references (including Hilty 2003).

The English name of *Chamaeza nobilis* is changed to "Striated Antthrush," in preference to "Noble Antthrush" (the name employed by Ridgely and Tudor 1994), to accord with most references.

What is presently considered *Grallaria rufula* (Rufous Antpitta) almost certainly comprises more than one species. *Cajamarcae* of n. Peru seems particularly distinct, on account of plumage differences and its markedly different song; it could be called Cajamarca Antpitta.

N. K. Krabbe, D. J. Agro, N. H. Rice, M. Jácome, L. Navarrete, and F. Sornoza (*Auk* 116[4]: 882–890, 1999) described *Grallaria ridgelyi* (Jocotoco Antpitta) as a new (and very distinct) species, found very locally in the Andes of extreme se. Ecuador.

S. Mayer (*Auk* 115[4]: 1072–1073, 1998) suggested recognizing *Hylopezus auricularis* (Masked Antpitta) of n. Bolivia as a species separate from *H. macularius* (Spotted Antpitta), primarily on the basis of its very different song. Further work may demonstrate that other taxa currently still treated as races of *H. macularius* may also deserve specific status.

The English name of *Hylopezus dives* is changed to "Thicket Antpitta," in preference to "Fulvous-bellied Antpitta" (the name employed in Ridgely and Tudor 1994, and in many earlier references). This is in accord with the 1998 AOU Check-list.

We recognize *Grallaricula leymebambae* (Leimebamba Antpitta) of the Peruvian and Bolivian Andes as a species separate from *G. ferrugineipectus* (Rusty-breasted Antpitta), based on its widely disjunct distribution and different voice; the latter is found in the Andes of Venezuela and n. Colombia.

M. Irestedt, J. Fjeldså, U. S. Johansson, and P. G. P. Ericson (*Molec. Phylogen. and Evol.* 23: 499–512, 2002) are followed in considering the four species in the genus *Melanopareia* and the *Teledromas* gallito as a separate family, the Melanopareiidae.

We follow P. Coopmans, N. K. Krabbe, and T. S. Schulenberg (*Bull. B.O.C.* 121[3]: 208–213, 2001) in separating *Scytalopus latrans* (Blackish Tapaculo) of the n. Andes as a species from *S. unicolor* (Unicolored Tapaculo) of nw. Peru.

We follow N. K. Krabbe and T. S. Schulenberg (2003) for the species-level taxonomy of the *Scytalopus* tapaculos, and for virtually all of their English names. Many taxa previously treated at

the subspecific level were raised to species rank therein, primarily on the basis of vocalization differences. These species are:

Scytalopus parvirostris (Trilling Tapaculo)
Scytalopus acutirostris (Tschudi's Tapaculo)
Scytalopus atratus (Northern White-crowned Tapaculo)
Scytalopus micropterus (Long-tailed Tapaculo)
Scytalopus meridanus (Mérida Tapaculo)
Scytalopus spillmanni (Spillmann's Tapaculo)
Scytalopus fuscicauda (Lara Tapaculo)
Scytalopus canus (Paramo Tapaculo)
Scytalopus affinis (Ancash Tapaculo)
Scytalopus altirostris (Neblina Tapaculo)
Scytalopus urubambae (Vilcabamba Tapaculo)
Scytalopus simonsi (Puna Tapaculo)
Scytalopus zimmeri (Zimmer's Tapaculo)
Scytalopus superciliaris (White-browed Tapaculo)

In addition, no less than seven *Scytalopus* species have been recently described (and more are yet forthcoming). As of 2005, these new species are the following:

Scytalopus parkeri (Krabbe and Schulenberg 1997), found in the Andes of se. Ecuador.
Scytalopus stilesi (A. M. Cuervo, C. D. Cadena, N. K. Krabbe, and L. M. Renjifo, *Auk* 122[2]: 445–463, 2005), found in the Cen. Andes of Colombia.
Scytalopus rodriguezi (N. K. Krabbe, P. G. W. Salaman, A. Cortés, A. Quevedo, L. A. Ortega, and C. D. Cadena, *Bull. B.O.C.* 125[2]: 93–108, 2005), found on Andean slopes in the upper Río Magdalena valley of Colombia.
Scytalopus chocoensis (Krabbe and Schulenberg 1997), found in sw. Colombia and nw. Ecuador.
Scytalopus robbinsi (Krabbe and Schulenberg 1997), found in the Andes of sw. Ecuador.
Scytalopus schulenbergi (B. M. Whitney, *Wilson Bull.* 106[4]: 585–614, 1994), found in the Andes of se. Peru and w. Bolivia.
Scytalopus iraiensis (M. R. Bornschein, B. L. Reinert, and M. Pichorim, *Ararajuba* 6[1]: 3–36, 1998), found in e. Paraná in se. Brazil.

What has long been known as *Scytalopus speluncae* (Mouse-colored Tapaculo) apparently comprises two species, with *S. speluncae* now believed to be confined to the Serra do Espinhaço in Minas Gerais. The much more widespread form of the se. Brazil region was recently given the name *S. notorius* (M. A. Raposo, R. Stopiglia, V. Loskot, and G. M. Kirwan, *Zootaxa* 1271: 37–56, 2006).

We recognize *Phaeomyias tumbezana* (Tumbesian Tyrannulet) of w. Ecuador and nw. Peru as a species distinct from the wide-ranging *P. murina* (Mouse-colored Tyrannulet), on account of its strikingly different vocalizations.

We recognize *Zimmerius flavidifrons* (Loja Tyrannulet) of s. Ecuador as a species distinct from *Z. chrysops* (Golden-faced Tyrannulet) on account of its strikingly different vocalizations.

J. Alvarez A. and B. M. Whitney (*Wilson Bull.* 113[1]: 1–9, 2001) described *Zimmerius villarejoi* (Mishana Tyrannulet) as a new species, known only from ne. Peru.

J. M. C. da Silva (*Bull. B.O.C.* 116[2]: 109–113, 1996) is followed in recognizing *Phyllomyias urichi* (Urich's Tyrannulet) of ne. Venezuela as a distinct species, primarily on account of its enormous range disjunction from both *P. virescens* (Greenish Tyrannulet) and *P. reiseri* (Reiser's Tyrannulet).

We recognize *Stigmatura gracilis* (Caatinga Wagtail-Tyrant) and *S. bahiae* (Bahia Wagtail-Tyrant) as full species, split from *S. budytoides* (Greater Wagtail-Tyrant) and *S. napensis* (Lesser Wagtail-Tyrant) respectively. Both species range in caatinga scrub of ne. Brazil and, apart from being morphologically distinct (especially *S. bahiae*), differ vocally from their purported parent species.

Controversy continues in the *Serpophaga subcristata/munda* complex (White-crested/White-bellied Tyrannulets). R. J. Straneck (*Rev. MACN, Zool.*, 16: 51–63, 1993) recently suggested that *subcristata* and *munda* be considered conspecific. He also presented evidence of an additional species, to which he applied the name *S. griseiceps* (the name *griseiceps* having been based on a small series of specimens taken in the highlands of Cochabamba, Bolivia). S. K. Herzog (*Bull. B.O.C.* 121[4]: 273–277, 2001), however, came to the opposite conclusion, that *S. munda* was indeed a separate species from *S. subcristata* (though a few apparently intermediate specimens exist). S. K. Herzog and J. M. Barnett (*Auk* 121[2]: 415–421, 2004) then confirmed that the specimens that had formed the basis of the description of *griseiceps* were actually juvenile examples of *S. munda*, so that name then became a junior synonym of *munda* and the "new" species of Straneck had no applicable name. It still does

not—a publication that will provide one is in preparation—and hence this still undescribed taxon cannot be treated here.

K. J. Zimmer and A. Whittaker (*Wilson Bull.* 112[1]: 51–66, 2000) are followed in separating *Inezia caudata* of n. South America as a separate species from *I. subflava* of Amazonia, on the basis of their very different voices. The expanded species was formerly known as the Pale-tipped Tyrannulet. Zimmer and Whittaker (op. cit.) suggested calling these two species the Pale-tipped Inezia and the Amazonian Inezia, and we do so here; this necessitates changing the group name for the two other *Inezia* species as well.

K. J. Zimmer, A. Whittaker, and D. C. Oren (*Auk* 118[1]: 56–78, 2001) described *Suiriri islerorum* (Chapada Suiriri) as a new species, found in s.-cen. Brazil and ne. Bolivia. They called the new species the Chapada Flycatcher; we prefer to use the generic name *Suiriri* as its English group name. We also now favor considering *S. suiriri* (Chaco Suiriri) and *S. affinis* (Campo Suiriri) as separate species, not viewing the evidence for their conspecificity as having been demonstrated; they differ markedly, for flycatchers, in appearance, behavior, and voice.

Recent evidence (fide P. Coopmans) indicates that the form of *Elaenia chiriquensis* (Lesser Elaenia) found in sw. Colombia and nw. Ecuador, *brachyptera*, although not dissimilar morphologically from other races of the species (e.g., *albivertex*), differs strikingly in its primary vocalization. It likely merits full species status.

P. Coopmans and N. K. Krabbe (*Wilson Bull.* 112[3]: 305–312, 2000) described *Myiopagis olallai* (Foothill Elaenia) as a new species found locally in the east-slope foothills of Ecuador and Peru.

L. P. Gonzaga and J. F. Pacheco (*Bull. B.O.C.* 115[2]: 88–97, 1995) described *Phylloscartes beckeri* (Bahia Tyrannulet) as a new species found locally in Bahia, Brazil.

J. W. Fitzpatrick and D. F. Stotz (*Studies in Neotropical Ornithology Honoring Ted Parker*, Ornithol. Monogr. 48: 37–44, 1997) described *Phylloscartes parkeri* (Cinnamon-faced Tyrannulet) as a new species, found along the eastern base of the Andes in cen. and s. Peru.

We follow the 1998 AOU Check-list in merging the monotypic genus *Atalotriccus*, in which the Pale-eyed Pygmy-Tyrant of n. Colombia and Venezuela has long been placed, into the genus *Lophotriccus*.

M. Cohn-Haft, A. Whittaker, and P. C. Stouffer

(*Studies in Neotropical Ornithology Honoring Ted Parker,* Ornithol. Monogr. 48: 205–235, 1997) are followed in recognizing *Hemitriccus griseipectus* (White-bellied Tody-Tyrant, with *naumburgae*) of s. Amazonia as a separate species from *H. zosterops* (White-eyed Tody-Tyrant).

N. K. Johnson and R. E. Jones (*Auk* 118[2]: 334–341, 2001) described *Poecilotriccus luluae* (Lulu's Tody-Flycatcher) as a new species, found in a limited area on the east slope of the Andes in n. Peru south of the Río Marañón.

We revert to using the group name "flatbill" for the genus *Tolmomyias*. This name was employed early on (e.g., in *Birds of the Americas,* part 5) but then for reasons unknown was switched to the much less useful "flycatcher." Although not as extreme as seen in *Rhynchocyclus, Tolmomyias* bills are notably wide and flat,

T. S. Schulenberg and T. A. Parker III (*Studies in Neotropical Ornithology Honoring Ted Parker,* Ornithol. Monogr. 48: 723–731, 1997) described *Tolmomyias traylori* (Orange-eyed Flatbill) as a new species, found locally in w. Amazonia.

Based on its very different voice, we recognize trans-Andean *Tolmomyias flavotectus* as a species separate from Amazonian *T. assimilis* (the latter also likely comprises more than one species). *T. flavotectus* retains the English name "Yellow-margined Flatbill," with *T. assimilis* becoming "Zimmer's Flatbill."

We follow a suggestion of J. M. Bates, T. A. Parker III, A. P. Caparella, and T. J. Davis (*Bull. B.O.C.* 112[2]: 90–91, 1992) that *Tolmomyias viridiceps* be considered a separate species from *T. flaviventris,* based primarily on its notably different vocalizations. *T. flaviventris* becomes the Ochre-lored Flatbill, and *T. viridiceps* the Olive-faced Flatbill.

We consider the four main population groups of *Onychorhynchus* royal flycatchers as allospecies, rather than continuing to consider them as conspecific (as in Ridgely and Tudor 1994), in accord with a number of recent references, including the Comite Brasileiro de Registros Ornitológicos (2006). Though similar vocally, quite striking morphological differences exist among the four groups.

We use the generic name *Myiobius* as the group name for that distinctive genus of flycatchers (now Whiskered, Yellow-rumped, Sulphur-rumped, Black-tailed, and Tawny-breasted Myiobius instead of Flycatcher). The change was forced by one species, *M. mastacalis,* formerly having the same English name (Yellow-

rumped Flycatcher) as a fairly well-known Asian member of the Muscicapidae, *Ficedula zanthopygia* (e.g., Gill and Wright 2006).

We consider the three main population groups that compose *Myiobius barbatus* (Whiskered Myiobius) as allospecies (in addition *M. sulphureipygius,* Sulphur-rumped Myiobius, and *M. mastacalis,* Yellow-rumped Myiobius) rather than continuing to regard them as conspecific (as in Ridgely and Tudor 1994). As with the royal flycatchers, striking morphological differences and range disjunctions exist.

We rename *Mitrephanes phaeocercus* the Northern (rather than the Common) Tufted Flycatcher, preferring to restrict the use of the name "Common" to species that truly are so.

We recognize *Contopus punensis* (Tumbes Pewee) of w. Ecuador and nw. Peru as a species distinct from *C. cinereus* (Tropical Pewee) on the basis of its strikingly different primary vocalization. Further study may well show that some taxa still considered part of *C. cinereus* may also deserve full-species status.

The applicable species name of the Olive-sided Flycatcher was recently shown to be *cooperi* and not the long-used *borealis,* and the former has now come into current use (e.g., 1998 AOU Check-list).

It has been suggested that the population of what is considered to be *Cnemotriccus fuscatus* (Fuscous Flycatcher) in the Bolivian highlands may represent a separate, undescribed species-level taxon (Mayer 2000). Earlier it had been suggested that there might also be two species of "Fuscous Flycatchers" in se. Brazil. More study is needed.

J. García-Moreno, P. Arctander, and J. Fjeldså (*Condor* 100[4]: 629–640, 1998) are followed in recognizing *Ochthoeca nigrita* (Blackish Chat-Tyrant) of the Venezuelan Andes and *O. thoracica* (Maroon-belted Chat-Tyrant, with *angustifasciata*) of the Andes of Peru and Bolivia as species distinct from *O. cinnamomeiventris* (Slaty-backed Chat-Tyrant).

J. García-Moreno, P. Arctander, and J. Fjeldså (*Condor* 100[4]: 629–640, 1998) are followed in subsuming the genus *Silvicultrix* into *Ochthoeca.* The same authors recognize *O. spodionota* (Kalinowski's Chat-Tyrant) of s. Peru and Bolivia as a species distinct from *O. frontalis* (Crowned Chat-Tyrant), found farther north in the Andes.

The generic allocation of what we call *Agriornis murinus* (Lesser Shrike-Tyrant) has been the subject of considerable debate in recent decades.

It has been suggested that the species could be placed in either the genus *Xolmis* (e.g., Meyer de Schauensee 1966, 1970), *Agriornis* (e.g., Sibley and Monroe 1990, Ridgely and Tudor 1994), or *Neoxolmis* (e.g., Barnett and Pearman 2001). In color and pattern the species strongly resembles *Agriornis*, but in behavior it more resembles *Xolmis*, particularly two species (*rubetra, salinarum*) that have traditionally been classified in *Xolmis* but actually may better be transferred to *Neoxolmis* (long a monotypic genus for the Chocolate-vented Tyrant, *N. rufiventris*). It is clear that a thorough re-examination of the relationships in this complex is sorely needed.

R. T. Chesser (*Molec. Phylogen. and Evol.* 15[3]: 369–380, 2000) is followed in recognizing *Muscisaxicola griseus* (Plain-capped Ground Tyrant) of the Peruvian and Bolivian Andes as a species distinct from *M. alpinus* (Paramo Ground Tyrant) of the Andes of Colombia and Ecuador.

We follow J. M. C. da Silva and D. C. Oren (*Goeldiana Zool.* 16: 1–9, 1992) in regarding *Knipolegus franciscanus* (São Francisco Black Tyrant) of e. Brazil as a species separate from the widely disjunct *K. aterrimus* (White-winged Black Tyrant). The English name "Caatinga Black Tyrant," usually applied to it, is inaccurate; actually the species is *not* found in the caatinga.

We recognize the trans-Andean population of the genus *Sirystes* as a species (Western Sirystes, *S. albogriseus*) separate from widespread cis-Andean populations (*S. sibilator*, Eastern Sirystes). This is based especially on their strikingly different vocalizations.

The English name of *Xenopsaris albinucha* is changed to "White-naped Xenopsaris" in preference to simply "Xenopsaris," as in Ridgely and Tudor (1994), to accord with most references.

Following Fitzpatrick (2004) and most recent references, we subsume the genus *Platypsaris*, in which three becard species have sometimes been placed (including in Ridgely and Tudor 1994) into the genus *Pachyramphus*.

We follow the IOC Standing Committee on English Names (Gill and Wright 2006) and various other recent authors in employing the group name "schiffornis" for members of the genus *Schiffornis*, and not "mourner."

B. M. Whitney, J. F. Pacheco, and R. Parrini (*Ararajuba* 3: 43–53, 1995) are followed in recognizing *Neopelma chrysolophum* (Serra do Mar Tyrant-Manakin) as a separate species from *N. aurifrons* (Wied's Tyrant-Manakin).

J. A. Mobley and R. O. Prum (*Condor* 97[3]: 650–662, 1995) demonstrated that the enigmatic, monotypic genus *Neopipo*, long considered a piprid (Cinnamon Manakin), is most closely related to the tyrannid genus *Terenotriccus*; they also recommend transferring it to the Tyrannidae. Mobley and Prum (op. cit.) suggest the English name "Cinnamon Tyrant." We suggest, however, calling the species the Cinnamon Neopipo (in accord with Hilty 2003 and others), because the group name of "Tyrant" will likely cause confusion with the Cinnamon Flycatcher (*Pyrrhomyias cinnamomeus*).

Prum (1992) recommended merging the genus *Chloropipo*, in which four manakin species were formerly placed (including in Ridgely and Tudor 1994), into the genus *Xenopipo*.

G. Coelho and W. Silva (*Ararajuba* 6[2]: 81–84, 1998) described as a new species the stunning Araripe Manakin (*Antilophia bokermanni*), found only in s. Ceará in ne. Brazil.

We recognize the striped manakins found locally in nw. South America as a species (Western Striped Manakin, *Machaeropterus striolatus*) separate from those found in far distant e. Brazil (Eastern Striped Manakin, *M. regulus*), on the basis of their totally different voices and their extreme range disjunction. This is in agreement with Snow (2004). In addition, it has been suggested that *aureopectus* of the tepuis and a single site in Peru may deserve species status (L. O. Rodríguez and D. K. Moscovits, eds., Perú: Biabo Cordillera Azul, Rapid Biological Inventories Report 2, Chicago, IL).

Prum (1992) recommended separating the crowned manakins formerly placed in the genus *Pipra* into the genus *Lepidothrix*, and this is followed here. Prum (op. cit.) also recommended separating *P. pipra* into the monotypic genus *Dixiphia*, and although this may be correct, the evidence for it seems to be less strong, and we retain that species in *Pipra*.

Following the evidence presented by G. Bromfield, W. N. Ritchie, V. Bromfield, J. Ritchie, and A. B. Hennessey (*Cotinga* 21: 63–67, 2004), we recognize *Phibalura boliviana* (Palkachupa Cotinga), found only in a very limited area in the Andes of w. Bolivia, as a species distinct from *P. flavirostris* (Swallow-tailed Cotinga), of the se. Brazil region.

We recognize the Andean population of *Laniisoma*, *L. buckleyi* (Andean Laniisoma), as a species distinct from birds found in far distant se. Brazil, *L. elegans* (Brazilian Laniisoma), based on plumage characters and its different song.

M. B. Robbins, G. H. Rosenberg, and F. Sornoza M. (*Auk* 111[1]: 1–7, 1994) described *Doliornis remseni* (Chestnut-bellied Cotinga) as a new species, found very locally in the Andes of w. Colombia and e. Ecuador.

We follow the evidence presented by R. O. Prum, N. H. Rice, J. A. Mobley, and W. W. Dimmick (*Auk* 117[1]: 236–241, 2000) in separating two piha species (*subalaris* and *cryptolophus*, Gray-tailed and Olivaceous Pihas) into their own genus. Based on morphological features this pair of pihas was transferred out of the genus *Lipaugus*, in which they were long placed, into the genus *Lathria* (R. O. Prum, *Occ. Papers Mus. Zool. Univ. Mich.* 723: 1–44, 1990). Prum subsequently (*Ibis* 143[2]: 307–309, 2001) determined that the name *Lathria* was not available, and proposed as a replacement the new name *Snowornis*.

A. M. Cuervo, P. G. W. Salaman, T. M. Donegan, and J. M. Ochoa (*Ibis* 143[3]: 353–368, 2001) described *Lipaugus weberi* (Chestnut-capped Piha) as a new species, found in the Central Andes of Antioquia, Colombia.

Populations of the Green Jay found disjunctly in n. Middle America are recognized as a species (*Cyanocorax luxuosus*, Green Jay) separate from those of the Andes (*C. yncas*, Inca Jay). The two groups have strikingly different habitats, vocalizations, and breeding strategies.

F. H. Sheldon and D. W. Winkler (*Auk* 110[4]: 798–824, 1993) are followed in merging the monotypic genus *Phaeoprogne*, in which the Brown-chested Martin has long been placed, into *Progne*.

Progne elegans (Southern Martin) and *P. murphyi* (Peruvian Martin) are considered species separate from the extralimital *P. modesta* (Galápagos Martin), following the 1983 and 1998 AOU Check-lists, though not some other recent authors (e.g., Ridgely and Tudor 1989, Sibley and Monroe 1990). Given the narrowly defined species limits in *Progne* martins currently accepted in North and Middle America and the West Indies, this seems the most consistent treatment.

Following the 1998 AOU Check-list and most other recent authors, the generic name for the American Cliff and Chestnut-throated Swallows is changed from *Hirundo* to *Petrochelidon*. Following Gill and Wright (2006), and because of several Old World swallows, the English name

of *P. pyrrhonota* must be changed from simply "Cliff Swallow" to "American Cliff Swallow."

Tachycineta stolzmanni (Tumbes Swallow) of extreme sw. Ecuador and nw. Peru is recognized as a separate species from Mangrove Swallow (*T. albilinea*) of Middle America, based on its highly disjunct range, smaller size and smaller bill, and on new information concerning habitat and plumage differences (cf. M. B. Robbins, G. H. Rosenberg, F. Sornoza M., M. A. Jácome, *Studies in Neotropical Ornithology Honoring Ted Parker*, Ornithol. Monogr. 48: 609–612, 1997).

Tachycineta meyeni has been shown to be the applicable scientific name for the Chilean Swallow, and not the formerly widely used *T. leucopyga* (cf. Sibley and Monroe 1990).

F. H. Sheldon and D. W. Winkler (*Auk* 110[4]: 798–824, 1993) recognized the monotypic genus *Pygochelidon* for the Blue-and-white Swallow (*P. cyanoleuca*), separating it from the genus *Notiochelidon* in which it had long been placed (e.g., Meyer de Schauensee 1966, 1970; Ridgely and Tudor 1989). This course was followed in the 1998 AOU Check-list (in which the extralimital *murina* and *flavipes* were not considered). Turner (2004), however, continued to retain all these species in *Notiochelidon*, and this is the course followed here.

The generic placement of the Tawny-headed Swallow reverts from being placed in the genus *Stelgidopteryx* (e.g., Ridgely and Tudor 1989; Sibley and Monroe 1990) to the previously used monotypic genus *Alopochelidon*. This is based on the male's lack of serration on the outer web of its outermost primary, and on its different voice (more like that of *Tachycineta*; pers. obs.). Its placement in a monotypic genus is in accord with Turner (2004).

The genus for the Andean Swallow is changed from *Hirundo* (which also has been placed in *Petrochelidon*) to *Haplochelidon*; cf. K. C. Parkes (*Auk* 110[4]: 947–950, 1993). This species' relationships remain uncertain; Parkes (op. cit.) suggested that it might be better placed in *Stelgidopteryx*, but we do not find this persuasive.

R. T. Brumfield and J. V. Remsen, Jr., (*Wilson Bull.* 108[2]: 205–227, 1996) are followed in separating what was long known as *Cinnycerthia peruana* (Sepia-brown Wren) into three allospecies: from north to south, *C. olivascens* (Sepia-brown Wren) from Colombia to n. Peru; *C. peruana* (Peruvian Wren) in Peru; and *C. fulva* (Fulvous Wren) of s. Peru and Bolivia. Brumfield and Remsen (op. cit.) suggested the English name "Sharpe's Wren" for *C. olivascens,* but we prefer to retain "Sepia-brown Wren" for this relatively well-known species (also the darkest, most sepia, in the complex). Brumfield and Remsen (op. cit.) suggested the English name "Superciliated Wren" for *C. fulva,* having overlooked that *Thryothorus superciliaris* has long gone by that name.

F. Vuilleumier, M. LeCroy, and E. Mayr (*Bull. B.O.C.* 112A: 296, 1992) suggest that the recently described *Thryothorus eisenmanni* (Inca Wren) might be better treated as the southernmost subspecies of *T. euophrys* (Plain-tailed Wren). We favor, however, continuing to regard it as a full species.

R. T. Brumfield and A. P. Capparella (*Condor* 98[3]: 547–556, 1996) suggest that *Troglodytes musculus,* found from s. Mexico south into South America, should be regarded as a species (Southern House Wren) distinct from *T. aedon,* which ranges in North America and n. Mexico (Northern House Wren). Though the 1998 AOU Check-list continued to regard all forms in the complex as conspecific, we consider the evidence Brumfield and Capparella presented persuasive, and thus treat *T. musculus* as an allospecies of *T. aedon.*

We follow R. W. Woods (*Bull. B.O.C.* 113[4]: 195–207, 1993) in recognizing *Troglodytes cobbi* (Cobb's Wren) of the Falkland Islands as a species distinct from *T. musculus* (Southern House Wren) of the mainland.

P. G. W. Salaman, P. Coopmans, T. M. Donegan, M. Mulligan, A. Cortés, S. L. Hilty, and L. A. Ortega (*Ornitol. Colomb.* 1: 4–21, 2003) described *Henicorhina negreti* (Munchique Wood Wren) as a new species, found very locally in the W. Andes of Cauca, Colombia.

We follow most recent authors in merging the genus *Platycichla* (in which two thrush species, *leucops* and *flavipes,* were formerly placed) into the wide-ranging *Turdus* genus.

We suspect that the southern (dark) population, *anthracinus,* presently considered conspecific with the Chiguanco Thrush (*Turdus chiguanco*), will prove to be a separate species from *T. chiguanco*'s paler populations found to the north. More work in the contact zone needs to be done, and the relationship of *T. chiguanco* with *T. fuscater* (Great Thrush), especially in Bolivia, presents additional complications. Should it be split, southern birds would become *T. anthracinus* (Coal-black Thrush).

Two *Turdus* thrushes have long gone by the English name "Bare-eyed Thrush," the American *T. nudigenis* and the African *T. tephronotus.* Sibley and Monroe (1990) proposed changing the name of the American species to "Yellow-eyed Thrush," a suggestion we are loath to follow, for it is the bare ocular area, not the eye itself, that is yellow. The bare ocular areas of both species are equally large and striking, and both are relatively well-known species. We therefore follow, with some reluctance, the IOC Standing Committee (Gill and Wright 2006) in adding "American" to the familiar name, hence "American Bare-eyed Thrush."

Turdus daguae (Dagua Thrush) of w. Colombia and w. Ecuador is considered a separate species from *T. assimilis* (White-throated Thrush) of Mexico to w. Panama, based mainly on its very different vocalizations (totally lacking the White-throated's mimidlike phraseology) but also on certain morphological considerations. The song of *T. daguae* actually resembles that of cis-Andean *T. albicollis* (White-necked Thrush) more than it does *T. assimilis.*

It seems likely that what is presently considered the Tropical Gnatcatcher (*Polioptila plumbea*) consists of at least two species; they differ from each other far more than do the populations formerly united as *P. guianensis* (Guianan Gnatcatcher), recently proposed as separate species. Populations east of the Andes and in Venezuela would remain as the Tropical Gnatcatcher (*P. plumbea*), and trans-Andean (and Middle American) birds would best be called the White-faced Gnatcatcher (*P. bilineata*). Complications arise, however, in certain cis-Andean populations (some of which sing very differently), as well as in a lack of precise knowledge concerning possible contact zones in n. Colombia. Hence, we feel we are precluded at this time from making this change. On the other hand, *P. maior* (Marañón Gnatcatcher) of the upper Río Marañón valley in nw. Peru differs notably on the basis of its large size, minimal sexual dimorphism, and voice; therefore, we do consider it a distinct species here.

B. M. Whitney and J. J. Alvarez (*Wilson Bull.* 117[2]: 113–207, 2005) described *Polioptila clementsi* (Iquitos Gnatcatcher) as a new species, known only from a white-sand forest near Iquitos in ne. Peru. The same authors also urged recognition of two taxa previously considered subspecies of *P. guianensis* (Guianan Gnatcatcher) as full species: *P. facilis* (Rio Negro Gnatcatcher) and *P. paraensis* (Pará Gnatcatcher).

R. J. Straneck (*Rev. Museo Arg. Cienc. Nat. "Bernardino Rivadavia"* 14[6]: 95–102, 1987) demonstrated that *Anthus chacoensis* is a valid species distinct from the morphologically very similar Yellowish Pipit (*A. lutescens,* of which it was described as a race), based especially on its entirely different song and flight display. *A. chacoensis* long went by the name "Chaco Pipit," though now that the species has become better known it is clear that it never occurs in the chaco. That name being so misleading, we call it the Campo Pipit.

S. I.. Olson (*Wilson Bull.* 106[1]: 1–17, 1994) provided a thorough review of the status of *Vireo gracilirostris* (Noronha Vireo), supporting its treatment as a full species.

P. G. W. Salaman and F. G. Stiles (*Ibis* 138[4]: 610–619, 1996) described *Vireo masteri* (Chocó Vireo) as a new species found very locally in the W. Andes of Colombia and recently in extreme nw. Ecuador as well.

E. O. Willis (*Wilson Bull.* 103[4]: 559–567, 1991) demonstrated that *Hylophilus amaurocephalus* (Gray-eyed Greenlet) of e. Brazil should be recognized as a species separate from *H. poicilotis* (Rufous-crowned Greenlet) of the se. Brazil region. The isolated populations in Bolivia and adjacent Mato Grosso are believed to be allied to *H. amaurocephalus* but deserve further study.

Despite their plumage similarity, it is likely that the Guianan and Amazonian populations of the Lemon-chested Greenlet (*Hylophilus thoracicus*) represent a separate species from the geographically far-removed population in se. Brazil. In this case, the English name "Lemon-chested Greenlet" should remain with the much more widespread *H. griseiventris* of Amazonia and the Guianas, and *H. thoracicus* of se. Brazil would be called the Rio de Janeiro Greenlet.

We have opted to follow various recent references (e.g., Curson et al. 1994) in employing the much more accurate group name "whitestart" rather than the long-used "redstart" for the genus *Myioborus*. All members of the genus flash ("start") white in the tail, not red.

B. P. Escalante-Pliego (*Acta 20 Congr. Internat. Ornithol.*: 333–341, 1990) is followed in considering *Geothlypis auricularis* (with *peruviana;* Black-lored Yellowthroat) of sw. Ecuador and nw. Peru, and *G. velata* of s.-cen. South America, as species separate from *G. aequinoctialis* (Masked Yellowthroat) of n. South America, based on substantial variation in their allozymes. The extralimital *G. chiriquensis* (Chiriquí Yellowthroat) of Costa Rica and Panama also warrants being considered an allospecies in the complex. No English name appears to have been proposed for *G. velata*. As

it is so similar in appearance to *G. aequinoctialis,* we opt to give it a geographic modifier; it is the southernmost-ranging *Geothlypis,* so we call it the Southern Yellowthroat.

The boreal migrant *Dendroica aestiva* (Yellow Warbler) and the resident *D. petechia* (Mangrove Warbler, including the *erithachorides* group of the West Indies and n. Venezuela) are considered separate species, following genetic data presented by N. Klein and W. M. Brown (*Evolution* 48: 1914–1932, 1994). There are also consistent plumage as well as behavioral and vocal differences between the two groups. Taxonomic treatment of the three groups has varied over the last few decades, though usually all taxa have been considered conspecific.

Based especially on their totally different songs, the pair of highly disjunct taxa that formerly comprised *Basileuterus chrysogaster* (Golden-bellied Warbler) are here treated as separate species, with *B. chlorophrys* of sw. Colombia and w. Ecuador being called the Chocó Warbler (its distribution encompassing much of that region), and *B. chrysogaster* of s. Peru and extreme w. Bolivia being called the Cuzco Warbler (its distribution centering on that Peruvian department).

Based on their highly disjunct ranges and strikingly different vocalizations, we consider *Basileuterus roraimae* (Roraiman Warbler) of the tepuis a separate species from *B. bivittatus* (Two-banded Warbler) of the Andes from s. Peru to nw. Argentina, in agreement with Hilty (2003).

We suspect that what is now considered to be the nominate group of *Basileuterus culicivorus* (Golden-crowned Warbler), ranging in Middle America, will prove, on the basis of its very different song, to be a separate species from South American populations presently considered conspecific.

Basileuterus hypoleucus (White-bellied Warbler), despite appearing superficially very different on account of its whitish underparts, seems closely related to the *auricapillus* group of what is now considered *B. culicivorus* (Golden-crowned Warbler) and has virtually identical behavior and vocalizations. There are apparently some intermediate specimens (Sick 1993), and it is possible that *hypoleucus* may prove to be better considered as conspecific with *B. culicivorus*. Recent field work, however, has verified that there are a few sites where they are sympatric, and so we continue to maintain them as distinct species.

Basileuterus delatrii (Chestnut-capped Warbler), found from Guatemala south into nw.

South America, is considered a separate species from *B. rufifrons* (Rufous-capped Warbler) of Mexico and adjacent Guatemala; this is based primarily on their very different songs (cf. J. W. Hardy et al., *Voices of Neotropical Wood Warblers,* 1994; Howell and Webb 1995). The 1998 AOU Check-list, however, continues to treat them as conspecific.

We continue to treat the two species Buff-rumped and Riverbank Warblers, sometimes considered to constitute the genus *Phaeothlypis* (e.g., the 1998 AOU Check-list and Gill and Wright 2006), as better placed in the genus *Basileuterus.* Our treatment was recently supported by molecular data (I. J. Lovette and E. Bermingham, *Auk* 119[3]: 694–714, 2002).

Basileuterus rivularis has long gone by the English name "River Warbler" in the Neotropical literature, although a sylviid warbler of Europe, *Locustella fluviatilis,* also carries that name. To avoid employing another awkward construct such as "American River Warbler," we call the South American species the Riverbank Warbler, in accord with Dickinson (2003) and Gill and Wright (2006).

W. J. Bock (*Neotropical Ornithology,* AOU Monograph no. 36, P. A. Buckley et al., eds., pp. 319–332, 1986) and Sibley and Monroe (1990) suggested recognizing the genus *Diglossopis* for four species of flowerpiercers: *Diglossa caerulescens, D. glauca, D. indigotica,* and *D. cyanea.*

The English name of *Diglossa glauca* is changed to "Golden-eyed Flowerpiercer" from "Deep-blue Flowerpiercer." Although many flowerpiercers are some shade of blue, *glaucus* is unique in the genus in having a conspicuous golden yellow iris.

The forms comprising *Conirostrum cinereum* (Cinereous Conebill) are perhaps worthy of specific separation. *Littorale* of w. Peru and n. Chile is replaced at higher elevations in the Peruvian Andes by the distinctly different nominate race; we are not aware that intergradation between these two taxa has been demonstrated, and the distribution pattern is typically one of full species. *Fraseri* of the Andes in Ecuador and s. Colombia is even more divergent in plumage. If split, *C. fraseri* could be called Fraser's Conebill, *C. littorale* the Littoral Conebill, and monotypic *C. cinereus* could remain the Cinereous Conebill.

Dacnis egregia (with *aequatorialis;* Yellow-tufted Dacnis) of w. Ecuador and w. Colombia (mainly in the Río Magdalena valley) is treated as a separate species from *D. lineata* (Black-faced Dacnis) of Amazonia and the Guianas, based on its different coloration, more prominent pectoral tuft, and disjunct distribution.

The monotypic genus *Erythrothlypis* (Scarlet-and-white Tanager) is so radically different from *Chrysothlypis* (Black-and-yellow Tanager) of s. Central America (also monotypic) that we now conclude that the two are best *not* merged (as first done, with no explanation, in J. L. Peters' *Checklist of the Birds of the World,* vol. 13). Should the two genera be merged, then likely both should be placed in *Hemithraupis.*

It remains possible that the two strikingly different groups presently united as *Tangara cayana* (Burnished-buff Tanager) are separate species, as suggested by Haverschmidt and Mees (1994). The little-known race *huberi* of Ilha Marajó in the mouth of the Amazon is, however, described as intermediate in at least some characters. If split, northern birds would become *T. cayana* (Rufous-crowned Tanager), southern birds *T. flava* (Stripe-bellied Tanager).

Though it has been suggested (e.g., Sick 1993) that *Tangara peruviana* (Black-backed Tanager) of se. Brazil is merely a morph of the more wide-ranging *T. preciosa* (Chestnut-backed Tanager), recent information concerning their different breeding distributions and habitats demonstrates that this view is no longer tenable.

F. Vuilleumier, M. LeCroy, and E. Mayr (*Bull. B.O.C.* 112A: 297, 1992) suggest that *Tangara phillipsi* (Sira Tanager) might be better treated as the southernmost subspecies of *T. heinei* (Black-capped Tanager). Given its wide range disjunction and quite marked plumage dissimilarities, however, we agree with the taxon's describers that *phillipsi* is better regarded as a southern allospecies of *T. heinei.*

What is still considered an isolated, distinct race of *Tangara velia* (Opal-rumped Tanager) found in e. Brazil is perhaps better regarded as a separate species, *T. cyanomelaena* (Silver-breasted Tanager).

We recognize *Tangara brasiliensis* (White-bellied Tanager) of se. Brazil as a species distinct from the widespread *T. mexicana* (Turquoise Tanager) of Amazonia. Though long considered a separate species (e.g., in Hellmayr's *Birds of the Americas*), *brasiliensis* was merged with *T. mexicana,* with no explanation, in *Birds of the World* (vol. 13), and this treatment has been followed subsequently.

J. García-Moreno, J. Ohlson, and J. Fjeldså (*Molec. Phylogen. and Evol.* 21[3]: 424–435, 2001) are followed in separating *Hemispingus auricu-*

laris of the Peruvian Andes as a separate species from *H. atropileus* (Black-capped Hemispingus) of the Andes from sw. Venezuela to northernmost Peru. We employ the English name "White-browed Hemispingus" for *H. auricularis*.

J. García-Moreno, J. Ohlson, and J. Fjeldså (*Molec. Phylogen. and Evol.* 21[3]: 424–435, 2001) also are followed in recognizing *Hemispingus piurae* (with *macrophrys*) of nw. Peru and adjacent Ecuador (Piura Hemispingus) as a species separate from *H. melanotis* (Black-eared Hemispingus). *H. ochraceus* (Western Hemispingus) of sw. Colombia and w. Ecuador was not analyzed in that paper, but we conclude that it too merits treatment as a full species.

Based on their stunningly different song (cf. recordings in Mayer 2000), it seems very likely that the Blue-winged Mountain Tanagers found in the Andes of Bolivia and extreme s. Peru should be treated as a separate species from taxa found farther north in the Andes (whose song is nowhere near as loud or complex; cf. recordings in Krabbe and Nilsson 2003). Neither form seems to respond to the other's song (RSR, pers. obs.), but whether they come into contact in s. Peru seems still to be unknown. If split, the former would become *Anisognathus flavinuchus* (Bolivian Mountain Tanager), leaving northern birds as *A. somptuosus* (Blue-winged Mountain Tanager).

The studies of K. J. Burns (*Auk* 115[3]: 621–634, 1998) suggest that *Piranga lutea* and the extralimital (Middle American) *P. hepatica* (Northern Hepatic Tanager) should be recognized as species distinct from *P. flava*. The English names proposed in Ridgely and Tudor (1989), "Lowland Hepatic Tanager" for *P. flava* and "Highland Hepatic Tanager" for *P. lutea*, are employed here. Haverschmidt and Mees (1994) propose possible species status for birds found on the tepuis in the Guianas, *haemalea;* if this course is followed, we would suggest that it go by the English name "Tepui Hepatic Tanager."

Ramphocelus icteronotus (Lemon-rumped Tanager) and *R. flammigerus* (Flame-rumped Tanager) are treated as closely related allospecies rather than conspecific. The two were long considered to be full species (e.g., Meyer de Schauensee 1966, 1970), but the discovery of a narrow band of apparent hybridization caused them to be treated as conspecific (Isler and Isler 1987, Ridgely and Tudor 1989, Sibley and Monroe 1990). Given the apparently very limited nature of that hybridization, and the recognition that two similar taxa in Central America are

now considered to be full species (S. J. Hackett, *Mol. Gen. Evol.* 5: 368–382, 1996; 1998 AOU Check-list), it seems is more appropriate to treat *R. flammigerus* and *R. icteronotus* as separate specific entities. We follow Hilty and Brown (1986) in employing the more distinctive English name "Lemon-rumped Tanager" for *R. icteronotus*, rather than the more generally used "Yellow-rumped Tanager."

Chlorothraupis frenata (Olive Tanager) of foothills on the east slope of the Andes is considered a separate species from *C. carmioli* (Carmiol's Tanager) of Nicaragua to extreme nw. Colombia, based on its different behavior and voice as well as its widely disjunct distribution.

We have changed the English name of *Neothraupis fasciata* to "Shrike-like Tanager" from the long used but singularly prosaic name "White-banded Tanager." This very distinctive species' overall pattern and color scheme is strikingly reminiscent of numerous typical shrikes (*Lanius* spp.).

The Cone-billed Tanager was long known from only a single specimen collected in 1938 in Mato Grosso, Brazil. It was finally rediscovered in 2004 by B. Carlos and others at Emas National Park in se. Goiás. By voice and ♀ plumage (the latter formerly unknown), the species appears to be most closely related to *Dolospingus fringilloides* (White-naped Seedeater) and not, as had been supposed, to *Conothraupis speculigera* (Black-and-white Tanager). We therefore revert to the genus in which the species was originally described, *Rhynchothraupis*. As yet only a tiny population is known.

The Streaked Saltators of mainland South and Central America are considered a species separate from birds found on the Lesser Antilles, following G. Seutin, J. Brawn, R. E. Ricklefs, and E. Bermingham (*Auk* 110[1]: 117–126, 1993). Mainland birds retain the English name "Streaked Saltator" but become *Saltator striatipectus;* West Indian birds retain the scientific name *S. albicollis* and are called the Lesser Antillean Saltator.

Recent evidence continues to support treating *Saltator maxillosus* (Thick-billed Saltator) as a species separate from *S. aurantiirostris* (Golden-billed Saltator). Their voices differ; also, cf. J. M. C. da Silva (*Bull. B.O.C.* 110[4]: 171–175, 1990).

What has long been called *Saltator atricollis* (Black-throated Saltator) is atypical for the genus in a number of respects, and we suspect it is actually not a saltator at all. It may be more closely allied to certain emberizid finches (such as *Embernagra*).

Recent biochemical evidence (cf. J. W. Tamplin, J. W. Demastes, and J. V. Remsen, Jr., *Wilson Bull.* 105[1]: 93–113, 1993) suggests that the genus *Pitylus* (Slate-colored and Black-throated Grosbeaks) is closely related to *Saltator* and is best merged therein. This change was accepted in the 1998 AOU Check-list, with the English group name "grosbeak" being retained.

A new generic name for the distinctive Yellow-shouldered Grosbeak was recently erected, *Parkerthraustes* (J. V. Remsen, Jr., *Studies in Neotropical Ornithology Honoring Ted Parker,* Ornithol. Monogr. 48: 89–90, 1997).

The English name of *Rhodospingus cruentus* is changed to "Crimson-breasted Finch" from "Crimson Finch." This shift was required to avoid a homonymous situation with an Australian estrildid finch, *Neochmia phaeton,* also called Crimson Finch. Sibley and Monroe (1990) suggested naming *Rhodospingus* the Crimson Finch-Tanager, but this seems confusingly similar to the long-established English name "Tanager Finch" for *Oreothraupis arremonops*.

M. Lentino and R. Restall (*Auk* 120[3]: 600–606, 2003) described *Amaurospiza carrizalensis* (Carrizal Seedeater) as a new species from the lower Río Caroni in Bolívar, Venezuela.

The larger members of the genus *Oryzoborus* continue to present taxonomic problems. We follow Sibley and Monroe (1990) in considering the black-billed populations of w. Amazonia as a full species (*O. atrirostris,* Black-billed Seedfinch), leaving the Great-billed (*O. maximiliani*) as occurring only in e. South America. In addition, on biogeographic and morphological grounds we now place the trans-Andean taxon *occidentalis* as a race of *O. crassirostris* and not of *O. maximiliani*.

Sick (1993) is followed in considering what was formerly called *Sporophila ardesiaca* (Dubois's Seedeater) of se. Brazil as a subspecies of *S. nigricollis* (Yellow-bellied Seedeater). Others (e.g., E. O. Willis and Y. Oniki, *Bull. B.O.C.* 113[1]: 27, 1993) have suggested that the *ardesiaca*-type plumage could be the result of hybridization between *S. nigricollis* and *S. caerulescens* (Double-collared Seedeater). In any case, it now seems clear that *ardesiaca* should not be regarded as a species.

F. G. Stiles (*Ornitol. Neotrop.* 7[2]: 75–127, 1996) is followed in treating trans-Andean *Sporophila corvina* (formerly called *S. aurita;* Variable Seedeater) and Amazonian *S. murallae* (Caquetá Seedeater) as separate species from eastern Amazonian *S. americana* (Wing-barred Seedeater). They differ in size, plumage details, and in some facets of behavior, and their songs appear to differ as well.

What was long called *Sporophila insulata* (Tumaco Seedeater), having only recently been rediscovered in coastal sw. Colombia (P. G. W. Salaman, *Cotinga* 4: 33–35, 1995), has now been shown (F. G. Stiles, *Ornitol. Neotrop.* 15(1): 17–30, 2004) to be better considered only a subspecies or color morph of *S. telasco* (Chestnut-throated Seedeater).

No less than four English names have been proposed for *Sporophila zelichi:* White-collared Seedeater (Narosky and Yzurieta 2003), Narosky's Seedeater (Ridgely and Tudor 1989, Sibley and Monroe 1990), Zelich's Seedeater (Canevari et al. 1991), and Entre Ríos Seedeater (Collar et al. 1992). The first is already in wide use for the Middle American species *S. torqueola,* so is obviously not a good choice. The two patronyms (the first for its describer, the second for its discoverer) seem in opposition to each other. Apparently, the species breeds mainly in Entre Ríos in ne. Argentina, which convinces us that the geographic modifier proposed by Collar et al. (1992) is the preferred choice.

M. A. Raposo and R. Parrini (*Bull. B.O.C.* 117[4]: 294–298, 1997) are followed in considering *Arremon semitorquatus* (Half-collared Sparrow) of se. Brazil as a species distinct from *A. taciturnus* (Pectoral Sparrow).

M. A. Raposo (*Ararajuba* 5: 1–9, 1997) described *Arremon franciscanus* (Sao Francisco Sparrow) as a new species, found in interior s.-cen. Brazil.

J. García-Moreno and J. Fjeldså (*Ibis* 141[2]: 199–207, 1999) are followed in recognizing *Atlapetes canigenis* (Cuzco Brushfinch) of Cuzco, Peru, as a species separate from *A. schistaceus* (Slaty Brushfinch) of the n. Andes.

J. García-Moreno and J. Fjeldså (*Ibis* 141[2]: 199–207, 1999) are followed in recognizing *Atlapetes forbesi* (Apurímac Brushfinch), found very locally in s. Peru, as a species separate from *A. rufigenis* (Rufous-eared Brushfinch) of nw. Peru.

T. Valqui H. and J. Fjeldså (*Ibis* 141[2]: 194–198, 1999) described *Atlapetes melanops* (Black-spectacled Brushfinch) as a new species, found very locally in the Andes of s. Peru. In the original article these authors overlooked that the species name *melanops* was preoccupied, and thus the species was later renamed *Atlapetes melanopsis* (T. Valqui H. and J. Fjeldså (*Ibis* 144[2]: 347, 2002).

J. V. Remsen, Jr., and W. S. Graves, IV (*Auk* 112[1]: 225–236, 1995) are followed in separating into the genus *Buarremon* three brushfinch species (*torquatus, atricapillus,* and *brunneinuchus*) formerly placed in *Atlapetes.* These authors considered *atricapillus* (with *tacarcunae* and *costaricensis*) conspecific with *B. torquatus.* We, however, maintain our previously stated opinion (Ridgely and Tudor 1989; R. A. Paynter, Jr., *Bull. Mus. Comp. Zool.* 148[7]: 323–369, 1978) that in the absence of information to the contrary, their pattern of altitudinal segregation warrants their continued treatment as separate species.

J. García-Moreno and J. Fjeldså (*Ibis* 141[2]: 199–207, 1999) are followed in recognizing *Atlapetes rufinucha* as comprising three species: *A. latinuchus* (Rufous-naped Brushfinch), *A. melanolaemus* (Gray-eared Brushfinch), and *A. rufinucha* (Bolivian Brushfinch). *A. terborghi* (Vilcabamba Brushfinch), recently described as a race of *A. rufinucha* (J. V. Remsen, Jr., *Proc. Biol. Soc. Wash.* 106[3]: 429–435, 1993), was also raised to species rank by García-Moreno and Fjeldså (op. cit.); we do likewise. García-Moreno and Fjeldså's (op. cit.) suggestion of "Black-faced" as an English name for *A. melanolaemus* seems unfortunate given that many brushfinches have faces that are equally black; in fact, the ear-coverts of *melanolaimus* are decidedly gray, a feature we prefer to highlight in the name "Gray-eared Brushfinch" for the species. As for the well-known *A. latinuchus* of the n. Andes, we favor simply continuing to call that species Rufous-naped Brushfinch and not saddle it (as García-Moreno and Fjeldså do) with the name "Northern Rufous-naped Brushfinch." As for *A. rufinucha,* we shorten their long name "Bolivian Rufous-naped Brushfinch" to simply "Bolivian Brushfinch."

J. García-Moreno and J. Fjeldså (*Ibis* 141[2]: 199–207, 1999) are followed in recognizing *Atlapetes crassus* of w. Colombia and w. Ecuador as a species distinct from *A. tricolor* (Tricolored Brushfinch) of the east slope of the Andes in s. Peru. As the range of *crassus* encompasses much of the Chocó region, we opt to call *A. crassus* the Chocó Brushfinch.

We change the name of *Atlapetes flaviceps* of Colombia's Cen. Andes to "Yellow-headed Brushfinch"; it formerly went by the name "Olive-headed Brushfinch." The head color of adults in this species is now known (fide F. G. Stiles) to be bright yellow, not olive.

H. Lloyd, B. Walker, C. Aucca C., and F. Schmitt (*Cotinga* 23: 48–51, 2005) suggest that instead of "Short-tailed Finch" (the English name the species was long known by), a much more appropriate name for *Idiopsar brachyurus* would be "Andean Boulder Finch." We agree.

The finch *Melanodera melanodera* long went by the name "Black-throated Finch" (*Birds of the Americas,* vol. 13, part 11; Meyer de Schauensee 1966, 1970) and was so named in Ridgely and Tudor (1989). An Australian estrildid finch, *Poephila cincta,* has also long been named "Black-throated Finch," and as a result Sibley and Monroe (1990) adopted the English name "Canary-winged Finch" for *M. melanodera.* This evocative name (originally suggested to B. Monroe by RSR) is eminently appropriate for the mainland population of the species but is less so for birds on the Falkland Islands (which have less yellow in their wings). As a result, we use the name "White-bridled Finch" for the species, as suggested by Barnett and Pearman (2001) and in contradistinction to the Yellow-bridled Finch, *M. xanthogramma.*

We agree with Barnett and Pearman (2001) that the genus *Compsospiza* is best retained for the two mountain finch species, *C. baeri* (Tucumán Mountain Finch) and *C. garleppi* (Cochabamba Mountain Finch). The genus had long been recognized as distinct but was merged, without explanation, into *Poospiza* in *Birds of the World* (vol. 13), which was then followed by Ridgely and Tudor (1989) and other recent authors. The monotypic genus *Poospizopis* seems even more distinct from *Poospiza;* it too was merged with no explanation into *Poospiza* in *Birds of the World* (vol. 13). We favor resurrecting it for *P. caesar* (Chestnut-breasted Mountain Finch).

Though currently classified as polytypic species, both *Sicalis flaveola* (Saffron Finch) and *S. luteola* (Grassland Yellowfinch) may each consist of more than one specific unit. Despite their more or less similar songs, various other factors make us question whether the widely disjunct southern group of *S. flaveola* (*pelzelni,* with *brasiliensis*) is actually conspecific with the much brighter nominate (with *valida*) northern group. That pair seem to differ from each other at least as much as does the southern group of *S. luteola* (*luteiventris,* presumably with *flavissima*) from more northern forms of *S. luteola.* Additional study may demonstrate that splitting is justified.

J. I. Hernandez-Prieto and J. V. Rodriguez-

Mahecha (*Caldasia* 15: 655–664, 1986) present evidence supporting the continued recognition of *Molothrus armenti* (Bronze-brown Cowbird) of n. Colombia as a species separate from the disjunct *M. aeneus* (Bronzed Cowbird) of sw. United States and Middle America.

S. M. Lanyon (*Science* 255: 77–79, 1992) and K. P. Johnson and S. M. Lanyon (*Auk* 116[3]: 759–768, 1999) are followed in subsuming the monotypic genus *Scaphidura*, in which the Giant Cowbird was long placed, into *Molothrus*. This was accepted by the AOU Check-list Committee (*Auk* 117[3]: 853, 2000).

What was formerly called *Molothrus badius* (Bay-winged Cowbird) has been shown (S. M. Lanyon, *Science* 255: 77–79, 1992) to be only distantly related to the other cowbirds, and the species therefore needs to be removed from that genus. The generic name *Agelaioides* is available; Jaramillo and Burke (1999) place it there, and we do as well. K. P. Johnson and S. M. Lanyon (*Auk* 116[3]: 759–768, 1999) suggest that its affinities lie with what has long been called *Oreopsar bolivianus* (Bolivian Blackbird), and that *badius* should be transferred to that genus. P. E. Lowther (*Bull. B.O.C.* 121[4]: 280–281, 2001) pointed out, however, that the name *Agelaioides* had priority over *Oreopsar;* further complicating the situation, a subspecies of *badius* is named *bolivianus,* resulting in a homonymous situation. Lowther (op. cit.) therefore proposed a new specific name for the Bolivian Blackbird, *oreopsar,* employed here.

As it is now known not to be a true cowbird, Jaramillo and Burke (1999) suggest that *Agelaioides badius* (formerly *Molothrus badius;* see above) be called simply the "Baywing," and not the Bay-winged Cowbird. *Fringilloides* of ne. Brazil may merit full species status; if split, it could be called the Pale Baywing, and *A. badius* the Common Baywing.

The monotypic genus *Xanthopsar* has been resurrected for the distinctive species *flavus* (Saffron-cowled Blackbird), based on various considerations, including its mitochondrial DNA (cf. S. M. Lanyon, *Evolution* 48: 679–693, 1994). The species was for a time placed in the genus *Agelaius* (e.g., L. S. Short, *Bull. Amer. Mus. Nat. Hist.* 154[3]: 165–352, 1975, followed by Ridgely and Tudor 1989).

S. M. Lanyon and K. E. Omlund (*Auk* 116[3]: 629–639, 1999) suggested that five South American blackbird species formerly placed in the genus *Agelaius* (*icterocephalus, xanthophthalmus, thilius, cyanopus,* and *ruficapillus*) be transferred to the genus *Chrysomus*. Subsequently it was suggested (P. E. Lowther, R. Fraga, T. S. Schulenberg, and S. M. Lanyon, *Bull. B.O.C.* 124[3]: 171–177, 2004) that three of these species deserved to be further separated generically, into *Agelasticus: xanthophthalmus, cyanopus,* and *thilius.*

The English name for *Macroagelaius imthurni* was originally "Golden-tufted Grackle" (e.g., Meyer de Schauensee 1966, 1970; Meyer de Schauensee and Phelps 1978). Ridgely and Tudor (1989) suggested associating the species with the closely related *M. subalaris* of the Colombian Andes, calling both of the species mountain grackles. Being restricted to the tepuis, *M. imthurni* became the Tepui Mountain Grackle. As the golden pectoral tufts are unique to *imthurni,* however, Hilty (2003) suggested calling *M. imthurni* the Golden-tufted Mountain Grackle. This seems acceptable and is done here.

We recognize the three principal forms of troupials as separate species, following Sibley and Monroe (1990) and Jaramillo and Burke (1999), though the evidence for doing so still is not overwhelming (see discussions in Ridgely and Tudor 1989 and Jaramillo and Burke 1999). Molecular data suggest that the troupials may not be congeneric with the true orioles. As for their English names, it seems worthwhile to associate all three as troupials. *Icterus icterus* requires a modifier, rather than being called simply the Troupial, as in Jaramillo and Burke (1999); as the species' range largely coincides with Venezuela, we opt to call it the Venezuelan Troupial. *I. icterus* also happens to be the Venezuelan national bird.

The 1998 AOU Check-list is followed in once again considering *Icterus bullockii* (Bullock's Oriole) of w. North America as a species separate from *I. galbula* (Baltimore Oriole). For a time (e.g., 1983 AOU Check-list) these had been considered conspecific under the name *I. galbula,* Northern Oriole. Only *I. galbula* occurs in South America.

Trans-Andean *Cacicus microrhynchus* (Scarlet-rumped Cacique) is now generally treated (e.g., Jaramillo and Burke 1999; Ridgely and Greenfield 2001; Hilty 2003) as a species separate from *C. uropygialis* (Subtropical Cacique) of the Andes. This is based on their differing distributions, vocalizations, and morphology.

Based on their notably different vocalizations (and also certain plumage characters), it appears quite possible that what is currently considered to be the trans-Andean population of *Cacicus cela* (Yellow-rumped Cacique) should be treated as a separate species, *C. vitellinus.*

Based especially on their quite different vocalizations (also plumage characters), we recognize two species of mountain caciques: Northern Mountain Cacique (*Cacicus leucoramphus,* with *peruvianus*) ranging in the Andes south to cen. Peru, and Southern Mountain Cacique (*Cacicus chrysonotus*) ranging in s. Peru and Bolivia.

We favor emphasizing the distinct characters of the Chestnut-headed and Casqued Oropendolas by continuing to recognize their monotypic genera, *Zarhynchus* and *Clypicterus,* respectively. Both genera have often (including Ridgely and Tudor 1989) been merged into *Psarocolius. Zarhynchus* has a markedly large bill (especially in proportion to its relatively small size, for an oropendola), swollen frontal shield, and unusually long wings; its display differs strikingly from *Psarocolius* (not leaning forward on its perch). *Clypicterus* is an unusually shaped oropendola with stocky proportions and relatively broad wings, and it has a unique swollen casque on its forehead.

Evidence is accumulating that the Amazonian and Andean populations of *Psarocolius angustifrons* (Russet-backed Oropendola) may be better considered separate species, though because some of the contact zones between the two remain little studied, we continue to regard them as conspecific. Should they be split, Amazonian birds can be known as the Black-billed Oropendola (*P. angustifrons*) and Andean birds as *P. alfredi* (Andean Oropendola). It has even been suggested (Jaramillo and Burke 1999) that *P. alfredi* might itself be composed of more than a single species.

Jaramillo and Burke (1999) are followed in considering *Psarocolius yuracares* (Olive Oropendola) and *P. bifasciatus* (Pará Oropendola) as separate (though doubtless closely related) species. The nature of their presumed contact zone remains poorly known.

BIBLIOGRAPHY

Aleixo, A. 2002. Molecular systematics and the role of the "Várzea" — "Terra-Firme" Ecotone in the diversification of *Xiphorhynchus* woodcreepers (Aves: Dendrocolaptidae). *Auk* 119(3): 621–640.

American Ornithologists' Union. 1983. *Checklist of North American Birds*, 6th ed. Washington, D.C.: American Ornithologists' Union.

———. 1998. *Check-list of North American Birds*, 7th ed. Washington, D.C.: American Ornithologists' Union.

Barnett, J. M., and M. Pearman. 2001. *Lista Comentada de las Aves Argentinas/Annotated Checklist of the Birds of Argentina.* Barcelona: Lynx Edicions.

BirdLife International. 2000. *Threatened Birds of the World.* Barcelona and Cambridge: Lynx Edicions and BirdLife International.

Canevari, M., P. Canevari, G. R. Carrizo, G. R. Carrizo, G. Harris, J. R. Mata, and R. J. Straneck. 1991. *Nueva Guia de las Aves Argentinas.* Buenos Aires: Fundación Acindar.

Collar, N. J., L. P. Gonzaga, N. K. Krabbe, A. Madroño Neito, L. G. Naranjo, T. A. Parker III, and D. C. Wege. 1992. *Threatened Birds of the Americas: The ICBP.IUCN Red Data Book.* Cambridge: International Council for Bird Preservation.

Comite Brasileiro de Registros Ornitológicos. 2006. *Lista das Aves do Brasil. Versão 15/7/2006.*

Couve, E., and C. Vidal. 2003. *Birds of Patagonia, Tierra del Fuego and Antarctic Peninsula, The Falkland Islands and South Georgia/ Aves de Patagonia, Tierra del Fuego y Península Antártica, Islas Malvinas y Georgia del Sur.* Punta Arenas, Chile: Editorial Fantástico Sur Birding.

Curson, J., D. Quinn, and D. Beadle. 1994. *Warblers of the Americas: An Identification Guide.* Boston: Houghton Mifflin Co.

Dickinson, E. C. (ed.). 2003. *The Howard and Moore Checklist of the Birds of the World*, 3rd ed. Princeton: Princeton University Press.

Fitzpatrick, J. W. 2004. Family Tyrannidae (Tyrant-Flycatchers). Pp. 170–462 in del Hoyo, J., A. Elliott, and D. A. Christie, eds. *Handbook of the Birds of the World.* Vol. 9,

Cotingas to Pipits and Wagtails. Barcelona: Lynx Edicions.

Fjeldså and Krabbe. 1990. *Birds of the High Andes.* Copenhagen: Zoological Museum, University of Copenhagen.

Gill, F., and M. Wright, on behalf of the International Ornithological Congress. 2006. *Birds of the World, Recommended English Names.* Princeton: Princeton University Press.

Guyra Paraguay. 2005. *Atlas de las Aves de Paraguay.* Asunción, Paraguay.

Haverschmidt, F., and G. F. Mees. 1994. *Birds of Suriname.* Paramaribo, Suriname: VACO.

Hellmayr, C. E. (in part with C. B. Cory or B. Conover). 1918–1938. *Catalogue of Birds of the Americas.* Field Mus. Nat. Hist., Zool. Ser., vol. 13, parts 1–11.

Hilty, S. L. 2003. *Birds of Venezuela.* Princeton: Princeton University Press.

Hilty and Brown. 1986. *A Guide to the Birds of Colombia.* Princeton, N.J.: Princeton University Press.

Howell, S. N. G., and S. W. Webb. 1995. *A Guide to the Birds of Mexico and Northern Central America.* Oxford: Oxford University Press.

Isler, M. L., and P. R. Isler. 1987. *The Tanagers: Natural History, Distribution, and Identification.* Washington, D.C.: Smithsonian Institution Press.

Jaramillo, A. 2003. *Birds of Chile.* Princeton: Princeton University Press.

Jaramillo, A., and P. Burke. 1999. *New World Blackbirds: The Icterids.* Princeton: Princeton University Press.

Krabbe, N. K., and J. Nilsson. 2003. *Birds of Ecuador, DVD-ROM.* Westernieland, The Netherlands: Bird Songs International BV.

Krabbe, N. K., and T. S. Schulenberg. 1997. *Studies in Neotropical Ornithology Honoring Ted Parker*, Ornithol. Monogr. 48: 47–88.

———. 2003. Family Rhinocryptidae (Tapaculos). Pp. 748–787 in del Hoyo, J., A. Elliott, and D. A. Christie, eds. *Handbook of the Birds of the World.* Vol. 8, Broadbills to Tapaculos. Barcelona: Lynx Edicions.

Marantz, C. A., A. Aleixo, L. R. Bevier, and M. A. Patten. 2003. Family Dendrocolaptidae (Woodcreepers). Pp. 358–447 in del Hoyo, J., A. Elliott, and D. A. Christie, eds. *Handbook of the Birds of the World.* Vol. 8, Broadbills to Tapaculos. Barcelona: Lynx Edicions.

Mayer, S. 2000. *Birds of Bolivia 2.0, CD-ROM.* Westernieland, The Netherlands: Bird Songs International BV.

Meyer de Schauensee, R. 1966. *The Species of Birds of South America with Their Distribution.* Narberth, Pa.: Livingston Publishing Co.

———. 1970. *A Guide to the Birds of South America.* Wynnewood, Pa.: Livingston Publishing Co.

Meyer de Schauensee, R., and W. H. Phelps, Jr. 1978. *A Guide to the Birds of Venezuela.* Princeton: Princeton University Press.

Narosky, T., and D. Yzurieta. 2003. *Birds of Argentina and Uruguay,* 15th Ed. Buenos Aires: Vasquez Mazzini Editores.

Peters, J. L. 1931–1986. *Check-list of the Birds of the World.* Vols. 7–15 (many vols., or parts thereof, have different authors). Cambridge, Mass.: Museum of Comparative Zoology.

Prum, R. O. 1992. Syringeal morphology, phylogeny, and evolution of the Neotropical manakins (Aves: Pipridae). *Amer. Mus. Novitates* 3043: 1–65.

Remsen, J. V. 2003. Family Furnariidae (Ovenbirds). Pp. 162–357 in del Hoyo, J., A. Elliott, and D. A. Christie, eds. *Handbook of the Birds of the World.* Vol. 8, Broadbills to Tapaculos. Barcelona: Lynx Edicions.

Remsen, J. V., C. D. Cadena, A. Jaramillo, M. Nores, J. F. Pacheco, M. B. Robbins, T. S. Schulenberg, F. G. Stiles, D. F. Stotz, and K. J. Zimmer. 2007. A classification of the bird species of South America. American Ornithologists' Union.

Ridgely, R. S., and P. J. Greenfield. 2001. *The Birds of Ecuador.* Vols. 1–2. Ithaca, N.Y.: Cornell University Press.

Ridgely, R. S., and J. A. Gwynne. 1989. *A Guide to the Birds of Panama, with Costa Rica, Nicaragua, and Honduras,* 2d ed. Princeton: Princeton University Press.

Ridgely, R. S., and G. Tudor. 1989. *The Birds of South America.* Vol. 1. Austin: University of Texas Press.

———. 1994. *The Birds of South America.* Vol. 2. Austin: University of Texas Press.

Salaman, P. G. W., T. M. Donegan, and A. M. Cuervo. 1999. Ornithological surveys in Serranía de los Churumbelos, southern Colombia. *Cotinga* 12: 29–39.

Sibley, C. G., and B. L. Monroe, Jr. 1990. *Distribution and Taxonomy of Birds of the World.* New Haven: Yale University Press.

Sick, H. 1993. *Birds in Brazil: A Natural History.* Princeton: Princeton University Press.

Snow, D. W. 2004. Family Pipridae (Manakins). Pp. 110–169 in del Hoyo, J., A. Elliott, and D. A. Christie, eds. *Handbook of the Birds of the World.* Vol. 9, Cotingas to Pipits and Wagtails. Barcelona: Lynx Edicions.

Stotz, D. F., R. O. Bierregaard, M. Cohn-Haft, P. Petermann, J. Smith, A. Whittaker, and S. V. Wilson. 1992. The status of North American migrants in central Amazonian Brazil. *Condor* 94[3]: 608–621.

Turner, A. K. 2004. Family Hirundinidae (Swallows and Martins). Pp. 602–685 in del Hoyo, J., A. Elliott, and D. A. Christie, eds. *Handbook of the Birds of the World.* Vol. 9, Cotingas to Pipits and Wagtails. Barcelona: Lynx Edicions.

Wege, D. C., and A. J. Long. 1995. *Key Areas for Threatened Birds in the Neotropics.* Cambridge, United Kingdom: BirdLife International.

Wetmore, A. 1973. The Birds of the Republic of Panama, Part 3, Dendrocolaptidae (Woodcreepers) to Oxyruncidae (Sharpbills). *Smiths. Misc. Coll.,* Vol. 150. Part 3.

Wetmore, A., R. A. Pasquier, and S. L. Olson. 1984. The Birds of the Republic of Panama, Part 4, Hirundinidae (Swallows) to Fringillidae (Finches). *Smiths. Misc. Coll.,* Vol. 150, Part 4.

Zimmer, K. J., and M. L. Isler. 2003. Family Thamnophilidae (Typical Antbirds). Pp. 448–731 in del Hoyo, J., A. Elliott, and D. A. Christie, eds. *Handbook of the Birds of the World.* Vol. 8, Broadbills to Tapaculos. Barcelona: Lynx Edicions.

INDEX TO ENGLISH NAMES

White-browed, 302, Pl. 10(16)
White-collared, 311, Pl. 14(1)
White-eyed, 309, Pl. 13(3)
White-throated. *See* Foliage-gleaner, Tepui
Fruitcrow
  Bare-necked, 512, Pl. 71(1)
  Crimson, 512, Pl. 71(4)
  Purple-throated, 512, Pl. 71(2)
  Red-ruffed, 512, Pl. 71(3)
Fruiteater
  Band-tailed, 505, Pl. 68(3)
  Barred, 504, Pl. 68(1)
  Black-chested, 505, Pl. 68(4)
  Fiery-throated, 506, Pl. 68(9)
  Golden-breasted, 505, Pl. 68(6)
  Green-and-black, 504, Pl. 68(2)
  Handsome, 505, Pl. 68(7)
  Masked, 505, Pl. 68(5)
  Orange-breasted, 505
  Red-banded, 506, Pl. 68(10)
  Scaled, 503, Pl. 67(5)
  Scarlet-breasted, 506, Pl. 68(8)

Gallito
  Crested, 393, Pl. 39(5)
  Sandy, 393, Pl. 39(6)
Gnatcatcher
  Creamy-bellied, 550, Pl. 84(5)
  Guianan, 550, 694, Pl. 84(6)
  Iquitos, 551, 694
  Marañón, 550, 694
  Masked, 551, Pl. 84(7)
  Pará, 550, 694
  Rio Negro, 550, 694
  Slate-throated, 551
  Tropical, 550, 694, Pl. 84(4)
  White-faced, 694
GNATCATCHERS AND GNATWRENS, 549
Gnateater
  Ash-throated, 388, Pl. 38(5)
  Black-bellied, 388, Pl. 38(8)
  Black-cheeked, 387, Pl. 38(4)
  Chestnut-belted, 388, Pl. 38(6)
  Chestnut-crowned, 387, Pl. 38(1)
  Hooded, 388, Pl. 38(7)
  Rufous, 387, Pl. 38(3)
  Slaty, 387, Pl. 38(2)
GNATEATERS, 387
Gnatwren
  Collared, 549, Pl. 84(2)
  Long-billed, 549, Pl. 84(3)
  Tawny-faced, 549, Pl. 84(1)
Goldfinch
  European, 681
  Lesser, 681, Pl. 121(10)

Grackle
  Carib, 670, Pl. 118(1)
  Colombian Mountain, 671
  Golden-tufted Mountain, 670, 700, Pl. 118(3)
  Great-tailed, 670, Pl. 118(2)
  Red-bellied, 671, Pl. 118(4)
  Tepui Mountain. *See* Grackle, Golden-tufted
    Mountain
  Velvet-fronted, 666, Pl. 117(1)
Grassfinch
  Duida, 662
  Lesser, 662, Pl. 115(10)
  Wedge-tailed, 662, Pl. 115(9)
Grassquit
  Black-faced, 630
  Blue-black, 630, Pl. 107(1)
  Dull-colored, 631, Pl. 107(3)
  Sooty, 630, Pl. 107(2)
  Yellow-faced, 631, Pl. 107(4)
Graveteiro
  Pink-legged, 281, 685, Pl. 6(1)
Graytail
  Double-banded, 298, Pl. 10(2)
  Equatorial, 298, Pl. 10(3)
Greenfinch
  European, 681
Greenlet
  Ashy-headed, 558, Pl. 85(13)
  Brown-headed, 559
  Buff-cheeked, 559, Pl. 85(15)
  Dusky-capped, 559, Pl. 85(14)
  Golden-fronted, 559, Pl. 85(16)
  Gray-chested, 558, Pl. 85(12)
  Gray-eyed, 558, 695
  Lemon-chested, 558, 695, Pl. 85(10)
  Lesser, 559, Pl. 85(18)
  Olivaceous, 558
  Rio de Janeiro, 695
  Rufous-crowned, 557, 695, Pl. 85(8)
  Rufous-naped, 559, Pl. 85(17)
  Scrub, 558, Pl. 85(9)
  Tawny-crowned, 560, Pl. 85(19)
  Tepui, 558, Pl. 85(11)
Grosbeak
  Black-backed, 628, Pl. 106(8)
  Black-headed, 629
  Black-throated, 629, 698, Pl. 106(12)
  Blue, 632
  Blue-black, 631, Pl. 107(7)
  Glaucous-blue, 632, Pl. 107(9)
  Golden-bellied. *See* Grosbeak, Southern Yellow
  Red-and-black, 629, Pl. 106(10)
  Rose-breasted, 628
  Slate-colored, 629, 698, Pl. 106(11)
  Southern Yellow, 628, Pl. 106(9)

Sharpe's. *See* Wren, Sepia-brown
Song, 535, Pl. 79(10)
Sooty-headed, 530, Pl. 78(3)
Southern House, 534, 694, Pl. 79(5)
Speckle-breasted, 531, Pl. 78(9)
Stripe-backed, 528, Pl. 77(6)
Stripe-throated, 530, Pl. 78(8)
Superciliated, 531, Pl. 78(13)
Tepui, 533
Thrush-like, 527, Pl. 77(3)
Tooth-billed, 532, Pl. 79(2)
Whiskered, 529, Pl. 78(1)
White-breasted Wood, 534, Pl. 79(6)
White-headed, 528, Pl. 77(5)
Wing-banded, 536, Pl. 79(13)
WRENS, 527
Wren-Spinetail
Bay-capped, 280, Pl. 5(12)

Xenops
Great, 300, Pl. 10(10)
Plain, 301, Pl. 10(14)
Rufous-tailed, 300, Pl. 10(12)

Slender-billed, 301
Streaked, 301, Pl. 10(13)
Xenopsaris
White-naped, 482, 692, Pl. 62(1)

Yellowfinch
Bright-rumped, 658, Pl. 114(6)
Citron-headed, 658, Pl. 114(7)
Grassland, 657, 699, Pl. 114(5)
Greater, 658, Pl. 114(10)
Greenish, 658, Pl. 114(9)
Orange-fronted, 657, Pl. 114(3)
Patagonian, 658, Pl. 114(11)
Puna, 658, Pl. 114(8)
Raimondi's, 657
Stripe-tailed, 657, Pl. 114(4)
Yellowthroat
Black-lored, 563, 695
Common, 563
Masked, 563, 695
Olive-crowned, 563, Pl. 86(10)
Southern, 563, 695, Pl. 86(9)

INDEX TO SCIENTIFIC NAMES

murinus, Agriornis, 455, 692
murinus, Thamnophilus, 334
murphyi, Progne, 521, 693
muscicapinus, Hylophilus, 559
Muscigralla, 461
Muscipipra, 463
Muscisaxicola, 458
musculus, Troglodytes, 534
mustelina, Hylocichla, 538
mustelinus, Certhiaxis, 285
Myadestes, 537
Myiarchus, 471
Myiobius, 447
Myioborus, 561
Myiodynastes, 476
Myiopagis, 419
Myiophobus, 445
Myiornis, 428
Myiotheretes, 456
Myiotriccus, 447
Myiozetetes, 474
Mymornis, 369
Myornis, 395
myotherinus, Myrmoborus, 359
Myrmeciza, 364
Myrmoborus, 359
Myrmochanes, 362
Myrmorchilus, 358
Myrmothera, 382
Myrmotherula, 340
mystacalis, Cyanocorax, 518
mystacalis, Diglossa, 575
mystacalis, Thryothorus, 529
mystaceus, Platyrinchus, 440

naevia, Sclateria, 362
naevioides, Hylophylax, 361
naevius, Hylophylax, 360
nana, Grallaricula, 385
napensis, Stigmatura, 408, 690
Nasica, 316
nationi, Atlapetes, 643
nattereri, Anthus, 552
nattereri, Hylopezus, 384
nattereri, Lepidothrix, 496
nattereri, Pipra. *See* nattereri, Lepidothrix
nattererii, Cotinga, 507
necopinus, Xiphorhynchus. *See* kienerii, Xiphorhynchus
negreti, Henicorhina, 534, 694
nematura, Lochmias, 313
Nemosia, 586
nengeta, Fluvicola, 467
Neochelidon, 523

Neoctantes, 358
Neopelma, 488
Neopipo, 490
Neothraupis, 622
Neoxolmis, 461
Nephelornis, 577
nicefori, Thryothorus, 532
nidipendulus, Hemitriccus, 433
niger, Neoctantes, 358
nigerrimus, Knipolegus, 466
nigrescens, Cercomacra, 356
nigrescens, Contopus, 450
nigricans, Cercomacra, 356
nigricans, Sayornis, 452
nigricans, Serpophaga, 409
nigricapillus, Formicarius, 374
nigricapillus, Thryothorus, 530
nigricauda, Myrmeciza, 368
nigriceps, Saltator, 625
nigriceps, Thamnophilus, 331
nigriceps, Todirostrum, 436
nigriceps, Turdus, 544
nigricollis, Phoenicircus, 514
nigricollis, Sporophila, 635
nigrifrons, Phylloscartes, 425
nigripes, Dacnis, 579
nigrirostris, Cyclarhis, 555
nigrita, Ochthoeca, 453, 691
nigrocapillus, Phyllomyias, 407
nigrocincta, Tangara, 594
nigrocinereus, Thamnophilus, 331
nigrocristatus, Anairetes, 414
nigrocristatus, Basileuterus, 571
nigrofumosus, Cinclodes, 271
nigrogularis, Icterus, 673
nigrogularis, Ramphocelus, 614
nigromaculata, Phlegopsis, 371
nigropectus, Biatas, 329
nigrorufa, Poospiza, 654
nigrorufa, Sporophila, 640
nigroviridis, Tangara, 588
nitidissima, Chlorochrysa, 587
nitidus, Cyanerpes, 581
niveigularis, Tyrannus, 479
nobilis, Chamaeza, 375
notabilis, Anisognathus, 607
Notiochelidon, 523, 693
notorius, Scytalopus, 689
novacapitalis, Scytalopus, 400
novaesi, Philydor, 308
noveboracensis, Seiurus, 568
nuchalis, Campylorhynchus, 528
nuchalis, Grallaria, 380
nudiceps, Gymnocichla, 368